TREATMENT OF CHILDHOOD DISORDERS

Edited by
ERIC J. MASH
University of Calgary

and

RUSSELL A. BARKLEY
University of Massachusetts Medical Center

THE GUILFORD PRESS
New York   London

With gratitude and appreciation
to my good friend and teacher, Leif G. Terdal
E.J.M.

With gratitude and appreciation to my mentors,
Donald K. Routh, Douglas G. Ullman, James E. Hastings
R.A.B.

© 1989 The Guilford Press
A Division of Guilford Publications, Inc.
72 Spring Street, New York, NY 10012

Printed in the United States of America

Last digit is print number: 9 8 7 6 5 4 3 2

Library of Congress Cataloging-in-Publication Data

Treatment of childhood disorders/edited
   by Eric J. Mash, Russell A. Barkley.
        p. cm.
   Includes bibliographies and index.
   ISBN 0-89862-743-5
   1. Child psychopathology. 2. Child psychotherapy. I. Mash, Eric
J. II. Barkley, Russell A., 1949–   .
   [DNLM: 1. Affective Disorders—in infancy & childhood.
2. Behavior Therapy—in infancy & childhood. 3. Child Behavior
Disorders—therapy. 4. Child Development Disorders—therapy. WS
350.6.T784]
   RJ499.T835 1989
   618.92'8914—dc19
DNLM/DLC
for Library of Congress   88-24464
                                                             CIP

CONTRIBUTORS

SANDRA T. AZAR, PhD, Department of Psychology, Clark University, Worcester, Massachusetts

RUSSELL A. BARKLEY, PhD, Department of Psychiatry, University of Massachusetts Medical Center, Worcester, Massachusetts

BILLY A. BARRIOS, PhD, Department of Psychology, University of Mississippi, University, Mississippi

JENNIFER H. COUSINS, PhD, Department of Medicine, Baylor College of Medicine, Houston, Texas

KEITH A. CRNIC, PhD, Department of Psychology, Pennsylvania State University, University Park, Pennsylvania

KENNETH A. DODGE, PhD, Department of Psychology and Human Development, Vanderbilt University, Nashville, Tennesee

MICHAEL J. DOLGIN, PhD, University of Southern California School of Medicine and Children's Hospital of Los Angeles, Los Angeles, California

JAN FAUST-CAMPANILE, PhD, Department of Psychology, Nova University, Ft. Lauderdale, Florida

JOHN FOREYT, PhD, Department of Medicine, Baylor College of Medicine, Houston, Texas

SHARON L. FOSTER, PhD, Department of Psychology, West Virginia University, Morgantown, West Virginia

SUSAN M. JAY, PhD. University of Southern California School of Medicine and Children's Hospital of Los Angeles, Los Angeles, California

ALAN E. KAZDIN, PhD., Department of Psychiatry, Western Psychiatric Institute and Clinic, University of Pittsburgh School of Medicine, Pittsburgh, Pennsylvania

MARY KENNING, PhD, Department of Psychology, University of Nebraska at Lincoln, Lincoln, Nebraska

ERIC J. MASH, PhD. Department of Psychology, University of Calgary, Calgary, Alberta, Canada

JILL K. MCGAVIN, PhD, Department of Psychology, University of Houston and Houston Child Guidance Center, Houston, Texas

ROBERT J. MCMAHON, PhD, Department of Psychology, University of Washington, Seattle, Washington

CRIGHTON NEWSOM, PhD, Department of Psychology, Muscatatuck Center, Butlerville, Indiana

STAN L. O'DELL, PhD, Department of Psychology, University of Mississippi, University, Mississippi

MOLLY REID, PhD, Department of Psychiatry and Behavioral Sciences, University of Washington, Seattle, Washington

ARNOLD RINCOVER, PhD, Behavioral Research, Surrey Place Centre, Toronto, Ontario, Canada

ARTHUR L. ROBIN, PhD, Department of Pediatrics, Wayne State University School of Medicine, Detroit, Michigan

H. GERRY TAYLOR, PhD, Department of Pediatrics, Rainbow Babies & Children's Hospital, Case Western Reserve University School of Medicine, Cleveland, Ohio

C. EUGENE WALKER, PhD, Department of Psychiatry and Behavioral Sciences, University of Oklahoma Health Sciences Center, Oklahoma City, Oklahoma

KAREN C. WELLS, PhD, Department of Psychiatry and Behavioral Sciences, George Washington University Medical School and Children's Hospital National Medical Center, Washington, DC

DAVID A. WOLFE, PhD, Department of Psychology, University of Western Ontario, London, Ontario, Canada

PREFACE

This book represents the culmination of several years of planning, preparation, and editing in an effort to develop a book that would be scholarly, yet applied, and would address a perceived void in the literature for an advanced text on the empirically based treatment of child psychopathological disorders. It is an outgrowth of prior work in developing the second edition of Mash and Terdal's *Behavioral Assessment of Childhood Disorders* (Guilford Press, 1988), and the desire to have a companion volume on treatments for childhood disorders. The exceptional chapters prepared for the Assessment volume convinced us that greater attention needed to be given to providing a review of those empirically established treatments for each disorder that are so closely entwined with the extensive assessment strategies that are now in existence. Authors were chosen, many from the earlier volume, who had established international reputations in both research and clinical practice for each childhood disorder. Their mission was to prepare a chapter that provided a summary and critique of the existing treatments for each disorder, to propose new directions for treatment research, and to discuss critical issues surrounding the treatments under review.

Given the plethora of treatments available for children, an effort was made to focus attention only on those that had some scientifically established basis for their efficacy with a given disorder, or that could be readily extrapolated from such an empirical foundation. This task was made all the more arduous by our desire to have greater clinical detail provided on each treatment than simply making passing reference to the name of the therapy and where it might be found in the literature. Even with these relatively circumscribed purposes, the volume is quite lengthy owing to the myriad of promising treatments now available for these disorders. Nevertheless, we believe these goals have been admirably accomplished by the writers and trust the reader will share this opinion having once digested the contents.

Any effort to capture the dynamic nature of the literature on empirically derived treatments for children is akin to taking a still photo of a brief moment in the life of a family. Ever evolving, changing rapidly, often fluid in its transitions over time, yet punctuated by moments of rapid restructuring or growth, treatment research and practice changes with virtually every new issue of relevant scientific journals. Nevertheless, we believe that the singular expertise of our authors and their extensive experience with their respective disorders has greatly aided us, for a time anyway, to capture the current scope and future directions of treatments for childhood disorders.

Our gratitude is owed to many who assisted us with this task, foremost among whom are the respective authors who tolerated our editorial excesses and eccentricities well, producing superb overviews of their respective fields. While completing this project Eric Mash held a Sabbatical Fellowship from the University of Calgary and was a Visiting Professor at the Crippled Children's Division of the Oregon Health Sciences University. The support of these two institutions is gratefully acknowledged. We are also grateful to Rowena Howells, Managing Editor at Guilford Press, for her attention to detail, expedience, and stewardship of the project throughout the production process. We thank Seymour Weingarten, Editor-in-Chief, Guilford Publications, and our friend for his continuing support and acceptance of this, and other, projects. Each of us owes much to the other for the lively, stimulating, and informative debates that occurred around reviewing each chapter, sometimes accentuated by a mutual weakness to sample some of Oregon's fine wines and wineries. Finally, our respective families deserve acknowledgment for their unselfishly permitting us time, often outside of our work schedules, to bring this project to fruition. Their support of our labors is deeply appreciated.

Eric J. Mash
Russell A. Barkley

CONTENTS

PART I

INTRODUCTION

1

TREATMENT OF CHILD AND FAMILY DISTURBANCE: A BEHAVIORAL–SYSTEMS PERSPECTIVE

ERIC J. MASH
University of Calgary

The behavioral, psychological, social, and learning problems for which children are referred to professionals for help are numerous and varied (Achenbach, 1982; Mash & Terdal, 1981a, 1988a; Quay & Werry, 1986). Adaptational difficulties that lead to referral frequently reflect developmentally and/or situationally inappropriate or exaggerated expressions of behavior that may at times also occur in children who are not referred (Achenbach & Edelbrock, 1981). As a result, decisions concerning the evaluation and treatment of any child are heavily embedded within the child's social and cultural milieu, and are always the result of ongoing judgments that are either made or not made by significant individuals in the child's environment, usually parents and teachers (Mash & Terdal, 1981b, 1988b). The professionals who evaluate and treat disturbed children and their families come from a variety of disciplines and backgrounds. They include psychologists, educators, pediatricians, child psychiatrists, social workers, speech and language pathologists, physical and occupational therapists, day care specialists, nurses, and others. It is not surprising, therefore, that a tremendous number and diversity of treatments for children and families exist (Johnson, Rasbury,

& Siegel, 1986), with some conservative estimates listing well over 200 different varieties of psychosocial intervention alone (Kazdin, 1988b).

Given the heterogeneity of circumstances surrounding the identification, referral, evaluation, and treatment of children with problems, it is believed that these activities are best depicted as ongoing decision-making/problem-solving processes (e.g., Evans & Meyer, 1985; Herbert, 1987; Kanfer & Schefft, 1988). These processes are directed at providing answers to such questions as these:

- Should this child's difficulties be treated?
- What are the projected outcomes in the absence of treatment?
- What type of treatment is likely to be most effective?
- Who is the best person to provide treatment?
- Which type of intervention is likely to be the most acceptable to the child, parents, and other family and community members?
- When should treatment be initiated and when should it be terminated?
- Is the intervention having its desired impact?

The ultimate goal of this iterative decision-making process should be to achieve effective solutions to the problems being faced by the child and his or her family and to enhance their long-term adjustments.

It is my view, and that of the authors represented in this book, that decisions concerning these and other related questions are best made when they are based on a consistently applied theoretical framework, well-established research findings relevant to both normal and deviant child and family functioning, empirically documented treatment procedures, and operational rules that are sensitive to the realities and changing demands of clinical practice. Although such an amalgamation of theory, research, and practice is more an ideal than a fact at the present time, current behavioral–systems perspectives seem to approximate this integration most closely, and it is these approaches upon which this volume is based. Behavioral approaches seem to be especially predominant with children, with approximately 50% of all clinical child and pediatric psychologists identifying with this orientation (O'Leary, 1984a). Nevertheless, we believe that the complexity of childhood disorders, the diversity of circumstances under which they occur, the evolving nature of behavioral treatments, and the current efforts to integrate and combine different therapy orientations (e.g., Kendall, 1982; Wolfe & Goldfried, 1988) and practices (i.e., medication and behavior therapy) would contraindicate a rigid adherence to *any* narrowly defined therapeutic perspective.

It is the purpose of this initial chapter to provide an overview of the recent developments, conceptual issues, and practical concerns associated with the treatment of child and family disturbances from a behavioral–systems perspective, and also to describe some of the more common features of this approach. The general themes that are raised in this introductory chapter are elaborated in the chapter discussions of specific child and family disorders that follow.

HISTORICAL ANTECEDENTS
AND EARLY DEVELOPMENTS

There have been several descriptions of the historical development of behavioral approaches to the treatment of children and families (e.g., Kazdin, 1978; O'Leary & Wilson, 1987; Ollen-

dick, 1986; Ollendick & Cerny, 1981; Ross, 1981). This development is briefly highlighted here. Although it is possible to find examples of the application of behavioral principles with children throughout the history of humankind, systematic behavioral applications are usually identified as beginning with the rise of behaviorism in the early 1900s, as reflected in the classic studies on the conditioning and elimination of children's fears (Jones, 1924; Watson & Rayner, 1920), and Pavlov's experimental research that established the foundations for classical conditioning. The period from 1930 to 1950 represented child behavior therapy's latency period, with a few reports in the 1930s describing the treatment of isolated problems such as bedwetting (Mowrer & Mowrer, 1938), stuttering (Dunlap, 1932), and fears (Holmes, 1936; Weber, 1936).

It was not until the 1950s and early 1960s that behavior therapy began to emerge as a systematic approach to the treatment of child and family disorders. The classic works of Wolpe (1958), Salter (1949), Lazarus (1958; Lazarus & Abramovitz, 1962), Eysenck (1960), Skinner (1953), and Bijou (Bijou & Baer, 1961) all contributed to behavior therapy's early development. Behavioral approaches during the 1950s and early 1960s were reactions to the then-dominant psychodynamic perspective. Most behavioral work with children was carried out with mentally retarded or severely disturbed youngsters for whom psychoanalytic practices were perceived as not being very effective. Much of this work took place in institutions or classrooms—settings that were thought to provide the kind of environmental controls needed to modify behavior effectively. Early case studies were designed primarily to demonstrate the applicability of one learning principle or another, and showed little concern for the clinical significance of treatment or its long-term impact on the child and family. As Wachtel (1977) has pointed out, many of the most prominent figures in the early behavior therapy movement were psychologists who were almost exclusively experimental researchers, with little or no clinical experience. In general, early case reports underestimated the complexity of clinical phenomena and did not communicate the subtleties necessary to understand and mediate the gap between laboratory principles and clinical applications (Kazdin, 1988a).

The case study phase of behavior modification is perhaps most clearly illustrated in the 1965 volume edited by Ullmann and Krasner, entitled *Case Studies in Behavior Modification.* The childhood behaviors treated in these case studies included phobias, thumb sucking, eliminative disturbances, tantrums, isolate behavior, crying, crawling, vomiting, hyperactivity, and cooperation. Most of these studies showed little attention to the larger social network in which these specific behavior problems occurred, or to issues such as generalization, follow-up, or the possible negative effects of treatment. With few exceptions, they also ignored or minimized developmental factors, cognitive variables, possible biological determinants, diagnostic considerations, the use of medications, and therapeutic processes such as resistance.

Early behavioral work with children and families was derived primarily from an operant/reinforcement tradition. A major development in the field involved the establishment of the *Journal of Applied Behavior Analysis* in 1968, which provided an outlet for treatment studies with children and also served to define and shape the field of applied behavior analysis (Baer, Wolf, & Risley, 1968). The establishment of journals such as *Behaviour Research and Therapy* and *Behavior Therapy,* and later *Child and Family Behavior Therapy, Behavior Modification, Journal of Behavior Therapy and Experimental Psychiatry,* and *Behavioral Assessment,* further legitimized and promoted behavioral applications in child clinical psychology.

Work during the late 1960s foreshadowed developments of the 1970s, as reflected in several noteworthy clinical research programs and publications. Tharp and Wetzel's (1969) *Behavior Modification in the Natural Environment* provided a model that redirected intervention into the community and provided a beginning systems framework for treatment. Mischel's (1968) *Personality and Assessment* focused attention on the importance of situations and established the conceptual foundations upon which behavioral assessment was built. Bandura's (1969) *Principles of Behavior Modification* and Kanfer and Phillips's (1970) *Learning Foundations of Behavior Therapy* placed behavioral approaches more squarely within a clinical context, broadened the range of principles upon which behavioral procedures were based, and laid the groundwork for the many cognitive applications that were to develop in the 1970s. Kanfer and Saslow's (1965, 1969) model for "behavioral diagnosis" established the complex network of factors that needed to be considered in treatment, and provided a beginning decision-making approach to treatment. Patterson's (Patterson, Ray, & Shaw, 1968) work with antisocial children extended the locus of behavioral intervention from the child to the family, and from the clinic to the home. The work of operant psychologists such as Lindsley, Bijou, Baer, Wolf, Risley, Hopkins, and many others refined many of the procedures and extended them across a range of settings, especially the classroom. Finally, Lovaas's (Lovaas, Freitag, Gold, & Kasorla, 1965) work with autistic children established the range of procedures to be used in working with developmentally disabled populations, and also provided the needed impetus for addressing such important issues as generalization, the use of aversive procedures in a clinical context, and ethical issues in behavior therapy more generally. Although there were undoubtedly other important developments during the late 1960s, the aforementioned seem especially noteworthy in retrospect.

It is difficult to place the events of the 1970s into a neat temporal perspective, partly as a function of the tremendous growth in behavioral applications. However, the continuing work of several investigators has served to establish the new conceptual and technological base for child and family behavior therapy. Patterson's (Patterson, Reid, Jones, & Conger, 1975) and Wahler's (1975) programs for antisocial children; Lovaas's work with autistic children (Lovaas, Koegel, Simmons, & Long, 1973); O'Leary's classroom interventions (O'Leary, Becker, Evans, & Saudargas, 1969); Meichenbaum's (1977) promotion of cognitive-behavior therapy; and the systematic interventions and ecological applications by operant psychologists in classroom, day care, group home, and work environments all served to shape the field. As described in the section that follows, further expansion and extensions of this work in the 1970s and 1980s moved behavioral applications into family treatment, health psychology, behavioral pediatrics, and environmental engineering. This has resulted in the integration of behavioral approaches with the more general field of clinical child psychology. The cumulative impact of Alan Kazdin's writings and research over the past decade has been enormous; his work has helped to bring behavioral approaches into mainstream clinical child psychology and to bridge the gap between work in child psychology and child psychiatry.

RECENT DEVELOPMENTS

A number of recent conceptual and methodological developments have shaped current behavioral approaches to the treatment of child and family disorders. These include the following:

1. A growing recognition of the need for a systems perspective to guide behavioral assessment and treatment (e.g., Kanfer & Schefft, 1988).
2. An increased developmental emphasis in the design and implementation of treatments (e.g., Harris & Ferrari, 1983; Kendall, Lerner, & Craighead, 1984).
3. An increased sensitivity to the importance of individual differences, including biological factors (e.g., Russo & Budd, 1987; Strayhorn, 1987), in moderating the effectiveness of treatment.
4. A heightened interest in the potential utility of clinical diagnosis and empirical classification as decision aids in formulating effective treatments (e.g., Achenbach & McConaughy, 1987; Harris & Powers, 1984).
5. A growing view of behavioral treatment as a clinical decision-making process (e.g., Evans & Meyer, 1985; Herbert, 1987; Kanfer & Busemeyer, 1982).
6. A greater emphasis on prevention (e.g., Peterson & Mori, 1985; Roberts & Peterson, 1984), including the development of individualized programs of early family intervention (e.g., Dunst & Trivette, in press; Dunst, Trivette, & Deal, in press).
7. A focus on the interrelated influences of child and family cognitions and affects on behavior, as assessed and treated within the context of ongoing social interactions (e.g., Lochman, 1987).
8. The continuing proliferation of behavioral practices in health care settings (e.g., Gross & Drabman, in press; Karoly, 1988; Routh, 1988).
9. A growing acceptance of the notion that individualized treatments should also be population-specific, focusing on parameters that are relevant to particular classes of childhood disorders (Lee & Mash, in press; Mash & Terdal, 1988b).

Behavioral–Systems Perspective

Perhaps the most striking development in child and family behavior therapy has been the increasing tendency to design and implement treatments utilizing an ecological–systems perspective on child and family functioning. This approach is consistent with a more general trend toward the use of systems models in other fields, such as developmental psychology (e.g., Bronfenbrenner, 1986; Fogel & Thelan, 1987) and biology. Many of the other developments that have occurred in child and family behavior therapy appear to be either directly or indirectly related to the adoption of a systems perspective. Although a thorough presentation of contemporary systems models for child and family treatment is beyond the scope of this chapter (see Steinglass, 1987, for an overview), concepts that are especially relevant for behaviorally based clinical practice include (1) the view of child and family disorders as constellations of interrelated response systems and subsystems; (2) the need to consider the entire situation when assessing the impact of any single variable; (3) the idea that similar behaviors may be the result of different sets of initiating factors; (4) a recognition that intervention is likely to lead to multiple outcomes, including readjustments of relationships within the family system (e.g., Brunk, Hengeller, & Whelan, 1987); and (5) the notion that family systems and subsystems possess dynamic properties and are constantly changing over time (Hollandsworth, 1986). As will be illustrated throughout this volume, all of these concepts have important implications for the manner in which treatments are selected, implemented, and evaluated.

Isolated elements of a systems formulation have characterized behavioral approaches to child and family treatment throughout their inception and development. For example, concepts such as situationism (Mischel, 1968), social learning (Bandura, 1969, 1986), reciprocity (Patterson, 1976, 1982), behavioral ecology (Willems, 1974), intervention in the natural environment (Tharp & Wetzel, 1969), response classes (Voeltz & Evans, 1982), keystone behaviors (Wahler, 1975), setting events (Wahler & Fox, 1981; Wahler & Graves, 1983), stimulus generalization (Stokes & Baer, 1977), and response generalization (Kazdin, 1982b) all suggest the complex interplay of variables associated with a systems orientation. However, it is only recently that explicit systems formulations have been brought to bear in child and family behavior therapy, both as a general therapeutic orientation (e.g., Alexander & Parsons, 1982; Robin & Foster, 1989) and in specific areas such as autism (Harris, 1984), school and learning problems (Evans & Meyer, 1985), and child abuse (Azar & Wolfe, Chapter 13, this volume).

Progression toward a systems perspective has resulted in a number of related developments in the behavioral treatment of child and family disorders, including (1) continued extension of behavioral practices into new areas; (2) increasing specialization; (3) a broadening of treatment goals; and (4) a growing recognition of the need for a multidisciplinary approach to treatment.

Extension into New Areas

The range of individual response systems (e.g., behavioral, cognitive, emotional, physiological), family subsystems (e.g., mother–child, father–child, marital, sibling), and settings (e.g., home, classroom, day care, outpatient clinics, hospitals, summer camps, workplace) encompassed by a systems perspective has promoted the extension of behavioral practices into new problems areas, with different populations, and in new settings. Perhaps the most visible extension has been in the area of pediatric health psychology (e.g., Dolgin & Jay, Chapter 10, this volume; Gross & Drabman, in press). The range of problems treated also continues to grow, as interventions have become increasingly sensitive to the interrelationships among the behavioral, emotional, and cognitive manifestations of most child and family disorders (e.g., Kendall, 1987). Recent applications in the areas of social competence (e.g., Lochman, 1988; Meyer, Cole, McQuarter, & Reichle, 1988), sexual abuse (e.g., Burke, Townsley, Messner, & Jackson, 1987; Hoier, Smith, Shawchuck, & Freeman, 1988; Wolfe & Wolfe, 1988), childhood and adolescent depression (e.g., Kazdin, Chapter 4, this volume), teenage drinking (e.g., Kline, Canter, & Robin, 1987), accident prevention (e.g., Peterson & Mori, 1985), and childhood anxiety dis-

orders (e.g., Barrios & O'Dell, Chapter 5, this volume; Last, 1988) illustrate this growth.

Increasing Specialization

Extension of behavioral practice into new areas has also been accompanied by increasing differentiation and specialization. Such specialization indicates a recognition of the unique developmental demands, setting events, controlling variables, and intervention requirements associated with particular age groups and problems. In referring to recent developments in child behavior therapy, Hersen and Van Hasselt (1987) noted that "the field has become more differentiated, with many of our colleagues specializing in the treatment of certain age groups and particular disorders. As time goes on we see fewer generalists in behavior therapy with children and adolescents" (p. xi). The chapters in this volume bear witness to the fact that the conceptual formulations, clinical procedures, and operational rules associated with different kinds of childhood disorders are quite different, and that effective intervention requires a thorough understanding of the specific parameters and empirical findings associated with particular clusters of problems and situations.

Broadening of Treatment Goals

The systems perspective in child and family behavior therapy has also had implications for the manner in which treatment goals are defined. Although behavioral programs were criticized for their overemphasis on management, compliance, and the short-term reduction of symptomatic distress (e.g., Winett & Winkler, 1972), recent applications have shown an increasing focus on the need to develop skills and competencies in both the child and his or her social environment, and on minimizing adverse outcomes through the use of prevention strategies (e.g., Wurtele, Marrs, & Miller-Perrin, 1987). As Blechman (1985) has stated, "Children with behavior problems deserve more in the way of treatment than training to conform quietly to the demands of poorly functioning homes and schools. Contemporary behavior therapy aspires to reshape the social environment, so that family and classroom foster children's social, emotional, and intellectual competence" (p. ix).

Current behavioral treatments are directed at

the family and/or peer group, and not just at the child. An increasing number of empirical studies support the notion that more effective treatment outcomes are achieved when treatment focuses on the child *and* on relevant family subsystems. For example, in treating conduct-disordered children, Dadds, Schwartz, and Sanders (1987) compared child management training alone with a combined child management training plus partner support training package, which focused on reducing marital conflict and improving communication and problem solving. Although there were no group differences immediately following treatment, the partner support condition was associated with better child and family outcomes at a 6-month follow-up for families in which there was marital discord.

These findings, and those from many other investigations to be discussed throughout this volume, all reinforce the notion that, to varying degrees, treatment goals should focus on building skills in the child and his or her social environment that will facilitate long-term adjustment, and not only on the elimination of problem behaviors and/or the reduction of subjective distress.

Multidisciplinary Perspective

The adoption of a systems viewpoint has also reinforced the need for a multidisciplinary perspective to the behavioral treatment of childhood disorders. As stated by Kanfer and Schefft (1988), "The systems approach implies the relevance of different knowledge bases, particularly the social and biological sciences. It is multidisciplinary, and effective treatment often requires familiarity with information that cuts across disciplines" (p. 19). The interlocking network of physical, behavioral, social, and learning difficulties that characterizes most childhood disorders necessitates a multidisciplinary approach to both treatment and prevention (e.g., Jason, Felner, Hess, & Moritsugo, 1987). The coordinated use of medication with the implementation of psychosocial interventions for children with attention deficit–hyperactivity disorders (e.g., Barkley, Chapter 2, this volume; Pelham & Murphy, 1986), autism (e.g., Schroeder, Gualtieri, & Van Bourgondien, 1986) or childhood depression (e.g., Kazdin, Chapter 4, this volume) illustrates this point, as does the integration of behavior management procedures with effective teaching strategies for learning-disabled children (e.g.,

Taylor, Chapter 9, this volume), or with required medical procedures in the case of chronically ill children (e.g., Johnson, 1988).

Developmental Emphasis

Early behavioral applications were decidedly insensitive to the need for incorporating developmental information into their assessments and treatments. This was due in part to their almost exclusive reliance on principles of learning such as positive reinforcement, negative reinforcement, extinction, and punishment, which were presumed to apply universally across all age groups and populations. Recent behavioral work has become increasingly sensitive to the developmental issues surrounding diagnosis (e.g., Peterson, Burbach, & Chaney, in press), assessment (e.g., Mash & Terdal, 1988b), and treatment (e.g., Harris & Ferrari, 1983; Kendall *et al.*, 1984; McMahon & Peters, 1985). Also, behavioral conceptualizations of child and family disturbance have increasingly attempted to describe, predict, and suggest ways to alter the progression of child and family disorders over time—for example, in the cases of antisocial children (e.g., Patterson, 1982), autistic children (e.g., Lovaas, 1987), or abusive families (e.g., Azar & Wolfe, Chapter 13, this volume). Although this increased developmental emphasis represents an exciting and needed direction in the field, the incorporation of developmental findings and principles into behavioral practice is a complex affair, and, to date, the degree to which it has been accomplished is rudimentary at best.

Part of the difficulty in achieving a clinical–developmental integration is in specifying precisely what such an integration would require. At its simplest level, and the one that has characterized behavioral approaches to date, a developmental emphasis involves some recognition that the child's age and gender may play a significant role in determining the methods of treatment that are likely to be most effective, and that normative information may facilitate clinical decision making by *suggesting* such things as what the boundaries for normal development are, when intervention is or is not required, and what constitute appropriate treatment goals. Normative information may also provide a basis for evaluating the clinical significance of change. For example, Kazdin, Esveldt-Dawson, French, and Unis (1987) found that even though a problem-solving skills training program was more effective than a relationship-oriented approach in treating conduct-disordered children, these children's adjustment was still outside the norms for a nonclinical population at a 1-year follow-up.

At a more complex level, a developmental emphasis would require the incorporation of developmental principles and findings into our conceptualizations of child and family psychopathology, such that treatments are sensitive not only to a child's age and sex but also to ongoing developmental *processes* as they unfold and interact with and within one or more dynamic and changing social systems. At this level, our treatments not only would be sensitive to developmental parameters, but would be *derived from* our knowledge of relevant developmental processes (e.g., early attachment; Peterson, 1987). However, the principles and processes that are deemed to be most important vary across developmental theories, and the empirical base describing these processes is just beginning to emerge from recent longitudinal investigations. In light of this, there is likely to be continued exploration of the boundaries for developmental applications in behavioral treatment. The establishment of a new journal, *Development and Psychopathology* (1989),* may help to provide the empirical base for some of these new interventions.

Within the field of developmental psychology, organizational–developmental positions that consider development as involving progressive reorganizations in response to changing environmental demands (e.g., Cicchetti & Braunwald, in press), and models that conceptualize early development in terms of the child's and family's coping reactions (e.g., Tronick & Gianino, 1986; Zeitlin, Williamson, & Rosenblatt, 1987), seem especially consistent with a behavioral perspective. Within these views, the origins for child and family disorders are seen as involving breakdowns in adaptational processes. For a variety of reasons, both the child and family fail to cope adequately with either normative or nonnormative events. These models consider adaptational outcomes in relation to the complex interaction between and among external events, perceptual and cognitive appraisals of such events, internal conditions (e.g., values, physical status, personality traits), external resources for coping (e.g., social support), decision-making processes, and preferred coping strategies.

*Published by Cambridge University Press.

Age

A common assumption in the treatment of children has been that interventions directed at younger children are likely to be more effective. In part, this is because younger children are presumed to be more malleable than older children, and because maladaptive patterns of behavior have had less time to become well established. Indirect support for this assumption comes from a meta-analysis carried out by Weisz, Weiss, Alicke, and Klotz (1987), who found a mean effect size of 0.92 for treatment studies with children aged 4–12, compared with a mean effect size of 0.58 for children aged 13–18. Although both common sense and clinical sensitivity would indicate that different approaches are required for children of different ages, few empirical studies have demonstrated specific behavioral procedures to be more or less effective with younger versus older children.

More importantly, the issue is not really one of differential effectiveness of the same treatment procedure at different ages, but rather the extent to which we can identify specific age-related developmental capacities and incorporate them into treatment in order to produce more effective outcomes. For example, at what ages can mental imagery be used in reducing fears, or can cognitive self-instruction be employed in regulating impulsive behavior? How might the application of a time-out procedure be different for 3- to 5-year-olds versus school-age children? How might explanations of procedures be adjusted to take into account a child's cognitive capabilities? In one study, Wurtele et al. (1987) found that participant modeling procedures were more effective than symbolic modeling procedures in teaching personal safety skills to kindergarten children, although this difference was not significant at a 6-week follow-up. These authors emphasized the importance of including active rehearsal in programs for young children, and noted that some prevention studies have found that young children may have difficulty understanding the abstract concepts involved in a cognitive approach.

Gender

Few studies have examined the general effectiveness of treatment as a function of the sex of the child. In a meta-analysis of treatment outcome studies with children, Casey and Berman (1985) found that the percentage of boys in the sample was negatively correlated with treatment outcome. However, in the Weisz, Weiss, Alicke, and Kotz (1987) study, the difference in the effect size for treatment studies with males (0.80) versus females (1.11) was not statistically significant. As is the case for age, the more important question is that of how information regarding sex differences in children might suggest different treatment strategies. To date, few behavioral treatment studies have directly addressed this question. However, many studies, have reported sex differences in the expression of childhood disorders that would suggest different courses of intervention for boys versus girls. To illustrate, a few of these studies are described below.

Moran and Eckenrode (1988) examined the relationship between social stress and depression in adolescent males and females. It was found that female early adolescents were significantly more affected by social stress than male agemates, but that older males and females were similarly affected. Other studies (e.g., Nolen-Hoecksema, Girgus, & Seligman, 1988) have shown peer popularity or rejection to be more highly correlated with depression in girls than in boys. Such findings suggest that interventions directed at enhancing peer relationships may be especially critical for young adolescent females.

Block and Gjerde (in press) found that the predictors at age 14 of depressive symptomatology at age 18 were quite different for boys versus girls. Fourteen-year-old girls subsequently expressing depressive tendencies were described as vulnerable, anxious, somaticizing, and showing generally low esteem. In contrast, 14-year-old boys who later showed high depressive symptomatology tended to show an early lack of concern for satisfying interpersonal relationships, and subsequent antisocial and hostile characteristics. Introspective concern with self-adequacy seemed to be a less salient tissue for boys. For boys, early intellective *in*competence predicted later depressive symptoms, whereas for girls early intellective competence predicted depressive symptomatology.

Block, Block, and Keyes (1988) found that the personality concomitants and antecedents of drug use differed somewhat as a function of gender and the drug used. At age 14, the use of marijuana was related to ego undercontrol,

while the use of harder drugs reflected an absence of ego resiliency, with undercontrol also being a contributing factor. For girls, adolescent drug use was related to both undercontrol and lower ego resiliency at 3 to 4 years of age; for boys, preschool undercontrol was a strong predictor of adolescent drug use, but there was no impact of ego resiliency. Early family environments that were characterized by an unstructured and laissez-faire atmosphere, with little pressure to achieve, were related to adolescent drug use in girls but not in boys. For boys only, drug use was related to an IQ decline from age 11 to 18.

There also may be sex differences in children's preferences for treatment agents. For example, Winter, Hicks, McVey, and Fox (1988) found that children's choices regarding the people (i.e., peers, parents, experts) they would consult for different types of problems varied as a function of the children's age and sex. Furthermore, in choosing consultants, females valued familiarity, whereas males valued expertise.

Although a number of the studies just described do not address treatment concerns directly, their findings do suggest that the focus of both treatment and prevention efforts needs to be different for boys and girls of different ages.

Norms

The uses of normative information in behavioral assessment have received extensive discussion (e.g., Edelbrock, 1984; Hartmann, Roper, & Bradford, 1979; Mash & Terdal, 1988b), and many of these uses parallel those for treatment. Briefly, such normative information is important in identifying problems, evaluating parental and teacher expectations, identifying difficulties that are likely to be chronic versus those that are common and transient, deciding when treatment is indicated, establishing treatment goals, suggesting different forms of treatment, and evaluating the clinical significance of change.

Normative information may also suggest possible goals for prevention studies. For example, Kline *et al.* (1987) reported that 15%–40% of junior and senior high school students may experience problems related to alcohol use, and found that measures of family functioning such as disengagement, poor communication, and family approval of alcohol were highly predictive of teenage drinking. Rubenstein, Heeren, Houssman, Rubin, and Stechler (1988) reported that 20% of the adolescents in their high school sample were suicidal, and virtually indistinguishable on all measures from their hospitalized suicidal sample. Of the high school sample of adolescents, 75% had received no therapeutic intervention in the year of their suicide attempt. Carlson, Asarnow, and Orbach (in press) reported that although rates of completed suicide were low prior to the age of 14 years, suicidal ideation and nonfatal suicide attempts were not uncommon in preadolescent children. Such ideation and nonfatal attempts have been noted prior to fatal suicides, and they sometimes occur in the context of depression. The normative information derived from the Rubenstein et al. and Carlson et al. studies suggests that there are significant numbers of unidentified and/or untreated suicidal adolescents in the public schools and that there is a need for early intervention and prevention programs in this area.

Recognition of Individual Differences

Behavioral approaches have shown an increasingly greater concern for individual differences in both inborn and/or acquired characteristics of both children and parents. Characteristics such as child temperament, personality disorder, or the generalized expectations of parents have been identified as possible mediators of treatment outcomes. In addition to basic biological differences (e.g., arousability, sensitivity to painful stimuli), background characteristics (e.g., intelligence, social status, or family configuration) may influence the child's and family's style of social problem solving, their attributional processes, and their reactions to specific types of treatment. For example, in the case of parents, generalized expectancies concerning what the future holds, referred to as "dispositional optimism or pessimism" (Scheier & Carver, 1985), could determine the success of behavioral parent training programs, to the extent that they influence the parental coping mechanisms that are invoked. Optimists focus on active problem solving in coping with stress, whereas pessimists focus on their feelings of distress, disengage from goal-directed activities, and give up their goals when obstacles intervene (Carver & Scheier, 1986). Maternal depression and anxiety, marital conflict, and

parenting self-esteem are examples of other important parent characteristics that have been shown to affect treatment outcomes.

One child characteristic that seems especially important for both treatment and prevention is intelligence, which appears to be an attenuating factor for many different kinds of problems. For example, Kandel et al. (1988) reported that in a group at high risk for criminality, seriously criminal cohort members evidenced lower IQ scores than cohort members with no criminal registration. Their interpretation was that within the high-risk group higher IQ led to school success and greater rewards, which in turn led to greater attachment to school and bonding to the conventional social order. Also, Schonfeld, Shaffer, O'Conner, and Portnoy (1988) have reported a direct link between deficiencies in cognitive functioning and conduct disorders in boys, and argue that the nature of this deficiency is one of acculturational learning broadly defined, rather than a narrowly focused social-cognitive deficit.

Clinical Diagnosis and Empirical Classification

Behavioral treatment approaches previously minimized the need for formal clinical diagnosis and/or assignment to groups based on empirical classification procedures. However, current work has gradually recognized the potential treatment benefits to be derived from the use of standardized diagnostic systems such as the revised third edition of the *Diagnostic and Statistical Manual of Mental Disorders* (DSM-III-R; American Psychiatric Association, 1987); multivariate classification strategies (e.g., Achenbach & McConaughy, 1987); and classification models based upon a developmental perspective (e.g., Garber, 1984). Such approaches are intended to supplement rather than to replace the individualized assessment information characteristic of a thorough behavioral analysis (Mash & Terdal, 1988b).

Many treatment programs have been instituted with poorly or globally defined groups of clients. Classification efforts focusing on the refinement and development of child and family subtypes have the potential for determining the types of treatments that are likely to be most effective for individuals and families showing particular constellations of characteristics. Categorization efforts thus far have attempted to subtype disturbed children on the basis of such dimensions as social withdrawal (e.g., Ledingham & Schwartzman, 1984), style of social information processing (e.g., Milich & Dodge, 1984), and peer social status (e.g., Lochman & Lampron, 1986).

The importance of differential diagnosis is also evident in some of the recent work on conduct-disordered children with and without hyperactivity. For example, Walker, Lahey, Hynd, and Frame (1987) found that children with DSM-III diagnoses of Conduct Disorder *and* Attention Deficit Disorder with Hyperactivity (ADD/H) showed a more diverse and serious pattern of antisocial behavior than children with a diagnosis of Conduct Disorder alone. Walker *et al.* (1987) suggest that when ADD/H (now classified in DSM-III-R as Attention Deficit–Hyperactivity Disorder, or ADHD) is present, the onset of conduct disorder is earlier, or the developmental progression from less serious to more serious antisocial behavior is more rapid.

Therapy as Clinical Decision Making

A number of writers have emphasized a clinical decision-making approach to behavioral intervention with disturbed children and families. In many ways, these viewpoints extend upon and formalize the everyday decision-making/problem-solving processes that are used by parents (e.g., Holden, 1985), teachers (Evans & Meyer, 1985), children (Urbain & Kendall, 1980), and adolescents (Tisdelle & St. Lawrence, 1988). The models presented by Kanfer and his associates (Kanfer & Busemeyer, 1982; Kanfer & Schefft, 1988), Evans and Meyer (1985), and Herbert (1981, 1987) have provided the most detailed accounts of this perspective thus far. In contrast to earlier behavioral approaches, which were concerned with the use of specific techniques derived from learning principles, decision-making approaches emphasize the flexible application and reapplication of these techniques over time. Decisions concerning the utilization of specific procedures are made within a broader clinical context that takes into account the phase of treatment; the cognitive activities and potential biases of the clinician (e.g., Kanfer, 1985; Tabachnik & Alloy, 1988); and the social context and values surrounding treatment. Although decision-making approaches are still developing, some of their more common features include an emphasis on the use of flexible

and ongoing decisional strategies (Kanfer & Busemeyer, 1982); a systems orientation (Evans, 1985); the development of generic strategies intended to optimize the effectiveness of more specific target-oriented tactics (Kanfer & Schefft, 1988); creation of a favorable therapeutic environment; identification and elaboration of decision points in treatment (e.g., seeking help, terminating treatment); client involvement in decision making; and a sensitivity to the varying needs of different treatment phases.

An emphasis on the flexible use of strategies as the medium in which behavioral techniques are to be applied is perhaps the major distinguishing feature of these approaches. As reflected in the following quotations, the concern is with process and not just with techniques. In describing their model of educational decision making, Evans and Meyer (1985) state:

> Our approach involves an extension and elaboration of standard behavior modification methods. It is a "second generation" of behavior modification in which the focus is no longer simply on the derivation of techniques from learning principles, but on how these principles may be most effectively adapted to the instructional situation and extended to deal with the total educational needs of the child. This volume is about educational programming, not just the design of isolated behavioral interventions; about clinical strategies and the values that influence clinical decisions, not just techniques that produce behavior change. (p. 2)

And Herbert (1987), in a practical manual for treating children's problems, states: "There is no one way of carrying out assessments and behavioural programmes. There is nothing preordained about the ordering of the steps suggested" (p. v).

Although the flexibility inherent in the approach being described here has some appeal, there are at present few guidelines concerning how clinical *strategies* are to be implemented from a behavioral perspective. As Kanfer and Schefft (1988) note, there are many descriptions of therapy methods (e.g., biofeedback, modeling, parent training, cognitive change methods, relationship enhancement methods), but "there are only a few books that offer clinicians a conceptually consistent framework for structuring each step of the change process, regardless of the specific treatment used" (p. xvi). Implicit in a probabilistic decision-making approach is the notion that there are many different ways to achieve the same treatment objective and that it is possible to identify alternative treatment goals and choices for the same client, depending on the circumstances. There is no proposed solution that can be rigidly adhered to, since each step in treatment is presumed to generate new information that requires ongoing adjustments in the program. In list of the many possible choices that are involved, further elaboration and empirical validation of the decision rules to be used in treatment are clearly needed, in much the same way that specific techniques have been described and validated. Although the desirability of such validation has been acknowledged, it remains to be seen whether systematic quantification of the complex judgmental process involved in treatment is even possible (Kanfer & Schefft, 1988).

Any decision rules in treatment are likely to be contextually specific, and there is a need to identify the parameters under which specific rules may or may not apply. I believe that the accumulated knowledge concerning specific childhood disorders represents a critical dimension for clinical decision making, and this view is reflected in the organization of the current volume. A host of other factors also contribute to the selection and sequencing of treatments for children and families, including characteristics of the family subsystems that are involved (e.g., child, parent–child, marital, sibling); the overt versus covert nature of the problem; characteristics of the primary agent of treatment (e.g., therapist, parent, child); the treatment setting (e.g., home vs. classroom); applicable psychological principles and techniques; and the therapist's orientation (Wolfe & Goldfried, 1988). Therapeutic decision making is an interactive process that incorporates information from each of these areas and more in formulating an overall intervention strategy.

Decision-making frameworks also emphasize the importance of adapting decision-making rules to the various phases of treatment (e.g., therapist's response to a missed first vs. a missed tenth treatment session), and several writers have delineated such phases. For example, Kanfer and Schefft (1988) describe seven phases of treatment: (1) role structuring and the creation of a therapeutic alliance; (2) developing a commitment for change; (3) the behavioral analysis; (4) negotiating treatment objectives and methods; (5) implementing treatment and maintaining motivation; (6) monitoring and evaluating progress; and (7) maintenance, generalization, and termination of treatment.

Herbert (1987) has presented three general phases. The first initial screening, involves explaining the therapist's role, identifying problems, identifying the child's and family's assets, specifying the desired outcomes, constructing a problem profile, teaching clients to think in antecedent–behavior–consequence (A-B-C) terms, and establishing problem priorities. The second phase, moving from data collection to problem formulation, includes specifying relevant situations, assessing the extent and severity of the problem, providing the client with appropriate materials, and determining the frequency and intensity of the problem. The third phase, intervention, involves planning treatment, formulating objectives, selecting procedures and methods, developing a treatment plan, working out practicalities of implementation, evaluating the plan, initiating the program, phasing out intervention, and conducting follow-up.

Conceptual models and decision guides to therapeutic choices within each of these phases for specific problems are just beginning to emerge in behaviorally oriented child and family interventions, and it is not possible in this brief introductory discussion to do justice to the many complexities involved. The interested reader may wish to consult Evans and Meyer (1985), Herbert (1987), and Kanfer and Schefft (1988) for particularly detailed accounts of how decisional models might be implemented in different types of therapeutic contexts.

Emphasis on Prevention

Behavioral approaches have shown a growing concern for both primary and secondary prevention programs for children and families (e.g., Rickel & Allen, 1987; Roberts & Peterson, 1984). Such programs have included interventions with high-risk populations directed at minimizing the likelihood of several known adverse outcomes (e.g., the sequelae associated with abusive family situations); interventions directed at reducing the future risk of specific problems, such as the abuse of alcohol or drugs; interventions designed to facilitate transitions and to minimize their negative impact (e.g., new school, foster placement); interventions intended to increase the child's and family's general adaptive competencies (e.g., early social skills training); and, interventions designed to increase ιne child's and family's overall health, safety, and physical well-being (Jason, 1980).

Some of the areas in which prevention efforts have been carried out include accident prevention (e.g., Christopherson, 1986; Mori & Peterson, 1986; Wright, Flagler, & Freidman, 1988), child abduction (e.g., Flanagan, 1986), sexual abuse (e.g., Harvey, Forehand, Brown, & Holmes, in press; Wurtele, Kast, & Kondrick, 1988; Wurtele et al., 1987), practicing safer sex (e.g., Gordon & Craver, 1988), and teaching emergency fire safety skills to blind children and adolescents (e.g., Jones, Sisson, & Van Hasselt, 1984).

In a recent prevention study, Markman, Floyd, Stanley, and Storaasli (1988) provided premarital intervention utilizing a cognitive–behavioral approach that included communication and problem-solving skills training, clarifying and sharing expectations, and sensual/sexual enhancement. Although there were no differences in self-reported relational quality at posttreatment, there were differences 1½ later that were maintained at 3 years. Markman *et al.* (1988) suggest that their premarital intervention served to reduce the declines in marital quality that occur in most relationships over time. Similar longitudinal studies involving premarital or prenatal interventions that focus on parent–child relationships and the prevention of possible child and family disorders are needed.

Although investigations of child and parent behaviors have typically employed causal models in which single factors are hypothesized to uniquely determine outcomes, a number of studies across a wide variety of domains, such as IQ (e.g., Sameroff, Seifer, Barocas, Zax, & Greenspan, 1987), behavior disorders (e.g., Rutter, Tizard, Yule, Graham, & Whitmore, 1976), and child abuse (e.g., Egeland, Jacobvitz, & Sroufe, 1988), have shown that combinations of risk factors provide the best prediction of outcome variables. In light of this, it follows that early prevention strategies should encompass multiple areas of child and family functioning. However, in considering a number of factors that have been shown to relate to child competence (e.g., maternal mental health, maternal anxiety, parental perspectives, maternal interactive behavior, maternal education, occupation of head of household, minority group status, family social support, family size, and stressful life events), Sameroff *et al.* (1987)

noted that there is a large difference between the number of variables affecting a child's competence and the number that can be changed by our interventions. Only stress is likely to change by itself (for better or for worse), and psychological interventions for the individual often come down to altering maternal interactive behavior and maternal anxiety.

The fact that early circumstances and early personality characteristics seem to foreshadow so many later childhood disorders reinforces the need for early intervention. For example, in a study by Block *et al.* (1988), personality dimensions such as undercontrol and ego resiliency at 3 and 4 years were predictive of adolescent drug use 10 or 11 years later. Lerner, Hertzog, Hooker, Hassibi, and Thomas (1988) analyzed data from the New York Longitudinal Study and found two separate dimensions of negative emotional behavior—aggression (aggression, undercompliance, disobedience) and affect (anxiety, dissatisfaction, depression)—both at ages 1–6 and at ages 7–12. There was a substantial amount of developmental stability in individual differences on these dimensions, with autoregressive coefficients of .97 and .91 for aggression and affect, respectively. Aggression at age 7–12 was the best predictor of adolescent adjustment problems. Affect did not predict social maladjustment independent of aggression. These and many other findings suggest that it is especially critical that interventions alter the course of early aggressive behavior, if later child maladjustment is to be prevented.

Cognition and Affect

Current behavioral interventions with children and families have given increased attention to cognitive and affective processes in treatment. The growth of cognitive-behavior therapy with children has continued unabated since the early 1970s, and this decade has also witnessed a greater concern for the affective components of child and family disorders, including child and maternal anxiety and depression, and the interactions between children and parents, peers, and spouses during emotionally charged social situations.

Cognitive-Behavior Therapy

There are now many descriptions of behavioral interventions that take both child (Harris,

Wong, & Keogh, 1985) and family (Foster & Robin, Chapter 14, this volume) cognitions into account. Although the long-term effectiveness of cognitive–behavioral interventions with children has yet to be determined (Lochman, 1988), and the concordance between cognitive–behavioral theory and cognitive-behavior therapy is not always clear (see Beidel & Turner, 1986, for a critique), a number of shared assumptions do seem to characterize current approaches:

1. Psychological disturbances are, in part, the result of faulty thought patterns that include distortions in both cognitive content (e.g., erroneous beliefs) and cognitive process (e.g., irrational thinking and faulty problem solving). A range of cognitive distortions and attributional biases have been identified in studies of depressed (e.g., Asarnow, Carlson, & Guthrie, 1987) and aggressive (Dodge, Chapter 6, this volume) children. For example, Lochman (1987) found that during social interaction, aggressive boys tended to minimize perceptions of their own aggressiveness and to perceive their partners as more aggressive than they were. There is also some evidence of the specificity of cognitive distortions across different child psychiatric populations (e.g., Siqueland, Kendall, Stoff, & Pollack, 1987). The presence of cognitive distortions in disturbed populations is suggestive, but there is a need for longitudinal studies that would establish causal relationships between early cognitive distortions and later childhood psychopathology.

2. A goal of treatment is to identify maladaptive cognitions and to replace them with more adaptive ones.

3. The manner in which children and parents think about their environment determines their reactions to it (Meichenbaum, 1977).

4. Cognitive appraisals need to be evaluated in the context of ongoing social interaction (Gottman & Levenson, 1986). For example, Lochman (1987) found that nonaggressive boys in the early stages of conflict tended to assume greater responsibility for aggression, and suggested that this attribution of greater self-blame might motivate their efforts to modulate the expression of hostility. In contrast, if aggressive boys blamed others, they might begin to justify their subsequent peer aggression and engage in conflict escalation.

5. Interventions need to take into account both the developmental continuities and

changes in children's cognitive appraisals over time (e.g., Lochman, 1988; Mahoney & Nezworski, 1985).

If cognitive approaches to treatment are to be systematically evaluated, it will also be important to improve our methodologies for assessing those cognitions that are being targeted for change—for example, attributional styles, cognitive errors, and irrational beliefs (e.g., Robins & Hinkley, in press)—and also to establish the relationship between cognitive changes and long-term behavioral outcomes.

Emotional Factors in Relationships

The progression in emphasis of behavioral treatments has been from behaviors, to cognitions, to emotions, to strategies that attempt to integrate information from all three areas. The more recent interest in affect has included the following, among other things:

1. The development and refinement of interventions for disturbances that are predominantly affective in nature, such as childhood and adolescent depression (e.g., Kazdin, Chapter 4, this volume) and anxiety (e.g., Barrios & O'Dell, Chapter 5, this volume; Last, 1988).

2. A concern for the way in which emotional processes (e.g., arousal) moderate the expression of other types of behavior, such as social aggression (e.g., Lochman, 1988).

3. A concern for the way in which the child's emotional status affects social-cognitive processes, such as attributions of causality (e.g., Dodge, Chapter 6, this volume).

4. A concern for the manner in which the emotional environment of the child's larger social system—for example, maternal depression (e.g., Patterson, 1982), maternal anxiety (e.g., Turner, Beidel, & Costello, 1987), maternal arousability (e.g., Wolfe & Bourdeau, 1987), or marital conflict (e.g., Gottman & Levenson, 1986)—affects the child's functioning.

The interest in affective processes has led to the development of such interventions as anger management and stress management training for both children and parents. It should be recognized that training (in child management, for example) that occurs under safe, sterile conditions may not simulate the real-life context in which these skills must be exercised. Parenting in relatively unhurried and unstressful circumstances, versus parenting in situations where the child or parent is stressed, irritable, or rushed, may require very different skills. Interventions are required that will generalize to the emotionally charged situations that often set the stage for family conflict (Foster & Robin, Chapter 14, this volume).

Population Specificity

Although behavioral interventions have maintained their idiographic focus on individuals, individual behaviors, and treatment individualization as the "categorical imperative" in therapy (Wolpe, 1986), there is an increasing sensitivity to the unique characteristics and treatment needs associated with particular populations of children and families (Mash & Terdal, 1988b). For example, Ollendick and Cerny (1981) stated that "although basic concepts of behavior therapy may not change across populations, the manner in which those concepts are applied to particular populations may vary considerably" (p. 3). While the latter part of this statement is undoubtedly true, it may well be that the basic concepts of behavior therapy (e.g., relevant principles, conceptual framework for treatment, model of childhood disorder) also vary from population to population. As will be illustrated throughout this volume, intervention models need to be directed at the specific child and family characteristics that have been shown to be important for different disorders. Training protocols for parents of retarded children (e.g., Baker, 1980), parents of defiant children (e.g., Barkley, 1987), or abusive parents (e.g., Azar & Wolfe, Chapter 13, this volume) are likely to be quite different, as are the social skills training programs employed with conduct-disordered (e.g., McMahon & Wells, Chapter 3, this volume) versus autistic (e.g., Newsom & Rincover, Chapter 8, this volume) children. An emphasis on populations rather than techniques in behavior therapy seems especially relevant for clinical practice, because, as noted by Kazdin (1988b, p. 3), "clinically, the major concern is not what the effects are of a particular treatment across a host of problem areas, but rather what the options are and what 'works' for a specific clinical problem."

CHILDHOOD DISORDERS

Consistent with a population-specific treatment focus, current behavioral approaches acknowledge the importance of considering specific clinical problems as representing constellations of child–environment symptoms that commonly occur together (Mash & Terdal, 1988b). Such an approach capitalizes on established bodies of knowledge concerning the expression, prevalence, etiology, prognosis, and prescribed treatments for specific problems, and attempts to use this information in order to design individualized programs of intervention.

The types of childhood problems that have most often been identified in clinical and empirical efforts at classification are reflected in the major headings and subheadings of DSM-III-R (American Psychiatric Association, 1987). These are presented in Tables 1-1 and 1-2. Although there are many unresolved conceptual and empirical issues surrounding all of the currently available classification system for childhood disorders (see Achenbach, 1985, or Mash & Terdal, 1988b, for a discussion of these issues), the DSM-III-R categories are useful in orienting the reader to the types of childhood disorders that will be discussed throughout this text. Further details concerning the descriptive characteristics for many of these problems are provided in the chapters that follow.

Within DSM-III-R, childhood disorders are grouped into two general classes with a number of subheadings for each. The first class, which is presented in Table 1-1, includes Developmental Disorders in which the primary disturbances are related to the acquisition of cognitive, language, motor, or social skills; it also includes Specific Developmental Disorders in which there is an inadequate development of specific academic, language, speech, or motor skills that is not due to demonstrable physical or neurological disorders, a Pervasive Developmental Disorder, Mental Retardation, or deficient educational opportunities.

The second class of childhood disorders, presented in Table 1-2, includes a variety of behavioral and emotional problems in which the child engages in actions that are disturbing to others and/or to himself or herself. Within DSM-III-R, several other categories are also appropriate for describing the problems of children and adolescents. These include Organic Mental Disorders; Psychoactive Substance

TABLE 1-1. DSM-III-R Categories for Developmental Disorders First Evident in Infancy, Childhood or Adolescence

Developmental Disorders

Mental Retardation
  Mild, Moderate, Severe, Profound, Unspecified
Pervasive Developmental Disorders
  Autistic Disorder
  Pervasive Developmental Disorder Not Otherwise Specified

Specific Developmental Disorders

Academic Skills Disorders
  Developmental Arithmetic Disorder
  Developmental Expressive Writing Disorder
  Developmental Reading Disorder
Language and Speech Disorders
  Developmental Articulation Disorder
  Developmental Expressive Language Disorder
  Developmental Receptive Language Disorder
Motor Skills Disorder
  Developmental Coordination Disorder
  Specific Developmental Disorder Not Otherwise Specified

Other Developmental Disorders

Developmental Disorder Not Otherwise Specified

TABLE 1-2. DSM-III-R Categories for Disorders First Evident in Infancy, Childhood, or Adolescence

Disruptive Behavior Disorders

Attention Deficit–Hyperactivity Disorder (ADHD)
Conduct Disorder
  Group
  Solitary Aggressive
  Undifferentiated
Oppositional Defiant Disorder

Anxiety Disorders of Childhood or Adolescence

Separation Anxiety Disorder
Avoidant Disorder of Childhood or Adolescence
Overanxious Disorder

Eating Disorders

Anorexia Nervosa
Bulimia Nervosa
Pica
Rumination Disorder of Infancy
Eating Disorder Not Otherwise Specified

Gender Identity Disorders

Gender Identity Disorder of Childhood
  Transsexualism
Gender Identity Disorder of Adolescence or Adulthood, Nontranssexual Type
Gender Identity Disorders Not Otherwise Specified

Tic Disorders

Tourette's Disorder
Chronic Motor or Vocal Tic Disorder
Transient Tic Disorder
Tic Disorder Not Otherwise Specified

Elimination Disorders

Functional Encopresis
Functional Enuresis

Speech Disorders Not Elsewhere Classified

Cluttering
Stuttering

Other Disorders of Infancy, Childhood, or Adolescence

Elective Mutism
Identity Disorder
Reactive Attachment Disorder of Infancy or Early Childhood
Stereotypy/Habit Disorder
Undifferentiated Attention Deficit Disorder

Abuse Disorders; Schizophrenia; Mood Disorders; Schizophreniform Disorder; Somatoform Disorders; Sexual Disorders; Adjustment Disorder; Psychological Factors Affecting Physical Condition; and Personality Disorders. For these problems, no special categories are given for children, because it is believed that the categories defined for adults are applicable across all ages.

Since the criteria for judging abnormality in children are to a large extent social in nature, what constitutes a problem, and the likelihood of referral for treatment, will depend greatly upon the norms and expectations of key individuals in the child's environment. Children are not accurate reporters of their own distress, especially when describing acting out types of difficulties such as social aggression. The discrepancy in what constitutes "normal" for different individuals is illustrated in the following extreme example reported by Donnellan (1988):

For two years the mother of a young man with autism would correct her son by saying, "Don't do that. It doesn't look normal." The son would stop the inappropriate behavior. Then she would add, "You want to look normal, don't you?" The son would say, "Yes."

Then one day, it occurred to the mother to ask her son, "Do you know what normal means?" "Yes," he said, and the mother was impressed. She pushed for his definition. He said, "It's the second button from the left on the washing machine."

NEED FOR EFFECTIVE INTERVENTIONS

In spite of frequently acknowledged inconsistencies in the manner in which childhood disorders are conceptualized, defined, diagnosed and assessed (Mash & Terdal, 1988a), epidemiological studies have been surprisingly consistent in their overall findings, reporting that between 5% and 15% of children and adolescents exhibit some type of emotional disturbance (e.g., U.S. Congress, Office of Technological Assessment, 1986). Although such incidence figures vary as a function of the child's age, sex, socioeconomic status, ethnicity, type of disorder, and geographical region, they do indicate a rather substantial need for effective child mental health services (Kazdin, 1988b). If preventive psychological and health-related services for high-risk populations, such as children who have been physically or sexually abused (e.g., Wolfe, 1988; Wolfe & Wolfe, 1988), infants with interactional disturbances (e.g., Peterson, 1987), learning-disabled youths (e.g., Interagency Committee on Learning Disabilities, 1987), chronically ill children (e.g., Johnson, 1988), or potential accident victims (e.g., Peterson & Mori, 1985), are also taken into account, this need would be considerably greater (e.g., Rickel & Allen, 1987).

It would also appear that most children who are in need of psychological services do not receive them (Kazdin, 1988b). Estimates indicate that only 20%–33% of children with clinically significant disturbances actually receive treatment (Knitzer, 1982), and that children with more severe dysfunctions may be slightly less likely to receive help (Sowder, 1975). On the other hand, the transient nature of many types of psychological disturbances during childhood would suggest that not all children exhibiting disorders are best served through the provision of specialized psychological services. For many children, community, school, and other health care services may adequately address the personal and social adjustment difficulties they are experiencing.

EFFECTIVENESS OF BEHAVIORAL TREATMENTS WITH CHILDREN

The growth, development, and effectiveness of behavioral treatments with children need to be considered in relation to empirical evidence regarding the efficacy of child therapies more generally, since it is not clear that behavioral procedures are more effective than alternative approaches (Ollendick, 1986). Kendall and Koehler (1985) have noted that there is comparatively little good controlled outcome research on any form of therapy for children, and Kazdin (1988b) states that "progress in the area of child treatment has been slow. There are many different treatments. . . . The great majority of these have not been shown to be effective. Even more regrettably, most of these techniques have never been carefully evaluated" (p. 9).

In an attempt to summarize research findings in this area, two meta-analytic studies are relevant. Casey and Berman (1985) included many descriptive features of treatment in their study and found significant durable treatment effects. Although these effects differed somewhat with the age of the child and the treatment method used, they were reliably greater than zero for most groups, most problems, and most methods. Type of treatment did not seem to make a difference in outcome. However, treatment differences when evident tended to favor the behavioral approaches.

Weisz, Weiss, Alicke, and Klotz (1987) also employed meta-analysis to investigate the effectiveness of psychotherapy with children and adolescents. They examined 108 well-designed outcome studies with participants aged 4–18. Findings showed that the average treated youngster was better adjusted than 79% of those not treated. These authors also found that behavioral treatments proved to be more effective than nonbehavioral treatments, regardless of the client's age, therapist's experience, or type of problem treated. The mean effect size for behavioral treatments was 0.88, compared with a mean effect size of 0.42 with nonbehavioral approaches. However, when comparisons were excluded in which the outcome measure was similar to the treatment procedure, this difference was nonsignificant. Weisz, Weiss, Alicke, and Klotz (1987) then reintroduced into their analysis those studies where inclusion of such outcome measures was deemed to be a fair test, and again found the behavioral procedures to be superior. These authors concluded that, overall, their findings make a case for the superiority of behavioral over nonbehavioral approaches in the treatment of children.

In considering the findings of the two meta-analyses that have been conducted, it is important to note that only studies involving group comparisons were included. This selection criterion probably underestimates the documented successes of behavioral procedures with children in studies employing single-subject research designs (e.g., Barlow & Hersen, 1984; Kazdin, 1982a). Since other forms of therapy have not received the rigorous empirical evaluations characteristic of the behavioral strategies in single-case studies, direct comparisons are not possible.

In general, the evaluation of treatment effectiveness with children is difficult because of the fact the comprehensive multifacted behavioral programs are more often the case than not, and it is difficult to evaluate the specific elements within such packages. Also, different aspects of the child's environment are involved in treatment, and changes may occur not only in the child, but also in other systems in which the child functions. These more general effects have not received sufficient attention. Moreover, in light of the rapid changes that take place during childhood, treatments that produce short-term effects are probably less meaningful in evaluating childhood disorders than they might be with adults (Kazdin, 1988b). Consequently, more studies of long-term adjustment following treatment are needed, although such studies are difficult to conduct (e.g., Mash & Terdal, 1980).

Finally, and perhaps most importantly, blanket claims concerning the general effectiveness of child and family behavior therapy make little sense. As Bornstein, Kazdin, and McIntyre (1985) have noted, "Behavior therapy is not a monolithic, monomethodological approach. The area incorporates widely diverse methods and techniques with differential efficacy. To draw reasonable conclusions, we must examine the individual literatures for each technique as it is applied to specific problems" (p. 837).

GENERAL FEATURES OF A BEHAVIORAL PERSPECTIVE

A behavioral perspective to the treatment of child and family disorders involves a problem-solving approach to treatment—one that is guided by a conceptual viewpoint and certain assumptions about child and family functioning, adheres to certain methodologies, and utilizes techniques that have empirical support and are evaluative, in the sense that they are self-corrective and constantly changing. Following a review of input from several major figures in the field of child behavior therapy and elsewhere, Ollendick (1986) concluded that the major points emphasized in definitions of a behavioral perspective to child treatment are these: "(1) principles of behavioral psychology, most notably principles of learning; (2) use of strategies or procedures that are methodologically sound and empirically validated; and (3) application of such principles and procedures to adjustment problems of children and adolescents" (p. 527).

It is now apparent that the principles upon which behavioral applications with children and families are based have become increasingly heterogeneous, and encompass elements from the areas of learning, developmental psychology, social psychology, cognitive psychology, and the neurosciences. The appropriateness of such a conceptual expansion has not gone uncontested (e.g., Levis, 1988), but the current state of affairs seems to be the result of a gradual 20-year evolution away from an ideological emphasis on principles of learning to a more pragmatic search for effective treatments, regardless of their theoretical origins (e.g., London, 1972). Although the development of a consistent conceptual framework is important for organizing behavioral research and practice with children and families, a framework that is based exclusively on the extrapolation of laboratory principles of learning to the clinical context seems far too narrow, and the current commitment in behavior therapy is more to empirical than to conceptual ties (e.g., Kazdin, 1988a). As noted by Ross (1981), "The touchstone of a behavioral technique is whether it has objective, observable referents that permit one to put its validity to empirical test—not whether it fits neatly into the procrustean bed of one theory or another" (p. 2).

Given that behavioral approaches are so thoroughly committed to a foundation of empiricism, the persistent contradictions between the vagaries of clinical practice and the rigor of laboratory–clinical research have been a continuing struggle. It is often the case that clinical realities require research-based treatment protocols to be altered or set aside in the interests of responsible practice. Some have suggested that the resolution of this paradox involves constructing a knowledge base for the therapeutic enterprise from *both* sources, although this is more easily said than done (Ross, 1981).

Interestingly, the epistemological alliance between clinic and laboratory, as reflected in a scientific orientation to the clinical situation, has been a double-edged sword for child and family behavior therapy. This alliance has embraced two premises, both of which have been challenged as providing a suitable model for practice.

Laboratory Research and Clinical Practice

The first premise is that behavioral clinical practice is based upon methods derived from empirically supported psychological principles including, but not restricted to, those derived from studies of learning. The validity of this premise has been challenged from within and from outside the field. For example, in his text on child behavior therapy, Ross (1981) stated, "It would be folly to assert that everything a behavior therapist does in the course of a treatment program, let alone in an individual treatment session, is explicitly and directly derived from empirically supported psychological principles" (p. 2). Similarly, Wachtel (1977), a psychoanalyst noted:

> The more sophisticated among behavior therapists recognize that there is often only a loose, analogic connection between the methods they use and the learning experiments on which the methods are purportedly based. The various models of learning derived from experimental research serve only as stimulating guiding metaphors for much of the clinical work in the behavioral tradition. . . . but they can be mischievous when the connection between clinic and laboratory is exaggerated or misconstrued for purposes of polemic or myth. (p. 8)

Wachtel went on:

> Behavior therapists are often effective precisely because they are *not* behavioristic in any narrowly construed way. In their clinical work they find it

necessary to make inferences and to concern themselves with what their patients want and feel as well as what they do. Most of the practicing behavior therapists with whom I have discussed this issue have acknowledged privately that what they actually do looks quite different from what one would expect from reading the literataure. (p. 8)

In support of this general view, findings from a survey by Morrow-Bradley and Elliot (1986) indicate that only a very small proportion of clinicians report using research findings as a basis for their practice.

Empiricism and Clinical Practice

The second premise is that behavioral clinical practice is closely wedded to empiricism, involving the collection of objective data prior to, during, and following treatment. However, guidelines for the uses of data collection in clinical practice are not readily available, and the extent to which such data collection facilitates meaningful outcomes in therapy has not been empirically documented. For example, Herbert (1987), in discussing his treatment manual for working with children and families, has stated:

> It [the manual] fails if it leads to some facile 'cookbook' application of techniques, or a mechanical insistence on numbers and measurement. The virtues of operationism can turn into quantiphrenia, which acts to the detriment of warm empathic interactions with parents and children. The emphasis on rigorous thinking and scientific assessment in this book is not meant to be at the expense of clinical art and sensitivity. 'Scientism,' a Pharasaical adherence to the letter rather than the spirit of the scientific method is to be avoided at all costs. (pp. 6–7)

PROTOTYPE FOR A BEHAVIORAL–SYSTEMS APPROACH

The basic model for the treatment of childhood disorders from a behavioral–systems perspective involves a blend of epistemological assumptions, psychological principles, research findings, specific techniques (literally hundreds), operational rules for the selection and implementation of these techniques in relation to specific problems and concerns, and the continuous evaluation of short- and long-term outcomes. Given the complexity of conditions and processes encompassed by this perspective, any single model that attempts to capture the complexities of therapeutic intervention will of necessity be an oversimplification. Although there are no necessary or defining characteristics of a behavioral–systems approach to intervention with children and families, the following conceptual, strategic, and procedural points, taken together, provide a general prototype for some of its more commonly occurring features.

Commitment to a Consistent Theoretical Framework

A behavioral perspective adheres to the general belief that good theory generates good practice, and that a consistent but flexible theoretical framework regarding behavior change principles and the nature and development of childhood disorders is needed to guide our intervention efforts (Bornstein & van den Pol, 1985; Herbert, 1987; Ollendick & Cerny, 1981). The epistemological framework for behavioral interventions has been changing and evolving. Although a general commitment to a variety of behavioral theories and models continues (e.g., instrumental, operant, respondent, drive reduction, mediational, observational/social learning, cognitive-behavior modification, applied behavior analysis), current approaches are perhaps best represented by a systems point of view. As noted by Kanfer and Scheff (1988), systems models provide the clinician with a perspective that will help to "guide decisions concerning what observations to make, what empirical data to select from various sciences, and at what systems level effective interventions should be conducted" (p. 19).

Within a general systems framework, the theoretical models being used to guide our treatments for disturbed children and families are becoming increasingly population-specific. For example, Patterson's (1986) performance model for social aggression suggests the importance of several molar and micro-level variables that are important to address in interventions with families of antisocial children. These include the extent to which the child is rejected or perceived as antisocial by others; the likelihood of the child's unprovoked negative behavior toward parents and siblings, and its duration; the extent to which parents monitor their children and spend time with them; and the parents' inept discipline, as reflected in their use of explosive forms of punishment, negative actions and reactions, and inconsistent/erratic behavior.

As will be illustrated throughout this volume, the theoretical models underlying various child and family problems suggest very different sets of variables that are important in treatment. The conceptual frameworks that guide our interventions with depressed, abused, mentally handicapped, chronically ill, or learning-disabled children are likely to be quite different from one population to another. Models of service delivery for handicapped children are typically based on teaching long-term management and coping strategies, whereas intervention models for many other childhood disorders are based on a curative or corrective view that we can go in, fix the problem, and then withdraw. It is becoming more apparent that many childhood disorders that were previously treated from a curative perspective (e.g., conduct disorders, ADHD) may be more appropriately considered from a chronic illness model of coping and long-term management (Barkley, Chapter 2, this volume; Kazdin, 1988b).

Conceptualization of Childhood Disorders

Although the number of child and family dysfunctions is large, a broad conceptualization of how such dysfunctions develop is needed in order to gather and organize information for assessment and treatment (Mash & Terdal, 1988b). What is observed and emphasized during assessment and treatment will depend on the therapist's assumptions concerning child and family development, including the importance ascribed to social context, sociocultural norms, and biological factors. In light of the multiple etiologies underlying any child or family problem, all of these determinants will be involved, although their relative emphasis may vary depending on the particular condition. Childhood disorders have been viewed as learned maladaptive habits, as physical defects and deficits, as failures in the adaptational process, and as system breakdowns. All of these views have some validity.

Most childhood disorders are best conceptualized as representing failures in adaptation on the part of the child and his or her social environment, and therapy is directed at corrective actions that will permit successful adaptation (or, in a preventive model, that will prevent or decrease the likelihood of future breakdowns). From a behavioral–systems perspective, childhood disorders are viewed as representing exaggerations, insufficiencies, handicapping combinations, situationally inappropriate behaviors, or developmentally atypical expressions of behavior that are common to all children at certain ages. For the most part, dysfunction is a matter of quantititative rather than qualitative variation in the expression of behavior, and the principles underlying the development and modification of normal and abnormal behaviors are presumed to be the same. As noted, there is also an increasing acceptance of the view of childhood problems as constellations of behavior, and not simply as isolated responses (Mash & Terdal, 1988b).

Importance of Reciprocal Influences

A behavioral–systems perspective recognizes the importance of the reciprocal influences that occur both within and between individuals (Bandura, 1986) Numerous studies have demonstrated reciprocity in parent–child and marital interactions (e.g., Houts, Shutty, & Emery, 1985; Patterson, 1982). At a more molar level, adult reactions are affected by the age, gender, physical attractiveness, and temperament of the child (Mash, 1984). Child characteristics will also influence parental disciplinary practices. For example, mothers may exhibit more helping and rewarding behavior toward an anxious child, and more controlling and restrictive behavior toward a conduct problem or hyperactive child. Unidirectional models of intervention that fail to recognize the reciprocal social influences that characterize most child and family disorders are not likely to be very effective.

Empirically Based Treatment and Clinical Sensitivity

In a relative sense, treatment from a behavioral perspective is based on empirical data and well-documented theories, rather than on an accumulation of clinical folklore and experience. As much as possible, the description and treatment of child and family disorders employ objectively defined terms and measurable operations, and are based on a quantitative analysis of actual performance (e.g., behavioral, cognitive, physiological), including a description of proximal and distal antecedent and consequent

events. Many writers have adopted the view that the analytic approach and empirical methodology that characterize behavioral interventions are far more important dimensions than the model of behavior change ascribed to.

In spite of the acknowledged importance of an empirical perspective, there is a growing appreciation of some of the difficulties inherent in such an approach. For example, in describing their systems-oriented approach, Kanfer and Shefft (1988) state:

> While parameters and details may vary across clients and treatment settings, the approach presented here has wide applicability. It presumes that an empirical knowledge base is indispensable. But there is simply not sufficient scientific knowledge available at present (or may never be) to guide a therapist's action in all detail. Therefore, the empirical knowledge base has to be supplemented by extrapolations from personal experience, subjective judgments, and the realities of the present situation. But whenever strategies and tactics derived from scientific principles *are* available, intuition and subjectivity should never be substituted for them. (pp xvii–xviii)

Thus, empirically grounded, behavioral intervention with children and families also constitutes a craft—one that involves "a subtle amalgam of art and applied science," and that requires careful study and supervised practice (Herbert, 1987, p. 6).

Combined Emphasis on Contemporaneous and Distal Controlling Events

From a behavioral–systems perspective, controlling variables that are contemporaneous and present in the immediate situation have been given special emphasis in assessment and treatment. This is in contrast to orientations that focus on historical or temporally remote events. This emphasis on contemporaneous influences reflects the view that such events are likely to be more accessible and therefore more easily incorporated into our change efforts. This is especially so when a primary emphasis is placed on external environmental events, as was the case with many of the early behavioral approaches. However, with the growing acceptance of cognitive mediators in behavior therapy, symbolic processes give historical events contemporaneous representation, and any designation of what is considered contemporaneous and what is not becomes arbitrary and often difficult to make.

In addition, numerous studies have established the important influence of extrasituational and temporally remote events on family functioning. External stressors such as marital discord (e.g., O'Leary, 1984b) or negative interactions with neighbors or friends (e.g. Wahler, 1980) may have direct effects on a mother's immediate reactions to her child's behavior. Behavioral intervention programs that do not take these and other such events within the child's larger social system into account have not proved to be very effective (Patterson, 1982). The combined emphasis on proximal and distal, micro-level and molar controlling events is evident in the intervention strategies presented throughout this volume.

Important Role of Assessment

Behavioral assessment and behavioral intervention are viewed as complementary and interactive. Initial invervention follows from a systematic behavioral or functional analysis that considers the different system parameters and levels that are likely to be important for a particular child or family. Behavioral analyses have typically involved a single-level and linear consideration of antecedents, behaviors, and consequences (A-B-C). Although this approach continues to have enormous heuristic value in organizing information for intervention, it is limited in describing complex system relationships and the possible organizing role of cognitions and plans. Grawe and his coworkers (as described in Kanfer & Schefft, 1988, pp. 181–182) have presented an adaptation of the A-B-C model, referred to as "vertical" or "hierarchical" behavioral analysis. In this model, behavior is seen as being organized at hierarchical levels; the top of the hierarchy consists of themes, or beliefs and motives, that are related to specific responses in a situation. Hierarchical behavioral analysis appears to be a promising approach to organizing assessment information within a behavioral–systems perspective.

Terdal and I (Mash & Terdal, 1981b, 1988b) have described child and family behavior assessment as involving a range of deliberate problem-solving strategies for understanding both disturbed and nondisturbed children and their social systems, including their families and peer groups. These strategies employ a flexible and ongoing process of hypothesis testing regarding the nature of the problem, its causes, likely outcomes in the absence of intervention, and the anticipated effects of various treatments. Such hypothesis testing should be based upon an understanding of the general theories, principles, and techniques of psychological assessment (e.g., Anastasi, 1988; Cronbach, 1984; Sattler, 1988); information concerning normal child and family development (e.g., Mussen, 1983); and knowledge of populations of children and families showing similar types of problems, including information about incidence, prevalence, developmental characteristics, biological factors, and system parameters (e.g, Achenbach, 1982; Quay and Werry, 1986).

We (Mash & Terdal, 1988b) have described a number of commonly occurring conceptual, strategic, and procedural features of behavioral assessment that, for the most part, parallel those associated with behavioral treatment. These include the following:

1. A conceptualization of personality and abnormal behavior that considers thoughts, feelings, and behaviors in specific situations, rather than as manifestations of global underlying traits or dispositions.
2. An idiographic and individualized focus on the child and family, rather than one that describes individuals in relation to group norms.
3. An emphasis on the importance of situational influences on behavior and the need to assess them in formulating effective treatments.
4. A recognition of the changes over time that often characterize child and family behavior.
5. A systems-oriented approach directed at describing and understanding the characteristics of children and families; the contexts in which these characteristics are expressed; and the structural organizations and functional relationships that exist between situations and behaviors, thoughts, and emotions.
6. An emphasis on contemporary controlling variables, in addition to the role of historical and more distal setting events.
7. A view of behaviors, cognitions, and affects as direct samples of the domains of interest, rather than as signs of some underlying or remote causes.
8. A focus on assessment information that is directly relevant to treatment, including

such activities as pinpointing goals; selecting targets for intervention; choosing, designing, or implementing interventions; and evaluating therapy outcomes.

9. A reliance on a multimethod approach involving the flexible use of different informants and a variety of procedures, including observations, interviews, and questionnaires.
10. The use of a relatively low level of inference in interpreting assessment findings.
11. An ongoing and self-evaluating approach to assessment, with the need for further assessment being dictated, in part, by the efficacy of methods in facilitating desired treatment outcomes.
12. The utilization of empirically validated assessment procedures.

The interested reader may wish to consult a number of comprehensive books and book chapters that review the underlying conceptual models and methods characteristic of behavioral assessment in general (e.g., Ciminero, Calhoun, & Adams, 1986; Hersen & Bellack, 1981; Mash & Hunsley, in press; Nelson & Hayes, 1986), and child and family behavioral assessment in particular (e.g., Bornstein & van den Pol, 1985; Mash & Terdal, 1981a, 1988a, in press; Ollendick & Hersen, 1984).

Continuous Evaluation of Outcomes

Although it is recognized that clinical practice dictates a priority on the discovery of a solution rather than the demonstration of a functional relation between treatment and performance, accountability has and continues to be a central characteristic of behavioral interventions with children and families. Single-subject designs, which are presumed to be more applicable in the clinical context, have been developed to document the relation between treatment and outcome (e.g., Barlow & Hersen, 1984).

Idiographic Emphasis

A behavioral–systems perspective recognizes that within groups of children showing common symptom clusters, variation among individuals is the norm. Individuals with the same disorder may have different etiologies that are represented both in past events and in current controlling conditions. For example, with hyperactivity, the etiology may involve organicity or parental overstimulation. One major implication for intervention is that different treatments

may be required for the same phenotypic expression of a disorder. Idiographic analyses permit this type of individualization of treatments for children within particular diagnostic categories.

Importance of Contextual Events

Behavioral approaches are especially sensitive to the impact of the situational context on behavior and the need to incorporate contextual information into treatment. Many studies have shown how context moderates the expression not only of behavior, but of cognitions and affects as well. For example, Asarnow et al. (1987) found that the negative biases of aged 8–13 children was not generalized across all situational contexts. Similarly, with aggressive boys, Lochman (1987) found that attributional processes were distorted only when a child was interacting with another boy who had a different behavioral status (e.g., nonaggressive with aggressive vs. aggressive with aggressive, or nonaggressive with nonagressive), and who was typically much more aggressive or nonaggressive than himself. Interventions need to be sensitive to these types of situational variations.

Within a systems framework for intervention, it is also important to identify the complex interrelationships between settings. For example, Pettit, Dodge, and Brown (1988) found that several dimensions of family experience were predictive of classroom social competence and problem solving. However, although early family experience with peers had a direct impact on peer outcomes, the impact of exposure to maternal values and expectations on social competence with peers was mediated by social problem-solving skills. Such findings suggest the need to consider family relationship factors when designing preventive interventions in the area of classroom social competence.

Context also moderates the effectiveness of treatment, as, for example, when intervention takes place in the home versus the classroom. Expectations and responses of family members, teachers, and the child's peers all interact in determining the expression of childhood disorders as well as the impact of various treatment strategies.

Family Involvement in Treatment

The behavioral–systems view often means that the child, family members, and other significant individuals will be actively involved in all phases of treatment. Koocher and Pedulla (1977) found that 94% of therapists reported seeing both parent and child, and 23% reported teacher involvement as well. Early behavioral views promoted the idea that the most effective change agents would be individuals in the child's environment, such as parents and teachers (Tharp & Wetzel, 1969). Although the "child as target" focus of this viewpoint is somewhat antagonistic to current systems formulations, it was seen as both conceptually relevant and economical, and it spawned a rich tradition in child behavior therapy of employing parents (e.g., Dangel & Polster, 1984), teachers (e.g., Alberto & Troutman, 1982), and peers (e.g., Strain, 1981) as change agents.

The assumption that individuals in the child's natural environment are likely to be the most effective change agents has not been systematically tested. However, the meta-analysis by Weisz, Weiss, Alicke, and Klotz (1987) suggested an interaction between the agent of intervention and the nature of the child's problem. It was found that paraprofessionals and graduate students were equally effective as therapists in the treatment of undercontrolled types of problems, such as aggression and impulsivity, but that professionals were more effective in treating disorders of overcontrol, such as phobias and shyness. Also, graduate students and paraprofessionals were more effective with younger than with older children, whereas this was not the case for professionals. These findings suggest that behavioral models of parent training may have differential applicability, depending on the nature of the disorder and the age of the child, although many other factors would also need to be considered in determining the primary agent of change.

A number of additional concerns must be dealt with when involving parents as therapists for their own children. As noted by Dunst and Trivette (in press), "The relationships between family resources, well-being, and adherence to prescribed regimens would indicate that before parents are asked to carry out child-level interventions, efforts to meet more basic family needs must be made in order for parents to have the time, energy, and personal investment to work with their own children in an educational or therapeutic capacity" (p. 41).

Importance of Cognitive Processes

Current practices emphasize that understanding the cognitive processes of both the child and significant others is essential to understanding and treating childhood disorders. Behavioral–systems interventions are based on developing new behaviors and response strategies, and this type of learning is mediated by the beliefs, perceptions, expectations, and attributions of children and their families (Herbert, 1987).

There has been an increasing emphasis on the role of social cognition in both the developmental and clinical literatures (e.g., Miller, 1988). In examining the link between family experience, social problem-solving skills, and children's social competence, Pettit et al. (1988) found that the strongest predictors of social competence were mothers' biased expectations (attributions of hostile intent). These authors suggest a developmental path running from maternal attitudes, values, and expectations to child social cognition to child social competence with peers. There seems to be a covert but pervasive influence of maternal attitudes, values, and expectations, and through verbal means mothers may exert a more subtle influence on their children than through other direct forms of control, such as harsh discipline. Pettit et al. (1988) hypothesize that through exposure to deviant maternal values, a child learns to process social information in a deviant way when interacting with peers, and then comes to be perceived by teachers and peers as socially incompetent. Putallaz (1987) reported that mothers' social values, as expressed in their advised solutions to a hypothetical situation involving their children being teased, were predictive of children's social status in the classroom. However, solutions involving other social situations, such as entry into a new group, were not predictive. Such findings reinforce the need for a contextually specific approach to cognitive as well as behavioral interventions.

Development of Operational Rules for Implementing Treatment

The availability of operational rules for interpreting principles, in formulating assessment and treatment strategies, is limited. However, the form that such rules might take has been suggested by several investigators. For example, in the context of early intervention, Dunst et al. (in press, pp. 2–3) have described four general operating rules, each specifying a pragmatic relationship between an outcome and the action that has the greatest probability of achieving a desired goal:

1. "To promote positive child, parent, and family functioning, base intervention efforts on family-identified needs, aspirations, and personal projects."
2. "To enhance successful efforts toward meeting needs, use existing family functioning style (strengths and capabilities) as a basis for promoting the family's ability to mobilize resources."
3. "To insure the availability and adequacy of resources for meeting needs, place major emphasis on strengthening the family's personal social network as well as promoting utilization of untapped but potential sources of informal aid and assistance."
4. "To enhance a family's ability to become more self-sustaining with respect to meeting their needs, employ helping behaviors that promote the family's acquisition and use of competencies and skills necessary to mobilize and secure resources."

In the context of educational interventions for handicapped learners, Evans, Meyer, Derer, and Hanashiro (1985) suggest that because of the limited availability of educational programming time in proportion to the learning needs of handicapped children, and because most excess behaviors can be effectively decreased by meeting educational needs rather than by behavior reduction procedures, "direct programming to modify a behavior should be considered a priority *only when unavoidable*" (p. 45).

Consideration of the Role of Biological Processes

The role of biologial processes, including basic maturational changes, has received increasing attention in behavioral approaches to the treatment of childhood disorders. Studies of the effects of endocrine products, metabolites, neurotransmitters, and genetic structures on behavioral predispositions have necessitated a reappraisal of several learning-based theories and treatment approaches (e.g., Kanfer & Schefft, 1988; O'Leary & Wilson, 1987). Genetically determined constitutional factors provide the medium in which psychological principles operate to produce both adaptive and maladaptive behavior. Biological determinants, biochemical disorders, or physical diseases frequently set limits on the skills a given child or family can learn; in turn, these limits influence decisions concerning the type of treatment that is likely to be most effective (Ross, 1981).

The possible involvement of organic illness in many forms of childhood disorder necessitates an active collaboration with medical specialists. Strayhorn (1987) has presented several general guidelines in assessing the possibility of organic illness (e.g., toxic, traumatic, infectious, idiopathic, neoplastic, nutritional, collagen vascular/autoimmune, congenital/hereditary, endocrine, vascular, metabolic, and degenerative). An organic contribution is seen as more likely when functioning is grossly impaired, when there is a loss of previous ability in intellectual functioning, when explanations based on other grounds are not readily available, and when there are physical complaints and symptoms in addition to psychological ones.

Current behavioral practices are based upon a wide net of research findings, including those emanating from the biological sciences. This has led to the identification of important organismic variables and to information concerning the manner in which such variables interact with environmental factors in determining behavioral outcomes. For example, the relationship between child temperament and the quality of early parent–child relationships may be mediated by social class, suggesting that early intervention with difficult infants may be more critical for low-socioeconomic-status families. Some longitudinal studies (e.g., Cohen, Velez, & Brook, in press), have found that pre- and perinatal problems, as well as illnesses, accidents, and hospitalizations in early childhood, pose a biological risk for future psychopathology in children. Interestingly, these studies have tended to find that biological risk factors such as perinatal and early somatic problems are nonspecific, placing a child at increased risk for all kinds of problems, including both externalizing and internalizing disorders as well as substance abuse. Implicit in such findings is the notion that experiential factors in the family may mediate the expression of the disorder and should therefore be targeted for intervention.

Concern for Treatment Generalization

Within a behavioral–systems framework, choices concerning the target of intervention, the agent of intervention, the setting in which intervention occurs, and the nature of the intervention should be based upon one's predictions concerning the generalizability of effects that can be achieved by intervening in one aspect of the family system versus another. The intent is to make choices that will maximize the impact of treatment throughout the relevant systems in which the child functions. Treatment generalization has been conceptualized as occurring across settings (e.g., clinic to home), across responses and response systems (e.g., from targeted to untargeted behaviors), and over time (e.g., durable effects). Findings from numerous investigations indicate that unless systematic steps are taken in treatment to promote generalization, it will not occur, and several writers have offered suggestions as to how generalization might be enhanced (e.g., Stokes & Baer, 1977). These suggestions have included the use of cognitive-behavior therapy procedures, the enlistment of mediators in the child's natural environment, the use of multicomponent treatment strategies that focus on several family subsystems (e.g., parent–child and marital), the employment of self-management programs, and the use of specific operant procedures such as fading. The emphasis on cognitive processes and self-control in treatment has been viewed as one way of increasing generalization, by providing internal regulators that will continue to operate across settings and time in the absence of external controls. However, to date, there is little evidence to support the notion that cognitive therapies do in fact produce more general or more durable treatment effects with children and families, relative to other forms of treatment.

Although follow-up studies have become increasingly common in the behavioral literature, there is still a great need for studies that evaluate the long-term impact of child and family interventions. Weisz, Weiss, Alicke, and Klotz (1987) reported the effects of child treatment to be durable, as reflected in average effect sizes of 0.79 and 0.93 at termination of treatment and follow-up, respectively. However, the follow-up periods in the studies that were included in their analysis were slightly less than 6 months on average. Complex issues surrounding the choice of follow-up intervals remain (e.g., Mash & Terdal, 1980), and the rapid developmental changes that characterize child and adolescent development make the assessment of long-term outcomes that much more difficult. A few investigators have suggested the possibility

of "sleeper effects" in treatment; that is, performance at follow-up may actually be better than that immediately following treatment. This improvement has been hypothesized to be a function of the cumulative benefits derived from the continuing use of skills that were learned during treatment and the positive impact that such skills might have on the child's social system. Further investigation of possible "sleeper effects" is needed, and in doing so, it will, be important to consider such posttreatment improvements against a baseline of growing maturity.

Several studies have found that treatments focusing on multiple family and school subsystems tend to produce more durable outcomes. For example, Dadds et al. (1987) found that child management training alone resulted in 6-month relapses in child problems, parent reports of difficulties, and marital dissatisfaction in families with marital discord. However, such relapses were less prevalent in families where child management training had been supplemented with partner support training in conflict resolution, communication, and problem solving. Epstein, Wing, Koeske, and Valoski (1987) found that at a 5-year follow-up of their diet management program, the children who had received combined parent and child training showed significantly greater weight reduction when compared to children who had been trained without their parents, or to controls. One third of the children in the parent and child training group were within 20% of normal weight, in comparison with only 5% of the controls.

Interest in Treatment Processes

A growing recognition of the importance of the general therapeutic milieu in moderating the effectiveness of behavioral techniques has resulted in a greater interest in understanding treatment processes (e.g., resistance, treatment termination). Although most forms of behavioral intervention require a cooperative therapeutic relationship with children, parents, and teachers, it is not always the case that these individuals are motivated for change (e.g., Chamberlain, Patterson, Reid, Kavanagh, & Forgatch, 1984). Consequently, there is a need for special strategies designed to increase client involvement in order to reduce the likelihood that premature intervention will lead to resistance and premature treatment termination (e.g., Ellis, 1985).

Kanfer and Schefft (1988) have described resistance and treatment noncompliance as representing a discrepancy between the client's behavior and the therapist's expectations. They also note that there are many sources of noncompliance that need to be examined, including such things as client anxieties and self-doubts (e.g., fear of the future, giving up a known life pattern for a new and possible worse state); client skill deficits; insufficient therapeutic structure or guidance; no motivation for change, due to secondary gain from symptoms; a countertherapeutic support network; and the client's lack of confidence in his or her ability to carry out therapeutic assignments. Understanding the different sources of therapeutic noncompliance will lead to different strategies for dealing with it in treatment.

Premature treatment termination has also been a concern in behavioral work with children and families. In the review of child treatment outcome studies conducted by Weisz, Weiss, Alicke, and Klotz (1987), the mean number of therapy sessions was 9.5. However, their findings supported the idea that more intensive forms of treatment may produce more beneficial effects. In light of this, understanding the factors surrounding treatment dropout and developing methods to minimize them are priorities in behavioral intervention. In a study by Weisz, Weiss, and Langmeyer (1987), dropouts and continuers in child psychotherapy were compared on a variety of child and family characteristics that included child demographic variables, therapist variables, child problems, and parent perception variables. Surprisingly, the two groups were virtually indistinguishable on the basis of these characteristics. Weisz, Weiss, and Langmeyer (1987) suggested that source of referral and caretaker symptomatology—factors that were not included in their study—may be more important factors in determining whether or not families drop out of treatment.

Emphasis on Self-Regulation, Self-Management, and Self-Control

A number of behavioral models for intervention have emphasized the importance of examining self-regulatory systems as the basis for treatment (e.g., Kanfer & Schefft, 1988; Karoly, 1981). Self-initiated, self-maintained, and self-corrective internal processes, including self-observation, self-monitoring, self-rein-forcement, imaging, planning, and decision making, have the potential for maintaining behavior over protracted periods of time, and by doing so can decrease the individual's dependence on environmental and biological factors. A self-management approach seems especially relevant for children and families, in that many of the disorders to be discussed in this volume represent a failure to develop (or a breakdown in) self-regulatory skills. Recent early-intervention models that have emphasized family needs assessment and concepts such as empowerment are consistent with the self-regulatory approach (e.g., Dunst, in press).

Self-management therapies are directed at teaching such processes as setting goals, evaluating norms and standards, monitoring and evaluating problem situations, planning, solving problems, examining choices, anticipating outcomes, employing self-reward and self-punishment, and understanding the relationships between cognitions and behavior. Appropriate use of these strategies assists the child and family in developing control over their behavior; over certain physiological reactions, such as anxiety, anger, and the experience of pain; and over-cognitive or imaginally mediated reactions, such as intrusive thoughts, negative self-appraisals, or undesirable urges (Kanfer & Schefft, 1988). Achieving such control is intended to make the child and family more proactive in their behavior, so that they are able to anticipate potentially conflictual situations, and have available a variety of mechanisms permitting them to cope effectively.

Concern for Ethical Standards

Criticism of some of the early behavior therapy procedures, especially the use of aversive controls, has led to a special concern for the development of ethical standards for behavioral intervention. Minimum ethical standards for practice have been presented and include such things as selecting treatment goals and procedures that are in the best interests of the client; making sure that client participation is active and voluntary; keeping records that document the effectiveness of treatments in achieving its objectives; protecting the confidentiality of the therapeutic relationship; and insuring the qualifications and competencies of the therapist (e.g., MacDonald, 1986). Guidelines for the responsible use of aversive procedures in behavioral intervention have also been developed (Favell et al., 1982), although the use of such tactics continues to be heatedly debated (see Newsom & Rincover, Chapter 8, this volume, for a discussion).

Use of Specific Techniques and Technology

The specific techniques that have been used in behavioral interventions for children and families are numerous; they are described in great detail throughout the chapters of this volume in relation to specific disorders. Some of the more commonly utilized general techniques are parent training; modeling and role playing; desensitization and its many variants; self-control and self-management methods; basic operant techniques, such as differential reinforcement, shaping, fading, punishment, and time out; cognitive change procedures, such as stress inoculation and teaching coping strategies; social skills training; token systems; behavioral contracting; and environmental engineering.

Although, as noted earlier, flexibility is required in the clinical context, efforts to describe behavioral programs in as precise and replicable a fashion as possible have resulted in the availability of many useful assessment and intervention technologies. These include detailed therapists' manuals for the assessment and treatment of a variety of child and family disorders (e.g., Barkley, 1987; Blechman, 1985; Evans & Meyer, 1985; Fleischman, Horne, & Arthur, 1983; Forehand & McMahon, 1981; Herbert, 1987; Kendall & Braswell, 1985); training materials and handouts for parents (e.g., Bernal & North, 1978); videotaped sequences of parent–child interaction (e.g., Wolfe & LaRose, 1986); computer simulations for training (e.g., Lambert, 1987); programs for data collection and treatment implementation utilizing microprocessors (e.g., Romancyzk, 1986); and filmed presentations of treatment programs (e.g., Houts, Whelan, & Peterson, 1987). Such technology is not presumed to be a substitute for sound clinical decision making, but it does permit the training, transmission, and further evaluation of empirically well-documented techniques and procedures. The availability of these technologies is viewed as an important distinguishing characteristic of the behavioral–systems approach to intervention.

Use of Multiple Indicators to Assess Treatment Outcomes

A behavioral–systems perspective recognizes the need to use multiple indicators to assess the impact of treatment. Such indicators include reduction in symptoms; improvements in adjustment at home, at school, or in the community; increases in self-reported happiness; evaluations of relatives and friends that things are better; and prevention of possible further deterioration in the child's and family's adjustment. A concern for the clinical significance of therapeutic change has increased. Not only is it important to demonstrate behavioral changes, but it is essential that the magnitude and quality of these changes place the child and family within the boundaries of developmental, sociocultural, and personal norms for adjustment.

Concern for Consumer Satisfaction and the Acceptability of Treatments

A number of studies have examined the acceptability to consumers of a variety of behavioral interventions, and the possible factors mediating such acceptance (e.g., Elliott, 1988; Kazdin, 1981, 1984; LeBow, 1982; McMahon & Forehand, 1983; Witt & Elliott, 1986). For example, Tarnowski, Kelly, and Mendlowitz (1987) examined pediatric nurses' acceptability ratings of six behavioral interventions. Accelerative interventions were rated as more acceptable than reductive treatments, and treatment acceptability varied as a function of behavior problem severity. The medical severity of the child's condition did not significantly influence ratings. Furey and Basili (in press) attempted to predict consumer satisfaction in parent training for noncompliant children, and noted the importance of predicting what consumer satisfaction is going to be in advance, rather than determining what satisfaction is after the fact. Although clients' rights to self-determination, ethical and legal considerations, and common sense would certainly dictate the use of client-preferred treatment procedures, it has also been assumed that procedures that are perceived as objectionable or offensive by children and families will not be very effective, and that procedures that are preferred over others are likely to be more effective. However, the relationships between acceptability and outcome are just beginning to be empirically investigated.

Need to Consider Cultural Factors in Assessment and Treatment

In light of the family's central importance as a social unit and transmitter of sociocultural values, it is especially critical that interventions concerned with child behavior, child rearing, and other family issues establish some degree of congruence between the therapy program and the sociocultural milieu in which it is carried out. Often the rules that govern behavior and expectations for children are more explicit than those describing social intercourse among adults. A consideration of treatment in relation to specific values, norms, expectations, and prescribed behaviors for different social classes within cultures; across families that vary in their religious belief systems; for new immigrants; and across cultures is essential. Although behavioral procedures have certainly been applied across many different cultures, cross-cultural assessment and treatment (Westermeyer, 1987) have received only minimal attention to date.

SUMMARY AND CONCLUSIONS

In this chapter, I have presented some of the major characteristics of a behavioral–systems perspective on the treatment of child and family disorders. The behavioral–systems perspective is depicted as a decision-making approach to treatment and prevention; it is based on a consistently applied theoretical framework, well-established research findings relevant to both normal and deviant child and family functioning, empirically documented treatment procedures, and operational rules that conform to the realities and changing demands of clinical practice. Recent developments in the field have included a growing systems emphasis; greater sensitivity to developmental factors; and an increased recognition of the importance of individual differences, biological determinants, and emotional and cognitive factors in treatment. A need for the further development of treatment strategies that are sensitive to specific clinical problems is emphasized. The population-specific chapter presentations that follow provide detailed discussions of many of the issues that have been highlighted in this introductory presentation.

Acknowledgments

During the preparation of this chapter, I was supported by a sabbatical leave fellowship from the University of Calgary, and was a visiting professor at the Oregon Health Sciences University. The administrative support of the Crippled Children's Division, and in particular David MacFarlane and Jerry Smith, greatly facilitated work on this project.

REFERENCES

Achenbach, T. M. (1982). *Developmental psychopathology* (2nd ed.). New York: Wiley.

Achenbach, T. M. (1985). *Assessment and taxonomy of child and adolescent psychopathology.* Beverly Hills, CA: Sage.

Achenbach, T. M., & Edelbrock, C. (1981). Behavior problems and competencies reported by parents of normal and disturbed children aged four through sixteen. *Monographs of the Society for Research in Child Development, 46* (1, Serial No. 188).

Achenbach, T. M., & McConaughy, S. H. (1987). *Empirically based assessment of child and adolescent psychopathology: Practical applications.* Newbury Park, CA: Sage.

Alberto, P. A., & Troutman, A. C. (1982). *Applied behavior analysis for teachers: Influencing student performance.* Columbus, OH: Charles E. Merrill.

Alexander, J. G., & Parsons, B. V. (1982). *Functional family therapy.* Monterey, CA: Brooks/Cole.

American Psychiatric Association. (1987). *Diagnostic and statistical manual of mental disorders: DSM-III-R* (3rd ed., rev.). Washington, DC: Author.

Anastasi, A. (1988). *Psychological testing* (6th ed.). New York: Macmillan.

Asarnow, J., Carlson, G. A., & Guthrie, D. (1987). Coping strategies, self-perceptions, hopelessness, and perceived family environments in depressed and suicidal children. *Journal of Consulting and Clinical Psychology, 55,* 361–366.

Baer, D. M., Wolf, M. M., & Risley, T. R. (1968). Some current dimensions of applied behavior analysis. *Journal of Applied Behavior Analysis, 1,* 91–97.

Baker, B. L. (1980). Training parents as teachers of their developmentally disabled children. In S. Salzinger, J. Antrobus, & J. Glick (Eds.). *The ecosystem of the sick child* (pp. 201–216). New York: Academic Press.

Bandura, A. (1969). *Principles of behavior modification.* New York: Holt, Rinehart & Winston.

Bandura, A. (1986). *Social foundations of thought and action: A social cognitive theory.* Englewood Cliffs, NJ: Prentice-Hall.

Barkley, R. A. (1987). *Defiant children: A clinician's manual for parent training.* New York: Guilford Press.

Barlow, D. H., & Hersen, M. (1984). *Single case experimental designs: Strategies for studying behavior change* (2nd ed.). New York: Pergamon Press.

Beidel, D. C., & Turner, S. M. (1986). A critique of the theoretical bases of cognitive-behavior theories and therapy. *Clinical Psychology Review, 6,* 177–197.

Bernal, M. E., & North, J. (1978). A survey of parent training manuals. *Journal of Applied Behavior Analysis, 11,* 533–544.

Bijou, S. W., & Baer, D. M. (1961). *Child development: Systematic and empirical theory.* New York: Appleton-Century-Crofts.

Blechman, E. A. (1985). *Solving child behavior problems at home and school.* Champaign, IL: Research Press.

Block, J., & Gjerde, P. F. (in press). Depressive symptomatology in late adolescence: A longitudinal perspective on personality antecedents. In J. E. Rolf, A. Masten, D. Cicchetti, K. Neuchterlein, & S. Weintraub (Eds.), *Risk and protective factors in the development of psychopathology*. Cambridge, MA: Harvard University Press.

Block, J., Block, J. H., & Keyes, S. (1988). Longitudinally foretelling drug usage in adolescence: Early childhood personality and environmental precursors. *Child Development, 59,* 336–355.

Bornstein, P. H., & van den Pol, R. A. (1985). Models of assessment and treatment in child behavior therapy. In P. H. Bornstein & A. E. Kazdin (Eds.), *Handbook of clinical behavior therapy with children* (pp. 44–74). Homewood, IL: Dorsey Press.

Bornstein, P. H., Kazdin, A. E., & McIntyre, T. J. (1985). Chartacteristics, trends, and future directions in child behavior therapy. In P. H. Bornstein & A. E. Kazdin (Eds.), *Handbook of clinical behavior therapy with children* (pp. 833–850). Homewood, IL: Dorsey Press.

Bronfenbrenner, U. (1986). Ecology of the family as a context for human development: Research perspectives. *Developmental Psychology, 22,* 723–742.

Brunk, M., Hengeller, S. W., & Whelan, J. P. (1987). Comparison of multisystemic therapy and parent training in the brief treatment of child abuse and neglect. *Journal of Consulting and Clinical Psychology, 55,* 171–178.

Burke, M. M., Townsley, R., Messner, S., & Jackson, J. (1987, November). *Short-term group therapy for sexually abused girls: A learning-theory-based treatment for negative affect*. Paper presented at the meeting of the Association for Advancement of Behavior Therapy, Boston.

Carlson, G., Asarnow, J. R., & Orbach, I. (in press). Developmental aspects of suicidal behavior in children. *Journal of the American Academy of Child and Adolescent Psychiatry*.

Carver, C. S., & Scheier, M. F. (1986, August). *Dispositional optimism: A theoretical analysis and implications for the self-regulation of behavior*. Paper presented at the annual meeting of the American Psychological Association, Washington, DC.

Casey, R. J., & Berman, J. S. (1985). The outcome of psychotherapy with chilren. *Psychological Bulletin, 98,* 388–400.

Chamberlain, P., Patterson, G. R., Reid, J. B., Kavanagh, K., & Forgatch, M. (1984). Observation of client resistance. *Behavior Therapy, 15,* 144–155.

Christophersen, E. R. (1986). Accident prevention in primary care. *Pediatric Clinics of North America, 33,* 925–933.

Cicchetti, D., & Braunwald, K. G. (in press). An organizational approach to the study of emotional development in maltreated infants. *Journal of Infant Mental Health*.

Ciminero, A. R., Calhoun, K. S., & Adams, H. E. (Eds.). (1986). *Handbook of behavioral assessment* (2nd ed.). New York: Wiley–Interscience.

Cohen, P., Velez, C. N., & Brook, J. S. (in press). Mechanisms of the relationship between perinatal problems, early childhood illness, and psychopathology in late childhood and adolescence. *Child Development*.

Cronbach, L. J. (1984). *Essentials of psychological testing* (4th ed.). New York: Harper & Row.

Dadds, M. R., Schwartz, S., & Sanders, M. R. (1987). Marital discord and treatment outcome in behavioral treatment of child conduct disorders. *Journal of Consulting and Clinical Psychology, 55,* 396–403.

Dangel, R. F., & Polster, R. A. (Eds.). (1984). *Parent training: Foundations of research and practice*. New York: Guilford Press.

Donnellan, A. M. (1988, February). Our old ways just aren't working. *Dialect* (Newsletter of the Saskatchewan Association for the Mentally Retarded).

Dunlap, K. (1932). *Habits: Their making and unmaking*. New York: Liveright.

Dunst, C. J. (Ed.). (in press). *Enabling and empowering families: Principles and guidelines for practice*. Cambridge, MA: Brookline Books.

Dunst, C. J., & Trivette, C. M. (in press). A family systems model of early intervention with handicapped and developmentally at-risk children. In D. Powell (Ed.), *Parent education and support programs: Consequences for children and families*. Norwood, NJ: Ablex.

Dunst, C. J., Trivette, C. M., & Deal, A. (in press). The individualized family service plan: Assessing and meeting family needs. In C. J. Dunst (Ed.), *Enabling and empowering families: Principles and guidelines for practice*. Cambridge, MA: Brookline Books.

Edelbrock, C. (1984). Developmental considerations. In T. H. Ollendick & M. Hersen (Eds.), *Child behavioral assessment: Principles and procedures* (pp. 20–37). New York: Pergamon Press.

Egeland, B., Jacobvitz, D., & Sroufe, L. A. (1988). Breaking the cycle of abuse. *Child Development, 59,* 1080–1088.

Ellis, A. (1985). *Overcoming resistance: Rational–emotive therapy with difficult clients*. New York: Springer Publishing Co.

Elliott, S. N. (1988). Acceptability of behavioral treatments: Review of variables that influence treatment selection. *Professional Psychology: Research and Practice, 19,* 68–80.

Epstein, L. H., Wing, R. R., Koeske, R., & Valoski, A. (1987). Long-term effects of family based treatment of childhood obesity. *Journal of Consulting and Clinical Psychology, 55,* 91–95.

Evans, I. M. (1985). Building systems models as a strategy for target behavior selection in clinical assessment. *Behavioral Assessment, 7,* 21–32.

Evans, I. M., & Meyer, L. H. (1985). *An educative approach to behavior problems: A practical decision model for interventions with severely handicapped learners*. Baltimore: Paul H. Brookes.

Evans, I. M., Meyer, L. H., Derer, K. R., & Hanashiro, R. Y. (1985). An overview of the decision model. In I. M. Evans & L. H. Meyer, *An educative approach to behavior problems: A practical decision model for interventions with severely handicapped learners* (pp. 43–61). Baltimore: Paul H. Brookes.

Eysenck, H. J. (Ed.). (1960). *Behavior therapy and the neuroses*. New York: Pergamon Press.

Favell, J. E., Azrin, N. H., Baumeister, A. A., Carr, E. G., Dorsey, M. F., Forehand, R., Foxx, R. M., Lovaas, O. I., Rincover, A., Risley, T. R., Romancyzk, R. G., Russo, D. C., Schroeder, S. R., & Solnick, J. V. (1982). The treatment of self-injurious behavior (AABT Task Force Report, Winter, 1982). *Behavior Therapy, 13,* 529–554.

Flanagan, R. (1986). Teaching young children responses to inappropriate approaches by strangers in public places. *Child and Family Behavior Therapy, 8,* 27–43.

Fleischman, M. J., Horne, A. M., & Arthur, J. L. (1983). *Troubled families: A treatment program*. Champaign, IL: Research Press.

Fogel, A., & Thelan, E. (1987). Development of early

expressive and communicative action: Reinterpreting the evidence from a dynamic systems perspective. *Developmental Psychology, 23,* 747–761.

Forehand, R. L., & McMahon, R. J. (1981). *Helping the noncompliant child: A clinician's guide to parent training.* New York: Guilford Press.

Furey, W. M., & Basili, L. (in press). Predicting consumer satisfaction in parent training for noncompliant children. *Behavior Therapy.*

Garber, J. (1984). Classification of child psychopathology: A developmental perspective. *Child Development, 55,* 30–48.

Gordon, J. R., & Craver, J. N. (1988, January). *Safer sex: A self help manual.* Unpublished manual, University of Washington School of Social Work.

Gottman, J. M., & Levenson, R. W. (1986). Assessing the role of emotion in marriage. *Behavioral Assessment, 8,* 31–48.

Gross, A. M., & Drabman, R. S. (in press). *Handbook of clinical behavioral pediatrics.* New York: Plenum.

Harris, K. R., Wong, B. L., & Keogh, B. K. (Eds.). (1985). Cognitive-behavior modification with children: A critical review of the state of the art [Special issue]. *Journal of Abnormal Child Psychology, 13,* 329–476.

Harris, S. L. (1984). The family of the autistic child: A behavioral systems view. *Clinical Psychology Review, 4,* 227–239.

Harris, S. L., & Ferrari, M. (1983). Developmental factors in child behavior therapy. *Behavior Therapy, 14,* 54–72.

Harris, S. L., & Powers, M. D. (1984). Diagnostic issues. In T. H. Ollendick & M. Hersen (Eds.), *Child behavioral assessment: Principles and procedfures* (pp. 38–57). New York: Pergamon Press.

Hartmann, D. P., Roper, B. L., & Bradford, D. C. (1979). Some relationships between behavioral and traditional assessment. *Journal of Behavioral Assessment, 1,* 3–21.

Harvey, P., Forehand, R., Brown, C., & Holmes, T. (in press). The prevention of sexual abuse: Examination of the effectiveness of a program with kindergarten-age children. *Behavior Therapy.*

Herbert, M. (1981). *Behavioural treatment of problem children: A practice manual.* London: Academic Press.

Herbert, M. (1987). *Behavioural treatment of children with problems: A practice manual* (2nd ed.). London: Academic Press.

Hersen, M., & Bellack, A. S. (Eds.). (1981). *Behavioral assessment: A practical handbook* (2nd ed.). New York: Pergamon Press.

Hersen, M., & Van Hasselt, V. B. (Eds.). (1987). *Behavior therapy with children and adolescents: A clinical approach.* New York: Wiley.

Hoier, T. S., Smith, G., Shawchuck, C., & Freeman, T. (1987, November). *Behavioral group treatment of sexually abused children: A pilot study.* Paper presented at the meeting of the Association for Advancement of Behavior Therapy, Boston.

Holden, G. W. (1985). Analyzing parental reasoning with microcomputer-presented problems. *Simulation and Games, 16,* 203–210.

Hollandsworth, J. G., Jr. (1986). *Physiology and behavior therapy.* New York: Plenum.

Holmes, F. B. (1936). An experimental investigation of a method of overcoming children's fears. *Child Development, 7,* 6–30.

Houts, A. C., Shutty, M. S., & Emery, R. E. (1985). The impact of children on adults. In B. B. Lahey & A. E.

Kazdin (Eds.), *Advances in clinical child psychology* (Vol. 8, pp. 267–307). New York: Plenum.

Houts, A. C., Whelan, J. P., & Peterson, K. (1987). Filmed versus live delivery of full-spectrum home training for primary enuresis: Presenting the information is not enough. *Journal of Consulting and Clinical Psychology, 55,* 902–906.

Interagency Committee on Learning Disabilities. (1987). *Learning disabilities: A report to the U.S. Congress.* Washington, DC: Department of Health and Human Services.

Jason, L. A. (1980). Prevention in the schools. In R. H. Price, R. F. Ketterer, B. C. Bader, & J. Morahan (Eds.), *Prevention in mental health: Research, policies, and practices.* Beverly Hills, CA: Sage.

Jason, L. A., Felner, R. D., Hess, R., & Moritsugo, J. N. (1987). *Prevention: Toward a multidisciplinary approach.* New York: Haworth Press.

Johnson, J. H., Rasbury, W. C., & Siegel, L. J. (1986). *Approaches to child treatment: Introduction to theory, research, and practice.* New York: Pergamon Press.

Johnson, S. B. (1988). Chronic illness and pain. In E. J. Mash & L. G. Terdal (Eds.), *Behavioral assessment of childhood disorders* (2nd ed., pp. 491–527). New York: Guilford Press.

Jones, M. C. (1924). A laboratory study of fear: The case of Peter. *Journal of Genetic Psychology, 31,* 308–315.

Jones, R. T., Sisson, L. A., & Van Hasselt, V. B. (1984). Emergency fire-safety skills for blind children and adolescents: Group training and generalization. *Behavior Modification, 8,* 267–286.

Kandel, E., Mednick, S. A., Kirkegaard-Sorensen, L., Hutchings, B., Knop, J., Rosenberg, R., & Schulsinger, F. (1988). IQ as a protective factor for subjects at high risk for antisocial behavior. *Journal of Consulting and Clinical Psychology, 56,* 224–226.

Kanfer, F. H. (1985). Target selection for clinical change programs. *Behavioral Assessment, 7,* 7–20.

Kanfer, F. H., & Busemeyer, J. R. (1982). The use of problem-solving and decision-making in behavior therapy. *Clinical Psychology Review, 2,* 239–266.

Kanfer, F. H., & Phillips, J. S. (1970). *Learning foundations of behavior therapy.* New York: Wiley.

Kanfer, F. H., & Saslow, G. (1965). Behavioral analysis: An alternative to diagnostic classification. *Archives of General Psychiatry, 12,* 529–538.

Kanfer, F. H., & Saslow, G. (1969). Behavioral diagnosis. In C. M. Franks (Ed.), *Behavior therapy: Appraisal and status* (pp. 417–444). New York: McGraw-Hill.

Kanfer, F. H., & Schefft, B. K. (1988). *Guiding the process of therapeutic change.* Champaign, IL: Research Press.

Karoly, P. (1981). Self-management problems in children. In E. J. Mash & L. G. Terdal (Eds.), *Behavioral assessment of childhood disorders* (pp. 79–126). New York: Guilford Press.

Karoly, P. (Ed.). (1988). *Handbook of child health assessment: Biopsychosocial perspectives.* New York: Wiley-Interscience.

Kazdin, A. E. (1978). *History of behavior modification.* Baltimore: University Park Press.

Kazdin, A. E. (1981). Acceptability of child treatment techniques: The influence of treatment efficacy and adverse side effects. *Behavior Therapy, 12,* 493–506.

Kazdin, A. E. (1982a). *Single-case research designs: Methods for clinical and applied settings.* New York: Oxford University Press.

Kazdin, A. E. (1982b). Symptom substitution, generalization, and response covariation: Implications for psychotherapy outcome. *Psychological Bulletin, 91,* 349–365.

Kazdin, A. E. (1984). Acceptability of aversive procedures and medication as treatment alternatives for deviant child behavior. *Journal of Abnormal Child Psychology, 12,* 289–302.

Kazdin, A. E. (1988a). Behavior therapy and the treatment of clinical dysfunction. *Contemporary Psychology, 33,* 686–687.

Kazdin, A. E. (1988b). *Child psychotherapy: Developing and identifying effective treatments.* New York: Pergamon Press.

Kazdin, A. E., Esveldt-Dawson, K., French, N. H., & Unis, A. S. (1987). Problem-solving skills training and relationship therapy in the treatment of antisocial child behavior. *Journal of Consulting and Clinical Psychology, 55,* 76–85.

Kendall, P. C. (1982). Integration: Behavior therapy and other schools of thought. *Behavior Therapy, 13,* 550–571.

Kendall, P. C. (1987). Ahead to basics: Assessments with children and families. *Behavioral Assessment, 9,* 321–332.

Kendall, P. C., & Braswell, L. (1985). *Cognitive–behavioral therapy for impulsive children.* New York: Guilford Press.

Kendall, P. C., & Koehler, C. (1985). Outcome evaluation in child behavior therapy: Methodological and conceptual issues. In P. H. Bornstein & A. E. Kazdin (Eds.), *Handbook of clinical behavior therapy with children* (pp. 75–122). Homewood, IL: Dorsey Press.

Kendall, P. C., Lerner, R. M., & Craighead, W. E. (1984). Human development and intervention in child psychopathology. *Child Development, 55,* 71–82.

Kline, R. B., Canter, W. A., & Robin, A. (1987). Parameters of teenage alcohol use: A path analytic conceptual model. *Journal of Consulting and Clinical Psychology, 55,* 521–528.

Knitzer, J. (1982) *Unclaimed children: The failure of public responsibility to children and adolescents in need of mental health services.* Washington, DC: Children's Defense Fund.

Koocher, G. P., & Pedulla, B. M. (1977). Current practices in child psychotherapy. *Professional Psychology: Research and Practice, 8,* 275–287.

Lambert, M. E. (1987). A computer simulation for behavior therapy training. *Journal of Behavior Therapy and Experimental Psychiatry, 18,* 245–248.

Last, C. G. (Ed.). (1988). Behavioral assessment and treatment of childhood anxiety disorders [Special issue]. *Behavior Modification, 12,* 163–310.

Lazarus, A. A. (1958). New methods in psychotherapy: A case study. *South African Medical Journal, 32,* 660–664.

Lazarus, A. A., & Abramovitz, A. (1962). The use of "emotive imagery" in the treatment of children's phobias. *Journal of Mental Science, 108,* 191–195.

LeBow, J. (1982). Consumer satisfaction with mental health treatment. *Psychological Bulletin, 91,* 244–259.

Ledingham, J. E., & Schwartzman, A. E. (1984). A 3-year followup of aggressive and withdrawn in childhood: Preliminary findings. *Journal of Abnormal Child Psychology, 12,* 157–168.

Lee, C. M., & Mash, E. J. (in press). Behaviour therapy. In B. Tonge, G. D. Burrows, & J. Werry (Eds.). *Handbook of studies on child psychiatry.* Amsterdam: Elsevier.

Lerner, J. V., Hertzog, C., Hooker, K. A., Hassibi, M., & Thomas, A. (1988). A longitudinal study of negative emotional states and adjustment from early childhood through adolescence. *Child Development, 59,* 356–366.

Levis, D. J. (1988). Integration of behavioral theory and practice. *the Behavior Therapist, 11,* 75.

Lochman, J. E. (1987). Self- and peer perceptions and attributional biases of aggressive and nonaggressive boys in dyadic interactions. *Journal of Consulting and Clinical Psychology, 55,* 404–410.

Lochman, J. E. (1988). *Effectiveness of a cognitive–behavioral intervention with aggressive boys.* Unpublished manuscript, Duke University Medical Center.

Lochman, J. E., & Lampron, L. B. (1986). Situational social problem-solving skills and self esteem of aggressive and nonaggressive boys. *Journal of Abnormal Child Psychology, 14,* 605–617.

London, P. (1972). The end of ideology in behavior modification. *American Psychologist, 27,* 913–920.

Lovaas, O. I. (1987). Behavioral treatment and normal educational and intellectual functioning in young autistic children. *Journal of Consulting and Clinical Psychology, 55,* 3–9.

Lovaas, O. I., Freitag, G., Gold, V. J., & Kasorla, I. C. (1965). Experimental studies in childhood schizophrenia: Analysis of self-destructive behavior. *Journal of Experimental Child Psychology, 2,* 67–84.

Lovaas, O. I., Koegel, R., Simmons, J. Q., & Long, J. S. (1973). Some generalization and follow-up measures on autistic children in behavior therapy. *Journal of Applied Behavior Analysis, 6,* 131–166.

MacDonald, L. (1986). Ethical standards for therapeutic programs in human services: An evaluation model. *the Behavior Therapist, 9,* 213–215.

Mahoney, M. J., & Nezworski, M. T. (1985). Cognitive–behavioral approaches to children's problems. *Journal of Abnormal Child Psychology, 13,* 467–476.

Markman, H. J., Floyd, F. J., Stanley, S. M., & Storaasli, R. D. (1988). Prevention of marital distress: A longitudinal investigation. *Journal of Consulting and Clinical Psychology, 56,* 210–217.

Mash, E. J. (1984). Families with problem children. In A. Doyle, D. Gold, & D. Moskowitz (Eds.), *Children in families under stress* (pp. 65–84). San Francisco: Jossey-Bass.

Mash, E. J., & Hunsley, J. (in press). Behavioral assessment: A contemporary approach. In A. S. Bellack, M. Hersen, & A. E. Kazdin (Eds.), *International handbook of behavior modification and therapy* (2nd ed.). New York: Plenum.

Mash, E. J., & Terdal, L. G. (1980). Follow-up assessments in behavior therapy. In P. Karoly & J. J. Steffan (Eds.), *The long-range effects of psychotherapy: Models of durable outcome* (pp. 99–147). New York: Gardner Press.

Mash, E. J., & Terdal, L. G. (Eds.). (1981a). *Behavioral assessment of childhood disorders.* New York: Guilford Press.

Mash, E. J., & Terdal, L. G. (1981b). Behavioral assessment of childhood disturbance. In E. J. Mash & L. G. Terdal (Eds.), *Behavioral assessment of childhood disorders* (pp. 3–76). New York: Guilford Press.

Mash, E. J., & Terdal, L. G. (Eds.). (1988a). *Behavioral assessment of childhood disorders* (2nd ed.). New York: Guilford Press.

Mash, E. J., & Terdal, L. G. (1988b). Behavioral assessment of child and family disturbance. In E. J. Mash & L.

G. Terdal (Eds.), *Behavioral assessment of childhood disorders* (2nd ed., pp. 3–65). New York: Guilford Press.

Mash, E. J., & Terdal, L. G. (in press). Assessment strategies in clinical behavioral pediatrics. In A. M. Gross & R. S. Drabman (Eds.), *Handbook of clinical behavioral pediatrics*. New York: Plenum.

McMahon, R. J., & Forehand, R. (1983). Consumer satisfaction in behavioral treatment of children: Types, issues, and recommendations. *Behavior Therapy, 14,* 209–225.

McMahon, R. J., & Peters, R. D. (Eds.). (1985). *Childhood disorders: Behavioral–developmental approaches.* New York: Brunner/Mazel.

Meichenbaum, D. (1977). *Cognitive behavior modification.* New York: Plenum.

Meyer, L. H., Cole, D. A., McQuarter, R., & Reichle, J. (1988). *Validation of a measure of social competence in children and young adults with mental retardation and other disabilities.* Unpublished manuscript, Division of Special Education and Rehabilitation, Syracuse University.

Milich, R., & Dodge, K. A. (1984). Social information processing in child psychiatric populations. *Journal of Abnormal Child Psychology, 13,* 471–490.

Miller, S. A. (1988). Parents' beliefs about children's cognitive development. *Child Development, 59,* 259–285.

Mischel, W. (1968). *Personality and assessment.* New York: Wiley.

Moran, P., & Eckenrode, J. (1988). *Social stress and depression during adolescence: Gender and age differences.* Unpublished manuscript, Department of Human Development and Family Studies, Cornell University.

Mori, L., & Peterson, L. (1986). Training preschoolers in home safety skills to prevent inadvertent injury. *Journal of Clinical Child Psychology, 15,* 106–114.

Morrow-Bradley, C., & Elliot, R. (1986). Utilization of psychotherapy research by practicing psychotherapists. *American Psychologist, 41,* 188–197.

Mowrer, O. H., & Mowrer, W. M. (1938). Enuresis: A method for its study and treatment. *American Journal of Orthopsychiatry, 8,* 436–459.

Mussen, P. H. (General Ed.). (1983). *Handbook of child psychology* (4th ed., 4 vols.). New York: Wiley.

Nelson, R. O., & Hayes, S. C. (Eds.). (1986). *Conceptual foundations of behavioral assessment.* New York: Guilford Press.

Nolen-Hoecksema, S., Girgus, J. S., & Seligman, M.E.P. (1988, March). *A longitudinal study of depression in pre-adolescents: Sex differences in depression and related factors.* Paper presented at the meeting of the Society for Research on Adolescence, Alexandria, VA.

O'Leary, K. D. (1984a). The image of behavior therapy: It's time to take a stand. *Behavior Therapy, 15,* 219–233.

O'Leary, K. D. (1984b). Marital discord and children: Problems, strategies, methodologies and results. In A. Doyle, D. Gold, & D. S. Moskowitz (Eds.). *Children in families under stress* (pp. 35–36). San Francisco: Jossey-Bass.

O'Leary, K. D., Becker, W. C., Evans, M. B., & Saudargas, R. A. (1969). A token reinforcement program in a public school: A replication and systematic analysis. *Journal of Applied Behavior Analysis, 2,* 3–13.

O'Leary, K. D., & Wilson, G. T. (1987). *Behavior therapy: Application and outcome* (2nd ed.). Englewood Cliffs, NJ: Prentice-Hall.

Ollendick, T. H. (1986). Behavior therapy with children and adolescents. In S. L. Garfield & A. E. Bergin (Eds.), *Handbook of psychotherapy and behavior change* (3rd ed., pp. 565–624). New York: Wiley.

Ollendick, T. H., & Cerny, J. A. (1981). *Clinical behavior therapy with children.* New York: Plenum.

Ollendick, T. H., & Hersen, M. (Eds.). (1984). *Child behavioral assessment: Principles and procedures.* New York: Pergamon Press.

Patterson, G. R. (1976). The aggressive child: Victim and architect of a coercive system. In E. J. Mash, L. A. Hamerlynck, & L. C. Handy (Eds.), *Behavior modification and families* (pp. 267–316). New York: Brunner/Mazel.

Patterson, G. R. (1982). *Coercive family process.* Eugene, OR: Castalia.

Patterson, G. R. (1986). Performance models for antisocial boys. *American Psychologist, 41,* 432–444.

Patterson, G. R., Ray, R. S., & Shaw, D. A. (1968). Direct intervention in families of deviant children [Special issue]. *Oregon Research Institute Research Bulletin, 8.*

Patterson, G. R., Reid, J. B., Jones, R. R., & Conger, R. E. (1975). *A social learning approach to family intervention: Families with aggressive children* (Vol. 1). Eugene, OR: Castalia.

Pelham, W. E., & Murphy, H. A. (1986). Attention deficit and conduct disorders. In M. Hersen (Ed.), *Pharmacological and behavioral treatment: An integrative approach* (pp. 108–148). New York: Wiley.

Peterson, L. (Ed.). (1987). Special series: Infant attachment and psychopathology. *Journal of Consulting and Clinical Psychology, 55,* 803–859.

Peterson, L., Burbach, D., & Chaney, J. (in press). Developmental issues in the diagnosis of child psychopathology. In C. G. Last & M. Hersen (Eds.), *Handbook of child psychiatric diagnosis.* New York: Wiley.

Peterson, L., & Mori, L. (1985). Prevention of child injury: An overview of targets, methods, and tactics for psychologists. *Journal of Consulting and Clinical Psychology, 53,* 586–595.

Pettit, G. S., Dodge, K. A., & Brown, M. M. (1988). Early family experience, social problem solving patterns, and children's social competence. *Child Development, 59,* 107–120.

Putallaz, M. (1987). Maternal behavior and children's sociometric status. *Child Development, 58,* 324–340.

Quay, H. C., & Werry, J. S. (Eds.). (1986). *Psychopathological disorders of childhood* (3rd ed.). New York: Wiley.

Rickel, A. U., & Allen, L. (1987). *Preventing maladjustment from infancy through adolescence.* Newbury Park, CA: Sage.

Roberts, M. C., & Peterson, L. (Eds.). (1984). *Prevention of problems in childhood: Psychological research and applications.* New York: Wiley.

Robin, A. L., & Foster, S. L. (1989). *Negotiating adolescence: A behavioral family systems approach to parent-adolescent conflict.* New York: Guilford Press.

Robins, C. J., & Hinkley, K. (in press). Social-cognitive processing and depressive symptoms in children: A comparison of measures. *Journal of Abnormal Child Psychology.*

Romancyzk, R. G. (1986). *Clinical utilization of microcomputer technology.* New York: Pergamon Press.

Ross, A. (1981). *Child behavior therapy: Principles, procedures and empirical basis.* New York: Wiley.

Routh, D. (Ed.). (1988). *Handbook of pediatric psychology.* New York: Guilford Press.

Rubenstein, J. L., Heeren, T., Houssman, D., Rubin, C., & Stechler, G. (1988, March). *Suicidal behavior in "normal" adolescents: Risk and protective factors.* Paper presented at the biennial meeting of the Society for Research in Adolescence, Alexandria, VA.

Russo, D. C., & Budd, K. S. (1987). Limitations of operant practice in the study of disease. *Behavior Modification, 11,* 264–285.

Rutter, M., Tizard, J., Yule, W., Graham, P., & Whitmore, K. (1976). Research report: Isle of Wight Studies, 1964–1974. *Psychological Medicine, 6,* 313–332.

Salter, A. (1949). *Conditioned reflex therapy.* New York: Capricorn.

Sameroff, A. J., Seifer, R., Barocas, R., Zax, M., & Greenspan, S. (1987). Intelligence quotient scores of 4-year-old children: Social-environmental risk factors. *Pediatrics, 79,* 343–350.

Sattler, J. M. (1988). *Assessment of children* (3rd ed.). San Diego, CA: Jerome M. Sattler.

Scheier, M. F., & Carver, C. S. (1985). Optimism, coping and health: Assessment and implications of generalized outcome expectancies. *Health Psychology, 4,* 219–247.

Schonfeld, I. S., Shaffer, D., O'Conner, P., & Portnoy, S. (1988). Conduct disorder and cognitive functioning: Testing three causal hypotheses. *Child Development, 59,* 993–1007.

Schroeder, S. R., Gualtieri, C. T., & Van Bourgondien, M. E. (1986). Autism. In M. Hersen (Ed.), *Pharmacological and behavioral treatment: An integrative approach* (pp. 89–107). New York: Wiley.

Siqueland, L., Kendall, P. C., Stoff, D., & Pollack, L. (1987). *Cognitive distortions and deficiencies in child psychiatric populations.* Unpublished manuscript, Department of Psychology, Temple University.

Skinner, B. F. (1953). *Science and human behavior.* New York: Macmillan.

Sowder, B. J. (1975). *Assessment of child mental health needs* (Vols. 1–8). McLean, VA: General Research Corporation.

Steinglass, P. (1987). A systems view of family interaction and psychopathology. In T. Jacob (Ed.), *Family interaction and psychopathology: Theories, methods, and findings* (pp. 25–65). New York: Plenum.

Stokes, T. F., & Baer, D. M. (1977). An implicit technology of generalization. *Journal of Applied Behavior Analysis, 10,* 349–367.

Strain, P. S. (Ed.). (1981). *The utilization of peers as behavior change agents.* New York: Plenum.

Strayhorn, J. M., Jr. (1987). Medical assessment of children with behavioral problems. In M. Hersen & V. B. Van Hasselt (Eds.), *Behavior therapy with children and adolescents: A clinical approach* (pp. 50–74). New York: Wiley.

Tabachnik, N., & Alloy, L. B. (1988). Clinician and patient as aberrant actuaries: Expectation-based distortions in assessment of covariation. In L. Y. Abramson (Ed.), *Social cognition and clinical psychology.* New York: Guilford Press.

Tarnowski, K. J., Kelly, P. A., & Mendlowitz, D. R. (1987). Acceptability of behavioral pediatric interventions. *Journal of Consulting and Clinical Psychology, 55,* 435–436.

Tharp, R. G., & Wetzel, R. J. (1969). *Behavior modification in the natural environment.* New York: Academic Press.

Tisdelle, D. A., & St. Lawrence, J. S. (1988). Adolescent interpersonal problem-solving skills training: Social validation and generalization. *Behavior Therapy, 19,* 171–182.

Tronick, E., & Gianino, A. (1986). Interactive mismatch and repair: Challenges to the coping infant. *Zero to Three, 6,* 1–6.

Turner, S. M., Beidel, D. C., & Costello, A. (1987). Psychopathology in the offspring of anxiety disorders patients. *Journal of Consulting and Clinical Psychology, 55,* 229–235.

Ullmann, L. P., & Krasner, L. (Eds.). (1965). *Case studies in behavior modification.* New York: Holt, Rinehart & Winston.

Urbain, E. S., & Kendall, P. C. (1980). Review of social-cognitive problem-solving interventions with children. *Psychological Bulletin, 88,* 109–143.

U.S. Congress, Office of Technology Assessment. (1986). *Children's mental health: Problems and services—a background paper.* Washington, DC: U.S. Government Printing Office.

Voeltz, L. M., & Evans, I. M. (1982). The assessment of behavioral interrelationships in child behavior therapy. *Behavioral Assessment, 4,* 131–165.

Wachtel, P. L. (1977). *Psychoanalysis and behavior therapy.* New York: Basic Books.

Wahler, R. G. (1975). Some structural aspects of deviant child behavior. *Journal of Applied Behavior Analysis, 8,* 27–42.

Wahler, R. G. (1980). The insular mother: Her problems in parent–child treatment. *Journal of Applied Behavior Analysis, 13,* 207–219.

Wahler, R. G., & Fox, J. J. (1981). Setting events in applied behavior analysis: Toward a conceptual and methodological expansion. *Journal of Applied Behavior Analysis, 14,* 327–338.

Wahler, R. G., & Graves, M. G. (1983). Setting events in social networks: Ally or enemy in child behavior therapy? *Behavior Therapy, 14,* 19–36.

Walker, J. L., Lahey, B. B., Hynd, G. W., & Frame, C. L. (1987). Comparison of specific patterns of antisocial behavior in children with conduct disorder with or without coexisting hyperactivity. *Journal of Consulting and Clinical Psychology, 55,* 910–913.

Watson, J. B., & Rayner, (1920). Conditioned emotional reactions. *Journal of Experimental Psychology, 3,* 1–14.

Weber, J. (1936). An approach to the problem of fear in children. *Journal of Mental Science, 82,* 136–147.

Weisz, J. R., Weiss, B., Alicke, M. D., & Klotz, M. L. (1987). Effectiveness of psychotherapy with children and adolescents: A meta-analysis for clinicians. *Journal of Consulting and Clinical Psychology, 55,* 542–549.

Weisz, J. R., Weiss, B., & Langmeyer, D. B. (1987). Giving up on child psychotherapy: Who drops out? *Journal of Consulting and Clinical Psychology, 55,* 916–918.

Westermeyer, J. (1987). Cultural factors in clinical assessment. *Journal of Consulting and Clinical Psychology, 55,* 471–478.

Willems, E. P. (1974). Behavioral technology and behavioral ecology. *Journal of Applied Behavior Analysis, 7,* 151–165.

Winett, R. A., & Winkler, R. C. (1972). Current behavior modification in the classroom: Be still, be quiet, be docile. *Journal of Applied Behavior Analysis, 5,* 499–504.

Winter, M. G., Hicks, R., McVey, G., & Fox, J. (1988). Age and sex differences in choice of consultant for various types of problems. *Child Development, 59,* 1046–1055.

Witt, J. C., & Elliot, S. N. (1986). Acceptability of class-room management procedures. In T. R. Kratochwill (Ed.), *Advances in school psychology* (pp. 251–288). Hillsdale, NJ: Erlbaum.

Wolfe, B. E., & Goldfried, M. R. (1988). Research on psychotherapy integration: Recommendations and con-clusions from an NIMH workshop. *Journal of Consulting and Clinical Psychology, 56,* 448–451.

Wolfe, D. A. (1988). Child abuse and neglect. In E. J. Mash & L. G. Terdal (Eds.), *Behavioral assessment of childhood disorders* (2nd ed., pp. 627–669). New York: Guilford Press.

Wolfe, D. A., & Bourdeau, P. A. (1987). Current issues in the assessment of abusive and neglectful parent–child relationships. *Behavioral Assessment, 9,* 271–290.

Wolfe, D. A., & LaRose, L. (1986). *Child videotape series* (Videotape). London, Ontario: University of Western Ontario.

Wolfe, V. V., & Wolfe, D. A. (1988). The sexually abused child. In E. J. Mash & L. G. Terdal (Eds.), *Behavioral assessment of childhood disorders* (2nd ed., pp. 670–714). New York: Guilford Press.

Wolpe, J. (1958). *Psychotherapy by reciprocal inhibition.* Stanford, CA: Stanford University Press.

Wolpe, J. (1986). Individualization: The categorical im-perative of behavior therapy practice. *Journal of Be-havior Therapy and Experimental Psychiatry, 17,* 145–153.

Wright, L., Flagler, S., & Friedman, A. G. (1988). Assess-ment for accident prevention. In P. Karoly (Ed.), *Hand-book of child health assessment: Biopsychosocial per-spectives* (pp. 491–518). New York: Wiley–Interscience.

Wurtele, S. K., Kast, L. C., & Kondrick, P. A. (1988). *Measuring young children's responses to sexual abuse prevention programs: The "what-if" situations test.* Un-published manuscript, Department of Psychology, Wash-ington State University.

Wurtele, S. K., Marrs, S. R., & Miller-Perrin, C. L. (1987). Practice makes perfect? The role of participant modeling in sexual abuse prevention programs. *Journal of Consulting and Clinical Psychology, 55,* 599–602.

Zeitlin, S., Williamson, G. G., & Rosenblatt, W. P. (1987). The coping with stress model: A counseling approach for families with a handicapped child. *Journal of Counseling and Development, 43,* 443–446.

PART II
BEHAVIOR DISORDERS

2

ATTENTION DEFICIT– HYPERACTIVITY DISORDER

RUSSELL A. BARKLEY
University of Massachusetts Medical Center

Numerous diagnostic labels have been given to clinically referred children having significant deficiencies in sustained attention, impulse control, and the regulation of activity level in response to situational demands (Whalen, in press). Recently, this disorder has been labeled "Attention Deficit–Hyperactivity Disorder" (ADHD) in the revised third edition of the *Diagnostic and Statistical Manual of Mental Disorders* (DSM-III-R; American Psychiatric Association, 1987). It has previously been referred to as "hyperkinesis," "hyperactive child syndrome," "minimal brain dysfunction," and earlier in this decade as "Attention Deficit Disorder (with or without Hyperactivity)" in DSM-III (American Psychiatric Association, 1980). Although confusing to many, this relabeling of the disorder every decade or so reflects a shifting emphasis in the primacy of certain symptoms within the disorder, based, in part, on the rapidly increasing abundance of research. To help the reader better appreciate this dynamic process, this chapter begins with a brief review of the history of ADHD; this is followed by a description of the nature of the disorder, its prevalence, developmental course, and etiologies. Suggestions for assessment of children with this disorder are then provided. Subsequently, various treatments for the disorder are reviewed.

OVERVIEW OF ATTENTION DEFICIT–HYPERACTIVITY DISORDER

History

In the middle 1800s, several reports described children who had developed significant problems with attention span, hyperactivity, and impulsivity following their recovery from various central nervous system diseases or injuries (see Ross & Ross, 1976; Taylor, 1986). However, one of the most complete descriptions of such children, and the first attempt to conceptualize the disorder, was presented by George Still (1902) in a series of published lectures to the Royal College of Physicians in England. Still described a group of children in his clinical practice who were quite aggressive, defiant, resistant to discipline, and highly emotional, and who showed little self-control. Many in this sample were also excessively active and poor at sustaining attention to tasks. Such children would probably now be viewed as having a mixture of ADHD, Oppositional Disorder, and Conduct Disorder, according to DSM-III-R (American Psychiatric Association, 1987).

Still (1902) believed that these children had serious deficiencies in the "volitional inhibition" of behavior and conceptualized the symptoms as arising from various types of "defects in moral control" (p. 1008). He argued that variation in moral control and volitional inhibition existed within the normal population as a result of both environmental and innate factors. However, he felt strongly that when such defects were seen to the severe degree observed in clinical samples, they were most often the result of biological factors rather than lack of adequate child rearing or training. He posited a possible hereditary transmission of these characteristics in some children, whereas in others it might be acquired as a result of central nervous system damage peri- or postnatally. In some cases, it could even be transient, corresponding with the acute phases of certain brain diseases or infections. More males than females displayed such problems in social behavior, and such children seemed to have a higher number of minor physical anomalies in their appearance.

During the next 35 years, few papers appeared on this subject in children, and those that did seemed to dwell more on motor restlessness (Childers, 1935; Levin, 1938) than on the disturbances in social conduct. More widespread interest in these children did not emerge until after World War II. At that time, the highly influential writings of Strauss, Lehtinen, and their colleagues (Strauss & Lehtinen, 1947) appeared, advocating that restless and inattentive behavior was *de facto* evidence of brain damage in children. These authors reasoned that if hyperactivity, inattention, and impulsivity could arise from brain damage, then all children manifesting such behaviors must be brain-injured, even where such a history was lacking. The term "minimal brain damage" was coined to refer to these children, and strict guidelines were advocated for their education. One such recommendation enduring to the present was to greatly reduce distractions in such children's classrooms, so as to focus their rather fragile attention on educational materials and activities. Despite little evidence for the efficacy of such a recommendation (Routh, 1978), much less for the existence of distractibility in these children (Douglas, 1983), the treatment remains commonplace today.

Emphasis on excessive motor activity as the *sine qua non* of the disorder continued through the 1950s and 1960s. An influential paper of that era by Laufer, Denhoff, and Solomons (1957) posited a possible defect in the filtering of stimuli in the central nervous system of hyperactive children, allowing excessive stimulation to reach the cortex. Later articles attempted to define the disorder as simply one of a daily rate of motor activity level significantly deviant from that of normal children (Chess, 1960; Werry & Sprague, 1970). Conclusions concerning brain damage as a cause of hyperactivity became less apparent over time, resulting in a shift in terminology from "minimal brain damage" to "minimal brain dysfunction" (Wender, 1971). Many scientific reports from this period focused on the objective measurement of various types of motor activity and the effects of stimulant medication upon them. Eventually, the link with neurological damage was dropped from the diagnostic terminology, and the disorder was now simply referred to as "hyperactive child syndrome" (Chess, 1960) or "Hyperkinetic Reaction of Childhood" (American Psychiatric Association, 1968). Nevertheless, the belief that brain damage was the major cause of the disorder remained strong until the 1970s, when a series of papers appeared refuting the syndromal nature of the disorder and its relationship to brain damage (Rie & Rie, 1980; Rutter, 1977).

By the mid-1970s, a growing body of evidence was suggesting that hyperactive children also had major deficits with sustained attention and impulse control (Douglas, 1972). Hyperactivity was eventually relegated to a role equivalent, or even secondary, to that of these problems with attention and impulsivity. In a series of reviews of the literature and her own research, Douglas (1972, 1980; Douglas & Peters, 1979) persuasively argued that the disorder consisted of impairments in (1) investment, organization, and maintenance of attention; (2) the inhibition of impulsive responding; (3) the modulation of arousal levels to meet situational demands; and (4) a strong tendency to seek immediate reinforcement (Douglas, 1983). Excessive motor activity was not seen as so much of a problem as was the regulation of activity level to situational demands (Routh, 1978). So influential was this shift in scientific and clinical thinking that the American Psychiatric Association (1980) relabeled the disorder as "Attention Deficit Disorder (with or without Hyperactivity)" in DSM-III. This essentially demoted the symptom of hyperactivity to that of an unnecessary or simply related characteristic of these children, yet one that could be used to create subtypes of the disorder based on its presence or absence.

At the same time, British scientists questioned the specificity of the disorder as separate from conduct disorders, noting that both seem to have similar symptoms, family histories, and developmental courses (Sandberg, Rutter, & Taylor, 1978; Shaffer, McNamara, & Pincus, 1974). At present, this debate appears to have diminished as a result of numerous factor-analytic studies of ratings of children's behavioral problems, which demonstrate separate yet overlapping dimensions for hyperactivity and conduct disorders (Achenbach & Edelbrock, 1983; Taylor, 1986). Research also suggests that hyperactive children may differ from defiant/aggressive children in having more developmental delays in language and motor skills, pervasiveness of overactivity across settings, and difficulties in sustained attention to boring, repetitive tasks (Milich, Loney, & Landau, 1982; Reeves, Werry, Elkind, & Zametkin, 1987; Werry, Reeves, & Elkind, 1987).

Early in the present decade, several scientists posited that the central deficiency in children with Attention Deficit Disorder was one of poor executive functioning, or self-regulation of behavior. Routh (1978) postulated that the core deficit was in the regulation of behavior to situational demands, whereas others conjectured impairments in self-directed instruction (Kendall & Braswell, 1985), self-regulation of arousal to environmental demands (Douglas, 1983), or rule-governed behavior (Barkley, 1981a, 1981b). This resembles a return to the earlier notions of Still (1902) that deficits in volitional inhibition and moral consciousness underlie the disorder.

Presently, the disorder has been relabeled yet again as "Attention Deficit–Hyperactivity Disorder" (ADHD) in the DSM-III-R (American Psychiatric Association, 1987), suggesting a re-emergence of the role of hyperactivity as a central feature of the disorder, equal in import to the other two. The subtyping scheme of "without Hyperactivity" has been eliminated in this revision—not because such children do not exist, but because it is unclear whether they represent a true subtype of this disorder or a separate diagnostic entity altogether (Carlson, 1986). The disorder is recognized as falling along a dimension of normal child behavior, but occupying the disordered extreme of this dimension relative to other children of the same mental age and sex.

Primary Symptoms

Children having ADHD, by definition, display difficulties with attention relative to normal children of the same age and sex. However, attention is a multidimensional construct that can refer to problems with alertness, arousal, selectivity, sustained attention, distractibility, or span of apprehension, among others (Hale & Lewis, 1979). Research to date suggests that ADHD children have their greatest difficulties with sustaining attention to tasks or vigilance (Douglas, 1983). These difficulties are sometimes apparent in free-play settings, as evidenced by shorter durations of play with each toy and frequent shifts in play across various toys (Barkley & Ullman, 1975; Routh & Schroeder, 1976). However, they are more dramatically seen in situations requiring the child to sustain attention to dull, boring, repetitive tasks (Luk, 1985; Milich et al., 1982; Ullman, Barkley, & Brown, 1978). The problem is not so much one of heightened distractibility, or the ease with which a child is drawn off task by extraneous stimulation. Instead, it appears to be one of diminished persistence in responding to tasks that have little intrinsic appeal or minimal immediate consequences for completion (Barkley, in press).

Intertwined with this difficulty in sustained attention is a deficiency in inhibiting behavior in response to situational demands, or impulsivity. Like attention, impulsivity is also multidimensional in nature (Milich & Kramer, 1985), and it remains unclear which aspects of impulsivity are impaired in ADHD children. The problem is often defined as a pattern of rapid, inaccurate responding to tasks (Brown & Quay, 1977), as measured by Kagan's Matching Familiar Figures Test (MFFT; Kagan, 1966). But, it may also refer to poor sustained inhibition of responding (Gordon, 1979), poor delay of gratification (Rapport, Tucker, DuPaul, Merlo, & Stoner, 1986), or impaired adherence to commands to regulate or inhibit behavior in social contexts (Kendall & Wilcox, 1979). Furthermore, factor-analytic studies (Achenbach & Edelbrock, 1983; Milich & Kramer, 1985) have failed to differentiate an impulsivity dimension from that measuring attention, calling into question its existence as a separate dimension of behavioral impairment in these children. If impulsivity is defined as poor sustained inhibition of responding, than it may simply be another facet of poor sustained attention, in that both involve persistence in responding.

Numerous studies have shown ADHD children to be more active, restless, and fidgety than normal children (Barkley & Cunningham, 1979; Porrino et al., 1983). As with poor sustained attention, however, there are significant situational fluctuations in this symptom (Jacob, O'Leary, & Rosenblad, 1978; Luk, 1985), implying that it is the failure to regulate activity level to setting or task demands that may be problematic in ADHD (Porrino et al., 1983; Routh, 1978). However, it has not been convincingly shown that hyperactivity distinguishes ADHD from other clinic-referred groups of children (Firestone & Martin, 1979; Sandberg et al., 1978; Shaffer et al., 1974). Recent studies suggest that it may be the pervasiveness of the hyperactivity across settings that separates ADHD from other diagnostic categories of children (Taylor, 1986).

Although the notion is not yet widespread, many have come to accept the idea that difficulties with adherence to rules and instructions may also be a primary deficit of ADHD children (American Psychiatric Association, 1987; Barkley, 1981a, 1982, in press). Care is taken here to exclude poor rule-governed behavior that may stem from sensory handicaps (i.e., deafness), impaired language development, or defiant or oppositional behavior. ADHD children have demonstrated significant problems in compliance with parental and teacher commands (Barkley, 1985; Whalen, Henker, & Dotemoto, 1980), with experimental instructions in the absence of the experimenter (Draeger, Prior, & Sanson, 1986), and with commands to defer gratification (Rapport, Tucker, et al., 1986). In fact, it has previously been argued that most prior research demonstrating impaired attention and impulse control in ADHD children actually demonstrated poor rule-governed behavior, in that all of these studies involved experimenter instructions to subjects. What the studies actually showed was that ADHD children had problems sustaining responding to experimenter rules and instructions, particularly when the instructions were not repeated or when the experimenter left the setting (Douglas, 1983; Draeger et al., 1986). Like the other symptoms, rule-governed behavior is a multidimensional construct having various components (Zettle & Hayes, 1982). It remains to be shown which of these are specifically impaired in ADHD children.

Diagnostic Criteria

Over the past decade, efforts have been made to develop more specific guidelines for the classification of children as ADHD. Although some guidelines appeared in the DSM-II (American Psychiatric Association, 1968) for the disorder Hyperkinetic Reaction of Childhood, these were quite vague. A more concerted effort at developing criteria appeared in the DSM-III (American Psychiatric Association, 1980), where quite specific recommendations were provided for Attention Deficit Disorder (with or without Hyperactivity). These criteria became widely adopted in research and clinical practice, despite their relative lack of empirical basis. In the recent revision of the DSM-III (American Psychiatric Association, 1987), an attempt was made in factor-analytic studies of child behavior rating scales to address this problem by selecting symptoms that appeared to cluster together into a single factor of hyperactivity, inattention, and impulsivity. The cutoff score was chosen that best differentiated ADHD children from other diagnostic groups, based upon a quasi-experimental field trial using a sample of more than 500 children. These criteria appear in Table 2-1 and will probably be even more widely endorsed than previous diagnostic guidelines.

It is recommended that additional criteria be followed (Barkley, 1982, 1987a, 1988a), particularly the use of well-standardized child behavior rating scales to establish the deviance of the child's ADHD symptoms; the requirement for relatively pervasive symptoms across most situations requiring sustained effort to relatively unappealing tasks; a duration of 12 months for the symptoms; and the adjustment of rating scale scores in view of the child's mental age (i.e., comparison to mental age norms).

Situational Variation

As already noted, all of the primary symptoms of ADHD show significant fluctuations across various settings and caregivers (Barkley, 1981a; Zentall, 1984). Some of the variables determining this variation have been delineated. First, the degree of "structure"—or, more spe-

TABLE 2-1. DSM-III-R Diagnostic Criteria for Attention Deficit–Hyperactivity Disorder

---

Note: Consider a criterion met only if the behavior is considerably more frequent than that of most people of the same mental age.

A. A disturbance of at least six months during which at least eight of the following are present:

(1) often fidgets with hands or feet or squirms in seat (in adolescents, may be limited to subjective feelings of restlessness)

(2) has difficulty remaining seated when required to do so

(3) is easily distracted by extraneous stimuli

(4) has difficulty awaiting turn in game or group situations

(5) often blurts out answers to questions before they have been completed

(6) has difficulty following through on instructions from others (not due to oppositional behavior or failure of comprehension), e.g., fails to finish chores

(7) has difficulty sustaining attention in tasks or play activities

(8) often shifts from one uncompleted activity to another

(9) has difficulty playing quietly

(10) often talks excessively

(11) often interrupts or intrudes on others, e.g., butts into other children's games

(12) often does not seem to listen to what is being said to him or her

(13) often loses things necessary for tasks or activities at school or at home (e.g., toys, pencils, books, assignments)

(14) often engages in physically dangerous activities without considering possible consequences (not for purpose of thrill-seeking), e.g., runs into street without looking

Note: The above items are listed in descending order of discriminating power based on data from a national field trial of the DSM-III-R criteria for Disruptive Behavior Disorders.

B. Onset before the age of seven.

C. Does not meet the criteria for a Pervasive Developmental Disorder.

Note. Adapted from *Diagnostic and Statistical Manual for Mental disorders* (3rd ed., rev.) by the American Psychiatric Association, 1987, Washington, DC: Author. Copyright 1987 by the American Psychiatric Association. Adapted by permission.

cifically, the extent to which caregivers make demands on ADHD children to restrict behavior—appears to affect the degree of deviance of the child's behavior from normal children. In free-play or low-demand settings, ADHD children are less distinguishable from normal children than in highly restrictive settings (Barkley, 1985; Jacob *et al.,* 1978; Luk, 1985; Routh & Schroeder, 1976). Second, ADHD children appear to be more compliant and less disruptive with their fathers than with their mothers (Tallmadge & Barkley, 1983; Tarver-Behring, Barkley, & Karlsson, 1985). Third, on tasks where instructions are repeated frequently to the ADHD child, problems with sustained responding are lessened (Douglas, 1980, 1983). Fourth, ADHD children display fewer behavioral problems in novel or unfamiliar surroundings, but increase their level of deviant behavior as familiarity with the setting increases (Barkley, 1977a). Finally, settings or tasks that involve a high rate of immediate reinforcement for compliance or punishment for noncompliance to instructions result in significant reductions in, or in some cases amelioration of, attentional deficits (Barkley, in press; Barkley, Copeland, & Sivage, 1980; Douglas, 1983; Douglas & Parry, 1983). Such dramatic changes in the degree of deviance of behavior across situations has led several scientists to question the notion that ADHD is actually a deficit in attention at all. Instead, they suggest that it may be more of a problem in the manner in which behavior is regulated by its effects or consequences (Barkley, in press; Draeger *et al.,* 1986; Haenlein & Caul, 1987; Prior, Wallace, & Milton, 1984)—in essence, that it may be a motivational deficit rather than an attentional one.

Prevalence and Sex Ratio

The consensus of opinion seems to be that approximately 3% of the childhood population has ADHD (American Psychiatric Association, 1987). Estimates vary between 1% and 20%, depending upon the rigor or strictness of the criteria used to define the disorder (Ross & Ross, 1982) and the degree of agreement required among parents, teachers, and professionals (Lambert, Sandoval, & Sassone, 1978). Rates of occurrence also fluctuate to a small degree across cultures (O'Leary, Vivian, & Nisi, 1985; Ross & Ross, 1982) and socioeconomic strata (Taylor, 1986). The proportion of males versus females manifesting the disorder varies considerably across studies, from 2:1 to 10:1 (American Psychiatric Association, 1980; Ross & Ross, 1982), with an average of 6:1 most often cited for clinic-referred samples of children. However, epidemiological studies find the proportion to be approximately 3:1 among nonreferred children displaying these symptoms (Trites, Dugas, Lynch, & Ferguson, 1979).

Onset, Course, and Outcome

Studies of the developmental course and outcome of ADHD children have been numerous (Thorley, 1984; Weiss & Hechtman, 1986) and can only be briefly summarized here. Although some ADHD children are reported to have been difficult in their temperament since birth or early infancy (Chamberlin, 1977; Ross & Ross, 1976), the majority appear to have been identified by their caregivers as deviant from normal between 3 and 4 years of age (Barkley, Fischer, Newby, & Breen, 1988; Ross & Ross, 1982). However, it may be several years later before such children are brought to the attention of professionals (Safer & Allen, 1976). During their preschool years, ADHD children are often excessively active, mischievous, noncompliant with parental requests, and difficult to toilet-train (Campbell, Schleifer, & Weiss, 1978; Hartsough & Lambert, 1985; Mash & Johnston, 1982). Parental distress over child care and management is likely to reach its zenith when the children are between 3 and 6 years of age, declining thereafter as the deficits in attention and rule following improve (Barkley, Karlsson, & Pollard, 1985; Mash & Johnston, 1983a).

By the time of entry into formal schooling (6 years of age), most ADHD children have become recognizably deviant from normal peers in their poor sustained attention, impulsivity, and restlessness. Difficulties with aggression, defiance, or oppositional behavior may now have emerged, if they did not earlier in development (Ross & Ross, 1982). ADHD children developing these conduct problems or antisocial behaviors are likely to veer into a more severe path of maladjustment in later years than are those ADHD children who do not develop aggressive/defiant behaviors or do so only to a limited degree. During these elementary school years, the majority of ADHD children have varying degrees of poor school performance, usually related to failure to finish assigned tasks

in school or as homework, disruptive behavior during class activities, and poor peer relations with schoolmates. Learning disabilities in areas of reading, spelling, math, handwriting, and language may also become manifest in a significant minority of ADHD children, and may require additional special educational assistance beyond that typically needed to manage the ADHD symptoms.

As teenagers, a small percentage of ADHD children will have "outgrown" their symptoms, in that they now fall within the broadly defined normal range in their symptom deviance. However, many, perhaps over 75% (Weiss & Hechtman, 1986), continue to have problems with school, home, or community adjustment. At home, family conflicts may now center around failure to accept responsibility for performing routine tasks, difficulties in being trusted to obey rules when away from home, and trouble with the problem-solving approaches that parents and ADHD adolescents attempt to use in resolving conflicts (e.g., authoritarianism, a high degree of emotion, excessive use of ultimatums, etc.). Among that subset of youngsters who had significant earlier problems with aggressive and oppositional behavior, delinquency and conduct disorder are more likely to develop as these adolescents spend greater amounts of unsupervised time in the community. Whether greater-than-normal substance abuse occurs within these years is debatable (Blouin, Bornstein, & Trites, 1978; Weiss, Hechtman, Perlman, Hopkins, & Wener, 1979), and may be related more to the presence of conduct disorder symptoms than to those of ADHD. One study (Weiss & Hechtman, 1986) seems to suggest that ADHD teenagers have a greater number of automobile accidents than normal teens, but this remains to be replicated. Up to 30% may fail to complete high school, and most fail to pursue college programs after high school (Weiss, Hechtman, Milroy, & Perlman, 1985). Certainly, the outcome of childhood ADHD in the adolescent years is far more negative than previous clinical lore has postulated, in that most ADHD children do not outgrow their symptoms by adolescence.

Less research exists on the outcome of ADHD children as young adults. What does exist suggests that at least 60% are continuing to have symptoms of ADHD; yet their adjustment to their employment setting may be adequate. Interpersonal problems continue to plague as many as 75%, and depression and low self-esteem are commonplace (Weiss *et al.*, 1985). Juvenile convictions and symptoms of adult antisocial personality may occur in 23%–45% (Farrington, Loeber, & van Kammen, 1987), and 27% or more may be alcoholic (Loney, Whaley-Klahn, Kosier, & Conboy, 1981). Hence, adult disorders that are the outcomes of earlier ADHD symptoms in childhood appear to exist; these range from residual ADHD symptoms that impair home or work adjustment (Wender, Reimherr, & Wood, 1981) to depression, substance abuse, and antisocial personality.

The adolescent and young adult outcomes of ADHD appear to be related to a varied set of predictors, chief among which are intelligence, socioeconomic status, degree of aggressiveness and oppositional behavior, poor peer relationships, emotional instability, and extent of parental psychopathology (Hechtman, Weiss, Perlman, & Amsel, 1984; Loney *et al.*, 1981; Paternite & Loney, 1980). Intensive, multimodal therapy in adolescence may produce beneficial effects on later outcome (Satterfield, Satterfield, & Cantwell, 1981), but lesser degrees of individual treatments, such as stimulant drug therapy alone, have only a marginal impact upon later outcome (Hechtman, Weiss, & Perlman, 1984; Paternite & Loney, 1980; Weiss & Hechtman, 1986).

Related Characteristics

Children with ADHD have a higher likelihood of having other medical, developmental, behavioral, emotional, and academic difficulties. Delays in intelligence, academic achievement, and motor coordination are more prevalent in ADHD children than in matched samples of normal children or even in siblings (Cantwell & Satterfield, 1978; Safer & Allen, 1976; Tarver-Behring *et al.*, 1985). Depression, low self-esteem, and poor peer acceptance are also more common in ADHD children (Johnston, Pelham, & Murphy, 1985; Weiss, Hechtman, & Perlman, 1978). It has been repeatedly shown that ADHD children have more minor physical anomalies, allergies, and accidental injuries than normal children (Hartsough & Lambert, 1985; Quinn & Rapoport, 1974; Trites, Tryphonas, & Ferguson, 1980).

Research on the family interactions of ADHD children, particularly those children who are also manifesting problems with op-

positional and defiant behavior, suggests that their symptoms produce significant alterations in family functioning. ADHD children have been shown to be less compliant, more negative, and less able to sustain compliance than normal children during task completion with their mothers (Barkley, Karlsson, & Pollard, 1985; Cunningham & Barkley, 1979; Mash & Johnston, 1982). Their mothers are more directive and negative, and less rewarding and responsive to their children's behavior, than mothers of normal children. There appears to be less conflict in the task-related interactions of older ADHD children than in those of younger age groups (Barkley, Karlsson, & Pollard, 1985; Mash & Johnston, 1982). However, older ADHD children remain deviant from same-age children in their noncompliance and parent–child conflicts. Studies evaluating the impact of stimulant medication on these interactions suggest that the greater directiveness and negative behavior of the mothers of ADHD children may be a reaction to their children's noncompliance and poor self-control than a cause of it (Barkley & Cunningham, 1978; Barkley, Karlsson, Pollard, & Murphy, 1985; Barkley, Karlsson, Strzelecki, & Murphy, 1984). Moreover, these conflicts in social interactions appear to exist in the relations of ADHD children with their fathers (Tallmadge & Barkley, 1983) and siblings (Mash & Johnston, 1983b), as well as with peers (Cunningham & Siegel, 1987) and teachers (Whalen *et al.*, 1980).

Etiologies

The proposed etiologies for ADHD are too numerous to review here in any detail. Brain damage was initially proposed as a chief cause of ADHD symptoms (Strauss & Lehtinen, 1947), but later reviews of the evidence suggest that fewer than 5% of ADHD children have neurological findings consistent with such an etiology. Possible neurotransmitter dysfunctions or imbalances have been proposed, resting chiefly on the responses of ADHD children to differing drugs; however, little direct evidence is available, and many of the studies are conflicting in their results (Shaywitz, Shaywitz, Cohen, & Young, 1983; Zametkin & Rapoport, 1986). Nevertheless, findings of decreased cerebral blood flow, frontal lobe deficits on neuropsychological tests, and various psychophysiological findings intimate some central nervous system mechanism in the development of ADHD symptoms (Chelune, Ferguson, Koon, & Dickey, 1986; Hastings & Barkley, 1978; Lou, Henriksen, & Bruhn, 1984).

Although various environmental toxins, such as food additives, refined sugars, and allergens (Feingold, 1975; Taylor, 1980), have been proposed as causal of ADHD, more rigorous investigations have failed to yield much supportive evidence (Conners, 1980; Gross, 1984; Mattes & Gittelman, 1981; Wolraich, Milich, Stumbo, & Schultz, 1985). Some evidence of a correlational nature exists to show that elevated blood lead levels in children may be related to excessive activity and inattention (David, 1974; de la Burde & Choate, 1972, 1974; Gittelman & Eskenazi, 1983), but a direct causal connection remains to be established. Maternal alcohol consumption and cigarette smoking during pregnancy (Denson, Nanson, & McWatters, 1975; Shaywitz et al., 1980; Streissguth et al., 1984) have both shown relationships with the degree of ADHD symptoms in the offspring of these mothers. It should be borne in mind, however, that the evidence is again correlational and does not establish cause.

One of the most exciting areas of research on etiologies has been the role of hereditary transmission of symptoms across generations. For many years, evidence has existed showing higher rates of psychopathology, particularly depression, alcoholism, conduct problems, and hyperactivity, among the biological relatives of ADHD children (Biederman et al., 1987; Cantwell, 1975). Other studies indicate that between 20% and 32% of parents and siblings of ADHD children also have the disorder (Biederman et al., 1986; Deutsch, Swanson, & Bruell, 1982). Such research continues to suggest a genetic predisposition to the disorder. Moreover, twin studies show greater concordance for ADHD symptoms between identical than between fraternal twins (O'Connor, Foch, Sherry, & Plomin, 1980; Willerman, 1973), further suggesting some role for genetics in the transmission of the disorder in some families.

A few environmental theories of ADHD have been proposed (Block, 1977; Willis & Lovaas, 1977), but have not received much support in the available literature. Most investigators endorse a biological predisposition to the disorder, much like that to mental retardation, in which a variety of neurological etiologies (e.g., pregnancy and birth complications, acquired brain damage, toxins, infections, and heredity) can give rise to the disorder through some disturbance in a final common pathway in the nervous system. Even so, such symptoms remain malleable to environmental influences and social learning. The actual severity of the symptoms, the types of secondary symptoms, and the outcome of the disorder are highly related to environmental as opposed to biological factors (Weiss & Hechtman, 1986).

Conceptualization of the Disorder

Although numerous studies have consistently demonstrated that ADHD children have deficits in sustained attention, impulse control, and the regulation of their activity levels, recent reviews question whether these are the fundamental behavioral disturbances in ADHD. The global and multidimensional nature of such constructs as attention, impulsivity, and activity level; the well-demonstrated situational variation in such ADHD symptoms; and the lack of testability of many of the theories of ADHD predicated on these constructs have led recent researchers to posit more specific behavioral impairments that may better account for the results of research in this area.

Different laboratories are beginning to converge on the notion that the manner in which behavior is regulated by its consequences may be the more fundamental problem in ADHD. Some hypothesize that ADHD children have greater-than-normal thresholds for arousal by stimulation; as environmental stimulation decreases, hyperactivity and inattention increase as means of compensating for this reduction so as to maintain an optimal level of central nervous system arousal (Zentall, 1985). Others have proposed that thresholds for reinforcement may be too high (Haenlein & Caul, 1987), leading to decreased persistence of responding to tasks (heightened boredom) in ADHD children. Quay (in press) has argued that ADHD may be due to decreased activity in the brain's behavioral inhibition system, such that punishment or its threat fails to inhibit and regulate behavior as well as in normal children. This may explain the symptoms of impulsivity and poor sustained attention to tasks where punishment is used to inhibit or maintain responding. Elsewhere (Barkley, 1981a, in press), I have indicated that several deficits may be involved: (1) decreased control by partial reinforcement schedules; (2) rapid habituation or satiation to behavioral consequences, or rapid extinction of responding; and (3) diminished regulation of behavior by rules. In any case, future conceptualizations of the disorder are likely to rely more heavily on motivational deficiencies, probably of physiological origin, than on attentional deficits in accounting for the behavioral symptoms of ADHD children. These theories provide for more testable hypotheses, coincide better with known neurophysiological effects of drugs used to treat the disorder, and offer better explanatory value for the tremendous situational fluctuations seen in ADHD symptoms.

Meanwhile, I have come to view ADHD as a developmental deficiency in the regulation and maintenance of behavior by its consequences. This deficiency gives rise to problems with inhibiting, initiating, or sustaining responses to tasks or stimuli, as well as with adhering to rules or instructions, particularly in situations where consequences for such behavior are delayed, weak, or nonexistent. The deficiencies are evident in early childhood and are probably chronic in nature. Although they may improve with neurological maturation, the deficits persist in comparison to same-age normal children, whose performance in these areas also improves with development. The disorder appears to have multiple etiologies, most of which are biological rather than environmental, with a final common pathway perhaps being their effects upon the prefrontal cortex and frontal–limbic connections of the central nervous system.

These apparently biological deficiencies in the regulation and maintenance of behavior emanate into the social ecology of the child's social interactions in the family, school, and community, resulting in increased controlling responses by caregivers and peers in return. Over time, as these controlling responses meet with little success in managing the ADHD child's behavioral problems, family members, peers, and classmates may come to reject the child, avoiding unnecessary interactions as a means of limiting conflict. In families where other factors (e.g., parental psychopathology, marital discord, or family hardships) result in inconsistent, unpredictable, coercive, or simply diminished efforts at child management, defiant, oppositional, and aggressive behaviors may increase in the ADHD child. Left untreated, these early antisocial behaviors appear to increase the risk of early and recurrent patterns of delinquent and antisocial conduct in the community, which may be maintained into young adulthood (Farrington *et al.*, 1987; Pat-

terson, 1982). Managed properly, these social interaction conflicts of ADHD children may be maintained at relatively low levels, such that difficulties with completing schoolwork may be the primary difficulty of such children during adolescence (Paternite & Loney, 1980).

ASSESSMENT

The overview of ADHD presented above argues for a comprehensive clinical assessment of ADHD children. By "comprehensive," I mean that such an assessment should rely on several informants, employ multiple settings, and use a variety of assessment methods that focus not only on the primary symptoms of ADHD, but also the child's academic and social functioning, as well as the integrity of his or her family environment. The increased risk of health problems, along with the classroom, family, and community problems, indicates the need for multidisciplinary assessment and management of ADHD children—incorporating psychologists, physicians, educators, and social workers. The specific information to be obtained in such assessments and greater detail on potentially useful instruments in doing so are reviewed elsewhere (Barkley, 1981b, 1988a). This section simply highlights those approaches of demonstrated utility in clinically assessing ADHD children.

Interviews

Besides the traditional interview typically used in clinical practice, structured psychiatric interviews have also come to be used in some major university clinics and teaching hospitals for the assessment of psychopathological symptoms in children. Many of these interviews were developed from classification systems such as the DSM-III, and provide an extensive item list that the examiner uses to query the respondent. Such interviews may yield more precise and quantifiable information about the various problems of ADHD children. Those employed in research on ADHD have been the Schedule for Affective Disorders and Schizophrenia for School-Age Children, (Puig-Antich & Chambers, 1978), the Diagnostic Interview for Children and Adolescents (Herjanic, Brown, & Wheatt, 1975), the Interview Schedule for Children (Kovacs, 1982), the Child Assessment Schedule (Hodges, McKnew, Cytryn, Stern, & Kline, 1982), and the Diagnostic Interview Schedule for Children (Costello, Edelbrock, Kalas, Kessler, & Klaric, 1982). They can be employed in interviews with both parents and children, and scored to yield the various diagnoses that may apply to a given case. Their limitations, however, are numerous (Edelbrock & Costello, 1984), not the least of which is their being immediately outdated by the publication of DSM-III-R (American Psychiatric Association, 1987). At present, such interview schedules may be more useful for research than for clinical practice.

Behavior Rating Scales

Standardized behavior checklists and rating scales have become an indispensable part of the assessment of ADHD children. Their convenience, applicability to multiple informants (e.g., parents, teachers, children), ability to gather information collapsed across long time intervals, and large pool of normative data have led to their widespread adoption in clinical practice. Numerous scales now exist (see Barkley, 1988b). Those having the greatest utility with ADHD children would seem to be the Child Behavior Checklist (Achenbach & Edelbrock, 1983); the Conners Parent and Teacher Rating Scales (Goyette, Conners, & Ulrich, 1978); the Werry–Weiss–Peters Activity Rating Scale (Werry & Sprague, 1970); the ADD-H Comprehensive Teacher Rating Scale (Ullmann, Sleator, & Sprague, 1984); the Self-Control Rating Scale (Kendall & Wilcox, 1979) and its modification by Humphrey (1982); and the Home and School Situations Questionnaires (Barkley & Edelbrock, 1987). Each of these permits comparison of the ADHD child against scores for normal same-age children to assist in establishing the degree of deviance of the ADHD symptoms, as well as the presence and pattern of other psychopathological dimensions. Such patterns may ultimately prove useful in creating more homogeneous subtypes of ADHD, as well as predicting response to treatment and later outcome.

For adolescents, I have found it useful also to obtain parent ratings on the type, frequency, and severity of conflictual issues between ADHD teens and their parents by using the Issues Checklist and Conflict Behavior Questionnaire (Robin, 1981). Such information can be invaluable in providing directions for behavioral family therapy with these adolescents.

I have also found it helpful to have teens not only rate their parents' behavior on these scales, but also rate their own behavioral problems using the Youth Self-Report Form of the Child Behavior Checklist (Achenbach & Edelbrock, 1987).

In view of the relatively high incidence of marital discord, major affective disorder, and general parental psychopathology among the parents of ADHD children, as well as the demonstrated bearing of these factors on treatment responsiveness and adolescent outcome, it is valuable to include parent self-report measures as part of the assessment of ADHD children. My colleagues and I have found the following scales to be useful in our research and clinical protocols: the Symptom Checklist-90, Revised (Derogatis, 1986), the Beck Depression Inventory (Beck, Rush, Shaw, & Emery, 1979), the Locke–Wallace Marital Adjustment Scale (Locke & Wallace, 1959), and the Life Stress subscale of the Parenting Stress Index (Abidin, 1983).

Laboratory Measures

After years of use in research, laboratory measures of sustained attention, impulsivity, and activity level are becoming more widely used in clinical practice, particularly in university clinics and medical centers where greater resources are available. As yet, many of these instruments either lack the appropriate normative data so essential for clinical diagnostic and assessment purposes, or have yet to have their reliability and validity adequately demonstrated. Nevertheless, such limitations are surmountable, and it is likely that laboratory tests of ADHD symptoms may in time become as popular in clinical assessment as are rating scales today.

Vigilance and Sustained Attention

One of the most widely used instruments for assessing vigilance has been the continuous-performance test (CPT). Numerous versions exist, but one recently marketed for clinical use has been the Gordon Diagnostic System (GDS; Gordon, 1983). This instrument is a small box containing a microchip programmed to administer both a vigilance and a delay task, believed to assess impulse control (see below). The child sits before the instrument and is instructed to watch a display screen where numbers appear at approximately one per second.

When the child sees a certain number combination (say, first 1, then 9), he or she is to press a blue button on the panel. Otherwise, the child is not to touch the button for any other number combinations. The task lasts approximately 9 minutes. Norms are available now for over 1,200 children between 3 and 17 years of age. CPTs such as this have been shown to be among the most reliable measures in discriminating ADHD children (Douglas, 1983) and the most sensitive to stimulant drug effects (Barkley, 1977b). However, several recent studies suggest that the GDS version may be sensitive to drug effects only at moderate to high doses of stimulant medication (Barkley et al., 1988). Although it shows some promise, the GDS requires further validation studies before it can be recommended as a diagnostic tool or measure of treatment response. Several other software programs now exist for assessing sustained attention, several of which have normative data, but they also suffer from a lack of validation research (see Swanson, 1985).

Impulsiveness

Several laboratory methods have been used in assessing impulsiveness in ADHD children. The best-known of these is the MFFT (Kagan, 1966). A longer version of the MFFT (Cairns & Cammock, 1978) has been developed for older children. Norms are available for 5- to 12-year-old children (Cairns & Cammock, 1984; Salkind & Nelson, 1980). The measure appears to significantly discriminate ADHD from normal children (Campbell, Douglas, & Morganstern, 1971), as well as aggressive versus nonaggressive ADHD groups (Milich, Landau, & Loney, 1981), and it is sensitive to stimulant drug effects (Barkley, 1977b). Impulsiveness has more recently been assessed by using a direct-reinforcement-of-latency task developed by Gordon (1983). The task involves a small metal box containing a microprocessor; a child is told to press a button, wait a while (usually 6 seconds), and then press the button again. If the child has waited longer than 6 seconds, a point is awarded for a successful delay. The child is to continue this procedure for approximately 8 minutes. The measure reportedly correlates positively with ratings of behavior problems from the Conners Parent and Teacher Rating Scales (Gordon, 1979), and significantly discriminated ADHD children from other clinic-referred children in one study (McClure & Gordon, 1984). However, it does not appear to be sensitive to stimulant drug effects (Barkley et al., 1988). Many studies have used the Porteus Mazes to evaluate planning and impulse control in ADHD children (Douglas, 1983). Although normative data are outdated for this instrument, it has been shown to successfully discriminate ADHD and normal children and to be sensitive to stimulant drug effects (Barkley, 1977b). A major problem with all of these instruments is their low intercorrelation, implying that each is measuring a different facet of impulsivity (Milich & Kramer, 1985).

Activity Level

Numerous measures of activity level have been employed in research with ADHD children, spanning a variety of types of activity, such as motion of arms, legs, or trunk; locomotion; total body movement; and so on (Barkley & Ullman, 1975; Tryon, 1984). Such instruments as actometers (modified wrist watches), pedometers, motion transducers, mercury switches, pneumatic pads, and sound-wave generators have been employed to evaluate these dimensions of activity (Porrino et al., 1983; Tryon, 1984). Their lack of normative data, low reliability in some cases, low intercorrelation, and poor relationship to parent and teacher ratings of activity level have argued against their use in clinical practice. The inability of these instruments to take into account important situational influences on activity level make them unlikely to contribute to decisions surrounding treatment planning.

Direct Observational Procedures

Various behavioral observation codes have been used with ADHD children for assessing their behavioral problems and interactions with others. Notable among these are the systems developed by Jacob et al. (1978) and Abikoff, Gittelman-Klein, and Klein (1977) for classroom observations, and by Roberts (1987) and Barkley et al. (1988) for clinic analogue situations. These coding systems record behaviors such as being off task, being out of seat, fidgeting, locomotion, vocalizations, and attention shifts—behaviors noted to occur far more often in ADHD than in normal children. Where interest is in assessing the conflicts frequently occurring between ADHD children and others, such as parents, teachers, and peers, coding systems such as the Response-Class Matrix (Mash & Barkley, 1987; Mash, Terdal, & Anderson, 1973), the Parent–Child Interaction Code (Barkley *et al.,* 1988; Forehand & McMahon, 1981), and the Parent–Adolescent Interaction Coding System (Robins, 1981) may prove useful.

TREATMENT APPROACHES

The large number of symptoms associated with ADHD, as well as the numerous other diagnoses and deficits seen to coexist with it, require that treatment be multidisciplinary as well as multimodal in nature if a significant improvement in the child's adjustment is to be obtained. A variety of treatments have been attempted with ADHD children over the past century—far too many to review here (see Ross & Ross, 1976, 1982, for reviews). Vestibular stimulation (Arnold, Clark, Sachs, Jakim, & Smithies, 1985), running (Hales & Hales, 1985), and biofeedback and relaxation training (Richter, 1984), among others, have been described as potentially effective in uncontrolled case reports, yet are lacking in well-controlled experimental replications. Many dietary treatments, such as removal of additives, colorings, or sugar from the diet or addition of high doses of vitamins, have proven very popular despite minimal scientific support (Conners, 1980; Haslam, Dalby, & Rademaker, 1984; Milich, Wolraich, & Lindgren, 1986). Certainly traditional psychotherapy and play therapy have not proven especially effective for ADHD (see Ross & Ross, 1976). Those treatments with some proven efficacy have been (1) psychopharmacological therapy; (2) direct application of behavior therapy techniques in the laboratory; (3) parent training in contingency management methods; (4) classroom applications of contingency management techniques; (5) cognitive–behavioral training of ADHD children; and (6) assorted combinations of these approaches. Besides these interventions, therapists should also be cognizant of the availability of special educational programs for ADHD children now mandated under U.S. federal law (Public Law 94-142). The determination of eligibility for such programs is often a major referral concern of parents or teachers.

None of the presently recommended treatments is at all curative of ADHD symptoms. Their value lies in the temporary reduction of symptom levels or in the reduction of related behavioral and emotional difficulties, such as defiance and conduct problems, depression and low self-esteem, or academic underachievement. When such treatments are removed, the level of ADHD symptoms appears to return to higher or pretreatment ranges of deviance. Their effectiveness in improving prognosis thus rests on their being maintained over long periods of time (often years). Even this practice, however, has only sparse research support (Satterfield *et al.,* 1981).

Psychopharmacological Therapy

Research suggests that at least two classes of psychotropic drugs have proven useful in the management of ADHD symptoms: the stimulants and the antidepressants. Use of each of these types of medications, however, has been founded on virtual chance discoveries of their effectiveness and not on any theoretical rationale (Bradley, 1937; Winsburg, Bialer, Kupietz, & Tobias, 1972). Until recently, it was not clear precisely how these medications affect brain function, although their sites and neurochemical modes of action have been relatively well understood for at least 10–15 years. It now appears that the stimulants achieve their effects on behavior (e.g., sustained attention, diminished impulsivity, etc.) by lowering the threshold for reinforcement in the nervous system and, perhaps, by prolonging the sensitivity to reinforcement beyond when satiation or habituation would have naturally occurred (Leith & Barrett, 1976, 1981; Stein, 1964). These findings, and others from psychophysiological studies and the effects of reinforcement on ADHD children, have been used to suggest that the behavioral deficit in ADHD may involve abnormally high thresholds for reinforcement (Haenlein & Caul, 1987). Others have proposed a decreased duration of sensitivity to reinforcement (rapid extinction or satiation to consequences) (Barkley, in press), or diminished activity in the behavioral inhibition system known to oppose the behavioral reinforcement system (Quay, in press). The direct rationale, then, for employing the stimulant medications with ADHD children may be that they directly, if only temporarily, redress these deficiencies in these behavioral regulation systems. Such motivational theories also suggest that to the extent that new medications alter these reinforcement and inhibitory brain functions, they should prove valuable in the management of ADHD.

Stimulant Medication

Since Bradley (1937) first described their successful use with behavior problem children, the stimulants have received an enormous amount of research—far more than any other known treatment for any childhood psychiatric disorder. The results overwhelmingly indicate that these medications are quite effective for the management of ADHD symptoms in most children older than 5 years. Between 4 and 5 years of age, the response rate is probably much less, and under 3 years of age, the drugs are not recommended for use. The effectiveness of these medications has led to their widespread use with ADHD children, with surveys suggesting that between 1% and 2.6% of the school-age population is treated with stimulants for ADHD symptoms (Gadow, 1981; Safer & Krager, 1983). There now appears to be a popular movement underway to restrict such large-scale use of behavior-modifying medications with children, similar to that which occurred in the late 1960s (Bacon, 1988; Williams, 1988). Nevertheless, with the recognition that these medications may be useful with ADHD adolescents and adults (Coons, Klorman, & Borgstedt, 1987a, 1987b; Mattes, Boswell, & Oliver, 1984), their frequency of prescription is only likely to increase.

The most commonly prescribed stimulants are methylphenidate (Ritalin), d-amphetamine (Dexedrine), and pemoline (Cylert). They are rapidly acting stimulants, producing effects on behavior within 30–45 minutes after oral ingestion and peaking in their behavioral effects within 2–4 hours. Their utility in managing behavior quickly dissipates within 3–7 hours, although minuscule amounts of the medication may remain in the blood for up to 24 hours (Cantwell & Carlson, 1978). Because of their short half-life, they are often prescribed in twice- or thrice-daily doses. Although these drugs were once used predominantly for school days, there is an increasing clinical trend toward usage throughout the week as well as during school vacations, particularly for children with more severe ADHD and conduct problems.

The behavioral improvements produced by the medications are in sustained attention, impulse control, and reduction of task-irrelevant activity, especially in settings demanding restraint of behavior (Barkley, 1977b; Cantwell & Carlson, 1978; Taylor, 1986). Generally noisy and disruptive behavior also diminishes with medication. As a result, ADHD children may become more compliant with parental and teacher commands, are better able to sustain such compliance, and often increase their cooperative behavior toward others with whom they may have to accomplish a task (Barkley et al., 1984; Cunningham, Siegel, & Offord, 1985; Whalen et al., 1980). The effects of stimulants on aggressive behavior are less clear-cut (Taylor, 1986). The quality of the children's handwriting may also improve with medication. Academic productivity, or the number of problems completed, and accuracy also increase—in some cases dramatically—as a function of medication (Pelham, Bender, Caddell, Booth, & Moorer, 1985; Rapport, DuPaul, Stoner, & Jones 1986). However, the effects of medication are highly individually unique (see Rapport, DuPaul, et al., 1986): Some children show maximal improvement at lower doses, whereas others are most improved at higher doses of medication. Much controversy remains over whether these immediate improvements in academic performance translate to greater gains in academic achievement (the level of difficulty of academic material mastered by the child) over longer-term use of the medications (Barkley & Cunningham, 1978). It seems best to conclude that the stimulants produce significant improvement in academic accuracy and productivity, but not in the achievement of ADHD children.

The most frequently occurring side effects of the stimulants are mild insomnia and appetite reduction, particularly at the noon meal (Barkley, 1977b). Temporary growth suppression may accompany stimulant treatment, but is not generally severe or common, and can be managed by insuring that adequate caloric and nutritional intake is maintained; this can be done by shifting the distribution of food intake to other times of the day when the child is more amenable to eating (Taylor, 1986). Some children become irritable and prone to crying late in the afternoon as their medication may be wearing off. This may be accompanied by an increase in hyperactivity. A small percentage of ADHD children may complain of stomachaches and headaches when treated with stimulants, but these tend to dissipate within a few weeks of beginning medication or can be managed by reducing the dose. In approximately 1%–2% of ADHD children treated with stimulants, motor or vocal tics may occur (Barkley, 1988c). In others where tics already exist, they can be exacerbated by stimulant treatment. Because of the possible risk of eliciting multiple tics or Tourette syndrome in such children by continuing stimulant therapy, it seems prudent to cease medication when such tics occur. After the tics subside, return to a lower dose of medication for a brief trial may be warranted to determine whether the tics will recur. If so, stopping stimulant treatment is recommended (Barkley, 1988c).

It has been difficult to establish any reliable predictors of response to stimulant medication in ADHD children. Those characteristics having the most consistent relationship to response have been pretreatment levels of poor sustained attention and hyperactivity (Barkley, 1976; Taylor, 1983). The greater from the norm a child's level on such factors is, the better the child's response to medication will usually be. Predictors of adverse responding have not been as well studied. What little research exists suggest that pretreatment levels of anxiety predict poor response to stimulants (Taylor, 1983).

The following issues should be involved in the decision to refer an ADHD child for medication: (1) the age of the child; (2) duration and severity of symptoms; (3) the risk of injury to the child (by either accident or abuse) posed by the present severity of symptoms; (4) the success of prior treatments: (5) the absence of a personal or family history of tics or Tourette syndrome; (6) relatively normal levels of anxiety; (7) the absence of substance abuse by the child's caregivers; and (8) the likelihood that the parents will employ the medication responsibly, in compliance with physician recommendations. Several suggested paradigms for evaluating stimulant drug response in individual cases have been recently reported (Barkley *et al.*, 1988; Pelham, 1987; Rapport, DuPaul, *et al.*, 1986).

Antidepressant Medication

Recently, clinicians have turned to the tricyclic antidepressants, such as imipramine and desipramine, for the management of ADHD symptoms, particularly in cases where stimulants are contraindicated (e.g., ADHD children with tics or Tourette syndrome). Less is known about the pharmacokinetics and behavioral effect of the antidepressants in children than is known about the stimulants. Often given twice daily (morning and evening), these medications are longer-acting than the stimulants. As a result, it takes longer to evaluate the therapeutic value of any given dose (Rapoport & Mikkelsen, 1978). Some research suggests that low doses of the tricyclics may mimic stimulants in producing increased vigilance and sustained attention and decreased impulsivity. As a result, disruptive and aggressive behavior may also be reduced. Elevation in mood may also occur, particularly in those children in who significant pretreatment levels of depression and anxiety exist (Pliska, 1987). Rapoport and Mikkelsen (1978) report that treatment effects may diminish over time, however; this may mean that the tricyclics cannot be used as long-term therapy for ADHD, as can the stimulants.

The most common side effects of the tricyclics are drowsiness during the first few days of treatment, dry mouth, constipation, and flushing. Less likely yet more important are the cardiotoxic effects, such as possible tachycardia or arrhythmia (and, in cases of overdose, coma or death) (Puig-Antich, Ryan, & Rabinovich, 1985). Some children may develop sluggish reactions in focusing of the optic lens that may mimic nearsightedness. The reaction is not permanent, dissipating when treatment is withdrawn. Skin rash is occasionally reported and usually warrants ceasing drug treatment.

In general, it seems that the tricyclic antidepressants may be useful in the short-term treatment of ADHD children when the stimulants cannot be used, or when significant mood disturbances accompany the ADHD symptoms (Donnelly & Rapoport, 1985; Pliska, 1987).

Behavior Therapy

The rationale for the use of behavior modification techniques with ADHD children has often been founded on the limitations and potential side effects of stimulant drug therapy (Mash & Dalby, 1978). By themselves, such arguments provide a nonspecific rationale for any form of intervention as an alternative to stimulant medication. More convincing is the argument that since referral of children for ADHD in part results from the social distress they have created for their caregivers, an intervention that attempts to change the interaction between children and their caregivers should be quite useful (Werry & Sprague, 1970). A variation on this theme provides an even more direct rationale for using behavioral interventions with ADHD children. Willis and Lovaas (1977) have proposed that ADHD reflects poor stimulus control of behavior by parental commands, resulting from the inconsistent or inadequate use of child management methods by the parents. Training parents in more consistent and effective child management should reduce, or even eliminate, the ADHD symptoms. However, such a theory of ADHD has been dismissed on the grounds that the inconsistent, negative, or punitive management techniques of some parents of ADHD children have been shown to be more a reaction to than a cause of their children's inappropriate behavior (Barkley, 1985). Also, some parents of ADHD children do not show such poor management skills. Parent training, moreover, does not eliminate all of the behavioral difficulties of ADHD children, nor do its effects generalize to no-treatment settings such as school, where ADHD symptoms may be equally problematic (see below). The evidence seems to be against the concept of "bad parenting" as a primary etiology of ADHD.

However, with the recent trend toward viewing ADHD as a potential problem in the children's response to motivational parameters in the environment, the most persuasive rationale for behavioral interventions with ADHD may now exist. As noted earlier, many researchers have speculated that ADHD children display somewhat unusual reactions to consequences, or fail to maintain their responding when the consequences for performance are weak, delayed, or unavailable. If ADHD is in fact a developmental delay in the regulation of behavior by its consequences, then interventions that directly alter the pattern, timing, or salience of such consequences by socially arranged means to improve ADHD symptoms should be the treatments of choice. Such procedures are precisely those provided by the behavior therapies. A logical extension of this argument holds, however, that such socially arranged means of addressing this dysregulation will not alter the underlying neurophysiological basis for it. These techniques must be employed across situations over extended time intervals (months to years), much as prosthetic devices (e.g., hearing aids, mechanical limbs, etc.) are employed to compensate for physically handicapping conditions. Premature removal of the socially arranged motivational programs can be predicted to result in an eventual return to pre-treatment levels of the behavioral symptoms. Also, use of the behavioral techniques in only one environment is unlikely to affect rates of ADHD symptoms in other, untreated settings unless generalization has been intentionally programmed to occur across such settings. The research reviewed below for the various behavioral techniques seems to support this interpretation.

Direct Application of Behavior Therapy Methods in the Laboratory

A number of studies have evaluated the effects of reinforcement and punishment, usually response cost, on the behavior and cognitive performance of ADHD children. These studies usually indicate that the performance of ADHD children on tasks measuring vigilance or impulse control can be immediately and significantly improved by the use of contingent consequences (Firestone & Douglas, 1975, 1977; Worland, 1976; North-Jones, & Stern, 1973). In some cases, the behavior of ADHD children approximates that of normal control children. However, none of these studies has examined the degree to which such changes generalize to the natural environments of the children, calling into question the clinical efficacy of such an approach. Given the findings of highly limited generalization of treatment effects for the classroom interventions described below, it is unlikely that behavioral techniques implemented only in the clinic or laboratory will carry over into the home or school settings of such children.

Another problem with past laboratory research has been its relatively exclusive focus on response consequences as a means of altering ADHD symptoms, as opposed to altering the stimuli that may control or set the occasion for ADHD symptoms. To their credit, recent investigators have begun examining stimulus control procedures. Zentall (1985), in her thorough review of the literature on situational factors related to ADHD symptoms, concludes that the degree of structure (e.g., task vs. free play), extent of shared attention (e.g., one-to-one vs. group settings), and presence or absence of an adult are not reliably associated with significant differences in the levels of ADHD symptoms. Instead, she argues that the difficulty of the task assigned to ADHD children, and especially the degree of enviromental stimulation, greatly determine the level of hyperactivity and inattention displayed by these children. In a series of ingenious studies, Zentall and her colleagues (see Zentall, 1985) have shown that increasing relevant intratask stimulation and novelty, and reducing task complexity, result in declines in ADHD symptoms. In contrast, extratask stimulation, especially during difficult or complex tasks, increases ADHD symptoms and proves more disruptive to the performance of these children on academic tasks. Perhaps related to this is the observation of Douglas (1983) that repeating task instructions frequently throughout a task enhances the performance of ADHD children to within normal limits in laboratory studies. Hence, an additional behavioral treatment of ADHD children besides altering response consequences would be to alter the stimulus properties of settings and especially of tasks assigned to ADHD children. Making tasks more novel and stimulating through the use of added color, motor participation by the children, frequent shifts in the nature of the task, increased rate of presentation of the material, frequent repetition of the task instructions, and greater enthusiasm and theatrics by the instructor during teaching of the task may make ADHD children more attentive, less active, and more productive in such tasks. Moreover, reducing the length of the task by creating smaller task units and providing frequent breaks from the task may also achieve improved task performance.

Another means of altering stimulus control parameters to enhance the task performance of ADHD children might be to increase the use of externally and concretely represented time limits and rules that are often associated with particular tasks. Such time limits and rules may be internally or cognitively represented in maintaining on-task behaviors. In ADHD children, however, such internal cues may be weak or inconsistently effective in mediating behavior. For instance, when normal children are assigned school tasks to complete and are orally given a time limit in which to do so, their perceptions of elapsed time (internal clocks?) and cognitive iteration of rules for on-task behavior (e.g., "Stay on-task, don't space out, don't bug others," etc.) may function to maintain task performance for adequate periods of time. It is possible that ADHD children are less influenced by such internal perceptions of time and self-statements or are inconsistently controlled by them, although this has never been experimentally examined. Even so, clinical experience with such children suggests that addressing these hypothesized difficulties may be fruitful. This could be achieved by the use of portable timers placed on children's desks and set to reflect the elapsed time available for task performance, or by placing the small "reminder" cards on their desks during individual desk work. Such "reminder" cards might list in bold print four or more rules for on-task behavior similar to the internal self-statements described above. I have employed a similar tactic of enhancing stimulus control by allowing an ADHD child to clip a small portable tape player to his or her belt with an earphone attached to permit the child to listen to "nag" tapes while performing individual desk assignments in class. These tapes are recorded by the parents and consist of periodic reminders ("Stay on task, finish your work, and don't daydream"), as well as reminders of how pleased the parents will be if the child completes that assignment on time. Clinical experience with these techniques, however, suggests that they must eventually be paired with a program of response consequences in order for adequate stimulus control to be maintained. Despite clinical anecdotes supporting the value of these methods, much research needs to be done, first to substantiate the existence of such deficits in ADHD children and then to test the efficacy of these stimulus control programs more rigorously.

Paniagua (1987) has also evaluated the contribution of stimulus control to the management of ADHD children. Using a method known as "correspondence training," he has attempted to establish greater control over ADHD symptoms by commands and rules previously stated publicly by the children. "Correspondence" refers to the degree of concordance between public statements by children as to what they will do and the actual behavior they subsequently display in that setting—in essence, the degree of agreement between "saying" and "doing." In this paradigm, ADHD children are requested to state publicly how they will behave in an immediately subsequent situation. Their behavior in that situation is then observed, after which they are reinforced or punished for the degree of correspondence. Results have suggested that under such conditions, ADHD children significantly reduce their levels of inattention and overactivity during task performance, as well as their levels of aggressive behavior during peer interactions. These preliminary findings with a small sample ($n = 3$) of 7- to 10-year-old

ADHD children are quite promising, suggesting that self-instruction followed by reinforcement for the degree of rule–behavior correspondence may be yet another way of improving the performance of ADHD children through stimulus manipulations. However, work by Hayes *et al.* (1985) suggests that such self-statements must be publicly made in order to be effective, as they serve as a form of public goal setting for which social consequences can be made contingent. Future research needs to show that the children's own statements are serving as the controlling stimuli in such paradigms, rather than the presence of the examiner during the task.

Training Parents in Contingency Management

Despite the plethora of research on parent training in behavior modification (Dangel & Polster, 1984), very few studies have examined the efficacy of this approach with children specifically selected for ADHD symptoms. What few studies exist can be interpreted with cautious optimism as supporting the use of behavioral parent training with ADHD children (Bidder, Gray, & Newcombe, 1978; Dubey, O'Leary, & Kaufman, 1983; Firestone, Kelly, Goodman, & Davey, 1981; O'Leary, Pelham, Rosenbaum, & Price, 1976; Pelham *et al.*, in press; Pollard, Ward, & Barkley, 1983). The treatment techniques used to date have primarily consisted of training parents in general contingency management tactics, such as contingent application of reinforcement or punishment following appropriate–inappropriate behaviors. Reinforcement procedures have typically relied on praise or tokens, whereas the punishment method has usually been loss of tokens or time out from reinforcement. Why these particular methods were chosen or what specific target behaviors they were used with have often gone unreported. At least one study (Bidder *et al.*, 1983) employed a shaping procedure to modify hyperactivity directly. ADHD children were required to sit for progressively longer periods of time while working on assigned tasks with their mothers, for which they were presumably reinforced.

Elsewhere (Barkley, 1981a), I have described a parent training program for ADHD children, the methods of which have been borrowed from research indicating their efficacy in managing defiant and oppositional children (Dangel & Polster, 1984; Forehand & McMahon, 1981). The rationale for the program is twofold. First, it is hypothesized that ADHD children may have a specific deficit in rule-governed behavior, or the stimulus control of behavior by commands, rules, and self-directed speech (Barkley, in press). Unlike a similar theory by Willis and Lovaas (1977), this one does not stipulate that the problem has arisen due to poor child management by parents, but instead proposes a neurophysiological deficiency underlying the problem with rules. Second, there exists a considerable overlap (as much as 70%) of ADHD symptoms and oppositional/defiant behavior, among clinic-referred ADHD children, and such children are recognized to have poorer adolescent and young adult outcomes (Paternite & Loney, 1980; Weiss & Hechtman, 1986). Hence, treatment must be provided for the oppositional/defiant behaviors, and the most useful vehicle for doing so seems to be parent training in behavioral techniques applied contingently for compliance–noncompliance.

The program consists of 10 steps, with 1- to 2-hour weekly training sessions provided either to individual families or in groups. Each step is described in detail elsewhere (Barkley, 1981a, 1987b), but is briefly presented below.

1. *Review of information on ADHD.* In the first session, the therapist provides a succinct overview of the nature, developmental course, prognosis, and etiologies of ADHD. Providing the parents with additional reading materials, such as a book for parents prepared by Wender (1987), can be a useful addition to this session. My colleagues and I have prepared a videotape that presents such an overview and can be loaned to parents for review at home and sharing with relatives or teachers, as needed. Such a session is essential in parent training to dispel a number of misconceptions parents often have about ADHD in children.

2. *The causes of oppositional/defiant behavior.* Next, parents are provided with an in-depth discussion of those factors identified in past research as contributing to the development of defiant behavior in children (see Forehand & McMahon, 1981; Patterson, 1982). Essentially, four major contributors are discussed: (a) child characteristics, such as health, developmental disabilities, and temperament; (b) parent characteristics similar to those described for the

child; (c) situational consequences for oppositional and coercive behavior; and (d) stressful family events. Parents are taught that where problems exist in child and parent characteristics and stressful family events, they increase the probability of the children displaying bouts of coercive, defiant behavior. However, the situational consequences for such defiance determine whether that behavior will be maintained or even increased in subsequent situations where commands and rules are given. Such behavior appears to primarily function as escape/avoidance learning, in which oppositional behavior succeeds in the child's escaping from aversive parent interactions and task demands, negatively reinforcing the child's coercion. As in the first session, this content is covered so as to correct potential misconceptions that parents have about defiance (e.g., it is primarily attention-getting in nature).

3. *Developing and enhancing parental attention.* Patterson (1982) has shown that the value of verbal praise and social reinforcement in families of oppositional children is greatly reduced, making it weak as a reinforcer for compliance. In this session, parents are trained in more effective ways of attending to child behavior so as to enhance the value of their attention to the child. The technique consists of verbal narration and occasional positive statements to the child, with attention being strategically deployed only when appropriate behaviors are displayed by the child. Parents are taught to ignore inappropriate behaviors, but to greatly increase their attention to ongoing prosocial and compliant child behaviors.

4. *Attending to child compliance.* This session extends the techniques developed in session 3 to instances when parents issue direct commands to children. Parents are trained in methods of giving effective commands, such as reducing question-like commands (e.g., "Why don't you pick up your toys now."), increasing imperatives, eliminating setting activities that compete with task performance (e.g., television), reducing task complexity, and so on. They are then encouraged to begin using more effective commanding style and to pay immediate positive attention when compliance is initiated by the child. As part of this assignment, parents are asked to increase the frequency with which they give brief commands to the child this week and to reinforce each command obeyed. Research suggests that these brief commands are more likely to be obeyed, thereby providing excellent training opportunities for attending to compliance.

5. *Establishing a home token economy.* As noted above, several researchers have hypothesized that ADHD children may require more frequent, immediate, and salient consequences for appropriate behavior and compliance in order to maintain it. If this is correct, then instituting a home token economy provides a means of addressing these difficulties by bringing more salient consequences to bear on child compliance than is typically the case. The parents list most of the child's home responsibilities and privileges and then assign values of points or chips to each. They are encouraged to have at least 12 to 15 reinforcers on the menu so as to maintain the motivating properties of the program. Generally, plastic chips are used with children, aged 8 or younger, as they seem to value the tangible features of the token. For children aged 9 or older, points recorded in a notebook seem sufficient.

During the first week of this program, the parents are not to fine the child or remove points for misconduct. The program is for rewarding good behavior only. Parents are also asked to be liberal in awarding chips to the child for even minor instances of appropriate conduct. However, chips are given only for obeying first requests. If a command must be repeated, it must still be obeyed, but the opportunity to earn chips has been forfeited. Parents are also encouraged to give bonus chips for good attitude or emotional regulation in the child. For instance, if a command is obeyed quickly, without complaint, and with a positive attitude, parents may give the child additional chips beyond those typically given for that job. Where this is used, parents are to note expressly that the awarding of the additional chips is for a positive attitude. Families are encouraged to establish and maintain such programs for at least 6–8 weeks, to allow for the newly developed interaction patterns spawned by such programs to become habit patterns in dealing with child compliance.

6. *Implementing time out for noncompliance.* Parents are now trained to use response cost (removal of points or chips) contingent on noncompliance. In addition, they are trained in an effective technique for time out from reinforcement, to be used with two serious forms of defiance that may continue to be problematic despite the use of the home token economy. These two misbehaviors are selected in con-

sultation with the parents and typically involve a type of command or household rule that the child continues to defy despite parental use of previous treatment strategies. Time out is limited to these two forms of misconduct so as to keep it from being used excessively during the next week.

The time-out procedure taught to parents often differs from that commonly used by them. First, the time out is to be implemented shortly after noncompliance by a child begins. Parents often wait until they are very upset with a child before instituting punishment, often repeating their commands frequently to a child in the interim. In this program, parents issue a command, wait 5 seconds, issue a warning, wait another 5 seconds, and then take the child to time out immediately should compliance not have begun to these commands or warnings. Second, children are not given control over the time-out interval, as they often are in many households. For instance, parents often place a child in time out, then say that the child can leave time out when he or she is quiet, when he or she is ready to do as the parents asked, or when a timer signals the end of the interval. In each of these cases, determination as to when the time-out interval ends is no longer under the parents' control. This program teaches parents simply to tell the child not to leave the time-out chair until given permission to do so. Three conditions must be met by the child before time out ends, and these are in a hierarchy: (a) The child must serve a minimum sentence in time out, usually 1 to 2 minutes for each year of his or her age; (b) the child must then become quiet for a brief period of time so as not to have disruption associated with the parents' approaching the time-out chair and talking to the child; and (3) the child must then agree to obey the command. Failure of the child to remain in time out until all three conditions are met is met with additional punishment. The consequence is tailored to meet parental wishes, but may consist of a fine within the home token system, two spanks on the buttocks, extension of the time-out interval an additional 5 or 10 minutes, or placement of the child in his or her bedroom. In the last case, toys or other entertaining activities are previously removed from the bedroom.

7. *Extending time out to additional noncompliant behaviors.* In this session, no new material is taught to parents. Instead, any problems with implementing time out are reviewed and corrected. Parents may then extend their use of time out to one or two additional noncompliant behaviors with which the child may still have trouble.

8. *Managing noncompliance in public places.* Parents are now taught to extrapolate their home management methods to troublesome public places, such as stores, church, and restaurants. Using a "think aloud–think ahead" paradigm, parents are taught to stop just before entering a public place, review two or three rules with the child that the child may previously have defied, explain to the child what reinforcers are available for obedience in the place, and then explain what punishment may occur for disobedience. Parents then enter the public place and immediately begin attending to and reinforcing ongoing child compliance with the previously stated rules. Time out or response cost is used immediately for disobedience.

Time out in a public place may require slight modification from its use at home. For instance, parents may be taught to stand the child against the wall farthest from the central aisle of a store to serve as the time-out location. If this is inconvenient, then taking the child to a restroom or having him or her face the side of a display cabinet may be adequate substitutes. If these are not possible, then taking the child outside the building to face the front wall or returning to the car can be used for time out. When none of these locations seem appropriate, parents can be trained to use a delayed-punishment contingency. In this case, the parent carries a small spiral notebook to the public place and, before entering the building, indicates that rule violations will be recorded in the book and the child will serve time out for them upon return home from this trip. I encourage parents to keep a picture of the child sitting in time out at home with this notebook and to show it to the child before entering the public building. This serves as a reminder to the child of what may be in store should a rule be violated. Whenever time out is used in a public place, it need not be for as long an interval as at home. I have found that half of the usual time-out interval may be sufficient for public misbehavior, given the richly reinforcing activities in public places from which the child has just been removed.

9. *Managing future misconduct.* By now, parents should have acquired an effective repertoire of child management techniques. The goal of this session is to get parents to think about how they may be implemented in the future if

some other forms of noncompliance develop. The therapist challenges the parents with misbehaviors they have not seen yet and asks them to explain how they might use their recently acquired skills to manage these problems.

10. *One-month review/booster session.* In what is typically the final session, the concepts taught in earlier sessions are briefly reviewed, problems that have arisen in the last month are discussed, and plans are made for their correction. Other sessions may be needed to deal with additional issues that persist but for most families, these 10 sessions appear adequate for improving rates of compliant behavior in ADHD children.

The program is intended for children aged 2 to 11 years for whom oppositional or defiant behavior is an issue. For teenagers with ADDH and oppositional behavior, I recommend the problem-solving communication training program developed by Robin and Foster (see Foster & Robin, Chapter 14, this volume). If a child's difficulties are purely those of ADHD, only sessions 1, 2, 5, and 6 need to be taught to provide the parents with a review of skills that can prevent the emergence of future oppositional behavior. Implementing the token system may not be necessary or may be used only for very circumscribed problems, such as doing homework.

As in other parent training programs (Dangel & Polster, 1984), several factors appear to mediate parents' success in acquiring these skills. These seem to be maternal depression, marital discord, severe parental psychopathology, maternal social isolation, and parental socioeconomic level. These problems apparently limit program success by interfering with the consistency and predictability of parental management of child behavior, as well as with the selection of consequences that parents may employ in reaction to misconduct. In troubled families, misconduct may not be disciplined as consistently, and thus it may succeed more often than in normal families. Moreover, the use of consequences may become more arbitrary, depending upon a parent's emotional state at the time consequences should be given. And perhaps the administration of reinforcers is diminished as a result of parental depression and distress. Whatever the mechanism, it is clear that the more serious these problems are within a family, the less likely it is that this program will effectively address the child's noncompliance.

Training Teachers in Classroom Management

Somewhat more research has been done on the application of behavior management methods in the classroom with ADHD children than on parent training. Moreover, there is a voluminous literature on the application of classroom management methods to disruptive child behaviors, many of which include typical ADHD symptoms. This research clearly indicates the effectiveness of behavioral techniques in the short-term treatment of academic performance problems in ADHD children.

As noted above in discussing laboratory applications of behavior therapy techniques, recent research suggests some promise in the use of stimulus control procedures with ADHD children, many of which can be readily adapted to the classroom. Reducing task length "chunking" tasks into smaller units to fit more within the child's attention span, and setting quotas for the child to achieve within shorter time intervals may increase the success of the ADHD child with academic work (see Ayllon & Rosenbaum, 1977). As Zentall (1985) has already documented, the use of increased stimulation within the task (e.g., color, shape, texture, rate of stimulus presentation) may enhance attention to academic tasks in ADHD children. Teaching styles may play an important role in how well ADHD children attend to lectures by a teacher. More vibrant, enthusiastic teachers who move about more, engage children frequently while teaching, and allow greater participation of the children in the teaching activity may increase sustained attention to the task at hand. Zentall has also shown that permitting ADHD children to move or participate motorically while learning a task may improve attention and performance. The use of written, displayed rules and timers for setting task time limits, as already described, may further benefit ADHD children in the classroom.

A number of studies have also shown that the contingent application of reinforcers for reduced activity level or increased sustained attention can rapidly alter the levels of these ADHD symptoms (see Ayllon & Roberts, 1974, for a discussion of issues in directly treating disruptive class behavior with contingencies; see also Schulman, Stevens, Suran, Kupst, & Naughton, 1978). Usually these programs incorporate token rewards, as some research suggests that praise may not be sufficient to increase or maintain normal levels of on-task behavior in hyperactive children (Pfiffner, Rosen, & O'Leary, 1985). Several studies have shown that rewards administered to the group, in which all children in class receive a reward contingent on the performance of one child, are as effective as individually administered rewards (Rosenbaum, O'Leary, & Jacob, 1975). One of the problems arising in such research, however, is the demonstration that simply reinforcing greater on-task behavior and decreased activity level does not necessarily translate into increased work productivity or accuracy (Marholin & Steinman, 1977). Since the latter are the ultimate goals of behavioral intervention in the classroom, these results are somewhat dismaying. Research now suggests that reinforcing the products of classroom behavior (i.e., number and accuracy of problems completed) not only results in increased productivity and accuracy, but also results indirectly in declines in off-task and hyperactive behavior (Ayllon, Layman, & Kandel, 1975; Ayllon, & Rosenbau, 1977; Marholin & Steinman, 1977; Pfiffner, Rosen, & O'Leary, 1985; Robinson, Newby, & Ganzell, 1981).

A serious limitation of these promising results has been the lack of follow-up on the maintenance of these treatment gains over time. In addition, none of these studies has examined whether generalization of behavioral control occurs in other school settings where no treatment procedures are in effect. Other studies employing a mixture of cognitive–behavioral and contingency management techniques have failed to find such generalization with ADHD children (Barkley et al., 1980), suggesting that improvements derived from classroom management methods are quite situation-specific and may not generalize or be maintained once treatment has been terminated.

The role of punishment in the management of classroom behavior in ADHD children has been less well studied. Pfiffner, O'Leary, Rosen, and Sanderson (1985) evaluated the effects of continuous and intermittent verbal reprimands and response cost on off-task classroom behaviors. They found that while each of these treatments significantly reduced disruptive and off-task behavior, the continuous use of response cost (loss of recess time) was most effective. Ayllon and Rosenbaum (1977) also reported on the initial success of adding response cost contingencies to an ongoing classroom token economy. However, after less than 1 week, disruptive behavior returned to baseline levels despite the punishment contingency.

In a later paper, Pfiffner and O'Leary (1987) determined that positive reinforcement for controlling ADHD behaviors in the classroom was not sufficient by itself to maintain improved behavior in these children unless punishment in the form of response cost was added to the program. The addition of response cost further increased rates of on-task behavior and academic accuracy. These gains in behavior could then be maintained by an all-positive program once the response cost procedure was gradually withdrawn. However, abrupt withdrawal of the punishment contingency resulted in declines in on-task behavior and accuracy, suggesting that the manner in which response cost techniques are implemented and then faded out of classroom management programs is important in the maintenance of initial treatment gains. In general, the efficacy of response cost procedures with ADHD children has been well documented (Firestone & Douglas, 1975, 1977; Rapport, Murphy, & Bailey, 1982).

What conclusions can be drawn from this literature indicate that contingency management methods can produce immediate, short-term improvement in the behavior, productivity, and accuracy of ADHD children in the classroom. Secondary or tangible reinforcers are more effective in reducing disruptive behavior and increasing performance than are attention or other social reinforcers. The use of positive reinforcement programs alone does not seem to result in as much improvement, nor does it maintain that improvement over time as well as does the combination of token reinforcement systems with punishment, such as response cost (i.e., removal of tokens or privileges). Such findings would be expected from the theories of ADHD discussed earlier, which suggest a decreased sensitivity to reinforcement in this disorder. What little evidence there is, however, suggests that treatment gains are unlikely to be maintained in these children once treatment has been withdrawn, and that improvements in behavior probably do not generalize to other settings where no treatment is in effect.

Two additional classroom management techniques may prove of value in treating ADHD children, but their effectiveness remains to be rigorously studied. One involves the use of a transmitter and receiver/counter for implementing an in-class token system. The device, known as the Attention Trainer,* consists of a small transmitter clipped to the belt of a teacher and a second counting device/receiver placed on the child's desk. The counter is turned on when the child is given an assignment to do at his or her desk. Every minute, the counter adds a point on the face of the device, and the cumulative points can be exchanged later for other rewards. Whenever the teacher sees that the child is off task or disrupting the class, she presses a button on the transmitter which activates a red light on top of the receiver and deducts a point from the face of the counter. This method of utilizing a combination of token reinforcement and response cost eliminates one of the major difficulties in implementing class token systems—the need for proximity of the teacher to the child to administer the contingencies. Rapport *et al.* (1982) compared this procedure to stimulant medication for improving attention and academic productivity of two ADHD children in a classroom setting. The response cost procedure was superior to methylphenidate alone in increasing both attention and productivity during academic tasks.

Another promising method deserving of further evaluation is the use of home-based contingencies for in-class behavior and performance. Atkeson and Forehand (1979) have reviewed this literature and find that the method offers some usefulness for managing disruptive classroom behavior, but that much more rigorous research is required to evaluate its promise. The method involves having a teacher rate a child's daily school performance one or more times throughout a school day. An example of one such rating card is shown in Figure 2-1 (Barkley, 1981a). These ratings are then sent home with the child for review by the parents. The parents dispense rewards or punishments (usually response cost) at home, contingent upon the content of these daily ratings. O'Leary *et al.* (1976) employed this procedure for 10 weeks with nine hyperkinetic children and documented significant improve-

*Available from Gordon Systems, Inc., P.O. Box 746, DeWitt, NY 13214.

NAME _____ DATE _____

Please rate this child in each of the areas listed below as to how he/she performed in school today using ratings of 1 to 5. 1 = excellent, 2 = good, 3 = fair, 4 = poor, 5 = terrible or did not do work.

CLASS PERIODS/SUBJECTS

AREAS	1	2	3	4	5	6
Participation						
Class Work						
Followed Rules						
Interaction with Other Children						
Teacher's Initials						

Place comments on back if desired

FIGURE 2-1. An example of a daily school report card used in conjunction with a home-based reinforcement program. From *Hyperactive Children: A Handbook for Diagnosis and Treatment* by R. A. Barkley, 1981, New York: Guilford Press. Copyright 1981 by Guilford Press. Reprinted by permission.

ments on teacher ratings of classroom conduct and hyperkinesis as compared to a no-treatment control group. Others have similarly found such home–school behavioral report cards to be useful, either alone or in combination with parent and teacher training in behavior management, in the treatment of ADHD children (Allyon, Garber, & Pisor, 1975; O'Leary & Pelham, 1978; Pelham *et al.*, in press)

In the procedure I employ, the child is rated on a scale from 1 ("excellent") to 5 ("terrible") in each area of behavior indicated on the card. Any behaviors problematic in class can be listed on the card. The teacher rates the child at least four or more times per day; in the case of middle or high school students, multiple teachers rate the child and initial the card. Space is provided for teacher comments. I also encourage the student to record homework for that evening on the back, and the teacher(s) should check to make sure it is accurately recorded before completing the ratings. At home, the parents review and discuss the ratings with the child and note the homework assignment for the evening. Where possible, a second set of school books is maintained at home, so as to avoid the problem common to ADHD children of not having all the materials they need for a given school assignment. The parents award points for ratings of 1 (15–25 Points), 2 (10–15 points), and 3 (5 points), and deduct points for ratings of

4 (minus 10–15 points) and 5 (minus 15–25 points). The total net points are then available for the child to purchase privileges from a reward menu maintained at home.

Although little research has been done on the subject, it is likely that certain aspects of the teacher and his or her philosophy of child behavior management contribute to the success or failure of any contingency management methods to be used in his or her class. In my experience, I have found that the two greatest hindrances to implementing these methods are the time available to the teacher for doing so and the teacher's attitude toward behavioral techniques in general. Many regular education classes have 22 to 26 children, making it difficult for a teacher to rigorously implement these procedures in what little time he or she may have for any individual child. This problem can be partly remedied by keeping the methods relatively simple or by having an aide assigned to the class temporarily to assist with the initial implementation of the program. Should this prove infeasible or ineffective, and should the severity of the child's ADHD symptoms warrant it, placement of the child in a smaller, special educational classroom for part or all of the school day may help. Special education teachers often have much more training and experience in contingency management methods, and typically have the time as well as the teacher assistants to implement them.

Overcoming an antagonistic philosophy held by a teacher is more difficult. Some teachers have had negative experiences with poorly designed behavioral techniques or simply feel that they are dehumanizing and mechanistic to children, failing to address the true, inner emotional disturbance. In such a case, I have often sought a change of classrooms for an ADHD child. In extreme circumstances, I recommend that the parents place the child in another school, where teachers may be more amenable to providing the additional time and special techniques ADHD children require to improve classroom adjustment. (See Barkley, 1981a for a more complete discussion of these and other issues.)

Cognitive–Behavioral Therapies

The limited space available here cannot permit justice to the burgeoning literature on cognitive–behavioral interventions for childhood behavioral problems, or specifically for ADHD.

The reader is referred to critical reviews (Harris, Wong, & Keogh, 1985), clinical texts (Kendall & Braswell, 1984), and chapters (Douglas, 1980) for a more thorough treatment of the subject. These therapies are generally attempts to combine the strategies developed from cognitive psychology for enhancing the acquisition of knowledge with the self-application of behavioral techniques (e.g., self-assessment, self-instruction, self-reinforcement, self-punishment, etc.). The particular appeal of this approach with ADHD children derives from its apparent focus upon some of the primary deficits of ADHD, such as poor organization in accomplishing tasks, difficulties with rules and instructions, deficient social skills, and impulsiveness (i.e., not "thinking" before one acts.) Furthermore, by having the child engage in his or her own self-regulated behavior modification program, one might circumvent the limited generalization of treatment effects over time and settings seen in more traditional contingency management programs.

Self-Monitoring. A relatively simple cognitive–behavioral treatment is to teach children to observe and record their own behavior. A particular problem behavior may be selected (off-task behavior, vocal noises, talk to classmates, etc.), and the child is instructed to record on a chart or diary occurrences of that behavior. Or, more commonly, a child may be instructed to record the appropriate behavior that the trainer is attempting to increase (on-task behavior, number of problems completed, raising one's hand for permission, etc.) Such procedures may be used alone or, more typically, may be combined with self-instruction and self-reinforcement for achieving desired changes in the target behavior.

Harris (1986) trained four learning-disabled children with serious attentional problems to monitor either their atention to tasks or their work productivity (number of problems completed). In self-monitoring on-task behavior, children were interrupted in their work periodically and asked to record whether they had been attending to their work or not during the previous interval. In the self-monitoring of production, children kept a written record of the amount of written spelling they had accomplished during a specified work period. Results indicated that both types of self-monitoring increased on-task behavior and work productivity for most children, whereas, self-monitoring of productivity appeared to be better than monitoring of on-task behavior in increasing work production for one child.

Using a more complicated treatment procedure, Varni and Henker (1979) compared the effects of self-monitoring of attention to academic work with self-instruction and self-reinforcement procedures in the treatment of three hyperactive boys. Treatment was instituted initially in a clinic setting and later in the children's regular school classroom for all three children. Self-monitoring consisted of recording the amount of time a child spent attending to task during a work period. Each boy awarded himself points for the length of time he spent attending to tasks. Although this would appear to be a form of self-reinforcement, these points could not be used to purchase any reinforcers. Under the self-reinforcement condition, however, these points could be exchanged for later privileges and rewards. Results indicated that self-monitoring did not improve the academic accuracy or productivity of these children in the clinic or at home, nor did it result in significant declines in behavioral observations of hyperactivity and inattention. The addition of a self-reinforcement contingency to self-monitoring program, however, did lead to significant improvements in these dependent measures. Self-instruction was of no benefit in improving work performance or hyperactivity.

We (Barkley, et al., 1980) combined group training in self-instruction with self-monitoring and self-reinforcement of on-task behavior during individual deskwork for six hyperactive children aged 7–10 years. Self-instruction training did not appear to reduce problem behaviors during the group instruction period. However, the combination of self-monitoring and self-reinforcement was effective in improving on-task behavior during individual deskwork periods. The degree of improvement was highly dependent upon the schedule of self-monitoring/reinforcement used and the age of the children. More frequent self-monitoring/reinforcement (mean variable interval, 1 minute) was superior to reduced schedules (mean variable interval, 3 minutes) in maintaining high levels of on-task behavior. In addition, older ADHD children were better able to maintain attention under conditions of reduced self-reinforcement than were younger children. It is not clear from this study, however, whether the self-monitoring or self-reinforcement was responsible for the improvement in attention to tasks, as the separate effects of each were not evaluated.

Several investigators have compared self-monitoring procedures to stimulant medication in treating children with ADHD. Hinshaw, Henker, and Whalen (1984a, 1984b) trained ADHD boys to monitor their social behavior, and then to reinforce themselves for meeting a specified criterion of improvement in the desired behaviors. Specifically, the target behaviors of interest in one study (1984a) were sharing, not fighting, and listening to adult direction; in the other study (1984b), the target was anger control during peer interactions. This treatment was compared to reinforcement by others and stimulant medication, used alone or combined with the self-evaluation procedures. The combination of the self-monitoring/reinforcement procedure with stimulant medication was superior to either treatment alone. Either self-monitoring/reinforcement or medication alone was also superior to reinforcement by others. Medication appeared to improve the accuracy of self-evaluations in these ADHD children. Anderson, Clement, and Oettinger (1981) compared stimulant drug treatment alone with self-monitoring/reinforcement alone in improving the performance of 12 ADHD boys on the Children's Checking Task, a measure of attention and vigilance. Unlike the findings of Hinshaw et al. (1984a), only the medication condition resulted in improvements on this task. Again, because self-reinforcement was combined with the self-monitoring procedures, the separate effects of each procedure could not be evaluated. Nevertheless, these studies suggest that the effect of self-monitoring/reinforcement may be highly dependent on the nature of the task or behavior chosen as the target of intervention. Moreover, self-monitoring alone may not be as beneficial as combining it with a self-reinforcement procedure.

Self-Reinforcement. As noted above, another cognitive–behavioral technique often used in research with ADHD children is self-reinforcement. This involves teaching children not only to monitor their behavior, but to evaluate how they have performed a given behavior or task and then to award themselves reinforcers (usually tokens or points) for their accomplishments. These tokens are later exchanged for a variety of privileges or rewards. Bowers, Clement, Fantuzzo, and Sorenson (1985) examined the effects of teacher-administered versus self-administered reinforcement in improving the attention of six ADHD children (aged 8 to 11 years) to their academic work. During individual performance of reading workbooks, a teacher was trained to administer points on a card at the child's desk for on-task behavior, using a variable-interval schedule of reinforcement. In the self-administered condition, the child self-administered a point and recorded this in a wrist counter, again using a variable-interval schedule. Teachers and children were cued as to when to evaluate and reinforce behavior by the use of a vibrotactile stimulator worn on the belt programmed to a variable-interval schedule (mean 81 seconds). Points earned were cashed in weekly for money. Results indicated that both treatments improved attention to task and accuracy of reading work, but that self-administered rewards were more effective in improving attention. Accuracy of work done appeared to be equivalent across the treatment conditions.

As described above, several other studies have found the combination of self-monitoring and self-reinforcement to be effective in improving on-task behavior, academic accuracy, hyperactivity, and peer interactions in ADHD children (Barkley *et al.*, 1980; Hinshaw et al., 1984a, 1984b; Varni & Henker, 1979), and that adding stimulant medication to the treatment package may further enhance treatment effects (Chase & Clement, 1985; Hinshaw et al., 1984a, 1984b). Only Anderson *et al..* (1981) have failed to find treatment effects for self-reinforcement, and this may be explained on the basis of the task they used (a paper-and-pencil vigilance test), which may not assess the same aspects of attention that are involved in on-task behavior to academic work.

Self-Instruction. Meichenbaum and Goodman (1971) are credited as being the first to apply self-instruction methods to hyperactive children. When these investigators trained the children to use self-directed verbalizations, improvements in performance on tasks measuring impulse control were achieved. Specifically, this type of training involved teaching the children to follow a set of self-directed instructions: to stop before beginning a task, repeat the instructions given, describe the nature of the task before them, verbalize how they might attempt the task, consider the likely consequences of that approach, and then decide which approach to follow. Then, while actually performing the

task, the children were trained to describe and reflect upon their performance and finally to evaluate their performance once complete. The therapist initially modeled these reflective, problem-solving steps, after which the children imitated the strategies while accomplishing various laboratory tasks.

These initially positive results were followed by a flurry of successful replications and extensions of the technique to classroom management and social skills (Bornstein & Quevillon, 1976; Douglas, Parry, Martin, & Garson, 1976; Kendall & Braswell, 1982; Kendall & Finch, 1978, 1979; Kendall & Wilcox, 1980). Unfortunately, more recent research has not found such promising results (Abikoff & Gittelman, 1986; Brown, Borden, Wynne, Schleser, & Clingerman, 1986; Brown, Wynne, & Medenis, 1985). There have been several failures to replicate Bornstein and Quevillon's (1976) initially successful reports of generalization of individualized training in school to classroom performance (Billings & Wasik, 1985; Friedling & O'Leary, 1979). These later studies suggest that children must be reinforced for demonstrating the self-instruction strategies in order to achieve or maintain treatment effects in classroom settings. Hence, self-reinforcement or reinforcement by others (which is often a part of self-instruction programs) may be the critical procedure that accounts for treatment effects, rather than self-instruction (Friedling & O'Leary, 1979). Others have not found generalization of the effects of special classroom group instruction to regular educational classrooms (Barkley *et al.*, 1980), or have found that improvement in attention or impulse control due to self-instruction does not generalize to measures of academic achievement and is highly dependent on level of cognitive development (Borden, Brown, Wynne, & Schleser, 1987; Brown *et al.*, 1985).

In view of these disappointing findings, others have questioned the actual ability of children to engage in self-control apart from external supervision, prompts, and reinforcement (Gross & Wojnilower, 1984; Hayes *et al.*, 1985). Improvements in cognitive–behavioral paradigms, these critics claim, are the result of the monitoring provided by adult supervisors, public goal setting by the children, arrangement of contingencies by adults to preclude cheating, and ultimate dispensation of the reinforcers by adults (e.g., cashing in self-administered points for rewards). Generalization of treatment effects to no-treatment settings has not been found, as originally hoped, and treatment effects over time have proven quite weak or nonexistent. The numerous methodological problems with the early research and more recent failures to replicate have led Abikoff (1985, 1987), in a critical review of these interventions for ADHD, to conclude that the effectiveness of such treatments for ADHD remains unproven.

It seems wise at present to continue to view self-instruction as promising for ADHD children, provided that it is combined with contingency management procedures to encourage performance of the strategies and assist with their generalization to nontraining settings.

Summary. In general, the cognitive–behavioral techniques described above appear to have some promise in the treatment of ADHD symptoms in the classroom (Whalen, Henker, & Hinshaw, 1985). Contrary to initial expectations, cognitive-behavioral techniques do not seem to free a child up from control by the social environment, but only shift the control by others to a slightly less direct form. Nevertheless, many caregivers see such a successful shift as a sign of increasing maturity, and therefore it may contribute to greater social acceptability for the child. Nor have these therapies circumvented the problem of situation specificity of treatment effects, which has plagued the contingency management methods for years. Where generalization to other settings or over time is desired, it must be actively programmed into the treatment. Where this occurs, generalization may follow (Harris, 1986). Kendall (personal communication, June 1987), a leading advocate of cognitive–behavioral treatments for impulsive children, has also argued that one should not forget the "behavioral" in the cognitive–behavioral paradigm; contingency management methods must be used in concert with metacognitive strategies so as to reinforce their usage and prompt their occurrence in other settings.

Others have noted that research must explore potential developmental limitations of these techniques, in view of their heavy reliance on linguistic competence and other developmental abilities that may not be sufficiently mature in young children to permit successful teaching or transfer of the learned skills (Cole & Kazdin, 1980). Underscoring this point are the findings of a recent study of such developmental considerations (Border *et al.*, 1987), which found results contrary to what one might expect. This study revealed that *older* children appeared to profit little from such instruction, as the skills taught may have been too elementary for children already in the developmental stage of formal operational thinking. In contrast, *younger* children appeared to benefit most from concrete instruction in using verbal strategies for behavioral control.

Combined Interventions

As should have been gathered from the discussion above, psychopharmacological and behavioral treatments are not, by themselves, completely adequate to address all of the difficulties likely to be presented by clinic-referred ADHD children. Optimal treatment is likely to be comprised of a combination of many of these approaches for maximal effectiveness. Some research studies have examined the utility of such treatment packages, with interesting results. It appears that in many studies, the combination of contingency management training of parents or teachers with stimulant drug therapies is generally little better than either treatment alone for the management of ADHD symptoms (Firestone *et al.*, 1981; Gadow, 1985; Pollard *et al.*, 1983; Wolraich, Drummond, Saloman, O'Brien, & Sivage, 1978). One study (Abikoff & Gittelman, 1984) found that classroom behavioral interventions may have mildly improved the deviant behavior of ADHD children, but did not bring such levels of behavior within the normal range. Medication, in contrast, rendered most children normal in classroom behavior. Where there is an advantage to behavioral interventions, it appears to be in reliably increasing rates of academic productivity and accuracy (Ayllon & Rosenbaum, 1977; Gadow, 1985; Wolraich *et al.*, 1978). Yet here, too, stimulant medication has shown some positive effects. Despite some failures to obtain additive effects for these two treatments, their combination may still be advantageous, given that the stimulants are not usually used in the late afternoons or evenings, when parents may need effective behavior management tactics to deal with the ADHD symptoms.

Several studies have examined the effects of combining stimulant medication with cognitive–behavioral interventions. Horn, Chatoor, and Conners (1983) examined the separate and combined effects of d-amphetamine and self-instructional training with a 9-year-old impatient ADHD child. The combined program was more effective in increasing on-task behavior during classwork and decreasing teacher ratings of ADHD symptoms. However, academic productivity was improved only by the use of direct reinforcement for correct responses. In contrast, using a group comparison design, Brown et al. (1986) and Brown et al. (1985) found no benefits of combined drug and cognitive–behavioral interventions over either alone on similar domains of functioning of ADHD children. Similarly negative results were found by Cohen, Sullivan, Minde, Novak, and Helwig (1981) for kindergarten-age ADHD children at a 1-year follow-up evaluation.

Some success for combined medication and self-evaluation procedures have been reported (Hinshaw et al., 1984a) when social skills such as cooperation have been the targets of intervention. Yet, when these same investigators attempted to teach anger control strategies to ADHD children to enhance self-control during peer interactions, no benefits of combined intervention were found beyond that achieved by self-control training alone (Hinshaw et al., 1984b). The self-control techniques were the most successful in teaching these children specific coping strategies to employ in provocative interactions with peers, which usually led to angry reactions from the ADHD children. Medication, in contrast, served only to lower the overall level of anger responses, but did not enhance the application of specific anger control strategies. These studies suggest that each form of treatment may have highly specific and unique effects on some aspects of social behavior but not on others.

Some investigators have evaluated the effects of behavioral parent training in contingency management, both alone and combined with self-control therapy (Horn, Ialongo, Popovich, & Peradotto, 1987), on home and school behavioral problems. The results failed to find any significant advantage for the combined treatments. Both self-control training and behavioral parent training alone improved home behavior problems, but neither resulted in any generalization of treatment effects to the school, where no treatment had occurred. Since a no-treatment group was not employed in this study, however, it is not possible to conclude that these effects were due to treatment rather than to nonspecific effects (e.g., maturation, therapist attention, regression effects, etc.).

Satterfield, Satterfield, and Cantwell (1980)

have attempted to evaluate the effects of individualized multi-modality intervention provided over extensive time periods (up to several years) on the outcome of ADHD boys. Interventions included medication, behavioral parent training, individual counseling, special education, family therapy, and other programs as needed by an individual. Results suggest that such an individualized program of combined treatments continued over longer time intervals can produce improvements in social adjustment at home and school, rates of antisocial behavior, substance abuse, and academic achievement.

CONCLUSION

ADHD appears to be a developmental disability in the domains of sustained attention, impulse control, and the regulation of activity level to situational demands. It arises during early childhood, is often relatively pervasive or cross-situational, and is typically chronic in nature. Future research may reveal an as-yet-unspecified deficit in the manner in which consequences regulate behavior, suggesting that the disorder may be one of motivation rather than attention. Present knowledge strongly points to a biological predisposition to the disorder, with multiple etiologies being implicated. Environmental influences appear to play a role in determining the severity of ADHD symptoms, the development of oppositional and defiant behavior as well as conduct problems, and the long-term prognosis for the disorder.

The assessment of ADHD children includes not only the traditional methods of parental and child interviews, but also standardized child behavior rating scales, psychometric measures of intelligence and achievement, and direct behavioral observations of the ADHD symptoms in natural or analogue settings. Promising laboratory measures of sustained attention may soon make it possible to evaluate ADHD symptoms more objectively in clinical settings. Even then, assessment is likely to require the use of multiple methods across several settings, incorporating the opinions of several caretakers (parents and teachers).

The treatment of ADHD requires expertise in many different treatment modalities, no single one of which can address all of the difficulties likely to be experienced by such children.

Among available treatments, stimulant medication, parent training in effective child management, classroom behavior modification methods, special educational placement, and (in some cases) self-control and social skills training appear to have the greatest efficacy or promise of such. Nevertheless, to be effective in altering prognosis, treatments must be maintained over extended time periods (months to years), with periodic reintervention after treatment termination.

REFERENCES

Abidin, R. R. (1983). *Parenting Stress Index*. Charlottesville, VA: Pediatric Psychology Press.

Abikoff, H. (1985). Efficacy of cognitive training interventions in hyperactive children: A critical review. *Clinical Psychology Review, 5*, 479–512.

Abikoff, H. (1987). An evaluation of cognitive behavior therapy for hyperactive children. In B. Lahey & A. Kazdin (Eds.), *Advances in clinical child psychology* (Vol. 10, pp. 171–216). New York: Plenum.

Abikoff, H., & Gittelman, R. (1984). Does behavior therapy normalize the classroom behavior of hyperactive children? *Archives of General Psychiatry, 41*, 449–454.

Abikoff, H., & Gittelman, R. (1985). Hyperactive children treated with stimulants: Is cognitive training a useful adjunct? *Archives of General Psychiatry, 42*, 953–961.

Abikoff, H., Gittelman-Klein, R., & Klein, D. (1977). Validation of a classroom observation code for hyperactive children. *Journal of Consulting and Clinical Psychology, 45*, 772–783.

Achenbach, T. M., & Edelbrock, C. (1983). *Manual for the Child Behavior Checklist and Revised Child Behavior Profile*. Burlington: University of Vermont, Department of Psychiatry.

Achenbach, T. M., & Edelbrock, C. (1987). *Manual for the Child Behavior Checklist Youth Self-Report*. Burlington: University of Vermont, Department of Psychiatry.

American Psychological Association. (1968). *Diagnostic and statistical manual of mental disorders* (2nd ed.) Washington, DC: Author.

American Psychological Association. (1968). *Diagnostic and statistical manual of mental disorders* (3rd ed.) Washington, DC: Author.

American Psychiatric Association. (1987). *Diagnostic and statistical manual of mental disorders* (3rd ed., rev.). Washington, DC: Author.

Anderson, E. C., Clement, P. W., & Oettinger, L., Jr. (1981). Methylphenidate compared with behavioral self-control in Attention Deficit Disorder: A preliminary report. *Developmental and Behavioral Pediatrics, 2*, 137–141.

Arnold, L. E., Clark, D. L., Sachs, L. A., Jakim, S., & Smithies, C. (1985). Vestibular and visual rotational stimulation as treatment for attention deficit and hyperactivity. *American Journal of Occupational Therapy, 39*, 84–91.

Atkeson, B. M., & Forehand, R. (1979). Home-based reinforcement programs designed to modify classroom behavior: A review and methodological evaluation. *Psychological Bulletin, 86*, 1298–1308.

Ayllon, T., Garber, S., & Pisor, K. (1975). The elimination of discipline problems through a combined school–home motivational system. *Behavior Therapy, 6*, 616–626.

Ayllon, T., Layman, D., & Kandel, H. (1975). A behavioral–educational alternative to drug control of hyperactive children. *Journal of Applied Behavior Analysis, 8*, 137–146.

Ayllon, T., & Roberts, M. (1974). Eliminating discipline problems by strengthening academic performance. *Journal of Applied Behavior Analysis, 7*, 71–76.

Ayllon, T., & Rosenbaum, M. (1977). The behavioral treatment of disruption and hyperactivity in school settings. In B. Lahey & A. Kazdin (Eds.), *Advances in clinical child psychology* (Vol. 1, pp. 83–118). New York: Plenum.

Bacon, J. (1988, February 17). What's the best medicine for hyperactive kids? *USA Today*, p. 4D.

Barkley, R. A. (1976). Predicting the response of hyperkinetic children to stimulant drugs: A review. *Journal of Abnormal Child Psychology, 4*, 327–348.

Barkley, R. A. (1977a). The effects of methylphenidate on various measures of activity level and attention in hyperkinetic children. *Journal of Abnormal Child Psychology, 5*, 351–369.

Barkley, R. A. (1977b). A review of stimulant drug research with hyperactive children. *Journal of Child Psychology and Psychiatry, 18*, 137–165.

Barkley, R. A. (1981a). *Hyperactive children: A handbook for diagnosis and treatment*. New York: Guilford Press.

Barkley, R. A. (1981b). Hyperactivity. In E. J. Mash & L. G. Terdal (Eds.), *Behavioral assessment of childhood disorders* (pp. 127–184). New York: Guilford Press.

Barkley, R. A. (1982). Specific guidelines for defining hyperactivity in children (Attention Deficit Disorder with Hyperactivity). In B. Lahey & A. Kazdin (Eds.), *Advances in clinical child psychology* (Vol. 5, pp. 137–180). New York: Plenum.

Barkley, R. A. (1985). The social interactions of hyperactive children: Developmental changes, drug effects, and situational variation. In R. McMahon & R. Peters (Eds.), *Childhood disorders: Behavioral–developmental approaches* (pp. 218–243). New York: Brunner/Mazel.

Barkley, R. A. (1987a). The assessment of Attention Deficit–Hyperactivity Disorder. *Behavioral Assessment, 9*, 207–233.

Barkley, R. A. (1987b). *Defiant children: A clinician's manual for parent training*. New York: Guilford Press.

Barkley, R. A. (1988a). Attention Deficit Disorder with Hyperactivity. In E. J. Mash & L. G. Terdal (Eds.), *Behavioral assessment of childhood disorders* (2nd ed., pp. 69–104). New York: Guilford Press.

Barkley, R. A. (1988b). Child behavior rating scales and checklists. In M. Rutter, A. H. Tuma, & I. S. Lann (Eds.), *Assessment and diagnosis in child psychopathology* (pp. 113–155). New York: Guilford Press.

Barkley, R. A. (1988c). Tic disorders and Gilles de Tourette syndrome. In E. J. Mash & L. G. Terdal (Eds.), *Behavioral assessment of childhood disorders* (2nd ed., pp. 552–585). New York: Guilford Press.

Barkley, R. A. (in press). The problem of stimulus control and rule-governed behavior in children with Attention Deficit Disorder with Hyperactivity. In J. Swanson & L. Bloomingdale (Eds.), *Attention deficit disorders*. New York: Pergamon Press.

Barkley, R. A., Copeland, A. P., & Sivage, C. (1980). A

self-control classroom for hyperactive children. *Journal of Autism and Developmental Disorders, 10*, 75–89.

Barkley, R. A., & Cunningham, C. E. (1978). Do stimulant drugs improve the academic performance of hyperkinetic children? A review of outcome research. *Journal of Clinical Pediatrics, 17*, 85–92.

Barkley, R. A., & Cunningham, C. E. (1979). Stimulant drugs and activity level in hyperactive children. *American Journal of Orthopsychiatry, 49*, 491–499.

Barkley, R. A., & Edelbrock, C. S. (1987). Assessing situational variation in children's behavior problems: The Home and School Situations Questionnaires. In R. Prinz (Ed.), *Advances in behavioral assessment of children and families* (Vol. 3, pp. 157–176). Greenwich, CT: JAI Press.

Barkley, R. A., Fischer, M., Newby, R., & Breen, M. (1988). Development of a multi-method clinical protocol for assessing stimulant drug responses in ADHD children. *Journal of Clinical Child Psychology, 17*, 14–24.

Barkley, R. A., Karlsson, J., & Pollard, S. (1985). Effects of age on the mother–child interactions of hyperactive children. *Journal of Abnormal Child Psychology, 13*, 631–638.

Barkley, R. A., Karlsson, J., Pollard, S., & Murphy, J. (1985). Developmental changes in the mother–child interactions of hyperactive boys: Effects of two doses of Ritalin. *Journal of Child Psychology and Psychiatry, 26*, 705–715.

Barkley, R. A., Karlsson, J., Strzelecki, E., & Murphy, J. (1984). Effects of age and Ritalin dosage on the mother–child interactions of hyperactive children. *Journal of Consulting and Clinical Psychology, 52*, 750–758.

Barkley, R. A., & Ullman, D. G. (1975). A comparison of objective measures of activity and distractibility in hyperactive and nonhyperactive children. *Journal of Abnormal Child Psychology, 3*, 231–244.

Beck, A. T., Rush, A. J., Shaw, B. F., & Emery, G. (1979). *Cognitive therapy for depression.* New York: Guilford Press.

Bidder, R. T., Gray, O. P., & Newcombe, R. (1978). Behavioural treatment of hyperactive children. *Archives of Disease in Childhood, 53*, 574–579.

Biederman, J., Munir, K., Knee, D., Armentano, M., Autor, S., Waternaux, C., & Tsuang, M. (1987). High rate of affective disorders in probands with attention deficit disorders and in their relatives: A controlled family study. *American Journal of Psychiatry, 144*, 330–333.

Biederman, J., Munir, K., Knee, D., Habelow, W., Armentano, M., Autor, S., Hoge, S. K., & Waternaux, C. (1986). A family study of patients with attention deficit disorder and normal controls. *Journal of Psychiatric Research, 20*, 263–274.

Billings, D. C., & Wasik, B. H. (1985). Self-instructional training with preschoolers: An attempt to replicate. *Journal of Applied Behavior Analysis, 18*, 61–67.

Block, G. H. (1977). Hyperactivity: A cultural perspective. *Journal of Learning Disabilities, 110*, 236–240.

Blouin, A. G., Bornstein, M. A., & Trites, R. L. (1978). Teenage alcohol abuse among hyperactive children: A five year follow-up study. *Journal of Pediatric Psychology, 3*, 188–194.

Borden, K. A., Brown, R. T., Wynne, M. E., & Schleser, R. (1987). Piagetian conservation and response to cognitive therapy in attention deficit disordered children. *Journal of Child Psychology and Psychiatry, 28*, 755–764.

Bornstein, P. H., & Quevillon, R. P. (1976). The effects of a self-instructional package on overactive preschool boys. *Journal of Applied Behavior Analysis, 9*, 179–188.

Bowers, D. S., Clement, P. W., Fantuzzo, J. W., & Sorensen, D. A. (1985). Effects of teacher-administered and self-administered reinforcers on learning disabled children. *Behavior Therapy, 16*, 357–369.

Bradley, W. (1937). The behavior of children receiving Benzedrine. *American Journal of Psychiatry, 94*, 577–585.

Brown, R. T., Borden, K. A., Wynne, M. E., Schleser, R., & Clingerman, S. T. (1986). Methylphenidate and cognitive therapy with ADD children: A methodological reconsideration. *Journal of Abnormal Child Psychology, 14*, 481–497.

Brown, R. T., & Quay, L. C. (1977). Reflection–impulsivity of normal and behavior-disordered children. *Journal of Abnormal Child Psychology, 5*, 457–462.

Brown, R. T., Wynne, M. E., & Medenis, R. (1985). Methylphenidate and cognitive therapy: A comparison of treatment approaches with hyperactive boys. *Journal of Abnormal Child Psychology, 13*, 69–88.

Cairns, E., & Cammock, T. (1978). Development of a more reliable version of the Matching Familiar Figures Test. *Developmental Psychology, 11*, 244–248.

Cairns, E., & Cammock, T. (1984). The development of reflection–impulsivity: Further data. *Personality and Individual Differences, 5*, 113–115.

Campbell, S. B., Douglas, V. I., & Morganstern, G. (1971). Cognitive styles in hyperactive children and the effect of methylphenidate. *Journal of Child Psychology and Psychiatry, 12*, 55–67.

Campbell, S. B., Schleifer, M., & Weiss, G. (1978). Continuities in maternal reports and child behaviors over time in hyperactive and comparison groups. *Journal of Abnormal Child Psychology, 6*, 33–45.

Cantwell, D. (1975). *The hyperactive child.* New York: Spectrum.

Cantwell, D., & Carlson, G. (1978). Stimulants. In J. Werry (Ed.), *Pediatric psychopharmacology* (pp. 171–207). New York: Brunner/Mazel.

Cantwell, E., & Satterfield, J. H. (1978). The prevalence of academic underachievement in hyperactive children. *Journal of Pediatric Psychology, 3*, 168–171.

Carlson, C. (1986). Attention Deficit Disorder without Hyperactivity: A review of preliminary experimental evidence. In B. Lahey & A. Kazdin (Eds.), *Advances in clinical child psychology* (Vol. 9, pp. 153–176). New York: Plenum.

Chamberlin, R. W. (1977). Can we identify a group of children at age two who are at risk for the development of behavioral or emotional problems in kindergarten or first grade? *Pediatrics, 59*, (Suppl.), 971–981.

Chase, S. N., & Clement, P. W. (1985). Effects of self-reinforcement and stimulants on academic performance in children with attention deficit disorder. *Journal of Clinical Child Psychology, 14*, 323–333.

Chelune, G. J., Ferguson, W., Koon, R., & Dickey, T. O. (1986). Frontal lobe disinhibition in attention deficit disorder. *Child Psychiatry and Human Development, 16*, 221–234.

Chess, S. (1960). Diagnosis and treatment of the hyperactive child. *New York State Journal of Medicine, 60*, 2379–2385.

Childers, A. T. (1935). Hyper-activity in children having behavior disorders. *American Journal of Orthopsychiatry, 5*, 227–243.

Cohen, N. J., Sullivan, J., Minde, K., Novak, C., &

Helwig, C. (1981). Evaluation of the relative effectiveness of methylphenidate and cognitive behavior modification in the treatment of kindergarten-aged hyperactive children. *Journal of Abnormal Child Psychology, 9,* 43–54.

Cole, P. M., & Kazdin, A. E. (1980). Critical issues in self-instruction training with children. *Child Behavior Therapy, 2,* 1–21.

Conners, C. K. (1980). *Food additives and hyperactive children.* New York: Plenum.

Coons, H. W., Klorman, R., & Borgstedt, A. D. (1987a). Effects of methylphenidate on adolescents with a childhood history of attention deficit disorder: I. Clinical findings. *Journal of the American Academy of Child and Adolescent Psychiatry, 26,* 363–367.

Coons, H. W., Klorman, R., & Borgstedt, A. D. (1987b). Effects of methylphenidate on adolescents with a childhood history of attention deficit disorder: II. Information processing. *Journal of the American Academy of Child and Adolescent Psychiatry, 26,* 368–374.

Costello, A., Edelbrock, C., Kalas, R., Kessler, M., & Klaric, S. (1982). *The NIMH Diagnostic Interview Schedule for Children (DISC).* Pittsburgh: Author.

Cunningham, C. E., & Barkley, R. A. (1979). The interactions of hyperactive and normal children with their mothers during free play and structured task. *Child Development, 50,* 217–224.

Cunningham, C. E., & Siegel, L. S. (1987). Peer interactions of normal and attention-deficit disordered boys during free-play, cooperative task, and simulated classroom situations. *Journal of Abnormal Child Psychology, 15,* 247–268.

Cunningham, C. E., Siegel, L. S., & Offord, D. R. (1985). A developmental dose response analysis of the effects of methylphenidate on the peer interactions of attention deficit disordered boys. *Journal of Child Psychology and Psychiatry, 26,* 955–971.

Dangel, R. F., & Polster, R. A. (1984). *Parent training.* New York: Guilford Press.

David, O. J. (1974). Association between lower level lead concentrations and hyperactivity. *Environmental Health Perspective, 7,* 17–25.

de la Burde, B., & Choate, M. (1972). Does asymptomatic lead exposure in children have latent sequelae? *Journal of Pediatrics, 81,* 1088–1091.

de la Burde, B., & Choate, M. (1974). Early asymptomatic lead exposure and development at school age. *Journal of Pediatrics, 87,* 638–642.

Denson, R., Nanson, J. L., & McWatters, M. A. (1975). Hyperkinesis and maternal smoking. *Canadian Psychiatric Association Journal, 20,* 183–187.

Derogatis, L. (1986). *Manual for the Symptom Checklist-90, Revised (SCL-90R).* Baltimore: Author.

Deutsch, C. K., Swanson, J. M., & Bruell, J. M. (1982). Over-representation of adoptees in children with the attention deficit disorder. *Behavioral Genetics, 12,* 231–238.

Donnelly, M., & Rapoport, J. L. (1985). Attention deficit disorders. In J. M. Weiner (Ed.), *Diagnosis and psychopharmacology of childhood and adolescent disorders* (pp. 178–198). New York: Wiley.

Douglas, V. I. (1972). Stop, look, and listen: The problem of sustained attention and impulse control in hyperactive and normal children. *Canadian Journal of Behavioural Science, 4,* 259–282.

Douglas, V. I. (1980). Higher mental processes in hyperactive children: Implications for training. In R. Knights &

D. Bakker (Eds.), *Treatment of hyperactive and learning disordered children* (pp. 65–92). Baltimore: University Park Press.

Douglas, V. I. (1983). Attention and cognitive problems. In M. Rutter (Ed.), *Developmental neuropsychiatry* (pp. 280–329). New York: Guilford Press.

Douglas, V. I., & Parry, P. A. (1983). Effects of reward on delayed reaction time task performance of hyperactive children. *Journal of Abnormal Child Psychology, 11,* 313–326.

Douglas, V. I., Parry, P., Martin, P., & Garson, C. (1976). Assessment of a cognitive training program for hyperactive children. *Journal of Abnormal Child Psychology, 4,* 389–410.

Douglas, V. I., & Peters, K. G. (1979). Toward a clearer definition of the attentional deficit of hyperactive children. In G. A. Hale & M. Lewis (Eds.), *Attention and the development of cognitive skills* (pp. 173–248). New York: Plenum.

Draeger, S., Prior, M., & Sanson, A. (1986). Visual and auditory attention performance in hyperactive children: Competence or compliance. *Journal of Abnormal Child Psychology, 14,* 411–424.

Dubey, D. R., O'Leary, S. G., & Kaufman, K. F. (1983). Training parents of hyperactive children in child management: A comparative outcome study. *Journal of Abnormal Child Psychology, 11,* 229–246.

Edelbrock, C. S., & Costello, A. (1984). Structured psychiatric interviews for children and adolescents. In G. Goldstein & M. Hersen (Eds.), *Handbook of psychological assessment* (pp. 276–290). New York: Pergamon Press.

Farrington, D. P., Loeber, R., & van Kammen, W. B. (1987, October). *Long-term criminal outcomes of hyperactivity–impulsivity–attention deficit and conduct problems in childhood.* Paper presented at the meeting of the Society for Life History Research, St. Louis.

Feingold, B. (1975). *Why your child is hyperactive.* New York: Random House.

Firestone, P. & Douglas, V. I. (1975). The effects of reward and punishment on reaction times and autonomic activity in hyperactive and normal children. *Journal of Abnormal Child Psychology, 3,* 201–216.

Firestone, P., & Douglas, V. I. (1977). The effects of verbal and material reward and punishers on the performance of impulsive and reflective children. *Child Study Journal, 7,* 71–78.

Firestone, P., Kelly, M. J., Goodman, J. T., & Davey, J. (1981). Differential effects of parent training and stimulant medication with hyperactives. *Journal of the American Academy of Child Psychiatry, 20,* 135–147.

Firestone, P., & Martin, J. E. (1979). An analysis of the hyperactive syndrome: A comparison of hyperactive, behavior problem, asthmatic, and normal children. *Journal of Abnormal Child Psychology, 7,* 261–273.

Forehand, R., & McMahon, R. (1981). *Helping the noncompliant child: A clinician's guide to parent training.* New York: Guilford Press.

Friedling, C., & O'Leary, S. G. (1979). Effects of self-instructional training on second- and third-grade hyperactive children: A failure to replicate. *Journal of Applied Behavior Analysis, 12,* 211–219.

Gadow, K. D. (1981). Prevalence of drug treatment for hyperactivity and other childhood behavior disorders. In K. D. Gadow & J. Loney (Eds.), *Psychosocial aspects of drug treatment* (pp. 13–70). Boulder, CO: Westview Press.

Gadow, K. D. (1985). Relative efficacy of pharmacological, behavioral, and combination treatments for enhancing academic performance. *Clinical Psychology Review, 5*, 513–533.

Gittelman, R., & Eskinazi, B. (1983). Lead and hyperactivity revisited. *Archives of General Psychiatry, 40*, 827–833.

Gordon, M. (1979). The assessment of impulsivity and mediating behaviors in hyperactive and non-hyperactive children. *Journal of Abnormal Child Psychology, 7*, 317–326.

Gordon, M. (1983). *The Gordon Diagnostic System*. Boulder, CO: Clinical Diagnostic Systems.

Goyette, C. H., Conners, C. K., & Ulrich, R. F. (1978). Normative data for Revised Conners Parent and Teacher Rating Scales. *Journal of Abnormal Child Psychology, 6*, 221–236.

Gross, M. D. (1984). Effects of sucrose on hyperkinetic children. *Pediatrics, 74*, 876–878.

Gross, A. M., & Wojnilower, D. A. (1984). Self-directed behavior change in children: Is it self-directed? *Behavior Therapy, 15*, 501–514.

Haenlein, M., & Caul, W. F. (1987). Attention deficit disorder with hyperactivity: A specific hypothesis of reward dysfunction. *Journal of the American Academy of Child and Adolescent Psychiatry, 26*, 356–362.

Hale, G. A., & Lewis, M. (1979). *Attention and cognitive development*. New York: Plenum.

Hales, D., & Hales, R. (1985). Using the body to mend the mind. *American Health, 15*, 27–31.

Harris, K. R. (1986). Self-monitoring of attentional behavior versus self-monitoring of productivity: Effects on on-task behavior and academic response rate among learning disabled children. *Journal of Applied Behavior Analysis, 19*, 417–423.

Harris, K. R., Wong, B. Y., & Keogh, B. K. (1985). Cognitive–behavior modification with children: A critical review of the state-of-the-art. *Journal of Abnormal Child Psychology, 13*, 329–467.

Hartsough, C. S., & Lambert, N. M. (1985). Medical factors in hyperactive and normal children: Prenatal, developmental, and health history findings. *American Journal of Orthopsychiatry, 55*, 190–201.

Haslam, R. H. A., Dalby, J. T., & Rademaker, A. W. (1984). Effects of megavitamin therapy on children with attention deficit disorders. *Pediatrics, 74*, 103–111.

Hastings, J. E., & Barkley, R. A. (1978). A review of psychophysiological research with hyperactive children. *Journal of Abnormal Child Psychology, 7*, 413–447.

Hayes, S. C., Rosenfarb, I., Wulfert, E., Munt, E. D., Korn, Z., & Zettle, R. D. (1985). Self-reinforcement effects: An artifact of social standard setting? *Journal of Applied Behavior Analysis, 18*, 201–214.

Hechtman, L., Weiss, G., & Perlman, T. (1984). Young adult outcome of hyperactive children who received long-term stimulant treatment. *Journal of the American Academy of Child Psychiatry, 23*, 261–269.

Hechtman, L., Weiss, G., Perlman, R., & Amsel, R. (1984). Hyperactives as young adults: Initial predictors of outcome. *Journal of the American Academy of Child Psychiatry, 23*, 250–260.

Herjanic, B., Brown, F., & Wheatt, T. (1975). Are children reliable reporters? *Journal of Abnormal Child Psychology, 3*, 41–48.

Hinshaw, S. P., Henker, B., & Whalen, C. K. (1984a). Cognitive–behavioral and pharmacologic interventions for hyperactive boys: Comparative and combined effects. *Journal of Consulting and Clinical Psychology, 52*, 739–749.

Hinshaw, S. P., Henker, B., & Whalen, C. K. (1984b). Self-control in hyperactive boys in anger-inducing situations. Effects of cognitive–behavioral training and of methylphenidate. *Journal of Abnormal Child Psychology, 12*, 55–77.

Hodges, K., McKnew, D., Cytryn, L., Stern, L., & Kline, J. (1982). The Child Assessment Schedule (CAS) diagnostic interview: A report on reliability and validity. *Journal of the American Academy of Child Psychiatry, 21*, 468–473.

Horn, W. F., Chatoor, I., & Conners, C. K. (1983). Additive effects of Dexedrine and self-control training: A multiple assessment. *Behavior Modification, 7*, 383–402.

Horn, W. F., Ialongo, N., Popovich, S., & Peradotto, D. (1987). Behavioral parent training and cognitive–behavioral self-control therapy with ADD-H children: Comparative and combined effects. *Journal of Clinical Child Psychology, 16*, 57–68.

Humphrey, L. L. (1982). Children's and teachers' perspectives on children's self-control: The development of two rating scales. *Journal of Consulting and Clinical Psychology, 54*, 624–633.

Jacob, R. G., O'Leary, K. D., & Rosenblad, C. (1978). Formal and informal classroom settings: Effects on hyperactivity. *Journal of Abnormal Child Psychology, 6*, 47–59.

Johnston, C., Pelham, W. E., & Murphy, H. A. (1985). Peer relationships in ADDH and normal children: A developmental analysis of peer and teacher ratings. *Journal of Abnormal Child Psychology, 13*, 89–100.

Kagan, J. (1966). Reflection–impulsivity: The generality and dynamics of conceptual tempo. *Journal of Abnormal Psychology, 71*, 17–24.

Kendall, P. C., & Braswell, L. (1982). Cognitive–behavioral self-control therapy for children: A components analysis. *Journal of Consulting and Clinical Psychology, 50*, 672–689.

Kendall, P. C., & Braswell, L. (1984). *Cognitive–behavioral therapy for impulsive children*. New York: Guilford Press.

Kendall, P. C., & Finch, A. J., Jr. (1978). A cognitive–behavioral treatment for impulsivity: A group comparison study. *Journal of Consulting and Clinical Psychology, 46*, 110–118.

Kendall, P. C., & Finch, A. J., Jr. (1979). Analyses of changes in verbal behavior following a cognitive–behavioral treatment for impulsivity. *Journal of Abnormal Child Psychology, 7*, 455–463.

Kendall, P. C., & Wilcox, L. E. (1979). Self-control in children: Development of a rating scale. *Journal of Consulting and Clinical Psychology, 47*, 1020–1029.

Kendall, P. C., & Wilcox, L. E. (1980). Cognitive–behavioral treatment for impulsivity: Concrete versus conceptual training in non-self-controlled problem children. *Journal of Consulting and Clinical Psychology, 48*, 80–91.

Kovacs, M. (1982). *The longitudinal study of child and adolescent psychopathology: I. The semi-structured psychiatric Interview Schedule for Children (ISC)*. Unpublished manuscript, Western Psychiatric Institute.

Lambert, N. M., Sandoval, J., & Sassone, D. (1978). Prevalence of hyperactivity in elementary school children as a function of social system definers. *American Journal of Orthopsychiatry, 48*, 446–463.

Laufer, M., Denhoff, E., & Solomons, G. (1957). Hyperkinetic impulse disorder in children's behavior problems. *Psychosomatic Medicine, 19,* 38–49.

Leith, N. J., & Barrett, R. J. (1976). Amphetamine and the reward system: Evidence for tolerance and post-drug depression. *Psychopharmacologia, 46,* 19–25.

Leith, N. J., & Barrett, R. J. (1981). Self-stimulation and amphetamine: Tolerance to d- and l-isomers and cross tolerance to cocaine and methylphenidate. *Psychopharmacology, 74,* 23–28.

Levin, P. M. (1938). Restlessness in children. *Archives of Neurology and Psychiatry, 39,* 764–770.

Locke, H. J., & Wallace, K. M. (1959). Short marital adjustment and prediction tests: Their reliability and validity. *Journal of Marriage and Family Living, 21,* 251–255.

Loney, J., Whaley-Klahn, M. A., Kosier, T., & Conboy, J. (1981, November). *Hyperactive boys and their brothers at 21: Predictors of aggressive and antisocial outcomes.* Paper presented at the meeting of the Society of Life History Research, Monterey, CA.

Lou, H. C., Henriksen, L., & Bruhn, P. (1984). Focal cerebral hypoperfusion in children with dysphasia and/or attention deficit disorder. *Archives of Neurology, 41,* 825–829.

Luk, S. (1985). Direct observations studies of hyperactive behaviors. *Journal of the American Academy of Child Psychiatry, 24,* 338–344.

Marholin, D., & Steinman, W. M. (1977). Stimulus control in the classroom as a function of the behavior reinforced. *Journal of Applied Behavior Analysis, 10,* 465–478.

Mash, E. J., & Barkley, R. A. (1987). Assessment of family interaction with the Response-Class Matrix. In R. Prinz (Ed.), *Advances in behavioral assessment of children and families* (Vol. 2, pp. 29–67). Greenwich, CT: JAI Press.

Mash, E. J., & Dalby, J. T. (1978). Behavioral interventions for hyperactivity. In R. L. Trites (Ed.), *Hyperactivity in children: Etiology, measurement, and treatment implications* (pp. 161–216). Baltimore: University Park Press.

Mash, E. J., & Johnston, C. (1982). A comparison of the mother–child interactions of younger and older hyperactive and normal children. *Child Development, 53,* 1371–1381.

Mash, E. J., & Johnston, C. (1983a). Parental perceptions of child behavior problems, parenting self-esteem, and mothers' reported stress in younger and older hyperactive and normal children. *Journal of Consulting and Clinical Psychology, 51,* 68–99.

Mash, E. J., & Johnston, C. (1983b). Sibling interactions of hyperactive and normal children and their relationship to reports of maternal stress and self-esteem. *Journal of Clinical Child Psychology, 12,* 91–99.

Mash, E. J., Terdal, L., & Anderson, K. (1973). The Response-Class Matrix: A procedure for recording parent–child interactions. *Journal of Consulting and Clinical Psychology, 40,* 163–164.

Mattes, J. A., Boswell, L., & Oliver, H. (1984). Methylphenidate effects on symptoms of attention deficit disorder in adults. *Archives of General Psychiatry, 41,* 1059–1063.

Mattes, J. A., & Gittelman, R. (1981). Effects of artificial food colorings in children with hyperactive symptoms. *Archives of General Psychiatry, 38,* 714–718.

McClure, F. D., & Gordon, M. (1984). Performance of disturbed hyperactive and nonhyperactive children on an objective measure of hyperactivity. *Journal of Abnormal Child Psychology, 12,* 561–572.

Meichenbaum, D., & Goodman, J. (1971). Training impulsive children to talk to themselves: A means of developing self-control. *Journal of Abnormal Psychology, 77,* 115–126.

Milich, R., & Kramer, J. (1985). Reflections on impulsivity: An empirical investigation of impulsivity as a construct. In K. Gadow & I. Bialer (Eds.) *Advances in learning and behavioral disabilities* (Vol. 3, pp. 117–150). Greenwich, CT: JAI Press.

Milich, R., Landau, S., & Loney, J. (1981, August). *The interrelationships among hyperactivity, aggression, and impulsivity.* Paper presented at the meeting of the American Psychological Association, Los Angeles.

Milich, R., Loney, J., & Landau, S. (1982). The independent dimensions of hyperactivity and aggression: A validation with playroom observation data. *Journal of Abnormal Psychology, 91,* 183–198.

Milich, R., Wolraich, M., & Lindgren, S. (1986). Sugar and hyperactivity: A critical review of empirical findings. *Clinical Psychology Review, 6,* 493–513.

O'Connor, M., Foch, T., Sherry, T., & Plomin, R. (1980). A twin study of specific behavioral problems of socialization as viewed by parents. *Journal of Abnormal Child Psychology, 8,* 189–199.

O'Leary, S. G., & Pelham, W. E. (1978). Behavior therapy and withdrawal of stimulant medication in hyperactive children. *Pediatrics, 61,* 211–216.

O'Leary, K. D., Pelham, W. E., Rosenbaum, A., & Price, G. H. (1976). Behavioral treatment of hyperkinetic children: An experimental evaluation of its usefulness. *Clinical Pediatrics, 15,* 510–515.

O'Leary, K. D., Vivian, D., & Nisi, A. (1985). Hyperactivity in Italy. *Journal of Abnormal Child Psychology, 13,* 485–500.

Paniagua, F. A. (1987). Management of hyperactive children through correspondence training procedures: A preliminary study. *Behavioral Residential Treatment, 2,* 1–23.

Paternite, C., & Loney, J. (1980). Childhood hyperkinesis: Relationships between symptomatology and home environment. In C. K. Whalen & B. Henker (Eds.), *Hyperactive children: The social ecology of identification and treatment* (pp. 105–141). New York: Academic Press.

Patterson, G. R. (1982). *Coercive family process.* Eugene, OR: Castalia.

Pelham, W. E. (1987). What do we know about the use and effects of CNS stimulants in the treatment of ADD? In J. Loney (Ed.), *The young hyperactive child: Answers to questions about diagnosis, prognosis, and treatment* (pp. 99–110). New York: Haworth Press.

Pelham, W. E., Bender, M. E., Caddell, J., Booth, S., & Moorer, S. H. (1985). Methylphenidate and children with attention deficit disorder. *Archives of General Psychiatry, 42,* 948–952.

Pelham, W. W., Schnedler, R. W., Bender, M. E., Nilsson, D. E., Miller, J., Budrow, M. S., Ronnel, M., Paluchowski, C. & Marks, D. A. (in press). The combination of behavior therapy and methylphenidate in the treatment of attention deficit disorders: A therapy outcome study. In L. Bloomingdale (Ed.), *Attention deficit disorders* (Vol. 3). New York: Pergamon Press.

Pfiffner, L. J., & O'Leary, S. G. (1987). The efficacy of all-positive management as a function of the prior use of negative consequences. *Journal of Applied Behavior Analysis, 20,* 265–271.

Pfiffner, L. J., O'Leary, S. G., Rosen, L. A., & Sanderson, Jr., W. C. (1985). A comparison of the effects of continuous and intermittent response cost and reprimands in the classroom. *Journal of Clinical Child Psychology, 14,* 348–352.

Pfiffner, L. J., Rosen, L. A., & O'Leary, S. G. (1985). The efficacy of an all-positive approach to classroom management. *Journal of Applied Behavior Analysis, 18,* 257–261.

Pliska, S. R. (1987). Tricyclic antidepressants in the treatment of children with attention deficit disorder. *Journal of the American Academy of Child and Adolescent Psychiatry, 26,* 127–132.

Pollard, S., Ward, E. M., & Barkley, R. A. (1983). The effects of parent training and Ritalin on the parent–child interactions of hyperactive boys. *Child and Family Behavior Therapy, 5,* 51–69.

Porrino, L. J., Rapoport, J. L., Behar, D., Sceery, W., Ismond, D. R., & Bunney, W. E. (1983). A naturalistic assessment of the motor activity of hyperactive boys. *Archives of General Psychiatry, 40,* 681–687.

Prior, M., Wallace, M., & Milton, I. (1984). Schedule-induced behavior in hyperactive children. *Journal of Abnormal Child Psychology, 12,* 227–244.

Puig-Antich, J., & Chambers, W. (1978). *The Schedule for Affective Disorders and Schizophrenia for School-Aged Children.* New York: New York State Psychiatric Institute.

Puig-Antich, J., Ryan, N., & Rabinovich, H. (1985). Affective disorders in childhood and adolescence. In J. Weiner (Ed.), *Diagnosis and psychopharmacology of childhood and adolescent disorders* (pp. 151–177). New York: Wiley.

Quay, H. C. (in press). The behavioral reward and inhibition systems in childhood behavior disorder. In L. M. Bloomingdale (Ed.), *Attention Deficit Disorders* (Vol. 3). New York: Pergamon Press.

Quinn, P. O., & Rapoport, J. L. (1974). Minor physical anomalies and neurologic status in hyperactive boys. *Pediatrics, 53,* 742–747.

Rapoport, J., & Mikkelsen, E. (1978). Antidepressants. In J. Werry (Ed.), *Pediatric psychopharmacology* (pp. 208–233). New York: Brunner/Mazel.

Rapport, M. D., DuPaul, G. J., Stoner, G., & Jones, J. T. (1986). Comparing classroom and clinic measures of attention deficit disorder: Differential, idiosyncratic, and dose–response effects of methylphenidate. *Journal of Consulting and Clinical Psychology, 54,* 334–341.

Rapport, M. D., Murphy, A., & Bailey, J. S. (1982). Ritalin versus response cost in the control of hyperactive children: A within-subject comparison. *Journal of Applied Behavior Analysis, 15,* 205–216.

Rapport, M. D., Tucker, S. B., DuPaul, G. J., Merlo, M., & Stoner, G. (1986). Hyperactivity and frustration: The influence of control over and size of rewards in delaying gratification. *Journal of Abnormal Child Psychology, 14,* 191–204.

Reeves, J. C., Weery, J., Elkind, G. S., & Zametkin, A. (1987). Attention deficit, conduct, oppositional, and anxiety disorders in children: II. Clinical characteristics. *Journal of the American Academy of Child Psychiatry, 26,* 133–143.

Richter, N. C. (1984). The efficacy of relaxation training with children. *Journal of Abnormal Child Psychology, 12,* 319–344.

Rie, H. E. & Rie, E. D. (1980). *Handbook of minimal brain dysfunction.* New York: Wiley.

Roberts, M. A. (1987). How is playroom behavior observation used in the diagnosis of attention deficit disorder?

In J. Loney (Ed.), *The young hyperactive child: Answers to questions about diagnosis, prognosis, and treatment* (pp. 65–74). New York: Haworth Press.

Robin, A. L. (1981). A controlled evaluation of problem-solving communication training with parent–adolescent conflict. *Behavior Therapy, 12,* 593–609.

Robinson, P. W., Newby, T. J., & Ganzell, S. L. (1981). A token system for a class of underachieving hyperactive children. *Journal of Applied Behavior Analysis, 14,* 307–315.

Rosenbaum, A., O'Leary, K. D., & Jacob, R. G. (1975). Behavioral intervention with hyperactive children: Group consequences as a supplement to individual contingencies. *Behavior Therapy, 6,* 315–323.

Ross, D. M., & Ross, S. A. (1976). *Hyperactivity: Research, theory, and action.* New York: Wiley.

Ross, D. M., & Ross, S. A. (1982). *Hyperactivity: Current issues, research, and theory* (2nd ed.). New York: Wiley.

Routh, D. K. (1978). Hyperactivity. In P. Magrab (Ed.), *Psychological management of pediatric problems* (pp. 3–48). Baltimore: University Park Press.

Routh, D. K., & Schroeder, C. S. (1976). Standardized playroom measures as indices of hyperactivity. *Journal of Abnormal Child Psychology, 4,* 199–207.

Rutter, M. (1977). Brain damage syndromes in childhood: Concepts and findings. *Journal of Child Psychology and Psychiatry, 18,* 1–21.

Safer, D. J., & Allen, R. (1976). *Hyperactive children.* Baltimore: University Park Press.

Safer, D. J., & Krager, J. M. (1983). Trends in medication treatment of hyperactive school children. *Clinical Pediatrics, 22,* 500–504.

Salkind, N. J., & Nelson, C. F. (1980). A note on the developmental nature of reflection–impulsivity. *Developmental Psychology, 16,* 237–238.

Sandberg, S. T., Rutter, M., & Taylor, E. (1978). Hyperkinetic disorder in psychiatric clinic attenders. *Developmental Medicine and Child Neurology, 20,* 279–299.

Satterfield, J. H., Satterfield, B. T., & Cantwell, D. P. (1980). Multimodality treatment. *Archives of General Psychiatry, 37,* 915–919.

Satterfield, J. H., Satterfield, B. T., & Cantwell, D. P. (1981). Three-year multimodality treatment study of 100 hyperactive boys. *Journal of Pediatrics, 98,* 650–655.

Schulman, J. L., Stevens, T. M., Suran, B. G., Kupst, M. J., & Naughton, M. J. (1978). Modification of activity level through biofeedback and operant conditioning. *Journal of Applied Behavior Analysis, 11,* 145–152.

Shaffer, D., McNamara, N., & Pincus, J. H. (1974). Controlled observations on patterns of activity, attention, and impulsivity in brain-damaged and psychiatrically disturbed boys. *Psychological Medicine, 4,* 4–18.

Shaywitz, S. E., Shaywitz, B. A., Cohen, D. J., & Young, J. G. (1983). Monoaminergic mechanisms in hyperactivity. In M. Rutter (Ed.), *Developmental neuropsychiatry* (pp. 330–347). New York: Guilford Press.

Stein, L. (1964). Self-stimulation of the brain and the central stimulant action of amphetamine. *Federation Proceedings, 23,* 836–850.

Still, G. F. (1902). Some abnormal psychical conditions in children. *Lancet, i,* 1008–1012, 1077–1082, 1163–1168.

Strauss, A. A., & Lehtinen, L. E. (1947). *Psychopathology and education of the brain-injured child.* New York: Grune & Stratton.

Streissguth, A. P., Martin, D. C., Barr, H. M., Sandman, B. M., Kirchner, G. L., & Darby, B. L. (1984). Intrauterine alcohol and nicotine exposure: Attention and reaction time in 4-year-old children. *Developmental Psychology, 20,* 533–541.

Swanson, J. M. (1985). Measures of cognitive functioning appropriate for use in pediatric psychopharmacology research studies. *Psychopharmacology Bulletin, 21,* 887–890.

Tallmadge, J., & Barkley, R. A. (1983). The interactions of hyperactive and normal boys with their mothers and fathers. *Journal of Abnormal Child Psychology, 11,* 565–579.

Tarver-Behring, S., Barkley, R., & Karlsson, J. (1985). The mother–child interactions of hyperactive boys and their normal siblings. *American Journal of Orthopsychiatry, 55,* 202–209.

Taylor, E. A. (1983). Drug response and diagnostic validation. In M. Rutter (Ed.), *Developmental neuropsychiatry* (pp. 348–368). New York: Guilford Press.

Taylor, E. A. (1986). Childhood hyperactivity. *British Journal of Psychiatry, 149,* 562–573.

Taylor, J. F. (1980). *The hyperactive child and the family.* New York: Random House.

Thorley, G. (1984). Review of follow-up and follow-back studies of childhood hyperactivity. *Psychological Bulletin, 96,* 116–132.

Trites, R. L., Dugas, F., Lynch, G., & Ferguson, B. (1979). Incidence of hyperactivity. *Journal of Pediatric Psychology, 4,* 179–188.

Trites, R. L., Tryphonas, H., & Ferguson, H. B. (1980). Diet treatment for hyperactive children with food allergies. In R. Knight & D. Bakker (Eds.), *Treatment of hyperactive and learning disordered children* (pp. 151–166). Baltimore: University Park Press.

Tryon, W. W. (1984). Principles and methods of mechanically measuring motor activity. *Behavioral Assessment, 6,* 129–140.

Ullman, D. G., Barkley, R. A., & Brown, H. W. (1978). The behavioral symptoms of hyperkinetic children who successfully responded to stimulant drug treatment. *American Journal of Orthopsychiatry, 48,* 425–437.

Ullmann, R., Sleator, E., & Sprague, R. (1984). A new rating scale for diagnosis and monitoring of ADD children. *Psychopharmacology Bulletin, 20,* 160–164.

Varni, J. W., & Henker, B. (1979). A self-regulation approach to the treatment of three hyperactive boys. *Child Behavior Therapy, 1,* 171–192.

Weiss, G., & Hechtman, L. (1986). *Hyperactive children grown up.* New York: Guilford Press.

Weiss, G., Hechtman, L., Milroy, T., & Perlman, T. (1985). Psychiatric status of hyperactives as adults: A controlled prospective 15-year follow-up of 63 hyperactive children. *Journal of the American Academy of Child Psychiatry, 24,* 211–220.

Weiss, G., Hechtman, L., & Perlman, T. (1978). Hyperactives as young adults: School, employer, and self-rating scales obtained during ten-year follow-up evaluation. *American Journal of Orthopsychiatry, 48,* 438–445.

Weiss, G., Hechtman, L., Perlman, T., Hopkins, J., & Wener, A. (1979). Hyperactives as young adults: A controlled prospective ten-year follow-up of 75 children. *Archives of General Psychiatry, 36,* 675–681.

Wender, P. H. (1971). *Minimal brain dysfunction in children.* New York: Wiley.

Wender, P. H. (1987). *The hyperactive child, adolescent, and adult.* New York: Oxford University Press.

Wender, P. H., Reimherr, F. W., & Wood, D. R. (1981). Attention deficit disorder ("Minimal brain dysfunction")

in adults. *Archives of General Psychiatry, 38,* 449–456.

Werry, J. S., Reeves, J. C., & Elkind, G. S. (1987). Attention deficit, conduct, oppositional, and anxiety disorders in children: I. A Review of research on differentiating characteristics. *Journal of the American Academy of Child and Adolescent Psychiatry, 26,* 133–143.

Werry, J. S., & Sprague, R. L. (1970). Hyperactivity. In C. G. Costello (Ed.), *Symptoms of psychopathology* (pp. 397–417). New York: Wiley.

Whalen, C. K. (in press). Attention deficit and hyperactivity disorders. In T. H. Ollendick & M. Hersen (Eds.), *Handbook of child psychopathology* (2nd ed.). New York: Plenum.

Whalen, C. K., Henker, B., & Dotemoto, S. (1980). Methylphenidate and hyperactivity: Effects on teacher behaviors. *Science, 208,* 1280–1282.

Whalen, C. K., Henker, B., & Hinshaw, S. P. (1985). Cognitive–behavioral therapies for hyperactive children: Premises, problems, and prospects. *Journal of Abnormal Child Psychology, 13,* 391–410.

Willerman, L. (1973). Activity level and hyperactivity in twins. *Child Development, 44,* 288–293.

Williams, L. (1988, January 15). Parents and doctors fear growing misuse of drug used to treat hyperactive kids. *Wall Street Journal,* p. 10.

Willis, T. J., & Lovaas, I. (1977). A behavioral approach to treating hyperactive children: The parent's role. In J. B. Millichap (Ed.), *Learning disabilities and related disorders* (pp. 119–140). Chicago: Year Book Medical.

Winsberg, B. G., Bialer, I., Kupietz, S., & Tobias, J. (1972). Effects of imipramine and dextroamphetamine on behavior of neuropsychiatrically impaired children. *American Journal of Psychiatry, 128,* 1425–1431.

Wolraich, M., Drummond, T., Saloman, M. K., O'Brien, M. L., & Sivage, C. (1978). Effects of methylphenidate alone and in combination with behavior modification procedures on the behavior and academic performance of hyperactive children. *Journal of Abnormal Child Psychology, 6,* 149–161.

Wolraich, M., Milich, R., Stumbo, P., & Schultz, F. (1985). The effects of sucrose ingestion on the behavior of hyperactive boys. *Pediatrics, 106,* 675–682.

Worland, J. (1976). Effects of positive and negative feedback on behavior control in hyperactive and normal boys. *Journal of Abnormal Child Psychology, 4,* 315–325.

Worland, J., North-Jones, M., & Stern, J. A. (1973). Performance and activity of hyperactive and normal boys as a function of distraction and reward. *Journal of Abnormal Child Psychology, 1,* 363–377.

Zametkin, A. J., & Rapoport, J. L. (1986). The pathophysiology of Attention Deficit Disorder with Hyperactivity: A review. In B. Lahey & A. Kazdin (Eds.), *Advances in clinical child psychology* (Vol. 9, pp. 177–216). New York: Plenum.

Zentall, S. (1984). Context effects in the behavioral ratings of hyperactivity. *Journal of Abnormal Child Psychology, 12,* 345–352.

Zentall, S. S. (1985). A context for hyperactivity. In K. Gadow (Ed.) *Advances in learning and behavioral disabilities* (Vol. 4, pp. 273–343). Greenwich, CT: JAI Press.

Zettle, R. D., & Hayes, S. C. (1982). Rule-governed behavior: A potential theoretical framework for cognitive–behavioral therapy. In Kendall, P. (Ed.) *Advances in cognitive–behavioral research* (Vol. 1, pp. 73–118). New York: Academic Press.

3

CONDUCT DISORDERS

ROBERT J. McMAHON
University of Washington

KAREN C. WELLS
George Washington University School of Medicine
Children's Hospital National Medical Center

Conduct disorders in children represent a broad range of "acting-out" behaviors, ranging from annoying but relatively minor behaviors such as yelling, whining, and temper tantrums to aggression, physical destructiveness, and stealing. Typically, these behaviors do not occur in isolation but as a complex or "class," and children displaying such behaviors have been labeled "oppositional," "antisocial," "socially agressive," and "conduct-disordered" by various authors (e.g., Patterson, 1974; Wahler, 1969a). In this chapter, we use the term "conduct disorders" to refer to this constellation of child behaviors.

Conduct disorders are the most frequently occurring child behavior disorders, not only with respect to clinic referrals for treatment, but in the general population as well (Quay, 1986b; Wells & Forehand, 1985). In their review of prevalence studies conducted with clinic-referred child populations, Wells and Forehand (1985) noted that 33%–75% of referrals were for conduct-disordered behaviors. The total proportion of clinic-referred cases consisting of conduct-disordered behaviors seems to be age-related, in that the proportion increases for older children (e.g., Wolff, 1971). Well-designed epidemiological studies in Great Britain and Canada suggest that the prevalence of conduct-

disordered behavior in the general population is on the order of 3%–4% (Rutter, Tizard, Yule, Graham, & Whitmore, 1976; Trites, Dugas, Lynch, & Ferguson, 1979).

Boys are consistently diagnosed as conduct-disordered more frequently than girls, regardless of age or sample studied (Wells & Forehand, 1985). Although there is some variability across studies, boys in the general population are two to three times as likely as girls to manifest conduct-disordered behavior, and three times as likely to present at clinics (Quay, 1986b).

With respect to the course of conduct disorders, it is important to differentiate between single behaviors engaged in by large numbers of nonreferred children (e.g. temper tantrums) and the constellation of behaviors that comprise conduct disorders. Developmental studies of nonreferred children indicate that these children may exhibit conduct-disordered behaviors at some point in their childhood and adolescence (Edelbrock, 1985; MacFarlane, Allen, & Honzik, 1954). For both clinic-referred and nonreferred children, the number of problem behaviors declines with age (e.g., Moore & Mukai, 1983). However, children with severe conduct disorders are likely to exhibit similar patterns of behavior into adulthood if left untreated, and they have an increased likelihood of engaging in delinquent and criminal behavior (Loeber, 1982; Olweus, 1979; Robins, 1966). In a review of studies assessing the stability of antisocial behavior, Loeber (1982) concluded that conduct-disordered children whose antisocial behavior had an earlier onset, was manifested in more than one setting, occurred at higher rates, and/or was manifested in several forms were at greatest risk for continued performance of these behaviors. In a review of 23 follow-up studies, Robins (1970) reported that approximately 40% of conduct-disordered children were diagnosed as having an antisocial or sociopathic personality disturbance as adults, compared to 10% of the adults who had not been thus diagnosed as children. As adults, not only are conduct-disordered children more likely to continue to engage in antisocial behavior; they are at increased risk for psychiatric impairment of various types, poor occupational adjustment, low educational attainment, marital distress/disruption, less social participation, and poor physical health (Kazdin, 1985).

There are a number of approaches in current use to describe and classify conduct-disordered children (McMahon, 1987). The *Diagnostic and Statistical Manual of Mental Disorders,* third edition, revised (DSM-III-R; American Psychiatric Association, 1987) describes two diagnostic categories (Conduct Disorder and Oppositional Defiant Disorder) that include conduct-disordered behaviors. The essential feature of Conduct Disorder is a "persistent pattern of conduct in which the basic right of others and major age-appropriate societal norms or rules are violated" (p.53). The pattern must have continued for at least 6 months, and at least 3 of the following 13 behaviors must have been present: stolen without confrontation of a victim (more than once); run away from home overnight (at least twice, or once without returning); lied; set fires; truant from school; broken into someone else's house, building, or car; deliberate destruction of others' property; physical cruelty to animals; forced someone into sexual activity; used a weapon (in more than one fight); initiated physical fights; stolen with confrontation of a victim; physical cruelty to people. The DSM-III-R lists three subtypes of Conduct Disorder. The Solitary Aggressive Type, which corresponds roughly to the DSM-III (American Psychiatric Association, 1980) subtype of Undersocialized Aggressive, is characterized by aggressive physical behavior in-

itiated by the child and usually directed toward both adults and peers. The Group Type, which corresponds somewhat to the DSM-III subtype of Socialized Nonaggressive, is characterized by conduct problems that occur mainly as group activities with peers. In contrast to its DSM-III counterpart, physical aggression may be manifested in the Group Type. Finally, the Undifferentiated Type is comprised of children with a diagnosis of Conduct Disorder whose pattern of behavior does not fit neatly into either of the other subtypes. The DSM-III-R notes that the Undifferentiated Type may be much more common that either of the other two subtypes.

The essential feature of Oppositional Defiant Disorder is a "pattern of negativistic, hostile, and defiant behavior without the more serious violations of the basic rights of others that are seen in Conduct Disorder" (American Psychiatric Association, 1987, p. 56). Thus, the Conduct Disorder category subsumes the Oppositional Defiant Disorder category. The pattern of behavior must have a duration of at least 6 months, and at least five of the following nine behaviors must have been present and have occurred frequently: loses temper; argues with adults; actively defies or refuses adult requests or rules; deliberately does things that annoy other people; blames others for his or her own mistakes; touchy or easily annoyed by others; angry and resentful; spiteful or vindictive; swears. The severity (mild, moderate, severe) of both Conduct Disorder and Oppositional Defiant Disorder is now noted in the DSM-III-R; it is based primarily on the number of different behaviors in which the child engages.

Because of the recent appearance of the DSM-III-R, its psychometric properties are not known, and so it is not possible to ascertain at this time whether the changes noted above with respect to the diagnostic catergories relevant to conduct disorders represent improvements over their DSM-III counterparts, which had low (and, in most cases, unacceptable) levels of interrater reliability (see Quay, 1986a). It is interesting to note that although earlier research (Werry, Methven, Fitzpatrick, & Dixon, 1983) found that only when the DSM-III categories of Conduct Disorder and Oppositional Disorder were combined did interrater reliability improve to near-acceptable levels, the DSM-III-R has maintained the distinction between the two disorders.

Multivariate statistical approaches to classification indicate that there are at least two subtypes of conduct-disordered children (Loeber & Schmaling, 1985a; Quay, 1986a, 1986b). For example, based on a meta-analysis of 22 studies with more than 11,000 children, Loeber and Schmaling (1985a) have proposed a bipolar unidimensional typology of conduct disorders. "Overt" conduct disorders include behaviors involving direct confrontation with or disruption of the environment (e.g., aggression, temper tantrums, argumentativeness), whereas "covert" conduct disorders include behaviors that occur behind the backs of adult caretakers (e.g., lying, stealing, alcohol/drug use). The two subtypes and their behavioral descriptors are presented in Table 3-1. It is interesting to note that both of the empirically derived syndromes include behaviors from the Conduct Disorder and Oppositional (Defiant) Disorder categories of the DSM-III and DSM-III-R; this again suggests that, the DSM-III-R to the contrary, there is no apparent justification for the separate classification of Oppositional Defiant and Conduct Disorders, at least as they are presently constituted (Wells & Forehand, 1985). Furthermore, the basis for differentiating two of the subtypes of Conduct Disorder in the DSM-III-R (i.e., whether the behavior

occurs alone or as a group activity with peers) is not replicated by the empirically derived subtypes.

Evidence is beginning to accumulate that indicates not only that the empirically derived subtypes of conduct disorders differ in terms of their primary behavioral characteristics, but that they may also have divergent developmental progressions (e.g., Edelbrock, 1985; Patterson 1986), differing individual and familial correlates (e.g., Loeber & Schmaling, 1985b; Patterson, 1982, Quay, 1986b), and differing prognoses (Moore, Chamberlain, & Mukai, 1979; Quay, 1986b). Children who engage in both overt and covert conduct-disordered behaviors seem to be particularly at risk for later difficulties (Loeber & Schmaling, 1985b; Patterson, 1986).

A substantial amount of research has focused on comparing the behavior of children referred to clinics for conduct-disordered behavior and their parents to the behavior of nonreferred children and their parents (e.g., Griest, Forehand, Wells, & McMahon, 1980; Patterson, 1976a, 1982). Most of this research has assessed overt forms of conduct-disordered behaviors (e.g., aggression, noncompliance, or a composite measure of overt conduct disorders); as predicted, the referred children demonstrate higher levels of these behaviors than do their nonreferred counterparts. The parents of clinic-referred conduct-disordered children generally demonstrate more commanding and critical behaviors toward their children; however, parents of clinic-referred and nonreferred children typically do not differ in the frequency of positive behaviors (e.g., verbal rewards) directed toward their children (see Rogers, Forehand, & Griest, 1981, for a review of these data).*

With respect to covert conduct disorders, the relatively little research that has been conducted has focused on children who steal, although researchers are also beginning to investigate other covert behaviors (e.g., lying, fire setting, and substance use). Most of the work on stealing has been conducted by Patterson and his colleagues. Children who steal exhibit levels of

TABLE 3-1. Overt and Covert Subtypes of Conduct-Disordered Behaviors

Overt	Covert
Disobedient	Disobedient
Sassy	Negative
Blames others	Lies
Brags	Destructive
Shows off	Steals
Irritable, cruel, fights	Sets fires
Loud, threatens	Bad companions, runs
Temper tantrums	away, truant, in a
Attacks people, jealous,	gang
sulks	Alcohol/drug abuse
Impulsive	
Argues, poor peer relations, teases	
Demanding	
Stubborn, moody	
Screams	
Hyperactive	

Note. Adapted from "Empirical Evidence for Overt and Covert Patterns of Antisocial Conduct Problems: A Meta-Analysis" by R. Loeber and K. B. Schmaling, 1985, *Journal of Abnormal Child Psychology, 13,* 337–352. Copyright 1985 by Plenum Publishing Corporation. Adapted by permission.

*However, Gardner (1987) recently demonstrated that the mother–child interactions of preschool-age conduct-disordered children were characterized by lower levels of positive interaction than were those of a nondeviant control sample. The conduct-disordered children were also more likely than the control children to be engaged in "doing nothing" or watching TV, as opposed to constructive solitary play.

aversive behavior that are comparable to those of nonreferred children, although children who engage in both stealing and social aggression are even more aversive than children who are socially aggressive but who do not steal (Loeber & Schmaling, 1985b; Patterson, 1982). It also appears that children who steal are older at time of referral than children referred for overt types of conduct disorders (Moore *et al.*, 1979; Reid & Hendricks, 1973) and are at greater risk for committing delinquent offenses as adolescents (Loeber & Schmaling, 1985b; Moore *et al.*, 1979).

Patterson (1982) has reported that the parents of stealers are more distant and less involved in interactions with their children than parents of nonreferred children or parents of socially aggressive children. The mothers and siblings of socially aggressive children are more coercive than their counterparts in nonreferred families or families in which the children steal. Loeber and Schmaling (1985b) found that families with socially aggressive children and those with children who both fought and stole were more likely to demonstrate poorer monitoring skills and to have rejecting mothers. Fathers of children who steal also appear to be less involved in the discipline process than fathers of socially aggressive or normal children (Loeber, Weissman, & Reid, 1983).

Lying, defined as a "verbal statement intended to deceive" (Stouthamer-Loeber, 1986, p. 268), may be one of the first covert conduct-disordered behaviors to appear (Edelbrock, 1985) and is highly correlated with stealing (especially in adolescents). For example, the correlations between lying and stealing in 4th-, 7th-, and 10th-grade boys were .39, .59, and .74, respectively (Stouthamer-Loeber & Loeber, 1986). Based on the finding of the meta-analytic study conducted by Loeber and Schmaling (1985a), Stouthamer-Loeber (1986) has concluded that although lying loads most heavily on the covert dimension of conduct disorders, it is also related (albeit less strongly) to overt conduct disorders. Lying did correlate significantly with fighting in a community sample of 4th-, 7th-, and 10th-grade boys (r's = .50–.65) (Stouthamer-Loeber & Loeber, 1986), particularly when it occurred in conjunction with stealing. Furthermore, early lying has been shown to be predictive of later recidivism (Loeber & Dishion, 1983).

Fire setting, although relatively rare, tends to be associated with other conduct-disordered behaviors. Recent investigations suggest that although only a relatively small proportion of conduct-disordered children engage in fire-setting behavior (e.g., 5% in Jacobson's [1985] outpatient sample in London), most, but not all, firesetters demonstrate other conduct-disordered behaviors (i.e., can be considered to display the "syndrome" of conduct disorders). For example, 74% of the fire-setting children in both outpatient (Jacobson, 1985) and inpatient (Kazdin & Kolko, 1986) samples received a diagnosis of Conduct Disorder. Although fire setting has typically been associated with other covert conduct-disordered behaviors such as lying and stealing (e. g., Loeber & Schmaling, 1985a), it has also been found to be associated with overt conduct-disordered behaviors such as aggression (Jacobson, 1985; Kolko, Kazdin, & Meyer, 1985).

It may be the case that conduct-disordered children who set fires are representative of the "versatile" group described by Loeber and Schmaling (1985b), who engage in both overt and covert forms of conduct-disordered behavior. Indirect support for this contention is provided by two findings. Vreeland and Waller (1980) reported that although 37 of 40 conduct-disordered fire-setting children referred to Oregon Social Learning Center (OSLC) also engaged in stealing, their aversive behavior scores from family interactions in the home were closer to those obtained by socially aggressive children than to those obtained by children identified primarily as stealers. It has also been demonstrated that conduct-disordered children who set fires are more extreme in their conduct-disordered behavior (Jacobson, 1985; Kolko *et al.*, 1985), similar to findings for versatile conduct-disordered children (Loeber & Schmaling, 1985b). Finally, the mothers of fire-setting children on an inpatient unit (most of whom were diagnosed as conduct-disordered) displayed greater psychiatric symptomatology, greater depression, and lower marital satisfaction than mothers of other children hospitalized on that unit (Kazdin & Kolko, 1986).

In addition to the behavioral differences noted in studies of parent–child interaction between parents of clinic-referred conduct-disordered children and their nonreferred counterparts, the parents of conduct-disordered children have more negative perceptions of their children's behavioral adjustment, and they experience more personal (e.g., depression, anxiety), interparental (marital), and extrafamilial (e.g., isolation) distress than parents of non-referred children (see Griest & Wells, 1983, for a review). In addition, they appear to experience higher frequencies of stressful events, both of a minor and of a more significant nature/ (Patterson, 1982, 1983). For example, investigations by Forehand and Patterson and their associates have supported the role of personal distress as one factor associated with mothers' misperceptions of their children: Not only does maternal depression seem to negatively bias the mothers' perception of the children, but the depression also adversely affects the mothers' parenting behavior (Forehand, Lautenschlager, Faust, & Graziano, 1986; Patterson, 1982). It also appears that for children who have been referred for the treatment of conduct-disordered types of behaviors, marital distress is positively related to parental perceptions of child maladjustment and to observed levels of child deviant behavior and parental negative behavior. These relationships seem to be stronger for boys than for girls (e.g., Rutter, 1970). Finally, Wahler and his associates have shown that maternal "insularity," which is defined as a "specific pattern of social contacts within the community that is characterized by a high level of negatively perceived coercive interchanges with relatives and/or helping agency representatives and by a low level of positively perceived supportive interchanges with friends" (Wahler & Dumas, 1984, p. 387), is positively related to negative parent behavior directed toward the child and oppositional child behavior directed toward the parent (Dumas & Wahler, 1985; Wahler, 1980) and is associated with poor maintenance of treatment effects (Dumas & Wahler, 1983; Wahler, 1980; Wahler & Afton, 1980). Thus, when a mother has a large proportion of aversive interactions outside the home, the interactions between the mother and her child in the home are likely to be negative as well.

In summary, parents of conduct-disordered children not only experience elevated levels of problem behaviors from their children, but they also emit higher levels of commanding and critical behaviors, as well as poor monitoring and disciplinary practices. Furthermore, they experience more personal, interparental, and extrafamilial distress, which most investigators

have postulated leads to the child behavior problems; however, sufficient data are not available to answer the directionality question at this time.

Conduct-disordered children may manifest a variety of skill deficits, including distorted attributional processes (e.g., Dodge, 1985), poor problem-solving skills (e.g., Lochman & Lampron, 1986; Richard & Dodge, 1982), lower levels of moral reasoning (Jurkovic, 1980), and difficulties in cognitive and affective perspective taking (e.g., Chandler, 1973). They also appear to be at risk for developing a wide variety of other behavior disorders and adjustment problems as well (Kazdin, 1985; Wells & Forehand, 1985). These include Attention Deficit–Hyperactivity Disorder (see Hinshaw, 1987), depression (especially in boys), academic problems (especially reading disabilities), and peer relationship difficulties. Although there has been little research beyond descriptive data that documents the frequent co-occurrence of conduct disorders with these other behavior problems, Patterson (1986) has proposed a social-learning-based model of conduct disorders that posits specific causal relationships between earlier conduct-disordered behavior and the subsequent development of depression, academic difficulties, and peer relationship problems.

The prevailing theoretical formulation concerning the development and maintenance of conduct-disordered behaviors has emphasized the primacy of familial socialization processes (Patterson, 1982, 1986). Patterson emphasizes the coercive, or controlling, nature of conduct-disordered types of behavior and has developed a coercion hypothesis to account for their development and maintenance. Negative reinforcement plays a particularly important role, in that coercive behavior on the part of one family member (parent or child) is reinforced when it results in the removal of an aversive event being applied to another family member. As this "training" continues over long periods, significant increases in the rate and intensity of these coercive behaviors occur as family member are reinforced by engaging in aggressive behaviors. Furthermore, the child also observes his or her parents engaging in coercive responses, and this provides the opportunity for modeling of aggression to occur (Patterson, 1982).

Patterson and his colleagues have recently expanded the coercion model by incorporating some of the more molar family influences described above and by recasting the model along developmental lines (Patterson, 1986). The overall model suggests a developmental progression from "basic training" in coercive processes via parent–child interactions within the home to the subsequent impact of the child's coercive and noncompliant behavior on self-concept, peer relationships, and academic skills. The model also describes variables such as parental psychopathology and stressors that are correlated with disruptions in parenting skills at different stages of these processes. Preliminary investigations have been supportive of the model as it applies to conduct-disordered boys in both home (e.g., Patterson & Bank, 1986; Patterson & Dishion, 1985) and school (Walker, Shinn, O'Neill, & Ramsey, 1987) settings, and it is currently being tested and revised in an ongoing longitudinal project (Patterson, 1986).

Other investigators have proposed descriptive models that describe various progressions or paths of conduct-disordered behaviors. Edelbrock (1985) has proposed a developmental model that suggests a four-step progression of conduct-disordered behaviors. In general, the four stages describe a progression from overt to covert types of behaviors, from minor to more serious behaviors, and (to a lesser extent) from problems within the home to problems within the school and community. Although the evidence for this model is somewhat preliminary at present because of a cross-sectional design and sole reliance on parental ratings of child behavior, the model does present a useful heuristic for continued research.

Loeber (in press) has proposed a model with three separate developmental paths that may culminate in delinquency and/or substance abuse. In the "aggressive/versatile" path, there is an early onset (i.e., preschool years) of aggressive conduct-disordered behaviors with a later appearance of covert conduct-disordered behaviors, followed by violent delinquent offenses and possibly property offenses as well. In the "nonaggressive/antisocial" path, covert nonaggressive behaviors such as lying and stealing appear in late childhood or early/middle adolescence and are followed by delinquent property offenses. For both paths, substance abuse is hypothesized to follow, rather than precede, the other conduct-disordered behaviors. The third path, "exclusive substance abuse," is postulated to begin in middle to late

adolescence and is not preceded by other conduct-disordered behaviors.

There also appears to be a specific developmental progression in stealing, with less serious forms of theft (e.g., theft at home) beginning earlier than more serious forms (e.g., vehicle theft, breaking and entering). In a reanalysis of interview data originally collected by Belson (1975) with 13- to 16-year-old boys, Loeber (in press) reported that the average age of onset for theft at home was 10 years, with increasingly serious forms of stealing appearing over the next 2½ years, culminating with an average age of onset of 12½ for vehicle theft and breaking and entering. Loeber's analyses also suggest that less serious forms of stealing continue as more serious theft is added to the adolescent's behavioral repertoire.

Much of the theoretical and empirical research has indicated that noncompliance (i.e., excessive disobedience to adults) is the keystone behavior in the development of both overt and covert forms of conduct-disordered behavior. Loeber and Schmaling (1985a) have found that noncompliance is positioned near the zero point of their unidimensional overt–covert scale of antisocial behaviors. Patterson's (1986) comprehensive theoretical model for the development and maintenance of conduct disorders has hypothesized not only that early child noncompliance is the precursor of severe manifestations of conduct-disordered behavior later in childhood and adolescence, but that it plays a role in the conduct-disordered child's subsequent academic and peer relationship problems as well. The data presented by Edelbrock (1985) indicate that noncompliance does appear very early in the progression of conduct disorders and continues to be manifested in subsequent stages. Furthermore, treatment research on behavioral generality has shown that when child noncompliance is targeted, there will often be concomitant improvement in other conduct-disordered behaviors (Russo, Cataldo, & Cushing, 1981; Wells, Forehand, & Griest, 1980).

Although social-learning-based models that emphasize family interaction patterns have been especially useful in conceptualizing the nature of conduct disorders and in suggesting assessment and treatment strategies, it is important to note that other, more biologically based factors may also contribute to the development and/or maintenance of conduct disorders. There is increasing evidence from twin and adoption studies to suggest that there may be a genetic predisposition to the development of conduct disorders (and/or criminal behavior) (e.g., Cloninger, Reich, & Guze, 1978; Jary & Stewart, 1985). That we are most likely dealing with a genetic predisposition is demonstrated by the findings of Cadoret, Cain, and Crowe (1983), who found that the likelihood of adolescents engaging in conduct-disordered behavior was greatly increased when both genetic and environmental influences were present.

Although the definitions of the constructs of "temperament" and "temperamental difficulty" appear to be in a state of flux among developmentalists (Goldsmith *et al.*, 1987), the role of child temperament (usually viewed as involving relatively stable innate personality characteristics; Plomin, 1981) has received increased attention from clinicians as a possible contributing factor to conduct disorders. Of particular interest is the "temperamentally difficult" child who, from very early in life, is intense, irregular, negative, and nonadaptable (Thomas, Chess, & Birch, 1968). Such a child is thought to be predisposed to the development of subsequent behavior problems, due to the increased likelihood of maladaptive parent–child interactions. Webster-Stratton and Eyberg (1982) have demonstrated moderate correlations between some dimensions of child temperament and parent reports of child conduct-disordered behavior (r's = .33–.48) and mother–child interactions (r's = .27–.47), and Olweus (1980) found that temperament contributed substantially to the prediction of aggressive behavior in adolescent boys. However, temperament variables did not contribute to the explanatory variance as much as did family variables such as maternal negativism and permissiveness of aggression.

Finally, some research has indicated that neurological abnormalities and/or history of head trauma are associated with extremely aggressive forms of conduct-disordered behavior (e.g., Shanok & Lewis, 1981). However, there is little evidence that these variables are significant contributors in the development of milder forms of conduct disorders.

ASSESSMENT

Historically, the behavioral assessment of conduct-disordered children has focused on a relatively narrow range of child behaviors and parental antecedents and consequences, with observational methods given primary importance (McMahon, 1987). As knowledge of the characteristics, causes, and correlates of conduct disorders has grown, it is apparent that the scope of behavioral assessment needs to be broadened as well. Primary areas to be assessed include child behavior per se and in an interactional context; other child characteristics (e.g., temperament); and familial and extrafamilial factors (e.g., parents' and teachers' perceptions of the child, parental personal and marital adjustment). In each of these areas, the particular methods (e.g., interviews, questionnaires, observations) that have proven to have the greatest utility with conduct-disordered children and their families are presented here. For a more extensive description and evaluation of these assessment methods, see McMahon and Forehand (1988).

Child Behavior Per Se and in An Interactional Context

In order to obtain an accurate representation of the referred child's conduct-disordered behavior, particularly with regard to its interactional aspects, the behavior therapist must rely on multiple assessment methods, including interviews with the parents, child, and other relevant parties (e.g., teachers); behavioral rating scales; and direct observations in the clinic, home, and/or school settings.

Behavioral Interviews

Because the etiology of child conduct disorders is conceptualized primarily in terms of parent–child interactions, the interview with the parent is of major importance. The primary purpose of the interview is to determine the nature of the typical parent–child interactions that are problematic, the antecedent stimulus conditions under which problem behaviors occur, and the consequences that accompany such behaviors. A number of interview formats are available to aid the therapist in structuring the information obtained from the parents. Some of the formats, such as those presented by Forehand and McMahon (1981) and Wahler and Cormier (1970), are structured around problematic situations (e.g., bedtime, sibling interactions), whereas others are structured according to different child behaviors (e.g., the Symptom Checklist; Patterson, Reid, Jones, & Conger, 1975). More recently, Patterson and his colleagues (e.g., Patterson & Bank, 1986) have developed a structured parent interview that includes questions regarding a broad range of theoretically relevant parenting behaviors (e.g., parental monitoring of the child, parental problem solving). However, this interview format has yet to be applied in a clinical setting, and its psychometric characteristics are relatively unknown.

When the presenting problems include classroom behavior, an interview with the child's teacher(s) is appropriate. Situationally formatted interview guides based on Barkley's (1981) School Situations Questionnaire or Wahler and Cormier's (1970) preinterview checklists can be employed in conjunction with specific questions related to the child's problem behaviors. Contextual factors, such as classroom rules of conduct, teacher expectations, and the behavior of other children in the classroom, are important as well.

An individual interview with the child may or may not provide useful content-oriented information, depending upon the age and/or developmental level of the child and the nature of the specific child behaviors. Children below the age of 10 may not be reliable reporters of their own behavioral symptoms (Edelbrock, Costello, Dulcan, Kalas, & Conover, 1985). Loeber and Schmaling (1985b) have suggested that when assessing overt types of conduct-disordered behaviors such as fighting, maternal and teacher reports may be preferable to child reports, since these children often underestimate their own aggressive behavior. Alternatively, because of the nature of covert types of conduct-disordered behaviors such as stealing, more valid reports are more likely to be obtained from the child.* However, even with younger children, informal interviews can be extremely useful, in that they can provide the therapist with an opportunity to assess the child's perception of why he or she has been brought to the clinic and can provide a preliminary evaluation of the child's cognitive, affective, and behavioral characteristics (Bierman, 1983).

*However, given the strong positive correlations between stealing and lying noted above, children who steal may not be veridical in their self-reports.

Behavioral Rating Scales

Behavioral rating scales are typically completed by parents or teachers in reference to the child's behavior or characteristics. They are very useful as screening devices, both for covering a broad range of conduct-disordered behaviors and for assessing the presence of other child behavior disorders. Behavioral rating scales are currently regarded as excellent measures of parental and teacher perceptions of the child, and as such, have been extensively employed as treatment outcome and social validation measures in treatment studies with conduct-disordered children and their families.

Although there are many excellent behavioral rating scales (McMahon, 1984), two have been recommended as most appropriate for clinical and research use with conduct-disordered children (McMahon & Forehand, 1988). The Child Behavior Checklist (CBCL; Achenbach & Edelbrock, 1983; Achenbach, Edelbrock, & Howell, 1987) is designed for use with children between the ages of 2 and 16. There are parallel forms of the CBCL for parents (including one form specifically for 2- and 3-year-olds), teachers, youths, and observers, although only the parent and teacher forms have been completely standardized.

The parent form of the CBCL currently consists of two different checklists: one that is completed by parents of children aged 4–16 (CBCL/4–16) and a newly developed checklist that is completed by parents of children ages 2–3 (CBCL/2–3) (Achenbach et al., 1987). The CBCL/4–16 includes both Social Competence and Behavior Problem scales, whereas the CBCL/2–3 includes only Behavior Problem scales. The CBCL scores are summarized on either the Revised Child Behavior Profile (RCBP) (for the CBCL/4–16) or the Child Behavior Profile for Ages 2–3 (for the CBCL/2–3). There are separate norms for boys and girls at three age levels (4–5, 6–11, 12–16) on the RCBP. Both profiles indicate the child's standing on various narrow-band and broad-band (Internalizing, Externalizing) syndromes. On the RCBP, the Externalizing broad-band syndrome includes conduct-disordered types of behavior problems on three narrow-band scales (Aggressive, Delinquent, Cruel), whereas the Child Behavior Profile for Ages 2–3 includes conduct-disordered types of behaviors on the Aggressive and Destructive narrow-band scales. The parent form of the CBCL has been shown to differentiate boys with a DSM-III diagnosis of Conduct Disorder from children with other diagnoses on an inpatient unit (Kazdin & Heidish, 1984), and to differentiate fire setters from non-fire setters with a group of inpatient conduct-disordered children (Kolko et al., 1985). It is also sensitive to changes resulting from parent training interventions for the treatment of conduct disorders (Webster-Stratton, 1984, 1985a). The teacher version of the CBCL and the Child Behavior Profile have yet to be evaluated specifically with conduct-disordered populations, but preliminary evidence supports the psychometric viability of the instrument (e.g., Edelbrock & Achenbach, 1984).

The Eyberg Child Behavior Inventory (ECBI; Eyberg, 1980) can be employed in situations in which the clinician wishes to focus solely on conduct-disordered behaviors. The ECBI is completed by parents and is intended for use with children aged 2–16. The 36 items describe specific conduct-disordered behaviors (primarily overt) and are scored on both a frequency-of-occurrence scale and a yes–no problem identification scale. Both scales have been shown to discriminate conduct-disordered children from other clinic-referred children and from normal children (Eyberg & Robinson, 1983a; Eyberg & Ross, 1978; Robinson, Eyberg, & Ross, 1980) and to be sensitive to behavioral treatment effects (e.g., Eyberg & Robinson, 1982; Webster-Stratton, 1984).

Behavioral Observation

As noted above, direct behavioral observation has long been the *sine qua non* of behavioral assessment of conduct-disordered children and their families, both for delineating specific patterns of maladaptive parent–child or teacher–child interaction and for assessing change in those interactions as a function of treatment. More recently, observational data have been compared with data gathered via other methods to assist the clinician in determining whether the focus of treatment should be on the adult–child interaction or on adult perceptual and/or personal adjustment issues. Space limitations preclude an extensive review of the many behavioral observation systems currently in use for assessing interactions with conduct-disordered children in the clinic, home, and school settings. Instead, the major systems employed with conduct-disordered children and their families in various settings are noted.

There are two structured observation procedures for assessing parent–child interactions in the clinic: the system developed by Forehand and his colleagues (Forehand & McMahon, 1981) and the Dyadic Parent–Child Interactional Coding System (DPICS; Eyberg & Robinson, 1983b). These observation systems are modifications of the assessment procedures developed by Hanf (1970) and are quite similar. Both systems place the parent–child dyad in standard situations that vary in the degree to which parental control is required, ranging from a free-play situation to one in which the parent directs the child's activity. In each system, a variety of parent and child behaviors are scored, many of which emphasize parental antecedents (e.g., commands) and consequences (e.g., praise, time out) for child compliance or noncompliance. Both systems have adequate psychometric properties; both have been extensively employed as treatment outcome measures; and both have been employed in the home setting as well.

Perhaps the best-known behavioral coding system designed for use in the home setting is the Family Interaction Coding System (FICS) developed by Patterson and his colleagues (Patterson, Ray, Shaw, & Cobb, 1969; Reid, 1978), which consists of 29 behavior categories used to describe social interactions among family members. The Total Aversive Behavior (TAB) score, which is a composite of 14 of those categories, has typically been reported as a measure of general coerciveness. The FICS has not only been shown to discriminate between clinic-referred and nonreferred children and their family members, but also among various subtypes of conduct-disordered children such as social aggressors and stealers. The FICS has been widely employed as a measure of treatment outcome and has been shown to be highly sensitive in this regard (see Patterson & Fleischman, 1979).

Wahler's Standardized Observation Codes system (Wahler, House, & Stambaugh, 1976) is similar to Patterson's FICS, although it includes a greater number of positive behaviors than do most of the other observation systems. Patterson and his colleagues (Dishion et al., 1984) have recently developed the Family Process Code (FPC), which includes reasonably broad coverage of prosocial as well as deviant behaviors, provides ratings of affect for each behavior that is coded, and records interactions in real time as opposed to intervals. Because of its recent appearance, the psychometric properties of FPC have not been extensively investigated, nor has it been employed as a treatment outcome measure.

The use of the preceding observation systems in the home setting for behavior therapists in clinical practice is desirable, but rare for obvious reasons. The coding systems are relatively complex and require lengthy periods to train observers and to maintain adequate levels of reliability. The observations themselves are usually lengthy as well. As a consequence, the use of structured clinical observations to assess parent–child interactions is recommended (McMahon & Forehand, 1988).

Behavioral observation systems designed specifically for assessing conduct-disordered types of behavior in the school setting have received relatively less attention. Both Patterson's and Forehand's systems have been adapted for use in the school (e.g., Breiner & Forehand, 1981; Harris, Kreil, & Orpet, 1977). Wahler et al.'s (1976) coding system was originally developed for use in both home and school settings, although it has not been used extensively in the latter setting. Adoption of one of these coding systems does have the advantage of facilitating cross-situational comparisons during the assessment process. Walker and his colleagues have developed several observation systems for assessing conduct-disordered behavior in various school settings (see Walker & Fabre, in press). Finally, preliminary data suggest that the Direct Observation Form (DOF) of the CBCL (Reed & Edelbrock, 1983) may represent a useful alternative to the observation systems described above. Yielding a total Behavior Problem score and a measure of on-task behavior, the DOF is relatively simple to use, discriminates between referred and nonreferred children in the classroom, and can be compared to other forms of the CBCL. A newly available Profile for the DOF yields On-Task, Internalizing, Externalizing, and Total Problem scores as well as scores for six narrow-band problem scales.

An alternative to placing independent observers in the home or school is to train significant adults in the child's environment to observe and record certain types of child behavior. An added advantage is the opportunity to assess low-rate behaviors such as stealing or

fire setting. The most extensively validated procedure of this type is the Parent Daily Report (PDR; Chamberlain & Reid, 1987; Patterson et al., 1975), a parent observation measure that is typically administered during brief telephone interviews. In the version reported by Patterson et al. (1975), the parent is asked which of 31 deviant child behaviors have occurred in the past 24 hours and the setting in which the behaviors occurred. In the Chamberlain and Reid (1987) version, the PDR consists of 33 deviant child behaviors and a single item referring to whether the parent has spanked the child in the past 24 hours. The setting in which the behavior occurs is not recorded in this version. The PDR has been employed on a pretreatment basis to assess the magnitude of behavior problems, to monitor the progress of the family during therapy, and to assess treatment outcome. Recent revision of the PDR has resulted in greater emphasis on parental disciplinary practices and the development of a parallel form for children (see Patterson & Bank, 1986).

A brief daily interview similar to the PDR for collecting parent report data on stealing has been developed by Jones (1974). The Telephone Interview Report on Stealing and Social Aggression (TIROSSA) has adequate test–retest reliability and is sensitive to the effects of treatment procedures designed to reduce stealing (Reid, Hinojosa Rivera, & Lorber, 1980). It is mentioned here because it is one of the few assessment instruments of any type to focus primarily on a covert, as opposed to an overt, form of conduct-disordered behavior.

Additional Child Characteristics

A brief developmental and medical history of the child should be obtained, usually as part of the initial behavioral interview with the parents. The purpose of this line of questioning with parents of conduct-disordered children is to determine whether there appear to be any medical factors that may be asssociated with the development or maintenance of the conduct-disordered behavior (e.g., neurological injury or disease), and whether the child's early temperament may have been a contributing factor in the development of a coercive style of parent–child interaction. If desired, child temperament may be assessed in a more formal manner by standardized parent interviews or parent-completed questionnaires (see Plomin, 1983, for a review), although they present difficulties in terms of lengthy administration and scoring procedures and/or problems with respect to the adequacy of their psychometric properties (e.g., Vaughn, Bradley, Joffe, Seifer, & Barglow, 1987).

As noted above, conduct-disordered children are at risk for manifesting additional behavior disorders, such as Attention Deficit–Hyperactivity Disorder and/or depression, as well as peer interaction problems and academic difficulties. Behavioral rating scales such as the CBCL (Achenbach & Edelbrock, 1983) that provide information about a wide variety of narrow-band behavior disorders can serve as useful screening devices, as can brief questions in the initial interview about these problems.

Familial and Extrafamilial Factors

McMahon and Forehand (1988) have delineated five areas that are relevant to the assessment of conduct-disordered children: parent and teacher perceptions of child adjustment, parent personal and marital adjustment, parental stress, maternal insularity, and parental satisfaction with treatment. As noted above, parental perception of the child, rather than child behavior per se, is the best predictor of referral for conduct-disordered types of behavior. The behavioral rating scales described previously are the most ready sources of such data; when examined in the context of behavioral observation data and the therapist's own impressions, they can be important indicators as to whether the informants (parents, teachers) appear to have a perceptual bias in their assessment of the referred child's behavior.

To assess the extent to which parents' personal and marital adjustment problems may be playing a role in the child's presenting behavior problems, a set of screening procedures that includes brief questions in the initial interviews with the parents and child and certain parental self-report measures can be utilized. Maternal depression has been the most widely investigated personal adjustment problem in parents of children with conduct disorders, and the Beck Depression Inventory (Beck, Rush, Shaw, & Emery, 1979) has been the most frequently employed measure. With respect to marital discord, the Marital Adjustment Test (Locke & Wallace, 1959) and the Dyadic Adjustment Scale (Spanier, 1976) have been the most widely used instruments with parents of conduct-disordered children, although there

is some preliminary evidence to suggest that the O'Leary–Porter Scale (Porter & O'Leary, 1980), which is designed to assess overt marital hostility, may be a better predictor of parent-reported child behavior problems than is the Marital Adjustment Test.

Parental exposure to stressors can be assessed by the OSLC Family Crisis List (Patterson, 1982, 1983) or the Parenting Stress Index (Loyd & Abidin, 1985). Although the Family Crisis List was developed specifically for use with the parents of conduct-disordered children, its psychometric properties have not been adequately evaluated. The Parenting Stress Index does have a reasonable psychometric foundation, but, to our knowledge, has not been employed specifically with the families of conduct-disordered children.

With respect to extrafamilial functioning, the Community Interaction Checklist (CIC; Wahler, Leske, & Rogers, 1979) is the only measure of its type to have been employed with conduct-disordered children and their families. The CIC is a brief interview designed to assess maternal insularity and is usually administered on multiple occasions. As noted above, classification as insular on the CIC is a strong predictor of poor maintenance of the effects of parent training interventions for conduct-disordered children (Dumas & Wahler, 1983; Wahler, 1980; Wahler & Afton, 1980).

Finally, it is important to assess the social validity of treatment with conduct-disordered children and their families. Parental satisfaction with treatment, which is one form of social validity, may be assessed in terms of satisfaction with the outcome of treatment, therapists, treatment procedures, and teaching format (McMahon & Forehand, 1983). At present, there is no single consumer satisfaction measure that is appropriate for use with all types of interventions for conduct-disordered children and their families. The Parent's Consumer Satisfaction Questionnaire (PCSQ; Forehand & McMahon, 1981; McMahon, Tiedemann, Forehand, & Griest, 1984) is an example of one such measure designed to evaluate parental satisfaction with a particular parent training program designed to modify child noncompliance and other conduct-disordered behaviors. Using the PCSQ, parents have generally reported high absolute levels of satisfaction with the various aspects of the parent training program, both at treatment termination and at various follow-up assessments (Baum & Forehand, 1981; McMahon, Forehand, & Griest, 1981; McMahon *et al.*, 1984). The PCSQ is also sensitive to differences in parental satisfaction across variations of this particular parent training program (McMahon, Forehand, & Griest, 1981; McMahon *et al.*, 1984), and has been employed with other parent training programs as well (Webster-Stratton, 1984).

An Assessment Model

It is readily apparent that a proper assessment of the conduct-disordered child must make use of multiple methods (e.g., behavioral rating scales, direct observation, interviews) completed by multiple informants (parents, teachers, the child himself or herself) concerning the child's behavior in multiple settings (e.g., home, school), and that the familial and extrafamilial context in which the child functions must also be assessed (McMahon, 1987). However, in cost-effectiveness terms, to conduct such a broad-based assessment with every child who is referred would be prohibitively expensive, and the incremental utility of each additional assessment measure or content area with respect to improving our treatment-selecting capabilities would be suspect as well (Mash, 1985).

A variation of the "multiple-gating" approach to assessment utilized by investigators at OSLC in the identification of children at risk for delinquency (e.g., Loeber, Dishion, & Patterson, 1984; Reid, Baldwin, Patterson, & Dishion, 1988) has been proposed as one strategy for dealing with this problem (McMahon, 1987). In this approach, less costly assessment procedures, such as brief interviews and behavioral rating scales, would be employed as screening instruments with all children who are clinic-referred for the treatment of conduct disorders. More expensive methods, such as observation in the home or school, would be used to assess that subgroup of children for whom the less expensive methods have indicated the desirability of further assessment. A similar sequential strategy could be followed in the assessment of other child characteristics and familial and extrafamilial factors, in that relatively low-cost methods such as interview questions (e.g., concerning the child's temperament or the parent's marital adjustment) and/or brief self-report measures such as the Beck Depression Inventory would be employed as screening measures. If additional assessment in

these areas were warranted, then a more thorough (and expensive) assessment could be conducted.

The ultimate goal of the assessment process is, of course, to facilitate selection of the most appropriate treatment strategy or strategies. McMahon (1987) has delineated several treatment selection issues facing the behavior therapist working with conduct disordered children. These include decisions as to:

> (a) when the "standard" parent training approach is beneficial; (b) when to intervene in additional areas such as other child disorders, parental personal or marital adjustment difficulties, child or parental perceptual biases, and/or extrafamilial functioning (e.g., insularity); and (c) if intervention is to take place in one or more of these areas, should it occur before, after, instead of, or concurrently with a parent training type of intervention? (p. 248)

Algorithms for matching clinic-referred families with specific interventions exist (e.g., Blechman, 1981; Embry, 1984), but they have been quite limited in scope, have not been closely tied to underlying assessment strategies, and have yet to be empirically tested. A comprehensive, empirically based treatment selection model for conduct-disordered children is sorely needed.

TREATMENT

Overview

As demonstrated in the preceding material, conduct disorders are multifaceted in the diversity of specific behaviors that are manifested, the ages of the children who engage in those behaviors, and the settings in which the behaviors occur. Not surprisingly, a plethora of therapies (behavioral and otherwise) have been developed to deal with the various manifestations of conduct disorders (e.g., Kazdin, 1985). In an attempt to impose some structure in our discussion of this array of interventions, we adopt the following organizational scheme. Behavioral treatments designed to deal with overt and covert conduct-disordered behaviors are discussed separately. Although noncompliance is characteristic of both overt and covert forms of conduct disorders, it has been typically dealt with in treatment programs designed to deal with overt conduct-disordered behaviors (e.g., Forehand & McMahon, 1981; Patterson *et al.*,

1975), and so is discussed in that section of the chapter. For each of the major subtypes of conduct disorders, we describe family-based interventions (e.g., parent training), community-based residential programs (e.g., Achievement Place), school-based interventions (e.g., classroom contingency management programs), and skills training approaches (e.g., social skills training, anger control training). For each type of program, interventions that are available for, and appropriate to, the preadolescent (3–12 years of age) and the adolescent (13 and older) are described. For each intervention, we describe the treatment approach and briefly review the empirical evidence concerning its effectiveness. Following the review of behavioral interventions for overt and covert conduct disorders, we discuss a number of issues related to the development, selection, and evaluation of these interventions, such as generalization and social validity, the prediction of outcome, and comparative efficacy.

Behavioral Interventions for Overt Conduct Disorders

The majority of behavioral interventions directed to conduct-disordered children have been designed for the treatment of overt, as opposed to covert, conduct disorders, probably because of the disruptive effects of those behaviors on parents, siblings, teachers, peers, and the like. Because current theoretical (e.g., Patterson, 1986) and empirical (e.g., Edelbrock, 1985; Loeber & Stouthamer-Loeber, 1986) writings indicate the primary role of the family in the development and maintenance of conduct disorders, we focus first on interventions directed at the conduct-disordered child in the context of the family.

Family-Based Interventions with Preadolescents

Behavioral approaches to treating conduct-disordered children in the family have typically been based on the "parent training" model of intervention (O'Dell, 1974). The underlying assumption of this model is that some sort of parenting skills deficit has been at least partly responsible for the development and/or maintenance of the conduct-disordered behaviors. The therapist instructs the parent in a variety of behavioral techniques (e.g., differential attention, time out), which the parent then uses to decrease the child's conduct-disordered behaviors while at the same time shaping more appropriate prosocial responses. Therapists usually employ a variety of teaching methods, including didactic instruction, modeling, behavioral rehearsal, shaping, and structured homework exercises, to instruct the parent. Parent training interventions have been successfully utilized in the clinic and home settings, have been implemented with individual families or with groups of families, and have involved some or all of the instructional techniques listed above. O'Dell (1985) has provided an extensive review of the myriad parametric considerations involved in parent training.

Although the short-term efficacy of behavioral parent training in producing changes in both parent and child behaviors has been demonstrated repeatedly (e.g., O'Dell, 1974), the generalization of those effects has been less consistently documented. Forehand and Atkeson (1977) discussed four major types of generalization relevant to parent training interventions with children. "Setting generalization" refers to the transfer of treatment effects to settings in which treatment did not take place (e.g., from the clinic to the home), whereas "temporal generalization" pertains to the maintenance of treatment effects following termination. "Sibling generalization" concerns the transfer of the newly acquired parenting skills to untreated siblings in the family, and the siblings' responding in the desired manner. "Behavioral generalization" refers to whether targeted changes in specific conduct-disordered behaviors are accompanied by improvements in other nontargeted behaviors.

Pertinent to the generalization of effects is the "social validity" of the intervention, which refers to whether therapeutic changes are "clinically or socially important" for the client (Kazdin, 1977, p. 429). Parent training interventions for the treatment of conduct-disordered children have demonstrated their generalizability and social validity to varying degrees—some quite impressively, others not at all. As a consequence of this emphasis on the generalization and social validity of treatment effects and the increased awareness of the multiple causal and maintaining factors of conduct disorders, the parent training model is being broadened to what is referred to as "behavioral family therapy" (Griest & Wells, 1983; Wells, 1985). Although still in its formative stages, the model is an attempt to acknowledge and incorporate into treatment the variety of child and parent variables that have been implicated in the development and maintenance of conduct disorders, such as parental personal adjustment and perceptions of the child, and child characteristics such as temperament and attributional style.

We have chosen to present several parent training/behavioral family therapy programs as examples of state-of-the-art family-based interventions for conduct-disordered children. Descriptions of the clinical procedures utilized in these programs are widely available, and each of the programs has been extensively evaluated.

The first parent training program is specifically designed to treat noncompliance in younger children (3–8 years of age). As noted above, noncompliance is regarded as a keystone behavior in the development and maintenance of conduct disorders. The program was originally developed by Hanf (Hanf, 1969, 1970; Hanf & Kling, 1973), but has been modified and subsequently evaluated by several independent groups of clinical researchers, including Forehand and his colleagues (Forehand & McMahon, 1981), Webster-Stratton (e.g., 1984), and Eyberg (e.g., Eyberg & Robinson, 1982). As presented by Forehand and McMahon (1981), the parent training program employs a controlled learning environment in which the parent is taught to change maladaptive patterns of interaction with the child. Sessions are conducted in a clinic setting with individual families rather than in groups. Treatment occurs in playrooms equipped with one-way mirrors for observation, sound systems, and "bug-in-the-ear" devices (Farrall Instruments) by which the therapist can unobtrusively communicate with the parent. A number of discrete parenting skills are taught to the parent by way of didactic instruction, modeling, and role playing. The parent also practices the skills in the clinic with the child while receiving prompting and feedback from the therapist by means of the bug-in-the-ear device. Finally, the parent employs these newly acquired skills in the home setting.

The treatment program consists of two phases. During the differential-attention phase of treatment (Phase I), the parent learns to break out of the escalating coercive cycle described above by increasing the frequency and range of social rewards and by reducing the frequency of competing verbal behavior. The parent is first taught to attend to and describe the child's appropriate behavior while eliminating commands, questions, and criticisms. The second segment of Phase I consists of training the parent to use verbal and physical rewards contingent upon compliance and other appropriate behaviors, and to ignore minor inappropriate behaviors. Homework is assigned in the form of daily 10-minute practice sessions with the child, using the skills taught in the clinic. The parent is also required to develop programs for use outside the clinic to increase at least two child behaviors using the new skills.

Phase II of the treatment program consists of training the parent to use appropriate commands and a time-out procedure to decrease noncompliant behavior exhibited by the child. The parent is taught to give direct, concise commands one at a time, and to allow the child sufficient time to comply.* If compliance is initiated, the parent is taught to reward or attend to the child. If compliance is not initiated, the parent learns to implement a 3-minute time-out procedure. Following time out, the command that originally elicited noncompliance is repeated. Compliance is followed by contingent attention from the parent. When the parent is able to administer time out perfectly in the clinic, he or she is instructed to begin using the procedure for noncompliance at home.

Progression to each new skill in the treatment program is determined by the use of behavioral and temporal (number of sessions) criteria. These criteria insure that the parent has attained an acceptable degree of competence in a particular skill before being taught additional parenting techniques, and allow for the individualization of the treatment program by allocating training time more efficiently. For complete details of this parent training program, see Forehand and McMahon (1981).

The Forehand and McMahon version of this parent training program has been extensively evaluated in terms of its short-term effectiveness, generalization, and social validity (see McMahon & Forehand, 1984). Short-term effectiveness and setting generalization from the clinic to the home have been demonstrated for both parent and child behaviors, as well as parents' perceptions of their children (e.g., Peed, Roberts, & Forehand, 1977). Furthermore, these improvements occur regardless of

---

*These commands are referred to as "alpha commands." "Beta commands" are those to which the child has no opportunity to demonstrate compliance because of vagueness or parental interruption (e.g., "Act your age").

families' socioeconomic status (Rogers, Forehand, Griest, Wells, & McMahon, 1981) or age of the children (within the 3- to 8-year-old age range) (McMahon, Forehand, & Tiedemann, 1985). Two studies have failed to find evidence for setting generality to the classroom, but there was also no evidence of a behavioral contrast effect, since there were no systematic increases or decreases in child deviant behavior in the classroom (Breiner & Forehand, 1981; Forehand et al., 1979).

The temporal generalization of this parent training program has been documented in several studies (Baum & Forehand, 1981; Forehand & Long, 1986; Forehand, Rogers, McMahon, Wells, & Griest, 1981; Forehand, Steffe, Furey, & Walley, 1983; Forehand et al., 1979), with follow-up assessments ranging from 6 months to 4½ years after treatment termination. More recently, Forehand and Long (1986) have demonstrated that, relative to a nonreferred "normal" sample, a sample of children who had participated in the parent training program 4½–10½ years earlier (and who were now between the ages of 11 and 15) were functioning well. Sibling generalization was demonstrated by Humphreys, Forehand, McMahon, and Roberts (1978), who showed that mothers employed the skills they had learned in the parent training program to untreated children in the home. Those children, in turn, responded by being more compliant to maternal directives. Finally, improvement in child compliance has been shown to be accompanied by decreases in other overt conduct-disordered behaviors, such as aggression, tantrums, destructiveness, and inappropriate verbal behavior (Wells, Forehand, & Griest, 1980).

The social validity of the Forehand and McMahon (1981) program has been assessed in several investigations. Child compliance and inappropriate behavior have improved to within the normal range by the end of treatment, although mothers' perceptions of the children's adjustment appear to lag behind the children's behavioral improvements (Forehand, Wells, & Griest, 1980). However, by 2 months after the conclusion of treatment, mothers' perceptions are consistent with the children's improved behavior and are comparable to those of mothers of "normal" children. High parental ratings of the acceptability of (Cross Calvert & McMahon, 1987) and satisfaction with (Baum & Forehand, 1981; Forehand et al., 1980; McMahon et al., 1984) the parent training program in general and its components have also been documented.

Several procedures have been evaluated as adjuncts to the basic treatment program. These include maternal (Wells, Griest, & Forehand, 1980) and child (Baum, Reyna McGlone, & Ollendick, 1986) self-control procedures; training the parents in the social learning principles underlying the parent training program (McMahon, Forehand, & Griest, 1981); and a multimodal treatment package ("parent enhancement therapy") designed to enhance general family functioning, which includes components related to parental perceptions of the child's behavior, marital adjustment, parental personal adjustment, and the parents' extrafamilial relationships (Griest et al., 1982). In general, these studies have supported the efficacy of these adjunctive procedures in enhancing the generalization and/or maintenance of treatment effects, over and above those gains obtained in the basic parent training program.

Two studies have compared the effects of this parent training program with other treatments for conduct-disordered children. Wells and Egan (1988) found that the parent training program was more effective than systems family therapy on observational measures of parent and child behaviors. The two treatment groups did not differ on parental self-report measures of personal (depression, anxiety) or marital adjustment. Baum et al. (1986) reported that a group version of the parent training program (with or without the child self-control adjunct noted above) was more effective at posttreatment and at a 6- to 8-month follow-up than a parent discussion group based on the Systematic Training for Effective Parenting (STEP) program (Dinkmeyer & McKay, 1976).

A second parent training program for young (3- to 8-year-old) conduct-disordered children, which includes some components of the Hanf (1969) and Forehand and McMahon (1981) programs, is the videotape modeling/group discussion (VMGD) program developed by Webster-Stratton (1981a, 1987). What is unique about this particular therapy program is its use of a standard package of 10 videotape programs of modeled parenting skills shown by a therapist to groups of parents. The 250 vignettes (each of which lasts approximately 2 minutes) include examples of parents interacting with their children in both appropriate and inappropriate ways. After each vignette, the therapist leads a discussion of the relevant interactions and solicits parental responses to the vignettes. In this particular program, the children do not attend the therapy sessions, although parents are given homework exercises to practice various parenting skills with their children. The videotapes and associated therapist manuals are commercially available (Webster-Stratton, 1987).

There have been three major treatment outcome studies evaluating the immediate and longer-term effects of this parent training approach. The first study (Webster-Stratton, 1981b, 1982a, 1982b), which employed a sample of nonreferred mothers, reported positive changes in mothers' and children's behaviors and maternal perceptions of the children's adjustment compared to a waiting-list control group at posttreatment. Mothers also reported high levels of satisfaction with the treatment program. At a 1-year follow-up, most of the parental perceptions and mother and child behaviors were maintained or continued to improve; however, there was a significant decrease in mothers' confidence in their parenting skills and perceived ability to manage their children's behavior problems.

In the second study, Webster-Stratton (1984) employed a sample of 35 mothers of clinic-referred conduct-disordered children. Mothers were randomly assigned to either the VMGD program, an individual parent training program, or a waiting-list control. The individual parent training program, the content of which was comparable to the VMGD program, employed one-to-one sessions with a therapist, a mother, and her child. In-session *in vivo* modeling and behavioral rehearsal (including feedback via the bug-in-the-ear) were employed in those sessions. Utilizing a variety of treatment outcome measures, including parent perception (CBCL, ECBI), parent report (PDR), observed parent and child behaviors (DPICS), and consumer satisfaction (a measure adapted from the PCSQ), Webster-Stratton documented positive changes in both treatment conditions compared to the waiting-list control condition at posttreatment. At a 1-year follow-up, most of these changes were maintained; in fact, the children's noncompliance and deviant behavior had continued to decrease. Parental satisfaction with treatment was also maintained at the 1-year follow-up. What is also of interest is that there were virtually no differences between the two treatment groups at posttreatment and at the follow-up. Given that therapist time per client was five times greater for the individual parent

training condition than for the VMGD condition, the latter program appears to represent a cost-effective alternative to the traditional parent training format of individual consultation with a single family, at least for families with young conduct-disordered children.

A component analysis of the VMGD program has recently been conducted with a sample of mothers and fathers of 114 conduct-disordered children (Webster-Stratton, Kolpacoff, & Hollinsworth, 1988). Parents were randomly assigned to either the VMGD program, self-administered videotape modeling (with no therapist feedback or group discussion), group discussion alone, or a waiting-list control condition. Each of the three treatment conditions was superior to the waiting-list control condition on most of the various outcome measures. Of major interest was the finding that, although the VMGD program appeared to be somewhat more effective than the other two treatment conditions, the self-administered videotape condition produced a variety of parental attitudinal and behavioral changes. However, its utility in leading to observable differences in actual child behavior was somewhat less clear, since differences from the control condition in child deviant behavior were noted only in interactions with fathers (but not mothers) in the self-administered videotape condition. Nevertheless, these findings again support the short-term effectiveness of Webster-Stratton's parent training program and suggest the power of the videotape modeling component.

As noted above, the work of Gerald Patterson and his associates at OSLC with conduct-disordered children and their families has been seminal in the development of the theoretical and empirical knowledge base concerning conduct disorders. Patterson's efforts over the past 20 years have also been extremely influential with respect to the development and evaluation of family-based intervention strategies for conduct-disordered children. Here, we briefly review Patterson's parent training program for preadolescent children (3–12 years of age) who engage in overt conduct disorders. OSLC intervention programs for children who steal and for adolescent delinquents are described later in the chapter.

The parent training program for preadolescent aggressive children is delineated in the treatment manual by Patterson et al. (1975) and has been recently summarized by Reid (1987). Prior to beginning treatment, parents are given a copy of either *Living with Children* (Patterson, 1976b) or *Families* (Patterson, 1975a). The rationale for assigning these programmed texts is that they will provide a conceptual background for the specific skills training in the therapy sessions and will facilitate generalization and maintenance. Parents complete a brief test on the reading material at the beginning of the first therapy session. Preliminary data suggest that for some families, simply reading the book may lead to a significant reduction in observed child deviant behaviors (Patterson, 1975b). After completion of the reading assignment and test, the next step is to teach the parents to pinpoint the problem behaviors of concern. This usually requires one to two treatment sessions; the rationale is that the parents must precisely define the target behaviors before they will be able to respond systematically to the behaviors. The parents then learn to track the child's behavior. Parents choose two or three behaviors (one of which is usually noncompliance) to observe for a 1-hour period each day for a week. An attempt is made to have both the mother and father track the behaviors. Once the parents are pinpointing and tracking child behavior appropriately, they are assisted in establishing a positive reinforcement system, using points for two or three positive behaviors. Backup reinforcers include privileges or treats, and are administered on a daily basis. Social reinforcement (i.e., praise) is provided to the child as he or she engages in each of the positive behaviors, and over time, the tangible reinforcers are faded. After the point system is well established and has been in place for a few weeks, the parents are taught to use a 5-minute time-out procedure for noncompliance or aggressive behavior. Response cost (e.g., loss of privileges) and work chores are also sometimes used with older children. As treatment progresses, parents become increasingly responsible for designing and implementing behavior management programs for various child behaviors. Problem-solving and negotiation strategies are taught to the parents at this point in treatment. Patterson and Chamberlain (1988) estimate that approximately 30% of therapy time is devoted to dealing with problems such as marital difficulties, parental personal adjustment problems, and family crises.

The parent training program for preadolescent conduct-disordered children has been extensively evaluated at OSLC and in community settings. Patterson, Cobb, and Ray (1973) treated 13 consecutive referrals of conduct-disordered boys and their families. Behavioral observation data from the FICS indicated that 9 of the 13 families demonstrated improvements equal to or greater than 30% reduction from baseline levels of observed deviant behavior. In subsequent replication studies, in which a total of 27 consecutive referrals were treated, similar effects were obtained (Patterson, 1974; Patterson & Reid, 1973). Improvements in maternal perceptions of the child's adjustment have also been reported, and there is evidence for generalization across settings, time (up to 1 year posttreatment), behavior, and siblings (e.g., Arnold, Levine, & Patterson, 1975; Horne & Van Dyke, 1983; Patterson, 1974; Patterson & Fleischman, 1979).

Early attempts by other investigators to replicate Patterson's procedures and methodology met with mixed results (Eyberg & Johnson, 1974; Ferber, Keeley, & Shemberg, 1974). The results of more recent studies have been more promising. Comparable findings to those reported by Patterson (1974) have been obtained in a mixed sample of stealers and social aggressors (Fleischman, 1981), and for a subset of social aggressors (Weinrott, Bauske, & Patterson, 1979). These families were treated by therapists who, although affiliated with Patterson, had not participated in the 1974 investigation and were not supervised by the OSLC staff during the course of the studies. Not only were positive treatment effects maintained at a 1-year follow-up, but standardization of treatment procedures and use of a group format in the replication studies reduced treatment time per family from 31 hours to 13–16 hours. Fleischman and Szykula (1981) conducted another replication study in a community setting with 50 families, and reported comparable improvements at posttreatment and at a 1-year follow-up.

The OSLC group has also conducted a number of comparison studies. Early investigations comparing the parent training program with an attention placebo (Walter & Gilmore, 1973) and a waiting-list control (Wiltz & Patterson, 1974) reported significant reductions in targeted deviant child behaviors, whereas there were no significant changes for the comparison groups. However, small sample sizes, short treatment intervals, and other methodological difficulties limited the significance of the findings. A more recent study (Patterson, Chamberlain, & Reid, 1982) randomly assigned 19 families to parent training or waiting-list control conditions. The control condition actually became a comparison treatment condition by default, since eight of nine families obtained treatment from various clinicians in the community. Treatment ranged from "eclectic" to behavioral in orientation. Observational data in the home indicated significant reductions in child deviant behavior for the parent training program only. However, both groups demonstrated significant improvements on the PDR with respect to frequency of parent-reported problem behaviors.

A large-scale comparative study is currently in progress at OSLC (Patterson & Chamberlain, 1988; Reid, 1987). Seventy families with conduct-disordered children (aged 6–12 years) have been randomly assigned to parent training ($n = 50$) or to a community agency employing eclectic family therapy ($n = 20$). Preliminary findings based on the first 34 families in the study indicate significant reductions in child deviant behavior for families in the parent training condition, but no significant reduction for children in the family therapy condition (Reid, 1987). Only mothers in the parent training condition have also demonstrated significant reductions in self-reported levels of depression.

Family-Based Interventions with Adolescents

Patterson and his colleagues have recently modified their parent training intervention for use with delinquent adolescents (Marlowe, Reid, Patterson, Weinrott, & Bank, 1988; Reid, 1987). Modifications include the following: (1) In addition to targeting prosocial and antisocial behaviors, parents also target any other behaviors that they believe put the adolescent at risk for further delinquency (e.g., class attendance, sassing the teacher, homework, spending time with "bad" companions, curfew violations, drug use); (2) there is a strong emphasis on parental monitoring/supervision of the adolescent, especially with respect to the adolescent's school attendance, behavior, and academic performance; (3) in lieu of the time-out procedure, punishment procedures include work details, point loss, restriction of free time, and restitution of stolen/damaged property; (4) the parents are asked to report legal offenses to juvenile authorities and then to act as advocates for the adolescent in court (as a way of decreasing the likelihood of the child's being removed from the home); and (5) there is greater involve-

ment of the adolescent in treatment sessions, especially with regard to the formulation and monitoring of behavioral contracts with the parents.

The relative efficacy of this approach to dealing with adolescents has been examined by Marlowe et al. (1988). Fifty-five chronically delinquent boys (mean age of 14, with an average of eight previous offenses) were randomly assigned to parent training or existing services provided by the court and community agencies. These services included behavioral–family systems therapy, and, for many of the adolescents, group counseling concerning drug use. The primary outcome measure was rate of official offenses as documented by the court, although home observation and PDR data were collected on families in the parent training condition (the court refused to permit the collection of treatment outcome data for the comparison condition). Families in the parent training condition received an average of 45 hours of treatment, half of which were over the phone. Nearly half of those families received additional booster sessions during follow-up as well.

During the treatment year, adolescents in the parent training condition evidenced a greater reduction in total and nonstatus (but not status) offense rates than the adolescents in the comparison condition. By the first year after treatment, however, offense rates for the two conditions were comparable, and remained so throughout the 3-year follow-up. Adolescents in the parent training condition also spent less time in institutions than their counterparts during the treatment year and first and second years of follow-up, at an estimated savings of over $100,000 over the 3-year period. There was no improvement in family interactions (as noted in the home observation data) as a function of treatment for the parent training condition, although parents did report significant decreases in targeted inappropriate behaviors (especially stealing) on the PDR. Despite these somewhat positive findings, Marlowe et al. are pessimistic as to the feasibility of this approach on a larger scale, given the extreme distress of the families and the high likelihood of therapist burnout. Instead, they argue for intervention with these families at an earlier stage, before the problems have increased to such severity and duration.

Another modification to the standard method of service delivery engineered by Patterson and his colleagues is the OSLC "Specialized Foster

Care" Model for working with adolescents who have been committed to state institutions for their delinquent behavior (Chamberlain, 1987). In this model, foster parents are selected from the community and provided with intensive training and supervision by the OSLC staff in behavior management strategies. A single adolescent is assigned to each foster family. The model includes a three-level point system in which the adolescent earns points for appropriate prosocial behaviors. Response cost procedures and daily feedback from the teacher concerning classroom behavior and achievement are part of the point system. During the first level, which lasts for 3 weeks, the adolescent earns points on a daily basis and is under constant supervision by the foster parents or the teacher. During Level Two, points are earned on a weekly basis, and at Level Three, daily ratings by the foster parents take the place of the point system. Foster parents are in daily phone contact with the OSLC staff; they receive ongoing monthly training sessions; and they participate in weekly staffings and regular meetings with school personnel. Weekly therapy sessions for the adolescent and his or her biological family are also conducted if a goal of treatment is for the adolescent to return to the family of origin. Preliminary data gathered over the first 3 years of the program with 39 male and female adolescent delinquents (mean age = 16 years) indicate that 75% completed the program. Of the adolescents who completed the program, 90% have not committed further violations of the law and are rated as living well-adjusted lives in the community.

Another family-based intervention for adolescents engaging in conduct disordered behaviors has been developed and evaluated by James Alexander and his colleagues at the University of Utah. "Functional Family Therapy" (FFT; Alexander & Parsons, 1982; Barton & Alexander, 1981) represents a unique integration and extension of family systems and behavioral perspectives. More recently, the model has also incorporated a cognitive perspective, especially with regard to attributional patterns within the family. In the early stages of the development of FFT, Alexander employed a "matching-to-sample" approach in which behavior patterns that distinguished deviant families from their nondeviant counterparts were first identified, and then etiologically significant subsets of those patterns were chosen as targets of intervention (Morris, Alexander, &

Waldron, 1988). Although early investigations of the efficacy of FFT were positive (see below), the model has been expanded to deal more successfully with those families more resistant to change.

In its current form, FFT consists of five components (Alexander, Waldron, Newberry, & Liddle, 1988). The introduction/impression phase is concerned with family members' expectations prior to therapy and in the initial sessions. Preliminary analogue investigations suggest the importance of identifying and modifying family members' blaming attributions in initial therapy sessions with families of delinquent adolescents (Alexander, Waldron, Barton, & Mas, 1987). In the assessment phase, the therapist identifies the behavioral, cognitive, and emotional expectations of each family member and the family processes in need of change (e.g., interpersonal functions such as closeness and distance). The goal of the induction/therapy phase is to modify the inappropriate attributions and expectations of family members. Various cognitive therapy techniques, especially relabeling, are employed. Relabeling is defined as the "verbal portrayal of any 'negative' family (or individual) behavior in a benign or benevolent light by describing the 'positive' antonym properties of the behavior, and by portraying family members as victims rather than perpetrators" (Morris et al., 1988, p. 112). This reattribution process among family members is seen as necessary, but not sufficient, for successful treatment. Actual behavior change must follow. In the behavior change/education phase, a variety of behavioral techniques are employed, including communication skills training, behavioral contracting, and contingency management. In the generalization/termination phase, the therapist's job is to facilitate maintenance of therapeutic gains while also fostering the family's independence from the therapy context through gradual disengagement. It is also during this phase that relevant extrafamilial factors (e.g., school, the legal system) are dealt with as necessary.

Most of the empirical research on the efficacy of FFT was conducted in the 1970s, prior to the inclusion of the cognitive therapy components described above. A series of three studies was conducted using a single sample of 86 status delinquents and their families (Alexander & Parsons, 1973; Klein, Alexander, & Parsons, 1977; Parsons & Alexander, 1973). Families were randomly assigned to FFT or to one of several comparison conditions (no treatment, client-centered counseling, or psychodynamic counseling). At the conclusion of treatment, families in the FFT condition performed better than families in the comparison conditions on a number of communication variables assessed in a 20-minute family discussion (e.g., greater equality in talk time, less silence, and increased interruptions). An examination of juvenile court records 6–18 months after treatment indicated that adolescents in the FFT condition had a significantly lower recidivism rate (26%), compared to adolescents in the no-treatment (50%), client-centered (47%), and psychodynamic (73%) counseling conditions (Alexander & Parsons, 1973). Within the FFT condition, a poorer outcome on the behavioral family interaction measures was associated with an increased likelihood of recidivism, thus lending direct support to the relationship between the two measures. Finally, Klein et al. (1977) reported a decreased probability of sibling involvement in the juvenile courts over a period of 2½–3½ years following the families' participation in FFT. Whereas only 20% of the siblings in the FFT condition had subsequent court contact, the percentages were 40%, 59%, and 63% for the no-treatment, client-centered counseling, and psychodynamic counseling conditions, respectively.

These earlier investigations focused on the families of adolescent delinquents with relatively minor status offenses. The current version of FFT, in conjunction with supportive adjuncts such as remedial education and job training, has recently been shown to be effective with multiply offending, previously incarcerated delinquents (Barton, Alexander, Waldron, Turner, & Warburton, 1985). In this investigation, adolescents who participated in FFT were less likely to be charged with committing an offense in the 15-month follow-up period than were adolescents placed in group homes (60% vs. 93%). FFT participants who did commit additional offenses committed significantly fewer offenses than adolescents in the group home condition.

Gordon, Arbuthnot, and their colleagues (Gordon, Arbuthnot, Gustafson, & McGreen, 1986; Gordon, McGreen, & Arbuthnot, 1984; and Gustafson, Gordon, & Arbuthnot, 1986, as cited in Gordon & Arbuthnot, 1987) have successfully employed a slightly modified version of FFT (longer treatment, treatment in the home

as opposed to clinic, and longer training and supervision of therapists) with a sample of 27 families with a delinquent adolescent. Recidivism rates for the FFT and comparison (probation-only) groups at a 2½-year follow-up were 11% and 67%, respectively. The FFT condition was also more cost-effective, and there were fewer court contacts by siblings in the FFT condition.

The "family–ecological systems" (FES) approach to treating conduct-disordered adolescents emphasizes both the interactional nature of adolescent psychopathology and the role of multiple systems in which the adolescent is embedded, such as the family, school, and peer group (Henggeler, 1982). Assessment and treatment are concerned with the adolescent as an individual, his or her role in the various systems, and the interrelationships among those systems. Therapists intervene at one or more levels as required, and employ a variety of therapy approaches, such as family therapy, school consultation, marital therapy, or individual therapy. Treatment techniques are similarly wide-ranging, and may include traditional family therapy procedures (e.g., paradoxical intent) as well as behavioral and cognitive–behavioral techniques (e.g., reinforcement, contingency contracting, self-instructions) (Schleser & Rodick, 1982).

Henggeler et al. (1986) have recently conducted a large-scale evaluation of the efficacy of FES with inner-city adolescent delinquents, most of whom were repeat offenders, and their families ($n = 57$). At the conclusion of treatment, parents in the FES condition reported fewer behavior problems on each of the scales of the Behavior Problem Checklist, whereas parents of adolescents in an alternative mental health services condition ($n = 23$) and in the normal control condition ($n = 44$) reported no change. Families in the FES condition had also improved at posttreatment on several observational measures of family interaction (based on a family discussion exercise), whereas the families in the alternative treatment condition either did not change or deteriorated on those measures from pretreatment to posttreatment.

It is unclear from the data reported by Henggeler et al. (1986) whether the improvements noted from pre- to posttreatment for the FES group represent significantly different patterns from those obtained in the alternative treatment conditions. Also, because the FES treatment approach emphasizes individually determined interventions directed at one or more systems and/or interrelationships among systems, which vary from adolescent to adolescent, it is not possible at this time to determine which of these treatment components are necessary or even helpful. Finally, the temporal generality of the approach needs to be assessed, not only with respect to family interaction measures and parental reports of behavior problems, but also in terms of recidivism and the impact of treatment on the extrafamilial systems that are targeted for treatment for at least some of these families. Nevertheless, the results of the Henggeler et al. (1986) investigation suggest that FES may be a promising intervention for dealing with conduct-disordered adolescents, and it is hoped that the emphasis on intervening at multiple levels will serve as heuristic inspiration for other clinician/researchers.

Community-Based Residential Programs for Adolescents

The prototypical behavioral community-based program for treating conduct-disordered adolescents is Achievement Place; the Achievement Place approach is currently known as the "Teaching-Family Model" (TFM; Willner, Braukmann, Kirigin, & Wolf, 1978). The first Achievement Place group home opened in Kansas in 1967; there are now more than 215 group homes employing this treatment model (Wolf, Braukmann, & Ramp, 1987). Each TFM group home is run by a young married couple, referred to as "teaching parents." The teaching parents undergo a rigorous 1-year training program and are certified by the National Teaching-Family Association. There are typically five to eight adolescents ranging from 12 to 16 years of age in each group home; most are adjudicated delinquents. While living in the group home, the adolescents attend local schools and are involved in community activities. The primary treatment components of TFM include a multilevel point system, self-government procedures (daily family conferences, a peer manager), social skills training, academic tutoring, and a home-based reinforcement system for monitoring school behavior. The average stay for a participant in the program is less than 10 months (Weinrott, Jones, & Howard, 1982).

The TFM approach to treating conduct-disordered adolescents has been extensively evaluated, both in terms of formative evalua-

tions of program components and with regard to treatment outcome. Formative evaluations have validated teaching procedures for social, academic, and self-care behaviors; vocational training procedures; the token reinforcement and self-government systems; and the home-based report card systems. These in-house evaluations have made extensive use of the assessment of social validity as a means of refining the program. Targets of those assessments have included the adolescents themselves; the teaching parents; and personnel in schools, juvenile courts, and social welfare agencies (see Willner et al., 1978, for a review).

The effectiveness of TFM has been assessed by its developers (e.g., Kirigin, Braukmann, Atwater, & Wolf, 1982), and by an independent evaluation team (Weinrott et al., 1982). Although the investigations differed in scope, the findings were similar. Kirigin et al. (1982) compared 13 TFM group homes with 9 "traditional" community-based residential programs. Court/police records were collected for the year preceding treatment, the period during treatment, and the year after treatment. During treatment, there was a lower percentage of TFM participants (both boys and girls) engaging in offenses, as well as fewer recorded offenses, than for participants in the other group homes. There was no difference between the two treatment conditions on these measures during the year following treatment. Consumer satisfaction ratings by the adolescent participants and by school personnel, as well as a composite measure of consumer satisfaction, favored the TFM group homes.

In an independent evaluation of the cost-effectiveness of TFM, Weinrott et al. (1982) examined 26 TFM group homes housing 354 adolescents and 25 community-based comparison programs (nearly all of which were group homes) that housed 363 adolescents. Data collection occurred at intake, during the treatment period, and for each of 3 years following treatment. The TFM programs were 22% less expensive than the comparison programs on a cost-per-youth basis and 7% cheaper on a per diem basis. To assess the relative effectiveness of the interventions, the programs were compared on four composite indices: deviant behavior (court records and self-reports of delinquent behavior), education, occupation, and social/personality. The two groups differed only on the education index, with the TFM approach being slightly more successful in slowing a decline in grade point average and in raising the percentage of courses passed. In a separate analysis, Howard, Jones, and Weinrott (1981, cited in Weinrott et al., 1982) found that TFM was perceived to be more effective than the comparison programs by various community groups (i.e., teachers, court workers, and social services personnel).

In summary, the TFM approach to treating adolescent delinquents appears to be more effective than comparison programs while the adolescents are active participants. However, once the adolescents complete treatment and leave the group home setting, those differences disappear. As noted by Weinrott et al. (1982), these findings may mean that the two treatment approaches are equally effective. The issue of whether TFM is better than either no intervention at all or institutional treatment has not been addressed. With respect to cost-effectiveness, TFM is cheaper than alternative group homes. However, both approaches are very expensive in that only 45% of the adolescents complete treatment, and by 2–3 years later, there are few meaningful differences between treatment completers and dropouts (Weinrott et al., 1982). Suggestions to decrease the costs associated with TFM have included better selection and training of the teaching parents (so that they stay with TFM longer than the current average of 18 months) and operating the group homes at capacity (Weinrott et al., 1982).

With respect to enhancing efficacy, TFM proponents have emphasized the necessity of a greater emphasis on the transition from the group home back to the family of origin and the use of treatment strategies to facilitate maintenance (Willner et al., 1978). More recently, it has been suggested by the developers of TFM that perhaps an alternative model of intervention is needed for at least some conduct-disordered adolescents (Wolf et al., 1987). Given the stability of conduct disorders, the fact that they tend to run in families, and the fact that short-term treatments such as TFM have often not been demonstrated to be effective over the long term, Wolf et al. have proposed a "long-term supportive family treatment" model. In this approach, specially trained foster parents (similar to the teaching parents in TFM) would provide care and treatment for a single adolescent, probably into early adulthood. As noted above, preliminary data gathered by Patterson and colleagues on a similar approach to that advocated by Wolf et al. is supportive (Chamberlain, 1987).

School-Based Treatment

A major problem in providing treatment (behavioral or otherwise) for conduct-disordered children in the school setting is the current definition of "serious emotional disturbance" in Public Law 94-142, which specifically excludes children who are "socially maladjusted but not emotionally disturbed" (Executive Committee of the Council for Children with Behavioral Disorders, 1987; Walker & Fabre, 1987). Thus, by federal mandate, many conduct-disordered children are technically ineligible for special education assistance.

In addition to this formalized exclusion of many conduct-disordered children from special education services, most of the behavior therapy research conducted in the school setting has failed to include a comprehensive assessment of children referred for school problems to ascertain whether they meet objective and/or clinical criteria for the diagnosis of conduct or oppositional disorder; behavior often is defined as "inappropriate" and worthy of modification if teachers and/or parents define it as such. Nevertheless, there is adequate reason to believe that this literature can provide useful guidelines for the treatment of conduct-disordered children in school settings. Although these children are often globally described as "disruptive," as "socially maladjusted," and as displaying "high rates of inappropriate behavior," an examination of the target behaviors that are the focus of treatment in these studies reveals such overt conduct-disordered behaviors as noncompliance to teacher requests or classroom rules, disturbing others, aggression, tantrums, and excessive verbal outbursts. The few investigations that have dealt with covert conduct-disordered behavior in the school are described later in the chapter.

Even if conduct-disordered behaviors are not occurring initially in the school setting, research on behavioral covariation and setting generality in behavioral treatment programs indicates that when conduct-disordered behavior is treated in the home environment, similar behavior in school may remain unchanged (Breiner & Forehand, 1981; Forehand et al., 1979; Wahler, 1969b), a behavioral contrast effect may occur, in which deviant school behavior *increases* as home disruption decreases (Johnson, Bolstad, & Lobitz, 1976; Wahler, 1975; Walker, Hops, & Johnson, 1975), or setting generalization may occur (e.g., Fellbaum, Daly, Forest, & Holland, 1985). Because it appears that most children do not show generalization of positive treatment effects to the school setting when conduct-disordered behavior is treated at home, it is necessary to monitor the school behavior of home-treated children throughout and following treatment to ascertain whether interventions specific to the school setting are needed. It is also necessary to have an armamentarium of treatment strategies available for school intervention once the need for treatment is identified.

In this section of the chapter, we highlight some of the major types of behavioral intervention that have been applied to overt conduct-disordered behaviors in the classroom. A comprehensive review of the myriad behavior therapy procedures that have been employed for these and related problems (such as academic achievement per se and peer relationship difficulties) is beyond the scope of this chapter. The reader is referred to Chapters 6 and 9 in this volume and to relevant reviews (e.g., Jones & Kazdin, 1981; Klein, 1979; O'Leary & O'Leary, 1977).

In their review of classroom behavior management strategies, O'Leary and O'Leary (1977) discuss the importance of teacher behavior in modifying disruptive classroom behavior of children. Many of the earliest studies in classroom behavior therapy focused on contingency arrangements in the interactions of teachers and students. For example, a number of studies have shown that teacher praise for appropriate behavior, especially when coupled with ignoring of inappropriate behaviors, can effectively reduce classroom disruption (Becker, Madsen, Arnold, & Thomas, 1967; Brown & Elliot, 1965). In these strategies, teachers are taught to notice instances of appropriate behavior that are the prosocial opposites of the child's target disruptive behaviors and to praise and otherwise reward the child when prosocial behaviors occur. For example, a child who frequently is noncompliant, noisy, and argumentative might receive a pat on the back, a smile, and a compliment (e.g., "You're doing a very nice job of working quietly at your desk") whenever he or she follows the teacher's work instructions without disrupting others. Although teachers often protest that "I routinely praise my students," naturalistic observation studies show that rates of positive teacher attention to prosocial behavior are surprisingly low, and may be insufficient for increasing and maintaining the prosocial behavior of conduct-disordered children who enter the classroom with problems in this domain (Strain, Lambert, Kerr, Stagg, & Lenkner, 1983; White, 1975).

Other elements of effective classroom management include the establishment of clear rules and directions; use of programmed instructional materials that pace the student's academic progress at his or her own rate; providing positive and corrective feedback; and, for disruptive behaviors that cannot be ignored, the use of reprimands, time out, and response cost procedures contingent upon the occurrence of conduct-disordered behavior. Although some studies demonstrate that each of these procedures alone can exert control over disruptive behaviors, clinically significant changes are most likely to occur when treatment strategies are combined. For example, O'Leary, Becker, Evans, and Saudargas (1969) showed that rules, structure, praising, and ignoring were only effective when combined with a token reinforcement program. Greenwood, Hops, Delquadri, and Guild (1974) demonstrated that rules alone produced no change in classroom behavior, whereas rules plus feedback plus individual and group contingencies systematically produced increases in appropriate behavior across three classrooms. When special education teachers stopped providing mild negative feedback (i.e., reprimands) to elementary-school-age students who had been functioning successfully with a combination of praise and reprimands, the students' academic and social behavior deteriorated (Acker & O'Leary, 1987; Pfiffner, Rosén, & O'Leary, 1985; Rosén, O'Leary, Joyce, Conway, & Pfiffner, 1984). Alternatively, use of reprimands alone successfully maintained academic and social behavior (e.g., Acker & O'Leary, 1987), as did praise plus tangible rewards (e.g., access to desired activities, such as reading comic books and playing musical instruments) (Pfiffner, Rosén, & O'Leary, 1985). Reprimands have been shown to be more effective than encouragement contingent upon off-task behavior (Abramowitz, O'Leary, & Rosén, 1987), but less effective than a combination of response cost procedures and reprimands applied on a continuous schedule

(Pfiffner, O'Leary, Rosén, & Sanderson, 1985).

Although instituting changes in teacher social behavior *can* be an effective approach for modifying children's aggressive behavior, there are a number of disadvantages to such an approach. First, some teachers resent the implication that somehow their behavior is responsible for some children's misconduct and are resistant to consultation regarding how to change their own social behavior. Other investigators have discussed the fact that changes in teacher social behavior alone may be effective with mildly disruptive children, but for children displaying more severely deviant classroom behavior, other, more powerful procedures are necessary (O'Leary et al., 1969; Walker, Hops, & Fiegenbaum, 1976). As noted earlier, several studies have shown empirically that changing teacher social behavior alone is not sufficient to change extremely disruptive child behavior. The effects of such strategies are enhanced by the addition of token reinforcement and more powerful, tangible rewards or activity reinforcers (O'Leary et al., 1969; Pfiffner, Rosén, & O'Leary, 1985).

For these reasons, investigators have turned their attention to the use of token reinforcement systems in the classroom. Token reinforcement programs typically involve three basic ingredients: (1) a set of instructions to the class about the behaviors that will be reinforced; (2) a means of making a potentially reinforcing stimulus (usually called a token) contingent upon behavior; and (3) a set of rules governing the exchange of tokens for backup reinforcers (O'Leary & Drabman, 1971). As such programs are applied to conduct-disordered children, teachers are often asked to target behaviors for inclusion in the system. Typical examples have been paying attention, remaining seated, raising hands before speaking, facing the front of the room, not running, not talking out, and accurately completing class assignments. Many of these behaviors are incompatible with the aggressive and oppositional behaviors of conduct-disordered children.

A variety of systems can be developed for the delivery of tokens to children; specific details should always be worked out with each individual classroom teacher, so that the system fits as smoothly as possible into ongoing classroom routine. For example, in special education classrooms with a small teacher-to-pupil ratio, the teacher(s) may be able to monitor and rate children's behavior every 10–15 minutes. In large classrooms, teachers may do well to rate behavior and dispense tokens at the end of each class. O'Leary et al. (1969) had the teacher rate children's behavior four times in an afternoon. Points ranging from 1 to 10, depending upon the degree of improvement, were entered into small notebooks placed on each child's desk. Points were exchangeable initially for prizes at the end of every day, and then were gradually faded to every 3 days. In one of our special education classrooms (Wells') for conduct-disordered children, students receive checkmarks every 10 minutes, and activity reinforcers are delivered immediately after class.

Token reinforcement programs have been evaluated singly and in combination with other classroom management strategies by a number of investigators (for reviews, see Kazdin, 1977; Kazdin & Bootzin, 1972; O'Leary & Drabman, 1971). In the first published study of the efficacy of a classroom token economy, O'Leary and Becker (1967) evaluated its use in an entire special education classroom of "disruptive" children. The system was highly effective in reducing average deviant behavior for the class. However, the token system was confounded with the simultaneous introduction of clear instructions and increased teacher attention. Therefore, in a subsequent study, O'Leary et al. (1969) systematically isolated these and other aspects of teacher social behavior before introducing a token economy. In this study, rules, educational structure, praising appropriate behaviors, and ignoring inappropriate behaviors were not effective in reducing disruptive behavior. However, the addition of a token reinforcement program resulted in substantial behavioral improvement. Walker et al. (1976) evaluated the effects of social reinforcement, token reinforcement, and response cost on the behavior of disruptive students. They found that combinations of variables were less effective in controlling behavior than was simultaneous introduction of all treatment variables.

A number of studies have investigated parameters of token reinforcement systems that enhance or diminish their effectiveness. For example, Kaufman and O'Leary (1972) and Iwata and Bailey (1974) examined the relative effects of reward versus response cost procedures in token economies. In the former procedure, students earn points for behavioral improvement; in the latter, they lose points for behavioral disruption. In both studies, no differences were found in the effectiveness of the two procedures. Stumpf and Holman (1985) found that experimenter-selected material reinforcers and child-selected activity reinforcers were equally effective in reducing disruptive behavior in the classroom while the token system was in effect. However, transfer to nontraining periods and maintenance after termination of the program occurred only for the group in which the experimenter selected and provided material reinforcers.

There may also be differences in the effectiveness of token programs when individual versus group contingencies are used. Pigott and Heggie (1986) reviewed 20 studies that directly compared these two strategies. In individual contingencies, individual children are reinforced solely on the basis of their own performance. In group contingencies, three or more children are reinforced on the basis of the overall performance of the group or a significant proportion thereof. Unlike previous authors, who generally have found no consistent differences across studies in individual versus group contingencies (e.g., Greenwood & Hops, 1981), Pigott and Heggie differentiated between studies according to target behavior. This strategy led to the conclusion that group contingencies were superior to individual ones when academic performance was the target behavior, whereas there was no consistent differential effect when social responses were the target behaviors. Group contingencies have been associated with an increase in verbal threats among classmates, however.

A number of investigators have examined the extent to which the effects of multicomponent treatment programs involving teacher training and token economies generalize across time and settings. In some of the earliest studies to examine these questions, little evidence for generalization was found. For example, O'Leary et al. (1969) and Kuypers, Becker, and O'Leary (1968) found no evidence of generalization from an afternoon classroom period in which token economies were in effect to a morning period in which no treatment procedures were in effect.

Walker and Hops (1976) found that some disruptive children who had been treated successfully with token economies and teacher training in an experimental classroom for 2 months displayed decreases in their levels of appropriate behavior (albeit not to baseline levels) when they were transferred back to their

regular public school classroom. On the other hand, there is some evidence that positive treatment effects will be maintained across time, although the duration of follow-up has ranged only from 3 to 12 weeks (Greenwood et al., 1974; Greenwood, Hops, & Walker, 1977; Walker & Hops, 1976). Treatment-acquired gains do not appear to generalize well from one academic year to the next when no attempts at facilitating generalization are implemented (Walker et al., 1975).

For all these reasons, Walker, Hops, and their colleagues have conducted a number of studies evaluating strategies to enhance generalization and maintenance of treatment effects acquired in multicomponent classroom programs. In one of their first studies, Walker and Buckley (1972) treated children for 2 months in a token economy classroom and then randomly assigned them to one of three maintenance strategies or a control group before returning them to their regular classrooms. In a "peer reprogramming" strategy, the target children's regular classroom peers were trained to support positive behavior and ignore minor disruption. In addition, target children earned points for appropriate behavior that were exchangeable for rewards for the entire class. In an "equating stimulus conditions" strategy, essential elements of the experimental classroom procedures were transferred directly to the children's regular classroom. In a "teacher training" condition, teachers learned general principles of behavior modification and were encouraged to implement programs in their own classrooms. Results of this study showed that peer reprogramming and equating stimulus conditions were significantly more effective than teacher training or no generalization programming in facilitating transfer of positive treatment effects to the regular classroom.

In a subsequent study, Walker et al. (1975) implemented a regular classroom maintenance program after 4 months of intensive treatment in a special classroom. In this study, classroom maintenance involved not only teacher training, but weekly meetings with the teachers in which feedback was provided regarding the level of the children's training. In addition, teachers earned credit hours as well as course grades contingent upon continued improvement in the children's behavior. The effects of the combined treatment (intensive treatment plus maintenance program) generalized to a significantly greater degree in the subsequent academic year than did treatment effects for subjects who did not receive maintenance strategies.

One of the most comprehensive systems for school-based behavior management is the four-component system developed by the Center at Oregon for Research in the Behavioral Education of the Handicapped (CORBEH) during the 1970s for children in mainstream kindergarten through fourth-grade classrooms (Walker & Fabre, in press; Walker, Hops, & Greenwood, 1984). Two of the four programs are specifically designed to deal with conduct-disordered behaviors such as acting-out disruptive behavior and social aggression. The other two programs address low academic survival skills and social withdrawal. Each program uses a teacher consultant (e.g., counselor, school psychologist) as the primary delivery agent, with control ultimately transferred to the classroom teacher and/or playground supervisor.

The Contingencies for Learning Academic and Social Skills (CLASS) program is designed to decrease disruptive behaviors in various school settings (i.e., classroom cafeteria, hallways, playground). Behavioral techniques include a token economy with a response cost component, contingency contracting, teacher praise, school and home rewards, and 1-day suspensions for certain serious acting-out behaviors (Walker & Hops, 1979). During the first week, the consultant implements the procedures; then the program is shifted to the classroom teacher. Over the next 5 weeks, the program is extended over the entire day, and there is a gradual fading from tangible rewards to social reinforcement in the natural environment. Because the child's progress through the program is performance-based, the actual length of the program varies from 6 to 10 weeks (Walker & Hops, 1979).

The Reprogramming Environmental Contingencies for Effective Social Skills (RECESS) program focuses on the remediation of social aggression with peers on the playground and in the classroom (Walker, Hops, & Greenwood, 1981). This 6-week package includes teaching the child to distinguish between appropriate and inappropriate social behavior, a token economy with a response cost component, praise for appropriate social interactions, group reward contingencies, and home-based reinforcement by the parents. Like the other CORBEH packages, RECESS includes built-in fading and maintenance procedures.

All of the CORBEH packages were developed and evaluated through a systematic three-phase process of component evaluation and package development in an experimental classroom, adaptation and standardization of package components, and field testing under normal conditions of use (Walker et al., 1984). The CLASS program has been implemented and evaluated with 119 children in this process in both urban and rural settings (Hops et al., 1978; Walker & Hops, 1979). Field trial evaluations indicate not only that the CLASS program was effective in increasing the level of appropriate behaviors among children in the classroom, compared to acting-out children who did not participate in the program, but that these effects were maintained at a 1-year follow-up (Hops et al., 1978). Furthermore, examination of student files 1½–3 years after the program indicated that students who had participated in the CLASS program were less likely to have been placed in special education settings. The CLASS program has also been successfully implemented in Costa Rica, although the magnitude of treatment effects was somewhat reduced (Walker, Fonseca Retana, & Gersten, 1988).

The RECESS program has also been extensively validated in experimental and field settings (Walker et al., 1981). This program is quite effective in reducing the rate of negative/aggressive social responses of the target children compared to untreated controls. However, empirical data with respect to its generalization once the program has ended is lacking. Walker and Hops (1979) and Walker et al. (1981) provide thorough discussions of issues that can prevent effective implementation of these programs.

Kent and O'Leary (1976) reported one of the few investigations to utilize a combined school-and home-based behavioral intervention package. A total of 32 second-, third-, and fourth-grade conduct-disordered children (who also had academic difficulties) were randomly assigned to treatment or no-treatment control conditions. Teachers were trained to increase positive attention and quiet reprimands and to eliminate threats. A home-based reinforcement system (see below), which included both academic and behavioral targets, was also implemented. Parents received training in differential attention and the restriction of privileges for child behavior in the home, and they participated in daily home tutoring. Intervention was limited to 20 hours of contact with the therapist. Observational measures of children's behavior in the classroom and teachers' perceptions of the children's adjustment indicated significant improvements from pre- to posttreatment only for children in the treatment condition. There was no group difference at posttreatment on academic achievement, as measured by grades and by a standardized achievement test. However, at a 6- to 9-month follow-up, the findings were reversed. There were no differences on the observational or teacher report measures between the two conditions, but children in the treatment condition displayed greater improvements in reading, social science, and math grades and obtained higher scores on the reading comprehension portion of the achievement test. There were no measures of parent or child behavior in the home, so it was not possible to assess the integrity or efficacy of the intervention in the home setting. Teachers and parents reported high levels of satisfaction with the therapists and the intervention.

In summary, it is clear that teacher training and teacher implementation of behavior therapy programs (such as token economies) in the classroom can significantly improve socially aggressive and disruptive behavior in the school environment, and in some cases can improve these children's academic achievement as well. In addition, maintenance and generalization strategies can be built into treatment to enhance the probability that treatment-acquired gains will transfer to other class periods and even into the next academic year. The problem with these programs is that they can be quite expensive in terms of the amount of consultant time necessary to train teachers to implement programs appropriately. In addition, the studies by Walker and his colleagues showed that weekly posttraining meetings with teachers may be necessary to maintain treatment-acquired gains. Teachers may not have the time to devote to the program and may be especially reluctant if only one or two children in the entire classroom require treatment. We have frequently heard the refrain, "I have 30 kids in my classroom—how can you expect me to devote all this time and effort to one child?" Therefore, although they are effective, these approaches may be most productive in special education classes in which the entire class needs and participates in treatment. For children in regular school classrooms, clinical researchers have turned their attention to other approaches. One of these involves the use of home-based daily reinforcement systems for classroom behavior.

The use of home-based reinforcement programs began to proliferate when some of the problems attendant on direct intervention with teachers in the classroom became apparent. With home-based reinforcement programs, a concerted effort is made to relieve the teacher of many of the aspects of managing a behavioral system, and to place some of the responsibility for implementation of the program on the parents and even on the child himself or herself. This not only has the effect of reducing the response cost to the teacher, but also involves the parents more directly and responsibly in ameliorating their child's behavior problems.

The first step in initiating a home-based reinforcement program is a decision as to the behaviors that will be targeted for monitoring and consequences. In work with conduct-disordered children, this may involve not only disruptive behaviors to be decreased, but also social, academic, or study behaviors to be increased. Usually, consultation with the teacher occurs to determine the relevant target behaviors for a particular child. Examples have ranged from the specific to the global (e.g., followed class rules, made acceptable use of class time, studied the whole period, completed assignment on time, showed "good behavior today," followed directions, stayed in seat, raised hand, got along with classmates). In addition, a monitoring interval is selected. Some studies have had teachers observe and rate children's behavior at frequent intervals. For example, Budd, Liebowitz, Riner, Mindell, and Goldfarb (1981) had teachers provide stickers on a token card every 4–8 minutes during structured activities in a special summer remedial program for children with serious acting-out behavior problems. On the other hand, Ayllon, Garber, and Pisor (1975) simply had teachers in a regular public school classroom give students a "good behavior letter" at the end of the day. Although no empirical studies exist of the most effective and efficient monitoring interval, clinical intuition dictates that children with severe, pervasive, and high-frequency behavior problems may need more frequent monitoring intervals.

Once the decisions described above are made, an index card or other reporting sheet listing the target behaviors is prepared, and the teacher monitors and rates the child's behavior daily on a card or sheet. Although in some research studies the experimenter has provided the teacher with the daily report form, the more common clinical situation is for parents to prepare the form listing the target behaviors, and to give it to the child each morning to take to school. It is the child's responsibility to keep track of the card, to approach the teacher for the ratings at the prespecified intervals, and then to take the card home at the end of the day. Back-up consequences are provided by the parent at home, contingent upon the child's meeting certain prearranged criteria. No excuses are accepted for failure to arrive home with the card (e.g., "I lost it"). Failure to produce a card at the end of the day results in loss of all rewards available in the system for that evening. The result is that children quickly learn not to "lose" their cards (Ayllon *et al.*, 1975).

Studies have varied in the extent to which the therapist or experimenter has consulted with the parents regarding the home backup reinforcers. Ayllon *et al.* (1975) had a single 2-hour meeting with parents, and in some cases only telephone contact. Parents were informed about the home-based reward system for their children, but no effort was made to teach them what to use as rewards and punishers. They were simply urged to use their own judgment in selecting rewards and sanctions that had worked for them in the past. At the other end of the spectrum, Schumaker, Hovell, and Sherman (1977) sent a therapist to students' homes to draw up lists of privileges and to negotiate systems for exchanging points earned at school for privileges at home. Weekly home visits occurred throughout the study, and twice-weekly telephone contact was made with each family. Although the procedure followed by Schumaker *et al.* may not be clinically feasible, the one followed by Ayllon *et al.* may not be sufficient or appropriate for some families. For example, in families in which rewards are scarce and punishment is impulsive, irrational, or abusive, therapists need to take greater responsibility for working out the details of the backup system of consequences with the parents in therapy sessions.

A number of studies have evaluated the efficacy of home-based reinforcement programs for school behavior problems (for a review, see Atkeson & Forehand, 1979). In one of the first series of studies, Bailey, Wolf, and Phillips (1970) evaluated their usefulness with predelinquent youths who had been remanded by the court to an Achievement Place group home treatment program. These boys displayed significant behavior problems in school and very poor academic achievement. Bailey *et al.* (1970) showed that the daily report system was

highly effective in reducing rule violations and increasing study behavior in a special summer school program. Moreover, they demonstrated that these effects were not due to nondifferential feedback or to feedback without backup reinforcement. In a second experiment, these investigators successfully transferred the system to the regular public school environment. However, backup reinforcers continued to be provided by highly trained teaching parents who were under the control of the investigators.

Subsequent studies have generally confirmed the positive effects of home-based reinforcement systems using the child's own parents. Consultation with the parents has ranged from minimal to extensive. Ayllon *et al.* (1975) implemented a home-based reinforcement system with disruptive third-graders in public school after a teacher-administered token system failed to effect sustained improvements in classroom behavior. The system involved one global daily report and minimal parent consultation regarding home consequences. Nevertheless, the system was highly effective in reducing classroom disruption. However, as mentioned earlier, we believe that it is incumbent upon behavior therapists to be more aware of and involved in the selection and implementation of home consequences if there is any suspicion of inappropriate or abusive disciplinary practices by parents.

Schumaker *et al.* (1977) also demonstrated the efficacy of a home-based reinforcement program involving daily report, praise, and home privileges in a multiple-baseline-across-subjects design, using "problem" junior high school students. In addition, these investigators showed that although praise alone may result in transient improvements in school behavior, the greatest, most sustained improvements are achieved when contingent privileges are provided at home. By contrast, Lahey *et al.* (1977) showed that praise alone delivered by parents contingent upon receipt of daily report cards was sufficient to improve the behavior of disruptive kindergarten students. The discrepancy in the results of these two studies is probably related to the different ages of the subject populations, in that parental praise is more likely to function as a powerful reinforcer for younger than for older students.

In a recent investigation of a home-based reinforcement system technology, Budd *et al.* (1981) examined its effectiveness as the predominant treatment mechanism for a combination of disruptive responses across several periods in a kindergarten class. The children were referred by community agencies for special treatment of serious acting-out behavior. The home-based reinforcement system was introduced in multiple-baseline fashion across three response classes in several structured activity periods. In contrast to the results with the kindergarten children in the Lahey *et al.* (1977) investigation, praise in the absence of home-based privileges was not sufficient to reduce the disruptive behavior of the kindergarten children in this study. However, in the Budd *et al.* investigation, praise was provided by teachers, whereas in the Lahey *et al.* study, praise was provided by parents. These results suggest that parental praise may be more important than teacher praise in work with young children, or that variables other than developmental ones may be operating. For example, the kindergarten children in the Budd *et al.* study appeared to be more seriously disordered than those in the Lahey *et al.* investigation. More serious behavior problems may warrant the use of more concrete backup reinforcers.

In terms of cognitive–behavioral approaches that specifically deal with conduct-disordered children in the classroom, there has been relatively little research. Populations have ranged from preschoolers (Bornstein & Quevillon, 1976) to junior high school students (e.g., Brigham, Hopper, Hill, de Armas, & Newsom, 1985); a variety of cognitive–behavioral interventions, including self-instruction training, goal setting, and interpersonal problem-solving training, have been examined, usually in combination with other cognitive–behavioral or behavioral techniques.

In a study that is frequently cited as supporting the efficacy of cognitive–behavioral therapy, Bornstein and Quevillon (1976) evaluated the effects of the Meichenbaum and Goodman (1971) self-instructional procedure with three preschool children who were "highly disruptive" in their Head Start program. Major problems included aggressive, violent temper outbursts and refusal to follow directions. The effects of treatment were assessed on only one target response: on-task behavior measured by trained observers. Results showed that self-instructional training resulted in immediate and significant increases in on-task behavior for all three children. Moreover, the results appeared to be maintained for 50 days after treatment termination.

Unfortunately, two subsequent attempts at systematic replication of this study have failed to produce the same results (Billings & Wasik, 1985; Friedling & O'Leary, 1979). In the first study (Friedling & O'Leary, 1979), hyperactive second- and third-graders served as subjects—a sample that was not identical to Bornstein and Quevillon's (1976) preschoolers. Subjects were seen for 90 minutes rather than 2 hours (as in Bornstein & Quevillon, 1976); otherwise, treatment procedures were identical. Nevertheless, no treatment effects were found for on-task behavior or academic measures. In the Billings and Wasik (1985) study, a great effort was made to replicate Bornstein and Quevillon's procedures as accurately as possible—an effort that included consultation with Bornstein. Nevertheless, the training failed to produce any major changes in classroom behavior for the children. Bornstein (1985) has recently postulated that a number of non-treatment-related variables may account for the inconsistent results across studies (e.g., therapist variables, IQ, race, gender, and a history of repeated failure and poor-quality relationships with adults). He calls for research aimed at identifying variables that predict success and failure with cognitive–behavioral therapy.

Two studies have employed comparisons of particular cognitive–behavioral interventions with more standard contingency management systems. Forman (1980) randomly assigned 18 aggressive third-, fourth-, and fifth-grade children to one of three group interventions: cognitive restructuring, which included elements of interpersonal problem solving, affective imagery, and verbal self-reinforcement; response cost, in which the teacher fined children for aggressive behavior by loss of activity privileges; or an attention placebo control condition, in which children were tutored in reading. The groups met for twelve 30-minute sessions. There were relatively few between-group differences on teacher ratings, teacher-recorded aggression, or independent observation measures of inappropriate behaviors and interactions. Those differences that did occur suggested that both the cognitive–behavioral and response cost procedures were more effective in decreasing aggressive behavior than the control condition, and that there was a tendency for the response cost procedure to lead to greater changes than the cognitive–behavioral intervention.

The assignment of three disruptive first-graders to monitor and reinforce their peers' appropriate behavior at noon recess resulted in decreases in the monitors' rates of negative interaction and increases in rates of positive interaction (Fowler, Daugherty, Kirby, & Kohler, 1986). However, the effects did not generalize to recess at other times of the day until the boys were appointed as peer monitors in those settings. Furthermore, adult monitoring of the children's behavior (as prescribed by the RECESS program) was more effective in eliminating negative behavior.

The potential utility of employing public goal setting to enhance on-task behavior in conduct-disordered children in the classroom has been noted by Lyman (1984). Six conduct-disordered boys aged 11–13 in residential treatment displayed significantly higher percentages of on-task behavior in the classroom when public (76%) as opposed to private (55%) posting of goals was employed. Although the students set somewhat lower goals for themselves in the public than in the private goal-setting condition (80% vs. 88%, respectively), this resulted in a closer match of stated goals and actual performance during the public goal-setting condition.

In a clinical replication series over a 3-year period, Brigham et al. (1985) implemented a self-management program with a total of 79 junior high school students with relatively mild conduct-disordered behaviors. The intervention consisted of eighteen 1-hour after-school classes over a 6-week period, in which the students were taught the principles of behavior analysis and completed a self-management project. Student participants received fewer detentions after the intervention, and this effect seems to have been maintained throughout the first year after participation in the self-management class. However, students with more severe conduct-disordered behaviors (e.g., "predelinquent") did not appear to be likely to benefit from the class.

Skills Training Approaches

As noted in an earlier section of this chapter, conduct-disordered children differ from their "normal" peers on a variety of behavioral, cognitive, and affective dimensions. The premise underlying a skills training approach to treating conduct-disordered children is that one or more of these differences represents a fundamental deficit, which, if remedied, will lead to improvements in the conduct-disordered child's functioning in several domains. There have been two basic skills training approaches. The earlier of the two represents a relatively straightforward behavioral approach, in which a specific behavioral skills deficit is identified, and then the child is trained to criterion. Social skills training (e.g., Spence & Marzillier, 1981) exemplifies this approach. The second approach relies on cognitive–behavioral methods and focuses on cognitive (e.g., interpersonal problem solving, moral reasoning) or affective (e.g., perspective taking) domains in addition to, or instead of, behavioral targets.

With respect to behaviorally oriented social skills training approaches, the majority of studies utilizing conduct-disordered samples have been with adolescent delinquents (see Goldstein & Pentz, 1984). Although many of these studies have demonstrated short-term improvements in specific social skills in analogue situations (role plays with the experimenter or a confederate), very few studies have examined the generalization of these effects to the real world. An exception is the well-designed investigation reported by Spence and Marzillier (1981), in which 76 adolescent male delinquents (aged 10–16) were randomly assigned to a social skills training group, an attention placebo group, or a no-treatment control group. The social skills training program was typical of those employed with this population and included twelve 1-hour sessions with groups of four youths. Training procedures included instructions, discussion, live and videotaped modeling, role plays, videotaped feedback, social reinforcement, and homework tasks. Skills taught were individually tailored to each adolescent, based on a needs assessment. Results of both multiple-baseline-across-behaviors and group comparison designs indicated specific improvements in many individual social skills on the analogue assessment tests for the social skills training group, but not for the attention placebo or no-treatment control groups. Furthermore, these improvements were maintained at a 3-month follow-up assessment. However, there was no evidence of generalized differential changes in social skills, according to staff ratings; self-report of social problems; observer ratings of friendliness, social anxiety, social skills, and employability; social workers' ratings of improvements in family, work, school, and social relationships; self-report of delinquent offenses; or police convictions.

Cognitive–behavioral skills training with conduct-disordered children and adolescents has addressed anger and aggression control (e.g., Camp, Blom, Hebert, & van Doorninck, 1977; Lochman, Lampron, Gemmer, & Harris, 1987), interpersonal problem solving (e.g., Kazdin, Esveldt-Dawson, French, & Unis, 1987a, 1987b), moral reasoning (e.g., Arbuthnot & Gordon, 1986), social perspective taking (e.g., Chandler, 1973), and combinations of these (Glick & Goldstein, 1987). Because anger arousal is a possible cognitive mediator of aggressive behavior, several cognitive–behavioral programs have focused on anger control with conduct-disordered children and adolescents. Most of these programs have utilized the school setting as the locus of training. The "Think Aloud" program developed by Camp *et al.* (1977) provided aggressive second-grade boys with six 30-minute sessions across 6 weeks and included interpersonal problem-solving games as well as the impersonal problem-solving tasks used by previous investigators. Camp *et al.* found improvements in tests of cognitive performance (similar to previous investigators), and also found improvements in teacher ratings of prosocial behavior. However, no improvement was found in teacher ratings of aggressive behavior, compared to ratings for no-treatment controls. Therefore, results were mixed with respect to classroom behavior.

Other investigators have also reported differential improvement for preadolescent aggressive children receiving cognitive–behavioral interventions, compared to children in no-treatment or attention placebo control groups, but typically only with analogue measures of anger control and/or aggression. Kettlewell and Kausch (1983) employed coping skills training, consisting of self-instruction training and behavioral rehearsal, with 7- to 12-year-old aggressive children in a summer day camp affiliated with a residential treatment facility. Compared to children in a no-treatment control group, children who received the coping skills training performed better on a task used during the training sessions and reported less anger on that task, received higher scores on some of the scales of an analogue problem-solving measure, and received fewer time outs for fighting. However, camp staff were not blind to treatment assignment, and measures of the frequency of verbal and physical aggression and peer ratings of aggression did not differ between the two groups. Garrison and Stolberg (1983) employed affective imagery training with third-, fourth-, and fifth-grade boys who had been labeled as "angry" because of high scores on the teacher form of the CBCL. Affective imagery training occurred in three 30- to 40-minute sessions during a 1-week period. The children were taught to associate physiological responses with various imagined emotionally laden events and to label the emotions. At the end of the intervention, children who had received the affect imagery training reported fewer anger-related cognitions on a self-report measure, compared to children in the attention placebo and no-treatment control conditions. However, the effect had begun to decay 1 week later. Teacher-recorded observations of aggressive behavior suggested a decrease for the boys in the treatment condition, but this may have been due to relatively higher baseline levels.

The most thoroughly evaluated approach to dealing with anger control in conduct disordered children has been developed by Lochman and his colleagues. Their "Anger Coping Program" is based on a secondary prevention model of intervention with young elementary school children; like other cognitive–behavioral approaches, it views the conduct-disordered child's aggressive behavioral responses as arising not from stimulus events directly, but from the child's cognitive processing (or lack thereof) and physiological arousal surrounding those events. Lochman's group's program is focused primarily on changes in those cognitive and physiological events that are evoked by frustrations, conflicts, problem situations, or perceived threats in the child's environment.

Lochman and colleagues have provided detailed descriptions of the Anger Coping Program model (Lochman *et al.*, 1987; Lochman, Nelson, & Sims, 1981). Briefly, the current program consists of 18 group therapy sessions of five children per group, led by two cotherapists. The children range in age from 9 to 12 years and are referred by teachers who are asked to nominate the most aggressive children in their classes. Treatment occurs in the school setting.

The program itself consists of group discussion during and following structured experimental, modeling, and behavioral rehearsal activities. The format includes the use of many hands-on materials and games, such as instant cameras, dominoes, puppets, decks of cards, and pictures of social problems from the Developing Understanding of Self and Others kit

(Dinkmeyer, 1973); videotape and camera equipment for modeling and role playing are also employed. The sessions begin with a general orientation to the group format and rules. They quickly advance to discussions and practice of problem-solving elements (identifying problems, generating alternatives, and evaluating solutions by identifying consequences), strategies for increasing physiological awareness, and learning to use self-talk during problem situations. Final sessions emphasize review and practice of typical social and school-related situations, utilizing all aspects of the cognitive strategies learned during the course of the program. Role playing and videotaped feedback are employed in these sessions.

Lochman and colleagues have conducted a series of studies aimed at evaluating the effects of this program (Lochman, 1985; Lochman, Burch, Curry, & Lampron, 1984; Lochman & Curry, 1986; Lochman et al., 1981). In their first uncontrolled study (Lochman et al., 1981), 12 children who participated in the cognitive–behavioral intervention showed significant decreases from pre- to posttreatment on teacher ratings of aggressiveness in the classroom and increases in on-task behavior. The children tended to have fewer acting-out behaviors on the Walker Problem Behavior Identification Checklist. A subsequent controlled evaluation (Lochman et al., 1984) confirmed that the cognitive–behavioral program was more effective than either goal setting alone or no treatment in reducing disruptive aggressive off-task behavior in the classroom. Also, the addition of a goal-setting strategy (in which children set daily behavioral goals that were monitored and reinforced by their teachers) to the cognitive intervention resulted in greater reductions in aggressive behavior than did the cognitive intervention alone (cf. Lyman, 1984). In a subsequent study looking at the parameters of treatment, Lochman (1985) found that longer-duration treatment (18 sessions) produced more significant changes in classroom behavior than did a 12-session intervention. On the basis of these two studies, Lochman has extended the standard program to 18 sessions and has incorporated a goal-setting strategy into the standard program. Finally, comparison of the 18-session version of the Anger Coping Program with an alternate version, in which the first six sessions focused on impersonal problem solving and academic tasks, indicated that the former was more effective in reducing disruptive

aggressive behavior in the classroom (Lochman & Curry, 1986). This research group is currently following the children into junior high school to ascertain the long-term effects of cognitive–behavioral intervention in preventing the usual developmental escalation to more serious forms of aggressive behavior in these children.

Feindler has developed a "Group Anger Control Training" program that is appropriate for conduct-disordered adolescents (Feindler, Ecton, Kingsley, & Dubey, 1986; Feindler, Marriott, & Iwata, 1984). In the Feindler et al. (1984) investigation, 36 junior high school students with a history of high rates of classroom and/or community disruption were randomly assigned to the treatment program or a no-treatment control condition. Students completed self-report measures of locus of control, means–ends problem solving, and impulsivity. Teachers completed ratings of self-control and kept daily records of fines incurred for aggressive behavior in an already ongoing contingency management system. The Group Anger Control Training program met for ten 50-minute sessions over 7 weeks. Students were taught to analyze provocation cues and anger responses, to provide alternative responses to provoking stimuli, and to control their own provocative behaviors. Control techniques included self-monitoring; self-imposed "time out" from anger-producing stimuli; and training in relaxation, assertiveness, and problem solving. The therapist utilized didactic instruction, modeling, behavioral rehearsal, and homework assignments as training procedures. The data collected at a 5-week follow-up provided minimal support for the efficacy of the treatment program. Students who received anger control training did perform better than the students in the no-treatment control condition, and teachers rated the former more highly on the self-control measure. However, there were no between-group differences on the behavioral fines or the other self-report measures.

This program was also adapted for use with male adolescent psychiatric inpatients, most of whom had been diagnosed as conduct-disordered (Feindler et al., 1986). Although there were significant posttreatment differences between the anger control and no-treatment control groups on the Matching Familiar Figures Test and child care staff ratings of self-control, the groups differed on only 3 of 11 behavioral measures in role-play tests at posttreatment. Daily records of discipline interactions on the ward indicated a significant decrease in general rule violations for the anger control training group and an increase in those violations for the control group. There were no group differences at posttreatment with respect to violations for physical aggression. Thus, the broad-based efficacy of this anger control training program for adolescents has yet to be clearly demonstrated.

The interventions just described employed training in interpersonal problem solving as a means of enhancing a broader array of social skills. Previous programs (e.g., Kendall & Braswell, 1985; Spivack, Platt, & Shure, 1976) have not focused specifically on conduct-disordered children. However, Kazdin et al. (1987b) have recently developed a "Problem-Solving Skills Training" (PSST) program specifically for preadolescents with antisocial behavior problems that is based on these two approaches. PSST is administered individually over 20 sessions, each of which lasts approximately 45 minutes. Although most of the sessions relate to interpersonal tasks, PSST also includes training in impersonal and academic tasks (cf. Lochman & Curry, 1986). Fifty-six children (aged 7–13) who were inpatients on a psychiatric unit were randomly assigned to PSST, a nondirective relationship therapy condition, or an attention placebo control condition. Parent and teacher ratings on both the behavior problem and social adjustment scales were collected at pre- and posttreatment and at a 1-year follow-up. PSST demonstrated a clear superiority over the relationship therapy and attention placebo control conditions on both parent and teacher ratings at posttreatment and the 1-year follow-up. Children in the PSST condition were also more likely to move to within or near the normal range on these measures, although it is important to note that most of the children in this group were still outside this range on measures of behavior problems in the home and school. In another investigation, Kazdin et al. (1987a) obtained similar results when PSST combined with a parent training intervention (the latter based on Patterson et al., 1975) was compared to an attention placebo control condition. These investigations are noteworthy among the skills training studies for their methodological sophistication, ratings in the natural environment (school and home), and 1-year follow-up. However, observational measures of behavior in both the training and natural settings are highly desirable; we hope that

they will be included in future evaluations of PSST.

Several investigators have attempted to address deficits in conduct-disordered adolescents' perspective-taking and moral reasoning skills. In an often-cited study, Chandler (1973) demonstrated differential improvement on analogue measures of perspective-taking ability by 11- to 13-year-old delinquent boys who had participated in a 10-week program in which role-taking ability was targeted. The youths wrote and acted in a series of skits involving interpersonal dilemmas common to their peer group. Each skit was repeated until each boy had played every role. Not only did perspective-taking ability improve, but the delinquent boys who had participated in treatment evidenced a greater reduction in offenses noted on police and court records over an 18-month follow-up period than did youths in the attention placebo and no-treatment control conditions.

With respect to moral reasoning, it has been demonstrated that higher levels can be facilitated by relatively brief (8–20 sessions) discussion groups composed of behavior-disordered (Arbuthnot & Gordon, 1986) or incarcerated delinquent (Gibbs, Arnold, Ahlborn, & Cheesman, 1984) adolescents. However, only Arbuthnot and Gordon have also included measures of behavioral functioning to assess whether changes in moral reasoning are associated with behavior change. Following participation in a "moral dilemma discussion group" that met for 45 minutes per week over 16–20 weeks in the school, behavior-disordered adolescents had fewer referrals to the principal for disciplinary reasons, were less tardy, had higher grades in the humanities and social sciences, and had fewer police or court contacts than adolescents in a no-treatment control condition. At a 1-year follow-up, these between-group differences were still evident, although both groups had virtually eliminated any police or court contacts. It should also be noted that there were no differences between the groups on teacher ratings of the adolescents' behavior, either at posttreatment or at the 1-year follow-up.

Several of the studies just described have employed cognitive–behavioral interventions to deal successfully with a number of specific behavioral, cognitive, and affective deficits in conduct-disordered children and adolescents. However, it is doubtful that remediation of any one of these deficits is sufficient by itself to institute clinically significant changes over a meaningful period of time in these children. Goldstein and his colleagues have developed a 10-week curriculum called "Aggression Replacement Training" (Goldstein, Glick, Reiner, Zimmerman, & Coultry, 1986), which combines interventions designed to enhance social skills (Structured Learning Training; Goldstein & Pentz, 1984), anger control (Anger Control Training; Feindler *et al.*, 1984), and moral reasoning (Moral Education). Preliminary evaluations in two juvenile correctional facilities suggested differential improvements on analogue measures of social skills (and sometimes on the moral development measure) for adolescents who participated in Aggression Replacement Training as opposed to those in either a brief-instruction or a no-treatment control group (Glick & Goldstein, 1987). Evidence for generalization to the community after release has been limited to global ratings completed by probation officers. Although evidence for this combined approach to treatment is preliminary, it does have the potential for facilitating improvement across a broad array of skills deficits, especially if it were to be combined with one of the family-based interventions described earlier in this chapter.

Behavioral Interventions for Covert Conduct Disorders

Whereas behavioral interventions for overt conduct-disordered behaviors have been extensively evaluated in home, school, and community settings, there is a paucity of data concerning interventions of any type for covert types of conduct-disordered behavior. This is due in part to the relatively weak data base concerning those behaviors (see above). However, the attention being given to some of these covert behaviors and their treatment is increasing. In this section of the chapter, we describe behavioral interventions that have been designed to treat stealing, lying, fire setting, and substance use.

Stealing

There is a consensus that the identification/labeling of stealing is the key to developing a successful intervention for this behavior (Barth, 1987; Miller & Klungness, 1986; Patterson *et al.*, 1975). Because of the low base rate and covert nature of stealing, firsthand, immediate detection of all stealing events by parents, teachers, or others is not a feasible goal. Therefore, stealing is operationally defined as "the child's taking, or being in possession of, anything that does not clearly belong to him [or her]" (Barth, 1987, p. 151). Table 3-2 contains an elaboration of this definition, as well as instructions for caregivers on how to respond to stealing behavior. Although adoption of this definition of stealing may result in instances in which the child is incorrectly labeled as having stolen, the alternative of not being able to treat the stealing behavior effectively is regarded as the greater of the two evils.

As indicated earlier in the chapter, the most systematic work on the treatment of covert conduct disorders has been conducted by Patterson, Reid, and their colleagues at OSLC with respect to family-based interventions for treating stealing. In addition to the definitional problems noted above, the failure of parents of children who steal to monitor their children's whereabouts or to be involved with the children to any great extent compounds the difficulty of designing effective family-based interventions. In order to address some of these problems, the OSLC group has developed a specialized approach to social-learning-based family therapy with children who display stealing and other covert conduct-disordered behaviors (Patterson *et al.*, 1975; Reid *et al.*, 1980). First, the standard OSLC parent training program for treating overt conduct-disordered behaviors is implemented, because these behaviors covary with the lower-rate covert behaviors in many children. Next, parents are taught to identify stealing using an operational definition similar to the one presented above, and to monitor its occurrence on a daily basis. Much discussion and role playing of these procedures occur in therapy sessions.

Once the operational definition of stealing is accepted by the parents (a process that can involve a great deal of therapy time), parents are taught to administer a mild consequence immediately contingent upon each and every suspected stealing event. The consequence (e.g., 1–2 hours of hard work around the home) is kept at a mild level because the child will be inaccurately accused from time to time. The implementation of this approach involves much support, telephone contact, and discussion. Check-in systems are instituted for families in which infrequent monitoring occurs. In addition, it would seem important to incorporate therapeutic strategies for involving fathers in the therapy process, given the relationship between uninvolved fathers and stealing (Reid, 1984).

Reid *et al.* (1980) evaluated the effectiveness of this modified approach to behavioral family therapy for 5- to 14-year-old conduct-disordered children referred for stealing. In this study, 28 families of conduct-disordered children who stole received treatment. The mean amount of therapist contact was 32 hours. Outcome measures consisted of parent reports of stealing on the TIROSSA, parent reports of other referral problems on the PDR, and the TAB summary score from the FICS in home observations conducted by trained independent observers. Results indicated significant decreases in parent-reported stealing events and other referral problems from pre- to posttreatment and at a 6-month follow-up. The TAB scores decreased nonsignificantly. However, as might be expected, aversive social behaviors in the families were not high to begin with in this sample of children who stole. A waiting-list control group, in which parent report data on stealing were collected at baseline, at the end of the parent training program for dealing with overt conduct disorders, and following the treatment package for stealing, indicated that significant reductions in parent-reported stealing did not occur until after the treatment for stealing was implemented. However, large differences in baseline levels of stealing limit the utility of this comparison.

In the Marlowe *et al.* (1988) investigation with chronic delinquent adolescents described earlier in the chapter, some empirical support was provided for the efficacy of this family-based approach with the subset of adolescents who engaged in both overt and covert conduct-disordered behaviors. Parent-reported stealing (as noted on the PDR) was reduced to zero at treatment termination.

Although the results of the Reid *et al.* (1980) and Marlowe *et al.* (1988) studies are suggestive, the effects of treatment on stealing were assessed from parental report measures. Given the problems these parents have with respect to effective monitoring of their children's behavior, future investigators should attempt to include some treatment component directed specifically to parental monitoring. Not only is this a worthwhile target of intervention in its own right, but effective monitoring of the child's

TABLE 3-2. Instructions to Caregivers for Defining and Providing Consequences for Stealing

1. The most important part of working to decrease stealing is *defining stealing as stealing. Stealing is defined as the child's taking, or being in possession of, anything that does not clearly belong to him [or her].* Parents, teachers, or other adults are the only judges. They may label an act as stealing by observing it, by having it reported to them, or by noticing that something is missing. There is no arguing about guilt or innocence. It is the child's job to be sure that he is not accused. The value of the object is irrelevant. Trading and borrowing are not permissible. Any "purchases" that the child brings home must be accompanied by a receipt. Otherwise they are to be returned and consequences instituted.
2. Once the behavior of stealing has been labeled, then the consequences are to be applied. Avoid discussions, shaming, or counseling.
3. *Every* stealing event must be so labeled and consequences given.
4. Avoid using excessive detective tactics (such as searches); just keep your eyes open, and investigate the origins of new property.
5. Consequences for stealing should be work restrictions and loss of privileges for the day of the stealing, and basic privileges only on the following weekend. There should be no other consequences such as humiliations or beatings. Special privileges can be earned again on the following day.
6. *Remember:* Stealing goes hand in hand with wandering and with your not knowing the whereabouts of your child. Check-in times are recommended if stealing is a problem.
7. Do not tempt your child. Keep items like those that your child has stolen in the past away from him or her. For example, avoid leaving your wallet or cigarette packs in view or unwatched.
8. Stealing may occur no matter how many possessions your child has, so giving him or her everything is not a successful approach to ending stealing. Your child should, however, have some way of earning his or her own money so that he or she may have a choice of things to buy.

Note. From "Assessment and Treatment of Stealing" by R. P. Barth, 1987, in B. B. Lahey and A. E. Kazdin (Eds.), *Advances in Clinical Child Psychology* (Vol. 10, pp. 137–170), New York: Plenum. Copyright 1987 by Plenum Publishing Corporation. Reprinted by permission.

behavior and whereabouts would seem to be a prerequisite for accurate recording on the TIROSSA and PDR. Another critical issue that must be addressed pertains to the generalizability of this intervention for stealing in other settings, such as the school or the community at large. Although there are effective treatment procedures for dealing with stealing in the school setting (see below), identifying and stopping stealing in public places such as stores is very difficult.

Henderson (1981, 1983) has developed an "Individualized Combined Treatment" (ICT) program for children and adolescents who report that they want to stop stealing. This approach has three broad components: (1) self-control of the internal environment; (2) adult or responsible-other control of the external environment; and (3) personalization of the program by the therapist. In the first component, Henderson teaches relaxation skills in an effort to countercondition internal arousal stimuli, which he maintains are often associated with stealing. In therapy sessions, the child is asked to imagine himself or herself in theft situations and then to relax and imagine walking away. In this way, relaxation and imagery are also conceptualized as self-control techniques, which are later extended to the external environment. Heart rate biofeedback is used to facilitate relaxation. Parents are asked to provide stealing opportunities or "traps" for the child in the home so that the child has an opportunity to practice self-control strategies. Bonuses in a reward system are provided for not stealing. The "traps" are gradually made less obvious and easier to take without being caught.

To provide external controls for not stealing, some system for monitoring "not stealing" must be implemented. Henderson (1981) advocates the use of a "not-stealing diary." Two types of entries are made in the diary: (1) any length of time that the stealer has been observed by a responsible adult not to have stolen; and (2) times of departure and arrival noted by responsible adults at both ends of a journey (e.g., from home to school). If the times logged in conform to appropriate travel time, then an assumption is made that no stealing has occurred. Daily time "not stealing" is computed, and nonstealing time is rewarded with backup privileges and activities. These reinforcers are selected so that they are related in some way to the child's motive for stealing (see Barth, 1987). For example, if the child seems to steal for "kicks," then an appropriate backup reinforcer might be a roller-coaster ride at an amusement park.

Henderson (1981, 1983) has presented descriptive data on 10 children (8–15 years of age) who were treated using the ICT program. Compared to 17 other children who were treated for stealing at the same clinic using a variety of other treatment procedures, only 20% of the children who received the ICT program were reported to have stolen in the 2-year period following treatment, whereas 60%–75% of the other children were reported to have stolen. Although the descriptive data on this approach to treatment are certainly encouraging, systematic evaluation of the program with appropriate controls needs to be undertaken.

Several case studies with an individual child or adolescent have reported the successful use of self-control training plus family contingency contracting (Stumphauzer, 1976), covert sensitization (Cautela, 1967), and response cost (loss of access to social contact with a preferred adult) (Wetzel, 1966).

A few studies have focused on the reduction of stealing in elementary school classrooms. Because of its relatively controlled and geographically confined nature, the classroom may be amenable to more systematic monitoring of stealing behavior and to the implementation of differential reinforcement procedures for not stealing than is the case when treatment is implemented in the home setting (cf. Reid, 1984). For example, with respect to the detection and monitoring of stealing, one teacher marked all of the target student's personal and school items with a green circle. Stealing was defined as "having items not marked with green circles on your person, desk, or supply box" (Rosen & Rosen, 1983, p. 58), and the teacher checked those areas every 15 minutes. In another study designed to reduce classroom-wide stealing, 10 standard items (e.g., nickels, Magic Markers, erasers) were placed around the classroom each day, and their presence or absence was noted at 15-minute intervals (Switzer, Deal, & Bailey, 1977).

The three studies that have examined procedures to reduce classroom stealing have all utilized some form of response cost for stealing and positive reinforcement for periods of nonstealing. Using a reversal design, Rosen and Rosen (1983) assessed the effects of token reinforcement and response cost on the stealing behavior of a 7-year-old boy in a self-contained behavior disorders classroom. Stealing was virtually eliminated while the treatment conditions were in place, and this effect was maintained throughout the 1-month follow-up period. Two studies utilized group contingencies to reduce stealing. Brooks and Snow (1972) employed a token reinforcement and response cost system in conjunction with a classroom-wide group contingency (15 minutes of extra free time) to reduce stealing in a 10-year-old boy. Switzer *et al.* (1977) compared the relative efficacy of a lecture by the teacher and a group contingency (10 minutes of free time) in reducing classroom-wide stealing in three second-grade classes. A multiple-baseline-across-classes design clearly demonstrated that the lecture was ineffective, whereas the group contingency had an immediate effect in reducing stealing. Although these procedures were conducted classroom-wide as opposed to focusing on a specific child, their use as adjuncts to an individualized set of contingencies (as in Brooks & Snow, 1972) should be considered in designing interventions for stealing by conduct-disordered children.

Although none of these studies formally assessed the generalization of treatment effects across settings or behaviors, anecdotal data indicated that there was a decrease in stealing of nontargeted items (Switzer *et al.*, 1977) and of disruptive acting-out behaviors (Rosen & Rosen, 1983). In the latter case, informal reports from the teacher and parents suggested decreases in stealing behavior in other areas of the school (e.g., cafeteria) and at home.

In their review of the treatment of nonconfrontative stealing in elementary-school-age children, Miller and Klungness (1986) raise some important issues that must be considered in the detection, monitoring, and treatment of stealing in the classroom. The use of unannounced theft probes (Switzer *et al.*, 1977) or systematic searches (Rosen & Rosen, 1983) raises important legal and ethical issues. The use of group contingencies has the potential for several undesirable side effects, such as increased negative peer pressure and/or rejection (Pigott & Heggie, 1986) and the possibility that children may eventually choose not to report stealing because they do not want to lose access to the reward. In the Switzer *et al.* (1977) investigation, peer sociometric ratings prior to and after the implementation of the group contingency and unobtrusive audiotaping of the children's conversations when the teacher left the classroom after each stealing incident did not indicate the presence of any of these negative effects. However, more systematic and practical methods of monitoring such potential negative side effects are essential.

Lying

To our knowledge, there have been no reports of formalized interventions (behavioral or otherwise) to deal with lying. Stouthamer-Loeber (1986) has suggested that younger children, whose lies are more transparent and easily detectable, should be easier to treat. She advocates an educational approach in which the parent instructs the child in the difference between what is true and not true, and provides training in empathy and/or perspective taking. For older children, she suggests an approach similar to that described above by Reid *et al.* (1980) for stealing. If the parent suspects that the child is lying, the child must prove that he or she is being truthful to avoid a negative consequence. Stouthamer-Loeber also stresses the necessity of focusing on increasing parental monitoring of the child in interventions designed to decrease lying.

Fire Setting

Given the potentially serious consequences of fire setting and the evidence that fire-setting children are at the extreme of the conduct disorder continuum in terms of the extent and severity of their antisocial behavior, the paucity of treatment outcome research is alarming. In a recent review, Kolko (1985) identified 15 case studies, of which 8 employed behavioral techniques. Behavioral procedures employed with fire-setting children have included response cost for fire play (e.g., Carstens, 1982; Holland, 1969), positive reinforcement (either social or tangible) for incompatible behaviors (e.g., Holland, 1969; Stawar, 1976), satiation (Jones, 1981; Welsh, 1971), structured imagery (Stawar, 1976), and graphing (Bumpass, Fagelman, & Brix, 1983). McGrath, Marshall, and Prior (1979) successfully employed a multicomponent package consisting of social skills training, overcorrection, covert sensitization, and instruction in fire safety with an 11-year-old boy. Kolko (1983) reported the successful use of negative practice, fire safety instruction, and token reinforcement with a 6-year-old developmentally disabled boy.

The limitations of case studies for the determination of treatment efficacy are numerous and well known, and are not reiterated here. A few specifics do bear mentioning. With the exception of Bumpass et al. (1983), who described the treatment of 29 fire setters with a graphing technique, all of the case studies were conducted with a single child. Follow-up data are absent or anecdotal. Furthermore, it is not possible to ascertain whether the fire-setting children treated in these case studies were conduct-disordered or not, although problems with noncompliance and aggression were mentioned by several authors (e.g., Carstens, 1982; Kolko, 1983). It has been suggested that targeting these high-rate, overt conduct-disordered behaviors in treatment may lead to decreases in fire setting (Kolko, 1985; Patterson, 1982).

The OSLC approach to the identification and treatment of stealing was modified in one instance to treat fire setting in a 4-year-old boy (Carstens, 1982). Fire setting was defined as previous evidence of fire play (e.g., burned matches), matches found out of their usual container, or actual contact with matches/lighters. A 1-hour work penalty was to be employed after each incidence of fire play. However, the parents reported immediate cessation of fire play and fire setting after imposition of the response cost system, so the work penalty was never implemented. Further investigation of this approach seems warranted, given its moderate success with the treatment of stealing and the possibility of treating stealing and fire setting simultaneously using the same treatment procedures.

Substance Use

As noted above, substance use (use of alcohol or other drugs) is often manifested by conduct-disordered youngsters, especially during adolescence (Dishion, Reid, & Patterson, 1988; Loeber, in press). Despite arguments (supported by current theoretical models and the empirical data base concerning the correlates of substance use in these individuals) that indicate the appropriateness of behavioral interventions (e.g., Bry, 1985; Dishion et al., 1988; Maisto & Carey, 1985), there has been a dearth of outcome research on interventions of any type. The few sources that have examined behavioral interventions have tended to be descriptive and/or based on very small samples (e.g., Bry, Conboy, & Bisgay, 1986; Teicher, Sinay, & Stumphauzer, 1976).

Teicher et al. (1976) described a pilot program for training community-based paraprofessionals to act as behavior therapists with the families of alcohol-abusing adolescents. Contingency contracting was the primary therapeutic technique. Bry et al. (1986) employed "Problem-Solving Communication Training" (see Foster & Robin, Chapter 14, this volume) with the families of three adolescents who had been referred because of drug use, parent–child conflict, and falling grades. The families were middle-class, and there was no indication that the adolescents were engaging in other conduct-disordered behaviors. Data were collected in a multiple-baseline-across-behaviors design, and indicated decreases in marijuana use and school failure at the end of a 15-month follow-up. Alcohol and tobacco use, which were not specifically targeted in treatment, did not change.

Although there has been very little activity with respect to the design and evaluation of behavioral interventions for adolescent substance use, several recent reviewers have provided quite consistent recommendations with respect to the focus and content of such interventions (Bry, 1985; Dishion et al., 1988; Maisto & Carey, 1985). The most specific guidelines have been presented by Dishion et al. Based on the large cross-sectional and longitudinal samples of 4th-, 7th-, and 10th-grade boys and their families described earlier in the chapter, they recommend that interventions designed to decrease substance use by adolescents target parental monitoring, the parents' own use of drugs, the adolescents' peer group, and the adolescents' social skills and antisocial behavior. A standard behavioral parent training program, in combination with an intervention targeting adolescents' social skills in relation to their peer group, is recommended. Parental monitoring, in particular, is viewed as an important focus of the parent training intervention, in that it may have both direct effects (by decreasing the number of opportunities to use drugs) and indirect effects (by decreasing exposure to a deviant peer group) on youth substance use. The "Life Skills Training Model" (Botvin, Baker, Renick, Filazzola, & Botvin, 1984), which is a school-based cognitive–behavioral prevention program that has been shown to reduce initiation to alcohol, tobacco, and marijuana, is presented as an exemplar of this type of approach. The program includes training in refusal skills, decision making, coping with anxiety, improving general social skills, and accurate information about substance use. Whether this component of Dishion *et al.'s* recommended treatment package could be employed effectively with conduct-disordered adolescents already engaging in substance use remains to be seen.

ISSUES IN TREATMENT EFFICACY

In this section of the chapter, we address some of the major issues pertaining to behavioral interventions with conduct-disordered children. These issues include generalization and social validity; predictors of outcome; and comparisons of the relative effectiveness of behavioral treatments with control conditions (no treatment, attention placebo, etc.) and with nonbehavioral forms of treatment.

Generalization and Social Validity

In an earlier section of the chapter, we have employed Forehand and Atkeson's (1977) classification of various types of generalization (setting, temporal, sibling, and behavioral) as an introduction to our evaluation of various family-based interventions with conduct-disordered children. With respect to such interventions with preadolescent children and their families (e.g., Forehand & McMahon, 1981; Patterson *et al.*, 1975; Webster-Stratton, 1987), there have been a number of investigations assessing the various types of generalization; these have, for the most part, supported the effectiveness of behavioral parent training programs.

Each of the three programs described earlier in the chapter has documented setting generalization from the clinic to the home for parent and child behavior and for parents' perception of the child's adjustment (e.g., Fleischman, 1981; Peed *et al.*, 1977; Taplin & Reid, 1977; Webster-Stratton, 1984). Temporal generalization of treatment effects has also been demonstrated over follow-up periods of at least 1 year (e.g., Baum & Forehand, 1981; Fleischman, 1981; Patterson & Fleischman, 1979; Webster-Stratton, 1984). Maintenance of treatment effects for the Forehand and McMahon (1981) parent training program has been demonstrated for up to 4½ years after treatment (Baum & Forehand, 1981), and a less rigorous

study done 4½–10½ years after treatment suggests that the children were functioning well compared to their peer group in terms of parent-, teacher-, and self-reported adjustment (Forehand & Long, 1986). Other parent training programs with young conduct-disordered children have also demonstrated long-term temporal generalization effects of 3 years or more (e.g., Daly, Holland, Forrest, & Fellbaum, 1985; Strain, Steele, Ellis, & Timm, 1982).

Relatively few investigators have assessed setting generalization from the clinic to the school. Although evidence of either generalization (e.g., Fellbaum *et al.*, 1985) or behavioral contrast effects (e.g., Johnson *et al.*, 1976; Wahler, 1975) has occasionally been found, no systematic effects have been reported for the Forehand and McMahon (1981) parent training program in two different studies (Breiner & Forehand, 1981; Forehand *et al.*, 1979). Based on this research, we suggest that when a child presents with problems in both the home and school settings, improvement in school functioning should not necessarily be expected to occur as a function of family-based intervention in the home; rather, intervening directly in the school will probably be required. Furthermore, therapists should monitor the child's behavior in the school regardless of whether this was an initial referral problem, because of the possibility of a behavioral contrast effect.

Both the Forehand and McMahon (1981) and Patterson *et al.* (1975) parent training programs have demonstrated sibling generalization at the end of treatment (Arnold *et al.*, 1975; Horne & Van Dyke, 1983; Humphreys *et al.*, 1978), and this generalization has been maintained at 6-month (Arnold *et al.*, 1975) and 1-year (Horne & Van Dyke, 1983) follow-ups for Patterson's program. However, it should be noted that many of the siblings in the Arnold *et al.* investigation had been directly involved in the actual treatment program.

Behavioral generalization from the treatment of child noncompliance to other deviant behaviors (e.g., aggression, temper tantrums) has been demonstrated for both the Forehand and McMahon (Wells, Forehand, & Griest, 1980) and Webster-Stratton (1984) parent training programs for younger conduct-disordered children, as well as by other parent trainers (e.g., Russo *et al.*, 1981). Significant reductions in the TAB score (which is a composite measure of observed coercive behaviors) and in PDR scores over the course of treatment suggest that

Patterson's parent training program for pre-adolescent conduct-disordered children also manifests behavioral generality (e.g., Fleischman, 1981; Fleischman & Szykula, 1981; Patterson, 1974), although it should be noted that Patterson and Reid (1973) did *not* find generalization of treatment effects from targeted to nontargeted observed deviant behaviors.

The social validity of family-based interventions with conduct-disordered children has been assessed by a number of methods, most often by some measure of consumer satisfaction completed by the parents (see McMahon & Forehand, 1983, for a review of consumer satisfaction in child behavior therapy). All three parent training programs for preadolescents have provided strong evidence of consumer satisfaction at posttreatment and/or follow-up periods of a year or more (e.g., Baum & Forehand, 1981; McMahon et al., 1984; Patterson et al., 1982; Webster-Stratton, 1984), and both the Forehand and McMahon (1981) and Patterson et al. (1975) programs have provided normative comparisons indicating that, by the end of treatment, child and/or parent behavior more closely resembles that in nonreferred families (e.g., Forehand et al., 1980; Patterson, 1974). The treatment acceptability of the former program has been recently demonstrated by Cross Calvert and McMahon (1987).

It is apparent that evidence for the generalization and social validity of family-based interventions with preadolescent conduct-disordered children is extensive and, for the most part, positive. A number of studies (most of them conducted by Forehand and his colleagues and by Sanders and Dadds and their colleagues) have examined the role of adjunctive treatments in facilitating generalization and/or social validity, over and above that obtained by standard parent training programs. Adjunctive treatments have included components designed to facilitate maternal self-control/self-management (Sanders, 1982; Sanders & Glynn, 1981; Wells, Griest, & Forehand, 1980); child self-control (Baum et al., 1986); parental knowledge of social learning principles (McMahon, Forehand, & Griest, 1981); generalization to specific settings in the home and community ("Planned Activities Training"; Sanders & Christensen, 1985; Sanders & Dadds, 1982); and marital support, communication, and problem solving ("Partner Support Training"; Dadds, Sanders, Behrens,

& James, 1987; Dadds, Sanders, & James, 1987; Dadds, Schwartz, & Sanders, 1987). The most comprehensive adjunct to date is Parent Enhancement Therapy (Griest et al., 1982), which, as noted above, includes components related to parental perceptions of the child's behavior, marital adjustment, parental personal adjustment, and the parents' extrafamilial relationships. The relative efficacy of these adjunctive treatments when employed in conjunction with the basic parent training programs lends support to the current movement toward a broader behavioral family therapy model of intervention (Griest & Wells, 1983).

With respect to other forms of behavioral intervention with conduct-disordered children and adolescents, less attention has been paid to generalization and social validity; when they have been assessed, they have often been found to be lacking. With respect to family-based treatments with adolescents, investigators have either failed to assess adolescent and parent behavior in the home (e.g., Alexander & Parson, 1973; Henggeler et al., 1986) or have failed to find changes in that setting (Marlowe et al., 1988). Marlowe et al. did find significant decreases in targeted delinquent and pre-delinquent behaviors as reported by parents on the PDR. Setting and temporal generalization have usually been assessed using some measure of recidivism, the use of which is fraught with methodological problems (cf. Gordon & Arbuthnot, 1987). Although Marlowe et al. (1988) found greater reductions in the rate of court-documented offense rates in the treatment year for adolescents who received parent training as opposed to standard mental health services, offense rates for the two conditions were comparable at each of the three follow-up years. Alexander and Parsons (1973) reported reduced recidivism rates at a 6- to 18-month follow-up for adolescents who had participated in FFT, compared to other forms of family therapy. FFT also appears to reduce the likelihood of subsequent court involvement by siblings of the identified client, thus providing some evidence of sibling generalization for this intervention (Gordon & Arbuthnot, 1987; Klein et al., 1977). The behavioral generalization and social validity of these interventions have not been formally assessed, although Marlowe et al. (1988) do provide some data for the cost-effectiveness of parent training, compared to other mental health services for these adolescents.

As noted above, treatment effects from community-based programs for adolescents, such as the TFM (Achievement Place), have not been found to show setting generalization to the home environment or temporal generalization when measures of recidivism are employed (Kirigin et al., 1982; Weinrott et al., 1982). Both of these investigations do indicate that TFM possesses a high degree of social validity in how it is perceived by program participants and members of the community. Weinrott et al. demonstrated that, although the TFM group homes may not have been more effective than alternative group homes, they were less costly. Furthermore, TFM has been an exemplar of the use of social-validational procedures in formative evaluations (see Willner et al., 1978).

To our knowledge, the setting generalization to the home of school-based interventions for conduct-disordered children has not been assessed. This is potentially of considerable import, given the previously noted findings of occasional generalization or behavioral contrast effects in the school as a function of family-based treatments. Even more restricted forms of setting generalization (e.g., generalization of effects from one class period to another) have usually not been assessed. The available evidence suggests that various school-based interventions often exert their effects only in those classes in which the procedures are implemented (e.g., Fowler et al., 1986; O'Leary et al., 1969; Walker & Hops, 1976), although use of experimenter-selected material reinforcers (as opposed to child-selected activity reinforcers) did facilitate setting generalization for a token system (Stumpf & Holman, 1985).

Temporal generalization has been largely ignored, except for the investigations by the CORBEH group (see also Brigham et al., 1985). The CORBEH studies have shown that multicomponent treatment packages do not generalize well from one academic year to the next when no generalization training is attempted (Walker et al., 1975). The CLASS program has demonstrated maintenance of treatment effects over a 1-year period, but weekly "booster" sessions may need to be held with the teachers during this period (Hops et al., 1978). The temporal generalization of the RECESS program has not been assessed, but Walker et al. (1981) note some anecdotal reports of decay of treatment effects when the program is eventually turned over to the school's playground supervisors. Shorter follow-up intervals (3–12 weeks) have been employed in investigations examining token economy and teacher contingency management interventions (Greenwood et al., 1974, 1977; Walker & Hops, 1976).

The issue of behavioral generalization of these school-based interventions for overt conduct disorders is a critical one. As noted above, we have purposely excluded those investigations that have directly targeted academic achievement per se, because they are dealt with in greater detail in other chapters. However, it is essential that investigators who elect to target overt conduct-disordered behaviors in the classroom examine the effects of their interventions not just on these behaviors, but also in terms of whether the intervention ultimately leads to adaptive changes in children's academic achievement, social adjustment, and so on (cf. Klein, 1979; Winett & Winkler, 1972). This issue has been largely ignored.

Similarly, the social validity of these school-based interventions has not received systematic attention. In one of the few studies to assess consumer satisfaction with the outcome of a school-based treatment for conduct-disordered children, Kent and O'Leary (1976) reported that both parents and teachers reported high levels of satisfaction with the outcome of treatment and with the therapists. The CLASS program appears to reduce demand for special educational services for its participants over at least a 3-year follow-up (Hops et al., 1978), and program consultants perceive their training and the program very positively (e.g., Walker et al., 1988).

While there have been relatively few investigations of generalization and social validity for multicomponent treatment packages employing token economies and teacher attention, virtually no research has been conducted on these topics with respect to home-based reinforcement systems (cf. Atkeson & Forehand, 1979) or school-based cognitive–behavioral interventions with conduct-disordered children.

With respect to skills training approaches to treating conduct-disordered children and adolescents, conclusions regarding the generalization of treatment effects are limited because of the already discussed reliance on analogue measures and settings to assess treatment efficacy. In the few studies that have assessed treatment outcome in naturalistic settings, generalization often either has not been assessed or has failed to occur (e.g., Spence &

Marzillier, 1981). Evidence of setting generalization to the classroom (Lochman et al., 1984), to psychiatric inpatient units (Feindler et al., 1986), and possibly to community functioning (Glick & Goldstein, 1987) for some of the anger control training interventions has been demonstrated, but maintenance of these effects has not been assessed. Temporal generalization of at least some treatment effects over 12- to 18-month follow-up periods has been demonstrated for perspective-taking skills (Chandler, 1973) and moral reasoning skills (Arbuthnot & Gordon, 1986) interventions.

The strongest demonstration of generalization for the skills training approaches has been presented by Kazdin et al. (1987b). Not only were children who participated in the PSST program while inpatients in a psychiatric unit rated more highly on both parent and teacher report measures after treatment than children in either relationship therapy or attention placebo control conditions, but this superiority was maintained at a 1-year follow-up. Similar findings were obtained when PSST was combined with a parent training intervention and compared to an attention placebo control condition (Kazdin et al., 1987a).

Evidence for social validity is similarly lacking, although some social skills researchers (e.g., Willner et al., 1978) have utilized social-validational techniques in a sophisticated manner in their development of teaching procedures for the skills training interventions. Kazdin et al. (1987a, 1987b) found that children in the PSST condition (alone or in combination with parent training) were more likely to move within or near the normal range on some of the parent and teacher report measures than were children in the other conditions, thus providing some evidence for the social validity of PSST.

A discussion of the generalization of treatment effects in dealing with covert conduct disorders is limited almost entirely to a few investigations that have dealt with stealing. A study by the OSLC group provides some limited evidence for setting, temporal, and behavioral generalization. Reid et al. (1980) noted parent-reported decreases in stealing and other referral problems at posttreatment and at a 6-month follow-up. However, decreases were not observed on the observational TAB measure. Furthermore, Moore et al. (1979) have presented data suggesting that children referred to OSLC for stealing (only some of whom completed treatment) were at great risk for being labeled as delinquent 2–9 years later. To our knowledge, no one has attempted to assess generalization or behavioral contrast effects of family-based treatments for stealing to other settings, such as the school or community. In school-based interventions for stealing, Rosen and Rosen (1983) reported maintenance of effects at 1 month for their single subject, and anecdotal reports of decreased stealing of non-targeted items (Switzer et al., 1977) and of disruptive acting-out behaviors (Rosen & Rosen, 1983) provide minimal support for behavioral generalization. In the latter study, informal teacher and parent reports also suggested a decrease in stealing in other areas of the school and at home. Finally, Bry et al. (1986) found no evidence of generalization to the non-targeted behaviors of alcohol and tobacco use as a result of their family-based approach to decreasing adolescent substance use.

Predictors of Outcome

We have described a broad spectrum of behavioral interventions for the treatment of conduct disorders in children and adolescents. These interventions have varied tremendously in their demonstrated efficacy, both in terms of immediate outcome and in terms of the generalization and maintenance of these effects. In this section of the chapter, we discuss various predictors of outcome, not only with respect to positive treatment effects, but also with respect to decreasing dropouts. As in other areas, most of the extant research has assessed predictors of outcome for intervention designed to treat overt conduct disorders, and most of that research has been carried out with family-based interventions for preadolescents (i.e., parent training). We have divided our review into child and family characteristics and characteristics of treatment (e.g., the nature of the referral, therapist characteristics).

Child Characteristics

A myriad of characteristics of the conduct-disordered child could conceivably affect outcome in a differential manner. These include the nature of the conduct disorder behavior (e.g., subtype, severity, duration); the child's age, sex, and race; and variables such as temperament, problem-solving abilities, attributional biases, and so on. With the few exceptions described here, there has been a dearth of research in this area. A particularly serious omission is the lack of data concerning aspects related to the nature of the conduct-disordered behavior. In terms of subtypes of conduct disorders, the best that can be garnered is indirect evidence that children referred for stealing have a poorer prognosis concerning delinquent behavior as adolescents than do children referred for aggressive behavior (Moore et al., 1979). However, the interpretability of these data is limited by the fact that only some of the children in these families actually received treatment.

Children whose families were classified as treatment "failures" (insufficient change in child and maternal deviant behavior and/or dropouts) exhibited more severe manifestations of overt conduct disorders, in that their behavior was more aversive and indiscriminate at baseline than that of children who succeeded in a parent training intervention (Dumas, 1984b). However, Fleischman (1981) did not find any difference between dropouts and completers of treatment in level of child aversive behavior, as observed by parents (i.e., PDR) or independent observers (TAB score). In contrast to the findings of Dumas (1984b), Lochman, Lampron, Burch, and Curry (1985) found that greater reductions in disruptive/aggressive off-task behavior in the classroom following their anger control intervention were predicted by higher initial rates of this behavior. This does not appear to have been merely due to regression to the mean, since boys in an untreated control group did not behave similarly.

Several investigators have found that relatively younger children are more likely to succeed in treatment (Strain et al., 1982; Strain, Young, & Horowitz, 1981) and that their families are less likely to drop out of parent training interventions (Fleischman, 1981; Scott & Stradling, 1987) than are older children and their families. However, McMahon et al. (1985) reported no differential treatment effects for their parent training program, either at posttreatment or at a 2-month follow-up, as a function of the children's age (which ranged from 3 to 8 years). Finally, based on Jacobson's (1985) descriptive investigation of child fire setters, it appears that younger children referred for fire setting (as well as children whose fire setting occurs in the presence of other conduct-disordered behaviors) have a poorer prognosis than do older children referred for this behavior. This finding is of interest, given the

results noted above for overt conduct disorders and the findings that, in general, interventions for conduct disorders seem to be more successful with preadolescents than with adolescents. Jacobson's findings may be partly a result of the fact that covert conduct disorders, for which we have less effective interventions, usually appear later in the developmental progression than do overt conduct disorders; thus, when fire setting appears at an early age, it may suggest a more serious manifestation of pathology (cf. Loeber, 1982).

Other individual-difference variables have been examined even less frequently. Strain et al. (1981, 1982) did not find children's sex or race to predict treatment outcome in the home at posttreatment or in the school and home at a 3- to 9-year follow-up. Most investigators have typically employed samples comprised entirely of boys (e.g., Patterson, 1974) or have failed to analyze their outcome data separately by sex of the children. Lochman et al. (1985) did find that lower initial levels of interpersonal problem-solving abilities and higher parental ratings of a child's somatization predicted a positive response on parental ratings of the child's aggression following participation in anger control training. With respect to cognitive interventions, Dodge (1985) has stressed the importance of the accurate identification and assessment of the particular processing deficits that are operating for an individual child. Attributional biases that arise from faulty formal information analysis should respond best to self-instructional interventions (e.g., Camp et al., 1977), whereas more affectively driven attributions indicate alternative interventions, such as extinguishing the negative affective response.

Family Characteristics

Characteristics that have been investigated include structural variables such as family composition (single-parent vs. two-parent households) and socioeconomic status; parental behavior, perceptions of the child's adjustment, and personal and marital distress; and extrafamilial characteristics such as insularity. O'Dell (1982) has delineated several other factors that may predict treatment outcome in parent training, such as parental personality traits (e.g., locus of control) and knowledge, attitudes, and beliefs (e.g., self-efficacy, parenting self-esteem). To our knowledge, none of these variables have been employed as predictors of treatment outcome.

With respect to parental behaviors, Dumas (1984b) reported that mothers classified as treatment "failures" (dropouts or inadequate improvement in child and maternal behaviors) were more aversive and indiscriminate at baseline than mothers who ultimately succeeded in the parent training program. Dropouts from this type of intervention have also been noted to emit higher rates of maternal commands (McMahon, Forehand, Griest, & Wells, 1981). Parental perceptions of children's adjustment prior to treatment have not been associated with treatment outcome (Dumas, 1984a; Dumas & Albin, 1986) or with dropout (McMahon, Forehand, Griest, & Wells, 1981), although maternal shifts to fewer blaming attributions and more specific and less global summary descriptions of the children have been shown to be associated with maintenance of treatment effects (at a 4-month follow-up) (Wahler & Afton, 1980).

The role of parental personal and marital distress in predicting treatment outcome is somewhat unclear. Maternal depression (as measured by the Beck Depression Inventory) has been shown to predict dropout (McMahon, Forehand, Griest, & Wells, 1981) and failure to participate in an 8-month follow-up assessment (Griest, Forehand, & Wells, 1981) for the Forehand and McMahon (1981) parent training program. However, maternal depression was not a significant predictor of treatment success at posttreatment or at a 1-year follow-up for Webster-Stratton (1985b). She did find that the occurrence of negative life events was a significant predictor of outcome, although the direction of prediction varied across different outcome criteria. Dumas and Albin (1986) found maternal report of psychopathological symptoms to account for 17% of the variance in predicting treatment outcome in their sample of 82 families.

For the most part, level of marital satisfaction has *not* been found to differentially affect treatment outcome and generalization at posttreatment or brief follow-up assessments (Brody & Forehand, 1985; Dadds, Schwartz, & Sanders, 1987; Forehand, Griest, Wells, & McMahon, 1982; Oltmanns, Broderick, & O'Leary, 1977). For example, Forehand et al. (1982) reported comparable improvements in parents' and children's behavior and in parental perceptions of the children's behavior at posttreatment and at a 2-month follow-up, regardless of level of marital satisfaction prior to treatment. However, Dadds, Schwartz, and Sanders (1987) failed to find maintenance of the effects of parent training at a 6-month follow-up for maritally distressed families; this suggests that, over longer periods of time, marital distress may ultimately impede temporal generalization.

Similarly, single-parent status has failed to emerge as a consistent predictor of treatment outcome when examined as an entity. Although a number of investigators have reported single-parent status to be associated with increased risk of dropping out of treatment (Oltmanns et al., 1977) or with a lack of treatment success (Dumas & Albin, 1986; Strain et al., 1981, 1982; Webster-Stratton, 1985a, 1985b), other investigators have failed to obtain similar results (e.g., Dumas & Wahler, 1983; Fleischman, 1981). In one investigation, single mothers were *less* likely to drop out than were married mothers (Scott & Stradling, 1987).

Lower socioeconomic status has been associated with subsequent dropout in at least one parent training program (McMahon, Forehand, Griest, & Wells, 1981), although for mothers who complete that program, socioeconomic status does not affect treatment outcome (Rogers et al., 1981). As noted earlier in this chapter, maternal insularity has been associated with failure to maintain improvements in parent and child behavior (Wahler, 1980; Wahler & Afton, 1980). In those earlier studies, insularity was confounded with socioeconomic disadvantage, in that all of the insular mothers were also highly disadvantaged. Dumas and Wahler (1983) conducted two studies in which they examined the relative predictive power of maternal insularity and socioeconomic disadvantage. The latter measure was a composite index comprised of six sociodemographic variables: family income, maternal education, family composition (one-parent vs. two-parent families), family size, source of referral, and area of residence. "Favorable" responders at a 1-year follow-up displayed reductions in aversive parent and child behaviors of at least 50% from baseline levels. The index of socioeconomic disadvantage and maternal insularity each contributed unique variance to predicting outcome, and together they accounted for 49% of the variance in both studies. Noninsular but disadvantaged families (or vice versa) had approximately a 50% chance of having a favorable outcome, whereas those mothers who were insular *and* disadvantaged were virtually assured of failure at the 1-year follow-up. Using a similar index of socioeconomic disadvantage, Webster-Stratton (1985b) also found this measure to be a strong predictor of outcome at posttreatment and at a 1-year follow-up for both parent and child behavior. Finally, in a study that employed causal modeling procedures, Dumas (1986) concluded that although parental perceptions of children were strongly influenced by characteristics of the children and the parents' own personal adjustment, treatment outcome was best predicted by a composite measure of socioeconomic disadvantage, which was also highly correlated with a composite measure of maternal and paternal psychopathology and family violence. It is interesting to note that use of a composite index seems to enhance predictability of treatment outcome, in that neither the individual measures making up the index (Dumas & Wahler, 1983) nor the commonly utilized combination of education and occupation (i.e., the Hollingshead index) (Webster-Stratton, 1985b) successfully predicted treatment outcome.

Therapist Characteristics

Only three sets of investigators have examined the role of therapist characteristics in predicting the outcome of behavioral interventions with conduct-disordered children or adolescents. Alexander, Barton, Schiavo, and Parsons (1976) examined the role of therapist characteristics in predicting outcome (as defined by completion of treatment and recidivism rate) for families that participated in FFT. Prior to the start of treatment, graduate student therapists were rated on a variety of characteristics that clustered into two dimensions. Relationship characteristics included affect–behavior integration, warmth, and humor, whereas Structuring characteristics included directiveness and self-confidence. The Relationship dimension accounted for 45% of the variance in predicting treatment outcome; the Structuring dimension accounted for an additional 15% of the variance. Additional research from this group suggests that therapist gender is associated with different verbal styles for mothers and adoles-

cents (but not fathers) in the first sessions of FFT (Mas, Alexander, & Barton, 1985).

Patterson and his colleagues have recently begun to examine the influence of therapist behaviors on parental noncooperation or "resistance" during treatment sessions with the parents of preadolescent conduct-disordered children. High levels of resistance in the first two therapy sessions were associated with subsequent dropout (Chamberlain, Patterson, Reid, Kavanagh, & Forgatch, 1984). Directive therapist behaviors of "teach" and "confront" increased the likelihood of parental noncooperative behavior within the session, whereas supportive and facilitative therapist behaviors had the opposite effect (Patterson & Forgatch, 1985). Patterson and Chamberlain (1988) have proposed a therapy process model (currently being tested), which postulates that these therapist behaviors play a secondary role to social (e.g., low socioeconomic status, insularity, agency referral), personal (e.g., depression, marital conflict), and child deviance factors in predicting parental noncooperativeness in the early stages of treatment, but play a primary role (along with child deviance) in predicting parental noncooperativeness in later stages of therapy. They have developed the Therapy Process Coding System, which is an adaptation of observation systems used in their earlier work, to assess therapist behavior and client cooperative and noncooperative behavior during therapy sessions. Should this model be validated, it would pose an intriguing paradox for behavioral family therapists: The directive therapist behaviors that seem to be intrinsic to behavioral parent training would also be those that predict parent noncompliance during treatment (Patterson & Forgatch, 1985). Patterson and Forgatch conclude that two sets of therapist skills are required: "standard" parent training skills, and relationship charcteristics (to use Alexander *et al.'s* [1976] term) to deal with parental noncompliance.

Researchers involved with TFM (Achievement Place) have also provided data with respect to the relationship of therapist (in this case, teaching-parent) behavior to treatment outcome (see Braukmann, Ramp, Tigner, & Wolf, 1984, for a review). As noted earlier, teaching parents undergo an intensive year-long training process. Use of the particular teaching behaviors (description, demonstration, use of rationales, providing opportunities for practicing behaviors, providing positive consequences) is positively correlated with higher levels of youth satisfaction and negatively correlated with self-reports of delinquency. Teaching parents' use of relationship-building behaviors such as joking, showing concern, and enthusiasm has also been shown to increase youths' satisfaction with the interactions (Willner et al., 1977).

Characteristics of Therapy

There has been even less research on the role of different aspects of the therapy process in predicting treatment outcome than in the other areas just reviewed. Chamberlain et al. (1984) found agency-referred families to be more resistant to therapy and thus more likely to drop out than were self-referred families (45% vs. 0% dropouts), but Dumas and Wahler (1983) reported that source of referral did not predict outcome except when it was included in the larger composite measure of socioeconomic disadvantage described above. Although Strain et al. (1981) found that families with a successful outcome attended more sessions than did treatment failures, Dumas and Albin (1986) reported that neither attendance nor completion of homework assignments was related to treatment outcome.

Lochman (1985) demonstrated that the 18-session version of his Anger Coping Program led to greater change in classroom behavior than did the 12-session version of the program. To our knowledge, this is the only investigation with conduct-disordered children that has systematically examined length of treatment as an independent variable, although Kazdin (1987) has suggested that parent training programs less than 10 hours in duration are less likely to be successful with this population.

Although there is some evidence that fathers' behavior and/or perceptions regarding their conduct-disordered children change as a function of participation in parent training interventions (e.g., Eyberg & Robinson, 1982; Taplin & Reid, 1977; Webster-Stratton, 1985a; Webster-Stratton et al., 1988), whether or not such participation enhances outcome is unclear. The relatively few studies to address this issue have generally not indicated the necessity of including the father in parent training; however, those studies suffer from a number of methodological weaknesses (small sample size, nonrandom assignment to groups, lack of follow-up data, reliance on self-report data) (Budd & O'Brien, 1982; Horton, 1984).

Comparison Studies

We divide our discussion of comparison studies into those comparing behavioral interventions with (1) no-treatment, waiting-list, attention placebo, or normal control conditions; and (2) nonbehavioral forms of treatment.

Control Conditions

Each of the three parent training programs described earlier in the chapter (Forehand & McMahon, 1981; Patterson et al., 1975; Webster-Stratton, 1987) has been positively evaluated in comparison with no-treatment and waiting-list control conditions (e.g., Peed et al., 1977; Webster-Stratton, 1984; Wiltz & Patterson, 1974) or an attention placebo condition (Walter & Gilmore, 1973). Furthermore, comparisons with groups of nonreferred "normal" children and their parents have indicated greater similarity in parent and child behaviors and/or parental perceptions of children after treatment (e.g., Forehand et al., 1980; Patterson, 1974). Other investigators have also reported the superiority of parent training over waiting-list control conditions (Bernal, Klinnert, & Schultz, 1980; Karoly & Rosenthal, 1977; Scott & Stradling, 1987), although Bernal et al. did not find any differences at posttreatment for parent and child behaviors observed in the home. However, nonrandom assignment to the waiting-list condition and other methodological difficulties limit the robustness of their findings.

Family-based interventions with adolescents have also demonstrated superiority over no-treatment control conditions. FFT (Alexander & Parsons, 1982) has been shown to lead to greater changes in family communication immediately after treatment and lower recidivism at 6–18 months posttreatment (Alexander & Parsons, 1973; Parsons & Alexander, 1973), as well as to a greater decrease in sibling involvement with the juvenile courts over a 2½- to 3½-year follow-up period (Klein et al., 1977). Parental perceptions of their adolescents' adjustment improved significantly as a function of FES therapy (Henggeler et al., 1986), whereas there was no change in a normal comparison group.

Several evaluations of school-based interventions with conduct-disordered children have employed control groups. For example, the comprehensive CLASS and RECESS programs developed by the CORBEH group have been shown to be effective compared to no-treatment control conditions (e.g., Hops et al., 1978; Walker et al., 1981, 1988), and Kent and O'Leary (1976) employed a no-treatment control group in their evaluation of a combined home–school intervention program. Forman (1980) noted greater improvements in child behavior in the classroom for both cognitive restructuring and response cost conditions, compared to an attention placebo condition.

Investigators evaluating skills training approaches to treating conduct-disordered children have, for the most part, done an exemplary job of including no-treatment and/or attention placebo comparison conditions in those evaluations. Both behavioral (e.g., Spence & Marzillier, 1981) and cognitive–behavioral (e.g., Lochman et al., 1984) interventions have consistently demonstrated superiority over the comparison conditions on a variety of measures. Unfortunately, as noted above, generalization of these effects to naturalistic settings and over time has occurred much less frequently. The setting and temporal generalization demonstrated by Kazdin et al.'s (1987a, 1987b) PSST program as compared to an attention placebo condition (and a nondirective relationship therapy intervention) is a notable exception.

The only study to employ a control condition in evaluating the effects of behavioral interventions for covert conduct disorders was Reid et al.'s (1980) investigation concerning stealing. Inclusion of a nonrandomly assigned subgroup of families that served as a waiting-list control group suggested that parental reports of decreased stealing were a function of the treatment program and not simply due to the passage of time.

Nonbehavioral Treatments

As evidence for the efficacy of various behavioral interventions with conduct-disordered children has accumulated, increased attention has been focused on the relative efficacy of these interventions compared to alternative, nonbehavioral treatments. Family-based interventions with preadolescents have been recently compared with family systems therapies (e.g., Patterson & Chamberlain, 1988; Wells &

Egan, 1988), the STEP program (Baum et al., 1986), client-centered therapy (Bernal et al., 1980), and available community mental health services (Patterson et al., 1982). With the exception of the Bernal et al. investigation, which indicated superiority of behavioral parent training over client-centered therapy on parent report measures at posttreatment but not at 6- and 12-month follow-ups, the other comparative investigations have supported the relative efficacy of behavioral parent training. It has been suggested (Wells & Forehand, 1985) that a critical factor distinguishing the Bernal et al. study from the other investigations was the former's utilization of a predetermined limited number of therapy sessions, which stands in marked contrast to the more flexible programs presented by Forehand and McMahon (1981) and Patterson et al. (1975).

Family-based interventions with adolescents have also been compared with a variety of alternative treatments. Both the OSLC program (Marlowe et al., 1988) and FES therapy (Henggeler et al., 1986) have been favorably compared with "existing mental health services" conditions, which provide the standard array of services available to delinquent adolescents in those communities. For example, in the Marlowe et al. investigation, these services included family therapy of an unspecified nature, and for many of the youths, group sessions concerning drug use. In a series of investigations examining the efficacy of FFT (Alexander & Parsons, 1973; Klein et al., 1977; Parsons & Alexander, 1973), both client-centered and psychodynamic counseling conditions were included. These alternative treatments proved to be no more effective (and sometimes less effective) than the no-treatment control condition with this sample of adolescent status offenders and their families. Barton et al. (1985) demonstrated that FFT had a lower recidivism rate for multiply offending adolescents over a 15-month follow-up period in comparison to an alternative treatment condition (primarily group homes), and Gordon and Arbuthnot (1987) have reported similar findings in comparing FFT to a probation-only condition.

Behavioral community-based residential programs such as TFM (Achievement Place; Willner et al., 1978) have not fared as well in comparison with their nonbehavioral counterparts, and have not, to our knowledge, been compared with no-treatment or attention placebo control conditions. As noted above, two different evaluations have indicated that the superiority of TFM over other types of group homes is limited, for the most part, to the period when the youths are active participants in the program (Kirigin et al., 1982; Weinrott et al., 1982).

There have been very few studies comparing nonbehavioral treatments with behavioral school-based or skills training approaches, or treatments for covert conduct disorders. Kazdin et al. (1987b) reported the superiority of PSST with inpatient children over a nondirective relationship therapy condition, both at treatment termination and at a 1-year follow-up. Children in the relationship therapy condition were rated by parents and teachers similarly to children in an attention placebo condition. Henderson (1983) presented descriptive data suggesting that children who received his behavioral ICT program engaged in stealing less frequently over a 2-year period than children who had received a variety of other interventions, singly or in combination (e.g., counseling, placement in a residential setting or special education class).

CONCLUSIONS

In this chapter, we have provided an overview of the characteristics of conduct-disordered children and their families, have outlined suggested treatment strategies and techniques, and have described and critically evaluated a variety of behavioral interventions. In this section of the chapter, we briefly summarize the most salient points of our review and provide some suggestions for future research.

It should be apparent that studies of family-based interventions with preadolescent conduct-disordered children (i.e., parent training, behavioral family therapy) not only comprise the largest and most sophisticated body of treatment research in this area, but have also presented the most promising results. Not only has immediate treatment outcome been quantified by changes in parents' and children's behavior and in parental perceptions of the children's adjustment in a large number of investigations, but generalization of such effects to the home, over reasonable follow-up periods (1 year posttreatment and longer), to untreated siblings, and to untreated behaviors has been demonstrated for many of these families as well. The

social validity of these effects has also been documented by a number of the parent training programs. Several of the most extensively validated parent training programs (Forehand & McMahon, 1981; Patterson et al., 1975; Webster-Stratton, 1987) provide commercially available therapist manuals and/or materials, which should aid in the dissemination of these programs and facilitate replication by investigators not associated with their original development and evaluation.

Investigators associated with these family-based interventions have begun to focus their attention on broadening the basic parent training model to enhance outcome and generalization. This has resulted in the assessment of a wide variety of variables in predicting the outcome of this type of intervention (the ongoing development and elaboration of which is now referred to as the behavioral family therapy model; Griest & Wells, 1983), as well as in the development of adjunctive treatment modules to deal with marital conflict, parental distress, and the like.

In contrast to family-based interventions with preadolescents, there is a smaller corpus of work with family-based treatments for conduct-disordered adolescents, and the findings have been less robust. Measures of family interaction in the home either have not been collected (e.g., Alexander & Parsons, 1973; Henggeler et al., 1986) or have failed to indicate treatment changes (e.g., Marlowe et al., 1988). Instead, laboratory-based measures of family interaction have been utilized, or there has been a heavy reliance on recidivism as a measure of treatment outcome. On these measures, however, behavioral family-based interventions have compared favorably to alternative forms of therapy (e.g., family systems, client-centered, and psychodynamic approaches; group homes) and to no-treatment control conditions. It should be noted that the most promising outcome data with this population, which come from FFT (Alexander & Parsons, 1982), have been collected primarily with families of delinquents who are status offenders. Also, the most recent revision of FFT, which has incorporated a cognitive perspective, has yet to be systematically evaluated.

Behavioral community-based residential programs, such as the TFM (Achievement Place; Willner et al., 1978), have not demonstrated their superiority to nonbehavioral interventions of this type in terms of reducing recidivism once adolescents have left the treatment setting. Although these results might be interpreted to mean that the two approaches are equally effective, a more pessimistic conclusion is that the TFM approach is not very effective in terms of temporal generalization. Systematic programming of aftercare services, involving ongoing social support strategies from family, peer, school, and community social networks (see Jenson, Hawkins, & Catalano, 1986), will probably be necessary if this and other residential programs are to have a meaningful impact on the course of conduct-disordered adolescents' behavior.

Evaluation of school-based interventions with conduct-disordered children has been hindered by a number of definitional and assessment problems. Although there have been dozens of studies documenting strategies for producing changes in "disruptive" or "acting-out" behavior in the classroom, it is unclear what proportion of the children in those studies were truly conduct-disordered. It is also important to begin to systematically examine the possibility of differential treatment effects, based on whether children's conduct-disordered behavior is expressed only in the school setting or both at school and at home (Loeber & Dishion, 1984), and to assess the possibility of generalization or behavioral contrast effects from the school to the home as a function of these school-based treatments. Attention must also be directed to evaluating the efficacy of interventions for reading disabilities and other academic difficulties specifically with conduct-disordered children.

Skills training approaches have been widely employed with conduct-disordered children and have focused on social skills, anger control, interpersonal problem solving, moral reasoning, and the like. Although evaluations of these interventions have often (but not always) demonstrated differential improvements on laboratory measures relative to no-treatment and/or attention placebo control conditions, most of the skills training approaches have failed to demonstrate a favorable outcome or evidence of generalization in more naturalistic settings. Lochman et al.'s (1987) anger coping program and Kazdin et al.'s (1987a, 1987b) PSST intervention are two promising exceptions that have marshaled somewhat greater support, although the former has yet to provide evidence of temporal generalization and the latter has relied exclusively on parent and teacher report.

However, it seems quite unrealistic to assume that altering a single skill deficit is likely to have a wide-ranging impact on youths with problems as pervasive as those typically seen in conduct-disordered populations. A more clinically defensible strategy would be the systematic evaluation of some of these interventions as adjuncts to family-based treatments (cf. Kazdin et al., 1987a), with particular attention being paid to the extent of the developmental progression of the conduct-disordered behaviors and the identification of particular deficits for individual children.

The most serious deficiency in the development of behavioral interventions for conduct-disordered children is the dearth of knowledge about the development, assessment, and treatment of covert conduct disorders, such as stealing, lying, fire setting, and substance use. Although there have been some recent advances in the conceptualization of stealing (Barth, 1987) and fire setting (Kolko & Kazdin, 1986), those models have yet to be translated into clinically useful assessment methods or treatment programs. There is little information that has been empirically evaluated to guide the clinician in the selection of treatment methods for these problems. The OSLC intervention to treat stealing (Reid et al., 1980) has not been well evaluated, and seems limited to stealing that comes to the attention of the parents. Patterson's (1986) recent longitudinal investigation would suggest that a more systematic approach to enhancing parental monitoring of the child might work to prevent the development of stealing in younger conduct-disordered children and to enhance the effectiveness of interventions to reduce stealing in youths who are just beginning to steal.

Not surprisingly, the issue of behavioral generalization from overt to covert conduct-disordered behaviors (and vice versa) has not been addressed, but it is a topic of importance for both theoretical and clinical reasons. Both Kolko (1985) and Patterson (1982) have suggested that targeting noncompliance or aggression in treatment may lead to decreases in fire setting. In line with the suggestion made in the preceding paragraph concerning parental monitoring, it may be that standard parent training programs for treating overt conduct-disordered behaviors *might* decrease stealing and other covert behaviors indirectly, as the parents become more effective monitors of their children's behavior.

It appears that, in general, behavioral interventions for the treatment of conduct disorders have been more effective with pre-adolescents than with adolescents. This finding is disheartening, but certainly not surprising. Conduct-disordered adolescents have moved farther in the developmental progression of the disorder; as a result, they present with a longer learning history of deviant behavior and typically with a broader repertoire of more serious conduct-disordered behaviors (often including those of a covert nature) than their younger counterparts. The difficulty of working with these adolescents has prompted some investigators to suggest the advisability of intervening prior to adolescence (e.g., with family-based modes of intervention) as a form of secondary prevention (e.g., Reid, 1987). This recommendation makes sense, given the strong evidence for the generalization and social validity of family-based interventions with pre-adolescent conduct-disordered children. However, despite evidence of temporal generalization, studies have not yet been conducted over a long enough time period to demonstrate that this (or any other) behavioral intervention changes the long-term negative prognosis for conduct-disordered children.

Some investigators have proposed a radical change in the way in which conduct disorders have been conceptualized, to one in which the disorder is viewed as a "social disability" (Wolf et al., 1987) or as analogous to a chronic physical disease (Kazdin, 1987). The treatment implications of such a chronic-disability model would involve a move away from single, relatively short-term interventions to multiple interventions provided sequentially throughout childhood and adolescence, and perhaps into early adulthood. The Specialized Foster Care program presented by Chamberlain (1987) is an example of this type of approach as it can be applied to conduct-disordered adolescents.

It is readily apparent that significant progress has been made and continues to be made in developing and evaluating a wide variety of interventions for treating conduct-disordered children. As the broader conceptual models of the development of conduct disorders (e.g., Patterson, 1986) and the analogous models of intervention (e.g., Griest & Wells, 1983; Kazdin, 1987) become more sophisticated and more extensively evaluated, our treatment efforts have the potential to prove more and more successful. However, a major stumbling block may prove to be the lack of a treatment selection model that is firmly based on the developmental and behavioral aspects of conduct disorders. In order to be of clinical utility, such a model must incorporate data about the subtype of conduct disorders (overt, covert, or mixed); the child's position on the developmental progression of conduct disorders; the presence or absence of various correlates or associated disorders (e.g., Attention Deficit–Hyperactivity Disorder, depression, reading disabilities, and peer relationship problems); and the child's "ecological niche" in family, school, peer, and community systems. In this way, we can begin to systematically assess the relative efficacy of various interventions (or, more likely, combinations of interventions) for particular types of conduct-disordered children as a function of their standing on these various dimensions.

Acknowledgments

Appreciation is gratefully extended to Lisa Moen and David Knipp for their assistance in the preparation of this chapter.

REFERENCES

Abramowitz, A. J., O'Leary, S. G., & Rosen, L. A. (1987). Reducing off-task behavior in the classroom: A comparison of encouragement and reprimands. *Journal of Abnormal Child Psychology, 15,* 153–163.

Achenbach, T. M., & Edelbrock, C. S. (1983). *Manual for the Child Behavior Checklist and Revised Child Behavior Profile.* Burlington: University of Vermont, Department of Psychiatry.

Achenbach, T. M., Edelbrock, C., & Howell, C. T. (1987). Empirically based assessment of the behavioral/emotional problems of 2- and 3-year-old children. *Journal of Abnormal Child Psychology, 15,* 629–650.

Acker, M. M., & O'Leary, S. G. (1987). Effects of reprimands and praise on appropriate behavior in the classroom. *Journal of Abnormal Child Psychology, 15,* 549–557.

Alexander, J. F., Barton, C., Schiavo, R. S., & Parsons, B. V. (1976). Systems–behavioral intervention with families of delinquents: Therapist characteristics, family behavior, and outcome. *Journal of Consulting and Clinical Psychology, 44,* 656–664.

Alexander, J. F., & Parsons, B. V. (1973). Short-term behavioral intervention with delinquent families: Impact on family process and recidivism. *Journal of Abnormal Psychology, 81,* 219–225.

Alexander, J. F., & Parsons, B. (1982). *Functional Family Therapy.* Monterey, CA: Brooks/Cole.

Alexander, J. F., Waldron, H. B., Barton, C., & Mas, C. H. (1987). *Minimizing blaming attributions and behaviors in conflicted delinquent families.* Manuscript submitted for publication.

Alexander, J. F., Waldron, H. B., Newberry, A. M., &

Liddle, N. (1988). Family approaches to treating delinquents. In E. W. Nunnally, C. S. Chilman, & F. M. Cox (Eds.), *Mental illness, delinquency, addictions, and neglect*. Newbury Park, CA: Sage.

American Psychiatric Association. (1980). *Diagnostic and statistical manual of mental disorders* (3rd ed.). Washington, DC: Author.

American Psychiatric Association. (1987). *Diagnostic and statistical manual of mental disorders* (3rd ed., rev.). Washington, DC: Author.

Arbuthnot, J., & Gordon, D. A. (1986). Behavioral and cognitive effects of a moral reasoning development intervention for high-risk behavior-disordered adolescents. *Journal of Consulting and Clinical Psychology, 54,* 208–216.

Arnold, J. E., Levine, A. G., & Patterson, G. R. (1975). Changes in sibling behavior following family intervention. *Journal of Consulting and Clinical Psychology, 43,* 683–688.

Atkeson, B. M., & Forehand, R. (1979). Home-based reinforcement programs designed to modify classroom behavior: A review and methodological evaluation. *Psychological Bulletin, 86,* 1298–1308.

Ayllon, T., Garber, S., & Pisor, K. (1975). The elimination of discipline problems through a combined school–home motivational system. *Behavior Therapy, 6,* 616–626.

Bailey, J. S., Wolf, M. M., & Phillips, E. L. (1970). Home-based reinforcement and the modification of predelinquents' classroom behavior. *Journal of Applied Behavior Analysis, 3,* 223–233.

Barkley, R. A. (1981). *Hyperactive children: A handbook for diagnosis and treatment*. New York: Guilford Press.

Barth, R. P. (1987). Assessment and treatment of stealing. In B. B. Lahey & A. E. Kazdin (Eds.), *Advances in clinical child psychology* (Vol. 10, pp. 137–170). New York: Plenum.

Barton, C., & Alexander, J. F. (1981). Functional Family Therapy. In A. S. Gurman & D. P. Kniskern (Eds.), *Handbook of family therapy* (pp. 403–443). New York: Brunner/Mazel.

Barton, C., Alexander, J. F., Waldron, H., Turner, C. W., & Warburton, J. (1985). Generalizing treatment effects of Functional Family Therapy: Three replications. *American Journal of Family Therapy, 13,* 16–26.

Baum, C. G., & Forehand, R. (1981). Long-term follow-up assessment of parent training by use of multiple-outcome measures. *Behavior Therapy, 12,* 643–652.

Baum, C. G., Reyna McGlone, C. L., & Ollendick, T. H. (1986, November). *The efficacy of behavioral parent training: Behavioral parent training plus clinical self-control training, and a modified STEP program with children referred for noncompliance*. Paper presented at the meeting of the Association for Advancement of Behavior Therapy, Chicago.

Beck, A. T., Rush, A. J., Shaw, B. F., & Emery, G. (1979). *Cognitive therapy of depression*. New York: Guilford Press.

Becker, W. C., Madsen, C. H., Arnold, C. R., & Thomas, D. R. (1967). The contingent use of teacher attention and praising in reducing classroom problems. *Journal of Special Education, 1,* 287–307.

Belson, W. A. (1975). *Juvenile theft: The causal factors*. London: Harper & Row.

Bernal, M. E., Klinnert, M. D., & Schultz, L. A. (1980). Outcome evaluation of behavioral parent training and client-centered parent counseling for children with conduct problems. *Journal of Applied Behavior Analysis, 13,* 677–691.

Bierman, K. L. (1983). Cognitive development and clinical interviews with children. In B. B. Lahey & A. E. Kazdin (Eds.), *Advances in clinical child psychology* (Vol. 6, pp. 217–250). New York: Plenum.

Billings, D. C., & Wasik, B. H. (1985). Self-instructional training with pre-schoolers: An attempt to replicate. *Journal of Applied Behavior Analysis, 18,* 61–67.

Blechman, E. A. (1981). Toward comprehensive behavioral family intervention: An algorithm for matching families and interventions. *Behavior Modification, 5,* 221–236.

Bornstein, P. H. (1985). Self-instructional training: A commentary and state-of-the-art. *Journal of Applied Behavior Analysis, 18,* 69–72.

Bornstein, P, H., & Quevillon, R. P. (1976). The effects of a self-instructional package on overactive preschool boys. *Journal of Applied Behavior Analysis, 9,* 179–188.

Botvin, G. J., Baker, E., Renick, N., Filazzola, A. D., & Botvin, E. M. (1984). A cognitive–behavioral approach to substance abuse prevention. *Addictive Behaviors, 9,* 137–147.

Braukmann, C. J., Ramp, K. K., Tigner, D. M., & Wolf, M. M. (1984). The Teaching-Family approach to training group-home parents: Training procedures, validation research, and outcome findings. In R. F. Dangel & R. A. Polster (Eds.), *Parent training: Foundations of research and practice* (pp. 144–161). New York: Guilford Press.

Breiner, J. L., & Forehand, R. (1981). An assessment of the effects of parent training on clinic-referred children's school behavior. *Behavioral Assessment, 3,* 31–42.

Brigham, T. A., Hopper, C., Hill, B., de Armas, A., & Newsom, P. (1985). A self-management program for disruptive adolescents in the school: A clinical replication analysis. *Behavior Therapy, 16,* 99–115.

Brody, G. H., & Forehand, R. (1985). The efficacy of parent training with maritally distressed and non-distressed mothers: A multimethod assessment. *Behaviour Research and Therapy, 23,* 291–296.

Brooks, R. B., & Snow, D. L. (1972). Two case illustrations of the use of behavior modification techniques in the school setting. *Behavior Therapy, 3,* 100–103.

Brown, P., & Elliot, R. (1965). Control of aggression in a nursery school class. *Journal of Experimental Child Psychology, 2,* 103–107.

Bry, B. H. (1985, November). *Family-based approaches to reducing adolescent substance use: Theories, techniques, and findings*. Paper presented at the Technical Review Meeting on Adolescent Drug Abuse: Analyses of Treatment Research, sponsored by the National Institute on Drug Abuse, Bethesda, MD.

Bry, B. H., Conboy, C., & Bisgay, K. (1986). Decreasing adolescent drug use and school failure: Long-term effects of targeted family problem-solving training. *Child and Family Behavior Therapy, 8(1),* 43–59.

Budd, K. S., Liebowitz, J. M., Riner, L. S., Mindell, C., & Goldfarb, A. L. (1981). Home-based treatment of severe disruptive behaviors: A reinforcement package for preschool and kindergarten children. *Behavior Modification, 5,* 273–298.

Budd, K. S., & O'Brien, T. P. (1982). Father involvement in behavioral parent training: An area in need of research. *the Behavior Therapist, 5,* 85–89.

Bumpass, E. R., Fagelman, F. D., & Brix, R. J. (1983). Intervention with children who set fires. *American Journal of Psychotherapy, 37,* 328–345.

Cadoret, R. J., Cain, C. A., & Crowe, R. R. (1983). Evidence for gene–involvement interaction in the development of adolescent antisocial behavior. *Behavior Genetics, 13,* 301–310.

Camp, B. W., Blom, G. E., Hebert, F., & van Doorninck, W. J. (1977). "Think Aloud": A program for developing self-control in young aggressive boys. *Journal of Abnormal Child Psychology, 5,* 157–169.

Carstens, C. (1982). Application of a work penalty threat in the treatment of a case of juvenile fire setting. *Journal of Behavior Therapy and Experimental Psychiatry, 13,* 159–161.

Cautela, J. R. (1967). Covert sensitization. *Psychological Record, 20,* 459–468.

Chamberlain, P. (1987, March). *The OSLC Specialized Foster Care Model.* Paper presented at the meeting of the Organizzato dalle Cattedre di Psicologia Clinica e delle Teorie di Personalita dell'Universita di Roma, Rome.

Chamberlain, P., Patterson, G., Reid, J., Kavanagh, K., & Forgatch, M. (1984). Observation of client resistance. *Behavior Therapy, 15,* 144–155.

Chamberlain, P., & Reid, J. B. (1987). Parent observation and report of child symptoms. *Behavioral Assessment, 9,* 97–109.

Chandler, M. J. (1973). Egocentrism and antisocial behavior: The assessment and training of social perspective-taking skills. *Developmental Psychology, 9,* 326–332.

Cloninger, C. R., Reich, T., & Guze, S. B. (1978). Genetic-environmental interactions and antisocial behaviour. In R. D. Hare & D. Schalling (Eds.), *Psychopathic behaviour: Approaches to research* (pp. 225–237). New York: Wiley.

Cross Calvert, S., & McMahon, R. J. (1987). The treatment acceptability of a behavioral parent training program and its components. *Behavior Therapy, 18,* 165–179.

Dadds, M. R., Sanders, M. R., Behrens, B. C., & James, J. E. (1987). Marital discord and child behavior problems: A description of family interactions during treatment. *Journal of Clinical Child Psychology, 16,* 192–203.

Dadds, M. R., Sanders, M. R., & James, J. E. (1987). The generalization of treatment effects in parent training with multidistressed parents. *Behavioural Psychotherapy, 15,* 289–313.

Dadds, M. R., Schwartz, S., & Sanders, M. R. (1987). Marital discord and treatment outcome in behavioral treatment of child conduct disorders. *Journal of Consulting and Clinical Psychology, 55,* 396–403.

Daly, R. M., Holland, C. J., Forrest, P. A., & Fellbaum, G. A. (1985). Temporal generalization of treatment effects over a three-year period for a parent training program: Directive Parental Counseling (DPC). *Canadian Journal of Behavioural Science, 17,* 379–388.

Dinkmeyer, D. (1973). *Developing understanding of self and others (DUSO).* Circle Pines, MN: American Guidance Service.

Dinkmeyer, D., & McKay, G. D. (1976). *Systematic training for effective parenting.* Circle Pines, MN: American Guidance Service.

Dishion, T., Gardner, K., Patterson, G., Reid, J., Spyrou, S., & Thibodeaux, S. (1984). *The Family Process Code: A multidimensional system for observing family interactions* (Oregon Social Learning Center Technical Report). (Available from Oregon Social Learning Center, 207 E. 5th Avenue, Suite 202, Eugene, OR 97401)

Dishion, T. J., Reid, J. B., & Patterson, G. R. (1988). Empirical guidelines for a family intervention for adolescent drug use. In R. H. Coombs (Ed.), *The family context of adolescent drug use.* New York: Haworth Press.

Dodge, K. A. (1985). Attributional bias in aggressive children. In P. C. Kendall (Ed.), *Advances in cognitive–behavioral research and therapy* (Vol. 4, pp. 73–110). New York: Academic Press.

Dumas, J. E. (1984a). Child, adult-interactional, and socioeconomic setting events as predictors of parent training outcome. *Education and Treatment of Children, 7,* 351–364.

Dumas, J. E. (1984b). Interactional correlates of treatment outcome in behavioral parent training. *Journal of Consulting and Clinical Psychology, 52,* 946–954.

Dumas, J. E. (1986). Parental perception and treatment outcome in families of aggressive children: A causal model. *Behavior Therapy, 17,* 420–432.

Dumas, J. E., & Albin, J. B. (1986). Parent training outcome: Does active parental involvement matter? *Behaviour Research and Therapy, 24,* 227–230.

Dumas, J. E., & Wahler, R. G. (1983). Predictors of treatment outcome in parent training: Mother insularity and socioeconomic disadvantage. *Behavioral Assessment, 5,* 301–313.

Dumas, J. E., & Wahler, R. G. (1985). Indiscriminate mothering as a contextual factor in aggressive-oppositional child behavior: "Damned if you do and damned if you don't." *Journal of Abnormal Child Psychology, 13,* 1–17.

Edelbrock, C. (1985). *Conduct problems in childhood and adolescence: Developmental patterns and progressions.* Unpublished manuscript.

Edelbrock, C. S., & Achenbach, T. M. (1984). The Teacher Version of the Child Behavior Profile: I. Boys aged 6–11. *Journal of Consulting and Clinical Psychology, 52,* 207–217.

Edelbrock, C., Costello, A. J., Dulcan, M. K., Kalas, D., & Conover, N. (1985). Age differences in the reliability of the psychiatric interview of the child. *Child Development, 56,* 265–275.

Embry, L. H. (1984). What to do? Matching client characteristics and intervention techniques through a prescriptive taxonomic key. In R. F. Dangel & R. A. Polster (Eds.), *Parent training: Foundations of research and practice* (pp. 443–473). New York: Guilford Press.

Executive Committee of the Council for Children with Behavioral Disorders. (1987). Position paper on definition and identification of students with behavioral disorders. *Behavioral Disorders, 13,* 9–19.

Eyberg, S. M. (1980). Eyberg Child Behavior Inventory. *Journal of Clinical Child Psychology, 9,* 29.

Eyberg, S. M., & Johnson, S. M. (1974). Multiple assessment of behavior modification with families: Effects of contingency contracting and order of treated problems. *Journal of Consulting and Clinical Psychology, 42,* 594–606.

Eyberg, S. M., & Robinson, E. A. (1982). Parent–child interaction training: Effects on family functioning. *Journal of Clinical Child Psychology, 11,* 130–137.

Eyberg, S. M., & Robinson, E. A. (1983a). Conduct problem behavior: Standardization of a behavioral rating scale with adolescents. *Journal of Clinical Child Psychology, 12,* 347–357.

Eyberg, S. M., & Robinson, E. A. (1983b). Dyadic Parent–Child Interaction Coding System: A manual. *Psychological Documents, 13,* (Ms. No. 2582)

Eyberg, S. M., & Ross, A. W. (1978). Assessment of child

behavior problems: The validation of a new inventory. *Journal of Clinical Child Psychology, 7*, 113–116.

Feindler, E. L., Ecton, R. B., Kingsley, D., & Dubey, D. R. (1986). Group anger-control training for institutionalized psychiatric male adolescents. *Behavior Therapy, 17*, 109–123.

Feindler, E. L., Marriott, S. A., & Iwata, M. (1984). Group Anger Control Training for junior high school delinquents. *Cognitive Therapy and Research, 8*, 299–311.

Fellbaum, G. A., Daly, R. M., Forrest, P., & Holland, C. J. (1985). Community implications of a home-based change program. *Journal of Community Psychology, 13*, 67–74.

Ferber, H., Keeley, S. M., & Shemberg, K. M. (1974). Training parents in behavior modification: Outcome of and problems encountered in a program after Patterson's work. *Behavior Therapy, 5*, 415–419.

Fleischman, M. J. (1981). A replication of Patterson's "Intervention for boys with conduct problems." *Journal of Consulting and Clinical Psychology, 49*, 342–351.

Fleischman, M. J., & Szykula, S. A. (1981). A community setting replication of a social learning treatment for aggressive children. *Behavior Therapy, 12*, 115–122.

Forehand, R., & Atkeson, B. M. (1977). Generality of treatment effects with parents as therapists: A review of assessment and implementation procedures. *Behavior Therapy, 8*, 575–593.

Forehand, R., Griest, D. L., Wells, K. C., & McMahon, R. J. (1982). Side effects of parent counseling on marital satisfaction. *Journal of Counseling Psychology, 29*, 104–107.

Forehand, R., Lautenschlager, G. J., Faust, J., & Graziano, W. G. (1986). Parent perceptions and parent–child interactions in clinic-referred children: A preliminary investigation of the effects of maternal depressive moods. *Behaviour Research and Therapy, 24*, 73–75.

Forehand, R., & Long, N. (1986, November). *A long-term follow-up of parent training participants.* Paper presented at the meeting of the Association for Advancement of Behavior Therapy, Chicago.

Forehand, R., & McMahon, R. J. (1981). *Helping the noncompliant child: A clinician's guide to parent training.* New York: Guilford Press.

Forehand, R., Rogers, T., McMahon, R. J., Wells, K. C., & Griest, D. L. (1981). Teaching parents to modify child behavior problems: An examination of some follow-up data. *Journal of Pediatric Psychology, 6*, 313–322.

Forehand, R., Steffe, M. A., Furey, W. A., & Walley, P. B. (1983). Mothers' evaluation of a parent training program completed three and one-half years earlier. *Journal of Behavior Therapy and Experimental Psychiatry, 14*, 339–342.

Forehand, R., Sturgis, E. T., McMahon, R. J., Aguar, D., Green, K., Wells, K., & Breiner, J. (1979). Parent behavioral training to modify child noncompliance: Treatment generalization across time and from home to school. *Behavior Modification, 3*, 3–25.

Forehand, R., Wells, K. C., & Griest, D. L. (1980). An examination of the social validity of a parent training program. *Behavior Therapy, 11*, 488–502.

Forman, S. G. (1980). A comparison of cognitive training and response cost procedures in modifying aggressive behavior of elementary school children. *Behavior Therapy, 11*, 594–600.

Fowler, S. A., Dougherty, B. S., Kirby, K. C., & Kohler, F. W. (1986). Role reversals: An analysis of therapeutic effects achieved with disruptive boys during their appointments as peer monitors. *Journal of Applied Behavior Analysis, 19*, 437–444.

Friedling, C., & O'Leary, S. G. (1979). Effects of self-instructional training on second- and third-grade hyperactive children: A failure to replicate. *Journal of Applied Behavior Analysis, 12*, 211–219.

Gardner, F. E. M. (1987). Positive interaction between mothers and conduct-problem children: Is there training for harmony as well as fighting? *Journal of Abnormal Child Psychology, 15*, 283–293.

Garrison, S. R., & Stolberg, A. L. (1983). Modification of anger in children by affective imagery training. *Journal of Abnormal Child Psychology, 11*, 115–129.

Gibbs, J. C., Arnold, K. D., Ahlborn, H. H., & Cheesman, F. L. (1984). Facilitation of sociomoral reasoning in delinquents. *Journal of Consulting and Clinical Psychology, 52*, 37–45.

Glick, B., & Goldstein, A. P. (1987). Aggression Replacement Training. *Journal of Counseling and Development, 65*, 356–362.

Goldsmith, H. H., Buss, A. H., Plomin, R., Rothbart, M. K., Thomas, A., Chess, S., Hinde, R. A., & McCall, R. B. (1987). Roundtable: What is temperament? Four approaches. *Child Development, 58*, 505–529.

Goldstein, A. P., Glick, B., Reiner, S., Zimmerman, D., & Coultry, T. (1986). *Aggression Replacement Training.* Champaign, IL: Research Press.

Goldstein, A. P., & Pentz, M. A. (1984). Psychological skill training and the aggressive adolescent. *School Psychology Review, 13*, 311–323.

Gordon, D. A., & Arbuthnot, J. (1987). Individual, group, and family interventions. In H. C. Quay (Ed.), *Handbook of juvenile delinquency* (pp. 290–324). New York: Wiley.

Greenwood, C. R., & Hops, H. (1981). Group-oriented contingencies and peer behavior change. In P. S. Strain (Ed.), *The utilization of classroom peers as behavior change agents* (pp. 189–260). New York: Plenum.

Greenwood, C. R., Hops, H., Delquadri, J., & Guild, J. (1974). Group contingencies for group consequences in classroom management: A further analysis. *Journal of Applied Behavior Analysis, 7*, 413–425.

Greenwood, C. R., Hops, H., & Walker, H. M. (1977). The durability of student behavior change: A comparative analysis at follow-up. *Behavior Therapy, 8*, 631–638.

Griest, D. L., Forehand, R., Rogers, T., Breiner, J. L., Furey, W., & Williams, C. A. (1982). Effects of Parent Enhancement Therapy on the treatment outcome and generalization of a parent training program. *Behaviour Research and Therapy, 20*, 429–436.

Griest, D. L., Forehand, R., & Wells, K. C. (1981). Follow-up assessment of parent behavioral training: An analysis of who will participate. *Child Study Journal, 11*, 221–229.

Griest, D. L., Forehand, R., Wells, K. C., & McMahon, R. J. (1980). An examination of differences between nonclinic and behavior-problem clinic-referred children and their mothers. *Journal of Abnormal Psychology, 89*, 497–500.

Griest, D. L., & Wells, K. C. (1983). Behavioral family therapy with conduct disorders in children. *Behavior Therapy, 14*, 37–53.

Hanf, C. (1969). *A two-stage program for modifying maternal controlling during mother–child (M-C) interaction* Paper presented at the meeting of the Western Psychological Association, Vancouver, British Columbia.

Hanf, C. (1970). *Shaping mothers to shape their children's behavior.* Unpublished manuscript, University of Oregon Medical School.

Hanf, C., & Kling, J. (1973). *Facilitating parent-child interactions: A two-stage training model.* Unpublished manuscript, University of Oregon Medical School.

Harris, A., Kreil, D., & Orpet, R. (1977). The modification and validation of the Behavior Coding System for school settings. *Educational and Psychological Measurement, 37,* 1121–1126.

Henderson, J. Q. (1981). A behavioral approach to stealing: A proposal for treatment based on ten cases. *Journal of Behavior Therapy and Experimental Psychiatry, 12,* 231–236.

Henderson, J. Q. (1983). Follow-up of stealing behavior in 27 youths after a variety of treatment programs. *Journal of Behavior Therapy and Experimental Psychiatry, 14,* 331–337.

Henggeler, S. W. (1982). The family–ecological systems theory. In S. W. Henggeler (Ed.), *Delinquency and adolescent psychopathology: A family–ecological systems approach* (pp. 1–10). Littleton, MA: Wright–PSG.

Henggeler, S. W., Rodick, J. D., Borduin, C. M., Hanson, C. L., Watson, S. M., & Urey, J. R. (1986). Multisystemic treatment of juvenile offenders: Effects on adolescent behavior and family interaction. *Developmental Psychology, 22,* 132–141.

Hinshaw, S. P. (1987). On the distinction between attentional deficits/hyperactivity and conduct problems/aggression in child psychopathology. *Psychological Bulletin, 101,* 443–463.

Holland, C. J. (1969). Elimination by the parents of firesetting behaviour in a 7 year-old boy. *Behaviour Research and Therapy. 7,* 135–137.

Hops, H., Walker, H. M., Fleischman, D. H., Nagoshi, J. T., Omura, R. T., Skindrud, K., & Taylor, J. (1978). CLASS: A standardized in-class program for acting-out children. II. Field test evaluations. *Journal of Educational Psychology, 70,* 636–644.

Horne, A. M., & Van Dyke, B. (1983). Treatment and maintenance of social learning family therapy. *Behavior Therapy, 14,* 606–613.

Horton, L. (1984). The father's role in behavioral parent training: A review. *Journal of Clinical Child Psychology, 13,* 274–279.

Humphreys, L., Forehand, R., McMahon, R., & Roberts, M. (1978). Parent behavioral training to modify child noncompliance: Effects on untreated siblings. *Journal of Behavior Therapy and Experimental Psychiatry, 9,* 235–238.

Iwata, B. A., & Bailey, J. S. (1974). Reward versus cost token systems: An analysis of the effects on students and teacher. *Journal of Applied Behavior Analysis, 7,* 567–576.

Jacobson, R. R. (1985). Child firesetters: A clinical investigation. *Journal of Child Psychology and Psychiatry, 26,* 759–768.

Jary, M. L., & Stewart, M. A. (1985). Psychiatric disorder in the parents of adopted children with aggressive conduct disorder. *Neuropsychobiology, 13,* 7–11.

Jenson, J. M., Hawkins, J. D., & Catalano, R. F. (1986). Social support in aftercare services for troubled youth. *Children and Youth Services Review, 8,* 323–347.

Johnson, S. M., Bolstad, O. D., & Lobitz, G. K. (1976). Generalization and contrast phenomena in behavior modification with children. In L. A. Hamerlynck, L. C.

Handy, & E. J. Mash (Eds.), *Behavior modification and families* (pp. 160–188). New York: Brunner/Mazel.

Jones, F. D. E. (1981). Therapy for firesetters. *American Journal of Psychiatry, 138,* 261–262

Jones, R. R. (1974). *"Observation" by telephone: An economical behavior sampling technique* (Oregon Research Institute Technical Report, Vol. 14, No. 1). Eugene: Oregon Research Institute.

Jones, R. T., & Kazdin, A. E. (1981). Childhood behavior problems in the school.. In S. M. Turner, K. S. Calhoun, & H. E. Adams (Eds.), *Handbook of clinical behavior therapy* (pp. 568–606). New York: Wiley.

Jurkovic, G. J. (1980). The juvenile delinquent as a moral philosopher: A structural–developmental perspective. *Psychological Bulletin, 88,* 709–727.

Karoly, P., & Rosenthal, M. (1977). Training parents in behavior modification: Effects on perceptions of family interaction and deviant child behavior. *Behavior Therapy, 8,* 406–410

Kaufman, K. F., & O'Leary, K. D. (1972). Reward, cost, and self-evaluation procedures for disruptive adolescents in a psychiatric hospital school. *Journal of Applied Behavior Analysis, 5,* 293–309.

Kazdin, A. E. (1977). *The token economy: A reveiw and evaluation.* New York: Plenum.

Kazdin, A. E. (1985). *Treatment of antisocial behavior in children and adolescents.* Homewood, IL: Dorsey Press.

Kazdin, A. E. (1987). Treatment of antisocial behavior in children: Current status and future directions. *Psychological Bulletin, 102,* 187–203.

Kazdin, A. E., & Bootzin, R. R. (1972). The token economy: An evaluative review. *Journal of Applied Behavior Analysis, 5,* 343–372.

Kazdin, A. E., Esveldt-Dawson, K., French, N. H., & Unis, A. S. (1987a). Effects of parent management training and problem-solving skills training combined in the treatment of antisocial child behavior. *Journal of the American Aademy of Child and Adolescent Psychiatry, 26,* 416–424.

Kazdin, A. E., Esveldt-Dawson, K., French, N. H., & Unis, A. S. (1987b). Problem-solving skills training and relationship therapy in the treatment of antisocial child behavior. *Journal of Consulting and Clinical Psychology, 55,* 76–85.

Kazdin, A. E., & Heidish, I. E. (1984). Convergence of clinically derived diagnoses and parent checklists among inpatient children. *Journal of Abnormal Child Psychology, 12,* 421–436.

Kazdin, A. E., & Kolko, D. J. (1986). Parent psychopathology and family functioning among childhood firesetters. *Journal of Abnormal Child Psychology, 14,* 315–329.

Kendall, P. C., & Braswell, L. (1985). *Cognitive–behavioral therapy for impulsive children.* New York: Guilford Press.

Kent, R. N., & O'Leary, K. D. (1976). A controlled evaluation of behavior modification with conduct problem children. *Journal of Consulting and Clinical Psychology, 44,* 586–596.

Kettlewell, P. W., & Kausch, D. F. (1983). The generalization of the effects of a cognitive–behavioral treatment program for aggressive children. *Journal of Abnormal Child Psychology, 11,* 101–114.

Kirigin, K. A., Braukmann, C. J., Atwater, J. D., & Wolf, M. M. (1982). An evaluation of Teaching-Family (Achievement Place) group homes for juvenile offenders. *Journal of Applied Behavior Analysis, 15,* 1–16.

Klein, N. C., Alexander, J. F., & Parsons, B. V. (1977). Impact of family systems intervention on recidivism and sibling delinquency: A model of primary prevention and program evaluation. *Journal of Consulting and Clinical Psychology, 45,* 469–474.

Klein, R. D. (1979). Modifying academic performance in the grade school classroom. In M. Hersen, R. M. Eisler, & P. M. Miller (Eds.), *Progress in behavior modification* (Vol. 8, pp. 293–321). New York: Academic Press.

Kolko, D. J. (1983). Multicomponent parental treatment of firesetting in a six year old boy. *Journal of Behavior Therapy and Experimental Psychiatry, 14,* 349–353.

Kolko, D. J. (1985). Juvenile firesetting: A review and methodological critique. *Clinical Psychology Review, 5,* 345–376.

Kolko, D. J., & Kazdin, A. E. (1986). A conceptualization of firesetting in children and adolescents. *Journal of Abnormal Child Psychology, 14,* 49–61.

Kolko, D. J., Kazdin, A. E., & Meyer, E. C. (1985). Aggression and psychopathology in childhood firesetters: Parent and child reports. *Journal of Consulting and Clinical Psychology, 53,* 377–385.

Kuypers, D. S., Becker, W. C., & O'Leary, K. D. (1968). How to make a token system fail. *Exceptional Children, 11,* 101–108.

Lahey, B. B., Gendrich, J. G., Gendrich, S. I., Schnelle, J. F., Gant, D. S., & McNees, M. P. (1977). An evaluation of daily report cards with minimal teacher and parent contacts as an efficient method of classroom intervention. *Behavior Modification, 1,* 381–394.

Lochman, J. E. (1985). Effects of different treatment lengths in cognitive behavioral interventions with aggressive boys. *Child Psychiatry and Human Development, 16,* 45–56.

Lochman, J. E., Burch, P. R., Curry, J. F., & Lampron, L B. (1984). Treatment and generalization effects of cognitive–behavioral and goal-setting interventions with aggressive boys. *Journal of Consulting and Clinical Psychology, 52,* 915–916.

Lochman, J. E., & Curry, J. F. (1986). Effects of social problem-solving training and self-instruction training with aggressive boys. *Journal of Clinical Child Psychology, 15,* 159–164.

Lochman, J. E., & Lampron, L. B. (1986). Situational social problem-solving skills and self-esteem of aggressive and nonaggressive boys. *Journal of Abnormal Child Psychology, 14,* 605–617.

Lochman, J. E., Lampron, L. B., Burch, P. R., & Curry, J. F. (1985). Client characteristics associated with behavior change for treated and untreated aggressive boys. *Journal of Abnormal Child Psychology, 13,* 527–538.

Lochman, J. E., Lampron, L. B., Gemmer, T. C., & Harris, S. R. (1987). Anger coping intervention with aggressive children: A guide to implementation in school settings. In P. A. Keller & S. R. Heyman (Eds.), *Innovations in clinical practice: A source book* (Vol. 6, pp. 339–356). Sarasota, FL: Professional Resource Exchange.

Lochman, J. E., Nelson, W. M., & Sims, J. P. (1981). A cognitive behavioral program for use with aggressive children. *Journal of Clinical Child Psychology, 10,* 146–148.

Locke, H. J., & Wallace, K. M. (1959). Short marital-adjustment and prediction tests: Their reliability and validity. *Marriage and Family Living, 21,* 251–255.

Loeber, R. (1982). The stability of antisocial and delinquent child behavior: A review. *Child Development, 53,* 1431–1446.

Loeber, R. (in press). Natural histories of juvenile conduct problems, substance use, and delinquency: Evidence for developmental progressions. In B. B. Lahey & A. E. Kazdin (Eds.), *Advances in clinical child psychology* (Vol. 11). New York: Plenum.

Loeber, R., & Dishion, T. S. (1983). Early predictors of male delinquency: A review. *Psychological Bulletin, 94,* 68–99.

Loeber, R., & Dishion, T. J. (1984). Boys who fight at home and school: Family conditions influencing cross-setting consistency. *Journal of Consulting and Clinical Psychology, 52,* 759–768.

Loeber, R., Dishion, T. J., & Patterson, G. R. (1984). Multiple gating: A multistage assessment procedure for identifying youths at risk for delinquency. *Journal of Research in Crime and Delinquency, 21,* 7–32.

Loeber, R., & Schmaling, K. B. (1985a). Empirical evidence for overt and covert patterns of antisocial conduct problems: A meta-analysis. *Journal of Abnormal Child Psychology, 13,* 337–352.

Loeber, R., & Schmaling, K. B. (1985b). The utility of differentiating between mixed and pure forms of antisocial child behavior. *Journal of Abnormal Child Psychology, 13,* 315–336.

Loeber, R., & Stouthamer-Loeber, M. (1986). Family factors as correlates and predictors of juvenile conduct problems and delinquency. In M. Tonry & N. Morris (Eds.), *Crime and justice* (Vol. 7, pp. 29–149). Chicago: University of Chicago Press.

Loeber, R., Weissman, W., & Reid, J. B. (1983). Family interactions of assaultive adolescents, stealers, and non-delinquents. *Journal of Abnormal Child Psychology, 11,* 1–14.

Loyd, B. H., & Abidin, R. R. (1985). Revision of the Parenting Stress Index. *Journal of Pediatric Psychology, 10,* 169–177.

Lyman, R. D. (1984). The effect of private and public goal setting on classroom on-task behavior of emotionally disturbed children. *Behavior Therapy, 15,* 395–402.

MacFarlane, J., Allen, L., & Honzik, M. (1954). *A developmental study of the behavior problems of normal children between 21 months and 14 years.* Berkeley: University of California Press.

Maisto, S. A., & Carey, K. B. (1985). Origins of alcohol abuse in children and adolescents. In B. B. Lahey & A. E. Kazdin (Eds.), *Advances in clinical child psychology* (Vol. 8, pp. 149–198). New York: Plenum.

Marlowe, H., Reid, J. B., Patterson, G. R., Weinrott, M. R., & Bank, L. (1988). *A comparative evaluation of parent training for families of chronic delinquents.* Manuscript submitted for publication.

Mas, C. H., Alexander, J. F., & Barton, C. (1985). Modes of expression in family therapy: A process study of roles and gender. *Journal of Marital and Family Therapy, 11,* 411–415.

Mash, E. J. (1985). Some comments on target selection in behavior therpay. *Behavioral Assessment, 7,* 49–64.

McGrath, P., Marshall, P. T., & Prior, K. (1979). A comprehensive treatment program for a fire setting child. *Journal of Behavior Therapy and Experimental Psychiatry, 10,* 69–72.

McMahon, R. J. (1984). Behavioral checklists and rating scales. In T. H. Ollendick & M. Hersen (Eds.), *Child behavioral assessment: Principles and procedures* (pp. 80–105). New York: Pergamon Press.

McMahon, R. J. (1987). Some current issues in the behavioral assessment of conduct disordered children and their families. *Behavioral Assessment, 9,* 235–252.

McMahon, R. J., & Forehand, R. (1983). Consumer satisfaction in behavioral treatment of children: Types, issues, and recommendations. *Behavior Therapy, 14,* 209–225.

McMahon, R. J., & Forehand, R. (1984). Parent training for the noncompliant child: Treatment outcome, generalization, and adjunctive therapy procedures. In R. F. Dangel & R. A. Polster (Eds.), *Parent training: Foundations of research and practice* (pp. 298–328). New York: Guilford Press.

McMahon, R. J., & Forehand, R. (1988). Conduct disorders. In E. J. Mash & L. G. Terdal (Eds.), *Behavioral assessment of childhood disorders* (2nd ed., pp. 105–153). New York: Guilford Press.

McMahon, R. J., Forehand, R., & Griest, D. L. (1981). Effects of knowledge of social learning principles on enhancing treatment outcome and generalization in a parent training program. *Journal of Consulting and Clinical Psychology, 49,* 526–532.

McMahon, R. J., Forehand, R., Griest, D. L., & Wells, K. C. (1981). Who drops out of treatment during parent behavioral training? *Behavioral Counseling Quarterly, 1,* 79–85.

McMahon, R. J., Forehand, R., & Tiedemann, G. L. (1985, November). *Relative effectiveness of a parent training program with children of different ages.* Paper presented at the meeting of the Association for Advancement of Behavior Therapy, Houston.

McMahon, R. J., Tiedemann, G. L., Forehand, R., & Griest, D. L., (1984). Parental satisfaction with parent training to modify child noncompliance. *Behavior Therapy, 15,* 295–303.

Meichenbaum, D., & Goodman, J. (1971). Training impulsive children to talk to themselves: A means of developing self-control. *Journal of Abnormal Psychology, 77,* 115–126.

Miller, G. E., & Klungness, L. (1986). Treatment of nonconformative stealing in school-age children. *School Psychology Review, 15,* 24–35.

Moore, D., Chamberlain, P., & Mukai, L. (1979). Children at risk for delinquency: A follow-up comparison of aggressive children and children who steal. *Journal of Abnormal Child Psychology, 7,* 345–355.

Moore, D. R., & Mukai, L. H. (1983). Aggressive behavior in the home as a function of the age and sex of control-problem and normal children. *Journal of Abnormal Child Psychology, 11,* 257–272.

Morris, S. B., Alexander, J. F., & Waldron, H. (1988). Functional Family Therapy. In I. R. H. Falloon (Ed.), *Handbook of behavioral family therapy* (pp. 107–127). New York: Guilford Press.

O'Dell, S. L. (1974). Training parents in behavior modification: A review. *Psychological Bulletin, 81,* 418–433.

O'Dell, S. L. (1982). Enhancing parent involvement in training: A discussion. *the Behavior Therapist, 5,* 9–13.

O'Dell, S. L. (1985). Progress in parent training. In M. Hersen, R. M. Eisler, & P. M. Miller (Eds.), *Progress in behavior modification* (Vol. 9, pp. 57–108). New York: Academic Press.

O'Leary, K. D., & Becker, W. C. (1967). Behavior modification of an adjustment class: A token reinforcement program. *Exceptional Children, 9,* 637–642.

O'Leary, K. D., Becker, W. C., Evans, M. B., & Saudargas, R. A. (1969). A token reinforcement program in a public school: A replication and systematic analysis. *Journal of Applied Behavior Analysis, 2,* 3–13.

O'Leary, K. D., & Drabman, R. (1971). Token reinforcement programs in the classroom: A review. *Psychological Bulletin, 75,* 379–398.

O'Leary, K. D., & O'Leary, S. G. (1977). *Classroom management: The successful use of behavior modification* (2nd ed.). New York: Pergamon Press.

Oltmanns, T. F., Broderick, J. E., & O'Leary, K. D. (1977). Marital adjustment and the efficacy of behavior therapy with children. *Journal of Consulting and Clinical Psychology, 45,* 724–729.

Olweus, D. (1979). Stability of aggressive reaction patterns in males: A review. *Psychological Bulletin, 86,* 852–857.

Olweus, D. (1980). Familial and temperamental determinants of aggressive behavior in adolescent boys: A causal analysis. *Developmental Psychology, 16,* 644–660.

Parsons, B. V., & Alexander, J. F. (1973). Short-term family intervention: A therapy outcome study. *Journal of Consulting and Clinical Psychology, 41,* 195–201.

Patterson, G. R. (1974). Interventions for boys with conduct problems: Multiple settings, treatments, and criteria. *Journal of Consulting and Clinical Psychology, 42,* 471–481.

Patterson, G. R. (1975a). *Families: Applications of social learning to family life* (rev. ed.). Champaign, IL: Research Press.

Patterson, G. R. (1975b). *Professional guide for* Families *and* Living with Children. Champaign, IL: Research Press.

Patterson, G. R. (1976a). The aggressive child: Victim and architect of a coercive system. In E. J. Mash, L. A. Hamerlynck, & L. C. Handy (Eds.), *Behavior modification and families* (pp. 267–316). New York: Brunner/Mazel.

Patterson, G. R. (1976b). *Living with children: New methods for parents and teachers* (rev. ed.). Champaign, IL: Research Press.

Patterson, G. R. (1982). *Coercive family process.* Eugene, OR: Castalia.

Patterson, G. R. (1983). Stress: A change agent for family process. In N. Garmezy & M. Rutter (Eds.), *Stress, coping and development in children* (pp. 235–262). New York: McGraw-Hill.

Patterson, G. R. (1986). Performance models for antisocial boys. *American Psychologist, 41,* 432–444.

Patterson, G. R., & Bank, L. (1986). Bootstrapping your way in the nomological thicket. *Behavioral Assessment, 8,* 49–73.

Patterson, G. R., & Chamberlain, P. (1988). Treatment process: A problem at three levels. In L. C. Wynne (Ed.), *The state of the art in family therapy research: Controversies and recommendations* (pp. 189–223). New York: Family Process Press.

Patterson, G. R., Chamberlain, P., & Reid, J. B. (1982). A comparative evaluation of a parent training program. *Behavior Therapy, 13,* 638–650.

Patterson, G. R., Cobb, J. A., & Ray, R. S. (1973). A social engineering technology for retraining the families of aggressive boys. In H. E. Adams & I. P. Unikel (Eds.), *Issues and trends in behavior therapy* (pp. 139–210). Springfield, IL: Charles C Thomas.

Patterson, G. R., & Dishion, T. J. (1985). Contributions of families and peers to delinquency. *Criminology, 23,* 63–79.

Patterson, G. R., & Fleischman, M. J. (1979). Maintenance of treatment effects: Some considerations concerning family systems and follow-up data. *Behavior Therapy, 10,* 168–185.

Patterson, G. R. & Forgatch, M. S. (1985). Therapist behavior as a determinant for client noncompliance: A paradox for the behavior modifier. *Journal of Consulting and Clinical Psychology, 53,* 846–851.

Patterson, G. R., Ray, R. S., Shaw, D. A., & Cobb, J. A. (1969). *Manual for coding of family interactions* (rev. ed.). New York: Microfiche Publications.

Patterson, G. R., & Reid, J. B. (1973). Intervention for families of aggressive boys: A replication study. *Behaviour Research and Therapy, 11,* 383–394.

Patterson, G. R., Reid, J. B., Jones, R. R., & Conger, R. E. (1975). *A social learning approach to family intervention: Vol. 1. Families with aggressive children.* Eugene, OR: Castalia.

Peed, S., Roberts, M., & Forehand, R. (1977). Evaluation of the effectiveness of a standardized parent training program in altering the interaction of mothers and their noncompliant children. *Behavior Modification, 1,* 323–350.

Pfiffner, L. J., O'Leary, S. G., Rosén, L. A., & Sanderson, W. C. (1985). A comparison of the effects of continuous and intermittent response cost and reprimands in the classroom. *Journal of Clinical Child Psychology, 14,* 348–352.

Pfiffner, L. J., Rosén, L. A., & O'Leary, S. G. (1985). The efficacy of an all-positive approach to classroom management. *Journal of Applied Behavior Analysis, 18,* 257–261.

Pigott, H. E., & Hèggie, D. L. (1986). Interpreting the conflicting results of individual versus group contingencies in classrooms: The targeted behavior as a mediating variable. *Child and Family Behavior Therapy, 7,* 1–14.

Plomin, R. (1981). Heredity and temperament: A comparison of twin data for self-report questionnaires, parental ratings and objectively assessed behavior. In L. Gedda, P. Parisi, & W. E. Nance (Eds.), *Progress in clinical and biological research: Vol. 69B. Twin research 3, Part B. Intelligence, personality, and development* (pp. 269–278). New York: Alan R. Liss.

Plomin, R. (1983). Childhood temperament. In B. B. Lahey & A. E. Kazdin (Eds.), *Advances in clinical child psychology* (Vol. 6, pp. 45–92). New York: Plenum.

Porter, B., & O'Leary, K. D. (1980). Marital discord and childhood behavior problems. *Journal of Abnormal Child Psychology, 8,* 287–295.

Quay, H. C. (1986a). Classification. In H. C. Quay & J. S. Werry (Eds.), *Psychopathological disorders of childhood* (3rd ed., pp. 1–34). New York: Wiley.

Quay, H. C. (1986b). Conduct disorders. In H. C. Quay & J. S. Werry (Eds.), *Psychopathological disorders of childhood* (3rd ed., pp. 35–72). New York: Wiley.

Reed, M. L., & Edelbrock, C. (1983). Reliability and validity of the Direct Observation Form of the Child Behavior Checklist. *Journal of Abnormal Child Psychology, 11,* 521–530.

Reid, J. B. (Ed.). (1978). *A social learning approach to family intervention: Vol. 2. Observation in home settings.* Eugene, OR: Castalia.

Reid, J. B. (1984, November). Stealing and other clandestine activities among antisocial children. In D. J. Kolko (Chair), *Child antisocial behavior research: Current status and implications.* Symposium conducted at the meeting of the Association for Advancement of Behavior Therapy, Philadelphia.

Reid, J. B. (1987, March). *Therapeutic interventions in the families of aggressive children and adolescents.* Paper presented at the meeting of the Organizzato dalle Cattedre di Psicologia Clinica e delle Teorie di Personalita dell'Universita di Roma, Rome.

Reid, J. B., Baldwin, D. V., Patterson, G. R., & Dishion, T. J. (1988). Observations in the assessment of childhood disorders. In M. Rutter, A. H. Tuma, & I. S. Lann (Eds.), *Assessment and diagnosis in child psychopathology* (pp. 156–195). New York: Guilford Press.

Reid, J. B., & Hendricks, A. F. C. J. (1973). A preliminary analysis of the effectiveness of direct home intervention for treatment of pre-delinquent boys who steal. In L. A. Hamerlynck, L. C. Handy, & E. J. Mash (Eds.), *Behavior change: Methodology, concepts, and practice* (pp. 209–220). Champaign, IL: Research Press.

Reid, J. B., Hinojosa Rivera, G., & Lorber, R. (1980). *A social learning approach to the outpatient treatment of children who steal.* Unpublished manuscript, Oregon Social Learning Center, Eugene.

Richard, B. A., & Dodge, K. A. (1982). Social maladjustment and problem solving in school-aged children. *Journal of Consulting and Clinical Psychology, 50,* 226–233.

Robins, L. N. (1966). *Deviant children grown up.* Baltimore: Williams & Wilkins.

Robins, L. N. (1970). The adult development of the antisocial child. *Seminars in Psychiatry, 2,* 420–434.

Robinson, E. A., Eyberg, S. M., & Ross, A. W. (1980). The standardization of an inventory of child conduct problem behaviors. *Journal of Clinical Child Psychology, 9,* 22–29.

Rogers, T. R., Forehand, R., & Griest, D. L. (1981). The conduct disordered child: An analysis of family problems. *Clinical Psychology Review, 1,* 139–147.

Rogers, T. R., Forehand, R., Griest, D. L., Wells, K. C., & McMahon, R. J. (1981). Socioeconomic status: Effects on parent and child behaviors and treatment outcome of parent training. *Journal of Clinical Child Psychology, 10,* 98–101.

Rosen, H. S., & Rosen, L. A. (1983). Eliminating stealing: Use of stimulus control with an elementary student. *Behavior Modification, 7,* 56–63.

Rosén, L. A., O'Leary, S. G., Joyce, S. A., Conway, G., & Pfiffner, L. J. (1984). The importance of prudent negative consequences for maintaining the appropriate behavior of hyperactive students. *Journal of Abnormal Child Psychology, 12,* 581–604.

Russo, D. C., Cataldo, M. F., & Cushing, P. J. (1981). Compliance training and behavioral covariation in the treatment of multiple behavior problems. *Journal of Applied Behavior Analysis, 14,* 209–222.

Rutter, M. (1970). Sex differences in children's responses to family stress. In E. J. Anthony & C. Koupernik (Eds.), *International yearbook for child psychiatry and allied disciplines: Vol. 1. The child in his family* (pp. 165–196). New York: Wiley.

Rutter, M., Tizard, J., Yule, W., Graham, P., & Whitmore, K. (1976). Research report: Isle of Wight studies, 1964–1974. *Psychological Medicine, 6,* 313–332.

Sanders, M. R. (1982). The generalization of parent responding to community settings: The effects of instructions, plus feedback, and self-management training. *Behavioural Psychotherapy, 10,* 273–287.

Sanders, M. R., & Christensen, A. P. (1985). A comparison of the effects of child management and planned activities training in five parenting environments. *Journal of Abnormal Child Psychology, 13,* 101–117.

Sanders, M. R., & Dadds, M. R. (1982). The effects of

planned activities and child management procedures in parent training: An analysis of setting generality. *Behavior Therapy, 13,* 452–461.

Sanders, M. R., & Glynn, T. (1981). Training parents in behavioral self management: An analysis of generalization and maintenance. *Journal of Applied Behavior Analysis, 14,,* 223–237.

Schleser, R., & Rodick, J. D. (1982). A comparison of traditional family therapy models and the family–ecological systems approach. In S. W. Henggeler (Ed.), *Delinquency and adolescent psychopathology: A family–ecological systems approach* (pp. 11–26). Littleton, MA: Wright–PSG.

Schumaker, J. B., Hovell, M. F., & Sherman, J. A. (1977). An analysis of daily report cards and parent-managed privileges in the improvement of adolescents' classroom performance. *Journal of Applied Behavior Analysis, 10,* 449–464.

Scott, M. J., & Stradling, S. G. (1987). Evaluation of a group programme for parents of problem children. *Behavioural Psychotherapy, 15,* 224–239.

Shanok, S. S., & Lewis, D. O. (1981). Medical histories of female delinquents: Clinical and epidemiological findings. *Archives of General Psychiatry, 38,* 211–213.

Spanier, G. B. (1976). Measuring dyadic adjustment: New scales for assessing the quality of marriage and similar dyads. *Journal of Marriage and the Family, 38,* 15–28.

Spence, S. H., & Marzillier, J. S. (1981). Social skills training with adolescent male offenders: II. Short-term, long-term, and generalized effects. *Behaviour Research and Therapy, 19,* 349–368.

Spivack, G., Platt, J. J., & Shure, M. B. (1976). *The problem solving approach to adjustment.* San Francisco: Jossey-Bass.

Stawar, T. L. (1976). Fable mod: Operantly structured fantasies as an adjunct in the modification of fire-setting behavior. *Journal of Behavior Therapy and Experimental Psychiatry, 7,* 285–287.

Stouthamer-Loeber, M. (1986). Lying as a problem behavior in children: A review. *Clinical Psychology Review, 6,* 267–289.

Stouthamer-Loeber, M., & Loeber, R. (1986). Boys who lie. *Journal of Abnormal Child Psychology, 14,* 551–564.

Strain, P. S., Lambert, D. L., Kerr, M. M., Stagg, V., & Lenkner, D. A. (1983). Naturalistic assessment of children's compliance to teachers' requests and consequences for compliance. *Journal of Applied Behavior Analysis, 16,* 243–249.

Strain, P. S., Steele, P., Ellis, T., & Timm, M. A. (1982). Long-term effects of oppositional child treatment with mothers as therapists and therapist trainers. *Journal of Applied Behavior Analysis, 15,* 163–169.

Strain, P. S., Young, C. C., & Horowitz, J. (1981). Generalized behavior change during oppositional child training: An examination of child and family demographic variables. *Behavior Modification, 5,* 15–26.

Stumpf, J., & Holman, J. (1985). Promoting generalization of appropriate classroom behaviour: A comparison of two strategies. *Behavioural Psychotherapy, 13,* 29–42.

Stumphauzer, J. S. (1976). Elimination of stealing by self-reinforcement of alternative behavior and family contracting. *Journal of Behavior Therapy and Experimental Psychiatry, 7,* 265–268.

Switzer, E. B., Deal, T. E., & Bailey, J. S. (1977). The reduction of stealing in second graders using a group

contingency. *Journal of Applied Behavior Analysis, 10,* 267–272.

Taplin, P. S., & Reid, J. B. (1977). Changes in parent consequences as a function of family intervention. *Journal of Consulting and Clinical Psychology, 45,* 973–981.

Teicher, J. D., Sinay, R. D., & Stumphauzer, J. S. (1976). Training community-based paraprofessionals as behavior therapists with families of alcohol-abusing adolescents. *American Journal of Psychiatry, 133,* 847–850.

Thomas, A., Chess, S., & Birch, H. G. (1968). *Temperament and behavior disorders in children.* New York: New York University Press.

Trites, R. L., Dugas, E., Lynch, G., & Ferguson, H. B. (1979). Prevalence of hyperactivity. *Journal of Pediatric Psychology, 4,* 179–188.

Vaughn, B. E., Bradley, C. F., Joffe, L. S., Seifer, R., & Barglow, P. (1987). Maternal characteristics measured prenatally are predictive of ratings of temperamental "difficulty" on the Carey Infant Temperament Questionnaire. *Developmental Psychology, 23,* 152–161.

Vreeland,, R. G., & Waller, M. B. (1980, September). *Social interactions in families of firesetting children.* Paper presented at the meeting of the American Psychological Association, Montreal.

Wahler, R. G. (1969a). Oppositional children: A quest for parental reinforcement control. *Journal of Applied Behavior Analysis, 2,* 159–170.

Wahler, R. G. (1969b). Setting generality: Some specific and general effects of child behavior therapy. *Journal of Applied Behavior Analysis, 2,* 239–246.

Wahler, R. G. (1975). Some structural aspects of deviant child behavior. *Journal of Applied Behavior Analysis, 8,* 27–42.

Wahler, R. G. (1980). The insular mother: Her problems in parent–child treatment. *Journal of Applied Behavior Analysis, 13,* 207–219.

Wahler, R. G., & Afton, A. D. (1980). Attentional processes in insular and noninsular mothers. *Child Behavior Therapy, 2(2),* 25–41.

Wahler, R. G., & Cormier, W. H. (1970). The ecological interview: A first step in out-patient child behavior therapy. *Journal of Behavior Therapy and Experimental Psychiatry, 1,* 279–289.

Wahler, R. G., & Dumas, J. E. (1984). Changing the observational coding styles of insular and noninsular mothers: A step toward maintenance of parent training effects. In R. F. Dangel & R. A. Polster (Eds.), *Parent training: Foundations of research and practice* (pp. 379–416). New York: Guilford Press.

Wahler, R. G., House, A. E., & Stambaugh, E. E. (1976). *Ecological assessment of child problem behavior: A clinical package for home, school, and institutional settings.* New York: Pergamon Press.

Wahler, R. G., Leske, G., & Rogers, E. S. (1979). The insular family: A deviance support system for oppositional children. In L. A. Hamerlynck (Ed.), *Behavioral systems for the developmentally disabled: Vol. 1. School and family environments* (pp. 102–127). New York: Brunner/Mazel.

Walker, H. M., & Buckley, N. K. (1972). Programming generalization and maintenance of treatment effects across time and across settings. *Journal of Applied Behavior Analysis, 5,* 209–224.

Walker, H. M., & Fabre, T. R. (1987). Assessment of behavior disorders in the school setting: Issues, problems, and strategies revisited. In N. G. Haring (Ed.),

Assessing and managing behavior disabilities (pp. 198–243). Seattle: University of Washington Press.

Walker, H. M., & Fabre, T. R. (in press). Antisocial behavior in young school aged children: Behavioral and ecological characteristics, screening and assessment procedures, and school accommodation and intervention strategies. In G. Adams (Ed.), *Behavior disorders: Theories and characteristics*. Englewood Cliffs, NJ: Prentice-Hall.

Walker, H. M., Fonseca Retana, G., & Gersten, R. (1988). Replication of the CLASS program in Costa Rica: Implementation procedures and program outcomes. *Behavior Modification, 12*, 133–154.

Walker, H. M., & Hops, H. (1976). Use of normative peer data as a standard for evaluating classroom treatment effects. *Journal of Applied Behavior Analysis, 9*, 159–168.

Walker, H. M., & Hops, H. (1979). The CLASS program for acting out children: R & D procedures, program outcomes, and implementation issues. *School Psychology Digest, 8*, 370–381.

Walker, H. M., Hops, H., & Fiegenbaum, E. (1976). Deviant classroom behavior as a function of combinations of social and token reinforcement and cost contingency. *Behavior Therapy, 7*, 76–88.

Walker, H. M., Hops, H., & Greenwood, C. R. (1981). RECESS: Research and development of a behavior management package for remediating social aggression in the school setting. In P. S. Strain (Ed.), *The utilization of classroom peers as behavior change agents* (pp. 261–303). New York: Plenum.

Walker, H. M., Hops, H., & Greenwood, C. R. (1984). The CORBEH research and development model: Programmatic issues and strategies. In S. C. Paine, G. T. Bellamy, & B. Wilcox (Eds.), *Human services that work: From innovation to clinical practice* (pp. 57–77). Baltimore: Paul H. Brookes.

Walker, H. M., Hops, H., & Johnson, S. M. (1975). Generalization and maintenance of classroom treatment effects. *Behavior Therapy, 6*, 188–200.

Walker, H. M., Shinn, M. R., O'Neill, R. E., & Ramsey, E. (1987). A longitudinal assessment of the development of antisocial behavior in boys: Rationale, methodology, and first-year results. *Remedial and Special Education 8*(4), 7–16, 27.

Walter, H. I., & Gilmore, S. K. (1973). Placebo versus social learning effects in parent training procedures designed to alter the behavior of aggressive boys. *Behavior Therapy, 4*, 361–377.

Webster-Stratton, C. (1981a). Modification of mothers' behaviors and attitudes through a videotape modeling group discussion program. *Behavior Therapy, 12*, 634–642

Webster-Stratton, C. (1981b). Videotape modeling: A method of parent education. *Journal of Clinical Child Psychology, 10*, 93–98.

Webster-Stratton, C. (1982a). The long-term effects of a videotape modeling parent-training program: Comparison of immediate and 1-year follow-up results. *Behavior Therapy, 13*, 702–714.

Webster-Stratton, C. (1982b). Teaching mothers through videotape modeling to change their children's behavior. *Journal of Pediatric Psychology, 7*, 279–294.

Webster-Stratton, C. (1984). Randomized trial of two parent-training programs for families with conduct-disordered children. *Journal of Consulting and Clinical Psychology, 52*, 666–678.

Webster-Stratton, C. (1985a). The effects of father involvement in parent training for conduct problem children. *Journal of Child Psychology and Psychiatry, 26*, 801–810.

Webster-Stratton, C. (1985b). Predictors of treatment outcome in parent training for conduct disordered children. *Behavior Therapy, 16*, 223–242.

Webster-Stratton, C. (1987). *The parents and children series*. Eugene, OR: Castalia.

Webster-Stratton, C., & Eyberg, S. M. (1982). Child temperament: Relationship with child behavior problems and parent–child interactions. *Journal of Clinical Child Psychology, 11*, 123–129.

Webster-Stratton, C., Kolpacoff, M., & Hollinsworth, T. (1988). Self-administered videotape therapy for families with conduct problem children: Comparison with two other cost-effective treatments and a control group. *Journal of Consulting and Clinical Psychology, 56*, 558–566.

Weinrott, M. R., Bauske, B. W., & Patterson, G. R. (1979). Systematic replication of a social learning approach to parent training. In P. O. Sjoden (Ed.), *Trends in behavior therapy* (pp. 331–351). New York: Academic Press.

Weinrott, M. R., Jones, R. R., & Howard, J. R. (1982). Cost-effectiveness of teaching family programs for delinquents: Results of a national evaluation. *Evaluation Review, 6*, 173–201.

Wells, K. C. (1985). Behavioral family therapy. In A. S. Bellack & M. Hersen (Eds.), *Dictionary of behavior therapy techniques* (pp. 25–30). New York: Pergamon Press.

Wells, K. C., & Egan, J. (1988). Social learning and systems family therapy for childhood oppositional disorder: Comparative treatment outcome. *Comprehensive Psychiatry, 29*, 138–146.

Wells, K. C., & Forehand, R. (1985). Conduct and oppositional disorders. In P. H. Bornstein & A. Kazdin (Eds.), *Handbook of clinical behavior therapy with children* (pp. 218–265). Homewood, IL: Dorsey Press.

Wells, K. C., Forehand, R., & Griest, D. L. (1980). Generality of treatment effects from treated to untreated behaviors resulting from a parent training program. *Journal of Clinical Child Psychology, 9*, 217–219.

Wells, K. C., Griest, D. L., & Forehand, R. (1980). The use of a self-control package to enhance temporal generality of a parent training program. *Behaviour Research and Therapy, 18*, 347–358.

Welsh, R. S. (1971). The use of stimulus satiation in the elimination of juvenile fire setting behavior. In A. M. Graziano (Ed.), *Behavior therapy with children* (pp. 283–289). Chicago: Aldine.

Werry, J. S., Methven, R. J., Fitzpatrick, J., & Dixon, H. (1983). The interrater reliability of DSM-III in children. *Journal of Abnormal Child Psychology, 11*, 341–354.

Wetzel, R. (1966). Use of behavioral techniques in a case of compulsive stealing. *Journal of Consulting and Clinical Psychology, 30*, 367–374.

White, M. A. (1975). Natural rates of teacher approval and disapproval in the classroom. *Journal of Applied Behavior Analysis, 8*, 367–372.

Willner, A. G., Braukmann, C. J., Kirigin, K. A., Fixsen, D. L., Phillips, E. L., & Wolf, M. M. (1977). The training and validation of youth-preferred social behaviors with child care personnel. *Journal of Applied Behavior Analysis, 10*, 219–230.

Willner, A. G., Braukmann, C. J., Kirigin, K. A., & Wolf, M. M. (1978). Achievement Place: A community model for youths in trouble. In D. Marholin (Ed.), *Child be-havior therapy* (pp. 239–273). New York: Gardner Press.

Wiltz, N. A., & Patterson, G. R. (1974). An evaluation of parent training procedures designed to alter inappropriate aggressive behavior of boys. *Behavior Therapy, 5,* 215–221.

Winett, R. A., & Winkler, R. C. (1972). Current behavior modification in the classroom: Be still, be quiet, be docile. *Journal of Applied Behavior Analysis, 5,* 499–504.

Wolf, M. M., Braukmann, C. J., & Ramp, K. A. (1987). Serious delinquent behavior as part of a significantly handicapping condition: Cures and supportive environ-ments. *Journal of Applied Behavior Analysis, 20,* 347–359.

Wolff, S. (1971). Dimensions and clusters of symptoms in disturbed children. *British Journal of Psychiatry, 118,* 421–427.

PART III

EMOTIONAL AND SOCIAL DISORDERS

4

CHILDHOOD DEPRESSION

ALAN E. KAZDIN
Western Psychiatric Institute and Clinic
University of Pittsburgh School of Medicine

Research on childhood depression has only begun to emerge within the last 15 years. Progress in the investigation of childhood disorders in general has been limited, due in part to the fact that classification and diagnosis of childhood dysfunctions have lagged behind parallel work with adults. In addition, prior conceptualizations of childhood depression thwarted empirical efforts until recently.

OVERVIEW OF THE DISORDER

Brief History

Psychoanalytic theory has dominated child clinical work over the last several decades. Variations of psychoanalytic theory asserted that depression as a disorder does not exist in children (e.g., Mahler, 1961; Rie, 1966). Certainly, some forms of depression were widely acknowledged. For example, Spitz (1946) discussed the reactions in infancy precipitated by separation from the mother. This reaction, referred to as "anaclitic depression," includes such signs as sadness, withdrawal, apprehension, weepiness, retarded reaction to external stimuli, slowed movement, dejection, loss of appetite and weight, and insomnia. Although many of these symptoms resemble the clinical picture of adult depression, anaclitic depression, as originally formulated, is not parallel to affective disorders in adults. Anaclitic depression is regarded as a result of the experience of object loss; adult depression goes beyond reactions to specific environmental events.

Depression as a clinical disorder in children, similar to major depression in adults, has not been considered possible in prominent psychoanalytic positions. Alternative explanations of the emergence of depression in adults have been advanced, including the views that depression results from inwardly directed aggression (Rochlin, 1965), from a conflict that arouses guilt (Beres, 1966), and from low self-esteem that stems from a discrepancy between the real and ideal self (Rie, 1966). In each of these views, depression depends on a well-developed superego. Because superego development is hypothesized not to mature until adolescence, the appearance of a full clinical syndrome of depression in childhood is precluded. The recent emergence of ego-analytic models makes it clear that depressive disorders can emerge in childhood (Anthony, 1975; Bemporad & Wilson, 1978). Depressive states and approximations of a depressive disorder can emerge at different ages and are considered to vary as a function of psychosexual development, experience, and perceptual and cognitive skills. Yet the dominant view has been that depression as a disorder does not exist in children.

In the early 1970s a second major conceptual position began to emerge, which acknowledged that depression can exist in children, but that its manifestations differ significantly from those of adult depression. The essential features, such as dysphoric mood and pervasive loss of interest, may not be present. Rather, this view proposes that there is an underlying depression that is manifested in several other symptoms or forms of psychopathology. Depression is said to be "masked" or expressed in "depressive equivalents." Children may be depressed, but their affective disorder can only be inferred from the presence of other complaints evident in childhood (Cytryn & McKnew, 1972, 1974; Glaser, 1968; Malmquist, 1977; Toolan, 1962). The symptoms that putatively mask depression have included the full gamut of problem behaviors evident in childhood. As a partial list, temper tantrums, hyperactivity, disobedience, running away, delinquency, phobias, somatic complaints, irritability, separation anxiety, and underachievement have been identified as depressive equivalents (see Kovacs & Beck, 1977).

The notion of masked depression is problematic, because there is no operational way to decide whether a particular symptom is or is not a sign of depression. Yet the idea that depression is masked at least acknowledges that depression can exist in children. The position has helped to foster research to see whether depressive symptoms are systematically associated with various other symptoms and whether depression can be assessed and detected in children apart from these other symptoms (Carlson & Cantwell, 1979). This research has suggested that depression can be identified through careful assessment, even though children who manifest symptoms of depression may have other behavioral problems as well.

The notions of masked depression and depressive equivalents are also historically very important, because they explicitly propose that depression in childhood may be evident in ways that differ from depression in adulthood. The differences among children, adolescents, and adults remain a topic of considerable discussion and research (Rutter, Izard, & Read, 1986). Yet the focus on developmental differences was made salient by the notion of masked depression.

Following on the heels of the notion of masked depression was another view that also emphasized possible developmental differences in the emergence and manifestations of depressive symptoms. This view suggests that symptoms of depression may emerge in children over the course of normal development but dissipate over time (Lefkowitz, 1980; Lefkowitz & Burton, 1978). A premise of this view is that if the clinical symptoms of depression are typical of childhood and if they remit with age, they should not be regarded as evidence of "psychopathology."

Epidemiological research has shown that many so-called "depressive equivalents," such as temper tantrums, fears, or enuresis, are relatively common over the course of childhood (e.g., Lapouse, 1966). These behaviors often are not diagnostically significant, because they are not necessarily related to adjustment in general, and they diminish over time (Lapouse, 1966; Werry & Quay, 1971). Even behaviors that relate more specifically to the syndrome of depression, as defined in current taxonomy, may be relatively common. For example, as a measure of sadness, crying has been shown to vary significantly as a function of age. At 6 years of age, approximately 18% of children are reported to cry two to three times per week; the percentage decreases markedly by puberty to 2% (Werry & Quay, 1971). Similarly, poor appetite, occasionally a symptom of depression, is relatively common in 5-year-old girls and boys (37% and 29%, respectively) but drops sharply by age 9 (9% and 6%, respectively) (MacFarlane, Allen, & Honzik, 1954).

The notion that depressive symptoms emerge over the course of development appears to be consistent with the available data. Yet the focus on isolated symptoms is not the issue. Evidence has failed to emerge to suggest that the syndrome is present as part of normal development. Nevertheless, the view directs attention to the fact that symptoms of depression may vary over the course of child development and fosters empirical research to map the developmental course of these symptoms.

The current view of childhood depression that guides contemporary research has been influenced by the third edition of the *Diagnostic and Statistical Manual of Mental Disorders* (DSM-III; American Psychiatric Association [APA], 1980). DSM-III has focused on the presenting symptoms and descriptive features of alternative disorders. In DSM-III, the essential features of depression are similar in children, adolescents, and adults (e.g., Annell, 1972; Cantwell, 1982; Puig-Antich & Gittelman, 1982). The criteria for delineating affective disorders are applied independently of age. Using DSM-III, research has clearly established that the diagnostic criteria developed with adult populations can be applied in unmodified form to diagnose affective disorders in children (e.g., Carlson & Cantwell, 1980; Chiles, Miller, & Cox, 1980; Kashani, Barbero, & Bolander, 1981; Kashani, Husain, et al., 1981; Puig-Antich, Blau, Marx, Greenhill, & Chambers, 1978).

The fact that depression as a clinical syndrome can be diagnosed in children, adolescents, and adults does not mean that the manifestations of the disorder are necessarily identical. DSM-III has recognized that there may be associated features for different ages and developmental levels. However, at present these differences are not well specified and are based on primarily clinical experience rather than solid empirical research.

Diagnosis of Depressive Disorders

In characterizing depression, it is important to distinguish depression as a *symptom* from depression as a *syndrome* or *disorder*. As a symptom, "depression" refers to sad affect and as such is a common experience of everyday life. As a syndrome or disorder, "depression" refers to a group of symptoms that go together. Sadness may be part of a larger set of problems that also includes loss of interest in activities, feelings of worthlessness, sleep disturbances, changes in appetite, and others.

There are many alternative diagnostic systems and different types of depressive syndromes or disorders that they cover (Carlson & Garber, 1985; McConville & Bruce, 1985). Alternative diagnostic systems that have been proposed include the Research Diagnostic Criteria (RDC; Spitzer, Endicott, & Robins, 1978), the *International Classification of Diseases* (World Health Organization, 1987), and the system of the Group for the Advancement of Psychiatry (1966). The major diagnostic system in use in the United States is the DSM. In the third edition (DSM-III; APA, 1980), a major advance was made in specifying diagnostic criteria for delineating alternative disorders. The general model of DSM-III was to specify a core or essential set of symptoms to delineate a particular disorder. Some number of symptoms from this set is required for a particular disorder to be diagnosed. Other criteria are included for disorders to be diagnosed, such as a particular duration of the symptoms and the absence of another condition (e.g., an organic disorder) that might explain the presence of symptoms.

Beginning in 1983, the diagnostic categories were re-evaluated to incorporate research findings on alternative disorders and experiences in applying the specific diagnostic categories. A revision of the DSM-III criteria has recently been published and is referred to as DSM-III-R (APA, 1987). In DSM-III-R, several changes were made in various disorders in terms of clarifying the criteria, changing subtypes, and deleting and adding alternative disorders.* For affective disorders, the changes were relatively minor.

Depression is part of a larger category referred to as Mood (rather than Affective) Disorders. The criteria for Major Depression in DSM-III-R are illustrated in Table 4-1. As in DSM-III, depressive symptoms may be included in other types of disorders as well. Table 4-2 enumerates several other categories of depressive disorders. In each of the disorders, there may be sad affect, loss of interest in the usual activities, and other symptoms. The severity, duration, and precipitants of the symptoms are major determinants of the type of depressive disorder that is defined.

Prevalence

A question of major interest obviously is the extent to which children experience depressive symptoms and mood disorder. Depression has been studied among "normal" (nonreferred) children and adolescents as well as in various clinic samples. Most research has addressed the prevalence of severe depressive symptoms by identifying subsamples of youths whose scores on self-report, parent report, and peer report inventories reflect relatively (i.e., statistically) extreme levels of depression.

For example, using a peer-based measure, Lefkowitz and Tesiny (1985) found severe depression (extreme scores exceeding two standard deviations above the mean) in 5.2% of a sample of over 3,000 normal third-, fourth-, and fifth-grade children. In another study, 7.3%

*For example, Identity Disorder was deleted from DSM-III-R because of the absence of information supporting its validity. Similarly, Attention Deficit Disorder without Hyperactivity was deleted as a subtype because this diagnosis was hardly ever made. New disorders also have been proposed. One example includes Cluttering, a disorder of speech fluency involving both the rate and rhythm of speech, resulting in impaired speech intelligibility. Expressive Writing Disorder also has been added to identify developmental disturbances in which writing skills are below expected levels of performance.

and 1.3% of high school students showed moderate and severe levels of depression, respectively, according to cutoff criteria developed with adults (Kaplan, Hong, & Weinhold, 1984). These and other studies utilize different methods of assessing depression and different criteria for defining extreme scores. In addition, even when extreme or optimal cutoff scores are used for various self-report and parent report measures, the children who are identified do not necessarily meet diagnostic criteria for depressive disorders (Kazdin, Colbus, & Rodgers, 1987). Thus, consistent information on the prevalence of depression as a disorder has been difficult to cull from many of the assessment studies.

Other studies have utilized specific diagnostic criteria to evaluate depression as a disorder. In the general population, approximately 2% have been identified as depressed in randomly selected child populations aged 7–12, according to DSM-III criteria (Kashani et al., 1983; Kashani & Simonds, 1979). In clinical populations, estimates have ranged from approx-

imately 2% to 60% (Kashani, Husain, et al., 1981), although estimates typically fall between 10% and 20% (Puig-Antich & Gittelman, 1982).

In adulthood, depression generally is more prevalent among women than among men. To date, research has typically found no sex differences in prevalence of depressive disorders in clinic and nonclinic samples of children (aged 6–12) (e.g., Kashani et al., 1983; Lefkowitz & Tesiny, 1985; Lobovits & Handal, 1985). On the other hand, research has suggested that among adolescents, the prevalence is greater in females than in males (e.g., Mezzich & Mezzich, 1979; Reynolds, 1985). Differences in severity of depression between males and females appear to begin in early adolescence and to increase over the next several years (Kandel & Davies, 1982). Yet differences in prevalence rates between adolescent males and females are not always found (Kaplan et al., 1984). Consequently, further work and large-scale epidemiological studies are still needed.

As for the overall prevalence rates for chil-

TABLE 4-1. DSM-III-R Criteria for Major Depression

A. *Inclusion Criteria:* At least five of the following symptoms have been present during the same two-week period; at least one of the symptoms was either (1) depressed mood, or (2) loss of interest or pleasure.
   (1) Depressed mood more of the day, nearly every day (either by subjective account, e.g., feels "down" or "low," or is observed by others to look sad or depressed)
   (2) Loss of interest or pleasure in all or almost all activities nearly every day (either by subjective account or is observed by others to be apathetic)
   (3) Significant weight loss or weight gain (when not dieting or binge-eating) e.g., more than 5% of body weight in a month) or decrease or increase in appetite nearly every day (in children consider failure to make expected weight gains)
   (4) Insomnia or hypersomnia nearly every day
   (5) Psychomotor agitation or retardation nearly every day (observable by others, not merely subjective feelings of restlessness or being slowed down) (in children under six, hypoactivity)
   (6) Fatigue or loss of energy nearly every day
   (7) Feelings of worthlessness or excessive or inappropriate guilt (either may be delusional) nearly every day (not merely self-reproach or guilt about being sick)
   (8) Diminished ability to think or concentrate, or indecisiveness nearly every day (either by subjective account or observed by others)
   (9) Thoughts that he or she would be better off dead or suicidal ideation, nearly every day; or suicide attempt
B. *Exclusion Criteria*
   (1) An organic etiology has been ruled out, i.e., either there was no new organic factor (or change in a pre-existing organic factor) that precipitated the disturbance, or the disturbance has persisted for at least one month beyond the cessation of the precipitating organic factor
   (2) Not a normal reaction to the loss of a loved one (Uncomplicated Bereavement)
   (3) At no time during the disturbance have there been delusions or hallucinations for as long as two weeks in the absence of prominent mood symptoms
   (4) Not superimposed on Schizophrenia, Schizophreniform Disorder, or Paranoid Disorder

---

Note. From *Diagnostic and Statistical Manual of Mental Disorders* (3rd ed., rev.) by the American Psychiatric Association, 1987, Washington, DC: Author. Copyright 1987 by the American Psychiatric Association. Reprinted by permission.

dren and adolescents, there remain rather large discrepancies in the currently available studies. The large discrepancies may result in part from the different ages that are studied. For example, using DSM-III diagnostic criteria, evidence suggests that young children (aged 1–6 years) referred for treatment may have markedly lower rates (1%) of major depression than children aged 9–12 (13%) (Kashani, Cantwell, Shekim, & Reid, 1982; Kashani, Ray, & Carlson, 1984). Also, differences in prevalence rates may be due to the different measures that are used, the difficulty in administering similar measures to children of different ages, and (perhaps most importantly) the different diagnostic criteria that are invoked. The clarity of prevalence data for depressive disorders among children is likely to improve with the increased use of standardized descriptive criteria for diagnostic purposes, the development of standard diagnostic interviews, and continued evidence that diagnoses can be invoked with acceptable reliability (e.g., Chambers *et al.*, 1985; Orvaschel, Puig-Antich, Chambers, Tabrizi, & Johnson, 1982).

Developmental Considerations

Within the DSM-III and DSM-III-R criteria, as noted earlier, the possibility of different symptoms' emerging as a function of age is acknowledged. Researchers occasionally have suggested that specific symptoms (e.g., separation anxiety, enuresis, conduct disorder) are likely to be associated with depression in children. However, no consistent pattern has emerged across studies to delineate age-specific criteria.

Multivariate studies of child symptoms suggest that there may well be developmental differences. For example, Achenbach and Edelbrock (1983) studied parent ratings on the Child Behavior Checklist (CBCL) of boys and girls in different age groups (4–5, 6–11, 12–16). A depression factor emerged in the factor analyses of CBCL ratings of all groups except boys and girls aged 12–16. For boys, no Depression factor emerged; for girls in this age range, the Depression factor clustered with items specifically related to withdrawal, being secretive, being shy and timid, and liking to be alone. For the groups where a Depression factor did

TABLE 4-2. DSM-III-R Diagnostic Categories Other than Major Depressive Disorder That Include Depressive Symptoms

---

Dysthymia

Essentially a mood disorder in which the symptoms of major depression are evident in less severe form. The symptoms may be chronic, lasting for at least 2 years (1 year for children and adolescents), during which there has been depressed mood most of the day more days than not.

Separation Anxiety Disorder

Many of the symptoms of depression, such as sadness, excessive worrying, sleep dysfunction, somatic complaints, apathy, and social withdrawal, may emerge as part of fear of separation from those to whom the child is attached. In such cases, the symptoms may be clearly associated with the theme of separation. For example, worrying may have a specific focus on worry about being away from the parent. Similarly, somatic complaints may occur to remain at home or to foster increased attention to the child.

Adjustment Disorder with Depressed Mood

Depressive symptoms may emerge as a reaction to an identifiable psychosocial stressor such as divorce of the parents, leaving friends during a move away from home, or serious illness of a parent. In such cases, the symptoms are in temporal proximity (within 3 months) of the stressor. The reaction is viewed as a maladaptive reaction because the person's functioning in everyday life is disrupted or because the symptoms are in excess of a "normal" or usually expected reaction. The symptoms are likely to remit after a period of adjustment with the new circumstances.

Uncomplicated Bereavement

Within DSM-III-R, bereavement resembles an Adjustment Disorder in terms of its association with a particular event. However, it is not listed as a disorder because it is considered as a normal reaction to the loss of a loved one. Bereavement is often associated with several depressive symptoms or a full depressive syndrome and temporary impairment in school and social functioning. Yet the reaction is not regarded as clinically significant unless the symptoms remain well beyond a "reasonable" period of adjustment or begin to recur with repeated episodes long after the loss.

Note. Adapted from *Diagnostic and Statistical Manual of Mental Disorders* (3rd ed., rev.) by the American Psychiatric Association, 1987, Washington, DC: Author. Copyright 1987 by the American Psychiatric Association. Adapted by permission.

emerge, the specific symptoms that clustered on this factor varied as a function of sex and age. For example, for boys aged 6–11, suicidal talk was associated with other symptoms of depression, although this was not the case at ages 4–5. For girls aged 6–11, anxiety and feeling persecuted were associated with other depressive symptoms; at ages 4–5, these symptoms were not part of the Depression factor. The results suggest that depressive symptoms may be organized quite differently as a function of age and gender.

To date, research has shown many similarities in the manifestations of depression among children and adults. Many cognitive attributes (e.g., attributional style, locus of control, hopelessness, cognitive distortion), biological correlates (e.g., responses to drug challenges, measures of endocrine functioning), and overt behaviors are similar among depressed children and adults (e.g., Kaslow, Rehm, & Siegel, 1984; Kazdin, Esveldt-Dawson, Sherick, & Colbus, 1985; Kazdin, Rodgers, & Colbus, 1986; Moyal, 1977; Puig-Antich, 1983; Seligman et al., 1984). In these studies, the search for developmental differences has encompassed a relatively broad age range (e.g., 6–14 years). Similarities in cognitive processes, symptoms of depression, and the correlates of depression among different age groups at this point have been the rule rather than the exception.

Differences have been found between depression in children and adults. First, data for adults indicate that depression is more prevalent in women than in men, at least in Western cultures. The female-to-male ratio of depressive disorder is approximately 2 : 1 (Whybrow, Akiskal, & McKinney, 1984). Studies of children have not revealed consistent sex differences in prevalence of major depression (Carlson & Cantwell, 1979; Kashani et al., 1982). On the other hand, sex differences have been found between depressed children that have not been evident with adults. For example, associations between depression and other characteristics (e.g., nonverbal behavior, unpopularity, somatic complaints) appear to be higher and more consistent among girls than among boys (Jacobsen, Lahey, & Strauss, 1983; Kazdin, Sherick, Esveldt-Dawson, & Rancurello, 1985).

Second, some of the serious concomitants of depression are clearly less evident in children. As a major case in point, suicide in children below the age of 12 is extremely rare (Hawton, 1985). Given its low base rate, suicide is less likely to be evident in children, whether or not they are depressed. On the other hand, suicidal ideation, threats, and attempts are not that rare among children and are often evident in patient samples, especially those with depressive disorder (Carlson & Cantwell, 1982; Pfeffer, Conte, Plutchick, & Jerrett, 1979). Third, biological correlates of depression are not identical for children and adults. For example, electroencephalographic (EEG) sleep patterns characteristic of depressed adults have not been found among depressed children (Goetz et al., 1983; Young, Knowles, MacLean, Boag, & McConville, 1982), although they have been found among depressed adolescents (Lahmeyer, Poznanski, & Srinath, 1983).

In general, the literature suggests a marked developmental continuity in depressive symptoms and many of its associated features. Some of the differences that have been found between depression in childhood and adulthood begin to demarcate discontinuities that warrant further study. The task is to identify the developmental course of alternative features of depression. Areas that appear to be discrepant at different age levels (e.g., EEG sleep patterns) point to the need to study the course of these characteristics and the point at which their concurrent association with depression may emerge.

ETIOLOGICAL MODELS: AN OVERVIEW

The literature on the etiology of affective disorders is complex because of the multiplicity of models and the different subtypes of depression to which they are directed (Beckham & Leber, 1985; Paykel, 1982a). Although the alternative models can be divided into several different approaches or schools of thought, they are highlighted here under two rubrics: namely, psychosocial and biological models. The models have been developed in the context of adult depression. They are important to highlight because they serve as the primary bases for treatment in both adult and child populations. Subsequent sections address the research on the characteristics of childhood depression and their treatment following from these models.

Psychosocial Models

Psychosocial models are approaches that emphasize intrapsychic, behavioral, cognitive, and interpersonal underpinnings of depression.

There are a number of different views, only some of which are sampled here.

Psychoanalytic Models

Psychoanalytic models focus on intrapsychic influences, beginning with Freud's emphasis on unsatisfied libidinal strivings, particularly object loss (e.g., as reflected in a parent who fails to fulfill the child's needs) (see Mendelson, 1982). The child's identification with the parents' values and ideals has also been accorded an important role. The self-criticism and self-rejection of depressed persons are attributed to the battle of the ego and superego, which reflects these values. The self-directed criticism and internal conflict reflect anger and hostility toward the parent (Freud, 1917/1957).

Freud's views served as a point of departure for several psychoanalytic positions among his followers (e.g., Abraham, Rado, and Bibring). Such factors have been identified as repeated disappointment in relation to one's parents, fixation at the oral stage, aggression turned inward, excessive craving for narcissistic gratification, loss of self-esteem resulting from the unsatisfied need for affection, feelings of helplessness, and others.

Behavioral Models

In general, the behavioral models focus on learning, environmental consequences, and skill acquisition and deficits (see Clarizio, 1985; Clarkin & Glazer, 1981). Symptoms of depression are considered to result from problems of interacting with the environment.

Lewinsohn (1974) has advanced the view that depression results from the loss or reduction of reinforcement from the environment. The person's behavior does not produce sufficient positive reinforcement from others, and the individual becomes passive, withdraws from interactions, and shows the affective and cognitive symptoms of depression. Alternatively, punishing and aversive consequences (unpleasant outcomes) may also result from person–environment interactions and lead to symptoms of depression.

A related behavioral model suggests that social skills deficits underlie depression. The view overlaps with the position advanced by Lewinsohn, because social skills deficits may lead to reduced or limited reinforcement from the environment. Social interactions are central sources of positive reinforcement that have been reduced in depressed persons. Social skills deficits may also cause depressed persons to fail to meet interpersonal demands and to suffer anxiety and lack of reinforcement.

Social interaction in the family may also play a significant role in the development of childhood depression. Studies of family interaction have shown that depressed mothers show higher dysphoric afffect and lower rates of happy affect in their interactions with other family members, and are less rewarding to their children (Biglan et al., 1985; Cole & Rehm, 1986; Hops et al., 1987). Less cohesion, expressiveness, and organization and more conflict are also evident in families with a depressed parent (Billings & Moos, 1983). Other research has suggested that parental resentment and rejection of the child, lack of affection, uninvolvement, and emotional detachment occur early in family life and contribute to subsequent depression on the part of the child (Crook, Raskin, & Eliot, 1981; Lefkowitz & Tesiny, 1984; Weissman, Paykel, & Klerman, 1972). The presence of depression in the home may be associated with family interactions that promote further dysfunction on the part of the child. The full range of interactions that may contribute to childhood depression, and causal connections between these interactions and depression, have not been established. Nevertheless, emerging evidence makes plausible the importance of intervening in maladaptive family processes to reduce the likelihood of childhood dysfunction in homes with a depressed parent.

Another model, referred to as a "self-control" model of depression (Rehm, 1977), focuses on the individual's maladaptive or deficient self-regulatory processes in coping with stress. The crucial self-regulatory processes include self-monitoring, self-evaluation, and self-reinforcement. Persons with deficits in these self-regulatory skills are likely to focus on negative events, to set overly stringent criteria for evaluating their performance, and to administer little reinforcement to themselves, among other characteristics. Treatment focuses on building specific self-control skills and utilizing these skills to promote adaptive behaviors (such as increased activities) and cognitive processes (such as positive attributions).

Cognitive Models

Cognitively based views of depression emphasize the perceptual and attributional styles and belief systems that underlie depressive symptoms. Beck's (1976) model emphasizes the importance of the "cognitive triad" of depression—namely, negative views of oneself, the world, and the future. The negative cognitions are considered to affect the person's judgment about the world and interpersonal interactions, and to account for affective, motivational, and behavioral symptoms of depression. Systematic errors in thinking, such as overgeneralizing specific events and misinterpreting experience in general, can be identified to reflect the pervasive focus on negative aspects of experience.

Seligman (1975) has proposed a "learned helplessness" model of depression. The model proposes that depression results from people's experiences and expectations that their responses do not influence events in their lives. Helplessness leads to passivity, social impairment, slowed activity, and other symptoms of depression. The model grew out of laboratory research showing that animals became helpless after exposure to unavoidable shock. When they could later escape from the shock, they failed to do so. The model was extended by focusing on the perceptions and attributions of depressed persons, who often feel they cannot influence their environment (Abramson, Seligman, & Teasdale, 1978). People's specific attributions about why they cannot control their environment (e.g., internal or external factors) and the pervasiveness of these influences (e.g., specific to a situation or general) affect the symptoms that may emerge (e.g., reduced self-esteem).

Another cognitively based position proposes that depression is related to deficits in interpersonal problem-solving skills (D'Zurilla & Nezu, 1982). Persons who are depressed, when compared to nondepressed controls, evince deficits in generating alternative solutions to social problems, engaging in means–ends thinking, and making decisions (Nezu & Ronan, 1985). Problem-solving skills, when present, appear to act as a buffer against the impact of negative life events (Billings & Moos, 1982). In response to negative events or stress and current problems of daily living, depressive symptoms are more likely to emerge because of deficits in problem-solving skills.

Socioenvironmental Views

Socioenvironmental models have focused on life events that may influence the onset or emergence of symptoms of depression. Such models are included here as psychosocial because it is not only a stressful event itself, but also the person's perception or cognitive appraisal of that event, that is important. The significance of stressful events as precursors to depressive symptoms is recognized in everyday life. Bereavement, for example, frequently includes multiple symptoms of depressive disorder linked specifically to death of a loved one. Moreover, the risk of suicide is greatly increased following death of a relative or spouse, suggesting that extremes of hopelessness and depression may follow stressful events (Bunch, 1972; MacMahon & Pugh, 1965).

Research has supported the role of stressful life events in depressive disorders. Persons who are depressed or who later meet criteria for depression report significantly more stressful life events than do matched controls (Paykel, 1982b). Although higher levels of stressful events characterize other patient groups (schizophrenics or medical patients), depression still seems to be associated with greater levels of such events. In addition, stressful events appear to precede by a few weeks or months the onset of an episode or relapse (Brown, Harris, & Peto, 1973; Paykel & Tanner, 1976). Attempts to identify the type of events that are uniquely related to depression (e.g., loss of a relative) and severity of the events (e.g., life-threatening) have not revealed consistent patterns.

Overall level of stressful events appears to be related to depression in children (e.g., Mullins, Siegel, & Hodges, 1985). Occasionally, specific events have been studied in relation to depression. One stressor in childhood that has been frequently implicated in later depression is loss of the parent (Brown, Harris, & Bifulco, 1985). In general, studying the impact of stressful events on children is difficult for several reasons, including the paucity of well-validated instruments; the possible differences in the impact of stressful events associated with age and stage of the child's development; and the factors often associated with the event (e.g., altered family interactions) that may be as important as or more important than the event itself (Compas, 1987; Johnson, 1986).

Biological Models

Psychosocial models of depression, particularly cognitive and behavioral models, have flourished and have generated a host of treatments. At the same time, remarkable progress has been made in biological views of the nature of depression. Assessment and treatment techniques have emerged from these models as well.

Biochemical Models

A number of biochemical agents have been implicated in depression, only a few of which can be mentioned here (see Usdin, Asberg, Bertilsson, & Sjoqvist, 1984). Research has focused on the identification of neurotransmitters that may underlie depression (see Zis & Goodwin, 1982). Different transmitters have been studied. Monoamines, especially catecholamines and indoleamines, have received attention in a variety of types of studies. The general view has been that affective disorders are characterized by a deficit (e.g., depression) or excess (e.g., mania) in one or more neurotransmitters or by an imbalance of these transmitters.

Neuroendocrine abnormalities have also been studied (e.g., Sachar, 1982). The focus has a broad-based rationale. Symptoms of depression include disturbances of mood, sex drive, sleep, appetite, and autonomic activity, which as a whole suggest dysfunction of the hypothalamus. Also, neurotransmitters (especially noradrenaline, serotonin, and acetylcholine), which have been implicated in depressive disorders, regulate the sorts of neuroendocrine agents that control pituitary function and hormonal responses. Different hormone systems have been studied. For example, depressed patients have been shown to hypersecrete cortisol and not to suppress cortisol secretion in response to drug challenge (administration of dexamethasone) (see Carroll, 1983). Also, hyposecretion of growth hormone has been found in response to insulin-induced hypoglycemia (Carroll, 1978). Growth hormone is believed to be mediated by neurotransmitters, which may be deficient among depressed patients.

Genetic Models

The genetic influences in depressive disorders have been established for some time. Close relatives of persons with major depression are more likely to have the disorder than are unrelated persons (see Depue & Monroe, 1979; Nurnberger & Gershon, 1982). The precise concordance varies with the criteria used to define depression, subtypes of depression, ages of the sample and relatives, and other factors. Different lines of evidence have supported the role of inheritance. The evidence from twin studies has been relatively consistent. Monozygotic twins show about 65% concordance for affective disorders, compared to approximately 14% for dizygotic twins (see Gershon, Targum, Kessler, Mazure, & Bunney, 1977). The strong familial ties of affective disorders have also been supported with studies of adoptees and with studies of parents and children of index populations (cf. Morrison, 1983).

The genetic evidence has helped foster diverse types of research, including the identification of subtypes of affective disorders, with their specific genetic loadings, biological correlates, family histories, and patterns of treatment response. Research has also explored biological markers (i.e., genetic, biochemical, or related characteristics that permit identification of who is at risk for affective disorders). Ideally, these markers consist of stable characteristics that can be detected whether or not a person is currently showing the symptoms of depression.

General Comments

The preceding discussion is intended only to highlight selected views of the causes of affective disorders. The list is by no means exhaustive (see Akiskal & McKinney, 1975). Different models might be presented (e.g., sociological, existential), as well as specific views within particular models (e.g., alternative neurotransmitters and endocrine systems, the modes of action through which stress is considered to promote depression).

The models overlap greatly. Many of the differences are not in the identification of specific factors, but in their relative weighting and in whether a given factor is accorded a causal role in generating depressive symptoms or is seen as a consequence or concomitant of some other source of influence. For example, life events and stressors are acknowledged as significant in cognitive, social skills, and biochemical models (e.g., Depue, 1979; Paykel, 1982a).

Few efforts have been made to integrate alternative views and to span different models (e.g., psychosocial, biological). As one example, Akiskal (1979; Akiskal & McKinney, 1975) has provided a biobehavioral model that integrates (1) genetic vulnerability; (2) developmental events (e.g., early object loss); (3) psychosocial events (e.g., life events as stressors); (4) physiological stressors (e.g., medical conditions, disease, results of childbirth); and (5) personality traits (e.g., stable characteristics that influence reactivity to stress). These influences are proposed to alter the central nervous system and to converge on a final common pathway that is implicated in the biological substrates of responses to environmental reinforcement. Figure 4-1 illustrates these influences, their possible pathway, and their integration. As illustrated in the figure, the common pathway is proposed to be in the diencephalon—an area selected because it mediates arousal, mood, motivation, and psychomotor functions (see Akiskal, 1979; Whybrow *et al.*, 1984). The idea of an integrated model is obviously attractive, if for no other reason than to acknowledge the legitimacy of alternative perspectives and areas of research. The model also suggests that the processes that lead to depression may be interrupted at different places.

Thus, many different treatment foci may be effective.

ASSESSMENT

Conceptualization of the nature, central features, and course of depression obviously can dictate the areas of functioning that need to be assessed and treated in individual patients. Thus, if social skills deficits are presumed to be critical to depression, the measure may focus on social behaviors. However, independently of the specific conceptual view, it is critical to conduct a broad-based assessment to describe the patient's dysfunction. "Broad-based assessment" refers here to the use of instruments that sample a wide range of areas of functioning and symptoms.

Diverse measures are available to sample a broad range of symptoms (Kazdin, 1988). As one example, psychiatric diagnostic interviews such as the Schedule for Affective Disorders and Schizophrenia for School-Age Children (K-

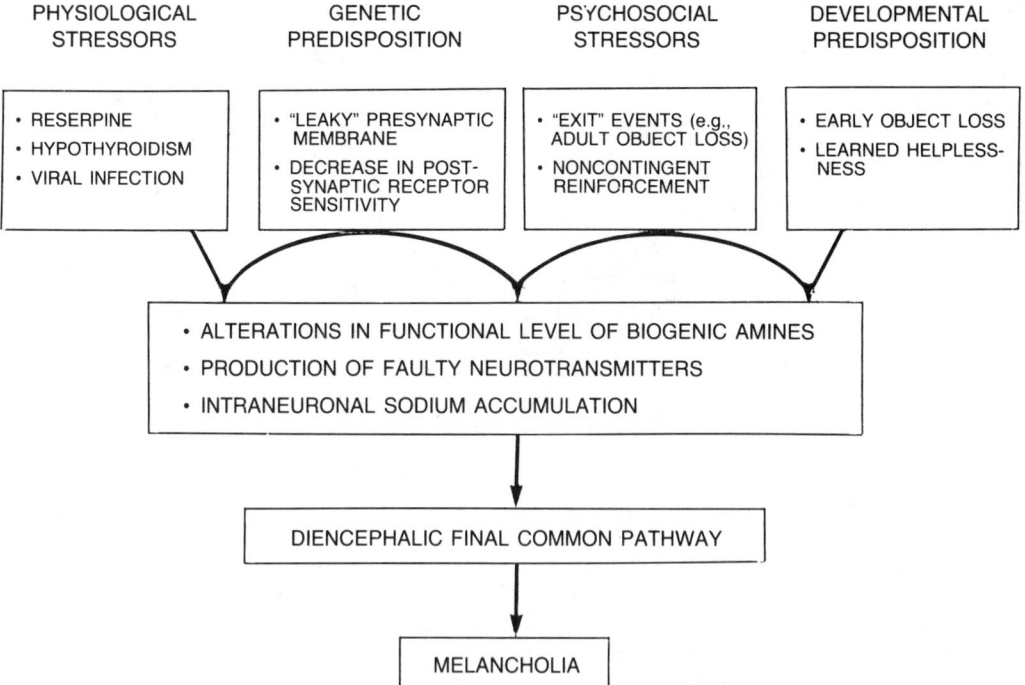

FIGURE 4-1. Diagrammatic representation of the biobehavioral model of depression. The model suggests that alternative biological and environmental or interpersonal factors have an impact on specific biological processes known to be implicated in depression. The final common pathway is proposed to be the diencephalon, which mediates arousal, mood, activation, and psychomotor functions. From "A Biobehavioral Approach to Depression" by H. S. Akiskal, 1979, in R. A. Depue (Ed.), *The Psychobiology of the Depressive Disorders* (pp. 409–437), New York: Academic Press. Copyright 1979 by Academic Press. Reprinted by permission.

SADS; Chambers *et al.*, 1985) might be used. This measure consists of a semistructured interview of both parents and child to identify the presence and severity of a broad range of symptoms. Based on the interview results, DSM-III diagnoses can be made for affective and several other disorders. The specific depressive symptoms that a particular child shows will be evident from the interview, but symptoms of other disorders are covered as well. Several other diagnostic interviews are available, including the Diagnostic Interview for Children and Adolescents (Herjanic & Reich, 1982), the Interview Schedule for Children (Kovacs, 1978), the Child Assessment Schedule (Hodges, McKnew, Cytryn, Stern, & Kline, 1982), and the Diagnostic Interview Schedule for Children (Costello, Edelbrock, & Costello, 1985). From these interviews, DSM-III diagnoses can be derived. Presumably, each will be revised to address the changes required to use DSM-III-R, the current psychiatric diagnostic system that has replaced DSM-III.

The purpose of the K-SADS is to yield a psychiatric diagnosis or categorical delineation of the child's problem. Many dimensional scales are available to sample a broad range of symptoms as well. For example, the Child Behavior Checklist (CBCL; Achenbach & Edelbrock, 1983) is a parent-completed measure where 118 items are rated on a scale of 0–2. Symptom areas (e.g., schizophrenia, withdrawal, aggressiveness, hyperactivity) have been derived from factor analyses completed separately for boys and girls of different age groups (e.g., 6–11, 12–16). Broad-band scales reflect more general types of behavioral patterns (internalizing, externalizing behaviors) and overall dysfunction (total behavior problems). Scales derived on an *a priori* basis and designed to measure social competence (participation in activities, social interaction, progress at school) are available as well. The information from the CBCL provides a profile of multiple areas of problem behaviors as well as prosocial functioning.

Current Measures of Depression

Assuming that a broad measure of dysfunction has been used to sample the range of potential symptoms, it is meaningful to focus more specifically on depression (Kazdin, 1988; Kazdin & Petti, 1982). Many measures of depression have been developed for children and adolescents. Table 4-3 enumerates many of the commonly used measures.*

Among the alternative assessment methods, self-report scales have dominated (see Table 4-3). Self-report is particularly important in assessing depression, given that key symptoms such as sadness, feelings of worthlessness, and loss of interest in activities reflect subjective feelings and self-perceptions. The most widely used measure is the Children's Depression Inventory (CDI; Kovacs, 1981), which assesses cognitive, affective, and behavioral signs of depression. Children select one of three alternatives that characterizes them within the last 2 weeks. For example, for one of the items, children are asked to choose one of the following statements: a. I am sad once in a while, b. I am sad many times, c. I am sad all of the time. Endorsement of the most extreme statement in each of the 27 items yield a total score for severity of depression.

The CDI has enjoyed widespread use in part because it is an offspring of the Beck Depression Inventory, the inventory most frequently used to measure depression among adults. Studies of the CDI have evaluated internal consistency; factor structure; test–retest reliability; alternative methods of test administration; gender and age differences; cutoff scores to delineate severe cases of depression; and correlates with other constructs such as self-esteem, hopelessness, and social behavior (e.g., Kazdin *et al.*, 1987; Kazdin, French, Unis, & Esveldt-Dawson, 1983; Nelson, Politano, Finch, Wendel, & Mayhall, 1987; Saylor, Finch, Baskin, Furey, & Kelly, 1984; Saylor, Finch, Spirito, & Bennett, 1984; Smucker, Craighead, Craighead, & Green, 1986).

Measures completed by significant others are often used to evaluate childhood depression. Ratings by others are important because they are likely to identify symptoms different from those identified by the child. Behavioral correlates of depression (e.g., irritability) and changes in eating and sleep patterns are readily evident to parents and less clearly reported by children. Here, too, many measures are available. In fact, almost all of the self-report measures have also been rephrased so that parents can report on the child's depression. Even if the same measure (e.g., the CDI) is used for the child, it is valuable to include ratings by parents as well. The reason is that child and parent ratings of the child's depression show little or no correlation (e.g., Kazdin, Esveldt-Dawson,

---

*For an examination of the characteristics of individual assessment techniques and their advantages and limitations, the reader is referred elsewhere (Kazdin, 1988).

Unis, & Rancurello, 1983). Yet, each source of information predicts performance in other domains. For example, child self-report of depressive symptoms, unlike parent reports, correlates significantly with hopelessness and with suicidal ideation and attempt (Kazdin, French, Unis, Esveldt-Dawson, & Sherick, 1983; Kazdin et al., 1986). In contrast, parent reports of depressive symptoms in the child are likely to correlate with overt behavioral signs of depression, such as afffect-related expression and social behavior (Kazdin, Esveldt-Dawson, et al., 1985).

Clinicians, teachers, and peers also may provide important information about the child. Clinician ratings can be completed using the Children's Depression Rating Scale (Poznanski, Cook, & Carroll, 1979; Poznanski et al., 1984), a measure adapted from the frequently used Hamilton Rating Scale for Depression for adults (Hamilton, 1967). The clinician rates symptom areas of depression on the basis of the child's verbal report and nonverbal behavior (e.g., appearance of sad affect). Ratings by teachers also have been used to assess child depression. Here too, self-report child depression measures are often used by changing the language of the items for teachers.

Ratings by peers have taken advantage of the nomination format often used for sociometrics.

The Peer Nomination Inventory of Depression (Lefkowitz & Tesiny, 1980) requires children within a group (e.g., a classroom) to nominate others for several specific characteristics. The requirement of having a peer group to provide nominations has limited the use of this measure in clinical settings. Also, the peer nomination format in general often raises ethical concerns associated with explicit peer identification of children as evincing negative or undesirable characteristics.

Apart from questionnaires and inventories, other measures have been used, such as direct observations of overt behavior when children engage in free play and nonverbal behavior as assessed while the child is being interviewed (Kazdin, Esveldt-Dawson, et al., 1985; Kazdin, Sherick, et al., 1985). These measures do not represent standardized codes that have been applied beyond the specific studies of interest. They do, however, convey the utility of developing direct behavioral observational measures that can discriminate depressed and nondepressed patient samples.

Measures of Related Constructs

A number of measures may be of interest or use because they address specific characteristics of depressive symptoms in greater depth, or be-

TABLE 4-3. Selected Measures of Depression for Children and Adolescents

Measure	Key reference
Self-report inventories	
Children's Depression Inventory	Kovacs & Beck (1977)
Short Children's Depression Inventory	Carlson & Cantwell (1979)
Child Depression Scale	Reynolds, Anderson, & Bartell (1985)
Children's Depression Adjective Checklist	Sokoloff & Lubin (1983)
Children's Depression Scale	Tisher & Lang (1983)
Self-Rating Scale	Birleson (1981)
Modified Zung Scale	Lefkowitz and Tesiny (1980)
Face Valid Depression Scale for Adolescents	Mezzich & Mezzich (1979)
Center for Epidemiological Studies—Depression Scale (child version)	Weissman, Orvaschel, & Padian (1980)
Beck Depression Inventory (modified for adolescents)	Chiles, Miller, & Cox (1980)
Reynolds Adolescent Depression Scale	Reynolds & Coats (1986)
Interviews	
Belleview Index of Depression (Revised)	Kazdin, French, Unis, & Esveldt-Dawson (1983)
Behavior Inventory for Depressed Adolescents	Chiles et al. (1980)
Children's Depression Rating Scale	Poznanski, Cook, & Carroll (1979)
Children's Affective Rating Scale	McKnew, (1979)
Other measures	
Peer Nomination Inventory for Depression	Lefkowitz & Tesiny (1980)

cause they address key areas that are likely to be influenced by depressive symptoms. The range of domains and measures is large, but major candidates for selection for a comprehensive assessment battery can be highlighted.

Low self-esteem or poor evaluations of personal worth are likely to be part of the symptom picture of depression and to play a role in alternative models of depression. A self-esteem scale such as the Self-Perception Profile for Children (Harter, 1985) may be useful. The scale assesses self-adequacy and personal competence in five specific domains: scholastic, social, athletic, physical appearance, and behavioral conduct. A global self-worth scale is also included to measure self-esteem more globally.

Perceived control over events is an important feature in alternative models of depression. "Control" refers to the capacity to influence or achieve an intended outcome, and includes the extent to which an outcome depends on someone's behavior and the competence of the individual to engage in the requisite behaviors (Weisz, Weiss, Wasserman, & Rintoul, 1987). One measure of control is the Multidimensional Measure of Children's Perception of Control (Connell, 1985). The measure examines the extent to which events are perceived as being controlled by the individual, by external sources, or by unknown sources of control. Evidence suggests that depression is related to low internal sources of control and perceptions of unknown sources of control (Weisz et al., 1987).

Cognitive distortion, which is related to perceived control, has been important in behavioral and cognitive views of depression. "Cognitive distortion" refers to negative cognitive "errors" in which the individual anticipates outcomes of events to be extremely negative (catastrophizing), assumes that a negative outcome will extend to other situations as well (overgeneralizing), or takes responsibility for negative events (personalizing). To assess these characteristics, the Children's Negative Cognitive Error Questionnaire has been developed (Leitenberg, Yost, & Carroll-Wilson, 1986). The measure includes brief vignettes that cover different types of cognitive distortions in everyday life. Children rate the extent to which each statement reflects their thinking. Cognitive distortion has been shown to relate to children's self-reports of depression, self-esteem, and anxiety.

Helplessness is an attributional style in which undesirable events are associated with depression when the person attributes them to internal, stable, and global causes. The Children's Attributional Style Questionnaire has been developed to measure these attributional characteristics among children (Seligman & Peterson, 1985). The measure lists numerous events and asks the child to identify one of two possible causes. The causes among the items vary to encompass different attributional styles, including internal versus external, stable versus unstable, and global versus specific categories. Results suggest that attributional style correlates with depression in children much as it does with adults (Seligman & Peterson, 1985).

Hopelessness, or negative expectations regarding the future, is especially relevant if there are signs of suicidal attempt or ideation. Hopelessness has been shown to correlate with suicidal behavior in adults and children (e.g., Beck, Kovacs, & Weissman, 1975; Kazdin, French, Unis, Esveldt-Dawson, & Sherick, 1983). The Hopelessness Scale for Children has been developed to assess whether the child views positive events as likely for the future (Kazdin et al., 1986). Total scores on the scale have been shown to correlate with depression, suicidal ideation and behavior, and diminished self-esteem.

Deficiencies in social behavior are often evident in depression. Social behavior is important to consider also because of the prominent place it has occupied in behavioral and cognitive models. A wide range of social behaviors has been shown to relate to depression among adults, including communication patterns, participation in activities, expressions of affect, eye contact, and others. Relatively few measures are available to assess a wide range of social behaviors in children. An exception is the Matson Evaluation of Social Skills with Youngsters (Matson, Rotatori, & Helsel, 1983). The scale is completed by children or adults and assesses a wide range of the child's skills in initiating social interaction, responding to others, making friends, expressing hostility, and other areas. Research has demonstrated the relation between depression and deficiencies in social functioning as reflected in alternative measures of social functioning (e.g., Blechman, McEnroe, Carella, & Audette, 1986; Kazdin, Esveldt-Dawson, et al., 1985).

Loneliness or perceived isolation from others is related to social behavior and likely to be relevant to depression. An easily completed self-report measure, the Loneliness Questionnaire, has been developed for school-age children (Asher, Hymel, & Renshaw, 1984; Asher & Wheeler, 1985). The measure includes 16 true–false items on which children indicate how difficult it is to make friends, how well liked they feel, and whether they have friends to play with or to talk with at school. Research has suggested that feelings of loneliness are related to peer rejection (Asher & Wheeler, 1985). The connection between rejection and loneliness raises the prospect of focusing on the peer social network as a means of influencing children's feelings about themselves.

Reinforcing events and activities are relevant for childhood depression, given the behavioral formulation attributing depression in part to a paucity of reinforcing experiences from the environment. Knowledge of these events can be used as a basis for developing specific activities in treatment. Perception of reinforcing events can be measured by the Children's Reinforcement Schedules (Cautela, Cautela, & Esonis, 1983). Three different forms are used, depending on the age of the children (kindergarten through sixth grade). A separate form is available for adolescents. In each of these child forms, children identify the extent to which they like potentially reinforcing events or activities (on a 3-point scale ranging from "dislike" to "like very much"). Sample items refer to liking to ride a bicycle, traveling to different places, and going to movies. As the authors of the scale acknowledge, reinforcers can only be identified by demonstrating that a particular event increases the frequency of a behavior when it is applied contingently. Nevertheless, the scales suggest rewarding activities that may be increased to reduce the symptoms of depression.

The assessment of pleasant and unpleasant activities has also been advanced by development of the Adolescent Activities Checklist (Carey, Kelley, Buss, & Scott, 1986). The measure is a self-report scale in which adolescents rate the occurrence and pleasantness of various activities (e.g., watching television, going out to eat). Initial evidence has suggested that depressed and nondepressed adolescents (nonclinic sample), as defined by performance on the Beck Depression Inventory, differ in their ratings of number of unpleasant activities but not on pleasant activities (Carey et al., 1986).

Life events, or factors in the environment that induce stress, are also relevant for the evaluation of depression. In the case of a child,

such events as a recent move, loss of friends, onset of serious illness or hospitalization, or separation of the parents may influence the child's affective symptoms and daily functioning (Trad, 1987). The magnitude or intensity of the event, the perceived valence of the event, and the number of events within a given period all may be important to an understanding of changes in the child's behavior. Indeed, studies of children and adolescents have shown relations between life stressors and change in life events and depression (e.g., Friedrich, Remas, & Jacobs, 1982; Mullins et al., 1985). Among alternative measures, the Life Events Record (Coddington, 1972) for children and the Life Events Checklist (Johnson & McCutcheon, 1980) for older children and adolescents have proved especially useful, although a variety of measures are available (Compas, 1987). Measures of life events correlate significantly with children's depression, personal problems, and adjustment (Compas, 1987; Johnson, 1986).

Because depression can influence virtually all facets of an individual's functioning, many other constructs and measures are relevant as well. Of special interest for children may be measures related to the family and the context in which the child develops. Thus, measures of interpersonal relationships and basic organizational structures in the family, as in the Family Environment Scale (Moos, Insel, & Humphrey, 1974); objective aspects of home life, as in the Home Environment Questionnaire (Laing & Sines, 1982); or stress in the home involving parent–child interactions, as in the Parenting Stress Index (Abidin, 1983), all may be of interest. Given the range of domains and measures that are potentially relevant to childhood depression, critical decisions will need to be made to delimit the battery.

Selection of Measures for Treatment

As evident from this overview of assessment, many options are available to evaluate childhood depression. Decisions of what to assess and with what instruments may be used on conceptualizations of treatment. However, several prior considerations are relevant for selecting a particular set of measures.

Need for Broad-Based Evaluation of Symptoms

For purposes of understanding the child's functioning, it is critical to include assessment methods that sample a wide range of symptoms. Depression can include any number of symptoms and symptom combinations; each symptom that comprises the constellation needs to be sampled systematically. In addition, it is quite possible (if not likely) that children with depression will show symptoms of other disorders as well, and that some of these may influence treatment decisions. Diagnostic instruments such as the K-SADS are designed to sample a broad range of symptom areas and provide a useful beginning for identifying the nature of the child's dysfunction. Dimensional scales (e.g., the CBCL) that give a profile of the child across a range of symptom areas are options as well.

Inclusion of Self-Report Measures

Given the nature of the symptoms, it is important to include different perspectives regarding the child's depression. Measures that include the child's own report recognize the importance of subjective experience in the symptom constellation. Other assessment methods (e.g., ratings by others, direct observations of overt behavior) do not correlate highly with self-report measures. Thus, the inclusion of self-report measures provides information that is not replaced by other assessment modalities.

Need to Sample Multiple Perspectives and Settings

The special role of self-report needs to be emphasized, given the subjective, affective, and cognitive components of depression; however, other perspectives are essential as well. Parent-completed measures are of special importance. Parents have access to large samples of behavior and play a major role in decisions about treatment (Achenbach & Edelbrock, 1983). Depressive symptoms also reflect a change in performance from the usual activities, which parents can readily identify. Depressive symptoms may include changes in eating, sleeping, and daily activities. Performance in the home is a primary place where these symptoms may be evident. Parent evaluations of the child's depression correlate with child functioning at home and at school. Other raters, such as teachers, peers, and clinicians, may obviously provide valuable information because of the different samples of performance they see or their unique perspectives.

Use of Measures with Established Norms and Cutoff Scores

Evaluation of the child's performance and functioning can be greatly facilitated by using measures with an established normative data base. Normative data, derived from large-scale studies of nonreferred children of different ages, can be very useful in interpreting the scores of individual cases. However, normative data are available for very few measures of childhood depression. The major exception is the CDI, which has now been examined in several studies with alternative community samples of different ages (e.g., Nelson et al., 1987; Saylor, Finch, Spirito, & Bennett, 1984; Smucker et al., 1986). The standing of the child in relation to same-age and same-sex peers facilitates evaluation of the severity of the problem and/or the magnitude of change over the course of treatment.

It is also useful to select measures for which information is available on the cutoff scores that define alternative levels of depression. Alternative cutoff scores might be drawn from the normative data to suggest that a specific score is, for example, at the 90th percentile for depression for children of a given age and sex. In the development of cutoff scores for a given measure, the score that distinguishes a particular level of dysfunction or percentile of youths may differ, depending upon who completes the measure. For example, we (Kazdin et al., 1987) found that cutoff scores to identify children with a diagnosis of depression (RDC) for each of four measures of childhood depression differed depending on whether the children or their parents completed the measure.

Investigators often define children as depressed when they attain an extreme score or surpass a particular cutoff for a measure such as the CDI. An extreme score on an inventory of depression is not tantamount to a diagnosis of depression using psychiatric diagnostic criteria (e.g., DSM or RDC). Studies comparing diagnoses with performance on various depression scales have shown that optimal cutoff scores that maximize classification accuracy have a high rate of false positives (those who are identified as depressed on the scale but who have not received a diagnosis of depression) and false negatives (those who are identified as *not* depressed on the measure but who have not received a diagnosis of depression) (Asarnow & Carlson, 1986; Kazdin et al., 1987; Lobovits & Handal, 1985). Thus, identifying an extreme group using cutoff scores may be quite useful for research or clinical purposes, but the group identified in this fashion may be different from that identified through diagnostic procedures.

Individualization of Assessment

The use of standardized measures has obvious advantages in terms of permitting comparison of the individual with normative data and providing a uniform way of surveying the full range of symptoms. However, for purposes of treatment, it may be useful as well to develop assessment techniques specific to the individual case. Individualized measures may be especially useful for purposes of treatment, where the focus may be on a few salient symptoms. The range of measures that may be relevant is unlimited. For example, it may be that specific cognitions or self-statements emerge over the course of a day and precipitate sad affect. Self-monitoring of these statements may be critical to evaluate treatment. Alternatively, diminished social interaction may be a major portion of the symptom picture. A specific measure may need to be developed to take into account the child's home, school, and social environment. Monitoring by others in the individual's life (e.g., at home) may be used to record social interactions. In general, there may be value in supplementing standardized measures with other measures directed more specifically toward the individual child's behavioral symptoms. Illustrations of such measures are provided in the discussion of specific treatment procedures.

TREATMENT STRATEGIES

Overview of Major Approaches

A large number of treatment strategies have been developed for the treatment of depression among adults (Clayton & Barrett, 1983; Paykel, 1982a). It is useful to highlight the major strategies in the context of adult depression, because the techniques have served as a point of departure for the treatment of children and adolescents.

Cognitive Therapy

The cognitive approach has been developed by Beck (1976) on the basis of his cognitive model of depression. As noted previously, the core of the model is the negative "cognitive triad," which refers to those characteristics that lead to depressive symptoms. The triad reflects the bias that depressed persons have in viewing themselves, the world, and the future negatively. The world is viewed in a way that is distorted through these negatively biased cognitive processes.

Cognitive therapy utilizes specific strategies that are designed to alter negatively biased cognitions (Beck, Rush, Shaw, & Emery, 1979). Depressed patients are trained to recognize the connections between their thoughts, affect, and behavior; to monitor their negative thoughts; to challenge their thoughts with evidence; and to substitute more reality-based interpretations for their usual cognitions. In addition to focusing on specific cognitions, assignments to engage in specific behaviors outside of treatment are provided.

Increase in Pleasant Activities

Depressive symptoms have been attributed to reduced activities, particularly reduced reinforcement from the environment (Lewinsohn & Arconad, 1981). Treatment focuses on increasing the level of pleasant activities in which depressed individuals engage. The purpose is to increase the amount of response-contingent reinforcement that will be associated with decreases in depressive symptoms. Treatments designed to increase activities include several ingredients, such as self-monitoring of activities and mood, identifying positively reinforcing activities that are associated with positive affect, increasing positive activities, and decreasing negative activities.

Social Skills Training

Depression also has been attributed to deficiencies in social skills. Social skills have been selected in part because social interaction is an area where the absence of positive reinforcement from the environment is likely to be evident. The objective of treatment is to increase the individual's ability to obtain reinforcement from others, as reflected both in increased interaction and in more rewarding interactions.

Social skills training consists of teaching individuals to engage in several concrete behaviors with others. Initiating conversation, responding to others, refusing requests of others, making requests, and similar behaviors are specific foci of training. Patients are usually treated individually and provided with instructions, modeling by the therapist, role playing, feedback, and planned activities in everyday life. Individual skills are taught and repeatedly practiced until the patients have learned the skills.

Self-Control Therapy

Self-control treatment is based on the view that depressed persons suffer from deficits in self-control strategies, including self-monitoring, self-evaluation, and self-reinforcement (Rehm, 1977). Depressive symptoms are considered to result from deficits in one or more of these areas and are reflected in attending to negative events, setting stringent self-evaluative criteria for performance, failing to attribute responsibility for behaviors in a realistic fashion, and providing insufficient self-reinforcement and/or too much self-punishment. The model integrates features of other models that emphasize cognitive processes, reinforcement, activity levels, and the role of learned helplessness.

Interpersonal Psychotherapy

Interpersonal psychotherapy is based on the view that development of depression occurs in an interpersonal context and is influenced by relationships with significant others (Weissman & Paykel, 1974). Interpersonal psychotherapy is based not on a narrow theoretical framework or therapeutic school, but rather on the general view and line of evidence that the social role performance of depressed patients is dysfunctional. The focus of treatment is on interpersonal relationships, social adjustment, and mastery of social roles. The processes or techniques of treatment usually include the nonjudgmental exploration of feelings, elicitation and active questioning on the part of the therapist, reflective listening, development of insight, discussion of emotionally laden issues, and direct advice.

Overview of the Evidence

Outcome studies of therapy techniques with adult depressed patients have been conducted

for several different treatments (see Beckham & Leber, 1985; Rehm & Kaslow, 1984; Weissman, 1984). In general, cognitive therapy, increased pleasant activities, social skills training, self-control therapy, and interpersonal psychotherapy, as major modalities of treatment, have effectively reduced symptoms of depression. These treatments have been superior to no-treatment, waiting-list, and minimal-treatment control conditions.

Much less clear are the outcome results regarding the relative efficacy of alternative techniques. Comparative studies have usually found no differences among various cognitive and behavioral treatments. Among the more provocative findings of comparative outcome studies is the evidence that cognitive therapy is more effective than antidepressant medication (Rush, Beck, Kovacs, & Hollon, 1977). Research from the large-scale National Institute of Mental Health collaborative study, completed only recently, compares cognitive therapy, interpersonal psychotherapy, and antidepressant medication and will provide critical data on the relative efficacy of alternative treatments. At present however, it is difficult to reach firm conclusions regarding the superiority of one psychosocial technique to another or to medication.

Several studies have examined the effects of combined psychotherapy and medication. The combination of interpersonal psychotherapy and medication has been shown to be more effective than either treatment alone (Klerman & Schechter, 1982). In some studies, psychotherapy and medication have reduced different symptoms. Psychotherapy tends to alter problems of living and social dysfunction, whereas medication alters the vegetative signs. The combined treatment provides broader coverage in the range of symptoms that are improved. Yet evidence has not invariably shown that the combination of psychosocial treatment and medication is more effective than the constituent treatments administered alone, nor that psychotherapy and medication affect different symptoms (Murphy, Simons, Wetzel, & Lustman, 1984; Simons, Garfield, & Murphy, 1984). As a general statement, the research on adult depression has already identified a number of treatments that produce therapeutic change. The improvements are reflected in depressive symptoms and social functioning at follow-ups of at least a year.

APPLICATIONS WITH CHILDREN

Extensions of Treatment Models to Children

The empirical work on the treatment of depressed children, if viewed from the standpoint of outcome studies alone, is quite sparse. Given the brief history of research on childhood depression, the paucity of work is quite understandable and no doubt will also be short-lived. Important lines of work that will serve as underpinnings for treatment research are derived from the models that have been developed from research on adults. The initial question of significance is the extent to which the models apply to children.

Evidence already has emerged attesting to the continuity of depressive symptoms and associated features among children, adolescents, and adults. To begin, evidence pertaining to biological markers (e.g., cortisol, growth hormone abnormalities) have shown several consistencies between depressed children and adults (Puig-Antich, 1985). Child research on biological markers has progressed largely because of the extrapolation of laboratory methods and biological assessment techniques developed from years of work with adults.

Research has shown that the model underlying Beck's (1976) cognitive therapy applies to children. Depressed children show the negative bias in their view of the world, themselves, and the future (e.g., Kazdin, French, Unis, & Esveldt-Dawson, 1983; Kazdin, French, Unis, Esveldt-Dawson, & Sherick, 1983). Thus, evidence supports the appearance of the cognitive triad that has served as the basis for cognitive therapy for depression among adults.

Cognitively based research has focused on helplessness and related processes. Attributional styles associated with helplessness, blame and externalized locus of conduct, as well as problem-solving deficits characteristic of adults, have been evident with children (e.g., Butler, Miezitis, Friedman, & Cole, 1980; Haley, Fine, Marriage, Moretti, & Freeman, 1985; Lefkowitz & Tesiny, 1980; Moyal, 1977; Seligman & Peterson, 1985; Seligman et al., 1984). Laboratory studies have begun to identify conditions that generate learned helplessness in children, the associated attributions, and procedures to overcome deterioration in performance on laboratory tasks associated with helplessness (Diener & Dweck, 1980; Dweck, 1975; Dweck & Reppucci, 1973). This work is significant in establishing the applicability of a helplessness model to children, although the goal has not been to address depression in clinical samples.

The social skills deficits evident in depressed adults have also been demonstrated in depressed children. More specifically, depressed children have shown deficits in their interactions with their families and peers (Puig-Antich et al., 1985a, 1985b). Depressed children engage in less social interaction and lower levels of expressiveness of affect and nonverbal behavior than do their nondepressed peers (Kazdin, Esveldt-Dawson, et al., 1985; Kazdin, Sherick, et al., 1985). On measures that evaluate a large number of social skills (e.g., making friends, initiating conversation), popularity, and participation in social activities, depressed children have shown clear deficits (e.g., Helsel & Matson, 1984; Kazdin et al., 1986; Vosk, Forehand, Parker, & Rickard, 1982). Thus the underpinnings of treatments aimed at social skills training are available with children.

Selected findings are beginning to emerge supporting other models that have been more thoroughly investigated with adults. For example, level of unpleasant activities and stressful life events also appear to be related to childhood depression, as they are to adult depression (Beck & Rosenberg, 1986; Carey et al., 1986). These and other findings have provided initial evidence regarding the applicability to children of several models developed from the study of adults. Among alternative models, extensions of psychoanalytic view to children have been conspicuously absent. This is unfortunate, because the conceptual bases of alternative manifestations of depression and potentially related concepts (e.g., shame, guilt, loss) have been well developed for adult depression. Recent extensions of theoretical notions to childhood depression have accelerated as well (e.g., Lewis, 1985), along with recommendations to deploy child psychoanalysis for treatment (e.g., Trad, 1987). Empirical research and treatment trials from psychoanalytic and psychodynamic perspectives would be important contributions to understanding mood disorders.

Similarly, the model underlying interpersonal psychotherapy for adults has not been well elaborated or well studied with children. Research on social skills and social interaction among depressed children, highlighted previously, conveys the importance of interpersonal interaction. However, the focus on roles and role satisfaction in the adult version of interpersonal psychotherapy has not been translated to children in current outcome research.

Findings indicating that alternative models developed with adult depression apply to children represent a significant point of departure for further understanding of depression and development of effective treatment and prevention strategies. Demonstrating commonalities across different ages does not, of course, mean that identical processes operate at different ends of the developmental spectrum. On the other hand, demonstration that core concepts apply to different ages is important. By implication, the research also suggests that treatments derived from such models warrant investigation with children.

Treatment Outcome Studies

Psychosocial Interventions

The previous discussion of approaches suggests that a large number of psychosocial techniques are available. To date, however, very few outcome studies have been reported with depressed children. Among controlled studies with children, initial investigations have drawn primarily upon cognitive–behavioral models.

For example, Butler et al. (1980) conducted a comparative outcome study for fifth- and sixth-grade school children identified through self-report measures of depression and teacher referral. Children received 10 sessions of either role play, cognitive restructuring, an attention placebo condition (discussion of teaching rather than depression-related topics), or no treatment. Role play focused on teaching interpersonal skills as well as problem-solving techniques. Cognitive restructuring focused upon maladaptive cognitions (à la Beck and Ellis). Although the outcome results appeared to favor role play, the differences among alternative groups are difficult to discern from the data analyses.

More recently, Reynolds and Coats (1986) compared a cognitive–behavioral treatment, relaxation, and a waiting-list control condition for treatment of depression among adolescents identified in the schools. Treatment was provided in 10 sessions over a 5-week period. Cognitive–behavioral subjects received training that emphasized self-control skills, including self-monitoring of positive activities and mood, self-evaluation, and self-reinforcement. In addition, cognitive distortions and faulty beliefs and assumptions were examined in the sessions. Homework activities were included to develop self-change plans and to increase behaviors and activities. Youths in the other treatment condition received relaxation training in their sessions and were assigned to practice relaxation for homework. In general, the results indicated that both active treatments were associated with reductions in depression after treatment and up to a 5-week follow-up. The treatments were not significantly different from each other in outcome.

Stark, Reynolds, and Kaslow (1987) evaluated self-control and behavioral problem-solving approaches in the treatment of children (aged 9–12) identified as moderately to severely depressed on the CDI. Treatments were administered in small groups (five children each) for 12 sessions over a 5-week period. Children in the self-control group received treatment modeled after Rehm's therapy for adults, in which self-monitoring, self-evaluation, and self-reinforcement were taught and applied through specific behavioral assignments. Children in the behavioral problem-solving group received training in problem-solving skills and self-improvements in pleasant activities. The treatments overlapped in a number of features, such as problem solving, self-monitoring, and homework assignments. Self-control therapy tended to be more highly structured, and the problem-solving approach tended to focus more on social relations. The results generally indicated that both treatments led to decreases in depressive symptoms; these two treatments were superior to a waiting-list control, but were not consistently different from each other. An 8-week follow-up suggested that the gains were maintained.

Social skills training has received attention in single-case reports (e.g., Calpin & Cinciripini, 1978; Molick & Pinkston, 1982; Petti, Bornstein, Delamater, & Conners, 1980). For example, we (Frame, Matson, Sonis, Fialkov, & Kazdin, 1982) evaluated the treatment of a hospitalized 10-year-old boy with a DSM-III diagnosis of Major Depression. Evaluation of the child revealed several prominent features, including avoidance of social interaction with others, as evident in poor eye contact, turning away from others, inaudible and constricted speech, and bland affect. These areas in turn served as the focus of treatment. The intervention was provided in individual sessions five times per week over a 5-week period. Before and during treatment, interviews were conducted with the child in order to assess the specific social behaviors noted above. The treatment consisted of training the child to interact in a variety of interpersonal situations. The therapist modeled specific social behaviors, encouraged the child to practice what was modeled, and provided praise and feedback as needed to improve socially appropriate interaction.

The training procedure was introduced across the different social behaviors at different points in time in order to meet the requirements of a multiple-baseline design. Figure 4-2 shows that marked changes occurred when treatment was introduced. The sequence of changes suggests that it was the intervention that accounted for the change, rather than any extraneous factors (e.g., contact with the therapist, repeated assessment, or exposure to social situations in training). A follow-up assessment, conducted 12 weeks after all training had been terminated, indicated that the gains were maintained. Unfortunately, posttreatment assessment did not evaluate the specific symptoms that led to the diagnosis of depression, nor did it examine whether the child continued to meet criteria for the diagnosis.

Single-case studies of behavioral techniques such as the one illustrated here can explore alternative treatments and carefully evaluate their impact. Yet the single-case studies for childhood depression conducted to date have suffered from many different problems. The studies have often confounded multiple treatments, failed to diagnose depression in a standardized manner, and used idiosyncratic measures without any standardized assessment. These studies have not clearly identified a treatment that alters depressive symptoms. For nonbehavioral psychosocial therapies, uncontrolled case studies have illustrated but not evaluated the effects of treatment of children (Bene, 1975; Sacks, 1977). Here single-case demonstrations as well as controlled studies are lacking.

Notwithstanding the beginnings of promising approaches, psychosocial interventions need a boost with strong tests of treatment. Initial outcome research reflects a rapid move to comparative outcome studies. The few tests currently available are quite weak because of very small sample sizes within alternative groups. For example, one study had 24 subjects across

three groups by the end of treatment, and 21 subjects by the end of a 5-week follow-up assessment (Reynolds & Coats, 1986). In addition, the group studies have not yet selected children who meet criteria (e.g., DSM-III, RDC) for major depression. In these methodological features, the work lags behind pharmacotherapy trials, highlighted below.

Pharmacotherapy

Several alternative medications have been used with adult depressed patients. Major types include monoamine oxidase inhibitors (e.g., phenelzine) and tricyclics (e.g., imipramine and amitriptyline), but other classes of medications have emerged as well (see Davidson, 1985; Kazdin, Rancurello, & Unis, 1987). The literature on the pharmacological treatment of depression in adults is vast. For example, over 200 placebo-controlled trials have appeared on tricyclic antidepressants alone (Elkins & Rapoport, 1983). Not all studies have shown favorable treatment effects, nor do all patients respond positively. Tricyclics have been estimated to be more effective than placebos in approximately 60%–75% of the studies (see Baldessarini, 1977; Elkins & Rapoport, 1983). However, the literature has gone well beyond establishing global effects for groups that receive active medication or placebo. Selective drug effects have been demonstrated, showing that some subtypes of depression (e.g., bipolar vs. unipolar, primary vs. secondary) are differentially responsive to alternative medications. Also, other variables (e.g., family history, presence of biological markers) have been identified that predict responsiveness to alternative medications. In general, research has progressed greatly on antidepressants for adults.

Many of the medications for adults have been applied to children with mood disorders. Most of the work to date has been with imipramine and amitriptyline. In the 1960s and 1970s, a number of uncontrolled trials appeared that suffered from such methodological problems as nonblind ratings or unsystematic assessment and poorly defined groups of children (e.g., Connell, 1972; Polvan & Cebiroglu, 1972). Studies with control groups began to appear, but also suffered from such problems as nonrandom assignment of children to groups, nonblind clinical ratings (e.g., Weinberg, Rutman, Sullivan, Pencik, & Dietz, 1973) or small sample sizes, and confounding with other treatments (e.g., Petti & Law, 1982). Notwithstanding these and other sorts of criticisms, the demonstrations have been relatively consistent in showing that imipramine and amitriptyline decrease depressive symptoms (see Weller & Weller, 1986).

Placebo-controlled and double-blind studies have begun to appear and have greatly advanced the knowledge about medication

effects. Puig-Antich and his colleagues have conducted ongoing studies of the effects of imipramine (see Puig-Antich & Weston, 1983). In one study, imipramine and placebo conditions yielded similar effects in the treatment of depressed children. However, significant differences emerged in the medication condition when the group was divided according to median plasma level of imipramine and de-

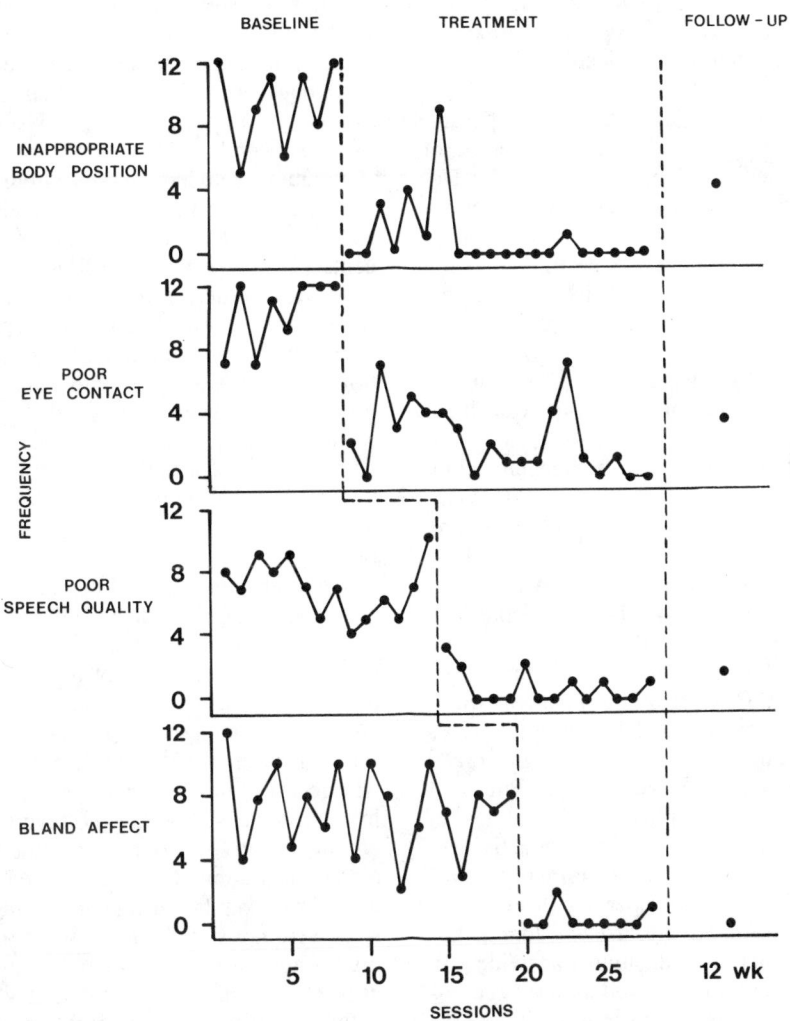

FIGURE 4-2. Frequency of social behaviors of a depressed boy as measured during assessment interviews. The treatment utilized modeling by the therapist, role playing, practice, feedback, and positive reinforcement to develop social interaction skills. The intervention was applied in a multiple-baseline design across the different behaviors. From "Behavioral Treatment of Depression in a Prepubertal Child" by C. Frame, J. L. Matson, W. A. Sonis, M. J. Fialkov, and A. E. Kazdin, 1982, *Journal of Behavior Therapy and Experimental Psychiatry, 3,* 239–243. Copyright 1982 by Pergamon Journals Ltd. Reprinted by permission.

sipramine (a major metabolite of imipramine). Children with higher levels of medication showed 100% response to treatment, whereas those with lower levels showed only 33% response. These results suggested that treatment effects are dependent upon a steady-state plasma level beyond a particular threshold. A subsequent report of this work continued to show that the plasma levels of imipramine and desipramine were related to clinical effects on depressive symptoms (Puig-Antich *et al.*, 1987). Other research on depressed children has shown that remission of symptoms depends upon plasma level of medication (Preskorn, Weller, & Weller, 1982).

Apart from plasma level, the study by Puig-Antich *et al.* (1987) indicated that subtype of depression mediated treatment effects. Depressed children with psychotic symptoms responded consistently less well to medication and required higher plasma levels of medication to evince treatment effects. Thus, both plasma level and type of depression were related to outcome.

The effects of imipramine often are reflected in diverse areas of performance. As a case illustration, Michelson, DiLorenzo, and Petti (1981) treated a 7-year-old boy hospitalized on an inpatient psychiatric service. Direct interviews revealed several symptoms, including dysphoria, helplessness, feelings of worthlessness, low self-esteem, and social withdrawal. The child met modified RDC for depression (see Weinberg *et al.*, 1973). Observations were made of the child's on-task and disruptive behavior in the classroom on the inpatient ward, as well as performance of daily activities across a wide spectrum of social, academic, meal, and free-play situations. For these latter areas of functioning, staff completed daily ratings of level of performance for 96 different activities.

After baseline observations, imipramine was provided to the child twice per day (leading to a maximum dose of 50 mg at each administration). The impact of medication was evident in classroom performance as well as across activities of daily living. Figure 4-3 shows the changes associated in classroom performance and activities during the phase in which imipramine was administered. During the follow-up phase, medication was no longer provided. Overall, the data suggest that the intervention altered diverse areas of performance.

Larger-scale applications have suggested a broad range of beneficial effects associated with symptomatic improvement of depression. For example, using amitriptyline or imipramine to treat depression in children (ages 5½–16), Wilson and Staton (1984) found improvements in neuropsychological functioning (right hemisphere and frontal lobe test performance). This included significant improvements in a number of subtests of the Wechsler Intelligence Scale for Children—Revised. In addition, symptomatic improvements were evident in a variety of externalizing and internalizing behaviors.

To date, tricyclic antidepressants such as imipramine have been the most widely studied medications for depression in children. Current results have suggested clear therapeutic effects, particularly for imipramine, when plasma levels fall within a specified range. The research to date has been largely restricted to the effects of imipramine with prepubertal children. Studies of adolescents do not provide parallel support. For example, Ryan *et al.* (1986) treated adolescents ($n = 34$) who met RDC for major depressive disorder. IMI was provided for a 6-week period. Fewer than 50% responded well to the medication. Moreover, symptom reduction was not associated with plasma levels of imipramine. These findings differ from data with both depressed prepubertal children and adult samples. The authors suggest that the high levels of sex hormones during adolescence may interfere with the antidepressant effects of imipramine.

For both child and adolescent populations, other medications no doubt will receive greater attention in the future. For example, mianserin, a tetracyclic antidepressant used to treat adult depressed patients, has also been used with children and adolescents (Dugas, Mouren, Halfon, & Moron, 1985). Eight youths (aged 8–19) who received the medication showed decreases in depressive symptoms on several measures within a relatively brief period (the first week) of administration. Gains continued to be evident throughout treatment. Interestingly, the results were not significantly different as a function of age (8–12 vs. 13–19) for either boys or girls. Thus, mianserin may be a viable alternative to imipramine for children and adolescents.

An important reason to explore alternative medications is the need to minimize side effects. For example, a study that evaluated nortriptyline for childhood depression (Geller, Perel, Knitter, Lycaki, & Farooki, 1983) found that fewer side effects and lower dose may be required to achieve therapeutic plasma levels, compared to imipramine.

Considerations and Limitations of Current Treatments

Use of Medications

To date, the greatest amount of research on treatment of childhood depression has been with medications. The weight of evidence in-dicates improvements in depressive symptoms following medication, particularly when medication (e.g., imipramine) achieves therapeutic levels of plasma concentrations. Although many researchers and clinicians consider the currently available evidence to indicate that medication is the treatment of choice,

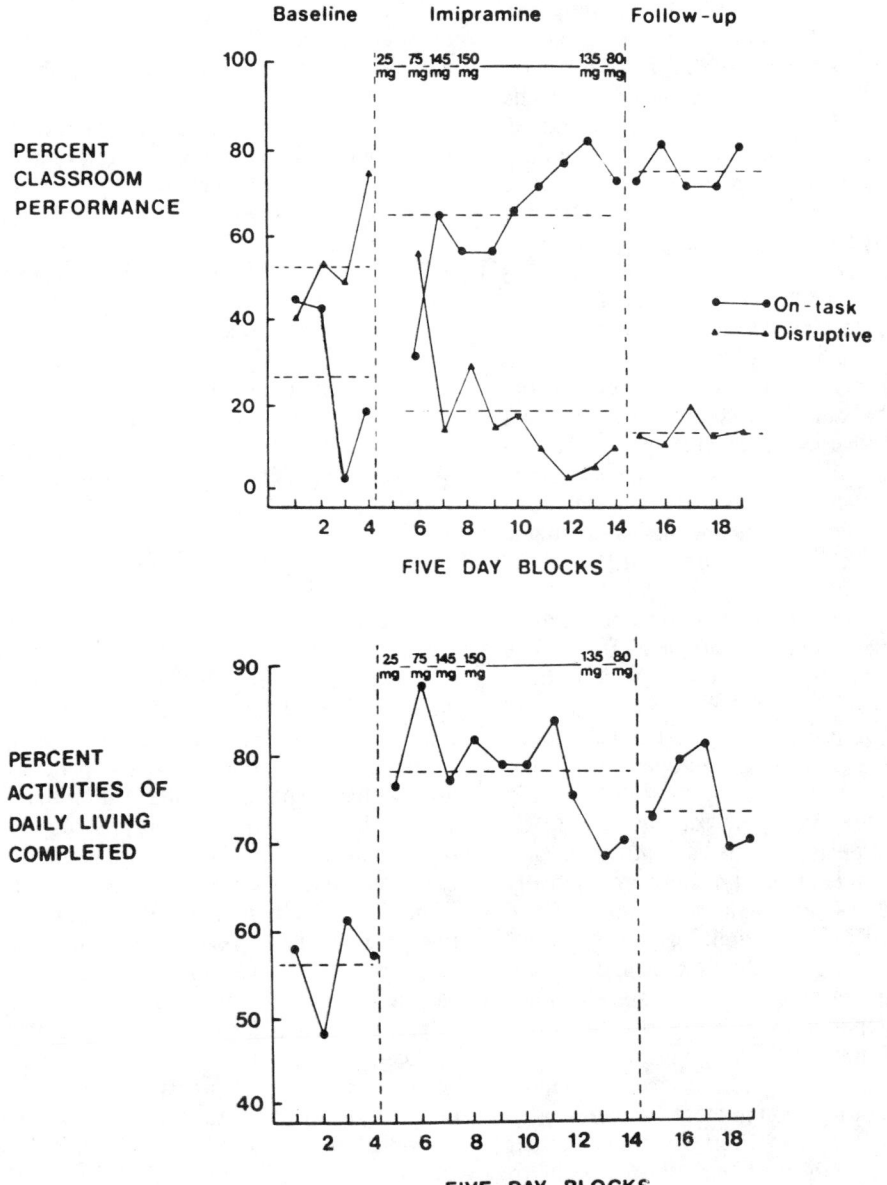

FIGURE 4-3. Mean percentage of on-task and disruptive classroom behavior *(upper panel)* and activities of daily living skills *(lower panel)* completed in 5-day blocks for each phase of the demonstration. From "Behavioral Assessment of Imipramine Effects in a Depressed Child" by L. Michelson, T. DiLorenzo, and T. Petti, 1981, *Journal of Behavioral Assessment, 3,* 253–262. Copyright 1981 by Plenum Publishing Corporation. Reprinted by permission.

several considerations must be borne in mind in deciding upon medication. To begin, the guidelines for administration of medications to children are not as well established as they are with adults. There are significant differences between adults and children in such characteristics as drug absorption and metabolism. Much less research is available in general on the pharmacokinetics of medications with children; consequently, greater caution needs to be exercised in their administration. Indeed, as of this writing the medication evaluated most frequently for treatment of depression in children (imipramine) has yet to receive approval from the Food and Drug Administration for this use.

Second, as already mentioned, medication has unclear effects in treating depression in adolescents. The Ryan *et al.* (1986) study has indicated that the therapeutic effects of imipramine usually achieved with children and adults are not as readily evident with adolescents. Alternative medications may be effective, but remain to be studied in controlled trials.

Third, concerns about side effects are increased with children. There is concern over the possible permanent effects that drugs may exert on growth, intelligence, and nonsymptomatic behaviors. The impact of medications on developmental changes raises issues not evident with adults. Apart from long-term effects, there are of course more temporary side effects. The severity of these effects can vary widely, from physiological changes undetectable to the child and of unclear or apparently no clinical significance (e.g., increased variability in heart rate or blood pressure), to minor discomfort (e.g., dry mouth) and to more severe consequences (e.g., seizures and death). In the case of cyclic antidepressants, side effects typically are relatively minor, such as dry mouth, sedation, blurred vision, and constipation. However, cardiovascular changes, reduced thresholds for seizures, cardiorespiratory arrest, and fatalities have been reported as well (see Kazdin *et al.*, 1987). Withdrawal of medication may produce side effects as well (e.g., headaches, abdominal pain, vomiting), although these can be avoided or minimized by tapering withdrawal rather than ceasing medication abruptly (Law, Petti, & Kazdin, 1981).

The adverse side effects place children at risk for problems beyond the symptoms that have led to treatment. No doubt the likely benefits are often worth the risks. Yet it is important to determine whether less risky interventions may

be substituted. In a review of medication effects for childhood depression, Rancurello (1986) concluded that 60% of children with major depressive disorder are likely to become free of symptoms when treated with placebo. If accurate, this would suggest that a significant proportion of children may improve without medication and thus avoid the risks associated with active drug treatment. Of course, this assumption requires that the short- and long-term effects of placebo and imipramine be equivalent.

The presence of side effects of medication raises practical issues that are relevant to the implementation, monitoring, and efficacy of treatment. The presence of such side effects may have important implications for treatment efficacy, since parents and children are less likely to comply with medication regimens if even mildly bothersome effects emerge. In treatment settings, such side effects can be closely monitored, and changes in treatment can be made in response to their appearance. Such flexibility is reduced slightly in outpatient treatment unless unusually close scrutiny is provided.

Need for Combined Treatments

At best, current research suggests that medications alone do not fully address the dysfunction of depressed children. In one study, depressed children showed marked deficiencies in communications with their mothers and in peer relations, compared to nondepressed patients and nonreferred children (Puig-Antich *et al.*, 1985a, 1985b). After recovery of depression from medication, mother–child interaction had improved, although it remained below the level of nonreferred children. In addition, peer relations had changed very little. These results suggest that medication may not affect significant areas of social functioning. The lack of response of individuals to commonly used medications for depression, or incomplete symptom reduction, prompts the need for additional if not different treatment. Occasionally, additional treatment takes the form of combinations of medications (Davidson, 1985). However, a more common view is the need to consider psychosocial interventions, either alone or in combination with medication.

Because social skills deficits have been proposed as a major characteristic of depressed patients (Lewinsohn, 1974), treatment may need to address this area directly. Research with adult patients has suggested that psychosocial treatments and medications offer unique and complementary advantages (see Klerman & Schechter, 1982). At present, too few studies have been conducted to identify the separate and combined effects of alternative treatments with children, or even the patterns of symptoms and social behaviors that are manifested over time among depressed children. Thus a strong case cannot be made for the use of combined treatment with children; research needs to proceed slowly, insofar as the use of medication with children raises special issues.

Psychosocial treatments are likely to contribute significantly, because the full range of depressive disorders is not likely to warrant medication or to be treated by persons in a position to prescribe medication. Mild forms of depression, even if clinically significant, are likely to be detected and treated in everyday life (e.g., at school, with peers). Interventions that can be utilized in such settings would be very helpful to professionals and paraprofessionals alike.

Extrapolations from the Literature on Adult Depression

The rapid progress in the investigation of childhood depression is due in large part to the extrapolation of conceptual views, assessment approaches, and laboratory techniques from the study of adult to the study of childhood depression. An obvious first step is to examine and explore models and treatment strategies that have proven to be useful in the context of adult dysfunction. Extrapolation of concepts and methods from the adult to the child disorder is important for many obvious reasons, not the least of which is identifying the boundaries of the continuity of dysfunction across the developmental spectrum.

Much of the work testing alternative models or proposing treatment alternatives for depressed children has been based largely on examining the literature with adults and extending these to children—a process referred to as "adultomorphism" (Ausubel, Sullivan, & Ives, 1980). Notwithstanding the continuities that have been identified already, it is important not to be too heavily wedded to the work on adult depression. It is useful to consider some of the obvious unique characteristics of children to which extrapolations of the adult literature can-

not be readily applied (see Digdon & Gotlib, 1985; Rutter et al., 1985). In the case of treatment, additional avenues beyond those applied routinely to adults may hold considerable promise. Distinguishing features of children are their living situation and the role of their parents in their daily lives. Because of the potential influence that parents can exert over their children, a family- or parent-based treatment warrants consideration.

Several avenues of work support the focus on the family (Burbach & Borduin, 1986). To begin, depressed children are more likely to come from homes with a depressed parent than children without such a diagnosis. Focus on the depression of a parent may have an impact on a child's symptoms as well. The impact may be through different parent–child interaction patterns. For example, in relation to the children, depressed parents display less affection and happy affect and show more problems in communicating, more dysphoric affect, and greater ambivalence toward their families (Hops et al., 1987; Weissman, et al., 1972). Families with a depressed parent are also characterized by less cohesion and expressiveness; more conflict; less emphasis on the development of independence, moral values, and religious values; and less participation in joint recreational activities (Billings & Moos, 1983). These characteristics may contribute to or exacerbate the symptoms that may subsequently emerge in a child. In either case, a focus on the functioning of the parents may have treatment or preventive implications for the child's depression.

Another point supporting a focus on the family is that parents may be utilized to alter their children's symptoms of depression. For example, parents can serve as trainers of their children, can structure activities, and can manage behavioral programs that promote participation in activities and social interaction. Parent management training has been well developed as a technique to manage externalizing behaviors, especially childhood aggression (Kazdin, 1985; Patterson, 1982). Parents are trained to implement alternative reinforcement and punishment techniques, to alter coercive child behaviors in the home, and to promote prosocial behavior. In applications of parent management training in families of aggressive children, many of the side effects of treatment would seem relevant to families with depression in one of the parents. Thus, in parent management training, decreases in maternal psychopathology, particularly depression, have been evident (e.g., Eyberg & Robinson, 1982; Forehand, Wells, & Griest, 1980; Patterson & Fleischman, 1979). Occasionally, marital satisfaction (Forehand, Griest, Wells, & McMahon, 1982) and parent perceptions of family cohesion (Karoly & Rosenthal, 1977) also have increased. These findings suggest that significant processes can be altered that may, in the homes of depressed parents, contribute to mood disorders in children.

School represents another unique situation for children that may be incorporated into treatment. Special influences such as peers can be incorporated into treatment to promote behaviors that may combat depressive symptoms in individual children. Here too, the contingencies under control of the teacher and the powerful influences of peers can be mobilized to alter specific behaviors.

The use of parents, teachers, and peers can draw upon models of treatment devised originally for adults. Thus, the focus of treatment (e.g., social skills, reinforcing or pleasant activities) may be retained, but parents and teachers may be used to serve as behavior change agents. Alternatively, it may be possible to develop new models of treatment based on closer scrutiny of the parental behavior that may influence the child's development of depressive symptoms. Depression of parents is already known to affect interaction patterns with their children (Hops *et al.*, 1987; Weissman & Paykel, 1974; Weissman *et al.*, 1972). Further study of depressed children may help identify patterns of interaction in the home that promote or exacerbate depressive disorders.

FINAL COMMENTS

The treatment of depression in children is an area that has very few empirical studies to its credit at this time. However, the status of this "nonliterature" is likely to change rapidly. The relevant background work has progressed relatively quickly. For example, research has consistently shown the utility of alternative diagnostic criteria applied to children. Patient samples can be identified in a reliable fashion for basic research on the characteristics of depressed children and, of course, for clinical trials of alternative treatments. Subtypes of depressive disorders can also be identified, as in work with adults. This raises the prospect of

evaluating interactions between treatment and alternative subtypes of dysfunction. The development and evaluation of several assessment techniques involving psychological as well as biological methods also provide critical background work for evaluating treatments. Years of work with adults have addressed many questions about the assessment of treatment outcome. Benefits of this work will no doubt extend to the newly emerging work with children. Finally, many different treatments have been effectively applied with adults. Extending these treatments to children no doubt involves many changes; however, treatment manuals provide an excellent beginning to modify treatment for work with children. In light of these considerations, it is likely that treatment research will increase greatly within the next few years.

Acknowledgments

Completion of this chapter was supported by a Research Scientist Development Award (MH00353) and by a grant (MH35408) from the National Institute of Mental Health.

REFERENCES

Abidin, R. R. (1983). *Parenting Stress Index—Manual.* Charlottesville, VA: Pediatric Psychology Press.

Abramson, L. Y., Seligman, M.E.P., & Teasdale, J. D. (1978). Learned helplessness in humans: Critique and reformulation. *Journal of Abnormal Psychology, 87,* 49–74.

Achenbach, T. M., & Edelbrock, C. S. (1983). *Manual for the Child Behavior Checklist and Revised Child Behavior Profile.* Burlington: University of Vermont, Department of Psychiatry.

Akiskal, H. S. (1979). A biobehavioral approach to depression. In R. A. Depue (Ed.), *The psychobiology of the depressive disorders* (pp. 409–437). New York: Academic Press.

Akiskal, H. S., & McKinney, W. T., Jr. (1975). Overview of recent research in depression: Integration of ten conceptual models into a comprehensive clinical frame. *Archives of General Psychiatry, 32,* 285–305.

American Psychiatric Association (APA). (1980). *Diagnostic and statistical manual of mental disorders* (3rd ed.). Washington, DC: Author.

American Psychiatric Association (APA). (1987). *Diagnostic and statistical manual of mental disorders* (3rd ed., rev.). Washington, DC: Author.

Annell, A. (Ed.). (1972). *Depressive states in childhood and adolescence.* Stockholm: Almqvist & Wiksell.

Anthony, E. J. (1975). Childhood depression. In E. J. Anthony & T. Benedek (Eds.), *Depression and human existence* (pp. 231–277). Boston: Little, Brown.

Asarnow, J. R., & Carlson, G. A. (1986). Depression Self-Rating Scale: Utility with child psychiatric inpatients. *Journal of Consulting and Clinical Psychology, 53,* 491–499.

Asher, S. R., Hymel, S., & Renshaw, P. D. (1984). Loneliness in children. *Child Development, 55,* 1456–1464.

Asher, S. R., & Wheeler, V. A. (1985). Children's loneliness: A comparison of rejected and neglected peer status. *Journal of Consulting and Clinical Psychology, 53,* 500–505.

Ausubel, D. P., Sullivan, E. V., & Ives, W. S. (1980). *Theory and problems of child development.* New York: Grune & Stratton.

Baldessarini, R. J. (1977). *Chemotherapy in psychiatry.* Cambridge, MA: Harvard University Press.

Beck, A. T. (1976). *Cognitive therapy and the emotional disorders.* New York: International Universities Press.

Beck, A. T., Kovacs, M., & Weissman, A. (1975). Hopelessness and suicidal behavior: An overview. *Journal of the American Medical Association, 234,* 1146–1149.

Beck, A. T., Rush, A. J., Shaw, B. F., & Emery, G. (1979). *Cognitive therapy of depression.* New York: Guilford Press.

Beck, S., & Rosenberg, R. (1986). The frequency, quality, and impact of life events in self-rated depressed, behavioral problem and normal children. *Journal of Consulting and Clinical Psychology, 54,* 863–864.

Beckham, E. E., & Leber, W. R. (Eds.). (1985). *Handbook of depression: Treatment, assessment, and research.* Homewood, IL: Dorsey.

Bemporad, J. R., & Wilson, A. (1978). A developmental approach to depression in childhood and adolescence. *Journal of the American Academy of Psychoanalysis, 6,* 325–352.

Bene, A. (1975). Depressive phenomena in childhood: Their open and disguised manifestations in analytic treatment. In *Studies in child psychoanalysis (Psychoanalytic Study of the child,* Monograph No. 5, pp. 33–46). New Haven, CT: Yale University Press.

Beres, D. (1966). Superego and depression. In R. M. Lowenstein, L. M. Newman, M. Scherr, & A. J. Solnit (Eds.), *Psychoanalysis: A general psychology* (pp. 479–498). New York: International Universities Press.

Biglan, A., Hops, H., Sherman, L., Friedman, L., Arthur, J., & Osteen, V. (1985). Problem-solving interactions of depressed women and their husbands. *Behavior Therapy, 16,* 431–451.

Billings, A. G., & Moos, R. H. (1982). Psychosocial theory and research on depression: An integrative framework and review. *Clinical Psychology Review, 2,* 213–237.

Billings, A. G., & Moos, R. H. (1983). Comparisons of children of depressed and nondepressed parents: A social-environmental perspective. *Journal of Abnormal Child Psychology, 11,* 463–486.

Birleson, P. (1981). The validity of depressive disorder in childhood and the development of a self-rating scale: A research project. *Journal of Child Psychology and Psychiatry, 22,* 73–88.

Blechman, E. A., McEnroe, M. J., Carella, E. T., & Audette, D. P. (1986). Childhood competence and depression. *Journal of Abnormal Psychology, 95,* 223–227.

Brown, G. W., Harris, T. O., & Bifulco, A. (1986). Long-term effects of early loss of parent. In M. Rutter, C. E. Izard, & P. B. Read (Eds.), *Depression in young people: Developmental and clinical perspectives* (pp. 251–296). New York: Guilford Press.

Brown, G. W., Harris, T. O., & Peto, J. (1973). Life events and psychiatric disorders: Part II. Nature of causal link. *Psychological Medicine, 3,* 159–176.

Bunch, J. (1972). Recent bereavement in relation to suicide. *Journal of Psychosomatic Research, 16,* 361–366.

Burbach, D. J., & Borduin, C. M. (1986). Parent–child relations and the etiology of depression: A review of methods and findings. *Clinical Psychology Review, 6,* 133–153.

Butler, L., Miezitis, S., Friedman, R., & Cole, E. (1980). The effect of two school-based intervention programs on depressive symptoms in preadolescents. *American Educational Research Journal, 17,* 111–119.

Calpin, J. P., & Cinciripini, P. M. (1978, May). *A multiple baseline analysis of social skills training in children.* Paper presented at the meeting of the Midwestern Association for Behavior Analysis, Chicago.

Cantwell, D. P. (1982). Childhood depression. In B. B. Lahey & A. E. Kazdin (Eds.), *Advances in clinical child psychology* (Vol. 5, pp. 39–93). New York: Plenum.

Carey, M. P., Kelley, M. L., Buss, R. R., & Scott, W.O.N. (1986). Relationship of acitivity to depression in adolescents: Development of the Adolescent Activities Checklist. *Journal of Consulting and Clinical Psychology, 54,* 320–322.

Carlson, G. A., & Cantwell, D. P. (1979). A survey of depressive symptoms in a child and adolescent psychiatric population. *Journal of the American Academy of Child Psychiatry, 18,* 587–599.

Carlson, G. A., & Cantwell, D. P. (1980). Unmasking masked depression in children and adolescents. *American Journal of Psychiatry, 137,* 445–449.

Carlson, G. A., & Cantwell, D. P. (1982). Suicidal behavior and depression in children and adolescents. *Journal of the American Academy of Child Psychiatry, 21,* 361–368.

Carlson, G. A., & Garber, J. (1986). Developmental issues in the classification of depression in children. In M. Rutter, C. E. Izard, & P. B. Read (Eds.), *Depression in young people: Developmental and clinical perspectives* (pp. 399–434). New York: Guilford Press.

Carroll, B. J. (1978). Neuroendocrine function in psychiatric disorders. In M. A. Lipton, A. DiMascio, & K. F. Killam (Eds.), *Psychopharmacology: A generation of progress* (pp. 487–497). New York: Raven Press.

Carroll, B. J. (1983). Neuroendocrine diagnosis of depression: The dexamethasone suppression test. In P. J. Clayton & J. E. Barrett (Eds.), *Treatment of depression* (pp. 1–30). New York: Raven Press.

Cautela, J. R., Cautela, J., & Esonis, S. (1983). *Forms for behavior analysis with children.* Champaign, IL: Research Press.

Chambers, W. J., Puig-Antich, J., Hirsch, M., Paez, P., Ambrosini, P. J., Tabrizi, M. A., & Davies, M. (1985). The assessment of affective disorders in children and adolescents by semistructured interview: Test–retest reliability. *Archives of General Psychiatry, 42,* 696–702.

Chiles, J. A., Miller, M. L., & Cox, G. B. (1980). Depression in an adolescent delinquent population. *Archives of General Psychiatry, 37,* 1179–1184.

Clarizio, H. F. (1985). Cognitive–behavioral treatment of childhood depression. *Psychology in the Schools, 22,* 308–322.

Clarkin, J. F., & Glazer, H. I. (Eds.). (1981). *Depression: Behavioral and directive intervention strategies.* New York: Garland–STPM.

Clayton, P. J., & Barrett, J. E. (Eds.). (1983). *Treatment of depression*. New York: Raven Press.

Coddington, R. D. (1972). The significance of life events as etiological factors in the diseases of children: A study of normal population. *Journal of Psychosomatic Research, 16*, 205–213.

Cole, D. A., & Rehm, L. P. (1986). Family interaction patterns and childhood depression. *Journal of Abnormal Child Psychology, 14*, 297–314.

Compas, B. E. (1987). Stress and life events during childhood and adolescence. *Clinical Psychology Review, 7*, 275–302.

Connell, J. P. (1985). A new multidimensional measure of children's perceptions of control. *Child Development, 56*, 1018–1041.

Connell, H. M. (1972). Depression in childhood. *Depression, Child Psychiatry and Human Development, 4*, 71–85.

Costello, E. J., Edelbrock, C. S., & Costello, A. J. (1985). Validity of the NIMH Diagnostic Interview Schedule for Children: A comparison between psychiatric and pediatric referrals. *Journal of Abnormal Child Psychology, 13*, 579–595.

Crook, T., Raskin, A., & Eliot, J. (1981). Parent–child relationships and adult depression. *Child Development, 52*, 950–957.

Cytryn, L., & McKnew, D. H. (1972). Proposed classification of childhood depression. *American Journal of Psychiatry, 129*, 149–155.

Cytryn, L., & McKnew, D. H. (1974). Factors influencing the changing clinical expression of the depressive process in children. *Anerican Journal of Psychiatry, 131*, 879–881.

Davidson, J. (1985). Nonresponse to tricyclic and MAOI drugs: What comes next? In A. Dean (Ed.), *Depression in multidisciplinary perspective* (pp. 173–193). New York: Brunner/Mazel.

Depue, R. A. (Ed.). (1979). *The psychobiology of the depressive disorders: Implications for the effects of stress*. New York: Academic Press.

Depue, R. A., & Monroe, S. M. (1979). The unipolar–bipolar distinction in the depressive disorders: Implications for stress–onset interaction. In R. A. Depue (Ed.), *The psychobiology of the depressive disorders* (pp. 23–53). New York: Academic Press.

Diener, C. I., & Dweck, C. S. (1980). An analysis of learned helplessness: II. The processing of success. *Journal of Personality and Social Psychology, 39*, 940–952.

Digdon, N., & Gotlib, I. H. (1985). Developmental considerations in the study of childhood depression. *Developmental Review, 5*, 162–199.

Dugas, M., Mouren, M. C., Halfon, O., & Moron, P. (1985). Treatment of childhood and adolescent depression with mianserin. *Acta Psychiatrica Scandinavica, 72*(Suppl. 320), 48–53.

Dweck, C. S. (1975). The role of expectations and attributions in the alleviation of learned helplessness. *Journal of Personality and Social Psychology, 31*, 674–685.

Dweck, C. S., & Reppucci, N. D. (1973). Learned helplessness and reinforcement responsibility in children. *Journal of Personality and Social Psychology, 25*, 109–116.

D'Zurilla, T. J., & Nezu, A. (1982). Social problem solving in adults. In P. C. Kendall (Ed.), *Advances in cognitive–behavioral research and therapy* (Vol. 1, pp. 202–274). New York: Academic Press.

Elkins, R., & Rapoport, J. L. (1983). Psychopharmacology

of adult and childhood depression: An overview. In D. P. Cantwell & G. A. Carlson (Eds.), *Affective disorders in childhood and adolescence: An update* (pp. 363–374). New York: Spectrum.

Eyberg, S. M., & Robinson, E. A. (1982). Parent–child interaction training: Effects of family functioning. *Journal of Clinical Child Psychology, 11*, 130–137.

Forehand, R., Griest, D. L., Wells, K., & McMahon, R. J. (1982). Side effects of parent counseling on marital satisfaction. *Journal of Counseling Psychology, 29*, 104–107.

Forehand, R., Wells, K. C., & Griest, D. L. (1980). An examination of the social validity of parent training program. *Behavior Therapy, 11*, 488–502.

Frame, C., Matson, J. L., Sonis, W. A., Fialkov, M. J., & Kazdin, A. E. (1982). Behavioral treatment of depression in a prepubertal child. *Journal of Behavior Therapy and Experimental Psychiatry, 3*, 239–243.

Freud, S. (1957). Mourning and melancholia. In J. Strackey (Ed. 2nd Trans.), *The standard edition of the complete psychological works of Sigmund Freud* (Vol. 14, pp. 243–258). London: Hogarth Press. (Original work published 1917).

Friedrich, W., Remas, R., & Jacobs, J. (1982). Depression and suicidal ideation in early adolescents. *Journal of Youth and Adolescents, 11*, 403–407.

Geller, B., Perel, J. M., Knitter, E. F., Lycaki, H., & Farooki, Z. Q. (1983). Nortriptyline in major depressive disorder in children: Response, steady-state plasma levels, predictive kinetics, and pharmacokinetics. *Psychopharmacology Bulletin, 19*, 62–65.

Gershon, E. S., Targum, S. D., Kessler, L. R., Mazure, C. M., & Bunney, W. E., Jr. (1977). Genetic studies and biologic strategies in the affective disorders. *Progress in Medical Genetics, 2*, 101–164.

Glaser, K. (1968). Masked depression in children and adolescents. In S. Chess & A. Thomas (Eds.), *Annual progress in child psychiatry and child development* (Vol. 1, pp. 345–355). New York: Brunner/Mazel.

Goetz, R. R., Goetz, D. M., Hanlon, C., Davies, M., Weitzman, E. D., & Puig-Antich, J. (1983). Spindle characteristics in prepubertal major depressives during an episode and after sustained recovery: A controlled study. *Sleep, 6*, 369–375.

Group for the Advancement of Psychiatry, Committee on Child Psychiatry. (1966). *Psychopathological disorders in childhood: Theoretical considerations and a proposed classification* (Vol. 6). New York: Author.

Haley, G., Fine, S., Marriage, K., Moretti, M., & Freeman, R. (1985). Cognitive bias and depression in psychiatrically disturbed children and adolescents. *Journal of Consulting and Clinical Psychology, 53*, 535–537.

Hamilton, M. A. (1967). Development of a rating scale for primary depressive illness. *British Journal of Social and Clinical Psychology, 6*, 278–296.

Harter, S. (1985). *Manual for the Self-Perception Profile for Children*. Denver, CO: University of Denver.

Hawton, K. (1985). *Suicide and attempted suicide among children and adolescents*. Beverly Hills, CA: Sage.

Helsel, W. J., & Matson, J. L. (1984). Assessment of depression in children: The internal structure of the Child Depression Inventory (CDI). *Behaviour Research and Therapy, 22*, 289–298.

Herjanic, B., & Reich, W. (1982). Development of a structured psychiatric interview for children: Agreement between child and parent on individual symptoms. *Journal of Abnormal Child Psychology, 10*, 307–324.

Hodges, K., McKnew, D., Cytryn, L., Stern, L., & Kline,

J. (1982). The Child Assessment Schedule (CAS) diagnostic interview: A report on reliability and validity. *Journal of the American Academy of Child Psychiatry, 21,* 468–473.

Hops, H., Biglan, A., Sherman, L., Arthur, J., Friedman, L., & Osteen, V. (1987). Home observations of family interactions of depressed women. *Journal of Consulting and Clinical Psychology, 55,* 341–346.

Jacobsen, R. H., Lahey, B. B., & Strauss, C. C. (1983). Correlates of depressed mood in normal children. *Journal of Abnormal Child Psychology, 11,* 29–40.

Johnson, J. H. (1986). *Life events as stressors in childhood and adolescence.* Newbury Park, CA: Sage.

Johnson, J. H., & McCutcheon, S. M. (1980). Assessing life stress in older children and adolescents: Preliminary findings with the Life Events Checklist. In I. G. Sarason & C. D. Spielberger (Eds.), *Stress and anxiety* (Vol. 7, pp. 111–125). Washington, DC: Hemisphere.

Kandel, D. B., & Davies, M. (1982). Epidemiology of depressive mood in adolescents: An empirical study. *Archives of General Psychiatry, 39,* 1205–1212.

Kaplan, S. L., Hong, G. K., & Weinhold, C. (1984). Epidemiology of depressive symptomatology in adolescents. *Journal of the American Academy of Child Psychiatry, 23,* 91–98.

Karoly, P., & Rosenthal, M. (1977). Training parents in behavior modification: Effects on perceptions of family interaction and deviant child behavior. *Behavior Therapy, 8,* 406–410.

Kashani, J. H., Barbero, G. J., & Bolander, F. D. (1981). Depression in hospitalized pediatric patients. *Journal of the American Academy of Child Psychiatry, 20,* 123–134.

Kashani, J. H., Cantwell, D. P., Shekim, W. O., & Reid, J. C. (1982). Major depressive disorder in children admitted to an inpatient community mental health center. *American Journal of Psychiatry, 139,* 671–672.

Kashani, J. H., Husain, A., Shekim, W. O., Hodges, K. K., Cytryn, L., & McKnew, D. H. (1981). Current perspectives on childhood depression: An overview. *American Journal of Psychiatry, 138,* 143–153.

Kashani, J. H., McGee, R. O., Clarkson, S. E., Anderson, J. C., Walton, L. A., Williams, S., Silva, P. A., Robins, A. J., Cytryn, L., & McKnew, D. H. (1983). Depression in a sample of 9-year old children. *Archives of General Psychiatry, 40,* 1217–1223.

Kashani, J. H., Ray, J. S., & Carlson, G. A. (1984). Depression and depression-like states in preschool-age children in a child development unit. *American Journal of Psychiatry, 141,* 1397–1402.

Kashani, J., & Simonds, J. F. (1979). The incidence of depression in children. *American Journal of Psychiatry, 136,* 1203–1205.

Kaslow, N. J., Rehm, L. P., & Siegel, A. W. (1984). Social-cognitive and cognitive correlates of depression in children. *Journal of Abnormal Child Psychology, 12,* 605–620.

Kazdin, A. E. (1985). *Treatment of antisocial behavior in children and adolescents.* Homewood, IL: Dorsey Press.

Kazdin, A. E. (1988). Childhood depression. In E. J. Mash & L. G. Terdal (Eds.), *Behavioral assessment of childhood disorders* (2nd ed., pp.). New York: Guilford Press.

Kazdin, A. E., Colbus, D., & Rodgers, A. (1987). Assessment of depression and diagnosis of depressive disorder among psychiatrically disturbed children. *Journal of Abnormal Child Psychology, 28,* 29–41.

Kazdin, A. E., Esveldt-Dawson, K., Sherick, R. B., & Colbus, D. (1985). Assessment of overt behavior and childhood depression among psychiatrically disturbed children. *Journal of Consulting and Clinical Psychology, 53,* 201–210.

Kazdin, A. E., Esveldt-Dawson, K., Unis, A. S., & Rancurello, M. D. (1983). Child and parent evaluations of depression and aggression in psychiatric inpatient children. *Journal of Abnormal Child Psychology, 11,* 401–413.

Kazdin, A. E., French, N. H., Unis, A. S., & Esveldt-Dawson, K. (1983). Assessment of childhood depression: Correspondence of child and parent ratings. *Journal of the American Academy of Child Psychiatry, 22,* 157–164.

Kazdin, A. E., French, N. H., Unis, A. S., Esveldt-Dawson, K., & Sherick, R. B. (1983). Hopelessness, depression and suicidal intent among psychiatrically disturbed inpatient children. *Journal of Consulting and Clinical Psychology, 51,* 504–510.

Kazdin, A. E., & Petti, T. A. (1982). Self-report and interview measures of childhood and adolescent depression. *Journal of Child Psychology and Psychiatry, 23,* 437–457.

Kazdin, A. E., Rancurello, M., & Unis, A. S. (1987). Childhood depression. In G. D. Burrows & J. S. Werry (Eds.), *Advances in human psychopharmacology* (Vol. 4 pp. 1–52.). Greenwich, CT: JAI Press.

Kazdin, A. E., Rodgers, A., & Colbus, D. (1986). The Hopelessness Scale for Children: Psychometric characteristics and concurrent validity. *Journal of Consulting and Clinical Psychology, 54,* 241–245.

Kazdin, A. E., Sherick, R. B., Esveldt-Dawson, K., & Rancurello, M. D. (1985). Nonverbal behavior and childhood depression. *Journal of the American Academy of Child Psychiatry, 24,* 303–309.

Klerman, G. L., & Schechter, G. (1982). Drugs and psychotherapy. In E. S. Paykel (Ed.), *Handbook of affective disorders* (pp. 329–337). New York: Guilford Press.

Kovacs, M. (1978). *Interview Schedule for Children* (ISC) (10th rev.). Pittsburgh: University of Pittsburgh School of Medicine.

Kovacs, M. (1981). Rating scales to assess depression in school aged children. *Acta Paedopsychiatrica, 46,* 305–315.

Kovacs, M., & Beck, A. T. (1977). An empirical clinical approach towards a definition of childhood depression. In J. G. Schulterbrandt & A. Raskin (Eds.), *Depression in children: Diagnosis, treatment, and conceptual models* (pp. 1–25). New York: Raven Press.

Lahmeyer, H. W., Poznanski, E. O., & Srinath, N. B. (1983). EEG sleep in depressed adolescents. *American Journal of Psychiatry, 140,* 1150–1153.

Laing, J. A., & Sines, J. O. (1982). The Home Environment Questionnaire: An instrument for assessing several behaviorally relevant dimensions of children's environments. *Journal of Pediatric Psychology, 7,* 425–449.

Lapouse, R. (1966). The epidemiology of behavior disorders in children. *American Journal of Diseases of Children, 111,* 594–599.

Law, W., Petti, T. A., & Kazdin, A. E. (1981). Withdrawal symptoms after graduated cessation of imipramine in children. *American Journal of Psychiatry, 138,* 647–650.

Lefkowitz, M. M. (1980). Childhood depression: A reply to Costello. *Psychological Bulletin, 87,* 191–194.

Lefkowitz, M. M., & Burton, N. (1978). Childhood depression: A critique of the concept. *Psychological Bulletin, 85,* 716–726.

Lefkowitz, M. M., & Tesiny, E. P. (1980). Assessment of childhood depression. *Journal of Consulting and Clinical Psychology, 48,* 43–50.

Lefkowitz, M. M., & Tesiny, E. P. (1984). Rejection and depression: Prospective and contemporaneous analyses. *Developmental Psychology, 20,* 776–785.

Lefkowitz, M. M., & Tesiny, E. P. (1985). Depression in children: Prevalence and correlates. *Journal of Consulting and Clinical Psychology, 53,* 647–656.

Leitenberg, H., Yost, L. W., & Carroll-Wilson, M. (1986). Negative cognitive errors in children: Questionnaire development, normative data, and comparisons between children with and without self-reported symptoms of depression, low self-esteem, and evaluation anxiety. *Journal of Consulting and Clinical Psychology, 54,* 528–536.

Lewinsohn, P. M. (1974). Clinical and theoretical aspects of depression. In K. S. Calhoun, H. E. Adams, & K. M. Mitchell (Eds.), *Innovative treatment methods of psychopathology* (pp. 63–120). New York: Wiley.

Lewinsohn, P. M., & Arconad, M. (1981). Behavioral treatment of depression: A social learning approach. In J. F. Clarkin & H. I. Glazer (Eds.), *Depression: Behavioral and directive intervention strategies* (pp. 33–67). New York: Garland–STPM.

Lewis, H. B. (1986). The role of shame in depression. In M. Rutter, C. E. Izard, & P. B. Read (Eds.), *Depression in young people: Developmental and clinical perspectives* (pp. 325–339). New York: Guilford Press.

Lobovits, D. A., & Handal, P. J. (1985). Childhood depression: Prevalence using DSM-III criteria and validity of parent and child depression scales. *Journal of Pediatric Psychology, 10,* 45–54.

MacFarlane, J. W., Allen, L., & Honzik, M. P. (1954). *A developmental study of the behavior problems of normal children between 21 months and 14 years.* Berkeley: University of California Press.

MacMahon, B., & Pugh, T. F. (1965). Suicide in the widowed. *American Journal of Epidemiology, 81,* 23–31.

Mahler, M. (1961). On sadness and grief in infancy and childhood. *Psychoanalytic Study of the Child, 16,* 332.

Malmquist, C. P. (1977). Childhood depression: A clinical and behavioral perspective. In J. G. Schulterbrandt & A. Raskin (Eds.), *Depression in children: Diagnosis, treatment and conceptual models* (pp. 33–59). New York: Raven Press.

Matson, J. L., Rotatori, A. F., & Helsel, W. J. (1983). Development of a rating scale to measure social skills in children: The Matson Evaluation of Social Skills with Youngsters (MESSY). *Behaviour Research and Therapy, 21,* 335–340.

McConville, B. J., & Bruce, R. T. (1985). Depressive illnesses in children and adolescents: A review of current concepts. *Canadian Journal of Psychiatry, 30,* 119–129.

McKnew, D. H., Jr., Cytryn, L., Efron, A. M., Gershon, E. S., & Bunney, W. E., Jr. (1979). Offspring of patients with affective disorders. *British Journal of Psychiatry, 134,* 148–152.

Mendelson, M. (1982). Psychodynamics of depression. In E. S. Paykel (Ed.), *Handbook of affective disorders* (pp. 162–174). New York: Guilford Press.

Mezzich, A. C., & Mezzich, J. E. (1979). Symptomatology of depression in adolescence. *Journal of Personality Assessment, 43,* 267–275.

Michelson, L., DiLorenzo, T., & Petti, T. (1981). Behavioral assessment of imipramine effects in a depressed child. *Journal of Behavioral Assessment, 3,* 253–262.

Molick, R., & Pinkston, E. M. (1982). Using behavioral analysis to develop adaptive social behavior in a depressed adolescent girl. In E. M. Pinkston, J. L. Levitt, G. R. Green, N. L. Linsk, & T. L. Rzepnicki (Eds.), *Effective social work practice* (pp. 364–375). San Francisco: Jossey-Bass.

Moos, R. H., Insel, P. M., & Humphrey, B. (1974). *Family, Work and Group Environment Scales.* Palo Alto, CA: Consulting Psychologists Press.

Morrison, H. L. (Ed.). (1983). *Children of depressed parents: Risk, identification, and intervention.* New York: Grune & Stratton.

Moyal, B. R. (1977). Locus of control, self-esteem, stimulus appraisal, and depressive symptoms in children. *Journal of Consulting and Clinical Psychology, 45,* 951–952.

Mullins, L. L., Siegel, L. J., & Hodges, K. (1985). Cognitive problem-solving and life event correlates of depressive symptoms in children. *Journal of Abnormal Child Psychology, 13,* 305–314.

Murphy, G. E., Simons, A. D., Wetzel, R. D., & Lustman, P. J. (1984). Cognitive therapy and pharmacotherapy. *Archives of General Psychiatry, 41,* 33–41.

Nelson, W. M., III, Politano, P. M., Finch, A. J., Jr., Wendel, N., & Mayhall, C. (1987). *Journal of the American Academy of Child and Adolescent Psychiatry, 26,* 43–48.

Nezu, A. M., & Ronan, G. F. (1985). Life stress, current problems, problem-solving, and depressive symptoms: An integrative model. *Journal of Consulting and Clinical Psychology, 53,* 693–697.

Nurnberger, J. I., & Gershon, E. S. (1982). Genetics. In E. S. Paykel (Ed.), *Handbook of affective disorders* (pp. 109–125). New York: Guilford Press.

Orvaschel, H., Puig-Antich, J., Chambers, W., Tabrizi, M. A., & Johnson, R. (1982). Retrospective assessment of prepubertal major depression with the Kiddie-SADS-E. *Journal of the American Academy of Child Psychiatry, 21,* 392–397.

Patterson, G. R. (1982). *Coercive family process.* Eugene, OR: Castalia.

Patterson, G. R., & Fleischman, M. J. (1979). Maintenance of treatment effects: Some considerations concerning family systems and follow-up data. *Behavior Therapy, 10,* 168–185.

Paykel, E. S. (Ed.). (1982a). *Handbook of affective disorders.* New York: Guilford Press.

Paykel, E. S. (1982b). Life events and early environment. In E. S. Paykel (Ed.), *Handbook of affective disorders* (pp. 146–161). New York: Guilford Press.

Paykel, E. S., & Tanner, J. (1976). Life events, depressive relapse and maintenance treatment. *Psychological Medicine, 6,* 481–485.

Petti, T. A., Bornstein, M., Delamater, A., & Conners, C. K. (1980). Evaluation and multimodality treatment of a depressed pre-pubertal girl. *Journal of the American Academy of Child Psychiatry, 19,* 690–702.

Petti, T. A., & Law, W. (1982). Imipramine treatment of depressed children: A double-blind pilot study. *Journal of Clinical Psychopharmacology, 2,* 107–110.

Pfeffer, C. R., Conte, H. R., Plutchik, R., & Jerrett, I. (1979). Suicidal behavior in latency age children. *Journal of the American Academy of Child Psychiatry, 18,* 679–692.

Polvan, O., & Cebiroglu, R. (1972). Treatment with psychopharmacologic agents in childhood depressions. In A.

L. Annell (Ed.), *Depressive states in childhood and adolescence* (pp. 467–472). Stockholm: Almqvist & Wiksell.

Poznanski, E. O., Cook, S. C., & Carroll, B. J. (1979). A depression rating scale for children. *Pediatrics, 64,* 442–450.

Poznanski, E. O., Grossman, J. A., Buchsbaum, Y., Banegas, M., Freeman, L., & Gibbons, R. (1984). Preliminary studies of the reliability and validity of the Children's Depression Rating Scale. *Journal of the American Academy of Child Psychiatry, 23,* 191–197.

Preskorn, S. H., Weller, E. B., & Weller, R. A. (1982). Depression in children: Relationship between plasma imipramine levels and response. *Journal of Clinical Psychiatry, 43,* 450–453.

Puig-Antich, J. (1983). Neuroendocrine and sleep correlates of prepubertal major depressive disorder: Current status of the evidence. In D. P. Cantwell & G. A. Carlson (Eds.), *Affective disorders in childhood and adolescence: An update* (pp. 211–227). New York: Spectrum.

Puig-Antich, J. (1986). Psychobiological markers: Effects of age and puberty. In M. Rutter, C. E. Izard, & P. B. Read (Eds.), *Depression in young people: Developmental and clinical perspectives* (pp. 341–381). New York: Guilford Press.

Puig-Antich, J., Blau, S., Marx, N., Greenhill, L. L., & Chambers, W. (1978). Prepubertal major depressive disorders: A pilot study. *Journal of the American Academy of Child Psychiatry, 17,* 695–707.

Puig-Antich, J., & Gittelman, R. (1982). Depression in childhood and adolescence. In E. S. Paykel (Ed.), *Handbook of affective disorders* (pp. 379–392). New York: Guilford Press.

Puig-Antich, J., Lukens, E., Davies, M., Goetz, D., Brennan-Quattrock, J., & Todak, G. (1985a). Psychosocial functioning in prepubertal major depressive disorders: I. Interpersonal relationships during the depressive episode. *Archives of General Psychiatry, 42,* 500–507.

Puig-Antich, J., Lukens, E., Davies, M., Goetz, D., Brennan-Quattrock, J., & Todak, G. (1985b). Psychosocial functioning in prepubertal major depressive disorders: II. Interpersonal relationships after sustained recovery from affective episode. *Archives of General Psychiatry, 42,* 511–517.

Puig-Antich, J., Perel, J., Lupatkin, W., Chambers, W. J., Tabrizi, M. A., King, J., Davies, M., Johnson, R., & Stiller, R. (1987). Imipramine in prepubertal major depressive disorders. *Archives of General Psychiatry, 44,* 81–89.

Puig-Antich, J., & Weston, B. (1983). The diagnosis and treatment of major depressive disorder in childhood. *Annual Review of Medicine, 34,* 231–245.

Rancurello, M. (1986). Antidepressants in children: Indications, benefits, and limitations. *American Journal of Psychotherapy, 40,* 377–393.

Rehm, L. P. (1977). A self-control model of depression. *Behavior Therapy, 8,* 787–804.

Rehm, L. P., & Kaslow, N. J. (1984). Behavioral approaches to depression: Research results and clinical recommendations. In C. M. Franks (Ed.), *New developments in behavior therapy* (pp. 155–229). New York: Haworth Press.

Reynolds, W. M. (1985). Depression in childhood and adolescence: Diagnosis, assessment, intervention strategies, and research. In T. R. Kratochwill (Ed.), *Advances in school psychology* (Vol. 4, pp. 133–189). Hillsdale, NJ: Erlbaum.

Reynolds, W. M., Anderson, G., & Bartell, N. (1985). Measuring depression in children: A multi-method assessment investigation. *Journal of Abnormal Child Psychology, 13,* 513–526.

Reynolds, W. M., & Coats, K. I. (1986). A comparison of cognitive–behavioral therapy and relaxation training for the treatment of depression in adolescents. *Journal of Consulting and Clinical Psychology, 54,* 653–660.

Rie, H. E. (1966). Depression in childhood: A survey of some pertinent contributions. *Journal of the American Academy of Child Psychiatry, 5,* 653–685.

Rochlin, G. (1965). *Griefs and discontents.* Boston: Little, Brown.

Rush, A. J., Beck, A. T., Kovacs, M., & Hollon, S. (1977). Comparative efficacy of cognitive therapy and pharmacotherapy in the treatment of depressed outpatients. *Cognitive Therapy and Research, 1,* 17–37.

Rutter, M., Izard, C. E., & Read, P. B. (Eds.). (1986). *Depression in young people: Developmental and clinical perspectives.* New York: Guilford Press.

Ryan, N. D., Puig-Antich, J., Cooper, T., Rabinovich, H., Ambrosini, P., Davies, M., King, J., Torrer, D., & Fried, J. (1986). Imipramine in adolescent major depression: Plasma level and clinical response. *Acta Psychiatrica Scandinavica, 73,* 275–288.

Sachar, E. J. (1982). Endocrine abnormalities in depression. In E. S. Paykel (Ed.), *Handbook of affective disorders* (pp. 191–201). New York: Guilford Press.

Sacks, J. M. (1977). The need for subtlety: A critical session with a suicidal child. *Psychotherapy: Theory, Research, and Practice, 14,* 434–437.

Saylor, C. F., Finch, A. J., Jr., Baskin, C. H., Furey, W., & Kelly, M. M. (1984). Construct validity for measures of childhood depression: Application of multitrait–multimethod methodology. *Journal of Consulting and Clinical Psychology, 52,* 977–985.

Saylor, C. F., Finch, A. J., Jr., Spirito, A., & Bennett, B. (1984). The Children's Depression Inventory: A systematic evaluation of psychometric properties. *Journal of Consulting and Clinical Psychology, 52,* 955–967.

Seligman, M.E.P. (1975). *Helplessness: On depression, development and death.* San Francisco: W. H. Freeman.

Seligman, M.E.P., & Peterson, C. (1986). A learned helplessness perspective on childhood depression: Theory and research. In M. Rutter, C. E. Izard, & P. B. Read (Eds.), *Depression in young people: Developmental and clinical perspectives* (pp. 223–249). New York: Guilford Press.

Seligman, M.E.P., Peterson, C., Kaslow, N. J., Tanenbaum, R. L., Alloy, L. B., & Abramson, L. Y. (1984). Attributional style and depressive symptoms among children. *Journal of Abnormal Psychology, 93,* 235–238.

Simons, A. D., Garfield, S. L., & Murphy, G. E. (1984). The process of change in cognitive therapy and pharmacotherapy for depression. *Archives of General Psychiatry, 41,* 45–51.

Smucker, M. R., Craighead, W. E., Craighead, L. W., & Green, B. J. (1986). Normative and reliability data for the Children's Depression Inventory. *Journal of Abnormal Child Psychology, 14,* 25–39.

Sokoloff, R. M., & Lubin, B. (1983). Depressive mood in adolescent, emotionally disturbed females: Reliability and validity of an adjective checklist (C-DACL). *Journal of Abnormal Child Psychology, 11,* 531–536.

Spitz, R. (1946). Anaclitic depression. *Psychoanalytic Study of the Child, 2,* 113–117.

Spitzer, R. L., Endicott, J., & Robins, E. (1978). Research Diagnostic Criteria: Rationale and reliability. *Archives of General Psychiatry, 35,* 773–782.

Stark, K. D., Reynolds, W. M., & Kaslow, N. (1987). A comparison of the relative efficacy of self-control therapy and a behavioral problem-solving therapy for depression in children. *Journal of Abnormal Child Psychology, 15,* 91–113.

Tisher, M., & Lang, M. (1983). The Children's Depression Scale: Review and further developments. In D. P. Cantwell & G. A. Carlson (Eds.), *Childhood depression* (pp. 181–203). New York: Spectrum.

Toolan, J. M. (1962). Depression in children and adolescents. *American Journal of Orthopsychiatry, 32,* 404–414.

Trad, P. V. (1987). *Infant and childhood depression: Developmental factors.* New York: Wiley.

Usdin, E., Asberg, M., Bertilsson, L., & Sjoqvist, F. (Eds.). (1984). *Advances in biochemical psychopharmacology: Vol. 39. Frontiers in biochemical and pharmacological research in depression.* New York: Raven Press.

Vosk, B., Forehand, R., Parker, J. B., & Rickard, K. (1982). A multimethod comparison of popular and unpopular children. *Developmental Psychology, 18,* 571–575.

Weinberg, W. A., Rutman, J., Sullivan, L., Pencik, E. C., & Dietz, S. G. (1973). Depression in children referred to an education diagnostic center. *Journal of Pediatrics, 83,* 1065–1072.

Weissman, M. M. (1984). The psychological treatment of depression: An update of clinical trials. In J.B.W. Williams & R. Spitzer (Eds.), *Psychotherapy research: Where are we and where should we go?* (pp. 89–103). New York: Guilford Press.

Weissman, M. M., Orvaschel, H., & Padian, N. (1980). Children's symptom and social functioning self-report scales: Comparison of mothers' and children's reports. *Journal of Nervous and Mental Disease, 168,* 736–740.

Weissman, M. M., & Paykel, E. S. (1974). *The depressed woman: A study of social relationships.* Chicago: University of Chicago Press.

Weissman, M. M., Paykel, E. S., & Klerman, G. L. (1972). The depressed woman as a mother. *Social Psychiatry, 7,* 98–108.

Weisz, J. R., Weiss, B., Wasserman, A. A., & Rintoul, B. (1987). Control-related beliefs and depression among clinic-referred children and adolescents. *Journal of Abnormal Psychology, 96,* 58–63.

Weller, R. A., & Weller, E. B. (1986). Tricyclic antidepressants in prepubertal depressed children: Review of the literature. *Hillside Journal of Clinical Psychiatry, 8,* 46–55.

Werry, J. S., & Quay, H. C. (1971). The prevalence of behavior symptoms in younger elementary school children. *American Journal of Orthopsychiatry, 41,* 136–143.

Whybrow, P. C., Akiskal, H. S., & McKinney, W. T. (1984). *Mood disorders: Toward a new psychobiology.* New York: Plenum.

Wilson, H., & Staton, R. D. (1984). Neuropsychological changes in children associated with tricyclic antidepressant therapy. *International Journal of Neuroscience, 24,* 307–312.

World Health Organization. (1987). *International classification of diseases, injuries, and causes of death* (10th ed., draft). Geneva: Author.

Young, W., Knowles, J. B., MacLean, A. W., Boag, L., & McConville, B. J. (1982). The sleep of childhood depressives. *Biological Psychiatry, 17,* 1163–1168.

Zis, A. P., & Goodwin, F. K. (1982). The amine hypothesis. In E. S. Paykel (Ed.), *Handbook of affective disorders* (pp. 175–190). New York: Guilford Press.

5

FEARS AND ANXIETIES

BILLY A. BARRIOS AND STAN L. O'DELL
University of Mississippi

Efforts to treat the fears and anxieties of children have always been of great interest to behavior therapists. Historically, such efforts have served to shape and validate the paradigm, theories, and techniques of behavior therapy. Behaviorism, the paradigm from which behavior therapy operates, owes much of its early survival to Mary Cover Jones's (1924a, 1924b) treatment of young Peter, Bobby, and Vincent's fear of rabbits. The success of her direct conditioning and social imitation treatments provided much-needed early support for the paradigm of behaviorism and the classical conditioning theory of emotional disorders (Watson & Rayner, 1920); the treatments themselves provided us with precursors to systematic desensitization (Wolpe, 1948, 1954, 1958) and modeling (Bandura, 1969, 1971), two of contemporary behavior therapy's most popular techniques. The popularity of desensitization and modeling also has its origin in the treatment of children's fears and anxieties. Successful applications of the techniques to the fears and anxieties of children contributed greatly to our early, if not our current, belief in the efficacy of desensitization and modeling and in the theories that underlie them (e.g., Bandura, Grusec, & Menlove, 1967; Lazarus, 1960; Lazarus & Rachman, 1957; Wolpe, 1958, 1961).

A great many other aspects of contemporary behavior therapy can be traced back in part, if not in full, to our attempts to treat the fears and anxieties of children. Among these are the field's interest in self-regulation and verbal mediation (e.g., Kanfer, Karoly, & Newman, 1975), in secondary and primary prevention (e.g., Peterson, Harmann, & Gelfand, 1980; Poser, 1976), and in psychological reactions to medical illness and medical procedures (e.g., Melamed & Siegel, 1975, 1980). The sundry techniques and interventions associated with each of these areas of interest also have certain ties to children's fears and anxieties. It is clear, then, that in our attempts to alter the fears and anxieties of children, we have also altered the nature and course of behavior therapy. In fact, it could be argued that most of our attempts to change children's fears and anxieties have been undertaken with just such a purpose in mind—to proclaim or promote a concept or theory or technique, rather than to alleviate or remediate a condition of clinical concern.

Though it may be true that most of our early attempts to treat the fears and anxieties of children had as their primary objective the promotion of a particular notion or technique, it certainly is not true of our most recent attempts. In our most recent efforts at treatment, the primary objective has been the alleviation of children's distress. This objective reflects a dramatic shift in our view of children's fears and anxieties: from that of convenient vehicle for the promulgation of ideas and techniques to that of legitimate problem condition worthy of concern and remediation (Gittelman, 1986; Johnson & Melamed, 1979; Morris & Kratochwill, 1983a; Ollendick, 1979). Though the two are not incompatible, we see the latter view as the more enlightened one and the one more likely to lead to an adequate understanding and treatment of children's fears and anxieties. It is, therefore, the view on which the present chapter is based.

The goal of the present chapter is to discuss in depth the subtleties and complexities of the behavioral treatment of children's fears and anxieties. Our discussion revolves around four issues: (1) the question of whether or not to treat the fears and anxieties of children; (2) the identification of a treatment focus once it has been determined that treatment is warranted; (3) the selection of the most appropriate intervention; and (4) the evaluation of that intervention. Preceding our discussion of these issues is a presentation of our working definition of children's fears and anxieties.

TERMINOLOGY AND SYMPTOMATOLOGY

Definitions

In reading the child therapy literature and conversing with child therapists, the following terms are encountered: "fear," "clinical fear," "avoidance behavior," "avoidance reaction," "anxiety," "anxiety state," "phobia," and "phobic reaction." In some instances, the terms are clearly meant to denote the same phenomenon; in other instances, the terms are clearly meant to denote distinctive phenomena. Often, though, it is not clear whether the terms are being used interchangeably or independently, or *why* they are being thus used. As such, we find considerable confusion and controversy surrounding the meaning and utility of the various terms.

Whether one chooses to use the term interchangeably or independently, the cornerstone concept or term appears to be that of "fear." Curiously enough, there appears to be good consensus on the definition of fear—that is, as a pattern of three types of reactions to a stimulus of perceived threat: (1) motor reactions, such as avoidance, escape, and tentative approach; (2) subjective reactions, such as verbal reports of discomfort, distress, and terror; and (3) physiological reactions, such as heart palpitations, profuse sweating, and rapid breathing (e.g., Marks, 1969; Morris & Kratochwill, 1983a, 1983c). "Anxiety," "phobia," "clinical fear," and so on are merely names ascribed to different manifestations of this pattern of reactions. Diffuse, moderate reactions to

no discernible threat are referred to as "anxieties" (e.g., Barrios, Hartmann, & Shigetomi, 1981; Jersild, 1954; Johnson & Melamed, 1979). Highly intense and persistent reactions to a stimulus posing little objective danger are referred to as "phobias" (e.g., Marks, 1969; Miller, Barrett, & Hampe, 1974). "Clinical fears" are said to be those that interfere with daily living or that have lasted for more than 5 months (Poznanski, 1973) or 2 years (Graziano, DeGiovanni, & Garcia, 1979). Other terms, such as "avoidance behavior" (e.g., Richards & Siegel, 1978) and "phobic reaction" (e.g., Morris, 1980), are applied to a subset of the overall pattern of reactivity.

In principle, the positing of different terms to denote different clinical phenomena may help serve a number of different functions. For example, the different terms may help in predicting the most efficacious course of treatment or the duration needed for a particular form of treatment. In practice, though, we see no compelling reason for adhering to the abovementioned distinctions among the terms "fear," "anxiety," "phobia," "clinical fear," and so on. Obvious problems of measurement notwithstanding, these distinctions have thus far proven to be of little worth: they have given rise to no new developments in theory or treatment. What is more, none of the distinctions are attended to in any of the current theorizing on emotions and emotional disorders (e.g., Delprato & McGlynn, 1984; Lang, 1984). For these reasons, then, we have elected to use the expression "fears and anxieties" in the material that follows. We use the terms "fear" and "anxiety" interchangeably, for we see them both as denoting a complex pattern of motor, subjective, and physiological reactions to a real or imagined threat (e.g., Lang, 1968, 1971, 1984; Rachman, 1977).

Within each category of reactions, responding may take many different forms. For example, escape, avoidance, trembling, flailing, crying, clinging, stuttering, swaying, rocking, and nail biting have all been cited as referents or symptoms of the motor component of children's fears and anxieties (Esveldt-Dawson, Wisner, Unis, Matson, & Kazdin, 1982; Fox & Houston, 1981; Glennon & Weisz, 1978; Katz, Kellerman, & Siegel, 1980; Melamed & Siegel, 1975). Reports of terror, doom, discomfort, impending harm, sadness, monsters, and self-denigration have all served as referents or symptoms of the subjective component. And increases in heart rate, pulse volume, respiration, skin conductance, and muscular tension have all served as referents for the physiological component (Giebenhain, 1985; Jay, Ozolins, Elliott, & Caldwell, 1983; Melamed, Yurcheson, Fleece, Hutcherson, & Hawes, 1978; Van Hasselt, Hersen, Bellack, Rosenblum, & Lamparski, 1979). Table 5-1 offers a further, albeit still partial, listing of the motor, subjective, and physiological symptoms of children's fears and anxieties.

Though diverse, the responses of each component have a shared feature. For those of the motor component, it is the feature of performance impairment; for those of the subjective component, it is psychological distress; and for those of the physiological component, it is somatovisceral arousal (cf. Lang, 1984). These three features act as boundaries for the numerous symptoms of children's fears and anxieties and lend some semblance of distinctiveness to the disorder. Because of the latitude of these boundaries, children vary from one another in the exact make up of their fear and anxiety reactions to a given context. And because of the varying task demands of different contexts, the

exact make up of a given child's fear and anxiety reactions varies from one threatening stimulus to another (Lang, 1984).

The motor, subjective, and physiological components of children's fear and anxiety reactions are at best loosely coupled. Several studies of children's responses to several different threatening stimuli attest to this (see Barrios, 1986). However, some data do present a very different view of the interrelationships among the response components. For example, there are data that show the response components to be virtually independent (e.g., Bradlyn, 1982). However, these data are clearly in the minority.

To summarize, our working definition of children's fears and anxieties is that of a complex pattern of motor, subjective, and physiological reactions to a real or imagined threat. Activity within each of the response categories may take many different forms, and activities from the different response categories may be only moderately related to one another. Thus, there may be considerable variation both between and within children: variation from child to child in the exact make up of the fear and anxiety reactions to the same stimulus, and variation within the same child in the exact

TABLE 5-1 A Subset of the Motoric, Physiological, and Subjective Responses of Children's Fears and Anxieties

Motoric responses	Physiological responses	Subjective responses
Avoidance	Heart rate	Thoughts of being scared
Gratuitous arm, hand, and leg movements	Basal skin responses	Thoughts of monsters
Trembling voice	Palmar sweat index	Thoughts of being hurt
Crying	Galvanic skin response	Images of monsters
Foot shuffling	Muscle tension	Images of wild animals
Screaming	Skin temperature	Thoughts of danger
Nail biting	Respiration	Self-deprecatory thoughts
Thumb sucking	Palpitations	Self-critical thoughts
Rigid posture	Breathlessness	Thoughts of inadequacy
Eyes shut	Nausea	Thoughts of incompetence
Avoidance of eye contact	Pulse volume	Thoughts of bodily injury
Clenched jaw	Headache	Images of bodily injury
Stuttering	Stomach upset	
Physical proximity	Stomachache	
White knuckles	Urination	
Trembling lip	Defecation	
	Vomiting	

Note. From "Fears and Anxieties" by B. A. Barrios and D. P. Hartmann, 1988, in E. J. Mash and L. G. Terdal (Eds.), *Behavioral Assessment of Childhood Disorders* (2nd ed., pp. 204). New York: Guilford Press. Copyright 1988 by The Guilford Press. Reprinted by permission.

make up of the fear and anxiety reactions to different stimuli.

Classification Schemes

Several systems for classifying the different fears and anxieties of children have been proposed; they range from intuitive to statistical in origin and from simple to intricate in nature. Those based on multivariate statistical procedures have fears and anxieties as part of a supraordinate class of problem behaviors. For example, in Quay's (1979) system, the problem behaviors of children cluster into four patterns: conduct disorder, anxiety–withdrawal, immaturity, and socialized aggression. Fears and anxieties as defined in this chapter are subsumed by the general pattern of anxiety–withdrawal, a pattern that has among its elements the following: anxiousness, fearfulness, tension, shyness, timidity, bashfulness, withdrawal, seclusiveness, social isolation, depression, aloofness, and secretiveness.

The taxonomic system of Achenbach (1985; Achenback & Edelbrock, 1978) is another factor-analysis-based classification scheme. Within this system, over 100 different problem behaviors reduce to nine distinct syndromes: schizoid or anxious, depressed, uncommunicative, obsessive–compulsive, somatic complaints, social withdrawal. hyperactive, aggressive, and delinquent. The nine distinct syndromes themselves cluster into two higher-order groupings: an Internalizing grouping comprised of the schizoid or anxious, depressed, uncommunicative, obsessive–compulsive, somatic complaints, and social withdrawal syndromes; and an Externalizing grouping comprised of the hyperactive, aggressive, and delinquent syndromes. Among those syndromes constituting the Internalizing grouping, the shared feature is an excess of anxious behaviors. Among those syndromes constituting the Externalizing grouping, the shared feature is an absence of appropriate anxious behaviors (Achenbach, 1985).

Very different from the factor-analytic systems, both in derivation and configuration, are the diagnostic categories of the American Psychiatric Association (1987). Founded on clinical observation and developed by committee consensus, the association's system devotes three categories solely to the fears and anxieties of children: Separation Anxiety Disorder, Avoidant Disorder, and Overanxious Disorder.

The disorders are similar in that they have anxiety as their predominant symptom; they are dissimilar in that the anxiety is linked to different situations. For Separation Anxiety Disorder, the situation is separation from a significant attachment figure. Excessive anxiety in this situation takes the form of three or more of the following: unrealistic worry about harm to attachment figure, unrealistic worry about harm to self, unrealistic worry about abandonment by attachment figure, persistent opposition to school attendance, persistent opposition to sleeping alone, persistent opposition to sleeping away from home, persistent opposition to being alone, recurrent nightmares involving separation, recurrent physical complaints in anticipation of separation, and recurrent distress in anticipation of and during separation. For Avoidant Disorder, the feared situation is social contact with strangers. Excessive anxiety in this situation takes the form of persistent avoidance of unfamiliar persons, persistent pleas or contact with familiar persons, and impaired peer relationships. For Overanxious Disorder, there is no identifiable situation to which the child's fears are linked. This generalized, persistent anxiety is expressed by the frequent occurrence of four or more of the following: unrealistic worry about the future, unrealistic worry about one's past behavior, unrealistic worry about one's competence, unfounded physical complaints, pleas for reassurance, marked self-consciousness, and marked physical tension.

Seven other psychiatric categories are pertinent to the classification of children's fears and anxieties: Agoraphobia without History of Panic Disorder, Social Phobia, Simple Phobia, Panic Disorder with Agoraphobia, Panic Disorder without Agoraphobia, Obsessive–Compulsive Disorder, and Post-Traumatic Stress Disorder. The three phobic disorders are alike in that the child's fear is linked to a particular stimulus; they differ in regard to the nature of the stimulus. For Agoraphobia without History of Panic Disorder, the feared stimulus is being alone or in a public place from which escape might be difficult or in which assistance might not be forthcoming, were an incapacitating or embarrassing symptom to arise. Examples of such public places are crowded stores, elevators, bridges, and buses; examples of such incapacitating or embarrassing symptoms are dizziness, heart palpitations, loss of bladder control, and loss of bowel control. For Social Phobia, the feared stimulus is being scrutinized by others or appearing foolish while in the presence of others. Examples of such social situations are writing, speaking, and eating in the presence of others. This fear of social situations is disruptive or distressing and is recognized as excessive or irrational. For Simple Phobia, the feared stimulus is any circumscribed object or situation other than those heretofore mentioned (e.g., separation from significant other, speaking in the presence of others) and those hereinafter mentioned (e.g., obsessions, trauma). Examples of such stimuli are animals, darkness, water, and heights. Fear of these stimuli is disturbing to the child or interferes with the development of the child and is recognized by the child as excessive or unreasonable.

At the heart of the two panic disorders is the unexpected occurrence of discrete episodes of intense fear. Such an episode is refered to as a "panic attack" and is comprised of a constellation of four or more physical and psychological symptoms (e.g., dizziness, sweating, chest pain, derealization, rumination over losing control). Because the panic attacks occur unexpectedly, this intense fear is not linked to any particular stimulus. In Panic Disorder with Agoraphobia, these discrete recurrent episodes of intense fear are accompanied by an intense fear of situations from which escape might be difficult or aid might not be forthcoming in the event of a panic attack. In Panic Disorder without Agoraphobia, these discrete recurrent episodes of intense fear are not accompanied by an intense fear of such situations.

Fear and anxiety are linked to specific stimuli in the two remaining psychiatric categories of Obsessive–Compulsive Disorder and Post-Traumatic Stress Disorder. In Obsessive–Compulsive Disorder, anxiety is tied to obsessions (i.e., recurrent repugnant thoughts, images, or impulses) or compulsions (i.e., regimented, useless behaviors) or both. The child recognizes that the obsessions are the products of his or her own mind, but may not recognize that the compulsions are excessive or unreasonable. Both, however, are a source of marked impairment in functioning. In Post-Traumatic Stress Disorder, anxiety is linked to a catastrophic event, such as rape, assault, combat, earthquake, or airplane crash. The catastrophic event is repeatedly symbolically relived through either play, dreams, or flashbacks. And the anxiety associated with the event is manifested in an increase in general arousal (e.g., hyper-

vigilance, heightened startle response) and a decrease in general responsiveness (e.g., detachment, diminished range of emotions, diminished interest in significant activities).

Other general systems of classification are based on subgroupings of fear contexts. The lists are based on either an intellectual or a statistical grouping of children's self-reported fears and anxieties. An example of the former is the scheme offered by Angelino, Dollins, and Mech (1956). From the reports of over 1,000 children, they reduced the fears and anxieties of children to the following stimulus categories: animals, personal appearance, personal conduct, personal health, physical safety, school, world events, natural events, and supernatural events. Using factor-analytic methods, Scherer and Nakamura (1968) and Ollendick (1983) arrived at sets of categories similar to each other and similar to those of Angelino and his colleagues (Angelino et al., 1956). Those of Scherer and Nakamura (1968) were the stimulus events of darkness, death, failure and criticism, home and school, physical illness, small animals, and social activities; those of Ollendick (1983) were the stimulus events of failure and criticism, injury and small animals, accidents and death, medical illness, and the unknown.

There are also classification schemes based upon parental reports. The system offered by Bandura and Menlove (1968) is one such scheme. From the parental ratings of their preschoolers, Bandura and Menlove (1968) collapsed the fears and anxieties of children into three groups: those related to small animals, those related to interpersonal events, and those related to events of nature. Another such scheme is the one proposed by Miller, Barrett, Hampe, and Noble (1972b). Using factor-analytic procedures, they sorted the fears and anxieties of children into three groups: those related to physical injury, those related to interpersonal events, and those related to natural and supernatural events.

Finally, there are classification schemes based upon theory. Classifying fears and anxieties according to the theoretical notion of "preparedness" (Seligman, 1971) is one such scheme. Stimuli of evolutionary significance in the phylogenetic history of the organism are referred to as "prepared," those of insignificance as "unprepared." Fears and anxieties to prepared stimuli are thought to be easier to learn and harder to unlearn than fears and anxieties to unprepared stimuli. Examples of prepared stimuli are snakes, spiders, heights, and darkness; examples of unprepared stimuli are flowers, mushrooms, and chocolate (Öhman, 1979; Rachman & Seligman, 1976).

Though fundamental to the practice of science, none of the classification systems described here appear to be at this time very functional to the practice of behavior therapy (*vis-à-vis* children's fears and anxieties). For classification to be helpful, it must predict the scope of impairments, the most efficacious treatment for those impairments, the duration of efficacious treatment, or the outcome of treatment. At present, there are few data showing any one of the schemes for classifying the fears and anxieties of children as predictive of any one of these relationships (e.g., Jacobs & Nadel, 1985; Morris & Kratochwill, 1983a). With more research, more support for the utility of the classification systems may accrue. However, until such research is conducted and such support is accrued, the various classification schemes are of little help in the treatment of children's fears and anxieties.

TO TREAT OR NOT TO TREAT

Fears and anxieties are part and parcel of both childhood and adulthood (see Campbell, 1986; Jersild, 1968; Lewis & Brooks, 1974). Some of these reactions are considered adaptive; others are considered maladaptive. In this section, we discuss several of the factors on which the judgment of a child's fears and anxieties as maladaptive and in need of treatment might be based. Specifically, these factors are the characteristics of the developing child, the characteristics of the fear context, and the characteristics of the family.

Developmental Characteristics

Research spanning some 50-odd years has consistently shown all children to have a large number of fears and anxieties. In the classic work by Jersild and Holmes (1935), mothers reported an average of four to five fears on the part of their 2- through 6-year-old children; they also reported one of these fears being displayed on the average of every 4–5 days. Two separate studies by Pratt (1945) of several hundred 4- through 16-year-olds found each child reporting an average of five to eight fears. Other studies

carried out over the last 30 years have found similar numbers of fears and anxieties for children of similar ages (e.g., Angelino *et al.*, 1956; Bamber, 1974; Eme & Schmidt, 1978; Kirkpatrick, 1984; Lapouse & Monk, 1959; Mauer, 1965; Nalven, 1970). Several studies have also estimated the frequency of children's fears and anxieties to be much higher. For example, 70% of the 540 fifth- and sixth-graders in Pinter and Lev's (1940) study identified themselves as having 10 or more worries. Over forty years later, in a replication of the Pinter and Lev (1940) investigation, Orton (1982) obtained comparable numbers of worries among his sample of 645 fifth- and sixth-graders. Ollendick's (1983) sample of 217 children aged 8 through 11 reported an average of 9 to 13 excessive fears, whereas the 99 children in Croake and Knoxs (1973) sample of 10-year-olds reported an average of 43 to 54 fears.

With increasing age, there are changes in the foci and possibly the frequency of children's fears and anxieties. The frequency issue is a matter of some contention, as there are findings suggesting both a decline and no decline in the number of fears and anxieties with increasing age. Early research tends to show a general decrease in the frequency of fears and anxieties with an increase in age; more recent research tends to show no change in frequency with age. For example, Holmes (1935) observed the reactions of 2- through 5-year-olds to strangers, darkness, and the like, and found that the younger the child, the greater the number of fears displayed. Similar age trends have been reported by MacFarlane, Allen, and Honzik (1954) for 2- through 14-year-olds; by Lapouse and Monk (1959) for 6- through 12-year-olds; by Bauer (1976) for 4- through 12-year-olds; and by Bamber (1974) for 12- through 18-year-old boys. No such age trends, though, have been reported by several other researchers (e.g., Angelino *et al.*, 1956; Barrios, Replogle, & Anderson-Tisdelle, 1983; Croake & Knox, 1973; Dunlop, 1952; Mauer, 1965; Ryall, Dietiker, 1979).

Whether their number declines or remains constant, the fears and anxieties of children do vary qualitatively with age. The prominent fears and anxieties of young infants differ from those of young children, and the prominent fears and anxieties of young children differ from those of older children. This shift in the objects of fears and anxieties continues through adolescence into adulthood (Kirkpatrick,

1984). For young infants, the objects or situations most commonly feared are heights; loss of physical support, and sudden, intense, and unpredictable stimuli such as loud noises (Ball & Tronick, 1971; Bronson, 1972; Jersild, 1954; Jersild & Holmes, 1935). For children 1, 2, and 3 years old, the common fear objects are strangers, loud noises, separation from caretakers, novel stimuli, and toileting activities (Jersild & Holmes, 1935; Miller et al., 1974). With preschoolers and first-graders, fears and anxieties take as their major foci animals, darkness, parental separation and abandonment, supernatural beings such as monsters and ghosts, and natural phenomena such as thunder and lightning (Bauer, 1976; Jersild & Holmes, 1935; Lapouse & Monk, 1959; Mauer 1965; Poznanski, 1973; Pratt, 1945). Older elementary school children continue to fear natural phenomena such as earthquakes, tornados, thunder, and lightning; most of their fears and anxieties, though, center around school-, health-, and home-related events. Among the school events that trouble children of this age group are test taking, poor grades, rejection by classmates, and reprimand by the principal; among the health events are physical injury and illness, death, and medical procedures; and among the home events are parental conflicts and parental punishment (Angelino et al., 1956; Croake & Knox, 1973; Eme & Schmidt, 1978; Lapouse & Monk, 1959; Nalven, 1970; Ollendick, 1983; Orton, 1982; Pinter & Lev, 1940; Scherer & Nakamura, 1968)). With adolescents, fears and anxieties related to school events, personal adequacy, and physical illness are most salient; economic, political, and sexual matters are also sources of great concern and worry (Angelino et al., 1956, Kirkpatick, 1984; Mauer, 1965; Pratt, 1945; Winker, 1949.)

The fears and anxieties of children vary not only with age, but also with sex and socioeconomic status. Irrespective of age, girls tend to report a greater number of fears and anxieties than boys do (e.g., Bamber, 1974; Croake, 1969; Croake & Knox, 1974; Kirkpatrick, 1985; Ollendick, 1983; Pratt, 1945; Ryall & Dietiker, 1979; Scherer & Nakamura, 1968). They also tend to differ from boys in the types of fears and anxieties they experience. Fears of animals and physical injury and illness are more common among girls than boys; fears of economic and academic failure are more common among boys than girls (e.g., Bamber, 1974; Kirkpatrick, 1984; Ollendick, 1983;

Orton, 1982; Pinter & Lev, 1940; Pratt, 1945; Scherer & Nakamura, 1968; Winder, 1949). Though some studies have found no differences between the fears and anxieties of boys and girls (e.g., Angelino et al., 1956; Eme & Schmidt, 1978; Mauer, 1965; Nalven 1970), these studies are in the minority.

With respect to socioeconomic status, the data are far more uniform. Children from lower-income families are similar to children from middle-income families in the frequency of their fears and anxieties, but dissimilar in the targets of their fears and anxieties. Though both groups are fearful of animals, lower-income children tend to be frightened of rats and roaches, whereas middle-income children tend to be frightened of poisonous insects. The same is true of the two groups' fears of economic misfortune: Lower-income children tend to be anxious and worried about necessities, whereas middle-income children tend to be anxious and worried about less essential items (e.g., Angelino et al., 1956; Nalven, 1970; Pinter & Lev, 1940; Pratt, 1945).

At present, no firm ties have been established between the fears and anxieties of childhood and other childhood behavioral problems (see Graziano, DiGiovanni, & Garcia, 1979; Morris & Kratochwill, 1983a). Many and sundry behavioral problems have been observed in isolated child cases of fears and anxiety; not a one, though, has been observed with any regularity across cases. For example, Poznanski (1973) noted the following among 18 children aged 4 through 12 with excessive fears: hyperactivity, encopresis, enuresis, obesity, learning difficulties, obsessive–compulsive tendencies, overdependency, somatic complaints, nightmares, and bed sharing. Of this list of associated problems, the least objectionable (bed sharing) emerged as the most common, occurring in slightly over one-third of the cases. Worth noting is the fact that over 10% of Poznanski's (1973) 28 nonfearful comparison children also exhibited bed sharing. Other studies of children fearful of the same object or of different objects have likewise failed to uncover any behavioral problems that are systematically related (e.g., Giebenhain, 1985; Graziano & Mooney, 1980; Lapouse & Monk, 1959; Miller, Hampe, Barrett, & Noble, 1971).

As information on the persistence of children's fears and anxieties has accrued, so have doubts accrued as to such fears and anxieties being short-lived. Much of the early research shows the fears and anxieties of children to be fairly fleeting; much of the recent research shows them to be far more stable. For example, three studies in the 1930s all report the life span of most childhood fears to be no greater than 12 weeks. Three-fourths of the fears of Jersild and Holmes's (1935) 2- through 5-year-olds were absent by the end of the study's 3-week assessment period. Virtually all of the fear and anxiety reactions of Slater's (1939) 2- and 3-year-olds abated by the end of 4 weeks. Of the fears of Hagman's (1932) child subjects, 54% disappeared completely by the end of 3 months. Two important series of studies in the early 1970s reinforced the view of children's fears and anxieties as transient. One was the epidemiological research of Agras and his colleagues (Agras, Chapin, & Oliveau, 1972; Agras, Sylvester, & Oliveau, 1969); the other was the treatment outcome research of Miller and his colleagues (Hampe, Noble, Miller, & Barrett, 1973; Miller, Barrett, Hampe, & Noble, 1972a). Agras and his colleagues questioned adult phobics as to the origins of their fears and carried out a 5-year follow-up on 10 child and adolescent phobics. Few of the adult phobics traced their fears back to childhood (Agras et al., 1969), and none of the child and adolescent phobics were fearful at the 5-year follow-up (Agras et al., 1972). Miller and his colleagues assigned 67 phobic children to 8 weeks of either reciprocal inhibition therapy, psychotherapy, or no treatment. At 6 weeks posttreatment, all groups evidenced significant reductions in phobic behavior (Miller et al., 1972a); at 2 years posttreatment, 80% of the children were symptom-free, and only 7% continued to be highly fearful (Hampe et al., 1973). The findings as a whole led to be conclusion that "the lifespan of phobias in children appears to be somewhere between two weeks and two years, with most phobias dissipating within one year of onset" (Hampe et al., 1973, p. 452).

More recent studies portray the fears and anxieties of children as being much more persistent. For example, the excessive fears of Poznanski's (1973) 28 child cases all had durations of 5 months to 1 or more years. The fears and anxieties of Eme and Schmidt's (1978) 27 fourth-graders were remarkably stable over a 1-year period, in terms of both absolute number and kind of fears. Moderate to marked stability has been reported for periods spanning 1 week (Ollendick, 1983; Ryall & Dietiker, 1979), 2 weeks (Giebenhain, 1985), 1 month (Barrios et al., 1983), and 3 months (Ollendick, 1983). Additional evidence for the persistence of children's fears and anxieties comes from the literature on adults' fears and anxieties. Comparisons of factor-analytic studies of children's fears with those of adult's fears show concern and agitation over physical injury and illness to be fairly constant throughout the life span (Miller et al., 1972b). Adults who display phobic reactions tend to report having more childhood fears than adults who display no such reactions (Solyom, Beck, Solyom, & Hugel, 1974), and adults who display the specific reaction of agoraphobia tend to report more childhood fears related to school than other adult phobics and nonphobics (Berg, 1976; Berg, Marks, McGuire, & Lipsedge, 1974).

Be they persistent or evanescent, the critical question is whether or not the fears and anxieties of children are serious enough to warrant our concern. Certainly the children themselves believe their fears and anxieties to be a serious matter; they report severe distress and discomfort over their reactions. Children do not, however, determine the problem status of their own behaviors. Adults make such determinations. And adults—parents, teachers, therapists, and theorists—have not acted consistently vis-à-vis children's fears and anxieties. For example, referrals to treatment agencies have been relatively few over the years—a statistic that would imply that children's fears and anxieties are not particularly bothersome either to the children or to their parents or to their teachers. Of 239 consecutive cases referred to the Maudsley Hospital Children's Department, only 10 were for fears (Graham, 1964). Of 547 cases referred to 19 child behavior therapists during a 6-month period, only 7% were for specific fear-related conditions (Graziano & DeGiovanni, 1979). And of all the child cases referred for psychological treatment irrespective of orientation, it is estimated that only 3%–4% are for fears and anxieties (Johnson & Melamed, 1979).

Despite the infrequency with which parents seek treatment services for their children's fears and anxieties, the availability of such services has increased steadily over the years. Most of the pediatric hospitals in the United States now offer some form of intervention to alleviate the fears and worries of children undergoing diagnostic and medical procedures (Peterson & Ridley-Johnson, 1980); in the past, such interventions were a rarity. The same is true of clinics specializing in the treatment of children's fears and anxieties. There are two obvious reasons for this proliferation in treatment services. One is the fact that when programs are offered for reducing children's fears and anxieties, adults make good use of these programs (e.g., Giebenhain, 1985; Hampe *et al.*, 1973; Peterson & Shigetomi, 1981)—a finding suggesting that the fears and anxieties of children are worrisome if not bothersome to adults. The second reason is that theorists now see children's fears and anxieties as being far more deleterious than they had previously been thought to be (e.g., Jacobs & Nadel, 1985; Rutter, 1981); as a consequence, they are now being studied more assiduously and treated more aggressively. All of this implies that the fears and anxieties of children are not to be dismissed outright as trivial and harmless.

In sum, fears and anxieties are quite common among children of all ages. They vary in number as a function of gender; they vary in foci as a function of gender, age, and socioeconomic status. Though many behavioral problems have been observed in fearful and anxious children, no behavioral problem has yet been systematically linked to fears and anxieties per se. The persistence and seriousness of children's fears and anxieties also have yet to be determined. At present, there are both data that suggest a decline in the frequency and intensity of fears and anxieties with increasing age, and data that suggest no such decline; there are both data suggesting that the fears and anxieties of children are of no great concern to adults, and data suggesting that they are indeed of considerable concern to adults. Given the uncertainty surrounding the course and criticalness of children's fears and anxieties, the cautious approach apparently would be to treat all cases. This may not, however, be the most efficacious approach for each individual case. Stimulus and familial considerations may advise a different course of action, such as treating a family member other than the fearful child. The nature and implications of these two classes of considerations—stimulus and familial—are discussed below.

Characteristics of the Fear Context

Earlier, we have defined fears and anxieties as collections of reactions to a perceived threat. The objective dangers posed by the stimulus are obviously a major determinant of the problem status of a child's fear reactions; thus, they are a major determinant of whether or not to treat the child's fear reactions. Perceived threat and concomitant responses that are in accord with the objective menace of the stimulus are seen as rational and adaptive; those that are in discord with the objective menace of the stimulus are seen as irrational and maladaptive (e.g., Marks, 1969; Miller *et al.*, 1974).

Given that we are dealing with a developing child, it is best that a developmental perspective be taken to judge the degree of mismatch between the perceived and actual dangers presented by the feared stimulus. Children of different ages have different repertoires of skills; as such, the same stimulus holds different demands and threats for children of different ages. Estimation of an object's actual danger should, therefore, be carried out from the vantage point of the developing child and not from the vantage point of the mature adult (e.g., parent, therapist). Specifically, this estimation of threat should be carried out from the perspective of the normative child for the age group in question. And this age-specific threat should serve as the background against which the rationality–irrationality and adaptiveness–maladaptiveness of the child's perceptions of threat are appraised.

Characteristics of the Family

The fears and anxieties of family members also constitute a factor in whether or not to treat the fears and anxieties of a child. Of the many studies that have examined the relationship between maternal anxiety and child anxiety, the vast majority have found a positive correlation between the two (see Peterson & Brownlee-Duffeck, 1984; Winer, 1982). The strength of this relationship does not, however, appear to be invariant across age and socioeconomic class. Stronger ties are evidenced for younger children than for older children (e.g., Klorman, Michael, Hilpert, & Sveen, 1979; Klorman, Ratner, Arata, King, & Sveen, 1978; Otto, 1974; Wright, Alpern, & Leake, 1973), and for children from lower socioeconomic strata than for children from higher socioeconomic strata (e.g., Robins, Robins, & Rawson, 1973).

Part of this evidence for a positive correlation between the fear reactions of the mother and the fear reactions of the child comes from treatment outcome studies. In several instances, incidental or intentional treatment of mothers' fears and anxieties occurred along with programmed treatment of the children's fears and anxieties. Fluctuations in the mothers' fear reactions were found to covary systematically with changes in the children's fear reactions. For example, Peterson and Shigetomi (1981) trained fearful children in the use of several techniques for coping with anxiety and pain. Among the techniques taught were comforting self-talk, cue-controlled relaxation, and pleasant imagery. Though the mothers of these children did not receive any direct training in the use of the coping techniques, they were actively incorporated into the training of the children in the use of these techniques. The mothers coached the children in proper execution of the skills, monitored the children's practice of the skills, and prompted the children as to when to draw upon the skills. The mothers reported reductions in their own anxiety and increments in their own self-confidence; these changes paralleled the changes observed in the children's reaction to the target situation. In a systematic replication of the Peterson and Shigetomi (1981) study, Zastowny, Kirschenbaum, and Meng (1981) had mothers undergo treatment for their own anxiety in addition to assisting in the treatment of their children's anxiety. Again, decrements in the children's fear reactions to the target situation were accompanied by decrements in the mothers' fear reactions to the same situation.

Though less researched than maternal anxiety, sibling anxiety has also been linked to the fears and anxieties of young children (cf. Winer, 1982). Observing an older sibling receiving treatment for his or her fears and anxieties has been shown to have a beneficial effect on the fears and anxieties of the younger brother or sister (e.g., Ghose, Giddon, Shiere, & Fogels, 1969). Having siblings accompany a child in the feared situation also has been shown to decrease the child's anxiety in that situation (e.g., Hawley, McCorkle, Witteman, & Van Ostenberg, 1974). Having siblings who have had repeated (presumably unpleasant) experiences with a stimulus has been found to increase the likelihood of a child's developing a fear towards the same stimulus (e.g., Bailey, Talbot, & Taylor, 1973).

Combined, these findings suggest that mothers and siblings exert some influence over the fear and anxiety reactions of children. Furthermore, they suggest that this influence over the fear and anxiety reactions may be greater for younger children. For the question of whether or not to treat the fears and anxieties of a young child, the implication is that it may be more expedient to treat the fears and anxieties of the mother and the siblings than to treat those of the child (e.g., Klesges, Malott, & Ugland, 1984). Such treatment of maternal and sibling anxiety may obviate the need for treatment of the child's anxiety or may serve as a prerequisite to more efficacious and enduring treatment of the child's anxiety.

The Decision Process

The question of whether or not to treat children's fears and anxieties overlaps with the general treatment decision issues involved in any child intervention. Unfortunately, as reflected by a virtual absence of this topic in most behavioral child therapy texts (Johnson, Rasbury, & Siegel, 1986; Morris & Kratochwill, 1983b; Ollendick & Cerny, 1981; Schwartz & Johnson, 1985), little empirical information or even expert opinion is available to guide such decisions. Mash and Terdal (1981) have summarized some literature on whether or not a child disorder should be treated and which problems should be targeted for intervention. Their suggestions are incorporated in the following discussion.

Several interrelated factors must be weighted in the decision concerning whether or not to treat a child's fear and anxiety. And this decision must, of course, be viewed as falling along a continuum. It may be useful to discuss briefly both extremes of this continuum. Of course, as previously discussed, adaptive fears to real threats should not be eliminated. Likewise, temporary fears that are developmentally normal or perhaps even necessary should be allowed to run their course. For example, attempting to eliminate the separation anxiety experienced by most infants late in their first year could be harmful to the mother–infant bonding process. As the child takes on new challenges and environments, many anxieties will have to be overcome and coping processes acquired. The important issue is that this fear or anxiety does not impede mastery of long-term adaptive behavior. There may also be instances when a fear need not be treated because future exposure to the feared stimulus is unlikely (e.g., anxiety over a medical procedure that will not recur). This, of course, assumes the absence of posttraumatic problems.

In certain instances, some type of intervention may be necessary when an adaptive fear or anxiety causes significant problems for others. For example, some parents may so alter their life style to help their children avoid even normal discomfort that maladaptive family patterns develop. Likewise, whenever the fear or anxiety reflects or produces other family problems or problems in other environments, treatment will likely be necessary. One spouse's aggravation over how the other spouse responds to the child's fears may exacerbate marital problems. Of course, in these latter instances, treatment may not focus primarily on the child's fear or anxiety, but on the problems of caretakers and siblings. These other child or family problems may push the treatment of the fear or anxiety to a relatively lower position in the treatment hierarchy.

On the other hand, some circumstances clearly warrant treatment. One can apply the standard rule of thumb that treatment is indicated whenever a problem significantly affects the current or future normal functioning of the child. Any fear or anxiety that threatens the normal developmental sequence, such as school phobia or strong social avoidance, should be treated. Evidence abounds that such a style foreshadows many types of adult problems (e.g., Gittelman, 1986; Solyom et al., 1974). The child's feelings must be strongly considered. Any time a child experiences strong, recurrent subjective distress, treatment is warranted. Whenever an unusually high number of even moderate fears is present, treatment is probably indicated.

A variety of other factors may play a role in the decision whether or not to treat. The motivation of the individuals involved, particularly the parents, must be considered, as must their skill level and resources. Even though the therapist may not feel that treatment is warranted, the feelings and opinions of the child, parents, and others (such as teachers) must be weighed in the decision. Also, the ethical issue of a child's right to effective treatment may emerge, should caretakers decline treatment that seems necessary. Thus, the treatment of children's fears and anxieties must be examined within a broad developmental, family systems, cultural, and ethical context. And decisions regarding whether or not to treat should be made with the child's general psychological functioning, family functioning, and environmental functioning in mind.

TREATMENT FOCUS AND DEVELOPMENT

Given that we have judged the fears and anxieties of a child to be problematic, our next task is to specify the focus and nature of our treatment. We do so by drawing upon our theory of children's fears and anxieties. Theory highlights for us the mechanisms that may be responsible for the origin and maintenance of fears and anxieties, and intimates to us the actions that may alter these mechanisms for the better. There is, however, no one behavioral theory of children's fears and anxieties. There are, in fact, many different accounts of the acquisition and perpetuation of children's fears and anxieties, all of which have emanated from the behavioral paradigm. In this section, we describe the six most prominent of these behavioral theories.

Respondent Conditioning Theory

According to the original formulation by Watson and Morgan (1917), fears and anxieties are acquired by means of Pavlovian conditioning. An unconditioned stimulus that reliably evokes the unconditioned response of fear follows in close proximity a conditioned stimulus that initially does not evoke such a response. Upon repeated pairings, the conditioned stimulus alone comes to elicit fear. Stimuli to which fear is displayed but for which there have been no direct pairings with an unconditioned stimulus are explained by the principle of stimulus generalization.

Though the demonstrations of fear induction through classical conditioning are numerous, so too are the criticisms of the respondent conditioning theory (e.g., Delprato & McGlynn, 1984; Eysenck, 1968, 1976; Rachman, 1977, 1978). Several attempts to replicate Watson and Rayner's (1920) results have failed to do so when objects other than a white rat have been used as conditioned stimuli (e.g., Bregman, 1934; English, 1929; Valentine, 1930). These studies along with more recent ones (e.g., Öhman, 1979) call into question the theory's equipotentiality premise—the premise that all neutral stimuli have an equal probability of becoming feared objects via respondent conditioning. Available data clearly show that this is not the case.

Other data pose other problems for the respondent conditioning theory. For example, according to the theory, trauma (e.g., the unconditioned stimulus) is crucial to the establishment of a fear reaction. In many cases of fears and anxieties, however, the individuals report no recollection whatsoever of a trauma (e.g., Rachman, 1977; Rimm, Janda, Lancaster, Nahl, & Dittmar, 1977). Moreover, the distribution of common fears and anxieties among children and adults is contrary to what one would predict from the theory (Rachman, 1977). Children have more traumatic interactions with needles, fire, and tricycles than they do with darkness, dogs, and imaginary creatures; yet fears of the latter are far more prevalent than fears of the former.

The respondent conditioning theory is also at a loss to explain how children develop fears and anxieties without directly encountering the conditioned and unconditioned stimuli. The theory deems such direct exposure necessary for the formation of a fear reaction, yet there is considerable evidence that simply observing another display a fear reaction may lead to the development of a fear reaction (e.g., Bandura, 1969, 1977b; Rachman, 1977). Finally, persistence of fear reactions poses yet another problem for the respondent conditioning theory. According to the theory, there should be a gradual diminution of the fear response to the repeated presentation of the conditioned stimulus in the absence of the unconditioned stimulus. From our discussion of the temporal stability of children's fears and anxieties, it is clear that not all fear reactions diminish upon repeated presentations of the conditioned stimulus without the unconditioned stimulus.

Revised Respondent Conditioning Theories

The respondent conditioning theory of fears and anxieties has undergone a number of revisions in order to overcome the weaknesses just described. The most notable of these are the revised formulations of Rachman (1977) and Seligman (1970, 1971). In Rachman's (1977) revision of the model, there are three possible routes by which fears and anxieties can be acquired: respondent conditioning, modeling, and verbal instruction. The model does away with the equipotentiality premise and inserts in its place the notion of hereditary determinants of fear—the notion that some stimuli are more biologically predisposed to becoming fear objects than others.

This notion of different stimuli having different potential as fear objects is the cornerstone of Seligman's (1970, 1971) revised respondent conditioning model—preparedness theory. According to preparedness theory, fears and anxieties to both stimuli of evolutionary significance and stimuli of evolutionary insignificance are acquired by the same general process of respondent conditioning. The two classes of fear reactions are thought to differ, though, in the speed with which they are acquired and the speed with which they are extinguished. Fear reactions to stimuli of evolutionary significance presumably are more easily established, severe, enduring, and resistant to treatment than are fear reactions to stimuli of evolutionary insignificance.

Though preparedness theory offers us an explanation for the unusual distributions of children's fears and anxieties, it has few clinical and experimental data to offer us in support of its major propositions. The work of Öhman and his colleagues (Fredrikson, Hugdahl, & Öhman, 1977; Hugdahl, Fredrikson, & Öhman, 1977; Hugdahl & Öhman, 1977; Öhman, Eriksson, & Olofsson, 1975; Öhman, Erixon, & Lofberg, 1975; Öhman, Fredrikson, Hugdahl, & Rimmo, 1976) is a case in point. Pictures of snakes, spiders, mushrooms, and flowers are paired with electric shock. Conditioned responses to the snakes and spiders develop more quickly and extinguish more slowly than conditioned responses to the mushrooms and flowers. Proponents of the theory attribute the differential rates of acquisition and extinction to differences in biological preparedness. In the phylogenetic history of humans, snakes and spiders were of greater evolutionary significance than mushrooms and flowers; therefore, we humans are more prepared to fear snakes and spiders than we are to fear mushrooms and flowers. The flaw in this line of reasoning and thus in this line of evidence is that it is not at all clear which stimuli should be thought of as biologically prepared and which as neutral (Delprato, 1980). For those stimuli thought to be biologically prepared, the clinical data are clearly not in line with the theory's predictions (DeSilva, Rachman, & Seligman, 1977; McNally & Reiss, 1982; Rachman & Seligman,

1976). Fear reactions to stimuli thought to be biologically prepared do not appear to be any more severe, enduring, or intractable than fear reactions to stimuli not thought to be biologically prepared.

Two-Factor Theory

Classical two-factor theory posits both respondent and instrumental conditioning in the origin and maintenance of fears and anxieties (Mowrer, 1939, 1947, 1960). Respondent conditioning is involved in the acquisition of fears and anxieties; instrumental conditioning is involved in their maintenance. Neutral objects and events are paired with an unconditioned stimulus, whereupon the neutral stimuli alone come to evoke visceral arousal (i.e., a fear response). This fear response gives rise to the instrumental behavior of avoidance, which leads to a reduction in visceral arousal, thereby reinforcing the act of avoidance and enhancing the probability of its recurrence.

Classical two-factor theory has had considerable impact on the practice of behavior therapy vis-à-vis fears and anxieties. This impact notwithstanding, it has come under a great deal of criticism in recent years (e.g., Bandura, 1969; Rachman, 1976; Seligman & Johnston, 1973). The most pertinent of these criticisms centers around the presumed role that fear plays in mediating avoidance and that fear reduction plays in reinforcing avoidance. From the theory, it follows that fear is necessary for the instigation of avoidance, and that fear reduction is necessary for the acquisition and perpetuation of avoidance. However, numerous findings call into question this hypothesized relationship between fear and avoidance behavior (see Bandura, 1969; Delprato & McGlynn, 1984). It has been demonstrated repeatedly that avoidance behavior can be acquired in the absence of fear (e.g., Auld, 1951; Wenzel & Jeffrey, 1967; Wynne & Solomon, 1955), that avoidance behavior can persist in the face of diminished respondent fear (e.g., Black, 1958; Brush, 1957; Solomon, Kamin, & Wynne, 1953), and that avoidance behavior can decrease in the face of undiminished respondent fear (e.g., Leitenberg, Agras, Butz, & Wincze, 1971).

Approach–Withdrawal Theory

To overcome the shortcomings described above, classical two-factor theory has undergone several revisions. Delprato and McGlynn (1984) have organized these various revisions into a loose conceptual framework, which they call approach–withdrawal theory. The theory is in essence a compilation of the views of such behavior theorists as D'Amato (1970), Denny (1971, 1976), Dinsmoor (1954, 1977), Gray (1971), Herrnstein (1969), Keehn (1966), and Schoenfeld (1950).

According to approach–withdrawal theory, fear acquisition begins with the pairing of a neutral stimulus with an unconditioned stimulus. During early trails, there is escape or withdrawal from the aversive stimulus. Upon repeated trials, the offset of the unconditioned stimulus is followed by a state of relaxation or relief, along with approach to a nonaversive area. Through backchaining, approach to the nonaversive area comes to occur before the onset of the unconditioned stimulus; thus, we have the establishment of avoidance behavior. The neutral or conditioned stimulus does not evoke fear, but instead functions as a cue for relaxation and approach behavior. When extinction is instituted (i.e., nonpresentation of the unconditioned stimulus), relaxation backchains to the conditioned stimulus, whereupon it competes with withdrawal and culminates in the elimination of the avoidance response (Delprato & McGlynn, 1984).

In approach–withdrawal theory, we have a solution to the dilemma of the persistence of avoidance behavior in the face of diminished respondent fear. Avoidance behavior is not seen as being maintained by fear reduction (as it is in classical two-factor theory), but is seen as being maintained by relaxation and approach, which are conceptualized as response-contingent safety cues. The presence or absence of respondent fear is therefore inconsequential to the occurrence or nonoccurrence of avoidance, for it is contingent approach to safety that sustains the avoidance response (Delprato & McGlynn, 1984; Denny, 1971).

An important aspect of approach–withdrawal theory is the prominence it assigns to positive reinforcement in the acquisition and maintenance of fears and anxieties. Orthodox respondent conditioning theory, revised respondent conditioning theories, and two-factor theory ascribe no such role to positive reinforcement. For years, though, our clinical observations have been telling us that in some instances of fears and anxieties, operant factors have been at work (e.g., Lazarus, Davison, & Polefka, 1965). In approach–withdrawal theory, we finally have a well-formulated model of fears and anxieties that recognizes their contribution.

Self-Efficacy Theory

According to Bandura (1977a, 1978, 1982), all fear and anxiety reactions are mediated by a central cognitive construct—self-efficacy expectations, or the conviction that one can interact adaptively with the feared object. These expectations emanate from four types of experiences: personal encounters with the target stimulus, vicarious encounters with the target stimulus, somatovisceral arousal experienced during encounters with the target stimulus, and verbal persuasion (Bandura, 1977a, 1978).

Perceptions of self-efficacy are thought to dictate the exact expression of fear and anxiety. The stronger the perceptions of self-efficacy, the less subjective distress, performance impairment, and autonomic agitation *vis-à-vis* the feared object. The stronger the perceptions of self-efficacy, the greater the perseverance and coping in the face of obstacles *vis-à-vis* the feared object. And the stronger the perceptions of self-efficacy, the greater the generalization of adaptive behavior to objects and situations beyond the feared object and feared situation (Bandura, 1977a, 1978).

Within this framework, treatment takes the form of modifying the fearful child's self-efficacy expectations. There are four general strategies for altering these expectations: performance accomplishments, vicarious experiences, emotional arousal techniques, and verbal exhortation (Bandura, 1977a). Performance-based treatments are presumed to be the most effective of the four strategies, for they are presumed to provide the most veridical information regarding performance capabilities. The other three strategies provide less dependable information regarding performance capabilities; therefore, they are less effective in altering perceptions of self-efficacy, which in turn makes them less effective in altering the fears and anxieties of children.

Bioinformational Theory

Lang's (1977, 1979, 1984) bioinformational theory of emotion also has fear being mediated by a cognitive construct—an affective image. The image is comprised of stimulus, response, and semantic propositions. Stimulus propositions are units of information concerning the features of the feared object or event; response propositions are units of information concerning the subjective, motor, and physi-ological components of the fear reaction; and semantic propositions are units of information concerning the meaning embodied in the stimulus–response sequence. When accessed and activated from the long-term store, the affective image dictates the exact form the fear reaction takes.

From the perspective of bioinformational theory, the treatment of fears and anxieties is a two-stage process: evocation of the affective image, followed by reorganization of its propositional network. The affective image may be evoked through either *in vivo* or *in vitro* exposure to the feared stimulus. Once accessed from long-term store, the image becomes amenable to change. It is at this point where the fear reaction too becomes amenable to change, for it is the affective image that mediates the expression of the fear reaction. The propositional network or the image is altered by providing new and more adaptive information regarding the properties of the feared stimulus, the responses to this stimulus, and the meaning of these responses to the stimulus. This new stimulus, response, and semantic information may be presented through any one of several different media or combinations of media. Among these are physiological feedback, verbal instruction, and kinesthetic feedback from direct and vicarious encounters with the feared simulus.

Summary

At present, no one behavioral theory of children's fears and anxieties has emerged as dominant. For, in large part, no one behavioral theory has been able to account for the emerging picture of the ecosystem of the fearful and anxious child. It is an ecosystem for which the following have been tentatively identified: genetic and familial patterns, mother–child interaction patterns, general parenting style, crisis parenting style, and information-processing style. A number of twin and family studies point to a genetic component in the development of children's fears and anxieties (for reviews, see Carey & Gottesman, 1981; Weissman, 1985). The two twin studies to date show significantly higher concordance rates of anxiety disorders among monozygotic twins than among dizygotic twins (Slater & Shields, 1969; Torgersen, 1978). And the five family studies to date show a high association between the anxiety disorders of children and the anxiety disorders of their parents (Cohen, Badal, Kilpatrick, Reed, & White, 1951; Weissman, Leckman, Merikangas, Prusoff, & Gammon, 1984; Wheeler, White, Reed, & Cohen, 1948). Studies of the family interaction patterns of anxious and fearful children show the mothers to be overprotective and restrictive in their general dealings with the children (e.g., Brown, 1979; Kagan & Moss, 1962; Lewis & Michalson, 1983), the parents to be overly lax and inconsistent in their general disciplining of the children (e.g., Venham, Murray, & Gaulin-Kremer, 1979), and the parents to be agitated and inept in their handling of childhood crisis situations (e.g., Melamed & Siegel, 1985; Robinson, 1978). Available research also points to a preferred social information-processing style on the part of fearful and anxious children. Specifically, the children display a marked preference for information avoidance as opposed to information seeking *vis-à-vis* their environment (e.g., Burstein & Meichenbaum, 1979; Knight *et al.*, 1979; Unger, 1982).

None of the behavioral theories described here mention any of these genetic, family, or personality variables in their accounts of the development of children's fears and anxieties. They may need to do so in order for us to achieve a fuller and richer understanding of the development and maintenance of children's fears and anxieties. They are, however, the theories that have given rise to an abundant supply of treatments. In the next section, we review the particulars and potency of each of these treatments.

BEHAVIORAL TREATMENTS

Our coverage of each behavioral intervention for children's fears and anxieties begins with a description of the procedure, followed by a review of the research on its efficacy. Though not comprehensive, our review of the research literature does span the years 1924 through 1985 and over 40 professional journals and books.

Systematic Desensitization and Its Variants

As a treatment for children's fears and anxieties, systematic desensitization consists of three basic steps: (1) The child is trained in deep muscle relaxation; (2) the child rank-orders from least distressing to most distressing several situations involving the feared stimulus; and

(3) the child imagines each one of the situations while in a relaxed state (see Hatzenbuehler & Schroeder, 1978; Morris & Kratochwill, 1983a, 1983c). This pairing of a state antagonistic to anxiety (i.e., relaxation) with imaginal representations of the feared stimulus begins with the least distressing situation and ends with the most distressing one. Progression from one hierarchy scene to another occurs when the child is able to imagine the feared situation and remain relatively calm.

Many variations of this basic procedure have been employed in the treatment of children's fears and anxieties. Game playing, story telling, feeding, maternal contact, therapist contact, and anger have all been used in the place of relaxation as the anxiety-antagonistic state. Slides, photographs, and toys of the feared stimulus have all been used in the place of imaginal representations of the feared stimulus. Whenever the actual feared stimulus has been used rather than some substitute, the treatment has been referred to as "*in vivo* desensitization." And whenever the imaginal scenario of the child confronting the feared stimulus has included support from the child's favorite superhero, the treatment has been referred to as "emotive imagery" (e.g., Lazarus & Abramovitz, 1962).

Table 5-2 in the Appendix presents a summary of the procedures and findings of 41 studies that have investigated the effectiveness of desensitization and its variants. Collectively, over 587 children were treated for over 18 different types of fear and anxiety reactions. The children ranged in age from 11½ months to 17 years; the fear and anxiety reactions ranged in duration from 2 weeks to 9 years. Among the most frequently treated fears and anxieties were those related to school, nighttime, small animals, separation, and test taking.

The vast majority of the studies had as their focus the effects of either systematic desensitization or *in vivo* desensitization; a small minority of the studies had as their focus the effects of either emotive imagery or some combination of systematic desensitization, *in vivo* desensitization, and other behavioral treatments. Uncontrolled case studies outnumbered true experiments by nearly three to one. Both types of investigations, though, consistently found systematic desensitization and its variants to be highly effective in reducing the fears and anxieties of children. These positive effects were evidenced across all three components of the fear reactions—subjective, motor, and physiological—and were maintained across intervals ranging in duration from 3 months to 2 years. Though limited, some evidence was also obtained for the generalization of these positive effects to other settings and other problematic behaviors (e.g., enuresis).

Prolonged Exposure and Its Variants

In prolonged exposure treatments, the child is asked from the outset to confront a threatening version of the feared stimulus, either real or imagined. This immediate, intense, and extended exposure to the feared stimulus may take one of four forms: imaginal flooding, *in vivo* flooding, implosion, and reinforced practice. In imaginal flooding, the child first constructs a list of situations involving the feared stimulus and rank-orders these situations from least distressing to most distressing. Beginning with an intermediate scene, the child imagines each situation, leading up to and including the most distressing one. For each situation, the child continues imagining the scene until he or she is no longer frightened of it. Successive scenes are handled in an identical fashion (e.g., Hersen, 1968). Very similar in format to imaginal flooding, *in vivo* flooding has the child construct a hierarchy of anxiety-eliciting situations involving the feared stimulus, select a situation at an intermediate point in the hierarchy, and confront that situation and all successive situations in the hierarchy in a systematic fashion. However, the situations that the child confronts are not images or photographs or slides, but the actual ones involving the actual feared stimulus (e.g., Kandel, Ayllon, & Rosenbaum, 1977; Kolko, 1984).

Of the two remaining prolonged exposure techniques, one (implosion) makes use of images of the feared stimulus; the other (reinforced practice) makes use of authentic versions of the feared stimulus. In implosion, the child imagines an unrealistic yet nevertheless horrific scenario involving the feared stimulus. The scenario is imagined again and again until the child ceases to be perturbed by it (e.g., Ollendick & Gruen, 1972; Smith & Sharpe, 1970). In reinforced practice, the child is rewarded for remaining in the presence of the feared stimulus for progressively longer periods of time. Initially, the child remains in the presence of the feared stimulus only for as long as is tolerable. Once this tolerance threshold is determined, the child is rewarded for remaining progressively longer in the presence of the feared stimulus (e.g., Leitenberg & Callahan, 1973; Luiselli, 1978).

Table 5-3 in the Appendix presents a summary of the procedures and findings of 11 studies that have examined the effectiveness of the four prolonged exposure treatments. Across all studies, a total of 72 children were treated for a total of 10 different types of fears and anxieties. The children ranged in age from 4 to 16 years; their fears and anxieties ranged in duration from 2 weeks to 3 years. Of the 10 different types of fear and anxiety reactions, the most commonly treated were those related to school and physical harm.

One-half of the studies had as their focus the therapeutic effects of imaginal and *in vivo* flooding; one-third, the therapeutic effects of reinforced practice; and one-fifth, the therapeutic effects of implosion. Though few of the studies were true experiments, all did find one or more of the four prolonged exposure treatments effective in reducing the fears and anxieties of children. Evidence of effectiveness was found across all three components of the fear reaction; evidence of maintenance of those effects was found across intervals ranging from 1 month to 8 years; and evidence of generalization of those effects was found across untreated settings and untreated behaviors.

Modeling and Its Variants

All forms of modeling therapies for children's fears and anxieties call for the observation of another person interacting adaptively with the feared stimulus (cf. Morris & Kratochwill, 1983a, 1983c). They differ from one another primarily in the directness of these observations and the rehearsal of the responses depicted in the observations. In live modeling, the fearful child directly observes a child or an adult interacting appropriately with the feared stimulus (e.g., Jones, 1924b; Ritter, 1968; White & Davis, 1974). In symbolic modeling, the fearful child observes a filmed or slide presentation of a child or an adult interacting appropriately with the feared stimulus (e.g., Bandura & Menlove, 1968; Ginther & Roberts, 1982; Hill, Liebert, & Mott, 1968; Melamed & Siegel, 1975). In covert modeling, the fearful child imagines a child or an adult interacting appropriately with the feared stimulus (e.g., Chertock & Bornstein, 1979). And in participant modeling, the fearful child first observes (either directly or indirectly) adaptive responding toward the feared stimulus, then practices duplicating those adaptive responses. This practice in adaptive responding is typically supplemented with guided instruction, support, and feedback from the therapist (e.g., Bandura, Blanchard, & Ritter, 1969; Lewis, 1974; Matson, 1983).

Each of the four major types of modeling therapies has a number of subtypes, based upon the nature and number of models employed. The single-model subtype makes use of only one child or adult in its demonstration of adaptive behavior toward the feared stimulus; the multiple-models subtype uses several different children or adults (e.g., Bandura & Menlove, 1968). In the similar-model(s) subtype, the fearful child observes a child or children of like age, gender, and race, whereas in the dissimilar-model(s) subtype, the fearful child observes a person or persons of discrepant age, gender, or race (e.g., Weissbrod & Bryan, 1973). The mastery-model(s) subtype has a person fearlessly interacting with the feared stimulus, whereas the coping-model(s) subtype has a person uneasily but successfully interacting with the feared stimulus (e.g., Klorman, Hilpert, Michael, LeGana, & Sveen, 1980; Kornhaber & Schroeder, 1975). Combinations of these six subtypes make up still other subtypes for each of the four major modeling treatments.

Table 5-4 in the Appendix provides a listing of the features and findings of 30 studies that have examined the effectiveness of modeling treatments for children's fears and anxieties. As a whole, the studies treated over 1,100 children suffering from nine different types of fears and anxieties. The children ranged in age from 1¾ years to 17 years; the anxiety reactions ranged in duration from several days to several months. Most common among the nine different types of fear reactions treated were those toward small animals, dental procedures, and medical procedures.

Approximately 50% of the studies had as their focus the effects of symbolic modeling, 20% the effects of participant modeling, and 30% the relative effects of two or more of the different modeling therapies. Virtually all of the studies employed experimental designs in their tests of the effects of the modeling therapies, and virtually all of the studies found the modeling therapies to be highly effective in reducing the fears and anxieties of children. Reductions

were evidenced across all three of the components of the fear state, across settings not targeted in treatment, and across problem behaviors not addressed in treatment. Maintenance of these reductions was evidenced across intervals ranging from 5 months to 1 year.

When compared to the control conditions of no treatment and attention placebo, the modeling treatments proved to be consistently more effective. And when compared to one another, the treatment of participant modeling proved to be consistently more effective than live, symbolic, and covert modeling. Few consistent findings, however, emerged from the comparisons among the six principal subtypes.

Several of the studies looked at the role that several child and parental characteristics may play in mediating treatment outcome. Two variables that were found to bear no relationship to treatment outcome were the therapeutic expectancies of the child (Mann, 1972) and the gender of the child (Bandura & Menlove, 1968; Ginther & Roberts, 1982; Ritter, 1968; Roberts, Wurtele, Boone, Ginther, & Elkins, 1981). Five variables that were found to bear a relationship to treatment outcome were the age of the child, the self-control of the child, the defensiveness of the child, the similarity of the child to the model, and the anxiety of the parent toward the feared stimulus. Specifically, the older the child, the more likely the child was to benefit from treatment (e.g., Gilbert et al., 1982; Melamed & Siegel, 1975; Peterson, Schultheis, Ridley-Johnson, Miller, & Tracy, 1984). The child high in self-control and low in defensiveness also was more likely to benefit from treatment than the child low in self-control and high in defensiveness (Klingman, Melamed, Cuthbert, & Hermecz, 1984). The more closely the child resembled the model in terms of age, fear level, and previous experience with the feared stimulus, the greater the probability of a positive treatment outcome (e.g., Klingman et al., 1984; Kornhaber & Schroeder, 1975; Melamed, Meyer, Gee, & Soule, 1976; Melamed et al., 1978). Apparently, observing a model who apprehensively approached the feared stimulus resulted in no better outcome than observing a model who boldly approached the feared stimulus (i.e., there was equivalence between the coping-model and mastery-model subtypes). However, observing a model who was similar to the child along all of these dimensions did appear to be associated with a more favorable outcome.

And, finally, the less fearful the parent was toward the stimulus the child feared, the more likely the child was to benefit from modeling therapy (Peterson *et al.*, 1984).

Information on these and other mediators of treatment outcome is obviously most pertinent to the task of treatment selection. Choosing the optimum treatment for a given fearful child obviously should be based upon such information, along with information on other conceptual and practical considerations. Precisely how these various bodies of information are assimilated, integrated, and utilized is discussed in a later section on treatment selection.

Contingency Management

Treatment of children's fears and anxieties by contingency management calls for the manipulation of the external events that follow the children's reactions. This manipulation of environmental consequences has taken many different forms (cf. Gelfand, 1978; Morris & Kratochwill, 1983a; Richards & Siegel, 1978). In some instances, the child has received a reward for interacting with the feared stimulus; in others, the child has had a reward rescinded for refusing to interact with the feared stimulus; and in still others, the child has been subjected to some combination of the two (e.g., Ayllon, Smith, & Rogers, 1970; Boer & Sipprelle, 1970). On some occasions, rewards have been dispensed for progressively bolder steps toward the feared stimulus; on other occasions, penalties have been imposed for failing to take such bold steps; and on still other occasions, some combination of the two sets of contingencies has been applied (e.g., Luiselli, 1978).

Table 5-5 in the Appendix offers a summary of the features and findings of the 15 studies that have examined the effectiveness of contingency management procedures. Across all studies, 55 children were treated for seven different types of fear and anxiety reactions. The children ranged in age from 3 to 15 years; the fears ranged in duration from 1 month to 5 years. Of the seven different types of fears and anxieties treated, the most common were those in regard to school and social situations.

Virtually all of the 15 studies had as their focus the therapeutic effects of contingency management per se, with the sole exception having as its focus the relative therapeutic effects of two different types of contingency management procedures. Approximately half of the studies were controlled in nature, and almost all of the studies reported successful fear reduction through contingency management treatments. Reductions were evidenced across subjective, motor, and physiological fear responses, and these reductions were evidenced across nontreated settings and nontreated fear stimuli. Maintenance of these reductions was evidenced across intervals ranging from 1 month to 1 year.

Self-Management

In self-management treatments for children's fears and anxieties, the focus is on manipulation of the children's subjective and physiological reactions to the feared stimuli (cf. Melamed, Klingman, & Siegel, 1984; Morris & Kratochwill, 1983a). To manipulate the children's subjective reactions to the feared stimuli, the children are taught adaptive ways of appraising an upcoming feared situation or adaptive ways of thinking about an ongoing feared situation or both (e.g., Fox & Houston, 1981; Peterson & Shigetomi, 1981). Adaptive ways of appraising an upcoming feared situation generally consist of viewing and construing the situation as less threatening; adaptive ways of thinking about an ongoing fear situation usually consist of saying to oneself that one can effectively handle the situation. To manipulate the children's physiological reactions to the feared stimuli, the children are typically instructed in deep muscle relaxation or creative visualization or both (e.g., Bankart & Bankart, 1983; Peterson & Shigetomi, 1981). The training in deep muscle relaxation generally entails learning how to relax one's muscles on cue; the training in creative visualization usually involves learning how to conjure up images of peacefulness and tranquility.

To date, nine studies have examined the effects of self-management treatments for children's fears and anxieties. A summary of their major features and findings is presented in Table 5-6 in the Appendix. Together, the studies examined 350 children ranging in age from 2½ years to 14 years and suffering from one of five different types of fears and anxieties— darkness, dental procedures, public speaking, school, or hospital procedures. Experimental designs were used in eight of the nine studies. Five of the studies compared the effects of self-management treatments to the effects of other behavioral treatments; four of the studies looked at the effects of self-management treatments in isolation.

Though the stated focus of self-management treatments is the modification of the subjective and physiological components of children's fear and anxiety reactions, the studies in general did not find self-management treatments to be effective in altering the subjective and physiological fear responses of children. The treatments were only found to be effective in reducing the motor fear responses of children. Maintenance of these reductions in motor fear responses was observed across intervals of 1 week, 1 year, and 2 years (Bankart & Bankart, 1983; Peterson & Shigetomi, 1982; Siegel & Peterson, 1981); spread of these reductions in motor fear responses was observed across untreated settings (Kanfer et al., 1975); and magnitude of these reductions in motor fear responses was observed to be greater than that produced by the control conditions of attention placebo and no treatment.

Several of the studies tested the validity of a number of the child and parental variables thought to possibly mediate treatment outcome. Among the child variables tested, no support was obtained for either age or gender as a mediator of treatment outcome (Nocella & Kaplan, 1982; Rosenfarb & Hayes, 1984; Siegel & Peterson, 1980). Support was, however, obtained for the variables of defensiveness and trait anxiety. As expected, the more defensive the child was, the less the child was found to benefit from self-management treatment (Fox & Houston, 1981). Not expected, though, was the finding that the higher the trait anxiety of the child, the less the child profited from self-management treatment (Fox & Houston, 1981). The sole parental variable examined was that of maternal anxiety toward the stimulus feared by the child, and it was found to bear a negative relationship to treatment outcome (Peterson & Shigetomi, 1981).

Compound Treatments

Various combinations of the aforementioned five techniques have been used to treat the fears and anxieties of children. Among the two-technique combinations that have been employed are desensitization plus contingency management, prolonged exposure plus contingency management, and modeling plus contingency management. Among the three-technique combinations that have been employed are desensitization plus modeling plus contingency management and desensitization plus prolonged exposure plus self-management. And of the possible four-technique combinations, the only one that has been employed is desensitization plus prolonged exposure plus modeling plus contingency management.

An example of a two-technique compound intervention is Graziano and associates' home-based program for nighttime fears (Graziano & Mooney, 1980; Graziano, Mooney, Huber, & Ignasiak, 1979). Mixing elements of self-management with contingency management, the program first calls for training in deep muscle relaxation, pleasant imagery, and courageous self-talk. Children practice each of the three self-control skills each night at bedtime and are rewarded by their parents for how well they perform the skills. Another example of a two-technique compound intervention is Esveldt-Dawson and associates' performance-based program for fear of school and/or strangers (Esveldt-Dawson et al., 1982). Mixing elements of modeling with contingency management, the program begins with verbal instruction and then moves to actual demonstration in adaptive ways of interacting with the feared stimulus. The children practice duplicating the modeled events and are systematically rewarded for closer approximations to criterion performance.

Two examples of three-technique compound interventions are the programs developed by Miller and associates (Miller et al., 1972a) and Barlow and Seidner (1983). Desensitization, modeling, and contingency management are combined in Miller and associates' treatment (Miller et al., 1972a); desensitization, prolonged exposure, and self-management are combined in Barlow and Seidner's (1983) treatment. The Miller et al. program first has parents dispensing rewards for nonfearful responding, then has the the child undergoing imaginal desensitization and participant modeling. In the Barlow and Seidner (1983) program, children frightened of being alone or away from home first receive training in relaxation-based panic management techniques, and then receive instruction in adaptive ways of construing the feared stimulus and their ability to deal with the feared stimulus. Finally, they interact with the actual feared stimulus for progressively longer periods of time.

The only four-technique compound intervention that we know of is the program developed by MacDonald (1975) to treat an 11-year-old boy's long-standing fear of dogs. In her treatment of the child, MacDonald (1975) employed two variants of desensitization: one in which the relaxed state was paired with images of the feared object, and one in which the relaxed state was paired with photographs of the feared object. To these two variants of desensitization, she added components of participant modeling, prolonged *in vivo* exposure, and contingency management. And for the final portion of the program, she had the parents rewarding progressively less fearful contact with dogs.

Table 5-7 in the Appendix summarizes the procedures and findings from the 18 studies that have examined the effectiveness of 11 different compound treatments for children's fears and anxieties. Across all studies, over 391 children ranging in age from 3 to 17 years were treated for over 11 different types of fears and anxieties, ranging from 3 weeks to 10 years in duration. Of the different fear and anxiety reactions treated, the most common were those toward school-related events, darkness, and social situations. Approximately three-fourths of the studies were concerned with the effects of two-technique compound treatments; the remaining ones examined the effects of three- and four-technique compound treatments.

Virtually all of the 18 investigations—10 of which were controlled experiments and 8 of which were uncontrolled case reports—found significant reductions in fear responding with virtually all of the compound treatments. These reductions in responding were evidenced only in the subjective and motoric components of the fear reaction (no study assessed responding in the physiological component of the fear reaction). Maintenance of these reductions in subjective and motor fear responses was evidenced across intervals ranging from 6 weeks to 4 years. And spread of these reductions in subjective and motor fear responses was observed across nontreated settings, nontreated fear stimuli, and nontreated problem behaviors.

In the many comparisons carried out between compound treatments and no treatment and between compound treatments and attention placebos, only one study failed to find the compound treatments superior to the two control conditions (i.e., Mayer *et al.*, 1971). In the few comparisons carried out between compound treatments and single-technique treatments, the compound interventions tended to be more effective than the single-technique treatments

(Miller & Kassinove, 1978; O'Connor, 1972). And in the only study to compare the effects of one compound intervention to those of another, the two treatments were found to be equivalent (Miller & Kassinove, 1978).

Only one study looked at the role that certain child and parental variables might play in mediating treatment outcome (Miller *et al.*, 1972a). Of the child variables examined, no support was obtained for gender, intelligence, socioeconomic status, and fear duration as mediators of treatment outcome. Support was, however, obtained for the child variable of age: The younger the child, the more the child profited from treatment. And support was obtained for the parental variable of motivation: The more highly motivated the parent, the more the child benefited from the compound intervention.

Summary

Though differences in methods and measures make cross-study comparisons among the different treatment groups difficult, a few general statements can be offered. Of the six behavioral treatments reviewed, desensitization, modeling, and compound interventions have been the most frequently employed with the greatest numbers of children.

Given that more children have been treated with desensitization, modeling, and compound interventions, it is not surprising that more different types of fears and anxieties have been treated with these three procedures than with the other three. The characteristics of these children and their fear reactions did not, however, radically differ from those treated with prolonged exposure, contingency management, and self-management. All six treatments were carried out with children of roughly equivalent ages suffering from fears of roughly equivalent chronicity.

Each of the six treatment procedures produced significant reductions in the fear and anxiety reactions of children. Desensitization, prolonged exposure, modeling, and contingency management did so across all three components of the various fear and anxiety reactions; compound interventions did so across the subjective and motor components of the reactions; and self-management did so only for the motor component of the reactions. Of the studies that conducted some type of follow-up assessment. a 1-year maintenance of effects was observed for modeling and contingency management, a 2-year maintenance of effects for desensitization and self-management, a 4-year maintenance of effects for compound interventions, and an 8-year maintenance of effects for prolonged exposure. Inequivalence in the length of these follow-up assessments precludes any statements about the equivalence or inequivalence of these maintenance effects. Longer follow-ups may have revealed continued maintenance of effects for each of the treatments, along with comparability of these effects among the treatments. Of the few studies that conducted an assessment of the spread of therapeutic effects to untreated settings and responses, such generalization was observed for virtually all of the treatments.

Very different treatment durations were reported for the six different procedures—a finding that leads us to believe that the different procedures may require different lengths of time to achieve their respective effects. The self-management and modeling treatments were of relatively brief duration; the prolonged exposure treatments were of intermediate duration; and the contingency management treatments, desensitization treatments, and compound interventions were of extended duration. For example, the self-management and modeling treatments ranged in duration from 15 minutes to 3 days and from 6 minutes to 20 days, respectively. The contingency management and desensitization treatments, on the other hand, ranged in duration from 16 to 100 days and from 8 days to 6 months, respectively.

Only a dozen or so studies directly compared the effects of the six treatment procedures to one another. Few in number, the studies varied in the treatments they compared, the children they treated, the fears they treated, and the methods they used to assess those fears. Thus, little can be concluded from these treatment comparisons. If we can conclude anything from these various studies, it is that more treatment does not necessarily mean better treatment. That is, more treatment (i.e., a compound intervention) does not necessarily lead to changes beyond those achieved through less treatment (i.e., any of the single-technique interventions). This is, of course, a conclusion that is very much open to doubt and that will continue to be so until treatment comparison studies of a more standardized nature are conducted.

In concluding, we should note that behavioral treatments are not the only treatments available for use with fearful and anxious children. Psychoanalytic, systems, and pharmacological interventions have been and continue to be viable treatment alternatives (e.g., Barker, 1984; Elmhirst, 1984; Gittelman & Klein, 1985; Herbert, 1984). Data on the effectiveness of these approaches are, however, quite equivocal as well as quite scarce. Take, for example, the literature on the use of tricyclic antidepressant compounds in the treatment of children's fears and anxieties. Of the four best-designed studies to date, two found the drug treatment to be superior to the placebo (Gittelman & Klein, 1971, 1973), and two found the drug treatment to be equivalent to the placebo (Berney et al., 1981; Rapoport, Elkins, & Mikkelsen et al., 1980). Much more research is obviously needed before a verdict can be reached on the effectiveness of pharmacological (as well as psychoanalytic and systems) treatments for children's fears and anxieties. Such research will certainly differ from research on the effectiveness of behavioral treatments for children's fears and anxieties along certain dimensions, but will parallel behavioral research along other dimensions. The section below on treatment evaluation should therefore be of interest to both behavioral and nonbehavioral readers.

TREATMENT SELECTION

Given the number of potentially successful interventions and their variations, the issue of treatment selection emerges. Of course, in the few previously discussed areas where evidence of differential effectiveness exists, this information must be weighed heavily. In addition, how the treatment will be evaluated must be considered; for example, whether the targeted change is primarily motor, subjective, or physiological could alter the type of intervention selected. Although there is as yet little empirical guidance, thoughtful consideration of the match between treatments and other factors should assist in the decision process.

As with any clinical intervention, a large number of factors may potentially interact with treatment selection. The following section briefly discusses the use of each of the six previously described techniques in conjunction with four additional factors: the nature of the fear and its stimulus; the characteristics of the child and parent; cost-effectiveness; and ethical considerations.

Systematic Desensitization

Systematic desensitization seems especially applicable when the fear is symbolic (such as fear of nuclear war), or when *in vivo* exposure to the feared stimulus is readily available and approachable in stages (such as fear of large dogs). Not all types of fears, however, can be easily translated into a hierarchy. Fears that do not easily lend themselves to segmentation (such as fears of test taking and speaking before a group) may require more challenging and more costly approaches to setting up effective hierarchies. Imagery and relaxation may require skills beyond those possessed by young children. Motivation and cooperation of the child and parent may have to be high for this technique. When imaginal exposure is sufficient, systematic desensitization would seem to be relatively cost-effective. Perhaps most important, the use of a gradual hierarchy reduces the risk of ethical problems when compared to more intense exposure or possibly coercive contingency management techniques.

Prolonged Exposure

In instances where a hierarchy is impractical, prolonged exposure may be applicable. Also, when treatment time must be reduced to the absolute minimum, this method could be indicated. When, for example, a child must undergo an emergency medical procedure, treatment time may be minimal. Both children and parents may, however, have strong feelings about cooperating with the higher levels of anxiety associated with prolonged exposure treatments. Thus, their attitudes and opinions may have to be considered (Gelfand, 1978; Graziano *et al.*, 1979). The biggest problems with this technique are probably ethical ones when the treatment is chosen by the parent or therapist on behalf of the child. Some parents advocate "sink or swim" approaches to dealing with their children's fears. It would seem, however, that a child has a right to a treatment that involves the least possible discomfort. The fact that escape must be eliminated also presents ethical problems.

Modeling

Modeling appears to have wide applicability, particularly with older children (Melamed *et al.*, 1984). Its use does present some problems.

Although the therapist, parent, or sibling may serve as a model, their validity in the eyes of the child may be limited. The presentation of convincing models dealing with fears similar to those of the child may be difficult and costly. When this technique can be used, however, it seems likely to have high face validity, to be acceptable to both the child and parent, and to present few ethical problems.

Contingency Management

The introduction of reinforcers and/or punishers into the treatment would seem to offer a variety of risks and advantages. They would seem most applicable when the fear stimulus and the fear response of interest are overt in nature. With imaginal stimuli or subjective responses, contingencies could promote false reporting by the child. Certainly, when the child's motivation to face the feared situation is low, contingencies could be extremely helpful. Assuming that higher motivation might facilitate treatment, contingencies could increase cost-effectiveness.

Sometimes parents have strong negative reactions to some reinforcers and punishers. These reactions could be particularly intense if there is also parental hesitancy to "push" the child into anxiety-provoking situations. Perhaps the most difficult aspect of contingency management, then, is that of its potential ethical problems. For example, offering strong reinforcers could encourage the child to experience more anxiety during treatment than is warranted. Ethical problems in the use of punishment seem obvious. Although few therapists might advocate the use of punishment to motivate a child to face a feared stimulus, they must deal with the fact that some parents do.

Self-Management

Self-management would seem to have few drawbacks and many advantages, at least with older children. It should be applicable whether the fear stimulus is real or imaginal and should allow *in vivo* application. Also, there should be few objections by the child or parent to its use and few ethical problems. However, depending on the type of self-management employed, the child will have to possess abilities involving abstraction, intellect, memory, data recording, and so on. Also, the work of Melamed and Peterson suggests that children high in the dispositional characteristic of self-control and low in defensiveness are most likely to benefit (Klingman *et al.*, 1984; Peterson & Tobler, 1984).

Compound Treatments

As treatments are combined, the relevant factors just described will, of course, all have to be considered.

Interactions with Other Treatments

The selection of the primary treatment method for fear and anxiety reduction will also have to consider a variety of factors that may interact with any child and family intervention. One primary dimension is whether the treatment will require more general treatment of the child or parent. For example, the parent may provide secondary gains for many fears, and these must be eliminated for successful treatment. Eliminating secondary gains may interact with maintenance effects when contingency management or even other techniques are employed. Also, the treatments described above do not deal with the elimination of recurrent causes of fears, such as parents who teach "neurotic styles" of functioning. How the selection of treatment techniques will interact with these complex individual and family factors is beyond the scope of this chapter and our knowledge. Be that as it may, the clinician must attempt to deal with these issues in a thoughtful manner.

TREATMENT EVALUATION

Evaluating the effectiveness of a treatment for children's fears and anxieties is every bit as complex as selecting a treatment. Multiple considerations enter into an overall evaluation of the treatment's worth. In this section, we discuss what is entailed in an assessment of the integrity, costs, and benefits of an intervention and what is involved in a determination of an intervention's effectiveness as a treatment for children's fears and anxieties.

Treatment Integrity

Before we ascertain the costs and benefits associated with a particular treatment, we must first ascertain whether or not the treatment has indeed been implemented. That is, we must first assess the integrity of the treatment—the

degree to which the treatment has been delivered as intended (Yeaton & Sechrest, 1981). As noted earlier, all treatments for children's fears and anxieties come with a protocol. The protocol specifies each of the tasks the therapist, the child, and (in some instances) the parent or teacher must perform in order for the treatment to be operative. Given the disagreements that exist in definition, classification, and explanation of children's fears and anxieties, one would expect to find widespread disagreement over the protocols' particulars. However, just the opposite is true: There is really little disagreement over what concrete, molar acts are needed for a treatment to be operative.

On the surface, then, assessing the integrity of a treatment is a rather straightforward affair. The actions of the therapist, the child, and (in some instances) the parent or the teacher are all monitored for their accordance with what the treatment protocol demands from each of them. For some interventions, the integrity of treatment hinges almost entirely upon the actions of one of these four persons: the therapist, child, parent, or teacher. For example, in contingency management, the child is either rewarded for progressive approach toward the feared object or punished for continued avoidance of the feared object, or both. The therapist, parent, or teacher is the person typically assigned to monitor the child's behavior and to dispense the rewards or punishers or both accordingly. Failure to carry out this assignment faithfully results in a corrupted version of the treatment. Another intervention whose integrity rests primarily upon the actions of a single person is the participant modeling treatment developed by Melamed and associates (Klingman *et al.*, 1984). According to its protocol, the child is to watch a film of a peer demonstrating various breathing and imagery techniques for coping with dental-related fear and anxiety. Time is allotted after each demonstration for the child to practice the technique. If the child neither views the modeling film nor practices the coping techniques during the designated times, a tainted version of the treatment has been administered.

The integrity of most of our treatments for children's fears and anxieties centers on the combined actions of the therapist, the child, and (in some instances) the parent or teacher. For example, in imaginal desensitization, the therapist's duties are to instruct the child in deep muscle relaxation techniques, to construct from the child's list of anxiety-provoking situations an anxiety hierarchy, to present each hierarchy scene to the child while he or she is in a relaxed state, and to present each anxiety-provoking scene upon mastery of the anxiety-provoking scene immediately below it in the hierarchy. For the child, the duties of imaginal desensitization are to follow the therapist's instructions to tense and relax various muscles, to compile a list of situations involving the feared stimulus, to rank-order the situations in terms of the fear they engender, to imagine each scene with great vividness while in a relaxed state, and to cease imagining the scene upon disruption of the relaxed state. For the treatment to be faithfully implemented, the therapist and the child must faithfully carry out their respective duties.

An example of an intervention whose integrity lies in the collective hands of the therapist, the child, and the parent is the self-control treatment developed by Peterson and associates (e.g., Peterson & Shigetomi, 1981; Siegel & Peterson, 1980, 1981). According to its protocol, the therapist has the assignment of demonstrating various techniques for coping with anxiety and alerting the child and the parent as to when it may be advantageous to use the techniques. The parent has the assignment of getting the child to practice the techniques and prompting the child as to when it is fitting to use the techniques. And the child has the assignment of simply complying with those parental instructions. If all three parties dutifully carry out their assignments, then it is safe to say that the treatment has been carried out as intended.

Though an assessment of treatment integrity is integral to an evaluation of treatment effectiveness, no study to date appears to have conducted such an assessment. From our vantage point, there appear to be two major reasons for our continuing failure to monitor the fidelity of our treatments for children's fears and anxieties. One is the crude and confused state of our assessment of the effects of our treatments—a matter that is discussed at greater length elsewhere. And the other is the complete absence of any instruments for measuring the integrity of our treatments. The two reasons are, of course, interrelated. Increased sensitivity to the inadequacies of our assessment of treatment outcome has prompted increased attention to and efforts at developing sound and sensitive measures of treatment outcome (Barrios & Hartmann, 1988; Barrios et al., 1981; Barrios & Shigetomi, 1985). Devoting more

and more attention and energy to the development of sound measures of treatment outcome has left us with less and less attention and energy to devote to the development of sound measures of treatment integrity. Obviously, a more equitable allocation of attention and energy is needed if we wish to systematically evaluate and cultivate our treatments for children's fears and anxieties.

Treatment Benefits

The benefits of treatment can be examined from one or more of the following three perspectives: the impact of treatment on the problem condition per se, the impact of treatment on other immediate problem conditions, and the impact of treatment on projected problem conditions. The former perspective focuses on the localized effects of treatment; the two latter perspectives focus on the generalized effects of treatment. Current thinking is that both types of perspectives are needed for a thorough analysis of the benefits of any treatment (e.g., Mash & Terdal, 1977; Stokes & Baer, 1977; Yates, 1981).

Problem Condition

Earlier, we have noted that children's fears and anxieties are seen as complex patterns of subjective, motor, and physiological responses. Given this conceptualization, assessment of children's fears and anxieties entails the assessment of multiple responses within and across the subjective, motor, and physiological response components (Barrios & Hartmann, 1988; Barrios & Shigetomi, 1985). Measurement of only a single response within each of the components or multiple responses within only one of the components offers an incomplete picture of the fear pattern, and thus constitutes an inadequate assessment of the problem condition. What is needed, then for an adequate assessment of treatment impact on the problem condition is the measurement of multiple responses within and across the multiple response components.

Also needed for an adequate assessment of the effects of treatment on the fear reaction per se is the measurement of that reaction across different settings and different time periods. Measurement across different settings allows for estimation of the benefits of treatment across different representations and presentations of the feared stimulus. Measurement across different time periods allows for estimation of the persistence of the benefits of treatment. Combined, the measurement of the fear reaction's complex response pattern and the measurement of that reaction across different settings and time periods make for a thorough assessment of treatment impact on the problem condition.

To date, the vast majority of our assessments have been less than thorough. Only 9 of the 124 outcome studies reviewed in the previous section monitored activity from all three of the response systems. As such, these 9 studies merit special mention. One is the treatment of a multiphobic child by Van Hasselt et al. (1979). Frightened by blood, heights, and school exams, the child received desensitization treatment for each of his fears. To assess the effects of desensitization on each of the fears, Van Hasselt and his associates collected measures of the child's subjective, motor, and physiological reactions to each stimulus. For the feared stimulus blood, degree of approach to a blood-soaked pillowcase served as a measure of motor responding; self-rating of discomfort during approach served as the measure of subjective responding; and heart rate and finger pulse volume during approach served as the measures of physiological responding. For heights, degree of ascent up a stepladder served as the measure of motor responding; self-rating of discomfort during ascent served as the measure of subjective responding; and heart rate upon ascent served as the measure of physiological responding. For school exams, trials to errorless performance on a memory task served as the measure of motor responding; self-rating of discomfort during the memory task served as the measure of subjective responding; and heart rate and finger pulse volume during the memory task served as the measures of physiological responding.

Nearly all of the remaining triple-response-system assessments have been carried out by either Melamed's research team or Peterson's research team. In their systematic studies of the effects of modeling treatments on children's fears of medical and dental procedures, Melamed and her associates gather several self-ratings of the children's discomfort during the procedures, observe the children's overt behavior during the procedure for several signs of anxiety, and monitor several of the children's physiological responses to the procedures

(Klingman et al., 1984; Melamed et al., 1976; Melamed & Siegel, 1975). In their systematic studies of the effects of self-control treatments on children's fears of medical and dental procedures, Peterson and her associates survey a very similar set of subjective, motoric, and physiological responses through use of a very similar set of methods (Peterson & Shigetomi, 1981; Siegel & Peterson, 1980, 1981).

As noted earlier, a thorough assessment of the localized effects of treatment calls not only for the measurement of the multiple components of fear, but also for the measurement of multiple responses within each of the components of fear. Few studies have followed this second directive. Most studies have limited their assessment of the subjective, motor, or physiological components of fear to a single response. Such studies tell us little about the benefits of treatment for the sundry responses within a single component of fear. However, a handful of studies have measured two or more responses from one or more of the response systems, and these studies likewise deserve mention. Some of them have already been described—the investigation by Van Hasselt et al. (1979), the investigations by Melamed and her associates (Klingman et al., 1984; Melamed et al., 1976; Melamed & Siegel, 1975; Melamed et al., 1978), and the investigations by Peterson and her associates (Peterson et al., 1984; Peterson & Shigetomi, 1981; Siegel & Peterson, 1980, 1981). One study that heretofore has not been described is the treatment of a multiphobic child by Esveldt-Dawson et al. (1982). In their assessment of the child's fear of school situations and strangers, Esveldt-Dawson and her associates observed the child for a host of motor signs of anxiety. Among the behaviors observed were eye contact, giggling, furrowing of the brow, grimacing, voice volume, speech fluency, and body posture. By tracking a host of responses rather than a single response, Esveldt-Dawson and her associates were better able to gauge the impact of their treatment on the motoric component of the child's fear reactions.

Two other guidelines for a thorough assessment of treatment impact on the problem condition are the measurement of responding to the feared stimulus across different settings and across different follow-up periods. To date, far more studies have complied with the second guideline than with the first. Two of the few studies that did assess the persistence of treatment benefits across variations in the testing situation are the investigations by Kanfer *et al.* (1975) and by Murphy and Bootzin (1973). Kanfer and his associates looked at the effects of their self-management treatment across two testing situations. The two testing situations were similar in that they both involved the presentation of the feared stimulus of darkness, but were dissimilar in that they utilized different modes of presentation. For one of the testings, the child was seated alone in a room with a device to control room illumination at his side. Left in total darkness, the child increased the lighting whenever he became uncomfortable. Time spent in total darkness was recorded. For the other testing, the child was again seated alone in a room with a device for controlling room illumination at his side. Left in a fully illuminated room, the child decreased the lighting to the lowest level he could tolerate. Degree of illumination was recorded. Murphy and Bootzin (1973) also carried out two assessments of the effects of their participant modeling treatment for fear of snakes. In one of the testings, the child approached and handled the snake. In the other testing, the child remained stationary while the snake was brought to him. In both situations, the degree of proximity to and contact with the snake was recorded.

Other Problem Conditions

Another element of a comprehensive assessment of the benefits of treatment is an assessment of the spread of treatment effects to untreated problem conditions. These untreated problem conditions may take the form of other fears and anxieties on the part of the child, other non-fear-related disturbances on the part of the child, fears and anxieties on the part of peers and family members, or non-fear-related disturbances on the part of peers and family members. Of the four types of problem conditions, the two most frequently inspected have been those of the treated child. Among the nontargeted fears and anxieties of the treated child that have been assessed are those to specific and nonspecific stimuli (i.e., generalized anxiety). And among the non-fear-related problems of the treated child that have been assessed are poor peer relations, poor family relations, and poor academic performance (e.g., Ayllon *et al.*, 1970; Barlow & Seidner, 1983; LeUnes & Siemsglusz, 1977).

The anxieties and non-fear-related troubles

of the treated child's peers, siblings, and parents make up the other two types of problem conditions. In their investigation of their treatment for agoraphobia, Barlow and Seidner (1983) examined the parents' interactions with the children along with the children's reactions to being alone and out of the home. This broadened assessment of treatment effects allowed Barlow and Seidner (1983) to check for improvements in parental behavior concomitant with improvements in children's approach behavior.

Projected Problem Conditions

The final element in a comprehensive assessment of treatment benefits is an assessment of the treatment's impact on projected problem conditions. This is, in essence, an assessment of the preventive effects of treatment. Of the many different problem conditions a treatment for children's fears and anxieties could possibly prevent, the most likely candidates are the future fears and anxieties of the children. They are, therefore, the problem conditions of primary interest to us in our examination of a treatment's preventive capabilities.

Though preventive research itself is a difficult undertaking (e.g., Gelfand & Hartmann, 1977; Roberts & Peterson, 1984), assessment of the preventive effects of our treatments for children's fears and anxieties need not be. Developmental data show the fears and anxieties of children of different ages to cluster around different stimuli. The common fear stimuli of each of the different age groups have been presented in an earlier section of this chapter. This breakdown of fear stimuli by age group can guide us in our assessment of the preventive effects of our treatments for children's fears and anxieties.

To date, no study has employed this strategy in its assessment of the preventive effects of a treatment for children's fears and anxieties. In fact, no study to date has examined the preventive effects of any of our treatments for children's fears and anxieties—certainly not the long-range, preventive effects we are referring to here. This gap in our assessment practices is one that obviously needs to be filled.

Treatment Costs

All treatments for children's fears and anxieties involve certain costs, the brunt of which are borne by the child, the parent, and the therapist. In general, the costs are of two types: financial and psychological. For the child, the financial costs of the treatment are almost always negligible, for almost always it is the parent who pays the fee for treatment services. The same cannot be said of the psychological costs of treatment for the child. All of our treatments for children's fears and anxieties call for the endurance of some discomfort, be it subjective or physiological or both; thus, all of our treatments involve some psychological costs for the child. For some of our treatments, such as desensitization and modeling, the amount of discomfort the child is asked to tolerate may be minimal; for other treatments, such as prolonged exposure and contingency management, the amount of discomfort the child is asked to tolerate may be substantial.

Another possible psychological cost to the child as a result of treatment is the stigmatization that accompanies being singled out as a child with a problem. This stigmatization may take the form of social rejection or social ridicule or both. For some of our treatments, such as desensitization and prolonged exposure, it may be very obvious that the child is being singled out as having a problem; for other treatments, such as group-administered modeling and self-management, it may not be so obvious. Treatments may differ, then, in terms of this particular psychological price that the child may be called upon to pay.

The treatment of children's fears and anxieties also involves certain costs—financial and psychological—for the parent and the therapist. For example, financially, the parent must part with some of his or her income to cover the fee for treatment services. And psychologically, the parent may incur some loss in the quality of his or her life as a result of participating in the treatment of the child. The therapist too sustains certain financial and psychological losses in treating the fears and anxieties of children. For example, in devoting time and energy to the treatment of a child's fears and anxieties, the therapist may have less time and energy to devote to more lucrative activities or to other professional and personal activities.

At its simplest, the evaluation of treatment effectiveness is seen as a comparison of treatment benefits to treatment costs. To date, no study has performed such a comparison, for to date no study has assessed the costs of treatment. The reasons for not doing so appear to be

two. One is the more pressing need to upgrade our assessment of the benefits of treatment (e.g., Barrios & Hartmann, 1988; Barrios et al., 1981; Barrios & Shiegetomi, 1985). Obviously, before we assess the costs of treatment, we had better be reasonably certain about the benefits of treatment. Most of our energies and efforts have gone toward achieving this certainty. The second reason is our unfamiliarity with the notion of treatment cost—its conceptualization and its assessment (Yates, 1985). Most of us are unacquainted with the different perspectives from which costs can be defined, the different methods by which costs can be assessed, and the different procedures by which costs and benefits can be compared. An assignment for the immediate future is for us to become better acquainted with the formulation and measurement of the concept of treatment costs.

Summary

Treatment evaluation is integral to our comprehension and remediation of children's fears and anxieties. Conscientious and meticulous evaluation of the effectiveness of our treatments provides us with insights into which of our theories of children's fears and anxieties would be best to develop and which would be best to discard, as well as similar insights about the treatments themselves. Unfortunately, our evaluation of our treatments has been neither conscientious nor meticulous. Only recently have we begun broadening our assessment of the fear condition such that it coincides with how we conceptualize the construct. Still awaiting us are the development of methods for assessing the integrity, the long-term benefits, and the costs of our treatments. Advances in our understanding and treating the fears and anxieties will also depend upon our attending to several other matters. In the chapter's final section, we discuss these matters.

SUMMARY AND RECOMMENDATIONS

Our review of behavioral treatment for children's fears and anxieties has revealed that we suffer from no shortage of techniques. We do, however, suffer from a shortage of guidelines and models that would faciliate advancements in our understanding and treatment of children's fears and anxieties. First and foremost, we lack a consensually agreed upon precise definition of "fear and anxiety." Heretofore we have defined "fear and anxiety" as a complex pattern of subjective, motor, and physiological responses. We have not, however, delineated the specific subjective, motor, and physiological responses that constitute the pattern. Consequently, many different combinations of responses to the same stimulus have shared the same "fear and anxiety" label. This liberal use of the label has enabled us to amass a sizeable literature on children's fears and anxieties, but has disabled us from clarifying what is meant by the label. For us to systematically study the pattern of children's fears and anxieties, we must first specify the exact content and configuration of the response pattern. In other words, we must render our current vague definition of children's fears and anxieties more explicit.

Related to this need for a more explicit response definition of children's fears and anxieties is the need for more explicit criteria for problematic fears and anxieties. Our practice has been to judge a child's fears and anxieties as problematic if the child's parent, teacher, or some other significant adult has judged the responding to be problematic. This has been a most unproductive practice. It has led to great variability in the types of responding designated as maladaptive and to little clarity in what constitutes maladaptive responding. For us to reliably identify fears and anxieties as problematic, we need operational definitions of problem fears and anxieties. The diagnostic criteria set forth by the American Psychiatric Association (1987) for Separation Anxiety Disorder, Avoidant Disorder, Overanxious Disorder, Agoraphobia without History of Panic Disorder, Social Phobia, Simple Phobia, Panic Disorder with and without Agoraphobia, Generalized Anxiety Disorder, Obsessive–Compulsive Disorder, and Post-Traumatic Stress Disorder are examples of such operational definitions. They may not, however, be the criteria we wish to use to identify the problem fears and anxieties of children. We may instead wish to use criteria that are more quantitative in nature—that specify the exact form and frequency of responding and that do so for each of the various age groups of childhood. Such diagnostic criteria could be consistent with the behavioral–developmental perspective advocated here and elsewhere (e.g.,

Barrios & Hartmann, 1988; Campbell, 1986; Campos & Barrett, 1984; Klinnert, Campos, Sorce, Emde, & Svejda, 1983). Such criteria, though, do not at this time exist. The task of devising them is ours.

Given the complex nature of children's fears and anxieties, we can address the pattern from any number of different directions. We can direct our treatment efforts at the responding of the subjective component, the motor component, the physiological component, or some combination of the three. We can direct our treatment efforts at the level of the fearful child or at the level of the family system of which the fearful child is an element. Our task is to select the optimum level at which to intervene and the optimum targets at which to aim our treatment efforts. We look to theory or data or both for help in performing this task. Contemporary behavioral theories of children's fears and anxieties have not been of much help, though, in carrying out the task of target behavior selection (Barrios & Hartmann, 1988; Barrios et al., 1981). For the most part, the theories offer few insights into the direction of influence from one element of the family system to another, or from one component of the fear pattern to another. For our purposes, we need behavioral theories that are truly developmental in nature (e.g., Barrios & Hartmann, 1988; Campbell, 1986). We need theories that specify the role parents and siblings play in the origin, maintenance, and modification of a child's fears and anxieties; we also need theories that specify the role responding in one component of the fear pattern plays in the instigation, perpetuation, and modification of responding in the other two components of the fear pattern.

Aside from theory, we can draw upon data to guide us in the selection of a target behavior. Data that would be of most help to us would be those on the interrelationships among the three components of the fear state—the degree of association among the three types of responding at any given point in time (i.e., concordance), and the rate of change among the three types of responding as a function of treatment (i.e., synchrony). Such data on the concordance and synchrony among the fear responses of adults are quite plentiful (e.g., Agras & Jacobs, 1981; Hodgson & Rachman, 1974; Rachman & Hodgson, 1974; Taylor & Agras, 1981; Vermelyea, Boice, & Barlow, 1984). Such data, though, are quite scarce for the fear responses of children (Barrios & Shigetomi, 1985). For target behavior selection in our treatment of children's fears and anxieties to be in any sense empirically based, we need more estimates of concordance and synchrony.

We are of the opinion, then, that having formal models for target behavior selection—be they theoretical or empirical in nature—is much preferable to having no such formal models for target behavior selection. We are of the same opinion regarding formal models for treatment selection and treatment evaluation. Unfortunately, at this time we find ourselves in possession of neither models for selecting a treatment nor models for evaluating a treatment. Instead, we find ourselves selecting a treatment for children's fears and anxieties largely on the basis of personal preference. A much more systematic approach would be for us to select a treatment along the lines recommended in this chapter (the requisite-matching model), or along the lines many have recommended for selecting a treatment for adults' fears and anxieties (the profile-matching model). In the latter model, a treatment is chosen on the basis of the profile of subjective, motor, and physiological fear responses (e.g., Heimberg, Gansler, Dodge, & Becker, 1987; Jerremalm, Jansson, & Öst, 1986; Öst, Jerremalm, & Johansson, 1981; Schwartz, Davidson, & Goleman, 1978; Trower, Yardley, Bryant, & Shaw, 1978). For example, for a fear profile in which subjective responses are predominant, the model advises us to apply a treatment whose predominant focus is the subjective component; for a fear profile in which motor responses are predominant, the model advises us to apply a treatment whose predominant focus is the motor component. For each possible profile of subjective, motor, and physiological responses, the model offers similar advice.

Both of these models for treatment selection have certain shortcomings. The requisite-matching model provides no guidelines for deciding when a treatment requisite has been met; the profile-matching model provides no guidelines for deciding between treatments with the same predominant focus. As significant as these shortcomings may appear, they pale in comparison to the shortcomings of a purely idiosyncratic approach to treatment seletion. Such an approach defies specification. If we are unable to specify the way in which we choose a treatment for children's fears and anxieties, we

are unable to evaluate and refine our selection process. It is for these reasons that we recommend the adoption of a more formalized approach to treatment selection.

More pressing than the need for formal models for target behavior and treatment selection is the need for formal models for treatment evaluation. To date, our efforts at evaluation have been largely haphazard. We have been incomplete and inconsistent in our assessment of the costs and benefits of our treatments. We have been divided in our efforts to amass a solid data base. A more unified front is obviously needed in regard to treatment evaluation. For there to be a consolidated approach to treatment evaluation, we must agree on three items (Mash, 1985). First, we must agree on the relevant dimensions that make up the concepts of treatment costs and treatment benefits. Second, we must develop sound measures for each of the relevant dimensions and agree to employ the measures in our studies of treatment effectiveness. And third, we must agree on a set of rules for integration of the data on costs and benefits. Arriving at some consensus on all three of these items will provide us with a coherent framework for assessing the worth of our treatments.

The keen interest now shown in children's fears and anxieties clearly differs from the interest shown in the past. Previously, children's fears and anxieties were seen as a convenient vehicle for testing the validity of our theories and techniques; the performance pattern was secondary to our interest in our theories and techniques. Today, children's fears and anxieties occupy a more prominent role; they are seen as a problem condition worthy of our attention and concern. And, as such, there is now a concerted effort to develop powerful programs for the prevention and remediation of children's fears and anxieties. For such efforts to prove successful, it is clear that we must first make strides in our conceptualization and assessment of the condition. Our hope is that this chapter has given us sufficient direction and motivation to take those steps—steps that will lead us to a more satisfying understanding and treatment of children's fears and anxieties.

REFERENCES

Achenbach, T. M. (1985). Assessment of anxiety in children. In A. H. Tuma & J. D. Maser (Eds.), *Anxiety and the anxiety disorders* (pp. 707–734). Hillsdale, NJ: Erlbaum.

Achenbach, T. M., & Edelbrock, C. S. (1978). The classification of child psychopathology: A review and analysis of empirical efforts. *Psychological Bulletin, 85,* 1275–1301.

Agras, W. S., Chapin, H. N., & Oliveau, D. C. (1972). The natural history of phobia. *Archives of General Psychiatry, 26,* 315–317.

Agras, W. S., & Jacobs, R. G. (1981). Phobia: Nature and measurement. In M. Mavissakalian & D. H. Barlow (Eds.), *Phobia: Psychological and pharmacological treatment* (pp. 35–62). New York: Guilford Press.

Agras, W. S., Sylvester, D., & Oliveau, D. C. (1969). The epidemiology of common fears and phobias. *Comprehensive Psychiatry, 10,* 151–156.

Allen, K., Hart, R., Buell, S., Harris, R., & Wolf, M. (1964). Effects of social reinforcement on isolate behavior of a nursery school child. *Child Development, 35,* 511–518.

American Psychiatric Association. (1987). *Diagnostic and statistical manual of mental disorders* (3rd ed, rev.). Washington, DC: Author.

Andrews, W. R. (1971). Behavioral and client-centered counseling of high school underachievers. *Journal of Counseling Psychology, 18,* 93–96.

Angelino, H., Dollins, J., & Mech, E. V. (1956). Trends in the "fears and worries" of school children as related to socio-economic status and age. *Journal of Genetic Psychology, 89,* 263–276.

Auld, F. (1951). The effects of tetraethylammonium on a habit motivated by fear. *Journal of Comparative and Physiological Psychology, 44,* 565–574.

Ayllon, T., Smith, D., & Rogers, M. (1970). Behavioral management of school phobia. *Journal of Behavior Therapy and Experimental Psychiatry, 1,* 125–138.

Bailey, P. M., Talhot, A., & Taylor, P. P. (1973). A comparison of maternal anxiety levels with anxiety levels manifested in child dental patients. *Journal of Dentistry for Children, 40,* 277–284.

Ball, W., & Tronick, E. (1971). Infant responses to impending collision: Optical and real. *Science, 171,* 818–820.

Bamber, J. H. (1974). The fears of adolescents. *Journal of Genetic Psychology, 125,* 127–140.

Bandura, A. (1969). *Principles of behavior modification.* New York: Holt, Rinehart & Winston.

Bandura, A. (Ed.). (1971). *Psychological modeling: Conflicting theories.* Chicago: Aldine–Atherton.

Bandura, A. (1977a). Self-efficacy: Toward a unifying theory of behavioral change. *Psychological Review, 84,* 191–215.

Bandura, A. (1977b). *Social learning theory.* Englewood Cliffs, NJ: Prentice-Hall.

Bandura, A. (1978). Reflections on self-efficacy. *Advances in Behaviour Research and Therapy, 1,* 237–269.

Bandura, A. (1982). Self-efficacy mechanism in human agency. *American Psychologist, 37,* 122–147.

Bandura, A., Blanchard, E. B., & Ritter, B. (1969). Relative efficacy of desensitization and modeling approaches for inducing behavioral, affective, and attitudinal changes. *Journal of Personality and Social Psychology, 13,* 173–199.

Bandura, A., Grusec, E., & Menlove, F. L. (1967). Vicarious extinction of avoidance behavior. *Journal of Personality and Social Psychology, 5,* 16–23.

Bandura, A., & Menlove, F. (1968). Factors determining vicarious extinction of avoidance behavior through symbolic modeling. *Journal of Personality and Social Psychology, 8,* 99–108.

Bankart, C. P., & Bankart, B. B. (1983). The use of song lyrics to alleviate a child's fears. *Child and Family Behavior Therapy, 5,* 81–83.

Barabasz, A. (1973). Group desensitization of test anxiety in elementary schools. *Journal of Psychology, 83,* 295–301.

Barker, P. (1984). Family dysfunction and anxiety in children. In V. P. Varma (Ed.), *Anxiety in children* (pp. 89–104). London: Croom Helm.

Barlow, D. H., & Seidner, A. L. (1983). Treatment of adolescent agoraphobics: Effects on parent–adolescent relations. *Behaviour Research and Therapy, 21,* 519–526.

Barrios, B. A. (1986). *Concordance and discordance among measures of children's fears and anxieties.* Unpublished manuscript, University of Mississippi.

Barrios, B. A. & Hartmann, D. P. (1988). Fears and anxieties. In E. J. Mash & L. G. Terdal (Eds.), *Behavioral assessment of childhood disorders* (2nd ed. pp. 196–262). New York: Guilford Press.

Barrios, B. A., Hartmann, D. P., & Shigetomi, C. (1981). Fears and anxieties in children. In E. J. Mash & L. G. Terdal (Eds.), *Behavioral assessment of childhood disorders* (pp. 259–304). New York: Guilford Press.

Barrios, B. A., Replogle, W., & Anderson-Tisdelle, D. (1983, December). *Multisystem–unimethod analysis of children's fears.* Paper presented at the meeting of the Association for Advancement of Behavior Therapy, Washington, DC.

Barrios, B. A., & Shigetomi, C. C. (1985). Assessment of children's fears: A critical review. In T. R. Kratochwill (Ed.), *Advances in school psychology* (Vol. 4, pp. 89–132), Hillsdale, NJ: Erlbaum.

Bauer, D. D. (1968). A case of desensitization and tutoring therapy. *Exceptional Child, 34,* 386–387.

Bauer, D. H. (1976). An exploratory study of developmental change in children's fears. *Journal of Child Psychology and Psychiatry, 17,* 69–74.

Bentler, P. M. (1962). An infant's phobia treated with reciprocal inhibition therapy. *Journal of Child Psychology and Psychiatry, 3,* 185–189.

Berg, I. (1976). School phobia in the children of agoraphobic women. *British Journal of Psychiatry, 128,* 86–89.

Berg, I., Marks, I., McGuire, R., & Lipsedge, M. (1974). School phobia and agoraphobia. *Psychological Medicine, 4,* 428–434.

Berney, T., Kolvin, I., Bhate, S. R., Garside, R. F., Jeans, J., Kay, B., & Scarth, L. (1981). School phobia: A therapeutic trial with clomipramine and short-term outcome. *British Journal of Psychiatry, 138,* 110–118.

Black, A. H. (1958). The extinction of avoidance under curare. *Journal of Comparative and Physiological Psychology, 51,* 519–524.

Blagg, N. R., & Yule, W. (1984). The behavioural treatment of school refusal: A comparative study. *Behaviour Research and Therapy, 22,* 119–127.

Boer, A. P., & Sipprelle, C. N. (1970). Elimination of avoidance behavior in the clinic and its transfer to the normal environment. *Journal of Behavior Therapy and Experimental Psychiatry, 1,* 169–174.

Bornstein, P. H., & Knapp, M. (1981). Self-control desensitization with a multi-phobic boy: A multiple baseline design. *Journal of Behavior Therapy and Experimental Psychiatry, 12,* 281–285.

Boyd, L. T. (1980). Emotive imagery in the behavioral management of adolescent school phobia: A case approach. *School Psychology Digest, 9,* 186–189.

Bradlyn, A. S. (1982). *The effects of a videotape preparation package in reducing children's arousal and increasing cooperation during cardiac catherization.* Unpublished doctoral dissertation, University of Mississippi.

Bregman, E. O. (1934). An attempt to modify the emotional attitudes of infants by the conditioned response technique. *Journal of Genetic Psychology, 45,* 169–198.

Bronson, G. W. (1972). Infants' reactions to unfamiliar persons and novel objects. *Monographs of the Society for Research in Child Development, 37*(3, Serial No. 148).

Brown, R. (1979). Beyond separation. In D. Hall & M. Stacey (Eds.), *Beyond separation.* London: Routledge & Kegan Paul.

Brown, R. E., Copeland, R. E., & Hall, R. V. (1974). School phobia: Effects of behavior modification treatment applied by an elementary school principal. *Child Study Journal, 4,* 125–133.

Brush, F. R. (1957). The effects of shock intensity on the acquisition and extinction of an avoidance response in dogs. *Journal of Comparative and Physiological Psychology, 50,* 547–552.

Buell, J., Stoddard, P., Harris, F. R., & Baer, D. M. (1968). Collateral social development accompanying reinforcement of outdoor play in a preschool child. *Journal of Applied Behavior Analysis, 1,* 167–173.

Burstein, S., & Meichenbaum, D. (1979). The work of worrying in children undergoing surgery. *Journal of Abnormal Child Psychology, 7,* 121–132.

Campbell, S. B. (1986). Development issues. In R. Gittelman (Ed.), *Anxiety disorders in childhood* (pp. 24–57). New York: Guilford Press.

Campos, J. J., & Barrett, K. C. (1984). Toward a new understanding of emotions and development. In C. E. Izard, J. Kagan, & R. B. Zajonc (Eds.), *Emotions, cognition, and behavior* (pp. 229–263). New York: Cambridge University Press.

Carey, G., & Gottesman, I. I. (1981). Twin and family studies of anxiety, phobic, and obsessive disorders. In D. F. Klein & J. G. Rabkin (Eds.), *Anxiety: New research and changing concepts* (pp. 117–136). New York: Raven Press.

Cavior, N., & Deutsch, A. M. (1975). Systematic desensitization to reduce dream-induced anxiety. *Journal of Nervous and Mental Disease, 161,* 433–435.

Chapel, J. L. (1967). Treatment of a case of school phobia by reciprocal inhibition. *Canadian Psychiatric Association Journal, 12,* 25–28.

Chertock, S. L., & Bornstein, P. H. (1979). Covert modeling treatment of children's dental fears. *Child Behavior Therapy, 1,* 249–255.

Clement, P. W., & Milne, D. C. (1967). Group play therapy and tangible reinforcers used to modify the behaviour of 8-year-old boys. *Behaviour Research and Therapy, 5,* 301–312.

Cohen, M. E., Badal, D. W., Kilpatrick, A., Reed, E. W., & White, P. D. (1951). The high familial prevalence of neurocirculatory asthenia (anxiety neurosis, effort syndrome). *American Journal of Human Genetics, 3,* 126–158.

Coyle, P. J. (1968). The systematic desensitization of reading anxiety: A case study. *Psychology in the Schools, 5,* 140–141.

Cradock, C., Cotler, S., & Jason, L. A. (1978). Primary prevention: Immunization of children for speech anxiety. *Cognitive Therapy and Research, 2,* 389–396.

Cretekos, C. J. G. (1977). Some techniques in rehabilitating the school-phobic adolescent. *Adolescence, 12,* 237–246.

Croake, J. W. (1969). Fears of children. *Human Development, 12,* 239–247.

Croake, J. W., & Knox, F. H. (1973). The changing nature of children's fears. *Child Study Journal, 3,* 91–105.

Croghan, L. M. (1981). Conceptualizing the critical elements in a rapid desensitization to school anxiety: A case study. *Journal of Pediatric Psychology, 6,* 165–170.

Croghan, L. M., & Musante, G. J. (1975). The elimination of a boy's high-building phobia by *in vivo* desensitization and game playing. *Journal of Behavior Therapy and Experimental Psychiatry, 6,* 87–88.

D'Amato, M. R. (1970). *Experimental psychology: Methodology, psychophysics, and learning.* New York: McGraw-Hill.

Davis, A. F., Rosenthal, T. L., & Kelley, J. E. (1981). Actual fear cues, prompt therapy, and rationale enhance participant modeling with adolescents. *Behavior Therapy, 12,* 536–542.

Delprato, D. J. (1980). Hereditary determinants of fear and phobias: A critical review. *Behavior Therapy, 11,* 79–103.

Delprato, D. J., & McGlynn, F. D. (1984). Behavioral theories of anxiety disorders. In S. M. Turner (Ed.), *Behavioral treatment of anxiety disorders* (pp. 63–122). New York: Plenum.

Denny, M. R. (1971). Relaxation theory and experiments. In F. R. Brush (Ed.), *Aversive conditioning and learning* (pp. 235–296). New York: Academic Press.

Denny, M. R. (1976). Post-aversion relief and relaxation and their implications for behavior therapy. *Journal of Behavior Therapy and Experimental Psychiatry, 7,* 315–321.

DeSilva, P., Rachman, S., & Seligman, M. E. P. (1977). Prepared phobias and obsessions: Therapeutic outcome. *Behaviour Research and Therapy, 15,* 65–77.

DiNardo, P. A., & DiNardo, P. (1981). Self-control desensitization in the treatment of a childhood phobia. *The Behavior Therapist, 4,* 15–16.

Dinsmoor, J. A. (1954). Punishment: I. The avoidance hypothesis. *Psychological Review, 61,* 34–46.

Dinsmoor, J. A. (1977). Escape, avoidance, punishment: Where do we stand? *Journal of the Experimental Analysis of Behavior, 28,* 83–95.

Doleys, D. M., & Williams, S. C. (1977). The use of natural consequences and a makeup period to eliminate school-phobic behavior: A case study. *Journal of School Psychology, 15,* 44–50.

Doyal, G. T., & Friedman, R. J. (1974). Anxiety in children: Some observations for the school psychologist. *Psychology in the Schools, 11,* 161–164.

Dunlop, G. (1952). *Certain aspects of children's fears.* Unpublished master's thesis, University of North Carolina at Raleigh.

Elmhirst, S. I. (1984). A psychoanalytic approach to anxiety in childhood. In V. P. Varma (Ed.), *Anxiety in children* (pp. 1–14). London: Croom Helm.

Eme, R., & Schmidt, D. (1978). The stability of children's fears. *Child Development, 49,* 1277–1279.

English, H. B. (1929). Three cases of the "conditioned fear response." *Journal of Abnormal and Social Psychology, 24,* 221–225.

Esveldt-Dawson, K., Wisner, K. L., Unis, A. S., Matson, J. L., & Kazdin, A. E. (1982). Treatment of phobias in a hospitalized child. *Journal of Behavior Therapy and Experimental Psychiatry, 13,* 77–83.

Evers, W. L., & Schwarz, J. C. (1973). Modifying social withdrawal in preschoolers: The effects of filmed modeling and teacher praise. *Journal of Abnormal Child Psychology, 1,* 248–256.

Eysenck, H. J. (1968). A theory of the incubation of anxiety/fear responses. *Behaviour Research and Therapy, 6,* 309–321.

Eysenck, H. J. (1976). The learning theory model of neurosis: A new approach. *Behaviour Research and Therapy, 14,* 251–267.

Faust, J., & Melamed, B. G. (1984). Influence of arousal, previous experience, and age on surgery preparation of same day or surgery and in-hospital pediatric patients. *Journal of Consulting and Clinical Psychology, 52,* 359–365.

Fox, J. E., & Houston, B. K. (1981). Efficacy of self-instructional training for reducing children's anxiety in evaluative situations. *Behaviour Research and Therapy, 19,* 509–515.

Franco, D. P., Christoff, K. A., Crimmins, D. E., & Kelly, J. A. (1983). Social skills training for an extremely shy young adolescent: An empirical case study. *Behavior Therapy, 14,* 568–575.

Fredrickson, M., Hugdahl, K., & Öhman, A. (1977). Electrodermal conditioning to potentially phobic stimuli in male and female subjects. *Biological Psychology, 4,* 305–314.

Freeman, B. J., Roy, R. R., & Hemmick, S. (1976). Extinction of a phobia of physical examination in a seven-year old mentally retarded boy: A case study. *Behaviour Research and Therapy, 14,* 63–64.

Garvey, W. P., & Hegrenes, J. R. (1966). Desensitization techniques in the treatment of school phobia. *American Journal of Orthopsychiatry, 36,* 147–152.

Gelfand, D. M. (1978). Behavioral treatment of avoidance, social withdrawal and negative emotional states. In B. B. Wolman, J. Egan, & A. O. Ross (Eds.) *Handbook of treatment of mental disorders in childhood and adolescence.* Englewood Cliffs, NJ: Prentice-Hall.

Gelfand, D. M., & Hartmann, D. P. (1977). The prevention of childhood behavior disorders. In B. B. Lahey & A. E. Kazdin (Eds.), *Advances in clinical child psychology* (Vol. 1, pp. 362–396). New York: Plenum.

Ghose, L. J., Giddon, D. B., Shiere, F. R., & Fogels, H. R. (1969). Evaluation of sibling support. *Journal of Dentistry for Children, 36,* 35–40.

Giebenhain, J. E. (1985). *Multi-channel assessment of children's fear of the dark.* Unpublished doctoral dissertation, University of Mississippi.

Giebenhain, J. E., & O'Dell, S. L. (1984). Evaluation of a parent-training manual for reducing children's fear of the dark. *Journal of Applied Behavior Analysis, 17,* 121–125.

Gilbert, B. O., Johnson, S. B., Spillar, R., McCallum, M., Silverstein, J. H., & Rosenbloom, A. (1982). The effects of a peer-modeling film on children learning to self-inject insulin. *Behavior Therapy, 13,* 186–193.

Ginther, L. J., & Roberts, M. C. (1982). A test of mastery versus coping modeling on the reduction of children's

dental fears. *Child and Family Behavior Therapy, 4,* 41–52.

Gittelman, R. (Ed.). (1986). *Anxiety disorders of childhood.* New York: Guilford Press.

Gittelman, R., & Klein, D. F. (1971). Controlled imipramine treatment of school phobia. *Archives of General Psychiatry, 25,* 204–207.

Gittelman, R., & Klein, D. F. (1973). School phobia: Diagnostic considerations in the light of imipramine effects. *Journal of Nervous and Mental Disease, 156,* 199–215.

Gittelman, R., & Klein, D. F. (1985). Childhood separation anxiety and adult agoraphobia. In A. H. Tuma & J. Maser (Eds.), *Anxiety and the anxiety disorders* (pp. 389–402). Hillsdale, NJ: Erlbaum.

Glennon, B., & Weisz, J. R. (1978). An observational approach to the assessment of anxiety in young children. *Journal of Consulting and Clinical Psychology, 46,* 1246–1257.

Graham, P., (1964). *Controlled trial of behavior therapy vs. conventional therapy: A pilot study.* Unpublished doctoral dissertation, University of London.

Gray, J. (1971). *The psychology of fear and stress.* New York: McGraw-Hill.

Graziano, A. M., & DeGiovanni, I. S. (1979). The clinical significance of childhood phobias: A note on the proportion of child-clinical referrals for the treatment of children's fears. *Behaviour Research and Therapy, 17,* 161–162.

Graziano, A. M., DeGiovanni, I. S., & Garcia, K. A. (1979). Behavioral treatment of children's fears: A review. *Psychological Bulletin, 86,* 804–830.

Graziano, A. M., & Mooney, K. C. (1980). Family self-control instruction for children's nighttime fear reduction. *Journal of Consulting and Clinical Psychology, 48,* 206–213.

Graziano, A. M., & Mooney, K. C. (1982). Behavioral treatment of "nightfears" in children: Maintenance of improvement at 2½- to 3-year follow-up. *Journal of Consulting and Clinical Psychology, 50,* 598–599.

Graziano, A. M., Mooney, K. C., Huber, C., & Ignasiak, D. (1979). Self-control instructions for children's fear-reduction. *Journal of Behavior Therapy and Experimental Psychiatry, 10,* 221–227.

Hagman, E. R. (1932). A study of fears of children of pre-school age. *Journal of Experimental Education, 1,* 110–130.

Hampe, E., Noble, H., Miller, L. C., & Barrett, C. L. (1973). Phobic children one and two years posttreatment. *Journal of Abnormal Psychology, 82,* 446–453.

Handler, L. (1972). The amelioration of nightmares in children. *Psychotherapy: Theory, Research, and Practice, 9,* 54–56.

Hatzenbuehler, L. C., & Schroeder, H. E. (1978). Desensitization procedures in the treatment of childhood disorders. *Psychological Bulletin, 85,* 831–844.

Hawley, B. P., McCorkle, A. D., Witteman, J. K., & Van Ostenberg, P. (1974). The first dental visit for children from low socioeconomic families. *Journal of Dentistry for Children, 41,* 376–381.

Heimberg, R. G., Gansler, D., Dodge, C. S., & Becker, R. E. (1987). Convergent and discriminant validity of the Cognitive–Somatic Anxiety Questionnaire in a social phobic population. *Behavioral Assessment, 9,* 379–388.

Herbert, M. (1984). Psychological treatment of childhood neuroses. In V. P. Varma (Ed.), *Anxiety in children* (pp. 172–193). London: Croom Helm.

Herrnstein, R. J. (1969). Method and theory in the study of avoidance. *Psychological Review, 76,* 49–69.

Hersen, M. (1968). Treatment of a compulsive and phobic disorder through a total behavior therapy program: A case study. *Psychotherapy: Theory, Research, and Practice, 5,* 220–225.

Hersen, M. (1970). Behavior modification approach to a school-phobia case. *Journal of Clinical Psychology, 26,* 128–132.

Hill, J. H., Liebert, R. M., & Mott, D. E. W. (1968). Vicarious extinction of avoidance behavior through films: An initial test. *Psychological Reports, 22,* 192.

Hodgson, R., & Rachman, S. (1974). Desynchrony in measures of fear: II. *Behaviour Research and Therapy, 12,* 319–326.

Holmes, F. B. (1935). An experimental study of the fears of young children. In A. T. Jersild & F. B. Holmes (Eds.), *Children's fears* (Child Development Monograph No. 20). Chicago: University of Chicago Press.

Holmes, F. B. (1936). An experimental investigation of a method of overcoming children's fears. *Child Development, 7,* 6–30.

Hugdahl, K., Fredrikson, M., & Öhman, A. (1977). "Preparedness" and "arousability" as determinants of electrodermal conditioning. *Behaviour Research and Therapy, 15,* 345–353.

Hugdahl, K., & Öhman, A. (1977). Effects of instructions on acquisition and extinction of electrodermal responses to fear relevant stimuli. *Journal of Experimental Psychology: Human Learning and Memory, 3,* 608–618.

Jackson, D. A., & Wallace, R. F. (1974). The modification and generalization of voice loudness in a fifteen-year-old retarded girl. *Journal of Applied Behavior Analysis, 7,* 461–471.

Jackson, H. J., & King, N. J. (1981). The emotive imagery treatment of a child's trauma-induced phobia. *Journal of Behavior Therapy and Experimental Psychiatry, 12,* 325–328.

Jacobs, W. J., & Nadel, L. (1985). Stress-induced recovery of fears and phobias. *Psychological Review, 92,* 512–531.

Jay, S. M., Ozolins, M., Elliott, C., & Caldwell, S. (1983). Assessment of children's distress during painful medical procedures. *Journal of Health Psychology, 2,* 133–147.

Jerremalm, A., Jansson, K., & Öst, L. G. (1986). Cognitive and physiological reactivity and the effects of different behavioral methods in the treatment of social phobia. *Behaviour Research and Therapy, 24,* 171–180.

Jersild, A. T. (1954). Emotional development. In L. Carmichael (Ed.), *Manual of child psychology* (2nd ed., pp. 833–917). New York: Wiley.

Jersild, A. T. (1968). *Child psychology* (6th ed.). Englewood Cliffs, NJ: Prentice-Hall.

Jersild, A. T., & Holmes, F. B. (Eds.). (1935). *Children's fears* (Child Development Monograph No. 20). Chicago: University of Chicago Press.

Johnson, J. H., Rasbury, W. C., & Siegel, L. J. (1986). *Approaches to child treatment: Introduction to theory, research, and practice.* New York: Pergamon Press.

Johnson, S. B., & Melamed, B. G. (1979). The assessment and treatment of children's fears. In B. B. Lahey & A. E. Kazdin (Eds.), *Advances in clinical child psychology* (Vol. 2, pp. 107–139). New York: Plenum.

Johnson, T., Tyler, V., Thompson, R., & Jones, E. (1971). Systematic desensitization and assertive training in the treatment of speech anxiety in middle-school students. *Psychology in the Schools, 8,* 263–267.

Jones, M. C. (1924a). The elimination of children's fears. *Journal of Experimental Psychology, 1,* 383–390.

Jones, M. C. (1924b). A laboratory study of fear: The case of Peter. *Pedagogical Seminar, 31,* 308–315.

Kagan, J., & Moss, H. A, (1962). *Birth to maturity.* New York: Wiley.

Kandel, H. J., Ayllon, T., & Rosenbaum, M. S. (1977). Flooding or systematic exposure in the treatment of extreme social withdrawal in children. *Journal of Behavior Therapy and Experimental Psychiatry, 8,* 75–81.

Kanfer, F. H., Karoly, P., & Newman, A. (1975). Reduction of children's fear of the dark by confidence-related and situational threat-related verbal cues. *Journal of Consulting and Clinical Psychology, 43,* 251–258.

Katz, E. R., Kellerman, J., & Siegel, S. E. (1980). Behavioral distress in children with cancer undergoing medical procedures: Developmental considerations. *Journal of Consulting and Clinical Psychology, 48,* 356–365.

Keehn, J. D. (1966). Avoidance responses as discriminated operants. *British Journal of Psychology, 57,* 375–389.

Keller, M. F., & Carlson, P. M. (1974). The use of symbolic modeling to promote social skills in preschool children with low levels of social responsiveness. *Child Development, 45,* 912–919.

Kellerman, J. (1980). Rapid treatment of nocturnal anxiety in children. *Journal of Behavior Therapy and Experimental Psychiatry, 11,* 9–11.

Kelly, C. K. (1976). Play desensitization of fear of darkness in preschool children. *Behaviour Research and Therapy, 14,* 79–81.

Kennedy, W. A. (1965). School phobia: Rapid treatment of fifty cases. *Journal of Abnormal Psychology, 70,* 285–289.

Kirkpatrick, D. R. (1984). Age, gender and patterns of common intense fears among adults. *Behaviour Research and Therapy, 22,* 141–150.

Kissel, S. (1972). Systematic desensitization therapy with children: A case study and some suggested modifications. *Professional Psychology, 3,* 164–168.

Klesges, R. C., Malott, J. M., & Ugland, M. (1984). The effects of graded exposure and parental modeling on the dental phobias of a four-year-old girl and her mother. *Journal of Behavior Therapy and Experimental Psychiatry, 15,* 161–164.

Klingman, A., Melamed, B. G., Cuthbert, M. I., & Hermecz, D. A. (1984). Effects of participant modeling on information acquisition and skill utilization. *Journal of Consulting and Clinical Psychology, 52,* 414–422.

Klinnert, M. D., Campos, J. J., Sorce, J. F., Emde, R. N., & Svejda, M. (1983). Emotions as behavior regulators: Social referencing in infancy. In R. Plutchik and H. Kellerman (Eds.), *Emotion: Theory, research, and experience* (Vol. 2, pp. 57–86). New York: Academic Press.

Klorman, R., Hilpert, P. L., Michael, R., LaGana, C., & Sveen, O. B. (1980). Effects of coping and mastery modeling on experienced and inexperienced pedodontic patients' disruptiveness. *Behavior Therapy, 11,* 156–168.

Klorman, R., Michael, R., Hilpert, P. L., & Sveen, O. B. (1979). A further assessment of predictors of the child behavior in dental treatment. *Journal of Dental Research, 58,* 2338–2348.

Klorman, R. Ratner, J., Arata, C. L., King, J. B., & Sveen, O. B. (1978). Predicting the child's uncooperativeness in dental treatment from maternal trait, state, and dental anxiety. *Journal of Dentistry for Children, 45,* 62–67.

Knight, R., Atkins, A., Eagle, C., Evans, N., Finklestein, J. W., Fukushima, D., Katz, J., & Weimer, H. (1979). Psychological stress, ego defenses, and cortisol productions in children hospitalized for elective surgery. *Psychosomatic Medicine, 41,* 40–49.

Kolko, D. J. (1984). Paradoxical instruction in the elimination of avoidance behavior in an agoraphobic girl. *Journal of Behavior Therapy and Experimental Psychiatry, 15,* 51–58.

Kondas, O. (1967). Reduction of examination anxiety and "stage-fright" by group desensitization and relaxation. *Behaviour Research and Therapy, 5,* 275–281.

Kornhaber, R. C., & Schroeder, H. E. (1975). Importance of model similarity on extinction of avoidance behavior in children. *Journal of Consulting and Clinical Psychology, 43,* 601–607.

Kuroda, J. (1969). Elimination of children's fears of animals by the method of experimental desensitization: An application of learning theory to child psychology. *Psychologia: An International Journal of Psychology in the Orient, 12,* 161–165.

Lang, P. J. (1968). Fear reduction and fear behavior: Problems in treating a construct. In J. M. Shlien (Ed.) *Research in psychotherapy* (Vol. 3, pp. 90–103). Washington, DC: American Psychological Association.

Lang, P. J. (1971). The application of psychophysiological methods to the study of psychotherapy and behavior modification. In A. E. Bergin & S. L. Garfield (Eds.), *Handbook of psychotherapy and behavior change* (pp. 75–125). New York: Wiley.

Lang, P. J. (1977). Fear imagery: An information processing analysis. *Behavior Therapy, 8,* 862–886.

Lang, P. J. (1979). A bio-informational theory of emotional imagery. *Psychophysiology, 16,* 495–512.

Lang, P. J. (1984). Cognition in emotion: Concept and action. In C. E. Izard, J. Kagan, R. B. Zajonc (Eds.), *Emotions, cognition, and behavior* (pp. 192–228). New York: Cambridge University Press.

Lapouse, R., & Monk, M. A. (1959). Fears and worries in a representative sample of children. *American Journal of Orthopsychiatry, 29,* 223–248.

Laxer, M., Quarter, J., Kooman, A., & Walker, K. (1969). Systematic desensitization and relaxation of high test-anxious secondary school students. *Journal of Counseling Psychology, 16,* 446–451.

Laxer, R. M., & Walker, K. (1970). Counterconditioning versus relaxation in the desensitization of test anxiety. *Journal of Counseling Psychology, 17,* 431–436.

Lazarus, A. A. (1960). The elimination of children's phobias by deconditioning. In H. J. Eysenck (Ed.), *Behavior therapy and the neuroses* (pp. 114–122). New York: Pergamon Press.

Lazarus, A. A., & Abramovitz, A. (1962). The use of "emotive imagery" in the treatment of children's phobias. *Journal of Mental Science, 108,* 191–195.

Lazarus, A. A., Davison, G. C., & Polefka, D. A. (1965). Classical and operant factors in the treatment of a school phobia. *Journal of Abnormal Psychology, 70,* 225–229.

Lazarus, A. A., & Rachman, S. (1957). The use of systematic desensitization in psychotherapy. *South African Medical Journal, 31,* 334–337.

Leitenberg, H., Agras, S., Butz, R., & Wincze, J. (1971). Relationship between heart rate and behavioral change during the treatment of phobias. *Journal of Abnormal Psychology, 78,* 59–68.

Leitenberg, H., & Callahan, E. J. (1973). Reinforced practice and reduction of different kinds of fears in adults and children. *Behaviour Research and Therapy, 11,* 19–30.

LeUnes, A., & Siemsglusz, S. (1977). Paraprofessional treatment of school phobia in a young adolescent girl. *Adolescence, 12,* 115–121.

Lewis, M., & Brooks, J. (1974). Self, others, and fear: Infants' reactions to people. In M. Lewis & L. A. Rosenblum (Eds.), *The origins of fear.* New York: Wiley.

Lewis, M., & Michalson, L. (1982). The measurement of emotional state. In C. E. Izard (Ed.), *Measuring emotions in infants and children* (pp. 178–207). London: Cambridge University Press.

Lewis, S. (1974). A comparison of behavior therapy techniques in the reduction of fearful avoidant behavior. *Behavior Therapy, 5,* 648–655.

Luiselli, J. K. (1978). Treatment of an autistic child's fear of riding a school bus through exposure and reinforcement. *Journal of Behavior Therapy and Experimental Psychiatry, 9,* 169–172.

MacDonald, M. L. (1975). Multiple impact behavior therapy in a child's dog phobia. *Journal of Behavior Therapy and Experimental Psychiatry, 6,* 317–322.

MacFarlane, J., Allen, L., & Honzik, M. (1954). *A developmental study of the behavior problems of normal children between twenty-one months and fourteen years.* Berkeley: University of California Press.

Mann, J. (1972). Vicarious desensitization of test anxiety through observation of videotaped treatment. *Journal of Counseling Psychology, 19,* 1–7.

Mann, J., & Rosenthal, T. L. (1969). Vicarious and direct counterconditioning of test anxiety through individual and group desensitization. *Behaviour Research and Therapy, 7,* 359–367.

Marks, I. (1969). *Fears and phobias.* New York: Academic Press.

Mash, E. J. (1985). Some comments on target selection in behavior therapy. *Behavioral Assessment, 7,* 63–78.

Mash, E. J., & Terdal, L. G. (1977). After the dance is over: Some issues and suggestions for follow-up assessment in behavior therapy. *Psychological Reports, 41,* 1287–1308.

Mash, E. J., & Terdal, L. G. (1981). Behavioral assessment of childhood disturbance. In E. J. Mash & L. G. Terdal (Eds.), *Behavioral Assessment of childhood disorders* (pp. 3–78). New York: Guilford Press.

Matson, J. L. (1981). Assessment and treatment of clinical fears in mentally retarded children. *Journal of Applied Behavior Analysis, 14,* 287–294.

Matson, J. L. (1983). Exploration of phobic behavior in a small child. *Journal of Behavior Therapy and Experimental Psychiatry, 14,* 257–260.

Mauer, A. (1965). What children fear. *Journal of Genetic Psychology, 106,* 265–277.

Mayer, G. E., Beggs, D. L., Fjellstedt, N., Forhetz, J., Nighswander, J. K., & Richards, R. (1971). The use of public commitment and counseling with elementary school children: An evaluation. *Elementary School Guidance and Counseling, 5,* 22–34.

McNally, R. J., & Reiss, S. (1982). The preparedness theory of phobias and human safety-signal conditioning. *Behaviour Research and Therapy, 20,* 153–159.

Melamed, B. G., Klingman, A., & Siegel, L. J. (1984). Childhood stress and anxiety: Individualizing cognitive behavioral strategies in the reduction of medical and dental stress. In A. W. Meyers & W. E. Craighead (Eds.), *Cognitive behavior therapy with children* (pp. 289–314). New York: Plenum.

Melamed, B. G., Meyer, R., Gee, C., & Soule, L. (1976). The influence of time and type of preparation on children's adjustment to hospitalization. *Journal of Pediatric Psychology, 1*, 31–37.

Melamed, B. G., & Siegel, L. J. (1975). Reduction of anxiety in children facing hospitalization and surgery by use of filmed modeling. *Journal of Consulting and Clinical Psychology, 43*, 511–521.

Melamed, R. G., & Siegel, L. J. (1980). *Behavioral medicine*. New York: Springer.

Melamed, R. G., & Siegel, L. J. (1985). Children's reactions to medical stressors: An ecological approach to the study of anxiety. In A. H. Tuma & J. Maser (Eds.), *Anxiety and the anxiety disorders* (pp. 369–388). Hillsdale, NJ: Erlbaum.

Melamed, R. G., Yurcheson, R., Fleece, E. L., Hutcherson, S., & Hawes, R. (1978). Effects of film modeling on the reduction of anxiety-related behaviors in individuals varying in level of previous experience in the stress situation. *Journal of Consulting and Clinical Psychology, 46*, 1357–1367.

Miller, L. C., Barrett, C. L., & Hampe, E. (1974). Phobias of childhood in a prescientific era. In S. Davids (Ed.), *Child personality and psychopathology* (pp. 89–134). New York: Wiley.

Miller, L. C., Barrett, C. L., Hampe, E., & Noble, H. (1972a). Comparison of reciprocal inhibition psychotherapy, and waiting list control for phobic children. *Journal of Abnormal Psychology, 79*, 269–279.

Miller, L. C., Barrett, C. L., Hampe, E., & Noble, H. (1972b). Factor structure of childhood fears. *Journal of Consulting and Clinical Psychology, 39*, 264–268.

Miller, L. C., Hampe, E., Barrett, C. L., & Nobel , H. (1971). Children's deviant behavior within the general population. *Journal of Consulting and Clinical Psychology, 37*, 16–22.

Miller, N., & Kassinove. H. (1978). Effects of lecture, rehearsal, written homework, and IQ on the efficacy of a rational–emotive school mental health program. *Journal of Community Psychology, 6*, 366–373.

Miller, P. M. (1972). The use of visual imagery and muscle relaxation in the counterconditioning of a phobic child: A case study. *Journal of Nervous and Mental Disease, 154*, 457–460.

Montenegro, H. (1968). Severe separation anxiety in two preschool children successfully treated by reciprocal inhibition. *Journal of Child Psychology and Psychiatry, 9*, 93–103.

Morris, R. J. (1980). Fear reduction methods. In F. H. Kanfer & A. P. Goldstein (Eds.), *Helping people change* (2nd ed., pp. 248–293). New York: Pergamon Press.

Morris, R. J., & Kratochwill, T. R. (1983a). Childhood fears and phobias. In R. J. Morris & T. R. Kratochwill (Eds.), *The practice of child therapy* (pp. 53–85). New York: Pergamon Press.

Morris, R. J., & Kratochwill, T. R. (1983b). *The practice of child therapy*. New York: Pergamon Press.

Morris, R. J., & Kratochwill, T. R. (1983c). *Treating children's fears and phobias: A behavioral approach*. New York: Pergamon Press.

Mowrer, O. H. (1939). A stimulus–response analysis of anxiety and its role as a reinforcing agent. *Psychological Review, 46*, 553–565.

Mowrer, O. H. (1947). On the dual nature of learning: A reinterpretation of "conditioning" and "problem solving." *Harvard Educational Review, 17*, 102–148.

Mowrer, O. H, (1960). *Learning theory and behavior*. New York: Wiley.

Muller, S. D., & Madsen, C. H. (1970). Group desensitization for "anxious" children with reading problems. *Psychology in the Schools, 7*, 184–189.

Murphy, C. M., & Bootzin, R. R. (1973). Active and passive participation in the contact desensitization of snake fear of children. *Behavior Therapy, 4*, 203–211.

Nalven, F. B. (1970). Manifest fears and worries of ghetto versus middle-class suburban children. *Psychological Reports, 27*, 285–286.

Neisworth, J. T., Madle, R. A., & Goeke, K. E. (1975). "Errorless" elimination of separation anxiety: A case study. *Journal of Behavior Therapy and Experimental Psychiatry, 6*, 79–82.

Ney, P. G. (1967). Combined therapies in a family group. *Canadian Psychiatric Association Journal, 12*, 379–385.

Ney, P. G. (1968). Combined psychotherapy and deconditioning of a child's phobia., *Canadian Psychiatric Association Journal, 13*, 293–294.

Nocella, J., & Kaplan, R. M. (1982). Training children to cope with dental treatment. *Journal of Pediatric Psychology, 7*, 175–178.

Obler, M., & Terwilliger, R. F. (1970). Pilot study on the effectiveness of systematic desensitization with neurologically impaired children with phobic disorders. *Journal of Consulting and Clinical Psychology, 34*, 314–318.

O'Connor, R. D. (1972). Relative efficacy of modeling, shaping, and the combined procedures for modification of social withdrawal. *Journal of Abnormal Psychology, 79*, 327–334.

Öhman, A. (1979). Fear relevance, autonomic conditioning, and phobias: A laboratory model. In P. O. Sjoden, S. Bates, & W. S. Dockens III (Eds.), *Trends in behavior therapy* (pp. 107–133). New York: Academic Press.

Öhman, A., Eriksson, A., & Olofsson, C. (1975). One-trial learning and superior resistance to extinction of autonomic responses conditioned to potentially phobic stimuli. *Journal of Comparative and Physiological Psychology, 88*, 619–627.

Öhman, A., Erixon, G., & Lofberg, I. (1975). Phobias and preparedness: Phobic versus neutral pictures as conditioned stimuli for human autonomic responses. *Journal of Abnormal Psychology, 84*, 41–45.

Öhman, A., Fredrikson, M., Hugdahl, K., & Rimmo, P. (1976). The premis of equipotentiality in human classical conditioning: Conditioned electrodermal responses to potential phobic stimuli. *Journal of Experimental Psychology: General, 105*, 331–337.

Ollendick, T. H. (1979). Fear reduction techniques with children. In M. Hersen, R. M. Eisler, & P. M. Miller (Eds.), *Progress in behavior modification* (Vol. 8, pp. 127–168). New York: Academic Press.

Ollendick, T. H. (1983). Reliability and validity of the Revised Fear Survey Schedule for Children (FSSC-R). *Behaviour Research and Therapy, 21*, 685–692.

Ollendick, T. H., & Cerny, J. A. (1981). *Clinical behavior therapy with children*. New York: Plenum.

Ollendick, T. H., & Gruen, G. E. (1972). Treatment of a bodily injury phobia with implosive therapy. *Journal of Consulting and Clinical Psychology, 38*, 389–393.

O'Reilly, P. P. (1971). Desensitization of fire bell phobia. *Journal of School Psychology, 9*, 55–57.

Orton, G. L. (1982). A comparative study of children's worries. *Journal of Psychology, 110,* 153–162.

Öst, L. G., Jerramalm, A., & Johansson, J. (1981). Individual response patterns and the effects of different behavioural methods in the treatment of social phobia. *Behaviour Research and Therapy, 19,* 1–16.

Otto, V. (1974). The behavior of children when visiting the dentist. *Svensk Tandlakare–Tidskright, 67,* 207–222.

Parish, T. S., Buntman, A. D., & Buntman, S. R. (1976). Effect of counterconditioning on test anxiety as indicated by digit span performance. *Journal of Educational Psychology, 68,* 297–299.

Patterson, G. R. (1965). A learning theory approach to the treatment of the school phobic child. In L. P. Ullman & L. Krasner (Eds.), *Case studies in behavior modification* (pp. 279–285). New York: Holt, Rinehart & Winston.

Peterson, L., & Brownlee-Duffeck, M. (1984). Prevention of anxiety and pain due to medical and dental procedures. In M. C. Roberts & L. Peterson (Eds.), *Prevention of problems in childhood: Psychological research and application* (pp. 267–308). New York: Wiley.

Peterson, L., Hartmann, D. P., & Gelfand, D. M. (1980). Prevention of child behavior disorders: A lifestyle change for child psychologists. In P. Davidson & S. Davidson (Eds.), *Behavioral medicine: Changing health lifestyles* (pp. 195–221). New York: Brunner/Mazel.

Peterson, L., & Ridley-Johnson, R. (1980). Pediatric hospital response to survey on prehospital preparation for children. *Journal of Pediatric Psychology, 5,* 1–7.

Peterson, L., Schultheis, K., Ridley-Johnson, R., Miller, D. J., & Tracy, K. (1984). Comparison of three modeling procedures on the presurgical and postsurgical reactions of children. *Behavior Therapy, 15,* 197–203.

Peterson, L., & Shigetomi, C. (1981). The use of coping techniques in minimizing anxiety in hospitalized children. *Behavior Therapy, 12,* 1–14.

Peterson, L., & Shigetomi, C. (1982). One-year follow-up of behavioral presurgical preparation for children. *Journal of Pediatric Psychology, 7,* 43–48.

Peterson, L., & Tobler, S. M. (1984). Self-regulated presurgical preparation for children. In B. Stabler (Chair), *Biobehavioral management of illness in children.* Symposium conducted at the meeting of the American Psychological Association, Toronto.

Phillips, D., & Wolpe, S. (1981). Multiple behavioral techniques in severe separation anxiety of a twelve-year-old. *Journal of Behavior Therapy and Experimental Psychiatry, 12,* 329–332.

Pinter, R., & Lev, J. (1940). Worries of school children. *Journal of Genetic Psychology, 56,* 67–76.

Pomerantz, P. B., Peterson, N. T., Marholin, D., & Stern, S. (1977). The *in vivo* elimination of a child's water phobia by a paraprofessional at home. *Journal of Behavior Therapy and Experimental Psychiatry, 8,* 417–421.

Poser, E. G. (1976). Strategies for behavioral prevention. In P. O. Davidson (Ed.), *The behavioral management of anxiety, depression and pain* (pp. 35–53). New York: Brunner/Mazel.

Poznanski, E. (1973). Children with excessive fears. *American Journal of Orthopsychiatry, 43,* 438–439.

Pratt, K. C. (1945). A study of the "fears" of rural children. *Journal of Genetic Psychology, 67,* 179–194.

Quay, H. C. (1979). Classification. In H. C. Quay & J. S. Werry (Eds.), *Psychopathological disorders of childhood* (2nd ed., pp. 1–42). New York: Wiley.

Rachman, S. J. (1977). The conditioning theory of fear-acquisition: A critical examination. *Behaviour Research and Therapy, 15,* 375–387.

Rachman, S. J. (1978). *Fear and courage.* San Francisco: W. H. Freeman.

Rachman, S. J., & Hodgson, R. (1974). Synchrony and desynchrony in fear and avoidance. *Behaviour Research and Therapy, 12,* 311–318.

Rachman, S. J., & Seligman, M. E. P. (1976). Unprepared phobias: "Be prepared." *Behaviour Research and Therapy, 14,* 333–338.

Rapoport, J., Elkins, R., & Mikkelsen, E. *et al.* (1980). Clinical controlled trial of chlorimipramine in adolescents with obsessive–compulsive disorder. *Psychopharmacology Bulletin, 16,* 61–63.

Richards, C. S., & Siegel, L. J. (1978). Behavioral treatment of anxiety states and avoidance behaviors in children. In D. Marholin II (Ed.), *Child behavior therapy* (pp. 274–338). New York: Gardner Press.

Rimm, D. C., Janda, L. H., Lancaster, D. W., Nahl, M., & Ditmar, K. (1977). An exploratory investigation of the origin and maintenance of phobias. *Behaviour Research and Therapy, 15,* 231–238.

Ritter, B. (1968). The group treatment of children's snake phobias using vicarious and contact desensitization procedures. *Behaviour Research and Therapy, 6,* 1–6.

Ritter, B. (1969). Treatment of acrophobia with contact desensitization. *Behaviour Research and Therapy, 7,* 41–46.

Roberts, M. C., & Peterson, L. (1984). Prevention models: Theoretical and practical implications. In M. C. Roberts & L. Peterson (Eds.), *Prevention of problems in childhood: Psychological research and applications* (pp. 1–39). New York: Wiley.

Roberts, M. C., Wurtele, S. K., Boone, R. R., Ginther, L. J., & Elkins, P. D. (1981). Reduction of medical fears by use of modeling: A preventive application in a general population of children. *Journal of Pediatric Psychology, 6,* 293–300.

Robins, C., Robins, W. V., & Rawson, H. E. (1973). Maternal anxiety and children's behavior during dental procedures. *Journal of the Missouri Dental Association, 53,* 47–55.

Robinson, C. M. (1978). Developmental counseling approach to death and dying education. *Elementary School Guidance and Counseling, 12,* 178–187.

Rosenfarb, I., & Hayes, S. C. (1984). Social standard setting: The Achilles heel of informational accounts of therapeutic change. *Behavior Therapy, 15,* 515–528.

Rutter, M. (1981). Stress, coping, and development: Some issues and some questions. *Journal of Child Psychology and Psychiatry, 22,* 323–356.

Ryall, M. R., & Dietiker, K. E. (1979). Reliability and clinical validity of the Children's Fear Survey Schedule. *Journal of Behavior Therapy and Experimental Psychiatry, 10,* 303–310.

Scherer, M. W., & Nakamura, C. Y, 91968). A fear survey schedule for children (FSS-FC): A factor analytic comparison with manifest anxiety (CMAS). *Behaviour Research and Therapy, 6,* 173–182.

Schoenfeld, W. N. (1950). An experimental approach to anxiety, escape, and avoidance behavior. In P. H. Hoch & J. Zubin (Eds.), *Anxiety* (pp. 70–99). New York: Grune & Stratton.

Schwartz, G. E., Davidson, R. J., & Goleman, D. J. (1978). Patterning of cognitive and somatic processes in the self-regulation of anxiety: Effects of meditation versus exercise. *Psychosomatic Medicine, 40,* 321–328.

Schwartz, S., & Johnson, J. H. (1985). *Psychopathology of childhood*. New York: Pergamon Press.

Seligman, M. E. P. (1970). On the generality of the laws of learning. *Psychological Review, 77*, 406–418.

Seligman, M. E. P. (1971). Phobias and preparedness. *Behavior Therapy, 2*, 307–320.

Seligman, M. E. P., & Johnston, J. C. (1973). A cognitive theory of avoidance learning. In F. J. McGuigan & D. B. Lumsden (Eds.), *Contemporary approaches to conditioning and learning* (pp. 69–110). Washington, DC: V. H. Winston.

Sheslow, D. V., Bondy, A. S., & Nelson, R. O. (1982). A comparison of graduated exposure, verbal coping skills, and their combination on the treatment of children's fear of the dark. *Child and Family Behavior Therapy, 4*, 33–45.

Siegel, L. J., & Peterson, L. (1980). Stress reduction in young dental patients through coping skills and sensory information. *Journal of Consulting and Clinical Psychology, 48*, 785–787.

Siegel, L. J., & Peterson, L. (1981). Maintenance effects of coping skills and sensory information on young children's response to repeated dental procedures. *Behavior Therapy, 12*, 530–535.

Slater, E. (1939). Responses to a nursery school situation of 40 children. *Monographs of the Society for Research in Child Development, 11*(No. 4).

Slater, E., & Shields, J. (1969). Genetical aspects of anxiety. *British Journal of Psychiatry, 3*, 62–71.

Smith, R. E., & Sharpe, T. M. (1970). Treatment of a school phobia with implosive therapy. *Journal of Consulting and Clinical Psychology, 35*, 239–243.

Solomon, R. L., Kamin, L. J., & Wynne, L. C. (1953). Traumatic avoidance learning: The outcomes of several extinction procedures with dogs. *Journal of Abnormal and Social Psychology, 48*, 291–302.

Solyom, I., Beck, P., Solyom, C., & Hugel, R. (1974). Some etiological factors in phobic neurosis. *Canadian Psychiatry Association Journal, 19*, 69–78.

Stokes, T. F., & Baer, D. M. (1977). An implicit technology of generalization. *Journal of Applied Behavior Analysis, 10*, 349–367.

Tahmisian, J. A., & McReynolds, W. T. (1971). Use of parents as behavioral engineers in the treatment of a school-phobic girl. *Journal of Counseling Psychology, 18*, 225–228.

Tasto, D. L. (1969). Systematic desensitization, muscle relaxation and visual imagery in the counterconditioning of a four-year-old phobic child. *Behaviour Research and Therapy, 7*, 409–411.

Taylor, C. B., & Agras, W. S. (1981). Assessment of phobia. In D. H. Barlow (Ed.), *Behavioral assessment of adult disorders* (pp. 181–208). New York: Guilford Press.

Torgerson, S. (1978)., The contribution of twin studies to psychiatric nosology. In W. E. Nance (Ed.), *Twin research: Part A. Psychology and methodology* (pp. 125–130). New York: Alan R. Liss.

Trower, P., Yardley, K., Bryant, B., & Shaw, P. (1978). The treatment of social failure: A comparison of anxiety-reduction and skills acquisition procedures on two social problems. *Behavior Modification, 2*, 41–60.

Ultee, C. A., Griffioen, D., & Schellekens, J. (1982). The reduction of anxiety in children: A comparison of the effects of 'systematic desensitization *in vitro*' and 'systematic desensitization *in vivo*.' *Behaviour Research and Therapy, 20*, 61–67.

Unger, M. (1982). *Defensiveness in children as it influences acquisition of fear-relevant information*. Unpublished master's thesis, University of Florida.

Valentine, C. W. (1930). The innate bases of fear. *Journal of Genetic Psychology, 37*, 394–420.

van der Ploeg, H. M. (1975). Treatment of frequency of urination by stories competing with anxiety. *Journal of Behavior Therapy and Experimental Psychology, 6*, 165–166.

Van Hasselt, V. B., Hersen, M., Bellack, A. S., Rosenblum, N. D., & Lamparski, D. (1979). Tripartite assessment of the effects of systematic desensitization in a multiphobic child: An experimental analysis. *Journal of Behavior Therapy and Experimental Psychiatry, 10*, 51–55.

Venham, L. L., Murray, P., & Gaulin-Kremer, E. (1979). Child-rearing variables affecting the preschool child's response to dental stress. *Journal of Dental Research, 58*, 2042–2045.

Vermilyea, J., Boice, R., & Barlow, D. H. (1984). Rachman and Hodgson (1974) A decade later: How do desynchronous response systems relate to the treatment of agoraphobia? *Behaviour Research and Therapy, 22*, 615–621.

Watson, J. B., & Morgan, J. J. B. (1917). Emotional reactions and psychological experimentation. *American Journal of Psychology, 28*, 163–174.

Watson, J. B., & Rayner, P. (1920). Conditioned emotional reactions. *Journal of Experimental Psychology, 3*, 1–14.

Weissbrod, C. S., & Bryan, J. H. (1973). Filmed treatment as an effective fear-reduction technique. *Journal of Abnormal Child Psychology, 1*, 196–201.

Weissman, M. M. (1985). The epidemiology of anxiety disorders: Rates, risks, and familial patterns. In A. H. Tuma & J. D. Maser (Eds.), *Anxiety and the anxiety disorders* (pp. 275–296). Hillsdale, NJ: Erlbaum.

Weissman, M. M., Leckman, J. F., Merikangas, K. R., Prusoff, B. A., & Gammon, G. D. (1983). Depression and anxiety disorders in parents and children: Results from the Yale family study. *Archives of General Psychiatry, 38*, 139–152.

Wenzel, B. M., & Jeffrey, D. W. (1967). The effect of immunosympathectomy on the behavior of mice in aversive situations. *Physiology and Behavior, 2*, 192–201.

Wheeler, E. O., White, P. D., Reed, E., & Cohen, M. E. (1948). Familial incidence of neurocirculatory asthenia ("anxiety neurosis," "effort syndrome"). *Journal of Clinical Investigation, 27*, 562.

White, W. C., Jr., & Davis, M. T. (1974). Vicarious extinction of phobic behavior in early childhood. *Journal of Abnormal Child Psychology, 2*, 25–32.

Winer, G. A. (1982). A review and analysis of children's fearful behavior in dental settings. *Child Development, 53*, 1111–1133.

Winker, J. B. (1949). Age trends and sex differences in the wishes, identifications, activities and fears of children. *Child Development, 20*, 191–196.

Wolpe, J. (1948). *An approach to the problem of neurosis based on the conditioned response*. Unpublished doctoral dissertation, University of Witwatersand, South Africa.

Wolpe, J. (1954). Reciprocal inhibition as the main basis of psychotherapeutic effects. *Archives of Neurology and Psychiatry, 72*, 205–226.

Wolpe, J. (1958). *Psychotherapy by reciprocal inhibition*. Stanford, CA: Stanford University Press.

Wolpe, J. (1961). The systematic desensitization treatment

of neuroses. *Journal of Nervous and Mental Disease, 132*, 189–203.

Word, P., & Rozynko, V. (1974). Behavior therapy of an eleven-year-old girl with reading problems. *Journal of Learning Disabilities, 7*, 551–554.

Wright, G. Z., Alpern, G. D., & Leake, J. L. (1973). The modifiability of maternal anxiety as it relates to children's cooperative behavior. *Journal of Dentistry for Children, 40*, 265–271.

Wynne, L. C., & Solomon, R. L. (1955). Traumatic avoidance learning: Acquisition and extinction in dogs deprived of normal peripheral autonomic function. *Genetic Psychology Monographs, 52*, 241–284.

Yates, A. J. (1981). Behavior therapy: Past, present, future—imperfect? *Clinical Psychology Review, 1*, 269–291.

Yates, B. T. (1985). Cost-effectiveness analysis and cost–benefit analysis: An introduction. *Behavioral Assessment, 7*, 207–234.

Yeaton, W. H., & Sechrest, L. (1981). Critical dimensions in the choice and maintenance of successful treatments: Strength, integrity, and effectiveness. *Journal of Consulting and Clinical Psychology, 49*, 156–167.

Yule, W., Sacks, B., & Hersov, L. (1974). Successful flooding treatment of a noise phobia in an 11-year-old. *Journal of Behavior Therapy and Experimental Psychiatry, 5*, 209–211.

Zastowny, T. R., Kirschenbaum, D. S., & Meng, A. L. (1981, November). *Coping skills training for children: Effects on distress before, during and after hospitalization for surgery*. Paper presented at the meeting of the Association of Advancement of Behavior Therapy, Toronto.

APPENDIX: SUMMARIES OF STUDIES ON THE BEHAVIORAL TREATMENT OF CHILDREN'S FEARS AND ANXIETIES

TABLE 5-2 A Summary of Desensitization Treatments for Children's Fears and Anxieties

Author(s)	Feared stimulus	Subjects	Research design	Treatment	Outcome
Barabasz (1973)	Test taking	5th- and 6th-graders ($n = 87$)	Experiment	Children assigned to one of two conditions: imaginal desensitization (5 sessions) or no treatment.	At posttest, desensitization superior to no treatment in terms of physiological and motor responses.
Bentler (1962)	Water	11½-mo-old with fear duration of approximately 2 wk	Case study	*In vivo* desensitization with game playing and maternal contact as the anxiety-antagonistic response. Treatment administered by the mother over a period of 1 mo.	At posttreatment, significant reductions in motor responses. At 6½-mo follow-up, maintenance of treatment gains.
Bornstein & Knapp (1981)	Separation, travel, illness	12-yr-old male with fear duration of 2 yr	Multiple baseline	Self-control imaginal desensitization administered for 4 days for each stimulus.	At posttreatment, significant reductions in subjective responses. Generalization of treatment gains to new settings and maintenance of treatment gains at 1-yr follow-up.
Cavior & Deutsch (1975)	Nighttime, nightmares	16-yr-old male with fear duration of 1 yr	Case study	Imaginal desensitization with relaxation as the anxiety-antagonistic response administered for 3 sessions.	At posttreatment, significant reductions in subjective and physiological responses. Generalization of treatment gains to new behaviors (social interaction) and maintenance of treatment gains at 6-mo follow-up.
Chapel (1967)	School	11-yr-old	Case study	Imaginal desensitization.	At posttreatment, significant reductions in fear.
Coyle (1968)	School, reading	14-yr-old female	Case study	Imaginal desensitization followed by *in vivo* desensitization, for a total of 11 sessions.	At posttreatment, significant reductions in motor responses. Maintenance of treatment gains at 3-mo follow-up.

TABLE 5-2 (*continued*)

Author(s)	Feared stimulus	Subjects	Research design	Treatment	Outcome
Croghan (1981)	School	17-yr-old female with fear duration of 5 yr	Case study	Imaginal desensitization with relaxation as the anxiety-antagonistic response administered for 12 sessions.	At posttreatment, significant reductions in subjective responses. Maintenance of treatment gains at 1-yr follow-up.
Croghan & Musante (1975)	Heights	7-yr-old male with fear duration of 6 mo	Case study	*In vivo* desensitization with game playing as the anxiety-antagonistic response administered for 6 sessions.	At posttreatment, significant reductions in motor responses. Generalization of treatment gains to other stimuli and maintenance of treatment gains at 1-yr follow-up.
DiNardo & DiNardo (1981)	Contamination	9-yr-old male with fear duration of 8½ mo	Case study	Self-control imaginal desensitization administered for 14 sessions.	At posttreatment, significant reductions in motor responses. Maintenance of treatment gains at 1-yr follow-up.
Doyal & Friedman (1974)	Test taking	5th-grade female	Case study	Imaginal desensitization with relaxation as the anxiety-antagonistic response administered for 10 sessions.	At posttreatment, significant reductions in subjective responses. Maintenance of treatment gains at 6-mo follow-up.
Freeman, Roy, & Hemmick (1976)	Physical exam	7½-yr-old retarded male with fear duration > 2 wk	Case study	*In vivo* desensitization with social contact as the anxiety-antagonistic response response administered for 11 sessions.	At posttreatment, significant reductions in motor responses. Generalization of treatment gains to other stimuli.
Garvey & Hegrenes (1966)	School	10-yr-old male with fear duration > 6 mo	Case study	*In vivo* desensitization with therapist contact as the anxiety-antagonistic response administered for 20 days.	At posttreatment, significant reductions in motor responses. Maintenance of treatment gains at 2-yr follow-up.
Jackson & King (1981)	Darkness, noises	5½-yr-old male with fear duration > 1 mo	Time series	Emotive imagery administered for 4 sessions.	At posttreatment, significant reductions in subjective and motor responses. Maintenance of treatment gains at 18-mo follow-up.
Jones (1924a)	Small animal	2¾-yr-old male	Case study	*In vivo* desensitization.	At posttreatment, significant reductions in subjective and motor responses. Generalization of treatment gains to other stimuli.
Kellerman (1980)	Nighttime	5-yr-old male with fear duration > 1 mo	Case study	*In vitro* and *in vivo* desensitization with anger as the anxiety-antagonistic response.	At posttreatment, significant reductions in motor responses. Maintenance of treatment gains at 24-mo follow-up.
	Separation, school, darkness	8-yr-old female	Case study	*In vitro* and *in vivo* desensitization with anger as anxiety-antagonistic response.	At posttreatment, significant fear reduction. Maintenance of treatment gains at 16-mo follow-up.
	Darkness	13-yr-old female with fear duration of 5 yr	Case study	*In vivo* desensitization with variety of behaviors as anxiety-antagonistic response.	At posttreatment, significant fear reduction. Maintenance of treatment gains at 9-mo follow-up.

TABLE 5-2 (*continued*)

Author(s)	Feared stimulus	Subjects	Research design	Treatment	Outcome
Kelley (1976)	Darkness	4- and 5-yr olds (*n* = 40)	Experiment	Children assigned to one of five conditions: *in vitro* desensitization, *in vitro* desensitization with noncontingent tangible reward, *in vitro* desensitization with contingent tangible reward, attention placebo, or no treatment. Treatment administered weekly over a 3-wk period.	At posttreatment, no group differences in motor and subjective responses.
Kissel (1972)	Small animal	11-yr-old female with fear duration of 9 yr	Case study	Imaginal and *in vitro* desensitization with therapist contact as the anxiety-antagonistic response administered for 6 sessions.	At posttreatment, significant reductions in motor responses.
Kondas (1967)	Public speaking	11- through 15-yr-olds (*n* = 23)	Experiment	Children assigned to one of four conditions: imaginal desensitization (12 sessions), autogenic training (7 sessions), imaginal desensitization without relaxation (4 sessions), or no treatment.	At posttreatment, all three treatments superior to no treatment in terms of subjective responses, with imaginal desensitization being most effective. Imaginal desensitization superior to the other three conditions in terms of physiological responses. At 5-mo follow-up, maintenance of subjective treatment gains for imaginal desensitization with and without relaxation.
Kuroda (1969)	Small animals	3- and 4-yr-olds	Experiment	Children assigned to one of two conditions: *in vivo* desensitization with game playing as the anxiety-antagonistic response or no treatment.	At posttreatment, *in vivo* desensitization superior to no treatment in terms of motor responses.
Laxer, Quarter, Kooman, & Walker (1969)	Test taking	9th- through 12th-graders (*n* = 89)	Experiment	Children assigned to one of three conditions: imaginal desensitization (30 sessions), relaxation (30 sessions), or no treatment.	At posttreatment, no group differences in terms of subjective and motor responses. Relaxation superior to no treatment in terms of responses to other stimuli.
Laxer & Walker (1970)	Test taking	Secondary school students (*n* = 110)	Experiment	Children assigned to one of six conditions: imaginal desensitization, relaxation, rehearsal, relaxation plus prolonged exposure, attention placebo, or no treatment. Treatment administered for 20 sessions.	At posttreatment, imaginal desensitization and relaxation superior to no treatment in terms of subjective responses. No group differences in terms of motor responses and fear responses to other stimuli.
Lazarus (1960)	Vehicles	8-yr-old male with fear duration of 2 yr	Case study	Imaginal and *in vivo* desensitization with eating as the anxiety-antagonistic response administered over a period of 6 wk.	At posttreatment, significant reductions in motor responses. Generalization of treatment gains to other settings.

TABLE 5-2 (*continued*)

Author(s)	Feared stimulus	Subjects	Research design	Treatment	Outcome
	Separation	9½-yr-old female with fear duration of 4 mo	Case study	Imaginal desensitization administered for 5 sessions.	At posttreatment, significant reductions in motor responses. Generalization of treatment gains to other settings and maintenance of gains at 15-mo follow-up.
	Small animals	3½-yr-old male with fear duration of 5 mo	Case study	Drug-assisted, *in vivo* desensitization administered over a 5-wk period.	At posttreatment, significant reductions in motor responses. Maintenance of treatment gains at 1-yr follow-up.
Lazarus & Abramovitz (1962)	Small animals	14-yr-old male with fear duration of 3 yr	Case study	Emotive imagery administered for 5 sessions.	At posttreatment, significant reductions in subjective responses. Maintenance of treatment gains at 1-yr follow-up.
	Darkness	10-yr-old male with fear duration of 1 yr	Case study	Emotive imagery administered for 3 sessions.	At posttreatment, significant reductions in subjective responses. Maintenance of treatment gains at 11-mo follow-up.
	School	8-yr-old female	Case study	Emotive imagery administered for 4 sessions.	At posttreatment, significant reductions in motor responses. Generalization of treatment gains to other problem behaviors (enuresis).
Lazarus & Rachman (1957)	Hospital	14-yr-old male with fear duration of 4 yr	Case study	Imaginal desensitization administered for 10 sessions.	At posttreatment, significant reductions in motor responses. Maintenance of treatment gains at 3-mo follow-up.
LeUnes & Siemsglusz (1977)	School	14-yr-old female with fear duration > 3 mo	Case study	*In vivo* desensitization with therapist contact as the anxiety-antagonistic response. Treatment administered by a paraprofessional over a 10-wk period.	At posttreatment, significant reductions in motor responses. Generalization of treatment gains to new behaviors (social interaction).
Mann & Rosenthal (1969)	Test taking	39 female and 32 male 12- through 14-yr-olds	Experiment	Children assigned to one of six conditions: individual imaginal desensitization, individual vicarious desensitization, group imaginal desensitization, group vicarious desensitization with group model, group vicarious desensitization with individual model, or no treatment. Treatment ranged from 6 to 8 sessions.	At posttreatment, no group differences in terms of subjective and motor responses.
Miller (1972)	Separation, death, school	10-yr-old female with fear duration > 8 wk	Case study	For fear of separation, imaginal desensitization administered over 12-wk period. For fear of dying, *in vivo* flooding administered after imaginal and *in vivo* desensitization proved unsuccessful. For fear of school, imaginal and *in vivo* desensitization administered.	At posttreatment, significant reductions in subjective and motor responses. Generalization of treatment gains to other problem behaviors (enuresis) and maintenance of treatment gains at 18-mo follow-up.

TABLE 5-2 (*continued*)

Author(s)	Feared stimulus	Subjects	Research design	Treatment	Outcome
Montenegro (1968)	Separation	6-yr-old male with fear duration > 1 yr	Case study	*In vivo* desensitization with eating as the anxiety-antagonistic response administered for 10 sessions.	At posttreatment, significant reductions in motor responses. Maintenance of treatment gains at 10-mo follow-up.
	Separation	3½-yr-old female with fear duration > 4 mo	Case study	*In vivo* desensitization with eating as the anxiety-antagonistic response, supplemented by a parent- and therapist-administered contingency management program. Treatment administered for 16 sessions.	At posttreatment, significant reductions in motor responses. Maintenance of treatment gains at 18-mo follow-up.
Muller & Madsen (1970)	School, reading	16 males and 12 females with average age 12 yr, 8 mo	Experiment	Children assigned to one of three conditions: imaginal desensitization (13 sessions) followed by *in vivo* desensitization (7 sessions), attention placebo (20 sessions), or no treatment.	At posttreatment, desensitization and attention placebo superior to no treatment in terms of subjective responses. No group differences in terms of motor responses. Generalization of subjective treatment gains to new stimuli for desensitization and placebo conditions.
Ney (1967)	School	13-yr-old	Case study	Imaginal desensitization.	At posttreatment, significant fear reduction.
Ney (1968)	Small animals	4½-yr-old	Case study	*In vivo* desensitization.	At posttreatment, significant reductions in motor responses.
O'Reilly (1971)	Noise	6-yr-old female with fear duration of 3 yr	Case study	*In vivo* desensitization with game playing and story telling as the anxiety-antagonistic response.	At posttreatment, significant reductions in motor responses.
Parish, Buntman, & Buntman (1976)	Test taking	39 males and 36 females ranging in age from 9 to 13 yr	Experiment	Children assigned to one of three conditions: *in vitro* desensitization with saying positive words as the anxiety-antagonistic response (4 sessions), attention placebo (4 sessions), or no treatment.	At posttreatment, *in vitro* desensitization superior to attention placebo and no treatment in terms of motor responses.
Phillips & Wolpe (1981)	Separation	12-yr-old male with fear duration of 2 yr	Case study	*In vivo* and imaginal desensitization administered for 88 sessions.	At posttreatment, significant reductions in subjective and motor responses. Maintenance of treatment gains at 2-yr follow-up.
Tasto (1969)	Noise	4-yr-old male	Case study	*In vivo* desensitization administered after imaginal desensitization proved unsuccessful. Treatment administered by parent for a total of 6 sessions.	At posttreatment, significant reductions in motor responses. Maintenance of treatment gains at 4-mo follow-up.
Ultee, Griffioen, & Schellekens (1982)	Water	12 males and 12 females ranging in age from 5 to 10 yr	Experiment	Children assigned to one of three conditions: *in vivo* desensitization (8 sessions), imaginal desensitization (4 sessions) plus *in vivo* desensitization (4 sessions), or not treatment.	At posttreatment, *in vivo* desensitization superior to imaginal plus *in vivo* desensitization and no treatment in terms of motor responses.

TABLE 5-2 (*continued*)

Author(s)	Feared stimulus	Subjects	Research design	Treatment	Outcome
van der Ploeg (1975)	School	14-yr-old male	Case study	Imaginal desensitization with story telling as the anxiety-antagonistic response administered for 15 sessions, supplemented with *in vivo* desensitization.	At posttreatment, significant reductions in subjective and motor responses. Maintenance of treatment gains at 18-mo follow-up.
Van Hasselt, Hersen, Bellack, Rosenblum & Lamparski (1979)	Blood, heights, test taking	11-yr-old male with fear duration > 3 yr	Multiple baseline	Imaginal desensitization administered over 16 wk.	At posttreatment, significant reductions in subjective and motor responses. No reductions in physiological responses. Generalization of treatment gains to new settings and maintenace of treatment gains at 6-mo follow-up.
Wolpe (1958)	Social situations	11-yr-old male	Case study	Imaginal desensitization administered for 8 sessions.	At posttreatment, significant fear reduction.
Wolpe (1961)	Social situations	Child of unknown age and gender	Case study	Imaginal desensitization.	At posttreatment, significant fear reduction.
		13-yr-old male	Case study	Imaginal desensitization.	At posttreatment, no fear reduction.
Word & Rozynko (1974)	School, reading	11-yr-old female	Case study	Imaginal desensitization administered for 9 sessions.	At posttreatment, significant reductions in subjective and motor responses. Maintenance of treatment gains at 1-yr follow-up.

TABLE 5-3 A Summary of Prolonged Exposure Treatments for Children's Fears and Anxieties

Author(s)	Feared stimulus	Subjects	Research design	Treatment	Outcome
Hersen (1968)	School, physical illness	12-yr-old male	Case study	Imaginal and *in vivo* flooding administered for 9 sessions, supplemented by contingency management program administered by parent.	At posttreatment, significant reductions in subjective and motor responses. Generalization of treatment gains to new behaviors and maintenance of treatment gains at 6-mo follow-up.
Johnson, Tyler, Thompson, & Jones (1971)	Public speaking	6th- through 8th-graders (*n* = 24)	Experiment	Children assigned to one of three conditions: reinforced practice (9 sessions), imaginal desensitization (9 sessions), or no treatment.	At posttreatment, reinforced practice and imaginal desensitization superior to no treatment in terms of subjective responses.
Jones (1924b)	Small animals	3-yr-old	Case study	*In vivo* flooding	At posttreatment, significant reductions in motor responses.
Kandel, Ayllon, & Rosenbaum (1977)	Social situations	4-yr-old male with fear duration > 2 wk	Multiple baseline	*In vivo* flooding administered for 11 sessions.	At posttreatment, significant reductions in subjective and motor responses. Maintenance of treatment gains at 5-mo follow-up.

TABLE 5-3 (*continued*)

Author(s)	Feared stimulus	Subjects	Research design	Treatment	Outcome
	Social situations	8-yr-old male with fear duration > 3 yr	Multiple baseline	*In vivo* flooding (1 session) followed by graduated *in vivo* exposure (11 sessions).	At posttreatment, significant reductions in motor responses. Maintenance of treatment gains at 9-mo follow-up.
Kennedy (1965)	School	25 males and females ranging in age from 4 to 16 yr	Case study	Prolonged exposure administered by the parent for an average period of 3 days.	At posttreatment, significant reductions in motor responses. Maintenance of treatment gains at 8-yr follow-up.
Kolko (1984)	Being alone, physical injury	16-yr-old female with fear duration > 6 mo	Case study	Graduated *in vivo* exposure administered over a period of 3 wk.	At posttreatment, significant reductions in subjective and motor responses. Maintenance of treatment gains at 9-mo follow-up.
Leitenberg & Callahan (1973)	Darkness	8 females and 6 males ranging in age from 5 to 6 yr	Experiment	Children assigned to one of two conditions: reinforced practice (8 sessions) or no treatment.	At posttreatment, reinforced practice superior to no treatment in terms of motor responses.
Luiselli (1978)	Vehicles	7-yr-old male with fear duration of 6 mo	Case study	Reinforced practice administered for 9 sessions.	At posttreatment, significant reductions in motor responses. Maintenance of treatment gains at 1-mo follow-up.
Ollendick & Gruen (1972)	Physical injury	8-yr-old male with fear duration of 3 yr	Case study	Implosion administered for 2 sessions.	At posttreatment, significant reductions in motor responses. Maintenance of treatment gains at 3-mo follow-up.
Smith & Sharpe (1970)	School	13-yr-old male with fear duration of 60 days	Case study	Implosion administered for 6 sessions.	At posttreatment, significant reductions in subjective, motor, and physiological responses. Generalization of treatment gains to new settings. Maintenance of treatment gains at 13-wk follow-up and generalization of gains to other feared stimuli and other problem behaviors (peer relations, academic performance).
Yule, Sacks, & Hersov (1974)	Noises	9-yr-old male	Case study	*In vivo* flooding administered (2 sessions) after *in vivo* desensitization (22 sessions) proved only partially successful.	At posttreatment, significant reductions in subjective and motor responses. Maintenance of treatment gains at 25-mo follow-up.

TABLE 5-4 A Summary of Modeling Treatments for Children's Fears and Anxieties

Author(s)	Feared stimulus	Subjects	Research design	Treatment	Outcome
Bandura, Blanchard, & Ritter (1969)	Small animals	Unknown number of 13- through 17-yr-olds	Experiment	Children assigned to one of four conditions: participant modeling (2 hr), symbolic modeling (2½ hr), imaginal desensitization (4½ hr), or no treatment.	At posttreatment, all three treatments superior to no treatment in terms of subjective, motor, and physiological responses. Participant modeling superior to imaginal desensitization in terms of subjective and motor responses. Symbolic modeling superior to imaginal desensitization in terms of subjective and physiological responses. Generalization of treatment gains to other fear stimuli for participant modeling and symbolic modeling. Generalization of treatment gains to new settings and maintenance of treatment gains at 1-mo follow-up.
Bandura & Menlove (1968)	Small animals	32 females and 16 males ranging in age from 3 to 5 yr	Experiment	Children assigned to one of three conditions: filmed modeling of single mastery model, filmed modeling of multiple mastery models, or attention placebo. Treatment films were 6 min in length and shown 4 times.	At posttreatment, no group differences in terms of motor responses. At 1-mo follow-up, filmed modeling of multiple mastery models superior to filmed modeling of single mastery model and attention placebo. Generalization of treatment gains to other fear stimuli.
Chertock & Bornstein (1979)	Dental treatment	Unknown number of 5- through 13-yr-olds	Experiment	Children assigned to one of three conditions: covert modeling with coping model, covert modeling with mastery model, or prolonged imaginal exposure.	At posttreatment, no group differences in terms of subjective and motor responses.
Davis, Rosenthal, & Kelley (1981)	Small animals	91 females ranging in age from 13 to 18 yr	Experiment	Children assigned to 1 of 12 variants of participant modeling. The treatments varied in terms of the immediacy of therapy (immediate vs. delayed), the types of treatment stimuli (*in vivo* vs. *in vitro*), and the type of rationale (rationale vs. no rationale). Treatment duration was 3 hr.	At posttreatment and 3-wk follow-up, immediate participant modeling with *in vivo* stimuli and rationale superior to others in terms of subjective and motor responses.
Evers & Schwarz (1973)	Social situations	8 males and 5 females ranging in age from 2 to 4½ yr	Experiment	Children assigned to one of two conditions: filmed modeling (23 min in length) or filmed modeling (23 min in length) plus teacher-administered contingency management (2 days).	At posttreatment, both treatments equally effective in reducing motor responses. Maintenance of treatment gains at 4-wk follow-up.

TABLE 5-4 (*continued*)

Author(s)	Feared stimulus	Subjects	Research design	Treatment	Outcome
Faust & Melamed (1984)	Medical treatment	4- through 17-yr-olds (*n* = 66)	Experiment	Children assigned to one of two conditions: filmed modeling (10 min in length) or attention placebo.	At posttreatment, filmed modeling superior to attention placebo in terms of motor responses.
Gilbert *et al.* (1982)	Medical treatment	15 females and 13 males ranging in age from 6 to 9 yr	Experiment	Children assigned to one of two conditions: filmed modeling (7½ min in length) or attention placebo.	At posttreatment, no group differences in terms of subjective, motor, and physiological responses.
Ginther & Roberts (1982)	Dental treatment	33 females and 27 males ranging in age from 4 to 12 yr	Experiment	Children assigned to one of three conditions: symbolic modeling with mastery model, symbolic modeling with coping model, or no treatment. Modeling treatments were 10 min in duration.	At posttreatment, no group differences in terms of subjective and motor responses to targeted and nontargeted stimuli.
Hill, Liebert, & Mott (1968)	Small animals	18 male preschoolers	Experiment	Children assigned to one of two conditions: filmed modeling with mastery model (11 min in length) or attention placebo.	At posttreatment, modeling superior to attention placebo in terms of motor responses.
Holmes (1936)	Darkness	14 children ranging in age from 39 to 54 mo	Case study	Participant modeling administered for 3 to 6 sessions.	At posttreatment, significant reductions in motor responses for 13 of the 14 children.
Jones (1924)	Small animals	30-mo-old male	Case study	Live modeling.	At posttreatment, significant fear reduction.
	Small animals	21-mo-old male	Case study	Participant modeling.	At posttreatment, significant fear reduction.
Keller & Carlson (1974)	Social situations	3- to 10-yr-olds (*n* = 19)	Experiment	Children assigned to one of two conditions: filmed modeling (4 min in length and shown 4 times) or attention placebo.	At posttreatment, filmed modeling superior to attention placebo in terms of motor responses. Maintenance of treatment gains at 3-wk follow-up.
Klesges, Malott, & Ugland (1984)	Dental treatment	4-yr-old female with fear duration of 1 yr	Case study	Filmed modeling plus participant modeling with the mother serving as the coping model. Treatment was administered for 6 sessions.	At posttreatment, significant reductions in subjective and motor responses. Maintenance of treatment gains at 6-mo follow-up.
Klingman, Melamed, Cuthbert, & Hermecz (1984)	Dental treatment	20 males and 18 females ranging in age from 8 to 13 yr	Experiment	Children assigned to one of two conditions: participant modeling (17 min in duration) or filmed modeling (17 min in length).	At posttreatment, participant modeling superior to filmed modeling in terms of subjective, motor, and physiological responses. Generalization of treatment gains to other stimuli and behaviors greater for participant modeling.
Klorman, Hilpert, Michael, LaGana, & Sveen (1980)	Dental treatment	34 males and 26 females ranging in age from 3 to 14 yr	Experiment	Children assigned to one of three conditions: filmed modeling with coping model (10 min in length), filmed modeling with mastery model (10 min in length), or attention placebo.	At posttreatment, no group differences in terms of motor responses.

TABLE 5-4 (*continued*)

Author(s)	Feared stimulus	Subjects	Research design	Treatment	Outcome
	Dental treatment	26 females and 20 males ranging in age from 4 to 13 yr	Experiment	Children assigned to one of three conditions: filmed modeling with coping model (10 min in length), filmed modeling with mastery model (10 min in length), or attention placebo.	At posttreatment, no group differences in terms of motor responses.
	Dental treatment	17 males and 13 females ranging in age from 4 to 12 yr	Experiment	Children assigned to one of three conditions: filmed modeling with coping model (10 min in length), filmed modeling with mastery model (10 min in length), or attention placebo.	At posttreatment, both modeling treatments superior to attention placebo in terms of motor responses.
Kornhaber & Schroeder (1975)	Small animals	50 female 2nd- and 3rd-graders	Experiment	Children assigned to one of five conditions: filmed modeling with adult mastery model, filmed modeling with child mastery model, filmed modeling with child coping model, filmed modeling with adult coping model, or no treatment. All filmed modeling treatments were 6–7 min in duration.	At posttreatment, filmed modeling with child models superior to other conditions in terms of motor responses. Filmed modeling with child coping model superior to no treatment and filmed modeling with adult mastery model in terms of subjective responses.
Lewis (1974)	Water	40 males ranging in age from 5 to 12 yr	Experiment	Children assigned to one of four conditions: participant modeling (18 min in duration), filmed modeling (8 min in length), rehearsal, or attention placebo.	At posttreatment, all treatments superior to attention placebo in terms of motor responses. Participant modeling superior to filmed modeling and rehearsal; rehearsal superior to filmed modeling. Generalization of treatment gains to new settings and maintenance of gains at 5-day follow-up.
Mann (1972)	Test taking	7th- and 8th-graders (n = 80)	Experiment	Children assigned to one of four conditions: filmed modeling with instructions to imitate, filmed modeling with instructions not to imitate, partial modeling film with instructions not to imitate, or no treatment. Treatment administered for 6 sessions.	At posttreatment, all three modeling treatments superior to no treatment in terms of subjective and motor responses. Maintenance of treatment gains at 4-wk follow-up.
Matson (1981)	Social situations	3 females ranging in age from 8 to 10 yr, with fear duration > 6 mo	Multiple baseline	Participant modeling administered by the parent over a period of 20 days.	At posttreatment, significant reductions in subjective and motor responses. Maintenance of treatment gains at 6-mo follow-up.

TABLE 5-4 (*continued*)

Author(s)	Feared stimulus	Subjects	Research design	Treatment	Outcome
Matson (1983)	Small animals	3-yr-old female with fear duration > 6 mo	Multiple baseline	Participant modeling administered by the parent for a total of 22 sessions.	At posttreatment, significant reductions in subjective and motor responses. Maintenance of treatment gains at 1-yr follow-up.
Melamed, Meyer, Gee, & Soule (1976)	Medical treatment	4- through 12-yr-olds (*n* = 48)	Experiment	Children assigned to one of four conditions: preoperative filmed modeling 1 wk in advance with full preparation, preoperative filmed modeling 1 wk in advance with minimal preparation, preoperative filmed modeling same day with full preparation, or preoperative filmed modeling same day with minimal preparation. Modeling film had a coping model and was 16 min long.	At posttreatment, all four treatments produced significant reductions in subjective, motor, and physiological responses. Generalization of treatment gains to other fear stimuli.
Melamed & Siegel (1975)	Hospital	4- through 12-yr-olds (*n* = 60)	Experiment	Children assigned to one of two conditions: filmed modeling with a coping model (16 min in length) or attention placebo.	At posttreatment, filmed modeling superior to attention placebo in terms of subjective, motor, and physiological responses. Generalization of treatment gains to other fear stimuli.
Melamed, Yurcheson, Fleece, Hutcherson, & Hawes (1978)	Dental treatment	4- through 11-yr-olds (*n* = 80)	Experiment	Children assigned to one of five conditions: lengthy modeling film of coping model (10 min), lengthy information film (10 min), brief modeling film of coping model (4 min), or attention placebo.	At posttreatment, both modeling films superior to other conditions in terms of subjective and motor responses.
Murphy & Bootzin (1973)	Small animals	1st- through 3rd-graders (*n* = 67)	Experiment	Children assigned to one of three conditions: active participant modeling, passive participant modeling, or no treatment. Treatment duration averaged 2 sessions.	At posttreatment, both participant modeling treatments superior to no treatment in terms of motor responses.
Peterson, Schultheis, Ridley-Johnson, Miller, & Tracy (1984)	Medical treatment	2- through 11-yr-olds (*n* = 44)	Experiment	Children assigned to one of four conditions: local modeling film (50 min in length), commercial modeling film (50 min in length), symbolic modeling (50 min in length), or information.	At posttreatment, all three modeling treatments superior to information in terms of motor responses. No group differences in terms of subjective responses.
Ritter (1968)	Small animals	28 females and 16 males ranging in age from 5 to 11 yr	Experiment	Children assigned to one of three conditions: participant modeling (3 sessions), live modeling (3 sessions), or no treatment	At posttreatment, both modeling conditions superior to no treatment in terms of motor responses. Participant modeling superior to live modeling. No group differences in terms of subjective responses to targeted and nontargeted stimuli.

TABLE 5-4 (*continued*)

Author(s)	Feared stimulus	Subjects	Research design	Treatment	Outcome
Ritter (1969)	Heights	Unknown number of 14- through 18-yr-olds	Experiment	Children assigned to one of three conditions: participant, modeling with physical support, participant modeling, or live modeling. All treatments administered in 1 session.	At posttreatment, both participant modeling conditions superior to live modeling in terms of motor responses. Participant modeling with physical support superior to participant modeling. No group differences in terms of subjective responses.
Roberts, Wurtele, Boone, Ginther, & Elkins (1981)	Hospital	7- through 12-yr olds (n = 36)	Experiment	Children assigned to one of two conditions: symbolic modeling with coping model (30 min in duration) or attention placebo.	At posttreatment, modeling superior to attention placebo in terms of subjective responses. Maintenance of treatment gains at 2-wk follow-up. No group differences in responses to nontargeted stimuli.
Weissbrod & Bryan (1973)	Small animals	25 male 4th- and 5th-graders	Experiment	Children assigned to one of five conditions: filmed modeling with same-age model and actual feared stimulus, filmed modeling with same-age model and replica of feared stimulus, filmed modeling with younger model and actual feared stimulus, filmed modeling with younger model and replica of feared stimulus, or attention placebo. Each modeling film 2½ min in length and shown 4 times.	At posttreatment, all modeling treatments superior to attention placebo in terms of motor responses. Modeling treatments with actual feared stimulus superior to modeling treatments with replica of feared stimulus. Maintenance of treatment gains at 2-wk follow-up.
White & Davis (1974)	Dental treatment	15 females ranging in age from 4 to 8 yr	Experiment	Children assigned to one of three conditions: live modeling with a mastery model, information, or no treatment. Treatment administered for 6 sessions.	At posttreatment, modeling and information superior to no treatment in terms of motor responses. Maintenance of treatment gains at 6-mo follow-up.

TABLE 5-5 A Summary of Contingency Management Treatments for Children's Fears and Anxieties

Author(s)	Feared stimulus	Subjects	Research design	Treatment	Outcome
Allen, Hart, Buell, Harris, & Wolf (1964)	Social situations	4-yr-old male	Reversal design	Contingency management program administered by teacher for 14 days.	At posttreatment, significant reductions in motor responses. Maintenance of treatment gains at 26-day follow-up.

TABLE 5-5 (*continued*)

Author(s)	Feared stimulus	Subjects	Research design	Treatment	Outcome
Ayllon, Smith, & Rogers (1970)	School	8-yr-old female with fear duration of 1 yr	Case study	Shaping program for school attendance plus home-based motivational program for child and mother. Program administered by mother for 1 mo.	At posttreatment, significant reductions in motor responses. Generalization of treatment gains to other problem behaviors (somatic complaints, academic performance, classroom behavior) and maintenance of treatment gains at 9-mo follow-up.
Boer & Sipprelle (1970)	Food	4-yr-old female with fear duration of 6 mo	Case study	Shaping program for the eating of solid foods administered for 7 sessions.	At posttreatment, significant reductions in motor responses. Generalization of treatment gains to other settings and fear stimuli and maintenance of treatment gains at 13-mo follow-up.
Brown, Copeland, School & Hall (1974)	School	11-yr-old male with fear duration of 2 yr	Changing criterion	Shaping program administered by principal for 17 days.	At posttreatment, significant reductions in motor responses. Maintenance of treatment gains at 1-yr follow-up.
Buell, Stoddard, Harris, & Baer (1968)	Social situations	3-yr-old female with fear duration ≥ 1 mo	Reversal	Contingency management program administered by teacher for 36 days.	At posttreatment, significant reductions in motor responses. Generalization of treatment gains to other social behaviors.
Clement & Milne (1967)	Social situations	11 males ranging in age from 8 to 9 yr	Experiment	Children assigned to one of three conditions: contingency management with tangible reward (14 sessions), contingency management with social reward (14 sessions), or no treatment.	At posttreatment, contingency management with tangible reward superior to other two conditions in terms of motor responses. No group differences in terms of subjective responses.
Cretekos (1977)	School	Male aged 13 yr, 10 mo, with fear duration of 5 yr	Case study	Teacher-assisted contract for school attendance implemented for 6 wk.	At posttreatment, significant reductions in motor and physiological responses.
Doleys & Williams (1977)	School	7-yr-old female with fear duration ≥ 2 yr	Case study	Teacher- and parent-assisted contingency management program administered for 16 days.	At posttreatment, significant reductions in motor responses. Maintenance of treatment gains at 4-mo follow-up.
Hersen (1970)	School	12½-yr-old male	Case study	Teacher- and parent-assisted contingency management program administered for 15 wk.	At posttreatment, significant reductions in motor responses. Maintenance of treatment gains at 6-mo follow-up.
Holmes (1936)	Heights	39-mo-old female, 51-mo-old male	Case study	Contingency management program administered for 9 to 11 sessions.	At posttreatment, significant reductions in motor responses for one of the two children.
Jackson & Wallace (1974)	Social situations	15-yr-old female with fear duration ≥ 3 mo	Reversal	Teacher-assisted contingency management program administered for 100 days.	At posttreatment, significant reductions in motor responses. No generalization of treatment gains to new settings.

TABLE 5-5 (*continued*)

Author(s)	Feared stimulus	Subjects	Research design	Treatment	Outcome
Neisworth, Madle, & Goeke (1975)	Separation	4-yr-old female with fear duration of 1 yr	Case study	Shaping and fading program administered for 7 sessions.	At posttreatment, significant reductions in motor responses. Maintenance of treatment gains at 6-mo follow-up.
Obler & Terwilliger (1970)	Vehicles, small animals	7- through 12-yr-olds (*n* = 30)	Experiment	Children assigned to one of two conditions: shaping program (10 sessions) or no treatment.	At posttreatment, shaping program superior to no treatment in terms of motor responses.
Patterson (1965)	School	7-yr-old male with fear duration ≥ 2 yr	Case study	Teacher- and parent-assisted shaping program administered for 23 sessions.	At posttreatment, significant reductions in motor responses. Maintenance of treatment gains at 3-mo follow-up.
Tahmisian & McReynolds (1971)	School	13-yr-old female with fear duration ≥ 1 yr	Case study	Parent-administered contingency management program carried out for 3 wk after imaginal desensitization proved unsuccessful.	At posttreatment, significant reductions in subjective and motor responses. Maintenance of treatment gains at 4-wk follow-up.

TABLE 5-6 A Summary of Self-Management Treatments for Children's Fears and Anxieties

Author(s)	Feared stimulus	Subjects	Research design	Treatment	Outcome
Bankart & Bankart (1983)	School	9-yr-old male with fear duration of 2 wk	Case study	Program of self-monitoring and coping self-talk administered for 2–3 days.	At posttreatment, significant reductions in motor responses. Maintenance of treatment gains at 2-yr follow-up.
Cradock, Cotler, & Jason (1978)	Public speaking	14-yr-old females (*n* = 40)	Experiment	Children assigned to one of three conditions: self-control (6 sessions), imaginal desensitization (6 sessions), or no treatment.	At posttreatment, self-control and imaginal desensitization superior to no treatment in terms of subjective responses. Self-control superior to imaginal desensitization. No group differences in terms of motor responses.
Fox & Houston (1981)	Public speaking	33 female and 23 male 4th-graders	Experiment	Children assigned to one of three conditions: coping self-talk (1 session), attention placebo (1 session), or no treatment.	At posttreatment, attention placebo and no treatment superior to coping self-talk in terms of subjective responses.
Kanfer, Karoly, & Newman (1975)	Darkness	30 males and 15 females ranging in age from 5 to 6 yr	Experiment	Children assigned to one of three conditions: coping self-talk, information, or attention placebo. All conditions administered for 1 session.	At posttreatment, coping self-talk superior to information and attention placebo in terms of motor responses. Information superior to attention placebo. Generalization of treatment gains to other settings.

TABLE 5-6 (*continued*)

Author(s)	Feared stimulus	Subjects	Research design	Treatment	Outcome
Nocella & Kaplan (1982)	Dental treatment	5- through 13-yr-olds (*n* = 30)	Experiment	Children assigned to one of three conditions: self-management program of relaxation and coping self-talk (1 session), attention placebo (1 session), or no treatment.	At posttreatment, self-management superior to attention placebo and no treatment in terms of motor responses.
Peterson & Shigetomi (1981)	Hospital	35 females and 31 males ranging in age from 2½ to 10½ yr	Experiment	Children assigned to one of five conditions: parent-assisted coping skills training, filmed modeling with a mastery model, coping skills training plus filmed modeling, information, or attention placebo. All conditions administered for 1 session.	At posttreatment, coping skills training and coping skills training plus modeling superior to filmed modeling in terms of motor responses. No group differences in terms of subjective and physiological responses.
Rosenfarb & Hayes (1984)	Darkness	19 males and 19 females ranging in age from 5 to 6 yr	Experiment	Children assigned to one of six conditions: program of coping self-talk administered in private, program of coping self-talk administered in public, modeling film shown in private, modeling film shown in public, attention placebo, or placebo film. All conditions administered for 1 session.	At posttreatment, coping self-talk administered in public and modeling film shown in public superior to other four conditions in terms of motor responses.
Sheslow, Bondy, & Nelson (1982)	Darkness	16 females and 16 males ranging in age from 4 to 5 yr	Experiment	Children assigned to one of four conditions: coping self-talk, *in vivo* desensitization, coping self-talk plus *in vivo* desensitization, or attention placebo.	At posttreatment, *in vivo* desensitization and coping self-talk plus *in vivo* desensitization superior to coping self-talk and attention placebo in terms of motor responses. No group differences in terms of subjective responses.
Siegel & Peterson (1980, 1981)	Dental treatment	42 children ranging in age from 42 to 71 mo	Experiment	Children assigned to one of three conditions: coping skills training, information, or attention placebo.	At posttreatment, coping skills training and information superior to attention placebo in terms of motor and physiological responses. No group differences in terms of subjective responses. At 1-wk follow-up, coping skills training and information superior to attention placebo in terms of motor responses. Information superior to coping skills training and attention placebo in terms of physiological responses. No group differences in terms of subjective responses.

TABLE 5-7 A Summary of Compound Treatments for Children's Fears and Anxieties

Author(s)	Feared stimulus	Subjects	Research design	Treatment	Outcome
Andrews (1971)	Test taking	48 male 10th- and 11th-graders	Experiment	Children assigned to one of three conditions: compound treatment of imaginal desensitization and contingency management, client-centered treatment, or no treatment. Treatments administered for 10 sessions.	At posttreatment, compound treatment superior to client-centered and no treatment in terms of subjective responses. No group differences in terms of motor responses.
Barlow & Seidner (1983)	Being alone	2 females and 1 male ranging in age from 15 to 17 yr; fear duration ranging from 14 mo to 4 yr	Case study	Parent-assisted compound treatment of desensitization, self-management, and prolonged exposure administered for 10 sessions.	At posttreatment, significant reductions in subjective and motor responses for two of the three children. Generalization of treatment gains to other problem behaviors (family relations) and maintenance of treatment gains at 6-mo follow-up.
Bauer (1968)	Mathematics	7th-grade male	Case study	Compound treatment of imaginal desensitization and modeling administered over a period of 4 mo.	At posttreatment, significant reductions in motor responses.
Blagg & Yule (1984)	School	33 males and 33 females ranging in age from 11 to 16 yr, with fear duration $\geq$ 3 days	Experiment with nonrandom assignment	Children received one of three treatments: compound treatment of parent-assisted contingency management and *in vivo* flooding (average duration of 2½ wk), inpatient hospitalization (average duration of 45 wk), or home tutoring and psychotherapy (average duration of 72 wk).	At posttreatment, compound treatment superior to hospitalization and home tutoring in terms of motor responses. Generalization of treatment gains to other fear stimuli and other problem behaviors (extraversion and neuroticism) and maintenance of treatment gains at follow-up of 3 yr, 10 mo.
Boyd (1980)	School	16-yr-old male with fear duration $\geq$ 3 wk	Case study	Compound treatment of emotive imagery and contingency management administered over a 3-wk period.	At posttreatment, significant reductions in motor responses.
Esveldt-Dawson, Wisner, Unis, Matson, & Kazdin (1982)	School, strangers	12½-yr-old female	Multiple baseline	Compound treatment of participant modeling and contingency management administered for 20 sessions.	At posttreatment, significant reductions in subjective and motor responses. Generalization of treatment gains to new settings and other fear stimuli and maintenance of treatment gains at 21-wk follow-up.
Franco, Christoff, Crimmins, & Kelly (1983)	Social situations	14-yr-old male	Multiple baseline	Compound treatment of participant modeling and contingency management administered weekly for 49 wk.	At posttreatment, significant reductions in subjective and motor responses. Maintenance of treatment gains at 3½-mo follow-up.
Giebenhain & O'Dell (1984)	Darkness	4 males and 2 females ranging in age from 3 to 11 yr, with fear duration $\geq$ 1 yr	Multiple baseline	Parent-administered compound treatment of self-management and contingency management carried out for 2 wk.	At posttreatment, significant reductions in motor responses. No changes in subjective responses. Maintenance of treatment gains at 12-mo follow-up.

TABLE 5-7 (*continued*)

Author(s)	Feared stimulus	Subjects	Research design	Treatment	Outcome
Graziano & Mooney (1980, 1982)	Darkness	18 males and 15 females ranging in age from 6 to 13½ yr, with fear duration from 1½ to 10¼ yr	Experiment	Children assigned to one of two conditions: parent-assisted compound treatment of self-management and contingency management (3 wk duration) or no treatment.	At posttreatment, compound treatment superior to no treatment in terms of motor responses. Maintenance of treatment gains at 3-yr follow-up.
Graziano, Mooney, Huber, & Ignasiak (1979)	Darkness	5 males and 2 females ranging in age from 8½ to 12¾ yr, with fear duration from 3 to 6 yr	Case study	Parent-assisted compound treatment of self-management and contingency management administered over a period of 3 to 19 wk.	At posttreatment, significant reductions in subjective and motor responses. Maintenance of treatment gains at 1-yr follow-up.
Handler (1972)	Nightmares	11-yr-old male	Case study	Compound treatment of imaginal flooding and participant modeling administered for 2 sessions.	At posttreatment, significant reductions in motor responses. Maintenance of treatment gains at 6-mo follow-up.
Lazarus, Davison, & Polefka (1965)	School	9-yr-old male with fear duration ≥ 4 yr	Case study	Compound treatment of *in vivo* desensitization, emotive imagery, and contingency management administered over a period of 4½ mo.	At posttreatment, significant reductions in motor responses. Generalization of treatment gains to other problem behaviors (family relations) and maintenance of treatment gains at 10-mo follow-up.
MacDonald (1975)	Small animals	11-yr-old male with fear duration of 8 yr	Case study	Parent-assisted compound treatment of desensitization, participant modeling, prolonged exposure, and contingency management administered for 16 sessions.	At posttreatment, significant reductions in subjective and motor responses. Generalization of treatment gains to other fear stimuli and maintenance of treatment gains at 2-yr follow-up.
Mayer et al. (1971)	School, test taking	5th- and 6th-graders (*n* = 54)	Experiment	Children assigned to one of five conditions: compound treatment of public self-management and contingency management, compound treatment of private self-management and contingency management, instruction, waiting list, or no treatment. Compound treatments administered weekly for 12 wk.	At posttreatment, no group differences in terms of subjective responses.
Miller, Barrett, Hampe, & Noble (1972b)	Varied from child to child; most common were school and darkness	37 males and females ranging in age from 6 to 15 yr	Experiment	Children assigned to one of three conditions: compound treatment of desensitization, modeling, and contingency management; psychotherapy; or no treatment. Treatment administered for 24 sessions.	At posttreatment, compound treatment and psychotherapy superior to no treatment in terms of motor responses. Generalization of treatment gains to other fear stimuli and maintenance of treatment gains at 14-wk follow-up.

TABLE 5-7 (*continued*)

Author(s)	Feared stimulus	Subjects	Research design	Treatment	Outcome
Miller & Kassinove (1978)	Generalized	4th-graders (*n* = 96)	Experiment	Children assigned to one of four conditions: self-management, self-management plus participant modeling, self-management plus participant modeling plus homework, or no treatment. Treatment administered daily for 12 wk.	At posttreatment, self-management plus participant modeling with and without homework superior to no treatment in terms of subjective responses.
O'Connor (1972)	Social situations	33 children	Experiment	Children assigned to one of four conditions: filmed modeling (23 min in length), filmed modeling plus contingency management, contingency management plus control film, or attention placebo. Contingency management treatments administered over period of 2 wk.	At posttreatment, all three treatments superior to attention placebo in terms of motor responses. Maintenance of treatment gains for two modeling treatments at 6-wk follow-up.
Pomerantz, Peterson, Marholin, & Stern (1977)	Water	4-yr-old male	Case study	Parent-administered program of contingency management and participant modeling. Treatment carried out for 11 sessions.	At posttreatment, significant reductions in motor responses. Maintenance of treatment gains at 6-mo follow-up.

6

PROBLEMS IN SOCIAL RELATIONSHIPS

KENNETH A. DODGE
Vanderbilt University

Historically, treatment of the problems of being unable to get along socially with other persons has not held a place of high esteem in American psychiatry and psychology. Certainly, in contrast with exotic disorders such as autism and Tourette syndrome, social incompetence has been viewed as commonplace, nonscientific, and mundane. The mental health profession has often abdicated responsibility for resolving these problems to popular writers, moral educators, and hucksters. Likewise, the educational system has not seen fit to place children's social skills on its priority list. Yet there is abundant evidence to indicate that positive peer relationships are necessary requisites for mental health and educational success (see Kupersmidt, Coie, & Dodge, in press, and Parker & Asher, 1987, for recent reviews). Recently, this evidence has begun to have an impact on psychiatric and educational systems, with the advent of social skills training programs. These programs have flourished in the last 15 years, along with the research evaluating their efficacy. In a recent review, Ladd and Asher (1985) report a growth curve that is geometric in its proportions. Like many bandwagons, however, the bandwagon for the social skills training movement has easily outdistanced the empirical evidence. The goals of this chapter are to describe some of the social skills interventions for children, to evaluate the scientific merit of these interventions, and to guide further inquiry in this area.

THE RATIONALE FOR FOCUSING ON SOCIAL RELATIONSHIP PROBLEMS IN CHILDREN

In order to provide a context for this review, the rationale for focusing on social relationship problems in children is described briefly. The rekindling of interest in social competence ("rekindling," because initial interest dates back at least to the days of ancient Greeks such as Demosthenes and Socrates; McFall & Dodge, 1982) came with the finding that measures of social competence are predictive of positive adjustment following psychiatric hospitalization. For example, Zigler and Phillips (1961) found that simple measures of competence such as marital and occupational status could be used to predict outcome in psychiatric patients. Jacobs, Muller, Anderson, and Skinner (1972, 1973) found that psychiatric patients who had positive social relationships (contrasted with those who did not) were relatively likely to respond favorably to treatment in a psychiatric ward and to fare well following release from the hospital. The consensus of these findings was that social competence indicators were positively correlated with favorable prognoses. Roff (1961, 1963) took this work a step further by demonstrating that measures of social interactions in childhood were predictive of psychiatric and maladjustment problems in later life. Children who had difficulty in getting along with peers at age 8 were at increased risk for bad-conduct discharges from military service 10–15 years later and for psychoses in young adulthood. Since then, the predictive relation between early social relationship problems and later maladjustment has been replicated in a variety of studies—with follow-back and follow-up designs; with measures of early peer relationships ranging from sociometrics (Cowen, Pederson, Babigian, Izzo, & Trost, 1973) to ratings made from child guidance clinic data (Robins, 1966); and with maladjustment outcomes including school dropout (Ullman, 1957), juvenile delinquency (Roff, Sells, & Golden, 1972), schizophrenia (Kohn & Clausen, 1955), neuroses (Roff, 1963), suicide (Stengel, 1971), and general psychiatric impairment (Cowen *et al.*, 1973).

Children with poor peer relationships not only are at risk for later psychological maladjustment, but also are known to be concurrently likely to have difficulties in academic performance at school (Buswell, 1953; Koch, 1933; Kohn, 1977) and to be overrepresented in referrals to child guidance clinics (Woody, 1969). Even though a child's level of social competence is not usually the primary focus of psychiatric inquiry, deficient peer relationships are a common feature of a number of child psychiatric disorders. Table 6-1 lists those diagnoses from the revised third edition of the *Diagnostic and Statistical Manual of Mental Disorders* (DSM-III-R; American Psychiatric Association, 1987) in which impairment in peer relationships is an explicit part of the diagnostic criteria. It is noted that these diagnoses range from Mental Retardation to Avoidant Personality Disorder, and from Conduct Disorder to Social Phobia. I hypothesize that social incompetence plays a role in a number of other disorders as well, and these are listed in Table 6-2. These disorders include those in which early social incompetence may predict later onset of a problem (such as Alcoholism), as well as those in which problems in social relationships are probably a part of the symptomatic syndrome (such as Academic Problem).

Even those socially rejected children who are not identified as having psychiatric problems are likely to report high levels of personal unhappiness and loneliness (Asher & Wheeler, 1985). At least half of rejected children are unable to resolve their difficulties on their own and remain socially rejected over several years (Coie & Dodge, 1983). Given the pervasiveness of these problems, it is perplexing why

parents and professionals do not typically refer rejected children for mental health interventions and why psychiatry as a profession has not acknowledged this domain of problems.

IDENTIFYING CHILDREN WITH PROBLEMS IN SOCIAL RELATIONSHIPS

Since the literature on social competence has origins in so many areas of research, there are few agreed-upon criteria for identifying the child who is experiencing problems in social relationships. Information about these problems has come from many sources, including teachers, parents, peers, adult observers, and the children themselves (Ladd & Asher, 1985). Estimates about the magnitude of these problems also vary. Peer informant data indicate that from 6% to 11% of all children in the third through sixth grades of elementary schools have not even a single friend in their classrooms (Gronlund, 1959; Hymel & Asher, 1977). The rate of friendlessness is slightly higher among boys than among girls, but this difference has not held up across all studies (Asher & Hymel, 1981; French & Tyne, 1982). About 12% of children meet criteria as socially rejected (Coie, Dodge, & Coppotelli, 1982). These criteria include relatively few peer nominations of a child as being liked and many nominations as being disliked. O'Connor (1969) used the rate of social interaction to identify targeted children and identified as many as one-third of all the children in a regular classroom. On the other hand, using a behavioral criterion of a rate of social interaction that was one standard deviation below the class mean for 3 consecutive days, Weinrott, Corson, and Wilchesky (1979) identified 1%–3% of a population as socially withdrawn. Clearly, both the kind of information gathered and the diagnostic criterion employed to identify children with peer relations problems have varied widely across studies.

At least four different sources of information have been used to diagnose problems in peer relations. At the most general level, teachers or other adults who are familiar with a child's behavior (such as parents) have simply nominated children who are having difficulties relating to peers. This is the most common route to identification, as demonstrated in the process of referral to child guidance and mental health clinics. Parents often refer their children for

TABLE 6-1 DSM-III-R Disorders in Which Social Incompetence Is Part of the Diagnostic Criteria

---

Mental Retardation (317.00 to 319.00)
"Concurrent deficits or impairments in adaptive functioning, i.e., the person's effectiveness in meeting the standards expected for his or her age by his or her cultural group in areas such as social skills . . ."

Autistic Disorder (299.00)
"[G]ross impairment in ability to make peer friendships (e.g., no interest in making peer friendships; despite interest in making friends, demonstrates lack of understanding of conventions of social interaction, for example, reads phone book to uninterested peer)"

Attention Deficit–Hyperactivity Disorder (314.01)
"[O]ften interrupts or intrudes on others, e.g., butts into other children's games"

Conduct Disorder (312.00 to 312.90)
"[O]ften initiates physical fights"

Oppositional Defiant Disorder (313.81)
"[O]ften deliberately does things that annoy other people, e.g., grabs other children's hats"

Avoidant Disorder of Childhood or Adolescence (313.21)
"Excessive shrinking from contact with unfamiliar people, for a period of six months or longer, sufficiently severe to interfere with social functioning in peer relationships"

Identity Disorder (313.82)
"Severe subjective distress regarding uncertainty about a variety of issues relating to identity, including . . . friendship patterns"

Reactive Attachment Disorder of Infancy or Early Childhood (313.89)
"Markedly disturbed social relatedness in most contexts, beginning before the age of five, as evidenced by . . . persistent failure to initiate or respond to most social interactions . . . [or] indiscriminate sociability"

Schizophrenia (295.10 to 295.95)
"During the course of the disturbance, functioning in such areas as work, social relations, and self-care is markedly below the highest level achieved before onset of the disturbance (or, when the onset is in childhood or adolescence, failure to achieve expected level of social development)"

Bipolar Disorder, Manic (296.40 to 296.46)
"Mood disturbances sufficiently severe to cause marked impairment in occupational functioning or in usual social activities or relationships with others"

Social Phobia (300.23)
"The avoidant behavior interferes with occupational functioning or with usual social activities or relationships with others"

Adjustment Disorder (309.00 to 309.90)
"The maladaptive nature of the reaction is indicated by . . . impairment in occupational (including school) functioning or in usual social activities or relationships with others"

Schizoid Personality Disorder (301.20)
"A pervasive pattern of indifference to social relationships . . . as indicated by . . . no close friends or confidants (or only one) other than first-degree relatives"

Schizotypal Personality Disorder (301.22)
"A pervasive pattern of deficits in interpersonal relatedness . . . as indicated by . . . no close friends or confidants (or only one) other than first-degree relatives"

Antisocial Personality Disorder (301.70)
"[I]s irritable and aggressive, as indicated by repeated physical fights or assaults"

Borderline Personality Disorder (301.83)
"A pervasive pattern of instability in mood, interpersonal relationships, and self-image"

Avoidant Personality Disorder (301.82)
"A pervasive pattern of social discomfort . . . as indicated by . . . no close friends or confidants (or only one) other than first-degree relatives"

Note. From *Diagnostic and Statistical Manual of Mental Disorders* (3rd ed., rev.) by the American Psychiatric Association, 1987, Washington, DC: Author. Copyright 1987 by the American Psychiatric Association. Reprinted by permission.

"behavior problems," which include an array of problems with compliance, aggression, and negative affect; however, the primary reason for referral is rarely an explicit focus on social incompetence (Woody, 1969). Children's social behavior has been evaluated more

TABLE 6-2 DSM-III-R Disorders in Which Social Incompetence Probably Plays a Role

DSM-III-R no.	Disorder Type
Disorders in which early social incompetence may predict later disorder	
303.90 and 305.00	Alcoholism (withdrawal, intoxication, etc.)
304 and 305	Substance Abuse Disorders (varied types)
295	Schizophrenia
297.10	Delusional (Paranoid) Disorder
302	Sexual disorders (paraphilias, dysfunctions)
312	Impulse Control Disorders (kleptomania, pyromania)
309	Adjustment Disorder
301	Personality Disorders (antisocial, paranoid, schizoid, schizotypal, avoidant, passive–aggressive)
Disorders in which social incompetence is probably a part of the disorder[a]	
315.00 to 315.80	Academic Skills Disorders (arithmetic, expressive writing, reading, articulation, expressive language, receptive language, coordination)
302.60	Gender Identity Disorder of Childhood
307.00	Stuttering
307.30	Stereotypy/Habit Disorder
300.22	Agoraphobia
V62.30	Academic Problem
V71.02	Childhood or Adolescent Antisocial Behavior
V62.81	Other Interpretational Problem

[a]In addition to the disorders listed in Table 6-1.

systematically through structured measures such as the Child Behavior Checklist (Achenbach & Edelbrock, 1981), the Walker Problem Behavior Identification Checklist (Walker, 1983), the Social Interaction Rating Scale (Hops, Walker, & Greenwood, 1979), and the Social Behavior Rating Scale (Greenwood, Walker, Todd, & Hops, 1979). These measures have been used to identify general problems in peer relations, as well as specific types of problem behaviors such as aggression and withdrawal. The validity of these measures has been demonstrated by their positive correlations with other assessments of peer relationship problems, including direct observations and referrals to mental health clinics. It is assumed that adults who know a child well are in a position to understand that child's social interactions with peers. However, a large portion of the peer culture is hidden from adults (Youniss, 1981), and adults' assessments may be biased by the child's academic performance or conduct toward adults (Coie, Dodge, & Kupersmidt, in press). The validity of adult rating instruments has proven far greater for general identification of problem children than for the identification of specific types of problems (for a review, see Hops & Greenwood, 1988).

A second source of information has been the peer group. Sociometric nominations as being liked or disliked have been used to identify three different groups of socially maladjusted children (Coie et al., 1982; Newcomb & Bukowski, 1983). The "socially rejected" child is identified as being liked by few or no peers as well as being disliked by many peers. The "socially neglected" child is liked by few peers as well, but is not highly disliked. The "controversial" child, on the other hand, is highly liked as well as highly disliked. All three groups may be targets for intervention, although longitudinal data have demonstrated that the low status of rejected children is more stable across 4 years than is the low status of neglected and controversial children (Coie & Dodge, 1983). In addition, the rejected child is clearly at risk for juvenile delinquency and school dropout, whereas the risk status of neglected and controversial children is less clear (Kupersmidt, 1983). Validity for the construct of rejected status has been demonstrated in a number of other ways, in addition to the predictive evidence concerning maladaptive outcomes. A high proportion of rejected children are known to behave deviantly toward peers, including high levels of aggression and inappropriate behaviors (Coie & Kupersmidt, 1983; Dodge, 1983; Dodge, Coie, & Brakke, 1982). They lack a variety of social-cognitive skills (Dodge, Murphy, & Buchsbaum, 1984; Feldman & Dodge, 1987), and they report high levels of loneliness (Asher & Wheeler, 1985). The rejected child is clearly a target for intervention aimed at improving social competence.

It is tempting to equate peer status groupings with particular psychiatric disorders. Rejected children are known to display (as a group) high rates of aggressive behavior, and neglected children have been thought of as shy and perhaps anxious, suggesting links to conduct disorders and anxiety or depressive disorders, respectively. The evidence suggests that these links are premature. Whereas conduct-disordered children are known to be likely to be socially rejected, a sizeable portion of rejected children are not conduct-disordered (displaying other behavior patterns instead) (Coie et al., in press). Likewise, neglected children are a heterogeneous group, with few coherent patterns that characterize the entire group.

A third source of information used to identify socially incompetent children has been direct observations by adults. Because aggressive behaviors occur relatively infrequently, but are often a major component of a child's peer relationship problems, direct observation of aggression may be too expensive as a screening procedure (Coie et al., in press). On the other hand, direct observations of the rate of social interaction have been used frequently to identify the socially withdrawn or isolated child (Greenwood, Walker, Todd, & Hops, 1981). Even though this identification procedure is fairly reliable, its validity has been called into question (Asher, Markell, & Hymel, 1981). Children with low rates of social interaction may display a wide variety of behaviors while not interacting with peers. These children are not necessarily socially rejected or neglected by peers. Most importantly, a review of the literature reveals that they are not at unusually high risk for later maladaptive outcomes (Asher et al., 1981). On the other hand, Rubin and Krasnor (1986) argue that children who consistently display low rates of social interaction over several years (particularly if their isolated play behavior is nondirected) may develop other signs of maladaptation and may be at social risk. Even if the rate of interaction is not an

empirically validated criterion for the identification of a child at social risk, it is quite possible that the rate of social interaction might be an appropriate target for intervention in a child identified on some other basis (such as peers' nominations or physical or intellectual handicap) (see Strain, 1983; Strain, Odom, & McConnell, 1984).

A fourth method of identifying socially maladaptive children has been self-report. Asher and Wheeler (1985) have developed a measure of reported loneliness and have found that about 10% of elementary school children report themselves to be unusually lonely. This measure has correlated highly with self-referrals for counseling (Williams, 1986). Even though the loneliness scale has not yet been used extensively to identify socially maladaptive children, its face validity suggests its potential.

IDENTIFYING TARGETS FOR INTERVENTION

Few of the procedures for identifying socially maladaptive children are helpful in identifying the behavioral patterns related to social maladaptation, and none are helpful in understanding the development and etiology of these problems. Even though a theory of social incompetence would seem to be a prerequisite for the development of treatments for these children, many interventions have proceeded without a systematic understanding of the nature of these problems. Often, the goals of intervention are determined intuitively or by their face validity. The goals (and techniques) therefore have varied widely across studies. One intervention may be targeted at increasing a child's rate of interaction with peers (e.g., O'Connor, 1969), whereas another is directed toward improving children's role-taking abilities (e.g., Chandler, Greenspan, & Barenboim, 1974). Comparisons across studies are virtually impossible without a theory (or at least a framework) of how these diverse goals might be relevant to effective peer relationships.

Several investigators have been developing such a framework over the past two decades. The theory began with the work of Goldfried and D'Zurilla (1969). These theorists argued that the process of identifying a socially incompetent individual begins with a judgment made by one person about another. Usually the judge is an expert (such as a teacher or a clinician). The four sources listed above as ways of identifying the socially incompetent child (i.e., adults, peers, direct observation by an impartial adult, and self-report) are four kinds of judges. This judgment process is distinguished from the identification of behavioral qualities that have led others to make a judgment of incompetence. Behavioral performance qualities thus constitute a second aspect of the theory.

Many behaviorally oriented investigators have gone about evaluating behavioral performance by counting the frequencies of various behaviors displayed by competent and incompetent children (Kelly, 1982). Those behaviors that incompetent children fail to display at adequate rates are called "behavioral deficits," whereas those behaviors that are over-represented are called "behavioral excesses." This is the rationale for targeting the rate of social interaction as a key behavior (e.g., Furman, Rahe, & Hartup, 1979). Of course, the validity of this procedure requires that the targeted behavior actually correlate with the judges' ratings of overall competence. Unfortunately, this empirical step is often bypassed. In fact, since rate of interaction does not correlate well with peers' sociometric evaluations, the empirical basis for targeting it as a focus of intervention is questionable (Asher et al., 1981). High rates of aggression, on the other hand, are clearly related to teachers', parents', and peers' evaluations, and are thus appropriate candidates for targeting (Asher et al., 1981; Dodge, 1983). Kelly (1982) has reviewed the behaviors associated with positive judgments of social competence and has identified the following behaviors as appropriate foci in intervention: social initiations (from Gottman, 1977; Gottman, Gonso, & Schuler, 1976; Strain, Shores, & Timm, 1977); asking and answering questions (Gottman, Gonso, & Rasmussen, 1975); greeting peers (LaGeca & Mesibov, 1979; LaGreca & Santogrossi, 1980); task participation (Hymel & Asher, 1977; Keller & Carlson, 1974; Oden & Asher, 1977); proximity (Evers & Schwarz, 1973; O'Connor, 1969); cooperation and sharing (LaGreca & Santogrossi, 1980; Oden & Asher, 1977); affective responsiveness (Hymel & Asher, 1977; LaGreca & Santogrossi, 1980); and praise to peers (LaGreca & Mesibov, 1979). This list is by no means exhaustive. In fact, it is not even systematically determined, since each

of the behaviors has been identified in separate studies (and not all by empirical means).

The approach of identifying specific behaviors that correlate with judgments of social competence is a tedious task, because the behavioral correlates of competence judgments are likely to vary across age, sex, and subcultural groups. Another major problem has been the failure to take into account the ecological system and context in which these behaviors occur. A high rate of a particular behavior may be appropriate in one context, but inappropriate in another. For example, we (Dodge, Coie, & Brakke, 1983) found that social initiations were positively correlated with positive peer status on the playground and negatively correlated in the classroom/work setting. Obviously, the task demands of the playground and work settings differ, and success in each setting requires responsiveness to these task demands. Taken further, this concept suggests that the identification of critical components of social competence should not begin with discrete behaviors that are simply to be counted; rather, the process should begin with the identification of critical social tasks (McFall, 1982). Analyses of these tasks will determine what behavioral patterns (not only frequencies, but also styles and sequences) are associated with success at the task. These patterns can then be targeted for intervention.

This approach has been taken in the creative work by Gottman (1983), who analyzed components of 5-year-old children's conversation during the critical task of friendship formation. He identified six behavioral patterns that empirically differentiated successful from unsuccessful outcomes (the outcomes being judgments by peers that a child was liked). These included the extent to which children (1) communicated clearly and in connected ways; (2) exchanged information; (3) established common play activities with their partners; (4) explored similarities and differences; (5) resolved conflicts; and (6) disclosed private information. Parker and Gottman (1985) recognized that a correlation between these patterns and successful outcomes would not necessarily indicate that these patterns were responsible for the outcomes, so they ingeniously manipulated these six patterns experimentally (through a talking doll that played with children). They presented children with dolls that either displayed these patterns or did not display these patterns. Indeed, children liked the "socially competent" dolls much more than the "incompetent" dolls. These six behavioral patterns are thus empirically based candidates for targeting in interventions aimed at improving children's friendship-making success.

The task-analytic approach holds great promise for the field. However, there is danger in arbitrarily (nonempirically) identifying which tasks are "critical," in the same way that it has been argued that critical behaviors should not be identified arbitrarily. Goldfried and D'Zurilla (1969) and McFall (1982) have suggested procedures for systematically identifying the critical tasks for particular populations so that social competence can be assessed within those task areas. The procedures include the following steps: (1) identifying the most relevant and critical life tasks for a population by systematically soliciting nominations from members of that population and "experts" who are knowledgeable about this population; (2) conducting a task analysis of the important components of successful behavior at each task; (3) obtaining a representative sample of an individual's performance at the task; (4) establishing task-specific criteria for evaluating performance; (5) evaluating the actual performance; and (6) interpretating the evaluation results. Freedman, Rosenthal, Donahoe, Schlundt, and McFall (1978) have used these steps to identify 44 critical situations for adolescent boys (e.g., confrontations with adult authorities, peer pressure, and academic failure situations), and they have found that juvenile delinquent boys performed less adequately in these situations than did socially competent boys. We (Dodge, McClaskey, & Feldman, 1985) have used a similar procedure with elementary-school-age aggressive boys and girls.

Once children are identified by judges as having problems in social relations, and once the particular deficient behavioral responses to specific tasks are identified, many clinicians are ready to attempt to train more competent behavioral responses. Reinforcement-oriented interventions are characterized by their focus at this level (Kelly, 1982). However, for complex patterns (e.g., exploring similarities and differences with a peer), simple reinforcement of a desired behavior may not be effective because the desired behavior is not in the child's repertoire. A number of theorists (e.g., Dodge, 1986; Ladd & Mize, 1983; McFall, 1982 have recognized that these complex behaviors may

occur as a function of component cognitive processes, such as the child's ability to recognize another's thoughts and the child's ability to anticipate the consequences of certain behaviors. These cognitive processes thus constitute yet another level at which intervention might be targeted. McFall (1982) has suggested a three-stage model of social information-processing steps that are crucial for socially competent performance at most tasks. These steps include accurate decoding (or interpretation) of social cues, effective decision making about a behavioral response, and skillful enactment of responses. Other models describe similar sets of component cognitive processes (e.g., Dodge, 1986; Rubin & Krasnor, 1986; Spivack, Platt, & Shure, 1976).

A large body of evidence has accumulated to indicate that these social-cognitive skills are indeed related to behavioral patterns and to positive judgments by others. For example, socially rejected children are known to be deficient at interpreting peers' intentions in provocation situations (Dodge et al., 1984), to make poor decisions regarding the solving of social problems (Asarnow & Callan, 1985; Pellegrini, 1985), and to be unskilled at enacting responses (Dodge et al., 1985). Ladd and Mize (1983), Rubin and Krasnor (1986), and I (Dodge, 1986) have reviewed the evidence in this area more thoroughly than is possible here.

A general model of the assessment and treatment of social competence thus includes at least three levels of assessment, including the evaluations of judgments of a person's competence (made by an "expert"), the identification of problematic social tasks and behaviors for a child, and the identification of social-cognitive skill deficits that may be related to the ineffective performance at those tasks. It also includes interventions that correspond to these three levels of assessment. This model of assessment and treatment focus is depicted in Figure 6-1. Interventions have variously focused on one or more of these three levels of assessment. Since the goal in all cases is to improve the judgments that others make, interventions have differing requirements to prove their efficacy. Interventions aimed at changing a child's behavioral patterns must demonstrate that the patterns change and that the judgments by others change in corresponding fashion. Interventions aimed at training social-cognitive skills must demonstrate that these skills do indeed improve, that skill enhancement leads to changes in behavioral patterns, and that the behavioral changes lead to improvements in judgments by others. Unfortunately, all hypothesized (or implied) steps of the change process are rarely analyzed in interventions. Process analyses are rarely conducted in any form. Those researchers who are conducting such analyses (e.g., Bierman, 1986) are therefore at the cutting edge of this field.

BEHAVIORAL INTERVENTIONS

Most interventions have been focused on either training social-cognitive skills or altering specific behavioral patterns (but not both). The techniques that have been used in the latter case

Stage 1—Identifying the socially incompetent child
A. Referral by parent, teacher, professional
B. Measurement of problematic peer relationships (sociometric assessment, behavior observation, etc.)

Stage 2—Identifying critical problematic social tasks for the child
A. Generation of a taxonomy of tasks by examination of the social ecology
B. Assessment of child's behavioral competence at each task (by rating, role-play, observation, etc.)
C. Listing of problematic areas and areas of strength for child

Stage 3—Identifying mechanisms related to situational social incompetence
A. Assessment of social-cognitive skills within problematic situations
B. Assessment of ecological system resources (for intervention planning; includes evaluation of classroom, family supports, etc.)

Stage 4—Improving social-cognitive skills
A. Didactic instruction, practice, feedback, etc., until criterial performance in skill is reached
B. Assessment of social-cognitive skills to verify improvement

Stage 5—Improving behavior in problematic social situations
A. Intervene to improve behavior (through social-cognitive skills enhancement or direct behavioral modification) until criterial performance is reached
B. Assessment of behavior within problematic social tasks to verify improvement

Stage 6—Improving social standing among peers
A. Intervene to improve peer status (through social-cognitive skills training, behavioral modification, or direct efforts to alter peer evaluations)
B. Assessment of peer status to verify improvement

FIGURE 6.1. A model of assessment and intervention for social incompetence.

are the ones familiar to any behavioral clinician: positive reinforcement, punishment, modeling, shaping, instruction, rehearsal, feedback, and so on (Ladd & Mize, 1983; Odom & DeKlyen, in press). Given the focus on behavioral change, interventions using these techniques have not been concerned with changing global aspects of children's peer status, but rather have targeted specific behaviors for enhancement or extinction. Most of the efforts have been directed toward enhancing the rate of social interaction (and specific positive behaviors such as eye contact, smiling, etc.) or inhibiting aggression and disruption.

Increasing the Rate of Social Interaction

A large group of researchers has targeted withdrawn children as the subject group and increasing their overall rate of interacting with peers as the behavioral goal of intervention, in spite of empirical evidence that this behavior is not a critical problem and the longitudinal evidence that withdrawn children are not at social risk (Asher *et al.*, 1981). An early, highly influential case study by Allen, Hart, Buell, Harris, and Wolf (1964) indicated that the contingent provision of adult attention (i.e., social reinforcement) in response to a 4-year-old withdrawn girl's social overtures to peers dramatically increased that girl's rate of social interaction from 20% to 60%. A later study by Hart, Reynolds, Baer, Brawley, and Harris (1968) demonstrated that the potent aspect of the intervention was the contingent nature of the adult's attention. Follow-ups by Baer and Wolf (1970) and Strain and Timm (1974) supported these findings.

Another approach has been taken by O'Connor (1969, 1972), who used symbolic modeling of reinforced social initiations on a 25-minute videotape to increase children's rate of interaction with peers immediately after the video presentation. The gains were greater than those achieved by children who had watched a nature film. Similar findings were obtained by Evers and Schwartz (1973) and Evers-Pasquale and Sherman (1975), and these effects were maintained for 6 weeks. However, Gottman (1977) failed to find enhancement effects after 8 weeks. The potential applications of a training procedure that is cost-efficient and transferrable to new settings (because it is on videotape) have led other researchers to examine this procedure further. This modeling strategy has the strongest positive effects on children who have a pre-existing interest in playing with peers (Evers-Pasquale & Sherman, 1975; Gresham & Nagle, 1980). Aspects of the modeling videotape may be crucial as well. Jakibchuk and Smeriglio (1976) found that a modeling film had a more positive effect on interaction rates when a child narrated the film from a first-person perspective than when an adult narrated the film from a third-person perspective. Presumably, when children are able to identify with the model (because the model is a peer or because they are motivated to learn), the effects of modeling are greater.

Another approach to increasing the rate of social interaction among isolated children is the peer-pairing technique of Furman et al. (1979). They paired isolated preschoolers with either a same-age or a younger companion for 20 play sessions of 10 minutes each. Both groups of isolated children increased their rate of social interaction subsequently, but those children who had been paired with a younger child increased their interactions at a greater rate than those children paired with a same-age child. The authors suggested that the gains experienced by the former children may have been due to the opportunity to initiate and practice social interaction in a safe setting that was afforded by interaction with a younger child.

Enhancing Specific Prosocial Behaviors

Recognizing that the rate of social interaction is distinct from the quality of that interaction, Cooke and Apolloni (1976) sought to enhance the frequency of four target behaviors in a group of socially withdrawn, learning-disabled children. The behaviors were smiling, sharing, positive physical contact, and verbal compliments. They used contingent social praise to enhance these behaviors successfully. In a similar study, Walker, Hops, Greenwood, and Todd (1979) used adult praise and tokens to enhance three types of social behavior in withdrawn children. The targeted behaviors were initiating interactions (called STARTS), responding to peers (called ANSWER), and extending the chain of interaction (called CONTINUE). Contingent reinforcement, either through tokens or verbal praise, thus seems to be effective in increasing the rates of specific prosocial behaviors. Even though most of the positive effects have been shown for socially withdrawn children, several investigators have shown that these behaviors (such as cooperation) can be enhanced in aggressive children as well (Brown & Elliott, 1965; Hart et al., 1968).

There are a number of problems with these studies and with the use of contingent reinforcement. Combs and Slaby (1978) point out that most of the studies have not included adequate follow-up assessments, so it is possible that the positive effects were short-lived. Ladd and Mize (1983) suggest that *decreases* in these behaviors may occur following the termination of systematic contingent reinforcement. Likewise, evidence of cross-setting generalization is lacking (Ladd & Mize, 1983). Also, it is not clear whether new behaviors are actually acquired by these procedures. Keller and Carlson (1974) tried to increase the rates of several behaviors in withdrawn children through symbolic modeling and found increases only in those behaviors that the children had exhibited most frequently prior to the treatment. That is, the treatment helped children to enhance behaviors already in their repertoires, but did little to help them acquire new behaviors. The administration of specific reinforcements by an adult has proved to be intrusive as well. Reinforcement by a teacher following an initial positive social behavior by a child may disrupt the ongoing social interchange among children and may actually be harmful to the peer interaction (Walker et al., 1979). Perhaps other methods can be developed that would allow for external reinforcements in a way that would not be so obtrusive (such as a "bug-in-the-ear" device).

Several procedures have been developed to enhance the generalization of the effects of these procedures. Fading adult reinforcement (Timm, Strain, & Eller, 1979) and booster training sessions (Paine et al., 1982) have been employed with some success. Following the lead of Wahler (1967), Strain and colleagues (Odom & Strain, 1984; Strain & Timm, 1974; Strain et al., 1977) have employed peers as the change agents. Others have employed group contingencies to reinforce the prosocial behavior of a specific child (Walker & Hops, 1973; Weinrott et al., 1979). Unfortunately, evidence for maintenance and generalization, even with these procedures, has been weak (Greenwood & Hops, 1981).

Inhibition of Aggressive Behaviors

Various punishment techniques have been employed to inhibit aggressive behaviors, which are thought to be responsible for some children's poor peer relations. Overt punishments, such as reprimands and physical strikes, have not proven very effective (see Kazdin, 1985). Time out from reinforcement has received far more support and is much more popular. Typically, following the display of an aggressive behavior, the child is removed from the environment and is restricted from access to positive reinforcers. Drabman and Spitalnik (1973) applied this procedure to a class of aggressive boys in a residential psychiatric setting. When a boy displayed an aggressive behavior, the teacher immediately identified the child and told the child to leave the classroom for 10 minutes. After 16 days, there were marked decreases in overall aggressive behaviors.

Problems of a lack of cross-setting generalization and poor maintenance of effects over time have been noted with these procedures, just as they have been noted in the prosocial behavior enhancement studies reviewed above. Similar attempts to fade contingencies gradually and to use group-oriented contingencies have been employed with aggressive behaviors (Drabman, Spitalnik, & Spitalnik, 1974; Speltz, Moore, & McReynolds, 1979). Kazdin's (1985) review of this literature reveals few lasting positive gains, however. Particularly noteworthy is his observation that inhibiting aggressive behaviors will do little to enhance positive peer relationships unless prosocial behaviors are enhanced as well. He has concluded that "the combined use of reinforcement and punishment appears to maximize the behavior change in operant conditioning programs" (1985, p. 145).

Conclusions

The success that clinical researchers have obtained in altering specific behaviors in children for at least a short period of time in a particular setting is remarkable. Though not theoretically complex, the positive reinforcement and punishment techniques are noteworthy in their power to alter behaviors. The problems of cross-setting generalization and maintenance over time are difficult ones that may be solved through fading, group contingencies, and other procedures. However, behavioral procedures have yet to be used in a way that has led to actual improvement in a child's peer relationships. The researchers have assumed that changes in specific behaviors will lead to changes in peer relationships, but this has yet to be demonstrated adequately. The most important indictment of these studies is that they have failed even to evaluate whether such changes occur. Ladd and Mize (1983) concluded that operant procedures have been generally unimpressive in changing peer relationships.

Several specific factors are likely to account for these failures. First, the selection of behaviors for modification has often been made without empirical justification. Frequency of initiation behaviors has been targeted in both withdrawn and aggressive children, even though it is not clear that these children fail to display adequate frequencies of these behaviors. In fact, it has been found (Dodge, Schlundt, Schocken, & Delugach, 1983) that socially rejected children display overly *high* frequencies of initiation attempts in their initial encounters with unfamiliar peers (relative to the number displayed by socially accepted children). Their problem is that they employ ineffective strategies during these initiation attempts. Only after repeated failures at initiation do rejected children withdraw and fail to initiate interaction. Clearly, merely increasing the rate of initiation attempts will not lead these children to experience social success. It is apparent that the quality of the initiation attempts is crucial to successful outcomes.

Second, even when behaviors have been targeted on an empirical basis, the application of empirical findings regarding a *group* of children will apply only loosely to individuals within that group. For example, rejected children have been found, as a group, to display disruptive and ineffective strategies when initiating play with peers, but not all rejected children display this pattern (Dodge, Schlundt, *et al.*, 1983). Therefore, targeting initiation behavior in an intervention for rejected children is appropriate for only a portion of the rejected children. Very few researchers have matched the treatment to specific characteristics of the children with whom they are intervening. One notable exception has been the work of Bornstein, Bellack, and Hersen (1977), who conducted detailed assessments prior to their intervention. These assessments led them to focus on different behaviors with different children. For example, three children were targeted for loudness of speech and one child for duration of speech.

Third, the behavioral approaches have failed to focus on component skills that may be responsible for specific behavior patterns. Ladd and Mize (1983) suggest that the failure to attend to these variables is responsible for the poor cross-setting generalization and poor maintenance of gains that have been experienced by operantly oriented clinicians. There have been several attempts to implement generalization in interventions with children who have attention deficit disorders, but these attempts have not been altogether promising. It is possible that the nature of the deficit experienced by these children (a cognitive deficit in attention and representation of stimuli) is precisely that which would inhibit generalization. A less pessimistic conclusion is that clinicians have not yet focused on the requisite skills for generalization. The general model of social competence described earlier in this chapter suggests that social-cognitive skills such as detection of intention cues social knowledge, social problem solving, and self-monitoring are requisites of competent social behavior. It may be that those interventions that attend to these skill variables will have success that is longer-lasting, because they provide a child with a skill that the child can bring to new situations. Since behavioral interventions are environmental manipulations, their impact on variables that are internal to the child may be minimal. It is this premise that has been the basis of a group of interventions called "social-cognitive skills training."

SKILLS TRAINING INTERVENTIONS

Even though social-cognitive skills training procedures have been formalized only recently, they have origins in work conducted several decades ago by Chittendon (1942). She taught children to display specific social behaviors (taking turns, sharing, and playing together) through skits enacted with dolls; more importantly, she also taught them how to recognize specific social goals and situations prior to teaching them the actual behaviors to display in these situations. Goal recognition is a social-cognitive skill. Her results were impressive, in that children exhibited less dominative behavior and more cooperative behavior in their classrooms, with the changes in dominative behavior lasting at the 1-month follow-up.

All social-cognitive skills training interventions are oriented toward enhancing one or more cognitive skills that are theoretically and/or empirically related to effective social behavior. The models of social information processing discussed earlier in this chapter (Dodge, 1986; McFall, 1982; McFall & Dodge, 1982) suggest that the following skills are candidates for intervention: (1) the accurate interpretation of social situations and others' intentions; (2) the generation and selection of appropriate and competent behavioral responses to specific situations; (3) the skillful enactment of behavioral strategies; and (4) the monitoring and adjustment of one's own behavior according to environmental demands. Ladd and Mize (1983) reviewed social-cognitive skills training interventions and classified them according to the type of skill that is the focus of intervention. They found that three kinds of skills have been targeted most frequently: (1) knowledge of specific behavioral strategies and the contexts in which those strategies should be displayed; (2) the ability to convert knowledge of social strategies into skillful social behaviors in interactions with peers; and (3) the ability to evaluate one's own performance and adjust it according to environmental demands. These three skill areas are very closely related to the last three skill areas identified in processing models. The processing skill of accurately interpreting social situations was omitted from the Ladd and Mize review simply because it has not been the target of very many interventions. One notable exception is the work of Chandler (1973; Chandler et al., 1974), who taught aggressive children to take the role of others in social interactions. He found positive outcomes, not only in enhanced performance at this skill but also in improved social adaptation, and these outcomes lasted at least a year. Since performance in the last three skill areas is contingent on an accurate appraisal of the social situation, it is unfortunate that more interventions have not focused on this skill.

Most skills training programs have attempted to enhance performance in one of the three areas identified as important by Ladd and Mize (1983). Those authors noted that, in general, those programs that emphasize all three areas have been the most successful in leading to improvements in peer relations. Three different traditions epitomize work in this area: social problem-solving training, anger coping training, and coaching.

Social Problem-Solving Training

Spivack and Shure (Shure & Spivak, 1978; Spivack et al., 1976; Spivack & Shure, 1974) have developed the most widely used program for teaching children social problem-solving skills. Their program for preschool children consists of 46 daily lessons that are oriented toward teaching children to generate novel and competent solutions to interpersonal dilemmas. The critical technique used to get children to think about social situations is called "dialoguing" (Shure, 1981). The essence of dialoguing, as stated by Shure (1980), is as follows:

> Instead of focusing on direct modification of behavior itself, children are taught skills that enable them to think through and solve problems so they can decide for themselves what and what not to do. When, for example, a child hits another child or grabs a toy, he is asked why he did that, what the other child did or said, and whether or not he thinks his action was a good idea. If he says the other child hit him back, the adult might say, "Hitting is one thing you can do," and then ask: "Can you think of something different you can do so he won't hit you back and you can have a chance to play with the toy?" (Shure, 1980, p. 55)

Through experience with a variety of tasks, ranging from nonsocial linguistic concepts to interpersonal conflicts, children are taught that problem solving is an important skill, as well as how to generate alternative solutions to problems. The approach has captured the attention of a number of investigators, because of its potential for effecting structural and procedural changes in children's social knowledge.

Major criticisms of the problem-solving programs of Spivack and Shure have been put forth recently. Krasnor and Rubin (1981; Rubin & Krasnor, 1986) have argued that the skills being taught (particularly the skill of generating *many* solutions to a problem) are not related to positive social adaptation. The Spivack and Shure approach has been to allow children to generate any kind of solution, without inhibiting this creativity by reprimanding children for generating inappropriate or harmful solutions. Critics argue that the freedom to generate inappropriate solutions may actually lead to incompetent behavior, whereas Spivack and Shure argue that the child's own evaluation skills will lead the child to reject inappropriate solutions from enactment. Another concern is that the program emphasizes the training of cognitive skills that are necessary in the latter stages of social information processing, to the neglect of skills at early stages, such as the child's perception and interpretation of social cues. A child's interpretation may bias subsequent processing and lead to affective responses (such as anxiety) that adversely affect later stages of processing. For example, if an emotionally vulnerable child is teased, the child may interpret the teasing peers as being mean (rather than as having fun) and may get upset and angry. This interpretation and its accompanying anger may lead the child to view the "problem" as one of how to get back at the peers rather than one of how to get the peers to be friendly. Clearly, problem definition (i.e., interpretation of the problem) is an important part of problem solving. The training programs might be enhanced by attention to this aspect of processing. Still another criticism has been directed at the failure to conduct nonbiased evaluations of treatment outcomes, since outcomes have sometimes been evaluated by teachers who are aware that a child has been a part of the training program. Of course, this intervention program is still evolving, so the investigators will have opportunities to alter their program and its evaluation according to the needs as they see them.

Anger Coping Training

Perhaps in response to the failure of the social problem-solving training programs to attend to children's interpretations and affect, Lochman and his colleagues have developed and evaluated components of an anger coping program for aggressive boys (Lochman, 1985; Lochman, Burch, Curry, & Lampron, 1984; Lochman, Lampron, Burch, & Curry, 1985; Lochman, Nelson, & Sims, 1981). This program integrates training in the interpretation of problems and the inhibition of impulsive responding with the traditional social problem-solving training program. The basis of the anger coping component of the program is the work of Novaco (1978) on anger control. In a 12-session intervention (Lochman et al., 1981), boys met for 45–60 minutes weekly in groups of four to six with two adult leaders. Groups were conducted at the boys' schools. The sessions focused on seven goals: (1) establishing behavioral management within the groups through rules and contingent reinforcements; (2) teaching boys to use self-statements to inhibit impulsive behavior; (3) teaching boys to identify problems and interpret social cues accurately; (4) encouraging boys to generate alternative solutions and to consider the consequences of the solutions to interpersonal problems (as in the Spivack and Shure program); (5) helping boys learn to control physiological arousal when angry through imitation of effective control displayed on videotapes; (6) helping boys plan and make their own videotape of effective anger control and problem solving; and (7) dialoguing, discussion, and role playing in order to encourage generalization of learned skills to classroom settings. Initial results indicated that second- and third-grade aggressive boys who participated in this program demonstrated reduced aggression on teachers' ratings (Lochman et al., 1981). Controlled studies have indicated that aggressive boys who participated in this program demonstrated greater reductions in aggressive classroom behavior (as observed directly by unbiased adults) and in aggression at home (as rated by parents), in contrast with nontreated controls and boys who participated in a minimal treatment (Lochman et al., 1984). In later work, Lochman has extended the program to 18 sessions and has incorporated a goal-setting component to the treatment. This component was responsible for enhanced generalization of effects. This 18-session program was also more effective in reducing aggression than a cognitively oriented treatment that did not emphasize applications in social situations (Lochman & Curry, 1986). The point of this last study is that the contexts in which cognitive processes are trained is important. Training cognitive skills at impersonal, academic-like tasks is not as effective in changing aggressive behavior as is cognitive training at social tasks.

Limits of the anger coping program include equivocal effects on children's sociometric scores, inadequate follow-ups, and a failure to match aspects of treatment to individual profiles of boys. Like the Spivack and Shure work, however, this work is an example of program development that is still evolving. Lochman has conducted several subanalyses of his program's efficacy that are impressive in their attention to details of the program's administration. For example, he has found that increasing the number of treatment sessions leads to improvements in children's on-task behavior, but has had minimal effects on aggression (Lochman, 1985). Also, he has found that his program is more effective with aggressive boys who are initially deficient in problem-solving skills than with aggressive boys who do not display these deficiencies (Lochman et al., 1985). This finding suggests the importance of matching the treatment to the characteristics of the client. That is, boys who are not deficient in problem-solving skills do not benefit greatly from treatments aimed at improving problem-solving skills. This is an obvious point; however, it is a rare treatment program that attends to this matching. Even Lochman's program has not included this matching.

Coaching

According to Ladd and Mize (1983), few interventions have emphasized all three of the training components that they see as essential aspects of a successful program (i.e., skill knowledge, skill performance, and maintenance/generalization of performance). Those interventions that do emphasize all of these components are called "coaching programs." The term has been selected carefully, for it implies that the coach nurtures, tutors, and mentors the child's skill development. It also emphasizes the skill-enhancing aspect of the intervention. The fundamental aspects of coaching have been outlined by McFall (1976) and were first explored by Gottman et al. (1976), who coached two unpopular third-grade girls in initiating friendships, giving and receiving positive social behaviors, and taking the listener's role. They used videotaped instructions to teach skill knowledge, used role plays and game-like tasks to enhance skill performance, and verbally encouraged generalization. The two girls received higher peer ratings following coaching (relative to two girls in an attention control condition), and these gains were maintained over 9 weeks.

Oden and Asher (1977) have systematized the coaching procedure and have evaluated it in a five-session controlled study with unpopular third- and fourth-graders. In their program, they focus on four behavioral areas that have been found to be critical to social acceptance (participation, cooperation, communication, and validation/support). During each of the first two sessions, children are instructed in each of these four areas (to teach skill knowledge); they practice performance of these skills in an interaction with a classmate; they review their performance with their coach; and they are encouraged to try out these skills in their classrooms (to foster generalization). Even though these four steps (instruction, rehearsal, review, and encouragement of generalization) characterize many behaviorally oriented interventions, the coaching procedure is unique in several respects. Most importantly, the coach emphasizes social skills concepts, rather than discrete behaviors. The coach follows a five-step procedure during the instruction of each concept that demonstrates this emphasis. These five steps are as follows: (1) The child is asked to define the concept (e.g., participation); (2) the child is asked to give examples of the concept; (3) the child is asked to give examples of the antithesis of the concept; (4) the child is asked for more examples and is asked to elaborate these ideas; and (5) the coach then provides additional exemplars. The child is thus undergoing concept learning, rather than the acquisition of discrete behaviors in the absence of a context. A second feature of this procedure is the nature of the relationship between the instructor and the child, as exemplified in the term "coach." The coach is a knowledgeable helper who has a script to follow, but who also attends to the child's particular assets and deficits. Another feature is that different classmate peers serve as partners during the practice, so that the child will be exposed to a variety of classmates, but also so that the classmates will get to see the child behave in a prosocially oriented way. In the last three sessions, coaches focus the child's learning on those areas where that child requires special help. Even though in the original coaching studies the skills coached were not matched to each child's pretreatment performance, the coaching did accommodate individual differences in this respect in the last three sessions. A treatment manual (Oden, Asher, & Hymel, 1977) was written to systematize the intervention.

The initial evaluation indicated that (1) coached children received more positive peer ratings at posttreatment than pretreatment; (2) the gains were greater than those achieved by children in a peer-pairing control condition; and (3) the gains were maintained over a 1-year follow-up. In later reflections, Asher (1984) hypothesized that the efficacy of coaching might have been due to changing the children's goals for peer interaction (from avoidance of peers to an interest in peers). Reorientation of goals presumably altered the children's cognitions in social situations and led to positive changes in social behavior. Direct observations did not detect any behavioral changes specific to the coached children, however.

Since that study, a number of investigators have attempted to refine the coaching procedure in various ways. Hymel and Asher (1977) contrasted the original coaching procedure with one that focused more directly on the individual skill needs of each child. Their attempts to match the treatment with a pretreatment assessment were thus more explicit than had been attempted previously (though the assessment was an informal one). The groups demonstrated equally substantial positive changes in peer ratings at posttreatment and at a 6-month follow-up; however, a peer-pairing control group also demonstrated positive changes. The changes, therefore, could not be attributed to a particular treatment, nor could regression to the mean be ruled out.

One puzzling aspect of the coaching evaluations by Oden and Asher (1977) had been the failure to detect behavioral changes in coached children. The hypothesis behind skills training is that the relation between enhanced social-cognitive skills and enhanced peer status is mediated by positive changes in social behavior. Ladd (1981) hypothesized that Oden and Asher's (1977) failure to detect behavioral changes might have been due to vagueness in defining the behavioral areas being coached and observed. He focused a coaching intervention and evaluation on three specific behavioral areas that had previously been found to represent the behavioral inadequacies of unpopular children (asking questions, leading, and offering support to peers). Ladd matched the focus of intervention to pretreatment deficiencies in these three areas by selecting for intervention only those children who were both unpopular and observed to be deficient in these three areas. Coached children demonstrated significant gains (relative to children receiving an attention control) in peer ratings and in direct observations of two of the three targeted behavioral areas. The hypothesized links between enhanced social-cognitive skills and enhanced social behavior, and between enhanced social behavior and positive sociometric change, were thus shown to be plausible.

Gresham and Nagle (1980) altered the coaching procedure by conducting the intervention in small groups of two or three (rather than individually) and by focusing on 11 different behavioral areas. They tried to determine the potent aspects of coaching by contrasting interventions that emphasized skill knowledge only (a film-mediated modeling condition), traditional coaching, and a combination of modeling and coaching. All three groups demonstrated gains in peer ratings; only the coached children decreased antisocial behaviors, however. Thus, there is partial support for the hypothesis that practice in behavioral enactment and attention to generalization (critical aspects of coaching) enhance the efficacy of intervention over the acquisition of skill knowledge only.

LaGreca and Santogrossi (1980) have made further use of videotape during coaching. Not only did they present models of appropriate behavior via videotape (in a manner similar to that used by O'Connor, 1969); they also videotaped the practice sessions of the coached children and played them back in a later session. This use of videotape followed from the creative work of Chandler (1973). LaGreca and Santogrossi found that the coached children (relative to controls) demonstrated enhanced social knowledge, better skill performance, and higher participation rates in the classroom, but they did not differ from controls in peer-related acceptance.

Conclusions

The social-cognitive skills training procedures have attempted to enhance generalization of the effects found in behavioral interventions by focusing on underlying processes that are hypothesized to be responsible for competent behavior. Descriptive and experimental studies (reviewed by Dodge, 1986; Rubin & Krasnor, 1986) have found that numerous social information-processing skills (e.g., problem solving, anger control, and social knowledge) are related to positive peer status, so the skills training procedures have focused on teaching children these skills. Successful outcomes have been reported in a large number of studies— enough to permit one to conclude that this general approach has merit. The potential for lasting effects that generalize to novel situations is obviously much greater for the skills training approaches than for the behavioral approaches. In fact, the operant approaches are based on a theory suggesting that generalization of effects to an environment in which reinforcements are not controlled in a desired manner is not even hypothesized. Since many socially rejected children are raised in environments in which deviant behaviors are modeled and reinforced (Pettit, Dodge, & Brown, 1987), short-term behavioral interventions are not likely to yield lasting and generalized effects for many children. The skills training approaches are directed at component skills that presumably guide behavioral performance across all situations, so maintenance and generalization may be more likely. The theory is intriguing, and the findings are encouraging.

The limits of these approaches thus far are obvious, however. The findings have not been uniformly favorable, nor have they been consistent. Some investigators report positive changes in behavioral performance with no change in peer perceptions, whereas other investigators (or the same persons in different studies) report the opposite. The role of the peer group in these interventions thus has not been resolved. Second, even though the theoretical model guiding this work posits a link between a child's skills deficits and his or her peer acceptance, few attempts have been made to match an intervention to an assessment of a child's needs. Third, skills training interventions assume a level of cognitive-developmental sophistication that may not be warranted for some children. In order for a child to benefit from most skills training interventions, which focus on *concepts* of social interaction and generic skills, the child must be capable of representational thought and concrete operations. Some groups of targeted children, such as preschoolers and mentally retarded children, may be incapable of benefiting from this intervention. Of course, it may be possible first to teach these children the skills that are prerequisites for effective social-cognitive skill acquisition. Through a thorough task analysis of the requisite skills for effective social interaction, one may become more cognizant of the kinds of skills that must be taught to a particular child. The general point here is that most interventions fail to take adequate account of the developmental level of a child in designing an intervention program. Greater attention to level of development is obviously needed. Fourth, little evidence has been reported that supports the theoretical model of social-cognitive skills as a mechanism of competent behavior and as a mediator of peer acceptance.

That is, few attempts have been made to link directly changes in skills to changes in behavior and peer acceptance. Such process research is badly needed in this area.

CURRENT AND FUTURE ISSUES IN SKILLS TRAINING RESEARCH

Four issues that highlight recent efforts in skills training research and that suggest directions for future efforts are discussed briefly here. These issues include the role of the peer group in skills training and behavioral change; the importance of matching interventions to children's profiles; and testing the skills model through process research and the role of emotion in skills training.

The Role of the Peer Group

Beginning with Wahler (1967), a number of researchers have noted the value of peers in altering the behavior of socially incompetent children. Wahler taught peers to direct attention to a targeted child contingently—that is, in response to specific behaviors. The outcome was positive change in the behavior of the targeted child. Since then, Strain and colleagues (Odom & Strain, 1984; Strain et al., 1977; Strain & Timm, 1974) have effectively used peers as behavior change agents for socially withdrawn children. Even though Odom and DeKlyen (in press) have noted that these studies have not typically found cross-setting changes in the targeted child's behavior and have not included sociometric ratings as measures of change, the point has been made that the peer group may be a powerful agent of behavioral control.

Another reason for attending to the peer group, of course, is that acceptance by the peer group is a defining characteristic of social competence. A number of studies (e.g., Hymel & Asher, 1977; LaGreca & Santogrossi, 1980) have reported positive changes in a child's behavioral performance through intervention without accompanying gains in peer acceptance. These findings make sense within the social skills model only if the concepts of time and peer group biases are added to the model. That is, it may be possible that the effects of skills training and behavioral improvements on peers' acceptance are delayed until the peer group can overcome its perceptual biases against rejected children. Biases (in the

form of stereotypes and negative evaluations in the absence of appropriate data) have been found toward rejected children in numerous studies (Dodge, 1980; Hymel, 1986; Koslin, Haarlow, Karlins, & Pargament, 1968). Once peers develop a perception of a child as socially incompetent, they may fail to detect changes in the child's behavior that may occur as a function of intervention. The power of these reputation effects is apparent to all children and is part of the reason why children fear social rejection so strongly, particularly in adolescence. They fear that rejection at one point in time may brand them as unacceptable for all time. Given the effects of reputation and expectations on children's social perceptions, this fear may not be totally unfounded. The hope of clinicians teaching children social skills has been, of course, that major, sustained behavioral changes in a child will eventually be recognized by the peer group. Given that actual behavioral changes may go undetected by peers (Campbell & Yarrow, 1961), some intervention researchers have attempted to alter peers' perceptions more directly by including the peer group in the design of the intervention.

The importance of intervening directly with the perceptions by the peer group may have been understood in the early coaching efforts by Asher, even though his writings do not emphasize this aspect. Asher gave each coached child an opportunity to interact in a supervised prosocial manner with each of six peers from his or her classroom. In all cases, this was an enjoyable experience for both the target child and the peer. Thus, the coaching experience was confounded with positive peer interaction. It is possible that a potent aspect of the coaching procedure is this positive contact, which enables the peer to come to a new perception of the target child. The contact alone cannot account for the effects, since one of the control conditions consisted of pairing the target child with a peer (though without coaching). Whether the peer contact is an essential aspect of coaching is not clear, however. Chandler's (1973) intervention also confounded social skills training with a positive peer group experience. In that study, children made videotapes in small groups as a way of teaching role-taking skills.

Bierman and Furman (1984) separated the effects of coaching and a peer group experience in a simple factorial experiment in which rejected children were randomly assigned to one of four treatment conditions: (1) individual coaching; (2) a peer group experience in which the target child participated with two nontarget peers in making films (following Chandler, 1973); (3) the peer group experience with coaching; and (4) no treatment. All treatments involved 10 sessions lasting 30 minutes each, so the length of treatment was controlled. The coaching intervention focused on training the conversational skills of self-expression, questioning, and leadership bids. Treatment efficacy was evaluated through performance on a dyadic task, observations of behavior in the classroom, and a written test. Other measures included peer ratings and observations of peer interaction rates.

The findings indicated remarkable specificity in the impact of interventions. The two groups that received coaching improved their conversational skills, whereas the other two groups did not demonstrate any change in these measures. The two groups that participated in a positive peer group experience received improved peer acceptance scores at the end of treatment, in contrast with the two groups that did not receive a peer group experience (even when peers who did not participate in the peer group experience were the only raters). The changes in peer acceptance were short-lived, however. A 6-week follow-up indicated that the children who received only the peer group experience (without coaching) returned to baseline in peer acceptance. The only group to demonstrate sustained improvements in both conversational skills and peer acceptance was the group receiving coaching plus a positive peer group experience. Coaching was thus found to be effective in improving rejected children's conversational skills, but coaching in the context of a positive peer group experience was necessary to bring about sustained improvements in peer acceptance. Peer group experience by itself was not sufficient to account for these effects. This study very neatly demonstrates that intervention may be necessary at two levels in order to yield lasting changes. Rejected children may require a structured positive experience with their peer group in order to break down stereotypic and reputational barriers on the parts of both these children and their peers; however, such an experience is not sufficient to bring about lasting effects, since (presumably) their poor skills will again become evident to the peer group. Therefore, skills training may be an essential component of a program to enhance peer acceptance.

Matching Intervention with a Child's Skills Deficits

Two key features of the recent intervention studies by Ladd (1981) and Bierman and colleagues (e.g., Bierman, Miller, & Stabb, 1987) suggest the importance of matching treatments to skills profiles displayed by rejected children. First, children have been selected for an intervention on the basis of specific skill deficits that match the goals of the intervention. For example, Ladd (1981) designed a coaching intervention aimed at training three skills (asking questions, leading peers, and making supportive statements). He selected as participants only those rejected children who displayed behavioral deficits in these three areas. Thus, the intervention matched the needs of those children. By attending to the match between skills deficits and training offered, Ladd was successful in improving the social status of the coached children, and the improvements were maintained at a 4-week follow-up. The second feature is the degree of specificity found in the positive effects of skills training interventions. Coaching particular skills seems to lead to improvements in those skills and not necessarily to improvements in any other skill areas. If the trained skills have been related to the low social status of the targeted children, then enhancing those skills will lead to improvements in social status.

These features are exemplified in a study by Coie and Krehbiel (1984), in which they identified for treatment rejected boys who demonstrated poor academic achievement. Low achievement was thought to be related to off-task disruptive behavior, which in turn was thought to be related to the low social status experienced by these boys. They assigned these boys to one of four conditions: (1) an academic tutoring intervention; (2) a coaching intervention similar to Ladd's (1981); (3) academic tutoring plus coaching; or (4) a no-attention control. Since these rejected boys were all functioning poorly in academic skills, the academic tutoring intervention was most closely suited to their needs. In addition, the tutoring intervention focused even more specifically on those academic areas in which a particular child displayed deficits (see Wallach & Wallach, 1976, for a description of this matching). Findings indicated that the tutored children displayed higher academic achievement scores (demonstrating that the intervention was successful in its proximal goal). Tutored children also demonstrated lower rates of off-task behavior. Finally, these children received higher peer acceptance ratings, which were maintained at the 1-year follow-up. The closeness of the matching of the type of intervention to the type of skill deficit displayed by a child may be responsible for these impressive long-term gains in peer acceptance.

These matching studies suggest a strategy for assessment and treatment planning that, to my knowledge, has not yet been systematically implemented and evaluated. The strategy is as follows. Once the incompetent child is identified (through peer assessments, direct observations, or any other means), the clinician conducts an assessment of the behavioral domains in which the child displays deviant behavior. These domains are problematic tasks that the child is unable to accomplish effectively (e.g., entering a group of peers, listening to a peer, and engaging cooperatively in a turn-taking game). Next, the clinician identifies the important skill components of effective behavior at each of these tasks (e.g., accurately interpreting peers' intentions, generating competent responses to the task, and anticipating consequences of various behaviors) and conducts a comprehensive assessment of these skills. Once the social-cognitive skills are identified within specific behavioral domains, the clinician's task is to teach these skills to the targeted child, through coaching or whatever other means. Adjunctive components of a treatment, such as peer group involvement, may be added. Posttreatment evaluation is conducted by means of a backward movement through these steps. That is, first, the clinician assesses the social-cognitive skills that have been trained, to assure that the treatment has been effective in reaching its most proximal goal. Next, the clinician assesses the child's behavior in the critical domains, to evaluate the degree to which the skills training has led to changes in social behavior. Finally, the clinician evaluates the child's social status, to determine whether behavioral changes have led to improved social relationships and status.

Testing the Skills Model through Process Research

The stages of assessment, treatment, and evaluation proposed above are predicated on hypotheses concerning the processes of change during skills training. In most studies, these processes are not evaluated directly; that is, the clinician evaluates only the global impact of the treatment on a child's status. Clearly, the clinician must evaluate each step in the hypothesized chain, in order to be confident of the skills model and to be sure that the treatment is operating in its proposed manner. Therefore, examination of these processes of change is a high priority for researchers in this area, propelling this kind of research to the leading edge of the field.

A recent study by Bierman (1986) exemplifies this kind of work. She re-evaluated the data that she and Furman had collected (Bierman & Furman, 1984), with the goal of testing several hypotheses concerning the processes involved in change in that study. These data included behavioral performance measures during treatment sessions, peer responses during treatment, behavior in the classroom, and sociometric assessments. First, she found that children who were coached in conversational skills improved their display of these skills from the 6th to the 10th sessions of treatment, beyond any changes displayed by children who received a different treatment. Next, she found that coached children received more positive behavioral responses from peers during the last treatment sessions than did children in a different treatment, and that the peer responses for the coached children became more positive from the 6th to the 10th sessions. Following the hypothesized chain, she next found that enhanced skill at conversation was directly related to more positive responses from peers during treatment. Also, enhancement of conversational skills and positive peer responses during treatment were significantly and positively correlated to improvements in children's social-interactive behavior in the lunchroom peer group. Finally, improvements in conversational skills and in peer responses during treatment were positively correlated with sociometric scores received at posttreatment and at follow-up. These findings held for ratings received from the peers involved in the treatment, as well as for ratings from other peers who were not involved in treatment. The chain of hypothesized processes of change was thus supported almost completely. These findings constitute strong support for the skills training mechanism of positive change in treatment, and therefore for a social skills model of social competence.

Considering the Role of Emotion in Skills Training

Thus far, the current presentation of children's social-interactive behavior and interventions to enhance social skills has lacked attention to a child's transient emotional state. These processes have been described as if affective factors, such as self-efficacy, emotional states, and social anxiety, are minimally important. Such a conclusion is obviously incorrect. A child's self-efficacy probably plays a reciprocally influential role in social performance, in that social failures can both reduce self-esteem and be the consequence of low self-esteem. Likewise, a child's emotional state has been shown to play an influential role in the performance of socially competent behavior. Negative emotional states, such as anxiety, anger, and fear, can have an adverse impact on a child's accuracy of problem solving and cognitive performance (Masters, Felleman, & Barden, 1981), and may interfere with a child's learning of social skills as well. Understanding a child's emotional state during social skills training thus may be an essential aspect of effective intervention.

A recent study (Dodge & Somberg, 1987) illustrates this point. We hypothesized that aggressive children would be particularly vulnerable to the adverse impact of a negative emotional state. We examined the social-cognitive performance of aggressive and nonaggressive children under conditions of relaxation and emotional anxiety. The condition of emotional anxiety was manipulated experimentally through an induction that led children to believe that they were about to interact with a peer who might cause a conflict with them. This induction was carried out because it is in these circumstances that children are typically called on to perform in peer interactions. Assessment (and training) of social skills in relaxed circumstances may not adequately represent the actual conditions under which performance occurs. The measure of social-cognitive performance was a measure of children's accuracy at the detection of intention cues using videotaped stimuli. Under the relaxed conditions, the nonaggressive children performed slightly more accurately than did the aggressive children, as had been found in previous studies (Dodge et al., 1984). Under the anxiety-provoking condition, however, the difference in performance between the two groups became significantly greater. That is, the anxiety-arousing stimulus had no discernible impact on the performance of nonaggressive children, whereas it had a clear adverse impact on performance of aggressive children. Thus, the social performance of aggressive children may be hindered under conditions of negative emotional states.

These findings suggest that interventions designed to enhance social skills must attend to the emotional circumstances in which children will be called on to acquire and perform these skills. Most interventions are carried out in "safe" and sterile environments (such as the therapy room). Such an intervention may not have effects that generalize to the emotionally charged playground settings of children's peer interactions. Interventions must be developed that can be implanted on the playground, or at least must have effects that will generalize to emotionally charged circumstances. Very little research effort has been devoted to this problem, so it is an area on which attention should be focused in the future.

FINAL COMMENT

It seems reasonable to conclude that multicomponent interventions are most likely to yield lasting positive changes in children's social status. Operantly oriented interventions may lead to behavioral changes in the environment in which the contingencies are applied, but because these interventions do not teach children more general concepts, cross-setting generalization has been disappointing. Likewise, interventions aimed solely at the peer group may lead to temporary improvements in peers' acceptance of a child, but when the peers learn that the target child has not changed in his or her behavior, those peers will renew their rejection of that child. Lasting success has been reported for some skills training interventions, particularly when the peer group has also been involved. Thus, the most successful interventions have been those in which both the rejected child and the peer group are targeted for treatment.

Examination of the process of change during intervention has led to conclusions that are consistent with a skills model of social rejection. That is, those children who improve in basic social skills during treatment are the ones who are most likely to improve in peer status. Of course, numerous alternative explanations could be applied to these findings (including the notion that skills changes co-occur with status changes but are not responsible for the changes). Still, process research of this kind is quite likely to clarify the nature of social relationships problems among children, and therefore this kind of research is also quite likely to yield important findings concerning the nature of behavioral and status changes during treatment. This kind of research ought to become the standard in the field.

REFERENCES

Achenbach, T. M., & Edelbrock, C. (1981). Behavioral problems and competencies reported by parents of normal and disturbed children aged four through sixteen. *Monographs of the Society for Research in Child Development*, 46, (Serial No. 188).

Allen, K. E., Hart, B., Buell, J. S., Harris, F. R., & Wolf, M. M. (1964). Effects of social reinforcement on isolate behavior of a nursery school child. *Child Development*, 35, 511–518.

American Psychiatric Association. (1987). *Diagnostic and statistical manual of mental disorders* (3rd ed., rev). Washington, DC: Author.

Asarnow, J. R., & Callan, J. W. (1985). Boys with peer adjustment problems: Social cognitive processes. *Journal of Consulting and Clinical Psychology*, 53, 80–87.

Asher, S. R. (1984, October). *Social skills training with unpopular children*. Colloquium delivered at Indiana University, Bloomington.

Asher, S. R., & Hymel, S. (1981). Children's social competence in peer relations: Sociometric and behavioral assessment. In J. D. Wine & M. D. Smye (Eds.), *Social competence* (pp. 125–157). New York: Guilford Press.

Asher, S. R., Markell, R. A., & Hymel, S. (1981. Identifying children at risk in peer relations: A critique of the rate-of-interaction approach to assessment. *Child Development*, 52, 1239–1245.

Asher, S. R., & Wheeler, V. (1985) Children's loneliness: A comparison of rejected and neglected peer status. *Journal of Consulting and Clinical Psychology*, 53, 500–505.

Baer, D. M., & Wolf, M. M. (1970). The entry into natural communities of reinforcement. In R. Ulrich, T. Stachnek, & J. Mabry (Eds.), *Control of human behavior*. (Vol. 2, pp. 319–324). Glenview, IL: Scott, Foresman.

Bierman, K. L. (1986). Process of change during social skills training with preadolescents and its relation to treatment outcome. *Child Development*, 57, 230–240.

Bierman, K. L., & Furman, W. F. (1984). The effects of social skills training and peer involvement on the social adjustment of preadolescents. *Child Development*, 55, 151–162.

Bierman, K. L., Miller, C. L., & Stabb, S. D. (1987). Improving the social behavior and peer acceptance of rejected boys: Effects of social skills training with instructions and prohibitions. *Journal of Consulting and Clinical Psychology*, 55, 194–200.

Bornstein, M. R., Bellack, A. S., & Hersen, M. (1977). Social skills training for unassertive children: A multiple baseline analysis. *Journal of Applied Behavior Analysis*, 10, 183–195.

Brown, P., & Elliott, R. (1965). Control of aggression in a nursery school class. *Journal of Experimental Child Psychology*, 2, 103–107.

Buswell, N. M. (1953). The relationship between the social structure of the classroom and the academic success of the pupils. *Journal of Experimental Education*, 22, 37–52.

Campbell, J. D., & Yarrow, M. R. (1961). Perceptual and behavioral correlates of social effectiveness. *Sociometry*, 24, 1–20.

Chandler, M. J. (1973). Egocentrism and antisocial behavior: The assessment and training of social perspective-taking skills. *Developmental Psychology*, 9, 326–332.

Chandler, M. J., Greenspan, S., & Barenboim, C. (1974). Assessment and training of role-taking and referential communication skills in institutionalized emotionally disturbed children. *Developmental Psychology*, 10, 546–553.

Chittendon, G. F. (1942). An experimental study in measuring and modifying assertive behavior in young children. *Monographs of the Society for Research in Child Development*, 7. (Serial No. 31).

Coie, J. D., & Dodge, K. A. (1983). Continuity of children's social status: A five-year longitudinal study. *Merrill–Palmer Quarterly*, 29, 261–282.

Coie, J. D., Dodge, K. A., & Coppotelli, H. (1982). Dimensions and types of social status: A cross-age perspective. *Developmental Psychology*, 18, 557–570.

Coie, J. D., Dodge, K. A., & Kupersmidt, J. (in press). Group behavior and social status. In S. R. Asher & J. D. Coie (Eds.), *Peer rejection in childhood: Origins, consequences, and modifications*. New York: Cambridge University Press.

Coie, J. D., & Kupersmidt, J. (1983). A behavior analysis of emerging social status in boys' groups. *Child Development*, 54, 1400–1416.

Coie, J. D., & Krehbiel, G. (1984). Effects of academic tutoring on the social status of low-achieving, socially rejected children. *Child Development*, 55, 1465–1478.

Combs, M. P., & Slaby, D. A. (1978). Social skills training with children. In B. Lahey & A. Kazdin (Eds.), *Advances in clinical child psychology* (Vol. 1, pp. 161–121). New York: Plenum.

Cooke, T. P., & Apolloni, T. (1976). Developing positive social–emotional behaviors: A study of training and generalization effects. *Journal of Applied Behavior Analysis*, 9, 65–78.

Cowen, E. L., Pederson, A., Babigian, H., Izzo, L. D., & Trost, M. A. (1973). Long-term follow-up of early detected vulnerable children. *Journal of Consulting and Clinical Psychology*, 41, 438–446.

Dodge, K. A. (1980). Social cognition and children's aggressive behavior. *Child Development*, 51, 162–170.

Dodge, K. A. (1983). Behavioral antecedents of peer social status. *Child Development*, 54, 1386–1399.

Dodge, K. A. (1986). A social information processing model of social competence in children. In M. Perlmutter (Ed.), *Minnesota Symposiom in Child Psychology* (Vol. 18, pp. 77–125). Hillsdale, NJ: Erlbaum.

Dodge, K. A., Coie, J. D., & Brakke, N. P. (1983). Behavior patterns of socially rejected and neglected pre-adolescents: The roles of social approach and aggression. *Journal of Abnormal Child Psychology, 10*, 389–410.

Dodge, K. A., McClaskey, C. L., & Feldman, E. (1985). A situational approach to the assessment of social competence in children. *Journal of Consulting and Clinical Psychology, 53*, 344–353.

Dodge, K. A., Murphy, R. R., & Buchsbaum, K. (1984). The assessment of intention-cue detection skills in children: Implications for developmental psychopathology. *Child Development, 55*, 163–173.

Dodge, K. A., Schlundt, D. G., Schocken, I., & Delugach, J. D. (1983). Social competence and children's sociometric status: The role of peer group entry strategies. *Merrill–Palmer Quarterly, 29*, 309–336.

Dodge, K. A., & Somberg, D. (1987). Hostile attributional biases in aggressive boys are exacerbated under conditions of threat. *Child Development, 58*, 213–224.

Drabman, R., & Spitalnik, R. (1973). Social isolation as a punishment procedure: A controlled study. *Journal of Experimental Psychology, 16*, 236–249.

Drabman, R., Spitalnik, R., Spitalnik, K. (1974). Sociometric and disruptive behavior as a function of four types of token reinforcement programs. *Journal of Applied Behavior Analysis, 7*, 93–101.

Evers, W., & Schwarz, S. A. (1973). Modifying social withdrawal in preschoolers: The effects of filmed modeling and teacher praise. *Journal of Abnormal Child Psychology, 1*, 248–256.

Evers-Pasquale, W., & Sherman, M. (1975). The reward value of peers: A variable influencing the efficacy of filmed modeling in modifying social isolation in preschoolers. *Journal of Abnormal Child Psychology, 3*, 179–189.

Feldman, E., & Dodge, K. A. (1987). Social information processing biases and deficits in rejected and neglected boys and girls. *Journal of Abnormal Child Psychology, 15*, 211–227.

Freedman, B. J., Rosenthal, L., Donahoe, C. P., Jr., Schlundt, D. G., & McFall, R. M. (1978). A social–behavioral analysis of skill deficits in delinquent and nondelinquent adolescent boys. *Journal of Consulting and Clinical Psychology, 46*, 1448–1462.

French, D. C., & Tyne, T. F. (1982). The identification and treatment of children with peer-relationship difficulties. In J. P. Curran & P. M. Monti (Eds.), *Social skills training: A practical handbook for assessment and treatment* (pp. 280–312). New York: Guilford Press.

Furman, W., Rahe, D. F., & Hartup, W. W. (1979). Rehabilitation of socially withdrawn preschool children through mixed-age socialization. *Child Development, 50*, 915–922.

Goldfried, M. R., & D'Zurilla, T. J. (1969). A behavioral-analytic model for assessing competence. In C. D. Spielberger (Ed.), *Current topics in clinical and community psychology* (Vol. 1, pp. 151–196). New York: Academic Press.

Gottman, J. M. (1977). The effects of a modeling film on social isolation in preschool children: A methodological investigation. *Journal of Abnormal Child Psychology, 5*, 69–78.

Gottman, J. M. (1983). How children become friends. *Monographs of the Society for Research in Child Development, 48*, (3 Serial No. 201).

Gottman, J. M., Gonso, J., & Schuler, P. (1976). Teaching social skills to isolated children. *Journal of Abnormal Child Psychology, 4*, 179–197.

Gottman, J. M., Gonso, J., & Rasmussen, B. (1975). Social interaction, social competence, and friendship in children. *Child Development, 46*, 709–718.

Greenwood, C. R., & Hops, H. (1981). Group-oriented contingencies and peer behavior change. In P. Strain (Ed.), *The utilization of classroom peers as behavior change agents* (pp. 189–259). New York: Plenum.

Greenwood, C. R., Walker, H. M., Todd, N. M., & Hops, H. (1979). Selecting a cost-effective screening measure for the assessment of preschool social withdrawal. *Journal of Applied Behavior Analysis, 12*, 639–652.

Greenwood, C. R., Walker, H. M., Todd, N. M., Hops, H. (1981). Normative and descriptive analysis of preschool freeplay social interaction rates. *Journal of Pediatric Psychology, 4*, 343–367.

Gresham, F. M., & Nagle, R. J. (1980). Social skills training with children: Responsiveness to modeling and coaching as a function of peer orientation. *Journal of Consulting and Clinical Psychology, 18*, 718–729.

Gronlund, N. E. (1959). *Sociometry in the classroom.* New York: Harper & Brothers.

Hart, B. M., Reynolds, N. J., Baer, D. M., Brawley, E. R., & Harris, F. R. (1968). Effects of contingent and noncontingent social reinforcement on the cooperative play of a preschool child. *Journal of Applied Behavior Analysis, 1*, 73–76.

Hops, H., & Greenwood, C. R. (1988). Social skills deficits. In E. J. Mash & L. G. Terdal (Eds.), *Behavioral assessment of childhood disorders* (2nd ed., pp. 263–316). New York: Guilford Press.

Hops, H., Walker, H. M., & Greenwood, C. R. (1979). PEERS: A program for remediating social withdrawal in school. In L. A. Hamerlynck (Ed.), *Behavioral systems for the developmentally disabled in school and home environments* (pp. 48–88). New York: Brunner/Mazel.

Hymel, S. (1986). Interpretations of peer behavior: Affective bias in childhood and adolescence. *Child Development, 57*, 431–445.

Hymel, S., & Asher, S. R. (1977, April). *Assessment and training of isolated children's social skills.* Paper presented at the biennial meeting of the Society for Research in Child Development, New Orleans. (ERIC Document Reproduction Service No. ED 136-930)

Jacobs, M. A., Muller, J. J., Anderson, J., & Skinner, J. R. (1972). Therapeutic expectations, premorbid adjustment, and manifest distress levels as predictors of improvement in hospitalized patients. *Journal of Consulting and Clinical Psychology, 39*, 455–461.

Jacobs, M. A., Muller, J. J., Anderson, J., & Skinner, J. R. (1973). Prediction of improvement in coping with pathology in hospitalized psychiatric patients: A replication study. *Journal of Consulting and Clinical Psychology, 40*, 343–349.

Jakibchuk, Z., & Smeriglio, V. L. (1976). The influence of symbolic modeling on social behavior of preschool children with low levels of social responsiveness. *Child Development, 47*, 838–841.

Kazdin, A. E. (1985). *Treatment of antisocial behavior in children and adolescents.* Homewood, IL: Dorsey Press.

Keller, M. F., & Carlson, P. M. (1974). The use of symbolic modeling to promote social skills in children with low levels of social responsiveness. *Child Development, 45,* 912–919.

Kelly, J. A. (1982). *Social-skills training: A practical guide for interventions.* New York: Springer.

Koch, H. L. (1933). Popularity among preschool children: Some related factors and a technique for its measurement. *Child Development, 4,* 164–175.

Kohn, M. (1977). *Social competence, symptoms, and underachievement in childhood: A longitudinal perspective.* Washington, DC: V. H. Winston.

Kohn, M., & Clausen, J. (1955). Social isolation and schizophrenia. *American Sociological Review, 20,* 265–273.

Koslin, B. L., Haarlow, R. N., Karlins, M., & Pargament, R. (1968). Predicting group status from members' cognitions. *Sociometry, 31,* 64–75.

Krasnor, L. R., & Rubin, K. H. (1981). The assessment of social problem-solving skills in young children. In T. Merluzzi, C. Glass, & M. Genest (Eds.), *Cognitive assessment* (pp. 452–476). New York: Guilford Press.

Kupersmidt, J. (1983, April). *Predicting delinquency and academic problems from childhood peer status.* Paper presented at the biennial meeting of the Society for Research in Child Development, Detroit.

Kupersmidt, J., Coie, J. D., & Dodge, K. A. (in press). Predicting disorder from peer social problems. In S. R. Asher & J. D. Coie (Eds.), *Peer rejection in childhood: Origins, consequences, and intervention.* New York: Cambridge University Press.

Ladd, G. W. (1981). Effectiveness of a social learning method for enhancing children's social interactions and peer acceptance. *Child Development, 52,* 171–178.

Ladd, G. W., & Asher, S. R. (1985). Social skills training and children's peer relations. In L. L'Abate & M. Milan (Eds.), *Handbook of social skills training and research* (pp. 219–244). New York: Wiley.

Ladd, G. W., & Mize, J. (1983). A cognitive–social learning model of social skill training. *Psychological Review, 90,* 127–157.

LaGreca, A. M., & Mesibov, G. B. (1979). Social skills intervention with learning disabled children: Selecting skills and implementing training. *Journal of Clinical Child Psychology, 8,* 234–241.

LaGreca, A. M., & Santogrossi, D. A. (1980). Social skills training with elementary school students: A behavioral group approach. *Journal of Consulting and Clinical Psychology, 48,* 220–227.

Lochman, J. E. (1985). Effects of different treatment lengths in cognitive behavioral interventions with aggressive boys. *Child Psychiatry and Human Development, 16,* 45–56.

Lochman, J. E., Burch, P. R., Curry, J. F., & Lampron, L. B. (1984). Treatment and generalization effects of cognitive–behavioral and goal-setting interventions with aggressive boys. *Journal of Consulting and Clinical Psychology, 52,* 915–916.

Lochman, J. E., & Curry, J. F. (1986). Effects of social problem-solving training and self-instruction training with aggressive boys. *Journal of Clinical Child Psychology, 15,* 159–164.

Lochman, J. Ed., Lampron, L. B., Burch, P. R., & Curry, J. F. (1985). Client characteristics associated with behavior change for treated and untreated aggressive boys. *Journal of Abnormal Child Psychology, 13,* 527–538.

Lochman, J. E., Nelson, W. M., III, & Sims, J. P. (1981). A cognitive behavioral program for use with aggressive children. *Journal of Clinical Child Psychology, 10,* 146–148.

Masters, J. C., Felleman, E. S., & Barden, R. C. (1981). Experimental studies of affective states in children. In B. Lahey & A. E. Kazdin (Eds.), *Advances in clinical child psychology* (Vol. 4, pp. 91–114). New York: Plenum.

McFall, R. M. (1976). *Behavioral training: A skill-acquisition approach to clinical problems.* Morristown, NJ: General Learning Press.

McFall, R. M. (1982). A review and reformulation of the concept of social skills. *Behavioral Assessment, 4,* 1–33.

McFall, R. M., & Dodge, K. A. (1982). Self-management and interpersonal skills learning. In P. Karoly & F. H. Kanfer (Eds.), *Self-management and behavior change: From theory to practice* (pp. 353–392). New York: Pergamon Press.

Newcomb, A. F., & Bukowski, W. M. (1983). Social impact and social preference as determinants of children's peer group status. *Developmental Psychology, 9,* 856–867.

Novaco, R. W. (1978). Anger and coping with stress: Cognitive behavioral intervention. In J. P. Foreyt & D. P. Rathjen (Eds.), *Cognitive behavioral therapy: Research and application* (pp. 135–173). New York: Plenum.

O'Connor, R. D. (1969). Modification of social withdrawal through symbolic modeling. *Journal of Applied Behavior Analysis, 2,* 15–22.

O'Connor, R. D. (1972). Relative efficacy of modeling, shaping, and the combined procedures for modification of social withdrawal. *Journal of Abnormal Psychology, 79,* 327–334.

Oden, S. L., & Asher, S. R. (1977). Coaching children in social skills for friendship making. *Child Development, 48,* 495–506.

Oden, S. L., Asher, S. R., & Hymel, S. (1977). *Procedures for coaching isolated children in social skills.* Unpublished manuscript.

Odom. S. L., & DeKlyen, M. (in press). Social withdrawal in childhood. In G. Adams (Ed.), *Behavior disorders: Theory and characteristics.* Englewood Cliffs, NJ: Prentice-Hall.

Odom, S. L., Strain, P. S. (1984). Peer-mediated approaches to promoting children's social interaction: A review. *American Journal of Orthopsychiatry, 54,* 544–557.

Paine, S. C., Hops, H., Walker, H. M., Greenwood, C. R., Fleishman, D. H., & Guild, J. J. (1982). Repeated treatment effects: A study of maintaining behavior change in socially withdrawn children. *Behavior Modification, 6,* 171–199.

Parker, J. G., & Asher, S. R. (1987). Predicting long term outcomes from peer rejection: Studies of dropping out, delinquency, and adult psychopathology. *Psychological Bulletin, 102,* 357–389.

Parker, J. G., & Gottman, J. M. (1985, April). *Making friends with an extraterrestrial: Conversational skills and friendship formation in young children.* Paper presented at the biennial meeting of the Society for Research in Child Development, Toronto.

Pellegrini, D. (1985). Social cognition and competence in middle childhood. *Child Development, 56,* 253–264.

Pettit, G. S., Dodge, K. A., & Brown, M. (1988). Early family experience, social problem solving patterns, and children's social competence. *Child Development, 59,* 107–120.

Robins, L. N. (1966). *Deviant children grown up*. Baltimore: Williams & Wilkins.

Roff, M. (1961). Childhood social relations and young adult bad conduct. *Journal of Abnormal and Social Psychology, 65,* 333–337.

Roff, M. (1963). Childhood social interactions and young psychosis. *Journal of Clinical Psychology, 19,* 152–157.

Roff, M., Sells, S. B., & Golden, M. (1972). *Social adjustment and personality development in children.* Minneapolis: University of Minnesota Press.

Rubin, K. H., & Krasnor, L. R. (1986). Social-cognitive and social behavioral perspectives on problem solving. In M. Perlmutter (Ed.), *Minnesota Symposium on Child Psychology* (Vol. 18, pp. 1–65). Hillsdale, NJ: Erlbaum.

Shure, M. B. (1980). Real-life problem solving for parents and children: An approach to social competence. In D. P. Rathjen & J. P. Foreyt (Eds.), *Social competence: Interventions for children and adults* (pp. 54–68). New York: Pergamon Press.

Shure, M. B. (1981). Social competence as a problem-solving skill. In J. D. Wine & M. D. Smye (Eds.), *Social competence* (pp. 158–188). New York: Guilford Press.

Shure, M. B., & Spivack, G. (1978). *Problem-solving techniques in child-rearing.* San Francisco: Jossey-Bass.

Speltz, M. L., Moore, J. E., & McReynolds, W. T. (1979). A comparison of standardized and interdependent group contingencies in a classroom setting. *Behavior Therapy, 10,* 219–226.

Spivack, G., Platt, J. J., & Shure, M. B. (1976). *The problem-solving approach to adjustment: A guide to research and intervention.* San Francisco: Jossey-Bass.

Spivack, G., & Shure, M. B. (1974). *Social adjustment of young children: A cognitive approach to solving real-life problems.* San Francisco: Jossey-Bass.

Stengel, E. (1971). *Suicide and attempted suicide.* Harmondsworth, England: Penguin.

Strain, P. S. (1983). Identification of social skills curriculum targets for severely handicapped children in mainstreamed preschools. *Applied Research in Mental Retardation, 4,* 369–382.

Strain, P. S., Odom, S. L., & McConnell, S. R. (1984). Promoting social reciprocity of exceptional children: Identification, target skill selection, and interventions. *Remedial and Special Education, 5,* 21–28.

Strain, P. S., Shores, R. E., & Timm, M. A. (1977). Effects of peer social initiations on the behavior of withdrawn preschool children. *Journal of Applied Behavior Analysis, 10,* 189–198.

Strain, P. S., & Timm, M. A. (1974). An experimental analysis of social interaction between a behaviorally disordered preschool child and her classroom peers. *Journal of Applied Behavior Analysis, 7,* 583–590.

Timm, M. A., Strain, P. S., & Eller, P. H. (1979). Effects of systematic, response dependent fading and thinning procedures on the maintenance of child–child interaction. *Journal of Applied Behavior Analysis, 12,* 208.

Ullman, C. A. (1957). Teachers, peers, and tests as predictors of adjustment. *Journal of Educational Psychology, 48,* 257–267.

Wahler, R. G. 91967). Child–child interactions in free field settings: Some experimental analyses. *Journal of Experimental Child Psychology, 5,* 278–293.

Walker, H. M. (1983). *Walker Behavior Problem Identification Checklist, revised 1983.* Los Angeles: Western Psychological Services.

Walker, H. M., & Hops, H. (1973). The use of group and individual reinforcement contingencies in the modification of social withdrawal. In L. Hamerlynck, L. Handy, & E. Mash (Eds.), *Behavior change: Methodology, concepts, and practice* (pp. 269–307). Champaign, IL: Research Press.

Walker, H. M., Hops, H., Greenwood, C. R., & Todd, N. (1979). Differential effects of reinforcing topographic components of free play social interaction: Analysis and direct replication. *Behavior Modification, 3,* 291–321.

Wallach, M. A., & Wallach, L. (1976). *Teaching all children to read.* Chicago: University of Chicago Press.

Weinrott, M. R., Corson, L. A., & Wilchesky, M. (1979). Teacher mediated treatment of social withdrawal. *Behavior Therapy, 10,* 281–294.

Williams, G. (1986, November). *Advances in identifying sub-groups of rejected and neglected children.* Paper presented at the meeting of the Merrill–Palmer Society, Detroit.

Woody, R. (1969). *Behavioral problem children in the schools: Recognition, diagnosis, and modification.* New York: Appleton-Century-Crofts.

Youniss, J. (1981). *Parents and peers in social development.* New York: Cambridge University Press.

Zigler, E., & Phillips, L. (1961). Social competence and outcome in psychiatric disorder. *Journal of Abnormal and Social Psychology, 63,* 264–271.

PART IV

DEVELOPMENTAL DISORDERS

7

MENTAL RETARDATION

KEITH A. CRNIC
Pennsylvania State University

MOLLY REID
University of Washington

Perhaps no other childhood disorder has contributed as much to the development of behavioral interventions with children as has mental retardation. There are obvious reasons for this, including the large population of children with the disorder; the range of behavioral deficits and excesses apparent in the disorder itself; and the amenability of environmental contexts such as schools and institutions to the use of such techniques. A voluminous literature describes the range of behavioral techniques that are available and effective across settings and problems. General overviews and specific portions of this literature have been summarized on various occasions (Keogh & Whitman, 1983; Matson & McCartney, 1981; Scibak, 1983; Whitman & Johnston, 1987; Whitman, Scibak, & Reid, 1982). Some of these reviews have a rather narrow focus in relation to the behavioral methodologies reported, preferring to deal primarily with operant processes. Within this volume, however, behavioral intervention methodologies are considered to encompass a more varied range of empirically validated procedures operating within an ecological systems perspective (Bronfenbrenner, 1979; Ramey, Campbell, & Finkelstein, 1979).

A systems perspective is particularly useful when considering the treatment of children with mental retardation, as research has clearly indicated that children with mental retardation do not comprise a homogeneous group (Knopf, 1979), and that the impact of the disorder is not limited to the affected child. Rather, both the child and the entire family structure are affected, with the relationships between the child and the various family subsystems (including siblings) being both reciprocal and multidirectional (Crnic, Friedrich, & Greenberg, 1983). The retarded child's cognitive, behavioral, and affective abilities affect the family's functioning, and the family in turn affects the course of the retarded child's adjustment. Therefore, it is important to treat the child in combination with the system by planning multimethod interventions that facilitate positive change throughout the system (Dunst & Trivette, in press).

Together with the narrow focus of much of the previous work involving behavioral interventions with retarded children, there has also been a lack of a clear unifying conceptual model for planning the interventions to be conducted. Operant theory has clearly guided the majority of the work accomplished to date, and such work has proven successful in promoting behavior change for a range of problems and contexts relevant to children with mental retardation. The major shortcoming in this work, however, has been the lack of a conceptual interactive model of child *and* environment functioning to guide programming for maintenance and generalization of the positive changes produced by the techniques employed. Issues of maintenance and generalization are of critical concern with retarded children, as the change produced by behavioral interventions must be evaluated in relation to its durability over time and flexible application across contexts.

In this chapter, following a brief overview of the disorder of mental retardation in childhood, we present a conceptual model for planning and implementing behavioral interventions with retarded children, with a specific focus on issues of maintenance and generalization in the context of a more general systems approach. Broad and empirically based behavioral interventions that are applicable across a variety of problems specific to retardation are reviewed and discussed with specific reference to their utility within this working model. This is followed by a discussion of applied research involving behavioral interventions within the family context. Of particular interest are family interventions and the use of family members (both parents and siblings) as therapists for retarded children. Finally, we present a case analysis illustrating the process of behavioral intervention with retarded children from an ecological perspective, utilizing the conceptual model of maintenance–generalization discussed.

OVERVIEW OF MENTAL RETARDATION DURING CHILDHOOD

Mental retardation during childhood has been a focus of concern since the early 1800s (Kanner, 1964), and recent evidence suggests that it was the object of scientific attention as early as 1614 (Woolfson, 1984). In part, this early attention was a function of the discrete nature of the disorder when conceptualized as a purely cognitive deficit. Nevertheless, current conceptualizations of the disorder suggest that mental retardation during childhood is not a discrete

disorder, as these children do not constitute a homogeneous group sharing similar cognitive, behavioral, social, emotional, and educational characteristics (Knopf, 1979). There is wide variability both within and across classifications of retardation; the variation is much the same as that within the normal population. Nevertheless, a number of specific deficits and behavioral problems are often associated with the disorder.

Definition

There are various approaches to defining mental retardation, with the major approaches falling into one of two categories: (1) definitions that rely solely on intellectual deficit (Zigler, Balla, & Hodapp, 1984); and (2) those that incorporate intellectual, social, and developmental deviations into their criteria (Grossman, 1983). At present, the most widely accepted definition falls into the latter category and was developed by the American Association on Mental Deficiency (AAMD; Grossman, 1983). Within this definition, mental retardation involves significantly subaverage intellectual functioning existing concurrently with deficits in adaptive behavior, both of which are first manifested during the developmental period (before age 18 years). The major problems associated with mental retardation are impaired cognitive ability and similar deficits in social and adaptive skills, measured within the developmental context. The diagnosis of Mental Retardation in the revised third edition of the *Diagnostic and Statistical Manual of Mental Disorders* (DSM-III-R; American Psychiatric Association, 1987) incorporates the entire set of AAMD diagnostic criteria.

Further differentiation within the disorder of mental retardation comes from specific classification schemes that separate children based on the degree of impairment in functional behavioral abilities (Grossman, 1983). Given the disparity and range of abilities and deficits apparent in retarded children, classification systems have proved most useful in conceptualizing the nature and severity of the disorder. They have also been helpful in distinguishing between subgroups for purposes of deciding on the level and intensity of services to be provided (Crnic, 1988). Like the major definition of the disorder, the major classification system was developed by the AAMD (Grossman, 1983) and is based entirely upon the severity of the disabilities present. The AAMD classification system includes four major categories of mental retardation: "mild," "moderate," "severe," and "profound." Table 7-1 (from Crnic, 1988) provides intellectual and behavioral descriptors for each classification. Classification systems are also available that are based on more educational or etiological models. The educational model, which is likewise based on severity, involves two major categories: "educable" and "trainable" mental retardation. These are roughly equivalent to the AAMD classifications of mild and moderate retardation (Robinson & Robinson, 1976). Etiological models (e.g., Zigler *et al.*, 1984) differentiate retarded from normal performance on the basis of whether organicity (e.g., microcephaly, diffuse encephalopathy) is present or not. Such etiological models are based on data that indicate differences in cognitive performance between retarded children with and without organic impairment. Each classification system is meaningful only to the degree that it is relevant to the treatment approaches being considered for a particular child and his or her family.

Prevalence

Estimates of the prevalence and incidence of mental retardation during childhood vary. Generally, figures range from 1% to 3% of the population (Robinson & Robinson, 1976). This can be somewhat misleading, however, as this figure only accounts for those children with IQ scores below 70. There is a sizeable portion of the population with IQ scores between 70 and 85 who can also be considered to have intellectual deficits. These children often demonstrate behavioral and social problems similar to those of children with IQs below 70. The prevalence of retardation is also known to vary in

TABLE 7-1. Classification of Mental Retardation by IQ Scores and Behavioral Competencies

Degree of retardation	IQ Scores by test standard deviations[a]		Behavioral competencies	
	15	16	Preschool (0–5)	School age (6–18)
Mild	55–69	52–67	Can develop social and communication skills; minimal retardation in sensory–motor area, often not distinguished until later ages.	Can learn academic skills up to sixth grade; can be guided toward social conformity.
Moderate	40–54	36–51	Can talk or learn to communicate; poor social awareness; fair motor skills, profits from self-help skill training; requires some supervision.	Can profit from training in social and occupational skills; unlikely to progress beyond second-grade level; some independence in familiar places possible.
Severe	25–39	20–35	Poor motor development and minimal language skill; generally cannot profit from training in self-help; little communication.	Can learn to talk or communicate; can be trained in elemental self-help skills; profits from systematic habit training.
Profound	Under 25	Under 20	Gross retardation, with minimal capacity for functioning in sensory–motor areas; requires intense care.	Some motor development present; may respond to very limited range of training in self-help.

[a]The major intelligence test have standard deviations of either 15 points (e.g., Bayley Scales, Stanford–Binet) or 15 points (e.g., Wechsler Scales). With these differences, the IQ scores by category differ correspondingly.
Note. From "Mental Retardation" by K. A. Crnic, 1988, in E. J. Mash and L. G. Terdal (Eds.), *Behavioral assessment of childhood disorders* (2nd ed., pp. 317–354). New York: Guilford Press. Copyright 1988 by The Guilford Press. Reprinted by permission.

relation to a number of factors. It is more prevalent with increasing age (Mercer, 1973); in males (Mumpower, 1970); in minority groups (Mercer, 1970), although this may well reflect bias in the assessment instruments; in lower-socioeconomic-status groups (Robinson & Robinson, 1976); and in geographic regions where services are scarce (Knopf, 1979).

Etiological Considerations

Little is known about the exact etiology of many forms of retardation. Nevertheless, a great deal of research has focused on conditions associated with retardation. In general, distinctions have been made among those etiological conditions that are primarily genetic, those that are primarily physical and environmental (e.g., the result of toxic agents in the environment), and those that are primarily psychosocial in nature. Genetic disorders associated with retardation are varied, and include chromosomal abnormalities as well as dominant and recessive gene disorders. Physical factors associated with mental retardation are generally operative during the prenatal and perinatal periods, but operate to some degree during postnatal development as well. There is a tremendous range in the physical factors that have been found to be associated with retardation, but some examples include maternal nutritional history, drug ingestion, maternal disease, parental age, prematurity, anoxia, maternal infection, infant head trauma, exposure to neurotoxins (e.g., lead), and later central nervous system (CNS) infections or trauma.

Of particular significance to the present chapter are those etiological concerns that are primarily psychosocial in nature. Robinson and Robinson (1976) have noted a number of psychological and familial factors that have been shown to be related to child intellectual functioning, including family structure and size, parental deprivation, early verbal stimulation provided to children, poor parent–child relationships, and environmental characteristics of the home. A fair amount of "transactional" research (Sameroff & Chandler, 1975; Sameroff & Seifer, 1983) also suggests that children's developmental outcomes are related to their ongoing and changing interactions with their parents and social environments. Some recent research with high-risk premature infants has indicated that more positive parenting, family functioning, and parent–child relationships predict better social competence of these children

(Crnic & Greenberg, 1984, 1987). All of these considerations have specific implications for behavioral interventions with mentally retarded children, because they suggest that various parameters of the social environment, particularly relationships between the retarded children and their caregivers, can affect both developmental outcomes (e.g., cognitive and linguistic) and behavioral functioning (e.g., more positive interaction styles and social competence) in these children.

Behavioral Problems in Retarded Children

An issue of some importance for behavioral interventions with retarded children is the frequency with which they exhibit associated behavior problems or psychiatric impairments (Matson & Barrett, 1982). Recent research indicates that retarded children are more likely to exhibit deviant behavior than are children in the general population (Jacobson, 1982a, 1982b; Koller, Richardson, Katz, & McLaren, 1982), although estimates of the prevalence of behavior problems in this population vary. The studies by Jacobson (1982a 1982b) provide perhaps the most reliable estimates of the occurrence of behavior problems and psychiatric disturbance in retarded children. He surveyed over 8,000 retarded children in New York ranging from infancy to adolescence, and found that 9.8% had significant psychiatric impairment. Subsequently, he examined the presence of specific behavior problems in those groups of retarded children who were diagnosed as developmentally disabled (DD) and those who were dually diagnosed as having both mental retardation and psychiatric impairment. A large number of behaviors were divided into four problem categories on the basis of major salient features and severity: (1) cognitive, which included major thought disorders, hallucinations, and delusions; (2) affective, which included significant depression and dysphoric affect; (3) major behavior problems, including physical aggression or assault, property destruction, coercive sexual behavior, and self-injurious behavior (SIB); and (4) minor behavior problems, which included hyperactivity, tantrums, stereotypies, verbal abusiveness, and substance abuse. The findings for retarded children and adolescents are summarized in Table 7-2. Children dually diagnosed had more frequent behavior problems across all categories than did the DD children, although the behavior problems most frequent for the dually diagnosed children were also most frequent for the DD children. The groups were equivalent in the types of problems present, but differed somewhat in the frequency and degree to which these were seen. Across the two groups, the presence of behavior problems was related to age (younger children had fewer problems), degree of retardation (fewer problems in the mild and profound categories), and living context (fewer problems with those children living at home).

When one is considering associated problems with mental retardation during childhood, a systems perspective necessitates attention to potential problems within a child's family that may be a function of the presence of the retardation. A review of parent, sibling, and family functioning (Crnic et al., 1983) suggests that parents, siblings, and the family as a unit are all at risk for significant difficulties, although such difficulties are not a necessary outcome of having a retarded child in the family. Parents are at risk for depression and various forms of emotional distress, less satisfaction with parenting and less positive attitudes toward the retarded child, increased social isolation, and less facilitative interactions with the retarded child. Siblings also appear at risk for specific behavior problems, but female siblings appear to be at greater risk than males. The family system is also at greater risk for dysfunctions such as lack of cohesiveness and disharmony. These potential difficulties are important for several reasons. It is clear that how the family and its individual members function influences the course of the retarded child's development (Mink, Nihira, & Meyers, 1983; Nihira, Meyers, & Mink, 1980), and that how the child functions influences the family. Behavioral approaches that do not assess the impact of problems on the family, or plan for interventions that are directed at the context in which the problem occurs, may prove only marginally or partially successful.

The ensuing sections of this chapter describe specific strategies that reveal the complexity of the process of behavioral intervention from a systemic point of view, and present a review of behavioral intervention research with retarded children and their families. Succeeding sections (1) describe the diversity of needed services, which creates challenges for behavioral interventions with mentally retarded children; (2) review basic behavioral techniques relevant to work with this population; (3) present a conceptual approach to behavioral intervention, based on the need to enhance maintenance and generalization of treatment effects with retarded children within a system's context; (4) outline the steps to accomplish the treatment plan with-

TABLE 7-2. Percentage of Behavior Problem Types as a Function of Age and Intellectual Level

Age within level of intellectual functioning	n (Cases)	Percentage without problem behaviors	Behavior type[a]			
			Cognitive	Affective	Major	Minor
Mild mental retardation						
0–12	708	60	11	14	14	61
13–21	818	45	5	26	19	50
Moderate mental retardation						
0–12	640	53	8	19	14	59
13–21	1,163	40	7	22	24	47
Severe mental retardation						
0–12	652	46	5	15	17	63
13–21	1,208	35	6	14	30	50
Profound mental retardation						
0–12	1,056	62	4	19	22	55
13–21	2,539	43	4	15	33	48

[a]Among individuals with a problem behavior reported only.
Note. From "Problem Behavior and Psychiatric Impairment within a Developmentally Disabled Population: I. Behavior Frequency" by J. W. Jacobson, 1982, Applied Research in Mental Retardation, 3, 121–139. Copyright 1982 by Pergamon Press, Inc. Reprinted by permission.

in such a conceptualization; (5) review relevant studies of behavioral interventions for specific problem areas within the conceptual approach presented; and, finally, (6) present a case study demonstrating the application of such a theoretically based but empirically validated approach to behavioral intervention with mentally retarded children.

DIVERSITY OF NECESSARY SERVICES

As noted previously, mentally retarded children differ widely in ability and social/behavioral skill from one another, and are likely to require services that vary along a number of dimensions as well. Understanding the issues raised by this diversity is a prerequisite to clarifying the subsequent therapeutic process. Several issues are illustrated below.

Defining the Focus of Treatment

It is necessary to consider what the primary focus of the treatment process will be: habilitative, social, or emotional. In previous decades, primary emphasis has been on educational and rehabilitative services for the retarded, teaching self-help, independent, or semi-independent community living skills, and specific vocational skills (Keogh & Whitman, 1983). Although these emphases have led to the development of rudimentary self-help skills as well as complex vocational skills, they have not addressed the critical problem of the high prevalence of psychiatric disturbance in retarded children. The lack of treatment emphasis on the emotional difficulties of retarded children, coupled with the high incidence of such problems, has contributed to the growing realization that the emotionally disturbed mentally retarded may be one of the most underserved populations in the country (Reiss, Levitan, & McNally, 1982). Therefore, behavioral interventions with these children are likely to require attention not only to adaptive and cognitive deficits, but also to emotional issues that are qualitatively similar to but more prevalent than those experienced by nonretarded children.

Children's Level of Cognitive and Social Functioning

Due both to their cognitive limitations and to their life histories, retarded children adapt and

react to environmental events differently than do nonretarded children (Zigler & Hodapp, 1986). The scope of behavioral interventions must therefore be carefully matched with a child's ability (both cognitive and social) if he or she is to benefit. Classifications of retardation provide only a rough estimate of ability level, necessitating careful and multidimensional approaches to assessing the range of children's skills and deficits. Planning for behavioral interventions involves making individual appraisals of retarded children's cognitive and social strengths and weaknesses. Given the variability in these children, the assumptions made are likely to vary widely, underscoring the need for careful assessment. Such considerations are further addressed in the later section on assessment.

Selecting Goals

The problems of retarded children that require behavioral intervention will range from specific difficulties with academic, social, or vocational skills to complicated and extensive response deficiencies, such as a lack of interpersonal relatedness. Because many of these problems are likely to be complex in nature, the planned behavioral intervention must assist parents, teachers, and/or staff to select realistic treatment goals. Although only one area of difficulty may be targeted for intervention at any one time, other related or collateral behaviors will need to be selected for observation both before and after treatment (Schroeder, Mulick, & Schroeder, 1979). From a systems perspective, clinical utility is determined not only by the change in the target behavior, but by the benefits to the child's overall performance and the ecology within which the child operates. An example of the importance of identifying collateral behaviors for the purpose of determining undesirable side effects is illustrated by the work of Rollings, Baumeister, and Baumeister (1977). In this study, attempts to reduce stereotypic behavior by overcorrection were associated with increases in SIBs.

Ecological Approaches and Child Involvement

The ecological context for the intervention must be determined. Behavioral interventions with retarded children are likely to be carried out in various settings, most notably the home, school, residential facilities, and institutions. Furthermore, such interventions often involve relationships between ecological contexts (e.g., home and school). Behavioral interventions with retarded children may focus on modifying specific behaviors in the child, providing parent training to manage the retarded child and/or other system influences (e.g., siblings of the retarded child who show difficulties in adjustment), or conducting observations aimed at recommending changes in the child's classroom environment. Where to focus the specific intervention and with whom are the key intervention questions. Although the foci are likely to vary with the specific nature of the problem, behavioral interventions with retarded children typically focus simultaneously on several different levels of target behavior in order to strengthen the behavior change (Stokes & Baer, 1977). In addition, specifically engaging the retarded child in the treatment process, to the degree to which the child can be engaged has been found to be important for the maintenance and generalization of the treatment effects (Kestner & Borkowski, 1979; Schleser, Meyers, & Cohen, 1981).

The range in ability level and treatment needs with retarded children presents major challenges for behavioral interventions. Meeting these challenges requires a clear understanding of behavioral principles, as well as a conceptual orientation to guide their use.

Developmentally Sensitive Interventions

With the recent emergence of the field of developmental psychopathology (Cicchetti, 1984), there has come the understanding that children's adaptive and behavioral problems must be conceptualized within a developmental framework. Development implies change, and behaviors that are appropriate or inappropriate at one age or stage may not be so at another. Within a developmental framework, the continuity of behavior problems across childhood and the definition of deviance with respect to age, context, developmental tasks, and the process of development over time are especially critical issues.

Developmental processes in behavioral and adaptive problems are a particularly salient issue for populations of retarded children. Interventions must be planned that are consistent with a child's developmental level, regardless of chronological age. Kendall, Lerner, and Craighead (1984) have recently presented a comprehensive discussion of treatment efficacy in relation to children's developing physical, psychological, and behavioral characteristics. They note that treatment effectiveness across various interventions (including cognitive–behavioral, social skills, and parent training strategies) is dependent upon the correspondence between the child's developmental characteristics and the intervention requirements. Interventions that do not take account of a child's developmental level and trajectory are not likely to result in successful change. For example, implementing cognitive control strategies with school-age retarded children is not likely to be successful unless such children have reached at least the concrete operational cognitive stage (Kendall et al., 1984).

BEHAVIORAL METHODOLOGIES USED WITH THE DEVELOPMENTALLY DELAYED

The behavioral approach most commonly used with retarded children is that of applied behavior analysis (Baer, Wolf, & Risley, 1968), the central tenets of which are that (1) the appropriate focus of study is observable behavior; (2) behavior is a function of consequences; and (3) the primary focus of intervention is on the conditions maintaining the presence or absence of a behavior. The key techniques, which include reinforcement, shaping, punishment, and extinction, will not be discussed here, since they are detailed in elsewhere throughout this volume. However, two "hybrid" behavioral approaches that have been developed in part to extend and enhance the outcomes of behavioral interventions are briefly discussed. These "hybrid" approaches are cognitive–behavioral interventions and behavioral family therapy.

Cognitive–Behavioral Procedures

Although the basic operant procedures mentioned above have been found to be successful in the short run, the absence of maintenance and generalization of newly learned skills has led to the expansion of behavioral treatments to include cognitive–behavioral training (Meichenbaum, 1977). Cognitive–behavioral methods have been used to modify a wide range of behaviors. Although there are many variants of cognitive–behavioral treatments, they have in common the emphasis on using thought processes and verbalizations as mediators in problem-solving situations (Brown, 1978; Meichenbaum, 1977). Self-instruction training and correspondence training are two types of cognitive–behavioral procedures. Self-instruction training is an interactive learning process in which the individual is taught to solve a problem while at the same time being provided with informative prompts that facilitate successful task completion (Belmont & Butterfield, 1977; Kendall & Braswell, 1985). Correspondence training is a cognitive–behavioral procedure that emphasizes establishing antecedent verbal control of motor behavior by reinforcing children for doing what they say they will do (Whitman *et al.*, 1982).

Behavioral Family Therapy

The reciprocity in relationship between the child's behavior and that of other family members has led to a recent emphasis on incorporating family interventions with the use of behavioral methodologies (cf. Crnic *et al.*, 1983). Behavioral family therapy is a hybrid that includes any or all of the following: discussions of family feelings and goals, an overview of child development, training in behavioral modification techniques, and the learning of new styles of interaction (Tymchuk, 1983).

Although behavioral therapy has been an effective tool for modifying behavior, there are a number of problems that its technology fails to solve (MacMillan & Forness, 1973). For this reason, it is generally held that in treating the mentally retarded, more is needed than a knowledge of operant techniques. Therapists who work with retarded children are encouraged to keep abreast of research in the field of developmental psychology, especially research dealing with factors (e.g., individual and family) that enhance children's cognitive and social growth at various ages. In addition, it is important that therapists working with retarded children be aware that a major criticism of behavioral treatments is the tendency of retarded children to abandon newly learned behaviors when therapy is withdrawn.

The acuteness of retarded children's problems with generalization has led to expansions in the field (noted above), as well as to the inclusion of "generalization-enhancing princi-

ples" such as intervening on the level of executive functioning (Brown & Campione, 1977) and considering metacognitive components (Flavell & Wellman, 1977). The challenge encountered when trying to intervene meaningfully in retarded children's lives underscores the importance of using a conceptual orientation to guide interventions.

CONCEPTUAL ORIENTATION

A conceptualization for guiding interventions with retarded children is needed that incorporates (1) issues in behavioral training with retarded children, especially issues concerning the maintenance and generalization of treatment effects; and (2) a systems approach, which views the child within the context of his or her environment (i.e., family, school, larger community). Maintenance and generalization are key elements in the conceptual orientation to be put forth here. "Maintenance" is typically the child's ability to perform the trained skill on a similar task at a short interval after training has ceased. Although important in its own right, maintenance is considered a necessary but not a sufficient condition for generalization (Borkowski & Cavanaugh, 1979). "Generalization" is the ability to appropriately use what was previously taught in new situations. Generalization reflects the scope and richness of a behavioral training program (Brown, 1978). The failure to generalize is given such emphasis because generalization is perhaps the best test of *usefulness* of what has been taught.

In its simplest form, the working model consists of three levels of cognitive functioning:

1. A biologically based "architectural" system constitutes the fundamental "hardware" of the system, such as registering information and responding to sensory input. The architectural system is rooted in the biological history of the organism and, as such, is fixed or relatively impervious to direct change. However, the functioning of the architectural system can be indirectly influenced by focusing intervention efforts on the more modifiable components— namely, executive and metacognitive functioning.

2. "Executive functioning" represents environmentally rooted components, including activities such as retrieving knowledge from long-term memory, enlarging the knowledge

base, and mediating problem solving. Control processes, such as those depicted under executive functioning, have been found to be relatively impoverished in retarded individuals (cf. Ellis, 1979). However, these control processes are somewhat modifiable through training, and successful intervention presumably allows the retarded child to utilize available architectural resources better.

The executive skills training that modifies control processes can be roughly divided into two types (a) training *specific* skills and behavioral repertoires, and (b) training more *general* self-regulatory skills. An example of training a specific skill would be training a child to reduce out-of-seat behaviors while working on math. An example of training a more general skill would be teaching a verbally mediated attentional routine that is not welded to a specific task but, instead, can be used across multiple situations.

3. "Metacognition" is the self-reflective ability to appropriately use the specific and general skills (Borkowski, Ryan, Kurtz, & Reid, 1983). The inclusion of general self-regulatory skills and metacognitive training in treatment programs with the retarded is based on the belief that it *cannot* be assumed that transfer is an automatic product of training, especially in individuals with impoverished executive control and metacognitive processes. This is clearly demonstrated in the review of behavioral interventions with retarded children that follows in later sections. For this reason, generalization needs to be trained along with new behavioral repertoires and skills through instruction on "when," "where," "why," and "how" the skill can be appropriately applied (Brown, Bransford, Ferrara, & Campione, 1983; Kurtz, Reid, Borkowski, & Cavanaugh, 1982). These components are bidirectionally related to one another as well as to motivation.

Motivation, often explained in terms of self-attributions (cf. Weisz, 1981), is perceived as providing the energy that motivates the system. The importance of focusing on children's attributions when implementing self-control training was recently demonstrated by Reid and Borkowski (1985). In this case, underachieving, hyperactive children who received combined attribution *plus* self-control training showed not only more improved attributional beliefs, but also significantly greater maintenance and generalization of skills over a long-term follow-up than children who received the self-control training without the attributional emphasis. The three major components of the theory and their relation to ecological factors are depicted in Figure 7-1.

A reason for the use of such a conceptualization by those who struggle with the transfer problems of retarded children is that it captures the difficulty retarded children have in using simple learning strategies (e.g., anticipating consequences and monitoring progress) that nonretarded children have been found to use without instruction (Campione & Brown, 1978). In addition, it provides a theoretical rationale for combining specific and general training, or "for giving the retarded child enough of the program so that he/she will successfully carry it out" (Belmont, 1978). Interestingly, although executive skills are not necessarily generated by the conceptual approach described above, cognitive–behavioral, self-instruction, and correspondence training all encourage incorporating "executive" types of skills into behavioral treatment packages to facilitate transfer. Some of the skills include general self-control strategies, using verbal rehearsal to guide behaviors, and training self-control steps in combination with more traditional behavioral interventions.

The working model set forth in this chapter goes one step further and combines individual functioning (as described above) with a systems approach that shows the child in interaction

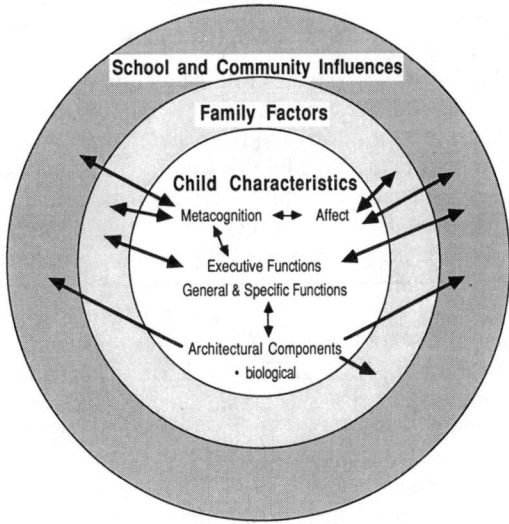

FIGURE 7-1. A working model of child and family functioning.

with significant others in his or her environment (see Figure 7-1). The rationale for such combined concepts comes from research showing that children influence and are influenced by their families (Bell, 1968; Crnic et al., 1983; Nihira et al., 1980), as well as from behavior therapists who have pointed out that a parent training component is necessary to maintain what is learned in the school and clinic (Berkowitz & Graziano, 1972; Tymchuk, 1983). This model shows reciprocal interactions between the child's functioning, the child's family, and other aspects of the child's environment. However, several points need to be emphasized.

First, a one-way interaction is depicted between the child's biologically rooted, architectural system and the family, because at this point in time, even though the parents have contributed to the child's genetic makeup, in most instances the family cannot directly improve the child's perceptual and sensory capacities. The inability to alter fixed capacities in the child may cause profound distress in many parents. In addition, the degree of physical impairment is at times directly related to family adjustment (Crnic et al., 1983). There are, however, reciprocal interactions between the family and the more modifiable executive and metacognitive components, showing that although the parents cannot alter fixed capacities, they can help the child to use his or her available resources more effectively. Families that facilitate this are typically adept at incorporating the child into predictable routines and patterns.

The arrow from the child's functioning to the family indicates that the child's improved skill level has a positive influence on the family system. In turn, the family's improved attitudes may influence the child's affect, which (if the feedback is made explicit to the child) may increase the probability of future choices to use skills (metacognition). Similar interactive sequences can be outlined for teachers in the child's school and staff–child relationships in institutions. Ecological variables (e.g., parental employment, parental social support, and community policies and resources), which are described by Bronfenbrenner (1979), are shown in the present orientation as affecting the child through their impact on the parents and schools. Stressful ecological events and difficult child characteristics may be additive problems for parents, setting in motion a negative spiral that

is seriously debilitating to both family coping and child functioning.

Although there are few behavioral interventions that utilize the entire working model as described above, several studies illustrate key aspects of this conceptual orientation. One such example is the systematic research on self-regulation in trainable mentally retarded children, in which children were taught to modify their own behaviors, set standards, evaluate themselves, and deliver self-rewards (Litrownik, Freitas, & Franzini, 1978; Litrownik, White, McInnis, & Licht, 1984). This work supports giving such children general problem-solving skills, rather than a skill that is appropriate to only a specific task. Another example is the PATHS program for severely retarded and profoundly deaf children (Greenberg, Kusche, Gustafson, & Calderon, 1985). In this intervention, the social-cognitive deficits resulting from the children's severe sensory handicaps are addressed through comprehensive training designed to enhance self-control, emotional awareness, and interpersonal problem solving. This intervention is also a good example of the utilization of a series of innovative and creative training techniques (i.e., drama, story telling, imagery). Tymchuk (1979) has also presented an example of an intervention that takes into account the mentally retarded child's family environment. In his work, he suggests compiling a "parent profile" based on parental attitudes, marital adjustment, parental knowledge of resources, and parent–child interaction observations, through which the intervention can be planned.

CLINICAL PRINCIPLES

A number of principles follow from the working model described above; these can be considered as guidelines when designing interventions for retarded children.

1. Effective behavioral change results from a well-planned intervention in which the therapist takes into account the retarded child's developmental stage, his or her strengths and weaknesses, and the people and resources in the child's environment.

2. The retarded child needs to be perceived as an active learner, rather than as a passive recipient of behavioral procedures. Wherever

possible, the child should be encouraged to be actively involved in the change process.

3. The attentional and processing difficulties of retarded children suggest the utilization of highly salient training techniques. Therapists working with retarded children are encouraged to rely more on the rich oral traditions rather than ones requiring reading, using repetitive statements, game-like tasks, story telling, and dramatization (Brown, 1978; Greenberg *et al.*, 1985; Robinson & Robinson, 1976). In addition, the use of simple self-monitoring techniques and the use of attractive stimuli (e.g., brightly colored pictures, star charts) are encouraged to hold the children's attention (Douglas, 1974a; Mahoney & Mahoney, 1976).

4. Generalization is a complex process that is *not* assumed to be an automatic by-product of treatment. The behavior therapist is encouraged to incorporate generalization-enhancing principles into behavioral treatments with the retarded. These principles are derived from research in applied behavioral analysis (Stokes & Baer, 1977), strategy training (Borkowski & Cavanaugh, 1979; Brown, 1978; Reid & Borkowski, 1987), parent training (Baker, 1984) and other areas of psychology (cf. Schleser *et al.*, 1981). Examples of these factors can be found in Table 7-3, as well as in some of the empirical studies reviewed later.

STAGES IN CLINICAL INTERVENTION

Stage 1: Assessment

Assessment is the initial step within the behavioral intervention process. There have been several recent attempts at explicating the process of behavioral assessment with retarded children (Crnic, 1988; Ollendick & Hersen, 1984; Rojahn & Schroeder, 1983), all emphasizing a multidimensional approach. Variability within the population of mentally retarded children makes an idiographic approach to behavioral assessment with these children critical to the identification of characteristics that lead to meaningful diagnoses, behavioral intervention planning, and treatment evaluation. An idiographic behavioral assessment approach is directed at a specific child, within specifically relevant settings, and measures individual target behaviors. Yet mental retardation during childhood is a condition that requires a multimodal and systems approach to behavioral assessment across cognitive, affective, behavioral, social, adaptive, and ecological domains (Crnic, 1988; Whitman & Johnston, 1987). Such an approach emphasizes the need to measure behavior using more than an observational approach, and often includes the use of standardized testing (including testing the limits), interviewing, and questionnaire or rating scales.

TABLE 7-3. Factors That Facilitate the Maintenance and Generalization of Newly Learned Behaviors and Skills

1. The reinforcement of new skills and behaviors should be transferred to natural contingencies (Bornstein & Quevillon, 1976).

2. Multiple exemplars, or training across sufficient settings, conditions, or persons, should be used to avoid having the skill welded to a particular situation or task (Brown, 1978; Stokes & Baer, 1977).

3. "Cognitive flexibility," such as when, where, why, and how the new behavior or skill can be applied to new situations, should be trained (Belmont & Butterfield, 1977).

4. One should do more than "train and hope"; instead, one should directly train and reinforce the occurrence of generalization through elaborative feedback (Brown, 1978; Goetz & Baer, 1973; Kennedy & Miller, 1976).

5. Training should facilitate overlearning and increase the child's active engagement in the treatment through semantic involvement or the extent of mental transformations required, such as having the child use imagery, elaboration, comparisons, and contrasts (Borkowski, Johnston, & Reid, 1985; Robinson & Robinson, 1976).

6. Training should directly address maladaptive attributions that interfere with the motivation to use skills persistently on new and difficult tasks (Balla & Zigler, 1979; Reid & Borkowski, 1985).

7. The reciprocal relationships between mentally retarded children and others in their environment require that the needs of both the children and their families be addressed in order to effect durable change across contexts (Crnic, Friedrich, & Greenberg, 1983).

8. The inclusion of parent components in behavioral training programs directly affects family functioning and indirectly influences child functioning, resulting in greater maintenance of parenting skills and more improved child behaviors than the use of behavioral interventions alone (Griest *et al.*, 1982).

The process of behavioral assessment relevant to subsequent intervention is best conceptualized within the "S-O-R-K-C" model originally proposed by Kanfer and Saslow (1969). This model highlights the need to assess the dimensions of the problem at hand in relation to specific parameters involving the following: (1) S, or the stimulus or antecedent conditions relevant to the behavior of concern; (2) O, the developmental and biological status of the organism (i.e., the child); (3) R, the response or behavior of concern; (4) K, the contingency, or schedules of reinforcement; and (5) C, the consequent events that influence the behavior of concern. Assessment within the S-O-R-K-C model allows for the identification of intervention concerns across both behaviors and contexts, and specifies possible intervention targets.

In planning intervention procedures with retarded children, assessment usually begins with a comprehensive developmental behavioral interview (Crnic, 1988), which identifies developmental and behavioral histories, past and present schedules of medications, current behavioral concerns and their antecedents and consequents, and the impact of these concerns on relevant developmental contexts. Strategies for conducting these interviews vary somewhat (Barkley, 1981; Kanfer & Saslow, 1969; O'Leary & Johnson, 1979; Roberts & LaGreca, 1981), but serve the purpose of identifying the specific concerns to be followed up with more specific assessments.

In addition to the flexibility offered by an interview process, standardized or normalized rating scales and questionnaires may be administered to target specific deficits as well as strengths. Within populations of mentally retarded children, several are specifically relevant. A number of measures of adaptive behavior exist, including the AAMD Adaptive Behavior Scale (Nihira, Foster, Shellhaas, & Leland, 1974); the revised Vineland Adaptive Behavior Scales (Sparrow, Balla, & Cicchetti, 1984); the Behavior Inventory for Rating Development (Sparrow & Cicchetti, 1984); and the Wisconsin Behavior Rating Scale (Song et al., 1980). Choosing among these scales for the most appropriate is a matter of child age, psychometric properties, and specific behaviors of interest (Crnic, 1988). There are also a number of standard measures for assessing psychiatric or behavior problem status, including the Child Behavior Checklist (Achenbach & Edelbrock, 1983), the Personality Inventory for Children (Wirt, Lachar, Klinedinst, & Seat, 1977), and the Eyberg Child Behavior Inventory (Eyberg, 1980). These measures, however, do not include specific norms for retarded children. Measures of both adaptive behavior and behavior problems are also generally useful for the assessment of social skills in retarded children.

A systems model also requires system measurements. In populations of retarded children, this generally includes measures of stresses within environmental contexts (Beckman, 1983; Wikler, 1981) and measures of family functioning (Crnic et al., 1983). The Questionnaire for Resources and Stress (Holroyd, 1974) and its short forms (e.g., Friedrich, Greenberg, & Crnic, 1983) provide one such measure detailing stresses, whereas the Family Environment Scale (Moos & Moos, 1981) offers one sound questionnaire approach to family system measurements. Although this list is certainly not exhaustive, the measures are easily used, are applicable across developmental contexts, and can be given both before and after intervention to assess change. Their primary value, however, is in the identification of specific problem behaviors that may require intervention.

Although significantly subaverage intellectual functioning is a major diagnostic criterion of retarded children, it is not always necessary to assess intellectual functioning in order to plan or evaluate behavioral interventions. Choosing to carry out standardized intellectual evaluations will depend upon the issues identified as problematic. Intellectual evaluation may, however, be particularly useful when concerns involve cognitive skills; academic planning; and behavioral skills important to such functions as attention, impulsivity, learning strategies, ability to follow instructions, and others (Nelson, 1974). In these cases, standardized tests of cognitive and academic ability may well prove to be useful samples of behavior obtained under rigorous conditions. Within assessment contexts, it may also at times be advantageous to abandon standardization while giving these tests, when questions arise that can only be answered by manipulating contingencies or antecedents. This process of "testing the limits" of retarded children's performances can serve to further identify cognitive and behavioral strengths and weaknesses that can be used in subsequent intervention planning. Examples can be found in studies showing how applications of reinforcement principles to correct performances on standardized tests resulted in higher scores on such measures (Johnson, Bradley-Johnson, McCarthy, & Jamie, 1984; Saigh & Payne, 1979, Young, Bradley-Johnson, & Johnson, 1982).

Once specific target behaviors have been identified through interviews, rating scales, or testing, the major assessment strategy relevant to behavioral intervention planning and evaluation is specific observation of the behavior(s) of interest in the contexts or settings of interest. Again, observations should follow the S-O-R-K-C model, and can be accomplished for any behavior or set of behaviors identified. Basically, within an intervention context, assessment requires measurement not only during a baseline or "diagnostic" phase, but also during treatment. The simplest form of such measurement is that in which the target behavior is observed as it occurs naturally (along with its antecedent and consequent events). This is generally referred to as the "A-B-C" model, in which A refers to antecedents, B to the behavior of interest, and C to its consequences. Through such data collection across time and ecological contexts, greater validity is achieved, and more effective interventions can be designed and evaluated (Bates & Hanson, 1983). Observational strategies vary widely, and many are available (Rojahn & Schroeder, 1983). Basically, they provide data on both the frequency and duration of the behaviors of interest, recorded continuously or in intervals, with the client alone or in interaction, and for single or multiple behavioral events (Rojahn & Schroeder, 1983).

Finally, assessment should plan for the maintenance and generalization of the behavior(s) identified and treated. Assessment planning should therefore ideally include measures of the behavior(s) to be treated, possible collateral behaviors and side effects, and the contexts for transfer; multiple behaviors that may be collateral should also be assessed, as well as behaviors across contexts that are systematically related. Although it may not be feasible to include each of these aspects, consideration should be given to those most likely to be relevant to the context in which treatment will take place.

Stage 2: Treatment Design and Implementation

At the completion of the assessment, the behavior therapist should have a number of hypotheses about the following: (1) the child's strengths and weaknesses, (2) the child's affective/motivational functioning (including a list of the goals the child will work for), (3) the child's relationships with significant others in his or her environment, and (4) the parents' or others' ability to collaborate in treatment. Since children typically present with more than one behavioral or emotional difficulty, the next step is to determine the goals for the present treatment.

Determining Treatment Goals

A number of decision guidelines exist for addressing problems in treatment. For example, ethical and practical reasons dictate that seriously aggressive behaviors or SIBs be addressed first. In addition, on some occasions the family is in a state of crisis when they bring in the child for treatment, due to both child and ecological factors (e.g., severe aggressive behavior or growing social rejection). When the family is in a state of crisis, the parents themselves may be the initial focus of treatment, and child behaviors that are exacerbating family stress may need to be targeted before other changes can realistically be made. If the referral has not been precipitated by an emergency, then the treatment goals may be selected on the basis of which behaviors are the most troublesome to the child (Bates & Hanson, 1983; Beck, 1983); which behavioral changes have been requested by the parents (Sulzer-Azaroff & Mayer, 1977); or which behavioral changes will be the most clinically useful (e.g., will bring the retarded child's behaviors more in line with those of normal peers) (Kazdin, 1977). It is important to be realistic with the child and parents and let them know that only one or perhaps two behaviors should be addressed in the initial treatment, even though general skills will also be taught. In many instances, effective change of even one problem area requires careful attention to multicomponent treatment packages (e.g., treating impulsive behaviors by working with the child, the child's family, and the school environment).

Gathering Baseline Data

Once the goals of the treatment have been determined, specific data need to be collected in regard to the targeted behavior. This will require a functional analysis of the behavior, including measures of the frequency, duration, antecedents, and consequences of the behavior, as well as the context in which it occurs. Functional analysis to determine baseline performance is discussed elsewhere in this volume, as well as in numerous previous reviews (Barkley, 1981; Kazdin & Straw, 1976; Whitman & Johnston, 1987), and is not discussed again in detail here.

Designing the Treatment

Once the goals of treatment have been established and a functional analysis has been done, then the next step is to select an appropriate intervention. This includes deciding the best way to bring about change, determining the means to maintain and generalize the effects of the treatment, and deciding the manner in which generalization will be tested after the completion of therapy.

Of course, there may be numerous ways to proceed with treatment design, and the particular decision in any individual case will depend upon a combination of factors, including child age, parental competency, contexts in which the behavior occurs, family resources, therapist resources, and others.

Behavioral programs for mentally retarded children have undergone many changes since their introduction in the early 1960s. Whereas earlier programs focused on teaching severely and profoundly retarded children basic self-help skills, recent programs have focused on teaching more advanced and refined skills, such as academic and community living skills, to all levels of retarded children. As mentioned earlier, it is this very "range" in abilities and services that makes it difficult to follow a simple set of rules when treating mentally retarded children. Instead, a working model is recommended as a guide to thinking through the various aspects of the problems at hand. In this way, the "goodness of fit" can be enhanced between the treatment package and the needs/resources of the child and his or her family and community.

Within the conceptual orientation presented here, the intervention should involve the child (through the use of star charts, self-monitoring, verbally mediated strategies, etc.) whenever possible, as well as the child's parents and the school. In addition, generalization should be specifically planned for and trained.

Stage 3: Monitoring Treatment

Monitoring the treatment process is important in order to determine whether change has occurred in the specified direction. The same methods as those used in establishing the baseline can be employed. However, in order to minimize the problems of intrusiveness at this stage in the intervention, rating scales are often used. During the intervention process, it is important to make necessary modifications and to transfer contingencies to the natural environment when necessary. For example, if positive praise has been paired with tangible reinforcers, then the tangible reinforcers need to be gradually removed.

Assessment of Maintenance and Generalization

Booster sessions are generally recommended after the monitoring stage and before the measurement of maintenance and generalization (Borkowski & Cavanaugh, 1979). This usually involves meeting with the retarded child and/or parents and teachers and assessing the training, while the therapist provides support but utilizes fewer prompts. In addition to repeating and thus reinforcing the original training, the booster session should also be designed to transfer more control to the child, parents, and natural contingencies.

A short interval after the final booster session (1–2 weeks, depending on the child/treatment), durability or maintenance should be assessed in a situation or task similar to that of training. The purpose of this session is to assess whether the child has maintained the new skills in his or her repertoire. The next step is to assess generalization. It is important to note that generalization does not imply indiscriminate repetition of the trained behavior; instead, it refers to the "clinical usefulness" of what was taught (Bornstein, Bach, & Anton, 1982). In other words, can the child access and transfer the new behavior in *appropriate* new situations? The type of task used to measure the retarded child's flexible use (generalization) will depend on the scope of the initial treatment. The breadth of transfer can be assessed in tasks and situations involving both "near" generalization (generalization in contexts similar to that in which the child has been treated) and "far" generalization (generalization in contexts dissimilar to the one in which treatment has occurred).

Although generalization is the best test of the usefulness of what has been taught, behavior therapists working with mentally retarded children know that even with well-planned interventions, this is painfully difficult to achieve. If the child does not demonstrate "near" or "far" generalization, it is useful to review the treatment package from the perspective of the working model. For example, did the child's attributional beliefs interfere? Were insufficient environmental baseline data gathered during treatment planning? Did problems at home or school exist that overshadowed the treatment? Did the treatment overestimate the child's abilities, lacking sufficient thoroughness and explicitness? It is not unusual for the child to show maintenance of the new skills, but to have incomplete knowledge of how to appropriately transfer these new behaviors. When this occurs, it is helpful to emphasize generalization directly (by having the child perform the behaviors/skills in new situations) and then to provide specific feedback about its usefulness (Brown, 1978).

BEHAVIORAL INTERVENTIONS

Behavior Problems

Behavioral interventions have been successfully employed with a wide range of behavior problems in mentally retarded children across a number of environmental contexts, but the preponderance of work has been accomplished on two major and related behavioral correlates of retardation: stereotypies and SIB. However, behavioral interventions have also proved successful with problems involving physical aggression, various inappropiate behaviors (e.g., stripping, inappropriate vocalizing), vomiting, pica, noncompliance, and other minor conduct problems.

Stereotypic behaviors in retarded children, defined as repetitive acts with invariant topography and no apparent function, are found in great proportions of retarded individuals (Repp & Barton, 1980; Repp, Barton, & Gottlieb, 1983). In a recent review of behavioral interventions for stereotypies, LaGrow and

Repp (1984) found 60 studies describing various behavioral approaches to decreasing the occurrence of stereotypies in varying retarded populations. Approaches found to be successful included four major types: (1) manipulation of the setting or antecedent events, (2) application of aversive procedures, (3) application of positive procedures, and (4) manipulation of sensory stimulation.

Manipulating antecedent events alters the setting conditions that promote stereotypies or increases opportunities for competing behaviors to occur. Drugs are one means by which antecedents can be manipulated (e.g., Schalock, Foley, Toulouse, & Stark, 1985), and the use of drugs in behavioral interventions with retarded children is discussed in a subsequent section. A number of intervention studies have manipulated environmental opportunity for stereotypies, generally by having the subject either alone or with other people or by having toys or other objects available for play. Generally, results from these studies suggest that having objects present decreases the occurrence of stereotypic responding (Berkson & Mason, 1963; Horner, 1980; Moseley, Faust, & Reardon, 1970), as does having an opportunity to interact with adults (Berkson & Mason, 1963; Moseley *et al.*, 1970). Several studies, however, found increased stereotypic responding when opportunities for social interaction increased (Baumeister & Forehand, 1970; Hutt & Hutt, 1965). LaGrow and Repp (1984) concluded that manipulating antecedent events (exclusive of drug use) was only minimally effective, although they did note that increasing manipulable objects and adult-initiated social interaction is a low-cost intervention applicable across various settings and may in fact assist in maintenance effects when used in combination with more effective aversive and positive control techniques. A useful and potentially effective intervention may also be the use of exercise, which has been found to reduce stereotypic responding in a retarded adolescent (Baumeister & MacLean, 1984).

Suppressing stereotypies through aversive techniques has generally proven quite effective, although many of the techniques have undesirable side effects or are of questionable ethical use. A number of aversive techniques have been applied, including electric shock (Forehand & Baumeister, 1976); physical restraint (Bitgood, Crowe, Suarez, & Peters, 1980; Shapiro, Barrett, & Ollendick, 1980); aversive physical consequences such as a slap (Koegel & Covert, 1972) or water mist sprayed in the face (Bailey, Pikrzywinski, & Bryant, 1983); and even the use of aversive music (Greene, Hoats, & Hornick, 1970). The Greene et al. (1970) study was particularly interesting in that distorted music was played contingently, and maintenance was planned through the use of an intermittent schedule of follow-up during which distorted music was played. Overcorrection, a technique requiring the practice of alternate forms of responding, has received more recent attention than any other form of suppressive or punishment technique, and has generally proven to be effective in reducing stereotypies in retarded children (Barrett & Linn, 1981; Martin, Weller, & Matson, 1977); at times, it has been shown to be more effective than differential reinforcement techniques (Denny, 1980; Luiselli, Helfin, Pemberton, & Reisman, 1977). Unfortunately, overcorrection has also been found to be associated with increases in untreated stereotypies or previously unobserved SIB (Doke & Epstein, 1975; Rollings et al., 1977).

Because stereotypic behavior is not injurious, ethical considerations arise as to the use of punishment techniques for these concerns. Positive procedures involving differential reinforcement of other (DRO) and differential reinforcement of incompatible (DRI) behaviors have also proven effective. Although the use of DRO and DRI alone has been successful with stereotypies, these techniques appear to be most effective when used in combination with other techniques, such as physical restraint, introduction of toys in the environment, or overcorrection (Barkley & Zupnick, 1976; Horner, 1980; Luiselli, Pemberton, & Heflin, 1978). For example, Luiselli et al. (1978) studied the effectiveness of DRI plus overcorrection on a hand stereotypy of a 10-year-old retarded boy, and also measured the side effects on three similar behaviors that were not consequated. The DRI (social praise and food) increased the targeted hand response and reduced the associated unconsequated responses significantly. Adding the overcorrection response further reduced the stereotypy, and follow-up at 2 months and at 3½ months indicated that stereotypic responding was totally eliminated. It seems most likely that combining features of positive and aversive control may be the most powerful and successful intervention, particularly with regard to subsequent maintenance and generalization.

SIB is behavior that results in physical injury to one's own body (Tate & Baroff, 1966), and primarily differs from stereotypy in that it results in physical harm. The two are clearly similar in function, and frequently co-occur. As such, it is not surprising that treatment strategies for SIB are similar to those for stereotypies and have resulted in similar findings, except that punishment procedures may be more acceptable in light of the potentially harmful nature of the behavior. Various aversive control techniques have been applied, including shock (Yeakel, Salisbury, Greer, & Marcus, 1970), contingent presentation of aromatic ammonia or citric acid (Altman, Havik, & Cook, 1978; Baumeister & Baumeister, 1977; Mayhew & Harris, 1979), aversive tickling (Greene & Hoats, 1971), and overcorrection (Azrin, Gottlieb, Hughart, Wesolowski, & Rahn, 1975). Although these techniques are generally successful, they are often also found to have undesirable side effects or show little maintenance or generalizability. Time-out procedures, or variations of such an approach, have shown a fair degree of success and represent the least objectionable form of punishment with SIB. Studies of time out are difficult to evaluate, given that time-out intervals vary considerably across studies (Keogh & Whitman, 1983).

There appears to be particular promise in the facial screening procedure developed by Lutzker (1978) and systematically assessed by Singh and colleagues with retarded children showing SIB (Singh, 1980; Winton, Singh, & Dawson, 1984). The Winton et al. (1984) study showed that facial screening (using a bib tied at the neck and left to hang on the child's chest until SIB is exhibited, at which time the bib is then pulled up over the face and held at the back of the head for 1 minute) was impressively effective at reducing retarded children's SIB to near-zero rates during the intervention. Furthermore, maintenance was enhanced by instructing institutional staff to use the facial screening intervention, and SIB was measured to be at near-zero rates up to 10 months after the intervention. Facial screening appears to be a particularly successful technique and avoids many (though not all) of the ethical problems and potentially negative side effects associated with other punishment techniques.

DRO and DRI have also been used with SIB

in retarded children, with some indications of success. Again, these are typically used in combination with some form of negative control, such as overcorrection (Azrin *et al.*, 1975; De-Catanzaro & Baldwin, 1978) or verbal reprimands (Repp & Deitz, 1974), and there are indications that DRI may be more effective than DRO techniques in suppressing SIB (Tarpley & Schroeder, 1979). Negative reinforcement was used by Favell, McGimsey, and Jones (1978) in the form of removal of restraints within a DRO program, and this was found to successfully decrease SIB. Lockwood and Bourland (1982) described a procedure involving introduction of toys (modifying antecedent events) along with DRO for two retarded adolescents exhibiting severe finger biting and face slapping. They found that toy introduction was not always sufficient, and that the DRO in combination with the toys (attached to the wheelchairs of these nonambulatory adolescents) produced the reduction in SIB.

Aggressive and destructive acting out is a relatively frequent problem with retarded children, and again a combination of reinforcement and response-contingent deceleration techniques has proven effective in decreasing such behaviors (Luiselli, Myles, Evans, & Boyce, 1985; Luiselli & Reisman, 1980). Yet there have been major difficulties in demonstrating both maintenance and generalization with aggressive behavior in retarded children, regardless of the techniques employed (Luiselli, Myles, & Littman-Quinn, 1983). Nevertheless, time out and DRO procedures in combination have been successful in modifying aggressive and destructive behaviors (Foxx, Foxx, Jones, & Kiley, 1980; Vukelich & Hake, 1971). Luiselli *et al.* (1983) recently described a program of DRO and time out with a 15-year-old retarded boy whose target behaviors were aggression and destruction. After baseline observations, token reinforcement of appropriate behavior was introduced, followed several days later by the addition of time out for aggressive behavior and later for both aggressive and destructive behavior. These procedures were carried out in his classroom. A second phase, identical to that used in the classroom, was begun in the subject's residential cottage 1 month later. Results indicated that only with the combination of DRO and time out was either aggression or destruction successfully eliminated in either setting. Disappointingly, no generalization

effects were found either across behaviors (decreases in aggression did not lead to decreases in untreated destruction) or across settings (decreases in aggressive and destructive behavior in the classroom did not generalize to the cottage without specific programming in the cottage).

Interventions similar to those described above have also been employed with problems of vomiting and rumination (Foxx, Snyder, & Schroeder, 1979; Marholin, Luiselli, Robinson, & Lott, 1980; pica (Bucher, Reykdal, & Albin, 1976), drooling (Drabman, Cordua y Cruz, Ross, & Lynd, 1979), air swallowing (Holburn & Dougher, 1985), and numerous other minor behavior problems similar to those of nonretarded children (Keogh & Whitman, 1983). Lacking in these intervention programs are systematic plans for generalization and maintenance of the target behaviors, and this may be the major reason why so little improvement is found on follow-up measurement.

Social Skills

Social skills deficits are often found in retarded children, and in fact are generally part of the adaptive skill deficits diagnostic of the disorder during childhood. Social skills training or interventions with mentally retarded children and adolescents have typically involved some combination of procedures proposed in Bellack and Hersen's (1979), general model of social skills training, which includes instruction, modeling, role play, social reinforcement, and practice. Most of this work has been accomplished with more severely and profoundly retarded children; the mildly and moderately retarded have received relatively little research attention (Keogh & Whitman, 1983).

Many of the interventions aimed at social skills training of retarded children have focused on interpersonal play skills or various communication strategies (Singh & Winton, 1983). Social play is particularly important, as social development can be facilitated through this modality with retarded children (Wehman, 1977). A number of studies have proven the efficacy of combining various behavioral techniques for increasing play skills in retarded children, and promising maintenance has been achieved as well. Paloutzian, Hasazi, Striefel, and Edgar (1971) used modeling and imitation training to develop social interactions in a group of 10 severely retarded children. Generalization was promoted by pairing different children with each other and with different trainers during the training. These authors noted anecdotally that increases in social interactive play were also seen on the children's ward, suggesting generalization across contexts. Several other studies provide similar evidence that combining modeling and social and primary reinforcement procedures increases social play with retarded children, and that the gains obtained through this training are maintained (Cone, Anderson, Harris, Goff, & Fox, 1978; Morris & Dolker, 1974). The Cone et al. (1978) study further found that physical and verbal prompts for cooperative play, reinforced with candy, increased cooperative and associated play, although generalization across settings required specific training. However, decreases were observed in self-stimulatory behavior without other specific interventions.

Recent work by Strain and his colleagues (Gable, Hendrickson, & Strain, 1978; Odom, Hoyson, Jamieson, & Strain, 1985; Strain, 1975, 1977, 1983) has shown that positive social interactions of retarded children can be increased and represent important targets for intervention; this is particularly true of behaviors that involve play, organizing, sharing, appropriate showing of affection, and giving assistance (Strain, 1983). In one study (Strain, 1975), antecedent conditions were manipulated to increase the social play of a group of eight retarded children. Preceding a free-play period in the children's classroom, a story was read, and the children were then encouraged to take the role of a character in the story. Role-taking behaviors were socially praised, and this resulted in increased positive social interactions and taking of turns, although the effects were generally short-lived in the free-play setting. Gable et al. (1978) produced somewhat better results with an intervention program combining physical and verbal prompting with DRO to increase approach and cooperative responses in two multiply handicapped children. Increases were found for social approach, cooperative play, and nonaggressive contact, and generalization occurred across settings with no intervention. Of specific interest was the additional result that direct generalization training using reinforcement techniques resulted in further increases in the original target behaviors. Several other studies support the findings by Strain and his colleagues, with most

indicating that combinations of prompts, modeling, and reinforcement are the most effective techniques and are best at promoting generalization (Burney, Russell, & Shores, 1977; Mayhew, Enyart, & Anderson, 1978; Peterson, Austin, & Lange, 1979).

Conversational skills are an important component of social skills and have been a focus of intervention efforts with retarded children and adolescents. Intervention plans have typically involved a combination of techniques, including instructions, modeling, rehearsal, and reinforcement, and have resulted in positive increases in asking and answering questions (Bray, Biasini, & Thrasher, 1983; Neef, Walters, & Egel, 1984; Warren, Baxter, Anderson, Marshall, & Baer, 1981); self-disclosure and information seeking about others; and choosing appropriate conversational topics (Nelson, Gibson, & Cutting, 1973). Particularly noteworthy is the study by Warren et al. (1981), in which eight retarded adolescents were trained in asking appropriate questions within a modeling and reinforcement paradigm for approximately 30 months. Training was successful in developing appropriate question-asking skills. Most importantly, the effects of this training program generalized well on their own or with simple exposure to a peer model or a brief review of the training program. This suggests that generalization and maintenance of some social skills can be enhanced by using a comprehensive approach in which time is allowed for skill development, accompanied by specific procedures for maintenance and generalization.

It appears that various behavioral interventions can be successfully employed to increase the social skills of retarded children. Yet the studies are weak in respect to plans for generalization and maintenance, with the few notable exceptions mentioned above. It is apparent that both generalization and maintenance can be established if plans for such are built into the intervention program. Another major weakness in the area of interventions for social skills is the social and ecological validity of the skills being treated (Singh & Winton, 1983). Singh and Winton note that the skills that have been addressed, although slightly problematic with populations of retarded children, have basically been chosen for their ease in assessment and programming rather than on the basis of social need or validity. This limitation in the research literature requires that subsequent interventions be tied to the individual assessment process.

Furthermore, the assessment must include measurements across the ecological contexts and deficits that are relevant to a particular child. As Romer and Heller (1983) suggest, social skills need to be considered from a social-ecological context that takes into account the impact and possible utilization of social networks in the development and maintenance of social skills in retarded children.

Adaptive and Self-Help Skills

Adaptive or self-help skill deficits constitute another of the major diagnostic criteria for mental retardation during childhood. Not surprisingly, behavioral interventions with retarded children have also been developed to increase adaptive skills where deficits exist. Adaptive abilities comprise feeding, dressing, toileting, personal hygiene, and skills generally associated with independent functioning (e.g., managing money, using telephones, and telling time).

Generally, behavioral interventions aimed at developing independent feeding skills have been directed toward the use of particular utensils and general dining skills or toward decreasing inappropriate mealtime behaviors (e.g., throwing food). These interventions typically employ techniques involving faded guidance, chaining (forward or backward), or a combination of both (Azrin & Armstrong, 1973; O'Brien & Azrin, 1972; Richman, Sonderby, & Kahn, 1980). Another successful approach to the teaching of feeding skills used positive practice overcorrection and time out for incorrect responding (Stimbert, Minor, & McCoy, 1977). However, the training of six retarded children to reach optimal levels required many more training sessions than have other techniques that have been reported. Combining faded guidance, positive practice, and continuous reinforcement in analogue feeding situations rather than during real mealtimes proved to be a particularly effective procedure with retarded children (Richman et al., 1980), and somewhat faster than similar procedures used during real mealtimes. The analogue situation within the children's classroom allowed for four training sessions during the day, rather than just the one lunch period for real mealtimes, and avoided the common problem of food satiation noted in feeding studies. Retarded children in the analogue situation were

also found to generalize their skills to the real lunch period.

Studies of interventions for dressing skills with retarded children are few, but have primarily involved procedures of verbal prompting, modeling, fading, and positive reinforcements (Whitman & Johnston, 1987). Two early studies of dressing interventions with retarded children (Colwell, Richards, McCarver, & Ellis, 1973; Martin, Kehoe, Bird, Jensen, & Darbyshire, 1971) indicated that simple combined fading and shaping procedures were successful in teaching undressing, and that combined fading, reinforcement, and time out effectively taught more sophisticated dressing skills to retarded girls. A recent study by Jarman, Iwata, and Lorentzson (1983) demonstrated that multiple self-care skills could be increased with a specific intervention involving the use of token reinforcement contingent on single responses, followed by a condition of token reinforcement contingent on chained responses. Six self-care skills were the focus of the intervention, all of which made up the morning routine at a residential facility serving adolescents and adults. The skills included toileting, showering, dressing, brushing teeth, cleaning the bed area, and removing bedding. Results showed that first under the single-response and later under the chained-response intervention, retarded adolescents were able to increase their rates of performance to near optimal level for each of the six skills. Interestingly, Jarman et al. (1983) emphasize the importance not only of variables related to client behaviors, but also of those related to staff members who carry out the interventions. This is a particularly significant notation, as it offers preliminary indications that a systems understanding is necessary in implementing behavioral interventions with retarded children.

Toilet training has received perhaps the greatest attention within the area of self-help skills with retarded children, and was among the earliest applications of behavioral interventions with this population (Keogh & Whitman, 1983). The classic behavioral intervention for this skill, developed by Azrin and Foxx (1971), involved the use of two mechanical signal devices: a pants alarm, and a toilet bowl alarm that signaled appropriate elimination. In addition, Azrin and Foxx included time out for accidents along with overcorrection techniques, and found that severely retarded children could be rapidly trained in appropriate toileting skills.

Several studies have replicated these results with various samples of retarded children (Raborn, 1978; Smith, 1979; Song, Song, & Grant, 1976) and have produced successful results, although at a somewhat slower rate than that reported by Azrin and Foxx (1971). These studies were limited to severely and profoundly institutionalized retarded children, in cases where the use of a signal device was both necessary and manageable. For noninstitutionalized retarded children with lesser degrees of retardation, such devices are not always necessary and can be difficult to manage by parents or other therapists in more natural environments. Azrin and Foxx (1974) also developed a methodology for toilet-training normal and noninstitutionalized or mildly to moderately retarded children. In this procedure, combined techniques of modeling and imitation, faded guidance, prompting, DRO, positive practice, and overcorrection were used to demonstrate that toilet training can be accomplished in very short duration. The popular book *Toilet Training in Less Than a Day* (Azrin & Foxx, 1974) specifically details this procedure for parents, with some distinct alterations noted for parents of mildly to moderately retarded children. These changes include a greater use of faded manual guidance; modification in the imitation contexts by eliminating or de-emphasizing the "doll that wets"; and, where appropriate, de-emphasizing social acceptability by omitting the "friends who care" procedures. Of interest is the finding that when this training method was used, generalization effects were noted in decreased enuresis as well (Azrin & Foxx, 1971).

Interventions with other adaptive behavior deficits also indicate the range and breadth of behavior approaches to skill development. Telephone-dialing skills were taught to moderately retarded children by managing stimulus conditions (Leff, 1974) and pairing numbers with colors on the phone. Over 90% of the retarded children in the study learned to dial correctly, although maintenance data did not clearly establish that such a technique alone was capable of establishing this skill in a lasting way. Telephone skills are potentially important in emergency situations, and the social validity of this skill training is clear (Risley & Cuvo, 1980). A number of behavior interventions have been successfully employed to teach money management skills to retarded children. A series of studies by Cuvo (Borakove & Cuvo, 1976; Lowe & Cuvo, 1976; Miller, Cuvo, & Borakove, 1977), using modeling, verbal instruction and praise, found that coin summation and equivalence could be learned by retarded adolescents and children. Summing and equivalence have only marginal ecological validity as adaptive skills, but a subsequent study (Cuvo, Veitch, Trace, & Konke, 1978) showed that modeling and reinforcement procedures were successful in teaching retarded adolescents to make change. Furthermore, gains in making change were maintained over a 2-week maintenance interval. Similar results were obtained in a study teaching grocery-shopping skills to adolescents, using role modeling, verbal instruction, mnemonic training, and reinforcement specifically focusing on maintenance and generalization of these skills (Aeschleman & Schladenhauffen, 1984).

The ability to tell time is an important adaptive skill, yet one of the most difficult for retarded children to learn. Acting on the time cues is an even more complex behavior requiring greater abstract cognitive ability (Partington, Sundberg, Iwata, & Mountjoy, 1979). A recent intervention paradigm using a clock agenda combination device, along with verbal instruction, modeling, physical guidance, and social praise, successfully increased time telling with four retarded children, as well as the ability to meet scheduled appointments on the basis of telling time (Smeets, Lancioni, & Van Lieshout, 1985). Unfortunately, data on maintenance and generalization were not included, but this study does provide evidence that relatively complex adaptive skills are amenable to specific behavioral technologies even in the absence of basic cognitive prerequisites for the skill.

Academic Skills

Several different behavioral approaches have been taken to intervening in the academic skill deficits of retarded children. They include (1) programming the environment to meet retarded children's difficulties with processing and perceptual efficiency; (2) eliminating inappropriate behaviors that compete with learning in the classroom; and (3) using direct training strategies to enhance attention, problem solving, and remembering.

The deficits in processing and attending that characterize retarded children (Ellis, 1979) directly limit their ability to learn in new situations. For this reason, professionals training retarded children often seek to alter aspects of the environment or the task in order to reduce the information load. Examples include reducing the irrelevant task dimensions or making the material to be learned more salient. Attempts to maximize aspects of the task to fit the children's strengths and weaknesses facilitate improved use of attentional skills as well as indirectly improving perceptual efficiency. As an example, Mercer and Snell (1977) outline several teaching implications of the Zeaman and House (1963) theory of attention, which include (1) reducing the number of irrelevant dimensions; (2) including the learner's dimension bias in planning tasks; (3) increasing the number of relevant dimensions; (4) reinforcing attention to relevant dimensions; and (5) making relevant cues distinctive. Research by Switzky (1973) and Zeaman, House, and Orlando (1958) provides support for educational efforts to make relevant cues more distinctive. Switzky's research indicates that discrimination learning in retarded children can be enhanced by varying both the shape and brightness of the stimuli. Similarly, Zeaman et al. (1958) found that novel stimuli of a positive or negative nature increased the saliency of training and resulted in improved performance. Another suggestion for improving the saliency of the training is to encourage teachers to use attractive stimuli to focus and maintain attention (Douglas, 1974b). During training and treatment, it is typically recommended that irrelevant distractions be reduced in order to emphasize the important elements. However, after the treatment is mastered, then the "inoculation process" needs to begin, in which the retarded child is slowly introduced to distracting stimuli (Borkowski & Konarski, 1980).

Another way of helping the retarded child utilize his or her processing capabilities most effectively is to eliminate the inappropriate behaviors that interfere with learning. These competing behaviors range from innocuous self-stimulatory behaviors to more disruptive hyperactive behaviors (being out of seat), and from these to dangerous classroom behaviors such as aggression and SIB (Borkowski & Konarski, 1980). A well-developed behavioral technology exists for using behavior modification principles with a wide range of disruptive classroom behaviors; the techniques involved have been described earlier in this chapter. Although behavior modification techniques are an integral part of classroom management, a

relevant criticism is that the behavioral improvements of retarded children typically do not generalize to other teachers and classrooms unless specifically reinforced. In addition, behavioral changes such as reduction in out-of-seat behavior indicate improved compliance in retarded children, but not necessarily enhanced learning (Borkowski & Konarski, 1980).

The incentive to use strategy-training procedures developed from work showing that retarded children do not readily demonstrate the strategies or skills typically employed by their nonretarded peers (Brown et al., 1983). In addition, teaching strategies to retarded children, such as strategies for remembering and learning, was found to bring about improvements in performance (Belmont, 1978; Borkowski & Cavanaugh, 1979). For example, Whitman et al. (1982) found that a self-instruction program utilizing an attention-focusing strategy produced improvements in attention, as well as general gains in the quantity and quality of classroom work. Brown (1978) has described strategies as methods (or activities) undertaken by the learner to render the novel more familiar.

Strategies have been successfully used to train a variety of skills such as attention (Whitman et al., 1982), self-control (Reid & Borkowski, 1987), and self-checking (Brown, Campione, & Barclay, 1979), as well as actual academic content such as mathematics (Johnston, Whitman, & Johnson, 1980) and vocabulary (Dorry & Zeaman, 1975). In addition, comprehensive programs exist that rely heavily on strategy training to create "support systems" to help the retarded child utilize available processing resources most effectively. Two examples of such programs are found in the work of Feuerstein (1979) and Ross and Ross (1978). Strategy training represents a type of "executive skill training" and, as such, is more amenable to generalization across tasks (if this is built into a program) than the treatments that are aimed solely at isolated behaviors. Strategies should be selected for their clinical usefulness to the child's overall development. Furthermore, other aspects of the working model presented earlier should be taken into consideration in strategy implementation, such as the child's affect (especially if the child's approach to learning is characterized by a "learned helplessness" orientation) and the potential influence of others (child's family, teachers) on the child's continued use of the new skills across tasks and contexts.

Another approach aimed at enhancing the cognitive skills and development of at-risk children is exemplified by the early intervention programs (e.g., the North Carolina Abecedarian Project and Head Start). These programs have a *preventive* focus, in the sense that their objective is to provide assistance (both educational and physical) to infants and mothers in order to alleviate environmental influences that contribute to low IQ, such as poor nutrition, lack of health services, insufficient knowledge about child development, and poor educational stimulation.

The Abecedarian Project is an ongoing early intervention program that was established in 1972. In this project children are identified through a High-Risk Index (cf. Ramey & Smith, 1977), which includes such risk factors as mother's and father's educational status, family income, maternal and paternal IQ, father's absence, and other familial characteristics. These high-risk children are randomly assigned to a experimental group (i.e., intervention) or a control group. Both groups of children receive free nutritional supplements and health care. However, only the children in the experimental group receive the intensive early intervention program at the day care facility, which begins at 3 months of age and continues until the children are ready for school.

The intervention focuses on teaching the children a wide variety of skills. From 3 months to 3 years of age, the children receive a program consisting of over 300 items in language, motor, social, and cognitive skills. From 3 to 5 years of age, the areas of math, music, prereading, and reading are emphasized. Children participate in this systematic, child-directed program for 6–8 hours per day, 50 weeks of the year.

The focus of the Abecedarian intervention efforts has been on high-risk children themselves, rather than on their mothers, fathers, siblings, or families. As a consequence, most of the results of the program pertain to the children themselves. The primary findings thus far have indicated that the children receiving the intervention have more advanced cognitive skills (as evidenced by higher IQ scores) and greater social competency than control children. A secondary finding has been that the mothers of children in the intervention group have also been affected by the day care program. That is, although mothers were not a direct target of the intervention, the mothers of children in the intervention group were found to have more education than the mothers of control children, even though maternal education had been equivalent at the time when children first entered the day care program. In addition, job attainment of the mothers in the intervention group also seems to have been positively affected by the children's placement in full-time day care.

In summary, the early intervention programs are not based on the premise that all mental retardation can be "cured" with appropriate environmental interventions, especially cases in which children have known brain damage or physical abnormality. However, for children who have experienced adverse environmental contexts, changing the environment has been found to alter the outcome greatly (Heber, 1978; Ramey & Haskins, 1981). According to Figure 7-1, these early intervention programs are an example of intervening at the ecological levels of community and school services in order to help the parents and children.

PHARMACOLOGICAL INTERVENTIONS

Psychoactive drugs are widely used as a form of treatment with retarded individuals. In fact, the extensiveness of drug usage suggests that the mentally retarded may be the most medicated group in society (Aman & Singh, 1983). The actual number of individuals on medication varies, depending on the related factors of age, severity of cognitive and behavioral deficits, and placement. Older individuals in institutions tend to have more severe and debilitating behavioral problems requiring medication than those who remain in nuclear families. However, antisocial behaviors are quite common across all groups; if these are not addressed, through either behavior intervention or medication, they will result in eventual institutionalization (Mulick & Schroeder, 1980).

Surveys of institutionalized residents suggest that between 40% and 50% are receiving psychotropic medication at any given time (Aman & Singh, 1983; Cohen & Sprague, 1977; Lipman, 1970). A study of 3,306 trainable mentally retarded children and adolescents attending special classes in public school found that 19% received medication, with 12% receiving anticonvulsant medication and 7% receiving psychotropic drugs (Gadow & Kalachnik, 1981).

Stimulants were reported to be the most commonly used behavior modification drug. Given the large numbers of mentally retarded individuals on medication and the pervasive effects of drugs on behavioral adjustment, learning, and physical health, it behooves clinicians working with the retarded to be familiar with the commonly prescribed medications.

Drug research with the retarded is difficult to review because of numerous methodological difficulties, which have undoubtedly contributed to the often-noted equivocal findings (Sprague & Werry, 1971). These problems include the absence of suitable control groups, placebos, and standard measures of drug effects. The failure to include learning variables when examining the influence of medication is particularly troublesome. Learning is a major problem with the retarded, yet the drug dosages used for behavioral control have often been found to interfere with sensitivity to reinforcement, as well as with various aspects of the children's cognitive performance (e.g., short-term memory) (Sprague & Sleator, 1977).

The main types of medication used with the mentally retarded are antipsychotics, antiepileptics, and stimulant medications. Antipsychotics, including chlorpromazine, thioridazine, and haloperidol, are the most frequently prescribed medications for aggression, destructiveness, hyperactivity, and antisocial behaviors in adults, and to a lesser degree in adolescents and children (Aman & Singh, 1983). Although antipsychotics are often prescribed, methodological difficulties and conflicting findings prevent any general conclusions about their efficacy. For example, reviews of the uncontrolled studies suggest that antipsychotics, especially chlorpromazine, produce a reduction in problem behaviors in mentally retarded children (Lipman, DeMascio, Reatig, & Kirson, 1978; Sprague & Werry, 1971). However, data from more recent and better-controlled studies challenge these earlier reviews and suggest that chlorpromazine may actually exacerbate problem behaviors in some children (Marholin, Touchette, & Stewart, 1979). Individualized child × medication assessments need to be undertaken to determine whether a child is an optimal responder or a nonresponder, since high dosages have been found to worsen the behaviors of nonresponders dramatically (Singh & Aman, 1981). Dose-response effects have been found for some of the antipsychotics (thioridazine), with low dosages (2.5 mg/kg) being sufficient to reduce self-stimulatory behaviors and higher dosages (5.9 mg/kg) reducing aggressive behaviors in known responders.

When one is providing behavioral treatment for a mentally retarded child who is on antipsychotic medication, it is important to know the child's medication status, including dosage (mg/kg) and length of time on medication. The complexity of child × medication × dosage interactions necessitates that the clinician be sensitive to whether the child is an optimal responder or a nonresponder, and to the possibility that the drug dosage prescribed to suppress inappropriate behavior is interfering with the learning that is required in the behavioral intervention. Although the behavioral therapist is not in a position to prescribe medication, he or she is typically in a good position to observe and assess the influence of medication on the child and should be in contact with the child's physician when appropriate. In addition, it is imperative that parents as well as professionals working with the child be aware of the possible physiological side effects of antipsychotics. These side effects include (1) anticholinergic effects (dry mouth, blurred vision, reduced gastric motility, and mental confusion); (2) alpha-adrenergic blockage (flushing of the skin); and (3) dopaminergic effects (such as tardive dyskinesia, which is a drug-induced movement disorder).

Anticonvulsant drugs or antiepileptics, such as phenytoin, phenobarbital, and Tegretol, are most commonly prescribed for the suppression of seizures. However, surveys of institutions for the retarded have suggested that from 19% to 59% of the individuals on anticonvulsants have no clinical evidence of a seizure disorder (Kaufman & Katz-Garris, 1979). In these cases, they appear to be on the medication because of purported claims that anticonvulsants reduce behavior disorders. Despite the usage of anticonvulsants for psychotropic purposes, research has been unable to establish any cognitive, behavioral, or emotional benefits. Conversely, high dosages have been associated with psychomotor deterioration (Conners, Kramer, Rothschild, Schwartz, & Stone, 1971) and behavioral disturbance (Ounsted, 1955; Schain, 1979). Wolf and Forsythe (1978) found that 42% of the children treated with phenobarbital developed a behavioral disturbance, compared to 18% who received no treatment. The increases in behavioral problems for children on anticonvulsants have been widely reported, and behavioral therapists working with mentally retarded children should be vigilant in looking for this reaction when children are brought in for treatment. All drugs are capable of producing untoward effects, but the toxic effects of antiepileptics may be particularly troublesome. Present research suggests that dosages of anticonvulsants for mentally retarded children should be kept to the actual minimum necessary for seizure control (Aman, 1983; Conners & Werry, 1979).

Stimulant medications, although seldom used with mentally retarded adults, have been found to be the most common behavior-modifying drugs prescribed for trainable mentally retarded children in special public school placements (Gadow & Kalachnik, 1981). The most commonly used psychostimulants are methylphenidate (Ritalin), dextroamphetamine (Dexedrine), and magnesium pemoline (Cylert). Unlike many other psychotropic drugs, which appear to cause CNS depression, stimulants have been found to enhance short-term improvements on attention, memory, and discrimination tasks (Douglas, 1974a; Reid & Borkowski, 1984). However, despite these short-term benefits, studies of hyperactive children receiving long-term stimulant medication have generally been unable to document any academic gains due to pharmacotherapy alone (Aman, 1978; Barkley & Cunningham, 1978). Stimulant medication is typically prescribed for mildly to moderately retarded children for the same reasons it is used with hyperactive and learning-disabled nonretarded children—that is, to address problems with inattention, distractibility, and excessive activity that interfere with learning. Stimulants have not been recommended for more severely retarded adults (Aman, 1983). Furthermore, although beneficial effects of stimulants on attentional factors have been shown for some hyperactive children, its efficacy with mildly to moderately retarded children has not been clearly documented because of the paucity of research in this area. For example, research with nonretarded hyperactive children suggests that moderate dosages of methylphenidate significantly increase overall information-processing efficiency, even when the effects of overt, on-task attentional behaviors are statistically removed (Reid & Borkowski, 1984). Tests of general IQ have repeatedly been found to be insensitive to drug manipulation in the retarded (Sprague & Werry, 1971). Research is

needed with mentally retarded children that looks at the impact of medication dosages on the more specific cognitive correlates of performance (Aman & Singh, 1983).

Although the side effects of stimulant medication are significantly less than those of many other psychoactive drugs, it is still important that the behavior therapist working with mentally retarded children be aware of them. The most frequent side effects include insomnia, decreased appetite, abdominal pain, and headaches (Cantwell & Carlson, 1978). As with the other medications, high dosages may interfere with optimal cognitive functioning (Sprague & Sleator, 1977), although this issue remains controversial.

Several other drugs not included in the discussion above also bear mentioning. Specifically, imipramine, an antidepressant, is the most commonly prescribed medication for enuresis in both retarded and nonretarded children. Also, lithium carbonate, an antimanic drug, has recently received some support for the treatment of chronic hyperactivity, aggression, and SIB (Cooper & Fowlie, 1972; Goetzl, Grunberg, & Berkowitz, 1977; Lion, Hill, & Madden, 1975).

Increasingly, medications are being used in combination with behavioral programs (the "pills plus skills" approach). For example, methylphenidate is often used in conjunction with behavioral training programs that are designed to increase children's attention to tasks (Whalen, Henker, & Hinshaw, 1985). However, when medication is combined with behavioral interventions, several issues need to be considered. First, the dosage needs to be monitored, to insure that the drug does not increase sluggishness or in any way interfere with the optimal cognitive functioning required for the child to perform the new behavioral skills (see Sprague & Sleator, 1977). The second concern involves the child's own perceptions or attributions regarding the medication. If the child thinks that the medication is *necessary* for him or her to successfully perform the new behavioral skills, then the child may not be likely to continue to perform the difficult new skills when medication is discontinued.

When the goal of the combined medication plus behavioral intervention approach is to eventually withdraw the medication and have the child continue to perform the newly acquired behavioral skills, then it is important during training to stress the importance of the child's own efforts, rather than just the medication, in bringing about success. There is not much research on retarded children's perceptions about being on medication. However, the attributions of other children on medication, such as hyperactive children, have indicated that the children's perceptions and misconceptions about drug usage are important to take into consideration when implementing interventions (see Whalen & Henker, 1980).

In summary, because of the high numbers of mentally retarded individuals on medication, it is not uncommon for therapists to be designing behavioral interventions for children who are on one of the medications mentioned above. For this reason, it is important to be aware of the child's dosage, time on medication, and behaviors while off medication, as well as some of the positive and negative effects of each of the pharmacological treatments. Also, studies that combine psychopharmacological and behavioral interventions may provide powerful treatments across settings, but remain to be systematically assessed (Brown, Borden, Wynne, Schleser, & Clingerman, 1986).

PARENT AND FAMILY TRAINING

Many of the behavioral interventions that have thus far been described for dealing with retarded children's skills or behaviors were delivered in institutional, residential, or school settings by staff members, teachers, or other professionals. Furthermore, they have involved children with more serious retardation. Yet it is clear that mildly to moderately retarded children who live at home are also in need of behavioral interventions for the various behavior problems and skill deficits they may have. Generally, the primary mechanism for treating these needs has been through training parents, as well as other family members, as therapists or teachers for their retarded children.

Parent intevention has begun to receive systematic treatment in the general literature on retarded children (Baker, 1984; Tymchuk, 1983), although it appears that there has been some confusion regarding the intent of parent training. Often, the teaching of intervention and parenting skills is considered as an intervention for parents or families, rather than as a technique for intervening with the retarded child in his or her primary developmental context. Providing parents with training in various approaches to dealing with child behavior no doubt increases parental effectiveness, but the intent is often to focus more on subsequent changes in the child's behavior than on changes in the parent or family. Indeed, whether this corresponds to more optimal parenting as a rule is still an empirical question and one specifically related to generalization of parent training interventions. Nevertheless, there is some indication from the studies available that parent training is effective and may indeed generalize to some additional aspects of parenting and family functioning (Baker, 1984; Karoly & Rosenthal, 1977).

Studies of parent training with retarded children have involved either case studies with single family–child units, or studies in which groups of parents are trained with various techniques to intervene with their retarded children. Individual case studies have indicated that parents can be effectively trained to use a variety of behavioral techniques, including modeling, time out, reinforcement, overcorrection, and general contingency management, to intervene in such areas as dressing skills (Adubato, Adams, & Budd, 1981), noncompliance (Budd, Green, & Baer, 1976; Casey, 1978; Forehand, Cheney, & Yoder, 1974; Johnson, Whitman, & Barloon-Noble, 1978), eating skills (White, 1982), acting-out or disruptive behavior (Brehony, Benson, Solomon, & Luscomb, 1980; Frazier & Schneider, 1975; Gerrard & Saxon, 1973), and even SIB (Barnard, Christophersen, & Wolf, 1976). Generally, results have been quite positive, and many of the interventions have produced acceptable maintenance of skill over time. For example, Brehony et al. (1980) trained the parents of a 7-year-old retarded boy who showed acting-out behaviors and difficulties in attention span. The boy's behavior significantly limited the family's ability to go on outings (e.g., to restaurants), as his behavior was a consistent source of stress and difficulty in management. The parents were provided with twelve 30-minute sessions focusing on consistent responding, the use of verbal control (a firm "No!" to inappropriate behavior), and praise and touch for appropriate or desired behaviors. Substantial decreases were found in the boy's noncompliance and throwing, while his ability to attend and behave appropriately in social settings increased dramatically over the 12 sessions. Observational follow-up 2 months later by independent observers indicated that the target behaviors were maintained. Another parent training study (Cowart, Iwata, & Poynter, 1984) found that training individual parents with a multicomponent program that included written instructions, role playing, and performance feedback resulted not only in increased target skills of their children, but also in maintenance of these skills over time and generalization to the teaching of other skills in the home.

Group interventions with parents of retarded children have likewise shown that dramatic treatment effects can be obtained, and many of the studies also provide information on parental change as well as that of the child (Baker, 1984). The group interventions vary widely in regard to the specificity and breadth of training offered, but most focus on strategies in which parents are taught to observe, identify, and intervene with specific target behaviors of their retarded children. Parent group training programs have proven effective in intervening with various problems associated with retarded children, including noncompliance and behavior problems (Breiner & Beck, 1984; Brightman, Baker, Clark, & Ambrose, 1982; Tavormina, 1975), self-help and adaptive skills (Baker, Heifetz, & Murphy, 1980; Feldman, Manella, & Varni, 1983), academic skills (Fry, 1977), and parent–child interactions (Diament & Colletti, 1978; Sandler, Coren, & Thurman, 1983). Many of these studies have likewise measured increases in parent knowledge (Brightman *et al.*, 1982); skills in applying this knowledge to specific child behaviors (Hudson, 1982); changes in interaction patterns (Sandler *et al.*, 1983), and even changes in parental attitudes, marital satisfaction, and family cohesion (Forehand & King, 1977; Karoly & Rosenthal, 1977; Scovern *et al.*, 1980). This last point is of particular interest in demonstrating that behavioral interventions can have system effects that require attention and measurement.

Exemplifying particularly well formulated and successful parent training programs is the Parents as Teachers Project (Baker, 1980). This project was specifically developed to train parents of retarded children to deal effectively with a range of skill deficits and behavior problems common to this population. Parenting training is accomplished over 10 sessions, each 2 hours in duration, with groups of fewer than 10 families. The sessions focus on specific problem areas (self-help, behavior problems, and play and language skills); behavioral objectives are developed, skills are broken down, and contingency management involving both positive and negative consequences is taught. Parents are also taught cognitive strategies to intervene with interfering thoughts related to teaching or behavior management, substituting more positive success-oriented thoughts. The training model incorporates role playing, demonstrations, videotaped feedback, and ongoing consultation as major training techniques; there is also a written manual covering skill areas involved in the training process. This program has reported consistent success across measurement domains of positive change in both retarded children's skills and parent's skills, as well as increases in parental knowledge about child rearing and retardation (Baker & Clark, 1983).

The results of these parent training projects seem to indicate clearly that parents can be effective change agents for their retarded children, and that parents also gain from the training. Interestingly, parent training has also been tried with retarded parents—a group whose children are at considerable risk for developmental problems and/or abuse (Feldman, Case, Towns, & Betel, 1985; Schilling, Schinke, Blythe, & Barth, 1982). A recent study by Budd and Greenspan (1985) indicated that parent training programs for retarded parents were judged by behavioral therapists to be more elaborate, more directive, and longer than typical programs for nonretarded parents; fewer than half the families described showed improvement on referral problems, and continued training was judged necessary to accomplish goals and to achieve generalization and maintenance. A specific procedure to teach more effective parent–child skills to retarded parents was recently reported by Peterson, Robinson, and Littman (1983). The program sought to teach parents to use their attention effectively to reinforce prosocial behavior in their children. In eight sessions, parents were taught to describe play activity, praise prosocial behavior, reflect the child's language, and avoid using commands, through the use of modeling, role playing, practice, and weekly consultation. Results indicated that the parents decreased their directiveness and increased positive verbal responsiveness, although only the decrease in directiveness was maintained at a 1-month follow-up. Unfortunately, the child behaviors measured in this study occurred so infrequently that it was not possible to assess whether changes in parent behavior resulted in changes in child behavior. Nevertheless, this study suggests that specific interventions with retarded parents can produce some successful changes, and such training merits further work.

Several intervention studies have taken an alternative tack by training siblings in behavior management techniques so that these might be applied during their interactions with their handicapped brothers or sisters (Bennett, 1973; Colletti & Harris, 1977; Schreibman, O'Neill, & Koegel, 1983). The results of these studies suggest that siblings can be taught effective management techniques and are capable of modifying their retarded siblings' behavior. However, Crnic and Leconte (1986) have noted that ethical issues associated with such training need to be considered. There is a fair amount of evidence to suggest that greater caretaking demand on siblings of retarded children is associated with greater maladjustment in the nonretarded siblings (Crnic *et al.*, 1983; Crnic & Leconte, 1986). Programs that seek to increase the caretaking responsibility of nonretarded siblings may well increase the risk of specific behavior problems in those siblings. Therefore, these programs need to consider the ethics of such an approach for individual siblings.

LIMITATIONS OF PREVIOUS INTERVENTIONS

The behavioral intervention studies reviewed in the previous sections demonstrate that applications of empirically derived behavior techniques can be successful in dealing with a range of difficulties presented by retarded children. Nevertheless, these studies have some limitations, particularly in relation to the conceptualization presented earlier in this chapter.

An issue of some importance is the clinical usefulness of the intervention being described and studied. Bornstein *et al.* (1982) have discussed the significance of this issue, and noted that if the application of behavioral principles is to be meaningful, the intervention techniques must have clinical utility. That is, they must be reasonable, and they must be put into practice by clinicians working in various settings. Some of the studies reviewed above were conducted more to demonstrate the technology than to provide a useful model of clinical service. In these studies, issues of maintenance and generalization were not of major concern and were rarely measured. Furthermore, although

most of the studies could demonstrate the clinical utility of the techniques assessed, many did not plan for or measure changes with a follow-up procedure. Therefore, many of the techniques described appear to have been successful in treating the behavior(s) of focus while the intervention was in progress, but it is unknown whether or not treatment effects were durable and were maintained over time. In addition, most of the studies did not attempt to assess whether the skills generalized to other meaningful situations in important and related ecological contexts. Clearly, planning and conducting clinically meaningful behavioral interventions with retarded children and their parents require careful planning and a consideration of the broader social context in which the children must function over time.

Another area in which many of the studies of behavioral intervention with retarded children have been deficient is in the measurement of possible side effects of aversive procedures or drugs. The issue of possible side effects needs to be carefully considered in planning interventions, and system effects will require more attention than they are presently being given. Measurement of collateral behaviors should be considered in all behavioral interventions, but especially when aversive or drug treatments are being planned.

Finally, the major shortcoming of the research on behavioral interventions with retarded children is that it has not reflected a systems approach. The studies that have involved specific approaches to training parents of retarded children to be effective teachers and interveners (e.g., Baker, 1980) begin to approach a more system-oriented model when consideration is given to general parenting skills as well as specific intervention techniques. Typically, however, the intervention is aimed at the specific behavior in question (e.g., noncompliance), without consideration of how that behavior functions within the context in which it occurs. More attention needs to be given during the assessment, intervention, and follow-up phases to the child as well as to the system in which the child operates (family, group home, school, institution). The retarded child's functioning cannot be separated from the context if the behavior in question is to be understood, successfully treated, and maintained. Furthermore, treatments must at times intervene on a systems level, which would add to empirically based intervention models.

INTERVENTIONS IN THE
FAMILY SYSTEM

Within the framework of this chapter, and the conceptual model as presented, there is a need to consider interventions that are focused on the family system. As emphasized throughout this chapter, there is a growing awareness that the family and the retarded child constitute a reciprocal system, in which the functioning of one family member affects the functioning of the others (Baker, 1984; Crnic et al., 1983; Mink et al., 1983; Nihira et al., 1980). Within the scope of the interventions described thus far, there has been little emphasis on the family as a system. The work that has focused on parent training has begun to deal with one aspect of the system; indeed, some studies have noted collateral changes within the family system (e.g., improved parent–child relationships with other children within the family) as a function of more positive parenting and behavior of the retarded child, (Forehand & King, 1977; Karoly & Rosenthal, 1977; Scovern et al., 1980). But, again, these were not interventions that were specifically aimed at the family unit as a whole. It is somewhat surprising to find that so little effort has been directed at various aspects of family functioning, given the historical emphasis on pathology-based models of family functioning and general indications that families with retarded children experience increased stresses. Family members are also at greater risk for social and emotional dysfunction, less positive attitudes toward child rearing, and less cohesive and harmonious functioning (Crnic et al., 1983). Furthermore, in relation to behavioral interventions that focus specifically on the behavior of the retarded child, family systems theory would predict that change in the behavior of one family member may well result in concomitant changes in the system as a whole to accommodate the change in the member (Minuchin, 1974). At times, such changes in the family system may not be functional, as when harmony in the marital relationship is dependent upon disruptive child behavior. At times, marital difficulties may be less of a focus when there is a disruptive behavior problem with a child. When that problem no longer exists, the marital difficulties may again become a focus.

Although little has been done specifically to address the broader concerns of the family unit, there have been recent attempts to incorporate such thinking into behavioral interventions relevant to families of retarded children. One such approach, termed "parent enhancement therapy," is described by Griest et al. (1982). Behavioral training is provided to parents much as in the various parent training studies noted earlier. However, this program adds to this basic process by making specific consultation available to parents in regard to their own personal adjustment, the parents' marital relationship, relationships with significant others outside the family context, and their attitudes toward their children. Griest et al. (1982) reported that this intervention, used with families with noncompliant children, resulted in better-maintained parent behavior management skills and greater child compliance than did the behavioral consultation alone. Such an approach seems particularly amenable to the needs of families with retarded children.

Family therapy, within a variety of theoretical and practical applications, is another potentially useful means of providing appropriate services aimed at meeting the needs of the family system (Baker, 1984; Tymchuk, 1983). However, to date there have been no reports of the systematic study of family therapy with families of retarded children. In part, this may reflect theoretical notions within family systems research, which seek etiologies within the specific pathology of the family context. This approach does not appear immediately applicable to the etiology of retardation; however, if families are viewed as reciprocal and transacting systems, then the approach would appear to have much potential for this population.

Although mainstream behavioral research has produced little intervention work within the family context, educational models have attempted to fill this void (Fewell & Vadasy, 1986). One particularly novel program is the Supporting Extended Family Members project (Vadasy, Fewell, Meyer, & Greenberg, 1985). In this program, fathers and siblings of retarded preschool-age children receive a specific program of support, information, and guided interaction with their retarded children/siblings. Biweekly meetings are held in which each of the three components are facilitated by the program staff. Participation is not time-limited within this program. Vadasy et al. (1985) reported that fathers who had been enrolled in this program for at least 1 year reported less stress and depression than did newly enrolled fathers, fewer family problems, and more satisfaction with their extrafamilial support systems. In addition, fathers who had been in the program longer reported greater self-esteem than did new enrollees. In regard to system effects, Vadasy *et al.* also measured mothers' levels of stress and self-esteem, even though mothers were not the specific targets of the intervention protocol. Mothers of families that had been in the program for a year reported less stress associated with their handicapped children and greater self-esteem. These findings suggest that programs that specifically target familial attributes have utility in regard to the general status of the family system. The next step for such young programs is the assessment of the long-term relationship between more positive family functioning and the behavioral and developmental status of the child.

Together, the results described in relation to individual interventions directed toward the behavioral and skill attributes of the retarded child, the training of parents to manage the behavior and skill of the retarded child, and the few studies related to interventions within the family system are important in regard to concerns involving maintenance and generalization of intervention successes. Using intervention protocols that emphasize each aspect of this matrix (child–parent–family) seems most likely to maximize the maintenance of the gains obtained and to provide the best context for generalization to occur.

SUMMARY

Behavioral interventions have proven particularly amenable to use and effective with the variety of problems common to children with mental retardation. In most cases, the interventions proven most successful have involved combinations of techniques and specific planning for maintenance and generalization. Yet it is clear that both maintenance and generalization of the skills taught or behaviors eliminated have been limited at best. We have suggested that the reasons for this limitation involve the lack of a specific plan for such within the intervention; the general lack of a conceptual model to guide planning for maintenance and generalization; and the failure to consider behavioral interventions within a system approach, particularly within the family. In this chapter, we have presented a conceptual framework to serve as a working model for guiding behavioral interventions with retarded children; we have focused specifically on multi-method approaches, plans for maintenance and generalization, and considerations of the ecological system within which the child operates. The case illustration that follows demonstrates an approach to behavioral intervention that incorporates many of the elements of the described model.

CASE ILLUSTRATION

Paul, aged 7 years and 2 months, was a student in a special education classroom; he was referred to a developmental clinic by his parents on the recommendation of his pediatrician. The pediatrician had concerns regarding his overall developmental status and his apparently high activity level. The parents also were concerned with his developmental status, but his mother, Linda, was most concerned about his noncompliant and aggressive behavior.

History

A developmental interview provided the following information. Paul, the family's only child, had been previously assessed as a preschooler, and found to be functioning in the mildly retarded to borderline range of intelligence, with a significant delay in language skills. He was born small for his gestational age (full-term), and had had numerous difficulties in feeding and growth during his infancy and early years. He had attended several special preschool placements; however, his parents had pulled him out of them, as they felt he was too "normal" to be in such programs, and placed him in normal preschools. When he struggled in these settings, they again sought special placements. Both parents noted that behavioral concerns had been ongoing for several years, although this was particularly an issue for Linda. Both parents worked full-time, the father as an engineer and the mother as a social worker.

Assessment

The developmental interview with the parents suggested that Paul continued to have some delays in cognitive and language development, as well as in his fine and gross motor skills. Self-help skills appeared to be near an age-appropriate level, but still delayed, according to his parents' report. This delay was complicated, however, by his significant noncompliance with dressing and feeding. Of greatest concern to his parents was his behavior, which they described as willfully negative and noncompliant, impulsive, aggressive, and unpredictable. These behaviors occurred more often with Linda than with Robert (the father), but were a concern across the family context. Paul refused to follow directions or commands, would run away when given instructions, would scream and kick if coerced into following commands, and would physically strike his parents when angry or become destructive with toys or furnishings in the house. These behaviors were a particular source of concern when Paul was in public settings with his parents, especially Linda. Linda described him as being an embarrassment, because of both his behavior and his developmental status. She was frank in her admission that she just did not like him and was unsure of her ability to accept him because of his intellectual deficit. His father, Robert, did not find him an embarrassment, and their discussion about Paul during the interview suggested that some significant marital discord was present.

Paul was administered the Wechsler Intelligence Scale for Children—Revised (WISC-R), as well as other tests of development germane to various disciplines concerned with language and motor skill. Results indicated that he was functioning in the mildly retarded range of intelligence (IQ = 69), with concomitant delays in language and motor skill areas. His parents were asked to complete the Child Behavior Checklist; to count the frequency of noncompliant, impulsive, and aggressive events that they observed with Paul over the course of a week; and to note the situation that precipitated each event and how they responded. A call to Paul's teacher at school indicated that behavior was less an issue at school than at home, although at times he was considered to be noncompliant and impulsive. Aggression was not seen as an issue in his school setting. The teacher agreed to interval-sample the frequency of occurrence of noncompliance and impulsive behavior on 2 different days over the school week. The results of the behavioral observations at home indicated that noncompliance, aggression, and impulsivity were high-frequency events (see Figure 7-2), were generally preceded by a request for some performance, and usually resulted in inconsistent responses (e.g., prolonged arguing, a time out, or giving in by the parent). The same behaviors occurred less frequently at school, even though they were observable more often than the teacher wished and usually followed some request for action or performance.

The parents were asked to complete the Marital Adjustment Inventory and the Family Environment Scale. Results from these scales indicated a high degree of marital disharmony, noted especially by Linda, and the family system functioning was noted to be particularly noncohesive, nonexpressive, disorganized, and

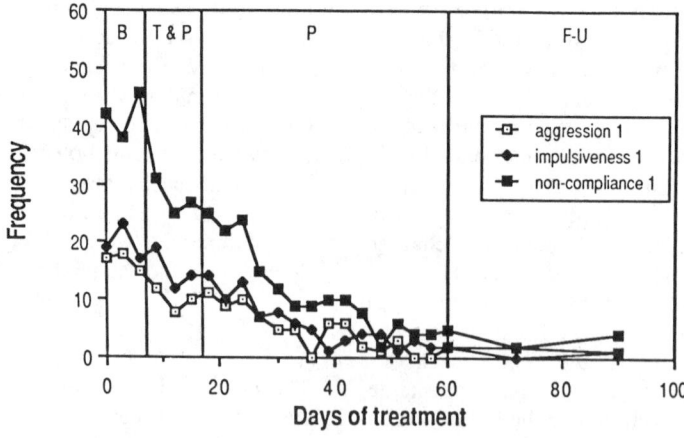

FIGURE 7-2. Multiple-baseline behavioral intervention with Paul and his family. B—baseline; T & P—therapist and parent training condition; P—parent only condition; F-U—follow-up; 1—all data collected in home.

conflictual. Despite these findings, the parents agreed to undertake systematic behavioral interventions to deal with the various behavior problems presented by Paul, as well as to participate in marital therapy.

Intervention

To intervene with Paul's behavior, a multiple-baseline system was established to monitor instances of noncompliance, impulsiveness, and aggression at home. In the first segment of the intervention ("T & P" in Figure 7-2), the therapist worked individually with Paul in training cognitive modification strategies, and trained the parents in the use of the same strategies as well as basic contingency management, reinforcement, and time out. With the therapist, Paul was taught to use self-statements to control his impulsive and aggressive outbursts (when requested to do something, he would say "wait" before responding and come up with alternatives to inappropriate refusals) through instruction, modeling, role play, practice, and reinforcement. In addition, Paul was taught to use a star chart to record instances of using these self-control steps and to bring the chart in to the subsequent sessions. The parents were taught basic contingency management techniques (emphasizing clear rules and positive approaches), the use of modeling for self-statements, and the use of the child's chart in a specific token system that was established for continuous reinforcement of compliance and reflection. Short time outs were instituted for any aggressive or impulsive behavior. This first phase of the intervention required five sessions over a 2-week period, and succeeded in significantly reducing Paul's behavior problems at home (see Figure 7-2). Following this, a parent-only condition ("P" in Figure 7-2) was planned, in which the parents continued to be provided with specific management techniques, general information on learning principles, and reinforcement for their efforts. The therapist met weekly with the parents to discuss progress.

In the meetings with Paul's mother during the parent training, it was clear that she did not feel motivated to exert the effort with the program. She noted that she did not feel that Paul was worth the effort, because of his developmental status and the unlikelihood that he would ever be "normal." She noted when questioned that she did have thoughts about beating Paul and did fear abusing him. She did not care for her husband or their marriage, either, and sometimes wished that both Paul and her husband would disappear. Although Linda appeared clearly depressed over her life condition, she refused individual therapy for herself, but did agree to a referral for a support group of parents at risk for abusing their children. Futhermore, she had agreed to marital intervention and had begun this process. The focus of the parent training changed somewhat, to include cognitive modification techniques with Linda regarding the self-statements she made about Paul and her interpretations about his development and behavior. Paul's teachers at school were also enlisted to model and make positive statements about Paul.

Under the conditions of the combined system approach to intervention with this family (parent training, marital therapy, support group for parents at risk to abuse, and enlisting the school personnel), Paul's behavior showed slow but dramatic change over the next weeks and months (see Figure 7-2). Parent training continued twice weekly over the next month, and instances of noncompliance, impulsiveness, and aggression became infrequent. Interval-sampling behavior observations by Paul's teacher also noted decreases in noncompliance and impulsiveness as well, suggesting that these skills had generalized to another setting without specific intervention. Booster sessions were scheduled with Linda and Paul over the next month, and Paul's behavior continued to improve. At 3 months after the beginning of treatment, Linda completed the Marital Adjustment Inventory and the Family Environment Scale. Although dramatic changes were not observed on the Marital Adjust Inventory, scores were more positive. In contrast, the Family Environment Scale showed great improvement, indicating that Linda's perception of the family's overall functioning was much more positive. Also, the gains seen in Paul's behavior had been maintained at levels near those reached during active intervention, and Linda was much more positive in her statements about him. Furthermore, his teachers had reported that he was doing better both behaviorally (specific incidences of noncompliance and impulsiveness had decreased by 85% and 78%, respectively) and academically in school.

This case clearly describes the necessity of using a combined systems and individual-functioning approach, such as the one described in the preceding sections. Without intervention at both the child and system levels, it is unlikely that the intervention program would have been successful. It also reflects the cognitive and behavioral difficulties typical of retarded children, as well as problems found in family adjustment (including depression, marital distress, embarrassment, and family conflict). Factors that enhance maintenance and generalization as presented in the model were also included, such as treating the child within a family systems context (including a parent component); emphasizing executive skills in the self-control and self-monitoring training; and transferring reinforcement for improved behaviors to the naturalistic home environment.

REFERENCES

Achenbach, T. M., & Edelbrock, C. (1983). *Manual for the Child Behavior Checklist and Revised Child Behavior Profile.* Burlington: University of Vermont, Department of Psychiatry.

Adubato, S. A., Adams, M. K., & Budd, K. S. (1981). Teaching a parent to train a spouse in child management techniques. *Journal of Applied Behavior Analysis, 14,* 193–205.

Aeschleman, S. R., & Schladenhauffen, J. (1984). Acquisition, generalization and maintenance of grocery shopping skills by severely mentally retarded adolescents. *Applied Research in Mental Retardation, 5,* 245–258.

Altman, K., Havik, S., & Cook, J. (1978). Punishment of SIB in natural settings using contingent aromatic ammonia. *Behaviour Research and Therapy, 16,* 85–96.

Aman, M. G. (1978). Drugs, learning, and the psychotherapies. In J. S. Werry (Ed.), *Pediatric psychopharmacology: The use of behavior modifying drugs in children* (pp. 79–108). New York: Brunner/Mazel.

Aman, M. G. (1983). Psychoactive drugs in mental retardation. In J. L. Matson & F. Andrasik (Eds.), *Treatment issues and innovations in mental retardation* (pp. 455–513). New York: Plenum.

Aman, M. G., & Singh, N. N. (1983). Pharmacological intervention. In J. L. Matson & J. A. Mulick (Eds.), *Handbook of mental retardation* (pp. 317–337). New York: Pergamon Press.

American Psychiatric Association. (1987). *Diagnostic and statistical manual of mental disorders* (3rd ed., rev.). Washington, DC: Author.

Azrin, N. H., & Armstrong, P. M. (1973). The "minimeal": A method for teaching eating skills to the profoundly retarded. *Mental Retardation, 11,* 9–13.

Azrin, N. H., & Foxx, R. (1971). A rapid method of toilet training the institutionalized retarded. *Journal of Applied Behavior Analysis 4,* 89–99.

Azrin, N. H., & Foxx, R. M. (1974). *Toilet training in less than a day.* New York: Simon & Schuster.

Azrin, N. H., Gottlieb, L., Hughart, L., Wesolowski, M. D., & Rahn, J. (1975). Eliminating self-injurious behaviour by educative procedures. *Behaviour Research and Therapy, 13,* 101–111.

Baer, D. M., Wolf, M. M., & Risley, T. R. (1968). Some current dimensions of applied behavior analysis. *Journal of Applied Behavior Analysis, 1,* 91–97.

Bailey, S. L., Pikrzywinski, J., & Bryant, L. E. (1983). Using water mist to reduce self-injurious and stereotypic behavior. *Applied Research in Mental Retardation, 4,* 229–241.

Baker, B. L. (1980). Training parents as teachers of their developmentally disabled children. In S. Salzinger, J. Antrobus, & J. Glick (Eds.), *The ecosystem of the "sick" child* (pp. 201–216). New York: Academic Press.

Baker, B. L. (1984). Intervention with families with young, severely handicapped children. In J. Blacker (Eds.), *Severely handicapped young children and their families* (pp. 319–375). New York: Academic Press.

Baker, B. L., & Clark, D. B. (1983). The family setting: Enhancing the retarded child's development through parent training. In K. T. Kernan, M. J. Begab, & R. B. Edgerton (Eds.), *Settings and the behavior and study of retarded persons.* Baltimore: University Park Press.

Baker, B. L., Heifetz, L. J., & Murphy, D. (1980). Behavioral training for parents of retarded children: One year follow-up. *American Journal of Mental Deficiency, 85,* 31–38.

Barkley, R. A. (1981). Hyperactivity. In E. J. Mash & L. G. Terdal (Eds.), *Behavioral assessment of childhood disorders* (pp. 127–184). New York: Guilford Press.

Barkley, R. A., & Cunningham, C. E. (1978). Do stimulant drugs improve the academic performance of hyperkinetic children? A review of outcome research. *Clinical Pediatrics, 17,* 85–92.

Barkley, R. A., & Zupnick, S. (1976). Reduction of stereotypic body contortions using physical restraint and DRO. *Journal of Behavior Therapy and Experimental Psychiatry, 7,* 167–170.

Barnard, J. D., Christopherson, E. R., & Wolf, M. M. (1976). Parent-mediated treatment of children's self-injurious behavior using overcorrection. *Journal of Pediatric Psychology, 1,* 56–61.

Barrett, R. P., & Linn, D. (1981). Treatment of stereotyped toe-walking with overcorrection and physical therapy. *Applied Research in Mental Retardation, 2,* 13–21.

Bates, P. E., & Hanson, H. B. (1983). Behavioral assessment. In J. L. Matson & S. E. Bruening (Eds.), *Assessing the mentally retarded* (pp. 27–63). New York: Grune & Stratton.

Baumeister, A. A., & Baumeister, A. A. (1977). Suppression of repetitive self-injurious behavior by contingent inhalation of aromatic amonia. *Journal of Autism and Childhood Schizophrenia, 8,* 71–77.

Baumeister, A. A., & Forehand, R. (1970). Social facilitation of body rocking in severely retarded patients. *Journal of Clinical Psychology, 26,* 303–305.

Baumeister, A. A., & MacLean, W. E. (1984). Deceleration of self-injurious and stereotypic responding by exercise. *Applied Research in Mental Retardation, 5,* 385–393.

Beck, S. (1983). Overview of methods. In J. L. Matson & S. E. Bruening (Eds.), *Assessing the mentally retarded* (pp. 3–26). New York: Grune & Stratton.

Beckman, P. J. (1983). The influence of selected child characteristics on stress in families of handicapped infants. *American Journal of Mental Deficiency, 88,* 150–156.

Bell, R. Q. (1968). Reinterpretation of the direction of

effects in studies of socialization. *Psychology Review,* 75, 81–95.

Bellack, A. S., & Hersen, M. (Eds.), (1979). *Research and practice in social skills training.* New York: Plenum.

Belmont, J. M. (1978). Individual differences in memory: The cases of normal and retarded development. In M. Gruneberg & P. Morris (Eds.), *Aspects of memory* (pp. 153–185). London: Methuen.

Belmont, J. M., & Butterfield, E. C. (1977). The instructional approach to developmental cognitive research. In R. V. Kail, Jr., & J. W. Hagen (Eds.), *Perspectives on the development of memory and cognition* (pp. 437–481). Hillsdale, NJ: Erlbaum.

Bennett, C. W. (1973). A four-and-a-half year old as a teacher of her hearing impaired sister: A case study. *Journal of Communication Disorders,* 6, 67–75.

Berkowitz, B., & Graziano, A. (1972). Training parents as behaviour therapists: A review. *Behaviour Research and Therapy,* 10, 297–317.

Berkson, G., & Mason, W. A. (1963). Stereotyped movements of mental defectives (Part. 3): Situation effects. *American Journal of Mental Deficiency,* 68, 409–412.

Bitgood, S. C., Crowe, M. J., Suarez, Y., & Peters, R. D. (1980). Immobilization: Effects and side effects on stereotyped behavior in children. *Behavior Modification,* 4, 187–208.

Borakove, L. S., & Cuvo, A. J. (1976). Facilitative effects of coin displacement on teaching coin summation to mentally retarded adolescents. *American Journal of Mental Deficiency,* 81, 350–356.

Borkowski, J. G., & Cavanaugh, J. C. (1979). Maintenance and generalization of skills and strategies by the retarded. In N. R. Ellis (Ed.), *Handbook of mental deficiency* (2nd ed., pp. 569–617). Hillsdale, NJ: Erlbaum.

Borkowski, J. G., Johnston, M. B., & Reid, M. (1985). Metacognition, motivation, and controlled performance. In S. J. Ceci (Ed.), *Handbook of cognitive, social, and neuropsychological aspects of learning disability* (pp. 147–173). Hillsdale, NJ: Erlbaum.

Borkowski, J. G., & Konarski, E. A. (1980). Educational implications of efforts to train intelligence. *Journal of Special Education,* 14, 32–50.

Borkowski, J. G., & Konarski, E. A. (1980). Educational implications of efforts to train intelligence. *Journal of Special Education,* – .

Borkowski, J. G., Ryan, E. B., Kurtz, B. E., & Reid, M. K. (1983). Metamemory and metalinguistic development: Correlates of children's intelligence and achievement. *Bulletin of the Psychonomic Society,* 21(5), 393–396.

Bornstein, P. H., Bach, P. J., & Anton, B. (1982). Behavioral treatment of psychopathological disorders. In J. L. Matson & R. P. Barrett (Eds.), *Psychopathology in the mentally retarded* (pp. 70–82). New York: Grune & Stratton.

Bornstein, P. H., & Quevillon, R. P. (1976). The effects of a self-instructional package on overactive preschool boys. *Journal of Applied Behavior Analysis,* 9, 179–188.

Bray, N. W., Biasini, F. J., & Thrasher, K. A. (1983). The effect of communicative demands on request-making in the moderately and severely mentally retarded. *Applied Research in Mental Retardation,* 4, 13–27.

Brehony, K. A., Benson, B. A., Solomon, L. J., & Luscomb, R. L. (1980). Parents as behavior modifiers: Intervention for three problem behaviors in a severely retarded child. *Journal of Clinical Child Psychology,* 9, 213–216.

Breiner, J., & Beck, S. (1984). Parents as change agents in the management of their developmentally delayed children's noncompliant behaviors: A critical review. *Applied Research in Mental Retardation,* 5, 259–278.

Brightman, R. P., Baker, B. L., Clark, D. B., & Ambrose, S. A. (1982). Effectiveness of alternative parent training formats. *Journal of Behavior Therapy and Experimental Psychiatry,* 13, 113–117.

Bronfenbrenner, U. (1979). *The ecology of human development: Experiments by nature and design.* Cambridge, MA: Harvard University Press.

Brown, A. L. (1978). Knowing when, where, and how to remember: A problem in metacognition. In R. Glaser (Ed.), *Advances in instructional psychology* (Vol. 1, pp. 77–165). Hillsdale, NJ: Erlbaum.

Brown, A. L., Bransford, J. D., Ferrara, R. A., & Campione, J. C. (1983). Learning, remembering, and understanding. In J. H. Flavell & E. M. Markman (Vol. Eds.), *Handbook of child psychology* (4th ed.): *Vol. 3. Cognitive development* (pp. 77–167). New York: Wiley.

Brown, A. L., & Campione, J. E. (1977). Training strategic study time apportionment in educable retarded children. *Intelligence,* 1, 94–107.

Brown, A. L., Campione, J. C., & Barclay, C. R. (1979). Training self-checking routines for estimating test readiness: Generalization from list learning to prose recall. *Child Development,* 50, 501–512.

Brown, R., Borden, K. A., Wynne, M. E., Scleser, R., & Clingerman, S. R. (1986). Methylphenidate and cognitive therapy with ADD children: A methodological reconsideration. *Journal of Abnormal Child Psychology,* 14, 481–497.

Bucher, B., Reykdal, B., & Albin, J. (1976). Brief physical restraint to control pica. *Journal of Behavior Therapy and Experimental Psychiatry,* 1, 137–140.

Budd, K. S., Green, D. R., & Baer, D. M,.(1976). An analysis of multiple misplaced parental social contingencies. *Journal of Applied Behavior Analysis,* 9, 459–470.

Budd, K. S., & Greenspan, S. (1985). Parameters of successful and unsuccessful interventions with parents who are mentally retarded. *Mental Retardation,* 23 (6), 269–273.

Burney, J. D., Russell, B., & Shores, R. E. (1977). Developing social responses in two profoundly retarded children. *The AAESPH Review,* 2, 117–124.

Campione, J. C., & Brown, A. (1978). Towards a theory of intelligence: Contributions from research with retarded children. *Intelligence,* 2, 279–304.

Cantwell, D. P., & Carlson, G. A. (1978). Stimulants. In J. S. Werry (Ed.), *Pediatric psychopharmacology: The use of behavior modifying drugs in children* (pp. 171–207). New York: Brunner/Mazel.

Casey, L. (1978). Development of communication behavior in autistic children: A parent program using signed speech. *Devereux Forum,* 12, 1–15.

Cicchetti, D. (1984). The emergence of developmental psychopathology. *Child Development,* 55, 1–7.

Clark, D. B., & Baker, B. L. (1983). Predicting outcome in parent training. *Journal of Consulting and Clinical Psychology,* 51, 309–311.

Cohen, M. N., & Sprague, R. L. (1977). *Survey of drug usage in two Midwestern institutions for the retarded.*

Paper presented at the Gatlinburg Conference on Research in Mental Retardation, Gatlinburg, TN.

Colletti, G., & Harris, S. L. (1977). Behavior modification in the home: Siblings as behavior modifiers, parents as observers. *Journal of Abnormal Child Psychology, 5,* 21–30.

Colwell, C. N., Richards, E., McCarver, R. B., & Ellis, N. R. (1973). Evaluation of self-help habit training of the profoundly retarded. *Mental Retardation, 11,* 14–18.

Cone, J. D., Anderson, J. A., Harris, F. C., Goff, D. K., & Fox, S. R. (1978). Developing and maintaining social interaction in profoundly retarded young males. *Journal of Abnormal Child Psychology, 6,* 351–360.

Conners, C. K., Kramer, R., Rothschild, G. H., Schwartz, L., & Stone, A. (1971). Treatment of young delinquent boys with diphenylhydantoin sodium and methylphenidate. *Archives of General Psychiatry, 24,* 156–160.

Conners, C. K., & Werry, J. S. (1979). Pharmacotherapy. In H. C. Quay, & J. S. Werry (Eds.), *Psychopathological disorders of childhood* (2nd ed., pp. 336–386). New York: Wiley.

Cooper, A. F., & Fowlie, H. C. (1972). Control of gross self-mutilation with lithium carbonate. *British Journal of Psychiatry, 122,* 370–371.

Cowart, J. D., Iwata, B. A., & Poynter, H. (1984). Generalization and maintenance in training parents of the mentally retarded. *Applied Research in Mental Retardation, 5,* 233–244.

Crnic, K. A. (1988). Mental retardation. In E. J. Mash & L. G. Terdal (Eds.), *Behavioral assessment of childhood disorders* (2nd ed., pp. 317–354). New York: Guilford Press.

Crnic, K. A., Friedrich, W. N., & Greenberg, M. T. (1983). Adaptation of families with mentally retarded children: A model of stress, coping, and family ecology. *American Journal of Mental Deficiency, 88,* 125–138.

Crnic, K. A., & Greenberg, M. T. (1984, April). *Social interaction and developmental competence of preterm and full-term infants from birth to 24 months: Predicting outcomes.* Paper presented at the International Conference on Infant Studies, New York.

Crnic, K. A., & Greenberg, M. T. (1987). Transactional relationships between perceived family style, risk status, and mother–child interactions in two year olds. *Journal of Pediatric Psychology, 12,* 343–362.

Crnic, K. A., & Laconte, J. M. (1986). Understanding sibling needs and influences. In R. R. Fewell & P. F. Vadasy (Eds.), *Families of handicapped children: Needs and supports across the life span* (pp. 75–98). Austin, TX: Pro-Ed.

Cuvo, A. J., Veitch, V. C., Trace, M. W., & Konke, J. L. (1978). Teaching change computation to the mentally retarded. *Behavior Modification, 2,* 531–548.

DeCatanzaro, D. A., & Baldwin, G. (1978). Effective treatment of self-injurious behavior through a forced cue exercise. *American Journal of Mental Deficiency, 82,* 433–439.

Denny, M. (1980). Reducing self-stimulatory behavior of mentally retarded persons by alternative positive practice. *American Journal of Mental Deficiency, 84,* 610–615.

Diament, C., & Colletti, G. (1978). Evaluation of behavioral group counseling for parents of learning-disabled children. *Journal of Abnormal Child Psychology, 6,* 385–400.

Doke, L. A., & Epstein, L. H. (1975). Oral overcorrection: Side effects and extended applications. *Journal of Experimental Child Psychology, 20,* 496–511.

Dorry, G. W., & Zeaman, D. (1975). The use of a fading technique in paired-associate teaching of a reading vocabulary with retardates. *Mental Retardation, 11,* 3–6.

Douglas, V. I. (1974a). Differences between normal and hyperkinetic children. In C. K. Conners (Ed.), *Clinical use of stimulant drugs in children* (pp. 12–23). Amsterdam: Elsevier.

Douglas, V. I. (1974b). Sustained attention and impulse control: Implications for the handicapped child. In *Psychology and the handicapped child* (DHEW Publication No. OE 73-0500). Washington, DC: U.S. Government Printing Office.

Drabman, R. S., Cordua y Cruz, G. C., Ross, J., & Lynd, S. L. (1979). Suppression of chronic drooling in mentally retarded children and adolescents: Effectiveness of a behavioral treatment package. *Behavior Therapy, 10,* 46–56.

Dunst, C. J., & Trivette, C. M. (in press). A family systems model of early intervention with handicapped and developmentally at-risk children. In D. Powell (Ed.), *Parent education and support programs: Consequences for children and families.* Norwood, NJ: Ablex.

Ellis, N. R. (Ed.), (1979). *Handbook of mental deficiency: Psychological theory and research* (2nd ed.). Hillsdale, NJ: Erlbaum.

Eyberg, S. M. (1980). Eyberg Child Behavior Inventory. *Journal of Clinical Child Psychology, 9,* 29.

Favell, J. E., McGimsey, J. F., & Jones, M. (1978). The use of physical restraint in the treatment of self-injury and as positive reinforcement. *Journal of Applied Behavior Analysis, 11,* 225–242.

Feldman, M. A., Case, L., Towns, F., & Betel, J. (1985). Parent Education Project: I. Development and nurturance of children of mentally retarded parents. *American Journal of Mental Deficiency, 90,* 253–258.

Feldman, W. S., Manella, K. J., & Varni, J. W. (1983). A behavioral parent training program for single mothers of physically handicapped children. *Child: Care, Health, and Development, 9,* 157–168.

Fewell, R. R., Vadasy, P. F. (Eds.). (1986). *Families of handicapped children: Needs and supports across the life span.* Austin, TX: Pro-Ed.

Feuerstein, R. (1979). *The dynamic assessment of retarded performance.* Baltimore: University Park Press.

Flavell, J. H., & Wellman, H. M. (1977). Metamemory. In R. V. Kail, Jr., & J. W. Hagen (Eds.), *Perspectives on the development of memory and cognition* (pp. 3–33). Hillsdale, NJ: Erlbaum.

Forehand, R., & Baumeister, A. A. (1976). Deceleration of aberrant behavior among retarded individuals. In M. Hersen, R. M. Eisler, & P. M. Miller (Eds.), *Progress in behavior modification* (Vol. 2, pp. 223–227). New York: Academic Press.

Forehand, R., Cheney, T., & Yoder, P. (1974). Parent behavior training: Effects on the noncompliance of a deaf child. *Journal of Behavior Therapy and Experimental Psychiatry, 5,* 281–283.

Forehand, R., & King, H. E. (1977). Noncompliant children: Effects of parent training on behavior and attitude change. *Behavior Modification, 1,* 93–108.

Foxx, G. L., Foxx, R. M., Jones, J. R., & Kiley, D. (1980). Twenty-four hour social isolation: A program for reducing the aggressive behavior of a psychotic-like adult. *Behavior Modification, 4,* 130–144.

Foxx, R. M., Snyder, M. S., & Schroeder, F. (1979). A

food satiation and oral hygiene punishment program to suppress chronic rumination by retarded persons. *Journal of Autism and Developmental Disorders, 9,* 399–412.

Frazier, J. R., & Schneider, H. (1975). Parental management of inappropriate hyperactivity in a young retarded child. *Journal of Behavior Therapy and Experimental Psychiatry, 6,* 245–247.

Friedrich, W. N., Greenberg, M. T., & Crnic, K. (1983). A short-form of the Questionnaire on Resources and Stress. *American Journal of Mental Deficiency, 88,* 41–48.

Fry, L. (1977). Remedial reading using parents as behaviour technicians. *New Zealand Journal of Educational Studies, 12,* 29–36.

Gable, R. A., Hendrickson, J. M., & Strain, P. S. (1978). Assessment, modification, and generalization of social interaction among severely retarded, multihandicapped children. *Education and Training of the Mentally Retarded, 13,* 279–286.

Gadow, K. D., & Kalachnik, J. (1981). Prevalence and pattern of drug treatment for behavior and seizure disorders of TMR students. *American Journal of Mental Deficiency, 85,* 588–595.

Gerrard, K. R., & Saxon, S. A. (1973). Preparation of a disturbed deaf child for therapy: A case description in behavior shaping. *Journal of Speech and Hearing Disorders, 38,* 502–509.

Goetz, E. M., & Baer, D. M. (1973). Social control of form diversity and the emergence of new forms in children's block building. *Journal of Applied Behavior Analysis, 6,* 105–113.

Goetzl, J., Grunberg, F., & Berkowitz, B. (1977). Lithium carbonate in the management of hyperactive aggressive behavior of the mentally retarded. *Comprehensive Psychiatry, 18,* 599–606.

Greenberg, M. T., Kusche, C. A., Gustafson, R. N., & Calderon, R. (1985). The PATHS Project: A model for the prevention of psychosocial difficulties in deaf children. In G. B. Anderson & D. Watson (Eds.), *Habilitation and rehabilitation of deaf adolescents: 1984 conference proceedings* (pp. 64–88). Washington, DC: Gallaudet College Press.

Greene, R. J., & Hoats, D. L. (1971). Aversive tickling: A simple conditioning technique. *Behavior Therapy, 2,* 389–393.

Greene, R. J., Hoats, D. L., & Hornick, A. J. (1970). Music distortion: A new technique for behavior modification. *Psychological Record, 20,* 107–109.

Griest, D. L., Forehand, R., Rogers, T., Breiner, J., Furey, W., & Williams, C. A. (1982). Effects of parent enhancement therapy on the treatment outcome and generalization of a parent training program. *Behaviour Research and Therapy, 20,* 429–436.

Grossman, H. (1983). *Manual on terminology and classification in mental retardation.* Washington, DC: American Association on Mental Deficiency.

Heber, F. R. (1978). Sociocultural mental retardation: A longitudinal study. In D. Forgays (Ed.), *Primary prevention of psychopathology* (Vol. 2). Hanover, NH: University Press of New England.

Holburn, C. S., & Dougher, M. J. (1985). Behavioral attempts to eliminate air-swallowing in two profoundly mentally retarded clients. *American Journal of Mental Deficiency, 89,* 524–536.

Holroyd, J. (1974). The Questionnaire on Resources and Stress: An instrument to measure family response to a handicapped family member. *Journal of Community Psychology, 2,* 92–94.

Horner, R. D. (1980). The effects of an environmental "enrichment" program on the behavior of institutionalized profoundly retarded children. *Journal of Applied Behavior Analysis, 13,* 473–792.

Hudson, A. M. (1982). Training parents of developmentally handicapped children: A component analysis. *Behavior Therapy, 13,* 325–333.

Hutt, C., & Hutt, S. (1965). Effects of environmental complexity on stereotyped behavior of children. *Animal Behavior, 13,* 1–4.

Jacobson, J. W. (1982a). Problem behavior and psychiatric impairment within a developmentally disabled population: I. Behavior frequency. *Applied Research in Mental Retardation, 3,* 121–139.

Jacobson, J. W. (1982b). Problem behavior and psychiatric impairment within a developmentally disabled population: II. Behavior severity. *Applied Research in Mental Retardation, 3,* 369–381.

Jarman, P. H., Iwata, B. A., & Lorentzson, A. M. (1983). Development of morning self-care routines in multiply handicapped persons. *Applied Research in Mental Retardation, 4,* 113–122.

Johnson, C. M., Bradley-Johnson, S., McCarthy, R., & Jamie, M. (1984). Token reinforcement during WISC-R administration: II. Effects on mildly retarded, black students. *Applied Research in Mental Retardation, 5,* 43–53.

Johnson, M. R., Whitman, T. L., & Barloon-Noble, R. (1978). A home-based program for a pre-school behaviorally disturbed child with parents as therapists. *Journal of Behavior Therapy and Experimental Psychiatry, 9,* 65–70.

Johnston, M. B., Whitman, T. L., & Johnson, M. (1980). Teaching addition and subtraction to mentally retarded children: A self-instructional program. *Journal for Applied Research in Mental Retardation, 1,* 141–160.

Kanfer, F. H., & Saslow, G. (1969). Behavioral diagnosis. In C. M. Franks (Ed.), *Behavioral therapy: Appraisal and status* (pp. 417–444). New York: McGraw-Hill.

Kanner, L. (1964). *A history of the care and study of the mentally retarded.* Springfield, IL: Charles C Thomas.

Karoly, P., & Rosenthal, M. (1977). Training parents in behavior modification: Effects on perceptions of family interaction and deviant child behavior. *Behavior Therapy, 8,* 406–410.

Kaufman, K. R., & Katz-Garris, L. (1979). Epilepsy, mental retardation, and anticonvulsant therapy. *American Journal of Mental Deficiency, 84,* 256–259.

Kazdin, A. E. (1977). Assessing the clinical or applied significance of behavior change through social validation. *Behavior Modification, 1,* 427–452.

Kazdin, A. E., & Straw, M. L. (1976). Assessment of behavior of the mentally retarded. In M. Hersen & A. S. Bellack (Eds.), *Behavioral assessment: A practical handbook* (pp. 337–368). New York: Pergamon Press.

Kendall, P. C., & Braswell, L. (1982). Cognitive-behavioral self-control therapy for children: A components analysis. *Journal of Consulting and Clinical Psychology, 50,* 672–689.

Kendall, P. R., Lerner, R. M., & Craighead, W. E. (1984). Human development and intervention in childhood psychopathology. *Child Development, 55,* 71–82.

Kendall, P. C., & Braswell, L. (1985). *Cognitive behavior for impulsive children.* New York: Guilford.

Kennedy, B. A., Miller, D. J. (1976). Persistent use of verbal rehearsal as a function of information about its value. *Child Development, 47,* 566–569.

Keogh, D., & Whitman, T. (1983). Mental retardation in children. In M. Hersen, V. B. Van Hasselt, & J. L. Matson (Eds.), *Behavior therapy for the developmentally and physically disabled* (pp. 205–246). New York: Academic Press.

Kestner, J., & Borkowski, J. G. (1979). Children's maintenance and generalization of an interrogative learning strategy. *Child Development 50*, 485–494.

Knopf, I. J. (1979). *Childhood psychopathology: A developmental approach.* Englewood Cliffs, NJ: Prentice-Hall.

Koegel, R., & Covert, A. (1972). The relationship of self-stimulation to learning in autistic children. *Journal of Applied Behavior Analysis, 5*, 381–387.

Koller, H., Richardson, S. A., Katz, M., & McLaren, J. (1982). Behavior disturbance in childhood and the early adult years in populations who were and were not mentally retarded. *Journal of Preventive Psychiatry, 1*, 453–468.

Kurtz, B. E., Reid, M. K., Borkowski, J. G., & Cavanaugh, J. C. (1982). On the reliability and validity of children's metamemory. *Bulletin of the Psychonomic Society, 19*, 137–140.

LaGrow, S. J., & Repp, A. C. (1984). Stereotypic responding: A review of intervention research. *American Journal of Mental Deficiency, 88*, 595–609.

Leff, R. B. (1974). Teaching the TMR to dial the telephone. *Mental Retardation, 12*, 12–13.

Lion, J. R., Hill, J., & Madden, D. J. (1975). Lithium carbonate and aggression: A case report. *Diseases of the Nervous System, 36*, 97–98.

Lipman, R. S. (1970). The use of psychopharmacological agents in residential facilities for the retarded. In F. J. Menolascino (Ed.), *Psychiatric approaches to mental retardation* (pp. 387–398). New York: Basic Books.

Lipman, R. S., DiMascio, A., Reatig, N., & Kirson, T. (1978). Psychotropic drugs and mentally retarded children. In M. A. Lipton, A. DiMascio, & K. F. Killam (Eds.), *Psychopharmacology: A generation of progress* (pp. 1437–1449). New York: Raven Press.

Litrownik, A. J., Freitas, J. L., & Franzini, L. (1978). Self-regulation in retarded persons: Assessment and training of self-monitoring skills. *American Journal of Mental Deficiency, 82*, 499–506.

Litrownik, A. J., White, K., McInnis, E. T., & Licht, B. G. (1984). A process for designing self-management programs for the developmentally disabled. *Analysis and Intervention in Developmental Disabilities, 4*, 189–197.

Lockwood, K., & Bourland, G. (1982). Reduction of self-injurious behaviors by reinforcement and toy use. *Mental Retardation, 20*, 169–173.

Lowe, M. L., & Cuvo, A. J. (1976). Teaching coin summation to the mentally retarded. *Journal of Applied Behavioral Analysis, 9*, 483–489.

Luiselli, J. K., Helfin, C. S., Pemberton, B. W., & Reisman, J. (1977). The elimination of a child's in-class masturbation by overcorrection and reinforcement. *Journal of Behavior Therapy and Experimental Psychiatry, 8*, 201–204.

Luiselli, J. K., Myles, E., Evans, & Boyce, D. A. (1985). Reinforcement control of severe dysfunctional behavior of blind, multihandicapped students. *American Journal of Mental Deficiency, 90*, 328–334.

Luiselli, J. K., Myles, E., & Littman-Quinn, J. (1983). Analysis of a reinforcement/time-out treatment package to control severe aggression and destructive behaviors in a multihandicapped rubella child. *Applied Research in Mental Retardation, 4*, 65–78.

Luiselli, J. K., Pemberton, B. W., & Helfin, C. S. (1978). Effects and side-effects of a brief overcorrection procedure in reducing multiple self-stimulatory behavior: A single case analysis. *Journal of Mental Deficiency Research, 22*, 287–293.

Luiselli, J. K., & Reisman, J. (1980). Some variations in the use of differential reinforcement procedures with mentally retarded children in specialized treatment settings. *Applied Research in Mental Retardation, 1*, 277–288.

Lutzker, J. R. (1978). Reducing self-injurious behavior by facial screening. *American Journal of Mental Deficiency, 82*, 510–513.

MacMillan, D. L., & Forness, S. R. (1973). Behavior modification: Savior or savant? In R. K. Eyman, C. E. Meyers, & G. Tarjan (Eds.) *Sociobehavioral studies in mental retardation* (pp. 197–210). Washington, DC: American Assocaition on Mental Deficiency.

Mahoney, M. J., & Mahoney, K. (1976). Self-control techniques with the mentally retarded. *Exceptional Children, 42*, 338–339.

Marholin, D., Luiselli, J. K., Robinson, M., & Lott, I. T. (1980). Response contingent taste-aversion in treating ruminative vomiting of institutionalized profoundly retarded children. *Journal of Mental Deficiency Research, 24*, 47–56.

Marholin, D., Touchette, P. E., & Stewart, R. M. (1979). Withdrawal of chronic chlorpramazine medication: An experimental analysis. *Journal of Applied Behavior Analysis, 12*, 159–171.

Martin, G. L., Kehoe, B., Bird, E., Jensen, V., & Darbyshire, M. (1971). Operant conditioning in dressing behavior of severely retarded girls. *Mental Retardation, 9*, 27–31.

Martin, J., Weller, S., & Matson, J. (1977). Eliminating object transferring by a profoundly retarded girl by overcorrection. *Psychological Reports, 40*, 779–782.

Matson, J. L., & Barrett, R. P. (Eds.). (1982). *Psychopathology in the mentally retarded.* New York: Grune & Stratton.

Matson, J. L., & McCartney, J. R. (Eds.). (1981). *Handbook of behavior modification with the mentally retarded.* New York: Plenum.

Mayhew, G. L., Enyart, P., & Anderson, J. (1978). Social reinforcement and the naturally occurring responses of severely and profoundly retarded adolescents. *American Journal of Mental Deficiency, 83*, 164–170.

Mayhew, G. L., & Harris, F. C. (1979). Decreasing self-injurious behavior. *Behavior Modification, 3*, 322–336.

Meichenbaum, D. (1977). *Cognitive behavior modification.* New York: Plenum.

Mercer, C. D., & Snell, M. E. (1977). *Learning theory research in mental retardation: Implications for teaching.* Columbus, OH: Charles E. Merrill.

Mercer, J. R. (1970). Sociological perspectives on mild mental retardation. In M. C. Haywood (Ed.), *Sociocultural aspects of mental retardation.* New York: Appleton-Century-Croft.

Mercer, J. R. (1973). *Labelling the mentally retarded.* Berkeley: University of California Press.

Miller, M. A., Cuvo, A. J., & Borakove, L. S. (1977). Teaching naming of coin values: Comprehension before production versus in production alone. *Journal of Applied Behavior Analysis, 10*, 735–736.

Mink, I. T., Nihira, K., & Meyers, C. E. (1983). Taxonomy of family lifestyles: I. Homes with TMR. *American Journal of Mental Deficiency, 37,* 484–497.

Minuchin, S. (1974). *Families and family therapy.* Cambridge, MA: Harvard University Press.

Moos, R. H., & Moos, B. (1981). *Revised Family Environment Scale.* Palo Alto, CA: Consulting Psychologists Press.

Morris, R. J., & Dolker, M. (1974). Developing cooperative play in socially withdrawn retarded children. *Mental Retardation, 12,* 24–27.

Moseley, A., Faust, L., & Reardon, D. M. (1970). Effects of social and nonsocial stimuli on the stereotyped behaviors on retarded children. *American Journal of Mental Deficiency, 74,* 809–811.

Mulick, J. A., & Schroeder, S. R. (1980). Research relating to management of antisocial behavior in mentally retarded persons. *Psychological Record, 30,* 397–417.

Mumpower, D. L. (1970). Sex ratios found in various types of referred exceptional children. *Exceptional Children, 36,* 621–622.

Neef, N. A., Walters, J., & Egel. A. L. (1984). Establishing generative yes/no answers in developmentally disabled children. *Journal of Applied Behavior Analysis, 17,* 453–460.

Nelson, R. O. (1974). An expanded scope for behavior modification in school settings. *Journal of School Psychology, 12,* 276–287.

Nelson, R. O., Gibson, F., & Cuttings, D. S. (1973). Video taped modeling: The development of three appropriate social responses in a mildly retarded child. *Mental Retardation, 11,* 24–28.

Nihira, K., Foster, R., Shellhaas, M., & Leland, H. (1974). *AAMD Adaptive Behavior Scale, 1974 revision.* Washington, DC: American Association on Mental Deficiency.

Nihira, K., Meyers, C. E., & Mink, I. T. (1980). Home environment, family adjustment, and the development of mentally retarded children. *Applied Research in Mental Retardation, 1,* 5–24.

O'Brien, F., & Azrin, N. H. (1972). Developing proper mealtime behaviors of the institutionalized retarded. *Journal of Applied Behavior Analysis, 5,* 389–399.

Odom, S. L., Hoyson, M., Jamieson, B., & Strain, P. S. (1985). Increasing handicapped preschoolers' peer social interactions: Cross-setting and component analysis. *Journal of Applied Behavior Analysis, 18,* 3–16.

O'Leary, K. D., & Johnson, S. B. (1979). Psychological assessment. In H. C. Quay & J. S. Werry (Eds.), *Psychopathological disorders of childhood* (2nd ed., pp. 210–246). New York: Wiley.

Ollendick, T. H., & Hersen, M. (1984). *Child behavioral assessment: Principles and procedures.* New York: Pergamon Press.

Ounsted, C. (1955). The hyperkinetic syndrome of epileptic children. *Lancet, ii,* 303–311.

Paloutzian, R. F., Hasazi, J., Streifel, J., & Edgar, C. L. (1971). Promotion of positive social interaction in severely retarded young children. *American Journal of Mental Deficiency, 75,* 519–524.

Partington, J. W., Sundberg, L. M., Iwata, B. A., & Mountjoy, P. T. (1979). A task-analysis approach to time telling instruction for normal and educably impaired children. *Education and Treatment of Children, 2,* 17–29.

Petersen, G. A., Austin, G. J., & Lang, R. P. (1979). Use of teacher prompts to increase social behavior: Generalization of effects with severely and profoundly retarded

adolescents. *American Journal of Mental Deficiency, 84,* 82–86.

Peterson, S. L., Robinson, E. A., & Littman, I. (1983). Parent–child interaction training for parents with a history of mental retardation. *Applied Research in Mental Retardation, 4,* 329–342.

Raborn, J. D. (1978). Classroom applications of the Foxx-Azrin toileting program. *Mental Retardation, 16,* 173–174.

Ramey, C. T., Campbell, F. A., & Finkelstein, N. W. (1979). Course and structure of intellectual development in children at high-risk for developmental retardation. In P. H. Brooks, R. Spencer, & C. McCauley (Eds.), *Learning and cognition in the mentally retarded* (pp. 419–432). Hillsdale, NJ: Erlbaum.

Ramey, C. T., & Haskins, R. (1981). A modification of intelligence through early experience. *Intelligence, 5,* 5–20.

Reid, M. K., & Borkowski, J. G. (1984). Effects of methylphenidate (Ritalin) on information processing in hyperactive children. *Journal of Abnormal Child Psychology, 12,* 169–186.

Reid, M. K., & Borkowski, J. G. (1985, April). *Attribution and self-control training with hyperactive children.* Paper presented at the biennial meeting of the Society for Research in Child Development, Toronto.

Reid, M., & Borkowski, J. G. (1987). Causal atributions of hyperactive children: Implications for teaching strategies and self-control. *Journal of Educational Psychology, 79,* 296–307.

Reiss, S., Levitan, G. W., & McNally, R. J. (1982). Emotionally disturbed mentally retarded people. *American Psychologist, 37,* 361–367.

Repp, A. C., & Barton, L. E. (1980). Naturalistic observations of institutionalized retarded persons: A comparison of licensure decisions and behavioral observations. *Journal of Applied Behavior Analysis, 13,* 333–341.

Repp, A. C., Barton, L. E., & Gottlieb, J. (1983). Naturalistic studies of institutionalized retarded persons: II. The effects of density on the behavior of profoundly or severely retarded persons. *American Journal of Mental Deficiency, 87,* 441–447.

Repp, A. C., & Deitz, S. M. (1974). Reducing aggressive and self-injurious behavior of institutionalized retarded children through reinforcement of other behaviors. *Journal of Applied Behavior Analysis, 7,* 313–325.

Richman, J. S., Sonderby, T., & Kahn, J. (1980). Prerequisite vs. *in vivo* acquisition of self-feeding skill. *Behaviour Research and Therapy, 18,* 327–332.

Risley, T. R., & Cuvo, A. (1980). Training mentally retarded adults to make emergency telephone calls. *Behavior Modification, 4,* 513–526.

Roberts, M. C., & LeGreca, A. M. (1981). Behavioral assessment. In C. E. Walker (Ed.), *Clinical practice of psychology: A practical quide for mental health professionals* (pp. 293–346). New York: Pergamon Press.

Robinson, N. M., & Robinson, H. B. (1976). *The mentally retarded child* (2nd ed.). New York: McGraw-Hill.

Rojahn, J., & Schroeder, S. K. (1983). Behavioral assessment. In J. L. Matson & J. A. Mulick (Eds.), *Handbook of mental retardation* (pp. 227–243). New York: Pergamon Press.

Rollings, J. P., Baumeister, A., & Baumeister, A. (1977). The use of overcorrection procedures to eliminate stereotyped behaviors in retarded individuals. *Behavior Modification, 1,* 29–46.

Romer, D., & Heller, T. (1983). Social adaptation of men

tally retarded adults in community settings: A social-ecological approach. *Applied Research in Mental Retardation, 4,* 303–314.

Ross, D. M., & Ross, S. A. (1978). *Pacemaker primary curriculum.* Belmont, CA: Fearon.

Saigh, P. A., & Payne, D. A. (1979). The effect of type of reinforcer and reinforcement schedule on performance on EMR students on four selected subtests of the WISC-R. *Psychology in the Schools, 16,* 106–110.

Sameroff, A. J., & Chandler, M. J. (1975). Reproductive risk and the continuum of caretaking casualty. In F. D. Horowitz, M. Hetherington, S. Scarr-Salapatek, & G. Siegel (Eds.), *Review of child development research* (Vol. 4, pp. 187–244). Chicago: University of Chicago Press.

Sameroff, A. J., & Seifer, R. (1983). Familial risk and child competence. *Child Development, 54,* 1254–1268.

Sandler, A., Coren, A., & Thurman, S. K. (1983). A training program for parents of handicapped preschool children: Effects upon mother, father and child. *Exceptional Children, 49,* 355–358.

Schain, R. J. (1979). Problems with the use of conventional anti-convulsant drugs in mentally retarded individuals. *Brain and Development, 1,* 77–82.

Schalock, R. L., Foley, J. W., Toulouse, A., & Stark, J. A. (1985). Medication and programming in controlling the behavior of mentally retarded individuals in community settings. *American Journal of Mental Deficiency, 5,* 503–509.

Schilling, R. F., Schinke, S. P., Blythe, B. J., & Barth, R. P. (1982). Child maltreatment and mentally retarded parents: Is there a relationship? *Mental Retardation, 20,* 201–209.

Schlesser, R., Meyers, A. W., & Cohen, R. (1981). Generalization of self-instructions: Effects of general versus specific context, active rehearsal, and cognitive level. *Child Development, 52,* 335–340.

Schreibman, L., O'Neill, R. E., & Koegel, R. L. (1983). Behavioral training for siblings of autistic children. *Journal of Applied Behavior Analysis, 16,* 129–138.

Schroeder, S. R., Mulick, J. A., & Schroeder, C. S. (1979). Management of severe behavior problems of the retarded. In N. R. Ellis (Ed.), *Handbook of mental deficiency* (2nd ed., pp. 618–649). Hillsdale, NJ: Erlbaum.

Scibak, J. W. (1983). Behavioral treatment. In J. L. Matson & J. A. Mulick (Eds.), *Handbook of mental retardation* (pp. 339–350). New York: Pergamon Press.

Scovern, A. W., Bukstel, L. H., Kilmann, P. R., Laval, R. A., Busemeyer, J., & Smith, V. (1980). Effects of parent counseling on the family system. *Journal of Counseling Psychology, 27,* 268–275.

Shapiro, E., Barrett, R., & Ollendick, T. (1980). A comparison of physical restraint and positive practice overcorrection in treating stereotypic behavior. *Behavior Therapy, 11,* 227–233.

Singh, N. N. (1980). The effects of facial screening on infant self-injury. *Journal of Behavior Therapy and Experimental Psychiatry, 11,* 131–134.

Singh, N. N., & Aman, M. G. (1981). Effects of thioridazine dosage on the behavior of severely mentally retarded persons. *American Journal of Mental Deficiency, 85,* 580–587.

Singh, N. N., & Winton, A. S. W. (1983). Social skills training with institutionalized severely and profoundly mentally retarded persons. *Applied Research in Mental Retardation, 4,* 383–398.

Smeets, P. M., Lancioni, G. E., & Van Lieshout, R. W. (1985). Teaching mentally retarded children to use an experimental device for telling time and meeting appointments. *Applied Research in Mental Retardation, 6,* 51–70.

Smith, P. S. (1979). A comparison of different methods of toilet training the mentally handicapped. *Behaviour Research and Therapy, 17,* 33–43.

Song, A. Y., Jones, S. E., Lippert, J., Metzgen, K., Miller, J., & Borreca, C. (1980). *Wisconsin Behavior Rating Scale.* Madison: Central Wisconsin Center for the Developmentally Disabled.

Song, A. Y., Song, R. H., & Grant, P. A. (1976). Toilet training in the school and its transfer in the living unit. *Journal of Behavior Therapy and Experimental Psychiatry, 7,* 281–284.

Sparrow, S. S., Balla, D. A., & Cicchetti, D. V. (1984). *Vineland Adaptive Behavior Scales* (rev. ed.). Circle Pines, MN: American Guidance Service.

Sparrow, S. S., & Cicchetti, D. V. (1984). The Behavior Inventory for Rating Development (BIRD): Assessments of reliability and factorial validity. *Applied Research in Mental Retardation, 5,* 219–231.

Sprague, R. L., & Sleator, E. K. (1977). Methylphenidate in hyperkinetic children: Differences in dose effects on learning and social behavior. *Science, 198,* 1274–1276.

Sprague, R. L., & Werry, J. S. (1971). Methodology of psychopharmacological studies with the retarded. In N. R. Ellis (Ed.), *International review of research in mental retardation* (Vol. 5, pp. 148–219). New York: Academic Press.

Stimbert, V. E., Minor, J. W., & McCoy, J. F. (1977). Intensive feeding training with retarded children. *Behavior Modification, 1,* 517–529.

Stokes, T., & Baer, D. (1977). An implicit technology of generalization. *Journal of Applied Behavior Analysis, 10,* 394–397.

Strain, P. (1975). Increasing social play of severely retarded preschoolers with socio-dramatic activities. *Mental Retardation, 13,* 7–9.

Strain, P. S. (1977). Effects of peer social initiations on withdrawn preschool children: Some training and generalization effects. *Journal of Abnormal Child Psychology, 5,* 445–455.

Strain, P. S. (1983). Identification of social skill curriculum targets for severely handicapped children in mainstream preschools. *Applied Research in Mental Retardation, 4,* 369–382.

Sulzer-Azaroff, R., & Mayer, G. R. (1977). *Applying behavior analysis procedures with children and youth.* New York: Holt, Rinehart & Winston.

Switzky, H. N. (1973). Cue distinctiveness, learning, and transfer in mentally retarded persons. *American Journal of Mental Deficiency, 78,* 277–285.

Tarpley, H. D., & Schroeder, S. R. (1979). Comparison of DRO and DRI on rate of suppression of self-injurious behavior. *American Journal of Mental Deficiency, 84,* 188–194.

Tate, B. G., & Baroff, G. S. (1966). Aversive control of self-injurious behaviour in a psyhctoic boy. *Behaviour Research and Therapy, 4,* 281–287.

Tavormina, J. B. (1975). Relative effectiveness of behavioral and reflective group counseling with parents of mentally retarded children. *Journal of Consulting and Clinical Psychology, 43,* 22–31.

Tymchuk, A. (1979). *Parent and family therapy.* New York: Spectrum.

Tymchuk, A. (1983). Interventions with parents of the mentally retarded. In J. L. Matson & J. A. Mulick (Eds.), *Handbook of mental retardation* (pp. 369–380). New York: Pergamon Press.

Vadasy, P. F., Fewell, R. R., Meyer, D. J., & Greenberg, M. T. (1985). Supporting fathers of handicapped young children: Preliminary findings of program effects. *Analysis and Intervention in Developmental Disabilities, 5,* 125–137.

Vukelich, R., & Hake, D. F. (1971). Reduction of dangerously aggressive behavior in a severely retarded resident through a combination of positive reinforcement procedures. *Journal of Applied Behavior Analysis, 4,* 215–225.

Warren, S. F., Baxter, D. K., Anderson, S. R., Marshall, A., & Baer, D. M. (1981). Generalization of question-asking by severely retarded individuals. *Journal of the Association for the Severely Handicapped, 6,* 15–22.

Wehman, P. (1977). *Helping the mentally retarded acquire play skills: A behavioral approach.* Springfield, IL: Charles C Thomas.

Weisz, J. R. (1981). Learned helplessness in black and white children identified by their schools as retarded and nonretarded: Performance deterioration in response to failure. *Developmental Psychology, 17,* 499–508.

Whalen, C. K., & Henker, B. (1980). *Hyperactive children: The social ecology of identification and treatment.* New York: Academic Press.

Whalen, C. K., Henker, B., & Hinshaw, S. P. (1985). Cognitive–behavioral therapies for hyperactive children: Premises, problems, and prospects. *Journal of Abnormal Child Psychology, 13,* 391–410.

White, A. J. R. (1982). Outpatient treatment of oppositional non-eating in a deaf retarded boy. *Journal of Behavior Therapy and Experimental Psychiatry, 13,* 251–255.

Whitman, T. L., & Johnston, M. B. (1987). Mental retardation. In M. Hersen & V. B. Van Hasselt (Eds.), *Behavior therapy with children and adolescents: A clinical approach* (pp. 184–223). New York: Wiley.

Whitman, T. L., Scibak, J. W., & Reid, D. H. (1982). *Behavior modification with the severely and profoundly retarded: Research and applications.* New York: Academic Press.

Wikler, L. (1981). Chronic stress of families of mentally retarded children. *Family Relations, 30,* 281–288.

Winton, A. S. W., Singh, N. N., & Dawson, M. J. (1984). Effects of facial screening and blindfold on self-injurious behavior. *Applied Research in Mental Retardation, 5,* 29–42.

Wirt, R. D., Lacher, D., Klinedinst, J. K., & Seat, P. D. (1977). *Multidimensional description of child personality.* Los Angeles: Western Psychological Services.

Wolf, S. M., & Forsythe, A. (1978). Behavior disturbance, phenobarbital, and febrile seizures. *Pediatrics, 61,* 728–731.

Woolfson, R. C. (1984). Historical perspective on mental retardation. *American Journal of Mental Deficiency, 89,* 231–235.

Yeakel, M. H., Salisbury, L. L., Greer, S. L., & Marcus, L. F. (1970). An appliance for auto-induced adverse control of self-injurious behavior. *Journal of Experimental Child Psychology, 10,* 159–164.

Young, R. M., Bradley-Johnson, S., & Johnson, C. M. (1982). Immediate and delayed reinforcement on WISC-R performance for mentally retarded students. *Applied Research in Mental Retardation, 3,* 13–20.

Zeaman, D., & House, B. J. (1963). The role of attention in retardate discrimination learning. In N. R. Ellis (Ed.), *Handbook of mental deficiency* (pp. 159–223). New York: McGraw Hill.

Zeaman, D., House, B. J., & Orlando, R. (1958). Use of special training conditions in visual discrimination learning with imbeciles. *American Journal of Mental Deficiency, 63,* 453–459.

Zigler, E., Balla, D., & Hodapp, R. (1984). On the definition and classification of mental retardation. *American Journal of Mental Deficiency, 89,* 215–230.

Zigler, E., & Hodapp, R. M. (1986). *Understanding mental retardation.* New York: Cambridge University Press.

8

AUTISM

CRIGHTON NEWSOM
Muscatatuck Center

ARNOLD RINCOVER
Surrey Place Centre

Autistic children are relatively rare and present an unusual constellation of severe problems when first seen in early childhood by a professional. The most definitive characteristic is an extreme failure in socialization: Autistic children show little interest in other human beings, including members of their own families, and are quite content to remain alone for long periods of time. The basic problem seems to go beyond skill deficiencies (although these play a part) to a lack of motivation to seek out play, affection, or any other form of social interaction with parents, siblings, and peers. A second area of obvious deficiency is language. About half of such children do not speak or use gestures, but show only primitive communicative acts, such as taking an adult by the hand to the door to have it opened or throwing a tantrum to coerce an adult to stop making a demand. The other half may use some meaningful words, but will also frequently echo the words or phrases of others without understanding them. Most autistic children will be found to be mentally retarded when assessed with intelligence tests and adaptive behavior scales, and they show considerable scatter across cognitive and developmental domains. The children's social, communication, and learning disabilities result in a very limited, rigid behavioral repertoire, largely dominated by stereotyped, self-stimulatory behaviors and disruptive, aggressive, and self-injurious behaviors. On the other hand, motor development is often normal or only mildly delayed, and a few autistic children will show some nearly age-appropriate, "splinter" skills within a circumscribed area, such as music (Newsom, Hovanitz, & Rincover, 1988; Rutter & Schopler, 1987; Wing & Attwood, 1987).

Not surprisingly, such children have proved sufficiently challenging clinically and theoretically to have attracted considerable attention from all the helping professions, most notably psychology, medicine, and education. This chapter presents a small but very significant part of the total effort to understand and help autistic children, focusing on current clinical practices in selected areas. The approach taken here is a pragmatic, strategic one, focusing on the procedures most commonly used to address such important problems as the severe social and communication deficiencies of autistic children. Wherever possible, variations of and alternatives to established procedures are presented, along with some of the relevant theoretical issues.

First, an overview of autism briefly describes the history of its study and some issues in diagnosis, etiology, and prognosis. Procedures used during the initial stage of treatment for teaching attention and managing disruptive behaviors are presented next. Then procedures for treating two of the cardinal features of autism, social unrelatedness and communication deficiencies, are considered in sufficient depth to indicate the various strategies available and the special difficulties in each area. Approaches to working with families are addressed next, including parent training and mention of some of the problems that arise in families with such severely handicapped children. A description of some very recent and important work in the area of early intervention follows, indicating the importance of the timing, intensity, and extent of treatment. Finally, the chapter concludes with a brief look at some current directions in the analysis and management of problem behaviors and some general conclusions and implications of current research.

Important, extensive areas that cannot be addressed adequately here include behavioral assessment procedures, recently addressed in some detail elsewhere (Newsom et al., 1988), and educational programming (see the books by, e.g., Cohen & Donnellan, 1987; Koegel, Rincover, & Egel, 1982; Sailor & Guess, 1983). Three points regarding terminology should be made. First, to simplify presentations of procedures, we usually refer to all intervention agents simply as "teachers," whether they are customarily psychologists, classroom teachers, speech pathologists, student therapists, or parents. This honorable if insufficiently appreciated term is meant to reflect Skinner's (1968) conception of the crucial role played by anyone in a teaching role as the designer of the contingencies of reinforcement under which learning occurs. Where we specifically discuss other roles, such as "clinician" or "parent," we use those terms. Second, where it is necessary to relate procedures or variations to children of different levels of functioning, we refer to "lower-functioning" or "higher-functioning" children, because greater precision is either impossible or, more often, is irrelevant to the execution or the effects of the procedure. The former term refers to children who lie in the severely and profoundly retarded ranges of intellectual and adaptive functioning and whose speech is absent or noncommunicative prior to treatment. "Higher-functioning" children are those in the mildly and moderately retarded

ranges, who usually have some communicative phrase speech. Finally, gender pronouns are randomly alternated to avoid awkward constructions.

OVERVIEW

Historical Roots

There are a few scattered reports of apparently autistic children prior to the 1940s (reviewed by Wing, 1976), including the famous case of the Wild Boy of Aveyron (Itard, 1801/1962). However, such children were usually not distinguished from retarded children in the 19th century and were considered to have childhood versions of adult psychoses, typically schizophrenia, in the early 20th century (Kanner, 1965). Kanner (1943) was the first to note a number of features that seemed to differentiate these children from retarded and schizophrenic children. These features included extreme social isolation; obsessive insistence on the preservation of sameness in everything, including daily routines and their own stereotyped behavior patterns; muteness or noncommunicative speech, along with speech abnormalities such as delayed echolalia and pronoun reversal; excellent rote memory; concrete, literal thought processes; generally normal physical development; and apparently normal intellectual potential—all combined with well-educated, aloof, obsessive parents from the higher social classes (Kanner, 1943). Kanner initially believed that the condition was due to some innate inability to establish a social relationship and named the syndrome "early infantile autism" (Kanner, 1943). Later he suggested that the etiology might lie in an interaction between a biological predisposition in the children and detached, mechanical child-rearing practices on the part of the parents, who themselves seemed to have a mild form of the disorder (Kanner, 1954). Eventually, he returned to focus on the notion of an inborn defect, leaning toward the possibility of a genetically based biochemical abnormality (Kanner, 1971).

Infantile autism soon became a popular and overextended diagnosis (Kanner, 1965). During the 1950s, most clinicians ignored Kanner's (1943) initial observation that the appearance of autism in early infancy seemed to point to innate causal factors, and instead, offered thoroughgoing psychogenic theories and prescribed some form of long-term psychotherapy for both the children and the parents (e.g., Despert, 1951; Mahler, 1952; Rank & McNaughton, 1950; Szurek, 1956). Other, more scientific investigators continued to pursue the possibility of physiological causes and attempted to establish some organization among autism and the many other conditions believed to be variants of "childhood schizophrenia" (e.g., Bender, 1955; Eisenberg, 1956; Fish, 1957).

The current era in autism took shape during the 1960s, when several lines of research and treatment that are still prominent were established. Basic facts about the characteristics of autistic children were gathered in epidemiological and medical studies (Lotter, 1966; Rutter & Lockyer, 1967; Schain & Yannet, 1960). These studies showed that most autistic children were, in fact, also mentally retarded; that they came from all social classes; and that a small but significant percentage had either "hard" or "soft" signs of neurological impairment, such as infantile spasms, epileptic seizures, or seriously delayed developmental milestones. Cognitive researchers began to identify deficits in basic perceptual, attentional, conceptual, and linguistic processes, again suggesting the likelihood of some type of neurological dysfunction (Hermelin & O'Connor, 1964; Pronovost, Wakstein, & Wakstein, 1966; Tubbs, 1966). Objective studies of parents failed to find evidence of significant psychopathology (Pitfield & Oppenheim, 1964; Rutter & Brown, 1966). Finally, behavioral and educational researchers found that some of the problem behaviors of autistic children that had proven most intractable to psychodynamic therapies, such as self-injury, mutism, and echolalia, could be understood and treated effectively with procedures derived from operant learning theory (Ferster, 1961; Hewett, 1965; Lovaas, Berberich, Perloff, & Schaeffer, 1966; Lovaas, Freitag, Gold, & Kassorla, 1965; Risley & Wolf, 1967).

The emerging data from these and numerous other studies rapidly forced a complete reconceptualization of the problem of autism, culminating in a book, a paper, and a film that epitomized the findings of the decade. Rimland (1964) reviewed most of the existing literature to date in a book that effectively terminated any further serious consideration of psychogenic hypotheses. Rutter (1968) marshaled the basic research to argue that autism was best conceived as a disorder of cognitive and perceptual

deficits affecting the comprehension of language. Lovaas (1969) presented his innovative behavioral teaching procedures and their results in a dramatic film that showed that autistic children could learn verbal imitation and converstional speech. Most of the major developments of the 1970s and 1980s, including the general acceptance of autism as a developmental disability instead of an emotional disorder (Ritvo & Freeman, 1978), the exponential growth in basic and applied research (DeMyer, Hingtgen, & Jackson, 1981), the estabishment of classroom educational programs (Wilcox & Thompson, 1980), and the development of effective early intervention projects (Simeonsson, Olley, & Rosenthal, 1987), owe a considerable intellectual debt to the work represented in these three sources.

Nature and Diagnosis

Autistic and other children with Pervasive Developmental Disorders as defined by the revised third edition of the *Diagnostic and Statistical Manual of Mental Disorders* (DSM-III-R; American Psychiatric Association [APA], 1987) can be conceptually located within a hypothetical continuum of pervasiveness (or extent) and severity of disability (cf. Cohen, Paul, & Volkmar, 1986). At the "most pervasive" end of the continuum fall profoundly retarded, cerebral-palsied children, who exhibit a fairly uniform pattern of profound impairments across the domains of intellectual, adaptive, social, language, and motor functioning. At the "least pervasive" end of the continuum lie children with specific developmental disorders, characterized by much less severe impairments in only one or a few related area(s), such as expressive language or both expressive and receptive language. Most children classified as having Pervasive Developmental Disorders fall between these two extremes, showing an uneven pattern of impairments. Autistic children tend to show, for example, mild motor impairment combined with mild to severe impairments in nonverbal intellectual skills, and moderate to profound impairments in social behavior, language, and adaptive behavior (Ornitz, Guthrie, & Farley, 1977; Rutter, 1983; Sigman & Ungerer, 1981; Wing, 1981a). The unevenness in the development of autistic children suggests that different areas of functioning can develop relatively independently of one another—a possibility supported by several lines of developmental and neurophysiological research (Tanguay, 1984). The conceptual implication of this view is that it is less useful to try to distinguish various clinical syndromes that are presumed to reflect underlying diseases than it is to characterize patterns of strengths and weaknesses and use these as a basis for individualizing treatment and searching for specific etiological factors (Tanguay, 1984). Such a position dovetails well with the consistent behavioral theme that the conceptualization of a child's problem as a "disorder" called "autism" is unproductive in research and treatment efforts, particularly in comparison with an alternative strategy, the analysis and treatment of individual classes of behavior (Ferster, 1961; Lovaas, 1971; Newsom, Carr, & Lovaas, 1979). However, these conceptualizations have not yet influenced current nosologies based on clinical phenomenology, which focus instead on certain similarities across a broad range of children.

Diagnostic Criteria and Differential Diagnosis

The current diagnostic criteria for the Pervasive Developmental Disorders (APA, 1987) appear in Table 8-1. Two categories are provided: Autistic Disorder, considered the prototype of the spectrum of pervasive disorders (Cohen et al., 1986); and a little-studied residual category, Pervasive Developmental Disorder Not Otherwise Specified, for children who seem to meet the general description of Pervasive Developmental Disorders in DSM-III-R but not all the criteria for Autistic Disorder, including children previously diagnosed as having Childhood Onset Pervasive Developmental Disorder (APA, 1980; Sparrow et al., 1986). Only two categories have been provided because virtually no progress has been made in detecting reliable patterns among the pervasively disordered children who do not quite fit the definition of autism, although some interesting conceptual and analytic efforts in this direction are continuing (e.g., Cohen et al., 1986; Dahl, Cohen, & Provence, 1986; Siegel, Anders, Ciaranello, Bienenstock, & Kraemer, 1986; Sparrow et al., 1986; Tanguay, 1984). It should be noted that in the list of criteria for Autistic Dirorder there is no criterion requiring an early age of onset, as appeared in previous diagnostic formulations (APA, 1980; Ritvo & Freeman, 1978; Rutter,

1978), although an onset after 36 months is considered sufficiently unusual that it should be noted (see item D in Table 8-1). The early-onset criterion was omitted because of the arbitrariness involved in selecting a cutoff age and the difficulties in establishing age of onset with any degree of precision in most cases (APA, 1987). Furthermore, some recent research suggests that age of onset fails to discriminate between autistic children and those with other pervasive developmental disorders in statistical cluster analyses (Dahl et al., 1986). However, this finding is in apparent contradiction with the results of a study by Prior, Perry, and Gajzago (1975), who found that the most efficient sorting of a large group of pervasively disordered children relied primarily on age of onset, with children having onsets prior to 2 years of age distinguishable from those with later onsets along a number of dimensions. In practice, the nature and severity of a child's behavioral characteristics are to determine which of the two diagnostic categories is applied, regardless of age of onset.

In making diagnostic distinctions between autistic and other children, the crucial area of focus is the developmental level and quality of the child's social functioning (item A in Table 8-1). The abnormalities in communication (item B) and behaviors indicating a rigid, stereotyped repertoire (item C) overlap with those seen in other diagnostic groups, such as aphasic and retarded children. The following considerations apply.

1. The social unrelatedness of autistic children at the beginning of treatment may be profound, but it is not absolute. There can be considerable variability across behaviors considered to indicate social development. For example, the parents of nearly all young autistic children will report that the children avoid eye contact, ignore people, and are aloof and emotionally distant (Lotter, 1966; Volkmar, Cohen, & Paul, 1986). However, as many as half of such children are reported to cuddle when held, to smile responsively at their mothers and to be aware of the mothers' absence (Volkmar et al., 1986). Most autistic children form real, if limited and deviant, relationships with familiar people as they grow older (Rumsey, Rapoport, & Sceery, 1985; Wing & Attwood, 1987). It is therefore necessary to sample a range of social behaviors to get a clear picture of the extent and severity of the child's social unrelatedness.

2. A child's level of social functioning

should be below her tested developmental level or mental age (MA) for her to be diagnosed as autistic (APA, 1987; Rutter, 1985). At the low end of the intelligence continuum, the social deficits of autistic children can be difficult to distinguish from those of severely and profoundly retarded children. Usually, however, even a profoundly retarded child will show social behaviors that are commensurate with his MA such as eye contact, smiling, and social approach (Wing, 1981a). One way of addressing this problem quantitatively is to compare a child's tested MA with her age-equivalent scores on the Socialization subdomains of the Vineland Adaptive Behavior Scales (Sparrow, Balla, & Cicchetti, 1984). Volkmar et al. (1987) found that autistic children functioned at a significantly lower level in the subdomains of Interpersonal Relationships, Play and Leisure Time, and Coping Skills than their overall MAs would predict.

3. At the high end of the intelligence continuum, it can be difficult to distinguish between autistic children and children with markedly "atypical" personalities (Sparrow et al., 1986), Aspergers syndrome (Wing, 1981b), Schizoid or Schizotypal Personality Disorders (APA, 1987; Wolff & Barlow, 1979), and Schizophrenia (APA, 1987; Burd & Kerbeshian, 1987; Kydd & Werry, 1982). In general, autistic children seem to differ from such children by having a lower overall level of cognitive functioning, academic achievement, and language development (Sparrow et al., 1986; Wing, 1981a, b; Wing & Gould, 1979); showing somewhat better gross and fine

TABLE 8-1 DSM-III-R Criteria for Pervasive Developmental Disorders

---

Autistic Disorder

At least eight of the following sixteen items are present, including at least two items from A, one from B, and one from C. Consider a criterion to be met *only* if the behavior is abnormal for the person's developmental level.

A. Qualitative impairment in reciprocal social interaction as manifested by the following:
   (The examples within parentheses are arranged so that those listed first are more likely to apply to younger or more handicapped persons with this disorder and those listed later to older or less handicapped persons.)

   (1) marked lack of awareness of the existence or feelings of others (e.g., treats a person as if he or she were a piece of furniture; does not notice another person's distress; apparently has no concept of the need of others for privacy)
   (2) no or abnormal seeking of comfort at times of distress (e.g., does not come for comfort even when ill, hurt, or tired; seeks comfort in a stereotyped way, e.g., says "cheese, cheese, cheese" whenever hurt)
   (3) no or impaired imitation (e.g., does not wave bye-bye; does not copy mother's domestic activities; mechanical imitation of others' actions out of context)
   (4) no or abnormal social play (e.g., does not actively participate in simple games; prefers solitary play activities; involves other children in play only as "mechanical aids")
   (5) gross impairment in ability to make peer friendships (e.g., no interest in making peer friendships; despite interest in making friends, demonstrates lack of understanding of conventions of social interaction, for example, reads phone book to uninterested peer)

B. Qualitative impairment in verbal and nonverbal communication, and in imaginative activity, as manifested by the following:
   (The numbered items are arranged so that those listed first are more likely to apply to younger or more handicapped persons with this disorder and those listed later to older or less handicapped persons.)

   (1) no mode of communication, such as communicative babbling, facial expression, gesture, mime, or spoken language
   (2) markedly abnormal nonverbal communication, as in the use of eye-to-eye gaze, facial expression, body posture, or gestures to initiate or modulate social interaction (e.g., does not anticipate being held, stiffens when held, does not look at the person or smile when making a social approach, does not greet parents or visitors, has a fixed stare in social situations)
   (3) absence of imaginative activity, such as playacting of adult roles, fantasy characters, or animals; lack of interest in stories about imaginary events
   (4) marked abnormalities in the production of speech, including volume, pitch, stress, rate, rhythm, and intonation (e.g., monotonous tone, questionlike melody, or high pitch)

motor coordination (Sparrow *et al.*, 1986; Wing, 1981b); and usually showing earlier onset than children with Schizophrenia and lacking their hallucinations and delusions (Kolvin, Ounsted, Humphrey, & McNay, 1971). Children who do not meet the criteria for Autistic Disorder, Schizoid or Schizotypal Personality Disorder, or Schizophrenia are diagnosed as having Pervasive Developmental Disorder Not Otherwise Specified. It should be noted that there is considerable controversy as to where and even whether lines should be drawn between these groups (Cohen *et al.*, 1986; Petty, Ornitz, Michelman, & Zimmerman, 1984). Petty *et al.*(1984) discuss cases in which children were accurately diagnosed as autistic prior to the age of 5 years, then met the criteria for schizophrenia by the age of 10 or 12, indicating that autism and schizophrenia may not be distinct entities as previously believed (Kolvin,

1971; Rutter, 1972). Additional aspects of diagnosis have recently been discussed elsewhere (Denckla, 1986; Newsom *et al.*, 1988; Rutter & Schopler, 1987).

Prevalence

The exemplary epidemiological studies of Lotter (1966) and Wing, Yeates, Brierley, and Gould (1976) indicate that autism occurs at a rate of 4.5–4.8 per 10,000 children. The ratio of males to females is about 3.5:1.

Etiology

There seems to be general consensus that autism is a developmental disorder, implying a neurological cause or, more likely, causes (Ritvo & Freeman, 1978; Rutter & Schopler, 1987). Most basic researchers now view autism

TABLE 8-1 (*continued*)

---

(5) marked abnormalities in the form or content of speech, including stereotyped and repetitive use of speech (e.g., immediate echolalia or mechanical repetition of television commercial); use of "you" when "I" is meant (e.g., using "You want cookie?" to mean "I want cookie"); idiosyncratic use of words or phrases (e.g., "Go on green riding" to mean "I want to go on the swing"); or frequent irrelevant remarks (e.g., starts talking about train schedules during a conversation about sports)

(6) marked impairment in the ability to initiate or sustain a conversation with others, despite adequate speech (e.g., indulging in lengthy monologues on one subject regardless of interjections from others)

C. Markedly restricted repertoire of activities and interests, as manifested by the following:

(1) stereotyped body movements, e.g., hand-flicking or -twisting, spinning, head-banging, complex whole-body movements

(2) persistent preoccupation with parts of objects (e.g., sniffing or smelling objects, repetitive feeling of texture of materials, spinning wheels of toy cars) or attachment to unusual objects (e.g., insists on carrying around a piece of string)

(3) marked distress over changes in trivial aspects of environment, e.g., when a vase is moved from usual position

(4) unreasonable insistence on following routines in precise detail, e.g., insisting that exactly the same route always be followed when shopping

(5) markedly restricted range of interests and a preoccupation with one narrow interest, e.g., interested only in lining up objects, in amassing facts about meteorology, or in pretending to be a fantasy character

D. Onset during infancy or childhood
Specify if childhood onset (after 36 months of age).

Pervasive Development Disorder Not Otherwise Specified

This category should be used when there is a qualitative impairment in the development of reciprocal social interaction and of verbal and nonverbal communication skills, but the criteria are not met for Autistic Disorder, Schizophrenia, or Schizotypal or Schizoid Personality Disorder. Some people with this diagnosis will exhibit a markedly restricted repertoire of activities and interests, but others will not.

Note. From *Diagnostic and Statistical Manual of Mental Disorders* (3rd ed., rev., pp. 38–39) by the American Psychiatric Association, 1987, Washington, DC: Author. Copyright 1987 by the American Psychiatric Association. Reprinted by permission.

as the "final common pathway" of a number of different possible etiologies, including biochemical, metabolic, electrophysiological, and structural abnormalities (Coleman & Gillberg, 1985; Rutter, 1988). For example, various studies have implicated abnormal serotonin or dopamine levels (e.g., Cohen, Caparulo, & Shaywitz, 1978), phenylketonuria (Lowe, Tanaka, Seashore, Young, & Cohen, 1980), epilepsy (e.g., Deykin & MacMahon, 1979), ventricular enlargement (e.g., Prior, Tress, Hoffman, & Boldt, 1984), and brain stem abnormalities (e.g., Gillberg, Rosenhall, Johansson, 1983). However, the proportion of cases in which a neurological cause of any kind can be definitely identified is only a "tiny minority" (Rutter & Schopler, 1987), and it is not at all clear how the few physiological abnormalities that have been found are related to the children's overt behaviors.

The very slow rate of progress in identifying physiological abnormalities is usually explained by noting that the defects in autistic children must be quite subtle, and our tools for investigating brain structure and function are not yet powerful enough to detect them (Rutter & Schopler, 1987). There may also be other, more fundamental problems that stand in the way of progress; these stem from the failure to establish subclassifications of the heterogeneous population of children now diagnosed as autistic. Tanguay (1984) has argued that the "syndrome" of autism is largely "man-made" and lacks what he terms descriptive, etiological, and therapeutic validity. It lacks descriptive validity because it overlaps with other diagnostic categories and because it includes such an exteme range of symptoms and handicaps (Freeman et al., 1981; Wing, 1981a). It lacks etiological validity because even in those few cases where specific etiological factors have been found in association with autistic behaviors, the factors have been extremely varied and usually include abnormalities that also cause mental retardation and probably other developmental disorders. The diagnosis lacks therapeutic validity because it provides only vague implications about treatment (Tanguay, 1984). Tanguay (1984) suggests that the solution is a reconceptualization of childhood disorders in terms of developmental psychology and neurophysiology—that is, as showing various types and degrees of dissociation between different cognitive processes that can ultimately be related to variations in the development of their corresponding neural systems.

Lovaas and Smith (in press) also question the validity and usefulness of autism as a meaningful syndrome, noting that the selection of a group of children according to a list of originally arbitrary characteristics has led to the reification of the characteristics into a hypothetical disease that may not exist. They suggest that lack of progress in identifying neurological causes of autistic behaviors results from the methodology of most basic research. Because neurologically oriented researchers cannot ethically manipulate the independent variables of greatest interest in the central nervous system to determine their causal status, they do correlational and descriptive research. Such designs make it difficult to specify cause-and-effect relationships and to rule out confounding variables (Lovaas & Smith, in press).

Differential Prognosis and General Treatment Strategies

Predictions of outcome are hazardous at best with such a heterogeneous population. It is difficult to draw overall conclusions from existing outcome studies because they span different eras of treatment and educational opportunity, report different predictor and criterion variables, vary greatly in the amount of detail provided about diagnosis and treatment, and seldom extend beyond adolescence (DeMyer et al., 1973; Eisenberg, 1956; Fenske, Zalenski, Krantz & McClannahan, 1985; Freeman, Ritvo, Needleman, & Yokota, 1985; Gillberg & Steffenburg, 1987; Howlin & Rutter, 1987; Kanner, 1973; Lotter, 1974; Lovaas, 1987; Rutter, Greenfeld, & Lockyer, 1967). However, if we look at the longer-term (but generally older) studies among those just cited (DeMyer et al., 1973; Eisenberg, 1956; Gillberg & Steffenburg, 1987; Rutter et al., 1967), 1%–2% of autistic individuals became normal in the sense that there was "little difference between them and children who had never been diagnosed as autistic" (DeMyer et al., 1973, p. 221). About 10% had what was judged to be a "good" outcome; that is, they achieved near-normal functioning in language and/or social behavior and made satisfactory progress in school or work, but usually displayed peculiarities of speech or personality (Rutter et al., 1967). Another 20% had "fair" outcomes, or continued to make social and educational progress in spite of a significant handicap, such as lack of speech. About 70% had "poor" or "very poor" outcomes, with limited progress in all areas and major remaining handicaps.

If we concentrate on the more recent studies and one objective short-term measure, successful placement in a normal classroom, the main factor in determining outcome was whether or not the children received intensive, behaviorally oriented intervention programs before the age of 5 years. In the absence of such intervention, only 0%–11% of autistic children achieved normal placements (DeMyer et al., 1973; Fenske et al., 1985; Freeman et al., 1985; Howlin & Rutter, 1987; Kanner, 1973; Lotter, 1974; Lovaas, 1987). With such intervention, two studies showed that 44% (Fenske et al., 1985) and 47% (Lovaas, 1987) of the children achieved such placements. Early intervention studies are discussed in some detail in a later section of this chapter.

The practical usefulness of all the figures just mentioned for making individual predictions is difficult to determine. On the one hand, the recent emergence and gradual dissemination of effective early intervention programs, community-referenced educational curricula, supported employment opportunities, and varied community living options (Falvey, 1986; Koegel, Rincover, & Egel, 1982; Simeonsson et al., 1987; Sailor & Guess, 1983) greatly complicate any attempt to project the status in 15 or 20 years of the autistic toddler seen today and suggest optimism. On the other hand, these new developments are still not widely available; in addition, there are disturbing findings such as those by Green et al. (1986) that in the "average" special education classroom (of 43 studied) for severely handicapped children, the children were on task less than half (44%) of the designated instructional time, and almost two-thirds of their on-task time involved nonfunctional tasks (i.e., tasks that did not involve natural materials and/or age-appropriate skills). Such an environment would seem to stand little chance of making much difference in the findings of the older outcome studies described above.

The most general conclusion that emerges from both early and more recent follow-up studies is that autistic children can be divided into two large groups based on intelligence (Lotter, 1974; Lovaas & Smith, in press; Rutter, 1988).

The first group is composed of those in the severely and profoundly retarded ranges of intelligence; the second is made up of those in the normal and mildly through moderately retarded ranges. The prognosis for the first group remains limited at the present time, with most individuals requiring sheltered living and work arrangements throughout life. Prognosis tends to be especially poor if, in addition to very low intelligence, there is a lack of any communicative speech by 5 years of age, profound unresponsiveness to sounds, profound social unrelatedness, clear evidence of neurological impairment (e.g., epilepsy, definitely abnormal electroencephalogram), chromosomal abnormalities, or significantly delayed motor milestones (DeMyer et al., 1973; Eisenberg, 1956; Gillberg & Steffenburg, 1987; Lotter, 1974; Rutter et al., 1967).

The most appropriate treatment strategy for children in the first group emphasizes the acquisition of behaviors that will make the children's lives less difficult than they would otherwise be and allow them to function as independently as possible. The main objectives include self-care skills, a reasonable degree of compliance with instructions and simple rules, basic social and affectional behaviors, communication of needs and wants, appropriate play, and the reduction of harmful behaviors. In later childhood and adolescence, a steadily increasing emphasis on domestic living and work-related skills is most appropriate in preparation for supervised living and work environments. In working with parents, the clinician must walk the narrow path between undue pessimism and unwarranted optimism. Communications that focus excessive attention on a child's deficiencies or that, on the other hand, raise expectations for dramatic improvement are to be avoided. The main jobs are to teach the parents how to teach basic skills, how to control inappropriate behaviors, and how to solve the inevitable practical problems that arise within the family and between the family and educational and other service providers. Equally important is the informal modeling of the celebration of progress, however slow and incremental at times, and the simple enjoyment of the child's unique and attractive characteristics.

For the second group of children, those in the normal to moderately retarded ranges, outcome is highly variable and more open to modification (Lotter, 1978; Lovaas & Smith, in press;

Rutter, 1988). As might be expected, this group accounts for those who achieve normal or near-normal outcomes (DeMyer *et al.*, 1973; Freeman *et al.*, 1985; Lovaas & Smith, in press; Rutter *et al.*, 1967). The general treatment strategy for young autistic children in this group should therefore assume the nature of a "total push" approach, in which time is of the essence, in order to take maximum advantage of the plasticity of neurological and behavioral processes early in life (Huttenlocher, 1988; Rincover, Taggart, Hyde, Cardella, & Baranyai, 1985). In addition to the objectives just mentioned for lower-functioning children, there are additional emphases on age-appropriate verbal language, social interaction with normal peers, and behaviors and skills expected in normal preschool and elementary classrooms (Lovaas, 1981; Lovaas & Smith, in press; Rincover *et al.*, 1985; Strain, Hoyson, & Jamieson, 1985). Extensive parent training and support are crucial and should be made available to every family interested in participating. The children most likely to achieve normal or near-normal functioning will show rapid learning during the first 3 or 4 months (Lovaas & Smith, in press). For the many older children and adolescents in this group who have not received such intensive early intervention, and for those who receive it but do not attain normal classroom placements, appropriate treatment emphases are successful functioning in their special education classes and the steady elaboration of their language, social, community, and vocational skills. Outcomes can be expected to be highly variable, depending on the child, the quality of his education, and the opportunities available in adulthood.

INITIAL TREATMENT

There are two main tasks at the beginning of treatment. First, the child is taught certain basic skills that are prerequisites to more complex behaviors. These "learning-readiness" skills include behaviors such as sitting in a chair, attending to the teacher (making eye contact), and looking at task materials. Concurrently, behaviors that interfere with learning, such as tantrums, aggression, and noncompliance, are minimized. These two treatment objectives occur in parallel because they are interdependent: Initial teaching efforts will not progress very far unless some control of disrup-

tive behaviors is accomplished, and the reduction of disruptive behaviors requires the strengthening of alternative behaviors if it is to endure. Conceptually, initial treatment programs establish some basic rules of social interaction that, if neglected, result in disruptions and delays in all subsequent treatment efforts.

Learning-readiness training and early behavior management efforts also seem to have more subtle but equally important effects on both the child and the teacher. For the child, initial treatment programs establish adults as sources of consistent positive and negative consequences, often for the first time in the child's life. They also teach the child how to learn from the social environment by introducing very clear stimulus–response–consequence cycles as the basic framework of many future teaching interactions. For the teacher, especially if she is a parent, initial treatment programs provide some satisfaction and self-confidence in finally gaining some control over the child's behavior, which does much to alleviate feeelings of inadequacy (Lovaas, 1981; Schreibman, Koegel, Mills, & Burke, 1984).

Basic procedures for teaching appropriate sitting in a chair, sitting at a table, and attending to the teacher and to task materials are presented by Lovaas (1981) and Kozloff (1974). Procedures for teaching visual attention to adults can serve here as a good example of how learning-readiness skills are taught.

Teaching Attention

Teaching a child who rarely attends to others to look at an adult's face upon request is a simple but important early goal in treatment. Eye contact does not guarantee attention, of course, but does make it more probable than when it is absent. In addition to making the child more socially accessible, eye contact also facilitates learning to attend to materials during table tasks and observing the teacher's behavioral models in imitation and speech training. Eye contact is relatively easy to teach, which makes eye contact training a good first program for parents and students because they are likely to be successful very quickly.

With autistic children who already make at least some spontaneous eye contact, it may be sufficient to use differential reinforcement to increase the rate of eye contact, providing praise and/or edibles when it occurs and ignoring its nonoccurrence (Brooks, Morrow, & Gray, 1968; McConnell, 1967). In many autistic children, however, the rate of eye contact is negligible and rarely occurs on request. Therefore, eye contact is usually taught through "discrete-trial" procedures after the child has been taught the prerequisite behaviors of sitting quietly with hands down in the lap. Discrete-trial methodology (Koegel, Russo, Rincover, & Schreibman, 1982) is a simple but very fundamental teaching methodology employed in one form or another in virtually every training activity with autistic children. Its importance lies in its "parsing" of the continuous flow of ordinary adult–child interactions into highly distinctive (discrete) events that are more easily discriminated by the child. The essential components of each training trial are the following:

1. The teacher presents a brief, highly discriminable stimulus (instruction or question).
2. The instruction is followed by a prompt (an additional stimulus that insures a correct response) if the child needs one to execute the correct response. This is an optional component that is eliminated as soon as the child begins to respond correctly on her own.
3. The child responds correctly or incorrectly.
4. The teacher provides an appropriate consequence (reinforces correct responses; ignores, reprimands, or corrects incorrect responses) (Koegel, Russo, et al., 1982).

Eye contact training illustrates the use of these components very clearly. The teacher starts a trial by saying "Look," then prompts the child to look by holding an edible reward near the bridge of his (the teacher's) nose or beside one eye. Because of the natural variability in the child's eye movements, her gaze will move from the edible to the teacher's face, and she is rewarded at that moment. Over trials, the edible as a prompt is faded (gradually moved farther and farther away from the teacher's face) to shift stimulus control of eye contact from the prompt to the teacher's instruction. Alternatively, instead of fading the prompt spatially, the teacher can delay its presentation for increasing durations after the command. The objective is simply to establish 2–3 seconds of eye contact on request at a fairly reliable level, such as 80% of requests. Two or three seconds are sufficient for the child to see the teacher's next verbalization or motor behavior; there is no

need to teach the child to stare for long durations (Mirenda, Donnellan, & Yoder, 1983).

The most common problem that occurs during eye contact training is that the child fixates on the edible being used as a prompt and does not shift her gaze to the teacher's face. One way around this problem is to stop prompting eye contact and, instead, to shape it. After each command, the teacher waits for the child to look in the general direction of the face and reinforces any such glances that occur within about 5 seconds. As trials continue, successively closer approximations to looking directly at the face immediately after the command are differentially reinforced. A second alternative is to use a negative reinforcement technique in which eye contact serves as a response to escape a midly aversive prompt. After presenting the instruction, the teacher holds the child's head to orient the child's face toward his, then releases it as soon as eye contact occurs (Altman & Krupshaw, 1982). A third alternative that can be attemped as a last resort is to use a mild punishment technique for failing to look on command in conjunction with positive reinforcement for looking. Foxx (1977) used a procedure termed "functional movement training" (2–5 minutes of prompted head movements) as an aversive consequence for not looking, along with edibles and praise as reinforcers for looking on command. The combined procedures were found to be more effective than positive reinforcement alone. The major disadvantage of escape and punishment procedures is that they may elicit incompatible emotional behaviors, such as struggling, whining, or aggression, during the early trials (Altman & Krupshaw, 1982; Foxx, 1977). Therefore, such procedures should not be used until there is ample evidence of the failure of less restrictive procedures.

Once eye contact begins to occur reliably in one-to-one training sessions, it is generalized across persons and settings through "incidental-teaching" (Hart & Risley, 1975) procedures to make it a functional social and educational skill. At home, the child is required to make eye contact during interactions with parents and siblings just before being allowed access to naturally occurring reinforcers, such as opening the refrigerator door, turning on the television, or going outside (Kozloff, 1974; Lovaas, 1981). Similarly, in subsequent teaching programs, the child is required to look at the teacher's hand and body movements during motor imitation training, at the teacher's mouth or hands during verbal or signed communication training, and at objects or pictures during discrimination tasks.

Management of Mild Problem Behaviors

The relatively mild interfering behaviors encountered early in treatment typically include tantrums, yelling, screaming, throwing or destroying objects, and aggression and self-injury at rates and intensities that are disruptive but not physically dangerous.

One useful approach to treatment is suggested by the fact that autistic children are frequently described at "negativistic" or "noncompliant" in teaching situations (Volkmar, 1986). Defining the problem of disruptive behavior as noncompliance leads to procedures that attempt to reduce disruptive behaviors indirectly by strengthening compliance as a class of appropriate alternative behaviors (Craighead, O'Leary, & Allen, 1973; Striefel, Wetherby, & Karlan, 1978). Russo, Cataldo, and Cushing (1981) conducted compliance training with developmentally disabled children by presenting one of three simple commands ("Come here," "Sit down," "Stand up") along with an appropriate gesture every 30–45 seconds during 10-minute sessions. If a child complied with the instruction within 5 seconds, he received a hug, praise, and an edible reward. Noncompliance and disruptive behaviors were ignored. With unusually disruptive children, instead of ignoring noncompliance, it is more effective to physically prompt the child through the behavior, without reinforcing it (Neef, Shafer, Egel, Cataldo, & Parrish, 1983; Parrish, Cataldo, Kolko, Neef, & Egel, 1986). The Russo *et al.* (1981) procedure not only increased the children's rates of compliance, but also resulted in substantial reductions of their disruptive behaviors, such as self-injury, aggression, and inappropriate crying. Replications and extensions of this finding have established that compliant behaviors and disruptive behaviors are inversely related response classes; strengthening one class of behaviors reduces the other class indirectly (Neef *et al.*, 1983; Parrish *et al.*, 1986).

An understanding of a common motivation for disruptive behaviors in teaching situations has facilitated the development of additional treatments. Several studies (Carr & Durand, 1985a; Carr & Newsom, 1985; Carr, Newsom, & Binkoff, 1976, 1980) found that tantrums, aggression, and self-injury are far more likely to occur when demands (instructions, requests, questions) are presented to autistic children than when no demands are made, and that these disruptive behaviors cease abruptly when a clear signal is given that no more demands will be made. Weeks and Gaylord-Ross (1981) replicated these findings and found, in addition, that disruptive behaviors are more likely to occur during difficult tasks than easy ones. These findings can be explained by Patterson's (1976) coercion hypothesis to account for the development of disruptive behavior in conduct-disordered children. Patterson found that high levels of disruptive behaviors (yelling, whining, crying, noncompliance) in such children often follow parents' commands and cease when the children's disruptive behaviors result in the parents' termination of their commands. Over a period of time, the children learn to repeat or escalate the intensity of their disruptive (coercive) behaviors because, whenever the parents do withdraw the commands, the children's coercive behaviors are strengthened through negative reinforcement (the termination of an aversive stimulus). Similarly, with autistic children, teachers' demands can function as aversive stimuli that the children try to escape by engaging in disruptive behaviors. If the teachers do allow the children to escape their demands by terminating them, the disruptive behaviors are strengthened through negative reinforcement. This scenario is especially likely with young autistic children, who may have had no experience with the relatively high rates of demands that occur in teaching situations.

The conceptualization of disruptive behaviors as escape behaviors maintained by negative reinforcement helps to generate interventions aimed at controlling coercive interactions (Carr & Newsom, 1985). First, any operation that serves to attenuate the aversive properties of a demand situation should result in a decrease of problem behaviors. The aversiveness of the demands in the teaching situation can be attenuated by creating a "positive context" of engaging, playful social interaction between demand presentations (Carr *et al.*, 1976) and by using highly preferred foods, toys, and sensory stimuli as reinforcers (Carr & Newsom, 1985; Carr *et al.*, 1980; Rincover & Newsom, 1985).

A second intervention suggested by an escape conceptualization involves a variant of extinction and is similar to the compliance training procedure described above (Russo *et al.*, 1981). Specifically, if the disruptive behavior has been maintained by the negative reinforcement of successful escape, then it follows that if the child is not permitted to escape following the disruptive behavior, the behavior should become nonfunctional and decrease. Escape extinction (Catania, 1968) can be arranged by "working through" the child's disruptive behavior—that is, continuing to present demands and prompts at a steady pace regardless of the child's behavior (Carr et al., 1980; Plummer, Baer, & LeBlanc, 1977). Because the child's behaviors no longer function as means to escape the teacher's demands, they tend to extinguish. A corollary of the escape hypothesis is that any treatment procedure that allows escape to occur contingent upon a disruptive behavior (e.g., time out) is contraindicated. Carr *et al.* (1980) found that time out can worsen escape-motivated problem behaviors by negatively reinforcing them

Finally, if the preceding approaches fail to reduce disruptive behaviors to a level at which learning can occur, it may become necessary to use an aversive consequence to punish disruptive behaviors. For example, a sharp, startling reprimand combined with brief restraint of the hands may eliminate the problem very quickly, especially in young children who are not accustomed to consistently applied punishment (Ackerman, 1980; Lovaas, 1981). If such mild punishers do not work fairly rapidly, however, they should be discontinued because they may become reinforcers if the child habituates to their aversive properties (i.e., the child seems to "enjoy" provoking emotional reactions from adults). Consideration of other behavior reduction strategies should be pursued (Axelrod & Apsche, 1983; Evans & Meyer, 1985; Matson & DiLorenzo, 1984; Whitman, Scibak, & Reid, 1983).

Initial treatment can last from an hour to a few weeks of daily sessions, depending on the child's level of functioning, extent of disruptive behaviors, and the teacher's skill. Certainly, by the end of the first month all children should be able to sit in a chair for 15–20 minutes at a time, look at the teacher on request, follow a few simple instructions reliably, and display very low rates of disruptive behavior. Subsequent training is devoted primarily to early social and communication skills, but self-help skills (eating, washing, toileting, dressing) and independent play should also be addressed in order to help children become more independent and to improve their ability to function well during unstructured times of the day.

SOCIAL BEHAVIORS

Kanner characterized the profound social unrelatedness of autistic children as an "*inability to relate themselves* in the ordinary way to people and situations from the beginning of life" (Kanner, 1943, p. 242; italics in original). Kanner considered the unrelatedness to be one of two fundamental disorders (along with an "obsessive desire for the maintenance of sameness") that together could account for all the other symptoms of autism. However, the extent to which social unrelatedness is primary or is secondary to other impairments, such as language or cognitive deficits, has been a matter of some controversy since Kanner first described autism (Fein, Pennington, Markowitz, Braverman, & Waterhouse, 1986; Rutter, 1983). Unfortunately, there are no theories with sufficient support to provide a convincing explanation of this most characteristic deficit of autistic children (Fein *et al.*, 1986). Experimental evidence has, however, ruled out the early hypothesis that the social unrelatedness results from the personalities or child-rearing practices of the parents (Cantwell & Baker, 1984; Koegel, Schreibman, O'Neill, & Burke, 1983; McAdoo & DeMyer, 1978; Wolff & Morris, 1971).

Strategies of Remediation

Four general strategies have been employed in efforts to remediate the social unrelatedness of autistic children. The first strategy attempts to increase the rate of existing social behaviors indirectly with procedures that are useful primarily early in treatment for establishing a simple level of rapport. The second strategy attempts to establish the social behaviors of other persons as generalized conditioned reinforcers, so that their attention and praise can subsequently strengthen and maintain a wide range of social behaviors. The third and most frequently used strategy is a skill-building approach concerned with the direct teaching of such social behaviors as imitation, cooperative play, and conversational language. The fourth and most recent strategy is the employment of normal or mildly handicapped peer confederates to initiate and maintain appropriate social interactions with autistic children.

Indirect Interventions for Building Rapport

Even very withdrawn autistic children will occasionally make eye contact or approach an adult (Hermelin & O'Connor, 1963). There are some simple procedures that are useful for increasing a number of existing social behaviors and establishing a rudimentary level of rapport early in treatment.

In an early, uncontrolled study, DeMyer and Ferster (1962) had teachers begin working with autistic children by participating in their ongoing activities, in order to habituate the children to physical closeness and to identify potential social and activity reinforcers, which were then used contingently to strengthen simple social, affectionate, and play behaviors. Subsequent studies have included some aspects of this approach. One technique is simply to imitate a child's toy manipulations. Doing so results in increased eye contact, touches, and vocalizations directed at the teacher (Dawson & Adams, 1984; Tiegerman & Primavera, 1981, 1984). Another technique is to prompt the child to engage in play with a preferred toy, as determined by prior assessment of the amount of time the child spends playing with various toys. Play with preferred toys is accompanied by decreased social avoidance behavior (e.g., gaze aversion, head hanging, moving away) in comparison to play with nonpreferred toys (Koegel, Dyer, & Bell, 1987). Finally, with higher-functioning children, having parents help with "homework" (e.g., printing letters) brought from school has been shown to lead to increased positive verbal interactions between the parents and the children (Wildman & Simon, 1978).

Given the difficulty often encountered in fading prompts with autistic children (Rincover & Koegel, 1975), it might be interesting to see whether any of the foregoing procedures could constitute alternative ways of increasing simple social behaviors at the beginning of a skill-teaching program. That is, once the rate of a simple social behavior (e.g., eye contact or physical proximity) has been increased indirectly through techniques like those just described, it might be possible to bring it under reinforcement control and shape it into a new, more complex social behavior without the use of prompting.

Establishing Social Reinforcers

The strategy of attempting to condition the attention, praise, and smiles of other persons as functional social reinforcers was conceived in the early 1960s, when autism was still considered to be primarily a disorder of social relatedness, with learning and communication deficiencies seen as secondary to the social deficiencies. Given this assumption, it was logical to expect that normalizing a child's responsiveness to social reinforcers might subsequently enable the everyday social environment to build and modify many important behaviors quite naturally through ordinary social interactions (Lovaas, Freitag, et al., 1966). We now know that even when social reinforcers can be established or the need for them is bypassed through the use of powerful arbitrary reinforcers, solving the motivational problem is not enough. Serious deficiencies in perception, language, and learning remain and must be addressed with specific teaching procedures. However, the effort to establish social reinforcers is still very worthwhile, because it facilitates subsequent teaching by adults and renders the child able to learn some social skills informally from siblings and peers (Lovaas, 1987; Nordquist, Twardosz, & McEvoy, 1982).

Four ways of establishing the behaviors of other persons as social reinforcers for autistic children have been attempted. Lovaas, Freitag, et al. (1966) reported that pairing an adult's praise (the word "good") with food delivery in a classical conditioning paradigm failed to establish the word as a conditioned reinforcer for two profoundly retarded, extremely asocial autistic boys, apparently because they failed to attend to the word. Two other procedures designed to insure attention to adults were more successful. Lovaas, Freitag, et al. (1966) established the word "good" as a conditioned positive reinforcer by making it a discriminative stimulus for edible reinforcement. Each child was rewarded if he approached an adult within 3 seconds after the adult said, "Good," and was not rewarded if he approached at other times. Over trials, the schedule of the edible reward was thinned to variable ratio 20 for one boy and 15 for the other. The acquired reinforcing properties of the word were demonstrated in sessions showing its ability to maintain an arbitrary response when presented contingent on responding. Lovaas, Freitag, *et al.* (1966) suggested that discriminative stimulus training succeeded where classical conditioning had failed because it forced the children to attend in order to get the food. The investigators did not discuss generalization to other settings or persons, but concluded elsewhere that the procedure was excessively time-consuming in relation to the limited gains it produced (Lovaas, Schaeffer, & Simmons, 1965). However, it seems important to note that the subjects in this study were more profoundly retarded than most autistic children, and it remains possible that the procedure might be more efficient and generalizable with higher-functioning and/or younger autistic children.

In a second study with the same subjects (although published earlier), Lovaas, Schaeffer, and Simmons (1965) found that requiring the boys to approach adults on command in order to escape or avoid electric shock on the soles of the feet had three beneficial effects. First, the adults' commands ("Come here," "Hug me") became discriminative stimuli that were complied with very reliably. Second, the adults acquired reinforcing properties as the result of being paired with shock termination. The children approached and hugged the adults in shock situations and increased their rates of an arbitrary response (pressing a lever) when that response produced visual access to the adults. Third, the adults' verbal reprimands became conditioned punishers; the word "No!" would stop a response instead of being ignored. However, generalization of these effects to the same adults in locations not associated with shock and to other adults was minimal. Consequently, the benefits of the procedure were considered insufficient to outweigh ethical concerns about its continued use.

The failure of the procedures just discussed to produce extensive gains in the children studied had the effect of discouraging any further attempts to solve the problem of social unrelatedness in a single stroke of expert conditioning; instead, emphasis shifted to teaching important classes of social behavior directly, as described in the next section. However, nearly 20 years after the Lovaas group's studies, the idea of establishing others' behaviors as conditioned reinforcers by making them discriminative for primary reinforcers reappeared in the form of a procedure similar to the language generalization technique known as "incidental teaching" (Hart & Risley, 1975). Nordquist *et al.* (1982) investigated procedures designed for a school setting that incorporated discriminative stimulus training as part of an effort to make peers' and teachers' behaviors effective social reinforcers for autistic children. The Nordquist *et al.* (1982) procedure was used with autistic boys 4 and 6 years of age and consisted of two phases. In the first phase, "affection activities," one autistic child was grouped with five or six nonhandicapped children and two teachers for a 15-minute period each day for 5–10 weeks. The activities emphasized expressing affection by smiling, hugging, tickling, and patting. A different set of nonhandicapped children participated each day to promote generalization. In the second phase, "incidental teaching," whenever one of the autistic children wanted something during the school day, he had to find a nonhandicapped peer and interact with the peer briefly in order to obtain the object or to join the activity. For example, if the autistic child wanted to swing, he had to find a nonhandicapped child and ask her to push or ride with him on the swing. If he wanted a piece of bread at lunch, he had to ask a nonhandicapped child to pass it to him. This phase lasted 7 weeks for one child and 29 weeks for the other. Note that this type of incidental teaching constituted discriminative stimulus training: The autistic children had to attend to peers to obtain reinforcement. Both of the subjects of this study, who rarely interacted with peers during baseline observations, showed increased social interactions and participation in activities after affection activities were introduced, and still greater increases when the incidental-teaching requirement was added. Although the level and quality of the autistic children's social interactions did not match those of the normal peers, the increases were substantial and generalized across settings and peers. These results provided indirect support for the authors' conclusion that the reinforcement value of the normal peers was enhanced when they were made discriminative for access to a variety of pre-existing reinforcers.

The Nordquist *et al.* (1982) procedure can serve as a valuable adjunct to the direct teaching of social behaviors to insure their generalization, just as incidental teaching of language skills is used to generalize speech learned in one-to-one sessions (Carr, 1985; Halle, 1982).

It would be most interesting to see whether even greater gains could be achieved by using the procedure with very young autistic children over a period of years, with gradually increasing criteria for duration and complexity of social behaviors. Taggart and Rincover (1985) have found that the establishment of social reinforcers is much easier to accomplish with very young autistic children than with older children, as is described later in the section on early intervention.

Direct Teaching of Social Behaviors

Social behaviors that have been taught directly to autistic children include eye contact (discussed above), imitation and observational learning, expressing affection, social play, and more complex interactions involving conversation.

Imitation and Observational Learning

The fundamental importance of imitation in human learning was stated years ago by Bandura (1962), who noted that the acquisition of complex acts such as social and linguistic behaviors would be extremely time-consuming and difficult if each of the components of such behaviors had to be learned individually and then chained together. This argument acquires special force in work with autistic and other developmentally disabled children. If shaping, prompting, and reinforcement were the only techniques available for teaching such children, severe limitations in the extent of their progress would occur simply as a function of the limited amount of time available for teaching countless individual behaviors and combining them into meaningful sequences and patterns of complex behaviors. The importance of imitation in the acquisition of social behaviors by autistic children is indicated by the finding that imitative ability correlates more highly with other social behaviors than do intelligence and chronological age (CA) (Dawson & Adams, 1984).

Imitation is normally taught through discrete-trial procedures, with the child's task being to reproduce the topography of the teacher's modeled behavior on each trial (Hingtgen, Coulter, & Churchill, 1967; Lovaas, Freitas, Nelson, & Whalen, 1967; Metz, 1965). Most teachers begin with simple motor movements involving the hands and arms, such as raising the arms, clapping hands, and touching the nose

(Baer, Peterson, & Sherman, 1967; Lovaas, 1981). Such behaviors lie roughly in the middle of a hypothetical easy-to-difficult series that begins with gross motor movements (e.g., standing up, sitting down, bending over); progresses through arm and hand movements; and ends with fine motor movements of the hands, fingers, and face (in preparation for subsequent training in toy play, manual signing, or verbal imitation). If the child fails to progress with simple arm and hand movements, it may be sufficient simply to switch to whole-body gross motor movements, which may be easier for the child to discriminate and to copy (Kozloff, 1974).

An alternative to starting imitation training with body movements is to begin by using objects and toys that are easy for a child to manipulate appropriately and whose manipulation is functional in producing an effect on the environment. DeMyer et al. (1972) found that autistic children were more successful at imitating behaviors that lay below their tested MAs and that involved object manipulation (e.g., stacking blocks, banging a spoon, covering a doll) than they were at imitating behaviors that were at or above their MAs and that involved only body movements (e.g., hopping on one foot, clapping, wiggling a thumb). The investigators speculated that object-related behaviors were easier to imitate because the object used on each trial remained in view as a prompt for the appropriate imitative manipulation. Furthermore, Guess, Keogh, and Baer (1977) found that object manipulations producing an immediate effect were learned more rapidly than similar movements with no obvious functionality. For example, squeezing a plastic bottle of liquid into a pan was acquired sooner than squeezing an empty bottle. Finally, Lovaas et al. (1967) noted anecdotally that toys that produced salient visual and auditory stimulation seemed to capture attention and to provide intrinsic reinforcement for their manipulation. The combination of these observations suggests that the selection of the initial behaviors to use in imitation training might well be made by first determining the autistic child's MA, then selecting object manipulations that normally occur at MA levels below that of the autistic child and that produce an interesting effect or provide rich sensory feedback.

During the initial imitation training trials, most autistic children must be manually prompted to reproduce the teacher's model. Subsequently, the major problem in imitation training becomes that of fading the prompt. Some suggestions for dealing with prompt dependency include the following. First, the prompt can be made less salient to the child by having an assistant who is sitting behind the child do the prompting (Lovaas, 1981). Second, prompt fading should begin on the trial immediately after a full prompt is first used, in order to minimize the child's exposure to the full prompt. Third, various ways of fading the prompt can be attempted, such as gradually reducing the force of the prompt (Baer et al., 1967; Furnell & Thomas, 1976; Metz, 1965; Rincover & Koegel, 1975); moving its location up the child's arm away from the hand in small increments (Striefel & Wetherby, 1973); or delaying the prompt after the teacher's model for progressively increasing durations in 1-second steps (Handen & Zane, 1987; Striefel, Bryan, & Aikins, 1974).

A different and more subtle approach to teaching imitation is Keogh, Guess, and Baer's (1977) Fast Motor Imitation Program, published in Baer (1978). Some of the key early steps in this program appear in Table 8-2. As the steps of the table indicate, the initial behavioral models include highly effective visual prompts for imitation: The teacher offers the child something she wants (e.g., candy), and the child takes the candy with a reaching response that closely approximates the teacher's model. Manual prompting and its attendant prompt-fading difficulties are thus avoided from the outset of training. The steps shown in Table 8-2 teach the child to imitate a variety of arm movements. Subsequent steps develop imitative object manipulations involved in appropriate toy play (Baer, 1978). The success of this highly innovative procedure with individuals who have failed to learn through other imitation training procedures (Baer, 1978) may be due to a number of features, including beginning with a response (reaching) that is already in the child's repertoire; the use of a "within-stimulus" prompt (the edible in the teacher's hand; cf. Schreibman, 1975); the direct relationship between the response and the acquisition of the reinforcer (Koegel & Williams, 1980); and the ease with which the edible as a prompt can be removed without loss of the behavior.

After the child has acquired several imitative behaviors, new behaviors modeled by the teacher will be learned in progressively fewer trials, eventually requiring only one demonstration (Baer et al., 1967; Lovaas et al., 1967; Metz, 1965). When the child begins to imitate novel behaviors on their first presentation by the teacher, training focuses on making imitation durable (resistant to extinction) and generalizing imitation to other situations and persons. Resistance to extinction is established by gradually thinning the schedule of edible reinforcement and replacing edibles with praise and other natural consequences of imitation (Bucher & Bowman, 1974; Furnell & Thomas, 1981). To generalize imitation across other persons, the child is taught to imitate novel adults and peers by having them conduct imitation training as described above and then use modeling to teach the child new behaviors with naturally reinforcing consequences, such as play skills, getting a glass of juice, or putting on a coat to go outside (Kozloff, 1974; Lovaas, 1981).

A recent extension of efforts to generalize imitation across persons appears in studies concerned with what is termed "observational learning" because the procedures used are related to the procedures used to study "observational" or "vicarious" learning in normal children (Bandura, 1969). In these studies, autistic children learn social, language, or academic skills by observing a peer model who already performs the skill competently, instead of learning via direct instruction from the peer or a teacher. Training in observational learning is usually conducted by having a normal peer confederate (or another autistic child who already knows the target behavior) sit next to the autistic child, model a behavior that has been instructed by the teacher, and receive a reward while the autistic child watches. The autistic child is then given an opportunity to perform the same behavior to determine whether observational learning has occurred. A variation of this approach is to teach the child to observe and to reinforce a particular behavior in another child before being tested for observational learning of that behavior (Brown & Holvoet, 1982). Behaviors taught through observational learning procedures have included appropriate toy play (Tryon & Keane, 1986), beginning academic skills (Egel, Richman, & Koegel, 1981), simple vocational workshop skills (Brown & Holvoet, 1982), and some language skills (Charlop, Schreibman, & Tryon, 1983; Coleman & Stedman, 1974). For example, Charlop et al. (1983) paired autistic children

TABLE 8-2 Initial Steps of the Fast Motor Imitation Program

Step 1:

Hand candy to the child with hand placed as near to the child's front as possible for easy acceptance by the child. As you offer the candy, instruct the child to "Take this." The child must take the candy with a hand response on the same side; that is, the child's response mirrors the teacher's. (For example, if the child is right-handed, offer the candy with your left hand, and vice versa if the child is left-handed.)

Step 2:

(a) Hand candy to the child with hand deviating from straight-on location a little to the left. Offer the candy with your left hand; the child takes the candy with his right hand.

(b) Hand candy to the child with hand deviating from straight-on location a little to the right. Offer candy with your right hand; the child takes it with his left.

(c) Hand candy to the child with hand deviating from straight-on location a little higher. If the child is right-handed, offer the candy with your left, and vice versa.

(d) Hand candy to the child with hand deviating from straight-on location a little lower. If the child is right-handed, offer the candy with your left, and vice versa.

Include some straight-on offerings along with these deviations. Offerings in each position (high, low, left, right, straight) should occur an equal number of times and should be presented in random order. Gradually increase the size of the deviations in steady increments until the child is reaching for the hand with the candy as high, low, and wide as he can successfully reach.

Step 3:

Introduce offerings in a high-up position, gradually increasing the height of the offerings until both you and the child are standing.

Step 4:

Introduce four one-step moves, two to the left and two to the right, thus requiring the child to step to the left or right to reach the hand with the candy. When stepping left, hold the candy in your left hand, and vice versa.

Step 5:

Introduce four trials in which the candy is concealed in the hand presenting the model. Open your fist when the child touches your hand.

Step 6:

Introduce trials in which a second step is chained to the first. Increase the frequency of two-step moves until they are as frequent as one-step moves. At this point, one-third of the trials should be one-step moves, another one-third should be two-step moves, and the remaining one-third should be made up of other model presentations.

Step 7:

Introduce four trials in which the candy is kept hidden. Show the child the candy, shake it in cupped hands, then hide it in the hand that is not performing the model. Thus, the child is not sure whether the candy is in the model hand or the other hand. When the child matches the model hand motion (and step, if included), hold the child's hand in the correct matching position with the model hand, and quickly bring your other hand (with candy) forward, close to the child's other hand to evoke the reaching for candy response by the child's other hand. Let the candy show as this is done to stimulate the child's reaching for it with his other hand. Continue until the child is no longer resisting (trying to pull away) with the held hand and is matching all moves satisfactorily.

Step 8:

Start deviating the placement of the hand delivering the candy, so that the child is finally matching a two-hand chain: a randomly located first-hand motion, with or without one or two steps to a side, followed by a randomly located other-hand motion that, when matched, obtains the candy.

Note. From "The Behavioral Analysis of Trouble" by D. M. Baer, 1978, in K. E. Allen, V. A. Holm, & R. L. Schiefelbusch (Eds.), *Early Intervention—A Team Approach* (pp. 87–89), Baltimore: University Park Press. Copyright 1978 by University Park Press. Reprinted by permission.

who had not learned certain receptive labeling skills with autistic peers of about the same CA who had learned the skills. On each of 20 trials, the autistic peer model performed the correct response on a task and was rewarded while the untrained child watched. The teacher then presented the same task to the untrained child without reinforcement to determine whether she had learned it. Each previously untrained child learned the task after observing the peer model for one or two blocks of 20 trials and showed generalization and maintenance of correct responding with a new teacher in a different setting. Optimal procedures for teaching observational learning to autistic children remain to be discovered, but there is suggestive evidence that the previous acquisition of generalized imitation facilitates observational learning (Egel *et al.*, 1981).

Expressing Affection

Teaching an autistic child to express affection in simple ways enables him to reciprocate the affection received from parents, siblings, teachers, and peers. The question of whether an autistic child really feels the emotions that normally accompany affectionate behaviors is a reasonable one, but is probably unanswerable. The child's affectionate behaviors do look stilted early in treatment, but become much more natural (and presumably genuine) later on. The assumptions made in teaching such behaviors are simply that changes in attitudes and feelings often follow changes in overt behavior rather than preceding them, and that a child should at least be given some means for expressing affection if she wishes to do so.

Initially, the child can be taught to give a hug or a kiss on request through manual prompting and edible reinforcement procedures (Lovaas, 1981). At a more advanced level, a hug can become a discriminative stimulus for verbalizations of affection (e.g., "I like you," for teachers and classmates; "I love you," for family members). Charlop and Walsh (1986) showed that such sentences could be taught through verbal modeling immediately after a hug and maintained as the verbal model was gradually delayed. The sentences generalized across relevant persons and settings but, appropriately, not to strangers. The direct teaching procedure was superior to a procedure in which a trained autistic peer modeled the behavior while an untrained subject watched. Social validation questionnaires indicated that after the training the children's parents and siblings rated them as more social and affectionate.

Research in the area of affectionate behaviors is just beginning with autistic children. However, behavioral procedures for teaching the expression of affection to withdrawn normal and mildly handicapped children are well developed (Twardosz & Jozwiak, 1981), and adaptations of such procedures may be found to be very useful with many autistic children.

Social Play and Recreation Skills

Most of the work in the area of play and recreation with autistic and other severely handicapped individuals has been concerned with solitary play with toys. Numerous studies have shown that solitary play can be taught through modeling and imitation procedures similar to those described in the preceding section (Lovaas, 1981; Lovaas *et al.*, 1967); through observational learning with a normal peer model (Tryon & Keane, 1986); and through prompting and reinforcement with either edibles or the intrinsic sensory reinforcers available in some toys (Eason, White, & Newsom, 1982; Koegel, Firestone, Kramme, & Dunlap, 1974; Rincover, Cook, Peoples, Packard, 1979; Santarcangelo, Dyer, & Luce, 1987). Although such procedures are effective in teaching independent, appropriate play behaviors, the acquisition of such behaviors is not typically followed by spontaneous social play among autistic children or between autistic children and normal peers (Romanczyk, Diament, Goren, Trunell, & Harris, 1975). Two general strategies for increasing social play have been pursued: One strategy is to teach social play directly (Brady *et al.*, 1984; Romanczyk *et al.*, 1975); the other is to teach peers to initiate play interactions, as described later in the section on peer-mediated interventions.

In their study of social play, Romanczyk *et al.* (1975) taught autistic children to engage in social toy play with their autistic peers in classroom play groups. Every 30 seconds, two of the children were rewarded with edibles and praise if they were playing with a peer. If a child was not playing socially, he was placed next to another child, and a hand was placed on the toy the other child was playing with. After social play had increased to a high level, the prompts were faded by decreasing their frequency over eight sessions. Social play declined when prompts were completely removed and declined again when reinforcement was withdrawn, but remained at a level above its original baseline. The main advantage of the Romanczyk *et al.* (1975) procedure is that it can be used in group situations, without extensive one-to-one intervention.

In an effort to teach play interactions that would generalize across peers who were not involved in the training, Brady *et al.* (1984) used a multiple-exemplar strategy (Stokes & Baer, 1977) with an autistic adolescent. The adolescent was prompted to initiate and to continue toy play interactions with three normal peers who were introduced sequentially at 9-day intervals. During training with the second peer, the adolescent's interactions with five other normal peers began to increase and increased further during training with the third peer. Interactions continued to occur after training was discontinued, and there was some generalization to an untrained (playground) setting.

Other studies on the direct teaching of social play behaviors, although conducted with socially withdrawn, severely retarded persons, deserve mention because they are directly applicable to autistic children. Singh and Millichamp (1987) used prompting to teach profoundly retarded adults to engage in social toy play, which generalized to a new setting and was maintained over a 12-month follow-up period. Keogh, Faw, Whitman, and Reid (1984) taught severely retarded adolescents to play table games with one another by using verbal instructions, modeling of game behaviors and self-instructions, prompting, and contingent praise for correct game behaviors and self-instruction. Finally, Luyben, Funk, Morgan, Clark, and Delulio (1986) used prompting and reinforcement to teach severely retarded adults to make correct soccer kicks as a first step in learning a team sport.

Complex Social Interactions

As autistic children and adults increasingly receive exposure to normal peers in school, work, and community environments, investigators have turned their attention to teaching the skills needed for more complex interactions than those described above. Such interactions involve verbal and motor behaviors in reciprocal stimulus–response chains, in which the autistic person both initiates social interactions and responds appropriately to the behaviors of another person. However, the designation of the types of interactions studied thus far as "complex" is meant in a relative sense only. Although more complex than the social play described in the preceding section, the procedures presented here address only the simplest kinds of extended social interactions seen in normal individuals. Nevertheless, some of the interaction skills that have been taught are more complex than would have been thought possible a few years ago, and they constitute important groundwork for future extension and elaboration.

Most social interactions in normal persons involve conversation. Elementary conversational skills can be taught to autistic children who have previously learned some expressive speech by beginning with answers to simple questions, such as "What's your name?", "How are you?", and "How old are you?" (Lovaas, 1977). A child is taught through prompting and fading to give a two-part response that answers the question and then returns the question to the teacher in order to extend the interaction. For example, in response to the question, "How are you?", the child is taught to say, "Fine, thanks. How are you?" As the child's ability to recall and describe experiences increases, longer responses are included in the same format. The teacher may ask, "What did you do this morning?" and the child is rewarded for describing several experiences, then asking the same question of the teacher.

At a somewhat higher level of complexity, questions to which the child does not know the answer are intermixed with questions the child can answer (Lovaas, 1977). The child is taught to say, "I don't know," to the former questions; to ask a second adult the question; then to repeat the answer to the teacher. In the presence of the mother, for example, the teacher may ask, "What are you having for dinner tonight?" The child says, "I don't know," then asks the mother, "What are we having for dinner?" The mother answers and the child repeats the answer to the teacher. In essence, the child learns to discriminate between questions to which she does and does not know the answer, then either to answer the question or to engage in a simple social interaction with another person in order to learn the answer that will be reinforced.

For higher-functioning autistic individuals with good expressive speech and imitation skills, procedures like those developed with nonautistic moderately and mildly retarded persons may be used to improve conversational skills (e.g., Haring, Roger, Lee, Breen, & Gaylord-Ross, 1986; Kelly & Drabman, 1977; Wildman, Wildman, & Kelly, 1986). These studies describe the use of instructions, verbal models, rehearsal, and contingent praise to teach such skills as initiating conversations, responding to others' statements, asking questions, giving compliments, and maintaining self-disclosure statements at an appropriate level. Some of these procedures have been used informally with mildly retarded and nonretarded autistic adults (Mesibov, 1984).

Gaylord-Ross, Haring, Breen, and Pitts-Conway (1984) noted that a complete social exchange can be divided into initiation, elaboration, and termination phases. Because many autistic persons have limited language for elaborating interactions, these investigators adopted the strategy of structuring social interactions around leisure objects that could be shared with nonhandicapped peers in a context of brief verbal exchanges. This strategy of letting the objects carry the burden of the interaction was enhanced by selecting items that would be interesting to the normal peers, including hand-held video games, an earphone radio, and a pack of gum. Gaylord-Ross *et al.* (1984) implemented this strategy with a two-phase approach. First, two moderately retarded, autistic adolescent boys were taught to manipulate the three leisure items correctly. Second, social interactions appropriate to each item were trained with the assistance of normal peers from the public high school where the autistic boys were students. For each item, a training script was devised that included phrases and sentences for each of the social initiation, elaboration, and termination components of the interaction. Training sessions continued until each autistic boy had been exposed sequentially to six different peers as multiple exemplars of the normal students at the school. A stringent evaluation of the training was conducted by measuring the number and durations of social interactions initiated by the autistic boys with normal peers in the school courtyard during daily breaks. The peers who had assisted in the training were not present. Both participants showed large increases in these measures of generalized social interaction over baseline conditions, when no interactions occurred. In a second experiment in this study (Gaylord-Ross *et al.*, 1984), with a higher-functioning autistic adolescent, similar results were obtained even though the two training phases were collapsed into one phase and only a single peer assisted in training. Noteworthy additional findings were that all three of the autistic students interacted more with familiar than with unfamiliar peers and that two of the boys frequently initiated interactions that did not include the leisure objects. Both of these unprogrammed results suggest that the social interactions of the autistic boys resembled those of their normal peers.

Training scripts and sequentially introduced normal peers were also employed by Breen, Haring, Pitts-Conway, and Gaylord-Ross (1985) to teach four autistic adolescents to engage in appropriate social interactions during breaks at job sites. The autistic participants learned to make a cup of coffee, greet a coworker, offer coffee to the coworker, ask, "What's new?", and respond to the coworker's statements. Confederate "coworkers" (high school students) were progressively added until probes in the actual break rooms at the work setting showed that interactions generalized to at least three natural coworkers.

Peer-Mediated Interventions

The fourth major strategy for remediating the social unrelatedness of autistic children is to teach normal or mildly handicapped peers to engage in appropriate social interactions with them. There are several reasons for adopting this approach. A practical reason is that the use of peer mediators can extend social interventions to multiple children concurrently once the peers are trained—a benefit that is especially important in group settings such as classrooms (Strain, 1980). A second reason derives from the findings that the immediate effect of adult reinforcement for social interaction may be an interruption of the interaction for a while (Strain, 1980), and that adult-mediated reinforcement may produce frequent but brief interactions that do not resemble natural, extended interactions in normal children (Walker, Greenwood, Hops, & Todd, 1979). A third reason—one that becomes increasingly important as more autistic children are educated in integrated schools—is that generalization and maintenance of social skills should be more likely if exemplars of the normal peers in such settings are involved in the intervention. Research has shown that the mere exposure of handicapped children to normal peers through integrated classroom placements does not result in significant observational learning by the handicapped children (Guralnick, 1976; Snyder, Appolloni, & Cooke, 1977).

Peer Initiation Procedure

The peer mediation procedure that has received the most study is the peer initiation model of Strain, Shores, and their colleagues, who originally developed the procedure for children who were normal but socially withdrawn (Strain, 1977; Strain, Shores, & Timm, 1977). As used with autistic children, several preliminary sessions are devoted to training a peer confederate to initiate toy play interactions. The teacher plays the role of an autistic child and uses instructions, modeling, and praise to teach the peer. On half the trials, the teacher complies with the peer's toy play initiations; on the other half, the teacher ignores the initiations in order to prepare the child for behaviors likely to occur with the autistic child. The peer is taught to persist until the teacher finally complies (Odom, Hoyson, Jamieson, & Strain, 1985; Ragland, Kerr, & Strain, 1978; Strain, 1983; Strain, Kerr, & Ragland, 1979). In some studies, practice with an autistic child while the teacher provides instructions and feedback to the peer is also a component of training (e.g., Odom & Strain, 1986; Shafer, Egel, & Neef, 1984). The content of peer initiation training typically includes some or all of the following types of interactions, derived empirically from observations of normal preschool children at play (Tremblay, Strain, Hendrickson, & Shores, 1981):

1. Play organizer: Verbalizations or responses to verbalizations in which the child specifies an activity, suggests an idea for play, or directs another child to engage in a play behavior.
2. Share: Offers or gives an object to another child or accepts an object from another child.
3. Share request: Asks another child to give an object to the speaker.
4. Assistance: Helps another child complete a task or desired action.
5. Compliment: Verbal statement indicating praise, affection, or attraction.
6. Affection: Hugging, patting, kissing, or holding hands.

The initial extensions of the peer initiation model to autistic children showed that the procedure was rapidly effective in bringing about increases in their social play. Ragland et al. (1978) taught a normal conduct-disordered 10-year-old boy to initiate toy play interactions with three autistic children. Each autistic child showed large increases in social play with the peer confederate. Strain et al. (1979) compared the relative efficacy of social play initiations by a peer confederate with a condition in which the peer prompted two autistic children to play with each other and praised them for doing so. The two procedures resulted in substantial and equal increases in social interaction.

In these initial studies, little generalization of social interaction occurred in settings where the peer did not initiate interactions (i.e., reversals to baseline in Ragland et al., 1978, and Strain et al., 1979) or where only autistic children were present (Strain et al., 1979). Therefore, subsequent research has addressed assessment and procedural variables that might enhance generalization.

The finding that little generalization was seen in situations where only autistic children were present suggested that the social responsiveness of the peers in the assessment setting is related to generalization—a possibility investigated by Strain (1983). Four autistic children were exposed to the peer initiation procedure, and generalization of their social interactions was assessed in two conditions. In segregated generalization sessions, the autistic children were observed in a school gym with six other severely developmentally disabled children. In integrated generalization sessions, the autistic children were observed in the gym with 24 normal second-graders. Generalization of social interaction occurred only in the integrated sessions. Additional data indicated the likely reason for the advantage of the integrated condition: The normal peers both initiated interactions with the autistic children and responded positively to their initiations far more frequently than did the handicapped peers. In the segregated setting, the autistic children's social behaviors underwent extinction. As Strain (1983) notes, these findings indicate the need for the assessment of social functioning to be conducted in responsive environments, and they raise serious questions about the effects of placement in handicapped-only classrooms on the social development of autistic children.

A variation of the peer initiation training model as discussed thus far was investigated by Shafer *et al.* (1984). Instead of having the peer work with an adult in a role-playing format during training, Shafer *et al.* (1984) taught the peer to interact directly with an autistic child. In each training session, the experimenter first modeled toy play interactions with the autistic child while the peer watched, then coached the peer while the peer interacted with the autistic child. After training, each of the four autistic children in the study was observed in a free-play setting with the peer trainer and two untrained nonhandicapped peers. Three of the four autistic children showed large increases in social behavior directed toward peer trainers, and two showed increased social behavior toward untrained peers. The one autistic child who failed to show increased interactions with his peer trainer did show increases when the experimenter removed one of the untrained peers, who frequently interrupted interactions. Two other noteworthy findings emerged from the Shafer *et al.* (1984) study. First, increases were seen in the durations as well as the frequencies of the social interactions between the autistic children and their peer trainers. Second, generalization to a new setting with new toys and new, untrained peers occurred, but was not maintained over sessions until the peer trainer and the autistic child repeated the earlier training with the new toys and the peer trainer was taught to reinforce play interactions more consistently than he had previously.

Peer initiation training that includes practice with autistic children has been combined with the multiple-exemplar approach by Brady, Shores, McEvoy, Ellis, and Fox (1987) in an effort to improve generalization of social interactions across normal peers. Two autistic boys were the recipients of the intervention. For the first subject, one nonhandicapped sixth-grader was given peer initiation training and practice with autistic children not in the study. Ten days later, a second nonhandicapped peer underwent the same training. For the second autistic subject, three peers were trained in sequence 12 days apart. The first autistic boy showed increases in play initiations and durations of interactions with untrained peers after the introduction of the second peer trainer. The second autistic boy, however, showed very little generalization to untrained peers, although he did increase initiations and durations of in-

teractions with his three peer trainers. This boy was more socially withdrawn than the first boy, showing no interactions with any peer during baseline observations. In line with Strain's (1983) findings, neither autistic boy generalized social interactions to other autistic children who were not part of the intervention.

The studies reviewed to this point indicate that, for autistic children who exhibit few or no initiations during baseline, generalized social interactions are composed almost entirely of responses to peers' initiations. For such children, peer initiation training alone is insufficient to increase their initiation rates significantly. The peer initiation procedure is not a skill-building technique, but a way of increasing the performance of existing social skills by providing increased social initiations as prompts (Strain, 1983). The problem of lack of generalization could be greatly diminished if autistic children could be trained to initiate appropriate interactions and thus to be less dependent on peers' initiations. Therefore, some investigators have have addressed ways of increasing autistic children's social initiations. One approach is to teach initiation behaviors directly, as described earlier in the sections on direct teaching of play and recreation skills (e.g., Brady *et al.*, 1984) and complex interactions (e.g., Gaylord-Ross *et al.*, 1984). In a recent variant of this approach, McEvoy *et al.* (1988) conducted group affection activities similar to those used by Nordquist *et al.* (1982) with an integrated group of autistic and normal children. They found that two of the three autistic children increased social initiations during the activities and during free-play sessions that included untrained peers. Another approach is to teach a peer confederate to respond appropriately to initiations by an autistic child, then to prompt the autistic child to initiate (Odom & Strain, 1986). Over time, it should be possible to fade the teacher's prompts (cf. Timm, Strain, & Eller, 1979), and, as Odom and Strain (1986) suggested, to shift stimulus control from the teacher's prompts to natural elements of the social and physical environments (i.e., the child's peers and the toys). A third strategy that has not yet been tried is suggested by observational learning studies on teaching autistic children to imitate normal peers' academic and linguistic behaviors (e.g., Charlop *et al.*, 1983; Egel *et al.*, 1981). This approach would entail teaching generalized imitation to autistic children prior to exposing them to the peer initiation procedure, to see whether they would then be more likely to acquire social initiation skills through observation.

Other aspects of the peer initiation model that have been investigated include the generalization of the peer confederates' interactions across settings; the role of teacher prompts and rewards in maintaining peer confederates' interactions; and characteristics of the peers. Odom et al. (1985) found that peer confederates' initiations did not generalize from one classroom activity to two others until the peers were trained in the context of the other activities. It may be significant that the peers in this study were younger (4–5 years old) than those in the Strain (1983) study (7–9 years old), who did show generalized initiations across settings. Furthermore, Odom et al. (1985) found that a token reinforcement system for the peer confederates was not necessary to maintain their initiations, but that verbal prompts from the teacher were. Those who work with preschool-age children should be prepared to conduct peer training in multiple settings and to provide prompts to peers to continue their initiations over time.

Some characteristics that are desirable in the peers employed in peer initiation programs have been studied. Odom and Strain (1984) suggested that reliable compliance with adult instructions, age-appropriate social and play skills, and regular attendance are important. In one of their studies, two peer confederates had to be withdrawn from the study when they failed to comply with the teacher's instructions to play with an autistic child. Furthermore, the peer should be capable of being directive and persistent in attempting to get an autistic child to play. McHale and Boone (1980) found it helpful to encourage directiveness by frankly instructing peers to "be bossy." Sasso and Rude (1987) have recently found that the social status of the peer confederate (as measured by sociometric ratings from classmates) affects the interaction levels of both severely handicapped children and untrained normal peers exposed to a peer initiation procedure. More play initiations and positive responses were seen in the handicapped and untrained normal peers when the handicapped children were paired with high-status than with low-status trained peers. The high-status peers were apparently more socially skillful than the low-status peers and served as more effective models for their un-

trained peers. Finally, it may be important in some settings to employ peer trainers who are naturally "thick-skinned," or can be taught to be impervious to untrained peers' taunts for playing with socially deviant children (Shafer et al., 1984) and to the negative behaviors that some autistic children may exhibit when interrupted by peer initiations early in the course of the intervention (Ragland et al., 1978).

Sibling-Mediated Procedures

In some families with autistic children, there are siblings who are willing to become peer trainers if given the opportunity. As Schreibman, O'Neill, and Koegel (1983) noted, siblings can play an important role as facilitation agents for an autistic child's social interactions with other children in the neighborhood, and can provide continuity between school and home for educational programs. Applied research with siblings as teachers of autistic children has concentrated so far on conducting behavior management procedures (Colletti & Harris, 1977) and teaching play and classroom skills (Schreibman et al., 1983). However, James and Egel (1986) have developed a procedure for training siblings of severely retarded children to teach social play, and their procedure is directly applicable to families with autistic children. Each of three siblings was taught play training skills by first observing the experimenter while she modeled instructions, prompts, and praise with the handicapped child. Then the sibling practiced with the child and received feedback from the experimenter. To increase the probability of social initiations by the handicapped children, the siblings also received training in incidental teaching (Hart & Risley, 1975). Through modeling and role playing, the siblings learned to withhold a desired toy until the handicapped child requested it and to prompt a request if necessary. These procedures resulted in increased reciprocal social play interactions (initiations followed by responses within 3 seconds) in three normal sibling–handicapped child dyads that were maintained over a 6-month follow-up period. When an untrained peer was added to each dyad, the handicapped children responded to their play initiations, but did not initiate interactions with them.

A small note of caution should be considered in working with the siblings of autistic children. Although our experience has been that siblings usually respond very positively to the opportunity to learn better ways of interacting with their autistic siblings, some siblings perceive themselves as having greater caretaking and supervision responsibilities than children whose siblings are not handicapped (Farber & Ryckman, 1965). Therefore, sibling training programs should be designed with attention to the need to avoid adding to that burden (James & Egel, 1986). Helpful in this regard are schedules negotiated with a sibling to avoid conflicts with other activities and letting the sibling establish some of the treatment priorities based on his own problems in living with the autistic sibling.

This review of strategies for addressing the social unrelatedness of autistic children, whether it is caused by neurological (Fein et al., 1986) or cognitive (Rutter, 1983) deficiencies, indicates that many aspects of social functioning can be improved through appropriate teaching methods. Although a promising start has been made, the social domain is large and complex, and is extensively interwoven with the domains of language and affect. Therefore, more extensive improvements in social functioning will undoubtedly require attention to behaviors in all three domains concurrently. Furthermore, the attainment of a significant level of social competence would seem to require the ability to use learned social skills discriminatively and flexibly, according to specific social contexts. The development of this ability will probably entail complex treatment strategies that include both direct training in such key skills as observational learning and the extensive involvement of peers as trainers and models in a number of settings.

COMMUNICATION

The development of procedures for establishing and improving language in autistic children was foreshadowed by conceptual (Skinner, 1957) and experimental (e.g., Isaac, Thomas, & Goldiamond, 1960; Rheingold, Gewirtz, & Ross, 1959; Salzinger, 1959) developments indicating that language, like many other classes of behavior, could be conceptualized as operant behavior—that is, behavior related to contingencies of reinforcement. An equally important influence was work showing the extensive influence of imitation in the normal acquisition of social behaviors (Bandura, 1962; Bandura &

Walters, 1963). Soon after, systematic procedures for teaching some elements of language to autistic and retarded children began to appear (Baer et al., 1967; Hewett, 1965; Kerr, Meyerson, & Michael, 1965; Lovaas, Berberich, et al., 1966; Risley & Wolf, 1967). These early procedures, concerned primarily with imitative speech in laboratory situations, have been refined and expanded over the years to include procedures for developing a variety of abstract linguistic forms and functions in natural environments (see reviews by Goetz, Schuler, & Sailor, 1979; Guess, 1980; Halle, 1982; and Warren & Rogers-Warren, 1980). The full scope of this technology is far beyond what can be reviewed here; however, the procedures used in establishing and improving early language skills in nonverbal autistic children are described here in some detail as we discuss verbal imitation, receptive labeling (comprehension), expressive labeling (naming), incidental teaching (used primarily to generalize language), and sign language.

Currently, the two major strategies for establishing a basic repertoire of expressive language where there is none are operant speech training (Guess, Sailor, & Baer, 1978; Lovaas, 1977, 1981) and the type of sign language training in which signs are paired with spoken words, often referred to as "total" or "simultaneous" communication training (Carr, Binkoff, Kologinsky, & Eddy, 1978; Creedon, 1973; Schaeffer, 1980). In both cases, the initial goals are to teach the child to use the names of five or six objects, actions, and persons that are meaningful in his everyday life, then to generalize those words across persons and settings while continuing to learn additional words. Operant speech training procedures commonly used to establish an initial repertoire of verbal labels are described first, followed by procedures used to establish signed labels.

Operant Speech Training

In operant speech training, the teaching of expressive labels is usually preceded by training in appropriate sitting, attending, compliance to simple commands, motor imitation, verbal imitation, and receptive labeling, conducted in the order just listed. The first three of these skills (sitting, attending, compliance) are usually considered to be necessary prerequisites to all further learning and have been discussed above in the section on initial treatment. The status of motor imitation as a prerequisite to the acquisition of verbal imitation and other language skills is less clear. In general, studies have shown that training in motor imitation is neither necessary (e.g., Kerr et al., 1965; Lovaas, Berberich, et al., 1966) nor sufficient (e.g., Baer et al., 1967; Garcia, Baer, & Firestone, 1971) for the acquisition of verbal imitation. However, the particular class of motor responses trained may be a factor worth investigating experimentally: Specific training in oral motor imitation (mouth and tongue movements) appears to facilitate verbal imitation in clinical studies through response generalization (Hingtgen et al., 1967; Sloane, Johnston, & Harris, 1968). Therefore, although motor imitation training prior to language training may not be necessary in all cases, most experienced clinicians recommend it (e.g., Guess et al., 1978; Kozloff, 1974; Lovaas, 1981), and it should definitely be undertaken if the child shows slow progress during verbal imitation training.

Verbal Imitation

Verbal imitation training is appropriate for mute children and those echolalic children whose echolalia is sporadic and inconsistently controlled by adult verbalizations (Risley & Wolf, 1967). Verbal imitation is usually taught in the following sequence of phases: (1) The child's existing level of vocalizations is increased; (2) vocalizations are shaped to occur with a short latency after the teacher's vocalizations; (3) vocalizations are shaped to sound like the teacher's vocalizations; and (4) the complexity of the child's vocalizations is increased by reinforcing the imitation of words or, if necessary, shaping simple sounds into words (Lovaas, 1981).

The teacher begins by creating a relaxed, pleasant atmosphere as free of aversive control as possible (tantrums and self-stimulatory behaviors should be well controlled by this point in training). Every 10 seconds or so, the teacher verbalizes a word or phoneme already present in the child's vocal repertoire, then reinforces any vocalization the child makes (Guess et al., 1977). If the child does not vocalize, vocalizations may be induced by various indirect prompts, such as tickling, caressing, or pressing on the stomach (Lovaas, 1981; Schell, Stark, & Giddan, 1967). If these fail, a return to motor imitation training, focusing on mouth and tongue movements, facial expressions, and

blowing air, may help (Hingtgen et al., 1967; Lovaas, 1981; Sloane et al., 1968). Alternatively, an attempt can be made to chain a vocal sound to a motor response the child imitates reliably, then to fade the motor response (Baer et al., 1967).

Once the level of the child's vocalizations has been increased, they are then shaped to occur immediately after the teacher's vocalizations and to sound like the teacher's vocalizations. The teacher presents a word, then reinforces any vocalization occurring within 3 seconds. Over trials, vocalizations closer in time to the teacher's vocalizations are differentially reinforced until the child reliably makes an immediate (within 1 second) response to each vocalization by the teacher. Phonological matching is taught by shaping the child's articulation to match the teacher's model. The teacher presents a simple phoneme (such as "ah") and differentially reinforces closer and closer approximations to it as trials progress. If necessary, visual or manual prompts are used initially to help the child make the correct sound, then faded (Lovaas, 1981). A description of useful prompts for most English phonemes appears in Kozloff (1974, pp. 266–272). Next, a second sound that is visually and acoustically distinct from the first (such as "mm") is introduced and shaped similarly; trials with the two sounds are then randomly intermixed. At this point, most children show a decline in correct responding for a few sessions (Lovaas, 1977). Up to this point, the child could be successful by responding to the teacher's model as a simple "go" signal, indicating when it was time to produce the phoneme being practiced in a particular block of trials. The teacher's random alternation of the two sounds constitutes an auditory discrimination task in which the child must shift from one sound to the other whenever the teacher does in order to maximize reinforcement. Discrimination training is a crucial part of many aspects of early language training, because it forces the child to attend to differences in the teacher's verbalizations. It is sometimes helpful to exaggerate an acoustic feature of one of the phonemes as a prompt by, for example, presenting one at a higher volume or pitch than the other, then gradually fading it back to a normal presentation. Training continues in this sequence of shaping a new phoneme until it is well articulated, then intermixing it with previous phonemes until the child imitates about 10 phonemes accurately and reliably when they are presented in random order.

Once the child has a small fund of phonemes including both vowels and consonants, training in the imitation of words begins. The teacher starts by presenting as a model a word that consists only of phonemes the child can produce easily and that is highly functional in the child's daily life. For example, if "uh" and "p" have been acquired, the first word might be "up" for a child who likes to be picked up. If the child produces at least a rough approximation of the word, further trials are devoted to shaping closer approximations. On the other hand, if the child produces only very poor approximations, forward or backward chaining is used to combine two phonemes into a word. For example, in forward chaining, a series of correct trials with only the first phoneme can be interspersed with occasional trials with both phonemes until the child begins to chain the two phonemes. Alternatively, the component sounds of the word can be presented on alternating trials for a few trials; then a trial is delayed to see whether the child will produce the second sound as a response chained to the first sound (Lovaas, 1981). In backward chaining, several trials with only the second phoneme are interspersed with trials with both phonemes until the child begins to chain them. If the word is a two-syllable word, forward or backward chaining techniques are used to chain the two syllables together. Forward chaining seems to work best with homogeneous chains (two identical syllables— e.g., "mama," "bye-bye"), whereas backward chaining seems to work best with heterogeneous chains (two different syllables—e.g., "cookie," "daddy") (Lovaas, 1981). Excellent models of specific techniques used in shaping sounds into words are available in Lovaas and Leaf's (1981) videotapes, which also demonstrate the shaping of certain qualitative aspects of speech (e.g., volume, pitch, intonation).

After the first word is mastered, a second word is taught; then trials with the two words are randomly intermixed until the child responds discriminatively on each trial. After the first three or four words, acquisition of each new word requires progressively fewer trials; that is, acquisition is positively accelerated (Hewett, 1965; Lovaas, Berberich, et al., 1966). Eventually, the child acquires 3–10 new

words a session and demonstrates generalized verbal imitation, imitating new words on their first presentation (Lovaas, 1977). However, the rate of acquisition across children is highly variable; some take weeks or months to learn the first 10 words, whereas others take only a few hours (Lovaas, 1977). The causes of this variability in rate of acquisition are not well known, but rate of acquisition may be related to level of comprehension, frequency of spontaneous vocalizations, and initial extent of vocal imitation (Carr, Pridal, & Dores, 1984; Howlin, 1981). In some cases, especially with children who babble frequently prior to treatment, the process of acquiring words can be accelerated by starting with the phonemes most frequently used spontaneously by the children and chaining them into words (Koegel & Traphagen, 1982). The improvement in learning efficiency presumably results from the fact that little or no shaping of the children's articulation is required; hence, discrimination training can begin very early in training.

Although verbal imitation training gives a child a basic repertoire of words, they are under the stimulus control of the teacher's models, not their actual referents in the natural environment, and therefore may have no function for the child beyond maintaining the flow of reinforcers from the teacher. Therefore, control must be shifted from the teacher to the objects, persons, and actions to which the words refer if they are to be meaningful. Most often, the child is first taught to make motor responses to the words in a receptive-labeling program, then to say the words in response to presentations of their referents in an expressive-labeling program. Note that the reverse sequence— expressive labeling before receptive labeling— is also justifiable. Studies have shown that normal toddlers acquire some language expressively before they do receptively (e.g., Chapman & Miller, 1975; Lahey, 1974), and various investigators have taught expressive verbal and signed labels to autistic and retarded children prior to their acquisition of receptive labels (e.g., Carr et al., 1978; Lovaas, Berberich, et al., 1966; Schaeffer, 1980). Guess et al. (1976) advocate starting with expressive language because it capitalizes on the motivation provided by the instrumental function of language. We describe receptive labeling first here, simply because doing so facilitates the presentation of a number of aspects of discrimination training in general with autistic children.

Receptive Labeling

It is usually most effective to begin receptive training with highly preferred foods, toys, and other objects that lend themselves to repeated presentations. The teacher begins by presenting the item (e.g., a cup of juice) and telling the child, "Juice" (later varied as "Get juice," "Drink juice," "Where's the juice?," etc., as the child is able to deal with more complex instructions). If the child touches or picks up the cup of juice, he is rewarded with a sip of the juice and the teacher's praise. If the child does not respond, the teacher provides an imitative prompt (picks up the cup) or a manual prompt (moves the child's hand to the cup). The stimulus item is removed for a brief intertrial interval, then presented again with the same command. The prompt is faded over trials, until the child responds reliably to the verbal command. Next, a second item (e.g., a preferred toy) is taught the same way, with praise and a few seconds of play with the toy being the reinforcement. After the child responds correctly and reliably to each item presented alone, the two items are presented simultaneously on each trial. The teacher names one or the other item in random order across trials and rewards the child for touching the named item on each trial.

Responding correctly to random presentations of the two objects is a difficult task for most autistic children, because it constitutes a "conditional" discrimination task (Lashley, 1938). On a given trial, either of the objects may be the correct choice, depending on which object is named by the teacher. Two cross-modal stimulus control relationships must be established: the auditory and visual stimuli associated with object 1, and the different auditory and visual stimuli associated with object 2. Faced with learning such a complex discrimination solely through trial-and-error procedures, most autistic children ignore the teacher's verbalizations and respond overselectively to one of the positions (right or left) (Wasserman, 1969) or to one of the objects (Stark, Giddan, & Meisel, 1968). Some basic approaches to minimizing these tendencies are the following. The left–right positions of the items are randomly alternated to reduce the probability that the child will respond simply on the basis of position. If the child does show a position bias,

often it can be broken up by requesting only the item on the opposite side until the child finally shifts (Newsom & Simon, 1977). Another way of dealing with a position bias is to shape responding to the nonpreferred side by gradually moving the item from the preferred to the nonpreferred side in small steps over trials (Lovaas, 1981). Third, three objects may be presented on each trial to insure that position-based responding is reinforced an average of only 33% of the trials instead of the 50% possible with two objects (Lovaas, 1977). If the child shows a bias toward a particular item, requesting only the nonpreferred item for several consecutive trials may prompt the child to shift. If not, removing the object for a few trials will break the pattern at least temporarily.

Along with these alterations in random sequencing of trials, the literature on discrimination training with developmentally disabled children indicates the value of employing several other procedural variables:

1. The child's correct responses should secure a reward naturally related to the response, rather than being reinforced with an unrelated reward arbitrarily selected by the teacher (Janssen & Guess, 1978; Koegel & Williams, 1980; Saunders & Sailor, 1979; Williams, Koegel, & Egel, 1981). For example, in the description above, the child's correct response to "Juice" results in drinking a sip of the juice, and the response to the name of the toy terminates in playing with the toy. As these examples suggest, the first items taught should be items that already function as reinforcers for the child (Goetz et al., 1979). If such response–reinforcer relationships cannot be arranged (e.g., tasks involving nonconsumable or nonmanipulable items) and arbitrary reinforcers, such as edibles, must be used, each training object should be associated with a different, specific reinforcer (Litt & Schreibman, 1981).

2. Intertrial intervals should be kept relatively brief (1–4 seconds), in order to minimize forgetting and distracting behaviors (Dunlap, Dyer, & Koegel, 1983; Koegel, Dunlap, & Dyer, 1980).

3. Trials should continue at a steady pace in spite of mildly disruptive behaviors. Stopping trials when such behaviors occur allows the child to escape the task momentarily, which increases their future probability of occurrence through the negative reinforcement of task escape (Carr et al., 1980; Plummer et al., 1977).

Various prompting and prompt-fading procedures can be tried to bring the child's responses under discriminative instructional control, such as modeling the correct response with an identical set of objects just before the child responds, then fading the model across trials (Lovaas, 1981; Zane, Handen, Mason, & Geffin, 1984); pointing to the correct object immediately after the instruction early in training, then fading the prompt by delaying its presentation in 1-second increments after the instruction (Godby, Gast, & Wolery, 1987; Striefel et al., 1974); maximizing acoustic differences between the two words by prolonging one of the words, repeating it, or saying it more loudly, then gradually fading out the emphasis (Hyde & Rincover, 1985; Striefel et al., 1978; Striefel & Wetherby, 1973); or requiring the child to wait for 3–5 seconds after the instruction before making a response (Dyer, Christian, & Luce, 1982) or to verbalize the critical cue in the teacher's instruction before responding (Koegel, Dunlap, Richman, & Dyer, 1981).

If the foregoing tactics fail to result in learning, a combined auditory–visual prompting and fading program developed by Witt and Wacker (1981) for two-choice discriminations can be attempted. In their procedure, two teachers are used during the early training trials, each teacher paired with one of the objects. Thus, on half the initial trials, one of the teachers holds one of the objects, shakes it, and names it in a low, deep, staccato voice; on the other half of the trials, the other teacher shakes the second object and names it in a loud, high-pitched, drawn out voice. Gradually, the visual prompts (movement of the objects and mouth movements) are reduced while the auditory prompts remain constant. Next, visual prompts are eliminated (the teachers face away from the child); then one teacher provides both of the auditory prompts. Finally, only one teacher is present (facing the child) and gradually fades the auditory prompts to normal volume, pitch, and duration of voicing. This sequence was successful in teaching a two-choice object discrimination to severely and profoundly retarded children who had failed to learn under a visual-only fading procedure, and it resulted in rapid acquisition of subsequent receptive-labeling tasks trained in trial-and-error fashion.

Once the child has learned six words, two types of generalization training are begun (Lovaas, 1981). First, different exemplars of each object are used to teach generalization within classes of objects while maintaining discriminations between classes of objects, or simple concepts. Second, the child is taught to identify the objects in different settings and with different individuals, in order to render the receptive language functional in natural environments. Frequently throughout the day, other teachers, parents, and siblings require the child to "get" or "find" or "show me" the objects she has just learned to identify. Such specific training in generalization across multiple settings and persons is crucial to making language functional for autistic children, as they typically fail to generalize (Rincover & Koegel, 1975) or maintain (Koegel & Rincover, 1977) newly acquired behaviors without it.

Expressive Labeling

When the child has learned to identify about 10 objects receptively, expressive training with the same objects begins (Lovaas, 1981). The teacher places the first object on the table and, when the child looks at it, says its name as a verbal prompt for the child to name it. Over trials, the verbal prompt is faded by reducing its volume and/or delaying its presentation, in order to shift stimulus control from the teacher's verbal model to the sight of the object. The name of a second object is taught the same way; then the two objects are presented in random order across trials until the child is able to name each object correctly without prompting on several consecutive trials. In subsequent training, the name of each new object is first taught in isolation, then trials with the new object are intermixed with trials with the previously trained objects for discrimination training. As in verbal imitation training and receptive labeling, acquisition of each new expressive label after the first three or four is positively accelerated, but the rate of acquisition is highly variable across children (Lovaas, 1977).

Most of the techniques for enhancing acquisition of receptive labeling are also used in expressive training. Thus, natural instead of arbitrary reinforcers are used whenever possible; training trials are conducted at a steady pace with brief intertrial intervals; and verbal prompts can be faded along dimensions such as loudness and duration. After the child has learned to name two or three items, answering simple questions (e.g., "What's this?") and verbalizing basic requests (e.g., "I want ___," "Gimme ___") are taught, in order to make the newly acquired labels more useful in ordinary verbal interactions. After requests have been taught through imitation, the teacher's model can be faded by delaying its presentation to shift control of the child's sentence from the model to the sight of the object, in order to make the child's requests more spontaneous (Charlop, Schreibman, & Thibodeau, 1985). The importance of teaching basic request forms early in training is that they facilitate generalization because they allow the child to use language to obtain reinforcers in the natural environment. Thus, requests ("mands" in Skinner's [1957] terminology) are more immediately and generally functional for an autistic child than are descriptive statements ("tacts"), which are largely maintained by social attention—a very weak reinforcer for autistic children early in treatment (Goetz *et al.*, 1979).

Generalization training begins when the child has mastered about six labels, and is again concerned with generalization within classes of similar items and with functional usage of the labels in natural settings (Lovaas, 1981). Special efforts to promote generalization across environments are necessary, because the tight control over attention and responding that is often required to teach beginning speech seems to combine with the overly selective attention that is characteristic of many autistic children (Lovaas, Koegel, & Schreibman, 1979) to result in their frequent failure to generalize speech to settings and persons not involved in the original training (Handleman, 1979; Harris, 1975; Rincover & Koegel, 1975). Two main strategies for promoting generalized language usage have been explored. Traditionally, investigators have exported discrete-trial methodology from treatment rooms to the natural environment, with only minor changes to accommodate some of the differences between clinic and home settings. Thus, considerable effort over the years has gone into developing effective training programs for parents, teachers, peers, and siblings, as described elsewhere in this chapter (e.g., Harris, 1983; Koegel, Schreibman, Britten, Burke, & O'Neill, 1982; Kozloff, 1973, 1979; Lovaas, 1981, 1987). More recently, investigators have attempted to minimize problems of generalization by insuring that the child's speech is immediately functional in producing frequent and varied reinforcing effects in everyday environments. This is accomplished by conducting brief teaching interactions requiring the child to use words to obtain natural reinforcers and to complete daily routines. The result has been the development of a group of procedures known collectively as "incidental teaching" after the name of the first of these procedures to be studied (Hart & Risley, 1968, 1974, 1975).

Incidental Teaching

Incidental-teaching procedures vary in detail and specific purpose, but they share four features that differentiate them from the discrete-trial language training procedures just described:

1. Discrete-trial training is a massed-trials approach controlled and paced by the teacher; incidental-teaching episodes consist of only one trial or a few trials at a time that are usually initiated by the child.
2. Discrete-trial training occurs in time-limited, one-to-one sessions away from distractions; incidental teaching occurs intermittently throughout the day in naturalistic, everyday environments such as classrooms and homes.
3. In discrete-trial training, the training stimuli are often teacher-selected objects, and the reinforcers may be arbitrary events (e.g., food and praise); in incidental teaching, the training stimuli are child-selected items, and the reinforcer is access to the item.
4. With autistic children, discrete-trial methods are typically employed to teach the child new language *forms;* incidental-teaching procedures are employed to teach new language *functions*—that is, to help the child use language forms to influence others or to elaborate acquired forms in order to communicate better (Carr, 1985; McGee, Krantz, & McClannahan, 1985).

Each of the most commonly used incidental-teaching procedures—mand–model (Rogers-Warren & Warren, 1980), delay (Halle, Marshall, & Spradlin, 1979), and incidental teaching (Hart & Risley, 1975)—is most appropriate at a different stage of generalization training (Halle, 1982). The mand–model technique (Rogers-Warren & Warren, 1980) facilitates the generalization of speech acquired in one-to-one sessions to natural settings by increasing the number and range of opportunities for the child to use it. Therefore, the mand–model technique is especially appropriate for children who rarely or never initiate newly acquired speech in natural environments. The teacher begins by providing a variety of attractive materials for play. When a child approaches an item, the teacher instructs (mands) the child to request the item verbally or to describe it (e.g., "Tell me what you want" or "Tell me what this is"). If the child gives an appropriate verbal response, the teacher praises the child and gives the item to the child. If the child fails to respond or gives an inadequate response, the teacher elaborates the instruction (e.g., "Tell me the whole sentence" or "I have red and green paper; tell me what you want") and/or models a satisfactory response for the child to imitate, then reinforces a correct imitation of the model with praise and access to the item.

Although the mand–model technique increases the usage of newly acquired words and phrases in the natural environment and can be used to teach new words, it has the potential disadvantage of maintaining the child's reliance on an adult for prompts for speech usage (Anderson, 1982). A technique for shifting stimulus control from the teacher's prompts to environmental cues is the delay procedure (Halle, Baer, & Spradlin, 1981; Halle et al., 1979). The delay procedure can be used whenever the child needs assistance or wants an item. Instead of instructing or modeling an appropriate response, the teacher looks at the child and waits silently for 5–15 seconds. If the child makes an appropriate response during the delay, it is reinforced with assistance or the desired item. If an incorrect response or no response occurs, the teacher models the word or phrase and reinforces the child's correct imitation. The delay procedure teaches the child to respond to nonverbal cues: To determine what verbalization is appropriate to the situation, the child must attend to cues in the environment (e.g., a desired object, the start of an activity, the teacher's arrival with cups of juice) in addition to the teacher's delay. Eventually, the objects and events are themselves sufficient to cue appropriate speech (Halle, 1982).

The main limitation of the delay technique is that although it teaches the child to initiate speech independently, it lacks procedures for elaborating the child's speech. Incidental-teaching procedures (Hart & Risley, 1975) have the objective of teaching elaborated adult language forms. An incidental-teaching occasion begins with the child's verbal or nonverbal request (calling the teacher's name, reaching for an object just beyond reach, struggling with clothing, crying, etc.). The teacher first attempts to prompt an appropriate verbal response by approaching the child, making eye contact, and adopting a questioning look. If the child does not respond to the teacher's focused attention, the teacher adds a general verbal cue, such as "What do you want?" or "What is this?" If the child does not respond to the general verbal cue, one of three levels of prompting is used, depending on the child's level of language ability: (1) a request for imitation, used when the child has not yet mastered the appropriate response ("Say, 'I want the ball' "); (2) a request for partial imitation ("Say, 'I want . . .' "); or (3) a request for the appropriate response ("You need to tell me what you want"). The variety and extent of the child's language learning depends on the teacher's skill in providing appropriate prompts and in maximizing the frequency of incidental-teaching interactions (Halle, 1982). To increase the frequency of opportunities, the teacher places desired materials out of reach on a shelf but in sight of the child, and keeps the incidental-teaching interactions brief and comfortable for the child (Hart & Risley, 1974, 1975).

Recent modifications of incidental-teaching procedures have indicated that they can be used to teach initial speech skills as well as to generalize existing skills. McGee, Krantz, Mason, and McClannahan (1983) taught receptive labels to autistic adolescents living in a group home by conducting a few training trials at the start of each of the tasks in a lunch-making routine. Prior to beginning each task in the routine (e.g., making sandwiches, preparing snacks, bagging the items), each adolescent was requested to hand the teacher one of the items used in the task from an array of five objects on the kitchen counter. Gestural prompts were used as needed, and praise was delivered for correct responses. Completion of the receptive-labeling tasks for a set of objects enabled the adolescent to proceed with the corresponding lunch preparation activity. The procedure resulted in rapid acquisition of receptive labels that had not been learned when access to the lunch preparation routine was noncontingent. A variation of the McGee et al. (1983) procedure is the "behavior chain interruption" procedure of Goetz, Gee, and Sailor (1985), in which a training trial is inserted into the middle of a regularly occurring chain of behaviors in the child's daily life (e.g., making toast, removing and hanging up a coat, brushing teeth). At a predetermined step in the chain, the child is interrupted and asked, "What do you want?" The child has to give a correct response to continue the chain; if the child is incorrect, the teacher provides a model for the child to imitate. This procedure seems to be effective because it takes advantage of an autistic child's typically strong motivation to complete a well-established routine once having started it (Goetz et al., 1985).

Koegel, O'Dell, and Koegel (1987) recently presented a procedure that involved the one-to-one sessions typical of the discrete-trial format, yet loosened the structure of such training through the use of incidental-teaching techniques in order to operationalize some correlates of normal language acquisition. These included "turn taking," the speaker–listener exchanges occurring in normal communication; "shared control," the sharing of attention, materials, and tasks (Snow, 1977); and "natural" consequences for speaking, such as access to desired objects or events (Bloom & Lahey, 1978). Koegel, O'Dell, and Koegel (1987) termed their procedure a "natural language teaching paradigm" that consisted of the following techniques, used with two mute autistic children in a clinic setting:

1. Instead of the teacher selecting the training objects (toys) arbitrarily, the child selected one from a pool of objects by looking at, touching, or pointing at the object.
2. Instead of drilling the child on one object in massed trials until mastery, the teacher changed the object whenever the child selected a different object.
3. Instead of instructing the child to label the object, the teacher played with the object and modeled its name; if the child failed to imitate, the teacher simply played with the object and modeled its name again.
4. Any verbal response, not just a correct response or an approximation, was reinforced.
5. Reinforcement consisted of praise and the opportunity to play with the object instead of praise and edibles.

Both children studied, who had failed to learn very many imitative verbalizations during previous discrete-trial training sessions, showed substantial increases in imitation, spontaneous vocalizations, and generalized imitation after natural language teaching began.

Although this study is an encouraging example of the cross-disciplinary research necessary for theoretical convergence to occur, two problems should be mentioned to indicate the difficulty of doing such research. First, the natural language teaching approach was compared with a discrete-trial expressive-labeling condition, not with verbal imitation training (which, given the subject descriptions, would seem to have been more appropriate); thus, it is not clear whether the increased imitation observed in the natural language teaching condition was superior to what would have occurred with verbal imitation training like that described earlier in this section. Second, the range of responses accepted as correct imitations seems quite broad. A correct imitation could be the same word spoken by the teacher or "an approximation including a phoneme that occurred in the word and could be differentiated from a self-stimulatory vocalization" (Koegel, O'Dell, & Koegel, 1987, p. 192). Thus, the data showing increases in "imitations" may include a high percentage of relatively rough approximations.

On balance, the Koegel, O'Dell, and Koegel (1987) procedure might best be considered useful for increasing the rate of a child's existing vocalizations and teaching some new imitative approximations. Koegel and colleagues attributed the success of the procedure to the combination of several established learning variables, such as direct reinforcement with the training objects (Saunders & Sailor, 1979), the reinforcement of all communicative attempts (Koegel & Egel, 1979), and task variation (Dunlap, 1984). The study is valuable in showing that developmental concepts can serve a heuristic role in suggesting some novel arrangements of behavioral variables.

A systematic replication of the natural language teaching paradigm makes the same point. Laski, Charlop, and Schreibman (1988) showed that parents could be successfully taught to use procedures like those used by Koegel, O'Dell, and Koegel (1987), with corresponding increases in their children's imitations and answers to questions. The main value of the procedure seemed to be its ability to increase the frequency of existing speech, although the investigators noted anecdotally that novel words and phrases also occurred.

Subsequent language training depends on the outcome of the attempt to establish verbal language. Young children who acquire labeling should receive further training that is informed by knowledge of normal development. Training in early semantic relationships focuses on possessives ("Billy's coat," "my car"), locatives ("on the plate"), noun–action phrases ("Mommy sits"), and action–object phrases ("drink juice"). Early morpheme rules include the "-s" suffix for plurals and possessives and the present progressive and past tenses ("-ing," "-ed") (Howlin & Rutter, 1987; Lovaas, 1977). Examples of the advanced language skills taught to autistic children include the use of prepositions and pronouns (Lovaas, 1977; McGee et al., 1985; Sailor & Taman, 1972); speaking in compound sentences (Stevens-Long & Rasmussen, 1974); answering "yes" and "no" appropriately (Hung, 1980; Neef, Walters, & Egel, 1984); asking questions (Hung, 1977); recalling past events (Lovaas, 1977); engaging in simple conversations (Breen et al., 1985; Gaylord-Ross et al., 1984; Lovaas, 1977; see section above on complex social interactions); and reducing excessive echolalia (McMorrow, Foxx, Faw, & Bittle, 1987; Palyo, Cooke, Schuler, & Apolloni, 1979; Risley & Wolf, 1967; Schreibman & Carr, 1978).

Older children, adolescents, and adults should be given training in language skills that are immediately useful in home, school/job, and community settings (Guess, Sailor, Keogh, & Baer, 1976). Necessary words can be taught in conjunction with training other skill areas—for example, by teaching students the names of various appliances during domestic skill training and simple greeting rituals while training community skills (Sailor & Guess, 1983).

In very general terms, the outcomes that can be expected from operant speech training with autistic children appear to depend primarily on the children's initial language level. Howlin (1981) reviewed 70 studies published between 1964 and 1980, involving 125 cases. Of children who were initially mute or using only simple vocalizations, 23% remained mute, 60% developed spontaneous use of single words, and 17% developed spontaneous phrase speech. Children initially using single words were divided about equally between those using single words spontaneously (52%) and those developing spontaneous phrase speech (48%). The best outcomes occurred with initially echolalic children; over 83% of these children advanced to appropriate, spontaneous phrase speech. For individuals who remain mute in spite of speech training, treatment efforts usually shift to sign language.

Sign Language Training

The basic techniques for teaching signing are similar to those used to teach speech. A typical program for teaching initial receptive sign labeling through simultaneous communication training is that developed by Carr and Dores (1981). The teacher starts with two objects on the table and signs the name of one of the objects while simultaneously saying its name. Correct responses (touching the named object) are reinforced with praise and edibles; incorrect responses are reprimanded. The position of the objects on the table and the names signed and spoken by the teacher vary randomly across trials. Training continues until the child is able to respond correctly to both of the teacher's sign–word stimuli during randomly intermixed trials. One new object is added each time the child masters the current words. Prompting and fading procedures like those described earlier in connection with receptive speech are used if needed.

If the child fails to learn receptive discriminations with training like that described by Carr and Dores (1981), certain modifications studied by Pridal (1982) have been found to be helpful with severely and profoundly retarded autistic children. Pridal (1982) found that learning is greatly enhanced when (1) the initial signs are iconic (i.e., consist of movements like those normally used to manipulate the object); (2) the teacher simply signs the name of the object, without simultaneously saying its name; (3) the child is required to imitate (rehearse) the teacher's sign before touching one of the objects; (4) the objects used in initial training are limited to those found in preliminary assessments to be highly reinforcing; and (5) the reinforcer for identifying the correct object is a few seconds of play with it.

Expressive signing is similarly taught through procedures similar to those used in operant speech training. The efficiency of learning will be enhanced if, before beginning sign training, the teacher minimizes any hand-related self-stimulatory behaviors so that it is easy to tell when the child makes the correct sign or a close approximation. It also is very helpful if the child has acquired generalized motor imitation, as modeling is the primary teaching technique. Even so, manual prompts may still be necessary to refine the topographies of the child's signs so that they more closely resemble the signs being taught (Carr, 1981).

Training in expressive labeling is carried out in three steps (Carr *et al.*, 1978). In Step 1, the teacher shows an object to the child and says the name of the object, then manually prompts the child to make the sign by molding the hand and fingers into the correct sign configuration while repeating the name of the object. Step 2 is identical to Step 1, except that the teacher gradually fades the manual prompt until the child is able to make the sign independently. By the end of Step 2, the teacher merely holds up the object while saying its name, and the child produces the correct sign for the object. Rough approximations are acceptable at this stage as long as they are reliably discriminable by the teacher. In Step 3, a new sign is introduced and trained as in Steps 1 and 2. Trials with the previous sign are interspersed with trials with the new sign at a ratio of about 1:3 to practice the old sign and facilitate the discrimination between the two signs. Step 3 is repeated with a new sign each time the child shows mastery of the current signs, according to a criterion such as 10 correct trials in a row during randomly intermixed trials. Carr *et al.* (1978) found that this procedure was sufficient to teach a basic sign-labeling vocabulary to severely retarded autistic children.

Other noteworthy findings were the following. First, as is the case with operant speech training, rates of acquisition showed considerable variability across the children, indicating that signing is not a panacea for severely retarded autistic children who fail to learn speech. The four children studied by Carr *et al.* (1978) required from 948 to 7,669 trials to learn to produce five signs reliably and discriminatively. Initial acquisition may be much faster if a child is only moderately or mildly retarded or has some imitative skills prior to sign training (e.g., Barrera & Sulzer-Azaroff, 1983; Bonvillian & Nelson, 1976; Remington & Clarke, 1983). Second, Carr *et al.* (1978) found that sign acquisition showed positive acceleration across signs, just as speech acquisition shows positive acceleration across words. Third, in relation to the question of whether simultaneous communication teaches receptive speech as well as signs, Carr *et al.* (1978) found that for three of their four subjects, signing was controlled by the visual stimuli of the training objects and not by the auditory stimuli of the spoken word. The fourth child, who produced signs equally well in response to either the sight of the object or the sound of its name, was the

only child with some simple vocal imitation ability. The importance of this finding for predicting what is learned during simultaneous communication training has been explored further and is discussed below when we consider how to decide which communication modality to teach.

One way of improving the efficiency of the Carr *et al.* (1978) procedure might be to conduct motor imitation training prior to or concurrently with sign training, just as verbal imitation training is conducted prior to speech training (Carr, 1981). Furthermore, procedural refinements like those used by Pridal (1982) to enhance receptive signing, such as using signs that are iconic and training objects that are strongly reinforcing, could be expected to enhance expressive sign learning. An alternative to the procedures developed by Carr and his colleagues for teaching initial expressive signs has been described by Schaeffer (1980). Although the procedure has not been evaluated as rigorously as that of Carr *et al.* (1978), it is interesting because it is reminiscent of the behavior chain interruption strategy (Goetz *et al.*, 1985), described in the section on incidental teaching. The teacher begins by holding out a desired edible and waiting. When the child reaches for the food, the teacher catches the hand and moves it into position to make the sign for the edible, molds the hand and moves it through the sign, then gives the child the edible. The teacher's manual prompts are gradually faded over many trials, until the child makes the sign independently. Subsequent signs can be taught similarly by interrupting reaching for other reinforcers.

After the child can reliably use signs to label about 10 reinforcing objects and events, spontaneous usage is taught and generalized. Spontaneous signing requires that signs occur in situations where objects, instructions, and prompts are absent; the only relevant stimulus should be an attending adult. A procedure for teaching spontaneity has been developed by Carr and Kologinsky (1983), who taught three autistic boys to use signs spontaneously by conducting training in a room where highly preferred food and toy reinforcers were concealed in a bag. During the first session, a teacher approached a child, made eye contact, and presented a sign for one of the 10 reinforcers. When the child imitated the sign, he was given the reinforcer. Then the teacher made eye contact again but did not present a prompt. If the child signed within 5 seconds, he received the reinforcer; if not, the teacher presented a partial imitative prompt to evoke the sign. Training continued until the child spontaneously initiated the sign on two consecutive trials without prompts. The same procedure was repeated for each of the remaining nine reinforcers in turn. During subsequent training sessions, the teacher approached the child, made eye contact, and waited for him to sign. Each time the child signed, the teacher delivered the relevant reinforcer. This procedure was found to be effective in establishing frequent, spontaneous signed requests for varied reinforcers in each of the boys within two sessions (Carr & Kologinsky, 1983). Informal observations of the patterns of signing within each session indicated that spontaneous signing was used in a natural way. For example, if the child signed for a salty snack early in the session, he would later begin signing for fluids; signing for food items early in a session would often be followed by signing for toys after the child was apparently satiated. In a second experiment in the same study, Carr and Kologinsky (1983) showed that generalization across settings and adults could be established by prompting and reinforcing signing in multiple settings and with several different teachers, then fading out the prompts while continuing reinforcement for spontaneous signing.

Procedures for teaching more advanced signing skills may be introduced as soon as the child has acquired a small vocabulary of signs. One example of the development of a signing procedure to teach a complex performance is the study by Carr, Kologinsky, and Leff-Simon (1987) concerned with generative action–object phrases. Children were first taught the sign for an action ("move," "point to," or "hold"), then taught to combine the action sign with an object sign (e.g., "chair," "ball," "apple") in order to produce a complete phrase (e.g., "move chair"). After learning to combine the action sign with two to eight objects, the children began to generate novel phrases consisting of the action sign combined with the sign for a new object. Carr et al. (1987) noted that such descriptive phrases can be linked to other signing skills to produce simple conversations during incidental teaching interactions in natural settings. For example, if a child looks at or points to a carton of milk, the teacher can pour a glass of milk and ask the child, "What am I doing?" After the child signs "Pour milk," the

teacher praises the child and asks, "What do you want?" When the child signs, "Want milk," the child is given the milk.

Speech Training or Sign Training?

The advent of simultaneous communication training during the 1970s as a major alternative to verbal language training for autistic children has resulted in the need to consider both strategies in planning communication interventions. Unfortunately, there are no brief assessment procedures that allow us to match clients to intervention strategies with any degree of certainty about the outcome. Verbal language is the norm for communication in society, and its acquisition would insure the widest possible audience both within and outside of treatment settings—a factor important in generalization and maintenance. Therefore, most clinicians retain a preference for verbal training and make the decision in accordance with the children's performance during a trial of verbal training. They expose all autistic children to verbal training for a period of time, then substitute or add simultaneous communication training for those whose progress is so slow that the possibility of developing spontaneous, useful speech is too remote to justify continuing verbal training (Bonvillian, Nelson, & Rhyne, 1981; Lovaas, 1981; Owens & House, 1984). This performance-based approach is fair to the children, who get a chance to demonstrate how much potential for spoken language they possess, and it provides valid data that help to justify a switch to sign training if the children fail to acquire useful speech.

The principal disadvantage of the performance-based approach is that it can take considerable time. With conventional speech therapy conducted for an hour or less a day, it is usually recommended that a child receive at least a year of treatment before a decision about changing the modality is made (Owens & House, 1984; Shane, 1980). Even with intensive operant training that is conducted at the rate of 1–4 hours a day (not counting incidental-teaching episodes occurring outside of formal training sessions), it is recommended that verbal training continue for at least 3 months before changing to sign training (Lovaas, 1981). Three months may not be an unduly long time span for initial assessment in an area as important as language, but a year does seem to be. In both cases, however, it would clearly be desirable to have a more efficient means of assessment if one is possible.

A second difficulty with the performance-based approach is that objective criteria for judging whether or not a child's progress is "too slow" are not yet available. However, some clinical rules of thumb can be applied. On the basis of his experience with dozens of autistic children, Lovaas (1981) has observed that if the child is over 6 years of age when treatment starts, vocalizes only simple vowel sounds and no "difficult" consonants (e.g., K, G, L), and fails to learn to imitate at least five sounds during the first 3 months of treatment, further progress in verbal training will continue to be slow and consideration should be given to sign training. Carr (1981), in addition, notes that there are some autistic children who acquire fairly good receptive language but whose verbal articulation remains so poor that no one can understand them; hence, expressive sign training would be appropriate for them.

One way of making the performance-based approach to assessment more efficient is to conduct verbal and simultaneous communication training concurrently in an alternating-treatments design (Barlow & Hayes, 1979). The child is exposed to both a verbal training session and a simultaneous communication session each day for 3–4 weeks. The training modality that produces the more rapid rate of acquisition of words then becomes the treatment method used in subsequent training sessions (Barrera, Lobato-Barrera, & Sulzer-Azaroff, 1980; Barrera & Sulzer-Azaroff, 1983; Brady & Smouse, 1978). For such an assessment to be valid, it is crucial that the words used in the two types of training sessions be equated for difficulty. Barrera and Sulzer-Azaroff (1983) have presented a rigorous procedure for selecting the words that includes equating words on the basis of their difficulty of pronunciation, number of syllables, and potential reinforcing value; and pretesting the child with a variety of objects to eliminate any that can already be identified either receptively or expressively.

The ideal alternative to the performance-based approach would be a relatively brief assessment based on the child's presenting behaviors that would predict which training modality would ultimately produce the best outcome. Some potential predictor variables that may become a part of a more efficient assessment procedure are gradually being identified.

Howlin and Rutter (1987) followed 12 initially mute children for 18 months and examined differences between 7 who acquired at least some communicative speech and 5 who remained noncommunicative in spite of operant speech training. Children who later acquired speech showed some spontaneous imitation of sounds or gestures and some comprehension of spoken language. The children who remained mute rarely showed spontaneous imitation and were severely limited in both verbal and nonverbal comprehension.

The predictive value of imitation has been established experimentally by Carr and his associates (Carr & Dores, 1981; Carr et al., 1984). Carr et al. (1984) found that mute children who were "good" verbal imitators (i.e., could imitate 74% or more of a list of 50 simple consonant–vowel sounds) later learned to respond correctly to receptive-labeling discrimination tasks whether they were given vocal-only training or sign-only training, whereas children who were "poor" imitators (imitated 20% or fewer of the sounds) learned the discriminations with sign training but not with verbal training. Carr and Dores (1981) found that, during simultaneous communication training, good imitators responded correctly to either the sign or the spoken word when learning receptive labels, whereas poor imitators learned only the signs. Remington and Clarke (1983) replicated these findings with expressive-labeling tasks. These results suggest that autistic children with little or no verbal imitative ability are functionally deaf when presented with simultaneous visual and auditory stimuli, attending to only the visual cues, as the research on stimulus overselectivity would suggest (Lovaas et al., 1979). Similarly, Rutter et al. (1967) found that mute children who failed to acquire speech were "profoundly unresponsive to sounds" in early childhood. Nishimura, Watamaki, Sato, and Wakabayashi (1987) found that babbling in such children either never developed or disappeared by 4.5 years of age, as it tends to do in organically deaf children (Bloom & Lahey, 1978). Carr and Dores (1981) do, however, caution that auditory inattention should not be considered to be irremediable. Specific training in verbal imitation is sometimes successful with such children and may lead to verbal speech (Howlin, 1981; Lovaas, 1977; Schaeffer, 1980). Yet the Carr and Dores findings (Carr & Dores, 1981; Carr et al., 1984) strongly suggest that mute children who are poor verbal imitators are *initially* more likely to learn language with simultaneous communication training or sign-only training than with verbal training.

The Carr and Dores (1981) and Carr et al. (1984) studies also speak to the question of the value of simultaneous communication training in promoting verbal language in mute autistic children. Some investigators have suggested that the pairing of speech with signs has a facilitative effect on the emergence of verbal language (e.g., Creedon, 1975; Miller & Miller, 1973; Schaeffer, 1980). The evidence suggests that this occurs in only about 25% of cases and that the speech that is acquired is very limited (Carr, 1979). The studies by Carr and his associates indicate that simultaneous communication training can produce either of two distinct patterns of receptive-language acquisition in autistic children, predictable on the basis of the children's verbal imitation ability at the start of training. A facilitative effect of simultaneous communication training on verbal language is far more likely to occur in children with good verbal imitation skills than in those with poor verbal imitation skills.

Until we have a well-developed assessment methodology for selecting the most appropriate modality for teaching communication, one logical alternative to starting with either verbal or sign training is to combine the two approaches. Schaeffer, Kollinzas, Musil, and McDowell (1977) conducted training in verbal imitation and, in separate sessions, training in simultaneous communication with three autistic boys (two of whom were mute and one echolalic). After 3–4 months of training, the children spontaneously began to produce approximations of words while they signed; thereafter, they were required to sign and speak simultaneously. After 9 months, words spoken in the absence of signing began to occur. At this point, the boys were told not to sign, and verbalizations without signs were differentially reinforced. All three children eventually produced spontaneous phrase speech (Schaeffer, 1980).

Finally, the decision about which approach to use in communication training should always be subject to change. The child's progress as determined by regular, objective assessments should indicate whether the child should continue to receive the type of training she is currently receiving or should be exposed to another approach. If some type of sign language train-

ing is contemplated, either of two kinds of reactions from parents commonly occur. Some parents will expect sign language training to promote verbal language automatically. Whether or not it does seems to depend on a child's initial verbal imitation skills, as just discussed. Other parents will be concerned that sign language training will hinder verbal language development that would otherwise occur. At the present time, there is no evidence that it does. If the only realistic alternative is no communication at all, then certainly sign language training is worth the attempt. If it fails, efforts should shift to another augmentative system that permits practical communication, such as picture boards or cards (McDonald, 1980). Blissymbols (McNaughton & Kates, 1980) and plastic chip systems (Carrier, 1976) have such limited audiences that they should be considered choices of last resort.

WORKING WITH FAMILIES

Historically, behavioral work with the families of autistic children was motivated primarily by their requests for help in dealing with disruptive and dangerous behaviors occurring in the home (e.g., Risley, 1968; Wetzel, Baker, Roney, & Martin, 1966). Somewhat later, it became apparent that language and other behaviors established so laboriously in clinics and classrooms would not generalize to the home unless parents were taught to use the same behavioral techniques (Kozloff, 1973; Lovaas, Koegel, Simmons, & Long, 1973). Most recently, another source of motivation has become evident—that of helping the family to cope with the additional stress imposed on the family as a system by the presence of a severely handicapped child (Harris, 1983; Donnellan & Mirenda, 1984; Kozloff, 1979). Thus, the work of the clinician who works with autistic children has steadily broadened over time from a focus on behavior management consultation to include parent training and counseling.

Parent Training

Although training programs for the parents of autistic children differ considerably in methods and scope, they usually involve some combination of lectures, readings, practice with feedback, tests for mastery of didactic materials, home visits for demonstrations and consultations, telephone consultations, and follow-up contacts. They may also include group discussion sessions to deal with practical problems and may provide arrangements for such services as respite care or brief residential treatment. The content of the lectures typically includes simple recording and graphing methods; the concept of contingencies of reinforcement in analyzing the functional causes of behaviors; elementary behavior modification principles, such as reinforcement, shaping, punishment, prompting, fading, chaining, generalization, and maintenance; and methods for teaching specific skills, such as eye contact, imitation, speech, play, and self-care skills (e.g., Harris, 1983; Koegel, Schreibman, et al., 1982; Kozloff, 1979).

The importance of teaching parents basic principles as well as specific techniques derives from studies of the immediate and generalized effects of parent and teacher training. Koegel, Glahn, and Nieminen (1978) demonstrated that although parents were able to learn how to teach a specific behavior to their autistic children after observing an experienced therapist do it, the parents were unable to teach other behaviors not demonstrated by the therapist. When children exhibit isolated skill deficits or problem behaviors, training parents or teachers in specific skills may be sufficient. However, when confronted with the multiple behavior deficits and excesses of autistic children, parents need to become "generative" teachers—that is, teachers capable of applying basic principles to practical problems and deriving logical treatments.

Koegel, Russo, and Rincover (1977) conducted a study on this point with special education teachers that is also relevant to work with parents. Koegel et al. (1977) found that teaching behavioral principles, as opposed to training specific techniques for specific skill deficits, resulted in greater generalization of teaching effectiveness. Eleven teachers of autistic children participated in a 4-week training program that consisted of videotapes illustrating correct and incorrect applications of behavioral teaching principles, literature on these principles, direct modeling, and practice with feedback. The teaching skills emphasized in the program were the basic discrete-trial instructional methods described earlier in the section on initial treatment. Direct observation of the teachers prior to training showed that the teachers generally exhibited these skills less than 50% of the time. After training, each teacher correctly used

the five procedures at least 90% of the time regardless of the child or the task involved, and all of the children made progress on the target behaviors assigned during the sessions.

Representative studies of the effects of parent training programs for families of autistic children indicate some of the advantages of parent training, as well as some of the unsolved problems in this area. Koegel, Schreibman, and their colleagues compared the effects of home-based treatment provided by parents who were given 25–50 hours of training in behavior modification with the effects of outpatient clinic treatment provided by trained students for 4–5 hours per week for a year (Koegel, Schreibman, et al., 1982; Schreibman et al., 1984). The main findings were that both groups of children showed increases in several categories of appropriate behavior (speech, play, and social behaviors) and decreases in inappropriate behaviors (tantrums, self-stimulation, echolalia, and noncompliance) during measurements taken while they were with their primary treatment providers (i.e., the mothers for the parent training group, the therapists for the clinic group). However, the children in the clinic group showed no generalization to their mothers (who had not been trained). During in-home observations of appropriate responses to parental questions and instructions, only the children in the parent training group showed improvement. Analyses of activity diaries showed that only the parents in the parent training group significantly increased the amounts of time engaged in recreation and leisure activities over the course of the year (Koegel, Schreibman, et al., 1982).

Harris and her colleagues have provided 10-week training courses for small groups of parents for many years in connection with their educational program at Rutgers (Harris, 1983; Harris & Boyle, 1985). In studies of some of these groups, measures obtained at posttreatment showed significant improvements in the parents' behavior modification skills and in the children's language, with initially verbal children progressing to a greater extent than initially mute children (Harris, Wolchik, & Milch, 1982). At a 1-year follow-up, the children had maintained their gains but had not shown further improvement, apparently due to the parents' discontinuation of structured teaching programs (Harris, Wolchik, & Weitz, 1981). In a multiple-regression analysis of parental predictors of change in children, Milch (1983) found that the parents' skillfulness at two of the more sophisticated behavioral techniques (shaping and recognition of the need for prompts) were predictive of the children's progress in language. In addition, the number of behavior management and academic programs the parents had in effect and the number of hours that both mothers and fathers spent working with their children were predictive of the children's progress at a 3-month follow-up (Milch, 1983). In a 4- to 7-year follow-up with 30 families, it was found that the parents whose children were in behaviorally oriented educational programs were more likely to continue to use behavior modification techniques than the parents whose children attended schools that were not behavioral (Harris, 1986a, 1986b).

In London, Howlin and her colleagues conducted a home-based parent training program for 16 families of high-functioning autistic boys aged 3–10 years (mean 6 years), whose nonverbal IQs ranged from 60 to over 120 (mean 87) (Howlin & Rutter, 1987). Treatment extended over an 18-month period; two matched control groups were provided with outpatient treatment "relatively infrequently" for 6 and 18 months, respectively. The parents of the experimental group were visited by psychologists for 2–3 hours weekly or biweekly during the first 6 months and monthly during the last 12 months. Mothers were individually trained to teach basic language skills and manage behavior problems in their autistic children. Counseling on various practical problems and family stresses was done as needed, and occasional respite services were provided. Psychometric, questionnaire, and observational measures of parent and child behaviors were recorded at 6-month intervals. Some of the main findings at 18 months were the following:

1. Children in the treatment group showed significantly fewer problem behaviors (tantrums, aggression, and problems with eating, sleeping, and toileting) and ritualistic and obsessional behaviors. There were no significant differences in stereotypies, hyperactivity, or mood abnormalities.

2. The treatment group showed significantly more social responsiveness to parents, other adults, and peers, and a developmentally higher level of simple play with objects (including "pretend" play), but not more imaginative play or self-initiated interactive play with peers.

3. Analyses of audiotapes of the children's speech showed that the children in the treatment group were significantly superior to their matched controls in quantity and communicativeness of speech (higher number of comprehensible utterances and percentage of communicative utterances), but were not significantly different in linguistic level (number of phrases and morphemes, standardized language test scores), except that the treatment children had more verb transformations. In general, then, functional language *use* increased with treatment to a far greater degree than language *complexity*. The echolalic children in both the treatment and control groups improved in the use of phrase speech to about the same degree. However, the treated echolalic children, unlike the controls, showed decreased spontaneous echolalia and increased verbal imitation ("prompted echoes"). Individual differences were important in language outcome for the mute children. Mute children whose tested language age was at least 12 months, who had a few words or sounds, who demonstrated at least some verbal comprehension, and who showed some play activities were more likely to progress to communicative phrase speech than those whose language age was 6 months or less, with no words, word approximations, or communicative gestures.

4. There were no significant differences in IQ, which declined a few points in both groups. At age 18, one of the treatment group children was in a private, regular school; all the others were in segregated residential placements or lived at home and attended schools or sheltered workshops for autistic or retarded people. Among the controls at age 21, one had a regular job while living at home; the rest were in residential placements or attended sheltered schools or workshops.

These negative results regarding IQ and placements are surprising, given the high mean intelligence level of the treatment sample. Although only post hoc speculation about why the treatment group failed to achieve a better long-term outcome is possible, such an exercise may be instructive. In addition to the high unemployment rate in Great Britain for young adults cited by Howlin and Rutter (1987), we note three additional plausible factors. First, only two of the treatment group children were still very young (under 4 years of age) when treatment began. Second, the intervention was deliberately not very intensive. Weekly visits lasted only 6 months. Only 20–30 minutes a day were spent in structured one-to-one teaching sessions, with most of the children's training coming in brief incidental-teaching interactions spread across the day. Finally, the investigators had no control over what happened in their absence from the homes or in the special education classes most of the children attended. The likely significance of these factors will become apparent when we describe the UCLA early intervention project later.

5. In an independent follow-up study of the parents after completion of the project, Holmes, Hemsley, Rickett, and Likierman (1982) found that the 16 treatment group mothers reported that concrete methods of dealing with problems had been suggested to them; that they were able to talk productively about general family stresses during treatment; that the program was not unduly demanding or intrusive into family life; and that their children's behavior improved during and after the program. However, only half the mothers felt that the treatment techniques had helped them cope with new problems, and only five had used them to teach new skills.

In summary, parent training programs clearly have beneficial and worthwhile effects on both parents and their autistic children, and are generally well received by parents. In the absence of maintaining contingencies from outside the home, however, it appears that most parents eventually drop structured teaching sessions for one reason or another, such as illness, employment, other demands on their time, and meeting the needs of other family members (Harris, 1986b; Holmes et al., 1982). In spite of this, the children appear to maintain their gains for at least a year (Harris et al., 1981), perhaps because parents continue to use effective reinforcement and behavior management techniques informally. The long-term outcome in terms of an autistic individual's residential situation and employment prospects in early adulthood, however, may not be appreciably altered (Howlin & Rutter, 1987). Howlin and Rutter's (1987) conclusion reflects not a weakness of parent training efforts so much as an indication of the need for a more comprehensive intervention in such a serious disorder.

Parent Counseling

In addition to teaching parents better ways of interacting with their autistic child, work with a family typically entails providing guidance and assistance in dealing with various other problems related to living with a severely handicapped child (DeMyer, 1979; Donnellan & Mirenda, 1984; Harris, 1983; Kozloff, 1979; Schopler & Mesibov, 1984). Kozloff (1984) has noted that along with teaching parents learning principles and behavior management skills, those who conduct parent training programs should recognize that the family will also have four other broad sets of needs to be addressed. One set occurs soon after the diagnosis and consists of the problems each family member has in coming to grips with the long-term implications for family life of having a severely handicapped child (or sibling). A second set of needs revolves around the expectations other family members have for the autistic child and the roles they provide for the child in the family. Questions in this area include the following: "How should I feel about this child and what can I expect of him?"; "What roles should he play—alien? cross to bear? increasingly competent child?"; and "What are my roles—disciplinarian? teacher? attendant?" A third set of needs concerns the family as part of a larger social system, reflected in questions that ask, in essence, "How do I balance my obligations to the family, my work, and myself?" and "How do we become involved in a supportive network of other families in the same situation?" The final set of needs consists of practical treatment issues: "Where, specifically, do we start? What do we do next? What do I do when there are problems?"

Harris (1983) has provided a useful discussion of the actual difficulties most families face at some point and productive ways of helping them to deal with them. We can only mention some of these problems briefly in the context of this chapter, because of the scarcity of empirical intervention studies with this population of parents and the fact that many of the problems are the same as those treated in the general child and family clinical literature. Mentioning the problems will at least sensitize the clinician to the scope of issues that often arise in working with the families of autistic children.

Pragmatic Problems

The pragmatic problems confronting parents often arise from a lack of community resources, difficulty in locating appropriate services due to a lack of knowledge, and similar practical concerns. Some of these include dealing with school systems that are not committed to providing optimal educational services to autistic children; finding health service providers who are able and willing to work with a handicapped child; managing finances to cope with extra expenses, such as uninsured medical expenses and summer programs; finding free time away from the daily demands of rearing an autistic child; and making a decision about residential care as the autistic adolescent grows older. In this area, the clinician's experience in the community can be invaluable if it includes knowledge of (1) how particular school systems operate; (2) contact persons for support networks such as parents' associations; (3) capable health providers, lawyers, and financial planners; (4) sources of respite care, including other parents and college students; and (5) the available alternatives among residential providers and their relative quality in meeting the needs of autistic adults.

Emotional Problems

Problems such as depression, guilt, anger, and feelings of inadequacy affect all parents of autistic children to a greater or lesser degree at various times (DeMyer, 1979; Harris, 1983). Such problems require careful assessment to determine their seriousness and source. The main questions are whether they are normal reactions to living with a very difficult child or are due to something else, such as marital, work, or other problem areas. An estimate of severity and chronicity is necessary to decide whether supportive counseling should be followed up by a recommendation for more specific therapy.

Interpersonal Problems

The presence of an autistic child inevitably has an impact on the extended family system. As a consequence, there may be marital problems including lack of mutual support, withdrawal from family involvement, sexual problems, and other issues (DeMyer, 1979; Harris, 1983). Problems involving normal siblings can include a sibling's feeling resentment or embarrassment about the autistic sibling; not being allowed to go places or do things because the autistic sibling cannot participate; being given too much responsibility for the care of the autistic sibling or too little guidance in how to interact appropriately with the sibling; and not receiving a fair share of the parents' attention (Harris, 1983; McHale, Simeonsson, & Sloan, 1984). Grandparents, friends, colleagues at work, and even strangers encountered in the community can create problems with uninvited advice and criticism. Helping families to cope with such problems may well involve several different levels of intervention, which again should flow from an adequate assessment of the exact nature and scope of the difficulties. The possibility that relatively simple interventions can have important extra benefits should not be overlooked. For example, in the area of sibling relationships, Schreibman et al. (1983) found that teaching normal siblings how to teach play skills to their autistic siblings led to measurable improvements in the normal siblings' attitudes and feelings toward their autistic siblings.

Finally, it is important to avoid an exclusive emphasis on the negative aspects of the presence of a handicapped child in the family, which are stressed in most research. It should be kept in mind that the child can make some important positive contributions, such as helping the parents to learn love, patience, acceptance, and discriminations between the important and trivial aspects of life (Turnbull, Blue-Banning, Behr, & Kerns, 1986). Bristol (1984) has identified successful coping strategies used by parents of autistic children that should be encouraged. The strategies ranked as most important by the parents fell into the following categories: (1) helping the child, expressed in the statements "learning how to help my child improve" and "believing that my child's program has my family's best interests in mind"; (2) controlling the meaning of the child's disability by endowing it with a higher significance ("believing in God") or making positive comparison with the "worse" past and the "better" present and future ("telling myself that I have many things I should be thankful for"; "believing that my child will get better"); (3) seeking spousal support ("talking over personal concerns and feelings with my spouse"); (4) focusing on the family ("building a closer relationship with my spouse"; "trying to maintain family stability"; "doing things with my children"); and (5) engaging in self-development through the cultivation of interests and activities not directly related to the child ("developing myself as a person").

Parent training and counseling programs can achieve the short-term benefit of improved child behavior in the home and general family functioning that they are designed to achieve (Kolko, 1984). However, it is equally clear that, as usually conducted, they can only do so much to alter the course of an autistic child's life. Something more is needed to achieve major long-term benefits. A few investigators have addressed the possibility that intensive early intervention may provide the additional therapeutic efficacy needed.

EARLY INTERVENTION

The logic of early intervention with autistic children extends beyond the well-known observation that considerable neurological development continues for years after birth (Jacobson, 1978). It is also apparent that the brain can exhibit considerable plasticity in overcoming early insults (Huttenlocher, 1988), and that the development and maintenance of cortical synaptic connections in the young child are influenced by sensory input; in other words, "to a certain extent experience determines the anatomy of the system" (Huttenlocher, 1988, p. 105). Directly relevant are scattered reports of recovery to normal levels of intellectual, linguistic, social, and educational or vocational functioning in individual cases of children who were clearly autistic (DeMyer et al., 1973; Gajzago & Prior, 1974; Groden, Domingue, Chesnick, Groden, & Baron, 1983; Kanner, 1973; Rimland, 1964). Such reports encourage the idea that more autistic children might attain a good long-term outcome if appropriate treatment were provided early enough and intensively enough.

Currently, intensive early intervention programs tend to be either home-based (Groden et al., 1983; Lovaas, 1987; Lovaas & Smith, in press) or classroom-based (Fenske et al., 1985; Rincover et al., 1985; Strain et al., 1985). Such a categorization is convenient but only partly accurate; in both types of programs there is extensive carryover between home and classroom or day care environments. Some programs involving good experimental controls are described to illustrate what can be accomplished.

The UCLA Autism Project

In 1970, Lovaas and his colleagues at the UCLA Psychology Department began treating very young (under 4 years of age) autistic children in their homes by teaching the parents to be the primary therapists, with the direction and help of graduate and undergraduate students who worked along with them in the homes (Lovaas, 1987; Lovaas & Smith, in press). The children in this intensive treatment group of 19 children received at least 40 hours a week of one-to-one treatment. The children in a control group of 19 children (control group 1), who could not be served by the project because of the distance of their homes from UCLA or an insufficient number of uncommitted staff members at the time of referral, attended special education classes and received 10 or fewer hours a week of one-to-one treatment. A second, no-contact control group (control group 2) consisted of 21 children from a larger group being followed at the UCLA Medical School during the same time period in a long-term study of cognitive and language characteristics (Freeman et al., 1985). Most of these children also attended special education classes. All the children's tested MA scores were normalized to 30 months to adjust for variations in CA at the time of testing, according to the following formula: prorated mental age (PMA) = MA/CA × 30. The mean PMA of the intensive treatment group was 18.8 months; in control group 1 it was 17.1, and in control group 2 it was 17.6 (statistically insignificant differences). Converted to ratio IQ estimates, the intensive treatment group mean was 63; the control group 1 mean was 57, and the control group 2 mean was 59 (Lovaas & Smith, in press). Measures of language, play, self-stimulatory behaviors, and problem behaviors showed no significant differences between the intensive treatment group and control group 1.

Treatment was conducted for at least 2 years, and longer for some children who needed more help. During the first year, the parents were trained in an apprenticeship model, working with experienced graduate students for a minimum of 10 hours a week in the home. Undergraduate students worked with each child in the home for 20–30 hours a week. The program for the intensive treatment group was that described in Lovaas (1981). The first phase of treatment was devoted to teaching imitation, simple toy play, self-help skills, and affectionate behaviors. Disruptive, self-stimulatory, and self-injurious behaviors were eliminated through shaping appropriate alternative behaviors, extinction, time out, and (as a last resort) a loud reprimand sometimes paired with a slap on the thigh. Studies conducted with samples of the children (Ackerman, 1980; McEachin & Leaf, 1984) indicated that if only positive reinforcement was used in treatment, only minor reductions occurred in problem behaviors, and small and unstable gains were achieved in appropriate language and play behaviors, over varying time periods up to 2 years. The introduction of punishment for self-stimulatory, aggressive, and noncompliant behaviors resulted in rapid and stable reductions in inappropriate behaviors and rapid, stable increases in appropriate behaviors.

The second phase of treatment emphasized expressive speech and complex language, interactive play with peers, and closely supervised exposures to normal nursery school settings. The third phase focused on teaching observational learning, classroom skills, and understanding cause–effect relationships and social rules. When the children were ready to enter preschool, the parents selected teachers who already imposed some structure on the children in the preschool and would collaborate closely with the mothers regarding the autistic children's treatment and progress. When the children were old enough for kindergarten, as many as possible were placed in regular kindergartens in public schools, with the autism diagnosis withheld to avoid placement in a special education program. After kindergarten, placement was left up to school personnel.

The main outcome data were obtained when the children were 6–7 years old (Lovaas, 1987). Table 8-3 shows the distribution of educational placements and IQs for the three groups of children. Of the 19 subjects in the intensive treatment group, 9 (47%) were educationally and intellectually normal. They had successfully completed the first grade, had been recommended for promotion by their teachers to a regular second-grade class, and scored at or above average on standardized IQ tests. In contrast, none of the children in control group 1 obtained a regular class placement, and only one of the children in control group 2 did so. Only two children (11%) in the intensive treatment group were still classified as autistic; they had been placed in classes for autistic/retarded children and scored in the severely to profoundly retarded range (IQ < 30). In the control groups, 53% (11 children in control group 1 and 10 in control group 2) were in autistic/retarded classes.

The only pretreatment measure showing a

significant difference between the children in the intensive treatment group who had a normal outcome and those who did not was PMA (although it did not predict outcome very well in individual cases). The PMA was 20.9 months at intake for the 9 children who became normal (roughly equivalent to a ratio IQ of 70; range 43–83), significantly higher than that of the 10 who did not (PMA = 17.0, equivalent to a ratio IQ of 58) (Lovaas & Smith, in press). The children's initial response to treatment seemed to be a better predictor of outcome than PMA. A systematic study has not yet been done, but children who learned motor and verbal imitation and receptive commands at a faster rate during the first 3 months of treatment were far more likely to have a normal outcome than children who did not (Lovaas & Smith, in press). McEachin (1987) conducted a long-term follow up of the normal-outcome children when their average age was 14 and compared them with a group of normal adolescents of the same age on measures of intelligence, adaptive behavior, and personality. The normal-outcome

TABLE 8-3 Educational Placements and IQs of Experimental and Control Groups in the UCLA Autism Project

	Normal[a]	Aphasic[b]	Autistic/ retarded[c]
Experimental			
Number	9	8	2
Mean IQ	107	70	30
IQ range	94–120	56–95	—
Control group 1			
Number	0	8	11
Mean IQ	—	74	36
IQ range	—	30–120	20–73
Control group 2			
Number	1	10	10
Mean IQ	99	67	44
IQ range	—	49–81	35–54

Note. From "Behavioral Treatment and Normal Educational and Intellectual Functioning in Young Autistic Children" by O. I. Lovaas, 1987, Journal of Consulting and Clinical Psychology, 55, p. 7. Copyright 1987 by the American Psychological Association. Reprinted by permission.
[a] Normal first-grade classroom.
[b] Aphasic, language-delayed, language-handicapped, learning-disabled classroom.
[c] Autistic or mentally retarded classroom.

children showed some significant differences from the normal controls on some of the personality items, but scored overall in the normal range on the tests. Residual deficits in language use or social behavior in some of the children were minor and not noticeable to school personnel.

A few of the conclusions that Lovaas and Smith (in press) have drawn from their findings are directly relevant to treatment. First autistic children seem to be constituted of two groups, one with the potential to become normal-functioning and one with a less favorable prognosis. Children with higher MAs are more likely to fall into the former group, but initial response to intensive behavioral treatment seems to be a better way of estimating prognosis. For children in the lower-functioning group, the main focus early in treatment might be on self-help skills, which would allow them to become as independent as possible. With this group, unlike the higher group, the use of aversive procedures (except, presumably, for dangerous behaviors unresponsive to other treatments) would not be justified because they would not be likely to lead to long-term benefits.

In addition to intensive teaching, the use of aversive consequences for maladaptive behaviors seems to be a key ingredient in the success of higher-functioning children, but even with higher-functioning children, regular use of aversive consequences would not be ethically justifiable unless they were in a treatment program as intensive as that provided to the intensive treatment group in the study. In less intensive programs, such as those provided to the control groups, there is insufficient training in appropriate alternative behaviors to justify the use of strong punishers (Lovaas & Smith, in press).

The main variable accounting for the success of nearly half the children treated was the intensity of treatment, quantified as 40 hours a week of one-to-one teaching but involving much more in qualitative terms. All the significant people in the autistic children's lives (parents, siblings, peers, teachers) administered comprehensive training across all of the children's environments (home, neighborhood, school) under the supervision of experts in behavioral treatment. Generalized improvement required addressing many domains of behavior instead of one or two domains, such as language or cognitive skills. Thus, ideal educational services for young autistic children would include teaching at home and in the community in close collaboration with the parents by someone skilled in behavioral methods, who addresses many areas of functioning concurrently (Lovaas & Smith, in press).

School-Based Programs

Fenske et al. (1985) compared outcomes for nine children who entered their comprehensive behavioral treatment program prior to age 5 (mean, 4.1 years) and nine who entered after age 5 (mean, 8.4 years). The program includes a day school, group homes for children in need of residential intervention, parent training, transition programs for children approaching discharge, and postdischarge follow-up services. Six of the nine younger children achieved successful placements in either regular classrooms in public schools (four children) or in special education classrooms in public schools (two children). Only one child in the older group achieved a regular classroom public school placement; the other eight remained in treatment. The advantages of early treatment for the younger children accrued in spite of the fact that the six older children who were testable had higher MAs (mean, 4.9 years) at entry than the younger children, only one of whom was testable (2.2 years), and were in the treatment program for a much longer period of time (6.0 years vs. 3.8 years).

Strain et al. (1985) provided an integrated preschool program for six autistic and "autistic-like" children who were 2.5–4.4 years of age at entry and scored in the mildly to severely retarded ranges of intelligence. Ten nonhandicapped peers were extensively involved in peer-mediated instruction with the autistic children, as described earlier. The parents of the autistic children received 12 hours a week of training in behavioral methods, in order to extend instruction into the home. After 2 years of treatment, the children showed increases in eight developmental domains of the Learning Accomplishment Profile (LeMay, Griffin, & Sanford, 1977) to normal levels for their CAs. The domains were Comprehension, Naming, Object Play, Matching, Counting, Writing, Gross Motor, and Fine Motor. Observational measures showed that the autistic children engaged in positive social interactions as frequently as their nonhandicapped classmates and were equivalent in measures of language, on-task behavior, and deviant behaviors.

Rincover *et al.* (1985) have studied the initial gains of a group of seven young autistic children in their behavioral preschool program at Surrey Place Centre in Toronto. The children were 2.5–3.5 years of age upon entering the program, and their MAs ranged from 1.1 to 1.9 years. Six children were functionally mute, vocalizing only vowel sounds; the remaining child was echolalic, parroting two or three words without any apparent meaning. All of the children engaged in tantrums or self-stimulatory, aggressive, or self-injurious behaviors. The program emphasized reduction of maladaptive behaviors, social development, and language. Each child had four individualized (or small-group) 30-minute language training sessions each day, two concerned with expressive speech and two with receptive language.

During the 9–15 months of treatment for these seven children, their MAs increased an average of 14 months, social ages an average of 18 months, expressive language an average of 12 months, and receptive language an average of 17 months. Inappropriate, self-stimulatory, and self-injurious behaviors were virtually eliminated in six of the seven children, and decreased substantially in the seventh child. Five of the seven children were placed in integrated day care or preschool programs. Standardized follow-up measures continue to be obtained; however, all of the children appear to be functioning well.

The results revealed that the younger autistic children improved substantially more than older autistic children (7–16 years old) who were matched to the younger children on MA and other characteristics and received the same treatment (Rincover *et al.*, 1985). It appeared that early intervention was beneficial not because more time was spent with the younger children, nor because the younger children were functioning at a higher cognitive level. Some reasons why the improvements may have occurred are indicated by two process studies concerned with the establishment of social reinforcers and stimulus generalization. Previously, in the section on social behaviors, we have described the difficulties in establishing social reinforcers in autistic children in the context of studies conducted with older children. Taggart and Rincover (1985) investigated whether social reinforcers could be developed in very young retarded and autistic children. Several novel tasks were selected for the preschool-age

and the older (control group) children, and these were taught in sessions using only praise as a consequence for correct responding. At first, the children did not learn despite hundreds of trials, showing that praise did not function as a reinforcer, just as was found by Lovaas, Freitag, *et al.* (1966). After about 2 months of treatment, however, every one of the seven preschool children was learning a variety of new tasks when praise alone was used as the reinforcer; none of the older children were learning any of their tasks with praise only. Moreover, it was found that a wide variety of praise statements were effective with new as well as familiar trainers, both at home and at school, enabling the natural social environment to strengthen and maintain many important behaviors.

The second study assessed whether generalization of treatment gains was acquired faster by younger than by older children. Much has been written about the need to program generalization, since it does not normally occur as a by-product of simply teaching new behaviors to developmentally disabled children (Horner, Dunlap, & Koegel, 1988; Stokes & Baer, 1977). It is noteworthy, however, that most generalization research has been conducted with children in middle childhood or later. Cardella and Rincover (1985) investigated whether younger developmentally delayed children would show more generalization of newly trained skills than older, matched children. Each of six younger (2.5–3.4 years) and older (5.4–10 years) children were taught both a new expressive (e.g., "What's this?") and receptive ("Find the ———") language task. Nearly all of the younger children generalized both tasks to new settings and new staff members, while only one of the older children showed any generalization. The results suggest that there may be a critical period for generalization, with younger children showing substantially more generalization. These experiments on social reinforcement and generalization suggest some fundamental process variables that bear further study in accounting for the relative superiority of early over later intervention with autistic and other developmentally disabled children. They may be the behavioral correlates of the neurological plasticity assumed to underlie the beneficial effects obtained.

In the aggregate, the findings of these early intervention programs seem to justify the following conclusions. Measured intelligence in autistic children can be significantly increased instead of remaining stable, as is usually found (DeMyer *et al.*, 1981; Freeman *et al.*, 1985; Howlin & Rutter, 1987), and about 40%–50% of autistic children can succeed in regular classes at age-appropriate grade levels in public schools, again contrary to the usual findings (DeMyer *et al.*, 1973; Freeman *et al.*, 1985; Howlin & Rutter, 1987). For these outcomes to occur, the following conditions seem to be necessary: (1) The child is functioning in the normal through moderately retarded ranges of intelligence; (2) treatment begins at an early age (2–4 years); and (3) the treatment is behaviorally oriented, intensive, and extensive (in terms of hours per day of direct instruction, involvement of well-trained peers and family members, and consistency across home and educational environments).

BEHAVIOR ANALYSIS AND MANAGEMENT

The extensive scope of the literature on the analysis and management of severe problem behaviors in autistic and other severely handicapped children precludes detailed discussion of specific treatment procedures (e.g., see the books by Axelrod & Apsche, 1983; Evans & Meyer, 1985; Koegel, Rincover, & Egel, 1982; Matson & DiLorenzo, 1984; Whitman *et al.*, 1983). Instead, we mention briefly three of the most important directions this area is currently taking.

Functional Analysis

Improved methods for assessing the causes of problem behaviors are emerging as greater attention is being addressed to the need to improve treatment effectiveness, generality, and durability by manipulating the most relevant variables. A treatment derived logically from the assessment can often be implemented with gains in timeliness and accountability as well.

One emerging approach is concerned with obtaining information on the correlates of a problem behavior throughout the individual's waking hours instead of in just a few situations. The attempt is to map problematic situations to facilitate the search for events functionally related to the behavior. For example, Touchette, MacDonald, and Langer (1985) have demonstrated the value of collecting data across the day in 30-minute intervals on problem behaviors, so that they can be related to the events regularly occurring during those intervals. Instead of attempting to count each response, the data collector simply marks each interval to indicate whether or not the behavior occurred and, perhaps, whether it was a major or minor episode according to a rule for discriminating between the two (which can be as simple as, e.g., "two or fewer responses" vs. "three or more responses" for some purposes). Over a period of a few weeks, such a chart takes on the appearance of a scatter plot, with time intervals on one axis and days on the other. Inspection of the scatter plot reveals any patterns in the behavior during times of day and on different days of the week or month. Investigation of the activities and persons associated with different levels of the behavior can suggest changes that might reduce the problem behavior. A scatter plot is also useful even if no patterns in the behavior emerge, because the lack of patterning should eliminate some initial hypotheses and suggest consideration of the possibilities that (1) there is a lack of structure in the environment (Touchette *et al.*, 1985, Case 3); (2) the behavior is not under reliable stimulus control, but instead is maintained by an erratic schedule of intermittent reinforcement or by its sensory consequences (Lovaas, Newsom, & Hickman, 1987; Rincover, 1978); or (3) the behavior results from randomly occurring environmental factors (e.g., the presence of substitute staff members) or noncyclical, randomly occurring physical problems (e.g., infections, toothaches, headaches).

Another growing trend in the assessment of problem behaviors is the use of functional analysis procedures in analogue situations that permit a high degree of control over variables that may influence a behavior. Functional analysis methods have been used in laboratory settings for many years with autistic children for the study of such behaviors as self-injury (Carr *et al.*, 1976; Lovaas & Simmons, 1969; Rincover & Devany, 1982), self-stimulatory behavior (Lovaas, Litrownik, & Mann, 1971; Rincover, 1978), aggression (Carr *et al.*, 1980), tantrums (Carr & Newsom, 1985), and other behaviors. In these and many related studies, only one or two variables (e.g., social attention, adult demands, sensory extinction) were compared with a control or baseline condition. Increasingly, investigators are studying the effects of several variables in combinations of assessment conditions that are scheduled according to reversal designs (Baer, Wolf, & Risley, 1968) or alternating-treatments designs (Barlow & Hayes, 1979). One condition serves as a control condition, and several additional conditions sample variables that may be related to the behavior under study.

For example, Iwata, Dorsey, Slifer, Bauman, and Richman (1982) created four assessment conditions based on the experimental literature on the motivation of self-injurious behavior. The variables assessed were contingent attention (Lovaas & Simmons, 1969), self-stimulation (Favell, McGimsey, & Schell, 1982; Rincover & Devany, 1982), and adults' demands (Carr et al., 1976), in comparison with a control condition designed to minimize self-injury by including high levels of reinforcement and play materials. Each condition was conducted for two 15-minute sessions (a total of eight randomly ordered sessions a day in a simultaneous treatment design) until responding stabilized or 12 days of sessions were completed. Despite the differences between subjects in overall levels of self-injury, most individuals showed higher rates of self-injury in one condition than in the others, although the patterns of several suggested that their self-injury served multiple functions. The procedure is easily adapted to the assessment of other problem behaviors and has recently been used to evaluate aggression (Mace, Page, Ivancic, & O'Brien, 1986), pica (Mace & Knight, 1986), and stereotypy (Stanley, 1985).

Carr and Durand (1985a) developed and validated an analogue assessment procedure for identifying two common antecedents of various problem behaviors (e.g., aggression, tantrums, object destruction, self-injury) of autistic and other developmentally disabled children in classrooms. Their procedure examined the effects of manipulating the level of adult attention and the level of task difficulty in separate conditions. Unlike the Iwata et al. (1982) procedure described above, Carr and Durand (1985a) used a reversal design, leaving each condition in force in repeated sessions across several days. Three distinctive patterns of motivation were implicated in the data. Two children's disruptive behaviors were escape-motivated, another child's were attention-seeking, and for a fourth child, both attention seeking and escape were factors. Support for the validity of these conclusions appeared in a second experiment in the Carr and Durand (1985a) study. There they showed that teaching each child a verbal phrase relevant to his motivation as an appropriate alternative response reduced disruptive behavior; teaching an irrelevant phrase did not. For example, escape-motivated children were successfully taught to say, "I don't understand," to prompt assistance from the teacher instead of engaging in disruptive behaviors. On the other hand, teaching these children a verbal attention-seeking response ("Am I doing good work?") did *not* result in less disruptive behavior, because it was irrelevant to the motivation of their behavior. Exactly the reverse occurred with attention-seeking children. Similar assessment and validation procedures have been applied to non-contextual, "psychotic" speech (Durand & Crimmins, 1987) and self-stimulatory behavior (Durand & Carr, 1987).

Emphasis on Function over Form

Multiple-condition analogue procedures like those just described not only help with immediate treatment concerns, but also indicate the value of reconceptualizing problem behaviors in terms of their functional relationships to other events, instead of in ways that simply describe the topographical or emotional aspects of such behaviors. One result of such a reconceptualization will ultimately be a more useful way of classifying problem behaviors— specifically, in terms of their functions (e.g., escape, attention seeking, self-stimulation) instead of their topographies (e.g., self-injury, aggression, tantrum). Efforts in this direction will require the study of more individuals and problem behaviors than have been studied to date, but work in this area is progressing at a steady pace (e.g., Durand, 1986; Durand & Crimmins, 1988; Iwata et al., 1982).

The general outline of a functional classification system might take the form of three general classes: positively reinforced behaviors (those maintained by attention and tangible reinforcers, as well as those maintained by their automatic sensory consequences); negatively reinforced behaviors (those that function to help a child escape or avoid aversive stimuli); and elicited or "emotionally induced" (Segal, 1972) behaviors (those that occur as a reaction to an aversive stimulus without subsequently coming under reinforcement control, such as pain-elicited aggression [Hutchinson, 1977] and self-injury in response to painful medical conditions [Carr, 1977]). A somewhat different proposal has been made by Carr and Durand (1985a, 1985b), who focus on problem behaviors mediated by the social environment. They suggest classifying problem behaviors in the categories of escape behavior (controlled by negative reinforcement processes) and attention-seeking behavior (controlled by positive reinforcement processes). Carr and Durand (1985b) have noted that, just as most problem behaviors have been found to serve multiple social functions, researchers who study language have observed that communicative acts serve multiple functions (Halliday, 1975; Skinner, 1957). Carr and Durand (1985b) argue that the similarity between problem behaviors and communicative acts may not be fortuitous, but an indication that problem behaviors may also be forms of communication.

Support for the communication hypothesis of problem behaviors comes from the developmental literature as well as the literature on developmental disabilities. For example, analyses of infant crying show a significant negative correlation between infants' communication and crying by the end of the first year (Bell & Ainsworth, 1972). Such evidence led Bruner (1979) to conclude that infant cries may be a primitive form of communication from which speech eventually emerges. In the literature on developmental disabilities, Casey (1978) found that after the parents of four autistic children were trained to reinforce their children's spontaneous sign language, communicative signing increased and problem behaviors such as tantrums, aggression, and self-injury decreased. Talkington, Hall, and Altman (1971) compared matched groups of communicative and noncommunicative retarded individuals with respect to several measures of aggression and found that the noncommunicative group received substantially higher ratings of aggression. The authors suggested that aggression was serving a function for the noncommunicative individuals that speech served for the communicative individuals. Finally, in an experimental instead of a correlational study, Carr and Durand (1985a) found that teaching disruptive children a communicative phrase related to the motivation of their disruptive behaviors eliminated those behaviors, as described above.

The value of viewing problem behaviors as primitive communicative acts offers the promise of more effective and durable treatments than are possible when functional aspects of the behavior are not addressed, and, instead, problem behaviors are viewed simply as deviant behaviors that are symptoms of an underlying disorder. The implication of the communication hypothesis for long-term treatment development is that children with problem behaviors should be provided with an appropriate communicative response that serves the same function as the problem behavior. A "replacement" rather than a "suppression" strategy can be expected to lead to more general and longer-lasting results. Although there are situations that require rapid suppression of dangerous or harmful behaviors, such measures should be viewed as temporary only (Carr, 1988; Carr & Durand, 1985b; Durand, 1986).

On Nonaversive Intervention

The advocacy of nonaversive approaches to the treatment of problem behaviors has recently reached the status of a movement, including professional (Guess, Helmstetter, Turnbull, & Knowlton, 1987; Sobsey, 1987), political (Meyer, 1988b), and philosophical (Turnbull, Guess, et al., 1986) dimensions. Such debate is hardly new (e.g., Roos, 1972) and is having the desirable effects of spurring the development of additional nonaversive procedures (Bellamy, 1988); encouraging clinicians to look beyond immediate antecedents and consequences at broader ecological and systemic shortcomings contributing to problem behaviors (Evans & Meyer, 1985; Meyer, 1988a); and provoking thought about ethical issues at a deeper level than is customary (Guess et al., 1987: Turnbull, Guess, et al., 1986). However, the current debate includes two new themes that take extreme positions. One theme is that aversive procedures are always morally wrong and should therefore never be used (Turnbull, Guess, et al., 1986). The other theme is that the technology of nonaversive treatment is sufficiently well developed to make aversive procedures largely or completely obsolete (Meyer, 1988a; Sobsey, 1987). Although a full discussion of these propositions is impossible here, some points can be noted.

1. Turnbull, Guess, et al. (1986) review various religious doctrines, philosophical ethical systems, and professional association standards, and by their own account fail to find unequivocal support for the proposal that aver-

sive interventions (defined as those causing pain or discomfort) are always immoral. However, the position is eventually justified by combining the reciprocity test of several religious and ethical systems ("What is right is what we want for ourselves and therefore want for others") with two assumptions: that aversive procedures are generally of doubtful efficacy, harming the therapist as well as the recipient; and that there are always effective positive alternatives available. Surely few would disagree with the reciprocity test; it can, in fact, be used to justify the use of aversive interventions in those situations in which the two assumptions made by the authors are incorrect. The existence of such situations is evident both in the literature on punishment and in the informed opinions of many professionals with extensive experience in treating severe problem behaviors with both positive and aversive interventions (e.g., Axelrod & Apsche, 1983; Favell, 1983; Favell, Azrin, et al., 1982; Foxx, 1982; Lovaas & Smith, in press; Matson & DiLorenzo, 1984; Newsom, Favell, & Rincover, 1983). At a more fundamental level, the methodology of the Turnbull, Guess, et al. (1986) article is questionable. The attempt to derive generalizable ethical precepts applicable to every case from universal philosophical principles conflicts with the recognition within philosophy that most ethical questions involving practical human affairs are best approached from a "case ethics" perspective—one that considers the relevant variables present in actual situations (Toulmin, 1988). Such an approach is common in medical ethics and judicial rulings, for example. Applied to the treatment of problem behaviors in autistic and other developmentally disabled persons, this approach involves consideration of such situational variables as the nature of the risks posed by the behavior, the person's level of functioning, previous treatment history and currently available alternative treatments, the parents' feelings, and the number of staff members available and their expertise in implementing behavioral procedures correctly. An ethically and morally correct decision seems more likely to flow from attention to these and other relevant factors than from an exclusive focus on general precepts.

2. The position that nonaversive interventions are sufficient to treat all or most severe problem behaviors successfully (Meyer, 1988a; Sobsey, 1987) may be a prescient view of the future, but as a subjective judgment about the current state of research and practice, it has limited empirical support at the present time (Berkman & Meyer, 1988; Evans & Meyer, 1985; Guess et al., 1987; LaVigna & Donnellan, 1986). Moreover, although nonaversive treatment successes will undoubtedly be reported at an increasing rate over the coming years, the desirability of nonaversive interventions may be more open to question than is usually thought if "nonaversive" is interpreted to mean strictly positive reinforcement approaches. (We should note that if "aversive" includes procedures that cause "discomfort" [Turnbull, Guess, et al., 1986], many very mild punishers as well as extinction can be deemed objectionable.) There is, for example, research showing that in normal children punishment enhances imitation, social approach, compliance, academic performance, and responsiveness to positive reinforcement (Nordquist & McEvoy, 1983; Pfiffner & O'Leary, 1987; Wahler, 1969; Wahler & Nordquist, 1973). More directly relevant are studies with autistic children showing that the acquisition of appropriate behaviors may be slow and unstable even with consistent positive reinforcement and that problem behaviors may not decrease until punishment is used (Ackerman, 1980; Koegel & Covert, 1972; Koegel et al., 1974; McEachin & Leaf, 1984). Finally, a number of important, desirable side effects of punishment are reported in studies with autistic children, such as increased attention, social interaction, appropriate play, imitation, learning, and positive emotional behaviors (Newsom et al., 1983). These effects can often be produced solely through the use of positive reinforcement, of course, but sometimes they cannot be (e.g., Ackerman, 1980; McEachin & Leaf, 1984). In the aggregate, these lines of research seem to caution that a completely nonaversive approach is capable of precluding or delaying unnecessarily the attainment of important treatment goals. At the very least, it can be concluded that ethical issues in this area are more complex than they often appear.

3. Finally, it is important to recognize that abuses of aversive interventions can and do occur; therefore, it is incumbent on clinicians to know and follow relevant guidelines on the use of such procedures (e.g., Favell, Azrin, et al., 1982; Hannah, Christian, & Clark, 1981; Matson & DiLorenzo, 1984). The use of such procedures requires conscientious trials of nonaversive treatments; a convincing demon-

stration of their inadequacy; provision of competent training in functionally equivalent alternative behaviors; informed consent and active participation by the parents to the extent possible; a system of valid, objective, daily data collection; direct supervision by an experienced behavioral psychologist; and periodic, unbiased peer review. Adherence to such practices does not insure the morality of aversive procedures, but it does greatly increase accountability, a prerequisite to the ethical use of any treatment procedure.

CONCLUSIONS

A few very general conclusions seem to emerge from this review of behavioral approaches to the treatment of autistic children. They apply to theoretical, treatment, and service delivery aspects of this field.

1. The variety of procedures described in this chapter may suggest a great increase in the complexity of the behavioral treatment of autistic children. To some extent this is true, but the increase is largely due to an increase in the range and complexity of the problems to which fairly basic teaching techniques are applied. The basic elements of teaching—giving instructions, lending assistance with prompts when necessary, providing appropriate consequences depending on the quality or quantity of the child's response, gradually withdrawing the assistance to establish independent responding—appear in one form or another in all the procedures described here. What has changed over the last 25 years are the situations in which these elements are applied (homes, classrooms, playgrounds, and other community settings in addition to treatment rooms); the instructional formats in which they are used (various naturalistic and incidental-teaching interactions in addition to formal discrete-trial sessions); and the complexity of the behaviors they have been used to teach (observational learning, social interaction, spontaneous verbal and signed language, etc., in addition to eye contact and verbal imitation).

2. The most distinctive characteristic of autistic children, social unrelatedness, can be addressed in meaningful ways at various levels of complexity. The more extensive improvements require changes in the children's social environment as well as direct treatment of specific

social deficits. The involvement of normal peers in integrated settings appears to be essential to the maintenance and elaboration of age-appropriate social behaviors (Strain, 1983). Unfortunately, society's typical treatment models (segregated classrooms, group homes, and developmental centers) have yet to incorporate many changes that would facilitate social development. However, models of service delivery are subject to selection by consequences, just as species, individual behaviors, cultural practices, and scientific theories are (Kuhn, 1962; Skinner, 1981). We can therefore expect that most existing models will eventually change to more closely resemble behaviorally oriented home-based programs (Lovaas, 1987), educational programs (Rincover et al., 1985; Strain et al., 1985) and combined residential–educational programs (Christian, 1983; Fenske et al., 1985). Those models that do not change will probably replicate the decline of the state institutional model over the last two decades (Scheerenberger, 1986).

3. Operant speech training is sometimes criticized for its apparent neglect of cognitive and developmental variables believed to be important in normal language acquisition (e.g., Seibert & Oller, 1981; Yoder & Calculator, 1981). Two observations (among many that could be offered) seem pertinent.

a. Linguistic input, modeling, imitation, and reinforcement are all correlates of normal language development (deVilliers & deVilliers, 1978) that are used routinely and effectively in behavioral language interventions. Although a large number of other correlates of normal language acquisition have been discovered, it is not yet known which are critical and should be included in remediation efforts and which are clinically insignificant. Thus, the key questions are these: (i) Which other correlates are both causal and important? (ii) Which of those that are causal and important are also manipulable? and (iii) How can they be manipulated most effectively in treatment?

b. Fortunately, theoretical conflict between psycholinguists and behaviorists may give way to some convergence (Carr, 1985). Some psycholinguists have "discovered the operant," in Segal's (1975) phrase, increasingly sharing traditional behavioral concerns with the functional or pragmatic aspects of language in its social context (Bates, 1976; Halliday, 1975). At the same time, behaviorists have documented and addressed the limitations of their language teaching efforts (Harris, 1975; Lovaas, 1987; Lovaas et al., 1973) and have sought new ideas in various places, including the developmental psycholinguistic literature (Koegel, O'Dell, & Koegel, 1987; Laski et al., 1988). Although complete convergence is still a long way off because of large differences in scientific epistemology, goals, methods, and language, some attempts at meaningful conversation are taking place.

4. Work with an autistic child and her family frequently presents the problem of balancing efforts toward the child and efforts toward the rest of the family system. At different times the priorities change, necessitating considerable sensitivity and flexibility. One approach is to deliberately minimize changes in family life, but this solution may serve neither the child nor the family very well. Lovaas and Smith (in press) noted that by providing several volunteer students for the autistic child in each family they worked with, the parents had an additional 20–30 hours a week free to take care of other family members and attend to personal needs. Thus, an intensive program does not necessarily entail either a stressful or an expensive one.

5. Although there are no pivotal behaviors that, when taught, produce rapid, widespread change, there are what might be called "keystone" behaviors (Rincover, 1981) operating on a smaller scale that produce additional gains beyond those achieved directly. For example, teaching either functionally incompatible behaviors, such as compliance to instructions (Russo et al., 1981), or functionally equivalent behaviors, such as communicative phrases relevant to the function of a problem behavior (Carr, 1988; Carr & Durand, 1985b), automatically produces corollary improvements in disruptive behaviors. Similarly, acquisition of functionally incompatible appropriate play skills reduces self-stimulatory behaviors (Eason et al., 1982), especially if the toys provide sensory stimulation functionally equivalent to that involved in the self-stimulatory behaviors (Favell, McGimsey, & Schell, 1982; Rincover et al., 1979). Such findings indicate the value of analyzing the contingencies of reinforcement surrounding the behaviors of autistic children and the measurement of the multiple effects of treatments (Newsom et al., 1983).

6. The behavioral approach to the treatment of autistic children can reach a considerable distance down the intelligence continuum, into the severely and profoundly retarded ranges, and achieve some remarkable effects. However, it seems that to bring about recovery to normal or near-normal functioning, behavioral treatment needs some help from nature in the form of a central nervous system still open to major modifications with sufficiently intensive and well-timed interventions. A medical analogy is apt: The successful treatment of many diseases requires some help from nature in the form of a reasonably healthy immune system. However, it is also true that this conclusion tells us more about the current state of our technology than about preordained limits on the children's progress. Advances in our understanding of behavioral and neurological processes show no signs of slowing down, suggesting the possibility of major changes in our work with autistic children in the future. Importantly, as this chapter has shown, there is much that can be done now.

REFERENCES

Ackerman, A. B. (1980). The role of punishment in the treatment of preschool-aged autistic children: Effects and side effects. Unpublished doctoral dissertation, University of California at Los Angeles.

Altman, K., & Krupshaw, R. (1982). Increasing eye contact by head-holding. Analysis and Intervention in Developmental Disabilities, 2, 319–327.

American Psychiatric Association (APA). (1980). Diagnostic and statistical manual of mental disorders (3rd ed.). Washington, DC: Author.

American Psychiatric Association (APA). (1987). Diagnostic and statistical manual of mental disorders (3rd ed., rev.). Washington, DC: Author.

Anderson, S. (1982). Programming language teaching opportunities in an SMH classroom: An analysis of teacher and child behavior. Unpublished doctoral dissertation, University of Kansas.

Axelrod, S., & Apsche, J. (Eds.). (1983). The effects of punishment on human behavior. New York: Academic Press.

Baer, D. M. (1978). The behavioral analysis of trouble. In K. E. Allen, V. A. Holm, & R. L. Schiefelbusch (Eds.), Early intervention—a team approach (pp. 57–93). Baltimore: University Park Press.

Baer, D. M., Peterson, R. F., & Sherman, J. A. (1967). The development of imitation by reinforcing behavioral similarity to a model. Journal of the Experimental Analysis of Behavior, 10, 405–416.

Baer, D. M., Wolf, M. M., & Risley, T. R. (1968). Some current dimensions of applied behavior analysis. Journal of Applied Behavior Analysis, 1, 91–97.

Bandura, A. (1962). Social learning through imitation. In M. R. Jones (Ed.), Nebraska Symposium on Motivation-1962 (pp. 211–269). Lincoln: University of Nebraska Press.

Bandura, A. (1969). Principles of behavior modification. New York: Holt, Rinehart & Winston.

Bandura, A., & Walters, R. H. (1963). *Social learning and personality development*. New York: Holt, Rinehart & Winston.

Barlow, D., & Hayes, S. (1979). Alternating treatment designs: One strategy for comparing the effects of two treatments in a single subject. *Journal of Applied Behavior Analysis, 12*, 199–210.

Barrera, R. D., Lobato-Barrera, D., & Sulzer-Azaroff, B. (1980). A simultaneous treatment comparison of three expressive language training programs with a mute autistic child. *Journal of Autism and Developmental Disorders, 10*, 21–37.

Barrera, R. D., & Sulzer-Azaroff, B. (1983). An alternating treatment comparison of oral and total communication training programs with echolalic autistic children. *Journal of Applied Behavior Analysis, 16*, 379–394.

Bates, E. (1976). *Language and context: The acquisition of pragmatics*. New York: Academic Press.

Bell, S. M., & Ainsworth, M. D. S. (1972). Infant crying and maternal responsiveness. *Child Development, 43*, 1171–1190.

Bellamy, T. (1988, September). *Federal initiatives and policies related to community-referenced research*. Paper presented at the conference on Community-Referenced Behavior Management Techniques, Santa Barbara, CA.

Bender, L. (1955). Twenty years of clinical research on schizophrenic children with special reference to those under six years of age. In G. Caplan (Ed.), *Emotional problems of early childhood* (pp. 503–515). New York: Basic Books.

Berkman, K. A., & Meyer, L. H. (1988). Alternative strategies and multiple outcomes in the remediation of severe self-injury: Going "all out" nonaversively. *Journal of the Association for Persons with Severe Handicaps, 13*, 76–86.

Bloom, L., & Lahey, M. (1978). *Language development and language disorders*. New York: Wiley.

Bonvillian, J. D., & Nelson, K. E. (1976). Sign language acquisition in a mute autistic boy. *Journal of Speech and Hearing Disorders, 41*, 339–347.

Bonvillian, J. D., Nelson, K. E., & Rhyne, J. M. (1981). Sign language and autism. *Journal of Autism and Developmental Disorders, 11*, 125–137.

Brady, D. O., & Smouse, A. D. (1978). A simultaneous comparison of three methods for language training with an autistic child: An experimental single case analysis. *Journal of Autism and Childhood Schizophrenia, 8*, 271–279.

Brady, M. P., Shores, R. E., Gunter, P., McEvoy, M. A., Fox, J. J., & White, C. (1984). Generalization of an adolescent's social interaction behavior via multiple peers in a classroom setting. *Journal of the Association for Persons with Severe Handicaps, 9*, 278–286.

Brady, M. P., Shores, R. E., McEvoy, M. A., Ellis, D., & Fox, J. J. (1987). Increasing social interactions of severely handicapped autistic children. *Journal of Autism and Developmental Disorders, 17*, 375–390.

Breen, C., Haring, T., Pitts-Conway, V., & Gaylord-Ross, R. (1985). The training and generalization of social interaction during breaktime at two job sites in the natural environment. *Journal of the Association for Persons with Severe Handicaps, 10*, 41–50.

Bristol, M. M. (1984). Family resources and successful adaptation to autistic children. In E. Schopler & G. B. Mesibov (Eds.), *The effects of autism on the family* (pp. 289–310). New York: Plenum.

Brooks, B. D., Morrow, J. E., & Gray, W. F. (1968).

Reduction of autistic gaze aversion by reinforcement of visual attention responses. *Journal of Special Education, 2*, 307–309.

Brown, F., & Holvoet, J. (1982). Effect of systematic peer interaction on the incidental learning of two severely handicapped students. *Journal of the Association for the Severely Handicapped, 7*, 19–28.

Bruner, J. (1979). Learning how to do things with words. In D. Aaronson & R. W. Rieber (Eds.), *Psycholinguistic research* (pp. 265–284). Hillsdale, NJ: Erlbaum.

Bucher, B., & Bowman, E. A. (1974). The effects of a discriminative cue and an incompatible activity on generalized imitation. *Journal of Experimental Child Psychology, 18*, 22–33.

Burd, L., & Kerbeshian, J. (1987). A North Dakota prevalence study of schizophrenia presenting in childhood. *Journal of the American Academy of Child and Adolescent Psychiatry, 26*, 347–350.

Cantwell, D. P., & Baker, L. (1984). Research concerning families of children with autism. In E. Schopler & G. B. Mesibov (Eds.), *The effects of autism on the family* (pp. 41–63). New York: Plenum.

Cardella, D., & Rincover, A. (1985, March). *Early intervention for autistic and retarded children: I. Generalization of treatment gains*. Paper presented at the conference of the Ontario Chapter of the American Association on Mental Deficiency, Toronto.

Carr, E. G. (1977). The motivation of self-injurious behavior: A review of some hypotheses. *Psychological Bulletin, 84*, 800–816.

Carr, E. G. (1979). Teaching autistic children to use sign language: Some research issues. *Journal of Autism and Developmental Disorders, 9*, 345–359.

Carr, E. G. (1981). Sign language. In O. I. Lovaas (Ed.), *Teaching developmentally disabled children* (pp. 153–161). Baltimore: University Park Press.

Carr, E. G. (1985). Behavioral approaches to language and communication. In E. Schopler & G. B. Mesibov (Eds.), *Communication problems in autism* (pp. 37–57). New York: Plenum.

Carr, E. G. (1988). Functional equivalence as a mechanism of response generalization. In R. H. Horner, G. Dunlap, & R. L. Koegel (Eds.), *Generalization and maintenance* (pp. 221–241). Baltimore: Paul H. Brookes.

Carr, E. G., Binkoff, J. A., Kologinsky, E., & Eddy, M (1978). Acquisition of sign language by autistic children: I. Expressive labelling. *Journal of Applied Behavior Analysis, 11*, 489–501.

Carr, E. G., & Dores, P. A. (1981). Patterns of language acquisition following simultaneous communication with autistic children. *Analysis and Intervention in Developmental Disabilities, 1*, 347–361.

Carr, E. G., & Durand, V. M. (1985a). Reducing behavior problems through functional communication training. *Journal of Applied Behavior Analysis, 18*, 111–126.

Carr, E. G., & Durand, V. M. (1985b). The social-communicative basis of severe behavior problems in children. In S. Reiss and R. Bootzin (Eds.), *Theoretical issues in behavior therapy* (pp. 219–254). New York: Academic Press.

Carr, E. G., & Kologinsky, E. (1983). Acquisition of sign language by autistic children: II. Spontaneity and generalization effects. *Journal of Applied Behavior Analysis, 16*, 297–314.

Carr, E. G., Kologinsky, E., & Leff-Simon, S. (1987). Acquisition of sign language by autistic children: III.

Generalized descriptive phrases. *Journal of Autism and Developmental Disorders, 17,* 217–229.

Carr, E. G., & Newsom, C. (1985). Demand-related tantrums: Conceptualization and treatment. *Behavior Modification, 9,* 403–426.

Carr, E. G., Newsom, C. D., & Binkoff, J. A. (1976). Stimulus control of self-destructive behavior in a psychotic child. *Journal of Abnormal Child Psychology, 4,* 139–153.

Carr, E. G., Newsom, C. D., & Binkoff, J. A. (1980). Escape as a factor in the aggressive behavior of two retarded children. *Journal of Applied Behavior Analysis, 13,* 101–117.

Carr, E. G., Pridal, C., & Dores, P. A. (1984). Speech versus sign comprehension in autistic children: Analysis and prediction. *Journal of Experimental Child Psychology, 37,* 587–597.

Carrier, J. K. (1976). Application of a nonspeech language system with the severely language handicapped. In L. L. Lloyd (Ed.), *Communication assessment and intervention strategies* (pp. 523–548). Baltimore: University Park Press.

Casey, L. O. (1978). Development of communicative behavior in autistic children: A parent program using manual signs. *Journal of Autism and Childhood Schizophrenia, 8,* 45–59.

Catania, A. C. (1968). *Contemporary research in operant behavior.* Glenview, IL: Scott, Foresman.

Chapman, R., & Miller, J. (1975). Word order in early two and three word sentences. *Journal of Speech and Hearing Research, 18,* 355–371.

Charlop, M. H., Schreibman, L., & Thibodeau, M. G. (1985). Increasing spontaneous verbal responding in autistic children using a time delay procedure. *Journal of Applied Behavior Analysis, 18,* 155–166.

Charlop, M. H., Schreibman, L., & Tryon, A. S. (1983). Learning through observation: The effects of peer modeling on acquisition and generalization in autistic children. *Journal of Abnormal Child Psychology, 11,* 355–366.

Charlop, M. H., & Walsh, M. E. (1986). Increasing autistic children's spontaneous verbalizations of affection: An assessment of time delay and peer modeling procedures. *Journal of Applied Behavior Analysis, 19,* 307–314.

Christian, W. P. (1983). A case study in the programming and maintenance of institutional change. *Journal of Organizational Behavior Management, 5,* 99–153.

Cohen, D. J., Caparulo, B. K., & Shaywitz, B. A. (1978). Neurochemical and developmental models of childhood autism. In G. Serban (Ed.), *Cognitive defects in the development of mental illness* (pp. 66–100). New York: Brunner/Mazel.

Cohen, D. J., & Donnellan, A. M. (Eds.). (1987). *Handbook of autism and pervasive developmental disorders.* New York: Wiley.

Cohen, D. J., Paul, R., & Volkmar, F. R. (1986). Issues in the classification of pervasive and other developmental disorders: Toward DSM-IV. *Journal of the American Academy of Child Psychiatry, 25,* 213–220.

Coleman, M., & Gillberg, C. (1985). *The biology of the autistic syndromes.* New York: Praeger.

Coleman, S. C., & Stedman, J. M. (1974). Use of a peer model in language training in an echolalic child. *Journal of Behavior Therapy and Experimental Psychiatry, 5,* 275–279.

Colletti, G., & Harris, S. L. (1977). Behavior modification in the home: Siblings as behavior modifiers, parents as

observers. *Journal of Abnormal Child Psychology, 5,* 21–30.

Craighead, W. E., O'Leary, K. D., & Allen, J. S. (1973). Teaching and generalization of instruction-following in an "autistic" child. *Journal of Behavior Therapy and Experimental Psychiatry, 4,* 171–176.

Creedon, M. P. (1973, March). *Language development in nonverbal autistic children using a simultaneous communication system.* Paper presented at the meeting of the Society for Research in Child Development, Philadelphia.

Creedon, M. P. (1975). *Appropriate behavior through communication.* Chicago: Michael Reese Medical Center, Dysfunctioning Child Center.

Dahl, E. K., Cohen, D. J., & Provence, S. (1986). Clinical and multivariate approaches to the nosology of pervasive developmental disorders. *Journal of the American Academy of Child Psychiatry, 25,* 170–180.

Dawson, G., & Adams, A. (1984). Imitation and social responsiveness in autistic children. *Journal of Abnormal Child Psychology, 12,* 209–226.

DeMyer, M. K. (1979). *Parents and children in autism.* Washington, DC: V. H. Winston.

DeMyer, M. K., Alpern, G. D., Barton, S., DeMyer, W. E., Churchill, D. W., Hingtgen, J. N., Bryson, C. Q., Pontius, W., & Kimberlin, C. (1972). Imitation in autistic, early schizophrenic, and non-psychotic subnormal children. *Journal of Autism and Childhood Schizophrenia, 2,* 264–287.

DeMyer, M. K., Barton, S., DeMyer, W. E., Norton, J. A., Allen, J., & Steele, R. (1973). Prognosis in autism: A follow-up study. *Journal of Autism and Childhood Schizophrenia, 3,* 199–246.

DeMyer, M. K., & Ferster, C. B. (1962). Teaching new social behavior to schizophrenic children. *Journal of the American Academy of Child Psychiatry, 1,* 443–461.

DeMyer, M. K., Hingtgen, J. N., & Jackson, R. K. (1981). Infantile autism reviewed: A decade of research. *Schizophrenia Bulletin, 7,* 388–451.

Denckla, M. B. (1986). New diagnostic criteria for autism and related behavioral disorders: Guidelines for research protocols. *Journal of the American Academy of Child Psychiatry, 25,* 221–224.

Despert, J. L. (1951). Some considerations relating to the genesis of autistic behavior in children. *American Journal of Orthopsychiatry, 21,* 335–350.

deVilliers, J. G., & deVilliers, P. A. (1978). *Language acquisition.* Cambridge, MA: Harvard University Press.

Deykin, E. Y., & MacMahon, B. (1979). The incidence of seizures among children with autistic symptoms. *American Journal of Psychiatry, 136,* 1310–1312.

Donnellan, A. M., & Mirenda, P. L. (1984). Issues related to professional involvement with families of individuals with autism and other severe handicaps. *Journal of the Association for the Severely Handicapped, 9,* 16–25.

Dunlap, G. (1984). The influence of task variation and maintenance tasks on the learning and affect of autistic children. *Journal of Experimental Child Psychology, 37,* 41–46.

Dunlap, G., Dyer, K., & Koegel, R. L. (1983). Autistic self-stimulation and intertrial interval duration. *American Journal of Mental Deficiency, 2,* 194–202.

Durand, V. M. (1986). Self-injurious behavior as intentional communication. In K. D. Gadow (Ed.), *Advances in learning and behavioral disabilities* (Vol. 5, pp. 143–157). Greenwich, CT: JAI Press.

Durand, V. M., & Carr, E. G. (1987). Social influences on

"self-stimulatory" behavior: Analysis and treatment application. *Journal of Applied Behavior Analysis, 20,* 119–132.

Durand, V. M., & Crimmins, D. B. (1987). Assessment and treatment of psychotic speech in an autistic child. *Journal of Autism and Developmental Disorders, 17,* 17–28.

Durand, V. M., & Crimmins, D. B. (1988). Identifying the variables maintaining self-injurious behavior. *Journal of Autism and Developmental Disorders, 18,* 99–117.

Dyer, K., Christian, W. P., & Luce, S. C. (1982). The role of response delay in improving the discrimination performance of autistic children. *Journal of Applied Behavior Analysis, 15,* 231–240.

Eason, L. J., White, M. J., & Newsom, C. (1982). Generalized reduction of self-stimulatory behavior: An effect of teaching appropriate play to autistic children. *Analysis and Intervention in Developmental Disabilities, 2,* 157–169.

Egel, A. L., Richman, G. S., & Koegel, R. L. (1981). Normal peer models and autistic children's learning. *Journal of Applied Behavior Analysis, 14,* 3–12.

Eisenberg, L. (1956). The autistic child in adolescence. *American Journal of Psychiatry, 112,* 607–613.

Evans, I. M., & Meyer, L. H. (1985). *An educative approach to behavior problems.* Baltimore: Paul H. Brookes.

Falvey, M. A. (1986). *Community-based curriculum.* Baltimore: Paul H. Brookes.

Farber, B., & Ryckman, J. (1965). Effects of severely mentally retarded children on family relationships. *Mental Retardation Abstracts, 2,* 2–17.

Favell, J. E. (1983). The management of aggressive behavior. In E. Schopler & G. Mesibov (Eds.), *Autism in adolescents and adults* (pp. 187–222). New York: Plenum.

Favell, J. E., Azrin, N. H., Baumeister, A. A., Carr, E. G., Dorsey, M. A., Forehand, R., Foxx, R. M., Lovaas, O. I., Rincover, A., Risley, T. R., Romanczyk, R. G., Russo, D. C., Schroeder, S. R., & Solmck, J. V. (1982). The treatment of self-injurious behavior. *Behavior Therapy, 13,* 529–554.

Favell, J. E., McGimsey, J. F., & Schell, R. M. (1982). Treatment of self-injury by providing alternate sensory activities. *Analysis and Intervention in Developmental Disabilities, 2,* 83–104.

Fein, D., Pennington, B., Markowitz, P., Braverman, M., & Waterhouse, L. (1986). Toward a neuropsychological model of infantile autism: Are the social deficits primary? *Journal of the American Academy of Child Psychiatry, 25,* 198–212.

Fenske, E. C., Zalenski, S., Krantz, P. J., & McClannahan, L. E. (1985). Age at intervention and treatment outcome for autistic children in a comprehensive intervention program. *Analysis and Intervention in Developmental Disabilities, 5,* 49–58.

Ferster, C. B. (1961). Positive reinforcement and behavioral deficits in autistic children. *Child Development, 32,* 437–456.

Fish, B. (1957). The detection of schizophrenia in infancy. *Journal of Nervous and Mental Disease, 125,* 1–24.

Foxx, R. M. (1977). Attention training: The use of overcorrection avoidance to increase the eye contact of autistic and retarded children. *Journal of Applied Behavior Analysis, 10,* 489–499.

Foxx, R. M. (1982). *Decreasing behaviors of severely retarded and autistic persons.* Champaign, IL: Research Press.

Freeman, B. J., Ritvo, E. R., Needleman, R., & Yokota, A. (1985). The stability of cognitive and linguistic parameters in autism: A five-year prospective study. *Journal of the American Academy of Child Psychiatry, 24,* 459–464.

Freeman, B. J., Ritvo, E. R., Schroth, P. C., Tonick, I., Guthrie, D., & Wake, L. (1981). Behavioral characteristics of high- and low-IQ autistic children. *American Journal of Psychiatry, 138,* 25–29.

Furnell, J. R. G., & Thomas, G. V. (1976). Stimulus control of generalized imitation in subnormal children. *Journal of Experimental Child Psychology, 22,* 282–291.

Furnell, J. R. G., & Thomas, G. V. (1981). Intermittent reinforcement of imitation in subnormal children: Effect on resistance to extinction. *Behavior Analysis Letters, 1,* 117–122.

Gajzago, C., & Prior, M. (1974). Two cases of "recovery" in Kanner syndrome. *Archives of General Psychiatry, 31,* 264–268.

Garcia, E., Baer, D. M., & Firestone, I (1971). The development of generalized imitation within topographically determined boundaries. *Journal of Applied Behavior Analysis, 4,* 101–113.

Gaylord-Ross, R. J., Haring, T. G., Breen, C., & Pitts-Conway, V. (1984). The training and generalization of social interaction skills with autistic youth. *Journal of Applied Behavior Analysis, 17,* 229–247.

Gillberg, C., Rosenhall, U., & Johansson, E. (1983). Auditory brainstem responses in childhood psychosis. *Journal of Autism and Developmental Disorders, 13,* 181–195.

Gillberg, C., & Stffenburg, S. (1987). Outcome and prognostic factors in infantile autism and similar conditions: A population-based study of 46 cases followed through puberty. *Journal of Autism and Developmental Disorders, 17,* 273–287.

Godby, S., Gast, D. L., & Wolery, M. (1987). A comparison of time delay and system of least prompts in teaching object identification. *Research in Developmental Disabilities, 8,* 283–306.

Goetz, L., Gee, K., & Sailor, W. (1985). Using a behavior chain interruption strategy to teach communication skills to students with severe disabilities. *Journal of the Association for Persons with Severe Handicaps, 10,* 21–30.

Goetz, L., Schuler, A., & Sailor, W. (1979). Teaching functional speech to the severely handicapped: Current issues. *Journal of Autism and Developmental Disorders, 9,* 325–343.

Green, C. W., Reid, D. H., McCarn, J. E., Schepis, M. M., Phillips, J. F., & Parsons, M. B. (1986). Naturalistic observations of classrooms serving severely handicapped persons: Establishing evaluative norms. *Applied Research in Mental Retardation, 7,* 37–50.

Groden, G., Domingue, D., Chesnick, M., Groden, J., & Baron, G. (1983). Early intervention with autistic children: A case presentation with pre-program, program and follow-up data. *Psychological Reports, 53,* 715–722.

Guess, D. (1980). Methods in communication instruction for severely handicapped persons. In W. Sailor, B. Wilcox, & L. Brown (Eds.), *Methods of instruction for severely handicapped students* (pp. 195–225). Baltimore: Paul H. Brookes.

Guess, D., Helmstetter, E., Turnbull, H. R., & Knowlton, S. (1987). *Use of aversive procedures with persons who are disabled: An historical review and critical analysis* (Monograph 2, No. 1, of the Association for Persons with Severe Handicaps). Seattle: The Association for Persons with Severe Handicaps.

Guess, D., Keogh, W., & Baer, D. (1977). *Imitation training for difficult to teach severely handicapped children: An analysis of new procedures*. Topeka: State of Kansas Department of Social and Rehabilitation Services.

Guess, D., Sailor, W., & Baer, D. (1978). *Functional speech and language training for the severely handicapped*. Lawrence, KS: H & H Enterprises.

Guess, D., Sailor, W., Keogh, W. J., & Baer, D. M. (1976). Language development programs for severely handicapped children. In N. G. Haring & L. J. Brown (Eds.), *Teaching the severely handicapped* (Vol. 1, pp. 301–324). New York: Grune & Stratton.

Guralnick, M. J. (1976). The value of integrating handicapped and non-handicapped preschool children. *American Journal of Orthopsychiatry, 42*, 236–245.

Halle, J. W. (1982). Teaching functional language to the handicapped: An integrative model of natural environment teaching techniques. *Journal of the Association for the Severely Handicapped, 7*, 29–37.

Halle, J. W., Baer, D. M., Spradlin, J. E. (1981). Teachers' generalized use of delay as a stimulus control procedure to increase language use in handicapped children. *Journal of Applied Behavior Analysis, 14*, 389–409.

Halle, J. W., Marshall, A., & Spradlin, J. E. (1979). Time delay: A technique to increase language use and facilitate generalization in retarded children. *Journal of Applied Behavior Analysis, 12*, 431–439.

Halliday, M. A. K. (1975). *Learning how to mean*. New York: Elsevier.

Handen, B. L., & Zane, T. (1987). Delayed prompting: A review of procedural variations and results. *Research in Developmental Disabilities, 8*, 307–330.

Handleman, J. S. (1979). Generalization by autistic-type children of verbal responses across settings. *Journal of Applied Behavior Analysis, 12*, 273–282.

Hannah, G. T., Christian, W. P., & Clark, H. B. (1981). *Preservation of client rights*. New York: Free Press.

Haring. T. G., Roger, B., Lee, M., Breen, C., & Gaylord-Ross, R. (1986). Teaching social language to moderately handicapped students. *Journal of Applied Behavior Analysis, 19*, 159–171.

Harris, S. L. (1975). Teaching language to nonverbal children—with emphasis on problems of generalization. *Psychological Bulletin, 82*, 565–580.

Harris, S. L. (1983). *Families of the developmentally disabled: A guide to behavioral intervention*. New York: Pergamon Press.

Harris, S. L. (1986a). Brief report: A 4- to 7-year questionnaire follow-up of participants in a training program for parents of autistic children. *Journal of Autism and Developmental Disorders, 16*, 377–383.

Harris, S. L. (1986b). Families of children with autism: Issues for the behavior therapist. *The Behavior Therapist, 9*, 175–177.

Harris, S. L., & Boyle, T. D. (1985). Parents as language trainers of children with autism. In E. Schopler & G. B. Mesibov (Eds.), *Communication problems in autism* (pp. 207–227). New York: Plenum.

Harris, S. L., Wolchik, S.A., & Milch, R. E. (1982). Changing the speech of autistic children and their parents. *Child and Family Behavior Therapy, 4*, 151–173.

Harris, S. L., Wolchik, S. A., & Weitz, S. (1981). The acquisition of language skills by autistic children: Can parents do the job? *Journal of Autism and Developmental Disorders, 11*, 373–384.

Hart, B., & Risley, T. R. (1968). Establishing use of descriptive adjectives in the spontaneous speech of disadvantaged preschool children. *Journal of Applied Behavior Analysis, 1*, 109–120.

Hart, B., & Risley, T. R. (1974). The use of preschool materials for modifying the language of disadvantaged children. *Journal of Applied Behavior Analysis, 7*, 243–256.

Hart, B., & Risley, T. R. (1975). Incidental teaching of language in the preschool. *Journal of Applied Behavior Analysis, 8*, 411–420.

Hermelin, B., & O'Connor, N. (1963). The response and self-generated behavior of severely disturbed children and severely subnormal controls. *British Journal of Social and Clinical Psychology, 2*, 37–43.

Hermelin, B. & O'Connor, N. (1964). Effects of sensory input and sensory dominance on severely disturbed children and on subnormal controls. *British Journal of Psychology, 55*, 201–206.

Hewett, F. M. (1965). Teaching speech to an autistic child through operant conditioning. *American Journal of Orthopsychiatry, 35*, 927–936.

Hingtgen, J. N., Coulter, S. K., & Churchill, D. W. (1967). Intensive reinforcement of imitative behavior in mute autistic children. *Archives of General Psychiatry, 17*, 36–43.

Holmes, N., Hemsley, R., Rickett, J., & Likierman, H. (1982). Parents as cotherapists: Their perceptions of a home-based behavioral treatment for autistic children. *Journal of Autism and Developmental Disorders, 12*, 331–342.

Horner, R. H., Dunlap, G., & Koegel, R. L. (1988). *Generalization and maintenance*. Baltimore: Paul H. Brookes.

Howlin, P. A. (1981). The effectiveness of operant language training with autistic children. *Journal of Autism and Developmental Disorders, 11*, 89–105.

Howlin, P. A. & Rutter, M. (1987). *Treatment of autistic children*. New York: Wiley.

Hung, D. W. (1977). Generalization of "curiosity" questioning behavior in autistic children. *Journal of Behavior Therapy and Experimental Psychiatry, 8*, 237–245.

Hung, D. W. (1980). Training and generalization of yes and no as mands in two autistic children. *Journal of Autism and Developmental Disorders, 10*, 139–152.

Hutchinson, R. R. (1977). By-products of aversive control. In W. K. Honing & J. E. R. Staddon (Eds.), *Handbook of operant behavior* (pp. 415–431). Edgewood Cliif, NJ: Prentice-Hall.

Huttenlocher, P. R. (1988). Developmental neurobiology: Current and future challenges. In F. J. Menolascino & J. A. Stark (Eds.), *Preventive and curative intervention in mental retardation* (pp. 101–111). Baltimore: Paul H. Brookes.

Hyde, L., & Rincover, A. (1985, March). *Early intervention for autistic and retarded children: III. Within-stimulus prompt fading for auditory discriminations*. Paper presented at the conference of the Ontario Chapter of the American Association on Mental Deficiency, Toronto.

Isaac, W., Thomas, J., & Goldiamond, I. (1960). Application of operant conditioning to reinstate verbal behavior in psychotics. *Journal of Speech and Hearing Disorders, 25*, 8–12.

Itard, J. M. G. (1962). *The wild boy of Aveyron* (G. Humphrey & M. Humphrey, Trans.). New York: Appleton-Century-Crofts. (Original work published in 1801)

Iwata, B. A., Dorsey, M. F., Slifer, K. J., Bauman, K. E., & Richman, G. S. (1982). Toward a functional analysis of self-injury. *Analysis and Intervention in Developmental Disabilities, 2,* 3–20.

Jacobson, M. A. (1978). *Developmental neurobiology* (2nd ed.). New York: Plenum.

James, S. D., & Egel, A. L. (1986). A direct prompting strategy for increasing reciprocal interactions between handicapped and nonhandicapped siblings. *Journal of Applied Behavior Analysis, 19,* 173–186.

Janssen, C., & Guess, D. (1978). Use of function as a consequence in training receptive labeling to severely and profoundly retarded individuals. *AAESPH Review, 3,* 246–258.

Kanner, L. (1943). Autistic disturbances of affective contact. *The Nervous Child, 2,* 217–250.

Kanner, L. (1954). To what extent is early infantile autism determined by constitutional inadequacies? In D. Hooker & C. C. Hare (Eds.), *Genetics and the inheritance of integrated neurological and psychiatric patterns* (pp. 378–385). Baltimore: Williams & Wilkins.

Kanner, L. (1965). Infantile autism and the schizophrenias. *Behavioral Science, 10,* 412–420.

Kanner, L. (1971). Follow-up study of eleven autistic children originally reported in 1943. *Journal of Autism and Childhood Schizophrenia, 1,* 119–145.

Kanner, L. (1973). How far can autistic children go in matters of social adaptation? In L. Kanner (Eds.), *Childhood psychosis: Initial studies and new insights* (pp. 189–213). Washington, DC: V. H. Winston.

Kelly, J. A., & Drabman, R. S. (1977). The modification of socially detrimental behavior. *Journal of Behavior Therapy and Experimental Psychiatry, 8,* 101–104.

Keogh, B., Guess, D., & Baer, D. (1977). *Fast Motor Imitation Program.* Lawrence: University of Kansas, Department of Human Development and Family Life.

Keogh, D. A., Faw, G. D., Whitman, T. L., & Reid, D. H. (1984). Enhancing leisure skills in severely retarded adolescents through a self-instructional treatment package. *Analysis and Intervention in Developmental Disabilities, 4,* 333–351.

Kerr, N., Meyerson, L., & Michael, J. (1965). A procedure for shaping vocalizations in a mute child. In L. P. Ullman & L. Krasner (Eds.), *Case studies in behavior modification* (pp. 366–370). New York: Holt, Rinehart & Winston.

Koegel, R. L., & Covert, A. (1972). The relationship of self-stimulation to learning in autistic children. *Journal of Applied Behavior Analysis, 5,* 381–388.

Koegel, R. L., Dunlap, G., & Dyer, K. (1980). Intertrial interval duration and learning in autistic children. *Journal of Applied Behavior Analysis, 13,* 91–99.

Koegel, R. L., Dunlap, G., Richman, G. S., & Dyer, K. (1981). The use of specific orienting cues for teaching discrimination tasks. *Analysis and Intervention in Developmental Disabilities, 1,* 187–198.

Koegel, R. L., Dyer, K., & Bell, L. K. (1987). The influence of child-preferred activities on autistic children's social behavior. *Journal of Applied Behavior Analysis, 20,* 243–252.

Koegel, R. L., & Egel, A. L. (1979). Motivating autistic children. *Journal of Abnormal Psychology, 88,* 418–426.

Koegel, R. L., Firestone, P. B., Kramme, K. W., & Dunlap, G. (1974). Increasing spontaneous play by

suppressing self-stimulation in autistic children. *Journal of Applied Behavior Analysis, 7,* 521–528.

Koegel, R. L., Glahn, T. J., & Nieminen, G. S. (1978). Generalization of parent training results. *Journal of Applied Behavior Analysis, 11,* 95–109.

Koegel, R. L., O'Dell, M. C., & Koegel, L. K. (1987). A natural language teaching paradigm for nonverbal autistic children. *Journal of Autism and Developmental Disorders, 17,* 187–200.

Koegel, R. L., & Rincover, A. (1977). Research on the difference between generalization and maintenance in extra-therapy responding. *Journal of Applied Behavior Analysis, 10,* 1–12.

Koegel, R. L., Rincover, A., & Egel, A. L. (Eds.). (1982). *Educating and understanding autistic children.* San Diego: College-Hill Press.

Koegel, R. L., Russo, D. C., & Rincover, A. (1977). Assessing and training teachers in the generalized use of behavior modification with autistic children. *Journal of Applied Behavior Analysis, 10,* 197–205.

Koegel, R. L., Russo, D. C., Rincover, A., & Schreibman, L. (1982). *Assessing and training teachers.* In R. L. Koegel, A. Rincover, & A. L. Egel (Eds.), *Educating and understanding autistic children* (pp. 178–202). San Diego: College-Hill Press.

Koegel, R. L., Schreibman, L., Britten, K. R., Burke, J. C., & O'Neill, R. E. (1982). A comparison of parent training to direct child treatment. In R. L. Koegel, A. Rincover, & A. L. Egel (Eds.), *Educating and understanding autistic children* (pp. 260–279). San Diego: College-Hill Press.

Koegel, R. L., Schreibman, L., O'Neill, R. E., & Burke, J. C. (1983). The personality and family-interaction characteristics of parents of autistic children. *Journal of Consulting and Clinical Psychology, 51,* 683–692.

Koegel, R. L., & Traphagen, J. (1982). Selection of initial words for speech training with nonverbal children. In R. L. Koegel, A. Rincover, & A. L. Egel (Eds.), *Educating and understanding autistic children* (pp. 65–77). San Diego: College-Hill Press.

Koegel, R. L., Williams, J. A. (1980). Direct versus indirect response–reinforcer relationships in teaching autistic children. *Journal of Abnormal Child Psychology, 8,* 537–547.

Kolko, D. J. (1984). Parents as behavior therapists for their autistic children: Clinical and empirical considerations. In E. Schopler & G. B. Mesibov (Eds.), *The effects of autism on the family* (pp. 145–162). New York: Plenum.

Kolvin, I. (1971). Studies in the childhood psychoses: I. Diagnostic criteria and classification. *British Journal of Psychiatry, 118,* 381–384.

Kolvin, I., Ounsted, C., Humphrey, M., McNay, A. (1971). Studies in the childhood psychoses: II. The phenomenology of childhood psychoses. *British Journal of Psychiatry, 118,* 385–395.

Kozloff, M. A. (1973). *Reaching the autistic child: A parent training program.* Champaign, IL: Research Press.

Kozloff, M. A. (1974). *Educating children with learning and behavior problems.* New York: Wiley.

Kozloff, M. A. (1979). *A program for families of children with learning and behavior problems.* New York: Wiley.

Kozloff, M. A. (1984). A training program for families of children with autism: Responding to family needs. In E. Schopler & G. B. Mesibov (Eds.), *The effects of autism on the family* (pp. 163–186). New York: Plenum.

Kuhn, T. S. (1962). *The structure of scientific revolutions.* Chicago: University of Chicago Press.

Kydd, R. R., & Werry, J. S. (1982). Schizophrenia in children under 16 years. *Journal of Autism and Developmental Disorders, 12,* 343–357.

Lahey, M. (1974). Use of prosody and syntactic markers in children's comprehension of spoken sentences. *Journal of Speech and Hearinig Research, 17,* 656–668.

Lashley, K. S. (1938). Conditional reactions in the rat. *Journal of Psychology, 6,* 311–324.

Laski, K. E., Charlop, M. H., Schreibman, L. (1988). Training parents to use the natural language paradigm to increase their autistic children's speech. *Journal of Applied Behavior Analysis, 21,* 391–400.

LaVigna, G. W., & Donnellan, A. M. (1986). *Alternatives to punishment: Solving behavior problems with nonaversive strategies.* New York: Irvington.

LeMay, D., Griffin, P., & Sanford, A. (1977). *Learning Accomplishment Profile: Diagnostic edition.* Chapel Hill, NC: Chapel Hill Training–Outreach Project.

Litt, M. D., & Schreibman, L. (1982). Stimulus-specific reinforcement in the acquisition of receptive labels by autistic children. *Analysis and Intervention in Developmental Disabilities, 1,* 171–186.

Lotter, V. (1966). Epidemiology of autistic conditions in young children: I. Prevalence. *Social Psychiatry, 1,* 124–137.

Lotter, V. (1974). Factors related to outcome in autistic children. *Journal of Autism and Childhood Schizophrenia, 4,* 263–277.

Lotter, V. (1978). Follow-up studies. In M. Rutter & E. Schopler (Eds.), *Autism: A reappraisal of concepts and treatment* (pp. 475–495). New York: Plenum.

Lovaas, O. I. (1969). *Behavior modification: Teaching language to psychotic children* [Film]. New York: Appleton-Century-Crofts.

Lovaas, O. I. (1971). General discussion. In D. W. Churchill, G. D. Alpern, M. K. DeMyer (Eds.), *Infantile autism: Proceedings of the Indiana University Colloquium* (pp. 104–118). Springfield, IL: Charles C Thomas.

Lovaas, O. I. (1977). *The autistic child: Language development through behavior modification.* New York: Irvington.

Lovaas, O. I. (Ed.). (1981). *Teaching developmentally disabled children.* Baltimore: University Park Press.

Lovaas, O. I. (1987). Behavioral treatment and normal educational and intellectual functioning in young autistic children. *Journal of Consulting and Clinical Psychology, 55,* 3–9.

Lovaas, O. I., Berberich, J. P., Perloff, B. F., & Schaeffer, B. (1966). Acquisition of imitative speech by schizophrenic children. *Science, 151,* 705–707.

Lovaas, O. I., Freitag, G., Gold, V. J., & Kassorla, I. C. (1965). Experimental studies in childhood schizophrenia: Analysis of self-destructive behavior. *Journal of Experimental Child Psychology, 2,* 67–84.

Lovaas, O. I., Freitag, G., Kinder, M. I., Rubenstein, B. D., Schaeffer, B., & Simmons, J. Q. (1966). Establishment of social reinforcers in two schizophrenic children on the basis of food. *Journal of Experimental Child Psychology, 4,* 109–125.

Lovaas, O. I., Freitas, L., Nelson, K., & Whalen, C. (1967). The establishment of imitation and its use for the development of complex behaviour in schizophrenic children. *Behaviour Research and Therapy, 5,* 171–181.

Lovaas, O. I., Koegel, R. L., & Schreibman, L. (1979). Stimulus overselectivity in autism: A review of reseach. *Psychological Bulletin, 86,* 1236–1254.

Lovaas, O. I., Koegel, R. L., Simmons, J. Q., & Long, J. S. (1973). Some generalization and follow-up measures on autistic children in behavior therapy. *Journal of Applied Behavior Analysis, 6,* 131–166.

Lovaas, O. I., & Leaf, R. B. (1981). *Teaching developmentally disabled children* [Videotapes]. Baltimore: University Park Press.

Lovaas, O. I., Litrownik, A., & Mann, R. (1971). Response latencies to auditory stimuli in autistic children engaged in self-stimulatory behavior. *Behaviour Research and Therapy, 9,* 39–49.

Lovaas, O. I., Newsom, C., & Hickman, C. (1987). Self-stimulatory behavior and perceptual reinforcement. *Journal of Applied Behavior Analysis, 20,* 45–68.

Lovaas, O. I., Schaeffer, B., & Simmons, J. Q. (1965). Building social behavior in autistic children by use of electric shock. *Journal of Experimental Research in Personality, 1,* 99–109.

Lovaas, O. I., & Simmons, J. Q. (1969). Manipulation of self-destruction in three retarded children. *Journal of Applied Behavior Analysis, 2,* 143–157.

Lovaas, O. I., & Smith, T. (in press). Intensive behavioral treatment with young autistic children. In B. B. Lahey & A. E. Kazdin (Eds.), *Advances in clinical child psychology* (Vol. 11). New York: Plenum.

Lowe, T. L., Tanaka, K., Seashore, M. R., Young, J. G., & Cohen, D. J. (1980). Detection of phenylketonuria in autistic and psychotic children. *Journal of the American Medical Association, 243,* 126–128.

Luyben, P. D., Funk, D. M., Morgan, J. K., Clark, K. A., & Delulio, D. W. (1986). Team sports for the severely retarded: Training a side-of-the-foot soccer pass using a maximum-to-minimum prompt reduction strategy. *Journal of Applied Behavior Analysis, 19,* 431–436.

Mace, F. C., & Knight, D. (1986). Functional analysis and treatment of severe pica. *Journal of Applied Behavior Analysis, 19,* 411–416.

Mace, F. C., Page, T. J., Ivancic, M. T., & O'Brien, S. (1986). Analysis of environmental determinants of aggression and disruption in mentally retarded children. *Applied Research in Mental Retardation, 7,* 203–221.

Mahler, M. S. (1952). On child psychosis and schizophrenia: Autistic and symbiotic infantile psychoses. *Psychoanalytic Study of the Child, 7,* 286–305.

Matson, J. L., & DiLorenzo, T. M. (1984). *Punishment and its alternatives.* New York: Springer.

McAdoo, W. G., & DeMyer, M. K. (1978). Personality characteristics of parents. In M. Rutter and E. Schopler (Eds.), *Autism: A reappraisal of concepts and treatment* (pp. 251–267). New York: Plenum.

McConnell, O. L. (1967). Control of eye contact in an autistic child. *Journal of Child Psychology and Psychiatry, 8,* 249–255.

McDonald, E. T. (1980). Early identification and treatment of children at risk for speech development. In R. L. Schiefelbusch (Ed.), *Nonspeech language and communication* (pp. 49–79). Baltimore: University Park Press.

McEachin, J. J. (1987). *Outcome of autistic children receiving intensive behavioral treatment: Psychological status 3 to 12 years later.* Unpublished doctoral dissertation, University of California at Los Angeles.

McEachin, J. J., & Leaf, R. B. (1984, May). *The role of punishment in the motivation of autistic children.* Paper presented at the annual convention of the Association for Behavior Analysis, Nashville, TN.

McEvoy, M. A., Nordquist, V. M., Twardosz, S., Heckaman, K. A., Wehby, J. H., & Denny, R. K. (1988). Promoting autistic children's peer interaction in an integrated early childhood setting using affection activities. *Journal of Applied Behavior Analysis, 21*, 193–200.

McGee, G. G., Krantz, P. J., Mason, D., & McClannahan, L. E. (1983). A modified incidental-teaching procedure for autistic youth: Acquisition and generalization of receptive object labels. *Journal of Applied Behavior Analysis, 16*, 329–338.

McGee, G. G., Krantz, P. J., & McClannahan, L. E. (1985). The facilitative effects of incidental teaching on preposition use by autistic children. *Journal of Applied Behavior Analysis, 18*, 17–31.

McHale, S., & Boone, W. (1980). Play between autistic and nonhandicapped children: An innovative approach to mainstreaming. *Pointer, 24*, 28–33.

McHale, S. M., Simeonsson, R. J., & Sloan, J. L. (1984). Children with handicapped brothers and sisters. In E. Schopler & G. B. Mesibov (Eds.), *The effects of autism on the family* (pp. 327–342). New York: Plenum.

McMorrow, M. J., Foxx, R. M., Faw, G. D., & Bittle, R. G. (1987). Cues–pause–point language training: Teaching echolalics functional use of their verbal labeling repertoires. *Journal of Applied Behavior Analysis, 20*, 11–22.

McNaughton, S., & Kates, B. (1980). The application of Blissymbolics. In R. L. Schiefelbusch (Ed.), *Nonspeech language and communication* (pp. 303–321). Baltimore: University Park Press.

Mesibov, G. B. (1984). Social skills training with verbal autistic adolescents and adults: A program model. *Journal of Autism and Developmental Disorders, 14*, 395–404.

Metz, J. R. (1965). Conditioning generalized imitation in autistic children. *Journal of Experimental Child Psychology, 2*, 389–399.

Meyer, L. H. (1988a). [Review of *Severe behavior disorders in the mentally retarded: Nondrug approaches to treatment*]. *Journal of the Association for Persons with Severe Handicaps, 13*, 54–57.

Meyer, L. (1988b). TASH joins with other organizations to protest electric shock device. *TASH Newsletter, 14*, 1–3.

Milch, R. E. (1983). *A comparison of 10 and 20 week behavioral training programs for parents of autistic children*. Unpublished doctoral dissertation, Rutgers University.

Miller, A., & Miller, E. E. (1973). Cognitive-developmental training with elevated boards and sign language. *Journal of Autism and Childhood Schizophrenia, 3*, 65–85.

Mirenda, P. L., Donnellan, A. M., & Yoder, D. E. (1983). Gaze behavior: A new look at an old problem. *Journal of Autism and Developmental Disorders, 13*, 397–409.

Neef, N. A., Shafer, M. S., Egel, A. L., Cataldo, M. F., & Parrish, J. M. (1983). The class specific effects of compliance training with "do" and "don't" requests: Analogue analysis and classroom application. *Journal of Applied Behavior Analysis, 16*, 81–99.

Neef, N. A., Walters, J., & Egel, A. L. (1984). Establishing generative yes/no responses in developmentally disabled children. *Journal of Applied Behavior Analysis, 17*, 453–460.

Newsom, C., Carr, E. G., & Lovaas, O. I. (1979). The experimental analysis and modification of autistic behavior. In R. S. Davidson (Ed.), *Modification of behavior pathology* (pp. 109–187). New York: Gardner Press.

Newsom, C., Favell, J. E., & Rincover, A. (1983). The side effects of punishment. In S. Axelrod & J. Apsche (Eds.), *The effects of punishment on human behavior* (pp. 285–316). New York: Academic Press.

Newsom, C., Hovanitz, C. A., & Rincover, A. (1988). Autism. In E. J. Mash & L. G. Terdal (Eds.), *Behavioral assessment of childhood disorders* (2nd ed., pp. 355–401). New York: Guilford Press.

Newsom, C. D., & Simon, K. M. (1977). A simultaneous discrimination procedure for the measurement of vision in nonverbal children. *Journal of Applied Behavior Analysis, 10*, 633–644.

Nishimura, B., Watamaki, T., Sato, M., & Wakabayashi, S. (1987). The criteria for early use of nonvocal communication systems with nonspeaking autistic children. *Journal of Autism and Developmental Disorders, 17*, 243–253.

Nordquist, V. M., & McEvoy, M. A. (1983). Punishment as a factor in early childhood imitation. *Analysis and Intervention in Developmental Disabilities, 3*, 339–357.

Nordquist, V. M., Twardosz, S., & McEvoy, M. A. (1982, November). *A naturalistic approach to the problem of establishing social reinforcers in autistic children*. Paper presented at the convention of the Association of Advancement of Behavior Therapy, Los Angeles.

Odom, S. L., Hoyson, M., Jamieson, B., & Strain, P. S. (1985). Increasing handicapped preschoolers' peer social interactions: Cross-setting and component analysis. *Journal of Applied Behavior Analysis, 18*, 3–16.

Odom, S. L., & Strain, P. S. (1984). Peer-mediated approaches for promoting children's social interaction: A review. *American Journal of Orthopsychiatry, 54*, 544–557.

Odom, S. L., & Strain, P. S. (1986). A comparison of peer-initiation and teacher-antecedent interventions for promoting reciprocal social interaction of autistic preschoolers. *Journal of Applied Behavior Analysis, 19*, 59–71.

Ornitz, E. M., Guthrie, D., & Farley, A. J. (1977). The early development of autistic children. *Journal of Autism and Childhood Schizophrenia, 7*, 207–229.

Owens, R. E., & House, L. I. (1984). Decision-making processes in augmentative communication. *Journal of Speech and Hearing Disorders, 49*, 18–25.

Palyo, W. J., Cooke, T. P., Schuler, A. L., & Apolloni, T. (1979). Modifying echolalic speech in preschool children: Training and generalization. *American Journal of Mental Deficiency, 83*, 480–489.

Parrish, J. M., Cataldo, M. F., Kolko, D. J., Neef, N. A., & Egel, A. L. (1986). Experimental analysis of response covariation among compliant and inappropriate behaviors. *Journal of Applied Behavior Analysis, 19*, 241–254.

Patterson, G. R. (1976). The aggressive child: Victim and architect of a coercive system. In E. J. Mash, L. A. Hamerlynck, & L. C. Handy (Eds.), *Behavior modification and families* (pp. 267–316). New York: Brunner/Mazel.

Petty, L., Ornitz, E. M., Michelman, J. D., & Zimmerman, E. G. (1984). Autistic children who later become schizophrenic. *Archives of General Psychiatry, 41*, 129–135.

Pfiffner, L. J., O'Leary, S. G. (1987). The efficacy of all-positive management as a function of the prior use of negative consequences. *Journal of Applied Behavior Analysis, 20,* 265–271.

Pitfield, M., & Oppenheim, A. M. (1964). Child rearing attitudes of mothers of psychotic children. *Journal of Child Psychology and Psychiatry, 5,* 51–57.

Plummer, S., Baer, D. M., & LeBlanc, J. M. (1977). Functional considerations in the use of procedural time-out and an effective alternative. *Journal of Applied Behavior Analysis, 10,* 689–706.

Pridal, C. G. (1982, May). *Teaching sign language to low functioning autistic children.* Paper presented at the conference of the Association of Behavior Analysis, Milwaukee.

Prior, M., Perry, D., & Gajzago, C. (1975). Kanner's syndrome or early-onset psychosis: A taxonomic analysis of 142 cases. *Journal of Autism and Childhood Schizophrenia, 5,* 71–80.

Prior, M. E., Tress, B., Hoffman, W. L., & Boldt, D. (1984). Computed tomographic study of children with classic autism. *Archives of Neurology, 41,* 482–484.

Pronovost, W., Wakstein, M. P., & Wakstein, D. J. (1966). A longitudinal study of speech behaviour and language comprehension of fourteen children diagnosed as atypical or autistic. *Exceptional Children, 33,* 19–26.

Ragland, E. U., Kerr, M. M., & Strain, P. S. (1978). Behavior of withdrawn autistic children: Effects of peer social initiations. *Behavior Modification, 2,* 565–578.

Rank, B., & McNaughton, D. (1950). A clinical contribution to early ego development. *Psychoanalytic Study of the Child, 5,* 53–65.

Remington, B., & Clarke, S. (1983). Acquisition of expressive signing by autistic children: An evaluation of the relative effects of simultaneous communication and sign-alone training. *Journal of Applied Behavior Analysis, 16,* 315–328.

Rheingold, H. L., Gewirtz, J. L., & Ross, H. W. (1959). Social conditioning of vocalizations in the infant. *Journal of Comparative and Physiological Psychology, 52,* 68–73.

Rimland, B. (1964). *Infantile autism.* New York: Appleton-Century-Crofts.

Rincover, A. (1978). Sensory extinction: A procedure for eliminating self-stimulatory behavior in psychotic children. *Journal of Abnormal Child Psychology, 6,* 299–310.

Rincover, A. (1981). Some directions for *Analysis and Intervention in Developmental Disabilities:* An editorial. *Analysis and Intervention in Developmental Disabilities, 1,* 109–115.

Rincover, A., Cook, R., Peoples, A., & Packard, D. (1979). Using sensory extinction and sensory reinforcement principles for programming multiple adaptive behavior change. *Journal of Applied Behavior Analysis, 12,* 221–233.

Rincover, A., & Devany, J. (1982). The application of sensory extinction procedures to self-injury. *Analysis and Intervention in Developmental Disabilities, 2,* 67–81.

Rincover, A., & Koegel, R. L. (1975). Setting generality and stimulus control in autistic children. *Journal of Applied Behavior Analysis, 8,* 235–246.

Rincover, A., & Newsom, C. D. (1985). The relative motivational properties of sensory and edible reinforcers in teaching autistic children. *Journal of Applied Behavior Analysis, 18,* 237–248.

Rincover, A., Taggart, D., Hyde, L., Cardella, D., & Baranyai, T. (1985, March). *An experimental preschool project for developmentally disabled children.* Paper presented at the conference of the Ontario Chapter of the American Association on Mental Deficiency, Toronto.

Risley, T. R. (1968). The effects and side effects of punishing the autistic behaviors of a deviant child. *Journal of Applied Behavior Analysis, 1,* 21–34.

Risley, T. R., & Wolf, M. (1967). Establishing functional speech in echolalic children. *Behaviour Research and Therapy, 5,* 73–88.

Ritvo, E. R., & Freeman, B. J. (1978). National Society for Autistic Children definition of the syndrome of autism. *Journal of Autism and Childhood Schizophrenia, 8,* 162–167.

Rogers-Warren, A., & Warren, S. F. (1980). Mands for verbalization: Facilitating the display of newly trained language in children. *Behavior Modification, 4,* 361–382.

Romanczyk, R. G., Diament, C., Goren, E. R., Trunell, G., & Harris, S. L. (1975). Increasing isolate and social play in severely disturbed children: Intervention and postintervention effectiveness. *Journal of Autism and Childhood Schizophrenia, 5,* 57–70.

Roos, P. (1972). Reconciling behavior modification procedures with the normalization principle. In W. Wolfensberger (Ed.), *The principle of normalization in human services* (pp. 136–148). Toronto: National Institute on Mental Retardation.

Rumsey, J. M., Rapoport, J. L., & Sceery, W. R. (1985). Autistic children as adults: Psychiatric, social, and behavioral outcomes. *Journal of the American Academy of Child Psychiatry, 24,* 465–473.

Russo, D. C., Cataldo, M. F., & Cushing, P. J. (1981). Compliance training and behavioral covariation in the treatment of multiple behavior problems. *Journal of Applied Behavior Analysis, 14,* 209–222.

Rutter, M. (1968). Concepts of autism: A review of research. *Journal of Child Psychology and Psychiatry, 9,* 1–25.

Rutter, M. (1972). Childhood schizophrenia reconsidered. *Journal of Autism and Childhood Schizophrenia, 2,* 315–337.

Rutter, M. (1978). Diagnosis and definition of childhood autism. *Journal of Autism and Childhood Schizophrenia, 8,* 139–161.

Rutter, M. (1983). Cognitive deficits in the pathogenesis of autism. *Journal of Child Psychology and Psychiatry, 24,* 513–531.

Rutter, M. (1985). Infantile autism and other pervasive developmental disorders. In M. Rutter & L. Hersov (Eds.), *Child and adolescent psychiatry* (2nd ed., pp. 545–566). Oxford: Blackwell.

Rutter, M. (1988). Biological basis of autism: Implications for intervention. In F. J. Menolascino & J. A. Stark (Eds.), *Preventive and curative intervention in mental retardation* (pp. 265–294). Baltimore: Paul H. Brookes.

Rutter, M., & Brown, G. (1966). The reliability and validity of measures of family life and relationships in families containing a psychiatric patient. *Social Psychiatry, 1,* 38–53.

Rutter, M., Greenfeld, D., & Lockyer, L. (1967). A five to fifteen year follow-up study of infantile psychosis: II. Social and behavioural outcome. *British Journal of Psychiatry, 113,* 1183–1199.

Rutter, M., & Lockyer, L. (1967). A five to fifteen year follow-up study of infantile psychosis: I. Description of sample. *British Journal of Psychiatry, 113,* 1169–1182.

Rutter, M., & Schopler, E. (1987). Autism and pervasive developmental disorders: Concepts and diagnostic issues.

Journal of Autism and Developmental Disorders, 17, 159–186.

Sailor, W., & Guess, D. (1983). *Severely handicapped students: An instructional design.* Boston: Houghton Mifflin.

Sailor, W., & Taman, T. (1972). Stimulus factors in the training of prepositional usage in three autistic children. *Journal of Applied Behavior Analysis, 5,* 183–190.

Salzinger, K. (1959). Experimental manipulation of verbal behavior: A review. *Journal of General Psychology, 61,* 65–94.

Santarcangelo, S., Dyer, K., & Luce, S. C. (1987). Generalized reduction of disruptive behavior in unsupervised settings through specific toy training. *Journal of the Association for Persons with Severe Handicaps, 12,* 38–44.

Sasso, G. M., & Rude, H. A. (1987). Unprogrammed effects of training high-status peers to interact with severely handicapped children. *Journal of Applied Behavior Analysis, 20,* 35–44.

Saunders, R., & Sailor, W. (1979). A comparison of three strategies of reinforcement on two-choice learning problems with severely retarded children. *AAESPH Review, 4,* 323–333.

Schaeffer, B. (1980). Spontaneous language through signed speech. In R. L. Schiefelbusch (Ed.), *Nonspeech language and communication* (pp. 421–446). Baltimore: University Park Press.

Schaeffer, B., Kollinzas, G., Musil, A., & McDowell, P. (1977). Spontaneous verbal language for autistic children through signed speech. *Sign Language Studies, 17,* 287–328.

Schain, R. J., & Yannet, H. (1960). Infantile autism: An analysis of 50 cases and a consideration of certain neurophysiologic concepts. *Journal of Pediatrics, 57,* 560–567.

Scheerenberger, R. L. (1986). *Public residential services for the mentally retarded, 1985* (Publication of the National Association of Superintendents of Public Residential Facilities for the Mentally Retarded). Madison: Central Wisconsin Center for the Developmentally Disabled.

Schell, R. E., Stark, J., & Giddan, J. J. (1967). Development of language behavior in an autistic child. *Journal of Speech and Hearing Disorders, 32,* 51–64.

Schopler, E., & Mesibov, G. B. (Eds.). (1984). *The effects of autism on the family.* New York: Plenum.

Schreibman, L. (1975). Effects of within-stimulus and extra-stimulus prompting on discrimination learning in autistic children. *Journal of Applied Behavior Analysis, 8,* 91–112.

Schreibman, L., & Carr, E. G. (1978). Elimination of echolalic responding to questions through the training of a generalized verbal response. *Journal of Applied Behavior Analysis, 11,* 453–463.

Schreibman, L., Koegel, R. L., Mills, D. L., & Burke, J. C. (1984). Training parent–child interactions. In E. Schopler & G. Mesibov (Eds.), *The effects of autism on the family* (pp. 187–205). New York: Plenum.

Schreibman, L., O'Neill, R. E., & Koegel, R. L. (1983) Behavioral training for siblings of autistic children. *Journal of Applied Behavior Analysis, 16,* 129–138.

Segal, E. F. (1972). Induction and the provenance of operants. In R. M. Gilbert & J. R. Millenson (Eds.), *Reinforcement: Behavioral Analyses* (pp. 1–34). New York: Academic Press.

Segal, E. F. (1975). Psycholinguistics discovers the op-

erant: A review of Roger Brown's *A first language: The early stages. Journal of the Experimental Analysis of Behavior, 23,* 149–158.

Seibert, J. M., & Oller, D. K. (1981). Linguistic pragmatics and language intervention strategies. *Journal of Autism and Developmental Disabilities, 11,* 75–88.

Shafer, M. S., Egel, A. L., & Neef, N. A. (1984). Training mildly handicapped peers to facilitate changes in the social interaction skills of autistic children. *Journal of Applied Behavior Analysis, 17,* 461–476.

Shane, H. C. (1980). Approaches to assessing the communication of non-oral persons. In R. L. Schiefelbusch (Ed.), *Nonspeech language and communication* (pp. 197–224). Baltimore: University Park Press.

Siegel, B., Anders, T. F., Ciaranello, R. D., Bienenstock, B., & Kraemer, H. C. (1986). Empirically derived subclassification of the autistic syndrome. *Journal of Autism and Developmental Disorders, 16,* 275–293.

Sigman, M., & Ungerer, J. (1981). Sensorimotor skills and language comprehension in autistic children. *Journal of Abnormal Child Psychology, 9,* 149–165.

Simeonsson, R. J., Olley, J. G., Rosenthal, S. L. (1987). Early intervention for children with autism. In M. J. Guralnick & F. C. Bennett (Eds.), *The effectiveness of early intervention for at-risk and handicapped children* (pp. 275–296). New York: Academic Press.

Singh, N. N., & Millichamp, C. J. (1987). Independent and social play among profoundly mentally retarded adults: Training, maintenance, generalization, and long-term follow-up. *Journal of Applied Behavior Analysis, 20,* 23–34.

Skinner, B. F. (1957). *Verbal behavior.* New York: Appleton-Century-Crofts.

Skinner, B. F. (1968). *The technology of teaching.* New York: Appleton-Century-Crofts.

Skinner, B. F. (1981). Selection by consequences. *Science, 213,* 501–504.

Sloane, H. N., Johnston, M. K., & Harris, F. R. (1968). Remedial procedures for teaching verbal behavior to speech deficient or defective young children. In H. N. Sloane, & B. D. MacAulay (Eds.), *Operant procedures in remedial speech and language training* (pp. 77–101). Boston: Houghton Mifflin.

Snow, C. E. (1977). The development of conversation between mothers and babies. *Journal of Child Language, 4,* 1–22.

Snyder, L., Apolloni, T., & Cooke, T. P. (1977). Integrated settings at the early childhood level: The role of nonretarded peers. *Exceptional Children, 43,* 262–266.

Sobsey, D. (1987). Non-aversive behavior management: The verdict is in. *News & Notes: A Quarterly Newsletter of the American Association on Mental Retardation, 1,* 2–8.

Sparrow, S. S., Balla, D., & Cicchetti, D. (1984). *Vineland Adaptive Behavior Scales.* Circle Pines, MN: American Guidance Service.

Sparrow, S. S., Rescorla, L. A. Provence, S., Condon, S. O., Goudreau, D., & Cicchetti, D. V. (1986). Follow-up of "atypical" children. A brief report. *Journal of the American Academy of Child Psychiatry, 25,* 181–185.

Stanley, A. E. (1985). *Toward a functional analysis of stereotypy.* Unpublished doctoral dissertation, Claremont Graduate School, Claremont, CA.

Stark, J., Giddan, J. J., & Meisel, J. (1968). Increasing verbal behavior in an autistic child. *Journal of Speech and Hearing Disorders, 33,* 42–47.

Stevens-Long, J., & Rasmussen, M. (1974). The acquisition of simple and compound sentence structure in an autistic child. *Journal of Applied Behavior Analysis, 7,* 473–479.

Stokes, T. F., & Baer, D. M. (1977). An implicit technology of generalization. *Journal of Applied Behavior Analysis, 10,* 349–367.

Strain, P. S. (1977). Effects of peer social initiations on withdrawn preschool children: Some training and generalization effects. *Journal of Abnormal Child Psychology, 5,* 445–455.

Strain, P. S. (1980). Social behavior programming with severely handicapped and autistic children. In B. Wilcox & A. Thompson (Eds.), *Critical issues in educating autistic children and youth* (pp. 179–206). Washington: U.S. Department of Education, Office of Special Education.

Strain, P. S. (1983). Generalization of autistic children's social behavior change: Effects of developmentally integrated and segregated settings. *Analysis and Intervention in Developmental Disabilities, 3,* 23–34.

Strain, P. S., Hoyson, M. H., & Jamieson, B. J. (1985). Normally developing preschoolers as intervention agents for autistic-like children: Effects on class deportment and social interactions. *Journal of the Division for Early Childhood, 9,* 105–115.

Strain, P. S., Kerr, M. M., & Ragland, E. U. (1979). Effects of peer-mediated social initiations and prompting/reinforcement procedures on the social behavior of autistic children. *Journal of Autism and Developmental Disorders, 9,* 41–54.

Strain, P, S., Shores, R. E., & Timm, M. A. (1977). Effects of peer initiations on the social behavior of withdrawn preschool children. *Journal of Applied Behavior Analysis, 10,* 289–298.

Striefel, S., Bryan, K. S., & Aikins, D. A. (1974). Transfer of stimulus control from motor to verbal stimuli. *Journal of Applied Behavior Analysis, 7, 123–135.

Striefel, S., & Wetherby, B. (1973). Instruction-following behavior of a retarded child and its controlling stimuli. *Journal of Applied Behavior Analysis, 6,* 663–670.

Striefel, S., Wetherby, B., & Karlan, G. (1978). Developing generalized instruction-following behavior in severely retarded people. In C. E. Meyers (Ed.), *Quality of life in severely and profoundly mentally retarded people* (pp. 267–326). Washington: American Association on Mental Deficiency.

Szurek, S. A. (1956). Psychotic episodes and psychotic maldevelopment. *American Journal of Orthopsychiatry, 26,* 519–543.

Taggert, D., & Rincover, A. (1985, March). *Early intervention for autistic and retarded children: Developing social reinforcers in autistic and retarded children.* Paper presented at the conference of the Ontario Chapter of the American Association on Mental Deficiency, Toronto.

Talkington, L. W., Hall, S., & Altman, R. (1971). Communication deficits and aggression in the mentally retarded. *American Journal of Mental Deficiency, 76,* 235–237.

Tanguay, P. E. (1984). Toward a new classification of serious psychopathology in children. *Journal of the American Academy of Child Psychiatry, 23,* 373–384.

Tiegerman, E., & Primavera, L. (1981). Object manipulation: An interactional strategy with autistic children. *Journal of Autism and Developmental Disorders, 11,* 427–438.

Tiegerman, E., & Primavera, L. H. (1984). Imitating the autistic child: Facilitating communicative gaze behavior.

Journal of Autism and Developmental Disorders, 14, 27–38.

Timm, M. A., Strain, P. S., & Eller, P. H. (1979). Effects of systematic response-dependent fading and thinning on the maintenance of child–child interaction. *Journal of Applied Behavior Analysis, 12,* 308.

Touchette, P. E., MacDonald, R. F., & Langer, S. N. (1985). A scatter plot for identifying stimulus control of problem behavior. *Journal of Applied Behavior Analysis, 18,* 343–351.

Toulmin, S. (1988). The recovery of practical philosophy. *American Scholar, 57,* 337–352.

Tremblay, A., Strain, P. S., Hendrickson, J. M., & Shores, R. E. (1981). Social interactions of normally developing preschool children: Using normative data for subject and target behavior selection. *Behavior Modification, 5,* 237–253.

Tryon, A. S., & Keane, S. P. (1986). Promoting imitative play through generalized observational learning in autisticlike children. *Journal of Abnormal Child Psychology, 14,* 537–549.

Tubbs, V. K. (1966). Types of linguistic disability in psychotic children. *Journal of Mental Deficiency Research, 10,* 230–240.

Turnbull, A. P., Blue-Banning, M., Behr, S., & Kerns, G. (1986). Family research and intervention: A value and ethical examination. In P. R. Dokecki & R. M. Zaner (Eds.), *Ethics of dealing with persons with severe handicaps* (pp. 119–140). Baltimore: Paul H. Brookes.

Turnbull, J. R., Guess, D., Backus, L. H., Barber, P. A., Fiedler, C. R., Helmstetter, E., & Summers, J. A. (1986). A model for analyzing the moral aspects of special education and behavioral interventions: The moral aspects of aversive procedures. In P. R. Dokecki & R. M. Zaner (Eds.), *Ethics of dealing with persons with severe handicaps* (pp. 167–210). Baltimore: Paul H. Brookes.

Twardosz, S., & Jozwiak, W. (1981). The expression of affection: Suggestions for research with developmentally disabled children. *Analysis and Intervention in Developmental Disabilities, 1,* 217–238.

Volkmar, F. R. (1986). Compliance, noncompliance, and negativism. In E. Schopler & G. B. Mesibov (Eds.), *Social behavior in autism* (pp. 171–188). New York: Plenum.

Volkmar, F. R., Cohen, D. J., & Paul, R. (1986). An evaluation of DSM-III criteria for infantile autism. *Journal of the American Academy of Child Psychiatry, 25,* 190–197.

Volkmar, F. R., Sparrow, S. S., Goudreau, D., Cicchetti, D. V., Paul, R., & Cohen, D. J. (1987). Social deficits in autism: An operational approach using the Vineland Adaptive Behavior Scales. *Journal of the American Academy of Child and Adolescent Psychiatry, 26,* 156–161.

Wahler, R. G. (1969). Oppositional children: A quest for parental reinforcement control. *Journal of Applied Behavior Analysis, 2,* 159–170.

Wahler, R. G., Nordquist, V. M. (1973). Adult discipline as a factor in childhood imitation. *Journal of Abnormal Child Psychology, 1,* 40–56.

Walker, H. M., Greenwood, C. R., Hops, H., & Todd, N. (1979). Differential effects of reinforcing topographic components of social interaction. *Behavior Modification, 3,* 291–321.

Warren, S. F., & Rogers-Warren, A. (1980). Current perspectives in language remediation. *Education and Treatment of Children, 3,* 133–152.

Wasserman, L. M. (1969). *Discrimination learning in autistic children.* Unpublished doctoral dissertation, University of California at Los Angeles.

Weeks, M., & Gaylord-Ross, R. (1981). Task difficulty and aberrant behavior in severely handicapped students. *Journal of Applied Behavior Analysis, 14,* 449–463.

Wetzel, R. J., Baker, J., Roney, M., & Martin, M. (1966). An operant analysis of child–family interaction: Outpatient treatment of autistic behaviour. *Behaviour Research and Therapy, 4,* 169–177.

Whitman, T. L., Scibak, J. W., & Reid, D. H. (1983). *Behavior modification with the severely and profoundly retarded.* New York: Academic Press.

Wilcox, B., & Thompson, A. (Eds.). (1980). *Critical issues in educating autistic children and youth.* Washington, DC: U.S. Department of Education, Office of Special Education.

Wildman, B. G., Wildman, H. E., & Kelly, W. J. (1986). Group conversational skills training and social validation with mentally retarded adults. *Applied Research in Mental Retardation, 7,* 443–458.

Wildman, R. W., & Simon, S. J. (1978). An indirect method for increasing the rate of social interaction in an autistic child. *Journal of Clinical Psychology, 34,* 144–149.

Williams, J. A., Koegel, R. L., & Egel, A. L. (1981). Response–reinforcer relationships and improved learning in autistic children. *Journal of Applied Behavior Analysis, 14,* 53–60.

Wing, J. K. (1976). Kanner's syndrome: A historical introduction. In L. Wing (Ed.), *Early childhood autism* (2nd ed., pp. 3–14). New York: Pergamon Press.

Wing, L. (1981a). Language, social, and cognitive impairments in autism and severe mental retardation. *Journal of Autism and Developmental Disorders, 11,* 31–44.

Wing, L. (1981b). Asperger's syndrome: A clinical account. *Psychological Medicine, 11,* 115–129.

Wing, L., & Attwood, A. (1987). Syndromes of autism and atypical development. In D. J. Cohen & A. M. Donnellan (Eds.), *Handbook of autism and pervasive developmental disorders* (pp. 3–19). New York: Wiley.

Wing, L., & Gould, J. (1979). Severe impairments of social interaction and associated abnormalities in children: Epidemiology and classification. *Journal of Autism and Developmental Disorders, 9,* 11–29.

Wing, L., Yeates, S. R., Brierley, L. M., & Gould, J. (1976). The prevalence of early childhood autism: Comparison of administrative and epidemiological studies. *Psychological Medicine, 6,* 89–100.

Witt, J. C., & Wacker, D. P. (1981). Teaching children to respond to auditory directives: An evaluation of two procedures. *Behavior Research of Severe Developmental Disabilities, 2,* 175–189.

Wolff, S., & Barlow, A. (1979). Schizoid personality in childhood: A comparative study of schizoid, autistic and normal children. *Journal of Child Psychology and Psychiatry, 20,* 29–46.

Wolff, W. M., & Morris, L. A. (1971). Intellectual and personality characteristics of parents of autistic children. *Journal of Abnormal Psychology, 77,* 155–161.

Yoder, D. E., & Calculator, S. (1981). Some perspectives on intervention strategies for persons with developmental disorders. *Journal of Autism and Developmental Disorders, 11,* 107–123.

Zane, T., Handen, B. L., Mason, S. A., & Geffin, C. (1984). Teaching symbol identification: A comparison between standard prompting and intervening response procedures. *Analysis and Intervention in Developmental Disabilities, 4,* 367–377.

9

LEARNING DISABILITIES

H. GERRY TAYLOR
Rainbow Babies & Children's Hospital
Case Western Reserve University School of Medicine

Children who do not learn at a normal rate for reasons other than general mental impairment, lack of opportunity, social–emotional disturbance, or sensory defect are referred to as "learning-disabled" (Hallahan & Bryan, 1981). In many ways, learning-disabled children are much like their nondisabled peers. Disabled learners may be no less intelligent than their classmates. At least initially, both groups have similar opportunities to learn. The major difference is that those with learning disabilities fail to benefit from conventional instruction and are therefore regarded as having special educational needs.

Given that billions of dollars are spent each year on special education programs for learning-disabled children, surprisingly little is known about program effectiveness (Farnham-Diggory, 1986). Formal attempts to measure program effects are uncommon, and methodologically sound research is rarer still (Keogh, 1983). The longitudinal data that are available suggest that existing programs fail to enable learning-disabled children to catch up with their peers academically (see "Remedial Programs," below). Some educators are beginning to question the value of special education classes altogether (Ysseldyke & Algozzine, 1983).

On the other hand, there are many useful methods for treating specific aspects of learning failure. The contention of this chapter is that effective treatment of learning-disabled children requires that multiple component needs be met simultaneously. Although some authorities are beginning to advocate more broad-based approaches to treatment (Schumaker, Deshler, & Ellis, 1986), multidimensional programs are rarely implemented in a way that would permit formal evaluation. The success of such programs, in any case, would be contingent on how well each of the several component problems was managed. For this reason, the present chapter focuses on component problems, and it reviews intervention methods that have proved effective in treating these problems. The emphasis of this chapter is on research-validated methods, since these procedures constitute the proper foundation for treatment recommendations. Following discussion of component problems and their treatment, issues to consider in formulating individual treatment plans are taken up. The final section of the chapter summarizes clinical demands, research needs, and major themes regarding treatment of children with learning problems.

THE FIELD OF LEARNING DISABILITIES

Interest in learning disabilities as a distinct clinical entity came to a head in 1963, with the establishment of the Association for Children with Learning Disabilities (Kirk, 1963). Pressure from this and other groups has been successful in bringing the dilemma of the learning-disabled child to light and in passing legislation mandating supplementary academic assistance. The learning disabilities movement is a natural consequence of North American values favoring the right to literacy for all citizens and equality of educational attainment (Kauffman, 1981; Resnick & Resnick, 1977). This movement also stems from the conviction that children with learning disabilities have much to gain from special education. The latter conviction seems to have originated from the acclaimed success of highly structured, individualized approaches to teaching brain-injured children. Exemplary methods include those of Strauss and Lehtinen (1947) and Cruickshank, Bentzen, Ratzeburg, and Tannhauser (1961). In view of the historical importance of this belief, critical appraisal of treatment strategies for children with learning disabilities is both timely and appropriate.

The concept of learning disabilities has been effective in providing a frame of reference for a common type of childhood problem. According to most estimates, between 5% and 15% of school-age children have learning disabilities. Males are more frequently identified than females, by a ratio of between 2:1 and 5:1 (Finucci & Childs, 1981). Incidence also varies as a function of cultural–familial and sociodemographic factors (Eisenberg, 1978; Rutter, 1978). Because prevalence estimates depend on sample characteristics as well as on the specific operational criteria used for identification, there is no "best" estimate. All one can conclude is that a substantial percentage of nonretarded school children have learning problems of the sort referred to by the concept.

The concept of learning disabilities has also brought about a greater awareness of the fact that learning problems are at least partially a function of characteristics intrinsic to the child, or of deficits in "one or more of the basic psychological processes involved in using spoken or written language" (U.S. Office of Education, 1968, p. 34). Research has established that the learning-disabled population manifests numerous deficits in psychological processing. Deficits have been reported in speech and language, visual–perceptual skills, sensory–motor abilities, use of cognitive strategies, and in memory, reasoning, and attentional capacities. Somewhat lower-than-average IQs are also typical of learning-disabled samples (Stanovich, 1986). Patterns of strengths and weaknesses vary considerably from child to child, and many children display multiple cognitive dysfunctions.

On balance, emphasis on basic psychological processes has had a healthy influence on the study of childhood learning problems. Assessment of basic psychological skills provides hints regarding cognitive factors that contribute to academic failure. Knowledge of these weaknesses is relevant both for treatment of the individual child and for research on subtypes of learning problems (Rourke, 1985; Torgesen, 1982). A further advantage of an emphasis on cognitive processes is that it encourages a broader view of the child. A child who has deficiencies in mental organization or memory, for instance, is likely to experience problems at home as well as at school. Problems may involve inability to remember directions or lack of independence in carrying out chores. Parents having difficulty managing these problems are receptive to sensible interpretations of their child's problems.

According to traditional definitions of learning disabilities, processing deficits are presumed to reflect "dysfunctions of the central nervous system" (U.S. Office of Education, 1968, p. 34). Review of the available evidence suggests that biological or genetic factors may indeed contribute to learning disabilities and other specific developmental disorders (Taylor & Fletcher, 1983). Learning problems can be predicted with some accuracy, based on skills present either before school begins or early in the child's educational career (Satz, Taylor, Friel, & Fletcher, 1978; Stevenson & Newman, 1986). These disabilities are present in many well-adjusted children, and are associated with various biological "marker" variables, including family histories of learning disabilities, electrophysiological irregularities, neurological "soft signs," and pre- and perinatal complications.

Nevertheless, the exact causes of learning disabilities are largely unknown. The relationship between biological markers and learning disabilities is only a weak one. There are many disabled learners for whom no markers are present; there are many other children with these markers who learn normally. Environmental factors appear to be just as relevant as the child's biological status (Keogh, 1982). Environmental contributors in addition to socioeconomic opportunity and cultural–familial makeup include lack of facility or willingness on the part of the school to accommodate to individual differences in learning aptitude. Unsupportive teachers or parents may unwittingly exacerbate a child's learning problem—to the extent that a relatively minor learning difficulty is transformed into a bona fide learning disability. Learning problems that some teachers take in stride as individual differences may be outside the range of tolerance of other teachers. How well the child compensates for intrinsic weaknesses will also affect the seriousness of the learning problems.

But those who founded the learning disabilities movement were more concerned with treatment than with etiology. The primary advantage of the concept of learning disabilities is that it forces us to confront the ineffectiveness of conventional instruction for many children who appear to have the potential to learn. The overriding interest of those who advocate the cause of disabled learners is in finding more effective ways to help these children gain academic competence.

DEFINITIONAL ISSUES

As indicated at the outset of this chapter, most definitions stipulate that learning disabilities are not secondary to generalized mental impairment, sensory disorders, emotional disturbance, or lack of opportunity. The learning disabilities themselves may be manifested in any number of ways. According to the original definition formulated by the National Advisory Committee on Handicapped Children, learning disabilities include "disorders of listening, thinking, talking, reading, writing, spelling, and arithmetic" (U.S. Office of Education, 1968, p. 34). The definition given by U.S. Public Law 94-142 (1977) lists problems in oral expression, listening comprehension, written expression, basic reading skill, reading comprehension, mathematics calculation, and mathematics reasoning (p. 65083). The latter definition also requires that it not be possible to meet the child's needs in the regular classroom. According to the National Joint Committee on Learning Disabilities (JCLD) (1983), learning disabilities involve problems in either the acquisition or application of communication and academic skills. The JCLD definition also makes it clear that other handicapping conditions may be present, so long as they do not constitute the primary basis of the learning problems. The *Diagnostic and Statistical Manual of Mental Disorders,* third edition, revised (DSM-III-R; American Psychiatric Association, 1987) refers to learning disabilities as Academic Skill Disorders (Developmental Arithmetic, Expressive Writing, and Reading Disorders). According to DSM-III-R, academic skills must be below expectations based on IQ and level of schooling, and they must significantly interfere with either academic achievement or day-to-day functioning.

These several definitions have been successful in focusing the attention of the public and the legal system on the dilemma of many essentially "normal" children who fail to respond to conventional instruction. None of the definitions, however, is totally satisfactory, at least for those professionals who study, evaluate, or treat disabled learners. Problems with existing definitions are essentially threefold. To begin with, current definitions do not acknowledge the fact that learning disabilities are to some degree dependent on our expectations of children (Smith, 1985). As long as there are variations in what we expect of children, any attempt to formulate a definition that is both operationally specific and universally applicable is doomed to failure (Ysseldyke & Algozzine, 1983). A second problem with existing definitions of learning disabilities is that they acknowledge neither the tremendous individual variation within groups of disabled learners, nor the importance of psychosocial, motivational, and environmental influences on learning problems (Keogh, 1982; Smith, 1985). Experience in conducting clinical assessments reveals that there is much individual variability in the severity of academic problems, accompanying cognitive deficits, and coping skills. Attempts to seek more homogeneous subgroupings of children within this broader category will be necessary if advances are to be made in identification procedures, treatment, and research.

A final issue relates to the fact that most definitions in current use exclude children who do not meet certain IQ requirements. IQ tests are useful in assessing cognitive strengths and weaknesses. Large differences in overall intelligence may indeed have implications regarding children's ability to profit from special help (Polloway, Epstein, Polloway, Patton, & Ball, 1986). There is also reason to believe that intelligence level is related to long-term prognosis (Horn, O'Donnell, & Vitulano, 1983; Rutter, 1978). Nevertheless, research comparing underachieving children who have at least normal

IQs with underachievers who do not meet this criterion has generally failed to reveal any meaningful differences (Deshler, Schumaker, Alley, Warner, & Clark, 1982; Stanovich, 1986). Other limitations of IQ scores are that they are not always good predictors of learning aptitude, and that psychometric intelligence is itself a function of learning history (Taylor, 1988). The very same skill deficits that underlie a given learning problem may contribute to poor performance on the IQ test. IQ tests simply provide too narrow a picture of children's competencies. The customary application of IQ test results to distinguish children with learning disabilities from other nonretarded low achievers seems particularly inappropriate. Many children with IQs in the 80s or even 70s have learning problems similar to those of children with higher IQs. Moreover, there is no empirical basis for the claim that children with IQs in the borderline to lower average ranges are less able to profit from remedial assistance than are those with higher IQs. Yet, in many school districts, children with lower IQs are disqualified from special educational programs. If the objective of identifying children with learning disabilities is to provide appropriate treatment for those children who are most likely to benefit from it, absolute levels of IQ and academic achievement must be viewed as parts of a much bigger picture.

LEARNING DISABILITIES RECONSIDERED

In light of the above-stated misgivings regarding the usual narrow conception of learning disabilities, it is essential that the assessment process be considered from as broad a perspective as possible (Taylor, 1988). Learning problems occur when children fail to meet expectations for academic achievement and productivity. These problems most likely reflect the influence of several sets of variables, including actual school-related skills and levels of academic achievement, cognitive and behavioral characteristics, and environmental and biological factors. It is essential that those who deal with children realize the complexity and diversity of learning problems, the fact that learning problems are influenced by environmental factors as well as by child characteristics, and the scope of developmental and behavioral difficulties associated with these problems (Keogh,

1982). The premise of this less restrictive conceptualization is that the sources of learning problems are best understood by means of multidimensional appraisals of children and of their interactions with family, school, and peers. Appropriate treatment is predicated on an appreciation of all contributing factors.

Children with behavior disorders so severe as to prevent even marginal adjustment in the classroom, who have been consistently absent from school, or who are experiencing acute adjustment reactions should not be expected to learn at a normal rate. A learning problem that accompanies such extreme conditions should be expected, and the child's learning difficulties should be regarded as secondary rather than primary symptoms. In keeping with the definition proposed by the JCLD, however, it is important to consider the possibility that these children may also have learning disabilities. Although appropriate treatment for children with other behavior disorders may begin with management of nonacademic issues, treatment of the learning problems themselves may eventually be in order.

In more typical cases of learning disabilities, a host of behavioral and environmental issues are part and parcel of the learning problems themselves. Learning disabilities frequently present as combinations of academic, cognitive, behavioral, motivational, and social disorders. Negative interactions between a child and others at home and at school, for example, may make it difficult for parents to know whether the child is really unable to perform or is simply maladjusted or unmotivated. The goal of assessment is to formulate hypotheses regarding the major factors responsible for a given child's learning problems.

The term "learning disabilities" is used in this chapter to refer to a relatively unrestricted set of learning problems in children for whom mental retardation, emotional disturbance, sensory defect, and lack of opportunity either are not present or do not fully account for the children's failure to learn. The problems to which the term refers are construed as the entire range of academic, cognitive, motivational, interpersonal, and behavioral difficulties facing these children. Failure to keep pace with the regular curriculum and lack of academic productivity are the major hallmarks of these disabilities. We may hope that future research will suggest more specific means by which to positively identify learning problems—means that will avoid reliance on the somewhat arbitrary exclusionary criteria in common use today.

COMPONENT PROBLEMS

According to the assessment model detailed in a companion chapter (Taylor, 1988), assessment of learning disabilities requires evaluation of each of several potential problem areas. The problem areas, summarized in Figure 9-1, comprise those biobehavioral systems that must be reviewed in any comprehensive assessment. Although a child may not evidence problems in all areas, any difficulties that do exist are considered relevant to the evaluation. Even if a particular deficit is not a sufficient antecedent for learning problems, it may either increase the child's vulnerability to learning failure or exacerbate pre-existing learning difficulties. Consideration of each problem area is also essential in planning treatment. Assessment techniques appropriate to evaluation of each problem area are summarized below.

Academic Achievement and School Performance

Academic deficits most commonly include failure to develop age- or grade-appropriate aptitudes in areas such as reading, spelling, math, and written expression. Deshler *et al.* (1982) have found that older children and adolescents with learning disabilities also have limited background knowledge in content areas and impoverished strategies for learning (e.g., poor listening skills, note-taking abilities, and study habits). Although academic deficits are usually pervasive, the fact that some children have relatively isolated academic difficulties makes it imperative to take a close look at component academic skills. Two dissociable reading subskills are decoding and comprehension. Components of spelling ability include knowledge of sound–symbol correspondences and orthography, recognition memory for written words, and the ability to employ spelling knowledge in the context of writing. Component math skills consist of memory for number facts, visual–spatial skills, the ability to carry out computational procedures, and appreciation of math concepts. Written expression requires penmanship, punctuation, vocabulary, and expression and organization of ideas. In each of these areas, it is important to assess speed and automaticity as well as accuracy. Standardized measures are available for most of these skills, although it is not clear how sensitive available measures are to treatment effects (Gittelman & Feingold, 1983; Lovett, Ransby, Hardwick, & Johns, in press). In cases where measures of a particular skill have not yet been standardized,

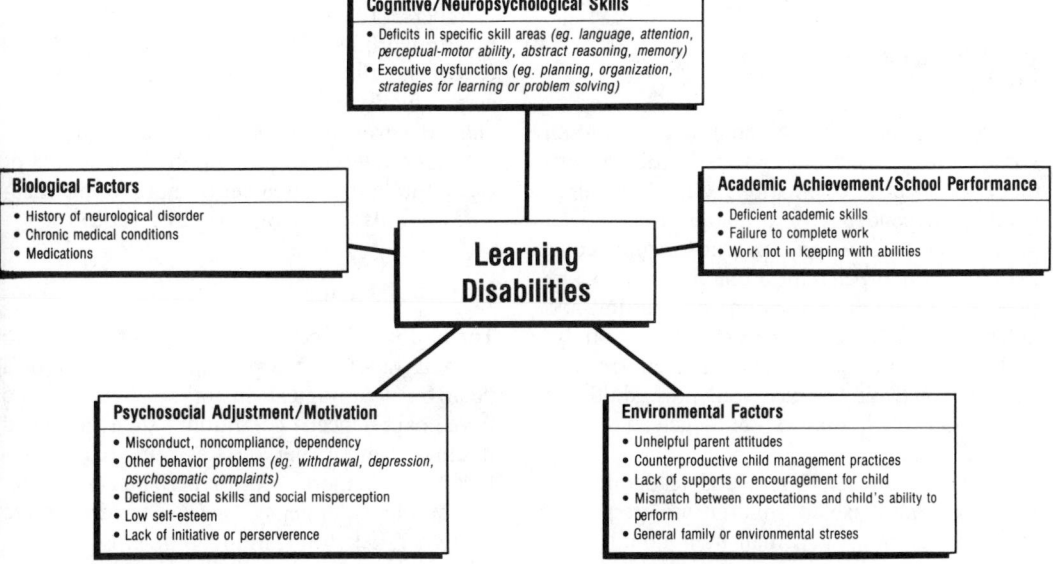

FIGURE 9-1. Problem areas to consider in evaluating learning disabilities: A biobehavioral systems model.

experimental procedures or systematic observations are useful.

Cognitive and Neuropsychological Skills

Cognitive deficits that frequently accompany learning problems include mild depressions in IQ, speech and language disorders, memory impairments, motor incoordination and other neurological "soft signs," visual–motor difficulties, attentional problems, weaknesses in abstract reasoning and problem solving, and failure to employ cognitive strategies such as rehearsal and comprehension monitoring as aids to learning. Because the examiner is interested in strengths as well as weaknesses, evaluations typically involve appraisal of a majority of these skill areas. The set of tests most appropriate for any given case will vary somewhat according to presenting problems. Clinicians' test repertoires will naturally evolve as new and improved test procedures are developed. In spite of recent doubts as to the value of diagnostic–prescriptive teaching, knowledge of individual differences in cognitive and neuropsychological functioning is relevant in planning treatment (Hartlage & Telzrow, 1983; Lyon, 1985). Advances in knowledge of those cognitive dimensions that underlie acquisition of academic skills will help to assure the relevance of cognitive and neuropsychological assessments.

Psychosocial Adjustment and Motivation

Psychosocial problems are common in children with learning disabilities. These problems include poor task orientation, classroom misconduct, dependency, and inappropriate social behaviors. Depression, psychosomatic complaints, or other behavior problems may also be present. Although interactions of learning and behavior difficulties have received little study, both kinds of problems may be present from an early age and may persist well into adulthood (Jorm, Share, Matthews, & Maclean, 1986; Spreen, 1982).

As a consequence of repeated academic failures, learning-disabled children are frequently more poorly motivated than their nondisabled classmates. Disabled learners tend to have lower self-esteem than their peers. They expect less of themselves, avoid challenges, and dislike school tasks. They attribute their difficulties to lack of ability rather than to insufficient effort and are often described as "helpless." Due to their failure experiences, these children seek less challenging tasks, become more dependent on help, or simply give up. Problems in these areas can be assessed informally through parent and teacher interviews, or more formally by means of standardized behavior checklists, sociometric assessments, or self-reports of attitudes or attributions.

Environmental Influences

Broad-based assessment of learning difficulties necessitates evaluation of all potential environmental influences. Relevant environmental considerations include sociodemographic status, cultural values, and child management practices. The mere presence of a learning disability predisposes a family to stress, social isolation, and reduced autonomy (Slater & Wikler, 1986). Misplaced blame, negativism, and parental feelings of guilt, anger, despair, or helplessness complicate effective treatment (Amerikaner & Omizo, 1984; Shapiro & Forbes, 1981). Adding to the burden on parents are concerns about the child's future, dependence on teachers and other professionals to make extra efforts on the child's behalf, and the substantial time and inconvenience involved in attending to the child's needs. These sacrifices may mean spending less time in preferred activities or with other family members. Teachers experience similar dilemmas in working with the child at school (Garis & Green, 1982). It is essential, therefore, to assess family relationships, parental attitudes, and environmental stresses and supports. Although interviews provide the best source of this information, a number of more formal measures are also available (Taylor, 1988).

Biological Factors

The biological factor of most direct relevance to learning failure is the presence or absence of a positive neurological history. Children who have experienced conditions such as head trauma, central nervous system (CNS) infections or tumors, pre- or perinatal neurological problems, epilepsy, or CNS irradiation are at higher risk for learning problems than are other children (Taylor, 1984). A positive neurological history may also have implications for the types of learning problems manifested by a child (Taylor, 1987). Children with actual brain disease can be justifiably labeled as learning-disabled, so long as their learning problems are not due to pervasive mental impairment.

Other medical problems having less direct effects on learning are chronic illnesses and defects in vision or hearing. Difficulties in managing an illness, incomplete correction of sensory defects, or medication side effects can lead to sensory impairment, fatigue, or physical discomfort that may interfere with learning. Available evidence fails to support speculations that learning disabilities are the direct result of increased intake of sugar or salicylates, vitamin deficiencies, low levels of environmental toxins, mild fluctuations in hearing due to otitis media, or visual dysfunctions such as poor fusional amplitudes (Barkley, 1981; Keogh & Pelland, 1985; Paradise, 1981). However, the child's overall medical status is a relevant concern.

Evaluation of a possible diagnosis of Attention Deficit–Hyperactivity Disorder (ADHD; American Psychiatric Association, 1987) also falls under the heading of biological influences. There is considerable overlap between attention deficits and learning disabilities (Douglas & Peters, 1979). Like learning disabilities, ADHD is presumed to be in part brain-related, and it is often treated with stimulant medications (see Barkley, Chapter 2, this volume). When a child is placed on medications for this condition, it is important to evaluate drug effects on cognitive and academic performance.

COMPONENT TREATMENTS

The multiple problems associated with learning disabilities are all potentially treatable. Interventions relevant to each component problem area are discussed in turn below.

Academic Achievement

Remedial Programs

The most common treatment for learning disabilities is placement in a special education class or tutorial setting. The major goal of special education programs is to facilitate development of academic skills. Teachers in these settings have fewer children to contend with, allowing for greater individualization of instruction. Teachers are also at liberty to use alternative instruction methods and materials. Because of the additional personnel, materials, and facilities involved, these programs are expensive to operate. According to data available in 1981 (Farnham-Diggory, 1986), the average cost per student of school programs for learning-disabilities approximates $4,000 per year. Given estimates of the number of children who participate in learning disabilities programs in the United States alone, expenditures exceed $6 billion each year. The precise cost varies with the manner in which school districts allocate funding and with the intensity of their programs.

In spite of the time, effort, and extra expense required for these programs, there is virtually no empirical support for their long-term effectiveness. Summarizing the findings of 25 studies of long-term academic changes in response to specialized teaching, Spache (1976) concludes that "remedial treatment apparently does not affect school progress appreciably over time" (p. 336). Other sources report short-term gains that wash out after active treatment has ended (Silberberg, Iversen, & Goins, 1973; Tobin & Pumfrey, 1976). Educational programs may mitigate many of the complications of learning failure by temporarily reducing children's frustration and by providing encouragement to develop strengths. Nevertheless, disabled learners remain well behind their peers academically, despite years of special assistance. For the bulk of these children, achievement levels plateau at about a fourth- or fifth-grade level by senior high school (Deshler et al., 1982). Persons with histories of learning disabilities are more likely than their peers to fail minimum academic competency exams, drop out of school, and experience later psychosocial and vocational difficulties (Deshler, Schumaker, & Lenz, 1984; Spreen, 1982).

Koppitz (1972–1973) carried out a 5-year follow-up study of a large group of children placed in a school-based learning disabilities program. At the end of the follow-up period, half of the children were still in the program. Another 25% of the group had moved, had been taken out of their placements by parents, or had been assigned to alternative educational programs. Only the remaining 25% had been transferred from the learning disabilities program back to their regular classrooms on a full-time basis. Special academic instruction, at least as provided in most school and clinic settings, fails to resolve either underachievement or associated behavioral problems (Gittelman & Feingold, 1983; McKinney & Feagans, 1984; Spreen, 1982).

Watered-down treatment is not a likely explanation for this phenomenon. Forell and Hood (1985) studied a group of children who, upon entrance to third grade, performed at either a preprimer or primer level on a test of reading recognition. At a follow-up assessment, the average grade placements for students in the preprimer and primer groups were the ninth and tenth grades, respectively. Both groups had received years of specialized, small-group reading instruction. Despite the help, follow-up achievement levels in reading and spelling were about 5 years below grade level for the preprimer group, and about 2 years below grade level for the primer group. Results suggest that children who make slow initial progress in reading fall further behind with age. According to Forell and Hood (1985), the most severely disabled children show limited benefits of instruction "as we know how to deliver it" (p. 113). Forell and Hood speculate that the limiting factors in such cases are inherent child characteristics (e.g., cognitive deficits). The fact that initial learning difficulties tend to be associated with decreased exposure to text and poor motivation may also help to explain poor treatment response in children who manifest serious initial learning failure (Stanovich, 1986).

The short-term benefits of academic remediation contrast markedly with these largely negative long-term outcomes. On average, children make twice as much academic progress with remediation as they do without it (Spache, 1976). Several investigations have documented that children with reading problems can make more progress when they are given special academic assistance (Balow, Fuchs, & Kasbohm, 1978; Silberberg et al., 1973; Tobin & Pumfrey, 1976).

Three recent studies of short-term instructional programs are particularly noteworthy. In the first part of a larger-scale study, Williams (1980) compared children assigned to a special learning disabilities program to a comparable group of children for which this program was not available. Treatment and comparison groups displayed equivalent pretreatment academic skills. The aim of the special program was to improve decoding skills. Children who participated in the program performed significantly better than the comparison children on several posttreatment reading measures. Findings were replicated in a second part of the study.

Gittelman and Feingold (1983) reported similar results in a study of a clinic-based program for disabled learners. The effectiveness of a word-decoding program was evaluated by comparing gains in treatment versus control subjects, and assignment to groups was randomized. The controls received nonspecific academic tutoring. Despite the fact that the groups did not differ in academic or other skills before treatment, posttreatment performances were in favor of the treatment group for nearly all of the reading measures employed.

In a third study, Lovett et al. (in press) randomly assigned children with specific reading disabilities to three groups. One group received training in word-decoding skills, a second in oral and written language skills, and a third in classroom survival skills (this last group served as an "attention control" group). Treatment sessions were held four times a week for 10 weeks. According to analyses of posttreatment performances (which were adjusted to take pretreatment achievement level into account), both experimental groups outperformed the controls on tests of word recognition and pseudoword spelling. The decoding skills group made greater gains in word recognition and word spelling than either of the other groups; however, the language skills group was superior in developing contextual reading skills (accuracy, rate, comprehension), vocabulary, knowledge, and semantic/syntactic abilities. The methodological sophistication of this and other recent studies offers persuasive evidence for the effectiveness of some forms of remedial therapy.

Remedial Principles

No one has yet developed the "ideal" remedial program. Judging from the findings of Lovett et al. (in press), program objectives may dictate what is taught and how it is taught. Methods that are effective in enhancing reading comprehension, for example, may differ from those that work best in developing word-decoding skills. But regardless of instructional objectives, there are a number of principles of remediation that apply more generally. These principles exemplify what most teachers would consider sound educational practice. They also enjoy substantial research support (Rosenshine, 1983). Adherence to these principles may be of some benefit to any child, but are likely to make the most difference for those children who fail to respond to conventional instruction (Snow, 1986). Each principle is briefly reviewed below.

Maximizing Engaged Instructional Time. In general, the more hours students spend in school, the more they achieve (Brophy, 1986). In a study of first-grade children who were at high risk for reading problems, Harris and Serwer (1966) found that time devoted to direct reading instruction was closely associated with achievements in word recognition and reading comprehension. Stallings (1975) also found a substantial association between academic achievement and instructional time. Based on their review of the literature, Guthrie, Seifert, and Kline (1977) concluded that at least 50 hours of special educational assistance are necessary if instruction is to have a significant impact on the achievement of learning-disabled children.

Time spent in a special educational class is not so critical as is time allocated for academic objectives, or "academic learning time" (Brophy, 1986). Process–product research on teacher practices shows that effective teachers require their students to spend substantial time on academic work, and they arrange for high rates of student success. What is most crucial for learning is the time devoted to presentation of information, student demonstration of ability, practice, feedback, and teacher follow-up. Given the importance of active involvement in academic work, any steps that can be taken to increase academic learning time bear close scrutiny (Schumaker *et al.*, 1986). Offering more individual or small-group remediation is only one way to increase instructional time. Other strategies are to organize regular classroom activities in a manner that maximizes time for academic learning, and to make judicious use of microcomputers. Microcomputers are increasingly available in classrooms. With appropriate choice of software programs, their use by students with learning problems affords ample opportunities for practice. Not all of this practice need be under direct teacher supervision. An added advantage of some of the more sophisticated software programs is that they incorporate many of the other instructional principles discussed in this section (Torgesen, 1986).

Providing Structure and Direction. One of the oldest and most often-cited principles for teaching a disabled learner is to structure and direct the child. It was this principle more than any other that distinguished the instructional approach of Strauss and Lehtinen (1947) from the more typical teaching methods of the time. Strauss and Lehtinen conceived of the brain-damaged child as "abnormally responsive to stimuli in his environment, reacting unselectively, passively, and without conscious intent" (p. 129). They felt that it was essential to provide the kind of structure that brain-damaged children were unable to provide for themselves. One of their educational recommendations was to place children in relatively unstimulating locations (e.g., a desk facing an empty wall) as a means of reducing distractions and enhancing concentration. They also recommended that study materials be simplified as much as possible. This could be accomplished, for example, by including only a few problems or words on a page at any given time, by simplifying the type of problem presented, or by structuring activities in a way that delimited the number of alternative responses. Remedial programs involved motor-based activities, the intention of which was to engage and motivate the child and to make the learning process more concrete. To avoid overloading the child, tasks were to be presented one element at a time, and the elements combined only after each separate element had been mastered. Memorization and automatization of skills were viewed as essential, but only in the last phase of the acquisition process.

The Strauss–Lehtinen approach was later extended to other groups of children, including those with hyperactivity and learning disabilities (Hallahan & Kauffman, 1976). There is, in fact, a high degree of similarity between this approach and a number of more recent programs for disabled learners (e.g., Feuerstein, Rand, Hoffman, & Miller, 1980; Rosner, 1979). Almost by definition, children with learning disabilities have difficulty acquiring information on their own. Discovery methods are of little use; children with learning problems benefit most from "direct teaching" (Brophy, 1986; Snow, 1986). The several elements of direct instruction are as follows: (1) explicit instruction and modeling; (2) controlled presentation and guided practice; (3) step-by-step progressions from subskill mastery to more complex learning objectives; (4) use of concrete aids and strategies that focus the learner's attention; and (5) monitoring of the learner's responses and informed feedback (Englert, 1984; Rosenshine, 1983).

The best example of a research program in which direct instructional methods were pitted against discovery learning is Project Follow-Through (Becker & Carnine, 1980). Follow-Through programs were administered to groups of children who entered kindergarten or first grade in the early 1970s. The programs were run under the direction of several model sponsors. Some of these sponsors focused on enhancing student motivation, others on parent education or language development, and still others on direct teaching of academic skills. One of the direct skill-building models—the direct instruction model—proved superior in promoting academic achievement. The most distinctive feature of this program was the high degree of structure and direct teaching it employed. Children were shown explicitly what to do; they were given much practice and corrective feedback; and they were led through a fixed sequence of instructional objectives.

The highly directed manner in which beginning reading is taught in programs that emphasize decoding skills may help to explain why these programs are often superior to other methods (Jorm & Share, 1983; Williams, 1985). Direct instruction in phonics seems to be particularly important for children who are having difficulty in the initial stages of learning how to read, and for learning-disabled children (Gettinger, 1982; Polloway et al., 1986; Wallach & Wallach, 1976). Phonic skills give readers a means by which to "unlock" unfamiliar words. These skills are separable from other elements of the reading process and can be taught explicitly. For children who have difficulty learning how to read, direct teaching of decoding skills may be a prerequisite for acquisition of more advanced levels of reading achievement (Stanovich, 1986).

Although few specific programs have been as well researched as these phonics-based methods, a number of the components of direct instruction have received separate validation. Bryant and his associates have shown that learning is more rapid and retention better when academic tasks are broken down into smaller parts or subtasks, and when each subtask is mastered before going on to the next (Bryant, Drabin, & Gettinger, 1981; Gettinger, Bryant, & Fayne, 1982). A study by Kauffman, Hallahan, Haas, Brame, and Boren (1978) underscores the importance of informed, or corrective, feedback. In this investigation, conditions in which the instructor highlighted differences between the child's misspelled words and the correct spelling facilitated spelling acquisition. Smith and Lovitt (1975) found that arithmetic computation improved when the teacher demonstrated the computational procedure and provided a written example for the children to follow. Similarly, Fleisher and Jenkins (1983) found that corrective feedback and directed practice with misread words improved word recognition skills.

Controlling stimulus presentation is another means of structuring the learning process. Schworm (1979) found that poor readers who received instruction in several specific spelling patterns (e.g., "ai," "ee") made more gains in reading words containing these spelling patterns than did poor readers who took part in a more standard remedial program. The children who received controlled instruction were also better able to generalize what they had learned in reading untrained spelling patterns. Rose (1984) showed that previewing reading passages—by having the teacher read the passage as the children followed along—improved subsequent oral reading performance in a group of poor readers. Bradley (1981) demonstrated that having children name the letters in words while writing them out was an effective way of teaching spelling—a method referred to as "simultaneous oral spelling." Findings by Thorpe and Borden (1985) suggest that multisensory presentations help to focus children's attention on the learning task.

Individualizing Instruction and Teaching to Mastery. Since individuals learn at different rates, structuring necessarily implies some degree of individualization. Guthrie, Martuza, and Seifert (1979) report that remedial programs involving low teacher–student ratios (from 1:1 to 1:4) result in greater student gains in reading achievement than do programs with higher ratios. Schwartz (1977) demonstrated that individual tutoring programs are preferable to group instruction. In the latter study, college student tutors provided effective individualized remedial help for adolescents with reading disabilities.

The principle of mastery learning is closely related to that of individualization. Advocates of mastery learning stress that teachers should establish a fixed minimum level of achievement, and that children should be given whatever instruction and practice is needed to reach this level. Obviously, some students will require more learning opportunities than others.

Findings reported by Gettinger and White (1979) suggest that the most adept learners in a given classroom master new learning tasks from six to nine times faster than the slowest learners. Bloom (1974, 1984) has estimated that as many as 80% of the students in a classroom may be able to achieve under mastery conditions what only the upper 20% can achieve with conventional instruction. According to Bloom, students who fail to master previously presented materials lack essential skills or knowledge for subsequent learning. Failing students also lose interest as a consequence of their failure to attain mastery, and they become less willing to put in the time and effort required for learning.

Bryant (1965) believes that overlearning is critical for attainment of mastery. A recent investigation of this issue by Ivarie (1986) provides support for Bryant's view. In the Ivarie study, two groups of fourth-graders practiced a paired-associate learning task to different levels of proficiency. Students for whom a higher proficiency rate was required showed better retention over a 90-day period than did students trained to the lower proficiency rate. Ivarie's provision of distributed rather than massed practice may have been an important element of her training procedure. Other research suggests that teachers must distribute practice if overlearning is to be beneficial (Gettinger *et al.*, 1982; Kratochwill, Demuth, & Conzemius, 1977).

Promoting Generalization and Transfer. Learning-disabled students are notoriously poor in applying skills they have practiced in isolation (Deshler, Alley, Warner, & Schumaker, 1981). Practice in reading or spelling word lists, for example, does not insure that the student will be able to read words correctly in the context of a paragraph, or spell words when writing a sentence. To facilitate generalization of subskills, a variety of stimuli and subskill applications is required. It is also helpful to discuss applications directly with the student (Stokes & Baer, 1977).

A study by Bryant, Fayne, and Gettinger (1980) illustrates how transfer activities can be incorporated into instruction. In this study, learning-disabled children were taught to identify the sounds of two vowel digraphs. Specific objectives were to teach the children (1) to sound out the digraphs; (2) to read lists of single-syllable words and nonsense syllables containing those digraphs; and (3) to apply this

knowledge in blending the sounds of novel words and in reading sentences composed of words that contained the digraphs. The lessons proved highly effective in teaching the children to read training words containing the digraphs, and to apply their decoding skills in reading new words. In addition to illustrating how training for transfer can be achieved, the "LD-efficient" method of Bryant and his colleagues offers excellent examples of stimulus control, distributed practice and review, and attention-focusing manipulations.

Providing Incentives Contingent on Academic Performance. Making incentives contingent on improved academic performance is yet another means for facilitating the acquisition process. A wealth of data indicates that children with learning difficulties respond well to incentive systems. These systems entail rewards that are contingent on certain pre-established performance criteria (e.g., number of correct responses or rate); or they involve response costs, in which case rewards are taken away for failure to meet such criteria. Typical rewards consist of tokens that can be exchanged for free time or for prizes, or teacher attention and praise. Children can also earn points or grades to be turned in for recognition, material reinforcers, or opportunities to engage in preferred activities. Incentive systems have been successfully used in teaching problem learners reading skills, handwriting, spelling, written expression, and arithmetic (Treiber & Lahey, 1983).

Contingencies are most effective when tied to academic products, such as the number of problems completed or response accuracy. Contingencies applied to on-task behaviors are of lesser value. Specifically, rewards and response costs that are based on how well a child performs academically result in both better academic performance and improved on-task behavior. On-task contingencies may lead to more on-task behaviors, but this latter type of contingency rarely translates into improved academic performance (Treiber & Lahey, 1983).

Although material rewards may be motivation-enhancing, the success of incentive systems is undoubtedly due to a host of factors. Delivering rewards and response costs implies that the educator has targeted specific behaviors for improvement, developed procedures for measuring these behaviors, and communicated expectations clearly and unequivocally (Kauffman, 1975). Reinforcement and response cost contingencies are commonly used in the context of a more encompassing approach to teaching known as applied behavior analysis (ABA). The goal of ABA is to gain stimulus control of the child's response—in this case, academic skill development. Rewards and response costs constitute only two ways of obtaining stimulus control. Other means include cueing, demonstration, modelling, feedback, and hierarchical teaching of subskills. Mastery learning and individualization of instruction are also important in ABA. The fact that the ABA approach incorporates so many principles of effective instruction may help to explain the long-standing success of ABA techniques in remediating disabled learners (Hallahan & Kauffman, 1976). Despite the limitations of these techniques, such as the potential for the child to become overly dependent on external rewards and to lose sight of learning as an intrinsically rewarding activity (Deshler, Schumaker, & Lenz, 1984), there is much to gain from their routine use.

Teaching to All Deficiencies. A final principle has to do with the need to help disabled learners improve in all areas of deficiency and to avoid exclusive focus on one single deficit (Guthrie & Seifert, 1978). This principle acknowledges the cumulative nature of academic skills, and the fact that higher-order abilities are heavily dependent on mastery and integration of lower-order subskills. Research showing that improvements in a targeted subskill (e.g., oral reading rate) often occur with little if any accompanying gains in other subskills (e.g., reading comprehension or oral reading accuracy) underscores the importance of this principle (Swanson, 1981).

One way to address multiple weaknesses is to teach practical skill applications and to use meaningful materials. Practice in reading meaningful materials enhances both reading and oral vocabulary (Stanovich, 1986). Because of severe difficulties experienced by many children and the need to take a learner one step at a time, it is easy to lose sight of longer-term instructional objectives. It is important, therefore, to remind oneself that the primary purpose of remedial teaching is to assist the child to become an independent learner—to read for meaning, write to communicate, and solve practical math problems. Requiring meaningful skill applications helps to assure that the educator will be aware of the entirety of the child's problems. Conversely, attending to each separate aspect of these problems makes it more likely that the child will profit from skill applications.

In summary, review of research on remedial teaching fails to uncover one best or preferred program for all disabled learners. Fortunately, a small number of instructional principles constitute a sound and reasonably well-validated instructional methodology. Principles of instruction by no means address all aspects of the learning-disabled child's problems. But they do provide guidance regarding ways in which to improve the effectiveness of remedial efforts. Regardless of those treatment strategies chosen to deal with other aspects of a child's disability, remedial principles are of central importance. These principles establish standards to follow in appraising current teaching strategies and in recommending methods to improve the child's educational program. As obvious as it might seem, it is necessary to emphasize that the way in which learning-disabled children are taught has a direct bearing on their educational development. Although children with learning problems have the most to gain from application of the instructional principles discussed in this section, nondisabled learners would probably benefit as well.

Cognitive and Neuropsychological Skills

Over the last few decades, considerable emphasis has been placed on techniques to remediate the psychological processing deficits believed to underlie learning disabilities. These methods include programs to enhance perceptual–motor and sensory skills, psycholinguistic abilities and auditory perception, and general cognitive processes (e.g., Delacato, 1963; Frostig & Horne, 1964; Kephart, 1971; Kirk & Kirk, 1971). Despite the popularity these programs have enjoyed for the last several decades, research reviews uniformly fail to find anything that would recommend their continued use (Arter & Jenkins, 1979; Kavale & Mattson, 1983; Newcomer & Hammill, 1976). Research on process-training procedures has not yielded unequivocal treatment effects. Neither the processing deficit itself nor academic achievement is clearly improved as a result of training.

A fundamental limitation of most previous approaches to process training is that they have been based on unfounded presumptions regarding the processing deficits that contribute to learning failure. Because so little is known about the psychological processes required for academic learning, previous process-training programs may have merely focused on the wrong set of abilities. More recently, investigators have stressed the need to study processes more clearly implicated in the acquisition of academic skills (Hartlage & Telzrow, 1983; Torgesen, 1979, 1982). More academically oriented process-training approaches have been successful in at least three specific areas.

On-Task Behavior

One academically relevant processing skill is the ability or willingness of children to attend to their schoolwork. Difficulties with remaining on task are common in children with learning disabilities (McKinney & Feagans, 1981). If children are unavailable for learning, their academic development will almost surely be compromised. Evidence reviewed earlier indicates that incentive systems applied to academic products may be a preferred means of getting children to pay more attention to their work. Nevertheless, some investigators consider attentional problems so central to learning failure that they recommend a more direct process-training approach.

Hallahan and his colleagues provide the best example of this approach to attentional problems. In one of their earlier investigations, Hallahan, Lloyd, Kosiewicz, Kauffman, and Graves (1979) developed a procedure for teaching on-task behaviors to a 7-year-old learning-disabled boy with attentional problems. To enhance the boy's on-task behaviors, he was assigned prescribed handwriting and math tasks to be carried out for a few minutes each day. During these tasks, the investigators played a recorder that emitted a beep at random intervals. At the sound of each beep, the child was asked to mark on a sheet whether or not he was paying attention. Training was conducted in four successive phases: baseline (Phase 1), self-monitoring with beeps as cues (Phase 2), self-monitoring without the beeps (Phase 3), and self-praise only (Phase 4). In Phase 3, the boy recorded his attention to task whenever he thought of asking himself whether he was attending. In Phase 4, he merely praised himself whenever he was aware of attending (i.e., he was not asked to record his self-observations). Dependent variables were on-task behavior (visual orientation to the task) and correct words or math answers written per minute. Results showed substantial increases in both on-task behavior and academic productivity when self-monitoring with cueing was employed. These improvements were maintained when the external supports of the beep and the response sheet were removed. Using a wrist counter in place of the recording sheet, Hallahan, Marshall, and Lloyd (1981) were subsequently able to improve other children's on-task behaviors during instructional interactions with teachers.

The success of this method demonstrates that academic productivity can in fact be elevated by focusing on on-task performance. Used in isolation, the self-monitoring technique is probably inadequate for treating children with serious attentional problems (see Barkley, Chapter 2, this volume). This technique may also be of little use for children who lack the basic skills to complete their assigned work, even if they were to become more attentive. The attention-disabled children for whom this strategy would seem most appropriate are those who have many of the prerequisite academic abilities and who are responsive to structuring.

A related self-monitoring procedure for inattentive learners requires that the child keep a self-rating log similar to the one shown in Figure 9-2. The purpose of the procedure is to teach children who are off task much of the time to track their own behaviors and to behave in ways more compatible with learning. The procedure itself is as follows. First, the teacher and child come to an agreement regarding behavioral objectives and rewards. Objectives might include remaining attentive to the teacher, doing seatwork independently, and refraining from distracting others. The rewards for meeting these objectives might be free time at the end of the day or access to a privileged activity. The teacher lists the objectives at the top of the self-rating sheet, and makes sure the child understands what each objective involves. For each of several class periods during the day, the child is asked to self-rate performance with respect to each of the objectives. Either numerical ratings or drawings of facial expressions can be used for this purpose (see Figure 9-2). Although the child's teacher may wish to monitor the ratings periodically to insure fidelity, completing the ratings and maintaining the rating log are essentially left up to the child. Rewards are earned by accummulating a criterion number of points by the end of the day. The criterion is usually set low initially, but can be adjusted upward toward more normal levels of expectation with regard to the child's behavior.

The advantages of this system are that it places emphasis on positive change, encourages children to take responsibility for their own behavior, and is easy for classroom teachers to implement. One limitation is that the procedure may be inappropriate for very young children or for adolescents; it is best suited for children in the middle and upper elementary grades. Another disadvantage is the fact that behavioral objectives are somewhat imprecise. Like Hallahan's procedures, this technique is likely to be most useful for children who are reasonably self-aware and academically competent (i.e., those individuals who are simply not working up to the best of their abilities in the classroom).

Language Skills

Language is a second skill area of direct relevance to academic learning. Although researchers have been generally critical of the value of psycholinguistic, auditory–perceptual, and language experience programs for children with learning disabilities (Arter & Jenkins, 1979), some types of language training seem to have special merit. There is now a large corpus of literature showing that phonological processing skills—such as those requiring auditory blending or segmentation of spoken words—are closely related to children's abilities to read and spell (Wagner & Torgesen, 1987). Weaknesses in these skills appear to obstruct reading acquisition. Moreover, young children with reading difficulties have been shown to profit more from programs that emphasize training in sound blending and oral word segmentation than they do from programs that do not include this type of remedial activity.

The possibility that some forms of language training can lead to improved academic achievement is further documented by Beck, Perfetti, and McKeown (1982). Beck et al. gave fourth-grade children extended training on word meanings. Instruction included practice with definitions and a variety of word association and word generation activities. Results showed that the training enhanced both vocabulary knowledge and reading comprehension. The children who participated in this study were not having any special learning problems. Nonetheless, the training effects observed suggest that vocabulary knowledge contributes to reading competency, and that vocabulary-building exercises may therefore benefit children with reading problems.

The findings of a study described earlier by Lovett et al. (in press) are also relevant to the issue of language training. One of the experimental conditions of this study was an oral and

Rating Scale

0 Points	1 Point	2 Points

Day	Class/Time Period					
Goals	**A**	**B**	**C**	**D**	**E**	**Points**
					Total	
Reward for reaching goal						

FIGURE 9-2. Self-rating daily log for improving on-task behaviors.

written language skills (OWLS) program. The OWLS program consisted of practice in vocabulary, structural and grammatical analysis of sentences, and discourse comprehension. Oral language instruction was a large component of the program, and emphasis was on language structures larger than the single word. Posttraining outcomes revealed that the OWLS program yielded significantly more gains in word recognition than a survival skills control condition.

Whether language-based programs can improve academic skills in all children is an open question. Language therapy may boost the language skills of some learning-disabled children (Semel & Wiig, 1981). What seems less clear is the effectiveness of such programs in facilitating academic development, especially in children with serious language disorders. Clinical experience with these children indicates that it makes little sense to attempt to remediate academic problems without first addressing the child's impaired language. Children who are not aware of word meanings, who cannot comprehend grammatical forms, or who show incomplete or inconsistent knowledge of word sounds can hardly be expected to make use of those skills in the domain of written language. More research is needed to establish how best to help language-disabled children develop both linguistic and academic competencies.

Cognitive Strategies

A third set of academically relevant processing skills consists of those that involve mental planning, organization, strategizing, metacognition, and other executive abilities. Executive dysfunctions are common in children with learning disabilities (Stanovich, 1986). Examples include inability to remember what is said or read, disorganized attempts at expression in writing and speaking, difficulties in comprehension, lack of ability to monitor errors, and poor study habits. Training in executive functions consists of teaching disabled learners to use more appropriate mental strategies. These strategies are not likely to rid children of weaknesses in specific cognitive skills (e.g., memory, language, attentional capacities). The purpose of training, rather, is to help students learn ways to compensate for these weaknesses.

The best-known technique for teaching cognitive strategies is cognitive-behavior modification (CBM). In CBM, children are taught a set of general procedures, such as self-verbalization of strategy rules. Other procedures, including the learning of the strategy itself, are specific to the task on which a child is receiving instruction. The basic elements of CBM include description of the specific mental steps to be employed, instructor modeling in the use of these steps, instructor-guided practice by the child, overt and then covert self-verbalization of the steps as the child performs the task, self-monitoring, and self-reinforcement. Self-instructional techniques have been used to teach math, copying, writing, memorization, reading comprehension, study skills, and problem solving (Ryan, Weed, & Short, 1986; Schumaker et al., 1986).

Although the importance of mental strategies for learning has been appreciated for some time, attempts to teach children explicit procedures for improving academic performance are of recent origin (Schumaker et al., 1986). Major contributions to research on cognitive training with disabled learners have been made by two research groups: Brown and her associates at the University of Illinois (Brown, Bransford, Ferrara, & Campione, 1983; Palincsar & Brown, 1984), and Deshler and his colleagues at the University of Kansas (Deshler, Warner, Schumaker, & Alley, 1983; Schumaker et al., 1986).

The approach of the University of Illinois group is best illustrated by the work of Palincsar and Brown (1984). In their series of studies, these investigators applied a method referred to as "reciprocal teaching" to facilitate reading comprehension skills. Regular seventh-grade students with reading comprehension difficulties were taught how to summarize each of several text passages, question themselves regarding the content of each passage, clarify information in the passage, and predict subsequent text information. Following teacher modeling of these activities, students were given guided practice. Practice consisted either of being supervised in processing a text passage or of supervising others in doing so. In the latter case, students took on the role of the "dialogue leader." Over the course of the training sessions, students became more proficient in assuming the role of dialogue leader, and their reading comprehension showed corresponding improvement. The students were also able to generalize their skills to classroom tests in social studies and science. Although the students who participated in this study had only limited academic weaknesses, a number of investigations have demonstrated the applicability of similiar procedures for children with learning disabilities (e.g., Ryan *et al.*, 1986; Wong & Jones, 1982).

The approach taken by the University of Kansas group is referred to as the "learning strategies intervention model" (Deshler *et al.*, 1983). This cognitive training approach was created to help learning-disabled adolescents meet the many practical demands of the regular secondary school curriculum. Deshler and his colleagues are the first to admit that learning-disabled adolescents are deficient in general knowledge, basic academic skills, and motivation. To rationalize their focus on cognitive strategies, Deshler *et al.* argue that these students are unlikely to make dramatic gains in basic academic skills after entry into secondary school, but that they are capable of mastering more efficient learning strategies. These investigators also point out that mastering these strategies is likely to bolster both classroom performance and motivation. Cognitive strategies developed and tested by the Kansas group range from ways in which to improve students' reading comprehension to helping them solve verbal math problems, study textbook chapters, take tests, monitor errors in written expression, organize and write paragraphs, paraphrase ideas, keep track of assignments, and listen and take notes. In summarizing their research on the learning strategies model, Deshler *et al.* report that most learning-disabled adolescents are able to apply these learning strategies to both ability-level and grade-level materials, and that the strategies result in significant improvements over baseline performance levels.

The approach taken by the Kansas group has been to train adolescents in a number of specific strategies. All strategy training follows a similar format. Training begins by having a student demonstrate how he or she typically carries out a particular task (e.g., studies for a test, reads for comprehension, or takes notes). The instructor discusses the shortcomings of the student's approach and presents the learning strategy appropriate to that task. Following modeling by the instructor and verbal rehearsal of the strategy by the student, the student is given guided practice in applying the strategy. Practice is first carried out with materials that are at the student's present ability level. After mastery is reached with these materials, the student moves on to grade-level materials similar to those encountered in daily schoolwork.

The major limitation of the learning strategies intervention model is the frequency with which students fail to make use of what they have learned outside of training. Failures of this sort are by no means unique to this model. Students commonly fail to apply the strategies they have been taught to settings or conditions other than those on which they have received practice (Brown & Campione, 1986). Ways to encourage generalization of task-specific skills include discussion and direct teaching of skill applications in a variety of settings, instruction in how to modify strategies in accordance with contextual demands, students' monitoring of their use of strategies, and cueing by the students' regular teachers (Deshler *et al.*, 1983; Schumaker & Deshler, 1984).

Teaching nonspecific executive strategies in combination with task-specific techniques is another way to foster generalization. An example of such a strategy is the SMART program (Deshler *et al.*, 1983). The acronym "SMART" reminds students what to do when faced with almost any complex task:

- S—set a goal (What am I being asked to do? What do I need to know beyond what I already know?)
- M—make a plan (What is my plan?)
- A—attempt a plan (Am I following my plan and working carefully?)
- R—review (Did I reach my goals?)
- T—try (What else might I try?)

Additional examples of programs aimed at improving executive functions are those described by Kendall and Braswell (1984) and by Feuerstein *et al.* (1980). As a rule, learning-disabled children tend to take a passive approach to learning (Torgesen, 1980). Teaching executive strategies offers children means for becoming more active learners. These strategies are most appropriate for children who do not adapt well in the classroom, who are mentally disorganized, or who have difficulties in abstract reasoning.

Psychosocial Adjustment and Motivation

Behavioral Management

Although children with learning disabilities are subject to the same range of behavior disorders as are other children, at least two behavioral concerns have a relatively direct bearing on academic development and deserve routine consideration in planning treatment. The first is failure to comply with basic rules of conduct at home and school. Noncompliance may take any of several forms. At home it may mean failure to get ready for school, come home on time, brush one's teeth, complete chores, or do homework. Noncompliance at school may consist of failure to stay in one's seat during work periods, raise one's hand before asking questions, or engage in teacher-directed work activities. For other children, simple noncompliance is compounded with disruptive behavior, refusal to comply with adult direction, or even antisocial acts. Because of ineffectual parental management, some children never learn the value of compliant behaviors. Consequences may include antisocial behavior and lowered academic achievement (Patterson, 1986). Other likely sources of behavior problems are the frustration associated with repeated academic failure, direct avoidance of schoolwork, and inability to follow through due to lack of memory, poor comprehension, or limited organizational skills.

Noncompliance is most often manifested when the child is expected to perform an academic task (e.g., homework or in-school assignment, listening during a lecture period). If such problems are restricted to the school setting, an in-school behavior program may suffice. Clear specification of rules of behavior, limits, and contingencies is essential to good classroom management (Good & Brophy, 1986). Reward-oriented behavior contracts are useful in encouraging more positive behaviors and in creating an atmosphere of cooperation. Time-out procedures and other restrictions on student activities are effective in dealing with overt transgressions, at least as long as the contingencies are clear to the child, consistently followed, and do not deprive the child of opportunities to become more appropriately engaged (Drabman & Spitalnik, 1973). It is not enough, however, to apply contingencies to misbehavior. Accommodating to the child's inherent limitations in performing school tasks is also imperative.

Improvements in behavior that occur as a result of school-initiated procedures will not automatically generalize to the home setting. Separate parent-administered contingencies may also be required. In some cases, it may be appropriate to have parents and teachers jointly participate in the management program. Parents, for example, may administer rewards based on the child's school performance. Joint programs assure that parents and teachers are not working at cross purposes, and that behavioral goals are similar across settings. Research indicates that cooperative programs of this sort can have beneficial results. But the hazards of this approach must also be appreciated. One limitation is that administration of rewards or punishments by parents for behaviors exhibited at school will, of necessity, be removed in time from the target behavior. Other shortcomings include the fact that parents and teachers sometimes have different standards or concerns, that good communication between school and home may be difficult to achieve, and that parent-administered contingencies may lead teachers to abrogate their responsibility for student management. Threats by teachers to inform parents regarding the child's behavior are unlikely to be as effective as direct action. Probably the most universally advisable system for increasing compliance in children is that in which parents and teachers have common general aims and strategies, but focus on behaviors over which they can gain independent control.

The second behavioral issue of frequent concern to parents and teachers is the tendency for learning-disabled children to seek help from others rather than to find solutions on their own (McKinney & Feagans, 1984). Dependency-seeking children benefit most from management systems that encourage them to work independently whenever possible and to make some of their own decisions. Giving these children models to follow and assigning tasks that are within their grasp are essential to the success of this approach. In such cases, behavior programs and direct teaching work hand in hand to instill confidence and encourage more independent action. One of the difficulties in managing dependency-seeking children is to decide which tasks they are capable of performing independently. In establishing appropriate expectations, gradual fading out of the support system is preferable to its abrupt withdrawal.

Behavioral management programs directed by parents or teachers occasionally need to be supplemented by individual or group therapy. According to Kaslow and Cooper (1978), individual therapy enables the learning-disabled child to 'feel safer ventilating, complaining, honestly telling what it has been like for him/

her and provides a time to simmer down and take stock" (p. 45). Group therapy can be of similar value and may provide disabled learners with opportunities to develop communication and social skills. Counselors and psychotherapists with appropriate training are valuable clinical resources. Such mental health professionals play important roles in helping family members to resolve destructive conflicts and in assisting families to find better ways of coping with their children's disabilities.

The well-established methods for treating behavior problems in children discussed elsewhere in this volume are just as applicable to disabled learners as to other children. Clinical experience suggests that treatment of behavior problems in this population is indeed necessary for successful academic intervention. Behavior treatment alone, however, is not likely to remedy most children's learning difficulties. In view of the fact that behavior problems frequently accompany learning disabilities, more formal study of the effects of behavioral therapies in conjunction with other treatment strategies would be of great interest.

Social Skills Training

The various difficulties that learning-disabled children and adolescents have in relating to others make social skills training highly relevant to their needs (La Greca, 1981; Schumaker & Hazel, 1984a). Efforts to help disabled learners become more socially competent consist of teaching them to use praise and compliments, to react appropriately to negative peer comments or actions, to sustain and reciprocate social conversations, and to engage in sharing and helping activities. Treatment procedures range from peer-initiated social interactions to cooperative group activities, behavior management procedures applied to the individual, and direct training through behavioral modeling and rehearsal (see Dodge, Chapter 6, this volume).

In their review of social skills training programs, Schumaker and Hazel (1984b) argue persuasively for the direct-training approach. A study by Hazel, Schumaker, Sherman, and Sheldon (1982) is a prototype of this approach. Hazel et al. taught groups of learning-disabled and nondisabled adolescents to give positive and negative feedback to their peers, accept negative feedback from their peers, resist peer pressure, negotiate with their peers, and solve personal problems. Each skill was described

and explained by group leaders, analyzed in terms of skill components, and modeled. After verbally rehearsing each of the steps needed to perform a skill, the students acted out simulations in front of the group and received feedback from other group members. Findings indicated that the learning-disabled group's performance on most of the social skills measures increased markedly as a result of the training. With the use of a multiple-baseline-across-skills design, the investigators demonstrated that mastery of a particular skill required direct training of the skill components.

As in the case of cognitive training, social skills acquired under simulated conditions do not necessarily transfer to the natural environment. Schumaker and Hazel (1984b) recommend that social skills programs be supplemented by procedures to assure that students apply what they have learned. Examples of such procedures include discussions with students regarding possible applications, reinforcement of student-initiated applications, and involvement of regular school personnel as facilitators.

A number of social skills curricula are presently available (Schumaker, Pederson, Hazel, & Meyen, 1983). Although these programs hold considerable promise for children with weaknesses in this area, benefits are as yet unclear. It is difficult to know which students are likely to gain the most from these programs, or to decide which particular social skills to train in order to improve social competence in a meaningful way (La Greca, 1981).

Motivational Enhancement

A requirement in common to all of the treatment strategies discussed thus far is an active and effortful involvement on the part of the disabled learner. As Licht and Kistner (1986) have aptly stated, "continued effort is even *more* essential for these children" (p. 227). Unfortunately, many learning-disabled children are unable to muster this extra effort. How can children with learning disabilities be encouraged to try harder, put more effort into coping with their problems, and have more confidence in themselves?

One method for enhancing motivation is referred to as "attribution retraining" (Dweck, 1986). The primary goal of this method is to teach children to attribute difficulties in learning to insufficient effort rather than to lack of ability, and to instill the attitude that effort and persistence pay off. According to Licht and Kistner (1986), it is important to choose training tasks in such a way that a child is exposed to a mixture of success and failure experiences. These authors also stress the need to teach children specific skills for improved performance on more difficult learning tasks (e.g., cognitive strategies, self-monitoring techniques). To enhance motivation further, Dweck (1986) recommends that the emphasis of instruction be on children's capacity to acquire new abilities, rather than on their ability to meet objective performance standards. According to Dweck, children are likely to expend more effort to obtain a learning goal than to meet a performance standard. In the latter case, children are likely to interpret failure as a sign of inability, and hence to give up more easily. Consistent with this recommendation, some researchers advise that any praise or reward given to children for improvements in academic work be relative to their past performances rather than to a fixed, pre-established performace level (Licht & Kistner, 1986).

Other motivational tactics are to reward students for doing well, involve them in planning their own programs, and set short-term goals for work completion (Bandura & Schunk, 1981; Feuerstein et al., 1980; Schumaker et al., 1986). Placing disabled learners in cooperative work groups with their nondisabled peers is also advantageous (Licht & Kistner, 1986; Snow, 1986). Cooperative group settings afford learning-disabled children an opportunity to engage successfully in academic work, and to observe the effective work habits of nondisabled peers. The division of labor may even allow learning-disabled members to show off some of their strengths. In light of the pervasiveness of motivational problems in the learning-disabled population, motivation-enhancing tactics deserve routine consideration in planning treatment. Working to improve student motivation is in many cases a precondition for successful implementation of other treatment strategies.

Environmental Factors

Numerous environmental factors besides teaching style influence children's motivation to learn. Parents or teachers who are overly critical of a child with learning disabilities instill an attitude of hopelessness. They are also likely to have a negative impact on any attempts the child might make to cope with learning problems. More supportive adults are those who encourage children to do their best and who use effective management and instructional techniques.

Individual teachers respond in distinct ways to the needs of children who are hard to teach (Brophy, 1983). Those teachers who hold to fixed standards tend to give more negative feedback and less praise to children with learning disabilities than to normal learners. More accommodating teachers administer positive feedback in accordance with individual standards of performance, rather than in relation to general standards for grade or age. Some teachers reward effort, whereas others place more emphasis on the final product. Secondary students in particular are rarely credited for effort, intent, or partial products (e.g., essays that express a good idea but contain improper grammar, punctuation, or misspelling) (Schumaker & Deshler, 1984). A rethinking of the ways in which the broader educational system deals with individual differences may be necessary in order to properly accommodate the needs of all children with learning problems (Kauffman, 1981; Schumaker et al., 1986; Wang, 1987).

Other important environmental variables to consider in planning treatment are parent attitudes and family stresses (Kaslow & Cooper, 1978). Children are likely to do better if their parents advocate for them in positive ways, collaborate with their teachers and with other professionals in arranging for appropriate educational programs, and use effective child management strategies (Smith, 1983). Children are at a disadvantage if their parents have low expectations of them or attribute any successes to luck or to the efforts of others (Pearl & Bryan, 1982). Other causes for concern are circumstances in which parents deny the seriousness of their child's problems; where they become overly protective of the child or are unable to see the child's problem from an objective point of view; or where they allow the child to become a scapegoat for other family problems, refuse to cooperate with teachers or other professionals, or fail to resolve conflicts within the family (Garis & Green, 1982; Kaslow & Cooper, 1978; Klein, Altman, Dreizen, Friedman, & Powers, 1981).

An important initial objective in working with parents is to clear up any misunderstandings concerning the child's abilities, future prospects, and current needs. Parents should be encouraged to deal with the child's problems one step at a time, and not to count on any sure or quick solutions. Performance expectations at home or school have to be set in accordance with the child's actual capacities. Those working with the child need to understand that what can be reasonably expected of the child will vary considerably across tasks. A given child, for example, may not be expected to read at grade level. But that same child may be encouraged to develop story-telling abilities, enter into discussions of lecture materials, or complete science projects. Breaking the "negative cycle" that is so often present is critical to the beginning stages of treatment. Many learning-disabled children, together with their parents and teachers, view their learning problems as insurmountable, or may blame themsleves. There may be little emphasis on strengths or on things that might be done to cope more effectively with a child's inherent weaknesses. Apart from whatever else is required to treat the child and family, putting the child's difficulties in proper perspective is of tremendous value in itself.

Finding ways for parents to become more positively engaged with their children is one way to achieve this end. A variety of parent-directed activities can be carried out at home. Cooking, playing card or word games, reading for pleasure, and writing letters to relatives or requests for free information are pleasurable ways to reinforce academic skills. Procedures like these help parents convey the message that learning is important but can also be fun (Golick, 1984).

Parents' involvement in their children's homework is quite another matter. Under some circumstances, parents can serve as effective tutors for their children (Shapiro & Forbes, 1981). More often than not, however, homework sessions with disabled learners are negative experiences for all concerned. Where conflict seems unavoidable, expectations of a child may be too high, or parents may want to find other ways of seeing that homework is completed (e.g., after-school tutoring by someone other than a parent). Problems of this sort should be discussed with the child's teacher. To be effective advocates, parents' foremost responsibilities are to understand their children's problems and do whatever possible to see that needs are met.

Biological Factors

Biological interventions constitute the last category of treatment options. Although there is nothing to be done in the way of direct neurological intervention, numerous therapies claim to reduce the problems of the learning-disabled child by means of direct manipulation of physical status or brain function. These include optometric procedures for improving binocular vision and ocular motor control, as well as training or medication intended to counter vestibular dysfunction, bring about improved sensory–motor integration, or in some way alter hemispheric organization (e.g., Ayres, 1978; Levinson, 1980). For the most part, research validating the effectiveness of these various physically oriented therapies is either absent or methodologically unsound (Keogh & Pelland, 1985; Kinsbourne & Caplan, 1979). Sensory difficulties due to impaired visual function, poor visual acuity, or significant uncorrected hearing loss will necessarily result in some difficulties in learning; correction of these problems will undoubtedly lead to improved learning. What is at issue is the claim that some presumed sensory or cortical impairment constitutes the major cause of learning disabilities, and that procedures to correct the impairment will "cure" many disabled learners. Claims such as these lack empirical support. Caution is advised in considering treatments that are based on unfounded theories or single-factor solutions.

As long as the child's general health is properly monitored, there are only three circumstances in which medical considerations are relevant to treatment. The first of these is the presence of a positive history of neurological disorder. Recent studies suggest that childhood neurological disease has its greatest effects on visual–motor skills, abstract reasoning, memory and learning, psychomotor efficiency, and performance on tasks that require planning or keeping track of several concurrent response demands (Taylor, 1987). Difficulties that brain-injured children have in learning are often quite different from those of children with more common forms of learning disability. These children may have acquired a substantial knowledge base (e.g., oral or reading vocabulary), especially if they have had many opportunities to learn or if brain damage was sustained later in childhood. Difficulties in abstract reasoning, poor modulation of attention, and mental disorganization may nevertheless have a dramatic impact on a child's ability to learn new material or work efficiently. In cases where neurological disease or injury has resulted in these latter forms of dysfunction, remediation may have to be more intensive than that required for most disabled learners. Direct teaching and individualization are especially critical for these children. Additional consideration must be given to ways in which the child and family have dealt with the disability. When disease or injury has occurred following a period of normal development, postmorbid changes in the child's behavior will need to be taken into account. The implications of any continuing handicaps, such as seizures, hearing impairment, or motor deficits, must also be considered. Finally, the examiner should be aware of the increased incidence of behavior disorders following neurological injuries (Rutter, 1981), to be sure that any problems of this nature are identified and treated.

The presence of a chronic medical disorder constitutes the second circumstance in which the medical condition of the child is relevant to treatment. Diabetes, asthma, and hyper- or hypo-thyroidism exemplify these disorders. The extent to which chronic medical conditions directly contribute to learning handicaps is not yet clear. Indirect effects of these conditions on learning are more certain. Lowered physical energy, distracting physical symptoms, medication effects, and stress associated with management issues may all have effects on school performance, and will exacerbate any pre-existing learning difficulties. Appropriate medical and psychological management of these problems is a precondition to effective treatment of such children's learning disability.

The presence of ADHD in a child with learning disabilities is the final circumstance in which intervention of a biological sort may merit consideration (Barkley, Chapter 2, this volume). In such a circumstance, the examiner must decide whether stimulant medications are an appropriate treatment option. Discussion of two issues that arise in treating learning-disabled children with stimulants is necessary to clarify the basis for making this decision.

The first issue has to do with the extent to which placement on stimulants can be expected to facilitate academic development in children with ADHD. A large body of research findings demonstrates that stimulants can significantly enhance academic productivity in children with ADHD. One would think that the immediate effects of stimulants—that is, enhanced attention, increased work output, and greater efficiency in learning novel material (Douglas, Barr, O'Neill, & Britton, 1986)—would necessarily lead to improved academic growth over time. These expected long-term gains have failed to materialize (Pelham, 1986); perhaps this is related to various methodological shortcomings of the research on this issue. For the present, therefore, recommendations regarding the use of stimulants for children with both learning disabilities and ADHD must be based on factors other than expectation of long-term academic gain. A more appropriate consideration is the possibility that immediate improvements in attention and work habits may enhance the child's self-esteem and the quality of social interactions with peers and teachers (Barkley, 1981).

The second issue relates to the appropriateness of stimulants for children whose learning problems are not accompanied by outright ADHD. This issue has been addressed most directly in studies by Gittelman on the effects of methylphenidate (Ritalin) versus a placebo on children with reading disabilities (Gittelman, 1983; Gittelman, Klein, & Feingold, 1983). In their investigations, Gittelman and her colleagues were not able to demonstrate any meaningful differences in reading performance as a function of drug condition. They also failed to find any practical advantage in combining stimulants with academic remediation. Gittelman (1983) concludes that support for the utility of stimulants with reading-disabled children is ambiguous and that any conclusions must await further studies in which larger groups are tested and the responses of individual children examined in greater detail. Pending such studies, Gittelman states that "it would be premature and ill-advised to recommend the use of methylphenidate in this patient group" (1983, p. 532).

In brief, current research suggests that stimulant medications can be useful adjuncts to treatment in cases where learning problems are accompanied by ADHD. In these cases, the most defensible strategy is to base recommendations for stimulant therapy on ADHD symptomatology only. Research findings to date fail to support the use of stimulants or other medications for learning-disabled children who do not also meet diagnostic criteria for ADHD.

TREATMENT APPLICATIONS

Individual Needs

The preceding discussion shows that there are many research-validated strategies for treating children with learning disabilities. Because disabled learners are by definition either underachieving or academically unproductive, recommendation for ways in which to improve such children's academic performance are always in order. Other treatment recommendations depend on what additional problems complicate the children's learning failure. Cognitive strategies training is often appropriate for children who are poorly organized or who take a passive approach to problem solving. Certain types of language or attentional problems can also be treated. Conduct problems, noncompliance, or dependency-seeking behaviors may call for behavior management. Similarly, attempts to increase social competency, motivation, and environmental supports are appropriate, given weaknesses in any of these areas.

One explanation for the fact that academic remediation has not led to documented long-term gains in academic function is that remedial help alone cannot hope to address the complex determinants of learning disabilities. Keogh and Barkett (1980) argue that interventions for hyperactive children have typically dealt with only one aspect of these children's problems (i.e., the behavioral, psychological, or educational component). Response to treatment for a given component problem does not tend to generalize to the other components. This same dilemma is encountered in treating learning disabilities. Effective treatment acknowledges the several factors that contribute to learning disabilities and addresses as many of these components as possible.

Children with learning disabilities vary markedly in their needs. Many disabled learners are well motivated and have no difficulties getting along with others. Obviously, these children do not require the same kind of interventions as do children who are poorly motivated or socially incompetent. Likewise, some disabled learners are good problem solvers and may not have much to gain from cognitive training (Deshler et al., 1982). The availability and practicality of various treatment options is another individual considertion that influences the type of program recommended for a child. Certain forms of treatment may be unavailable, unaffordable, or too demanding of the child's time. Treatment may have many, and often competing, objectives. Those responsible for planning intervention may want the child to interact better with peers, to develop academic competence, to acquire knowledge regarding content areas or earn credits toward graduation, to become self-confident, and to learn how to work and solve problems independently (Deshler, Schumaker, & Lenz, 1984). Depending on the child's age, interests, and priorities, it may be necessary to emphasize some goals more than others. Treatment plans have to be fitted to the individual child and circumstances. The approach to intervention that is best suited to the child's needs will be dictated by immediate priorities, long-term goals, and cost effectiveness (Schumaker et al., 1986; Wong, 1985).

A child's ability to profit from a given treatment mode must also be considered. Despite the scarcity of evidence for aptitude by treatment interactions (Arter & Jenkins, 1979), a number of recent findings indicate that certain student characteristics are indeed relevant in planning treatment. To illustrate, younger learning-disabled children with weaknesses in auditory and language skills seem to profit less from phonics instruction than do those with normal language abilities (Fox & Routh, 1975; Lovett, Warren, Ransby, & Borden, 1987; Lyon, 1985; Torneus, 1984). The preferred approach to reading instruction in such cases may be one that combines a highly graduated phonics method with other approaches to remedial reading. We may hope that a better understanding of the cognitive abilities that are most essential for academic learning will suggest ways in which to match treatment to type of disability (Torgesen, 1982).

However, knowledge of any single child characteristic will have only limited implications with regard to the total treatment plan. Any number of individual characteristics and circumstances need to be considered, and treatment must be planned accordingly. No matter how much a given child's problem is like that of another child, or how well test findings correspond to a subtype profile, recommendations must be highly individualized (Snow, 1986; Zigmond, 1978b).

General Guidelines for Making Treatment Recommendations

Despite the complexity of treatment considerations, a small set of guidelines is useful in formulating recommedations. These guidelines apply universally and help assure that treatment is both appropriate and comprehensive.

Emphasizing the Principles of Effective Instruction

Surveys of current instructional practice suggest that application of the remedial principles discussed earlier in this chapter is not routine (McKinney & Feagans, 1981). Many remedial programs often consist of the same type of instruction that is offered in regular classrooms, the only special provision being smaller group size (Licopoli, 1984; Thurlow, Ysseldyke, Graden, & Algozzine, 1983). One of the most serious violations of instructional principles is lack of sufficient academic learning time. Available estimates indicate that little more than 30 minutes of direct academic instruction may be available daily (Schumaker *et al.,* 1986; Thurlow *et al.,* 1982). Although nonoptimal teaching methods cannot be blamed for all cases of learning disabilities, these children have considerable potential to benefit from more consistent application of the instructional techniques discussed earlier in this chapter. Persons responsible for treatment plans would be well advised to evaluate current teaching methods and suggest changes in accordance with these principles.

Being Sensitive to All of a Child's Needs

A treatment program that addresses as many of a learner's problems as possible will be more effective in the long run than one that is focussed only on academic remediation. Comprehensive treatment requires a concerted effort to create conditions that will maximize the benefits of remediation. This means finding ways to help the child and family better cope with the child's disability, giving the child the necessary support and encouragement, enhancing the child's desire to learn, utilizing cognitive strategies that may result in more efficient learning, and resolving any behavioral or family problems that may prevent the child from devoting full effort to schoolwork.

Discussions of intervention programs usually make reference to one of three alternative approaches (Deshler, Schumaker, Lenz, & Ellis, 1984; Hartlage & Telzrow, 1983). The "remedial" approach emphasizes development of basic academic skills. The "tutorial" approach provides the student with extra assistance in learning the content presented in the regular curriculum. Study guides, tapes of lectures, oral or film presentations of chapter materials, and simplified or condensed written materials are illustrations of the tutorial method. And the "compensatory" approach focuses on ways to help the child keep up with the curriculum. Here the student is taught how to deal with the regular curriculum independently, without relying on tutorial assistance or special materials. Students learn ways to take notes, listen, write paragraphs, remember what they read, and study for tests that enhance their ability to meet classroom demands. The three approaches might be assigned different priorities, depending on the child's or adolescent's age and the school curriculum. Long-range goals, however, will nearly always entail improvements in academic skill, accumulation of content information, and acquisition of strategies that help the student to become more self-sufficient in learning and problem-solving activities. For this reason, the most appropriate intervention program will combine these three basic approaches.

Keeping the multiple aspects of learning problems in perspective helps to prevent treatment goals from becoming too narrowly focused. The focus of intervention may need to be expanded, for instance, in cases where impulsive children take undue time to complete their work for fear of making a mistake, or when children with decoding difficulties attempt to read by sounding out words in a letter-by-letter fashion. Although these children may be employing meaningful strategies, their behavior is in some ways maladaptive. To function adequately in the regular classroom, impulsive children need to learn to work efficiently as well as accurately. Decoding skills are important for children with reading difficulties, but reading comprehension will be jeopardized unless these children are also able to read with some fluency. A broad-based approach to treatment recognizes the child's overall needs.

Keeping the Developmental Context in Mind

Children are expected to learn different things at different points in their development. Needs consequently vary as a function of age. Much of the elementary curriculum is devoted to acquisition of academic skills. Learning content knowledge and passing required courses take on more value in secondary school (Schumaker & Deshler, 1984). Important transitions exist even within the elementary age range. Decoding skills are a major focus in early elementary school, whereas fluency and comprehension in reading and writing receive more emphasis later on (Guthrie & Seifert, 1978). Children with poor decoding skills require assistance in this area regardless of age, but reading comprehension deficits are of greater consequence for older children. Attempts to develop study skills and other learning strategies are also appropriate for the upper elementary student (Robinson, Braxdale, & Colson, 1985).

Examples of the importance of developmental context include age differences in response to praise, the greater tendency of older children to attribute their difficulties to inability as opposed to lack of effort, the special relevance of social skills and vocational training during adolescence, and the unique contribution older children can make in designing their own programs (Licht & Kistner, 1986; Schumaker *et al.*, 1986). As is the case in working with psychopathological disorders of childhood, the child's current needs are most clearly determined by "adaptational failures, defined in age-appropriate terms" (Sroufe & Rutter, 1984, p. 24). Intervention plans must recognize adaptational failures and propose strategies for dealing with them. In this sense, prescriptions for intervention should be present-oriented.

But long-term planning is also essential. Although the effects of early intervention on the incidence, severity, and longevity of learning problems are uncertain, existing data suggest that children with special needs should be recognized and treated as soon as possible (Schenck, Fitzsimmons, Bullard, Taylor, & Satz, 1980). The short-term effectiveness of programs to remediate cognitive and academic deficiencies in young children at risk for learning disabilities is well established (Becker & Carmine, 1980; Schenck *et al.*, 1980). Longer-term effects may require continuous, possibly intensive efforts over many years (Meyen & Lehr, 1980; Spache, 1976). Intervention must address a child's academic weaknesses while finding ways to minimize the delays in vocabulary development and acquisition of content knowledge that accompany academic failure (Stanovich, 1986). Working with learning-

disabled children is a long-term investment. Adequate planning requires attention to both immediate and future objectives (Keogh & Glover, 1980; Schumaker *et al.*, 1986).

Accommodating to the Individual Child's Level of Functioning

Regardless of the child's age, expectations must be realistic and in keeping with the individual child's capabilities. In concrete terms, this means providing graduated instructions, assigning reading or math materials that are below grade level, or lessening workloads. Unfortunately, responsible adults frequently feel that it is unfair to the disabled learner—or to the rest of the classroom—to make these adjustments. This "sink or swim" attitude toward management of such a child's problems stems either from a lack of resources or time, or from failure of parents or teachers to acknowledge the full extent of the child's learning handicap. Expecting children to perform tasks of which they are incapable not only generates frustration; this approach also yields little if any academic progress and may precipitate avoidance tactics and learned helplessness (Butkowsky & Willows, 1980).

Setting appropriate expectations is far from easy. To do so requires that persons working with a disabled learner be well acquainted with the child's capacities, as well as with general developmental considerations. Appropriate tasks are those in which the child can attain consistent success but that are also challenging (Brophy, 1986). Accommodating to the child's academic weaknesses will be facilitated by an appreciation of just how difficult it is for the child to contend with schoolwork. The concept of "mental energy" is useful in helping parents come to this realization. Mental energy, in this instance, refers to the effort that children have to put into their schoolwork to succeed. By virtue of their weaknesses, children with learning disabilities have to invest more mental energy in their work than do their peers to achieve the same objectives. As there is only a limited supply of such energy, children cannot be expected to work extra hard all day in school and then do the same all evening or weekend. Some balance of activities is necessary. An overriding goal of any treatment plan is to see that the child works constructively, avoids counterproductive activities, and resolves preoccupations or concerns that serve only to detract from efforts to learn (e.g., acting out in the classroom, excessive anxiety of frustration, preoccupation with family stresses).

Getting All Those Involved to Take Active Responsibility for the Child's Problems.

Treatment programs will work best if all persons who relate to a child are willing to make allowances and to take active responsibility for the child's problems. This includes regular teachers as well as remedial specialists. It is difficult for regular classroom teachers—especially those at the secondary level—to individualize instruction to the extent that is necessary for most disabled learners. Classrooms have large numbers of students, many of whom would benefit from individual help. But as long as disabled learners spend a majority of their day in regular classes, there is no substitute for accommodating to their needs in that setting.

Parents must also be active participants in the treatment program. Primary parental responsibilities are to effectively manage their child's behavior, to see that any issues that might interfere with the child's academic learning are resolved, and to foster an interest and confidence in learning. Personal experience suggests that active and appropriate parental involvement generally leads to a greater willingness on the part of school personnel to go out of their way on the child's behalf. Lastly, the child himself or herself needs to be given some responsibilities—for example, in setting instructional goals and choosing materials (Schumaker *et al.,* 1986). Other specific ways to promote a sense of personal responsibility are to encourage use of self verbalizations, spelling dictionaries, number lines, and computer editing of written documents.

Encouraging Development of Strengths While Working on Weaknesses

A common question posed by those who teach learning-disabled children is whether it is best to remediate weaknesses or to circumvent weaknesses by capitalizing on strengths. This question is most frequently posed by teachers of children who have severe difficulties acquiring decoding skills. The educator is forced in these instances to decide whether phonics instruction is truly useful for such children, or whether relatively more emphasis should be placed on language-based or sight word methods. A recent study by Lovett *et al.* (1987) suggests that the sight word approach may have some advantages over phonics instruction. It is difficult, however, to recommend that efforts at teaching decoding skills be totally abandoned, even for this subset of children. As previously noted, phonics-based approaches to early reading instruction have generally proved superior to other methods. The most obvious reason for direct instruction in phonics is that it makes sound–symbol relationships explicit. Knowledge of these relationships is necessary for decoding unfamiliar words and hence for building word recognition skills (Jorm *et al.,* 1986).

It is essential, however, that treatment not be too deficit-oriented. An emphasis on strengths is critical. Encouraging disabled learners to participate in activities or hobbies at which they show some facility contributes to improved self-confidence and provides a necessary break from the stressful academic tasks. The concept of mental energy is again appropriate here. Disabled learners must expend much effort if they are to successfully cope with their disabilities; they cannot be expected to put this amount of energy into all of their activities. Children who participate in some activities that are easy for them are more likely to view themselves as competent individuals and to return to their schoolwork with renewed vigor. An additional benefit is the opportunity for further skill development in areas where a child is most likely to excel. The child must also have opportunities to master content information, develop socialization skills, and acquire critical thinking abilities. Review of research on outcomes of childhood learning disorders indicates that many individuals continue to experience academic problems well into adulthood and despite considerable remedial assistance along the way (Bruck, in press; Forell & Hood, 1985). Notwithstanding the fact that academic progress may be facilitated by means of proper instructional techniques, ignoring strengths does the child a disservice. It is essential, therefore, that every effort be made to work on both strengths and weaknesses.

Making Learning Meaningful and Fun

However necessary it is to work on weaknesses, most learning-disabled children find academic tasks distressing. They view academic learning as something that has to be done, rather than as something that can be both useful and enjoyable. Games and other nonacademic activities are useful adjuncts to drill (Golick, 1984, 1986, 1987; Sanders, 1979). If children are to remain motivated, their efforts must also be accompanied by significant and meaningful change in their abilities (Dweck, 1986).

The several ways in which to encourage children to become more fluent and enthusiastic readers exemplify the types of activities that can make learning more meaningful. One simple technique is to have the child take turns with an adult in oral reading of alternate pages of a story (F. Hellstrom, personal communication, 1987). Another technique is to familiarize the child with the reading vocabulary contained in a given passage and then have the child reread the passage until fluency is achieved (Rashotte & Torgesen, 1985). A related procedure is to have the child listen to a tape recording of a passage and to follow along with the text as it is played until the passage is memorized. The child can then "read" the passage in a semirote fashion without playing the tape recording. According to Chomsky (1978), this "repeated listening" technique is particularly useful for dysfluent readers who have been overdrilled in phonics. A similar technique for developing written language skills is to have children tape-record their own orally presented stories. With teacher assistance, the children can then transcribe their own recordings. Further ways to make learning enjoyable include having children read restricted-vocabulary books covering topics or themes of special interest to them; or, in the case of learning-disabled adolescents, finding ways to improve reading vocabulary through use of content or textbook materials (Smith, 1983). Even those parents who find it impossible to help with homework assignments may take pleasure in working with children on these learning activities.

Educational Programs

The most common form of treatment is to place children in special educational classes at their schools—assuming, of course, that they meet the school's criteria for learning disabilities. Special educational options range from placements in special schools or rehabilitation centers to full- or part-time placements in special educational programs within the public school system (Lerner, 1981). Children in part-time programs receive special educational assistance individually or in small groups for a few hours per week. They are "mainstreamed" into regular classes for the remainder of the school day. In some school systems, programs for learning-disabled children are separate from those set up to serve children with other handicaps, such as mental retardation or social–emotional disturbance. In other systems, children with various disabilities are grouped together according to educational need rather than diagnosis. The two types of programs are referred to, respectively, as "categorical" and "noncategorical" placements.

Special educational assistance for children with learning disabilities is mandated in the United States by the Education for All Handicapped Children Act (U.S. Public Law 94-142, 1977). Public Law 94-142 requires that all children, regardless of their handicap, be given a free and appropriate education in the least restrictive educational environment. This law also requires that parents be involved in the planning of the child's program, and that planning be individualized in accordance with an individual educational plan (IEP).

Despite the appropriateness and good intentions of this legislation, the programs it has promulgated are often poorly conceptualized. According to Calfee (1982), "curriculum components are splintered collections of instructional objectives, and both teacher and student may find it difficult to see clear direction to the programs" (p. 174). As previously indicated, the effectiveness of many special education programs for the learning-disabled is in serious doubt (McKinney & Feagans, 1984; Short, Feagans, McKinney, & Appelbaum, 1986; Sindelar & Deno, 1978). The several shortcomings of resource room programs are well documented (Schumaker & Deshler, 1984; Zigmond, Levin, & Laurie, 1985). To begin with, skills taught do not always help the child to function within the regular classroom. Programs are often of limited intensity and do not meet multiple student needs. Students may miss important regular classroom instruction, and fragmented schedules tend to reduce instructional time. Regular teachers are frequently uninvolved. Finally, these programs offer no assistance to underachieving children who fail to qualify as learning-disabled.

Proposals to consider for improving the effectiveness of special education are as follows:

1. Providing greater specialization of instruction for all students (Algozzine & Ysseldyke, 1986; Good & Weinstein, 1986; Snow, 1986; Wang, 1987).
2. Encouraging more cooperative planning between learning disabilities specialists and regular classroom teachers (Zigmond, 1978a).
3. Arranging for cooperative learning groups and peer tutoring (Brown & Campione, 1986; Licht & Kistner, 1986; Nevin, Johnson, & Johnson, 1982; Slavin, Leavey, & Madden, 1984).
4. Implementing teacher training programs to assure that teachers are familiar with instructional principles and to establish more uniformity in teaching practice (Brophy, 1986).
5. Trying to meet as many of the disabled learners' needs as possible (Schumaker et al., 1986).

If schools are to offer truly comprehensive services, their programs must make provisions to enhance student motivation and independence (Deshler et al., 1983). Steps must be taken to assure that secondary school students acquire content knowledge without sacrificing continued efforts to improve their basic skills. This may involve supplementary out-of-school or summer programs, intensification of remedial services at school, or attempts to teach basic skills through content materials (Schumaker et al., 1986). Alternative curriculum models may be necessary for some students (Wiederholt & McEntire, 1980). Educators must make sure that students retain and apply what they learn, that regular teachers have adequate support to make classroom modifications, and that skills taught assist the child or adolescent in making a successful transition to the next stage of development (Deshler, Schumaker, Lenz, & Ellis, 1984; Schumaker et al., 1986; Zigmond, 1978a). Comprehensive treatment calls for commitment on the part of individual teachers, school administrators, and the community (Deshler, Schumaker, Lenz, & Ellis, 1984). Collaboration from parents is also

vital to program effectiveness (Bloom, 1984; Zigmond, 1978a).

The importance of cooperative and broad-based planning for disabled learners is becoming increasingly apparent (Budoff, 1975; Cordes, 1986). With implementation of programs such as those designed by Schumaker et al. (1986) and Zigmond (1978a), it may soon be possible to evaluate more comprehensive interventions. We may hope that these methods will have more far-reaching effects than the programs currently available at most schools.

DISCUSSION

Clinical Demands

Treatment of children with learning disabilities is a complex undertaking. Recommendations for treatment originate from a thorough assessment of children's learning difficulties, academic expectations, cognitive and behavioral attributes, and environmental and biological influences (Taylor, 1988). It is important to know not only what children can do, but how they and their parents and teachers are attempting to cope with current problems. The results of such evaluations permit the examiner to formulate hypotheses regarding potential sources of learning failure. Treatment plans follow from these hypotheses. In most cases, children have multiple needs. Deficits in specific cognitive areas are frequently compounded by low self-esteem, behavioral problems, family stress, or lack of sufficient individual attention at school. The individual or team of individuals in charge of the child's treatment plan must decide how best to address each problem. Some problems may be assigned higher priority initially, as in the case of a child whose behavioral problems preclude meaningful instructional interaction. But if treatment is to have a long-term impact, attention must eventually be paid to each contributing factor.

Professionals who work with this population must be aware of the multiple needs of learning-disabled children and of effective treatment methods. Clinical experience with families and schools is another valuable asset. Clinicians should be familiar with the special educational options available in their local school systems, and with other community resources. School personnel are often willing to make modifications to suit individual needs. It is essential that the professional responsible for planning treatment serve fundamentally as a child advocate. The ethical obligations of those who assume this role are to do whatever possible to see that (1) all of a child's needs are appreciated; (2) intervention is as appropriate and intensive as possible; (3) both immediate and long-range goals are kept in mind; (4) parents and teachers are fully informed as to plans for intervention; (5) these plans take the values of the child and family into account; and (6) the potential benefits of treatment are weighed against costs (e.g., sacrifices in time or money, diagnostic labeling of the child) (Schumaker & Hazel, 1984b).

Research Directions

There is much to be gained from systematic application of empirically validated treatment methods. At the same time, existing research falls far short of providing the kind of guidance needed to make clinical decisions. It is not as yet clear, for example, that social skills training generalizes in meaningful ways to the classroom, or that training in language or other cognitive abilities facilitates academic achievement. There are few formal studies of family interventions. Specific instructional programs are often accepted at face value, with no empirical evidence for their superiority over other methods. Although child characteristics vary markedly within samples of learning-disabled children, it is difficult to know which children will benefit most from a particular method. More attention needs to be paid to the particular demands of the tasks or settings in which the learner is engaged (Torgesen, 1979, 1982). Finally, there have been few investigations of multiple-component treatment programs. Future investigations must examine the effects of such programs on a range of educational, behavioral, and social outcomes (Keogh & Glover, 1980; Schumaker et al., 1986; Wong, 1985).

Relatively few experimentally based investigations of treatment effects were conducted prior to the 1970s (Bryan, 1974). A survey by Torgesen and Dice (1980) showed that only 17% of the studies of learning-disabled children published in major journals from 1976 to 1978 related to treatment methods. Although treatment issues are now considered to be of central importance to the field (Adelman & Taylor, 1986), most of the available literature on intervention is subject to numerous methodological limitations (see reviews by Gittelman,

1983; Hallahan & Cruickshank, 1973; Keogh, 1982; Torgesen & Dice, 1980; Yule, 1976).

Criteria for sound research in this area are as follows:

1. Procedures for sample selection must be specified, and important subject characteristics and "extrachild" factors must be reported (e.g., IQ and achievement levels, demographic information).
2. There must be some attempt to assess variability in response to treatment, and to study this variability as a function of individual-difference variables.
3. Treatment itself must be of sufficient intensity and duration to allow for the possibility of measurable treatment effects.
4. Investigators must examine maintenance effects following termination of treatment, and explore the impact of treatment on aspects of functioning besides those directly targeted in the intervention (e.g., effects on motivational status and behavior).
5. In group comparisons, subjects must be randomly assigned to treatment and control groups, and any pretreatment differences between these groups must be taken into account in evaluating treatment effects.
6. Appropriate procedures for statistical analysis of the data should be employed (e.g., use of multivariate procedures where indicated).
7. The reliability, sensitivity, and construct validity of measures chosen to assess change must be examined.
8. Experimental treatments must be compared against meaningful control conditions if treatment effects are to have clinical value.
9. In cases where intervention is successful, efforts must be made to discover what aspects of treatment are most essential.

Only a handful of studies in the current literature meet a majority of these requirements. Exemplary investigations are the previously cited studies by Williams (1980), Gittelman and Feingold (1983), Lovett et al. (in press), and Chan and Cole (1986). More research of this nature is needed if clinical recommendations are to have a scientific basis. We may hope that, because of their clinical relevance, more methodologically sophisticated treatment studies will narrow the gap between researcher and clinician (Keogh, 1977). Greater use of single-subject or small-group, multiple-baseline designs is in order, as are more comprehensive research programs that consider multiple aspects of learning disabilities (Deshler *et al.*, 1983; Guralnick, 1978; Kratochwill, Brody, & Piersel, 1979).

SUMMARY AND CONCLUSIONS

A significant proportion of the school-age population manifests academic achievement or productivity that is well below normal expectations. Notwithstanding active debate over which individuals appropriately qualify as learning-disabled, they are most fundamentally "hard to teach" (Rosner, 1979; Zigmond, 1978b). Many cognitive and other problems contribute to the failure that disabled learners experience when placed in regular classrooms. Most of these children require assistance not often available in the regular classroom, at least if they are to develop fully in areas of weakness and to capitalize on individual strengths. The major thesis of this chapter is that there are a variety of ways to promote academic development in learning-disabled children, and a body of research-validated methods on which to draw in planning intervention to better meet their needs. Much more research is necessary to refine treatment procedures and to examine the effects of combined methods. Although clinical judgment is essential in making recommendations that suit individual needs, several important conclusions can be made on the basis of information summarized in this review.

One theme is the current disregard for many research-validated instructional principles. Learning-disabled children often receive little extra instructional support. Nonacademic problems may be neglected altogether. The academic progress of many of these children would be greater if they were to receive more intensive and comprehensive assistance. Although more widespread application of the principles of effective instruction would not necessarily reduce differences between disabled learners and their nondisabled peers, it might well result in improved quality of education for both groups (Bloom, 1984; Kauffman, 1981; Good & Weinstein, 1986).

A related conclusion is that treatment strategies appropriate for children who meet strict diagnostic criteria for learning disabilities are equally applicable to many other underachievers. A common assumption among clinicians is that children whose underachievement is matched by lowered general intellect are doing as well as can be expected. Although such children may in fact be doing as well as can be expected, given the education provided them, the same may be said of the children who qualify as learning-disabled. Children who are formally identified as learning-disabled are not readily distinguished from other underachievers (Stanovich, 1986). It seems likely that similar factors contribute to learning failure in both groups, and that all underachievers would stand to benefit from the treatment strategies discussed in this chapter (Algozzine & Ysseldyke, 1986).

A further conclusion is that learning difficulties are in part a function of the *demands* placed on the learner (Smith, 1985). Regardless of how much special attention children receive, expecting them to perform tasks that are beyond their capabilities is not merely instructionally ineffective; it generates frustration, leads to loss of self-confidence, and may result in behaviors that are incompatible with learning. If children with learning disabilities are to cope actively with their weaknesses, they need to feel that their efforts will be worthwhile. For children who cannot cope with the regular curriculum, a supportive and flexible approach to teaching—as well as to parenting—is critical. Accommodating to the children's patterns of strengths and weaknesses reduces frustration and maximizes opportunities to learn. Parental involvement provides further assurances of an optimal response to intervention (Deshler, Schumaker, Lenz, & Ellis, 1984; Zigmond, 1978a).

Developmental context must also be kept in mind. Treatment methods and priorities suited for younger children do not necessarily apply to older children or adolescents. Appropriate treatment requires early recognition of a child's learning problems and long-term follow-up. At any given point in time, developmental tasks appropriate to the age of the child will dictate treatment objectives.

Finally, effective treatment plans must take all of a child's needs into account. Treatment programs are typically far too narrow in scope and intensity. Effective intervention requires application of the principles of effective instruction and of strategies for improving educationally relevant cognitive abilities, social skills, and motivational status. Consideration of environmental and biological factors is also essential to treatment. The limited nature of most current programs for disabled learners may help explain the seeming intractibility of their problems. Despite the sobering nature of the longer-term outcome studies conducted to date (Koppitz, 1972–1973; McKinney & Feagans, 1981; Satz *et al.*, 1978; Spreen, 1982), much can be done to promote positive outcomes. Learning problems can be successfully managed. Knowledge of the several aspects of these problems, appreciation of individual differences, tenacity of effort, and cooperative planning are all fundamental to this process.

REFERENCES

Adelman, H. S., & Taylor. L. (1986). Summary of the survey of fundamental concerns confronting the LD field. *Journal of Learning Disabilities, 19*, 391–393.

Algozzine, B., & Ysseldyke, J. E. (1986). The future of the LD field: Screening and diagnosis. *Journal of Learning Disabilities, 19*, 394–398.

American Psychiatric Association. (1987). *Diagnostic and statistical manual of mental disorders* (3rd ed., rev.). Washington, DC: Author.

Amerikaner, M. J., & Omizo, M. M. (1984). Family interaction and learning disabilities. *Journal of Learning Disabilities, 17*, 540–543.

Arter, J. A., & Jenkins, J. R. (1979). Differential diagnosis—prescriptive teaching: A critical appraisal. *Review of Education Research, 49*, 517–555.

Ayres, A. J. (1978). Learning disabilities and the vestibular system. *Journal of Learning Disabilities, 11*, 30–41.

Balow, B., Fuchs, D., & Kasbohm, M. (1978). Teaching nonreaders to read: An evaluation of the Basic Skill Centers in Minneapolis. *Journal of Learning Disabilities, 11*, 351–354.

Bandura, A., & Schunk, D. H. (1981). Cultivating competence, self-efficacy, and intrinsic interest through proximal self-motivation. *Journal of Personality and Social Psychology, 41*, 586–598.

Barkley, R. A. (1981). *Hyperactive children: A handbook for diagnosis and treatment.* New York: Guilford Press.

Beck, I., Perfetti, C. A., & McKeown, M. G. (1982). Effects of long-term vocabulary instruction on lexical access and reading comprehension. *Journal of Educational Psychology, 74*, 506–521.

Becker, W. C., & Carmine, D. W. (1980). Direct instruction: An effective approach to educational intervention with disadvantaged and low performers. In B. B. Lahey & A. E. Kazdin (Eds.), *Advances in clinical child psychology* (Vol. 3, pp. 419–473). New York: Plenum.

Bloom, B. S. (1974). Time and learning. *American Psychologist, 29*, 682–688.

Bloom, B. S. (1984). The search for methods of group instruction as effective as one-to-one tutoring. *Educational Leadership, 41*, 4–17.

Bradley, L. (1981). The organization of motor patterns for spelling: An effective remedial strategy for backward readers. *Developmental Medicine and Child Neurology, 23*, 83–91.

Brophy, J. E. (1983). Research on the self-fulfilling prophecy and teacher expectations. *Journal of Educational Psychology, 75*, 631–661.

Brophy, J. (1986). Teacher influences on student achievement. *American Psychologist, 41*, 1069–1077.

Brown, A. L., Bradford, J. D., Ferrara, R. A., & Campione, J. C. (1983). Learning, remembering, and understanding. In J. H. Flovell & E. E. Markman (Eds.), *Handbook of child psychology: Cognitive development* (4th edition, pp. 77–166). New York: Wiley.

Brown, A. L., & Campione, J. C. (1986). Psychological theory and the study of learning disabilities. *American Psychologist, 41*, 1059–1068.

Bruck, M. (in press). The long-term prognosis of children with learning disabilities. *Annals of Dyslexia.*

Bryan, T. H. (1974). Learning disabilities: A new stereotype. *Journal of Learning Disabilities, 7*, 304–309.

Bryant, N. D. (1965). Some principles of remedial instruction for dyslexia. *The Reading Teacher, 18*, 567–572.

Bryant, N. D., Drabin, I. R., & Gettinger, M. (1981). Effects of varying unit size on spelling achievement in learning disabled children. *Journal of Learning Disabilities, 14*, 200–203.

Bryant, N. D., Fayne, H. R., & Gettinger, M. (1980). *"LD efficient" instruction in phonics: Applying sound learning principles to remedial teaching* (Technical Report No. 1, Research Institute for the Study of Learning Disabilities). New York: Teachers College, Columbia University.

Budoff, M. (1975). Engendering change in special education practices. *Harvard Educational Review, 45*, 507–526.

Butkowsky, I. S., & Willows, D. (1980). Cognitive–motivational characteristics of children varying in reading ability: Evidence for learned helplessness in poor readers. *Journal of Educational Psychology, 72*, 408–422.

Calfee, R. (1982). Cognitive models of reading: Implications for assessment and treatment of reading disability. In R. N. Malatesha & P. G. Aaron (Eds.), *Reading disorders: Varieties and treatments* (pp. 151–176). New York: Academic Press.

Chan, L. K. S., & Cole, P. G. (1986). The effects of comprehension monitoring training on the reading competence of learning disabled and regular class students. *Remedial and Special Education, 7*(4), 33–40.

Chomsky, C. (1978). When you still can't read in third grade: After decoding, what? In S. J. Samuels (Ed.), *What research has to say about reading instruction* (pp. 13–30). Newark, DE: International Reading Association.

Cruickshank, W. M., Bentzen, F., Ratzeburg, F., & Tannhauser, M. A. (1961). *Teaching methods for brain-injured and hyperactive children.* Syracuse, NY: Syracuse University Press.

Delacato, C. H. (1963). *The diagnosis and treatment of speech and reading problems.* Springfield, IL: Charles C Thomas.

Deshler, D. D., Alley, G. R., Warner, M. M., & Schumaker, J. B. (1981). Instructional practices for promoting skill acquisition and generalization in severely learning disabled adolescents. *Learning Disability Quarterly, 4*, 415–421.

Deshler, D. D., Schumaker, J. B., Alley, G. R., Warner, M. M. & Clark, F. L. (1982). Learning disabilities in adolescent and young adult populations. *Focus on Exceptional Children, 15*, 1–12.

Deshler, D. D., Schumaker, J. B., & Lenz, B. K. (1984). Academic and cognitive interventions for LD adolescents: Part I. *Journal of Learning Disabilities, 17*, 108–117.

Deshler, D. D., Schumaker, J. B., Lenz, B. K., & Ellis, E. (1984). Academic and cognitive interventions for LD adolescents: Part II. *Journal of Learning Disabilities, 17*, 170–179.

Deshler, D. D., Warner, M. M., Schumaker, J. B., & Alley, G. R. (1983). Learning strategies intervention model: Key components and current status. In J. D. McKinney & L. Feagans (Eds.), Current topics in learning disabilities (Vol. 1, pp. 245–283). Norwood, NJ: Ablex.

Douglas, V. I., Barr, R. G., O'Neill, M. E., & Britton, B. G. (1986). Short-term effects of methylphenidate on the cognitive, learning and academic performance of children with attention deficit disorder in the laboratory and the classroom. Journal of Child Psychology and Psychiatry, 27, 191–211.

Douglas, V. I., & Peters, K. G. (1979). Toward a clearer definition of the attentional deficit of hyperactive children. In G. Hale & M. Lewis (Eds.), Attention and cognitive development (pp. 173–247). New York: Plenum.

Drabman, R. S., & Spitalnick, R. (1973). Social isolation as a punishment procedure: A controlled study. Journal of Experimental Child Psychology, 16, 236–249.

Dweck, C. S. (1986). Motivational processes affecting learning. American Psychologist, 41, 1040–1048.

Eisenberg, L. (1978). Definitions of dyslexia: Their consequences for research and policy. In A. L. Benton & D. Pearl (Eds.), Dyslexia: An appraisal of current knowledge (pp. 29–42). New York: Oxford University Press.

Englert, C. S. (1984). Effective direct instruction practices in special education settings. Remedial and Special Education, 5, 38–47.

Farnham-Diggory, S. (1986). Time, now, for a little serious complexity. In S. J. Ceci (Ed.), Handbook of cognitive, social and neuropsychological aspects of learning disabilities (pp. 123–158). Hillsdale, NJ: Erlbaum.

Feuerstein, R., Rand, Y., Hoffman, M., & Miller, R. (1980). Instrumental enrichment: An intervention program for cognitive modifiability. Baltimore: University Park Press.

Finucci, J., & Childs, B. (1981). Are there really more dyslexic boys than girls? In A. Ansara, N. Geschwind, A. Galaburda, M. Albert, & N. Gartrell (Eds.), Sex differences in dyslexia (pp. 1–9). Towson, MD: Orton Dyslexia Society.

Fleisher, L. S., & Jenkins, J. R. (1983). The effect of word—and comprehension—emphasis instruction on reading performance. Learning Disability Quarterly, 6, 146–154.

Forell, E., & Hood, J. (1985). A longitudinal study of two groups of children with early reading problems. Annals of Dyslexia, 35, 97–116.

Fox, B., & Routh, D. K. (1975). Phonemic analysis and synthesis as work attack skills. Journal of Educational Psychology, 68, 70–74.

Frostig, M., & Horne, D. (1964). The Frostig program for the development of visual perception. Chicago: Follett.

Garis, A. M. V., & Green, L. A. (1982). A structural family therapy approach to the treatment of learning disabilities. In W. M. Cruickshank & J. W. Lerner (Eds.), Learning disabilities: A coming of age (pp. 72–83). Syracuse, NY: Syracuse University Press.

Gettinger, M. (1982). Improving classroom behaviors and achievement of learning disabled using direct instruction. School Psychology Review, 11, 329–336.

Gettinger, M., Bryant, N. D., & Fayne, H. R. (1982). Designing spelling instruction for learning-disabled children: An emphasis on unit size, distributed practice, and training for transfer. Journal of Special Education, 16, 439–448.

Gettinger, M., & White, M. A. (1979). Which is the stronger correlate of school learning? Time to learn or measured intelligence. Journal of Educational Psychology, 71, 405–412.

Gittelman, R. (1983). Treatment of reading disorders. In M. Rutter (Ed.), Developmental neuropsychiatry (pp. 520–541). New York: Guilford Press.

Gittelman, R., & Feingold, I. (1983). Children with reading disorders: I. Effects of reading instruction. Journal of Child Psychology and Psychiatry, 24, 167–191.

Gittelman, R., Klein, D. F., & Feingold, I. (1983). Children with reading disorders: II. Effects of methylphenidate in combination with reading remediation. Journal of Child Psychology and Psychiatry, 24, 193–212.

Golick, M. (1984). A parent's guide to learning problems (rev. ed.). Montreal: Quebec Association for Children and Adults with Learning Disabilities.

Golick, M. (1986). Reading, writing, and rummy. Markham, Ontario: Pembroke.

Golick, M. (1987). Playing with words. Markham, Ontario: Pembroke.

Good, T. L., & Brophy, J. E. (1986). Educational psychology: A realistic approach (3rd ed.). New York: Longman.

Good, T. L., & Weinstein, R. S. (1986). Schools make a difference: Evidence, criticisms, and new directions. American Psychologist, 41, 1090–1097.

Guralnick, M. J. (1978). The application of single-subject research designs to the field of learning disabilities. Journal of Learning Disabilities, 11, 415–421.

Guthrie, J. T., Martuza, V., & Seifert, M. (1979). Impacts of instructional time in reading. In L. B. Resnick & P. A. Weaver (Eds.), Theory and practice of early reading. Hillsdale, NJ: Erlbaum.

Guthrie, J. T., & Seifert, M. (1978). Education for children with reading disabilities. In H. Myklebust (Ed.), Progress in learning disabilities (Vol. 4, pp. 223–255). New York: Grune & Stratton.

Guthrie, J. T., Seifert, M., & Kline, L. (1977). Clues from research on programs for poor readers. In S. J. Samuels (Ed.), What research says to classroom teachers (pp. 1–12). Newark, DE: International Reading Association.

Hallahan, D. P., & Bryan, T. (1981). Learning disabilities. In J. Kauffman & D. Hallahan (Eds.), Handbook of special education (pp. 141–164). Englewood Cliffs, NJ: Prentice-Hall.

Hallahan, D. P., & Cruickshank, W. M. (1973). Psychoeducation foundations of learning disabilities. Englewood Cliffs, NJ: Prentice-Hall.

Hallahan, D. P., & Kauffman, J. M. (1976). Introduction to learning disabilities. Englewood Cliffs, NJ: Prentice-Hall.

Hallahan, D. P., Lloyd, J., Kosiewicz, M. M., Kauffman, J. M., & Graves, A. W. (1979). Self-monitoring of attention as a treatment for a learning disabled boy's off-task behavior. Learning Disability Quarterly, 2, 24–32.

Hallahan, D. P., Marshall, K. J., & Lloyd, J. W. (1981). Self-recording during group instruction: Effects of attention to task. Learning Disability Quarterly, 4, 407–413.

Harris, A., & Serwer, B. (1966). The Craft Project: Instructional time in reading research. Reading Research Quarterly, 2, 27–57.

Hartlage, L. C., & Telzrow, C. F. (1983). The neuropsychological basis of educational intervention. Journal of Learning Disabilities, 16, 521–528.

Hazel, J. S., Schumaker, J. B., Sherman, J. A., & Sheldon, J. (1982). Application of a group training program in social skills and problem solving in learning disabled and non-learning disabled youth. Learning Disability Quarterly, 5, 398–408.

Horn, W. F., O'Donnell, J. P., & Vitulano, L. A. (1983). Long-term follow-up studies of learning-disabled persons. *Journal of Learning Disabilities, 16,* 542–555.

Ivarie, J. J. (1986). Effects of proficiency rates on later performance of a recall and writing behavior. *Remedial and Special Education, 7*(5), 25–30.

Jorm, A. F., & Share, D. L. (1983). Phonological recoding and reading acquisition. *Applied Psycholinguistics, 4,* 103–147.

Jorm, A. F., Share, D. L., Matthews, R., & Maclean, R. (1986). Behavior problems in specific reading retarded and general reading backward children: A longitudinal study. *Journal of Child Psychology and Psychiatry, 27,* 33–43.

Kavale, K., & Mattson, P. D. (1983). "One jumped off the balance beam": Meta-analysis of perceptual–motor training. *Journal of Learning Disabilities, 16,* 165–173.

Kaslow, F. W., & Cooper, B. (1978). Family therapy with the learning disabled child and his/her family. *Journal of Marriage and Family Counseling, 4,* 41–49.

Kauffman, J. M. (1975). Behavior modification. In W. M. Cruickshank & D. P. Hallahan (Eds.), *Perceptual and learning disabilities in children: Research and theory* (Vol. 2, pp. 395–444). Syracuse, NY: Syracuse University Press.

Kauffman, J. M. (1981). Historical trends and contemporary issues in special education in the United States. In J. M. Kauffman & D. P. Hallahan (Eds.), *Handbook of special education* (pp. 3–23). Columbus, OH, Charles E. Merrill.

Kauffman, J. M., Hallahan, D. P., Haas, K., Brame, T., & Boren, R. (1978). Imitating children's errors to improve their spelling performance. *Journal of Learning Disabilities, 11,* 217–222.

Kendall, P. D., & Braswell, L. (1984). *Cognitive–behavioral therapy for impulsive children.* New York: Guilford Press.

Keogh, B. K. (1977). Working together: A new direction. *Journal of Learning Disabilities, 10,* 478–482.

Keogh, B. K. (1982). Research in learning disabilities: A view of status and need. In J. P. Das, R. F. Mulcahy, & A. E. Wall (Eds.), *Theory and research in learning disabilities* (pp. 27–44). New York: Plenum.

Keogh, B. K. (1983). Classification, compliance, and confusion. *Journal of Learning Disabilities, 16,* 25.

Keogh, B. K., & Barkett, C. J. (1980). An educational analysis of hyperactive children's achievement problems. In C. K. Whalen & B. Henker (Eds.), *Hyperactive children: The social ecology of identification and treatment* (pp. 259–282). New York: Academic Press.

Keogh, B. K., & Glover, A. T. (1980). The generality and durability of cognitive training effects. *Exceptional Education Quarterly, 1,* 75–82.

Keogh, B. K., & Pelland, M. (1985). Vision training revisited. *Journal of Learning Disabilities, 18,* 228–236.

Kephart, N. (1971). *The slow learner in the classroom* (2nd ed.). Columbus, OH: Charles E. Merrill.

Kinsbourne, M., & Caplan, P. (1979). *Children's learning and attention problems.* Boston: Little, Brown.

Kirk, S. A. (1963). Behavioral diagnosis and remediation of learning disabilities. In *Proceedings of the annual conference on exploration in the problems of the perceptually handicapped child* (pp. 1–7). Evanston, IL: Fund for Perceptually Handicapped Children.

Kirk, S. A., & Kirk, W. D. (1971). *Psycholinguistic learning disabilities: Diagnosis and remediation.* Chicago: University of Illinois Press.

Klein, R. S., Altman, S. D., Dreizen, K., Friedman, R., & Powers, L. (1981). Restructuring dysfunctional parental attitudes toward children's learning and behavior at school: Family-oriented psychoeducational therapy—Part I. *Journal of Learning Disabilities, 14,* 15–19.

Koppitz, E. (1972–1973). Special class pupils with learning disabilities: A five-year follow-up study. *Academic Therapy, 8,* 133–139.

Kratochwill, T. R., Brody, G. H., & Piersel, W. C. (1979). Time-series research: Some comments on design methodology for research in learning disabilities. *Journal of Learning Disabilities, 12,* 257–263.

Kratochwill, T. R., Demuth, D. M., & Conzemius, W. C. (1977). The effects of over-learning on preschool children's retention of sight vocabulary words. *Reading Improvement, 14,* 223–228.

La Greca, A. M. (1981). Social behavior and social perception in learning-disabled children: A review with implications for social skills training. *Journal of Pediatric Psychology, 6,* 395–415.

Lerner, J. W. (1981). *Learning disabilities: Theories, diagnosis, and teaching strategies.* Boston: Houghton Mifflin.

Levinson, H. N. (1980). *A solution to the riddle: Dyslexia.* New York: Springer-Verlag.

Licht, B. G., & Kistner, J. A. (1986). Motivational problems of learning-disabled children: Individual differences and their implications for treatment. In J. K. Torgesen & B. Y. L. Wong (Eds.), *Psychological and educational perspectives on learning disabilities* (pp. 329–365). New York: Academic Press.

Licopoli, L. (1984). The resource room and mainstreaming secondary handicapped students: A case study. *Topics in Learning and Learning Disabilities, 3,* 1–15.

Lovett, M. W., Ransby, M. J., Hardwick, N., & Johns, M. S. (in press). Can dyslexia be treated: Treatment-specific and generalized treatment effects in dyslexics' response to remediation. *Brain and Language.*

Lovett, M. W., Warren, P. M., Ransby, M. J., & Borden, S. L. (1987). *Training the word recognition skills of dyslexic children: Treatment and transfer effects.* Paper presented at the meeting of the International Neuropsychological Society, Washington, DC.

Lyon, G. R. (1985). Educational validation studies of learning disability subtypes. In B. Rourke (Ed.), *Neuropsychology of learning disabilities* (pp. 228–253). New York: Guilford Press.

McKinney, J. D., & Feagans, L. (1981). *Learning disabilities in the classroom* (Grant No. G00-76-0522-4, Final Report to Bureau of Education for the Handicapped). Washington, DC: U.S. Office of Education.

McKinney, J. D., & Feagans, L. (1984). Academic and behavioral characteristics of learning disabled children and average achievers: Longitudinal studies. *Learning Disability Quarterly, 7,* 251–264.

Meyen, E. L., & Lehr, D. H. (1980). Perspectives of instructionally least restrictive environments: Instructional implications. *Focus on Exceptional Children, 12,* 108.

National Joint Committee on Learning Disabilities. (1983). Learning disabilities: Issues on definition (Position paper). *Learning Disability Quarterly, 6,* 42–44.

Nevin, A., Johnson, D. W., & Johnson, R. (1982). Effects of group and individual contingencies on academic performance and social relations of special need students. *Journal of Social Psychology, 116,* 41–59.

Newcomer, P. L., & Hammill, D. D. (1976). *Psycholinguistics in the schools.* Columbus, OH: Charles E. Merrill.

Palincsar, A. S., & Brown, A. L. (1984). Reciprocal teaching of comprehension-fostering and monitoring activities. *Cognition and Instruction, 1,* 117–175.

Paradise, J. L. (1981). Otitis media during early life: How hazardous to development? A critical review of the evidence. *Pediatrics, 68,* 869–873.

Patterson, G. R. (1986). Performance models for antisocial boys. *American Psychologist, 41,* 432–444.

Pearl, R. A., & Bryan, T. (1982). Mothers' attributions for their learning disabled child's successes and failures. *Learning Disability Quarterly, 5,* 53–57.

Pelham, W. E., Jr. (1986). The effects of psychostimulant drugs on learning and academic achievement in children with attention-deficit disorders and learning disabilities. In J. K. Torgesen & B. Y. L. Wong (Eds.), *Psychological and educational perspectives on learning disabilities* (pp. 259–296). New York: Academic Press.

Polloway, E. A., Epstein, M. H., Polloway, C. H., Patton, J. R., & Ball, D. W. (1986). Corrective reading program: An analysis of effectiveness with learning disabled and mentally retarded students. *Remedial and Special Education, 7*(4), 41–47.

Rashotte, C. A., & Torgesen, J. K. (1985). Repeated reading and reading fluency in learning-disabled children. *Reading Research Quarterly, 20,* 180–188.

Resnick, D. P., & Resnick, L. B. (1977). The nature of literacy: An historical exploration. *Harvard Educational Review, 47,* 370–385.

Robinson, S. M., Braxdale, C. T., & Colson, S. E. (1985). Preparing dysfunctional learners to enter junior high school: A transitional curriculum. *Focus on Exceptional Children, 18*(4), 1–12.

Rose, T. L. (1984). The effects of two prepractice procedures on oral reading. *Journal of Learning Disabilities, 17,* 544–548.

Rosenshine, B. (1983). Teaching functions in instructional programs. *Elementary School Journal, 83,* 335–351.

Rosner, J. (1979). *Helping children overcome learning difficulties: A step by step guide for parents and teachers* (2nd ed.). New York: Walker.

Rourke, B. P. (Ed.). (1985). *Neuropsychology of learning disabilities: Essentials of subtype analysis.* New York: Guilford Press.

Rutter, M. (1978). Prevalence and types of dyslexia. In A. L. Benton & D. Pearl (Eds.), *Dyslexia: An appraisal of current knowledge* (pp. 3–28). New York: Oxford University Press.

Rutter, M. (1981). Psychological sequelae of brain damage in children. *American Journal of Psychiatry, 138,* 1533–1544.

Ryan, E. B., Weed, K. A., & Short, E. J. (1986). Cognitive behavior modification: Promoting active, self-regulatory learning styles. In J. K. Torgesen & B. Y. L. Wong (Eds.), *Psychological and educational perspectives on learning disabilities* (pp. 367–398). New York: Academic Press.

Sanders, M. (1979). *Clinical assessment of learning problems: Model, process, and remedial planning.* Boston: Allyn & Bacon.

Satz, P., Taylor, H. G., Friel, J., & Fletcher, J. M. (1978). Some developmental and predictive precursors of reading disabilities: A six year follow-up. In A. L. Benton & D. Pearl (Eds.), *Dyslexia: An appraisal of current knowledge* (pp. 313–347). New York: Oxford University Press.

Schenck, B. J., Fitzsimmons, J., Bullard, P. C., Taylor, H. G., & Satz, P. (1980). A prevention model for children at risk for reading failure. In R. M. Knights & D. J. Bakker (Eds.), *Treatment of hyperactive and learning disordered children: Current research* (pp. 31–48). Baltimore: University Park Press.

Schumaker, J. B., & Deshler, D. D. (1984). Setting demand variables: A major factor in program planning for the LD adolescent. *Topics in Language Disorders Journal, 4,* 22–40.

Schumaker, J. B., Deshler, D. D., & Ellis, E. S. (1986). Intervention issues related to the education of LD adolescents. In J. K. Torgesen & B. Y. L. Wong (Eds.), *Psychological and educational perspectives on learning disabilities* (pp. 329–365). New York: Academic Press.

Schumaker, J. B., & Hazel, J. S. (1984a). Social skills assessment and training for the learning disabled: Who's on first and what's on second? Part I. *Journal of Learning Disabilities, 17,* 422–431.

Schumaker, J. B., & Hazel, J. S. (1984b). Social skills assessment and training for the learning disabled: Who's on first and what's on second? Part II. *Journal of Learning Disabilities, 17,* 492–499.

Schumaker, J. B., Pederson, C. S., Hazel, J. S., & Meyen, E. L. (1983). Social skills curricula for mildly handicapped adolescents: A review. *Focus on Exceptional Children, 16*(4), 1–16.

Schwartz, G. J. (1977). College students as contingency managers for adolescents in a program to develop reading skills. *Journal of Applied Behavior Analysis, 10,* 645–655.

Schworm, R. W. (1979). The effects of selective attention on the decoding skills of children with learning disabilities. *Journal of Learning Disabilities, 12,* 639–644.

Semel, E. M., & Wiig, E. H. (1981). Semel Auditory Processing Program: Training effects among children with language learning disabilities. *Journal of Learning Disabilities, 14,* 192–196.

Shapiro, S., & Forbes, R. (1981). A review of involvement programs for parents of learning disabled children. *Journal of Learning Disabilities, 14,* 499–504.

Short, E. J., Feagans, L., McKinney, J. D., & Appelbaum, M. I. (1986). Longitudinal stability of LD subtypes based on age- and IQ-achievement discrepancies. *Learning Disability Quarterly, 9,* 214–225.

Silberberg, N. E., Iversen, I. A., & Goins, J. T. (1973). Which remedial method works best? *Journal of Learning Disabilities, 6,* 547–557.

Sindelar, P., & Deno, S. (1978). The effectiveness of resource programming. *Journal of Special Education, 1971, 5,* 143–149.

Slater, M. A., & Wikler, L. (1986). "Normalized" family resources for families with a developmentally disabled child. *Social Work, 31,* 385–390.

Slavin, R. E., Leavey, M. B., & Madden, N. A. (1984). Combining cooperative learning and individualized instruction: Effects on student mathematics achievement, attitudes, and behaviors. *Elementary School Journal, 84,* 409–422.

Smith, C. R. (1983). *Learning disabilities: The interaction of learning, task, and setting.* Boston: Little, Brown.

Smith, C. R. (1985). Learning disabilities: Past and present. *Journal of Learning Disabilities, 18,* 513–517.

Smith, D. D., & Lovitt, T. C. (1975). The use of modeling techniques to influence the acquisition of computational arithmetic skills in learning disabled children. In E. Ramp & G. Semb (Eds.), *Behavior analysis: Areas of research and application* (pp. 283–308). Englewood Cliffs, NJ: Prentice-Hall.

Snow, R. E. (1986). Individual differences and the design of educational programs. *American Psychologist, 41,* 1029–1039.

Spache, G. (1976). *Diagnosing and correcting reading disabilities*. Boston: Allyn & Bacon.

Spreen, O. (1982). Adult outcome of reading disorders: In R. N. Malatesha & P. G. Aaron (Eds.) *Reading disorders: Varieties and treatments* (pp. 473–498). New York: Academic Press.

Sroufe, L. A., & Rutter, M. (1984). The domain of developmental psychopathology. *Child Development, 55*, 17–29.

Stallings, J. (1975). Implementation and child effects of teaching practices on Follow Through classrooms. *Monographs of the Society for Research in Child Development, 40*, (7–8, Serial No. 163).

Stanovich, K. E. (1986). Cognitive processes and the reading problems of learning disabled children: Evaluating the assumption of specificity. In J. K. Torgesen & B. Y. L. Wong (Eds.), *Psychological and educational perspectives on reading disabilities* (pp. 87–131). New York: Academic Press.

Stevenson, H. W., & Newman, R. S. (1986). Long-term prediction of achievement and attitudes in mathematics and reading. *Child Development, 57*, 646–659.

Stokes, T. F., & Baer, D. M. (1977). An implicit technology of generalization. *Journal of Applied Behavior Analysis, 10*, 349–367.

Strauss, A., & Lehtinen, L. (1947). *Psychopathology and education of the brain-injured child: Fundamentals and treatment* (Vol. 1). New York: Grune & Stratton.

Swanson, L. (1981). Modification of comprehension deficits in learning disabled children. *Learning Disability Quarterly, 4*, 189–202.

Taylor, H. B. (1984). Early brain injury and cognitive development. In C. R. Almli & S. Finger (Eds.), *Early brain damage: Research orientations and clinical observations* (Vol. 1, pp. 325–345). New York: Academic Press.

Taylor, H. G. (1987). Childhood sequelae of early neurological disorders: A contemporary perspective. *Developmental Neuropsychology, 3*, 153–164.

Taylor, H. G. (1988). Learning disabilities. In E. J. Mash & L. G. Terdal (Eds.). *Behavioral assessment of childhood disorders* (2nd ed., pp. 402–450). New York: Guilford Press.

Taylor, H. G., & Fletcher, J. M. (1983). Biological foundations of "specific developmental disorders": Methods, findings, and future directions. *Journal of Clinical Child Psychology, 12*, 46–65.

Thorpe, H. W., & Borden, K. S. (1985). The effect of multisensory instruction upon the on-task behaviors and word reading accuracy of learning disabled children. *Journal of Learning Disabilities, 18*(5), 279–286.

Thurlow, M., Ysseldyke, J., Graden, J., & Algozzine, B. (1983). Instructional ecology for students in resource and other classrooms. *Teacher Education and Special Education, 6*, 248–254.

Tobin, D., & Pumfrey, P. D. (1976). Some long-term effects of the remedial teaching of reading. *Educational Review, 29*, 1–12.

Torgesen, J. K. (1979). What shall we do with psychological processes? *Journal of Learning Disabilities, 12*, 514–521.

Torgesen, J. K. (1980). Conceptual and educational implications of the use of efficient task strategies by learning disabled children. *Journal of Learning Disabilities, 13*, 364–371.

Torgesen, J. K. (1982). The use of rationally defined subgroups in research on learning disabilities. In J. P. Das, R. F. Mulcahy, & A. F. Wall (Eds.), *Theory and research in learning disabilities* (pp. 111–131). New York: Plenum.

Torgesen, J. K. (1986). Computer-assisted instruction with learning-disabled children. In J. K. Torgesen & B. Y. L. Wong (Eds.), *Psychological and educational perspectives on learning disabilities* (pp. 417–435). New York: Academic Press.

Torgesen, J. K., & Dice, C. (1980). Characteristics of research on learning disabilities. *Journal of Learning Disabilities, 13*, 531–535.

Torneus, M. (1984). Phonological awareness and reading: A chicken and egg problem? *Journal of Educational Psychology, 76*(6), 1346–1358.

Treiber, F. A., & Lahey, B. B. (1983). Toward a behavioral model of academic remediation with learning disabled children. *Journal of Learning Disabilities, 16*, 111–116.

U.S. Office of Education. (1968). *First annual report, National Advisory Committee on Handicapped Children*. Washington, DC: U.S. Department of Health, Education and Welfare.

U.S. Public Law 94-142 (The Education for All Handicapped Children Act). (1977, December 29). *Federal Register*, pp. 65082–65085.

Wagner, R. K., & Torgesen, J. K. (1987). The nature of phonological processing and its causal role in the acquisition of reading skills. *Psychological Bulletin, 101*(2), 192–212.

Wallach, M., & Wallach, L. (1976). *Teaching all children to read*. Chicago: University of Chicago Press.

Wang, M. C. (1987). Toward achieving educational excellence for all students: Program design and student outcomes. *Remedial and Special Education, 8*(3), 25–34.

Wiederholt, J. L., & McEntire, B. (1980). Educational options for handicapped adolescents. *Exceptional Education Quarterly, 1*(2), 1–11.

Williams, J. P. (1980). Teaching decoding with an emphasis on phoneme analysis and phoneme blending. *Journal of Educational Psychology, 72*, 1–15.

Williams, J. P. (1985). The case for explicit decoding instruction. In J. Osborn, P. T. Wilson, & R. C. Anderson (Eds.), *Reading education: Foundations for a literate America* (pp. 205–213). Lexington, MA: Lexington Books.

Wong, B. Y. L. (1985). Issues in cognitive–behavioral interventions in academic skill areas. *Journal of Abnormal Child Psychology, 13*(3), 425–442.

Wong, B. Y. L., & Jones, W. (1982). Increasing metacomprehension in learning-disabled and normally-achieving students through self-questioning training. *Learning Disability Quarterly, 5*, 228–240.

Ysseldyke, J. E., & Algozzine, B. (1983). LD or not LD: That's the question. *Journal of Learning Disabilities, 16*, 29–31.

Yule, W. (1976). Issues and problems in remedial education. *Developmental Medicine and Child Neurology, 18*, 674–682.

Zigmond, N. (1978a). A prototype of comprehensive services for secondary students with learning disabilities. *Learning Disability Quarterly, 1*(1), 39–49.

Zigmond, N. (1978b). Remediation of dyslexia: A discussion. In A. L. Benton & D. Pearl (Eds.), *Dyslexia: An appraisal of current knowledge* (pp. 435–450). New York: Oxford University Press.

Zigmond, N., Levin, E., & Laurie, T. E. (1985). Managing the mainstream: An analysis of teacher attitudes and student performance in mainstream high school programs. *Journal of Learning Disabilities, 18*(9), 535–541.

PART V

HEALTH-RELATED PROBLEMS

10

PAIN MANAGEMENT IN CHILDREN

MICHAEL J. DOLGIN
SUSAN M. JAY
University of Southern California School of Medicine
Childrens Hospital of Los Angeles

The management of pain poses one of the most significant and complex challenges facing health professionals. Its significance lies in the fact that pain is the most universal and basic expression of human suffering, the minimization of which is the primary goal of the behavioral and biomedical sciences. Its complexity stems from the interaction of biological, psychological, and social influences that shape the pain experience. In spite of its significance, and perhaps because of its complexity, our understanding and management of pain have lagged in comparison to our abilities in other areas of health and behavior.

Interest in pediatric pain management is particularly recent, not only among behavioral practitioners, but within the overall health care community. In a review of the medical literature between 1970 and 1975, Eland and Anderson (1977) found 1,380 articles on pain, but only 33 dealing with pain in children. Of these, the majority were concerned with symptomatology and differential diagnosis of pediatric pain, with virtually no emphasis on assessment or treatment. The psychological literature since 1960 has also included substantial theory, research, and clinical applications in the area of adult pain management, but is limited, for the most part, to anecdotal reports and uncontrolled studies of pediatric pain (Jay & Elliott, 1983).

This neglect stands in apparent contradiction to our instinct to protect children from harm and discomfort, and stems in large part from myths, misinformation, and some measure of denial that have blurred our focus on pain in children (see Eland & Anderson, 1977; McCaffery, 1977). For example, it has been suggested that because of their immature nervous systems (e.g., incomplete myelinization), infants do not perceive pain with the same intensity as adults. The qualitative aspects of pain in very young children may be unclear because of their limited ability to communicate, but, as Eland and Anderson (1977) point out, "Anyone who has seen the restraint needed for an alert newborn undergoing simple operative procedures such as circumcision without general anesthesia has little doubt about the infant's ability to perceive pain" (p. 457). Still, many pediatric medical procedures are conducted without anesthesia or analgesia (Schechter, 1985; Swafford & Allan, 1968). Narcotic pain medications are used far less frequently in children than in adults (e.g., postoperatively), even though concerns about addiction and medical complications associated with their use have been demonstrated to be unfounded (Eland & Anderson, 1977; Porter & Jick, 1980).

Undertreatment of pain has also resulted from misconceptions regarding children's pain behavior. Caregivers may believe that the school-age child who refuses pain medication or remains physically active is not experiencing pain, when, for example, the child may be avoiding an aversive relief-promising injection and occupying himself or herself in distracting activities. In addition, professional accountability for pediatric pain management is often lacking (McCaffery, 1977). Systematic standards of care exist for such procedures as antibiotic administration and dressing changes, yet pain medication is usually dispensed at the caregiver's discretion. Parents may rely on medical staff to determine the extent and meaning of their child's pain behavior, whereas caregivers may expect parents to be the best interpreters of their child's pain. The least recognized authority is often the child.

Recent advances in behavioral medicine and the adoption of a biopsychosocial approach to problems in health and behavior have provided a foundation for a more encompassing conceptualization of pain and more innovative techniques for its management (Katz, Varni, & Jay, 1984; Masek, Russo, & Varni, 1984). The purpose of this chapter is to consider current behavioral approaches for assessing and managing pain in children, with particular attention to the role of developmental and contextual factors in their implementation. A theoretical framework for understanding and classifying pediatric pain problems is outlined, followed by a discussion of crucial issues and methods in pain assessment. Specific pain problems often encountered in pediatric populations are then discussed in terms of the clinical techniques that have empirically demonstrated the greatest utility.

DEFINITION AND CLASSIFICATION OF PEDIATRIC PAIN PROBLEMS

Definition and Conceptualization

The word "pain" is derived from the Latin "poena," meaning "punishment" or "penalty," suggesting that early civilizations viewed pain primarily within a philosophical context related to moral transgression (Degenaar, 1979). Although modern conceptualizations of pain

avoid such attributions, it is important to note that pain may be interpreted by the patient in these terms. This is particularly true of the child in the preabstract stages of cognitive development, for whom pain may be perceived as temporally noncontingent punishment for "bad" thoughts, impulses, and behavior (Varni, Katz, & Dash, 1982). In contrast to this philosophical perspective, pain has been defined simply and phenomenologically as "what the subject says hurts" (Parkhouse, Pleurvy, & Rees, 1979, p. 15).

Modern theory views pain as a complex psychophysiological phenomenon involving sensory, neurochemical, cognitive, affective, and motivational components that interact to produce a behavioral response to tissue damage or irritation, and that may be influenced by antecedent and consequent stimulus conditions (Jay & Elliott, 1983; Sanders, 1979; Varni et al., 1982). As Sanders (1979) points out, pain may be manifested, and subsequently measured, along three separate but interacting dimensions: overt, covert, and physiological. Overt pain responses include verbal and nonverbal pain behaviors, such as crying, grimacing, complaining, or requesting pain medication. These behaviors are observed by those surrounding the patient. Covert responses are the subjective thoughts, perceptions, attitudes, and images experienced by the patient, whose self-report is the primary data source for assessing this dimension of the pain experience. Physiological responses to pain are generally monitored with the aid of special equipment and/or procedures, and include changes in autonomic, pyramidal, and extrapyramidal functions, as well as biochemical responses. It is noteworthy that these changes may not be specific to the sensation of pain itself, but are indicative of the generalized arousal and cognitive–affective concomitants of the painful experience (e.g., fear, anxiety). Developmental factors in part determine the avenue via which pain may be expressed and assessed. Overt behaviors such as crying and flailing may be seen more often in infants and younger children, whereas self-reported covert feelings and perceptions are more accessible with older children and adolescents (Grunau & Craig, 1987; Johnson & Strada, 1986; Katz, Kellerman, & Siegel, 1980). This trimodal conceptualization offers an approach not only to the assessment of pain, but also to pain management strategies, which may be directed at modifying responses on any one or a combination of the overt, covert, and physiological dimensions.

In the past, researchers have tended to distinguish between "real" pain, defined by the presence of organic etiology, and "psychogenic" (i.e., nonorganically based) pain complaints (Sternbach, 1979). More recent formulations recognize that no direct one-to-one relationship exists between organic pathology and pain expression (Schechter, 1985). Athletes or soldiers who may be oblivious to injury, firewalkers who report little or no discomfort, and patients who sense phantom pain following limb amputation clearly illustrate this point.

We have adopted a model of pain that takes into account those variables that mediate the relationship between pain stimuli and responses (Figure 10-1). Pain stimuli involve some form of insult to body tissue, resulting in neurophysiological transmission of nociceptive impulses. Responses to these stimuli are determined by cognitive–affective variables, operant and environmental contingencies, familial and sociocultural factors, and constitutional makeup. Hence there is wide variability in individuals' perception of and responses to similar pain stimuli (Sternbach, 1979; Weisenberg, 1977). The resulting overt, covert, and physiological responses may therefore represent more than pain sensation. Indeed, some researchers prefer

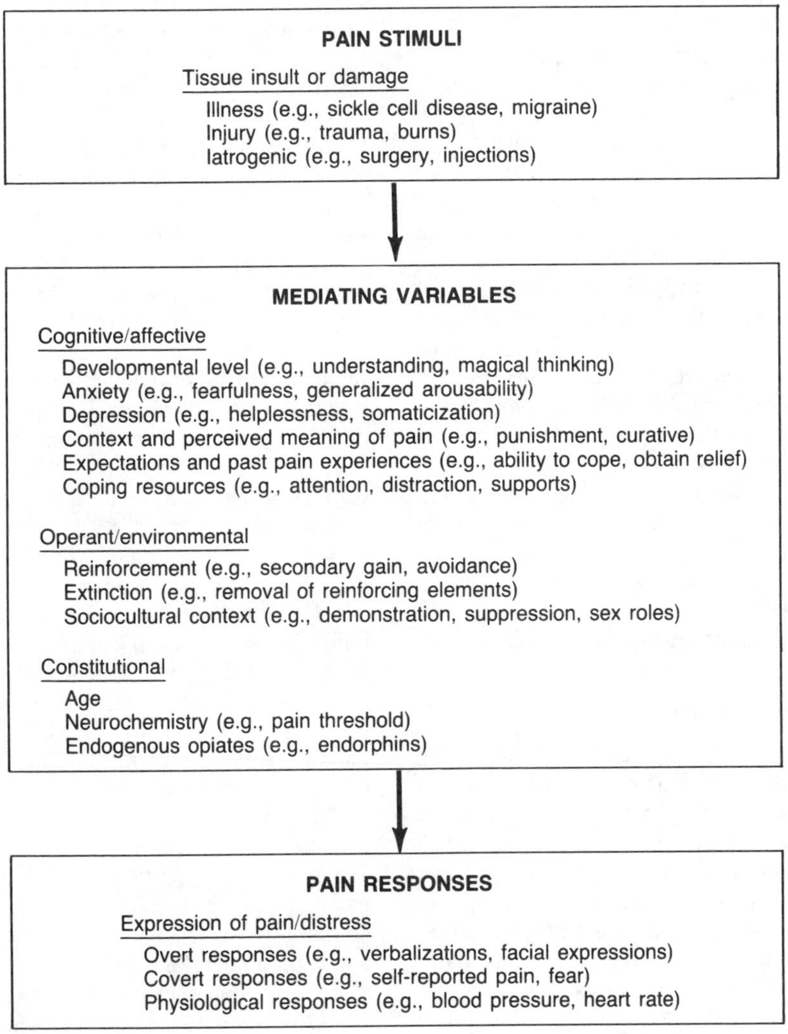

PAIN STIMULI

Tissue insult or damage

    Illness (e.g., sickle cell disease, migraine)
    Injury (e.g., trauma, burns)
    Iatrogenic (e.g., surgery, injections)

↓

MEDIATING VARIABLES

Cognitive/affective

    Developmental level (e.g., understanding, magical thinking)
    Anxiety (e.g., fearfulness, generalized arousability)
    Depression (e.g., helplessness, somaticization)
    Context and perceived meaning of pain (e.g., punishment, curative)
    Expectations and past pain experiences (e.g., ability to cope, obtain relief)
    Coping resources (e.g., attention, distraction, supports)

Operant/environmental

    Reinforcement (e.g., secondary gain, avoidance)
    Extinction (e.g., removal of reinforcing elements)
    Sociocultural context (e.g., demonstration, suppression, sex roles)

Constitutional

    Age
    Neurochemistry (e.g., pain threshold)
    Endogenous opiates (e.g., endorphins)

↓

PAIN RESPONSES

Expression of pain/distress

    Overt responses (e.g., verbalizations, facial expressions)
    Covert responses (e.g., self-reported pain, fear)
    Physiological responses (e.g., blood pressure, heart rate)

FIGURE 10-1 Conceptual model of pain.

the more general term "behavioral distress" when describing pain behavior, since it takes into account the cognitive and affective components that can rarely be isolated from the nociceptive component (Katz et al., 1980; Katz, Kellerman, & Siegel, 1981). The nature and impact of these mediating variables are addressed further in our discussion of pain assessment. Of importance here is the fact that pain management strategies may be directed at the pain stimuli (e.g., analgesia, anesthesia, medical/pharmacological intervention) or at the pain responses and their mediators (e.g., education, psychotherapy, behavioral intervention).

Classification

Pediatric pain problems have been classified into four major categories according to their origin or source: (1) pain associated with a disease state (e.g., hemophilia, sickle cell disease, cancer, juvenile rheumatoid arthritis); (2) pain associated with physical injury or trauma (e.g., burns, fractures, lacerations); (3) pain associated with medical procedures (e.g., injections, venapunctures, bone marrow aspirations, lumbar punctures, dental procedures); (4) pain associated with no identifiable physical injury or pathology (e.g., recurrent abdominal pain [RAP], headaches, limb pain) (Varni, 1983; Varni et al., 1982). These types of pain differ in their acuteness versus chronicity, the relative contributions of organic and psychological factors, the impact of anxiety on their expression, and the efficacy and feasibility of nonpsychological treatment (analgesia, anesthesia) in their management. Analysis of these dimensions will influence both intervention selection and outcome (Jay, 1985).

Acute versus Chronic Pain

Acute and chronic pain conditions have been distinguished in terms of their etiology, mechanisms, function, diagnosis, and implications for treatment (Bonica, 1979). Acute pain and its associated physiological, psychological, and behavioral responses result from noxious or tissue-damaging stimulation. Acute pain serves an adaptive function as a signal of organic damage or danger, and prompts protective and palliative action. A child's reaction following a burn from a hot stove illustrates this adaptive function. Similarly, acute pain such as severe headache, limb pain, toothache, or hemorrhage

prompts medical attention, and results in differential diagnosis and appropriate treatment.

In acute pain, the painful event (i.e., stimulus) and the pain behavior (i.e., response) parallel each other in terms of their onset, duration, and course. Possibly related to this contiguity, the major affective component of acute pain is fear, focused either on the pain itself or on its presumed source (Varni, 1983; Varni et al., 1982). The contribution of this anxiety is particularly evident in situations when the acutely painful event can be anticipated, as in the case of children undergoing repeated aversive medical procedures (e.g., venapunctures, debridement for burns, bone marrow aspirations, lumbar punctures, or cancer chemotherapy). Due to the characteristic anxiety associated with such acute distress, classically conditioned avoidance reactions and intensified behavioral distress are more likely to be observed both in anticipation of and during aversive medical procedures (Dolgin, Katz, McGinty, & Siegel, 1985; Katz & Rubinstein, 1984).

Chronic pain is pain that is either continuous, as in the case of progressive disease, or recurrent, as seen in chronic headache or RAP (Masek et al., 1984). At times, the pathogenic process underlying the pain experience may be readily identifiable, whereas in other instances the pain may be etiologically or clinically nondescript. Chronic pain in children is a less well-defined syndrome than in adults (Elliott & Jay, 1987; Jay, Elliott, & Varni, 1987). Indeed, the distinction between acute and chronic pain in children may at times be more semantic than real (e.g., recurrent painful hemorrhages in the hemophilia patient), and may have less relevance for children than for adults, in whom chronic disabling pain conditions (e.g., lower back pain) are more prevalent (Schechter, 1985; Varni et al., 1982). Still, chronic pain does occur in certain pediatric conditions, and useful parallels may be drawn from our knowledge of chronic pain in adults.

The active cognitive–affective components of acute and chronic pain differ (Varni et al., 1982). Whereas acute pain is usually accompanied by fear and anxiety, chronic pain is more commonly associated with depressive affect and symptomatology (e.g., depressed mood, sleep and appetite disturbances, inactivity), passivity and dependency, and what might best be described as a "helplessness" syndrome (Seligman, 1975). Consider, for example, the child who is experiencing chronic pain during the terminal phase of an illness, and in whom the fear component is outweighed by such factors as lethargy, apathy, withdrawal, and irritability.

Of major importance in chronic pain conditions are the operant environmental forces that shape and maintain the pain behavior, above and beyond the original nociceptive impulses and tissue damage (Varni, Bessman, Russo, & Cataldo, 1980). In its most pathological form, chronic pain behavior may serve no biological function at all, persisting only as a result of reinforcing psychological or environmental factors, even though it may have originally had some organic etiology (Bonica, 1977). This is frequently seen in children whose recurrent pain complaints result in secondary gains (avoidance of school, household chores, increased adult attention, etc.). In such cases, alteration of the reinforcing contingencies is an essential prerequisite to the treatment and resolution of the pain itself. Therefore, careful assessment of chronic pain behavior is necessary in order to determine the relative contributions of organic and operant factors (Elliott & Jay, 1987; Jay, 1985; Masek et al., 1984).

Behavioral interventions have been studied in virtually all of the pain categories and conditions mentioned thus far. Before discussing the specific techniques that have proven useful, we turn to an overview of pain assessment strategies, as these provide the basis on which treatment progress and outcome are evaluated.

BEHAVIORAL ASSESSMENT OF PEDIATRIC PAIN

Pain Perception versus Pain Behavior

Pain may be assessed along the lines that it is either subjectively experienced or objectively manifested by the child. Thus, an important distinction has been drawn between pain perception and pain behavior (Masek et al., 1984; Varni, 1983). How a child thinks and feels about a painful or potentially painful event (i.e., pain perception) is a function of various factors, including the child's developmental stage and interpretation of the event, past experiences in the same or similar circumstances, parental attitudes and modeling, self-directed coping strategies, and pain threshold (see Figure 10-1) (Jay & Elliott, 1983). Assessment methods that tap these cognitive and affective components of the pain experience, and self-

regulatory techniques aimed at modifying the perception of pain, have been most commonly applied in acute conditions. The measurement and modification of pain behavior (i.e., how the child expresses pain behaviorally) are of particular interest in chronic pain conditions, where environmental stimuli and reinforcement contingencies (social, familial, concrete) are central. Assessment of these behavioral excesses and deficits follows the principles of functional behavior analysis. Target behavioral goals are selected (e.g., reducing crying, grimacing, requests for pain medication; increasing mobility, self-care, communication; etc.). Antecedent events most likely to precipitate the occurrence of target behaviors are identified. Consequences of pain behavior are assessed in terms of their positive reinforcement properties (pain medication; social reward in the form of sympathy, attention, etc.) and negative reinforcement value (avoidance of school, chores, activity, etc.).

Assessment of Pain Perception

Pain perception is most directly measured through covert indices, such as self-reports of the child's distress, thoughts, feelings, and images during the pain-related situation (Katz et al., 1984). The subjective (verbal or nonverbal) nature of these measures must be kept in mind, since children and parents may underreport or overreport pain for a variety of reasons (Beales, 1979). Also, the meaning of "a little pain" or "a lot of pain" may not be the same for different individuals, based on their age, past experiences, and other factors. Thus, individual differences and lack of uniform measurement criteria make self-report data more useful for within-subject than for between-subject comparisons.

Developmental factors often dictate the selection of self-report measures. Unlike older children and adolescents, whose language skills better enable them to describe the quality and intensity of their pain in semantic terms, preschool-age children respond more readily to highly concrete and visual methods of communicating their pain. Katz and colleagues (Katz et al., 1980), in their studies of pediatric cancer patients undergoing bone marrow aspirations and lumbar punctures, assessed pain by showing children a visual representation of a "pain thermometer" with intervals of 0 (no hurt) to 100 (the worst hurt possible). Each child was instructed to point to the place that showed "how much you hurt." Anxiety was measured by asking the child to point to one of seven "fear faces," ranging from a broad smile to a severe frown, that showed "how scared you were during the bone marrow aspiration." Such representational scales can be applied clinically as well as for research purposes to other sensory and affective dimensions, such as nausea, sadness, and so on (Katz, Dolgin, & Zeltzer, 1987).

Self-report measures can be difficult and unreliable for children under 6 or 7 years of age. The use of complex visual representations requiring fine discrimination (e.g., 0–100 pain ratings) is developmentally inappropriate for very young children and may result in greater measurement error, as compared to simplified measures such as 5-point or even 3-point scales (e.g., faces), which are more useful with small children. However, even these more concrete and visually graphic scales may be inappropriate for preschool children who are still developing relativity ("more," "less") and numerical concepts. As Zeltzer and LeBaron (1986) point out, studies aimed specifically at determining the ages at which children can respond validly and reliably to these various self-report scales are needed. Their preliminary study (Zeltzer et al., 1988) indicates that variance in the ratings of somatic symptoms decreases with age and that there is an interaction between ratings of symptom severity and duration.

The Eland Color Tool is another self-report instrument for the assessment of pain in children (Eland, 1982; Eland & Anderson, 1977). Children designate the colors of eight crayons to represent different intensities of pain. Using a body outline, they then color in the areas where they experience pain, and differentiate current from previous hurts. Further controlled research is needed to establish the validity and reliability of this technique. Children as young as the preschool years enjoy using this technique, and it has been noted to identify pain symptoms that were previously unknown to caregivers.

Varni, Thompson, and Hanson (1987) constructed the Pediatric Pain Questionnaire (PPQ) to address the intensity and location of children's pain, as well as its sensory and emotive qualities. Situational variables associated with pain are elicited, and a comprehensive family history section addresses the child's and family's pain history, symptomatology, and management. This is particularly important when assessing a child's pain complaint within a systems context. In their review of personality factors and family characteristics associated with pediatric pain, Lavigne, Schulein, and Hahn (1986) describe evidence linking some pain syndromes, such as RAP, to families in which similar painful conditions or illnesses are common. Heredity, social modeling, reinforcement, or the use of somatic complaints as a vehicle to solving family conflicts must be considered in understanding the child's pain within the larger system context. Parent and child versions of the PPQ allow independent reporting and cross-validation. Although further reliability and validity studies are needed, the PPQ appears to be an excellent tool for guiding comprehensive intake evaluations with newly referred patients and families.

The Pediatric Pain Inventory (PPI), designed by Lollar, Smits, and Patterson (1982), utilizes a projective approach to assessing the child's experiences, expectations, feelings, and attitudes about pain. Twenty-four pictures depicting pain in medical, recreational, psychosocial, and daily living situations are presented to the child, and information regarding intensity, duration, causation, and management is elicited. A relatively new instrument, the PPI awaits wider use and further determination of its reliability and validity.

The ethical issues involved in inquiring about an individual's pain experience have received little discussion in the literature, but should be kept in mind. Conceivably, asking a child about his or her pain experience could draw unnecessary attention to the painful stimuli or sensations, and thereby add to the patient's distress. This might be particularly harmful for the patient who copes with pain by not thinking about it or by distraction (Zeltzer & LeBaron, 1986). Such considerations should be kept closely in mind, particularly when the inquiry is being made for the benefit of the caregiver, as is the case of clinical research situations.

Assessment of Pain Behavior

Overt pain expression evolves along a developmental continuum beginning in the neonatal period. In a review of studies analyzing the cries of human infants, Levine and Gordon (1982) found that pain cries were unique and qualitatively different from cries indicating hunger, fatigue, and other sensations. Various investigators have analyzed infants' pain behavior in terms of their facial expressions, posturing, and the acoustical properties of their cries during such procedures as immunizations or blood draws (Grunau & Craig, 1987; Johnson & Strada, 1986). Most developmental studies of pain behavior in infants show a trend from random, diffuse reactions in the first 6 months of life to more modulated, goal-directed behavior and indications of anticipatory distress by 12 months of age (Kagan, 1984). The response to and interpretation of the infant's pain behavior are also functions of contextual variables, such as the infant's real or perceived characteristics and who is making the observation. For example, Frodi, Lamb, Leavitt, and Donovan (1978) found that mothers and adolescent girls were behaviorally and emotionally more responsive to infant cries than fathers and adolescent boys. Labeling an infant "premature" resulted in greater physiological responses among both mothers and fathers.

Beginning in toddlerhood and continuing through childhood, language and purposeful physical behavior take a more central role in our assessment of pain behavior. Overt pain behavior is usually assessed by an individual other than the patient (parent, medical staff member, trained observer). Three general techniques have been described in pediatric studies: (1) global rating scales; (2) indirect measures; and (3) behavioral observation scales. Global rating scales have been used by nurses observing pediatric cancer patients undergoing painful medical procedures and chemotherapy (Jay, Ozolins, Elliott, & Caldwell, 1983; Katz et al., 1980; Katz, Dolgin, & Zeltzer, 1987). Expressions of pain and distress (e.g., crying, screaming, verbalizations of fear or pain) are rated on a 7-point Likert scale with 1 indicating "no distress at all" and 7 indicating "extreme, uncontrollable distress." These studies found nurses' global ratings of distress to be highly correlated with more sophisticated observational scales of distress. Global ratings have the advantage of being simple and straightforward, and therefore constitute the measure of choice where economic and personnel restrictions apply.

Indirect measures of pain involve documenting behaviors associated with either pain (e.g., requests for assistance, pain medication) or wellness (e.g., walking, playing, talking) (Fordyce, 1976). As discussed earlier, such indices may be potentially misleading in assessing children's pain. For example, a child may inhibit requests for medication in order to avoid the further discomfort of injections or pill taking. Also, children may be playful or active in an attempt to distract themselves from mild or moderate pain. Varni, Gilbert, and Dietrich (1981), in their behavioral treatment of a 9-year-old hemophiliac child's bleeding and arthritic pain, utilized a multimodal assessment of pain medications, physical therapy measures, school days missed, and hospitalizations. Although these indices reflect indirectly upon actual pain, their added value in assessing a child's overall level of functional independence should not be overlooked. This is particularly relevant in the management of chronic pain syndromes.

Observational scales constitute the most objective and reliable approach to the measurement of the occurrence, frequency, and intensity of overt pain behavior. These scales typically consist of checklists or inventories of operationally defined behaviors, and are completed by trained observers over a specified time period or painful event. Observational scales are best suited for acute or time-limited events such as aversive medical procedures, although an interval-sampling method could broaden their application to protracted or chronic pain (e.g., hourly samples). In addition to repeated within-subject measurements, their objectivity makes between-subject comparisons possible.

Two observational scales have been developed to assess children's pain and distress during bone marrow aspirations and lumbar punctures (Elliott, Jay, & Woody, 1987; Katz et al., 1980). The Procedure Behavior Rating Scale (PBRS) involves coding the occurrence–nonoccurrence of 11 distress-related behaviors (e.g., cry, scream, expressions of verbal pain). The Observational Scale of Behavioral Distress (OSBD) is a refined version of the PBRS and differs from the PBRS in that its behavioral categories are rated in continuous 15-second intervals rather than once over an entire phase of the procedure. The OSBD behaviors are also weighted according to the severity of the distress they represent (e.g., crying = 1.5, information seeking = 1.5, verbal expressions of pain or fear = 2.5, screaming = 4.0, flailing = 4.0). Both scales yield high interrater reliability and have proved useful in assessing developmental changes in pain behavior, as well as the effects of behavioral interventions in acute pain management. The PBRS is a simpler tool; the OSBD may be more precise when evaluating specific behaviors and their frequency or intensity. The effect of increased sophistication (e.g., time sampling, weighted scores) upon validity is open to question (Jay & Elliott, 1984). Developmentally, both measures show a decline in overt pain behavior with increasing age, suggesting rising pain thresholds and greater ability to modulate the pain experience with age. However, as LeBaron and Zeltzer (1984) point out, it is necessary to make sure that the behaviors included in such scales represent the range of pain behaviors from early childhood (e.g., crying, screaming) through adolescence (e.g., moaning, flinching) before conclusions regarding developmental trends in the nature or magnitude of pain expression can be made.

Pain diaries have been used extensively with adults, and increasingly with pediatric patients in recent years (Keefe, 1982; Masek *et al.*, 1984). Their application is particularly appropriate for chronic pain assessment. Daily (or more frequent) diary entries document pain levels and activity patterns, as well as antecedent and consequent events. Thus, pain diaries use self-report and/or observer (e.g., parent) report to record occurrence, intensity, and circumstances surrounding pain. Such information is valuable in treatment planning and evaluation. Sample items from one such diary used to assess pediatric migraine headache (Masek *et al.*, 1984) are as follows:

- Day/date
- Time of headache—start/stop
- Intensity—mild/moderate/severe/very severe
- Other people around (who?)
- Where were you (place?)
- Medicines taken for headache—type and amount
- Did you experience vomiting, sore eyes, or stomachache?
- School (classes)/activities missed because of headache
- What was going on before the headache?
- What did you do when you had the headache?

Diaries can be modified to fit specific pain problems or patient populations of interest. As with any self-report measure, their reliability may be questioned, and data should be cross-validated with other sources (e.g., parent reports).

Physiological and Neurochemical Assessment

Various physiological parameters have been studied in relation to pain, including increased respiration rate, increased muscle tension, elevated systolic and diastolic blood presssure, increased pulse rate, and skin resistance (Sternbach, 1974). However, several methodological limitations preclude the use of physiological indices as valid measures of pain. First, physiological responses supposedly indicative of pain reflect the same patterns of sympathetic arousal that characterize other affective states (e.g., anger, fear). A high level of physiological reactivity may be measuring the anxiety associated with the painful event, rather than the actual response to noxious sensation. Second, patterns and relationships between various physiological measures and pain experience have not been well established, because of the variability of responses elicited by different pain stimuli and because of wide individual differences in pain responses (Sternbach, 1974). Finally, overt (behavioral), covert (self-report), and physiological measures of pain and anxiety typically do not correlate highly, and studies have not determined which is the most valid (Jay & Elliott, 1988).

Few studies have employed physiological measures of pain in children. Melamed and Siegel (1975) found the palmar sweat index to be a useful measure of children's pre- and postoperative anxiety. Peterson and Shigetomi (1981) used pulse rate and skin temperature as measures of pre- and postoperative anxiety, but found that they did not correlate with other measures of anxiety, nor did they discriminate between treatment groups. Note that these studies did not focus on surgery-related pain at all. Jay, Elliott, Katz, and Siegel (1987) found heart rate just prior to bone marrow aspirations to be a predictive treatment outcome measure. Jay and Elliott (1988) found that the interrelationships between self-report, observational, and physiological response systems were mediated by the subjects' age. Observed distress and physiological arousal were highly correlated for children under 7 years of age, but not for older children; self-report measures were not correlated with physiological data for either age group.

Neurochemical measures constitute a new and exciting avenue for pain assessment. The recent identification of endogenous opiates (endorphins and encephalins) and their demonstrated activity in pain pathways in the spinal cord and brain have generated considerable interest and have increased our understanding of endogenous pain modulation (Varni *et al.*, 1982). Katz *et al.* (1982) measured beta-endorphin immunoreactivity in the cerebrospinal fluid of 70 children undergoing lumbar punctures. A significant correlation was found between endorphin concentrations and global nurse ratings of distress, suggesting that beta-endorphin in spinal fluid is reactive to stress, increasing as the child perceives higher levels of distress. Differences were also found in the endorphin concentrations of males and females; these may relate to gender differences in pain thresholds and tolerance. Although little research has been conducted to date on neurochemical assessment of pain, the integration of these parameters into behaviorally oriented studies promises to further our appreciation of the mind–body interaction and to promote interest in behavioral research among those with a more basic science orientation.

Summary

In summary, pediatric pain may be assessed along covert, observable, and physiological dimensions. When the focus of assessment and treatment is pain perception, covert measures are most appropriate. When pain behavior is being considered, direct and indirect measures of overt behavior should be employed. Clinically, this is rarely a dichotomous issue. For example, an intervention may have little observable impact on a patient's overt pain behavior, although the patient's self-report may indicate improved tolerance. This is not an uncommon occurrence in practice, and a unidimensional focus may obscure improvements on other levels of the pain experience. In addition to considering the purpose of the evaluation, the child's developmental level may also influence the assessment method chosen. In preverbal children, behavioral and physiological measures are particularly important, whereas self-reports of sensory and affective experiences become more meaningful as linguistic and cognitive capacities increase. For these reasons, a multidimensional assessment (e.g., self-report plus nurses' ratings) is recommended in most clinical situations, as well as for research purposes.

BEHAVIORAL TREATMENT OF CLINICAL PAIN PROBLEMS

The range of clinical interventions for pediatric pain management may be viewed within the conceptual framework for the classification of pain problems described earlier. Table 10-1 summarizes the techniques that have proven useful with various types of pain in children. Note that each class differs in terms of the preponderance of acute, chronic, or recurrent pain. Broadly speaking, these interventions can be reduced to self-regulatory and operant management strategies. The self-regulatory techniques (e.g., relaxation training, imagery, hypnosis, breathing exercises) modify physiological response to painful stimuli and offer a means for cognitive refocusing to alter pain perception. Operant managment primarily targets pain behavior through functional analysis

TABLE 10-1 Interventions in Pediatric Pain Management

Pain associated with a disease state
(acute, chronic)
   Relaxation training
   Breathing exercises
   Imagery
   Hypnosis
   Operant management

Pain associated with injury or trauma
(acute, chronic)
   Relaxation training
   Attention distraction
   Imagery
   Hypnosis
   Operant management

Pain associated with medical procedures
(acute)
   Procedural preparation
   Relaxation training
   Hypnosis
   Modeling
   Reinforcement
   Cognitive–behavioral "packages"

Idiopathic pain syndromes
(chronic, recurrent)
   Relaxation training
   Biofeedback
   Breathing exercises
   Hypnosis
   Operant management

and the selective reinforcement and extinction of well and pain behaviors, respectively. The discussion that follows elaborates on the application and effectiveness of these techniques.

Pain Associated with a Disease State

Hemophilia

Hemophilia is a congenital hereditary disorder of blood coagulation, characterized by recurrent internal bleeding episodes resulting from the absence of a plasma protein essential to the blood-clotting process. Hemorrhages are particularly common in the extremities and joints, where repeated bleeding episodes often result in an osteoarthritis-like condition with articular cartilage destruction, pathological bone formation, and impaired function (Sokoloff, 1975). Acute pain associated with hemorrhage provides an alerting signal that factor replacement and other treatment measures must be initiated, whereas chronic arthritic pain represents a potentially debilitating condition that serves no such adaptive function. Acute bleeding episodes can be controlled effectively through factor replacement therapy (i.e., infusion of the essential clotting factors following their separation from normal plasma); however, management of arthritic pain is more problematic, due to the limited usefulness of anti-inflammatory drugs and risks involved in the long-term use of narcotic analgesics (Varni & Gilbert, 1982). In addition, approximately 10% of the hemophiliac population is resistant to factor replacement because of the development of Factor VIII inhibitor, rendering bleeding episodes and their associated pain more severe and refractory to standard therapy.

Varni (1981a, 1981b) demonstrated the usefulness of behavioral self-regulation techniques in the management of chronic arthritic pain perception in five children with hemophilia. The treatment rationale was based on survey data from hemophilia patients and prior findings with patients with rheumatoid arthritis and osteoarthritis, indicating reductions in perceived arthritic pain associated with sensations of body warmth, as experienced during warm weather, hot showers, massage, or applications of heat-sensation-producing counterirritants (Varni 1983; White, 1973). Self-regulation skills training consisted of three sequential components, all of which tend to be associated with relaxation, vasodilation, increased peripheral blood flow, and warming sensations: (1) progressive muscle relaxation training, involving alternate tensing and relaxing of major muscle groups; (2) meditative breathing, with visualization of the word "relax" in warming colors; (3) guided imagery training, involving a multisensorial description (first by the therapist, and then by the patient) of a scene depicting warmth and freedom from discomfort, followed by further suggestions for smooth and gentle blood flow and bodily warmth. In order to provide a direct measure of warming, patients were monitored during treatment with a thermal biofeedback device, with the thermistor placed at the site of greatest arthritic pain. Home practice and individualization of cognitive strategies and imagery were encouraged.

Results showed significant improvements in arthritic pain, in terms of both painful days per week and daily pain ratings, between baseline and follow-up periods. Positive changes in mobility, sleep, and overall functioning were also noted. Medical charts and pharmacy records documented a consistent decrease across patients in analgesic consumption. Support for the treatment rationale was provided by the finding that surface skin temperature over the targeted arthritic joint increased for all patients by an average of 4.1°F from baseline levels. This suggests that increased body warmth may have been a mediating variable in the effectiveness of the self-regulation strategies. Interestingly, no treatment gains were found in terms of the average number of bleeding episodes, need for factor replacement therapy, or the intensity of pain associated with bleeding.

Varni et al. (1981) used a modified self-regulation training approach for the reduction of acute bleeding pain in a 9-year-old boy with Factor VIII inhibitor, for whom extended and high-dose narcotic use posed a serious management problem. The treatment and assessment protocol was similar to the one described earlier (Varni, 1981a, 1981b), with the exception that the guided imagery consisted of pleasant, distracting imagery rather than warming imagery. Average ratings of bleeding pain decreased from baseline levels of 7 (on a 10-point scale) to ratings of 2 at a 1-year follow-up. Measures of mobility, sleep, and psychosocial functioning also showed improvment. Number of hospitalizations, number of days in the hospital, and use of narcotics and analgesics were reduced. As with any multicomponent treatment package, the relative contributions of progressive relaxation, meditative breathing, guided imagery and suggestion are not isolated in these studies (Varni, 1981a, 1981b; Varni et al., 1981). Rather, it appears that they comprise a hypnotic-like intervention, the goals of which include distraction, refocusing of attention, imagery incompatible with pain and anxiety, and suggestions for pain relief (Hilgard, 1975).

Sickle Cell Disease

Sickle cell anemia is the most common hemoglobin disorder in the United States, affecting between 0.3% and 1.3% of American blacks. It is characterized by a malformation of red blood cells into sickle- or crescent-shaped cells, which leads to vaso-occlusion, increased blood viscosity, and impaired circulation. The resulting tissue anoxia and infarction are manifested clinically as pain (Lehamann et al., 1977). Pain crises occur intermittently, lasting from several days to several weeks, and are most frequently concentrated in the chest, abdomen, and bones (Schechter, 1985). Sickling crises are managed by keeping the patient warm, administering oxygen as needed, and giving blood transfusions (Lehmann et al., 1977). Morphine is the drug of choice for pain reduction, posing a concern about dependence in patients with frequent crises, although there have been no studies to date demonstarting addiction in these patients (Schechter, 1985).

Zeltzer, Dash, and Holland (1979) taught self-hypnosis to two adolescents with sickle cell disease; their rationale was that vasoconstriction and occlusion are major pathological features of the condition, and that therapy producing warmth and vasodilation would reduce the painful nature of the crises. Following hypnotic induction using eye fixation and progressive relaxation techniques, patients were led through guided imagery centering around pleasant, pain-free scenes, with suggestions of body warmth and vasodilation. Patients were instructed to utilize these skills at the perceived onset of sickling crises. Each patient's peripheral skin temperature was periodically monitored using a thermal biofeedback unit with the thermistor attached to the patient's index finger, although no direct feedback was given to the patient. Results indicated significant reductions in both the frequency and intensity of painful crises over an 8-month follow-up period. Analgesic need decreased, as did number of out

patient visits, hospitalizations, and total number of hospitalized days. In support of the therapeutic rationale, peripheral skin temperature increased during self-hypnosis, as measured by the thermal biofeedback device. This study, like the ones described earlier in reference to chronic and acute pain in hemophilia, illustrates the secondary impact of interventions aimed at reducing pain perception on pain behavior (e.g., need for medication, health care utilization).

Cancer

Childhood cancer is a relatively rare disease, with an incidence of 11 per 100,000 in the general population. Still, pediatric malignancies rank second only to accidents as the leading cause of death following the neonatal period (Silverberg, 1979). Contemporary multimodal therapy for children has resulted in dramatic improvements in survival rates (Siegel, 1980), converting what was a universally fatal group of diseases into chronic life-threatening conditions. Along with increased life expectancy, patients and families are faced with a new variety of adjustment problems—namely, those related to living with the disease and its treatment (Kellerman, 1980).

In contrast to adult cancers, chronic debilitating pain is relatively uncommon in pediatric oncology. This is primarily due to epidemiological differences between adult and childhood cancers. Whereas adult cancers are predominantly carcinomas or tumors involving specific organs, the modal pediatric malignancies (e.g., leukemias and lymphomas) are not painful malignancies per se, although they may be accompanied by joint pain, headaches, fatigue, and fever during periods of active disease. Chronic pain may be experienced by some children during the terminal phase of illness, when disseminated disease invades multiple organs and systems. Far more common is the acute pain and distress associated with invasive diagnostic and treatment procedures, such as bone marrow aspirations and the administration of emetogenic (i.e., nausea/vomiting-causing) chemotherapy (Jay, Elliott, & Varni, 1987). Behavioral interventions for aversive medical and surgical procedures are addressed in greater detail in a later section.

No controlled studies have been reported on behavioral treatment of chronic-disease-related pain in children with cancer (Jay, Elliott, &

Varni, 1987). Jay and Elliott (1983) discuss various considerations in the application of psychological approaches to such problems. For example, operant conditioning techniques aimed at extinguishing pain behaviors and reinforcing behaviors incompatible with pain have been applied successfully in the treatment of chronic adult and pediatric pain (e.g., Bonica & Fordyce, 1974; Sank & Biglan, 1974). Behavioral suppression of pain can be an important therapeutic goal, insofar as it facilitates normal activities and functioning. Jay and Elliott (1983) caution against the application of such procedures when the cooperation of family and staff members has not been secured and resistances have not been addressed, and they offer useful suggestions for introducing and implementing such programs. Importantly, they point out that with terminally ill children, intractable disease-related pain may be best managed by adequate doses of narcotic medication, and that operant conditioning is warranted only when a child's pain behavior is disproportionate to the level thought to be caused by organic factors, or reaches a level where the child's medical or emotional well-being is compromised. Likewise, they discuss considerations in the use of other treatment approaches, including family systems therapy, stress management, and hypnosis.

A number of investigators have reported anecdotal data suggesting the effectiveness of hypnosis for the control of chronic pain in children with cancer (LaBaw, Holton, Tewell, & Eccles, 1975; Miller, 1980). A variety of induction techniques are described, followed by imagery of fantasized scenes depicting comfort and distancing from pain (e.g., at the beach, on a mountain top, in one's own bed). Keane (1980) utilized symbolic imagery such as flipping a switch or removing a fuse to "turn off" pain in specific areas. For further discussion of the uses of hypnotic techniques, the reader is referred to Dash (1980) and to Gardner and Olness's (1981) comprehensive text on hypnosis with children.

Pain Associated with Injury or Trauma

Burns

Management of the burn patient poses a special challenge, since acute pain stems not only from the burn itself, but also from treatment procedures such as wound debridement, dressing changes, and physical therapy. Schechter (1985) notes the under-utilization of analgesia and anesthesia in the management of both burn and iatrogenic pain in children as compared to adult burn patients. However, even with appropriate administration of narcotic analgesics such as morphine, merperidine, and codeine, and psychotropic drugs such as diazepam, pain is rated in the moderate to severe range (Perry & Heidrich, 1982). Chronic pain syndrome may also result (e.g., from scar contractures).

Three behavioral studies have focused on the reduction of acute pain perception in pediatric burn patients. Wakeman and Kaplan (1978) treated child, adolescent, and adult burn patients using progressive deep muscle relaxation, dissociation, imagery involving pleasant scenes, and suggestions for pain control. Children and adolescents required significantly less pain medication subsequent to behavioral intervention, compared to a medication-only control group and to adults receiving behavioral intervention. Elliott and Olson (1983) reported on a stress management package that included distraction and attention refocusing, relaxation, imagery, and reinforcement, in their treatment of pediatric burn patients undergoing debridement and hydrotherapy. Significantly, the investigators found that "coaching" by the therapist during the painful procedure was essential in reducing children's distress levels. Kavanaugh (1983) developed an approach to nursing procedures with burned children that maximized patient control and predictability of aversive events, rather than the traditional approach that relies on verbal soothing, distraction, and pain medication. Specifically, patients were directed in the removal of their own dressings, assisted with debridement in limited ways, and were given a role in deciding when these procedures would occur. Nurses wore red aprons during debridement in order to increase predictability and to facilitate a less fearful relationship at those times when the aprons were not worn and no procedure was taking place. Using this approach, Kavanaugh (1983) documented less need for narcotic premedication, less resistance, and better psychological adaptation, compared to children treated more traditionally.

Varni et al. (1980) describe an operant approach to the management of chronic pain behavior in a 3-year-old child hospitalized for

10 months for treatment of second- and third-degree burn injuries. Prior to intervention, the patient exhibited a variety of chronic pain behaviors that interfered with her rehabilitation and strained her interaction with caregivers. Target pain behaviors were defined as crying (ranging in intensity from sobbing to screaming), verbal expressions of pain (e.g., "Ouch," "My leg/foot/stomach hurts"), and non verbal pain behavior (e.g., facial grimacing, avoidance behaviors).

Baseline data collected in three different settings (clinic, bedroom, and physical therapy room) confirmed that the frequency of these pain behaviors increased in the presence of adults and in demand situations, and decreased when the child was engaged in interesting/enjoyable activities, suggesting that secondary gain in the form of attention, sympathy, and avoidance were important maintaining factors. Treatment consisted of rearranging environmental contingencies so that social praise and a treat (e.g., candy) followed well behaviors such as helping to put on her splints, positive verbalizations, and increasing time intervals with no pain behaviors (1 minute, 5 minutes). Pain behavior was placed on extinction (i.e., ignored). Treatment was carried out along a multiple-baseline design across settings, with gradual shaping and fading of reinforcement. This program resulted in the reduction of the target pain behaviors in all three settings, as well as in improvements in rehabilitative measures (e.g., number of steps descended in physical therapy). Other clinically significant changes included increased participation in self-care, pride in accomplishments, and utilization of well behaviors as a means of securing social attention and praise.

This case illustrates the influence of socioenvironmental contingencies on chronic pain behavior. This formulation does not ignore possible organic causes underlying the child's pain, nor does it contraindicate expressions of empathy and concern by family members and caregivers on the patient's behalf. Operant techniques such as these utilize and manipulate socioenvironmental reinforcers in such ways as to maximize patterns of behavior and interaction that promote patient adaptation and rehabilitation. As Varni et al. (1982) point out, the therapeutic goal should not be the total suppression of pain expression, since such communication serves an essential function, but rather the shaping of well behavior in situations where pain behavior interferes with the child's long-term rehabilitation and psychosocial adjustment.

Minor Trauma

Injury and trauma constitute the leading cause of morbidity and mortality following the neonatal period (Silverberg, 1979). From a developmental perspective, the distress and anxiety associated with pain resulting from concrete, visible bodily harm may be greater than that experienced in relation to internal, more abstract pathological states, particularly for younger children (Beales, 1979). For example, the child with a minor laceration may exhibit greater distress than a child with internal disease-related pain that has no visible manifestations. Still, as Dolgin and Katz (1982) note, psychological considerations in emergency medicine are not viewed as "life or death" in importance and are easily overlooked, despite the fact that distinct emotional needs arise in the emergency situation and that, in the majority of cases, caregivers can take direct and effective measures to meet those needs without sacrificing any precepts of good medical care.

Andolsek and Novik (1980) reported the use of hypnotic techniques with four children aged 3–4 years who presented in the emergency room with injuries and/or lacerations. The hypnotic techniques involved giving the children some control over the situation and using images that transformed the meaning of the pain. For example, one 4-year-old was allowed to pop a balloon, and then was instructed to imagine the balloon popping while the physician incised and drained an abscess in her hand. This approach involved a distraction component, which further served to decrease the perception of pain during the procedure. Turk (1978) summarizes a number of useful attention-distracting techniques that can be used with older children who sustain injury or trauma. These include (1) focusing on physical characteristics of the environment (e.g., counting ceiling tiles); (2) focusing attention on mental exercises (e.g., doing mental arithmetic); (3) imagining scenes incompatible with the perception of pain (e.g., lying on a beach); (4) minimizing pain sensations (e.g., imagining the body part has been frozen or numbed; and (5) altering the context of the pain (e.g., imagining that the injury has been sustained in a football game or heroic act, but that one continues to function despite the pain).

Pain Associated with Medical Procedures

Painful medical procedures are a source of anxiety for clinical and nonclinical populations alike. Agras, Sylvester, and Oliveau (1969) found that 14% of the general population at age 20 reported injection phobias. Non-invasive medical procedures, such as X-rays and physical exams, can create significant distress in the general pediatric population. Because painful medical procedures are acute and generally predictable events, and because the sensory (nociceptive) and affective (anxiety) components are so intertwined, some investigators have adopted the more inclusive concept of "distress" as the focus of assessment and intervention (e.g., Jay, 1988; Katz et al., 1980).

Children with serious or chronic illnesses endure a variety of more intrusive procedures, including catheterizations, spinal taps, bone marrow aspirations, endoscopies, and so on. These children often consider repeated medical procedures more aversive than the threat of their disease itself, and this constitutes a primary reason for psychological referral (Kellerman & Katz, 1979; Zeltzer, Kellerman, Ellenberg, Dash, & Rigler, 1980). Furthermore, studies of pediatric cancer patients undergoing bone marrow aspirations and spinal taps indicate that in most cases a stable pattern of habituation is not evident (Katz et al., 1980; Kellerman, Zeltzer, Ellenberg, & Dash, 1983). Some patients develop symptoms of anticipatory distress that may include anxiety, somatic complaints, nausea and vomitting, avoidance, and resistance (Kellerman & Varni, 1982). The literature on medical, dental, and surgical procedures reflects a growing interest in these distress symptoms in recent years, and a comprehensive review is beyond the scope of this chapter. A more detailed discussion is presented by Jay (1988). What follows are highlights of the pertinent literature in terms of both clinical situations and approaches.

With regard to any medical procedure, the most fundamental intervention involves prior preparation of the child. This typically includes giving the child information about what will be done, letting the child handle equipment, having the child practice the procedure on a doll, introducing the child to medical personnel, and discussing fears and concerns. Such preparation serves multiple functions, including education, desensitization, modeling, reassurance, mastery, and trust. Fernald and Corry (1981) found that an empathic preparation (which was supportive and child-centered, and which described the sensations, anxieties, and reactions that might occur during an injection) produced less crying and better cooperation than a directive preparation (where the child was informed of what would occur and told to be big, brave, and still). In the empathic preparation, the child was assured that the injection was in no way a punishment, that anxiety was natural, and that crying was permissible. The directive preparation focused on the importance of cooperation and the negative consequences of noncompliance (e.g., prolonging the procedure). Preparation has proven useful in helping children cope with surgery and in reducing postoperative adjustment difficulties, and many hospitals offer programs to prepare children and parents for hospitalization and surgery prior to their admission (Peterson & Ridley-Johnson, 1980). However, the issues of individual coping styles and of how much preparatory information children actually want and need are matters for further investigation (Hubert, Jay, Saltoun, & Hayes, in press). For a review of the literature on preparation for medical procedures, see McCue (1980). Unfortunately, research studies on the efficacy of preoperative preparation suffer from numerous methodological flaws, such as inadequate measurement techniques and uncontrolled variables.

One exception is the study by Melamed and Siegel (1975), in which they demonstrated the effectiveness of filmed modeling in reducing children's anxiety concerning surgery. Children in the experimental group were shown a film entitled *Ethan Has an Operation,* which depicts a 7-year-old boy encountering various events associated with surgery, including admission, meeting his surgeon and anesthesiologist, having a blood test, exposure to hospital equipment, separation from mother, and scenes in the operating and recovery rooms. The child in the film narrates his feelings and thoughts as he coped with anxiety-provoking situations. Children in the control group saw a film unrelated to the hospital. Children in the experimental group exhibited less anxiety and fewer behavior problems, both pre- and postoperatively.

The beneficial effects of preparation can be enhanced by offering the child a coping skill he or she can actively use. *In vivo* systematic desensitization, combining relaxation training, modeling, and behavioral rehearsal, has been successfully employed with adult patients who showed high levels of anxiety associated with injections (e.g., Ferguson, Taylor, & Wermuth, 1978). Hypnosis, pleasant imagery, participant modeling, and *in vivo* desensitization have been reported as anxiety reduction strategies in case studies of children with needle phobias, and more systematic, data-based studies are needed. In one such case Dash (1981) treated severe needle phobia in a 5-year-old cardiac patient during three sessions of *in vivo* participant modeling, which involved pairing needles, syringes, and test tubes with the child's most valuable reinforcer (sugarless bubble gum). The needles were unwrapped and exposed gradually as the child unwrapped her gum. As the therapist then began handling the needles and placing them against his arm, the child gradually modeled his behavior without distress. The child was then hypnotized by use of a rapid induction consisting of eye fixations, deep breathing, and visualization of herself walking down a flight of stairs through a large door and entering her favorite place. The therapist also trained the nursing staff to assist the child in utilizing these skills when he was not present. Follow-up 2 and 24 months later indicated no further needle phobias or other problem behaviors. Peterson and Shigetomi (1981) also found that children who were taught active coping skills in addition to filmed modeling preparation were more calm and cooperative during tonsillectomies than children who had received either one of the interventions alone.

A number of studies have demonstrated the effectiveness of behavioral interventions in reducing pain and anxiety in children with cancer undergoing painful medical procedures. Conditioned anxiety in response to bone marrow aspirations and lumbar punctures occurs frequently in these patients, and contributes to the pain–anxiety–distress cycle. Most investigations have focused on hypnotic techniques (see Dash, 1980). Individual case studies (e.g., Ellenberg, Kellerman, Dash, Higgins, & Zeltzer, 1980; Gardner, 1976) provide in-depth accounts supporting the utility of hypnosis in reducing the perceived pain and anxiety in children and adolescents undergoing these procedures.

Studies employing hypnosis with larger groups of pediatric cancer patients also show significant improvements in procedure-related distress over baseline measurements (Hilgard & LeBaron, 1982; Kellerman *et al.*, 1983). Zeltzer and LeBaron (1982) found hypnosis to be superior to a nonhypnotic technique (i.e., supportive counseling). Katz, Kellerman, and Ellenberg (1987) compared hypnosis and nondirected play in a randomized study of 36 children with acute leukemia undergoing routine bone marrow aspirations. Self-report ratings of pain and fear, nurses' ratings of distress, and behavioral observations of distress were recorded. When the two interventions were compared, no significant differences were noted on any measure. Both groups reported improvements on self-report measures, with no demonstrable improvements in observed distress behavior. Intervention × sex interactions were significant for all dependent measures; that is, boys benefited more in the nondirected play condition, whereas, girls did better with hypnosis. Results were most apparent on self-report measures of pain and fear. The authors point out that this finding warrants future scrutiny, as it may reflect on the differential utility of active versus passive coping skills with boys and girls. These findings also underscore the advantages of multimodal assessment, since treatment gains were more evident on subjective (self-report) pain perception indices than on objective (observational) measures. Intervention may have an important impact on the patient's covert experience that may be obscured by an emphasis on achieving dramatic, visible improvements.

Jay, Elliott, Katz, and Siegel (1987) developed a multicomponent cognitive–behavioral intervention package designed to teach effective coping skills and reduce children's distress during bone marrow aspirations. The rationale for using a multidimensional intervention was to offer patients more than one strategy and to maximize the likelihood of therapeutic benefit. The package was based on the stress inoculation model described by Meichenbaum and Turk (1976) and incorporated filmed modeling, positive incentive, breathing exercises, emotive imagery, and behavioral rehearsal. Dependent measures included self-report, physiological, and observational data. A counterbalanced design with 56 children aged 3–14 with leukemia was used in order to compare the effectiveness of this behavioral package to that of oral sedation

(Valium) and a minimal-attention control condition.

Findings indicated that the cognitive–behavioral package was significantly more effective than the control condition in reducing children's observed distress, self-reported pain, pulse rate, and blood pressure. The results for the Valium condition were equivocal, with a reduction in blood pressure being the only significant difference from the other two conditions. There was some evidence suggesting that Valium was helpful in reducing anticipatory anxiety, but less helpful during the actual bone marrow aspiration—a logical finding, given that no information or coping skills were offered in the Valium condition. An additional advantage of the cognitive–behavioral package was its effectiveness with preschool as well as older children. Studies of hypnosis or other behavioral techniques generally do not address children under 7 years of age, despite the fact that these children exhibit significantly higher levels of distress (Jay et al., 1983).

The issue of parental distress during children's medical procedures must also be considered, especially for young children. The relationship between children's observed distress and parental anxiety has been documented (Jay et al., 1983). Jay and her colleagues are currently conducting a treatment outcome study of a stress inoculation program for parents whose children are undergoing bone marrow aspirations. Parent intervention involves filmed modeling, education, self-statement training, cognitive rehearsal, and relaxation training. Observational and self-report data regarding parent and child distress during the procedure are collected. Analysis of the interaction between parent and child distress, and of the effects of parental intervention on parent and child distress, should add to our understanding of systems influences in childhood pain and its management.

Idiopathic Pain Syndromes

Headache

Pediatric headache, the most common form of which is migraine headache, occurs in approximately 20% of school-age children and adolescents, with females outnumbering males by a 3:2 ratio (Oster, 1972). Research indicates that between 40% and 60% of these children contin-ue to suffer into adulthood (Billie, 1981). Organic etiological factors have been prominent in some studies, whereas other surveys point to socioenvironmental stressors as the most common precipitating factors (Billie, 1981; Millicap, 1978). Familial patterns are evident in many patients presenting with chronic headache; possibly these are related to an inherited trait of vasomotor instability and a vulnerable physiological system that may be predisposed to aggravation under stress. As with any such somatic complaint a thorough medical evaluation should be conducted prior to initiating any treatment program, particularly since recurrent headache may be a symptom of serious organic disease.

Treatment of pediatric migraine has improved over the past decade, in part because of advances in pharmacotherapy (which is not without its dose-limiting side effects), and in part because of the development and application of behavioral technologies for the management of both pain perception and pain behavior. As Masek et al. (1984) point out, pediatric migraine lends itself well to behavioral treatment, because its intermittent and recurrent nature allows for a functional analysis of the antecedents and consequences associated with its occurrence. Pain diaries are especially useful in assessing these factors (Joffe, Bakal, & Kaganov, 1982; Masek et al., 1984). For example, positive or negative stressors (e.g., exciting activities, competetive events, exams) may precipitate a headache; avoidance of demand activities and other secondary gain factors may then reinforce and maintain the behavior that accompanies the headache episode. Because the symptoms experienced during migraine headaches tend to be quite severe (e.g., pain, nausea, abdominal pain), and because of the extreme disruption imposed on routine activities and family functioning, motivation for behavioral intervention is often high, particularly since this approach involves self-regulation and control and may negate the need for an reliance on medication.

Olness and MacDonald (1981) presented case material on three children with migraine who did not respond well to pharmacological therapy. Positive results were obtained using self-hypnosis training and thermal biofeedback. Houts (1982) reported on an 11-year-old boy treated with cue-controlled relaxation and thermal biofeedback. Treatment consisted of 10 biofeedback training sessions, with a relaxation tape given for home practice. Results showed a decline in headache frequency during treatment compared to baseline levels, and these gains were maintained over a 1-year follow-up period. Labbe and Williamson (1983) used a multiple-baseline design across subjects in their treatment of three children aged 9–13. Treatment consisted of 10 sessions of thermal biofeedback coupled with autogenic training (imagining hands warming), and resulted in significant reductions in headache activity, which were maintained for all three patients at a 2-year follow-up. Diamond (1979) treated 32 pediatric migraine patients with a three-stage protocol, involving sequential training in thermal biofeedback with autogenic suggestion for warmth and relaxation, progressive muscle relaxation, and frontalis electromyographic (EMG) biofeedback. Home practice of relaxation and of hand-warming exercises was encouraged. Among the 32 patients, 226 responded with both decreased frequency and intensity of headache episodes, and an additional 3 patients showed a reduction of either headache frequency or severity. Lack of experimental control limits the interpretation of these findings in terms of the active treatment components.

Focusing solely on the operant control of pain behavior, Famsden, Friedman, and Williamson (1983) manipulated contingencies at school and at home in their treatment of a 6-year-old girl with migraine headaches. The program consisted of the child's teacher rewarding her with a preferred activity at the end of headache-free school days. Fewer than a predetermined number of headache-free days per week resulted in the child forfeiting one recess period. A similar program was introduced at home 6 weeks after the school program was initiated. Headache frequency decreased and was subsequently eliminated entirely while the program was implemented both at home and at school. These improvements were maintained over a 10-month follow-up period.

Masek (1982) used a multiple-baseline design across subjects in his treatment of 20 children with migraine headaches. Children were randomly assigned to one of four groups, with treatment beginning after either 3, 6, 9, or 12 weeks of baseline data collection. Treatment included frontalis EMG biofeedback training and meditative breathing. In addition, parents were given guidelines for managing their children during headache and pain-free periods.

These guidelines (which can be applied to parental management of any chronic childhood pain syndrome) included frequent approval for maintaining normal activity, encouraging the child to stay calm and practice relaxation exercises where feasible, and advocating regular school attendance and household responsibilities. Parents were also instructed in strategies for extinguishing pain behaviors, including ignoring excessive complaining or pain gesturing, enforcing strict compliance with medication regimens, discouraging avoidant behavior and suggesting alternatives (e.g., bed rest) during headache episodes, and avoiding excessive inquiry about the presence or status of a headache. Daily diaries provided data on headache frequency, intensity, and duration, as well as medication use. Eighteen children reported at least a 50% reduction in total hours of headache per week and in pain intensity.

A subsequent study by Fentress and Masek (1982) controlled for the effects of biofeedback by assigning pediatric migraine patients to three conditions: (1) frontailis EMG biofeedback, meditative breathing, and parental management instruction; (2) progressive muscle relaxation training, meditative breathing, and parental management instruction; and (3) waiting-list control group. Results indicated comparably significant reductions in headache frequency, intensity, and duration for both treatment groups as compared to the waiting-list control group.

The Fentress and Masek (1982) findings support what has been recognized for some time in the adult literature on chronic headache—namely, that the specific self-regulation technique employed does not appear to be critical to treatment outcome. Blanchard, Andrasik, Ahles, Teders, and O'Keefe (1980) hypothesize that the general effects of relaxation represent the final common pathway by which biofeedback and other self-regulation procedures achieve their therapeutic effect. Clinically, the choice of techniques should depend on the patient's preference and the therapist's level of comfort with each. As Varni, Jay, Masek and Thompson (1986) point out, pediatric migraine patients often tend to be bright, achievement-oriented individuals. Therefore, a combination of biofeedback training, which appeals to their interest and challenges their achievement orientation, and relaxation techniques, which provide a practical and readily transferable skill, is recommended in most cases. It is important to recognize that some patients may be uncooperative or unmotivated to assume control over their headaches, and may not exhibit the level of concern demonstrated by their parents or others. Significant emotional disturbance or family disruption may also hinder motivation or compliance. Initial feelings that treatment is silly or hopeless and could not possibly work must be addressed. Conversely, popular misconceptions of biofeedback as a quick and magical cure must be corrected.

Recurrent Abdominal Pain

RAP occurs in approximately 15% of school-age children and adolescents; like recurrent headache, it tends to be significantly more prevalent among girls than among boys (Oster, 1972). Pediatric RAP may be symptomatic of various medical conditions, and follow-up studies of children presenting with RAP reveal an increased incidence of gastrointestinal ailments and pain in adulthood, compared with a no-RAP control group (Christensen & Mortensen, 1975). Still, organic etiologies can be documented in only about 5% of children complaining of RAP (Apley, 1975; Maddison, 1977). Familial patterns are common, raising the question of genetic predisposition versus modeling of parental pain behavior (Christensen & Mortensen, 1975). Although thorough medical evaluation is warranted prior to initiation of any treatment program, it is significant that as many as 20% of children presenting with RAP may at some point undergo surgical or medical treatments of doubtful necessity (Stickler & Murphy, 1979).

Socioenvironmental factors, such as emotional stress (positive or negative), parental pressure for achievement, modeling, and avoidance of demanding tasks, have been implicated as precipitating or maintaining factors in childhood RAP (Adler, Katz, & Bongar, 1982; Berger, Honig, & Liebman, 1977). Despite the prevalence of RAP and the contribution of socioenvironmental variables to its occurrence, the literature contains only isolated case studies of behavioral treatment of children with RAP.

Sank and Biglan (1974) described a 10-year-old boy with a 2½-year history of RAP, with daily episodes lasting between 5–20 minutes and several hours. The child had been absent during 45 of the previous 72 school days. When an episode occurred, the child's mother would administer medication and massage, take his temperature, and stay with him. When he stayed home from school, the child was allowed to read, watch television, and get out of bed when he felt better. His mother would restrict her activities in order to attend to him. A behavioral shaping program was initiated, with reinforcement contingent on decreased pain frequency and intensity and on increased school attendence. Severe pain was managed by having the child remain in bed for that half-day, with access to school books only and no entertainment. Frequency, intensity, and duration of RAP episodes, as well as school attendence, were recorded during baseline, treatment, follow-up periods. These records showed a decline in daily pain intensity rating during the last 15 weeks of treatment, and a corresponding increase in school attendance to 92 of 107 posttreatment school days.

A similar case reported by Miller and Kratochwill (1979) involved a 10-year-old girl with RAP for whom repeated school absences, parental overindulgence, and unlimited access to television, play, and food during pain episodes were hypothesized to be maintaining factors in her pain complaints. A time-out procedure was instituted at home, whereby pain complaints resulted in rest periods with minimal stimulation, restricted entertainment, and limited social attention. Food was available only at mealtimes. When the child experienced pain at school, the time-out strategy was for her to remain in school resting quietly. A gradual reduction of RAP followed the initiation of treatment, first in the home, then at school. No pain complaints were reported at a 1-year follow-up.

These two case studies illustrate the usefulness of two complementary behavioral strategies, positive reinforcement (shaping) and time out (extinction), in the reduction of RAP behavior. Clinically, these strategies can be combined to form an especially potent treatment package. Insofar as school avoidance and school phobia are associated with RAP, an aggressive approach to returning the child to school as soon as possible, even before the RAP has been resolved, is advocated (Kellerman, 1981). Prolonged school absence leads to debilitating academic and social consequences of its own, and serves only to reinforce and intensify the anxiety–avoidance cycle, of which RAP is often a key characteristic.

Focusing on pain perception, Adler *et al.* (1982) discussed the use of hypnosis in reducing RAP associated with parental pressure and childhood athletics. Children were taught self-hypnosis with suggestions for self-control and stress management, and were instructed to use these techniques at the first perceived signs of RAP onset. Parental counseling concentrated on reducing parents' demands with regard to their children's athletic performance. Although there have been no empirical studies to verify this, it has been our own clinical experience that children with RAP tend to be perfectionistic, highly demanding of themselves, and sensitive to competition, failure, and criticism. In this respect, Adler *et al.* (1982) offer an approach that may be useful in cases where RAP represents an anxiety reaction and avoidance response to excessive parental or environmental demands.

SUMMARY AND CONCLUSIONS

The magnitude and significance of pediatric pain exceeds our current ability to control or eliminate it. Nevertheless, much progress has been made in our ability to conceptualize and assess pain multidimensionally, and to contribute to its amelioration in a variety of clinical conditions through the application of behavioral principles.

For the practitioner, this rich yet somewhat fragmented body of knowledge may be reduced to a few working principles. First, the distinction between pain perception and pain behavior, as well as their interaction, is useful in assessing the nature of the patient's pain problem and in selecting the appropriate treatment approaches. Second, having targeted one or both of these pain dimensions as the focus of intervention, current wisdom dictates that a multilevel assessment of the pain problem and of the effects of the intervention program be made. At the very least, this should involve some covert measures of subjective pain experience and some objective index of overt pain expression, since treatment gains (or lack thereof) on either dimension are of clinical significance. Simple self-report and caregiver ratings are easily obtained in most settings and are valuable sources of data.

Finally, the practitioner may extract from the current literature a number of therapeutic principles. The numerous case reports and treatment studies reviewed here share several common denominators that translate into guidelines for addressing pain problems in children. For example, the majority of reports focusing on pain perception in children utilize techniques (regardless of their labels) that involve elements of information, relaxation, and distraction. Whether the therapist chooses to help the patient achieve a more calm state via progressive muscle relaxation, breathing exercises, hypnotic induction, guided imagery, biofeedback, or gentle massage has generally not been shown to be critical to treatment outcome, and is probably best determined by the therapist's level of comfort and expertise and the patient's individual characteristics and preferences. Similarly, distraction may be achieved through guided imagery, biofeedback, video games, or music. Clearly, some techniques involve elements of both relaxation and distraction. The individualization of intervention programs—in terms of the relative weight given to each treatment component (e.g., relaxation, distraction, contingency management of well vs. pain behavior), and the specific techniques selected on the basis of sound therapeutic rationale to achieve these objectives—is most likely the critical factor in treatment outcome.

Much remains to be learned from future research. Our understanding of the cognitive, affective, physiological, and neurochemical aspects of the pain experience and their interactions is still primitive. Large-scale studies must replace our current reliance on data from small samples. New and innovative techniques for assessment and intervention must be developed and tested. Virtually nothing has been reported on treatment failures or on the indications and contraindications for specific techniques. Of particular interest in this regard are individual coping styles and other patient and milieu characteristics that might dictate treatment selection and predict outcome.

Behavioral research on pediatric pain represents a new and challenging area for the application of behavioral science principles to problems in health and illness. Indeed, it is characteristic of the graduation of psychological research and practice from mental health care to health care in general, and reflects the growth and promise of behavioral medicine and the biopsychosocial approach.

REFERENCES

Adler, R., Katz, E. R., & Bongar, B. (1982). Psychogenic abdominal pain related to excessive parental pressure in childhood athletics. *Psychosomatics, 23,* 1021–1023.

Agras, S., Sylvester, D., & Oliveau, D. (1969). The epidemiology of common fears and phobias. *Comprehensive Psychiatry, 10,* 151–156.

Andolsek, K., & Novik, B. (1980). Use of hypnosis with children. *Journal of Family Practice, 3,* 503–508.

Apley, J. (1975). *The child with abdominal pains.* Oxford: Blackwell Scientific.

Beales, J. G. (1979). Pain in children with cancer. In J. J. Bonica & W. F. White (Eds.), *Advances in pain research and therapy* (pp. 89–98). New York: Raven Press.

Berger, H. G., Honig, P. J., & Liebman, R. (1977). Recurrent abdominal pain: Gaining control of the symptom. *American Journal of Diseases of Children, 131,* 1340–1344.

Bille, B. (1981). Migraine in childhood and its prognosis. *Cephalagia, 1,* 71–75.

Blanchard, E. B., Andrasik, F., Ahles, T. A., Teders, S. J., & O'Keefe, D. (1980). Migraine and tension headache: A meta-analytic review. *Behavior Therapy, 11,* 613–631.

Bonica, J. J. (1977). Neurophysiologic and pathologic aspects of acute and chronic pain. *Archives of Surgery, 112,* 750–761.

Bonica, J. J. (1979). Introduction to management of pain of advanced cancer. In J. J. Bonica & V. Ventafridda (Eds.), *Advances in pain research and therapy* (Vol. 2, pp. 115–130). New York: Raven Press.

Bonica, J. J., & Fordyce, W. E. (1974). Operant conditioning for chronic pain. In J. J. Bonica, P. Procacci, & C. A. Pagni (Eds.), *Recent advances in pain* (pp. 275–284). Springfield, IL: Charles C Thomas.

Christensen, M. F., & Mortensen, O. (1975). Long-term prognosis in children with recurrent abdominal pain. *Archives of Disease in Childhood, 50,* 110–114.

Dash, J. (1980). Hypnosis for symptom amelioration. In J. Kellerman (Ed.), *Psychological aspects of childhood cancer* (pp. 215–230). Springfield, IL: Charles C Thomas.

Dash, J. (1981). Rapid hypno-behavioral treatment of a needle phobia in a five-year-old cardiac patient. *Journal of Pediatric Psychology, 6,* 34–42.

Degenaar, J. J. (1979). Some philosophical considerations in pain. *Pain, 7,* 281–304.

Diamond, S. (1979). Biofeedback and headache. *Headache, 19,* 180–184.

Dolgin, M. J., & Katz, E. R. (1982). *Psychological aspects of pediatric emergency care.* Unpublished manuscript.

Dolgin, M. J., Katz, E. R., McGinty, K., & Siegel, S. E. (1985). Anticipatory nausea and vomiting in pediatric cancer patients. *Pediatrics, 75,* 547–552.

Eland, J. M. (1982). Pain. In L. Hart, J. Reese, & M. Fearing (Eds.), *Concepts common to acute illness.* St. Louis: C. V. Mosby.

Eland, J. M., & Anderson, J. E. (1977). The experience of pain in children. In A. Jacox (Ed.), *Pain: A sourcebook for nurses and other health professionals* (pp. 253–273). Boston: Little, Brown.

Ellenberg, L., Kellerman, J., Dash, J. Higgins, G., & Zeltzer, L. (1980). Use of hypnosis for multiple symptoms in an adolescent girl with leukemia. *Journal of Adolescent Health Care, 1,* 132–137.

Elliott, C. H., & Jay, S. M. (1987). Chronic pain in children. *Behaviour Research and Therapy, 25,* 263–271.

Elliott, C. H., Jay, S. M., & Woody, P. (1987). An observational scale for measuring children's distress during medical procedures. *Journal of Pediatric Psychology, 12,* 543–551.

Elliott, C. H., & Olson, R. A. (1983). The management of children's behavioural distress in response to painful medical treatment for burn injuries. *Behaviour Research and Therapy, 21,* 675–683.

Fentress, D., & Masek, B. J. (1982). *Behavioral treatment of pediatric migraine.* Paper presented at the meeting of the Association for Advancement of Behavior Therapy, Los Angeles.

Ferguson, J. M., Taylor, C. B., & Wermuth, B. (1978). A rapid behavioral treatment of needle phobias. *Journal of Nervous and Mental Disease, 166,* 194–298.

Fernald, D. C., & Corry, J. J. (1981). Empathic versus directive preparation of children for needles. *Children's Health Care, 10,* 44–47.

Fordyce, W. E. (1976). *Behavioral methods for chronic pain and illness.* St. Louis: C. V. Mosby.

Frodi, A. M., Lamb, M. E., Leavitt, L. A., & Donovan, W. L. (1978). Fathers' and mothers' responses to infants' smiles and cries. *Infant Behavior and Development, 1,* 187–198.

Gardner, G. G. (1976). Childhood death and human dignity: Hypnotherapy for David. *International Journal of Clinical and Experimental Hypnosis, 24,* 122–139.

Gardner, G. G., & Olness, K. (1981). *Hypnosis and hypnotherapy with children.* New York: Grune & Stratton.

Grunau, R. V. E., & Craig, K. D. (1987). Pain expression in neonates: Facial action and cry. *Pain, 28,* 395–410.

Hilgard, E. R. (1975). The alleviation of pain by hypnosis. *Pain, 1,* 213–231.

Hilgard, J. R., & LeBaron, S. (1982). Relief of anxiety and pain in children and adolescents with cancer: Quantitative measures and clinical observations. *International Journal of Clinical and Experimental Hypnosis, 32,* 417–442.

Houts, A. C. (1982). Relaxation and thermal biofeedback treatment of child migraine headache: A case study. *American Journal of Clinical Biofeedback, 5,* 154–157.

Hubert, N., Jay, S. M., Saltoun, M., & Hayes, M. (in press). Approach–avoidance and distress in children undergoing preparation for painful medical procedures. *Journal of Child Clinical Psychology.*

Jay, S. M. (1985). Pain in children: An overview of psychological assessment and intervention. In A. Zeiner, D. Bendall, & C. E. Walker (Eds.), *Health psychology: Research and treatment issues* (pp. 167–196). New York: Plenum.

Jay, S. M. (1988). Invasive medical procedures: Management of pain and discomfort. In D. Routh (Ed.), *Handbook of pediatric psychology* (pp. 401–425). New York: Guilford Press.

Jay, S. M., & Elliott, C. H. (1983). Psychological intervention for pain in pediatric cancer patients. In G. B. Humphren (Ed.), *Adrenal and endocrine tumors in children* (pp. 123–154). Boston: Martinus Nijhoff.

Jay, S. M., & Elliott, C. H. (1984). Behavioral observation scales for measuring children's distress: The effects of increased methodological rigor. *Journal of Consulting and Clinical Psychology, 52,* 1106–1107.

Jay, S. M, & Elliott, C. H. (1988). *Multimodal assessment of children's distress during medical procedures.* Manuscript submitted for publication.

Jay, S. M., Elliott, C. H., Katz, E. R., & Siegel, S. E. (1987). Cognitive–behavioral and pharmacologic interventions for children undergoing painful medical procedures. *Journal of Consulting and Clinical Psychology*, 55, 860–865.

Jay, S. M., Elliott, C. H., & Varni, J. W. (1987). Acute and chronic pain in adults and children with cancer. *Journal of Consulting and Clinical Psychology*, 54, 601–607.

Jay, S. M., Ozolins, M., Elliott, C. H., & Caldwell, S. (1983). Assessment of children's distress during painful medical procedures. *Health Psychology*, 2, 133–147.

Joffe, R., Bakal, D. A., & Kaganov, J. (1982). A self-observation study of headache symptoms in children. *Headache*, 23, 20–25.

Johnson, C. C., & Strada, M. E. (1986). Acute pain response in infants: A multidimensional description. *Pain*, 24, 373–382.

Kagan, J. (1984). *The nature of the child*. New York: Basic Books.

Katz, E. R., Dolgin, M. J., & Zeltzer, L. K. (1987). Chemotherapy-related distress: Do adolescents have a harder time? *Journal of Adolescent Health Care*, 8, 303.

Katz, E. R., Kellerman, J., & Ellenberg, L. (1987). Hypnosis in the reduction of acute pain and distress in children with leukemia. *Journal of Pediatric Psychology*, 12, 379–393.

Katz, E. R., Kellerman, J., & Siegel, S. E. (1980). Behavioral distress in children with cancer undergoing medical procedures: Developmental considerations. *Journal of Consulting and Clinical Psychology*, 48, 356–365.

Katz, E. R., Kellerman, J., & Siegel, S. E. (1981). Anxiety as an affective focus in the clinical study of acute behavioral distress: A reply to Shacham and Dant. *Journal of Consulting and Clinical Psychology*, 49, 470–471.

Katz, E. R., & Rubinstein, C. L. (1984). *Parent–child communication prior to aversive medical procedures: Impact on anxiety, fear and pain behavior*. Unpublished manuscript.

Katz, E. R., Sharp, B., Kellerman, J., Marston, A. R., Hershman, J. N., & Siegel, S. E. (1982). Beta-endorphin and acute behavioral distress in children with leukemia. *Journal of Nervous and Mental Disease*, 170. 72–77.

Katz, E. R., Varni, J. W., & Jay, S. M. (1984). Behavioral assessment and management of pediatric pain. *Progress in Behavior Modification*, 18, 163–193.

Kavanaugh, C. (1983). Psychological intervention with the severely burned child: Report of an experimental comparison of two approaches and their effects on psychological sequelae. *Journal of the American Academy of Child Psychiatry*, 22, 145–156.

Keane, W. M. (1980, August). *Hypnosis with pediatric cancer patients: Giving control in an uncontrollable situation*. Paper presented at the meeting of the American Psychological Association, Montreal.

Keefe, F. J. (1982). Behavioral assessment and treatment of chronic pain: Current status and future directions. *Journal of Consulting and Clinical Psychology*, 50, 896–911.

Kellerman, J. (Ed.). (1980). *Psychological aspects of childhood cancer*. Springfield, IL: Charles C Thomas.

Kellerman, J. (1981). *Helping the fearful child*. New York: Warner Books.

Kellerman, J., & Katz, E. R. (1979) *Psychological referrals in pediatric hematology–oncology*. Unpublished manuscript.

Kellerman, J., & Varni, J. W. (1982). Pediatric hematology–oncology. In D. C. Russo, & J. W. Varni (Eds.), *Behavioral pediatrics: Research and practice* (pp. 67–100). New York: Plenum.

Kellerman, J., Zeltzer, L., Ellenberg, L., & Dash, J. (1983). Adolescents with cancer: Hypnosis for the reduction of acute pain and anxiety associated with medical procedures. *Journal of Adolescent Health Care*, 4, 85–90.

LaBaw, W., Holton, C., Tewell, K., & Eccles, D. (1975). The use of self-hypnosis by children with cancer. *American Journal of Clinical Hypnosis*, 17, 233–238.

Labbe, E. E., & Williamson, D. A. (1983). Temperature biofeedback in the treatment of children with migraine headaches. *Journal of Pediatric Psychology*, 8, 317–323.

Lavigne, J. V., Schulein, M. J., & Hahn, Y. S. (1986). Psychological aspects of painful medical conditions in children: II. Personality factors, family characteristics and treatment. *Pain*, 27, 147–169.

LeBaron, S., & Zeltzer, L. K. (1984). Assessment of acute pain and anxiety in children and adolescents by self reports, observer reports, and a behavior checklist. *Journal of Consulting and Clinical Psychology*, 52, 729–738.

Lehmann, H., Huntsman, R. S., Casey, R., Lang, A., Lorkin, P. A., & Comings, D. F. (1977). Sickle cell disease and related disorders. In J. W. Williams, E. Beutler, A. J. Ersler, & R. W. Rundles (Eds.), *Hematology*. New York: McGraw-Hill.

Levine, J. D., & Gordon, N. C. (1982). Pain in prelingual children and its evaluation by pain-induced vocalization. *Pain*, 14, 85–93.

Lollar, D. J., Smits, S. J., & Patterson, D. L. (1982). Assessment of pediatric pain: An empirical perspective. *Journal of Pediatric Psychology*, 7, 267–277.

Maddison, T. G. (1977). Recurrent abdominal pain in children. *Medical Journal of Australia*, 1, 708–710.

Masek, B. J. (1982). *Behavioral medicine treatment of pediatric migraine*. Paper presented at the meeting of the Society of Behavioral Medicine, Chicago.

Masek, B. J., Russo, D. C., & Varni, J. W. (1984). Behavioral approaches to the management of chronic pain in children. *Pediatric Clinics of North America 31*, 1113–1131.

McCaffery, M. (1977). Pain relief: Problem areas and selected nonpharmacological methods. *Pediatric Nursing*, 3, 11–16.

McCue, K. (1980). Preparing children for medical procedures. In J. Kellerman (Ed.), *Psychological aspects of childhood cancer* (pp. 238–256). Springfield, IL: Charles C Thomas.

Meichenbaum, D., & Turk, D. (1976). The cognitive-behavioral management of anxiety, anger, and pain. In P. O. Davidson (Ed.), *The behavioral management of anxiety, depression and pain* (pp. 1–34). New York: Brunner/Mazel.

Melamed, B. G., & Siegel, L. J. (1975). Reduction of anxiety in children facing hospitalization and surgery by use of filmed modeling. *Journal of Consulting and Clinical Psychology*, 43, 511–521.

Miller, A. J., & Kratochwill, T. R. (1979). Reduction of frequent stomachache complaints by time out. *Behavior Therapy*, 10, 211–218.

Miller, J. A. (1980). Hypnosis in a boy with leukemia. *American Journal of Clinical Hypnosis*, 22, 231–236.

Millicap, J. G. (1978). Recurrent headaches in 100 children: Electroencephelographic abnormalities and response to phenytoin (Dilantin). *Child's Brain*, 4, 95–105.

Olness, K., & MacDonald, J. (1981). Self-hypnosis and

biofeedback in the management of juvenile migraine. *Developmental and Behavioral Pediatrics, 2,* 168–170.

Oster, J. (1972). Recurrent abdominal pain, headache, and limb pains in children and adolescents. *Pediatrics, 50,* 429–436.

Parkhouse, J., Pleurvy, B. J., & Rees, J. M. (Eds.). (1979). *Analgesic drugs.* Oxford: Blackwell Scientific.

Perry, S., & Heidrich, G. (1982). Management of pain during debridement: A survey of U.S. burn units. *Pain, 13,* 267–280.

Peterson, L., & Ridley-Johnson, R. (1980). Pediatric hospital response to survey on prehospital preparation for children. *Journal of Pediatric Psychology, 5,* 1–7.

Peterson, L., & Shigetomi, C. (1981). The use of coping techniques to minimize anxiety in hospitalized children. *Behavior Therapy, 12,* 1–14.

Porter, J., & Jick, H. (1980). Addiction rare in patients treated with narcotics. *New England Journal of Medicine, 302,* 123–128.

Ramsden, R., Friedman, B., & Williamson, D. A. (1983). Treatment of childhood headache reports with contingency management procedures. *Journal of Clinical Child Psychology, 12,* 202–206.

Sanders, S. H. (1979). Behavioral assessment and treatment of clinical pain: Appraisal and current status. In M. Hersen, R. M. Eisler, & P. M. Miller (Eds.), *Progress in behavior modification* (Vol. 8, pp. 249–291). New York: Academic Press.

Sank, L. I., & Biglan, A. (1974). Operant treatment of a case of recurrent abdominal pain in a 10-year-old boy. *Behavior Therapy, 5,* 677–681.

Schechter, N. L. (1985). Pain and pain control in children. *Current Problems in Pediatrics, 15,* 1–67.

Seligman, M. E. P. (1975). *Helplessness: On depression, development, and death.* San Francisco: W. H. Freeman.

Siegel, S. E. (1980). The current medical outlook of childhood cancer: The medical background. In J. Kellerman (Ed.), *Psychological aspects of childhood cancer* (pp. 5–13). Springfield, IL: Charles C Thomas.

Silverberg, E. (1979). Cancer statistics. *CA: A Cancer Journal for Clinicians, 29,* 44–49.

Sokoloff, L. (1975). Biochemical and physiological aspects of degenerative joint disease with special reference to hemophilic arthropathy. *Annals of the New York Academy of Sciences, 240,* 285–290.

Sternbach, R. A. (1974). *Pain patients: Traits and treatment.* New York: Academic Press.

Sternbach, R. A. (1979). Clinical aspects of pain. In R. A. Sternbach (Ed.), *The psychology of pain.* New York: Raven Press.

Stickler, G. B., & Murphy, D. B. (1979). Recurrent abdominal pain. *American Journal of Diseases of Children, 133,* 484–486.

Swafford, L. I., & Allan, D. (1968). Pain relief in the pediatric patient. *Medical Clinics of North America, 52,* 131–136.

Turk, D. (1978). Cognitive behavioral techniques in the management of pain. In J. P. Foreyt & D. P. Rathjen (Eds.), *Cognitive behavior therapy* (pp. 199–227). New York: Plenum.

Varni, J. W. (1981a). Behavioral medicine in hemophilic arthritic pain management: Two case studies. *Archives of Physical Medicine and Rehabilitation, 62,* 183–187.

Varni, J. W. (1981b). Self-regulation techniques in the management of chronic arthritic pain in hemophilia. *Behavior Therapy, 12,* 185–194.

Varni, J. W. (1983). *Clinical behavioral pediatrics: An interdisciplinary biobehavioral approach.* New York: Pergamon Press.

Varni, J. W., Bessman, C. A., Russo, D. C., & Cataldo, M. F. (1980). Behavioral management of chronic pain in children: Case study. *Archives of Physical Medicine and Rehabilitation, 61,* 375–379.

Varni, J. W., & Gilbert, A. (1982). Self-regulation of chronic arthritic pain and long-term analgesic dependence in a hemophiliac. *Rheumatology and Rehabilitation, 22,* 171–174.

Varni, J. W., Gilbert, A., & Dietrich, S. L. (1981). Behavioral medicine in pain and analgesia management for the hemophiliac child with Factor VIII inhibitor. *Pain, 11,* 121–126.

Varni, J. W., Jay, S. M., Masek, B. J., & Thompson, K. L. (1986). Cognitive behavioral assessment and management of pediatric pain. In A. D. Holzman & D. C. Turk (Eds.), *Pain management: A handbook of treatment approaches* (pp. 168–192). New York: Pergamon Press.

Varni, J. W., Katz, E. R., & Dash, J. (1982). Behavioral and neurochemical aspects of pediatric pain. In D. C. Russo & J. W. Varni (Eds.), *Behavioral pediatrics: Research and practice* (pp. 177–224). New York: Plenum.

Varni, J. W., Thompson, K. L., & Hanson, V. (1987). The Varni–Thompson pediatric pain questionnaire: Chronic musculoskeletal pain in juvenile rheumatoid arthritis. *Pain, 28,* 27–38.

Wakeman, R. J., & Kaplan, J. Z. (1978). An experimental study of hypnosis in painful burns. *American Journal of Clinical Hypnosis, 21,* 3–12.

Weisenberg, M. (1977). Pain and pain control. *Psychological Bulletin 84,* 1008–1044.

White, J. R. (1973). Effects of a counterirritant on perceived pain and hand movements in patients with arthritis. *Physical Therapy, 53,* 956–960.

Zeltzer, L. K., Dash, J., & Holland, J. P. (1979). Hypnotically induced pain control in sickle cell anemia. *Pediatrics, 64,* 533–536.

Zeltzer, L. K., Kellerman, J., Ellenberg, L., Dash, J., & Rigler, D. (1980). Psychologic effects of illness in adolescence: II. Impact of illness in adolescents: Crucial issues and coping styles. *Journal of Pediatrics, 97,* 132–138.

Zeltzer, L. K., & LeBaron, S. (1982). Hypnosis and nonhypnotic techniques for reduction of pain and anxiety during painful procedures in children and adolescents with cancer. *Journal of Pediatrics, 101,* 1032–1035.

Zeltzer, L. K., & LeBaron, S. (1986). Assessment of acute pain and anxiety and chemotherapy-related nausea and vomiting in children and adolescents. In D. M. Dush, B. R. Cassileth, & D. C. Turk (Eds.), *Psychosocial assessment in terminal care* (pp. 75–98). New York: Haworth Press.

Zeltzer, L. K., LeBaron, S., Richie, D. M., Reed, D., Schoolfield, J., & Prihoda, T. J. (1988). Can children understand and use a rating scale to quantify somatic symptoms? Assessment of nausea and vomiting as a model. *Journal of Consulting and Clinical Psychology, 56,* 567–572.

11

OBESITY

JOHN P. FOREYT
JENNIFER H. COUSINS
Baylor College of Medicine

Obesity is a serious and increasingly prevalent problem in children and adolescents. Previous estimates of obesity were placed at 10%–15% for young children and at 15%–30% for adolescents (Colley, 1974; Garn & Clark, 1976; Hathaway & Sargent, 1962). More recent data suggest that these figures may be even higher. Comparing skinfold data from three national surveys conducted from 1963 to 1980, Gortmaker, Dietz, Sobol, and Wehler (1987) found a 54% increase in obesity in children and a 39% increase in adolescents over the last two decades. Depending on the age, sex, and race of the group studied, the prevalence of obesity among children and adolescents was found to increase by 17% to 306% during this time period. Defining obesity as triceps skinfolds greater than or equal to the 85th percentile of age and sex in the earlier and larger surveys, the National Health Examination Surveys (NHES) cycles 2 and 3, Gortmaker *et al.* estimated that 27% of children aged 6–11 and 22% of youths aged 12–17 in this country are obese. The increased skewedness of both skinfolds and weights in the upper percentiles of the population suggests that children and adolescents are becoming fatter and that the fatter individuals are becoming more obese (Gortmaker *et al.*, 1987).

Prevalence of obesity differs by sex, socioeconomic status, race, and ethnicity. Data from the NHES, collected from 1963 to 1970, and from the first and second National Health and Nutrition Examination Surveys (NHANES 1 and 2), collected from 1971–1974 and from 1976–1980, respectively, indicate that obesity among black boys continues to be substantially less prevalent than among white boys, whereas the prevalence of obesity among black girls was previously lower but is now similar to the rate for white girls (Gortmaker *et al.*, 1987). A recent survey of 868 Mexican-American children aged 6–17 years suggests that Mexican-American children tend to be shorter and heavier than their non-Hispanic peers (Malina, Zavaleta, & Little, 1987). Compared to data collected in 1972 from children of the same ages in the same community (Zavaleta & Malina, 1980), children of both sexes and all ages (except boys of 16 years) from the 1983 sample demonstrated significant increases in weight, body mass index, and skinfolds. Data assessing the growth and nutritional status of 2,056 black, white, and Hispanic children aged 5 to 12 years, of low socioeconomic status from the urban Northeast, indicate that black children are taller and heavier than whites or Hispanics, and that Hispanic girls are heavier than white girls (Scholl, Karp, Theophano, & Decker, 1987). Low socioeconomic status is consistently associated with smaller size and less fat in both boys and girls when compared with their peers of higher socioeconomic status, but these data are reversed for females in adolescence, when socioeconomic status becomes related to fatness level (Garn, 1986).

One of the difficulties in determining precise estimates of the prevalence of obesity within children and adolescents is the problem of defining obesity. "Obesity" refers to an excess of body fat, whereas "overweight" usually refers to an excess of weight. Determining what is an excessive amount of fat typically varies from study to study. As the literature reviewed above illustrates, definitions that depend on percentiles of the distribution may vary from sample to sample (depending on age, sex, race, or ethnicity) and from year to year. In general, weight or body fat may be considered excessive when it is associated with another physical symptom, such as hypertension, hyperlipidemia, or diabetes, or when it is associated with poor self-concept, peer interaction, or psychosocial development. It may require some judgment on the part of the clinician whether a child's or adolescent's weight or percentage of body fat is sufficiently excessive to require intervention.

There are a number of common factors involved in the development and maintenance of obesity in childhood and adolescence. Obesity is strongly associated with family membership. The child of one obese parent is more likely to be obese, and the child of two obese parents is even more likely to be so (Garn & Clark, 1976). Data from studies of twins (Stunkard, Foch, & Hrubec, 1986) and from a Danish adoption study (Stunkard, Sorensen, et al., 1986) indicate that heritability may account for a substantial proportion of the variance in obesity. Environmental factors also play a large role in determining fatness, however. Parents serve as models for children regarding attitudes toward food and eating behaviors. Parents also determine food availability and model exercise behavior as well. A causal relationship of television viewing has been proposed from data linking increased television viewing with increased prevalence rates of childhood and adolescent obesity (Dietz & Gortmaker, 1985). Other data also suggest that decreased physical activity may be involved in an increase in childhood obesity (U.S. Department of Health and Human Services, 1985). Weight and fatness have been associated with geographic region and seasonal variations (Dietz & Gortmaker, 1984), with children in the Northeast and Midwest heavier than their peers in the West, and with obesity more prevalent during the winter than the summer.

Contrary to earlier assumptions, obesity is not a condition likely to be "outgrown." Most obese children become obese adolescents, and most obese adolescents become obese adults (Abraham, Collins, & Nordsieck, 1971; Johnston & Mack, 1978; Weil, 1977; Zack, Harlan, Leaverton, & Cornoni-Huntley, 1979). Developmental data indicate that risk of adult obesity increases as the age of the obese child increases (Epstein, 1986). If overweight continues through adolescence, the odds against the child becoming a normal weight adult are 28 to 1 (Stunkard & Burt, 1967).

Obese children are at greater risk for a number of health problems, as well as difficulties in psychological and social adjustment. Childhood obesity has been associated with such cardiovascular risk factors as hypertension (Court, Hill, Dunlop, & Boulton, 1974; Londe, Bourgoignie, Robson, & Goldring, 1971) and elevated serum cholesterol and triglycerides (Clarke, Merrow, Morse, & Keyser, 1970; Lauer, Conner, Leaverton, Reiter, & Clark, 1975), and may lead to adult hypertension or hyperlipidemia. In addition, there is some evidence that childhood obesity makes an independent contribution to risk for cardiovascular disease (Kannel & Dawber, 1972; Miller & Shekelle, 1976). The presence of overweight in children has been shown to contribute to the occurrence of orthopedic difficulties (Mayer, 1970), hyperinsulinism (Drash, 1973), and impaired physical work capacity (Boulton, 1981).

Childhood obesity is also associated with developmental problems of a social and psychological nature. Contemporary American cultural values equate attractiveness, competence, and even intelligence with thinness. Although most, if not all, of the obese suffer from the consequences of such attitudes, children and adolescents are particularly vulnerable (Dwyer & Mayer, 1975).

In a survey of children's attitudes toward others, Lerner (1973) found that children indicated a desire to maintain greater personal distance from their overweight peers than from those of normal weight. Staffieri (1967, 1972) showed boys aged 6–10 and girls aged 7–11 silhouettes that were identical to each other except in body shape (thin, muscular, fat) and asked them to evaluate these drawings using a list of 39 adjectives. Even those who resembled the drawing described endomorphs negatively, disproportionately applying to them such adjectives as "stupid," "lazy," "mean," and "ugly." Prejudicial attitudes toward obese children are not limited to their peers. Similar attitudes toward obese youngsters have been observed among adults, even among health professionals (Goodman, Richardson, Dornbush, & Hastorf, 1963; Lerner, 1969).

Serveral studies have documented that ethnic differences in children's preferences for body type are slight. One series of studies found that although Mexican-American children assigned more positive traits to an average body type than an obese one, they chose the leaner type less consistently than either Amercian or Japanese children (Iwawaki, Lerner, & Chihara, 1977; Lerner & Korn, 1972; Lerner & Pool, 1972). In a recent study of Mexican-American children's attitudes about attractiveness and body type, none of the forty 6- to 12-year-old girls tested selected the larger than average body types as attractive (Hall & Cousins, 1987).

The social and psychological problems associated with childhood obesity do not lessen during adolescence; if anything, they appear to intensify. As with obese children, obese adolescents are often negatively viewed by their peers (Lerner & Korn, 1972; Worsley, 1981), by adults (Hendry & Gillies, 1978), and perhaps even by college admission boards (Canning & Mayer, 1966).

The pressure to conform to socially determined standards of appearance intensifies during adolescence, particularly among females (Allon 1980). Deviation from the "norm" of appearance is cause for concern and self-consciousness at some time for all adolescents, regardless of whether or not they are overweight. But for obese teenagers, these concerns may lead from feelings of unacceptability to more serious problems, such as self-condemnation and body image distortions (Monello & Mayer, 1963). These problems in turn may lead to the development of eating disorders, such as anorexia nervosa and bulimia (Cahnman, 1968; Dwyer, 1973; Miller, Coffman, & Linke, 1980).

ASSESSMENT

Assessment is an integral part of the behavioral treatment of obesity. Before intervention is begun, the collection of baseline information provides the foundation for goals, approach, length, and limitations of treatment (Foreyt & Goodrick, 1988). During treatment, assessment continues to play a vital role in determining program adherence and progress toward treatment goals. Finally, assessment provides the therapist, the child, and the family with the mechanism for the evaluation of treatment. Table 11-1 outlines the elements of a model for the assessment and treatment of obesity in children and adolescents.

Physical Measures

Obesity is an excess of body fat. Assessing obesity involves two steps: (1) measuring or estimating body fat, and (2) making a judgment regarding the extent to which body fat is excessive.

Several methods exist for the measurement of body fat. These are summarized below. Determining the extent to which body fat is excessive involves consideration of its effect on the present and future health status of the child and its effect on social and psychological functioning. Judging the extent to which a particular child's weight and body fat interfere with his or her physical and psychosocial health must be based on a thorough assessment of each of these aspects of the child's overall functioning (Foreyt & Goodrick, 1981).

Densiometry is the calculation of the percentage of fat from the amount of water displaced when the child is totally immersed in water. Densiometry is a useful measure of body fat, but it is also the most expensive and least convenient method. Nor is it free of questionable assumptions (Weil, 1977).

Skinfold measurement is a commonly used technique for approximating body fat. Several investigators (e.g., Franzini & Grimes, 1976; Grimes & Franzini, 1977; Weil, 1977) believe that skinfold measurement is the method of choice for assessing body fat, because the most common alternatives, such as height–weight tables, are less closely related to the concept of obesity as excess body fat. Others (e.g., Bray, 1976; Johnson & Stalonas, 1977) disagree, because of the difficulty in achieving adequate reliability and validity. Measurement error can be decreased through identifying the site more clearly by marking the skin (Bray, 1976), and standards for measuring triceps and subscapular skinfolds have been published (Tanner & Whitehouse, 1975). There are no normed conversion tables that approximate percentage of body fat from children's skinfolds, so the skinfold thickness itself is typically used. Triceps skinfold percentiles are available for boys and girls aged 6–17 years (Lauer *et al.*, 1975). Obesity standards (defined as one standard deviation above the mean) are also available for children aged 5–18 (Seltzer & Mayer, 1965). These data are based on measurements of Caucasian children, so caution should be exercised in applying them to children of other ethnic or racial backgrounds.

Body weight is also used frequently as an indirect measure of body fat. Because body weight is dependent on numerous factors other than body fat, particularly height, age, sex, body build, and composition (percentage of fat), it should not be assumed that the overfat are always overweight or that the reverse is always true. In spite of this qualification, several measures of body weight have proven to be

useful in assessing obesity. The most commonly used measures are absolute weight, relative weight, percentage of overweight, and the body mass index.

Absolute weight is useful because it is easily collected and understood. The degree of excess weight for height that is usually assumed to correspond to obesity in adults and sometimes children is 20% (Rowe, 1980). The validity of this figure for children and adolescents is questionable. Garn, Clark, and Guire (1975) investigated whether the overfat (85th percentile for triceps skinfold) were also the overweight (20% overweight) in a large sample of children and adults (aged 2–70 years). Although measures were generally in agreement for adults, they were not for children or adolescents. Many nonobese teenagers tended

TABLE 11-1. A Model for Assessment and Treatment of Childhood Obesity

Physical	Family-parents
Medical history	Is obesity evident in either or both parents? Do any of the other children in the family demonstrate signs of excess fat?
Particular physical factors causing or exacerbating the condition	
Age of onset of obesity	How does the family eat? Do they eat in a nutritionally sound manner?
Weight–height history	
Physical characteristics	Is food often used to reward or punish?
Height and weight	Who wants the child to lose weight—the parents or the child?
Percentage of fat	
Physical characteristics of parents	Goals
Psychosocial characteristics	Child's weight
Psychological	Child's eating behaviors
Self-esteem	Family eating behaviors
Cognitive development	Perceptions of self
Physical self-concept	Interactions with family and others
Introverted or extraverted?	Treatment characteristics
Withdrawn? Shy?	Treatment format
Social	Family context
Does the patient have close friends?	Cognitive–behavioral methodologies
Are they overweight?	Examination of the energy balance: energy intake versus energy expenditures
Does the patient participate in group activities with others of his or her age?	
How does the patient perceive himself or herself *vis-a-vis* his or her peers?	Nutrition awareness
	Exercise activity
How is the patient's weight perceived by his or her family?	Self-esteem
	Social interaction
Do the parents appear overprotective, or do they allow a reasonable degree of independence?	
How appropriate are the parents' and other family members' perceptions regarding the child's physical, social, and intellectual capabilities?	

Note. Adapted from "Cognitive–Behavioral Treatment of Childhood and Adolescent Obesity" by J. P. Foreyt and A. T. Kondo, 1983, in A. Ellis and M. E. Bernard (Eds.), *Rational–Emotive Approaches to the Problems of Childhood* (pp. 271–309). New York: Plenum. Copyright 1983 by Plenum Publishing Corporation. Adapted by permission.

to be greater than 20% overweight, and many obese children, by contrast, tended to be lighter. These results suggest that absolute weight and percentage of overweight should not be used singly in the assessment of juvenile obesity.

Relative weight is the percentage of the median weight for the child's age, sex, and height (Lauer et al., 1975; Wheeler & Hess, 1976). Normative data are available (see Foreyt & Goodrick, 1981). A disadvantage to using relative weight is that it does not take body build into account, so a normal child with a large frame may have a relative weight indicating obesity. Under 7 years of age, these weights may overestimate fatness (Weil, 1977). Percentage of overweight, calculated as (initial absolute weight/goal weight) $\times$ 100, is useful in treatment programs because it incorporates into the measure both initial absolute weight and goal weight. Goal weight is set as the median weight for children of the same age, sex, and height. The body mass index (weight/height^2) is also advised frequently because it relates most closely to measures of body fat (Bray, 1976; Michielutte, Diseker, Corbett, Schey, & Ureda, 1985).

Because no measure is capable of assessing obesity without error, we encourage researchers and practitioners to collect several measures of weight and body fat, including absolute weight, percentage of overweight, the body mass index, and triceps and subscapular skinfolds (Brownell, 1983; Brownell & Stunkard, 1980; Foreyt & Goodrick, 1981; Foreyt & Kondo, 1983). We also advise a medical history and examination in order to rule out underlying physical causes of obesity. The medical history and conversation with the child's physician can provide vital information concerning the child's experience with obesity, such as the age of onset and previous weight loss efforts.

Physical assessment of the child would not be complete without a similar, though much less intensive, physical assessment of the parents (Foreyt & Kondo, 1983). In particular, a determination should be made of the existence and extent of overweight in both parents. If overweight is present in both, then it may be suspected that the child has a physical and an environmentally derived tendency toward the condition. In this case, the child and the parents need to understand the presence of the familial tendency and the difficulty of the task before them.

Psychosocial Assessment

Part of the initial assessment should be used to examine the psychological status of the child. We find that determination of the child's self-esteem, personal capabilities, physical image, and social attractiveness is especially important. As described earlier, overweight children are the recipients of substantial prejudice in our society. It can be expected that most overweight children reflect such treatment in psychological symptomatology (Israel & Stolmaker, 1980). We find that many obese children and adolescents assume that weight loss will solve all of their problems, when in fact an improved physique does not automatically result in improved self-concept or social skills. Problems in psychological functioning and unrealistic expectations regarding the effects of weight loss should be identified and addressed during treatment (Giotto, 1980).

In conjunction with a psychological assessment, we also examine the child's social life and interactions. We collect parental reports concerning the child's behavior at school, in the home, and with friends. An outline of questions that can serve as the foundation for an exploration of the child's social life is given in Table 11-1.

Our final area of psychosocial assessment is the family of the child. We find that we need to have a reasonable understanding of the family's overall level of functioning. This may range from the relatively simple task of assessing the kinds and quantities of foods served in the household to the more complex task of uncovering the overt and covert messages that the parents give the child regarding his or her overweight.

With respect to this last point, it is important to determine whether it is the child or the parent who is most desirous of weight loss. If our interview reveals that the primary motivation for seeking treatment belongs to the parents, we will then structure a portion of the treatment to explore this matter.

We find that it is also important to assess the extent to which the family can be expected to support the child's treatment. Depending in part on their own experience with overweight, family members may differ regarding the extent to which they view the child's overweight as a problem in need of treatment, their role in supporting treatment, and their expectations regarding the effects of treatment.

BEHAVIORAL METHODOLOGIES

The goal of behavioral treatment for overweight is to change the child's eating behaviors and physical activity patterns to ones that are more adaptive. Behavioral treatment programs are designed to assist the child in developing more adaptive approaches to food and exercise by teaching self-control methodologies that are intended to become an important part of the child's life. Five methodologies are used most frequently in behavioral approaches: (1) self-monitoring; (2) stimulus control; (3) eating management; (4) contingency contracting; and (5) cognitive–behavioral strategies. A brief description of each technique follows and may also be found elsewhere (e.g., DeBakey, Gotto, Scott, & Foreyt, 1984; Foreyt & Kondo, 1983).

Self-Monitoring

Self-monitoring is an important aspect of most treatment programs. We ask the child, if old enough, to record the quantity and nature of food eaten, the time of ingestion, who shared the meal, where eating occurred, and the mood or feeling accompanying the event. We use this information as a diagnostic tool, working with the child and the parents to determine the presence of inappropriate eating patterns and related causative factors. We also use self-monitoring in the same manner to document aerobic activity and sedentary behavior, and to identify situational factors controlling exercise. With this information, we can tailor a treatment plan to the child's problematic eating and activity patterns. During treatment, self-monitoring serves the important function of helping to assess behavioral change. That is, at any time during treatment, we can compare the child's current eating behaviors with those of the pretreatment (baseline) period to determine the extent to which improvement has occurred. We find that most preadolescents and adolescents are able to monitor and record their own behaviors. For the very young, we ask the parents to record their child's eating on the basis of their own observations and their child's reports.

Stimulus Control

Stimulus control is the modification of factors that appear to serve as cues leading to inappropriate eating. These cues vary considerably among individuals. However, we find that the following are common sources of difficulty in our patients: (1) handling food frequently; (2) having high-calorie snacks in the household; (3) having food located throughout the house; and (4) eating while watching television, doing homework, or reading.

The particular stimuli causing difficulty may be determined through the child's personal assessment of the problem as well as through our examination of the child's eating records. Following this examination, we suggest specific alterations in the child's environment or daily routines so that the influence of the troublesome stimuli is effectively negated. For example, one of our patients, Laura, found that the presence in her home of snack foods, particularly chocolate chip cookies, was the source of much of her difficulty. We suggested two alternatives to Laura and her family: (1) that the parents not buy chocolate chip cookies (perhaps buying for other family members a type of cookie that Laura did not find as difficult to avoid); or (2) that they store the cookies in places or containers that reduced their availability, and perhaps thus their power of temptation. By taking either of these actions, the family would help Laura control the stimulus that led to inappropriate eating. In this case, the family began buying fig bars, which Laura disliked, rather than chocolate chip cookies.

Eating Management

Eating management techniques are applied to modify the act of eating. Some obese children as young as 1½ to 2 years of age have been found to eat more rapidly than their nonobese agemates (Drabman, Cordua, Hammer, Jarvie, & Horton, 1979). Many of these children may eat so rapidly that insufficient time is provided for satiation to reach cognitive awareness (Keane, Geller, & Scheirer, 1981). Our treatment of this pattern involves using techniques to slow a child's usual rate of eating. For example, we recommend that children practice chewing slowly and thoroughly, laying down their forks or spoons frequently, and taking extended pauses during their meals. We also encourage the parents to use these techniques, in order to provide a model for the child and to help decrease the eating rate of the family. An added advantage of this technique is that children and their parents often report that their enjoyment of food is increased, diminishing their desire to overeat.

Contingency Management

In many behavioral treatment programs, appropriate behaviors are rewarded and inappropriate behaviors either are punished or are systematically not reinforced. Operant conditioning forms the basis for contingency management. Research on operant conditioning suggests that behaviors that receive consequent rewards are likely to be strengthened, whereas those that are not reinforced or are punished are likely to be extinguished. Contingency contracting is applied to treatment programs to enhance the probability of desired eating or exercise behaviors while reducing those that are less desirable. The consequences of performing or not performing the behaviors may be administered by the child, family, friends, or therapist.

One example of contingency management was a contract made between Drew and his mother, which stated that failure to complete a daily eating record would be punished by the addition of one household chore the following day. In another case, Kelli determined that sitting in front of the television after school and in the evenings was a recurring and difficult problem. Kelli decided to reward herself with a trip to the shopping mall for each week in which daily television viewing did not exceed a specified amount of time (1 hour a night).

We believe that contingency contracts should focus on increasing adaptive and decreasing maladaptive behaviors associated with weight loss, rather than on weight loss itself. Rewarding or punishing children for achieving or not achieving particular weight loss goals may motivate them to use physically abusive techniques (e.g., laxatives, diuretics, self-induced vomiting, or short-term fasting) to achieve "success."

Cognitive–Behavioral Methodologies

The earliest behaviorally oriented programs typically presented a standard package of the above-described techniques for all children, but recent reviews of this research suggest that a more effective approach involves matching particular strategies to the individual (Brownell, 1979, cited in Coates & Thoresen, 1981; Coates & Thoresen, 1981; Epstein, 1986). As we have indicated earlier, the ultimate goal of the behavioral approach to the treatment of obesity is to replace the child's maladaptive eating and activity habits with adaptive approaches to food and exercise that will be incorporated into the child's life style. We feel that the source of many of these maladaptive behaviors are maladaptive cognitions and that the role of the therapist is to alter these cognitions to ones that are more adaptive (Foreyt & Goodrick, 1981).

We find that in treating overweight children, three areas are likely to be of primary importance: (1) food and eating, (2) self-image and self-esteem, and (3) social interactions. Both alone and in interaction, these problems tend to exacerbate the presenting problem of obesity. Thus, a comprehensive approach to the treatment of childhood obesity requires multiple interventions using a variety of cognitive and behavioral strategies.

The success of the particular cognitive strategy used with a child depends on the child's level of cognitive development (Cole & Kazdin, 1980). Because research on the appropriateness of the various cognitive interventions at different stages of cognitive development is just beginning, we believe that the therapist must rely on judgment and experimentation in the application of these techniques with a particular child.

A review of the cognitive–behavioral approach with children (Kendall, 1981) suggests several promising strategies. Modeling (e.g., Bandura, 1971) combined with a variation of self-instructional training (Meichenbaum, 1977) is one approach that has been used successfully to modify eating pace and to sensitize children to internal sensations associated with eating, such as hunger and fullness (Foreyt & Kondo, 1983). Because child self-control has been found to relate to long-term successful weight control (Cohen, Gelfand, Dodd, Jensen, & Turner, 1980), child self-control procedures (O'Leary & Dubey, 1979) have been incorporated into treatment programs (Epstein, Woodall, Goreczny, Wing, & Robertson, 1984).

Cognitive methodologies have also been used to treat problems of self-esteem and social interaction. For example, we ask children with low self-esteem to list their positive qualities and practice self-statements that acknowledge their capabilities, talents, and worth (Foreyt & Kondo, 1983). Other techniques that we have found useful in treating obesity in children and adolescents are role playing (Fagan, Long, & Stevens, 1975), problem solving (Mahoney & Mahoney, 1976), covert modeling (Cautela,

1971), cognitive restructuring (Ellis, 1962), and imagery (Homme, 1965).

REVIEW OF RESEARCH

Early behavioral interventions for weight loss in children typically involved the application of a standard set of techniques derived from research with adults. Although the results of these approaches compared favorably to alternate treatments and potentially dangerous traditional approaches (e.g., diets, fasting, hormones, and anorectic drugs), the outcomes have been modest at best (Brownell & Stunkard, 1980; Coates & Thoresen, 1981; Israel & Stolmaker, 1980). As we have indicated in the preceding section, an important recent innovation in the behavioral treatment of juvenile obesity is the use of cognitive–behavioral methodologies (Foreyt & Kondo, 1983).

A recent review (Foreyt, 1987) summarized a number of changes made in the treatment of obesity since the 1970s, many of which have influenced the treatment of obesity with children and adolescents. Several trends are of particular note: (1) the inclusion of exercise and physical activity interventions; (2) the development and evaluation of programs specifically for younger children; and (3) the introduction of social support, in the family and in other settings, in weight loss programs with children and adolescents.

Exercise and Physical Activity

It is a widely held belief that most obesity is caused by an imbalance between energy intake and energy expenditure. Until recently, however, most behavioral treatment programs for children placed considerably more emphasis on reducing caloric inputs than on increasing caloric expenditures (Foreyt & Goodrick, 1981). This focus appears to be changing. Reviews of recent research on the behavioral treatment of childhood obesity have recommended that greater emphasis be placed on energy output, both in the assessment and in the treatment of childhood obesity (Coates & Thoresen, 1981; Foreyt & Goodrick, 1981; Foreyt & Kondo, 1983; Israel & Stolmaker, 1980).

The precise role that exercise plays in the etiology of obesity in children is not fully understood (Brownell, 1982). Studies with children are divided almost evenly into those showing that obese children are less active than nonobese, and those finding no differences. Carrera (1967) found that only 4% of obese children were overeaters. Most were characterized by below-normal activity levels. Some studies have supported this observation (Corbin & Pletcher, 1968; Mayer, 1975; Rose & Mayer, 1968), but others have found no differences in activity (Brownell & Stunkard, 1980; Wilkinson, Parkin, Pearlson, Strong, & Sykes, 1977).

The different findings may result in part from the ways in which observations are made and energy output is defined (Brownell & Stunkard, 1980). For example, Waxman and Stunkard (1980) observed boys aged 6–13 in the home and at school. They found that overweight children were about as active as the nonoverweight at school, but were less active at home and at play. However, when measures of activity were converted to caloric expenditure (by measuring oxygen consumption), the obese boys, by virtue of their heavier weights, expended more calories through exercise than did thin boys.

Commenting on this research, Brownell (1982) has suggested that inactivity may be as much a consequence as a cause of obesity in children. Obesity in children has been linked consistently to low fitness levels (Epstein, Koeske, Zidansek, & Wing, 1983). Poor fitness may result both from inactivity and from the work "overload" caused by excess body weight. Simulating obesity by adding external weights to a thin person can produce the kind of impaired fitness performance found for obese individuals (Epstein et al., 1983; Hanson, 1973).

The addition of an exercise component to behavioral weight loss programs appears to have several beneficial effects. Exercise is thought to enhance weight loss by increasing calorie expenditure (Christakis et al., 1966; Epstein & Wing, 1980; Jokl, 1969) and via its effects on basal metabolism and appetite suppression (Mayer, 1968). Exercise appears to increase the loss of fat while minimizing the loss of lean tissue (McArdle, Katch, & Katch, 1981; Moody, Wilmore, Girandola, & Royce, 1972). Exercise in children and adolescents has also been found to have a positive influence on such health factors as blood pressure (Brownell, Kelman, & Stunkard, 1983) and on psychosocial functioning (Foreyt & Goodrick, 1988).

Our assessment of baseline caloric output is most frequently accomplished through a daily activity record. Usually the child alone (or, if too young, with the aid of the parents) monitors brief daily routines and more prolonged activities. Periods of inactivity are also sometimes monitored.

Exercise programs for children may take several forms (LeBow, 1984). Regular aerobic exercise is necessary for demonstrating appreciable effects of body fat and fitness level (Foreyt & Goodrick, 1981). However, because many overweight children are in poor physical condition, we find that it is usually best if they begin by gradually increasing the amount of exercise required by everyday activities (Brownell & Stunkard, 1980; Foreyt & Kondo, 1983). We do this by targeting a number of daily routines for modification. For example, if children live within a reasonable distance of school, we ask them to walk or ride a bike instead of taking a bus or riding in a car. Or we encourage them to assist with the daily household chores, such as running errands, mowing the grass, or vacuuming the carpet.

Adherence to the exercise program is an important consideration. Several excellent studies conducted by Epstein and colleagues investigated the long-term effects of different types of exercise programs on children's weight and exercise habits. In one study, Epstein, Wing, Koeske, Ossip, and Beck (1982) compared the effects of isocaloric life style and programmed aerobic exercise programs on weight loss in children 8–12 years of age. Results showed equal effects of life style and aerobic exercise during the initial 8-week treatment, with the aerobic program producing better fitness effects. However, by 6 months, and continuing to the 17-month follow-up, subjects in the life style group continued to lose weight and improve their fitness scores, whereas effects of the aerobic program deteriorated. The most probable reason for the differences found by the authors was better adherence in the life style group than in the aerobic group.

The comparison of life style versus aerobic exercise was replicated in a study that added a low-intensity calisthenics group to control for nonspecific aspects of participating in an exercise program (Epstein, Wing, Koeske, & Valoski, 1985). Each group also received a dietary intervention in addition to one of the three exercise interventions. The results of this study showed no differences in relative weight change at 12 months, but at 24 months the life style group (–18.0%) had lost significantly more than the programmed aerobic group (–6.8%) or the calisthenics group (–7.2%).

Findings from these and other studies indicate that exercise intensity is an important factor in predicting exercise nonadherence, particularly for children (Epstein et al., 1984). The inclusion of a variety of activities that children can incorporate into their lives may be a necessary condition for exercise to be continued after treatment. Increasing activity levels in a slow but progressive fashion allows for the development of skills and attitudes necessary for regular participation and enjoyment in more rigorous exercise.

Treatment for Young Children

Most research in childhood obesity has focused on preadolescent and adolescent obesity (Epstein, 1986). Only a few large-scale controlled studies of treatments for young children have been reported. One of the earliest studies compared the effectiveness of a "prudent diet" versus an untreated control for children between the ages of 3 months and 3 years (Piscano, Lichter, Ritter, & Siegal, 1978). Following treatment, only 1% of the treatment group was obese, compared to 29% of the control group.

More recently, Epstein and his colleagues (Epstein, 1986; Epstein, Valoski, Koeske, & Wing, 1986; Epstein, Wing, Woodall, et al., 1985; Epstein et al., 1984) modified a behavioral family-based treatment program originally developed and tested with preadolescents for use with 5- to 8-year-old children. In one study (Epstein, Wing, & Valoski, 1985), parents and children were randomly assigned to one of two treatment groups. Both received the same information on diet and exercise, but the behavioral group also received information on parent management and social learning principles. Parent management strategies were used to promote habit change, although children were given responsibility for some aspects of treatment (e.g., self-monitoring, goal setting, and self-reinforcement), depending on their age. Results indicated better weight loss for children in the behavioral intervention at 8 and 12 months, at which time 47% of the children were less than 20% over ideal weight. Children in the behavioral group had an average reduction of 25.3% in their percentage of overweight, 2.4 times the change observed for the instructional group (–11.2%).

In the same sample of obese 5- to 8-year-olds, Epstein and colleagues (Epstein *et al.*, 1984) investigated the effectiveness of behavioral treatment for increasing activity level. Children in the treatment group were alternately reinforced for increasing activity or sharing, and their activity levels were compared during treatment and reversal phases and to the activity levels of the control group. Behavioral observations of activity showed clear effects of the sequential treatment phases, and caloric expenditure was reliably increased both during and after the enhanced activity.

Among the youngest children reported in the behavioral literature were a group only 14–70 months old, with an average age of 4.1 years (Epstein *et al.*, 1986). Weight and growth were carefully monitored, as was nutrient intake during treatment. Parents also tended to be obese, with mothers averaging 38.4% and fathers 32.9% overweight. Participants attended 10 weekly and 10 monthly meetings over the course of the 1-year program. Parents and children were seen separately for instruction in diet, exercise, and behavioral principles. Results indicated significant differences in children's percentage of overweight, from an initial level of 42% to 26.8% after 2 months and to 22.5% after 6 months, with maintenance of the decreased relative weight at 1 year. A nonsignificant increase in height percentile during the year suggested that the growth changes were appropriate for the children's age.

Results of these and previous studies have prompted Epstein to develop a four-stage model for the treatment of childhood obesity that takes into consideration the child's age, developmental capabilities, and parental influence (Epstein, 1986). As children develop, responsibility for habit change is shifted from the parent to the child—from Stage 1 (ages 1–5), in which most or all responsibility is given to the parent, to Stage 4 (adolescents), in which responsibility is the adolescent's with appropriate support from the parents.

The Role of the Family

The Family's Role in Obesity

Epidemiological research indicates that a child's probability of being obese is 80% if both parents are obese and 40% if one parent is obese (Garn & Clark, 1976). Although genetic factors undoubtedly contribute to this association (see Stunkard, Foch, & Hrubec, 1986; Stunkard,

Sorensen, *et al.*, 1986), environmental variables are known to play a role as well (Baranowski & Nader, 1985a, 1985b). Garn and Clark (1976) have suggested that the mechanisms by which the family environment contributes to childhood obesity primarily involve "similarities in caloric intake, caloric expenditures, and attitudes toward food and eating" (p. 454).

A number of behavioral factors within the family may contribute to the development of obesity in children. One way in which parents influence children's eating habits is through the foods that they make available to them. Using multidimensional scaling techniques to investigate the salient dimensions of preschool children's food preferences, Birch (1979a, 1979b) found that 50% of the variance in preferences was explained by familiarity, twice that explained by the next most salient dimension, sweetness. These results were replicated in a second study, and the correlation between children's preferences and consumption (.80) was considerably higher than the relationship reported in studies using adult subjects. When the data were analyzed separately by age group, familiarity accounted for the greatest proportion of the variance in the preference of 3-year-olds, whereas sweetness was the most salient dimension for 4-year-olds.

Birch and her colleagues also demonstrated that children's food preferences are influenced by environmental conditions. In one study, children's attitudes toward specific foods changed from negative to positive following peer modeling (Birch, 1980). Preferences were also enhanced for novel foods by repeated exposure to the initially neutral foods (Birch & Marlin, 1982), by presenting foods as rewards, and by pairing the presentation of foods with adult attention (Birch, Zimmerman, & Hind, 1980). Conversely, when food was eaten in order to obtain a reward, decrements in preference were noted (Birch, Birch, Marlin, & Kramer, 1982). Because the use of sweets as rewards is a common practice in our culture, these results are worthy of attention. They suggest that the use of dessert as a reward for eating one's vegetables will have the opposite effect of that intended. Rather than teaching children to eat their vegetables, this practice may result in children's developing a greater preference for dessert and a lesser preference for vegetables.

Parental food prompts have also been related

to obesity in children. Waxman and Stunkard (1980) found that mothers gave larger food portions to their obese children than to their nonobese children. Observations in the homes of families with both obese and nonobese children indicated that parents encouraged their obese offspring to eat more frequently and gave them more food prompts than they did to their normal-weight children (Klesges et al., 1983; Klesges, Malott, Boschee, & Weber, 1986). Similarly, parents encouraged less physical activity in obese children than in their nonobese siblings (Klesges et al., 1984; Klesges et al., 1986).

Parents also serve as models for child behavior. Harper and Sanders (1975) compared the effectiveness of mothers and strangers as models on children's willingness to sample novel foods. Modeling was more effective for younger children than for older children, and mothers were more effective than strangers. Results also indicated that children were more likely to eat a novel food when the adult modeled eating than when the adult prompted the child to eat the food. Modeling also influences children's exercise behavior. Griffiths and Payne (1976) found that the energy expended on physical activity by children of obese parents was only half that expended by children of nonobese parents. This finding was independent of the children's own body weight.

The Family's Role in Treatment

Evidence of the influence of parents on children's eating and exercise patterns has encouraged researchers to investigate the role of the family in the treatment of childhood obesity. Results of these studies have produced mixed results, suggesting that the role of the family is more complex than initially assumed (Foreyt & Kondo, 1983).

The earliest behavioral studies to include family members (e.g., Aragona, Cassady, & Drabman, 1975; Kingsley & Shapiro, 1977; Wheeler & Hess, 1976) taught parents to implement changes in the diet and exercise habits of their children. Following Kingsley and Shapiro's finding of an unexpected effect of weight loss in mothers included in children's treatment, subsequent studies included parents in the weight loss process itself, and found significant relationships between child and parent weight change (Epstein & Wing, 1980; Epstein et al., 1982).

In order to compare the effects of modeling with the effects of support, Israel, Stolmaker, Sharp, Silverman, and Simon (1984) allowed parents of 8- to 12-year-olds to choose either a weight loss condition or a helper condition. Parents in the weight loss condition contracted to lose weight by following a program parallel to their child's (modeling), whereas parents in the helper condition focused on improving their supportive skills, monitoring, and contracting for rewards based on the performance of helping behaviors (support). The two conditions were equally successful in producing weight loss in subjects during treatment and at a 1-year follow-up, and both were superior to a waiting-list control. Developmental differences were observed, however: The weight loss condition produced better results for the younger subjects, whereas the supportive role appeared to improve weight loss in the older subjects.

Training parents in problem-solving techniques may also increase the effectiveness of behavioral interventions with obese children. Coyne, Meyers, and Clark (1985) compared obese 6- to 12-year-old overweight children who were given one of three treatments: a problem-solving intervention, a traditional behavioral intervention, or an instruction-only intervention. In the problem-solving condition, children and parents received nutrition information and behavioral weight loss methods, and the parents were instructed in problem-solving strategies that would facilitate the implementation and maintenance of the behavioral techniques. Subjects in the behavioral group received the same nutrition information and behavioral techniques without the problem-solving training, and those in the instruction-only condition received only the nutrition information. Results of the 3- and 6-month measurements indicated that subjects in the problem-solving condition achieved greater weight loss at 3 months and were more successful at maintaining weight loss at 6 months. Parental problem-solving skills may be especially beneficial in helping parents identify relapse situations and implement additional strategies to maintain treatment gains.

Studies with adolescents also indicate potentially beneficial effects of parental involvement. Coates and Thoresen (1981) compared three single-subject interventions, two of which involved family participation in behavioral strategies. The two experimental participants demonstrated significant weight loss, whereas the control subject gained. However, it was not clear whether family involvement or behavioral techniques were responsible for the weight loss. Using similar behavioral techniques, Coates, Killen, and Slinkard (1982) found no differences in weight loss between a group with parent participation and a group without such participation.

Brownell et al. (1983) demonstrated the importance of developmental issues in a study comparing three types of parent–child involvement in adolescent weight loss. In one group, parents and children were trained together; in another, parents and children were trained separately; and in a third, children were trained alone. Subjects in the parent–child separate training group achieved the greatest posttreatment weight loss, and maintained this weight loss at 1-year follow-up. Brownell et al. suggested that one of the reasons for the superior performance of the parent–child separate group involved the developmental process in adolescence of separating from the parent and establishing an independent identity. By meeting separately, the adolescents were allowed sufficient freedom from their parents, but also were provided with parents who were informed about and involved in resolving the weight problem.

Treatment in Other Settings

Another way in which social support has been used in the behavioral treatment of obesity is in the development of programs for school settings (Brownell, 1983). Several school programs with children and adolescents have demonstrated significant weight losses by combining nutrition education, exercise, behavior modification, peer counselors, and psychological support (e.g., Botvin, Cantlon, Carter, & Williams, 1979; Brownell & Kaye, 1982; Foster, Wadden, & Brownell, 1985; Lansky & Brownell, 1982; Zakus, Chin, Cooper, Makovsky, & Merrill, 1981).

One advantage of treating obesity in the schools is the large number of children who can be reached at a minimal cost to their families. Another advantage is the ability to involve many children in treatment before their obesity becomes severe. The problem may be better approached in an educational setting than in a medical setting (Seltzer & Mayer, 1965).

School-based programs have also been designed to facilitate the involvement and support of family and peers outside of the school (Brownell & Kaye, 1982).

In one school-based program, Lansky and Brownell (1982) found that different approaches may be needed for different children. They found that very obese adolescents achieved greater weight loss when given structured and systematic assignments and concrete incentives in a behavioral program, and did poorly in an exercise and nutrition instructional program lacking these elements. These elements may be less important to moderately overweight students. The long-term effectiveness of school-based programs, however, has not yet been addressed.

Summer camps are another context in which eating and exercise behavior change programs have been implemented (Brandt, Maschhoff, & Chandler, 1980; Epstein et al., 1984; Southam, Kirkley, Murchison, & Berkowitz, 1984). The advantages of a camp setting for weight loss are that it provides an excellent opportunity for intensive treatment and a supportive environment in which to practice changes in eating, exercise, and social behavior.

A program developed for use in either a 4-week or an 8-week day camp conducted by Southam et al. (1984) included four components: behavior modification, aerobic exercise, sports skills instruction, and an eating laboratory. In addition, counselors met with parents weekly to encourage a support system outside the program environment. At posttest, treatment improvements were noted in weight, percentage of overweight, and skinfold, with greater changes observed for the 8-week than for the 4-week group. Of equal note, the attrition rate was 0%, and daily attendance was high. The authors speculated that this was related to the high level of satisfaction with the program reported by campers and parents. A summer camp setting also may be an appropriate setting for the treatment of obesity in young (5- to 8-year-old) children, according to results obtained by Epstein and colleagues (Epstein et al., 1984; Epstein, Wing, Woodall, Penner, Kress, & Koeske, 1985). Further work is needed to investigate those aspects of treatment (e.g., the setting itself, the length of the sessions, the support of peers and family, or components of the program itself) that most closely relate to treatment outcome.

IMPLICATIONS AND CONCLUSION

Behavior therapy is a relatively recent approach in the treatment of obesity in children and adolescents. Results of the studies conducted in this field suggest few conclusions but many questions. Whereas behavioral programs appear to be more successful than previous approaches, results have been modest at best. Few children achieve goal weight, and findings are not always consistent regarding the effectiveness of various strategies. In addition, successful maintenance of weight loss has yet to be demonstrated on a consistent basis.

Several issues need to be addressed if the situation is to improve. We believe that one problem is the absence of developmental theory in most of the research on the treatment of obesity in children—a problem that characterizes much of child clinical work in general (Gelfand & Peterson, 1985). Rather than being developed for use with children, most of the behavioral techniques used in these programs were originally developed for use with adults, then modified for children. The studies that have addressed developmental issues have typically done so in a post hoc fashion. We find that a more appropriate and productive approach is to use the developmental literature to generate and test hypotheses regarding the effects of social and cognitive development on such treatment issues as compliance, comprehension of instructions, peer support, parental involvement, self-regulation, and outcome. Epstein's (1986) stage model of treatment for children is a first step in this direction. Prospective observational studies of childhood obesity are currently underway in several locations, and we may hope that they will contribute to a developmental understanding of this problem.

The inclusion of the family in weight loss programs for children shows great promise (Baranowski & Nader, 1985b). However, it also raises many issues that are only now beginning to be addressed in the behavioral weight loss literature. We think that the most serious problem inherent in family-based weight loss programs is the lack of a theoretical framework for guiding research and treatment. Using the family as the unit of study is a relatively recent development, and is most apparent in the family therapy literature.

In a family systems perspective, the family is viewed as a natural system, in which the behavior of any family member is seen as but one part of a series of interrelated and interactive processes within the family. Thus, symptomatic behavior of one member belongs not to the individual but to the whole family. In addition, such behavior is seen as serving some function for the family. Treatment requires changing the pattern of family interaction in which symptomatic behavior is embedded, and helping the family find another way of managing.

Investigations are few in which the family is the unit of study. Marshall and Neill (1977) report an example of a more systemic perspective on adult obesity in a study of the effects of intestinal bypass surgery on a group of extremely obese women. Weight loss was considerable, but equally dramatic was the degree of conflict and disruption observed in the women's marriages. The authors suggest that in these cases the obesity served an important function in stabilizing the marital system.

Several studies have investigated the characteristics of families in which there is an obese child or adolescent. Bromberg (1977) found that obese families made less unanimous and more chaotic decisions than nonobese families. Bullen, Monello, Cohen, and Mayer (1963) found a similar pattern of results in families of obese and nonobese adolescent girls. Hammar et al. (1972) found that families of obese adolescents were socially isolated, with members relying on each other for company, and that the obese adolescent occupied a "Cinderella-like" role in the family, serving as scapegoat for the frustrations and anger of parents and siblings. The results of these three studies should be viewed with caution, however, as each relied on self-report methods. The need for direct observational methods in the assessment of the family has been noted by family researchers (Cromwell, Olson, & Fournier, 1976), and such methods are necessary before conclusions can be drawn regarding any specific characteristics of obese families.

With a few exceptions (c.f., Barbarin & Tirado, 1984), family therapists and family researchers have paid little attention to obesity. However, they have shown great interest in the area of childhood psychosomatic disorders (Loader, 1985). Minuchin in particular has investigated families of psychosomatic children (Minuchin et al., 1975; Minuchin, Rosman, &

Baker, 1978). Although Minuchin has not written specifically on the subject of obesity, his work should be considered in this context, because obesity is often referred to as a psychosomatic disorder and fits in well with Minuchin's definition of this category of disease. Although there are probably predisposing biological factors, they appear to be less deterministic than recent theories have suggested, and within a systems perspective they should be conceptualized within the relationship context (Ganley, 1986).

Four characteristics in organization and functioning describe Minuchin's "psychosomatic family": (1) enmeshment, (2) overprotection, (3) rigidity, and (4) lack of conflict resolution. Members of these families tend to be overly interdependent, to be overly concerned for one another's welfare, to be fearful of change, and to rely on a variety of mechanisms to insure that conflicts are unacknowledged or unresolved. These interaction patterns have been hypothesized to encourage "the transformation of emotional conflicts into somatic symptoms" (Minuchin et al., 1975, p. 1033). The symptomatic child, and the symptom itself, have been found to play roles in diffusing family conflict and maintaining family homeostasis.

Minuchin views effective treatment of psychosomatic disorders as changing the pattern of family behavior, in addition to providing medical attention for the sick child. Using specifically developed family therapy techniques for these families, he has reported impressive results with cases of poorly controlled diabetes, asthma, and anorexia nervosa (Minuchin et al., 1975, 1978).

We feel that the lack of family studies of childhood obesity may be partially the result of researchers' unwillingness to tackle the methodological problems involved in the study of family functioning and family interaction. It is more likely, though, that the relative absence of family theory in the behavioral literature on obesity reflects fundamental differences in assumptions, methods, and goals that historically have separated behavioral and family systems perspectives. As a result, the family therapy literature has been neglected as a source of theoretical and practical ideas for health behavior change programs in families. The "role of the family" typically translates as the "role of the mother." Our recent reviews of this literature were unable to document a single controlled study in which entire families served as the focus for behavioral treatment of obesity (Foreyt & Cousins, 1987; Kondo & Foreyt, 1987).

Other challenges await the researcher and practitioner. Attrition has been a consistently difficult problem in weight loss programs, yet recent reports indicate that a good fit between treatment and subject can dramatically reduce the number of dropouts (e.g., Southam et al., 1984). Recent findings suggest that the more individualized the treatment, the greater the likelihood of success. On a related note, the degree of choice or control that subjects perceive themselves to have appears to have significantly positive effects on both immediate and long-term treatment outcome. The differences between short-term and long-term, or maintenance, strategies are just beginning to be explored with children and adolescents.

Obesity is a serious physical and psychological health hazard for children. Weight loss is a difficult endeavor, and for many an unsuccessful one. If we are to improve our modest treatment results to date, we believe that attention should be directed increasingly to the issues described above.

Acknowledgment

Preparation of this chapter was supported in part by Grant No. 1 R01 HL33954-02 from the National Heart, Lung and Blood Institute, National Institutes of Health, Bethesda, Maryland.

REFERENCES

Abraham, S., Collins, G., & Nordsieck, M. (1971). Relationship of childhood weight status to morbidity in adults. *Public Health Reports, 86,* 273–284.

Allon, N. (1980). Sociological aspects of overweight youth. In P. J. Collipp (Ed.), *Childhood obesity* (2nd ed., pp. 139–156). Littleton, MA: PSG.

Aragona, J., Cassady, J., & Drabman, R. S. (1975). Treating overweight children through parental training and contingency contracting. *Journal of Applied Behavior Analysis, 8,* 269–278.

Bandura, A. (1971). Psychotherapy based on modeling principles. In A. E. Bergin & S. L. Garfield (Eds.), *Handbook of psychotherapy and behavior change: An empirical analysis* (pp. 653–708). New York: Wiley.

Baranowski, T., & Nader, P. R. (1985a). Family health behavior. In D. Turk & R. Kerns (Ed.), *Health, illness and families: A life-span perspective* (pp. 51–80). New York: Wiley.

Baranowski, T., & Nader, P. (1985b). Family involvement in health behavior change programs. In D. Turk & R. Kerns (Eds.), *Health, illness and families: A life-span perspective* (pp. 81–107). New York: Wiley.

Barbarin, O. A., & Tirado, M. C. (1984). Family involvement and successful treatment of obesity: A review. *Family Systems Medicine, 2,* 37–45.

Birch, L. L. (1979a). Dimensions of preschool children's food preferences. *Journal of Nutrition Education, 11,* 77–80.

Birch, L. L. (1979b). Preschool children's food preferences and consumption patterns. *Journal of Nutrition Education, 11* 189–192.

Birch, L. L. (1980a). Effects of peer models' food choices and eating behaviors on preschoolers' food preferences. *Child Development, 51,* 489–496.

Birch, L. L., Birch, D., Marlin, D. W., & Kramer, L. (1982). Effects of instrumental consumption on children's food preferences. *Appetite, 3,* 125–134.

Birch, L. L., & Marlin, D. W. (1982). I don't like it; I never tried it: Effects of exposure on two-year-old children's food preferences. *Appetite, 3,* 353–360.

Birch, L. L., Zimmerman, S. I., & Hind, H. (1980). The influence of social-affective context on the formation of children's food preferences. *Child Development, 51,* 856–861.

Botvin, G. J., Cantlon, A., Carter, B. J., & Williams, C. L. (1979). Reducing adolescent obesity through a school health program. *Journal of Pediatrics, 95,* 1060–1062.

Boulton, J. (1981). Physical fitness in childhood and its relationships to age, maturity, body size, and nutritional factors. *Acta Paediatrica Scandinivica,* (Suppl. 284), 80–85.

Brandt, G., Maschhoff, T., & Chandler, N. S. (1980). A residential camp experience as an approach to adolescent weight management. *Adolescence, 15,* 807–822.

Bray, G. A. (1976). *The obese patient.* Philadelphia: W. B. Saunders.

Bromberg, D. R. (1977). Family dominance patterns and the decision-making process in obese and nonobese families. *Dissertation Abstracts International, 37,* 3597.

Brownell, K. D. (1981). Assessment of eating disorders. In D. H. Barlow (Ed.), *Behavioral assessment of adult disorders* (pp. 329–404). New York: Guilford Press.

Brownell, K. D. (1982). Obesity: Understanding and treating a serious, prevalent, and refractory disorder. *Journal of Consulting and Clinical Psychology, 50,* 820–840.

Brownell, K. D. (1983). New developments in the treatment of obese children and adolescents. *Psychiatric Annals, 13,* 878–883.

Brownell, K. D., & Kaye, F. S. (1982). A school-based behavioral modification, nutrition education and physical activity program for obese children. *American Journal of Clinical Nutrition, 35,* 277–283.

Brownell, K. D., Kelman, J. H., & Stunkard, A. J. (1983). Treatment of obese children with and without their mothers: Changes in weight and blood pressure. *Pediatrics, 71,* 515–523.

Brownell, K. D., & Stunkard, A. J. (1980). Behavioral treatment for obese children and adolescents. In A. J. Stunkard (Ed.), *Obesity* (pp. 415–437). Philadelphia: W. B. Saunders.

Bullen, B. A., Monello, L. F., Cohen, H., & Mayer, J. (1963). Attitudes towards physical activity, food and family in obese and nonobese adolescent girls. *American Journal of Clinical Nutrition, 12,* 1–11.

Cahnman, W. J. (1968). The stigma of obesity. *Sociological Quarterly, 9,* 283–299.

Canning, H., & Mayer, J. (1966). Obesity: Its possible effect on college acceptance. *New England Journal of Medicine, 275,* 1172–1174.

Carrera, F. (1967). Obesity in adolescence. *Psychosomatics, 8,* 342–349.

Cautela, J. R. (1971). Covert conditioning. In A. Jacobs & L. B. Sachs (Eds.), *The psychology of private events: Perspectives on covert response systems* (pp. 109–130). New York: Academic Press.

Christakis, G., Sajecki, S., Hillman, R. W., Miller, E., Blumenthal, S., & Archer, M. (1966). Effect of a combined nutrition education and physical fitness program on the weight status of obese high school boys. *Federation Proceedings, 25,* 15–19.

Clarke, R. P., Merrow, S. B., Morse, E. H., & Keyser, D. E. (1970). Interrelationships between plasma lipids, physical measurements, and body fatness of adolescents in Burlington, Vermont. *American Journal of Clinical Nutrition, 23,* 754–763.

Coates, T. J., Killen, J. D., & Slinkard, L. E. (1982). Parent participation in a treatment program for overweight adolescents. *International Journal of Eating Disorders, 1,* 37–48.

Coates, T. J., & Thoresen, C. E. (1981). Behavior and weight changes in three obese adolescents. *Behavior Therapy, 12,* 383–399.

Cohen, E. A., Gelfand, D. M., Dodd, D. K., Jensen, J., & Turner, C. (1980). Self-control practices associated with weight loss maintenance in children and adolescents. *Behavior Therapy, 11,* 26–37.

Cole, P. M., & Kazdin, A. E. (1980). Critical issues in self instruction training with children. *Child Behavior Therapy, 2,* 1–23.

Colley, J. R. T. (1974). Obesity in schoolchildren. *British Journal of Preventative and Social Medicine, 28,* 221–225.

Corbin, C. B., & Pletcher, P. (1968). Diet and physical activity patterns of obese and nonobese elementary school children. *Research Quarterly, 39,* 922–928.

Court, J. M., Hill, G. J., Dunlop, M., & Boulton, T. J. C. (1974). Hypertension in childhood obesity. *Australian Paediatric Journal, 10,* 296–300.

Coyne, T., Meyers, A., & Clark, L. (1985, November). *Behavioral treatment for obese children: Does parental problem solving solve the problem?* Paper presented at the meeting of the American Association of Behavior Therapists, Houston, TX.

Cromwell, R. E., Olson, D. H. L., & Fournier, D. G. (1976). Tools and techniques for diagnosis and evaluation in marital and family therapy. *Family Process, 15,* 1–49.

DeBakey, M. E., Gotto, A. M., Jr., Scott, L. W., & Foreyt, J. P. (1984). *The living heart diet.* New York: Raven Press.

Dietz, W. H., Jr., & Gortmaker, S. L. (1984). Factors within the physical environment associated with childhood obesity. *American Journal of Clinical Nutrition, 39,* 619–624.

Dietz, W. H., Jr., & Gortmaker, S. L. (1985). Do we fatten our children at the TV set? Obesity and television viewing in children and adolescents. *Pediatrics, 75,* 807–812.

Drabman, R. S., Cordua, G. D., Hammer, D., Jarvie, G. J., & Horton, W. (1979). Developmental trends in eating rates of normal and overweight preschool children. *Child Development, 50,* 211–216.

Drash, A. (1973). Relationship between diabetes mellitus and obesity in the child. *Metabolism, 22,* 337–344.

Dwyer, J. (1973). Psychosexual aspects of weight control and dieting behavior in adolescence. *Medical Aspects of Human Sexuality, 7,* 82–108.

Dwyer, J., & Mayer, J. (1975). The dismal condition: Problems faced by obese adolescent girls in American society. In G. R. Bray (Ed.), *Obesity in perspective* (DHEW Publication No. NIH 75-708, Vol. 2, Part 2, pp. 103–110). Washington, DC: U.S. Government Printing Office.

Ellis, A. (1962). *Reason and emotion in psychotherapy.* Secaucus, NJ: Lyle Stuart.

Epstein, L. H. (1986). Treatment of childhood obesity. In K. D. Brownell & J. P. Foreyt (Eds.), *Handbook of eating disorders: Physiology, psychology, and treatment of obesity, anorexia, and bulimia* (pp. 159–179). New York: Basic Books.

Epstein, L. H., Koeske, R., Zidansek, J., & Wing, R. R. (1983). Effects of weight loss on fitness in obese children. *American Journal of Diseases of Children, 137,* 654–657.

Epstein, L. H., Valoski, A., Koeske, R., & Wing, R. R. (1986). Family-based behavioral weight control in obese young children. *Journal of the American Dietetic Association, 86,* 481–484.

Epstein, L. H., & Wing, R. R. (1980). Aerobic exercise and weight. *Addictive Behaviors, 5,* 371–388.

Epstein, L. H., Wing, R. R., Koeske, R., Ossip, D., & Beck, S. (1982). A comparison of lifestyle changes and programmed aerobic exercise on weight and fitness changes in obese children. *Behavior Therapy, 13,* 651–665.

Epstein, L. H., Wing, R. R., Koeske, R., & Valoski, A. (1985). A comparison of lifestyle exercise, aerobic exercise, and calisthenics on weight loss in obese children. *Behavior Therapy, 16B,* 345–356.

Epstein, L. H., Wing, R. R., & Valoski, A. (1985). Childhood obesity. *Pediatric Clinics of North America, 32,* 363–379.

Epstein, L. H., Wing, R. R., Woodall, K., Penner, B. C., Kress, M. J., & Koeske, R. (1985). Effects of family-based behavioral treatment on obese 5-to-8-year-old children. *Behavior Therapy, 16,* 205–212.

Epstein, L. H., Woodall, K., Goreczny, A. J., Wing, R. R., & Robertson, R. J. (1984). The modification of activity patterns and energy expenditures in obese young girls. *Behavior Therapy, 15,* 101–108.

Fagan, S. A., Long, N. J., & Stevens, D. J. (1975). *Teaching children self control: Preventing emotional and learning problems in the elementary school.* Columbus, OH: Charles E. Merrill.

Foreyt, J. P. (1987). Issues in the assessment and treatment of obesity. *Journal of Consulting and Clinical Psychology, 55,* 677–684.

Foreyt, J. P., & Cousins, J. H. (1987). Obesity. In M. Hersen & V. B. Van Hasselt (Eds.), *Behavior therapy with children and adolescents: A clinical approach* (pp. 485–511). New York: Wiley.

Foreyt, J. P., & Goodrick, G. K. (1981). Childhood obesity. In E. J. Mash & L. G. Terdal (Eds.), *Behavioral assessment of childhood disorders* (pp. 573–599). New York: Guilford Press.

Foreyt, J. P., & Goodrick, G. K. (1988). Childhood obesity. In E. J. Mash & L. G. Terdal (Eds.), *Behavioral assessment of childhood disorders* (2nd ed., pp. 528–551). New York: Guilford Press.

Foreyt, J. P., Goodrick, G. K., & Gotto, A. M. (1981). Limitations of behavioral treatment of obesity: Review and analysis. *Journal of Behavioral Medicine, 4,* 159–174.

Foreyt, J. P., & Kondo, A. T. (1983). Cognitive-

behavioral treatment of childhood and adolescent obesity. In A. Ellis & M. E. Bernard (Eds.), *Rational–emotive approaches to the problems of childhood* (pp. 271–309). New York: Plenum.

Foster, G. D., Wadden, T. A., & Brownell, K. D. (1985). Peer-led program for the treatment and prevention of obesity in the schools. *Journal of Consulting and Clinical Psychology, 53,* 538–540.

Franzini, L. R., & Grimes, W. B. (1976). Skinfold measures as the criterion of change in weight control studies. *Behavior Therapy, 7,* 256–260.

Ganley, R. M. (1986). Epistemology, family patterns, and psychosomatics: The case of obesity. *Family Process, 25,* 437–451.

Garn, S. M. (1986). Family-line and socioeconomic factors in fatness and obesity. *Nutrition Reviews, 44,* 381–386.

Garn, S. M., & Clark, D. C. (1976). Trends in fatness and the origins of obesity: Ad hoc committee to review the ten-state nutrition survey. *Pediatrics, 57,* 443–456.

Garn, S. M., Clark, D. C., & Guire, K. E. (1975). Growth, body composition, and development of obese and lean children. In M. Winick (Ed.), *Childhood obesity* (pp. 23–46). New York: Wiley.

Gelfand, D., & Peterson, L. (1985). *Child development and psychopathology.* Beverly Hills, CA: Sage.

Giotto, M. I. (1980). The effect of peer support upon ideal weight attainment and the self-concept of adolescent girls involved in a multidimensional physical education program. *Dissertation Abstracts International, 40,* 4413A–4414A.

Goodman, N., Richardson, S. A., Dornbusch, S. M., & Hastorf, A. H. (1963). Variant reactions to physical disabilities. *American Sociological Review, 28,* 429–435.

Gortmaker, S. L., Dietz, W. H., Sobol, A. M., & Wehler, C. A. (1987). Increasing pediatric obesity in the United States. *Amerian Journal of Diseases of Children, 141,* 535–540.

Griffiths, M., & Payne, P. R. (1976). Energy expenditure in small children of obese and nonobese patients. *Nature, 260,* 698–700.

Grimes, W. B. & Franzini, L. R. (1977). Skinfold measurement techniques for estimating percentage body fat. *Journal of Behavior Therapy and Experimental Psychiatry, 8,* 65–59.

Hall, S. H., & Cousins, J. H. (1987). *Perceptual agreement between Mexican-American mothers and daughters in judgments of body size and attractiveness.* Manuscript submitted for publication.

Hammar, S. L., Campbell, M. M., Campbell, A., Moores, N. L., Sareen, C., Gareis, F. J., & Lucas, B. (1972). An interdisciplinary study of obesity. *Journal of Pediatrics, 80,* 373–383.

Hanson, J. S. (1973). Exercise responses following production of experimental obesity. *Journal of Applied Physiology, 35,* 587–591.

Harper, L. V., & Sanders, K. M. (1975). The effect of adults' eating on young children's acceptance of unfamiliar foods. *Journal of Experimental Child Psychology, 20,* 206–214.

Hathaway, M. L., & Sargent, D. W. (1962). Overweight in children: Relationship to height and age. *Journal of the American Dietetic Association, 40,* 511–515.

Hendry, L. B., & Gillies, P. (1978). Body type, body esteem, school, and leisure: A study of overweight, average, and underweight adolescents. *Journal of Youth and Adolescence, 7,* 181–195.

Homme, L. E. (1965). Perspectives in psychology: XXIV. Control of coverants, the operants of the mind. *Psychological Record, 15,* 501–511.

Israel, A. C., & Stolmaker, L. (1980). Behavioral treatment of obesity in children and adolescents. In M. Hersen, R. M. Eisler, & P. M. Miller (Eds.), *Progress in behavior modification* (Vol. 10, pp. 82–109). New York: Academic Press.

Israel, A. C., Stolmaker, L., Sharp, J. P., Silverman, W. K., & Simon, L. G. (1984). An evaluation of two methods of parental involvement in treating obese children. *Behavior Therapy, 15,* 266–272.

Iwawaki, S., Lerner, R. M., & Chihara, T. (1977). Development of personal space schemata among Japanese in late childhood. *Psychologia, 20,* 89–97.

Johnson, W. G., & Stalonas, P. (1977). Measuring skinfold thickness—A cautionary note. *Addictive Behaviors, 2,* 105–107.

Johnston, F. E., & Mack, R. W. (1978). Obesity, stature, and one year relative weight of 15-year-old youths. *Human Biology, 52,* 35–41.

Jokl, E. (1969). *Exercise, nutrition, and body composition.* Springfield, IL: Charles C. Thomas.

Kannel, W. B., & Dawber, T. R. (1972). Atherosclerosis as a pediatric problem. *Journal of Pediatrics, 80,* 544–554.

Keane, T. M., Geller, S. E., & Scheirer, C. J. (1981). A parametric investigation of eating styles in obese and nonobese children. *Behavior Therapy, 12,* 280–286.

Kendall, P. C. (1981). Cognitive behavioral interventions with children. In B. B. Lahey & A. E. Kazdin (Eds.), *Advances in clinical child psychology* (pp. 53–90). New York: Plenum Press.

Kingsley, R. G., & Shapiro, J. (1977). A comparison of three behavioral programs for the control of obesity of children. *Behavior Therapy, 8,* 30–36.

Klesges, R. C., Coates, T. J., Brown, G., Sturgeon-Tillisch, J., Moldenhauer-Klesges, L. M., Holzer, B., Woolfrey, J., & Vollmer, J. (1983). Parental influences on children's eating behavior and relative weight. *Journal of Applied Behavior Analysis, 16,* 371–378.

Klesges, R. C., Coates, T. J., Moldenhauer-Klesges, L. M., Holzer, B., Gustavson, J., & Barnes, J. (1984). The FATS: An observational system for assessing physical activity in children and associated parent behavior. *Behavioral Assessment, 6,* 333–345.

Klesges, R. C., Malott, J. M., Boschee, P. F., & Weber, J. M. (1986). Parental influences on children's food intake, physical activity and relative weight. *International Journal of Eating Disorders, 5,* 335–345.

Kondo, A. T., & Foreyt, J. P. (1987). A family perspective on weight loss and maintenance. *Health Values, 11,* 47–51.

Lansky, D., & Brownell, K. D. (1982). Comparison of school-based treatments for adolescent obesity. *Journal of School Health, 52,* 384–387.

Lauer, R. M., Conner, W. E., Leaverton, P. E., Reiter, M. A. & Clark, W. R. (1975). Coronary heart disease risk factors in school children: The Muscatine study. *The Journal of Pediatrics, 86,* 697–706.

LeBow, M. D. (1984). *Child obesity: A new frontier of behavior therapy.* New York: Springer.

Lerner, R. M. (1969). Some female stereotypes of male body build–behavior relations. *Perceptual and Motor Skills, 28,* 363–366.

Lerner, R. M. (1973). The development of personal space schemata toward body build. *Journal of Psychology, 84,* 229–235.

Lerner, R. M., Korn, S. J. (1972). The development of body-build stereotypes in males. *Child Development, 43,* 908–920.

Lerner, R. M., & Pool, K. B. (1972). Body build stereotypes: A cross-cultural comparison. *Psychological Reports, 31,* 527–532.

Loader, P. J. (1985). Childhood obesity: The family perspective. *International Journal of Eating Disorders, 4,* 211–225.

Londe, S., Bourgoignie, J. J., Robson, A. M., & Goldring, D. (1971). Hypertension in apparently normal children. *Journal of Pediatrics, 78,* 569–577.

Mahoney, M. J., & Mahoney, K. (1976). *Permanent weight control: A total solution to the dieter's dilemma.* New York: Norton.

Malina, R. M., Zavaleta, A. N., & Little, B. B. (1987). Body size, fatness, and leanness of Mexican American children in Brownsville, Texas: Changes between 1972 and 1983. *American Journal of Public Health, 77,* 573–577.

Marshall, J. R., & Neill, J. (1977). The removal of a psychosomatic symptom: Effects on the marriage. *Family Process, 16,* 273–280.

Mayer, J. (1968). *Overweight: Causes, cost, and control.* Englewood Cliffs, NJ: Prentice-Hall.

Mayer, J. (1970). Some aspects of the problem of regulating food intake and obesity. *International Psychiatry Clinics, 7,* 255–334.

Mayer, J. (1975). Obesity during childhood. In M. Winick (Ed.), *Childhood obesity* (pp. 73–80). New York: Wiley.

McArdle, W. D., Katch, F. I., & Katch, V. L. (1981). *Exercise physiology: Energy, nutrition, and human performance.* Philadelphia: Lea & Febiger.

Meichenbaum, D. (1977). *Cognitive behavior modification: An integrative approach.* New York: Plenum.

Michielutte, R., Diseker, R. A., Corbett, W. T., Schey, H. M., & Ureda, J. R. (1985). The relationship between weight–height indices and the triceps skinfold measure among children 5 to 12. *American Journal of Public Health, 74,* 604–606.

Miller, R. A., & Shekelle, R. B. (1976). Blood pressure in tenth-grade students: Results from the Chicago Heart Association pediatric heart screening project. *Circulation, 54,* 993–1000.

Miller, T. M., Coffman, J. G., & Linke, R. A. (1980). Survey on body image, weight, and diet of college students. *Journal of the American Dietetic Association, 77,* 561–566.

Minuchin, S., Baker, L. L., Rosman, B. L., Liebman, R., Milman, L., & Todd, T. C. (1975). A conceptual model of psychosomatic illness in children. *Archives of General Psychiatry, 32,* 1031–1038.

Minuchin, S., Rosman, B. L., & Baker, L. (1978). *Psychosomatic families: Anorexia nervosa in context.* Cambridge, MA: Harvard University Press.

Monello, L. F., & Mayer, J. (1963). Obese adolescent girls: An unrecognized "minority" group. *American Journal of Clinical Nutrition, 13,* 35–39.

Moody, D. L., Wilmore, J. H., Girandola, R. N., & Royce, J. P. (1972). The effects of a jogging program on the body composition of normal and obese high school girls. *Medicine and Science in Sports, 4,* 210–213.

O'Leary, S. G., & Dubey, D. R. (1979). Applications of

self-control procedures by children: A review. *Journal of Applied Behavior Analysis, 12,* 449–466.

Piscano, J. C., Lichter, H., Ritter, J., & Siegel, A. P. (1978). An attempt at prevention of obesity in infancy. *Pediatrics, 61,* 360–364.

Rose, H. E., & Mayer, J. (1968). Activity, calorie intake, fat storage, and the energy balance of infants. *Pediatrics, 41,* 18–29.

Rowe, N. R. (1980). Childhood obesity: Growth charts versus calipers. *Pediatric Nursing, 6,* 24–27.

Scholl, T. O., Karp, R. J., Theophano, J., & Decker, E. (1987). Ethnic differences in growth and nutritional status: A study of poor schoolchildren in southern New Jersey. *Public Health Reports, 102,* 278–283.

Seltzer, C. C., & Mayer, J. (1965). A simple criterion of obesity. *Postgraduate Medicine, 38,* A101–A107.

Southam, M. A., Kirkley, B. G., Murchison, A., & Berkowitz, R. I. (1984). A summer day camp approach to adolescent weight loss. *Adolescence, 19,* 855–868.

Staffieri, J. R. (1967). A study of social stereotype of body image in children. *Journal of Personality and Social Psychology, 7,* 101–104.

Staffieri, J. R. (1972). Body build and behavior expectancies in young females. *Developmental Psychology, 6,* 125–127.

Stunkard, A. J. (Ed.). (1980). *Obesity.* Philadelphia: W. B. Saunders.

Stunkard, A. J., & Burt, V. (1967). Obesity and body image: II. Age of onset in the body image. *American Journal of Psychiatry, 123,* 1443–1447.

Stunkard, A. J., Foch, T. T., & Hrubec, Z. (1986). A twin study of human obesity. *Journal of the American Medical Association, 256,* 51–54.

Stunkard, A. J., Sorensen, T. I. A., Hanis, C., Teasdale, T. W., Chakraborty, R., Schull, W. J., & Schulsinger, F. (1986). An adoption study of human obesity. *New England Journal of Medicine, 314,* 193–198.

Tanner, J. M., & Whitehouse, R. H. (1975). Revised standards for triceps and subscapular skinfolds in British children. *Archives of Disease in Childhood, 50,* 142–145.

United States Department of Health and Human Services. (1985). *Summary of findings from National Children and Youth Fitness Study.* Office of Disease Prevention and Health Promotion, Washington, DC: U.S. Government Printing Office.

Waxman, M., & Stunkard, A. J. (1980). Caloric intake and expenditure in obese boys. *Journal of Pediatrics, 96,* 187–193.

Weil, W. B., Jr. (1977). Current controversies in childhood obesity. *Journal of Pediatrics, 91,* 175–187.

Wheeler, M. E., & Hess, K. W. (1976). Treatment of juvenile obesity by successive approximation control of eating. *Journal of Behavior Therapy and Experimental Psychiatry, 7,* 235–241.

Wilkinson, P. W., Parkin, J. M., Pearlson, G., Strong, H., & Sykes, P. (1977). Energy intake and physical activity in obese children. *British Medical Journal, i,* 756.

Worsley, A. (1981). Teenagers' perceptions of fat and slim people. *International Journal of Obesity, 5,* 15–24.

Zack, P. M., Harlan, W. R., Leaverton, P. E., & Cornoni-Huntley, J. (1979). A longitudinal study of body-fatness in childhood and adolescence. *Journal of Pediatrics, 95,* 126–130.

Zakus, G., Chin, M. L., Cooper, H., Jr., Makovsky, E., & Merrill, C. (1981). Treating adolescent obesity: A pilot project in a school. *Journal of School Health, 51,* 663–666.

Zavaleta, A. N., & Malina, R. M. (1980). Growth, fatness, and leanness in Mexican American children. *American Journal of Clinical Nutrition, 33,* 2008–2020.

12

ENURESIS AND ENCOPRESIS

C. EUGENE WALKER
MARY KENNING
JAN FAUST-CAMPANILE
University of Oklahoma Health Sciences Center

F ew problems in child development concern parents more than their children's attainment of urinary and fecal continence, and few topics produce more advice or staunchly held opinions than that of proper toilet training. In Chamberlain's (1974) survey of 200 parents of preschool children asking their concerns about their children, toilet training led the list of reported worries. Parents often have questions about how and when to train and what to do if training is not progressing according to their expectations. They frequently express concern about the effects of training that is too strict, too lax, too late, or too early. As a result of their consternation, parents frequently seek the advice of professionals. Unfortunately, literature to guide parents or professionals in treating this problem is scarce, and authors often differ greatly in their recommendations (Walker, 1978).

Enuresis and encopresis represent behavioral deficits in achieving or maintaining control of eliminative functions. Both are distressing to parents and children, and for good reason. The child who has wetting or soiling accidents after entering school may feel isolated from peers who are not similarly afflicted. He or she may be teased or ostracized by classmates and adults who label incontinence as immature or infantile. The child will probably be restricted from certain activities, and enuretic children

especially may be excluded from overnight trips, camping, or sleepovers. Parents' anxiety and concern over the problem may color their view of the child or lead them to attribute accidents to planful passive aggression on the child's part.

Significant conflict may exist in the family about appropriate treatment or punishment of the child following accidents. Obviously, urinary or fecal incontinence can be quite detrimental to the child's development of appropriate self-esteem and emotional well-being. The present chapter focuses on diagnosis and effective treatment of these disorders.

ENURESIS

History

"Enuresis" is a word of Greek and Latin origin that means literally "to make water." The recognition of enuresis as a problem predates modern civilization. Glicklich (1951) reports that in 1500 B.C. a mixture of juniper berries, cypress, and beer was proposed as a remedy for the incontinence of urine. During the Middle Ages, the first book on diseases of children contained chapters on bedwetting and urinary incontinence, offering prescriptions such as groundhog flesh, the inside of a hen's stomach, and the ground cerebrum of a hare for the problem. Etiological theories offered at this time included pathology of the genital–urinary tract and neurogenesis. Often neurogenic theories implicated the sacral nerves, which were thought to require increased or decreased stimulation to prevent bedwetting. Treatments involved external medication and injections to this area of the back, as well as the more barbaric practice of burning blisters. It was originally believed that blistering would stimulate the sacral nerves, thereby decreasing enuresis. On the other hand, some believed that warmth from the bed might stimulate the sacral nerves and cause incontinence. As a result, various implements, including spikes and knotted ropes, were used to prevent children from lying on their backs during sleep. Rotating the body at different angles, including elevating the feet, pelvis, or genitals, was considered useful in retaining urine. Fortunately, more humane and effective treatment measures have been developed in the past 50 years.

Definition

"Urinary incontinence" is a general term used by many clinicians to describe voiding dysfunction, whether functional or organic in origin. "Functional enuresis" is a specific term for incontinence defined as urination in the clothing or bed beyond the age of when children should be toilet-trained and in the absence of organic pathology. According to the revised third edition of the *Diagnostic and Statistical Manual of Mental Disorders* (DSM-III-R; American Psychiatric Association, 1987), a diagnosis of Functional Enuresis requires the following: (1) repeated involuntary or intentional voiding by day or night in clothes or bed; (2) at least two such events per month for children between the ages of 5 and 6 and at least one event per month for older children; (3) chronological age at least 5 and mental age at least 4; and (4) not due to a physical disorder, such as diabetes, urinary tract infection, or seizures. The term "enuresis" may be used in cases where the incontinence is of organic origin, but many experts suggest restricting the term to cases of functional origin in order to avoid confusion.

There is much discord concerning the chronological age at which the condition can be appropriately diagnosed. The age of 5 as the earliest age for diagnosis by DSM-III-R represents a compromise between clinicians who have diagnosed the disorder in children as young as 3 and others who have deferred diagnosis until the child is 6 or 7.

The pattern of incontinence demonstrated by the child is also of interest and should be specified. "Diurnal enuresis" refers to daytime voiding in clothing. Children are considered diurnally enuretic if they continue wetting beyond the age of 3 or 4, although some clinicians would delay diagnosis until age 5 or 6. Wetting the bed at night is referred to as "nocturnal enuresis." Since normally developing children typically achieve nighttime control a year or two later than daytime control, nocturnal enuresis is not often diagnosed until age 5. Again, however, some clinicians would defer diagnosis until age 6 or 7 (de Jonge, 1973; Henderson, 1976). As noted, DSM-III-R uses age 5 as the criterion age for nocturnal and diurnal voiding accidents.

Enuresis can also be described as "primary" or "secondary," and clinicians are asked to record this information in following the DSM-III-R. In primary enuresis, also known as persistent or continuous enuresis, urinary continence lasting a year or more has not been accomplished. In secondary, discontinuous, or acquired enuresis, the child has been toilet-trained for at least a year and bladder control is subsequently lost. However, no difference in response to treatment is noted between the two types, and this distinction is largely for classification purposes (Walker, 1978).

Prevalence

Accurate estimates of the incidence and prevalence of enuresis are confounded by the lack of an established definition for this problem. However, reports estimate that about 15%–20% of 5-year-olds, 5% of 10-year-olds, and about 2% of 12- to 14-year-olds suffer from nocturnal enuresis (Lovibond & Coote, 1970; Oppel, Harper, & Rider, 1968). The rate decreases consistently until the late teen or adult years, when the percentage levels remain constant at about 1%–2% of the population (Doleys, 1977). Boys are twice as likely as girls to be nocturnally enuretic. More than 60% of nocturnally enuretic children wet the bed at least once a week or more (Verhulst *et al.*, 1985). Nighttime wetting most often occurs alone rather than in conjunction with diurnal enuresis or encopresis.

Diurnal enuresis is far less prevalent than nocturnal enuresis, with estimates reported at only about 3% of 6-year-olds in Britain and Sweden (Blomfield & Douglas, 1956; Hallgren, 1956). However, Hallgren (1956) also found that in as many as 50%–60% of the cases presenting with diurnal enuresis, nocturnal enuresis was present as well. There is some evidence suggesting that day wetting and night wetting are governed by separate psychological and physiological mechanisms. Thus, the two may readily occur independently of each other, and they appear to respond differently to treatment methods (Fielding, 1980).

When the incidence rates of primary and secondary enuresis are examined, it appears that primary enuresis accounts for approximately 85% of all cases (de Jonge, 1973). This percentage decreases with age, and only about 50% of 12-year-old enuretics have never accomplished bladder control (see Figure 12-1). As indicated by these statistics, primary nocturnal enuresis accounts for the majority of referrals in the treatment of urinary incontinence.

When enuresis is untreated, the spontaneous remission rate is 15% each year from ages 5 to 19 (Forsythe & Redmond, 1974). However, a study by Verhulst *et al.* (1985) suggested that this may be the mean remission rate primarily for boys. Results of their investigation indicate that the remission rate of enuresis is higher in girls, especially between the ages of 4 and 6, when it may reach as high as 44% to 71%. Bedwetting becomes rare in girls from the 11th year onward and in boys from the 13th year. Although it is apparent that most children eventually become continent, referring to remission as "spontaneous" illustrates the current paucity of information on the series of events that leads to dryness. The problem of who to treat, when, and how remains.

Etiology

Several etiological theories are thought to account for urinary incontinence. These fall into three main categories: medical–genetic disorders, emotional disturbance, and failure to learn. We discuss each of these in turn. As noted earlier in this chapter, the term "enuresis" is best reserved only for functional cases; however, sometimes the line between the two becomes unclear, as, for example, when an organic problem may hinder (though not prohibit) the learning process.

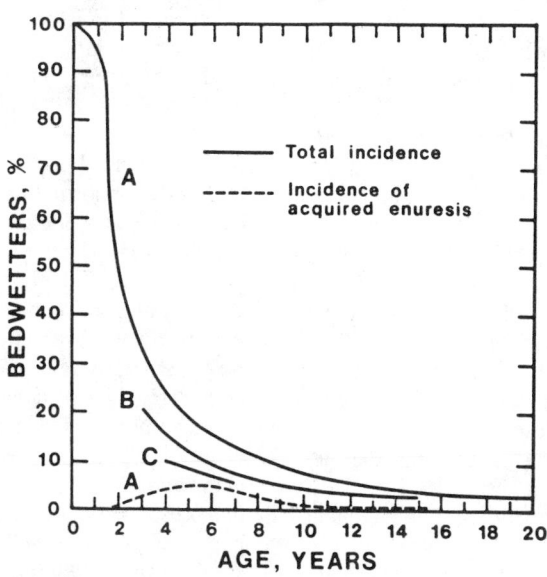

FIGURE 12-1 Incidence of enuresis. A, results from Crosby (1950); B, results from Bransby, Blomfield, and Douglas (1955); C, results from Hallgren (1956). Figure modified from Jones (1960). From *Behavior Therapy* by A. J. Yates, 1970, New York: Wiley. Copyright 1970 by John Wiley and Sons, Inc. Reprinted by permission.

Medical–Genetic Disorders

Included in the organic causes are a variety of acquired and congenital central nervous system lesions, as well as disorders in the neural innervation of the bladder. Structural problems of the genital–urinary system are a second organic factor in children's voiding dysfunctions. These include congenital insufficiencies of the sphincter or urine bypassing the sphincters altogether. Certain injuries or surgical procedures involving the urinary system also create structural disorders leading to incontinence. Bladder or urinary tract infections are a third category of organic factors causing urinary incontinence. The presence of infection may be signaled by fever, pain, burning on micturition, diurnal dribbling, excessive frequency or urgency of urination, or the passage of blood in the urine. Finally, chronic diseases may precipitate voiding dysfunction in children. Urinary incontinence may be found in diabetes mellitus, diabetes insipidus, seizure disorders, sickle cell disease, and possibly food allergies.

The actual incidence of clearly organic urinary incontinence is quite low. Although estimates vary, it is generally accepted that 90% or more of cases of urinary incontinence are caused by other than organic factors (Pierce, 1971). When medical factors cause incontinence, the child will most often present with other symptoms that strongly signal the presence of organic pathology. It is important for the nonmedical clinician to be certain that such factors have been ruled out by a competent medical examination.

In addition to cases clearly involving organic pathology, Doleys (1977) has suggested a medical–genetic theory of etiology that proposes several factors implying an organic basis for enuresis. These are the genetic, neuromaturational, and developmental lag hypotheses. Although these hypotheses are not well established by empirical data, they are briefly discussed here in turn.

The genetic component of the medical–genetic theory is represented by Bakwin (1973), who reported that monozygotic twins had a 68% concordance rate of enuresis, whereas dizygotic twins had a 38% concordance rate. Many studies report that a high percentage of parents, siblings, and relatives of enuretics are or were bedwetters themselves as children (Crosby, 1950; Young, 1963). Reports of a positive family history of enuresis in enuretic children have ranged from 44% to 55% (Baller, 1975). Also, in a study on an Israeli kibbutz where toilet training took place away from parents, Kaffman and Elizur (1977) found that 67% of enuretic children had enuretic siblings, compared to 22% of dry children. These studies provide evidence of a hereditary factor in voiding dysfunctions in children. However, this information is not sufficient to predict which children will be afflicted or the duration of time before remission occurs. Most genetic studies also have not ruled out the influence of environmental factors, such as ineffective family toilet-training habits (Walker, 1978).

The neuromaturational component of the medical–genetic theory views enuresis as a delay or deficit in higher cortical functioning (Crosby, 1950). Evidence for this hypothesis has been suggested by findings of electroencephalographic (EEG) abnormalities in enuretic children (Lovibond & Coote, 1970). However, data in this area are conflicting, and studies have reported widely diverse rates of abnormal EEGs among enuretics. These rates range from a high of 77% (Gunnarsen & Melin, 1951) to a low of 28% (Turton & Spear, 1953). Mikkelsen, Brown, Minichiello, Millican, and Rapoport (1982) found no significant differences in EEGs between enuretic children and a control group. In two carefully controlled studies by Poussaint and colleagues (Poussaint & Greenfield, 1966; Poussaint, Koegler, & Riehl, 1967), enuretics did not have an unusual incidence of EEG abnormalities, and children with EEG abnormalities did not have a statistically unusual incidence of urinary incontinence. As Salmon, Taylor, and Lee (1973) have pointed out, even if strong evidence of an association between EEG abnormalities and enuresis were discovered, it would account for only a small number of cases. Data from Finley and Perry (1973) concur with this assertion; these authors further propose that there may be different types of enuresis, some of which entail abnormal EEGs and others do not. Results of their research have suggested the existence of a particular syndrome of enuresis, involving both an abnormal EEG and the presence of an emotional disturbance. Certainly, further research in this area is needed to validate this hypothesis.

A related area of investigation in the neuromaturational component of the medical–genetic theory is that of sleep patterns. Common lore has long held that unusually deep sleep causes enuresis, and many parents describe their enuretic children as difficult to arouse during the night. However, Gillin *et al.* (1982) concluded from their research that enuresis is not a disorder of sleep arousal. Other scientific investigations of arousal time, sleep stages during enuretic events, and sleep structure have failed to yield consistent evidence on the role of sleep in enuresis (Boyd, 1960; Mikkelson & Rapoport, 1980). More research is needed in this area.

The final component of the medical–genetic theory suggests that enuretics suffer from a developmental lag in attaining mature bladder functioning. Wetting accidents therefore represent inadequate or incomplete development of urinary control. This has also been suggested as an explanatory factor for the higher incidence of enuresis among males. Since males are often slower than females in their rate of development throughout childhood and adolescence, it is possible that sex differences in the development of bladder control are a result of normal maturational delay. Despite the intuitive appeal of this explanation, MacKeith (1972) has argued that there is scant evidence to support deviations in the development of the neuromuscular system as a cause of enuresis. He argues that by age 5, most children have established sufficient neuromuscular coordination to control the bladder. Therefore, very few cases of enuresis can be accounted for by this explanation.

Emotional Disturbance

In the past, the most widely held etiological theory of enuresis has been that of emotional disturbance. According to this notion, enuresis is a symptom of underlying emotional dysfunction, psychological conflict, or anxiety (Pierce, 1971). Psychoanalytic theories have related enuresis to sexual conflict—specifically, to disturbances in which the process of urination symbolizes suppressed masturbation, ejaculation, or sexual identity confusion (Fenichel, 1946). Other authors have stressed the passive–aggressive and hostile aspects of disrupting the family and causing extra work for the mother (Solomon & Patch, 1969). Although some theories have not held that emotional disturbances are the cause of enuresis, they still maintain that the two most frequently occur together. Shaffer (1973), in a review of the literature, determined that there is evidence of an association between emotional disturbance

and enuresis. However, he pointed out that most enuretic children are psychiatrically normal and that enuretics displaying emotional disturbance demonstrate no consistent pattern of disturbance. Douglas (1973) has noted that when disturbance is found in enuretic children, it generally involves anxiety, family disruption (e.g., divorce or a death of a parent), or stressful life events (e.g., hospitalization, birth of a sibling, etc.). It is well known that increased urination is a physiological symptom of stress in humans. Therefore, heightened stress may cause enuresis in children, but the presence of enuresis is not necessarily the result of psychopathology. There is a tendency for the association between enuresis and emotional disturbance to be stronger in females (especially older ones) than in males (Rutter, Yule, & Graham, 1973). However, in the small number of cases where this association exists, it remains to be determined which factor is causal (Werry, 1967).

Failure to Learn

The final model regarding causes of enuresis is the learning theory approach. In order to achieve mature bladder functioning, children must gain cognitive control over the urination reflex. Parts of this reflex include contractions of the detrusor muscle within the wall of the bladder, along with relaxation of the internal and external sphincter muscles located between the neck of the bladder and the beginning of the urethra. Control of these reflexes is achieved in gradual stages and involves a wide range of prerequisite skills and discriminative tasks on the child's part before adequate control may be obtained (Azrin & Foxx, 1974; Brazelton, 1962; Muellner, 1960). Learning theory postulates that some children simply have difficulty learning to control the urination reflex, much as they might have trouble learning to swim, ride a bike, or read. Therefore, learning theory treatments are based on principles of learning and conditioning. As we discuss later in this chapter, behavioral interventions designed to promote mastery of this reflex have been found to be by far the most effective treatments for enuresis (Walker, Milling, & Bonner, 1988).

Assessment

Doleys (1979; Doleys & Dolce, 1982; Fielding & Doleys, 1988) has recommended a three-stage assessment for enuresis, including medical screening, clinical interview, and baseline behavioral recordings. The medical screening should be carried out by a physician and should evaluate neurological and urological abnormalities. A urine culture and urinalysis are standard procedures to rule out infection. Observation of the size and velocity of the urine stream, presence of daytime dribbling or blood in the urine, dysuria, polyuria, or urgency of urination may indicate that additional medical testing is necessary.

The clinical interview should solicit information about the history and current status of the child's incontinence. The nature of the problem must be examined thoroughly, including diurnal or nocturnal wetting, intermittent or daily incontinence, and primary or secondary status. The parents' attitude toward the enuresis, their responses to accidents, and the general family environment should be assessed. Prior attempts at toilet training, as well as parents' beliefs about current measures required to control the problem, must also be explored. Parents may believe that the child is actively attempting to create work for them or that the child's inability to obtain bladder control is a result of their improper parenting. They may also be at odds with each other over the correct solution to the problem, or each may believe that the other is responsible for the enuresis. Ascertaining the parents' reason for seeking treatment at the present time may give useful information on these attitudes and misperceptions. Whether bedwetting is maintained by reinforcing consequences such as parental indulgence or parental exasperation must also be investigated.

A brief family medical history, including inquiry about the presence of diabetes, renal diseases, and enuresis among family members, should also be obtained. Parents' motivation to pursue treatment may be influenced by whether or not they were themselves enuretic as children and the methods by which they attained bladder continence. Finally, a brief developmental history and a description of other current behavior problems are necessary. Current stressors in the child's life that may contribute to the difficulty should be noted. If serious psychopathology (e.g., a pervasive developmental disorder or attention deficit–hyperactivity disorder) is discovered, it is recommended that the treatment of enuresis be postponed until these problems are better controlled. In addition, behavior problems such as noncompliance may be severe

enough to hamper treatment and may need to be eliminated first. Other problems may also be involved. For example, Doleys (1977) has pointed out that children may be fearful of the dark or of the toilet and therefore avoid going to the bathroom at night. The astute clinician will routinely inquire about the presence of such behaviors, as they may be causally related to the enuresis.

The behavioral recording portion of the initial assessment provides precise information about the frequency and timing of enuretic events, size of the wet spot, and instances of appropriate bladder control. This also serves as a baseline for evaluating treatment. Although Doleys (1977) has recommended a 3-week baseline, recording for 7–14 days may be more feasible for routine clinical practice (Walker et al., 1988). Instructions on recording may be given by phone prior to the first clinical interview; this will allow parents to bring this information to the initial appointment. Estimates of average bladder capacity should also be obtained by asking parents to record the amount of urine passed by the child each time he or she voids over the recording period. A simple home measuring jar will be adequate to determine the amount in ounces. The total amount of urine passed divided by the total number of voids yields the mean functional bladder capacity. This information may be useful, since low functional bladder capacity may play a role in some cases of enuresis.

"Functional bladder capacity" refers to the ability of the bladder to retain a given volume of urine without producing an urge to void (rather than the actual physical size of the bladder, which is usually normal for the chronological age of the child). Studies indicate that many enuretic children pass the same amount of urine as nonenuretics, but do so in smaller quantities, at more frequent intervals, and with a greater sense of urgency (Wright, Schaefer, & Solomons, 1978). However, as Doleys (1978) has noted, not all enuretic children have decreased functional bladder capacity, and increased bladder capacity has not been demonstrated as necessary or sufficient to produce a reduction in enuresis. This information notwithstanding, the smaller functional bladder capacity of some enuretics may have implications for treatment.

During the baseline period, the parents should also be encouraged to check their child periodically through the night to determine when and how often wetting occurs. This information is important because early in treatment, children most often show a reduction in the number of wetting accidents per night or a decrease in the size of wet spots, rather than an overall reduction in the number of wet nights. If only global measures are obtained, treatment approaches may be abandoned prematurely. These behavioral recordings should be continued throughout treatment.

Before treatment begins, information on the relative frequency of enuresis in the general population and the stages children go through in learning to control the urine reflex should be shared with the parents and child. This provides reassurance that the child's problem is relatively common and not a result of hostility or lack of cooperation. Providing this information also serves to build rapport with the family and enhances cooperation with the chosen treatment protocol. Both parents and child should know that relapses in treatment are common and that booster treatment will easily remedy this problem if it occurs. Finally, parents should be encouraged to avoid shaming the child or using other forms of punishment.

Treatment

In light of the long history of ineffective and sometimes harmful actions suggested as cures. physicians and psychologists currently advocate patience and restraint in treating enuresis. Present measures include drug therapy and behavioral interventions (e.g., the urine alarm, dry bed training, urine retention training, and sphincter control exercises). Hypnotherapy is also utilized, although there is less research to support this approach. Finally, psychotherapy is sometimes employed, though no research is available to support such an approach.

Drug Therapy

Medication is one of the most popular treatments for enuresis. The drug most often utilized is imipramine hydrochloride (Tofranil), a tricyclic antidepressant. The basis for imipramine's action is still unknown, although its effectiveness has been primarily attributed to anticholinergic effects on the bladder (relaxing the detrusor muscle and inhibiting urination). Other proposed mechanisms for action include mood elevation, decreasing the depth of sleep, placebo effects, and strengthening voluntary control of the urethral sphincter.

Although many children show initially positive responses to imipramine, there is a high percentage of relapse when the drug is withdrawn. Fewer than 40% of enuretics are permanently cured by the drug (Blackwell & Currah, 1973). This does not represent a significant improvement over spontaneous remission rates. The benefits of the drug may also be compromised by the risks involved. A growing body of evidence documents negative side effects, such as increased pulse rate and diastolic blood pressure (Lake, Mikkelson, Rapoport, Zavadil, & Kopin, 1979). In addition, few drugs are as toxic or lethal in low doses as imipramine. Two other drugs, oxybutynin (Ditropan) and desmopressin, have recently grown in popularity for the treatment of enuresis. Although initial reports of their effectiveness have been encouraging (Schmitt, 1982), more research on side effects and long-term effectiveness is required to ascertain their value in treating enuresis.

Urine Alarm

The urine alarm or bell-and-pad method of treating enuresis involves a urine-sensitive pad placed in the child's bed and connected to a bell or buzzer, or sometimes to a light. The electrolytic effect of a few drops of urine completes a circuit, activating an alarm that continues to sound until manually turned off. Newer models of the alarm utilize smaller, credit-card-size pads attached directly to the child's underwear.*

Mowrer and Mowrer (1938) were the first to employ this system regularly, although variations of the bell and pad have existed for over 100 years. An early model used by Mowrer (1980) rigged the bed so that the child was dumped on the floor when the alarm was activated.

The urine alarm was initially conceptualized using a classical conditioning paradigm, in which bladder distension became associated with the sound of the awakening alarm. Eventually, bladder distension would then become a cue to awaken the child. However, more variables than the conditioned stimulus–unconditioned stimulus contingency appear to be operating, since most children treated with this method learn to sleep through the night rather

---

*Available from Palco Laboratories, 5026 Scotts Valley Drive, Scotts Valley, CA 95066.

than awakening to go to the bathroom. As Lovi-bond (1964) has suggested, operant principles may better explain this learning process. The child learns to avoid the aversive alarm by retaining urine and sleeping through the night or by awakening and using the bathroom prior to the alarm. Positive reinforcement for dry nights also plays an important role, as does attention from parents and the therapist. There may also be nonspecific factors active in the treatment of enuresis with the urine alarm. Baker (1969) and Doleys (1977) have noted positive changes us-ing self-recording and an inoperative alarm in the child's room.

Outcome studies on the effectiveness of the urine alarm have demonstrated that this system eliminates wetting in 70%–90% of the cases (Doleys, 1979; Lovibond, 1964; Lovibond & Coote, 1970; Sacks & DeLeon, 1983; Turner, 1973; Yates, 1970). Doleys (1977), in a review of the literature from 1960 to 1975, found that across all studies using the urine alarm, 75% of 628 patients were successfully treated in 5–12 weeks. However, 41% relapsed within 6 months of treatment. Retreatment with a shorter series of nights using the alarm produced suc-cessful reconditioning for 68% of these cases.

Despite the relatively high relapse rate, empirical studies confirm the urine alarm sys-tem as one of the most effective methods avail-able for treating enuresis. When compared to other forms of treatment, it has been found more efficacious than a placebo (Turner, Young, & Rachman, 1970; White, 1968), the presence of an inoperative alarm (Baker, 1969), verbal psychotherapy (DeLeon & Mandell, 1966; Novick, 1966; Werry & Cohrssen, 1965), retention control training (Fielding, 1980), or imipramine (Wagner, Johnson, Wal-ker, Carter, & Wittner, 1982).

Although relapse after treatment is a signifi-cant problem with the urine alarm, this may be successfully reduced by employing overlearn-ing procedures and intermittent reinforcement schedules. Overlearning requires the child to increase fluid intake prior to bedtime after dry-ness has been achieved but while the alarm procedure remains in use. Young and Morgan (1972) suggested that this process strengthens the newly learned response (bladder con-tinence) against extinction and generalizes con-trol to greater levels of bladder fullness. Using this procedure, these authors reduced the re-lapse rate with the urine alarm from 35% to 13%. Other studies have subsequently con-firmed reduction in relapse rate using overlearn-ing (Jehu, Morgan, Turner, & Jones, 1977; Taylor & Turner, 1975).

In the intermittent alarm procedure, the urine alarm is presented on a variable rather than a continuous schedule. That is, only 50%–70% of incontinent episodes are followed by the alarm instead of 100%. As is well known, condition-ing is more resistant to extinction when an in-termittent reinforcement schedule is utilized. Many studies (Abelew, 1972; Finley, Besser-man, Bennett, Clapp, & Finley, 1973; Finley, Rainwater, & Johnson, 1982; Finley & Wans-ley, 1976; Finley, Wansley, & Blenkarn, 1977; Turner et al., 1970) have demonstrated a signif-icantly lower relapse rate when the intermittent reinforcement schedule is utilized in conjunc-tion with the urine alarm.

The urine alarm apparatus can be purchased from the medical aids section of department store catalogs such as Montgomery Ward or Sears. Unfortunately, some of this equipment is not very sturdy in construction, and it tends to break down frequently. Equipment may also be leased from commercial companies, but the cost of leasing may be excessive, and supervi-sion of treatment is provided by nonprofession-als. Plans for constructing suitable equipment may be found in the literature (e.g., Finley & Smith, 1975; Fried, 1974; Kashinsky, 1974). Highly sophisticated equipment is available from Finley.*

Before the urine alarm procedure is im-plemented, the equipment should be explained in detail and demonstrated to the child. Cooperation and interest on the child's part can be increased by presenting the alarm as an aid in controlling the problem rather than as a magic cure. If a child indicates strong resistance or indifference, another method of treatment will probably yield better results.

While in use, the pad is placed inside a pillowcase or under a sheet to prevent minor electrical burns. The child should sleep with little or no underclothing below the waist. Fluids should not be restricted prior to bedtime, as this may limit the child's opportunity to prac-tice urine retention. Parents should be in-structed that this is a training procedure; there-fore, instant results should not be expected. However, wet spots will gradually lessen in size during the first week or two, dry nights will

---

*Dr. William Finley, Children's Medical Center, P.O. Box 35648, 3500 Skelly Drive, Tulsa, OK 74135.

probably be intermittent for the following 2–3 weeks, and consistent dryness should be accomplished in 6–8 weeks.

During implementation of the procedure, the alarm is turned on at bedtime by the child. When an accident occurs, the alarm will sound. Parents are instructed to go to the child's room to make sure he or she turns off the alarm and goes to the bathroom. To insure complete wakefulness, the child is also asked to wash his or her face with cold water. The bedding is then changed by the child with help from the parent, if needed, and the alarm is reset. This procedure is repeated each time the child wets.

Parents should be advised to carry out this program in a matter-of-fact way, without excessive praise or punishment. Charts are kept noting size of the wet spot, number of wets per night, and number of dry nights. The child should receive a small reward for each dry night.

Parents should be advised to clean the urine pad in soapy water after every night that a wetting accident occurs. Batteries and equipment require regular examination, as equipment easily becomes worn from use. A firm mattress should be used, as sagging can interfere with the operation of the alarm. If the child turns off the alarm or disconnects the equipment during the night, having a general discussion with the child, moving switches out of reach, or taping connections so that they cannot easily be removed is generally effective in eliminating the problem. If not, the decision to utilize the program should be reconsidered.

Treatment continues until the child achieves 14 consecutive dry nights. Thereafter, an overlearning procedure may be added. Depending upon the child's size and age, the child is encouraged to drink 10–32 ounces of a favorite liquid before bedtime. Wetting may resume, and some children may regress to their baseline number of accidents when exposed to the overlearning procedure. The parents and the child should be forewarned of this possibility, since renewed bedwetting after remission can be distressing to both. Treatment again continues until 14 consecutive dry nights are achieved.

The intermittent reinforcement schedule can be implemented by using an automated urine alarm designed to permit a ratio of nonreinforced trails. The 70% intermittent reinforcement schedule is most commonly chosen after a schedule of continuous reinforcement for the first seven wettings. It should be noted that the employment of overlearning or intermittent reinforcement schedules extends the duration of treatment but greatly reduces the rate of relapse. Equipment programmed for intermittent schedules may be obtained from Children's Medical Center in Tulsa, Oklahoma (see footnote, p. 430).

Doleys (1977) and Doleys and Dolce (1982) have pointed out that the most frequently cited reason for failure in the use of the bell and pad is parental noncompliance. This can be altered with careful instruction, regular feedback, and follow-up by a professional. Research by Fielding (1982) also indicates that children who are both diurnally and nocturnally enuretic may respond more slowly to treatment, and may relapse more quickly after dryness has been achieved. In these cases, it is important to encourage the parents and the child to persevere in their treatment efforts. As with all enuretic children, it is helpful if the parents and child prepare graphs of the data, perhaps with the assistance of the clinician; these allow both parents and child to see the small improvements during treatment. Parents should also be encouraged to contact the clinician for additional instruction if relapse occurs, and occasional phone calls to check on the child's progress are worthwhile.

Dry Bed Training

Azrin, Sneed, and Foxx (1974) developed a multidimensional approach to enuresis known as "dry bed training" (DBT). This approach uses operant conditioning principles to teach the child the responses necessary for remaining dry at night. Positive reinforcement for inhibiting urination, retention control training (see following section), positive practice, nighttime awakening, mild punishment, full cleanliness training, negative reinforcement, family encouragement, and a urine alarm are incorporated in this procedure. When DBT was first described, the authors recommended an in-home behavioral technician to manage the complicated program on the first night. Since then, a number of modifications have been made, including possible omission of the urine alarm and employment of increased office-based training for the parents and the child in place of the technician.

In the initial evaluation of DBT, 100% of the 24 children achieved the 14-day dryness criterion set by the authors, and none were reported to have relapsed at the 6-month follow-up

(Azrin *et al.*, 1974). Subsequent replications have yielded encouraging but less remarkable results. Doleys, Ciminero, Tollison, Williams, and Wells (1977) found that 8 of 13 subjects were dry following the completion of the 6-week program. At a 2-year follow-up, 5 of the 8 remained dry, while 2 were wetting four times per month and 1 six times. Griffiths, Meldrum, and McWilliam (1982) administered DBT to 11 children. Initially, 100% of the children achieved the dryness criterion at the end of 2 weeks, and at the 9-month follow-up, 73% were still dry.

Further research with DBT has attempted to examine which components of the program contributed to its success. Bollard and Woodroffe (1977) compared DBT with and without the urine alarm in a matched group of 10 children. They concluded that the urine alarm was a crucial variable, as none of the children in the nonalarm group reached the success criterion of 14 consecutive dry nights. Nettelbeck and Langeluddecke (1979) compared DBT with and without the urine alarm and a no-treatment control. DBT with the urine alarm was clearly the most effective intervention, and DBT without the alarm was much the same as the control condition. Bollard and Nettelbeck (1981) compared DBT with the alarm, DBT without the alarm, alarm only, and a no-treatment control. DBT with the alarm was most effective in achieving the dryness criterion and maintaining these gains during a 1-year follow-up. The alarm-only condition was more effective than DBT without the alarm, which was not significantly different from the control condition. Azrin and Thienes (1978) compared a modified version of DBT without the alarm and the traditional urine alarm procedure. Their results differed from those previously cited, in that DBT without the alarm was found to be more effective in achieving and maintaining dryness than the urine alarm alone. Thus, Azrin suggested that the alarm not be used. However, when Ross (1981) compared these results with those of the original Azrin *et al.* (1974) study, he discovered that with the urine alarm, the percentage of wet nights per week was lower overall and the dryness criterion was accomplished earlier in treatment.

Bollard and Nettelbeck (1982) compared combinations of various components: (1) waking schedule, (2) retention control training, and (3) positive practice with cleanliness training. Although none of the single components pro-

duced significant effects, the effects were cumulative when the components were added to the urine alarm. Thus, the urine alarm seems to represent the core of DBT, but the addition of other components significantly increases the effectiveness of the procedure as a treatment for enuresis.

The following is a general DBT protocol suggested for clinical use. It is based on the original DBT program, along with modifications suggested by Azrin, Theines-Hontos, and Besalel-Azrin (1979) and Keating, Butz, Burke, and Heimberg (1983). Training is begun by providing an overview of the procedure to the child and adults who will carry out the program. This allows both to decide whether they wish to participate in the demanding training procedures. Success of treatment is heavily dependent upon parents' receiving adequate supervision by a qualified professional.

On the first night of the intensive training portion of the program, parents and child review all aspects of the procedure. About an hour before bedtime, the child is given a glass of his or her favorite drink, and the urine alarm is placed in the child's bed. The child then performs 20 trials of positive practice. This entails the child's lying on the bed, counting to 50 (less for younger children), going to the bathroom, attempting to urinate, and returning to the bed. The child is also encouraged to note the dry bed and feel how comfortable it is. Just before retiring, the child attempts to consume more fluids and repeats the training instructions to the parents.

Every hour during the night, the parents gently awaken the child and prompt him or her to go to the bathroom. At the bathroom door, the child is asked whether he or she can retain urine for another hour. If so, the child is praised for his or her control and returned to bed without voiding. If not, the child urinates in the toilet, is praised for the correct toileting, and returns to bed. In the bedroom, parents call the child's attention to the dry sheets and praise the child for a dry bed. The child is given more fluids to drink and then goes back to sleep for another hour.

If a wetting accident occurs, parents shut off the alarm, wake the child, express mild displeasure, and rush the child to the bathroom to complete urination. The child then performs cleanliness training by changing pajamas, removing wet sheets, cleaning the mattress, getting clean sheets, remaking the bed, and appropriately disposing of the soiled linens. The child then performs 20 trials of positive practice as described above.

Following the evening of intensive training, the posttraining phase begins. In this second phase, the urine alarm is again utilized, but encouraging fluid intake is discontinued. If the child has a dry night, he or she is praised throughout the next day for this success. Significant others are encouraged to praise the child as well (e.g., grandparents, a favorite aunt or uncle, etc.). If an accident occurs during the night, 20 positive practice trials are performed prior to bedtime the next night. Just before the parents retire (11:00 P.M. to 12:00 midnight), they awaken the child and encourage him or her to urinate. After each dry night, the child is awakened a half hour earlier on the following evening. When the waking time follows bedtime by no more than an hour, it is discontinued. This phase ends when the child achieves dryness for seven consecutive nights.

In the final phase of training, the urine alarm and periodic awakening are discontinued. The child's bed should be inspected each morning by the parents. If a wetting accident has occurred during the night, the child is to change and remake the bed immediately. That evening, 20 trials of positive practice are performed. If two accidents occur in the same week, the second phase of training should be reinstituted until seven consecutive dry nights are again achieved.

It is worth noting that a general toilet-training program based on DBT procedures has been described in nontechnical language, so that parents are easily able to refer to a written guide (Azrin & Foxx, 1976). The use of this book should not be expected to replace contact with the clinician, as research has shown that parents are better able to manage this program if they are receiving professional supervision (Butler, 1976; Matson & Ollendick, 1977).

Urine Retention and Sphincter Control Exercises

Urine retention and sphincter control exercises were developed to assist children in gaining control over the urination reflex as well as increasing functional bladder capacity, which, as noted earlier in this chapter, is deficient in many enuretic children. In the retention control procedure, children are instructed to go to the bathroom when they feel the urge to urinate, but

are told to refrain from urinating for as long as possible. Initially, most children can inhibit the urgency for only a few seconds. However, with practice they can eventually refrain for several minutes or hours. Fluid intake may be increased to provide additional training opportunities as well as overlearning. Stanfield and Mellits (1968) found that of 83 enuretic children treated with this procedure, 19% were cured and 66% were reported improved. Kimmel and Kimmel (1970) used urine retention in conjunction with reinforcement. During their 15- to 20-day training period, each child was expected to increase the time of urine retention by 2–3 minutes daily. He or she was rewarded for increases in retention time, urination in the toilet, and dry nights. Paschalis, Kimmel, and Kimmel (1972), in treating 31 children with this method, reported that 15 were dry and another 8 showed significant improvement. Conversely, Doleys, Ciminero, et al. (1977) found no relationship between increased bladder capacity and changes in the frequency of enuretic events.

Sphincter control training has also been used in combination with retention control training (Walker, 1978). To accomplish this, the child is instructed to practice starting and stopping the stream of urine when voiding. The child should try to stop and start the flow of urine three to five times during each voiding. Rewards may be offered to encourage the process.

In using these methods, care should be taken not to force excessive amounts of fluid or to require the child to retain urine for unusually long periods of time. A cup or two of fluid per hour with retention encouraged up to 1–2 hours is well within safe limits. However, if the child shows signs of distress, these requirements should be lowered.

Although empirical support for this method is tentative, it represents a less intensive alternative that can be used with young children, especially those who exhibit excessive frequency and urgency in urination or who are known to have low functional bladder capacity. This method may also be employed with adolescents, who are generally resistant to methods requiring extensive supervision or control by parents.

Other Behavioral Techniques

Other procedures for treating enuresis have employed behavioral principles in a less complex manner than the programs outlined above. For example, Johnson and Thompson (1974) eliminated wetting accidents with one child by combining modeling via a younger sibling and reinforcement. Doleys (1977) noted improvement in enuresis simply as a result of self-monitoring and charting wetting accidents. Allgeier (1976) reported the successful use of a response cost program. Two subjects were monitored daily for nocturnal wetting and fined for failing to record daily. After 5 weeks, withdrawal of privileges followed wet nights. Wetting was eliminated in 18 weeks.

Parents frequently report the unsuccessful use of punishment to eliminate enuresis, and most professionals rightly discourage such approaches. However, punishment and differential reinforcement were applied by Tough, Hawkins, McArthur, and Ravenswaay (1971) in a case study raising ethical concerns. The two brothers described in the study were dipped in cold water after each wetting incident. Nighttime continence was achieved in 3 weeks.

Charting, self-monitoring, positive reinforcement, and encouragement are effective treatment methods with some children (Collins, 1973; Dische, 1971; White, 1968) and can be used in baseline behavioral recordings to prevent the use of more complex and time-consuming procedures with children who do not require them. Although more efficient when used in combination than singly, simple behavioral interventions may be attempted in situations where a more complex program cannot be carried out.

Fixed or random intervals of nighttime awakening followed by attempts to urinate in the toilet have been found effective in eliminating enuresis in some cases (Creer & Davis, 1975). Using a random awakening procedure, Young (1964) reported a reduction in wetting frequency in 67% of 58 children. However, only 10% became totally dry even with extended treatment. Although the mechanism by which this procedure works is not well defined, the desire to avoid the aversive characteristics of nighttime wakening may play a role. The method does appear to result in increased attention to cues for the onset of urination (Walker, 1978).

To implement this procedure, parents are instructed to awaken the child at intervals throughout the night and have him or her go to the bathroom to attempt urination. These intervals should be randomized, but should also include awakening at times when the child would generally need to urinate. The child may also be responsible for self-awakening, using an alarm clock he or she sets at various intervals. Lovibond (1964) and Morgan and Young (1972) have cautioned that the awakening procedure may promote nighttime wetting and teach the child dependence on being awakened, rather than promoting awareness of internal cues. This danger appears minimal, however, and if noted could be corrected by utilizing retention control training or other procedures.

Psychotherapy

Because enuresis in the past has been viewed as a symptom of psychopathology, verbal psychotherapy, play therapy, and family therapy have often been recommended as treatment. However, there is little evidence to support the emotional disturbance theory of the etiology of enuresis, and there are correspondingly few data to suggest that psychotherapy can produce a remission rate significantly different from that noted in no-treatment control groups (Friedman, 1968; Lovibond, 1964; Novick, 1966; Werry & Cohrssen, 1965).

Hypnotherapy

Hypnotherapy has also been used to treat enuresis. In hypnosis, children are given suggestions to hold urine, refrain from wetting, and use the toilet when necessary. Kohen, Olness, Corwell, and Heimel (1980) found that 44% of their sample of enuretic children achieved the dryness criterion of 30 consecutive nights using hypnosis. Similarly, Olness (1975) found that of 40 enuretic children treated with self-hypnosis, 31 had stopped wetting and 6 had reduced the frequency of accidents at follow-up. As it is not time-consuming, hypnotherapy may be combined with any of the behavioral interventions previously outlined, particularly if parents indicate a strong preference for it. However, there is no literature at present that documents the increased efficacy of behavioral interventions when used in conjunction with hypnosis in the treatment of enuresis.

Fluid Restriction

Restricting fluids after supper and having the child urinate just before bedtime are treatments often suggested. This method will have little effect except for mild cases or cases where the child is drinking excessive quantities of fluid.

In more severe cases, this method may only postpone a more effective solution to the problem. As Doleys (1977) suggests, this method deprives the child of opportunities to learn to inhibit voiding or use the toilet. Therefore, this technique interferes with behavioral interventions and should not be utilized in conjunction with such procedures.

Considerations in Choosing Treatment Procedures

In treating enuresis, there has not been careful research on choosing protocols best suited to individual patient variables. Therefore, information gained during assessment can be used in only a general way to plan suitable interventions. The behavioral methods outlined above clearly provide the most empirically sound procedures in treating enuresis.

A young child who exhibits excessive frequency and urgency of urination and who has not been previously treated may begin a program of retention training and sphincter control exercises. If unsuccessful, this may be followed by use of the urine alarm or DBT. The work of Fielding (1980, 1982) indicates that children who are both diurnally and nocturnally enuretic may respond more slowly to treatment and may relapse more quickly once continence is accomplished. Therefore, charting, self-monitoring, positive reinforcement, advice, and encouragement can be employed with the treatments listed above in order to help improve success rates.

In choosing any of these interventions, it is readily apparent that parents play a crucial role in the success or failure of the procedure. It is therefore critical that parents' beliefs about the best treatment be considered carefully and employed if possible. Parents should be provided with an adequate explanation if their suggestions are inappropriate to the situation.

The most frequently cited reason for treatment failure is parental noncompliance (Doleys, 1977; Doleys & Dolce, 1982). This can be altered with careful instruction, regular feedback, and follow-up by a professional. Parents should also be encouraged to contact the clinician for additional instructions if relapse occurs.

Ethical Issues

Several ethical issues are worth mentioning in the treatment of enuresis. If serious emotional disturbance is present, it is possible that attempts to treat enuresis will be upsetting to the child. As a result, treatment for this problem is best delayed until significant progress is achieved in the other area. It is crucial that organic causes of the disorder be ruled out by a competent medical examination. Embarking on a treatment course without establishing the functional nature of the disorder is inefficient at best and frustrating or harmful to the child at worst. Likewise, treating children younger than age 5 is a questionable professional practice. The spontaneous remission rate is sufficiently high up to this age to warrant giving the child more time before aggressive measures are employed. Instructions for parents in appropriate toilet-training methods are likely to be more successful in the majority of these cases. No treatment should be attempted without the consent and cooperation of the child and the parents. Punishment, other than mild overcorrection measures such as cleaning up and changing the bed, has no place in the treatment of enuresis. Finally, if a pad and bell or other equipment is to be used, the therapist must be certain that the equipment is safe and in good working condition.

Case Example

A 7-year-old boy, Will, was referred for treatment by his family physician after the parents voiced concern over his failure to develop nocturnal continence. According to his mother, Will had never achieved a consecutive month of dry nights and usually wet the bed one to two times per night, every night. Will's parents denied being enuretic as children, but both of Will's older brothers exhibited similar problems in achieving urinary control. Will's parents reported that his frequency of nighttime wetting was greater than that of his brothers, and so chose to pursue treatment with him. Will also wanted to attend Cub Scout camp during the upcoming summer, but was reluctant to do so because of the teasing he would receive from peers as a result of a wetting accident. His parents were quick to point out that Will was otherwise a normally developing child, and denied any connection between enuretic episodes and stressful life events. Neither observed Will as having greater frequency or urgency of urination than other children. They reported using fluid restriction, mild punishment, and inattention to wetting incidents as previous treatment strategies, with little success.

Will was referred to a urologist prior to assessment by the pediatric psychology service. No medical complications were detected. During the initial interview, Will's father requested hypnosis for his son "to help him control himself better." A plan using a pad and bell was established with the parents. It was agreed that hypnosis might also be used if the pad and bell proved unsuccessful. The equipment was demonstrated to Will and his parents, and they were given instructions as described in the present chapter. Will was fascinated by the equipment and eager to try it because he thought it would work and wanted the problem to be over. Will and his parents agreed on the following day as a start date, since, at the suggestion of the therapist, Will's parents had charted a baseline for wetting accidents during the week prior to their initial appointment.

During the second week of treatment, Will's parents noted that the size of the wet spots was significantly reduced from the baseline condition. In the third week, Will had his first dry night. Dry nights increased each week, and he achieved 14 consecutive dry nights in 9 weeks. He then began an overlearning procedure, drinking extra fluid prior to bedtime, and had three incontinent nights during this week. However, he quickly recovered and was incontinent only one night the following week. Will achieved the criterion of 14 consecutive dry nights 4 weeks after the overlearning procedure was begun. During treatment, the therapist maintained phone contact with the family, calling 1 week after the initial appointment and at 2-week intervals thereafter. Three months after the initial treatment, Will began to wet once or twice per week. The parents reinstituted the use of the pad and bell. With this, Will quit wetting the bed after about 10 days. A 6-month follow-up after the second course of pad-and-bell use indicated that Will had had only one wetting accident since discontinuing treatment.

ENCOPRESIS

The history of encopresis is similar to that of enuresis with respect to frequently utilized barbaric treatment methods. For example, the use of strong blows with the hand to the perineal tract was endorsed by Edward Henoch, a physician, in 1881; Henoch also threatened encopretic patients with a branding iron or electrical shock (Bellman, 1966). "Encopresis," as a term, was first utilized in 1925 by Pototosky, and in 1926 Weissenberg recommended its use as a counterpart to the term "enuresis" (Bellman, 1966; Taska & Young, 1982). In general, much less is known about encopresis than about enuresis, because there has been less research in this area. It is often humorously noted that researchers have generally kept some distance from patients who soil during the day, as compared to those who wet their beds at night. In the remaining portion of this chapter, we turn to a discussion of the research that has been done with this population.

"Fecal incontinence" is a broad category used to connote a number of fecal elimination problems both organically and nonorganically based. For a diagnosis of Functional Encopresis, DSM-III-R requires the following: (1) repeated, voluntary or involuntary passage of feces into places not appropriate for that purpose (e.g. clothing, floor); (2) at least one such event a month for at least 6 months; (3) chronological and mental age of at least 4; and (4) not due to any physical disorder, such as aganglionic megacolon (American Psychiatric Association, 1987). Like "enuresis," "encopresis" can be used for fecal incontinence due to organic causes, but it is probably best reserved for disorders of functional origin. A distinction may be made between "primary" and "secondary" encopresis, with primary encopresis being incontinence in those individuals who have reached the age of 4 without being continent for at least 1 year (American Psychiatric Association, 1987). Secondary encopresis is fecal incontinence in those individuals who have been previously continent for at least 1 year. Encopresis also may be diurnal or nocturnal. Diurnal encopresis is by far the more common; nocturnal encopresis is rare but does occur.

After a careful review of the literature, Walker (1978) identified three major categories of encopresis. The first and most common is retentive encopresis based on constipation. The second is a type that results from stress and resultant diarrhea, which appears to be related to irritable bowel syndrome and similar problems. The third and least frequently observed is manipulative soiling, where the child uses soiling incidents to manipulate the environment (e.g., to be excused to go home from school, to passively express anger toward the family, etc).

Prevalence

The reported prevalence of functional encopresis has varied among researchers, ranging from approximately 0.3% to 8% of children (Bellman, 1966; Doleys, Schwartz, & Ciminero, 1981; Levine, 1975; Newson & Newson, 1968). The fluctuations in the reported incidence of functional encopresis appear to result primarily from the definitions employed and the age ranges sampled. The frequency of encopresis in children decreases with age; hence encopresis appears to be infrequent after age 7 years (Knopf, 1979). However, Rutter (1975) reported a rate as high as 1.6% in a normal sample of 10- to 11-year-olds.

Most researchers and clinicians believe that encopresis is frequently underreported, since many parents do not report it unless specifically questioned about the presence of relevant symptoms. Encopresis is four to five times more common in males than females. Finally, approximately 50%–60% of all encopretic children have been formerly successfully toilet-trained; hence their encopresis is secondary or discontinuous.

Etiology

Fecal incontinence may result from numerous organic conditions involving structural anomalies or diseases of the bowel or sphincters as well as of the nervous system (e.g., meningomyelocele). A fairly common problem in children is aganglionic megacolon, known as Hirschsprung disease (Vaughan, McKay, & Behrman, 1979). Aganglionic megacolon is a congenital defect in which a segment of the colon lacks sufficient nerve innervation to function. As a result, fecal material becomes impacted above this point, producing an enlarged colon (megacolon). Severe cases are discovered shortly after birth; mild cases may go undetected until later in life. Treatment is surgical removal of the affected tissue and reconnection of the functional segments of the colon. Careful medical examination of cases of fecal incontinence is required to rule out such organic etiologies.

If the problem is determined to be functional in nature, it is properly designated by the term "functional encopresis." Two primary etiological theories have been postulated to account for functional incontinence or encopresis. Not surprisingly, one of these is a psychodynamic and the other a behavioral conceptualization.

The psychodynamic literature consists primarily of individual case analyses, with few systematic well-controlled etiological studies. Out of these theoretical dissertations have emerged several basic premises upon which psychodynamic practitioners have based their theories of encopretic etiology. These clinicians view encopresis as a symptom of emotional disturbance. Conflict has been identified as the primary catalyst leading to the onset of encopresis. Although this conflict has been described in a variety of ways, much of the psychodynamic literature has suggested that the conflict stems primarily from the mother–child relationship. The mothers of these children are generally described as excessively punitive, overcontrolling, domineering, perfectionistic, and lacking emotional warmth. As a result, they tend to be excessively strict and harsh in their attempts to toilet-train their children. The children's response to the mothers' controlling and coercive efforts is unconscious and includes soiling as an attempt to retaliate (Bemporad, Pfeifer, Gibbs, Cortner, & Bloom, 1971; Vaughn, 1961). Others working within a psychodynamic etiological framework have suggested that conflict leading to encopresis is derived from a stressful or fearful event, such as the arrival of a new sibling, separation from parents, or loss of a parent (Kanner, 1972).

Unfortunately, these notions about etiology are based almost exclusively on single-case reports and a few questionnaire studies. The available data do not support a strong causal relationship between psychological disturbances and encopresis in the majority of cases. Most encopretic children do not appear to be emotionally disturbed, and the majority of emotionally disturbed children are not encopretic. When the two conditions coexist, the causal relationship may go either way (encopresis may as easily lead to emotional stress as vice versa), or the occurrence of the two may be simple coincidence without causal relationship (both caused by other independent factors).

The behavioral theory of etiology employs a learning model of the acquisition and maintenance of encopretic behavior. Doleys and colleagues distinguish between those environmental contingencies responsible for primary encopresis and secondary encopresis. In primary encopresis, it is questionable whether the child has ever learned the necessary prerequisite skills for going to the bathroom (e.g., undressing, proper muscle contractions, etc.); whether the child has been properly reinforced for appropriate toileting behavior; and/or whether the child has learned to discriminate the appropriate physiological cues (e.g., rectal distention, sphincter relaxation) (Doleys et al., 1981; Ross, 1981). Secondary encopresis has been attributed to avoidance conditioning or inappropriate shaping/conditioning (e.g., parental attention following soiling) (Doleys et al., 1981; Ross, 1981). Avoidance conditioning may also occur as the result of painful elimination due to impacted stools (i.e., constipation), or as a result of toilet phobia wherein the toileting experience has been paired with aversive or frightening events (e.g., severe punishment during attempts to toilet-train, seeing blood in stools, etc).

Consideration of the three types of soiling noted by Walker (1978) reveals that retentive encopresis based on chronic constipation accounts for the vast majority of cases (80%–95%) referred for clinical intervention (Christopherson & Rapoff, 1983; Fitzgerald, 1975; Levine, 1975; Wright & Walker, 1978). Intuitively, one might be puzzled about how constipation can be a major cause of soiling. However, an understanding of the physiological mechanisms involved in constipation helps to clarify this issue.

Constipation may be the result of a number of factors or a combination of such characteristics as genetic predisposition, diet, previously painful bowel movements, and/or psychological states such as stress or depression. Once the constipation begins, there is a tendency for it to become a chronic condition, as children are often not aware of changes in their elimination patterns and hence do not attempt to help rectify the condition (e.g., by telling parents). Furthermore, it is difficult for parents to continuously monitor and be aware of these toileting habits, especially once the child reaches school age and is no longer at home for large portions of the day.

As a result of the constipation, fecal material becomes impacted in the bowel, such that normal peristaltic and mass movements are not able to evacuate feces fully from the bowel. Hence, fecal material continues to increase over time, with the result that the intestine becomes enlarged (producing psychogenic megacolon) and loses its muscle tone. In addition, the intestinal wall becomes thin as a result of stretching caused by the impacted material. All of these factors compromise the functioning of the bowel and create a chronic state of constipation.

As this impaction continues, the contents of the stomach, which are in fluid form, pass into the small intestine and make their way to the large intestine, where they form a pool above the point of the impacted fecal mass in the colon. This fluid material then seeps around the impacted mass and out through the anus, staining the child's clothes. The child does not generally realize that this has occurred, since the material has passively seeped out rather than being forcefully expelled by bowel contractions. This passive seepage is not accompanied by the usual sensation of having a bowel movement. The child only realizes that this type of defecation has occurred when he or she feels the wetness in the rectal area and/or on the clothing. At other times, large amounts of the impacted material may be explosively expelled, producing major soiling of the clothing. Neither the seepage nor the explosive bowel movements are under cortical control. Thus, chronic constipation may inhibit learning of bowel control in the child or interfere with the performance of previously learned toileting behavior.

The etiology of Walker's category of soiling due to chronic diarrhea or irritable bowel syndrome may be explained on the basis of a classical conditioning model, in which anxiety and stress become paired with gastrointestinal physiological responses, eventually resulting in diarrhea and soiling accidents. This is quite distinct from soiling due to constipation.

Walker's category of manipulative soiling follows an operant paradigm and is the result of successful (i.e., reinforced) manipulation of the environment. For example, a child may learn that one way to obtain parental attention (positive or, more than likely, negative) is to defecate in his or her undergarments. Hence the attention serves to reinforce the child for inappropriate toileting behavior, thereby maintaining the encopresis. Some children also appear to enjoy upsetting their parents by soiling. In addition, soiling behavior may be successful in helping a child escape or avoid unpleasant situations.

Social Factors

Since it is exceedingly rare for a behavior to occur in a social vacuum, it is important to consider the larger context in which encopretic behavior occurs, is maintained, and is alleviated. Hence, when one is assessing and treating encopretic behavior, the soiling should not be approached in isolation, but rather in a larger environmental context. Although the literature examining the role of peer/social variables in encopresis is, unfortunately, scant, there is general agreement that encopresis can be a significant hindrance to the social development of the child (Knopf, 1979; Walker, 1978). Encopretic children are subjected to teasing and even ostracism by their peers. For the encopretic manifesting irritable bowel syndrome, this additional peer stress can serve to exaggerate anxiety and the physiological reactivity to this anxiety, thereby maintaining the encopresis. In the case of the manipulative soiler, the child may actually view peer harassment as rewarding, with obvious detrimental effects on peer relationships.

Likewise, the other primary childhood social context, the family, needs to be explored for its impact upon the etiology, maintenance, and alleviation of encopretic symptoms. To date, there is relatively little literature available regarding the impact familial interactions have upon the encopretic child. The literature available is mostly comprised of case studies (see McColgan, Pugh, & Pruitt, 1985), and the theoretical underpinnings have not been operationalized for systematic study (Walker *et al.*, 1988). Family theorists suggest that the patient's encopresis actually represents a symptom of a larger family system malfunction (Bemporad *et al.*, 1971; Hoag, Norriss, Himeno, & Jacobs, 1971; McColgan *et al.*, 1985). Thus a disruptive family system may play a role in the etiology and maintenance of encopresis.

It is also likely that, irrespective of the factors contributing to the onset of encopresis, a child's soiling can be stressful for a family. Such stressors include embarrassment and the interruption of family activities by soiling accidents. In addition, the parents may perceive the soiling as a personal failure at being good parents and may apply undue pressure to the child to rectify the encopresis. It is not uncommon in clinical practice to discover that parents believe their children can control their soiling, and that they further believe the children are lying when they say that they cannot prevent it. Obviously, much more research is needed in this area.

Assessment

Prior to the implementation of a psychological treatment plan for encopresis, it is imperative that the patient be medically evaluated to rule out organic causes of fecal incontinence. Once organic factors have been ruled out, a thorough clinical interview should be conducted to determine more specifically the type of encopresis manifested, as well as the contributing and maintaining factors for the encopresis.

Initially, the clinician should determine whether or not the patient is experiencing serious emotional distress and the nature of any such problems. For those individuals with incapacitating psychological disorders, such as psychosis or very severe anxiety or depression, it is important to treat these problems first and then deal with the encopresis at a later date (Walker, 1978). However, if less severe adjustment problems are present, the clinician may choose to treat the encopretic problem first, because a general improvement in behavior and emotional status is often noted when soiling is eliminated.

Next, it is necessary to assess the variables directly involved in maintaining the encopretic behavior and to obtain information as to the type of encopresis present (retentive, diarrheic, manipulative). This information will dictate the manner in which the treatment protocol is designed and implemented.

Information from the medical examination, along with a careful interview of the parents and child regarding the frequency and nature of the stools, makes it possible to establish the type of soiling with considerable confidence. In addition, information concerning the child's learning history with respect to toileting behavior may help delineate the type of encopresis. Physical signs of constipation indicate retentive encopresis. Diarrheic soiling occurs in the context of significant situational stressors that precede soiling episodes, and in cases of manipulation soiling it is generally possible to identify factors that reinforce and thus maintain the behavior. An extended discussion of principles involved in tailoring treatment of encopresis to the etiology may be found in Walker and Shaw (1988).

Finally, the motivation of the parents and child to participate in treatment directed at resolving the problem must be assessed. All successful treatment approaches for encopresis require considerable effort and careful compliance by the child and family to eliminate the problem.

Treatment

The literature on the treatment of encopresis is scant, relative to that on the treatment of enuresis (Ross, 1981). Treatment methods have included one or a combination of the following: behavioral programs, biofeedback, cathartics, medications, dietary alterations, hypnosis, relaxation, psychotherapy (e.g., play therapy, dream analysis), and hospitalization. Since three distinctive types of encopresis have been identified, treatment should be tailored to account for the uniqueness of each of these elimination problems.

Retentive Encopresis

Because retentive encopresis or chronic constipation accounts for the vast majority of encopretic cases, this type is discussed first. Numerous treatment methods have been developed and utilized with this population. It appears however, that five primary treatment approaches for the chronically constipated emerge from the literature; these include medical, psychotherapeutic, hypnotic, biofeedback, and behavioral approaches.

Medical Approaches. Medical treatments for the retentive encopretic include exercise, dietary changes, and the use of enemas, suppositories, and laxatives (see Hein & Beerends, 1978; Parker & Whitehead, 1982). The rationale for utilizing such medical approaches is based on the need to cleanse the bowel of impacted feces and to produce regularity in bowel movements. Mineral oil is often used for this purpose, sometimes combined with an initial course of laxatives or enemas (Walker *et al.*, 1988). Once the bowel is evacuated, the enemas or laxatives are discontinued. The administration of mineral oil is continued for several weeks until regular bowel movements are established. It is then slowly decreased in dosage until completely faded out (Abrahamian & Lloyd-Still, 1984; Walker, 1978; Walker & Shaw, 1988). Since mineral oil inhibits the absorption of fat-soluble vitamins, the oil must be taken 2–3 hours after meals, or a multiple vitamin supplement must be taken as part of the treatment. In a recent follow-up study conducted by Abrahamian and Lloyd-Still (1984), 47% of their sample of pediatric patients were symptom-free following treatment with mineral oil and other laxatives; an additional 36% of the subjects had their encopresis controlled with the continued use of laxatives following the original course of treatment. Hein and Beerends (1978) successfully implemented a program that consisted of dietary control, enemas, bowel training, and parental consultation. A majority

of their sample ceased soiling (14 of 18), 3 were significantly improved, and only 1 subject failed to exhibit some reduction in symptoms.

Psychotherapy. Some of the earliest psychological interventions for encopresis included psychotherapy and play therapy. Generally, poor results have been reported for the use of such therapies (McTaggert & Scott, 1959; Pinkerton, 1958). Furthermore, Berg and Jones (1964), in their clinical case review, reported that the remission rate for patients receiving such traditional therapies did not differ markedly from that for those children who were not receiving therapy.

More recently, an emphasis has been placed upon the contributions of family therapy in conceptualizing and treating encopresis (see McColgan *et al.*, 1985; Protinsky & Kersey, 1983; Protinsky, Quinn, & Elliott, 1982). Family therapists often view the child's encopresis as a symptom of family dysfunction; as a result, the focus of intervention is geared toward ameliorating family problems. Unfortunately, most reports on this approach are case studies or poorly controlled investigations. Thus, no conclusions for family therapy as an efficacious treatment for encopresis can be drawn. Overall, psychotherapy as a treatment approach for encopresis appears to be of little value. Considering the role that constipation and megacolon play in encopresis, it is not surprising that insight-oriented talking therapy has little impact.

Hypnosis. The literature is sparse with respect to large-sample studies on the effectiveness of hypnosis in treating encopretic children. However, case studies and those utilizing small groups have consistently reported positive results in the use of hypnosis as a treatment technique for encopresis (Baer, 1961; Olness, 1976; Tilton, 1980). It appears that one of the most efficacious components in hypnosis is the self-control aspect (Gardner & Olness, 1981; Olness, 1976). Imagery is utilized in aiding the child to obtain bowel control, as he or she is instructed to visualize being the "boss" or being in control. Hypnotic suggestions emphasize the child's ability to control fecal elimination, as well as to retain feces between toiletings. In addition, the child is encouraged to use the toilet at regular intervals. Olness (1976) taught three of four preschoolers to appropriately retain and eliminate feces via autohypnosis. These preschoolers had previously undergone arduous medical and surgical interventions without success. In a case study reported by Goldsmith (1962), a 9-year-old girl treated with hypnosis was able to reduce her soiling episodes significantly. The evidence as to the utility of hypnosis appears to be promising; however, better-designed and better-controlled studies with larger subject samples are needed before any firm conclusions may be drawn.

Biofeedback. Biofeedback geared toward teaching sphincter control has been utilized successfully in the treatment of fecal incontinence secondary to organic disorders (Cerulli, Nikoomanesh, & Schuster, 1979; Engel, Nikoomanesh, & Schuster, 1974; Goldenberg, Hodges, Hersh, & Jinick, 1980; Wald, 1981; Whitehead, Parker, Masek, Cataldo, & Freeman, 1981). In fact, Whitehead *et al.* (1981) reported successful sphincter control in their patients with as little as 6 hours of training.

There are three distinct components in the use of biofeedback for treating encopresis: (1) exercising the external sphincter muscles, (2) training in discrimination of rectal sensations, and (3) synchronizing the internal and external sphincter responses (Latimer, Campbell, & Kasperski, 1984). It has been noted that sphincter control may be obtained without incorporating all three biofeedback components in the treatment protocol. For example, Latimer *et al.* (1984), obtained significant improvements in all eight of their subjects, but only one required all three procedures to alleviate the elimination difficulties.

Behavioral Programs. Over the years, considerable attention has focused on behavioral treatment methods for encopresis. Though much of the research in this area is based on single cases or small-sample studies, the results have been almost uniformly positive. The behavioral approach usually includes more than one intervention in an overall treatment plan. The primary foci of the behavioral programs include reinforcing appropriate behavior and mildly punishing soiling or inappropriate toileting behavior (Blechman, 1979; Bornstein *et al.*, 1983; Doleys, McWhorter, Williams, & Gentry, 1977; Walker, 1978; Wright & Walker, 1978). Although studies have been conducted utilizing either positive reinforcement or punishment alone, the literature suggests that the most successful outcome occurs when the two are combined (Azrin & Foxx, 1971, 1974; Doleys, McWhorter, *et al.*, 1977; Nilsson, 1976). In addition, some behavioral programs incorporate aspects of the medical approach

(e.g., enemas and laxatives) as well as other therapy techniques (e.g., paradoxical instructions, relaxation techniques).

Successful results have been reported in numerous single-case or small-sample research projects utilizing positive reinforcement alone to eliminate encopresis (e.g., Bach & Moylan, 1975; Bornstein *et al.*, 1983). Young and Goldsmith (1972), for example, successfully utilized positive reinforcement of an 8-year-old boy for his proper fecal elimination. Concurrently, the patient's accidents were ignored, and he was given the option to clean himself or not upon an encopretic event.

Occasionally, punishment has been used as the main treatment for encopresis. For example, Ferinden and Van Handel (1970) reported a case in which aversive consequences were employed to eliminate soiling. The child was required to clean his soiled clothes as well as himself with a potent soap and in cold water. Amelioration of symptoms occurred within 5 months. More recently, Rolider and Van Houten (1985) required a child to sit for increasing lengths of time on the toilet (up to 90 minutes) if no bowel movement occurred, and employed overcorrection for soiling. The absence of soiling was positively reinforced. Using a reversal design, the authors concluded that, in this particular case of a 12-year-old female with a 5-year history of soiling, the requirement of sitting on the toilet for increased lengths of time was the most effective measure.

Comprehensive behavior therapy programs have included periodic pants checks, frequent toileting, and positive practice, as well as the implementation of token systems and full cleanliness training (Azrin & Foxx, 1971, 1974). Foxx (1985) successfully treated a 5½-year-old girl who had both encopretic and enuretic disorders; feedback (i.e., progress charting or monitoring) and pants checks were employed, along with both positive and negative consequences. Doleys and his colleagues also were able to help eliminate soiling behavior in their encopretic sample within 15 weeks through the use of periodic pants checks, regular toileting, full cleanliness training, and the integration of a positive reinforcement system for desired toileting behaviors (Doleys & Arnold, 1975). Successful results have been noted with other similar protocols incorporating a variety of behavioral treatment components (e.g., Butler, 1977; Crowley & Armstrong, 1977).

Other comprehensive behavioral programs have combined medical interventions with behavioral techniques, with great success (Walker, 1978; Walker et al., 1988; Wright, 1973; Wright & Walker, 1976, 1977, 1978). These programs are based upon the premise that it is first necessary to have the bowel evacuated before behavioral control can be established over the elimination. Cathartics are employed initially to establish regularity. These are gradually withdrawn as elimination processes become regular and soiling diminishes. Positive reinforcements for appropriate defecation in the toilet and for each 24-hour soil-free period are utilized conjointly with mild punishment such as time out, fines, or loss of privileges after episodes of soiling. Research has demonstrated this to be a highly effective method for the treatment of encopresis (Christopherson & Rainey, 1976; Wright, 1975). When properly applied, the program has resulted in cessation of soiling in nearly 100% of cases (Wright, 1975; Wright & Walker, 1976). Only 15%–25% of the patients relapse, and these generally respond favorably to a second course of the same treatment. Approximately, 10%–15% of the cases are treatment failures because of noncompliance with the program (Wright, 1975).

Chronic Diarrhea or Irritable Bowel Syndrome

The treatment options for irritable bowel syndrome depart noticeably from the suggested regimens for the chronically constipated encopretic. Emphasis in treatment is placed on control of symptoms and reduction of stress and anxiety in the patient. Both medical and psychological treatment approaches may be utilized with the encopretic experiencing chronic diarrhea. Medicinal preparations can be divided into two categories: antidiarrheal agents and antianxiety drugs. Antidiarrheal agents are the more commonly employed of the two (Angelides & Fitzgerald, 1981). The use of antianxiety prescriptions does not appear to be common practice in treating children (Walker et al., 1988); hence much of the treatment emphasis has been placed upon the reduction of stress and its related anxiety through psychological interventions.

For example, hypnosis has been successfully utilized in the treatment of chronic diarrhea (Byrne, 1973). Behavioral and cognitive methods have also been proven to be effective.

Cohen and Reed (1968) and Hedberg (1973) were successful in their treatment of pediatric patients with chronic diarrhea through the use of systematic desensitization. Relaxation training and stress innoculation procedures have also been used to reduce the effects of stressors in the encopretic patient's life (Bernstein & Borkovec, 1973; Meichenbaum, 1977; Walker, Hedberg, Clement, & Wright, 1981). Finally, assertion training has also been utilized successfully in treating the encopretic with chronic diarhhea (Alberti & Emmons, 1974; Walker et al., 1981). In selecting a psychological intervention strategy, one must be sensitive to the individual characteristics of the child and his or her family, as well as the stressors the child encounters.

Manipulative Soiling

Since manipulative soiling is relatively uncommon compared to other types of encopresis, not much literature exists delineating treatment methods for the manipulative soiler. However, what is available suggests that treatment emphasis should be placed on the reduction of reinforcers for maladaptive soiling behavior, and on providing reinforcement for efficacious coping behaviors. Professionals have utilized basic family counseling principles (Gurman & Kniskern, 1981) and behavioral treatment programs (Ross, 1981; Walker et al., 1981) to accomplish this.

Ethical Issues in Treatment

There are several ethical considerations in treating the encopretic child. First, the psychologist must maintain a good working relationship with the physician. It is clear that one should not treat an encopretic without first being certain that all possible organic etiologies for the soiling have been ruled out. Good communication with the physician and ongoing medical evaluation are necessary for the safety of the patient. In contrast to the treatment of enuresis, which is often optional, the dangers of untreated chronic constipation and diarrhea mandate a more aggressive approach. Thus, encopresis should generally be treated at any age when it occurs, rather than waiting until the child is older. Ideally, treatment should not be attempted without the cooperation of the child; however, sometimes this may need to be weighed against the health hazards of not treating. Mild punishments are often used in encopresis treatment programs. These should be used only when necessary, and care should be taken to be sure the punishment is mild and safe. There is always a danger that child abuse may result from parents' overaggressive attempts to employ negative consequences in treating the encopretic child. All of these ethical concerns are best handled by careful supervision of the treatment and clear communication between the psychologist and all participants.

Case Example

Steven, a 6-year-old male, was referred for psychological services because of his frequent soiling episodes. The patient's pediatrician indicated that Steven had a history of chronic constipation for 2½ years without any known organic etiology. The psychologist's interview revealed that Steven soiled four to five times per day. His soiling was described by his mother as a paste-like stain on some occasions and as a very large bowel movement on other occasions. In addition, she noted that Steven did not use the toilet frequently, but that if prompted to, he would go (no fear avoidance of the toilet was noted). Stools passed in the toilet were of unusually large diameter for a child his age, hard, and foul in odor. Family evaluation indicated a stable family with no evidence of serious conflict or discord. Steven's parents were concerned about the encopresis, but were not punitive toward him when he had accidents. Steven did not exhibit symptoms of other behavioral problems. As a result of this evaluation, it was evident that Steven had functional retentive encopresis and psychogenic megacolon, as opposed to either chronic diarrhea or manipulative soiling.

Steven's parents were instructed to place him on a diet with high fiber content and minimal dairy products (milk, cheese, ice cream). Fortunately, Steven's pediatrician had already informed Steven's parents about the necessity for dietary changes. Simultaneously with this, he was placed on the protocol described by Wright and Walker (1977). Steven's parents were instructed to evacuate his colon via an enema the night prior to commencing with the protocol. In the morning, Steven was encouraged to defecate as soon as he awoke. His parents were told that he should not sit on the toilet for more than 5 minutes and that they should make his toileting experience as pleasant as possible.

Praise and significant rewards (e.g., small toys) were administered to Steven for having bowel movements in the toilet upon awakening. If Steven did not defecate, he was given a glycerin suppository, ate breakfast, and was instructed to ready himself for school. Prior to leaving for school, Steven was instructed to make a second attempt to have a bowel movement. If proper elimination occurred at this time, Steven was praised and given a small reward (e.g., chewing gum, stickers, a few pennies, etc.). If Steven was unable to have a bowel movement with the aid of the suppository, he was given an enema prior to going to school. No rewards were offered on those occasions when enemas were needed to produce defecation.

At the end of the day, Steven's parents were instructed to examine his clothing for staining. If Steven had not soiled, he received another reward (e.g., "Steven time," which was 30 minutes when either his mother or father would give him undivided attention and do anything he wanted to do). During the occasions he did soil, Steven received mild punishment, which included a 5-minute time out (sitting in a chair). Also, when Steven soiled, he was required to clean himself and his clothing thoroughly. His parents were instructed to be neutral and nonpunitive in their approach to Steven during the punishment and cleanliness period.

Steven's parents reported the need to use an enema the first 5 days and suppositories on approximately 10 days of the treatment protocol, but by the end of the 4 weeks Steven was able to defecate without the use of enemas or suppositories. The frequency of soiling episodes had diminished from the second week on. In the fifth week, Steven soiled only once and required no enemas or suppositories. By the end of the eighth week, Steven had not experienced soiling episodes for 3 weeks. At this point, he was taken to dinner at a local restaurant to celebrate successful completion of the program, and the protocol was discontinued. At a 3-month follow-up, Steven's parents reported maintenance of the behavior change, with no episodes of soiling during this time period.

REFERENCES

Abelew, P. H. (1972). Intermittent schedule of reinforcement applied to the conditioning treatment of enuresis. *Dissertation Abstracts International, 33,* 2799B–2800B.

Abrahamian, F. P., & Lloyd-Still, J. D., (1984). Chronic constipation in childhood: A longitudinal study of 186 patients. *Journal of Pediatric Gastroenterology and Nutrition, 3*, 460–467.

Alberti, R. E., & Emmons, M. L. (1974). *Your perfect right* (2nd ed.). San Luis Obispo, CA: Impact.

Allgeier, A. R. (1976). Minimizing therapist supervision in the treatment of enuresis. *Journal of Behavior Therapy and Experimental Psychiatry, 7*, 371–372.

American Psychiatric Association. (1987). *Diagnostic and statistical manual of mental disorders* (3rd ed., rev.). Washington, DC: Author.

Angelides, A., & Fitzgerald, J. F. (1981). Pharmacologic advances in the treatment of gastrointestinal diseases. *Pediatric Clinics of North America, 28*, 95–112.

Azrin, N. H., & Foxx, R. M. (1971). A rapid method of toilet training the institutionalized retarded. *Journal of Applied Behavior Analysis, 4*, 89–99.

Azrin, N. H., & Foxx, R. M. (1974). *Toilet training in less than a day*. New York: Simon & Schuster.

Azrin, N. H., & Foxx, R. M. (1976). *Toilet training in less than a day*. New York: Pocket Books.

Azrin, N. H., Sneed, T. J., & Foxx, R. M. (1974). Dry-bed training: Rapid elimination of childhood enuresis. *Behaviour Research and Therapy, 12*, 147–156.

Azrin, N. H., & Thienes, P. M. (1978). Rapid elimination of enuresis by intensive learning without a conditioning apparatus. *Behavior Therapy, 9*, 342–354.

Azrin, N. H., Thienes-Hontos, P. T., & Besalel-Azrin, V. (1979). Elimination of enuresis without a conditioning apparatus: An extension by office instruction of the child and parents. *Behavior Therapy, 10*, 14–19.

Bach, R., & Moylan, J. J. (1975). Parents administer behavior therapy for inappropriate urination and encopresis: A case study. *Journal of Behavior Therapy and Experimental Psychiatry, 6*, 239–241.

Baer, R. F. (1961). Hypnosis applied to bowel and bladder control in multiple sclerosis, syringomyelia, and traumatic transverse myelitis. *American Journal of Clinical Hypnosis, 4*, 22–23.

Baker, B. L. (1969). Symptom treatment and symptom substitution in enuresis. *Journal of Abnormal Psychology, 74*, 42–49.

Bakwin, H. (1973). The genetics of enuresis. In I. Kolvin, R. C. MacKeith, & R. Meadow (Eds.), *Bladder control and enuresis* (pp. 73–77). Philadelphia: J. B. Lippincott.

Baller, W. R. (1975). *Bedwetting: Origins and treatment*. New York: Pergamon Press.

Bellman, M. (1966). Studies on encopresis. *Acta Paediatrica Scandinavica, 170*, 1–137.

Bemporad, J. R., Pfeifer, C. M., Gibbs, L., Cortner, R. H., & Bloom, W. (1971). Characteristics of encopretic patients and their families. *Journal of the American Academy of Child Psychiatry, 10*, 272–292.

Berg, I., & Jones, K. V. (1964). Functional fecal incontinence in children. *Archives of Disease in Childhood, 39*, 465–472.

Bernstein, D. A., & Borkovec, T. D. (1973). *Progressive relaxation training: A manual for helping professionals*. Champaign, IL: Research Press.

Blackwell, B., & Currah, J. (1973). The psychopharmacology of nocturnal enuresis. In I. Kolvin, R. C. MacKeith, & S. R. Meadow (Eds.), *Bladder control and enuresis* (pp. 231–257). Philadelphia: J. B. Lippincott.

Blechman, E. A. (1979). Short and long-term results of positive home-based treatment of childhood chronic constipation and encopresis. *Child Behavior Therapy, 1*, 237–247.

Blomfield, J. M., & Douglas, J. W. B. (1956). Bedwetting: Prevalence among children age 4–7 years. *Lancet, i*, 850–852.

Bollard, J., & Nettelbeck, T. A. (1981). A comparison of dry-bed training and standard urine alarm conditioning treatment of childhood bedwetting. *Behaviour Research and Therapy, 19*, 215–226.

Bollard, J., & Nettelbeck, T. (1982). A component analysis of dry-bed training for treatment for bedwetting. *Behaviour Research and Therapy, 20*, 383–390.

Bollard, R. J., & Woodroffe, P. (1977). The effects of parent-administered dry-bed training on nocturnal enuresis in children. *Behaviour Research and Therapy, 15*, 159–165.

Bornstein, P. H., Balleweg, B. J., McLellarn, R. W., Wilson, G. C., Strum, C. A., Andre, J. C., & Van Den Pol, R. A. (1983). The bathroom game: A systematic program for the elimination of encopretic behavior. *Journal of Behavior Therapy and Experimental Psychiatry, 14*, 67–71.

Boyd, M. M. (1960). The depth of sleep in enuretic school children and in nonenuretic controls. *Journal of Psychosomatic Research, 4*, 274–281.

Bransby, E. R., Blomfield, J. M., & Douglas, J. W. B. (1955). The prevalence of bed-wetting. *Medical Officer, 94*, 5–7.

Brazelton, T. B. (1962). A child oriented approach to toilet training. *Pediatrics, 29*, 121–128.

Butler, J. F. (1976). The toilet training success of parents after reading *Toilet training in less than a day. Behavior Therapy, 7*, 185–191.

Butler, J. F. (1977). Treatment of encopresis by over correction. *Psychological Reports, 40*, 639–646.

Byrne, S. (1973). Hypnosis and the irritable bowel: Case history methods and speculation. *American Journal of Clinical Hypnosis, 15*, 263–265.

Cerulli, M. A., Nikoomanesh, P., & Schuster, M. M. (1979). Progress in biofeedback conditioning for fecal incontinence. *Gastroenterology, 76*, 742–746.

Chamberlain, R. W. (1974). Management of preschool behavior. *Pediatric Clinics of North America, 21*, 33–47.

Christophersen, E. R., & Rainey, S. K. (1976). Management of encopresis through a pediatric outpatient clinic. *Journal of Pediatric Psychology, 1*, 38–41.

Christophersen, E. R., & Rapoff, M. A. (1983). Toileting problems of children. In C. E. Walker & M. C. Roberts (Eds.), *Handbook of clinical child psychology* (pp. 593–615). New York: Wiley.

Cohen, S. I., & Reed, J. L. (1968). The treatment of "nervous diarrhea" and other conditioned autonomic disorders by desensitization. *British Journal of Psychiatry, 114*, 1275–1280.

Collins, R. W. (1973). Importance of the bladder-cue buzzer contingency in the conditioning treatment of enuresis. *Journal of Abnormal Psychology, 82*, 299–308.

Creer, T. L., & Davis, M. H. (1975). Using a staggered-wakening procedure with enuretic children in an institutional setting. *Journal of Behavior Therapy and Experimental Psychiatry, 6*, 23–25.

Crosby, N. D. (1950). Essential enuresis: Successful treatment based on physiological concept. *Medical Journal of Australia, 2*, 533–543.

Crowley, C. P., & Armstrong, P. M. (1977). Positive practice, over correction and behavior rehearsal in the treatment of three cases of encopresis. *Journal of Behavior Therapy and Experimental Psychiatry, 8,* 411–416.

de Jonge, G. A. (1973). Epidemiology of enuresis: A survey of the literature. In I. Kolvin, R. C. MacKeith, & S. R. Meadow (Eds.), *Bladder control and enuresis* (pp. 39–46). Philadelphia: J. B. Lippincott.

DeLeon, G., & Mandell, W. (1966). A comparison of conditioning and psychotherapy in the treatment of functional enuresis. *Journal of Clinical Psychology, 22,* 326–330.

Dische, S. (1971). Management of enuresis. *British Medical Journal, ii,* 33–36.

Doleys, D. M. (1977). Behavioral treatments for nocturnal enuresis in children: A review of the recent literature. *Psychological Bulletin, 84,* 30–54.

Doleys, D. M. (1978). Assessment and treatment of enuresis and encopresis in children. In M. Hersen, R. Eisler, & P. M. Miller (Eds.), *Progress in behavior modification* (Vol. 6, pp. 85–121). New York: Academic Press.

Doleys, D. M. (1979). Assessment and treatment of childhood enuresis. In A. J. Finch & P. C. Kendall (Eds.), *Chemical treatment and research in child psychopathology* (pp. 207–233). New York: Spectrum.

Doleys, D. M., & Arnold, S. (1975). Treatment of childhood encopresis: Full cleanliness training. *Mental Retardation, 13,* 14–16.

Doleys, D. M., Ciminero, A. R., Tollison, J. W., Williams, C. L., & Wells, K. C. (1977). Dry-bed training and retention control training: A comparison. *Behavior Therapy, 8,* 541–548.

Doleys, D. M., & Dolce, J. D. (1982). Toilet training and enuresis. *Pediatric Clinics of North America, 29,* 297–313.

Doleys, D. M., McWhorter, A. Q., Williams, S. C., & Gentry, W. R. (1977). Encopresis: Its treatment and relation to nocturnal enuresis. *Behavior Therapy, 8,* 77–82.

Doleys, D. M., Schwartz, M. S., & Ciminero, A. R. (1981). Elimination problems: Enuresis and encopresis. In E. J. Mash & L. G. Terdal (Eds.), *Behavioral assessment of childhood disorders* (pp. 679–710). New York: Guilford Press.

Douglas, J. W. B. (1973). Early disturbing events and later enuresis. In I. Kolvin, R. C. MacKeith, & S. R. Meadow (Eds.), *Bladder control and enuresis* (pp. 109–117). Philadelphia: J. B. Lippincott.

Engel, B. T., Nikoomanesh, P., & Schuster, M. R. (1974). Operant conditioning of rectosphincteric responses in the treatment of fecal incontinence. *New England Journal of Medicine, 290,* 646–649.

Fenichel, O. (1946). *The psychoanalytic theory of neurosis.* London: Routledge & Kegan Paul.

Ferinden, W., & Van Handel, D. (1970). Elimination of soiling behavior in an elementary school child through the application of aversive techniques. *Journal of School Psychology, 8,* 267–269.

Fielding, D. (1980). The response of day and night wetting children and children who wet only at night to retention control training and the enuresis alarm. *Behaviour Research and Therapy, 18,* 305–317.

Fielding, D. (1982). An analysis of the behaviour of day and night-wetting children: Towards a mode of micturition control. *Behaviour Research and Therapy, 20,* 49–60.

Fielding, R., & Doleys, D. (1988). Enuresis and encopresis. In E. J. Mash & L. G. Terdal (Eds.), *Behavioral assessment of childhood disorders* (2nd ed., pp. 586–626). New York: Guilford Press.

Finley, W. W., Besserman, R. L., Bennett, L. F., Clapp, R. K., & Finley, P. M. (1973). The effect of continuous, intermittent, and placebo reinforcement on the effectiveness of the treatment for enuresis nocturna. *Behaviour Research and Therapy, 11,* 289–297.

Finley, W. W., & Perry, R. R. (1973). Relationship of EEG findings to enuresis nocturna in children with psychiatric disorders. *Clinical Encephalography, 4,* 62–69.

Finley, W. W., Rainwater, A. J., & Johnson, G. (1982). Effect of varying alarm schedules on acquisition and relapse parameters in the conditioning treatment of enuresis. *Behaviour Research and Therapy, 20,* 69–80.

Finley, W. W., & Smith, H. A. (1975). A long-life, inexpensive urine-detection pad for conditioning of enuresis nocturna. *Behavior Research Methods and Instrumentation, 7,* 273–276.

Finley, W. W., & Wansley, R. A. (1976). Use of intermittent reinforcement in a clinical-research program for the treatment of enuresis nocturna. *Journal of Pediatric Psychology, 4,* 24–27.

Finley, W. W., Wansley, R. A., & Blenkarn, M. M. (1977). Conditioning treatment of enuresis using a 70% intermittent reinforcement schedule. *Behaviour Research and Therapy, 15,* 419–427.

Fitzgerald, J. F. (1975). Encopresis, soiling, constipation: What's to be done? *Pediatrics, 56,* 348–349.

Forsythe, W. I., & Redmond, A. (1974). Enuresis and spontaneous cure rate: A study of 1129 enuretics. *Archives of Disease in Childhood, 49,* 259–276.

Foxx, A. Z. (1985). The successful treatment of diurnal and nocturnal enuresis and encopresis. *Child and Family Behavior Medicine, 7,* 39–47.

Fried, R. (1974). A device for enuresis control. *Behavior Therapy, 5,* 682–684.

Friedman, A. R. (1968). Behavior training in a case of enuresis. *Journal of Individual Psychology, 24,* 86–87.

Gardner, G. G., & Olness, K. (1981). *Hypnosis and hypnotherapy with children.* New York: Grune & Stratton.

Gillin, J. C., Rapoport, J. L., Mikkelson, E. J., Langer, D., Vanskiver, C., & Mendelson, W. (1982). EEG sleep in enuresis: A further analysis and comparison with normal controls. *Biological Psychiatry, 17,* 947–953.

Glicklich, L. B. (1951). An historical account of enuresis. *Pediatrics, 8,* 859–876.

Goldenberg, D. A., Hodges, K., Hersh, T., & Jinick, H. (1980). Biofeedback therapy for fecal incontinence. *American Journal of Gastroenterology, 74,* 342–345.

Goldsmith, H. (1962). Chronic loss of bowel control in a nine year old child. *American Journal of Clinical Hypnosis, 4,* 191–193.

Griffiths, P., Meldrum, C., & McWilliam, R. (1982). Dry-bed training in the treatment of nocturnal enuresis in childhood: A research report. *Journal of Child Psychology and Psychiatry, 23,* 485–495.

Gunnarsen, S., & Melin, K. A. (1951). The electroencephalogram in enuresis. *Acta Pediatrica, 40,* 496–501.

Gurman, A. S., & Kniskern, D. P. (Eds.). (1981). *Handbook of family therapy.* New York: Brunner/Mazel.

Hallgren, B. (1956). Enuresis: I. A study with reference to morbidity risk and symptomatology. II. A study with reference to certain physical, mental and social factors possibly associated with enuresis. *Acta Psychiatrica Scandinavica, 31,* 379–436.

Hedberg, A. G. (1973). The treatment of chronic diarrhea by systematic desensitization: A case report. *Journal of Behavior Therapy and Experimental Psychiatry, 4,* 67–68.

Hein, H. A., & Beerends, J. J. (1978). Who should accept primary responsibility for the encopretic child? *Clinical Pediatrics, 17,* 67–70.

Henderson, W. (1976). A review of the current medical aspects of enuresis. *Journal of Pediatric Psychology, 4,* 15–16.

Hoag, S. M., Norriss, N. G., Himeno, E. T., & Jacobs, J. (1971). The encopretic child and his family. *Journal of the American Academy of Child Psychiatry, 10,* 242–256.

Jehu, D., Morgan, R., Turner, R., & Jones, A. (1977). A controlled trial of the treatment of enuresis in residential homes for children. *Behaviour Research and Therapy, 15,* 1–16.

Johnson, J. H., & Thompson, D. J. (1974). Modeling in the treatment of enuresis: A case study. *Journal of Behavior Therapy and Experimental Psychiatry, 5,* 93–94.

Jones, H. G. (1960). The behavioral treatment of enuresis nocturna. In H. J. Eysenck (Ed.), *Behavior therapy and the neuroses* (pp. 377–403). New York: Pergamon Press.

Kaffman, M., & Elizur, E. (1977). Infants who become enuretics: A longitudinal study of 161 kibbutz children. *Monographs of the Society for Research in Child Development, 42:2,* (Serial No. 170).

Kanner, L. (1972). *Child psychiatry* (4th ed.). Springfield, IL: Charles C Thomas.

Kashinsky, W. (1974). Two low cost micturition alarms. *Behavior Therapy, 5,* 698–700.

Keating, J. C., Butz, R. A., Burke, E., & Heimberg, R. G. (1983). Dry-bed training without a urine alarm: Lack of effect of setting and therapist contact with child. *Journal of Behavior Therapy and Experimental Psychiatry, 14,* 109–115.

Kimmel, H., & Kimmel, E. C. (1970). An instrumental conditioning method for the treatment of enuresis. *Journal of Behavior Therapy and Experimental Psychiatry, 1,* 121–123.

Knopf, I. J. (1979). *Childhood psychopathology: A developmental approach.* Englewood Cliffs, NJ: Prentice-Hall.

Kohen, D., Olness, K., Corwell, S., & Heimel, A. (1980, November). *500 pediatric behavioral problems treated with hypnotherapy.* Paper presented at the annual meeting of the American Society of Clinical Hypnosis, Minneapolis.

Lake, C. R., Mikkelson, E. J., Rapoport, J. L., Zavadil, A. P., & Kopin, I. J. (1979). Effects of imipramine on norepinephrine and blood pressure in enuretic boys. *Clinical Pharmacology and Therapeutics, 26,* 647–653.

Latimer, P. R., Campbell, D., & Kasperski, J. (1984). A components analysis of biofeedback in the treatment of fecal incontinence. *Biofeedback and Self-Regulation, 9,* 311–324.

Levine, M. D. (1975). Children with encopresis: A descriptive analysis. *Pediatrics, 56,* 412–416.

Lovibond, S. H. (1964). *Conditioning and enuresis.* New York: Macmillan.

Lovibond, S. H., & Coote, M. A. (1970). Enuresis. In C. G. Costello (Ed.), *Symptoms of psychopathology: A handbook* (pp. 373–396). New York: Wiley.

MacKeith, R. C. (1972). Is maturation delay a frequent factor in the origins of primary nocturnal enuresis? *Developmental Medicine and Child Neurology, 14,* 217–223.

Matson, J. L., & Ollendick, T. H. (1977). Issues in toilet training normal children. *Behavior Therapy, 8,* 549–553.

McColgan, E. B., Pugh, R. L., & Pruitt, D. B. (1985). Encopresis: A structural/strategic approach to family treatment. *American Journal of Family Therapy, 13,* 46–54.

McTaggert, A., & Scott, M. (1959). A review of twelve cases of encopresis. *Journal of Pediatrics, 54,* 762–768.

Meichenbaum, D. (1977). *Cognitive behavior modification.* New York: Plenum.

Mikkelsen, E. J., Brown, G. L., Minichiello, M. D., Millican, F. K., & Rapoport, J. L. (1982). Neurologic status in hyperactive, enuretic, encopretic and normal boys. *Journal of the American Academy of Child Psychiatry, 21,* 75–81.

Mikkelsen, E. J., & Rapoport, J. L. (1980). Enuresis: Psychopathology, sleep stage, and drug response. *Urologic Clinics of North America, 7,* 361–377.

Morgan, R. T. T., & Young, G. C. (1972). The treatment of enuresis: Merits of conditioning methods. *Community Medicine, 128,* 119–121.

Mowrer, O. H. (1980). Enuresis: The beginning work—what really happened. *Journal of the History of the Behavioral Sciences, 16,* 25–30.

Mowrer, O. H., & Mowrer, W. M. (1938). Enuresis—a method for its study and treatment. *American Journal of Orthopsychiatry, 8,* 436–459.

Muellner, S. R. (1960). Development of urinary control in children: A new concept in cause, prevention and treatment of primary enuresis. *Journal of Urology, 84,* 714–716.

Nettelbeck, T., & Langeluddecke, P. (1979). Dry-bed training without an enuresis machine. *Behaviour Research and Therapy, 17,* 403–404.

Newson, J., & Newson, E. (1968). *Four-year-old in the urban community.* London: Allen & Unwin.

Nilsson, D. E. (1976). Treatment of encopresis: A token economy. *Journal of Pediatric Psychology, 1,* 42–26.

Novick, J. (1966). Symptomatic treatment of acquired and persistent enuresis. *Journal of Abnormal Psychology, 71,* 363–368.

Olness, K. (1975). The use of self-hypnosis in the treatment of childhood nocturnal enuresis. *Clinical Pediatrics, 14,* 273–279.

Olness, K. (1976). Autohypnosis in functional megacolon in children. *American Journal of Clinical Hypnosis, 19,* 28–32.

Oppel, W. C., Harper, P. A., & Rider, R. V. (1968). Social, psychological, and neurological factors associated with nocturnal enuresis. *Pediatrics, 42,* 627–641.

Parker, L., & Whitehead, W. (1982). Treatment of urinary and fecal incontinence in children. In D. C. Russo & J. W. Varni (Eds.), *Behavioral pediatrics: Research and practice* (pp. 143–174). New York: Plenum.

Paschalis, A. P., Kimmel, H. D., & Kimmel, E. C. (1972). Further study of diurnal instrumental conditioning in the treatment of enuresis nocturna. *Journal of Behavior Therapy and Experimental Psychiatry, 3,* 253–256.

Pierce, C. M. (1971). Enuresis. In A. M. Friedman & H. I. Kaplan (Eds.), *The child: His psychological and cultural development* (Vol. 1, pp. 203–209). New York: Atheneum.

Pinkerton, P. (1958). Psychogenic megacolon in children:

The implications of bowel negativism. *Archives of Disease in Childhood, 33,* 371–380.

Poussaint, A. F., & Greenfield, R. (1966). Epilepsy and enuresis. *American Journal of Psychiatry, 122,* 1426–1427.

Poussaint, A. F., Koegler, R. R., & Riehl, J. R. (1967). Enuresis, epilepsy, and the electroencephalogram. *American Journal of Psychiatry, 123,* 1294–1295.

Protinsky, H., & Kersey, B. (1983). Psychogenic encopresis: A family therapy approach. *Journal of Clinical Child Psychology, 12,* 192–197.

Protinsky, H., Quinn, W., & Elliott, S. (1982). Paradoxical prescriptions in family therapy: From child to marital focus. *Journal of Marital and Family Therapy, 8,* 51–55.

Rolider, A., & Van Houten, R. (1985). Treatment of constipation-caused encopresis by a negative reinforcement procedure. *Journal of Behavior Therapy and Experimental Psychiatry, 16,* 67–70.

Ross, A. O. (1981). *Child behavior therapy.* New York: Wiley.

Rutter, M. (1975). *Helping troubled children.* Harmondsworth, England: Penguin Education.

Rutter, M., Yule, W., & Graham, P. (1973). Enuresis and behavioral deviance: Some epidemiological considerations. In I. Kolvin, R. C. MacKeith, & S. R. Meadow (Eds.), *Bladder control and enuresis* (pp. 137–150). Philadelphia: J. B. Lippincott.

Sacks, S., & DeLeon, G. (1983). Conditioning functional enuresis: Follow-up after retraining. *Behaviour Research and Therapy, 21,* 693–694.

Salmon, M. A., Taylor, D. C., & Lee, D. (1973). On the EEG in enuresis. In I. Kolvin, R. C. MacKeith, & S. R. Meadow (Eds.), *Bladder control and enuresis* (pp. 84–94). Philadelphia: J. B. Lippincott.

Schmitt, B. D. (1982). Nocturnal enuresis: An update on treatment. *Pediatric Clinics of North America, 29,* 21–36.

Shaffer, D. (1973). The association between enuresis and emotional disorder: A review of the literature. In I. Kolvin, R. C. MacKeith, & S. R. Meadow (Eds.), *Bladder control and enuresis* (pp. 118–136). Philadelphia: J. B. Lippincott.

Solomon, P., & Patch, V. D. (1969). *Handbook of psychiatry.* Los Altos, CA: Lange Medical.

Stanfield, B., & Mellits, E. D. (1968). Increase in functional bladder capacity and improvements in enuresis. *Journal of Pediatrics, 72,* 483–487.

Taska, R. J., & Young, D. A. (1982). Childhood encopresis and personality development. *Psychiatric Forum, 11,* 3–13.

Taylor, P. D., & Turner, R. K. (1975). A clinical trial of continuous, intermittent, and overlearning "bell and pad" treatments for nocturnal enuresis. *Behaviour Research and Therapy, 13,* 281–293.

Tilton, P. (1980). Hypnotic treatment of a child with thumbsucking, enuresis and encopresis. *American Journal of Clinical Hypnosis, 22,* 238–240.

Tough, J. H., Hawkins, R. P., McArthur, M. M., & Ravenswaay, S. V. (1971). Modification of enuretic behavior by punishment: A new use for an old device. *Behavior Therapy, 2,* 567–574.

Turner, R. K. (1973). Conditioning treatment of nocturnal enuresis: Present status. In I. Kolvin, R. C. MacKeith, & J. R. Meadow (Eds.), *Bladder control and enuresis* (pp. 195–210). Philadelphia: J. B. Lippincott.

Turner, R. K., Young, G. C., & Rachman, S. (1970). Treatment of nocturnal enuresis by conditioning techniques. *Behaviour Research and Therapy, 8,* 367–381.

Turton, E. C., & Spear, A. B. (1953). Electroencephalographic findings in 100 cases of severe enuresis. *Archives of Disease in Childhood, 28,* 316–320.

Vaughn, G. F. (1961). Constipation and encopresis: A children's psychiatrist's view. In R. C. MacKeith & J. Sandler (Eds.), *Psychosomatic aspects of pediatrics,* (pp. 9–12). London: Pergamon Press.

Vaughan, V. C., McKay, R. J., & Behrman, R. E. (1979). *Nelson textbook of pediatrics* (11th ed.). Philadelphia: W. B. Saunders.

Verhulst, F. C., Van Der Lee, J. H., Akkerhuis, G. W., Sanders-Woudstra, J. A., Timmer, F. C., & Donkhorst, I. D. (1985). The prevalence of nocturnal enuresis: Do DSM III criteria need to be changed? A brief research report. *Journal of Child Psychology and Psychiatry, 26,* 989–993.

Wagner, W., Johnson, S. B., Walker, D., Carter, R., & Wittner, J. (1982). A controlled comparison of two treatments for nocturnal enuresis. *Journal of Pediatrics, 101,* 302–307.

Wald, A. (1981). Biofeedback therapy for fecal incontinence. *Annals of Internal Medicine, 95,* 146–149.

Walker, C. E. (1978). Toilet training, enuresis, encopresis. In P. R. Magrab (Ed.), *Psychological management of pediatric problems* (Vol. 1, pp. 129–189). Baltimore: University Park Press.

Walker, C. E., Hedberg, A. G., Clement, P. W., & Wright, L. (1981). *Clinical procedures for behavior therapy.* Englewood Cliffs, NJ: Prentice-Hall.

Walker, C. E., Milling, L., & Bonner, B. (1988). Incontinence disorders: Enuresis and encopresis. In D. Routh (Ed.), *Handbook of pediatric psychology* (pp. 263–398). New York: Guilford Press.

Walker, C. E., & Shaw, W. (1988). Assessment of eating and elimination disorders. In P. Karoly (Ed.), *Handbook of child health assessment.* New York: Wiley.

Werry, J. S. (1967). Enuresis: A psychosomatic entity? *Canadian Medical Journal, 97,* 319–327.

Werry, J. S., & Cohrssen, J. (1965). Enuresis: An etiologic and therapeutic study. *Journal of Pediatrics, 67,* 423–431.

White, M. (1968). A thousand consecutive cases of enuresis: Results of treatment. *Medical Officer, 120,* 151–155.

Whitehead, W. E., Parker, L. H., Masek, B. J., Cataldo, M. F., & Freeman, J. M. (1981). Biofeedback treatment of fecal incontinence in patients with myelomeningocele. *Developmental Medicine and Child Neurology, 23,* 313–322.

Wright, L. (1973). Handling the encopretic child. *Professional Psychology, 4,* 137–144.

Wright, L. (1975). Outcome of a standardized program for treating psychogenic encopresis. *Professional Psychology, 6,* 453–456.

Wright, L., Schaefer, A., & Solomons, G. (1978). *Encyclopedia of pediatric psychology.* New York: Plenum.

Wright, L., & Walker, C. E. (1976). Behavioral treatment of encopresis. *Journal of Pediatric Psychology, 4,* 35–37.

Wright, L., & Walker, C. E. (1977). Treatment of the child with psychogenic encopresis. *Clinical Pediatrics, 16,* 1042–1045.

Wright, L., & Walker, C. E. (1978). A simple behavioural

treatment program for psychogenic encopresis. *Behaviour Research and Therapy, 16,* 209–212.

Yates, A. J. (1970) *Behavior therapy.* New York: Wiley.

Young, G. C. (1963). The family history of enuresis. *Journal of the Research Institute of Public Health, 26,* 197–201.

Young, G. C. (1964). A staggered-wakening procedure in the treatment of enuresis. *Medical Officer, 111,* 142–143.

Young, G. C., & Morgan, R. T. T. (1972). Overlearning in the conditioning treatment of enuresis. *Behaviour Research and Therapy, 10,* 419–420.

Young, I. L., & Goldsmith, A. O. (1972). Treatment of encopresis in a day treatment program. *Psychotherapy: Theory, Research, and Practice, 9,* 231–235.

PART VI
CHILDREN AT RISK

13

CHILD ABUSE AND NEGLECT

SANDRA T. AZAR
Clark University

DAVID A. WOLFE
University of Western Ontario

S ocial scientists have been actively investigating the causes and prevention of
child physical abuse for only a brief time
period, relative to other problems of childhood
(such as deprivation, retardation, or behavior
problems; Garmezy, 1983). This inattention
may primarily reflect both lay and professional
groups' lack of awareness regarding the psychological versus the physical impact of child
maltreatment. Throughout the first decade of
focused research on child abuse, the effects of
abuse on the child were typically described in
terms of physical injuries. Child abuse was considered a barbarous act, primarily because
abused children were helpless and were exposed to physical peril, and the medical profession assumed much of the responsibility for
examining the causal factors of abuse (see
Kempe & Helfer, 1972). Justifiably, the interest of medical researchers was largely focused
on the physical injuries that the children suffered, as well as on the underlying psychopathology or disturbance of the parents.

The focus on physical trauma from abuse
gave the problem visibility, yet a recognition of
the more hidden manner in which it can be
traumatic to children has emerged more slowly.
The pervasive effects on abused children's psychological and behavioral development that result from the many factors *accompanying* abuse

in families and affecting their behavior are less
understood and potentially more harmful to the
children's development. The growing interest
of behavioral scientists in the plight of abused
children has helped to identify the inadequately
met needs of these children (e.g., a stable home
environment, positive interactions with adults
and siblings, opportunities for learning prosocial behavior) that often coexist with abuse,
and that continue to affect the children's development if left unattended.

In this chapter, we present an overview of
the child, parent, and family factors that are
believed to cause or result from child abuse. A
conceptual model of abuse is presented to provide a theoretical basis for the development of
abusive behavior over time, and to assist treatment planners in the recognition of major family "symptoms" that foretell greater risk of
abuse. This model is accompanied by an assessment overview that focuses on the general
needs of the family and the specific needs of the
abusive parent and the abused child. Treatment
methods that have shown promise or have received empirical support with abusive families
are then discussed in detail. This discussion of
treatment is accompanied by a rationale for using behavioral approaches with abusive families, as well as decision rules and precautions
that have emerged from treatment efforts with

451

this population. Although this chapter is primarily limited to behavioral interventions that have received some empirical support, an effort is made to provide the reader with additional suggestions that hold promise for changing the patterns of behavior in abusive families that are most harmful to children's psychological development.

OVERVIEW OF THE PROBLEM

Conceptual Definition

A parent who abuses a child is often viewed by community members as being quite different or distinct from nonabusive parents. That is, abusive behavior is so inconceivable to many individuals that a false dichotomy surfaces inadvertently to separate and define "abusive" parents in relation to "normal" parents. However, such a clear distinction between abusive and nonabusive parents does not readily appear if one looks at the different styles of parenting in each community. A parent's behavior toward his or her offspring may change dramatically at any given moment in response to child- or to situation-related demands, and at times this behavior includes negative interactions. What most often distinguishes parents who have been reported for abuse from socioeconomically matched parents who have not, however, is the chronic and escalating pattern of conflict between the parents and their children, culminating in more and more serious injuries over time.

Rather than viewing child abuse and neglect as phenomena that are distinct and separate from other parental actions, therefore, the present approach to conceptualizing these problems focuses on a continuum model of parenting behavior (see Bell & Harper, 1977; Burgess, 1979). At one extreme of the continuum, are those practices considered to be most abusive and inappropriate for the child (e.g., blows with a dangerous object, burns, physical and emotional rejection, etc.); at the other extreme are methods that promote the child's social, emotional, and intellectual development. From this perspective, child abuse and neglect can be defined, for treatment purposes, in terms of the *degree to which a parent uses aversive or inappropriate control strategies with his or her child and/or fails to provide minimal standards of caregiving and nurturance* (Wolfe, 1987). Child abuse, accor-

dingly, is not viewed as being necessarily a symptom of an undefined personality disorder, but rather is conceptualized as the hypothetical extreme of aversive control to which a parent will go during interactions with his or her child without exercising restraint. The psychological mechanisms associated with such lack of control (e.g., thought processes, emotional responses) are receiving greater attention in recent studies; we may hope that this research will clarify the extent to which abusive behavior is a function of characteristics of the individual (e.g., personality disturbance) and situational factors (e.g., aversive child behavior, marital conflict, unmanageable stress) that foster such behavior.

The present definition of child abuse and neglect for treatment-planning purposes does not imply that the consequences to the child are not serious, for abusive acts are the fourth most common cause of death in the first 5 years of life (Standing Senate Committee on Health, Welfare, & Science, 1980). Rather, this viewpoint intends to draw attention toward those aspects of abuse that resemble "typical" parenting methods except in terms of their severity. Furthermore, this definition highlights not only the physically harmful methods that a parent may use, but highlights as well those methods that may be inadequate to meet the child's needs, such as a lack of physical attention, praise, or clear directives from the parent (Azar, 1986, 1987). This view of child abuse as an extreme disturbance of child rearing, therefore, emphasizes the nature of the socialization process (i.e., cultural values and norms) that permits the use of violence as a means of interpersonal control and problem solving. Maltreating families are ones in which the usual balances between reward and punishment and between discipline and affection have broken down. Thus, they are families that have ceased to function as facilitators of children's social and cognitive development and as arenas for socialization (Maccoby & Martin, 1983).

Incidence and Profile of Child Abuse and Neglect

The number of children who are officially reported to child protection agencies because of child abuse and neglect has increased each year, with over twice as many reports in recent years as was true 10 years ago (416,000 in 1976 vs.

929,000 in 1982; American Humane Association, 1984). However, the prevalence of child maltreatment has also been estimated on the basis of nationwide surveys of families across the United States, which provide contrasting viewpoints of the occurrence of this problem. Gelles and Straus (1987), for example, replicated their 1975 nationwide survey 10 years later, and found that the estimated rate of violence toward children (per 1,000) actually *declined* from 1975 to 1985. The most substantial decline was in the use of severe and very severe violence. Severe violence, defined as "kicking, biting, punching," "hitting or trying to hit with an object," "beating, threatening with a knife or a gun," or "using a knife or a gun over the past 12 months," declined from 140 cases per 1,000 in 1975 to 107 per 1,000 in 1985. The authors' index of very severe violence (which dropped the category "hit or tried to hit with something") declined from a rate of 36 per 1,000 to 19 per 1,000, which corresponds to a 47% decline in the rate of abusive violence over that reported in 1975.

Gelles and Straus (1987) suggest several reasons why the rate of child abuse, in particular, may actually be declining: (1) Family organization has changed, as reflected in the increase in the average age at first marriage and having a first child, as well as the decrease in the number of children per family and the number of unwanted children; (2) the economic climate in 1985 had improved over that of 1975, as shown by reductions in the unemployment and inflation rate; (3) there was a massive increase in public awareness of child abuse over this period; and (4) innovative prevention and treatment programs have been implemented. Therefore, the authors acknowledge that the past 10 years have successfully produced a change in consciousness, such that violence toward children is becoming inappropriate and intolerable. Their replication study, therefore, found a reduction in the estimated number of abused children from 1.5 million in 1975 to 705,000 in 1985. The prevalence of physical abuse based on these figures changed from 1 in 25 children in 1975 to 1 in 33 in 1985. Unfortunately, similar estimates of the incidence and prevalence of child neglect and related forms of maltreatment cannot be obtained from these survey findings.

A sociodemographic profile of families reported for child abuse and neglect illuminates many of the cultural and social forces that determine child-rearing methods and that at the same time may contribute to family discord and violence. Although maltreatment occurs in all socioeconomic groups, clinical reports, surveys, and official statistics consistently find that it is most likely to happen among the poor or disadvantaged (American Humane Association, 1984; Gelles, 1983). Studies of the representativeness of epidemiological data indicate that this finding does not appear to be a bias in reporting, especially since it has consistently emerged over the last 20 years of data gathering (National Center on Child Abuse and Neglect, 1981; Pelton, 1978). The child's parents are, for the most part, the perpetrators of physical abuse (97%), with the vast majority being the child's natural parents (American Humane Association, 1984). Another descriptive finding meriting particular concern is that abusive parents often begin their families at a younger age than the average in the population, with many being in their teens at the birth of their first child. This finding suggests they may be less prepared to raise children, given teenagers' maturity level and limited ability to develop social supports and economic security. Finally, official reports indicate that males are more likely than females to be the perpetrators of physical abuse, whereas females are more likely to be reported for neglect (American Humane Association, 1984).

Sociodemographic characteristics of children who are victims of maltreatment do not reveal that any particular subpopulation of children is more likely to be abused than any other. Girls and boys are reportedly maltreated at approximately the same rate, and all age groups are proportionately represented. One potentially important relationship between age and abuse, however, is reflected in the finding that the highest rates of physical injury occur among preschool children and adolescents (American Humane Association, 1984). This finding can be interpreted to mean that these younger and older age groups may receive harsher forms of punishment as a function of the developmentally related oppositional behavior that both groups display (LaRose & Wolfe, 1987). This interpretation is supported by findings indicating that abuse is commonly associated with child disciplinary situations that involve aversive child behaviors (e.g., noncompliance, disruption from the child, aggressive behavior, etc.) (Herrenkohl, Herrenkohl, & Egolf, 1983).

Theoretical–Conceptual Formulation

Distinctions among different theoretical formulations of child abuse have become less clear in recent years; this may reflect the fact that they share important commonalities and do not necessarily represent radically opposed viewpoints of abusive parents (Wolfe, 1985). The three major models of child abuse that were developed throughout the 1970s (i.e., the psychopathological, sociocultural, and social-interactional models) all reflect attempts to understand individual characteristics of abusive parents in relation to prior experience and current demands. One distinction that can be inferred from these explanations, however, is the amount of emphasis each model places on the parent as the principal cause of abuse, as opposed to situational circumstances or the broader sociocultural milieu.

The major theories of child abuse focus primarily on explanations as to *why* a parent may abuse a child, and *how* family process can develop into violent interactions (see Azar, 1987; Burgess, 1979; LaRose & Wolfe, 1987; Parke & Collmer, 1975, for discussion). Although it is beyond the scope of this chapter to expound on these theories, three tenets can be summarized to form a foundation for the current transitional model of abuse.

The first of these tenets relates to the importance of recognizing and studying the *context* of maltreatment, such as the nature of family life, environmental stressors affecting the family, and sociodemographic factors. The context of child maltreatment, as argued by sociocultural theorists, is typically one of social and economic family deprivation. Such deprivation may be the force that transforms predisposed, high-risk parents into abusive or neglectful parents (see Garbarino & Stocking, 1980). An increased degree of stress in the social environment of the abusive or neglectful parent increases the probability that family violence or gross neglect will surface as an attempt to gain control or cope with irritating, stressful events. According to this perspective, child maltreatment is not an isolated social phenomenon or a personality defect of the parent per se; rather, this view maintains that "normal" parents may be socialized into harmful child care practices through the interaction of cultural, community, and familial influences (Belsky, 1980; Parke, 1977). This tenet is supported by studies indicating that, for example, socioeconomic factors (e.g., unemployment, restricted educational and occupational opportunities, poor housing) account for a large proportion of the variance in rates of child abuse and neglect reports (Garbarino, 1976; Gil, 1970; Light, 1973). The context of maltreatment emerges as a critical factor in determining treatment goals and directions, as discussed later in this chapter.

The second major tenet drawn from child abuse theories relates to the ongoing social-interactional *process* between parent and child (within the context of the family and larger social structure). This process resembles similar processes that occur in normal and in clinically distressed parent–child relationships, such as the reciprocation of aversive behavior, reinforcement of inappropriate behavior, ineffective use of punishment, and conditioned emotional arousal. This interactional process approaches the etiology and maintenance of abuse in terms of the dynamic interplay among individual, family, and social factors in relation to both past (e.g., previous abuse as a child in the parent's history) and present (e.g., a demanding child) events that shape the parent–child relationship (Burgess, 1979; Parke & Collmer, 1975). Although parental characteristics are considered important determinants of an abusive episode, the emphasis is mostly upon the processes that define the relationship between the parent and child. These processes are not limited only to observable behavior, such as parental criticisms, child behavior problems, yelling, or displays of anger and aggression. The relevance of cognitive and affective processes, such as intelligence, attitudes, attributions for behavior, depression, and anger, also emerges in studies of how abusive parents process the stressful aspects of their environment.

The third tenet to be incorporated into the current model concerns the learning-based explanations for aggressive behavior that are implicit in the two previous explanations. Particularly relevant to an understanding of the escalation from punishment to abuse are the psychological processes linking mood states and emotional arousal to the disinhibition of aggression.

It comes as no surprise that an individual's

behavior can be greatly influenced by his or her mood and/or relative state of quiescence versus arousal. What is most salient to the study of child abuse, however, is the recognition that negative experiences with intimate others can have affective "tags" when stored in memory (see Bower, 1981). When these experiences are recalled at some later point in time, the recollection of the actual event may bias or overshadow the person's mood at the time. Thus, a parent's previous mood of distress and anger toward others or the child may be recalled by the child's current expression or behavior, even though it is not necessarily provocative. In turn, this association between mood and memory can lead to an overgeneralized (i.e., more angry, more aggressive) response by the parent. Presumably, the adult is responding to cues that have been previously associated with frustration and anger, and consequently the adult's behavior toward the child may be potentiated by these conditioning experiences (Berkowitz, 1983; Vasta, 1982).

Furthermore, the person's level of arousal and his or her beliefs about the *source* of the arousal play a critical role in determining the actual expression of aggression. An abusive parent, for example, may have been angered and aroused (i.e., hyperalert, tense, anxious, in a state of emotional reactivity) by a previous encounter with someone (employer, neighbor, motorist, etc.), which lowers his or her threshold for anger and aggression with others (family members). These feelings of anger create a need for justification, such as blaming others for causing him or her to feel angry, upset, and bothered, which in return encourages further anger and aggression (Averill, 1983). Because of the child's availability and lower-status position, he or she becomes a likely target for this blaming process. The resulting anger and arousal interferes with rational problem solving, such that the parent's awareness of the outcome of his or her actions is diminished and the disciplinary behaviors come under control of emotional and reflexive factors (Vasta, 1982). In this state, the physical punishment may be prolonged, and the act itself can become invigorating or cathartic (see Zillman, 1979).

How parents gradually acquire the preconditions that lead to the rather sudden onset of an abusive episode or chronic rejection and neglect remains a critical concern for treatment planning. Different approaches to intervention may be more relevant at different stages in the development of the preconditions of maltreatment. The manner in which child abuse and neglect risk factors become transformed over time into a harmful pattern is addressed by the following transitional model.

A Transitional Model of Child Abuse and Neglect

The theoretical course of the development of abusive and neglectful behavior has been conceptualized as shown in Figure 13-1. This figure provides an overview of major destabilizing and compensatory factors that are briefly reviewed in the following discussion. The model is based on the major proposition that the development of harmful child-rearing patterns follows a somewhat predictable course in the absence of intervention efforts or compensatory factors. This course of the development of the parent–child relationship is conceptualized here in terms of *stages* that signify the transition from milder to more harmful interactions over time (see Wolfe, 1987).

The initial stage (Stage 1) of the development of abusive patterns is relatively benign in comparison to later stages. It begins with the parent's own preparation (in terms of psychological and social resources, attributional style, modeling, and similar learning experiences from childhood) and current style of coping with daily demands that compete with the parenting role. Much of this preparation is assumed to be tied to the parent's own family of origin, as well as his or her psychological resources (e.g., IQ, stress tolerance, coping skills). Based on retrospective reports from abusive parents, the family of origin can be typified as a training ground for interpersonal violence and/or lowered social competence (see Kempe & Helfer, 1972; Spinetta & Rigler, 1972). This training is inadvertently accomplished through the modeling of aggressive problem-solving tactics and an external attributional style; rehearsal and reinforcement of aggressive behavior with siblings and peers (or, alternatively, the lack of effective punishment for such behavior); and the absence of opportunities to learn prosocial behavior, which presumably may lower the individual's frustration level or enable him or her to avoid anger-arousing situations.

Factors that play a critical role in mediating the expression of aggressive behavior once the individual becomes a parent can be identified from the related research on stress and coping (Folkman, 1984; Levine, 1983). In particular, the degree of control, feedback, and predictability that the parent perceives in relation to stressful life events can help to explain the parent's behavior. The significance of the parent's ability to cope with fluctuating levels of stressful life events (e.g., financial loss, marital conflict, high levels of ambient noise) cannot be understated. Stressful events play a critical role in provoking the onset of major health- and adjustment-related disorders (e.g., Brown & Harris, 1978; Rutter, 1983), and it is reasonable to assume that such events may provoke abusive behavior as well. Life events, moreover, are perceived as more stressful under circumstances in which persons believe they have little ability to make coping responses (i.e., low control and predictability), and receive poor feedback on their efforts to deal with the stressor (Levine, 1983). On a more positive note, however, these difficulties that emerge in some families may be counterbalanced by compensatory factors such as a supportive spouse; socioeconomic stability; success experiences at work, school, or similar activity; and adequate social supports and resources to draw upon for information and assistance (see Figure 13-1, right-hand side of each box).

Stage 2 represents the hypothetical point in the development of maltreatment at which the parent's previous attempts or methods of managing life stress or child behavior begin to fail

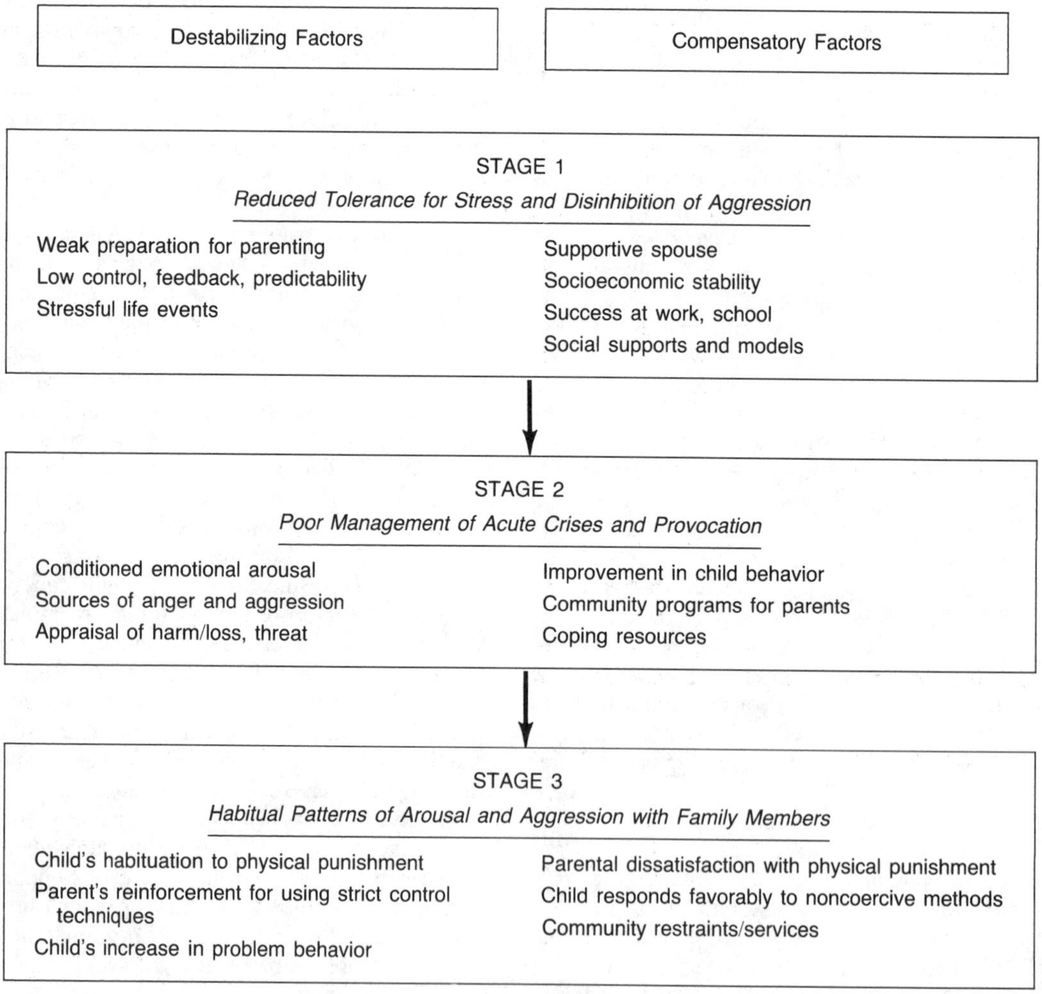

Destabilizing Factors	Compensatory Factors

STAGE 1

Reduced Tolerance for Stress and Disinhibition of Aggression

Weak preparation for parenting
Low control, feedback, predictability
Stressful life events

Supportive spouse
Socioeconomic stability
Success at work, school
Social supports and models

STAGE 2

Poor Management of Acute Crises and Provocation

Conditioned emotional arousal
Sources of anger and aggression
Appraisal of harm/loss, threat

Improvement in child behavior
Community programs for parents
Coping resources

STAGE 3

Habitual Patterns of Arousal and Aggression with Family Members

Child's habituation to physical punishment
Parent's reinforcement for using strict control
    techniques
Child's increase in problem behavior

Parental dissatisfaction with physical punishment
Child responds favorably to noncoercive methods
Community restraints/services

FIGURE 13-1. A transitional model of child abuse.

significantly. Negative feedback, and poor control and predictability of child behavior and family matters, serve to exacerbate the feelings of "losing control" that are frequently reported by abusive parents who are seen by professionals. It is at this juncture that the risk of child abuse, in particular, begins to increase. The parent may "step up" the intensity of power-assertive methods that he or she believes are necessary to re-establish a semblance of control. As mentioned previously, conditioned emotional responding may overtake the parent's rational behavior at this point. Feelings of extreme agitation and irritation that may have originated from other sources of anger (e.g., employer, neighbor, spouse) are attributed to the child, based on previous conditioning experiences that resemble the current perception of child provocation. As a consequence, when the child cries or fusses to seek attention or assistance, the parent may appraise the situation as one of harm, loss, or threat, leading him or her to conclude that excessive countermeasures are justified to gain control of the child's aversive behavior. As in Stage 1, the degree of stress experienced by the parent may be offset by compensatory factors, especially improvement in the child's behavior (through maturation, treatment, changes in family circumstances, etc.), the availability of community resources (e.g., day care, respite centers, educational programs for parents), and effective coping resources (e.g., problem-solving skills, social supports, physical energy and stamina, material assistance, and cognitive strategies that differentiate the child's immaturity from other stress-inducing events).

Beyond this crisis point represented by Stage 2, a habitual pattern of irritability, arousal, and/or avoidance of responsibility (e.g., failure to instruct or guide the child; emotional or physical rejection) may become established (Stage 3) and serves to maintain the use of excessive punishment and force or the reliance on inappropriate avoidance of responsibility. Provocative stimuli, such as child behavior problems, frustration, and emotional arousal, now become more commonplace, and the parent's response to such events escalates in intensity, duration, and frequency.

Parents who have reached this point often perceive that they are "trapped" into continuing to use harsh or extreme methods to control their children. This perception is somewhat accurate, in that some children habituate to the existing level of punishment intensity, so that more and more severe forms of discipline are required to attain the previous level of desired behavior (Friedman, Sandler, Hernandez, & Wolfe, 1981). In addition, the short-term consequences for the parent often serve to maintain such strict control methods. That is, the parent may sense a diminution of tension and irritation (i.e., negative reinforcement) following a coercive battle with the child, or he or she may be rewarded by the child's ultimate compliance to demands. However, these short-lived "gains" that the parent may sense are often negated by long-term negative effects that usually go undetected: The child's problem behavior increases, the child fails to acquire desirable behavior, and the mounting intensity of punishment or gross neglect heightens the risk to the child.

Unfortunately, the reversal of this process is aided by very few compensatory factors by Stage 3. The parent may become dissatisfied with the ineffectiveness of physical punishment and/or recognize the need to refrain from using such methods. Conversely, the child may begin to respond more favorably to parental directives, thus easing pressure on the parent. The probability of either of these occurring at this point is presumed to be low. Community efforts to curtail child abuse, however, may have an impact if the parent is warned of his or her intolerable behavior as soon as the crisis point has been reached, and services are immediately provided to augment the parent's coping resources and reduce the level of stress on the family. The common dilemma faced by treatment planners is most salient at this stage: Major efforts to change well-established patterns of family interactions must be introduced in such a manner that the parent will recognize that the benefits (e.g., a well-behaved child, more pleasant family interactions) outweigh the costs (e.g., efforts needed to learn different disciplinary methods, pronounced increases in child problem behavior in the short-term).

The task of professionals dealing with such distressed families is to interrupt this deterioration and to intervene in such a way as to restore the families' ability to cope with external demands and provide for the developmental and socialization needs of their children. Behavioral assessment and intervention approaches show much promise in assisting in this task.

TREATMENT ISSUES WITH CHILD-ABUSIVE FAMILIES

The Growth of Interest in Behavioral Approaches to Child Abuse Intervention

Behavioral strategies for treating child maltreatment have only recently become the object of empirical examination (Gambrill, 1983; Isaacs, 1982). Since the late 1970s, their use has grown rapidly, and the number of outcome studies documenting their effectiveness has been steadily increasing. This growth of interest in behavioral approaches has been fostered by a number of events. One major force has been the fact that early methods of treatment for abuse (e.g., lay counseling, psychotherapy, and provisions of support services) have been found to be inadequate. These methods have been criticized as being too narrow in scope to produce changes in the disturbed family interaction patterns that are central to the occurrence of abuse. Early treatment efforts with abusive families were based on psychodynamic theorizing regarding parental psychiatric deviancy (e.g., the belief that abusive parents are psychotic) (Steele & Pollock, 1968). This led to an initial focus on producing intrapsychic change in the parents (Williams, 1983). For example, Cohn and Miller's (1977) evaluation of federally funded programs of the National Center on Child Abuse and Neglect found that in 85% of abuse cases, only adult family members were being treated. It is now clear that only a small proportion of abusive parents (e.g., approximately 5%) are significantly psychiatrically disturbed (Steele, 1975), therefore, the foundation of traditional approaches has come into doubt.

In addition to problems with the etiological assumptions of traditional approaches, these approaches have not been demonstrated to be effective. Large-scale treatment studies employing traditional methods of lay counseling, parent education, support services, and psychotherapy have consistently shown high recidivism rates of abuse, both during and after treatment. Cohn's (1979) evaluation of 11 federally funded demonstration programs indicated that 30% of abusive parents seriously reabused their children *during* treatment. In another study with 328 families, Herrenkohl, Herrenkohl, Egolf, and Seech (1979) found that 66.8% of the families completing treatment had

incidents of reabuse that were verified. Even after cases had been closed, 18.5% of these parents were found to be reabusing their children. Such failures occurred despite the fact that one-fourth of the families had received over 3 years of treatment. Traditional approaches emphasizing personality change in the parents, therefore, were not addressing the problem.

Concurrently, as changes occurred in social attitudes toward child abuse, pressure was placed on the court system and on social service agency personnel to take action to maintain the family unit. This re-emphasis produced a move toward less court involvement (Reid, 1985) and fewer and shorter placements of children outside their homes. Social service agencies were called upon more frequently to provide effective, yet brief, interventions to change family interactions to insure the safety of the children. This promoted a search for treatments that were broader in scope than intrapsychic methods, and that would produce changes in parent–child interactions in a shorter time period.

Behavioral approaches fulfill this mandate directly. Intervention techniques for the kinds of deficits exhibited by abusive families are already well developed in the behavioral literature. For example, an extensive literature has described techniques for modifying parent–child interactions and has documented their effectiveness (e.g., Gordon & Davidson, 1981; Graziano, 1977; O'Dell, 1974) Similarly, effective approaches based on social learning theory also exist for training adults in stress management skills and anger control, as well as for modifying thought processes that interfere with behavioral goals.

The family characteristics of child abusers also make behavioral techniques attractive. First, many of these clients are cognitively low-functioning (Schilling & Schinke, 1984), making more traditional insight-oriented approaches less appropriate. Behavioral strategies can be designed to be concrete and problem-focused, and therefore may be better suited to the less intellectual client. The effectiveness of behavioral approaches with low-functioning clients has been well documented (Foxx, McMorrow, & Mennemeier, 1984; Foxx, McMorrow, & Schloss, 1983; Kazdin & Polster, 1973); thus, their feasibility with abusive and neglectful families is supported.

In addition to parental cognitive limitations, clients' expectations regarding what will take place in therapy are relevant to choosing treatment approaches. Expectations regarding the nature of and appropriate behavior for psychotherapy significantly influence the course of treatment along a number of dimensions, including duration (Garfield & Wolpin, 1963), attrition rates (Overall & Aronson, 1962), outcome (Lennard & Bernstein, 1960), patient discomfort (Baum & Felzer, 1964), and involvement in the therapeutic process (Kamin & Caughlin, 1963; Levitt, 1966; White, Fichtenbaum, & Dollard, 1964). Because maltreating patients typically are from lower socioeconomic backgrounds (American Humane Association, 1984), their expectations regarding treatment are believed to differ from those of middle-class clients (Aronson & Overall, 1966). They approach psychological treatment in much the same manner as they would medical help, expecting it to be closely tied to the "pain" they are experiencing and to involve a direct "prescription" by the therapist. Behavioral techniques have been suggested as being more consistent with such expectations than traditional dynamic therapies (Lorion, 1978). Techniques based on social learning theory are high in face validity and are action-oriented, permitting clients to work most on changing their parenting behavior (i.e., the behavior that got them into difficulty).

Another characteristic that makes behavioral approaches more attractive for this population is the fact that parents are often involuntary clients. Resistance to treatment is inevitable in such cases; it may involve a fear of being seen as "crazy," or anger at being told to do something against their will. Because behavioral treatments may be perceived as more "educational" in nature, such approaches may be less threatening, and thereby may make it easier to elicit cooperation from a family.

Some Limitations of Behavioral Strategies

All of the reasons described above make behavioral strategies attractive for treating abuse and neglect; however, there are some limitations in the use of these approaches as well. First, some abusive parents do suffer from long-standing personality disorder or specific severe disturbances (e.g., psychosis), which may respond best to long-term psychiatric treatment approaches or to pharmacological interventions. Such approaches should precede or replace behavioral treatment when necessary.

Second, the involvement of the legal system may complicate the use of behavioral procedures. For example, behavioral treatment often requires the close monitoring of family behavior (e.g., family observations in the home or laboratory). Such monitoring can lead families' legal counsel to recommend that they not participate in treatment, for fear the data may be used against them (Reid, 1985). In addition, court involvement may also impede client motivation. Extra care must be taken in structuring the therapeutic relationship in such cases, and some compromises may be necessary to overcome some of these problems. More attention is given to this area later in the chapter.

A third limitation in using behavioral methods is related to the requirement that parents practice new parenting strategies with their children. Many times, a maltreating parent who is referred for treatment does not have custody of the child (e.g., the child has been placed in foster care), and visitation rights may be so restricted or artificial that opportunities for practice with the child may be curtailed. Role playing and special supervised visitation arrangements may be viable interim solutions to this problem, followed by supervised rehearsal once the child has been returned to the family.

A fourth limitation is related to the social context of maltreating families. Behavioral approaches with family members may be inadequate to modify the families' lack of social and economic resources and may require collaborative efforts with social service agencies for vocational training and other programs.

Finally, a more general and less easily resolved limitation to the application of behavioral techniques with abusive families has to do with the state of our understanding of child abuse as a "behavioral" problem (Azar, Fantuzzo, & Twentyman, 1984). Behavioral interventions require a clear, empirically grounded understanding of the topography of the disorder to be treated (e.g., the antecedents and consequences that elicit and maintain the behavior). Although in our model we have presented some preliminary ideas regarding the relevant dimensions on which to assess a family (see Wolfe, 1988), detailed information is still relatively unavailable. Child maltreatment is a private event, and research documenting its topography is still in its infancy (Azar, Fantuzzo, & Twentyman, 1984). The assessment procedures we describe below can help in defining potential targets for treatment, but some of the most relevant dimensions may still be unknown. These issues are addressed throughout the remainder of this chapter.

ASSESSMENT WITH ABUSIVE AND NEGLECTFUL FAMILIES

The causes and outcomes of child maltreatment are entwined with the parent's childhood and early adult history, child-rearing skills, stressful events, social relationships, and features of the child, among others. In view of the complexity of this problem, behavioral assessment and treatment of abusive and neglectful families must be approached as a multistage process. Assessment typically begins with impressionistic data from reporting and referral sources, and then narrows toward the evaluation of more specific intervention needs. In addition, several aspects of assessing as well as treating abusive families are different from the assessment and treatment of other clinical populations (Wolfe, 1988), and are highlighted in this section and the one that follows.

Developing An Assessment Strategy

Several intermediate goals must be met prior to making case management decisions and initiating intervention with a maltreating family. In the following assessment strategy, these goals include two general concerns requiring initial screening and attention: (1) determining danger and risk to the child, and (2) identifying general strengths and problem areas of the family system. These are followed by more specific goals: (3) identifying parental needs *vis-à-vis* child-rearing demands, and (4) identifying child needs.

This assessment strategy has been summarized in Table 13-1, which specifies the purpose of assessment in view of decisions that must be made and precautions that must be heeded. In reference to the first two general assessment concerns listed, the examiner often must first address the degree of dangerousness or risk to the child that currently exists in the family, in order to assist the child protection agency and/ or courts in deciding on apprehension and alternative placement of the child, as opposed to having the child remain in his or her own home. This overriding concern of child protection is typically approached in conjunction with

other community professionals involved with the family (e.g., physicians, social workers, public health nurses), although the psychologist's role is critical in identifying the major strengths and problem areas of the family system. An interview with the parent(s) can begin to establish the significance of different etiological factors (e.g., parental background, the marital relationship, perceived areas of stress and support, and psychiatric or physical symptomatology) that may have a bearing on the parent's behavior toward the child.

Assessment findings that have more specific relevance to behavioral treatment emerge during the detailed identification of parental and child needs (see Table 13-1). At this point, the examiner is concerned with identification or development of possible treatment alternatives for the family, which requires more specialized assessment instruments and skills, as discussed below.

Assessing Parental Responses to Child-Rearing Demands

Child abuse is strongly linked to events that involve the child in some manner, despite the formidable influence of parental background, psychological functioning, and situational stressors (Wolfe, 1985). Therefore, the following assessment overview of the parent's typical daily behavior with his or her child includes self-report and observational procedures in reference to situations that may lead to parent–child conflict. This strategy involves an analysis of idiosyncratic arousal patterns, fluctuations in mood and affect, and characteristic response styles during everyday child-rearing situations.

The parent's emotional reactivity or displeasure in response to aversive environmental demands merits careful attention, because of the role it is believed to play as a mediator of anger and aggression (Averill, 1983; Berkowitz, 1983; Wolfe, 1985). Although abusive parents may be unwilling to acknowledge the full extent of their culpability, they are often willing to describe their feelings of anger and irritation that they believe are "provoked" by their children or family events. Therefore, feelings of anger, tension, and frustration can be identified most readily by asking parents to provide recent examples of irritating child behaviors, the circumstances in which they occurred, how they felt and interpreted the situation, and how they reacted. Similarly, mood and affect disturbances (e.g., depression, anxiety, agitation) that precede or follow incidences of parent–child conflict can be assessed in the context of the clinical interview or through standardized tests, such as the Symptom Checklist-90 (Derogatis, 1975), the Minnesota Multiphasic Personality Inventory (Hathaway & McKinley, 1951), the General Health Questionnaire (Goldberg & Hillier, 1979), or the Child Abuse Potential Inventory (Milner, 1986). Distorted views regarding what is appropriate to expect from children that might lead to frustration also may be examined using the Parent Opinion Questionnaire (Azar, Robinson, Hekimian, & Twentyman, 1984; Azar & Rohrbeck, 1986).

Alternatively, self-monitoring of annoyance, anger, or similar feelings that lead to conflict with the child can be achieved by using an "anger diary" (Wolfe, Kaufman, Aragona, & Sandler, 1981), in which the parent records his or her feelings of anger or frustration in response to incidents of child misbehavior, or by having the parent review videotapes from previous parent–child interactions in the clinic and identify changes in affect and/or irritation during an ongoing, realistic interchange with the child. This latter procedure holds promise for assessing each parent's distinctive pattern of emotional arousal and cognitive attributions in reference to typical situations involving his or her own child, especially if the child is young and his or her behavior is spontaneous during

TABLE 13-1. Child Abuse and Neglect Assessment Strategy: An Overview

Purpose	Pending decisions	Precautions
A. Determining dangerousness and risk to the child in cases of detected or undetected maltreatment	Apprehension Alternative placement of child	Removing and returning child to family is highly stressful Initial impression of family may be distorted
B. Identifying general strengths and problem areas of the family system Family background Marital relationship Perceived areas of stress and supports Symptomatology	Identification of major factors (antecedents, consequences, and individual characteristics) suspected to be operative within the family Directions for protective services, additional community support services	Involvement of too many professionals may overwhelm family "Crises" that family members report may change dramatically Parent–child problems may be embedded in chronic family problems (e.g., financial, marital) that resist change
C. Indentification of parental needs *vis-à-vis* child-rearing demands Child-rearing methods and skills Anger and arousal toward child Perceptions and expectations of children	Behavioral intervention planning and prioritization of needs	Parental behavior toward child may be a function of both proximal (e.g., child behavior) and distal (e.g., job stress) events Numerous treatment interferences must be identified (e.g., resistance, socioeconomic status, marital problems)
D. Identification of child needs Child behavior problems with family members Child adaptive abilities and cognitive and emotional development	Referral to school-based intervention Behavioral interventions (e.g., parent training) Returning child to family	Unclear or delayed expression of symptoms/impairments Child's behavior may be partially a function of recent family separation and change

clinic observations. Moreover, having parents review videotaped interactions with their children can be a valuable introduction to behavioral intervention, whereby parents are put in the role of observers and problem solvers in reference to their own situations.

Assessment of child-rearing methods that a parent uses on a daily basis with his or her child is critical for developing behavioral treatment objectives. Such assessment is aimed at determining the frequency and quality of parenting methods that favor the child's social and cognitive development, as well as identifying the functional relationships between parent and child behavior. There are several ways to approach this task (e.g., home vs. clinic setting; structured vs. "naturalistic" interactions), as well as a number of suitable observational systems for assessing interactions between members of aggressive families. Essentially, the observer is interested in assessing the major dimensions of parenting that may require intervention (e.g., verbal and physical positive behaviors, criticisms, commands, verbal and physical negative behaviors), as well as the affective "delivery" of these behaviors (e.g., voice tone, orienting the child to the task, age-appropriate language and directions, interest in the child's response). Although these latter affective dimensions have been poorly developed to date, researchers are attempting to devise methods for coding hostility, anger, and similar emotional expression that would be highly pertinent to the assessment of abusive families (e.g., Gottman & Levenson, 1985; Wolfe & Bourdeau, 1987).

Assessing the Needs of the Child

An investigation of the abused child's development and social behavior across settings is often necessary to determine his or her current needs, since abused children may display a wide range of behavioral and emotional symptomatology that varies according to their development. Although abused children are seldom found to display problem behaviors indicative of a clinical disorder (Azar, Barnes, & Twentyman, 1988; Friedrich, Einbender, & Leucke, 1983; Wolfe & Mosk, 1983), they are often described by their parents and teachers as being extremely "difficult" and annoying. These problems have been traced to the beginning of the parent–child relationship, in which an early "mismatch" between parental expectations and infant develop-

ment creates friction and discord. For example, findings from prospective studies have linked early attachment problems to patterns of declining developmental abilities over the first 2 years of life (e.g., speech and language, social interaction; Egeland & Farber, 1984; Egeland & Sroufe, 1981). Abused preschool children show further developmental delays related to the ability to discriminate emotions in others (Frodi & Smetana, 1984) and to their moral and social judgment (e.g., their ability to judge allocation of resources and fairness of rules; Smetana, Kelly, & Twentyman, 1984). Studies of abused children's social behavior with peers and adults have also indicated that they display more aggression toward peers (George & Main, 1979; Hoffman-Plotkin & Twentyman, 1984), as well as poor self-control and attentional ability (e.g., Gaensbauer & Sands, 1979).

Such behavior excesses and deficits on the part of a child are often the antecedents to physical abuse (Herrenkohl et al., 1983), in that the parent fails to respond appropriately to typical child behavior. Such findings, therefore, suggest that clinical assessment of the child must take into consideration both the parent's subjective perceptions of the child and other sources of objective information regarding the child's behavior and development (e.g., behavioral observations in the home or school). Major assessment questions can be formulated around two primary concerns: (1) child behavior problems with family members, and (2) child adaptive abilities and cognitive development. With older children (over age 6), self-reported symptoms, fears, and self-concept may also be assessed for treatment purposes.

Several well-validated and clinically useful parental report instruments for assessing the child's development and behavior are available as starting points for intervention planning; these include the Child Behavior Checklist (Achenbach & Edelbrock, 1983) and the Behavior Problem Checklist (Quay & Peterson, 1967). These instruments permit the clinician to obtain a broad spectrum of information as to the parent's perception of problem areas in the parent–child relationship. Parents are usually quite willing to provide such information, since they feel their behavior stems directly from their children's difficulties. Ancillary reports from other adults who know a child can provide further information regarding the accuracy of the parent's report and the child's adjustment at school or in the community (e.g., foster parents, social workers, school teachers). The child's adaptive abilities, in addition, can be initially screened through parental report instruments (e.g., Vineland Adaptive Behavior Scales; Doll, 1964) or interview to determine the child's current level of performance in important developmental areas (e.g., speech, social interaction, self-care, etc.). Remediation of deficits in these latter areas may become an important treatment objective, either singly or in combination with related behavioral approaches (to follow).

In addition to these sources of information, the child's own report can assist in understanding his or her overall functioning and can provide insight as to current fears or anxieties that might be quite disruptive. A semistructured child interview provides a good beginning point for eliciting the child's feelings and perceptions about the family. This interview should address what has happened to the child in the family, his or her feelings about these events, his or her perceptions of blame and responsibility, and his or her view of the future, along with related topics of school and family interests, dislikes, and concerns.

The child's "crisis adjustment," in particular, is very important in deciding immediate treatment directions. This adjustment can be further assessed, following the interview, with a short battery of tests. Instruments that measure the child's feelings of fear and anxiety include the Revised Fear Survey Schedule for Children (Ollendick, 1978) and the Children's Manifest Anxiety Scale—Revised (Reynolds & Richmond, 1978); unhappiness and depression can be assessed with the Children's Depression Inventory (Kovacs, 1983); and attitudes toward other family members, especially parents, can be assessed via the Parent Perception Inventory (Hazzard, Christensen, & Margolin, 1983). The Children's Impact of Traumatic Events Scale has also been recently developed specifically to assess the school-age child's attributions about victimization from family members, such as physical or sexual abuse, or exposure to marital violence (Wolfe & Wolfe, 1988). Children who attribute the traumatic event (i.e., being physically abused by a parent and/or being removed from the home) to stable and internal characteristics of their own, or to global characteristics of parents and families, may suffer more prolonged consequences from the trauma (e.g., guilt, self-blame, or intrusive thoughts) that impair their subsequent development (see Peterson & Seligman, 1983). Instruments specifically designed to assess the issues over which family conflict arises with adolescents may also be useful for this age group (see Foster & Robin, Chapter 14, this volume, for suggestions).

Given the difficulties inherent in self-report measures, assessment data should also be collected from individuals outside the family. Interviews with teachers and examination of school records may be especially useful in providing clues regarding the intensity and chronicity of the maltreatment and the areas where intervention may be required for the child. For example, prolonged absences from school may represent periods where injuries occurred and the child was kept home to prevent discovery. Frequent absences may also explain academic difficulties (Azar et al., 1988). Standardized teacher reports, such as the Teacher Report Form of the Child Behavior Checklist (Achenbach & Edelbrock, 1983), may also be used to collect data regarding behavior problems and social competence.

Finally, in cases of neglect, a medical examination of the child may be important to rule out specific physical conditions resulting from neglect that may interfere with the child's functioning and response to intervention. For example, severe anemia may produce apathetic behavior that may interfere with academic performance.

Determining Treatment Priorities

Once the child's abilities and needs are assessed, these findings can be integrated with those of the parent's report and observations of current behavior to establish treatment priorities for the family. In general, these priorities follow from the assessment directives outlined in Table 13-1. First and foremost, the feasibility of the parent and child's remaining together must be decided, and then treatment recommendations to support the family unit must be formulated. The second step in the treatment plan typically is to establish a timetable and hierarchy of priorities for addressing major parental and child needs that have been revealed by the assessment.

SPECIAL TREATMENT CONSIDERATIONS

Before discussing applications of behavioral techniques to the treatment of child abuse, a number of more general concerns that are relevant to any treatment approach to child abuse need to be addressed. These concerns fall under three general headings: the characteristics of maltreating parents, the characteristics of maltreated children, and contextual factors that influence the development of therapeutic relationships.

The Characteristics of Maltreating Parents

Abusive parents typically do not identify themselves as having a problem and are not self-referred for treatment (Azar & Twentyman, in press; Conger, 1982). Because most families commonly use corporal punishment as a means of controlling child behavior (O'Leary, 1985), some parents may believe (falsely) that society places no bounds or restraints on such techniques. Although all communities have established standards for deciding when such practices become labeled as abuse, it is not always clear when these limits have been violated. Rather, such judgments have been left to social services agencies and courts, and an involved parent is unlikely to agree with this designation (Conger, 1982).

This fundamental disagreement between "society's" judgment and that of the parent is important to keep in mind as the behavior therapist approaches treatment. The client has not volunteered himself or herself for treatment; as a result, resistance to treatment is usually high, and motivation for change is often an issue. This fact is shown clearly by the high treatment dropout rates found among abuse cases. For example, Reid (1985) reported a 45% dropout rate for parents who were not court-ordered into treatment. Similarly, in a study carried out by Wolfe, Aragona, Kaufman, and Sandler (1980), a 32% dropout rate for families court-ordered into treatment was found, but this rate increased to 87% when no court order was involved.

An active attempt needs to be made to address this issue before treatment can be started. One solution is for the therapist to help the family reframe the "problem" in terms of day-to-day difficulties that the parent can identify. "Child noncompliance," "poor ability to deal with stress," "vocational difficulties," and "lack of supports" may all be more easily accepted problem definitions than "abuse or neglect" for such a parent. Openness to such redefinition and acceptance by the therapist of the parent's way of seeing the problem is crucial to reducing resistance for two reasons. First, it may reduce the parent's fear of being evaluated and labeled as a "bad" parent by the therapist. Being labeled as a person who "has trouble handling your children" or as someone who "is very lonely" (e.g., without social supports) or "stressed" may be easier to accept. Second, such redefinition may serve to differentiate the therapist from the referral source (e.g., child protective services or the court system), whom the parent may see as the cause of the "trouble."

In developing this reformulation, care must be taken not to collude with the client in agreeing that no problem exists. A delicate balance must be achieved. For some clients, the only problem definition that they are initially willing to accept is that they are "in trouble" and that the therapist may help them to learn ways to interact with their children that will assist them in getting "out of trouble."

Lack of compliance with treatment may still occur despite such reformulations. Many maltreating families lead chaotic lives. Their many competing life crises may interfere with participation in treatment (e.g., eviction, spouse battering, legal troubles, etc.; Justice & Justice, 1976), and it is often difficult for treatment providers to compete with such urgent issues. The requirements of treatment may constitute one of the few stresses that they can easily avoid. In traditional treatments with child abusers, the use of lay therapists as adjuncts to formal psychotherapy has been seen as essential to produce treatment compliance by helping families with these life problems (see Kempe & Helfer, 1972). To date, the use of such support workers has not been mentioned in the behavioral literature. Their potential utility as an adjunct to behavior treatment is discussed later.

Incentives to improve participation and attendance have been cited by behaviorally oriented clinicians as being crucial with these families (Azar & Twentyman, in press; Conger, 1982; Wolfe, Kaufman, et al., 1981). However, although there is an extensive behavioral literature dealing with increasing client compliance, many of the typical behavioral techniques for handling treatment noncompliance were developed for more middle-class client populations, and therefore may not be feasible for maltreating families. The fact that many of these clients do not have telephones, for example, precludes the widespread use of telephone prompts, which have been shown to improve attendance for parent training sessions with other types of clients (Ayllon & Roberts, 1975). Initial monetary deposits, another commonly used technique to increase compliance in behavioral treatments (Hagen, Foreyt, & Durham, 1976), may represent a hardship for such families.

Other, more applicable suggestions have been made for improving motivation and treatment compliance with abusive parents. Ambrose, Hazzard, and Haworth (1980), for example, have suggested the use of tangible incentives, such as movie tickets, for treatment attendance. The provision of transportation and babysitting has also been seen as facilitating parents' attendance of treatment sessions (Azar & Twentyman, in press). Other researchers have suggested that parents be paid for the improvements that they make in interacting with their children (Fleischman, 1979), although the feasibility and acceptance of this approach with maltreating families are questionable.

Wolfe, Kaufman, et al. (1981) and Gambrill (1983) recommend the use of behavioral contracts to facilitate treatment compliance (Figure 13-2). Contracts have shown value with other difficult populations (Patterson, 1971). These investigators stress the importance of making clear the objectives and consequences of such contracts (both positive and negative), because maltreating families may initiate treatment only to avoid unpleasant consequences, or may expect unrealistic changes in return for their effort. In line with this, court ordering of treatment attendance may be more likely to encourage completion of treatment by the parents (Wolfe et al., 1980). Unfortunately, it must be noted that the court system is involved in only a small number of child abuse cases (14%; American Humane Association, 1981), and that this figure has been steadily declining since the mid-1970s. In addition, court-ordered treatment may have undesirable side effects that are detrimental to progress being made (e.g., hostility toward the therapist). Emphasizing a more positive approach, Conger (1982) suggests that the behavior therapist may contract with the parent to act as his or her advocate with the protective service agency or with the court if certain objectives are met, such as treatment attendance and acquisition of specific skills (Doctor & Singer, 1978).

Except for court orders, the effectiveness of each of these suggestions for improving treatment compliance has not yet been tested empirically. Although such incentives and assistance for complying with treatment may produce better attendance at sessions, they do not insure that clients will make the personal investment in treatment that is required for lasting behavioral changes. For example, a mother who had been court-ordered to "complete a behavioral parent training group" run by one of the authors conscientiously *attended* every session, but spent her time looking out the window each session and did not participate in group discussions. Even if such incentives result in clients' participating actively in treatment sessions, the self-attributions for change that have been shown to be crucial for maintaining treatment effects may be lacking. Once incentives are no longer present, old behaviors may quickly return.

The social isolation and poor relationship histories of the maltreating parent are final factors that need to be addressed as the therapeutic relationship begins. Wahler and his colleagues have shown that a combination of social isolation and socioeconomic disadvantage reduces the probability that parent–child interaction changes will occur and also limits their generalization over time (Wahler, 1980). Because of poor relationship skills, the parent may also act inappropriately toward the therapist (e.g., testing limits, making excessive demands, being overly dependent, etc.). In the initial stages of treatment, the therapist may need to define clearly the parameters of the relationship, and along the way inform the parent as to what is expected in such relationships. Studies of therapy preparation techniques with disadvantaged clients indicate that such efforts improve success (Heitler, 1973, 1976). This process can also be an important source of role modeling of relationship-building skills.

The Characteristics of Abused and Neglected Children

Specific treatment considerations involving the maltreated child have received little attention in the behavioral literature. In addition, treatment efforts to date have primarily focused on families of preschool- or elementary-school-age children, and little mention has been made of work with families of toddlers or adolescents. This is noteworthy, given that children are at greatest risk for abuse between the ages of 3 months and 3 years (Gambrill, 1983). Recent reports also suggest that a second peak in incidence rates occurs with adolescents (Farber & Joseph, 1985).

The characteristics of these younger and older age groups of abused children may explain their neglect in the behavioral literature. The participation of the young abused infant or toddler in treatment may be limited because of developmental considerations, and priority may be given to parental behavior changes. When an abuse report involves this age group, treatment commonly focuses on changing the parents' negative responses to normal developmental behavior, such as crying (e.g., Sandford & Tustin, 1974). In addition, given the greater vul-

90-DAY AGREEMENT BETWEEN (CLIENT) AND CHILD WELFARE AGENCY

I, (client), have stated my interest in receiving training in parent effectiveness and decreasing my use of physical punishment with my child. In order to work towards that goal, I agree to the following conditions:

1. I agree to attend the Child Management Program (CMP) at the University of South Florida for the entire 8-week program, at least 75% of the sessions (six out of eight).
2. I agree to discuss my child management problems and self-control difficulties with a staff member of this program in order to devise a treatment plan.
3. I agree to have a staff member visit me and my family in my home at prearranged times once a week, in order to continue instruction and application of the material presented in the group meetings.
4. I agree to rehearse these techniques with my child at home and attempt to my best ability to apply them at all times.
5. I agree to refrain from using any form of physical punishment (spanking, whipping, slapping, etc.) with my child during the period of this contract, in order to practice other forms of discipline that have been presented in the group. In the event that my child gets "out of hand" I will elicit the support of my counselor, , social worker, , or neighbor, _____, or will remove myself from the situation temporarily until I have regained my self-control.

I, (client), understand that failure to meet the terms of this agreement may result in written recommendations to the Juvenile Court of Hillsborough County for their involvement in the supervision of my child. The completion of the terms of this contract will result in a written statement recording that fact, which will be placed into my Health and Rehabilitative Services (HRS) file.

Signed,

_____   _____
Client   Date

I, (caseworker), acting on behalf of the Department of Health and Rehabilitative Services for the state of Florida, agree to assist (client) in her efforts to learn more effective child management techniques and decrease her use of physical punishment with her child. In order to work towards that goal, I agree to the following conditions:

1. I agree to refer (client) to the CMP and recommend her acceptance.
2. I agree to provide the CMP with any information that they request that would assist in their intervention with (client), per her signed release.
3. I agree to arrange transportation, upon request, for (client) so that she can attend the weekly meetings at the university.
4. I agree to supervise (client) by telephone and monthly visits until her goal has been accomplished.
5. I agree to place a written statement of the results of this contract into (client)'s HRS file upon its completion.

Signed,

_____   _____
Caseworker   Date

It is jointly understood and agreed between (client) and (caseworker) that this agreement will continue in effect for a period of 90 days and will be reviewed by _____ (date), to evaluate progress toward meeting the stated goals, in the event that this contract proves unsatisfactory for either party, modification may be jointly approved.

FIGURE 13-2. Sample contract. From *The Child Management Program for Abusive Parents* by D. A. Wolfe, D. Kaufman, J. Aragona, and J. Sandler, 1981, Winter Park, FL: Anna. Copyright 1981 by David Wolfe. Reprinted by permission.

nerability of this younger age group, the "treatment" of choice is more likely to be placement outside of the home when abuse occurs (Kempe & Helfer, 1972).

The explanation for the lack of treatment literature regarding abused adolescents focuses on different concerns. For this older age group, the consequences of maltreatment most often surface as disruptive behaviors, such as running away (Farber, McCoard, Kinast, & Baum-Faulkner, 1984) and delinquency (Lewis, Shanok, Pincus, & Glaser, 1979); such behaviors have probably acted to overshadow parental abuse as a focus of treatment. Clearly, additional investigations need to be conducted to address the behavioral treatment needs of younger and older groups of maltreated children.

Behavioral treatment efforts can involve the preschool- or elementary-school-age child in two ways: He or she may participate in parent–child interaction training, or may be treated in other settings, such as the day care center or school. To date, only the former approach has appeared in the literature. Although many of the issues that need to be considered in treating the maltreated child are no different from those typical of behavioral child treatment in general, child abuse cases have been said to have some unique features that need to be addressed. The majority of these issues have to do with the unusual experiences of these children in their relationships with caretakers. First, since abused children's history with adult figures typically has been negative, they may approach interactions with the therapist and other adults fearfully. One case report has described this as a posttraumatic stress reaction (Mann & McDermott, 1983). Hypervigilance has been commonly noted in such children when they encounter a new adult (Martin & Beezley, 1976), especially if the abuse was very recent. Therefore, developing trust may be the initial task of intervention work (Galdston, 1979). Such children, for example, may require greater control over what happens in treatment sessions, or may become anxious if left alone in a room with the therapist or another adult. Keeping the door open or allowing them to leave the session when they choose may be important in building a therapeutic relationship.

Along with hypervigilant behavior, aggression toward caregivers has been commonly observed among abused children (George & Main, 1979; Hoffman-Plotkin & Twentyman, 1984; Reidy, 1977). Thus, aggressive forms of behavior (e.g., temper tantrums, screaming, kicking) may occur either when the therapist is working alone with the child or in the presence of the parent. In such circumstances, the therapist's calm handling of the behavior is crucial to provide the child with a different experience (e.g., a desensitizing experience), as well as to role-model appropriate caretaking responses for the parent. Given the possibility of a parent's feelings of inadequacy or dogmatism regarding his or her parenting, care must be taken not to undermine the parent's role with the child when working with the dyad.

A third area of concern in undertaking treatment involving the child is how much belief to put in the child's reports of home interactions. Children in such families have learned not to report difficulties. Previous disclosures, for example, may have resulted in foster care placement—an event that a maltreated child may have perceived as punishment for "telling." The child's readiness and comfort for sharing information regarding home interactions should determine how much is asked of him or her in this regard. If disclosures of abuse are made, the child needs to be prepared for the actions that may be taken. This should be done at a level that is developmentally appropriate.

Observations of parent–child interaction also need to be approached with caution. In the authors' work, abusive parents have been observed to threaten or bribe their children to perform in a particular way during observational sessions, prior to arriving at the clinic for such sessions. The therapist must be alert to the stress that such observations place on the family and, ultimately, the child. For example, the therapist's presence in the home may intensify parental responses to child noncompliance (e.g., a parent may feel that the child is purposefully trying to make him or her "look bad"). The negative consequences may not be evident while the therapist is present, but may only erupt once he or she has left. Care needs to be taken to provide a "cooling-down" period in which any residual parental anger can be discussed and resolved. Such protections are essential to insure the safety of the child throughout the intervention.

Contextual Factors That Affect the Therapeutic Relationship

The last area of concern in approaching treatment with abusive and neglectful families relates to the development of a therapeutic relationship. The nature of child maltreatment and the referral source introduce a number of factors not present in most therapy situations. First and foremost, the behavior therapist may have personal reactions to the serious injury and neglect of children that, depending upon their intensity, may interfere with his or her ability to work effectively with an offender. Steele (1975) notes two reactions that most therapists have: (1) denial, or (2) a surge of anger and an urge to scold the parents. Obviously, both reactions can be destructive to establishing a therapeutic relationship. The assumptions underlying the behavioral approach may inhibit such negative reactions somewhat, however. By definition, abusive and neglectful behaviors are viewed as environmentally determined (e.g., learned) and are not viewed as something "intrinsically bad" about the parent. Treatment often involves predetermined, prescribed "behaviors" on the part of the therapist that help in guiding interactions with the family.

Referral of an abusive family by social service agencies or the court system often can result in a different kind of role strain for the behavior therapist. Two conflicting goals present themselves in the course of such treatment—therapeutic intervention with the family versus physical protection of the child. Training for accomplishing the latter is often lacking in the therapist's preparation and experience. Moreover, actions taken to accomplish protection for the child may negatively affect the family's chance of success in treatment. There is no easy solution to this conflict; rather, it requires cooperative effort with social service agencies that have responsibility for child protection (see Wolfe, Kaufman, et al., 1981).

Another area where role strain occurs is in the area of client confidentiality. The most important of these issues is the legal requirement to report abuse if it is suspected during the course of treatment. Given the figures cited earlier indicating a high rate of recidivism during treatment, the probability of the need to report is high. Most clinical reports emphasize the importance of discussing this legal requirement at the outset with parents (Azar & Twentyman, in press). This discussion can be resurrected if the necessity to report occurs. Clearly, although this precaution does not entirely alleviate the obstacles to maintaining a therapeutic relationship with such a client if reporting occurs, at the very least it defines overtly for the client the limitations of confidentiality.

If reporting of maltreatment becomes necessary, following certain steps may be helpful to minimize the effects on the therapeutic relationship. If possible, no report should be made without first informing the client. The client should be offered the option of making the report himself or herself or with the therapist's assistance, rather than the therapist's making it alone. These steps may reduce some of the anger at being "betrayed" and may act as a positive element in therapy. In making a self-referral, the client has also made a public statement of having a problem. Such public statements can act as motivators for change (e.g., as in Alcoholics Anonymous). Follow-up with the client in dealing with the authorities can also act to enhance the therapeutic relationship: The first time such a report was made, the client had to go through the process alone, and now the therapist is there to help him or her. In addition, such self-referral is often viewed as a hopeful sign by authorities and in less serious cases may actually lessen the repercussions of having reabused.

Court involvement adds other dimensions that can hamper treatment. Court-ordered treatment usually carries with it a requirement that the therapist report back to the court on the family's progress (i.e., the court is the client, and full disclosure of assessment findings is warranted). The parent needs to be made aware that this will take place at the beginning of treatment. If possible, when the time comes, the content of the report should be either shared with the parent or developed with his or her cooperation. Such behavior on the therapist's part will help to differentiate the therapist's role from that of the "authorities" and may facilitate cooperation.

The fact that the client is often "pushed" into treatment can also result in conflicting agendas for the treatment process. The parent and the therapist may differ in their goals for treatment. The parent's position may be "I want to get the social service agency off my back, so I'll come to sessions, but don't expect me to do anything." Here, the therapist needs to make his or her own position and the goals of intervention clear, and work out a compromise with the client that is within the bounds of treatment. Written contracts with the family, discussed earlier, may be useful in this regard to spell out clearly the expectations of the participants in therapy.

The social service agency's and the therapist's agendas may also conflict. The agency's goal in seeking treatment for the family may be to demonstrate that it has tried every possible alternative for reuniting the family before starting proceedings for permanent removal of the child, whereas the therapist may be working on the assumption that he or she must work to reunite the family. The reverse situation can also occur: The social service agency may have as a goal that the family be reunited, when the therapist does not see this as realistic. As with the parent, goals must be clearly specified before the treatment proceeds.

Working with children also may result in agenda conflict. A child may want to return to abusive parents, and the therapist may be given the task of dealing with the child's behavioral problems in adjusting to permanent removal. Conversely, a child may wish to remain with a foster family, and the therapist may be asked to help him or her adjust to being returned home. These conflicting agendas can produce role strain on the individuals involved. At the outset of therapy, therefore, the goals of the referral source, the family, the child, and the therapist need to be expressed and agreed upon.

The final two areas that need to be mentioned have to do with the value system of the therapist. The maltreating parent may come from a minority background or from a different social stratum than the therapist. Since "good parenting" can be thought of as a relativistic goal, the therapist must be careful not to generalize his or her own personal views on parenting to the families he or she is asked to treat. A culturally relativistic point of view has been advocated in the literature (Goodluck & Tuthill, 1983; Swinger, 1983); a therapist working from such a point of view attempts to define treatment goals in relation to cultural, community, and personal expectations and capabilities. In a similar manner, unrealistic expectations by the therapist and the family of what progress will be made should be anticipated. Highly stressed and disadvantaged families are slow to make detectable changes and require much patience. Families may also expect all of their problems to be handled by the therapist. Even with the elimination of maltreatment, parents in such families may still not be "ideal" parents or even

"ideal" clients. A goal that may be the most realistic is to help them to become *adequate* parents.

Each of these areas must be considered as the behavior therapist begins treating an abusive or neglectful parent and his or her family, as well as during the course of treatment. Failure to address each of these issues carefully may limit the progress that might be achieved through use of a behavioral approach.

TREATMENT DECISIONS RELATED TO CLIENTS, FORMAT, AND SUPPORT PERSONNEL

Parent versus Child Focus

Current treatments of child abuse and neglect by behavioral strategies have included a number of different cognitive and behavioral targets. Treatment outcome studies have been carried out with individual parents, children, parent–child dyads, families, and parent groups, both in the clinic and in the home setting. The greatest bulk of this work has focused on changing parent–child interaction patterns through the use of training in child management skills, role playing, and feedback. In addition to attempts to change parent–child interactions directly, other efforts have been aimed at broad-spectrum skill deficits associated with the occurrence of maltreatment. These have included systematic desensitization to increase tolerance for aversive child behavior, stress management and anger control training, and cognitive restructuring of distorted interpretations of child behavior. Combinations of these approaches have also been utilized. A few studies have tailored programs to the individual needs of clients, selecting as targets unique antecedent conditions specific to the parent involved (e.g., marital discord, migraines, alcohol use, etc.). Other potential targets have been discussed in descriptive reports of behavioral programs, such as vocational assistance, but empirical work has not yet been undertaken to document the usefulness of such targets.

As noted earlier, parental treatment has clearly been predominant in efforts to date, despite the occurrence of child behavioral and developmental problems resulting from parental inadequacies. The only child behavior that has been addressed with any frequency in the literature is noncompliance, but even this behavior has been approached through parent training. A number of reasons exist for this emphasis on parental treatment as the method of choice for intervention work, even where child disturbances are evident. Child behavior therapy in general has turned to parent training as the method of choice for intervention work, based on the assumption that parents are the most powerful change agents in a child's environment. Parents constitute a "continuous treatment resource" who can work conveniently where the problem exists (Johnson & Katz, 1973), and it has been demonstrated that many parents can easily master behavioral change techniques (Graziano, 1977). Furthermore, many child referral problems, even those of abused children, are well-defined enough to make such an approach applicable. In the general clinical child population, the use of parent training has been shown to be highly effective in producing favorable changes in child behavior across a number of problem areas (Gordon & Davidson, 1981; Graziano, 1977; O'Dell, 1974), and similar findings have been reported with abusive populations (Crozier & Katz, 1979). Furthermore, parent training may be more effective than individual child treatment for socioeconomically disadvantaged families (Love, Kaswan, & Bugenthal, 1972).

Despite this emphasis in the literature, treatment focusing on the child and his or her difficulties should be carefully considered. Such treatment may take priority over concerns about "blaming the victim"—that is, concerns that somehow treatment aimed at changing the child will result in reinforcing the belief that he or she is responsible for the maltreatment. As discussed earlier, the abused child has been shown to exhibit a wide range of behavioral and emotional problems. This maladaptive behavior has also been shown to extend beyond the home setting to include interactions with others (e.g., foster care parents, teachers, peers, etc.; George & Main, 1979; Hoffman-Plotkin & Twentyman, 1984; Reidy, 1977), and it may continue to be maintained in these settings despite changes in the family. Training efforts may need to be conducted in each of these settings to enhance the changes produced at home.

Content, Format, and Setting

The decision as to whether the abusing parent, the couple (if one exists), the parent–child dyad, or the child should be treated, as well as the structure and content of that treatment, should be made according to the specific needs of the family. Although parent training is the most commonly used strategy, this approach may not be the treatment of choice if parental or child characteristics or the family's situation indicates that child-rearing problems are not the biggest source of difficulty. An issue that arises during assessment is whether the child or children are actually exhibiting deviant behavior that warrants change, or whether the problem is primarily due to inappropriate expectations on the part of the parent(s). In the latter case, a cognitive–behavioral strategy to deal with such inappropriate perceptions may be the starting point of treatment (see following discussion).

It may also be decided that other significant parent-related problems need to be handled before changes in parent–child interactions are attempted. For example, a parent who has a significant alcohol problem may require treatment for that problem prior to working on parent–child interactional problems, since attempts to produce parenting changes may be doomed to failure because of the effects of alcohol abuse. Extreme marital conflict, another factor associated with maltreatment (Berger, 1980), may keep the parents from working together in a collaborative manner and may therefore result in lower priority being accorded to parent training. Similarly, if parents' stress level is high and resources are so low that they are incapable of altering their social environment, then the effectiveness of parent training strategies will also be severely limited unless support services can be provided (Gordon & Davidson, 1981). Finally, intrapersonal difficulties, such as severe depression, may limit parents' ability to benefit from parent training (Miller, 1975). In each of these scenarios, other problem areas may require treatment either before or simultaneously with behavioral interventions for parent–child problems. Despite these other treatment needs, however, it is important to reaffirm that in the majority of cases, treatment of abusive families must focus on the parent–child relationship and its context (e.g., the family, financial limits, alcohol usage, etc.).

If parent training is to be utilized, a decision needs to be made as to whether the parent will be seen individually or with other parents in a group. If parental deficit areas are highly specific, or if the parent is too low-functioning or socially avoidant to benefit from material presented in a group session, individual treatment may be preferred. Although no study has compared individual to group treatment with abusers, an extensive general psychotherapy literature has made such comparisons. Group treatment, for the most part, has been favored in such studies (Bedner & Kaul, 1978).

The use of groups in modifying parental behavior has a number of advantages (Rose, 1969). First, in a group, the parent can be exposed to a wider range of target behaviors and intervention strategies. Groups may also be more potent, in that other group members can act as role models and reinforcers of change in parenting behavior (Arnold, 1978). In addition, groups are more efficient in terms of staff time (Rinn, Vernon, & Wise, 1975; Rose, 1969). For maltreating parents who tend to be socially isolated (Salzinger, Kaplan, & Artemyeff, 1983), the group can also be a place where social skills can be informally attained and perhaps can act as the beginning of a social network. Several investigators who have used groups with child abusers have encouraged the formation of such relationships between group members by having them exchange phone numbers and providing refreshments or lunch outside of the session to promote social interactions (Azar, 1984; Barth, Blythe, Schinke, Stevens, & Schilling, 1983).

Both individual and group parent training have been employed with child abusers, and some researchers have used a combination of both methods. For example, Wolfe, Sandler, and Kaufman (1981) and Azar and Twentyman (1984) combined group parenting sessions with weekly individual home visits. The role of the home visitor was to promote generalization of the gains made during group sessions and to provide extra practice in the trained techniques. Both studies provide sound arguments, and supportive results, for combining individual and group training.

In addition to decisions regarding the structure of treatment, the choice of setting must also be made. Three different settings have been used with abusive families in research efforts to date: (1) the standard clinic office or educational group; (2) a controlled learning environment in the clinic; and (3) the home. As noted before, a combination of these settings has often been utilized (e.g., group didactic training and home practice sessions, or individual office discussions followed by practice in a structured laboratory analogue situation). The controlled learning environment can be equipped with a one-way mirror and a "bug-in-the-ear" transmitter device to guide parents through interactions with their children. Such a guided approach has been shown to produce rapid behavioral change with other clinical populations, as well as in two case studies involving an abusive mother (Crimmins, Bradlyn, St. Lawrence, & Kelly, 1984; Wolfe et al., 1982). This mode of treatment is especially suited for parents who need concrete demonstrations and feedback, but clearly requires extensive therapist time and effort to promote generalization to the home. Unfortunately, systematic, empirically based guidelines are not yet available on the impact of these structural and setting variables (Gordon & Davidson, 1981).

The Use of Lay Therapists and Support Services as Adjuncts to Treatment

"Lay therapists" or family support volunteers are commonly used in community-based therapies for child abuse and neglect (see Kempe & Helfer, 1972). These adjunct workers assist with the day-to-day crises while the family is in treatment. The goal of their work has been to allow the therapist more opportunity to focus on "therapeutic" issues, and to help reduce the family stress level enough to allow parents to work on therapeutic issues as well. The presence of a volunteer or "home aide" has also been assumed to help provide a social support network for the parent and to model social skills informally (Kempe & Helfer, 1972).

Other support services have also been provided to maltreating parents while they are involved in treatment, such as home aides, day care, respite care, and hotlines. The goal of each of these services has been to reduce the families' stress level to the point where the parents can work on behavioral changes. Although such support services may be beneficial to these families, their interactive effects with treatment need to be considered. The use of such services, for example, may influence clients' attributions for changes produced in treatment; therefore, support services need to be provided without encouraging a family to feel dependent upon them. Support workers need to be carefully trained to provide a structured learning atmosphere with the goal of increasing the family's effectiveness and operation. For instance, if a parent is having trouble with a landlord, the support worker might help the parent generate alternative solutions to the problem, have him or her decide on one alternative, role-play the response, and then have the client deal with the problem himself or herself. Such a process would promote skills that the client could use in future encounters with life stressors, whereas the worker's talking to the landlord for the family would only resolve the immediate difficulty. Support workers in the traditional literature have more often provided the latter function. In brief, support workers and services may be useful in facilitating treatment effects in behavioral interventions, although empirical work is needed to test their utility and effectiveness.

SPECIFIC BEHAVIORAL METHODS FOR TREATING FAMILIES

Once the treatment target areas, structure, and format have been decided upon the choice of specific behavioral methods remains. A limited number of standard cognitive and behavioral methods have been employed with child abusers to date, such as behavioral rehearsal, cognitive restructuring, feedback, skills training (e.g., parent training, anger and self-control training, and stress management training), and treatment of antecedent conditions. In addition to programs that focus on just one of these skill areas, a number of treatment programs have utilized a package approach that works on a number of target areas simultaneously. In many cases, however, the techniques being employed have been modified to meet the special needs of maltreating families. Therefore, each of these commonly used methods is discussed with specific consideration to their application with maltreating families. Several single-case and group studies involving behavioral efforts with child abusers have appeared in the literature. In addition, there have been two comparative treatment studies to date (Azar & Twentyman, 1984; Egan, 1983). Where appropriate, this

literature is touched upon, as well as its methodological problems. (The reader is referred to reviews by Gambrill, 1983, and Isaacs, 1982, for more details.) Although little empirical work has been directed at the behavioral treatment of neglected and of emotionally maltreated children, a short discussion of these areas is also presented. Finally, methods that seem promising but are not currently well developed in the literature are also mentioned, in anticipation that future efforts will be directed toward these areas (e.g., specific child treatments, behavioral consultation).

Parent-Focused Treatment

Modeling and Behavioral Rehearsal

Modeling and role playing of newly acquired behaviors are probably the most common components in behavioral treatments of child abuse in general and parent training in particular (see Denicola & Sandler, 1980; Smith, 1984; Wolfe, Kaufman, et al., 1981). These techniques have been demonstrated to be quite effective in producing changes in interpersonal interactions (Eisler, Hersen, & Agras, 1973; Twentyman & McFall, 1975). Goldfried and Davidson (1970) break down the use of role playing into four general stages: (1) preparation of the client (e.g., providing a rationale for use of the technique); (2) selection of target situations (e.g., generating a list of types of situations that might lead to troublesome interactions); (3) behavioral rehearsal proper (e.g., modeling of new behaviors by the therapist and practice by the client); and (4) carrying out of new role behaviors in real life. Although this combination of strategies is quite effective in training parenting skills (Flanagan, Adams, & Forehand, 1979; Nay, 1975), maltreating parents' feelings of inadequacy regarding their parenting behavior or general interpersonal skills may make them more reluctant than most clients to undertake role playing. The preparation stage, therefore, may be especially important. Presenting a clear rationale for conducting role plays is especially crucial with this population. Therapist modeling of role-playing behavior initially may also be useful in reducing parents' anxiety.

A treatment program developed by Barth et al. (1983) demonstrated how parents might gradually be worked into role playing. Examples of desirable child management approaches were first presented via videotape, followed by therapist modeling of the behaviors. Finally, parents were provided with scripts to follow in their initial role-play attempts, and they were praised for their effort. Such careful shaping of behavior is often necessary with this population of parents to facilitate involvement and behavior change.

In group interventions, asking other parents to act out particular parents' situations or to act as coaches in a role play may also reduce the pressure in using such a technique. A danger of using role plays with this population, however, is that on occasion inappropriate parental responses (e.g., coercive responses) may be volunteered by group members during coaching. Therapists must be careful to deal with such responses immediately; otherwise, parents are likely to incorporate such negative responses into their repertoires.

Feedback

An important component of role playing is the provision of feedback. Careful attention needs to be paid to the manner in which feedback is provided with this population, however. Given the nature of interactions within abusive families, parents are accustomed to giving and receiving negative feedback. If the therapist's approach to feedback is perceived as negative or harsh, parents have less opportunity to learn or benefit from their experience. In addition, maltreating parents are often sensitive to any comments about their child-rearing methods, and may leave treatment if sessions are too critical.

The feedback process during a role play serves two purposes. First, it helps in refining parents' response toward the desired goal behavior. Second, it models for the parents a different way of responding when faced with needing to correct the behavior of another. It is especially important, therefore, that feedback be presented in as positive a manner as possible (e.g., what a parent is doing right, not wrong). Initially, the frequency of praise for attempting or acquiring new parenting behaviors must be higher than with other populations, and/or commensurate with a parent's preference for certain forms of praise (e.g., some parents prefer quiet recognition, and others prefer a lot of attention and fanfare). The therapist can also model

acceptance of negative feedback by describing instances of self-criticism.

Cognitive Restructuring

A technique that has only recently been applied in treatment with child abusers is cognitive restructuring (Azar, 1984). This method addresses irrational or dysfunctional beliefs that may lead to inappropriate responses (e.g., misattributions, distorted beliefs) (Ellis, 1962; Meichenbaum, 1974; Novaco, 1975). Underlying the use of this technique is the assumption that maladaptive "cognitive sets" mediate the behavioral reactions of child abusers (Azar, 1986; Azar & Twentyman, 1986). Recent evidence has supported the idea that child abusers possess cognitive styles and belief systems that could play such a mediational role. For example, abusers have been shown to ascribe greater negative intentionality to their children's behavior than do normal parents, even when that behavior is within developmental norms (Larrance & Twentyman, 1983; Plotkin, 1983), and to have more unrealistic expectations of what is appropriate to expect in children's behavior (Azar, Robinson, Hekimian, & Twentyman, 1984; Azar & Rohrbeck, 1986). As noted earlier in our transitional model of child abuse and neglect, such appraisals can lead to an increased probability of aggression (Averill, 1983).

Cognitive restructuring involves, first of all, clients' recognition that their thoughts about situations and others affect their behavior. Once this relationship is acknowledged, clients are required to generate their own "personalized cognitions" regarding situations that are problematic. An example is a father's interpretation of his 2-year-old's unwillingness to go take a nap as an active attempt to devalue him as a parent (e.g., "He must think I'm really stupid"), rather than as an aspect of typical 2-year-old behavior. Those cognitions that are judged to be dysfunctional or self-defeating are then challenged by the therapist, and an attempt is made to replace them with ones that are more appropriate (e.g., "Here we go again—the 'terrible 2's.' I've just got to be patient"). Generating such "personalized" cognitions may be very difficult for a maltreating parent, however, and therefore a more active approach is required by the therapist than is typically used with other clinical populations. Role-playing problematic situations can help parents to identify their dysfunctional thoughts *in vivo*. Imagery techniques have also been employed (Azar, 1984). Extremely stressful situations, for example, can be described in which a potentially triggering child event is introduced. An example of such a vignette might be the following:

> Your landlord just came by and said that he is evicting you. Your welfare check that was due yesterday still hasn't arrived, and you and your boyfriend had a bad fight last night. You have on your new white dress that you saved for weeks to buy and your child comes up to you and despite telling him to be careful, he spills his Kool-Aid all over it. (Azar, 1984; p. 166)

Once a client has successfully imagined this situation (or a self-generated problem situation), questioning can take place regarding what the parent would be saying to himself or herself at that moment, and how these statements would affect his or her actions. The vignettes used can be designed to fit clients' particular situations, and dramatizations of examples they spontaneously provide can be particularly useful. Questioning can start with what a parent is feeling. Once a feeling is stated, the parent can then be questioned as to why the child's behavior made him or her feel that way or what it is that the parent expected of the child in this situation. It is also helpful to ask the parent whether other people in their lives make them feel the same way. One mother, for example, found conflict with her 3-year-old very difficult to take and perceived him as intentionally trying to make her feel "stupid." When she was asked about others in her life, it became clear that the child's father, her ex-boyfriend, used to belittle her in conflict situations, and that the boy looked very much like his father.

In building a rationale for going through this exercise, it is important for the therapist to model the process by sharing examples from his or her own experience in which cognitions made him or her respond in an inappropriate manner. The exact process of rational reevaluation can then be modeled, with alternative cognitive statements generated as solutions. If clients still have difficulty generating cognitions, the therapist may need to provide a list of examples. Common ones that have been observed in the authors' own work with abusers involve perceptions that others are intentionally trying to annoy the client (e.g., "She's trying to get to me"), self-deprecatory statements (e.g., "He must think I'm really stupid"), and ones involving a feeling of being at the end of one's rope (e.g., "I can't take any more"). Scripts that include such cognitive statements may also be helpful to provide material for cognitive training (Barth *et al.*, 1983). In group treatment, exercises designed to generate parents' ideas regarding their definitions of "good" parenting or a "good" child can also elicit what may be overly idealized parental expectations regarding themselves and those around them (Azar, 1984).

Once such statements and belief systems are identified, challenging them can then be undertaken. Parents can be questioned as to whether such self-statements help or hinder their job as parents (e.g., allow them to act as good teachers to their children). Beliefs that children's understanding and ability are similar to those of adults can also be disputed by using concrete demonstrations. For example, with parents of preschoolers, Piagetian conversation tasks can be shown in a group situation as concrete evidence that children do not think in the same way that adults do. The faulty belief systems and inappropriate self-statements can then be replaced with ones like these: "He's only 2," "He doesn't know any better," "It may feel like I can't take any more, but I can handle it. She's only a child. She doesn't know what I've been through today," or "It was an accident. Kids do these things."

The Use of Resources and Technology

Each of the techniques described above may be augmented by the use of other resources and technology. For example, concrete demonstrations of desired parenting methods may be especially important with this population, and recent technology is well suited for this purpose. For instance, coaching can be carried out through the use of a "bug-in-the-ear" transmitter and a one-way mirror. Such training allows for prompting, shaping, and reinforcement of new responses as they happen, which may be a more powerful training method than demonstration alone.

Videotaped observations of staged parenting situations (Barth *et al.*, 1983; LaRose & Wolfe, 1985) and of the clients and their children (Wolfe & Manion, 1984) may make therapist suggestions more salient to abusing parents. As treatment progresses, previous tapes of the parent and child can be replayed to illustrate to the client that progress has been made, and also to note how a relapse might appear.

Board games have been used to train retarded adults in social skills (Foxx *et al.*, 1983), and have also been employed in work with families. This technique has been adapted for use with low-functioning maltreating parents (Fantuzzo, Wray, Hall, Goins, & Azar, 1986). Using a common board game, "Sorry," parents make moves on the board dependent upon their responses to various parenting and social problem situations. More elaborate responses to situations are gradually shaped and socially reinforced.

In group programs, films may also be useful adjuncts to provide material for discussion. Commercially produced parenting films and audiotapes illustrating behavioral techniques, as well as the handling of general parenting and child development issues, are available. Table 13-2 provides a representative list of such films.

Skills Training

Skills training has been utilized with child abusers in three general areas: parent training, anger control, and stress management. In each case, standardized training packages employed with other populations have been employed, with modifications to meet the specific needs of this population.

Parent Training. Child management skills training with maltreaters has been described in the most detail in the literature. Standard parent training packages typically include the following: (1) teaching parents to track problem behaviors that they have selected in their children; (2) education in techniques based on social learning theory, such as the identification of antecedents and the use of reinforcement, extinction, time out, and punishment to change behavior (usually presented didactically); and (3) home application of techniques. Record keeping (e.g., charting of child behavior) is required, and reading often supplements didactic presentations.

The most basic of issues in undertaking parent training with child abusers is their willingness to give up physical forms of punishment and to utilize more positive means of control. Even if such a parent is willing to attempt a different approach, attending to the child's good behavior takes time to produce results, and the parent may become frustrated and harm the child. Rather than completely removing the

parent's only means of control, the therapist can establish a contractual agreement with the parent at the outset of such training to practice a nonphysical form of punishment for a specified period of time, thus allowing for a gradual shift in behavior (Wolfe, Kaufman, *et al.*, 1981).

The requirements of standard training packages may also be difficult for the typical abusing parent. The parent's chaotic life style, for example, may interfere with the consistent collection of data usually required in such programs, and therefore data collection procedures must often be simplified. Collecting data for one day or afternoon, rather than for a week, may be more practical with such families. With some parents, verbally reviewing over the phone what occurred in a given day may be the only way to collect such information consistently.

Training parents in the use of reinforcement and punishment techniques may also present problems. Parents' own state of economic and emotional deprivation, for example, may interfere with their use of reinforcement with their children. A clinical example of this occurred in a case where a child's bedwetting was the target of intervention. This behavior resulted in the mother's becoming angry and at times aggressive. When a reinforcement procedure was

TABLE 13-2. Parenting Films and Audiotapes

Films

Time Out: A Way to Help Children Behave Better (Hanson, 1971)

Who Did What to Whom? (Mager, 1972)

Parent's Magazine Filmstrips on Development[a]
1. "How an Average Child Behaves—From Birth to Age Five"
2. "Conflicts between Parents and Children—Daily Disagreements"
3. "The Effective Parent: The Parent as Teacher"
4. "The Effective Parent: Learning Away from Home"
5. "Conflicts between Parents and Children: Parents Expect . . . Children Want"

Child Behavior Equals You[b]

Audiotapes

The Family Living Series (Patterson & Forgatch, 1975)

---

[a]Available through *Parent's Magazine*, 685 Third Avenue, New York, NY 10017.

[b]Available through Audio Visual Services, Pennsylvania State University, University Park, PA 16802.

worked out for the family, it quickly became clear that despite the initial success of the program, the maltreating mother was sabotaging it by not using it consistently. It was only after a parental reward (i.e., special attention from her spouse) was systematically introduced contingent on her carrying out the program that progress was made. High levels of therapist encouragement are also needed initially to motivate such a parent to try the new techniques.

Even if a parent reports active use of the new techniques and desired improvement in the child's behavior, observation of the parent's application of the methods is needed. Manipulative behavior on the part of parents often occurs because of their legal status or because of a sincere desire to "please" the therapist.

Particular dangers exist in training abusive parents in behavioral punishment strategies. Because of the inappropriate judgment of such parents, there is a greater chance that they will misuse such techniques. Time-out procedures, such as placing a child in his or her room for misbehavior, need to be carefully reviewed and rehearsed with parents; otherwise, they may proceed to lock children in closets or other closed spaces. "Grandma's rule" (e.g., "If you do X, then Y will happen"; Becker, 1971) can easily be twisted into a new form of parental tyranny unless extreme caution is used in training. The types of behavior that are most appropriate for targeting in this technique should be carefully specified with each client. Extinction (e.g., ignoring negative child behavior), another commonly suggested behavioral child management technique, also can be hazardous, because this method usually results in an increase in a child's aversive behavior before a reduction occurs. Clients should be warned that this might take place, and cognitive coping strategies should be provided to get them through this stressful period. They also can be told to *interpret* this increase as a sign of success.

Single-case design studies employing primarily child management training (in which role modeling, rehearsal, and feedback were combined with bibliotherapy) with abusive parents have shown increases in positive parental behavior and decreases in negative behavior (Denicola & Sandler, 1980; Sandler, Van Dercar, & Milhoan, 1978; Wolfe & Sandler, 1981). Positive "spillover" in prosocial child behavior was also observed, as well as mainte-

nance of effects over periods ranging from 1 to 7 months. In addition, Wolfe et al. (1982) and Crimmins et al. (1984) showed similar effects when these techniques were combined with the use of a radio transmitter to communicate with abusive and neglectful mothers who were cognitively limited.

Overall, parent training efforts have shown success in changing interaction patterns in the abusing and neglectful parents studied. In addition, some limited data have suggested maintenance over time. Although this approach holds promise, some criticisms of the outcome studies in this area can be made. First, the clients typically treated either have been court-ordered into treatment or have been under some threat of losing custody of their children. Also, treatments have taken place in the home and been done by highly trained professionals (e.g., graduate students, psychologists). Neither of these parameters is typical in most treatment settings. Whether these techniques will work with less "motivated" clients and with more typical professionals and treatment settings is still open to question. Finally, with one notable exception (Wolfe, Sandler, & Kaufman, 1981), recidivism data have not been reported. Without this most crucial of outcome information, it is difficult to assess the usefulness of the techniques employed.

Anger Control Strategies.   Along with parenting skills training, instruction in self-control and anger control strategies is also useful with abusive parents, given their heightened arousal and poorer ability to cope with stress. Cognitive and behavioral techniques have been employed with other populations to reduce anger and to increase coping ability (Novaco, 1975). Such techniques have obvious applicability to this population of parents (Azar & Twentyman, 1984; Barth et al., 1983; Nomellini & Katz, 1983; Wolfe, Sandler, & Kaufman, 1981). The most common strategies include the following components: (1) early detection of physiological and cognitive cues associated with anger arousal; (2) replacing anger-producing thoughts with more appropriate cognitions; and (3) developing self-control skills to modulate the expression of anger in anger-eliciting situations.

Nomellini and Katz (1983), for example, employed these techniques in a set of three case studies. Treatment took place in parents' homes for six to eight 90-minute sessions; outcome data included home observations, pre–post scores on the Novaco Anger Scale, and self-monitoring of "angry urges" by the parents. During and after treatment, parents showed significant reductions in aversive behavior and "angry urges," as well as substantial decreases on the anger scale. Maintenance of effects was shown over follow-up periods ranging from 2 to 6 months. No recidivism data were reported, however, and changes in positive behavior were small, suggesting that anger control training may not be useful in producing changes in this area. Barth et al. (1983), in another study focusing on self-control, made extensive use of role playing with and without scripts and coaching. Parents were also instructed to reward themselves when they carried out the procedures at home. After eight group sessions, the treated parents showed significantly greater improvement in behavioral and cognitive responses during a role play and in response to videotaped situations than an untreated control group did. Positive changes were also found on paper-and-pencil measures of nervousness, calmness, and irritability. Unfortunately, the sources of subjects for the two groups differed (e.g., the treated parents were referred by child protective services, whereas the controls were recruited from a well-baby clinic program); this raises questions regarding comparability of the two groups. Despite this flaw, the study provides examples of innovative self-control techniques that can be employed with maltreating parents.

In addition to cognitive techniques, a few single-case studies have incorporated systematic desensitization, in which progressive muscle relaxation techniques are trained and hierarchies of aversive child behavior are created (Gilbert, 1976; Koverola, Elliot-Faust, & Wolfe, 1984; Sanders, 1978; Sandford & Tustin, 1974). One of these studies incorporated spouses' help in reinforcing new responses on the abusive parents' part (Gilbert, 1976). (Such supports in a parent's environment may be very useful to promote generalization of effects.) Generally, these studies have supported the usefulness of desensitization with abusive parents for reducing their intolerance for aversive or stressful child behavior, and, in one case, for increasing a mother's positive contact with her child (Gilbert, 1976). Some maintenance of behavioral effects was demonstrated, and in the one study where recidivism data were mentioned, no recidivism was found. However,

Koverola et al. (1984) found that interruptions caused by the many life stresses of the mother they treated resulted in a return to pretreatment functioning during follow-up. Such intervening factors, which are typical in such families, may therefore interfere with this technique's effectiveness. Although this initial single-case work appears promising, future work might evaluate effectiveness across a broader spectrum of parents using group designs.

A word of caution in using anger control techniques as the only form of treatment is also in order. There is evidence to suggest that training in anger control may not be sufficient to change a parent's behavior toward the child (Egan, 1983). Specifically, the parent may be less likely to engage in aggressive responses with the child, but this does not mean that he or she will respond in "appropriate" or optimal ways to the child's behavior. Over time, the child management situation may deteriorate to the point where the anger control techniques are insufficient to prevent abuse from occurring.

Stress Reduction Strategies. Stress reduction techniques are a third skills training approach employed with abusive parents. This type of training, like anger control, is usually included as part of a larger package of treatment. Training typically includes instruction in relaxation techniques and cognitive–behavioral methods of reducing stress. Parents are trained to recognize how their negative interpretations of situations lead them to become stressed, and to substitute stress-reducing self-statements for negative ones. They are also trained to perform actions to reduce their stress level (e.g., leave the situation, seek outside advice, increase resources). Parents may be required to read written material on stress reduction techniques between treatment sessions, and to keep notebooks on class material and do homework assignments (Egan, 1983). In some programs, parents have also been provided with relaxation tapes to practice this strategy between sessions (Wolfe, Sandler, & Kaufman, 1981). Since general coping abilities in this population may be low, situations for which techniques may be applicable should be broad, including parenting and nonparenting situations, to provide the maximal effect.

At least three outcome studies have included such training (Azar & Twentyman, 1984; Egan, 1983; Wolfe, Sandler, & Kaufman, 1981). Only one study used stress reduction techniques exclusively (Egan, 1983). Its effects appeared to be primarily in reducing parental negative feelings. In the 6-week group treatment employed in this study, some generalization occurred to interactions with the children, but not in improvement of child management techniques.

Stress reduction techniques and anger control training are subject to many of the same problems as parenting skills training (e.g., lack of client sophistication, manipulation, etc.), and modifications of presentation may be needed, depending upon the characteristics of the individuals being served. Home training has also been suggested as crucial to effectiveness with this population (Wolfe, Kaufman, et al., 1981).

Treatment of Antecedents of Abuse and Strategies for Addressing Neglect Issues

Along with addressing various general components of social learning models of child abuse, some outcome work has been directed to specific antecedent conditions (e.g., stressors) that might set up situations where maltreatment is more likely to occur. The outcome studies in this category have tailored the treatments to the specific needs of the families they were serving (e.g., attempted to isolate treatment targets that were most relevant to the families in question). Targets of such intervention have typically been multiple ones and have included depression, marital discord, migraine headaches, and vocational goals (Campbell, O'Brien, Bickett, & Lutzker, 1983; Conger, Lahey & Smith, 1981; Justice & Justice, 1978). Marital treatment, for example, has included use of behavioral techniques outlined by Jacobson (1978) and reciprocity counseling procedures (Azrin, Naster, & Jones, 1973). These studies, while showing positive effects, have employed limited designs (e.g., single cases or small sample sizes, no control group).

Neglect issues have also been the target of behavioral interventions, although with less frequency. These have included strategies for teaching parents home safety skills to "child-proof" their homes (Lutzker, 1984), meal planning and budgeting to improve the nutrition provided to children (Sarber, Halasz, Messmer, Bickett, & Lutzker, 1983), and symptom recognition skills to improve parents' ability to identify illness in their children and to make appropriate responses (Delgado & Lutzker, 1985). More work is needed in this area.

Multicomponent Treatment Approaches

Because no single deficit area predicts the occurrence of maltreatment in most families, recent behavioral efforts have evaluated the impact of multicomponent (package) approaches to treatment. Although this has been criticized as a "shotgun" strategy (Gambrill, 1983), it makes the most sense, given the complexity of the factors that lead to abuse. Packages can also be delivered in group formats by agencies that serve abusive families, thereby meeting the differing needs of a larger number of families at one time. Social services agencies usually have limited resources available to them, and the development of effective packages may therefore have the most utility. Furthermore, the urgency of the problem from a clinical perspective requires immediate changes to occur in an abusing family, and lengthy assessment periods to determine specific target areas may not be possible. A number of treatment studies have shown that such an approach may be quite effective in this regard.

Wolfe, Sandler, and Kaufman (1981) utilized a group treatment format that emphasized several behavioral methods in their "competency-based" program for abusive parents. Individual home-based sessions served as adjuncts to group training sessions. Eight abusive families from child protective services were provided with eight sessions of group training; another eight abusive families received the usual level of monitoring provided by the referring social service agency. Training focused on child management skills and anger control, taught through didactic instruction, problem solving, role modeling, rehearsal, self-control training, and in-home implementation. During observations of parent–child interactions in the home, treated subjects were found to use appropriate child management procedures (e.g., positive reinforcement, effective punishment and commands) significantly more than waiting-list controls. This difference was maintained at a 1-year follow-up, and the treated group was found to have no recurrences of abuse at that time (one abuse report occurred in the control group).

Two large-scale programs based on social learning theory, which operate in the community with large numbers of maltreating clients, have also been evaluated. Project 12-Ways, a large treatment program operating in a primarily rural area of Illinois, uses a variety of behavioral techniques to deal with child maltreatment (Lutzker & Rice, 1984). In-home services (treatment and training) are provided to families referred to the project by child protective services. Areas of treatment include parent–child training, stress reduction, self-control training, social support, assertiveness training, basic skills, uses of leisure time, health maintenance and nutrition, home safety, job placement, marital discord counseling, alcoholism referral, and money management. Selection of treatment provided is based on individual case needs. To evaluate the efficacy of the program, 50 abusive and neglectful families were randomly selected from 150 families served in 1 year of the program's operation. A comparison group of families was also selected from the same referral sources as the treated families. The families in both groups had at least one previous incident of abuse or neglect. The names of treated families were matched against state registry data of incidents of abuse and neglect to determine recidivism, both during treatment and after services were terminated. Data for control families were also determined for the same period. The results indicated that the program was successful in reducing multiple incidences of maltreatment in treated families relative to the control group, but not overall recidivism rates. Because of the variations in the specific treatments offered each individual family, solid conclusions regarding the effectiveness of any one type of treatment are difficult to draw from the results of this study.

In two interesting community studies, Szykula and Fleischman (1985) demonstrated the impact that intervention programs based on social learning theory might have on out-of-home placement of abused and neglected children. The families treated in the two studies were cases of a state child protective service and were selected because they were considered at risk for protective placement of their children outside the home because of abuse. Families all had children between the ages of 3 and 12 years of age. The client population was described as primarily white and of lower socioeconomic status, and about 50% were single parents. The treatment package employed social learning theory-based treatment (e.g., training parents in tracking problem behavior and using reinforcement and time-out procedures to modify behavior; problem-solving training; and cognitive self-control training to deal with anger, guilt, depression, and anxiety). Phone supervision of assignments was also employed. Each family received 15–25 hours of treatment-oriented contact time.

The first study carried out employed an ABA design, capitalizing on a natural 9-month break in the program's operation that occurred when staff members left. Agency statistics on out-of-home placements due to abuse were examined. They found that there was an 85% drop in such placements during the program's operation and that figures rebounded to previous levels during the 9-month break in the program. Out-of-home placements for reasons other than abuse showed no change over the entire period of study. There was also no recidivism for abuse among treated families during treatment and a 1-year follow-up. Unfortunately, the number of families involved was not reported. Assuming that sufficient numbers were involved, this adds further evidence for the efficacy of the social-learning-based approach to treatment. A noteworthy aspect of this program is that it employed bachelor's- and master's-level caseworkers as treatment agents, and thus provided a better demonstration of the utility of such techniques in typical treatment settings.

The second study reported by Szykula and Fleischman (1985) employed an experimental design with 48 abusive and neglectful families and the same package as described above, with out-of-home placement again used as the outcome measure. Families were first divided into two levels of severity, "less difficult" and "more difficult," based on review of each family's social history and case file. Less difficult cases ($n = 26$) had fewer than three reports of abuse, had no serious difficulty with housing or transportation, and had the children's conduct identified as a major problem. More difficult cases ($n = 22$) had three or more reports of abuse, had serious problems with unemployment, had consistent transportation and housing difficulties, and had been identified as having major problems outside of their relationship with their children (e.g., frequent fights with boyfriends or extended family, extreme feelings of anger and/or depression, and frequent difficulties with others in their community). Families within each difficulty level were randomly assigned to either social-learning-based training or a control condition that received standard social services (ranging from limited supervision to other forms of therapy available in the community). Outcome data indicated that the treatment package was most successful in significantly reducing out-of-home placement for the less difficult group (e.g., 1 of 13 of those receiving treatment vs. 5 of 13 of the controls), but not for the more difficult group (e.g., 7 of 11 of those receiving treatment vs. 5 of 11 for the control condition). In their conclusions, the authors point out that the success rates for the first study may have been due to differential referrals of less difficult cases. They also suggest that there is a need to refine methods of discriminating between families who will and those who will not benefit from social-learning-based treatments.

These studies suggest the viability of programmatic application of child abuse interventions based on social learning theory. Their findings suggest that such interventions may be effective in reducing the incidence of maltreatment and out-of-home placement of children. Packages also may allow the widespread dissemination of such methods. Because of the fact that multiple components have been employed, however, it cannot be determined which specific methods are responsible for packages' effectiveness. In addition, the studies suggest that widespread application of packages may not have utility for all abusive families. Future research needs to delineate the characteristics of the families for whom social-learning-based approaches are most applicable.

Comparative Treatment Effectiveness

Two studies have evaluated differential treatment effectiveness in order to specify methods that are most beneficial with this population. One focused on comparing different types of behavioral approaches (Egan, 1983), and the other compared two forms of cognitive–behavioral treatment to an insight-oriented intervention (Azar & Twentyman, 1984). Both studies included a waiting-list control condition.

Egan (1983) compared the impact of two behavioral strategies, using four study conditions: stress management training only ($n = 11$), child management only ($n = 11$), a combination of stress management and child management training ($n = 9$), and a waiting-list control group that received only social service monitoring ($n = 10$). Evaluation was conducted in part via paper-and-pencil measures of affect associated with life changes and perceptions of family cohesion and conflict: the Recent Events Survey (Sarason, Johnson, & Siegel, 1979); the State–Trait Anxiety Inventory (Spielberger, Gorsuch, & Lushene, 1970); and the Family Environment Scale (Moos, 1974). Evaluation also included observations of parent–child interaction patterns and parental reports of child management strategies in hypothetical child-rearing situations. Treatment took place weekly over a 6-week period, and families were evaluated prior to beginning treatment and at termination. Waiting-list controls received evaluations 6 weeks apart. The results indicated some differential treatment effects. Stress management training led to changes in the feelings of parents, and child management training produced changes in specific child management skills. Unfortunately, the manner in which analyses were carried out in this study (e.g., 21 multiple F tests instead of multivariate analyses) makes it difficult to evaluate the significance of the findings.

The second comparative treatment study was done by Azar and Twentyman (1984) with abusive and neglectful parents with children between the ages of 3 and 5 years. The effectiveness of a cognitive–behavioral package was compared to that of an insight-oriented approach using a short-term (10-week) group treatment format. The cognitive–behavioral package included (1) child management skills training; (2) cognitive restructuring; (3) stress management and anger control training; and (4) communications skills training. Four study conditions were used: (1) cognitive–behavioral group treatment with weekly home visits designed to promote generalization of treatment effects ($n = 13$); (2) cognitive–behavioral group treatment with weekly supportive home visits to control for the extra attention received in a home visit ($n = 16$); (3) insight-oriented group treatment with weekly supportive home visits ($n = 14$); and (4) a waiting-list control group that received the normal services provided by the local child protective services ($n = 16$). Home visitors were trained university undergraduates.

Evaluations of the abusing and neglectful mothers who participated were carried out prior to beginning treatment, at termination, and at a 2-month follow-up. Outcome measures included behavioral observations in the home and in the laboratory; paper-and-pencil measures of knowledge of child development, problem-solving ability, and unrealistic expectations of appropriate child behavior; and caseworker reports of parenting problems. Although differences were found between the two forms of cognitive–behavioral treatments on some of the paper-and-pencil and behavioral measures at posttreatment and follow-up, no differential treatment effects were found at pre–post test or at the 2-month follow-up. Significant effects for all treatments versus no treatment did occur at posttreatment on caseworker reports of parenting problems and at posttreatment and follow-up on maternal behavior in the home. A 1-year follow-up of the three treatment conditions indicated no recidivism for the group receiving cognitive–behavioral training with generalization training (0 out of 13 cases), but 37.5% recidivism (6 out of 16 cases) for the group receiving cognitive–behavioral training without the generalization training and 21.4% recidivism (3 out of 14 cases) for the insight-oriented group.

These two studies seem to provide support for the effectiveness of behavioral approaches to treating child abuse. In addition, Egan's (1983) results indicate that skill-specific responses can be produced with behavioral skills training. The results of Azar and Twentyman (1984), however, cast doubt on the differential effectiveness of behavioral versus other treatments, although the subjects receiving behavioral group training plus active home training did show no recidivism. The small sample sizes employed and the potential lack of homogeneity of client populations, the short-term nature of the treatment, and the age range of the children being studied (e.g., 3–5 years old) may account for the lack of differential treatment effects in this study. Future efforts might employ larger sample sizes, allowing for a test of the question of what treatment works best for which type of client.

Child–Focused Treatment

As noted earlier, outcome studies focusing on treatment of the abused child are almost nonexistent in the literature. Out of necessity, therefore, the discussion in this section is based on rather limited information. Three major categories of intervention are described: removal of the child from the home, developmental stimulation work, and behavioral consultation.

Foster Care Placement and Day Care

In the past, the most commonly employed "intervention" for the abused child was to remove him or her from the home. Two types of removal have occurred: foster care placement outside the home for a specified period of time, or day care placement for a limited number of hours each day.

Foster care placement was advocated as a means of dealing with child abuse for two reasons. First, it was assumed to remove the child from harm and provide a stable and therapeutic environment. Second, it was also believed to provide a brief time for the family to undergo rehabilitation before the child was returned. Foster care placement has, however, recently come under criticism for economic and social reason. The cost of placement outside the home is great (Green, 1976). Furthermore, although it has been assumed that the decision to place the child is made after specific consideration of the danger to the child, recent evidence suggests that the factors leading to such a decision are inconsistent across cases (Runyan, Gould, Trost, & Loda, 1981). More importantly, the therapeutic benefit of foster care to the child's development and recovery has also been questioned (Arvanian, 1975; Eisenberg, 1962; Geiser, 1973; Mass & Engler, 1959). For example, one study has indicated that the medical care of foster children is significantly neglected (Schor, 1982).

The assumption that placement is short-term in nature and will provide the child with a stable home environment has also not held up under evaluation. Multiple placements are fairly common for most foster care children (Knitzer & Allen, 1978; Wald, 1976), and placements have not been shown to be brief. Fanshel and Shinn (1978) found in their foster care study that 47.7% of the children placed in care because of abuse or neglect remained in care at the end of 5 years, with only 22.1% staying in care for less than 1 year. This may be considered a strong additional stress being placed on the maltreated child who finds himself or herself in the foster care system.

A final criticism involves the assumption that rehabilitation of the parent is occurring while the child is in placement. Early reports indicated that only limited treatment services were typically provided to parents (Mass & Engler, 1959; Stone, 1969), and treatment deliverers still tend to be inadequately trained and to carry heavy caseloads, making intervention spotty (Williams, 1983). In addition, parental contact with a child in foster care may be quite limited. Lack of contact may make return of the child home and unification of the family after foster placement a difficult transition for both parent and child. Children who have spent most of their lives in foster placement, after much litigation, are often being returned to parents they hardly know.

These criticisms have caused a reduction in the use of foster care. Laws have been enacted reducing the time period for which foster care can be used before permanent-placement planning needs to take place for a child. In addition, when foster care is used, these same laws require that specific plans for parental treatment be made.

The use of day care, at least for the young child, is often used as an alternative to foster placement. A number of clinical reports have described research day care centers specifically designed to deal with abused and neglected children (Martin, 1976). Such specially designed programs are rare, and more often than not maltreated children are placed in day care settings alongside nonmaltreated children, with no modifications.

Although the effects of such programs may be positive, difficulties may also arise from their use. Observational studies with abused and neglected children in such centers indicate that management problems may quickly become an issue. Staff members are unprepared to handle these children's emotional and behavioral difficulties. In addition, when exposed to an environment where the caretakers are more flexible and show higher levels of attention than those found in their own homes, the maltreated children may behave "differently" at home (e.g., they may become more demanding of attention and less compliant, and may also show a preference for the day care staff). Some of the new behaviors may be perceived negatively by parents and result in frustration and the potential for abuse. The maltreating parents may need preparation for such changes. One solution may be to integrate the parents into the day care program in some way. This can be accomplished by prearranged observation sessions of the program or by actual involvement of the parents in classroom activities. Either of

these solutions should always be accompanied by discussion between the parents and staff members or outside consultants regarding what the parents have observed, as well as perhaps some didactic instruction regarding classroom management of children. Such informal instruction can be a valuable adjunct to treatment of such parents.

The only systematic study of the impact of day care suggests that without modifications, the typical programs provided may indeed have a negative impact. Crittenden (1983) followed 22 children for 4 years after protective day care was sought. In 9 cases, adequate day care could not be arranged (e.g., because of lack of transportation, unavailability of openings, or insufficient funds). Although no differences between the groups that did and did not receive day care were found at the time of referral in child development, home environment, and maternal attachment, a 1-year follow-up the day care group surprisingly showed higher rates of out-of-home placement (13 out of 13 for the day care group vs. 6 out of 9 for the group not receiving day care). At the 4-year follow-up, no differences were found in placement figures for the two groups. Because this study did not employ random assignment, its results must be viewed with caution; the two groups may have differed in some systematic way. It does, however, raise questions regarding the assumption that day care will have a positive impact. Further research is needed to evaluate the impact of such services on maltreating families' functioning and child outcome.

Stimulation Training

Because of the nature of interactions within abusive and neglectful families (e.g., low levels of parent–child interaction), developmental delays are often noted among maltreated children. A child's developmental delays and associated lowered responsivity may further exacerbate disturbed family functioning (e.g., interaction with a delayed and unresponsive child is less reinforcing to the parent; Azar, 1986). Interventions, therefore, might be undertaken that increase parents' stimulation of their children.

A large literature exists describing programs designed to intervene with infants and young children whose environments are thought to provide inadequate resources for facilitating growth and development. The earliest of this work was conducted with infants and young children subjected to the understimulating environments of institutional care (e.g., orphanage residents). This early work resulted in large-scale efforts to increase the cognitive and social stimulation provided to children at risk because of the deprivation associated with poverty (e.g., the Head Start program). Although there is still much debate regarding the effectiveness of these efforts, there is some agreement regarding the positive impact of those programs that targeted changes in parents' behavior. Programs that attempted to teach parents to increase the stimulation they provided their children, in order to promote functioning and language skills, seemed to result in positive child outcomes (Karnes, Teska, Hodgins, & Badger, 1970; Levinstein, 1969).

The use of such intervention may be useful for abusive parents. Wolfe and his colleagues (Wolfe & Manion, 1984; Wolfe, Edwards, Manion, & Koverola, 1988), in describing a competency-based stimulation program for parents at risk for abuse, suggest that such training be aimed at increasing the positive nature of parent–child interactions (e.g., positive physical contact, positive child experiences, nonaversive control). Parents are shown through modeling, role playing, and feedback how to engage in daily activities with their children that serve to strengthen the children's areas of deficiency and to promote adaptive functioning. The activities they suggest are behaviorally specific and include developmentally appropriate language abilities (e.g., eye contact, responding to simple sounds or phrases, producing sounds, etc.) and social interaction abilities (e.g., following directions, engaging in play with parents, expressing affection and needs). Field, Widmayer, Stringer, and Ignatoff (1980), using a similar intervention with black teenage mothers who were high school dropouts showed that it was very effective in producing developmental gains in the children. Play behavior may be a particularly important behavior to teach abusive parents, in that low levels of this behavior have been associated with at-risk or "difficult" child status (Field, 1979). Further empirical work is needed to explore the effectiveness of stimulation programs with abusive parents.

Behavioral Consultation in Day Care, School, and Foster Care Settings

Although efforts are being directed at improving interactions in the home, inappropriate child behaviors that were acquired from an abusive and neglectful environment may be maintained by caretakers' reactions in other settings. Behavioral consultation with staff members in these other settings may be important to help support the changes made at home by the parents and to facilitate the overall adjustment of the children. Unfortunately, such consultation has not been discussed in the literature.

Two behaviors in particular may require intervention. High levels of aggressive behavior have been reported among maltreated children (George & Main, 1979; Hoffman-Plotkin & Twentyman, 1984; Reidy, 1977), as have high levels of socially withdrawn behavior (Martin, 1976). Reward programs to reduce aggressive behavior in school settings have been undertaken with other populations, using teachers and other staff members, and such programs may be useful for aggressive abused children. Day care staffers, for example, may be trained in the use of reinforcement, and reward the abused aggressive child for periods where he or she is behaving in a nonaggressive or prosocial way. "Time-out" procedures might also be employed by the staff for inappropriate behavior, in coordination with the parent's using it at home with the child.

Socially withdrawn behavior has also been handled using behavioral techniques, such as peer prompting of social initiations (Strain, Shores, & Timm, 1977; Strain & Timm, 1974). Fantuzzo, Azar, and Twentyman (1985) reported two studies using peer- and teacher-prompted social initiation strategies with maltreated, socially withdrawn preschoolers in a day care setting. Peer prompting in this report appeared to facilitate the interactions of the socially withdrawn target children, whereas adult prompting appeared to have negative effects. It may be important, therefore, in carrying out behavioral consultation, to design programs that take into consideration the special nature of these children's caretaking experiences.

Summary of Treatment Methods

In summary, the neglect of the child in treatment outcome research in this area is striking. Further work needs to be directed toward gathering information on how best to deal with the abused child's problems, as well as to enhance family functioning sufficiently to insure his or her safety and continued growth. In teaching new child-rearing skills to abusive parents, the behavior therapist must be aware of the contextual factors that interact with the family's acquisition of new parenting methods, and must also bear in mind the potential misuse of the material presented. Information the client has acquired during sessions needs to be consistently monitored, and careful evaluations of the parent's use of techniques need to be carried out if failures occur. The modifications needed for work with these families have not received much attention in the literature. The importance of such modifications in treatment effectiveness needs to be evaluated. Finally, few techniques for working with abused children have been reported. Such strategies clearly require attention in future research. Stimulation training and behavioral consultations are two approaches that might be explored further with this population of children.

CONCLUSIONS AND RECOMMENDATIONS FOR THE FUTURE

Behavioral approaches to treating child abuse have developed quickly over the past decade and show real promise as effective means of changing interaction patterns within abusive families. To date, most of this work has focused on changing the parents' behavior. Future work might be directed at alleviating the psychological consequences of abuse upon the children. Particularly important would be interventions aimed at families where the children are infants or adolescents. Even with treatments aimed at changing parents, child outcome, in both the short and the long term, needs to be assessed to determine the impact of families' functioning. In addition, because of the nature of the population, innovative techniques need to be developed, documented, and evaluated that will best meet these families' special needs.

Finally, preventive efforts that employ techniques based on social learning theory might be an important area for researchers to examine. If specific deficits are delineated, it may be possible to develop objectively defined risk indicators for early identification of individuals at risk to become child maltreaters. This might be done with mothers and fathers during pregnancy, or even earlier, during the high school years. For example, adolescents who are impulsive, aggressive, and socially isolated and who have poor parental role models themselves might be selected for preventive "preparenting" training programs. Such efforts to "enhance something positive" at an early stage in the development of the parent–child relationship hold considerable promise for the prevention of child maltreatment and its consequences (Helfer, 1982).

REFERENCES

Achenbach, T., & Edelbrock, C. S. (1983). *Manual for the Child Behavior Checklist and Revised Child Behavior Profile*. Burlington: University Associates in Psychiatry.

Ambrose, S., Hazzard, A., & Haworth, J. (1980). Cognitive–behavioral parenting groups for abusive families. *Child Abuse and Neglect, 4*, 119–125.

American Humane Association. (1981). *Annual report, 1980: National analysis of official child neglect and abuse reporting*. Denver, CO: Author.

American Humane Association. (1984). *Highlights of official child abuse and neglect reporting—1982*. Denver, CO: Author.

Arnold, E. L. (1978). *Helping parents help their children*. New York: Brunner/Mazel.

Aronson, H., & Overall, B. (1966). Treatment expectations of parents in two social classes. *Social Work, 11*, 35–41.

Arvanian, A. L. (1975). Dynamics of separation and placement. In N. B. Ebeling & D. A. Hill (Eds.), *Child abuse: Intervention and treatment* (pp. 45–62). Acton, MA: Publishing Science Group.

Averill, J. R. (1983). Studies on anger and aggression: Implications for theories of emotion. *American Psychologist, 38*, 1145–1160.

Ayllon, T., & Roberts, M. D. (1975). Mothers as educators for their children. In T. Thompson & W. S. Dockens (Eds.), *Applications of behavior modification* (pp. 107–137). New York: Academic Press.

Azar, S. T. (1984). *An evaluation of the effectiveness of cognitive behavioral versus insight oriented mothers groups with child maltreaters*. Unpublished doctoral dissertation, University of Rochester.

Azar, S. T. (1986). A framework for understanding child maltreatment: An integration of cognitive behavioural and developmental perspectives. *Canadian Journal of Behavioural Science, 18*, 340–355.

Azar, S. T. (1987, August). *A transactional model of child abuse*. Paper presented at the annual meeting of the American Psychological Association, New York.

Azar, S. T., Barnes, K. T., & Twentyman, C. T. (1988). Developmental outcomes in abused children: Consequences of parental abuse or a more general breakdown in caregiver behavior? *the Behavior Therapist, 11*, 27–32.

Azar, S. T., Fantuzzo, J., & Twentyman, C. T. (1984). An applied behavioural approach to child maltreatment: Back to basics. *Advances in Behaviour Research and Therapy, 6*, 3–11.

Azar, S. T., Robinson, D. R., Hekimian, E., & Twentyman, C. T. (1984). Unrealistic expectations and problem solving ability in maltreating and comparison mothers. *Journal of Consulting and Clinical Psychology, 52*, 687–691.

Azar, S. T., & Rohrbeck, C. A. (1986). Child abuse and unrealistic expectations: Further validation of the Parent Opinion Questionnaire. *Journal of Consulting and Clinical psychology, 54,* 867–868.

Azar, S. T., & Twentyman, C. T. (1984, November). *An evaluation of the effectiveness of behaviorally versus insight oriented group treatments with maltreating mothers.* Paper presented at the annual meeting of the Association for Advancement of Behavior Therapy, Philadelphia.

Azar, S. T., & Twentyman, C. T. (1986). Cognitive-behavioral perspectives on the assessment and treatment of child abuse. In P. C. Kendall (Ed.), *Advances in cognitive–behavioral research and therapy* (Vol. 5, pp. 237–267). New York: Academic Press.

Azar, S. T., & Twentyman, C. T. (in press). A cognitive behavioral approach to child maltreatment. In C. T. Twentyman & L. Siegel (Eds.), *Behavioral medicine.* New York: Springer.

Azrin, H. N., Naster, B. J., & Jones, R. (1973). Reciprocal counseling: A rapid learning based procedure for marital counseling. *Behaviour Research and Therapy, 11,* 365–383.

Barth, R. P., Blythe, B. J., Schinke, S. P., Stevens, P., & Schilling, R. F. (1983). Self-control training with maltreating parents. *Child Welfare, 62,* 313–324.

Baum, O. E., & Felzer, S. B. (1964). Activity in initial interviews with lower class patients. *Archives of General Psychiatry, 10,* 345–353.

Becker, W. C. (1971). *Parents are teachers.* Champaign, IL: Research Press.

Bedner, R. L., & Kaul, T. J. (1978). Experiential group research: Current perspectives. In S. L. Garfield & A. E. Bergin (Eds.), *Handbook of psychotherapy and behavior change* (2nd ed., pp. 769–815). New York: Wiley.

Bell, R. Q., & Harper, L. (1977). *Child effects on adults.* Hillsdale, NJ: Erlbaum.

Belsky, J. (1980). Child maltreatment: An ecological integration. *American Psychologist, 35,* 320–335.

Berger, A. (1980). The child abusing family: Part I. Methodological issues and parent-related characteristics of abusing families. *American Journal of Family Therapy, 8,* 53–66.

Berkowitz, L. (1983). Aversively stimulated aggression: Some parallels and differences in research with animals and humans. *American Psychologist, 38,* 1135–1144.

Bower, G. H. (1981). Mood and memory. *American Psychologist, 36,* 129–148 .

Brown, G. W., & Harris, T. (1978). *Social origins of depression: A study of psychiatric disorder in women.* London: Tavistock.

Burgess, R. L. (1979). Child abuse: A social interactional analysis. In B. B. Lahey & A. E. Kazdin (Eds.), *Advances in clinical child psychology,* (Vol. 2, pp. 142–172). New York: Plenum.

Campbell, R. V., O'Brien, S., Bickett, A. D., & Lutzker, J. R. (1983). In-home parent training of migraine headaches and marital counseling as an ecobehavioral approach to prevent child abuse. *Journal of Behavior Therapy and Experimental Psychiatry, 14,* 147–154.

Cohn, A. H. (1979). Essential elements of successful child abuse and neglect treatment. *Child Abuse and Neglect, 3,* 491–496.

Cohn, A. H., & Miller, M. K. (1977). Evaluating new modes of treatment for child abusers and neglectors: The experience of federally funded demonstration projects in the USA. *Child Abuse and Neglect, 1,* 453–458.

Conger, R. D. (1982). Behavioral intervention for child abuse. *the Behavior Therapist, 5,* 49–53.

Conger, R. D., Lahey, B. B., & Smith, S. S. (1981, July). *An intervention program for child abuse: Modifying maternal depression and behavior.* Paper presented at the Family Violence Research Conference, University of New Hampshire, Durham.

Crimmins, D. B., Bradlyn, A. S., St. Lawrence, J. S., & Kelly, J. A. (1984). A training technique for improving the parent–child interaction skills of an abusive-neglectful mother. *Child Abuse and Neglect, 8,* 533–539.

Crittenden, P. M. (1983). The effects of mandatory protective daycare on mutual attachment in maltreating mother–infant dyads. *Child Abuse and Neglect, 3,* 297–300.

Crozier, J., & Katz, R. C. (1979). Social learning theory treatment of child abuse. *Journal of Behavior Therapy and Experimental Psychiatry 10,* 213–220.

Delgado, A. E., & Lutzker, J. R. (1985, November). *Training parents to identify and report their children's illness.* Paper presented at the annual convention of the Association for Advancement of Behavior Therapy, Houston.

Denicola, J., & Sandler, J. (1980). Training abusive parents in cognitive behavioral techniques. *Behavior Therapy, 11,* 263–270.

Derogatis, L. R. (1975). *The SCL-90.* Baltimore: Clinical Psychometric Research.

Doctor, R. M., & Singer, E. M. (1978). Behavioral intervention strategies with child abusive parents: A home intervention program. *Child Abuse and Neglect, 2,* 57–68.

Doll, E. A. (1964). *Vineland Social Maturity Scale.* Circle Pines, MN: American Guidance Service.

Egan, K. (1983). Stress management and child management with abusive parents. *Journal of Clinical Child Psychology, 12,* 292–299.

Egeland, B., & Farber, E. A. (1984). Infant–mother attachment: Factors related to its development and changes over time. *Child Development, 55,* 753–771.

Egeland, B., & Sroufe, L. A. (1981). Attachment and early maltreatment. *Child Development, 52,* 44–52.

Eisenberg, L. (1962). The sins of the father: Urban decay and social pathology. *American Journal of Orthopsychiatry, 15,* 1–5.

Eisler, R. M., Hersen, M., & Agras, W. S. (1973). Effects of videotape and instructional feedback on nonverbal marital interactions: An analogue study. *Behavior Therapy, 4,* 551–558.

Ellis, A. (1962). *Reason and emotion in psychotherapy.* New York: Lyle Stuart.

Fanshel, D., & Shinn, E. B. (1978). *Children in foster care: A longitudinal investigation.* New York: Columbia University Press.

Fantuzzo, J. W., Azar, S. T., & Twentyman, C. T. (1985, November). *Child abuse and psychotherapy research: Merging social concerns.* Paper presented at the annual convention of the Association for Advancement of Behavior Therapy, Houston.

Fantuzzo, J. W., Wray, L., Hall, R., Goins, C., & Azar, S. T. (1986). Parent and social skills training for mentally retarded parents identified as child maltreaters. *American Journal of Mental Deficiency, 91,* 135–140.

Farber, E. D., & Joseph, J. A. (1985). The maltreated adolescent: Patterns of physical abuse. *Child Abuse and Neglect, 9,* 201–206.

Farber, E., McCoard, D., Kinast, C., & Baum-Faulkner,

D. (1984). Violence in families of adolescent runaways. *Child Abuse and Neglect, 8,* 295–299.

Field, T. (1979). Games people play with normal and high risk infants. *Child Psychiatry and Human Development, 10,* 41–48.

Field, T., Widmayer, S. M., Stringer, S., & Ignatoff, E. (1980). Teenage, lower class, black mothers and their preterm infants: An intervention and developmental follow-up. *Child Development 51,* 426–436.

Flanagan, S., Adams, H. E., & Forehand, R. (1979). A comparison of four instructional techniques for teaching parents to use time out. *Behavior Therapy, 10,* 94–102.

Fleischman, M. J. (1979). Using parenting salaries to control attrition and cooperation in therapy. *Behavior Therapy, 10,* 111–116.

Folkman, S. (1984). Personal control and stress and coping processes: A theoretical analysis. *Journal of Personality and Social Psychology, 46,* 839–852.

Foxx, R. M., McMorrow, M. J., & Mennemeir, M. (1984). Teaching social/vocational skills to retarded adults with a modified table game: An analysis of generalization. *Journal of Applied Behavior Analysis, 17,* 343–352.

Foxx, R. M., McMorrow, M. J., & Schloss, C. (1983). Stacking the deck: Teaching social skills to retarded adults with a modified table game. *Journal of Applied Behavior Analysis, 16,* 157–170.

Friedman, R., Sandler, J., Hernandez, M., & Wolfe, D. (1981). Child abuse. In E. J. Mash & L. G. Terdal (Eds.), *Behavioral assessment of childhood disorders* (pp. 221–255). New York. Guilford Press.

Friedrich, W. N., Einbender, A. J., & Luecke, W. J. (1983). Cognitive and behavioral characteristics of physically abused children. *Journal of Consulting and Clinical Psychology, 51,* 313–314.

Frodi, A., & Smetana, J. (1984). Abused, neglected, and nonmaltreated preschoolers' ability to discriminate emotions in others: The effects of IQ. *Child Abuse and Neglect, 8,* 459–465.

Gaensbauer, T. J., & Sands, K. (1979). Distored affective communication in abused/neglected infants and their potential impact on caretakers. *Journal of the American Academy of Child Psychiatry, 18,* 236–251.

Galdston, R. (1979). Preventing the abuse of little children. In D. G. Gil (Ed.), *Child abuse and violence* (pp. 340–353). New York: AMS Press.

Gambrill, E. D. (1983). Behavioral intervention with child abuse and neglect. In M. Hersen, R. M. Eisler, & P. M. Miller (Eds.) *Progress in behavior modification.* (Vol. 17, pp. 1–56). New York: Academic Press.

Garbarino, J. (1976). A preliminary study of some ecological correlates of child abuse: The impact of socioeconomic stress on mothers. *Child Development, 47,* 178–185.

Garbarino, J., & Stocking, S. H. (1980). *Protecting children from abuse and neglect.* San Francisco: Jossey-Bass.

Garfield, S. L., & Wolpin, M. (1963). Expectations regarding psychotherapy. *Journal of Nervous and Mental Disease, 137,* 353–362.

Garmezy, N. (1983). Stressors of childhood. In N. Garmezy & M. Rutter (Eds.), *Stress, coping, and development in children* (pp. 43–84). New York: McGraw-Hill.

Geiser, R. L. (1973). *The illusion of caring: Children in foster care.* Boston: Beacon Press.

Gelles, R. J. (1983). An exchange/social control theory. In D. Finkelhor, R. J. Gelles, G. T. Hotaling, & M. A. Strauss (Eds.), *The dark side of families* (pp. 151–165). Beverly Hills: Sage.

Gelles, R. J., & Straus, M. A. (1987). Is violence toward children increasing? A comparison of 1975 and 1985 national survey rates. *Journal of Interpersonal Violence, 2,* 212–222.

George, C., & Main, M. (1979). Social interactions of young abused children: Approach, avoidance and aggression. *Child Development, 50,* 306–318.

Gil, D. G. (1970). *Violence against children: Physical child abuse in the United States.* Cambridge, MA: Harvard University Press.

Gilbert, M. R. (1976). Behavioral approach to the treatment of child abuse. *Nursing Times, 72,* 140–143.

Goldberg, D. P., & Hillier, V. F. (1979). A scaled version of the General Health Questionnaire. *Psychological Medicine, 9,* 139–145.

Goldfried, M. R., & Davison, G. C. (1970). *Clinical behavior therapy.* New York: Holt, Rinehart & Winston.

Goodluck, C., & Tuthill, N. H. (1983, September). *Understanding Native American families.* Paper presented at the Sixth National Conference on Child Abuse and Neglect, Baltimore.

Gordon, S. B., & Davidson, N. (1981). Behavioral parent training. In A. F. Gurman & D. P. Kniskern (Eds.), *Handbook of family therapy* (pp. 517–555). New York: Brunner/Mazel.

Gottman, J. M., & Levenson, R. W. (1985). A valid procedure for obtaining self-report of affect in marital interaction. *Journal of Consulting and Clinical Psychology, 53,* 151–160.

Graziano, A. M. (1977). Parents as behavior therapists. In M. Hersen, R. M. Eisler, & P. M. Miller (Eds.), *Progress in behavior modification.* (Vol. 9, pp. 251–298). New York: Academic Press.

Green, A. H. (1976). A psychodynamic approach to the study and treatment of abusing parents. *Journal of the American Academy of Child Psychiatry, 15,* 414–429.

Hagen, R. L., Foreyt, J. P., & Durham, T. W. (1976). The dropout problem: Reducing attrition in obesity research. *Behavior Therapy, 7,* 463–471.

Hanson, R. (1971). *Time out: A way to help children behave better* [Film]. Detroit: Informatics.

Hathaway, S. R., & McKinley, J. C. (1951). *Minnesota Multiphasic Personality Inventory: Manual.* Minneapolis: University of Minnesota Press.

Hazzard, A., Christensen, A., & Margolin, G. (1983). Children's perceptions of parental behaviors. *Journal of Abnormal Child Psychology, 11,* 49–59.

Heitler, J. B. (1973). Preparation of lower-class patients for expressive group psychotherapy. *Journal of Consulting and Clinical Psychology, 41,* 251–260.

Heitler, J. B. (1976). Preparatory techniques in initiating expressive psychotherapy with lower-class unsophisticated patients. *Psychological Bulletin, 83,* 339–352.

Helfer, R. E. (1982). A review of the literature on the prevention of child abuse and neglect. *Child Abuse and Neglect, 6,* 251–261.

Herrenkohl, R. C., Herrenkohl. E. C., & Egolf, B. P. (1983). Circumstances surrounding the occurrence of child maltreatment. *Journal of Consulting and Clinical Psychology, 51,* 424–431.

Herrenkohl, R. C., Herrenkohl, E. C., Egolf, B., & Seech, M. (1979). The repetition of child abuse: How frequently does it occur? *Child Abuse and Neglect, 3,* 67–72.

Hoffman-Plotkin, D., & Twentyman, C. T. (1984). A

multimodal assessment of behavioral and cognitive deficits in abused and neglected preschoolers. *Child Development, 55,* 794–802.

Isaacs, C. D. (1982). Treatment of child abuse: A review of the behavioral interventions. *Journal of Applied Behavior Analysis, 15,* 273–294.

Jacobson, N. S. (1978). Specific and nonspecific factors in the effectiveness of a behavioral approach to the treatment of a marital discord. *Journal of Consulting and Clinical Psychology, 45,* 92–100.

Johnson, C. A., & Katz, C. (1973). Using parents as change agents for their children. *Journal of Applied Behavior Analysis, 14,* 131–200.

Justice, B., & Justice, R. (1978). Evaluating outcome of group therapy for abusing parents. *Corrective and Social Psychiatry and Journal of Behavioral Technology, 24,* 45–49.

Justice, R., & Justice, B. (1976). *The abusing family.* New York: Human Sciences Press.

Kamin, L., & Caughlin, J. (1963). Subjective experiences of outpatient psychotherapy. *American Journal of Psychotherapy, 17,* 660–668.

Karnes, M. B., Teska, J. A., Hodgins, A. S. & Badger, I. D. (1970). Educational intervention at home by mothers of disadvantaged infants. *Child Development, 41,* 925–935.

Kazdin, A. E., & Polster, R. (1973). Intermittent token reinforcement and response maintenance in extinction. *Behavior Therapy, 4,* 386–391.

Kempe, C. H., & Helfer, R. E. (1972). *Helping the battered child and his family.* Philadelphia: J. B. Lippincott.

Knitzer, J., & Allen, M. J. (1978). *Children without homes.* Washington, DC: Children's Defense Fund.

Kovacs, M. (1983, April). *The Children's Depression Inventory: A self-rated depression scale for school-aged youngsters.* Unpublished manuscript, University of Pittsburgh.

Koverola, C., Elliot-Faust, O., & Wolfe, D. A. (1984). Clinical issues in the behavioral treatment of a child abusive mother experiencing multiple life stressors. *Journal of Clinical Child Psychology, 13,* 187–191.

LaRose, L., & Wolfe, D. A. (1985). *A video-simulated stress procedure for parents* [Videotape]. London, Ontario: University of Western Ontario, Department of Psychology.

LaRose, L., & Wolfe, D. A. (1987). Psychological characteristics of parents who abuse or neglect their children. In B. B. Lahey & A. E. Kazdin (Eds.), *Advances in clinical child psychology* (Vol. 10, pp. 55–97). New York: Plenum.

Larrance, D. L., & Twentyman, C. T. (1983). Maternal attributions in child abuse. *Journal of Abnormal Psychology, 92,* 449–457.

Lennard, H. L., & Bernstein, A. (1960). *The anatomy of psychotherapy.* New York: Columbia University Press.

Levine, S. (1983). A psychobiological approach to the ontogeny of coping. In N. Garmezy & M. Rutter (Eds.), *Stress, coping, and development in children* (pp. 107–131). New York: McGraw-Hill.

Levinstein, P. (1969, April) *Cognitive growth in preschoolers through stimulation of verbal interaction with mothers.* Paper presented at the annual meeting of the American Orthopsychiatry Association, New York.

Levitt, E. E. (1966). Psychotherapy research and the expectancy-reality discrepancy. *Psychotherapy: Theory, Research, and Practice, 3,* 163–166.

Lewis, D. O., Shanok, S. S., Pincus, J. H., & Glaser, G.

H. (1979). Violent juvenile delinquents: Psychiatric, neurological, psychological, and abuse factors. *Journal of the American Academy of Child Psychiatry, 18,* 307–319.

Light, R. (1973). Abused and neglected children in America: A study of alternative policies. *Harvard Educational Review, 43,* 556–598.

Lorion, R. P. (1978). Research on psychotherapy and behavior change with the disadvantaged. In S. L. Garfield & A. E. Bergin (Eds.), *Handbook of psychotherapy and behavior change: An empirical analysis* (2nd ed., pp. 903–938). New York: Wiley.

Love, L. R., Kaswan, J., & Bugenthal, D. (1972). Differential effectiveness of three clinical interventions for different socioeconomic groupings. *Journal of Consulting and Clinical Psychology, 39,* 347–360.

Lutzker, J. R. (1984). Project 12-Ways: Treating child abuse and neglect from an ecobehavioral perspective. In R. F. Dangel & R. A. Polster (Eds.), *Parent training: Foundations of research and practice* (pp. 260–293). New York: Guilford Press.

Lutzker, J. R., & Rice, J. M. (1984). Project 12-Ways: Measuring outcome of a large in-home service for treatment and prevention of child abuse and neglect. *Child Abuse and Neglect, 8,* 519–524.

Maccoby, E. E., & Martin, J. A. (1983). Socialization in the context of the family: Parent–child interaction. In E. M. Hetherington (Vol. Ed.), *Handbook of child psychology* (4th ed.): *Vol. 4. Socialization, personality, and social development* (pp. 1–101). New York: Wiley.

Mager, R. F. (1972). *Who did what to whom?* [Film]. Champaign, IL: Research Press.

Mann, E., & McDermott, J. F. (1983). Play therapy for victims of child abuse and neglect. In C. E. Schaefer & K. J. O'Connor (Eds.), *Handbook of play therapy* (pp. 283–307). New York: Wiley.

Martin, H. P. (1976). *The abused child: A multidisciplinary approach to developmental issues and treatment.* Cambridge, MA: Ballinger.

Martin, H. P., & Beezley, P. (1976). Behavioral observations of abused children. *Developmental Medicine and Child Neurology, 19.* 373–387.

Mass, H. S., & Engler, R. (1959). *Children in need of parents.* New York: Columbia University Press.

Meichenbaum, D. H. (1974). *Cognitive behavior modification.* Morristown, NJ: General Learning Press.

Milner, J. S. (1986). *The Child Abuse Potential Inventory: Manual* (2nd ed.). Webster, NC: Psytec Corp.

Moos, R. E. (1974). *The Family Environment Scale.* Palo Alto, CA: Consulting Psychologists Press.

National Center on Child Abuse and Neglect. (1981). *Executive summary: National study of the incidence and severity of child abuse and neglect* (DHHS Publication No. OHDS 81-30329). Washington, DC: U.S. Government Printing Office.

Nay, W. R. (1975). A systematic comparison of instructional techniques for parents. *Behavior Therapy, 6,* 14–21.

Nomellini, S., & Katz, R. C. (1983). Effects of anger control training on abusive parents. *Cognitive Therapy and Research, 7,* 57–68.

Novaco, R. W. (1975). *Anger control: The development and evaluation of an experimental treatment.* Lexington, MA: Lexington Books.

O'Dell, S. (1974). Training parents in behavior modification: A review. *Psychological Bulletin, 81,* 418–433.

O'Leary, S. G. (1985, November). *It's time to stop avoid-*

ing punishment. Paper presented at the annual convention of the Association for Advancement for Behavior Therapy, Houston.

Ollendick, T. H. (1978). Reliability and validity of the Revised Fear Survey Schedule for Children (FSSC-R). *Behaviour Research and Therapy, 21,* 685–692.

Overall, B., & Aronson, H. (1962). Expectations of psychotherapy in lower socio-economic class patients. *American Journal of Orthopsychiatry, 32,* 271–272.

Parke, R. D. (1977). Socialization into child abuse: A social interactional perspective. In J. L. Tapp & F. J. Levine (Eds.), *Law, justice, and the individual in society: Psychological and legal issues* (pp. 183–199). New York: Holt, Rinehart & Winston.

Parke, R. D., & Collmer, C. W. (1975). Child abuse: An interdisciplinary analysis. In E. M. Hetherington (Ed.), *Review of child development research* (Vol. 5, pp. 509–590). Chicago: University of Chicago Press.

Patterson, G. R. (1971). *Families: Application of social learning theory to family life*. Champaign, IL: Research Press.

Patterson, G. R., & Forgatch, M. S. (1975). *The Family living series* [Audiotapes]. Champaign, IL: Research Press.

Pelton, L. H. (1978). Child abuse and neglect: The myth of classlessness. *American Journal of Orthopsychiatry, 48,* 608–617.

Peterson, C., & Seligman, M. E. P. (1983). Learned helplessness and victimization. *Journal of Social Issues, 39,* 103–116.

Plotkin, R. (1983). *Cognitive mediation in disciplinary action among mothers who have abused or neglected their children: Dispositional and environmental factors*. Unpublished doctoral dissertation, University of Rochester.

Quay, H. C., & Peterson, D. R. (1967). *Manual for the Behavior Problem Checklist*. Champaign: University of Illinois, Child Research Center.

Reid, J. B. (1985). Behavioral approaches to intervention and assessment with child abusive families. In P. H. Bornstein & A. Kazdin (Eds.), *Handbook of clinical behavior therapy with children* (pp. 772–802). Homewood, IL: Dorsey Press.

Reidy, T. J. (1977). The aggressive characteristics of abused and neglected children. *Journal of Clinical Psychology, 33,* 1140–1145.

Reynolds, C. R., & Richmond, B. O. (1978). What I think and feel: A revised measure of children's manifest anxiety. *Journal of Abnormal Psychology, 6,* 271–280.

Rinn, R. C., Vernon, J. C., & Wise, M. J. (1975). Training parents of behavior-disordered children in groups: A three years' program evaluation. *Behavior Therapy, 6,* 378–387.

Rose, D. (1969). A behavioral approach to the group treatment of parents. *Social Work, 14,* 12–29.

Runyan, D. K., Gould, C. L., Trost, D. C., & Loda, F. A. (1981). Determinants of foster care placement for the maltreated child. *American Journal of Pediatric Health, 71,* 706–710.

Rutter, M. (1983). Stress, coping, and development: Some issues and some questions. In N. Garmezy & M. Rutter (Eds.), *Stress, coping, and development in children* (pp. 1–41). New York: McGraw-Hill.

Salzinger, S., Kaplan, S., & Artemyeff, C. (1983). Mother's personal social networks and child maltreatment. *Journal of Abnormal Psychology, 92,* 68–72.

Sanders, W. (1978). Systematic desensitization in the treatment of child abuse. *American Journal of Psychiatry, 135,* 483–484.

Sandford, D. A., & Tustin, R. D. (1974). Behavioral treatment of parental assault on a child. *New Zealand Psychologist, 2,* 76–82.

Sandler, J., Van Dercar, C., & Milhoan, M. (1978). Training child abusers in the use of positive reinforcement practices. *Behaviour Research and Therapy, 16,* 169–175.

Sarason, I. G., Johnson, J. H., & Siegel, J. M. (1979). Assessing the impact of life changes: Development of the Life Experiences Survey. *Series in Clinical and Community Psychiatry, 6,* 131–149.

Sarber, R. E., Halasz, M. M., Messmer, M. C., Bickett, A. D., & Lutzker, J. R. (1983). Teaching menu planning and grocery shopping skills to a mentally retarded mother. *Mental Retardation, 21,* 101–106.

Schilling, R. F., & Schinke, S. P. (1984). Maltreatment and mental retardation. *Perspectives and Progress in Mental Retardation, 1,* 11–22.

Schor, E. L. (1982). The foster care system and health status of foster children. *Pediatrics, 69,* 521–528.

Smetana, J., Kelly, M., & Twentyman, C. (1984). Abused, neglected, and nonmaltreated children's conceptions of moral and social-conventional transgressions. *Child Development, 55,* 277–287.

Smith, J. E. (1984). Non-accidental injury to children: I. A review of behavioural interventions. *Behaviour Research and Therapy, 22,* 331–347.

Spielberger, C. D., Gorsuch, R. L., & Lushene, R. E. (1970). *State–Trait Anxiety Inventory manual*. Palo Alto, CA: Consulting Psychologists Press.

Spinetta, J. J., & Rigler, D. (1972). The child abusing parent: A psychological review. *Psychological Bulletin, 77,* 296–304.

Standing Senate Committee on Health, Welfare, and Science. (1980). *Child at risk*. Hull, Quebec: Minister of Supply and Services Canada.

Steele, B. F. (1975). Working with abusive parents: A psychiatric view. *Children Today, 4,* 3–5.

Steele, B. F., & Pollock, C. B. (1968). A psychiatric study of parents who abuse infants and small children. In R. Helfer & C. G. Kempe (Eds.), *The battered child* (pp. 414–463). Chicago: University of Chicago Press.

Stone, H. D. (1969). *Reflections on foster care: A report of a national survey of attitudes and practice*. New York: Child Welfare League.

Strain, P. S., Shores, R. E., & Timm, M. A. (1977). Effects of peer social initiations on the behavior of withdrawn perschool children. *Journal of Applied Behavior Analysis, 10,* 289–298.

Strain, P. S., & Timm, M. A. (1974). An experimental analysis of social interaction between a behaviorally disordered preschool child and her classroom peers. *Journal of Applied Behavior Analysis, 7,* 583–590.

Swinger, H. K. (1983, September). *Understanding black families*. Paper presented at the Sixth National Conference on Child Abuse and Neglect, Baltimore.

Szykula, S. A., & Fleischman, M. J. (1985). Reducing out-of-home placements of abused children: Two controlled studies. *Child Abuse and Neglect, 9,* 277–284.

Twentyman, C. T., & McFall, R. M. (1975). Behavioral training of social skills in shy males. *Journal of Consulting and Clinical Psychology, 43,* 384–395.

Vasta, R. (1982). Physical child abuse: A dual component analysis. *Developmental Review, 2,* 164–170.

Wald, M. S. (1976). Legal policies affecting children: A lawyer's request for aid. *Child Development, 47,* 1–5.

Wahler, R. G. (1980). The insular mother: Her problems in parental reinforcement control. *Journal of Applied Behavior Analysis, 2,* 159–170.

White, A. M., Fichtenbaum, L., & Dollard, J. (1964). Evaluation of silence in initial interviews with psychiatric clinic patients. *Journal of Nervous and Mental Disease, 139,* 550–557.

Williams, G. (1983). Child abuse reconsidered: The urgency of authentic prevention. *Journal of Clinical Child Psychology, 12,* 312–319.

Wolfe, D. A. (1985). Child–abusive parents: An empirical review and analysis. *Psychological Bulletin, 97,* 462–482.

Wolfe, D. A. (1987). *Child abuse: Implications for child development and psychopathology.* Newbury Park, CA: Sage.

Wolfe, D. A. (1988). Child abuse and neglect. In E. J. Mash & L. G. Terdal (Eds.), *Behavioral assessment of childhood disorders* (2nd ed., pp. 627–669). New York: Guilford Press.

Wolfe, D. A., Aragona, J., Kaufman, K., & Sandler, J. (1980). The importance of adjudication in the treatment of child abuse: Some preliminary findings. *Child Abuse and Neglect, 4,* 127–135.

Wolfe, D. A., & Bourdeau P. (1987). Current issues in the assessment of abusive and neglectful parent–child relationships. *Behavioral Assessment, 9,* 271–290.

Wolfe, D. A., Edwards, B., Manion, I., & Koverola, C. (1988). Early intervention for child abuse and neglect: A preliminary investigation. *Journal of Consulting and Clinical Psychology, 56,* 40–47.

Wolfe, D. A., Kaufman, D., Aragona, J., & Sandler, J. (1981). *The child management program for abusive parents.* Winter Park, FL: Anna.

Wolfe, D. A., & Manion, I. G. (1984). Impediments to child abuse prevention: Issues and directions. *Advances in Behaviour Research and Therapy, 6,* 47–62.

Wolfe, D. A., & Mosk, M. D. (1983). Behavioral comparisons of children from abusive and distressed families. *Journal of Consulting and Clinical Psychology, 51,* 702–708.

Wolfe, D. A., & Sandler, J. (1981). Training abusive parents in effective child management. *Behavior Modification, 5,* 320–335.

Wolfe, D. A., Sandler, J., & Kaufman, K. (1981). A competency-based parent training program for abusive parents. *Journal of Consulting and Clinical Psychology, 49,* 633–640.

Wolfe, D. A., St. Lawrence, J., Graves, K., Brehony, K., Bradlyn, D., & Kelly, J. (1982). Intensive behavioral parent training for a child abusive mother. *Behavior Therapy, 13,* 438–451.

Wolfe, D. A., & Wolfe, V. (1988). The sexually abused child. In E. J. Mash & L. G. Terdal (Eds.), *Behavioral assessment of childhood disorders* (2nd ed., pp. 670–716). New York: Guilford Press.

Zillman, D. (1979). *Hostility and aggression.* Hillsdale, NJ: Erlbaum.

PART VII

PROBLEMS OF ADOLESCENCE

14

PARENT–ADOLESCENT CONFLICT

SHARON L. FOSTER
West Virginia University

ARTHUR L. ROBIN
Wayne State University School of Medicine

Conflict between parents and adolescents, while not ubiquitous, occurs quite often as young children mature into adults (Montemayor, 1983). Deviant parent–teen communication patterns characterize some clinical populations, including teenagers who commit status offenses (Alexander, 1973) and other aggressive acts (Loeber & Dishion, 1984). Furthermore, disturbed family communication predicts the development of schizophrenic-spectrum disorders in late adolescence and the early 20s (Doane, West, Goldstein, Rodnick, & Jones, 1981).

Problematic family conflict is a relatively new area of research. The revised third edition of the *Diagnostic and Statistical Manual of Mental Disorders* (American Psychiatric Association, 1987) is the first to list a diagnostic category explicitly relevant to parent–adolescent conflict: Oppositional Defiant Disorder. This diagnosis requires age-inappropriate excesses in at least five of nine areas: losing temper, arguing with adults, defying rules or requests, deliberately annoying others, blaming others, seeming easily annoyed by others, appearing angry, seeming spiteful or vindictive, and swearing. Because this diagnosis is so new,

however, epidemiological information on its incidence and prevalence in adolescence is unavailable. Nor is its etiology or prognosis clear.

Adolescents experiencing severe conflict with parents could thus be a subset of the population of teenagers diagnosable with the label Oppositional Defiant Disorder. In addition, as previously indicated, parent–adolescent conflict and/or communication problems sometimes characterize other clinical populations (e.g., those with a conduct disorder). For the purposes of this chapter, we define clinically significant parent–adolescent conflict as characterized by one or more of the following: (1) repeated, unpleasant, predominantly verbal disagreements about one or more issues; (2) disputes that fail to produce workable agreements, resulting in repeated occurrence of the issues that elicit disputes; (3) negative, anger-laden exchanges over problem issues; and (4) feelings of dissatisfaction about family relations, the behavior of others, and/or unresolved issues. Nonproblematic conflict, in contrast, tends to be time-limited, results in resolution of disagreements, and is not accompanied by pervasive dissatisfaction with family relations.

When and how does family conflict reach

clinically significant proportions? We (Foster & Robin, 1988; Robin & Foster, 1989) hypothesize that the child's transition into adolescence, with its concomitant biological, cognitive, and social changes, disrupts ongoing family patterns. The adolescent's increased requests for autonomy, thought to be a major task of the adolescent years, precipitates this disruption. As the family attempts to restructure its interactions to deal with a changing member, conflict is likely to result.

Whether the conflict is relatively short-lived or escalates into acrimonious, unresolved, and pervasive disputes depends on four major factors, according to our model (Robin & Foster, 1989): the family's problem-solving skills, its communication patterns, belief systems of individual family members, and the structural and functional patterns that overlay these molecular components of interaction sequences. Maladaptive patterns in any of these domains increase the likelihood that the family will not resolve its disputes, resulting in recurring angry conflicts. Thus, each domain is assessed prior to initiating treatment for parent–adolescent conflict. Problems noted in each area during assessment form the basis for selecting a treatment approach, with the approach geared toward improving specific difficulties in problem-solving and communication skills, cognitive patterns, and/ or structural and functional patterns. In this chapter, we first discuss each of these dimensions and its assessment. We then turn to treatment strategies for modifying each component.

ASSESSING DIMENSIONS OF FAMILY CONFLICT

Assessment has two functions. The first involves collecting information on the topics and process of conflictual interaction between the parents and the teenager. The interview, direct observation of family discussions, data collection at home, and responses to questionnaires provide this information, which serves as a basis for formulating hypotheses about problematic family patterns and their antecedents and consequences. These hypotheses in turn underlie a treatment plan tailored to the family's difficulties.

The second function of assessment is to lay the groundwork for later intervention. As the first stage of therapy, assessment has the specific goals of engaging the family in treatment, developing goals for treatment, establishing a shared view of the problem, gaining the family's understanding of the rationale for the treatment approach, formulating a treatment contract, and establishing the sessions as a forum for productive communication about troublesome issues.

Conflictual Issues

At the heart of family conflict lie the specific issues that provoke disagreement. These are often the family's presenting problems, and can be assessed in several ways. Interview questions asking family members to describe what they argue about and the behaviors they would like other members to change provide information on topics likely to provoke discord. Observing the family during the interview to see which topics elicit different opinions gives further clues and may corroborate members' reports about conflictual issues. Asking members to keep daily records of topics, antecedents, and consequences of arguments at home is another way of isolating conflictual issues.

The Issues Checklist (IC; Foster & Robin, 1988; Prinz, Foster, Kent, & O'Leary, 1979; Robin & Foster, 1988b, 1989), specifically assesses topics parents and teens discuss. The IC contains a list of 44 topics of potential disagreement. Each respondent indicates whether the topic has come up during the past 4 weeks, then estimates how many times the topic arose and how angry on average the discussions were. Scores based on the number of issues endorsed, average anger reported for each endorsed topic, and average anger reported per discussion (i.e., a weighted frequency × intensity score) all significantly differentiate families seeking treatment for parent–adolescent relationship problems from those reporting satisfactory relations (Robin & Foster, 1989), with the average anger intensity per issue accounting for the greatest variance in distressed–nondistressed status.

The IC is particularly useful for assessing which issues family members report as being associated with greater and lesser degrees of anger, and can be used to select topics to discuss in treatment. However, agreement between distressed mothers and adolescents on the issues they report as having occurred and not occurred averages only about 68% (Robin & Foster, 1989). Thus, reports on the IC are best interpreted as potentially distorted appraisals of past events, subject to confirmation or disconfirmation with other assessment methods.

Problem-Solving and Communication Skills

Assessing topics of dispute gives information about the content of disagreements. Assessing the family's problem-solving and communication skills provides information about the ways in which family members communicate about these topics. Gathering information on these processes involves describing the positive and negative interactive behaviors and behavior sequences that family members commonly exhibit during conflictual exchanges. Descriptions of behaviors exhibited by individual family members are crucial for determining the targets of interventions geared at improving problem-solving and communication skills, whereas descriptions of sequences of exchanges among members are essential prerequisites for molecular functional analysis of family members' interlocking patterns.

Problem-solving skills are those verbal interactional behaviors hypothesized to facilitate arriving at a solution to a specific dispute. Conceptualizations of problem solving frequently involve the following steps (D'Zurilla & Goldfried, 1971): (1) recognizing the existence of a problem; (2) formulating the problem specifically, in a way that makes it solvable; (3) generating future-oriented solutions; (4) evaluating the solutions and selecting the one most likely to solve the problem; (5) planning and implementing the solution; and (6) observing the effects of the solution. In a family, this process translates into such interaction behaviors as making specific statements that define a problem, suggesting alternatives, evaluating those alternatives, negotiating compromises, and agreeing on a plan to try. Parents and teenagers seeking clinical assistance for family problems differ from their nonreferred counterparts both in outside observers' ratings of their overall effectiveness at solving problems (Prinz & Kent, 1978) and in the frequency with which problem specification, positive solutions, evaluation statements, and agreements occur in audiotaped discussions of current real problems (Robin & Weiss, 1980).

Communication skills facilitate the exchange of information among family members and thus

are crucial to successful conflict resolution. Poor communication skills increase the likelihood of misunderstandings, reciprocated negative exchanges, and angry feelings. Studies comparing families seeking treatment with nondistressed families point to the kinds of positive communication skills seen more often in less distressed families, including humor, approval, acceptance of responsibility (Robin & Weiss, 1980), and supportiveness (Alexander, 1973). These same studies point to communication behaviors more common to distressed parents and teens, including defensive statements (Alexander, 1973), commands, put-downs, and lack of response (Robin & Weiss, 1980). Clinicians point to the importance of other skills with less empirical backing, such as reflective listening, clear "I-statements," appropriate nonverbal posture and tone of voice, and acknowledgment (e.g., Gordon, 1970; Guerney, 1977). Table 14-1 presents a compendium of skills culled from the research and clinical literatures that can be used to describe family communication skills and difficulties.

Problem-solving and communication skills can be assessed in several ways. The therapist can both ask questions about the ways family members handle specific disputes at home and observe the behaviors they display in discussing these topics during the session; the therapist should recognize, however, that reports of process at home may be inaccurate and that observations in the therapy room in the therapist's presence may not be representative of discussions at home.

Several questionnaires assess dimensions of family problem solving and/or communication. The Conflict Behavior Questionnaire (CBQ; Prinz et al., 1979; Robin & Foster, 1988a, 1989) assesses various interactive behaviors, discriminates distressed from nondistressed parents and teenagers (Robin & Foster, 1989), and has shown pre–post changes as a function of intervention (Foster, Prinz, & O'Leary, 1983), but does not yield information about the specific problem-solving and communication behaviors described above. Instruments with items more directly relevant to these behaviors include the Parent–Adolescent Communication Scale (Barnes & Olson, 1985) and the Parent–Adolescent Relationship Questionnaire (PARQ; Robin, Koepke, & Moye, 1986). Unfortunately, both of these instruments are new and have only preliminary psychometric data.

Questionnaire assessments of family interac-

TABLE 14-1. Common Communication Targets with Parents and Adolescents

Problematic behavior	Possible alternative

Talking through a third person
  Example: "I'd like Susie to clean her room."
	Talking directly to another
	  Example: "Susie, I'd like you to clean your room."

Accusatory, blaming, defensive statements
  Example: "You make me so mad! You don't respect your curfew."
	I-statements ("I feel———when———happens")
	  Example: "I get angry when you come in after your curfew."

Putting down; zapping; shaming
  Example: "You'll never amount to anything."
	Accepting responsibility; I-statements
	  Example: "I worry about you when you get failing grades."

Interrupting	Listening; raising hand or gesturing when wanting to talk; using brief statements

Overgeneralization; catastrophizing; making extremist, rigid statements
  Example: "I don't like it that you never help out around here."
	Qualifying; making tentative statements ("sometimes," "maybe," etc.); accurate quantitative statements
	  Example: "I don't like it that you sometimes don't do your chores."

Lecturing; preaching; moralizing
  Example: "I need to convince you of the importance of getting along with your sister. Sibling relationships are very important in families, and without a good relationship with your sister, you can't have that. When I was young . . ."
	Making brief, explicit problem statements ("I would like———")
	  Example: "I would like you and Susie to fight less."

Talking in a sarcastic tone of voice	Talking in a neutral tone of voice
Avoiding eye contact	Looking at the person with whom one is talking
Fidgeting, moving restlessly, or gesturing while being spoken to	Sitting in a relaxed fashion; excusing self for being restless

Mind reading
  Example: "Mom just wants to spoil my fun."
	Reflecting, paraphrasing, validating
	  Example: "Mom, I feel like you don't want me to have fun. Is that right?"

Getting off the topic	Catching self and returning to the problem as defined; putting other problems on a future agenda for discussion

Commanding, ordering
  Example: "You must be in by 11 on weekends and 9 on weeknights."
	Suggesting alternative solutions
	  Example: "One idea is for you to come in at 11 on weekends and 9 on weeknights."

Dwelling on the past
  Example: "Last week you didn't do your homework at all." "That's not true! I did my homework on Monday, and didn't have any after that."
	Sticking to the present and future; suggesting changes that will solve the problem in the future
	  Example: "We need to work out a way for you to get your homework done on time."

Monopolizing the conversation	Taking turns making brief statements

Intellectualizing; speaking in abstractions
  Example: "The problem is your lack of respect for your parents."
	Speaking in simple, clear language that a teenager can understand; talking about the behavior that prompts the abstractions
	  Example: "I don't like it when you swear at us when you're angry."

Threatening
  Example: "If you don't stop lying, I'll tan your hide."
	Suggesting alternative solutions
	  Example: "One solution is to reduce your punishment if you tell the truth."

Humoring, discounting
  Example: "Getting a maid is a stupid idea."
	Reflecting, validating
	  Example: "Getting a maid would solve your problem, but I can't afford it."

TABLE 14-1. (*continued*)

Problematic behavior	Possible alternative
Words saying one thing, body language saying another	Matching words with feelings; being direct about feelings
"Psychologizing" Example: "I think he talks back to us because he is fundamentally insecure about being adopted."	Inquiring about situations that provoke the behavior and about the consequences of behavior Example: "Joe, what situations really make you lose your temper? What bothers you about these things?"
Remaining silent, not responding to what others say	Reflecting, validating, expressing negative feelings

Note. Adapted from "Problem-Solving Communication Training: A Behavioral–Family Systems Approach to Parent–Adolescent Conflict" by A. L. Robin and S. L. Foster, 1984, in P. Karoly and J. J. Steffen (Eds.), *Adolescent Behavior Disorders: Foundations and Contemporary Concerns* (pp. 195–240), Lexington, MA: D.C. Heath. Copyright 1984 by D.C. Heath. Adapted by permission of the authors and the publisher.

tion present problems in interpretation because of repeated findings that parents and teens often agree only moderately at best in their reports of family interaction patterns (e.g., Barnes & Olson, 1985; Robin & Foster, 1989). For this reason, more direct assessment of family conflict is essential. One way to assess problem-solving skills directly is to ask the family to discuss a particular issue in the therapist's absence and to audiotape or videotape the discussion for later observation. The issue selected may be hypothetical (e.g., asking family members to plan something together, to come to a consensus on responses to a questionnaire, or to solve a hypothetical problem as though it were their own). We prefer to select current, real issues of dispute, based on the assumption that this will enhance the generalizability of the behavior sample to discussions the family has at home. Issues endorsed as provoking high levels of anger intensity on the IC are good topics for discussion. Even with real problems, though, the discussion may or may not be similar to home discussions (Foster & Robin, 1988). Similarity can be assessed by asking family members to indicate immediately after the discussion how their discussion resembled and differed from those they customarily have about the issue at home. When family members report that communication in the clinic differed from their customary patterns, the therapist can speculate on what circumstances differentiated the clinic and home environments and might be responsible for the improved (or deteriorated) patterns.

Various systematic coding methods are available for scoring interaction samples. The modified Marital Interaction Coding System (MICS), developed by Robin and his colleagues (Robin, 1988; Robin & Weiss, 1980), based on Weiss, Hops, and Patterson's (1973) MICS, contains 23 exhaustive, mutually exclusive categories used to code sequentially within 30-second intervals all verbal behaviors emitted during a discussion. This code has several advantages: (1) Its categories include both general communication skills and components of the problem-solving process; (2) many of the categories and a global composite score relate strongly to distressed–nondistressed family status; (3) the system permits both sequential analysis and frequency estimates of individual categories; and (4) the global composite score correlates highly with global ratings of conflict and problem solving (Robin & Canter, 1984), as well as with a second code, the Interaction Behavior Code (IBC), which assesses problem-solving and communication behavior (Robin & Koepke, 1985). Liabilities of the modified MICS lie in the extensive observer training it requires (about 30–40 hours), low interobserver agreement on many categories despite extensive training (Robin & Foster, 1989), and the amount of time required to code and analyze even brief audiotapes.

Alternative coding systems rely on inferential judgments rather than trained observers' evaluations of specific utterances. The Community Members' Rating Scale (Robin & Canter, 1984) requires that several raters (parents, teenagers, or professionals) review a family discussion and then rate the presence of modified MICS categories, as well as making global ratings of problem-solving effectiveness, conflict, and positivity of communication. This scale requires little training (15–30 minutes), can be completed quickly, and with 13 to 15 raters yields reliable mean scores for individual categories, a composite score, and the global ratings. Global ratings and the composite score also correlate .81 or more with the modified MICS composite (Robin & Canter, 1984). However, agreement among pairs of raters is too low for specific categories (generally below .60) for the data from small numbers of raters to be used for selecting and evaluating specific communication skills. In addition, most ratings of specific categories correlate below .60 with their modified MICS counterparts (Foster & Robin, 1988).

Related problems of poor pairwise agreement despite good interrater reliability with four or more raters characterize the IBC (Prinz & Kent, 1978), another checklist that contains a series of communication skills, most of which are rated as either present or absent during a discussion. The IBC also includes Likert scales for rating problem-solving effectiveness, friendliness, and insults. Like the Community Members' Rating Scale, this instrument requires little training and can be completed quickly. Summary scores discriminate distressed from nondistressed mother–adolescent dyads on the basis of audiotaped discussions of real problems (Prinz et al., 1979), and summary positive and negative behavior scores and ratings correlate .50–.75 with the modified MICS composite score (Robin & Koepke, 1985). Interrater agreement for specific behaviors listed on the IBC has not been computed to date, however. The code is also insensitive to changes in frequency of behaviors, since most are scored using dichotomous occurrence–nonoccurrence ratings.

Generally poor agreement on specific categories of behavior, whether with systems like the modified MICS or with global inferential rating systems like the Community Members' Rating Scale, implies that different individuals do not label interactions in the same ways. This is particularly troublesome, since one of the major tasks of assessment is to describe repeated problematic interaction sequences. In the absence of unambiguous, consensual labels for family communication patterns, clinicians should at a minimum be aware that the ways in which they label particular behaviors may not match other professionals' or families' ways of categorizing the same re-

sponses. Such awareness should remind therapists to avoid confusion by asking what family members mean when they use generic terms like "put-down" and by explaining their own terminology.

Analyzing the sequences into which behaviors such as accusations, humor, and positive solutions fall is the second step in assessing family process. This involves describing the antecedents and consequences of characteristic interaction behaviors and arriving at descriptions of the common patterns that characterize family discussions. These descriptions include behavior of all involved family members, and provide the raw material for analyzing the functions of particular interactive behaviors, as will be discussed later.

Cognition

Thoughts influence interaction among family members by either facilitating or interfering with adaptive communication. Rigid, inflexible, and negatively biased thoughts about one's own and other family members' actions promote equally rigid, inflexible, and negative communication. Two studies (Robin et al., 1986; Vincent Roehling & Robin, 1986), using different questionnaires to assess beliefs, indicated that several cognitive themes discriminated distressed from nondistressed parents and teenagers in one or both studies. For parents and teens, these included "ruination" (unrealistic projection of catastrophic consequences following a particular event) and "malicious intent" (misattributing the cause of another's behavior to the conscious desire to make another family member suffer). Distressed parents were also more likely than their nondistressed counterparts to endorse beliefs revolving around "perfectionism" (excessively high standards for the teen's behavior) and "obedience" (excessive demands for the adolescent to follow parental demands unquestioningly), whereas distressed teens more strongly endorsed beliefs related to "fairness" (the idea that parental rules should always be reasonable according to the adolescent's standards) and "autonomy" (the belief that teenagers should be granted as much decision-making freedom as they wish). Two other beliefs failed to discriminate the groups—"self-blame" (appraising another's problems as one's own fault) and "approval" (excessive emphasis on the importance of other members' evaluations of one's own behavior)—possibly because these thoughts are more likely to produce guilt and conflict avoidance than anger-laden exchanges.

Thoughts can be assessed via interview questions, questionnaires, or methods such as *in vivo* thought sampling. Interview questions asking family members to recall what they thought about during recent conflicts can help to pinpoint any cognitions that members recall. The Family Beliefs Inventory (FBI; Vincent Roehling & Robin, 1986) provides a series of vignettes about potential parent–adolescent conflicts. After each vignette, the respondent indicates the degree to which he or she agrees with a series of statements, each representing either one of the irrational beliefs described above or a "filler" (less extreme) belief. The PARQ (Robin *et al.,* 1986) contains subscales that also assess these beliefs. FBI scores discriminated the responses of distressed and nondistressed fathers and teenagers, but not mothers (Vincent Roehling & Robin, 1986). Robin *et al.* (1986) found differences between clinic and nonclinic samples of mothers, fathers, and teens on the PARQ irrational belief scales.

As with questionnaires assessing communication and problem solving, the generalizability of family members' reports of their thoughts to what they actually think about during conflictual exchanges cannot be assumed. Thoughts can be assessed more directly by (1) asking members to describe their thoughts when they communicate with each other during the interview; (2) having them keep a log of their thoughts whenever they have a conflict at home; and/or (3) replaying on audiotape or videotape of a family discussion and asking family members periodically to report what they were thinking about (see Genest & Turk, 1981; Hollon & Bemis, 1981; and Kendall & Hollon, 1981, for reviews of similar strategies used with other populations).

Structural Patterns

The assessment methods described up to this point target molecular patterns of interaction. Structural patterns, in contrast, involve looking for more molar patterns that (1) characterize family relations across situations, and (2) are described by various topographically distinct behaviors. The structural concepts of "alignment" (including coalitions and triangulation)

and "cohesion," adapted from strategic and structural family therapies (e.g., Aponte & VanDeusen, 1981; Haley, 1976, 1980; Minuchin, 1974), are particularly relevant to parent–adolescent conflict.

Alignment

"Alignment" refers to how family members take sides or support one another in their interactions (Aponte & VanDeusen, 1981). In a "coalition," two family members support one another against another, as when two parents blame their family difficulties on their adolescent. With "triangulation," two members who disagree compete for the support of a third, who vacillates between the disagreeing parties (e.g., the "peacemaker" who carries messages between disputing family members). Cross-generational coalitions lead to increased conflict, because they undermine the more adaptive pattern in Western societies of parents working together as a team to grant autonomy gradually to the developing adolescent within the constraints of flexible but consistent limits. Triangulated patterns promote conflict because the two disputing members handle their disagreement indirectly through a third member, instead of directly with each other.

Assessment of alignment is complicated by the lack of construct and content validity evidence for measures of coalitions and triangulation. The PARQ (Robin *et al.,* 1986) contains scales assessing family members' reports of coalitions and triangulation, but scores on these scales failed to discriminate distressed from nondistressed parents and adolescents. Hypotheses about alignment can also be generated based on observations of who supports, blames, and seeks the support of other family members during the interview and during audiotaped discussions. Gilbert, Christensen, and Margolin (1984) have developed a coding system for systematically assessing dyadic alliances in taped interactions among parents and children, based on the content, affective quality, and weighting of the content category for each utterance. Alliance scores are computed for each dyad in the discussion, based on to whom or about whom each alliance-related speech act is directed. Although the system discriminates patterns of alliance in ways predicted by family systems theory, the content and construct validity of the system warrant further investigation.

Cohesion

A cohesion continuum can be used to describe the degree of closeness and contact among family members. "Enmeshed" families, at one end of the continuum, are described by overly close interaction patterns characterized by a lack of privacy, overconcern with the approval of other family members, interference in other members' affairs, and pressure to conform to family norms. Enmeshed patterns impede adolescent development because they stifle the adolescent's natural progression toward increased autonomy, with conflicts played down, avoided, or denied. At the other end of the continuum are "disengaged" families, whose members have little involvement in one another's affairs and minimal concern about one another's opinions. Parents in disengaged families may express only minor worry about serious problems exhibited by their adolescent (such as delinquent activities), impose inconsistent and ineffective contingencies, and/or fail to monitor their teenager's whereabouts (cf. Patterson & Bank, 1986). Disengaged families provide insufficient structure for the adolescent to move gradually from child to adult situations. Such a family is likely to display periodic bursts of high-intensity conflict, often triggered by the adolescent's getting in trouble with an outside agency; the family then returns to laissez-faire behavior when the trouble dies down.

Several questionnaires have scales purporting to assess cohesion, including the Family Environment Scale (Moos & Moos, 1983), the Family Adaptability and Cohesion Evaluation Scales—II (Olson & Portner, 1983), and the PARQ (Robin et al., 1986). The clinician can more directly assess aspects of cohesion in a sample of family communication using the Centripetal–Centrifugal Rating Scale (Kelsey-Smith & Beavers, 1981), with which raters evaluate tapes of family interactions along a variety of dimensions related to the cohesion continuum, such as closeness, scapegoating, and parental conflict. As with assessments of coalitions and triangulation, however, questions of content and construct validity have been insufficiently addressed in descriptions of these instruments.

Less formal assessment of cohesion can be conducted by observing family interaction patterns during the interview, with particular attention to patterns of closeness, support, reactions to approval and disapproval, speaking for others, and confrontation versus avoidance of conflictual topics. Family members' descriptions of behavior at home provide additional information.

Function

Formulating hypotheses about the functions of family members' behavior involves, first, describing common sequences of interaction surrounding conflictual issues, and, second, generating possible payoffs or reinforcers for the behaviors in question. Information about common sequences comes from assessment of communication and problem-solving behaviors, cognitive reactions, and behaviors related to structural domains, as well as from interview questions and other assessment tactics designed to ensure that the clinician has a complete picture of problematic interaction patterns. This should include information about subjective emotional reactions, which can serve as important links in interaction chains (e.g., when a parent "picks a fight" whenever he or she feels anxious about a personal issue).

The language of applied behavior analysis captures the functional relations among behaviors and their consequences: "positive and negative reinforcement," "punishment," and "avoidance." These can be supplemented by Patterson's (1982) descriptions of patterns of exchange, including "reciprocity" (an exchange of similar kinds of behavior, sometimes characterized as "like begetting like") and "coercion" (interlocking negative reinforcement conditions that support a sequence of often-escalating negative behaviors, as when a teenager's unpleasant wheedling provokes a parent to make a rule more lenient, thus stopping the wheedling while negatively reinforcing it).

Looking for consistent payoffs across types of interaction, using Alexander and his colleagues' concepts of "intimacy," "distance," and "regulation" (Alexander & Parsons, 1982; Barton & Alexander, 1981), can also be useful for characterizing the functions of family members' behavior. According to this scheme, individuals have characteristic preferences for closeness and emotional contact (intimacy), privacy and independence from others (distance), or some blend of closeness and independence (regulation). By looking for typical outcomes for each member when interactions involving a problem issue subside (which may be hours or days after the issue first arises), the clinician can postulate whether each member's behavior appears to produce intimacy, distance, or regulation, and can design a treatment plan to establish more adaptive methods for members to reach the same ends.

Functional analysis can address information described at varying levels of molecularity. As a general rule of thumb, molecular description is useful for selecting key targets for communication training, whereas more molar analysis helps the clinician to examine more general functions of the family's methods of handling conflict. For example, in the Anderson family, the mother generally begins a discussion by making a clear, specific statement of the problem, but then lectures at length about her resentment and negative feelings. The adolescent responds with counteraccusations, and the father criticizes the teen's backtalk. The teenager responds by telling his parents they never listen to him, and the conflict continues with a series of accusations and counteraccusations and parental attempts to reason with the teenager via lecturing, until the teenager finally says he will do whatever his parents wish.

Molecular analysis of this pattern would characterize it as a series of reciprocal, escalating negative exchanges in which the teenager's promises are negatively reinforced when both parents stop the accusations, and the parental accusations are eventually negatively reinforced when the teenager gives in (thus halting, at least temporarily, his unpleasantness and rebellion). Based on this formulation, communication training should involve teaching the teenager ways to stop parental accusations without having to make promises he has no intention of honoring. The parents, too, need ways of responding to negative adolescent communication that reduce the likelihood it will continue, as well as better methods of arriving at constructive resolutions to the problems that provoke disagreements.

Functional analysis at a molar level involves broadening the time frame to examine the functions of larger units of behavior. Moving back from the Andersons' molecular patterns might lead the clinician to see that both parents are busy professionals, that arguments are commonly instigated by the adolescent's getting in trouble at school, and that the arguments result in temporary improvements in the adolescent's behavior and in the parents' making a special effort to pay more attention to their son. After a

week of good behavior, the parents resume their normal patterns, and the son again engages in pretty troublemaking at school. Analysis at a more molar level suggests that the son's misbehavior and his part in the ensuing arguments are positively reinforced by parental attention, and that parental involvement is negatively reinforced when the son's misbehavior at school stops. As parental attention declines, antecedent conditions for misbehavior reappear, and the cycle begins again. Based on this analysis, the therapist might incorporate into the treatment plan ways to encourage positive interactions among the parents and the son, such that the son receives regular parental attention contingent upon something other than negative behavior. Such interactions should be rewarding for parents as well, so that their attention will be maintained and will not decline, as declines in attention seem to be antecedents for the teen's repeated misbehavior.

Family members' interactions are often more complex than those just described, and it is not unusual to be able to postulate several possible functions that a problem interaction pattern might serve. Therapists can evaluate these hypotheses by asking themselves which seem to apply most generally to family patterns, by formulating additional questions and tests to provide confirmatory or disconfirmatory information, and by initiating treatment plans based on the primary hypothesis. Although the success of a treatment plan does not prove that a hypothesis is "correct," failure to produce change implicates an incorrect or incomplete formulation of a family's difficulties as one possible explanation for a therapist's difficulties.

TREATMENT APPROACHES

After collecting sufficient assessment information, the therapist can formulate a treatment plan. This plan should be family-specific; should follow naturally from assessment (and thus make sense to family members); and should emphasize components of treatment directed toward those dysfunctional behaviors, cognitions, and structural and functional patterns revealed during the assessment. In our experience, six to eight weekly sessions (after the assessment phase) are usually sufficient for moderately distressed families with few pervasive cognitive distortions and structural problems; more severely distressed families may need up to 20 sessions. We recommend establishing a time-limited initial contract with a family that specifies the goals, nature, and logistics of treatment, at the conclusion of which the therapist and family together will assess the family's progress. This both encourages family members to use their time wisely and allows reluctant members to see that they are not committed to an unending course of therapy. Via the contract, the therapist communicates that treatment involves active participation by family members in learning new ways of interacting and in integrating those patterns into their daily interactions via homework assignments.

In the pages that follow, we describe different treatment elements that can be incorporated into a comprehensive treatment plan geared toward the family's major difficulties. Difficulties with problem-solving and communication skills are addressed via structured skills training in these areas. Cognitive restructuring interventions address cognitive distortions. Problematic structural patterns are altered either within the context of a skills training approach by organizing elements of treatment and homework to establish more adaptive structural patterns, or via methods borrowed from structural and strategic family therapies. Hypotheses generated from functional analyses should also guide treatment planning by alerting the therapist to build in sufficient positive consequences for behavior change to outweigh the factors currently maintaining problem behavior.

Different aspects of treatment are emphasized at different times, depending upon the nature of the family's problems. As problem areas cumulate, treatment becomes increasingly multifaceted. In general, problem-solving communication training (PSCT), cognitive restructuring, homework assignments, and supplemental interventions are the basic elements of the treatment approach. Structural and functional considerations direct the strategies used in implementing these specific procedures. For example, with triangulated patterns, the therapist may need to conduct PSCT and in the course of this instigate direct communication between disagreeing family members to decrease triangulation. When the family shows few deviant structural and functional patterns, skills training can be fairly straightforward. When grossly distorted structural patterns appear, negative reciprocity predominates, and

behavior appears to be maintained by pervasive patterns of negative reinforcement and avoidance, strategic deployment of treatment elements becomes more important.

Before we describe treatment components, three caveats are in order. First, we draw heavily upon approaches we have designed and researched for modifying problem-solving and communication skills and dysfunctional cognitions; however, we realize that others use different strategies to attack the same targets. Second, because controlled research has rarely evaluated specific "how-to" suggestions for dealing with implementation questions, many suggestions are based on experience rather than data. Finally, although we describe treatment as though all relevant members are always present in sessions, deviations sometimes occur. When the adolescent is extremely resistant and repeatedly refuses to participate, or when the family is extremely explosive, sessions with individual members may prove more fruitful until the therapist can resolve the session management difficulties. In addition, when severe marital problems or individual psychopathology (e.g., depression, substance abuse) are integrally related to parent–adolescent conflict, individual or marital treatment may be preferable as an alternative, precursor, or complement to family intervention.

Problem-Solving Communication Training

PSCT is a highly directive, skill-oriented intervention for teaching families to resolve specific disputes democratically and to communicate effectively about both the style and the substance of their interactions. A family is presented with a five-step outline of problem-solving steps; negative communication patterns are identified; and common issues of dispute are hierarchically ordered from least to most anger-producing. The therapist guides the family in applying the steps of problem solving to one specific dispute per session, correcting targeted negative communication patterns when they occur. As treatment progresses, more intense issues are discussed using the problem-solving format. To produce generalized change in the natural environment, the family members complete a variety of skill-building assignments between sessions, including written exercises, home problem-solving discussions, home communication exercises, and application of their new skills in daily interactions.

Problem Solving

Table 14-2 outlines the five steps of problem solving as they are presented to the parents and the adolescent. The first step, defining the problem, entails pinpointing the behaviors of the other members that create a problem for the speaker and indicating why these actions are troublesome. An adequate problem definition statement addresses actions, feelings, and situations in a concise, nonaccusatory fashion. A prototype problem definition statement might take the form, "I get upset when you do ———." As each family member defines the problem, the therapist prompts others to paraphrase the problem definitions to encourage verification and to emphasize that listening and understanding are important, even if a family member does not see the problem in the same way. Feedback, instructions, modeling, and behavior rehearsal are used to correct inadequate problem definitions and paraphrases.

After the problem has been defined, family members progress to the second step of problem solving (generating solutions) and take turns generating a variety of creative ideas to solve it. Three rules of brainstorming are introduced and enforced: (1) Defer evaluation of the solutions in order to encourage uncensored creativity; (2) quantity is more important than quality of ideas—through multiple suggestions, potentially effective ideas will emerge; (3) be creative—any ideas are acceptable as suggestions, and evaluation comes later. The therapist normally refrains from giving solutions unless the family is unable to generate a variety of ideas. In this case, the therapist can offer occasional suggestions, particularly in the form of strategies for generating solutions (e.g., changing the environment, offering a trade, changing the way family members think about an issue, providing positive or negative consequences). Solution listing continues until either the family members have listed at least eight ideas or their ideas go beyond their initial positions and the therapist judges them to have one or more solutions that all members are likely to find acceptable. The therapist typically asks the adolescent to write down the ideas—a task that maximizes attention and participation.

The third step of problem solving involves evaluating the solutions. The therapist instructs

the family in projecting the positive and negative consequences of implementing each solution. Each member assigns each solution a rating of plus or minus, with the rating recorded in writing. The therapist uses instructions and modeling to teach members perspective-taking skills, emphasizing whether each solution would solve the others' problems. Asking members to identify the pros and cons of each solution for all parties concerned is a useful way to prompt good evaluation statements. After the family members evaluate all solutions, they examine the ratings for a consensus. These agreements become the selected solution; otherwise,

TABLE 14-2 Problem-Solving Outline for Families

I. Define the problem.
    A. You each tell the others what they are doing that is a problem and why.
    B. You each paraphrase the others' statements of the problem to check out your understanding of what they said.

II. Generate alternative solutions.
    A. You take turns listing solutions.
    B. You follow three rules for listing solutions.
       1. List as many ideas as possible.
       2. Don't evaluate the ideas.
       3. Be creative and freewheeling; suggest crazy ideas.
    C. One person writes down the ideas on a worksheet.

III. Decide upon the best idea.
    A. You take turns evaluating each idea by:
       1. Saying what you think would happen if the family followed the idea.
       2. Give the idea a "plus" or "minus" and write the rating next to the idea.
    B. You select the "best" idea.
       1. Look for ideas rated "plus" by all.
         a. Select one idea.
         b. Combine several ideas.
       2. If none are rated "plus" by all, look for ideas rated "plus" by one parent and a teenager.

IV. Plan to implement the selected solution.
    A. You decide who will do what, when, where, and how.
    B. You write down the details on the bottom of the worksheet.

Note. From *Negotiating Parent–Adolescent Conflict: A Behavioral–Family Systems Approach* by A. L. Robin and S. L. Foster, 1989, New York: Guilford Press. Copyright 1989 by The Guilford Press. Reprinted by permission.

they negotiate a compromise. During this process, the therapist persuasively prompts parents and adolescents to generate and evaluate possible compromises. If negotiations bog down because of unreasonable beliefs or problems in family structure, suggestions given later in this chapter may help move the family ahead.

The agreed-upon solution then undergoes implementation planning, the fourth step of problem solving. The parents and adolescent specify who will do what, when, where, and how. This discussion culminates in specifying a home-based system for monitoring compliance with the solution(s), and the family is sent home to put the solution into effect.

Upon their return, the family members report to the therapist the results of trying the solution. If successful, the therapist praises their efforts, and they move ahead to a new problem. Otherwise, they recount step by step what happened, and the therapist and family go back through the steps of problem solving to find a more suitable solution. This process of evaluating the effectiveness of the solution and renegotiating if necessary is the final step of problem solving. The therapist short-circuits the normal tendency to become accusatory about unsuccessful implementations by reframing the failure as part of the learning process and helping the family to identify the stage of problem solving where the process became sidetracked. Approximately 20% of problems discussed during problem solving require renegotiation (Foster, 1978).

Communication Training

Communication training can either be conducted separately from problem-solving discussions or as an interlude in the problem-solving process, with skills selected on the basis of initial assessment data and members' subsequent communication during problem-solving sessions. Communication training generally begins after the first problem-solving session, because it is difficult for the family to attend both to following the problem-solving model for the first time and to correcting their communication. An exception occurs when a family communicates so poorly that the therapist judges that initial training in listening and making nonaccusatory statements is necessary for the family to achieve even marginal success at completing a problem-solving discussion in the session.

Separate sessions or portions of sessions that focus specifically on communication skills are useful when all family members need to learn similar skills and the skills require a good deal of rehearsal to master, and/or negative habits are deeply ingrained and will require considerable practice to overcome. During these sessions, the therapist introduces the skill(s) with a rationale. Table 14-1 summarizes common communication targets, and may be presented as is or in modified form to reasonably verbal families. Using a discrimination training format, the therapist can then present examples of communication responses (presented orally, via written examples, or via audiotape or videotape) to test the parents' and teenager's ability to discriminate positive from negative examples of the targeted skill. When family members are proficient at this, the therapist asks members to role-play the use of positive communication responses in a contrived conversation. Then the therapist announces that whenever the negative behaviors occur during the session, he or she will interrupt the conversation, give feedback, and ask the members to restate their points in a more constructive manner. To achieve lasting change in communication, the therapist must assertively apply the four-step procedure of feedback, instructions, modeling, and behavior rehearsal in a consistent fashion, targeting one or two negative patterns per session.

Stopping the action during a problem-solving discussion is useful when the therapist wishes to intervene briefly to correct a problem communication, then to return to the topic of discussion. Pointing out or asking a family member to identify how the problem-solving discussion is being sidetracked provides a useful way of showing family members the results of problem communication. This leads into a discussion in which the therapist either identifies an alternative way of communicating or prompts family members to do the same thing via Socratic questioning. Asking members first to replay the communication sequence using the new skill, then to resume the problem-solving discussion (with prompts to use the new skill as needed), completes this type of communication training. To minimize perceptions that the therapist is aligning against one member by singling out his or her communication, and to encourage the view that negative communication is an interactive problem, the therapist should provide dyadic or triadic communication feedback (e.g., coach both the speaker and the listener on how to change a problem interaction).

Generalization Strategies

Three types of homework assignments promote generalization. First, a written exercise for practicing problem-solving steps is given after the initial PSCT session; the therapist reviews family members' written responses with them during the next session. Second, the family is asked to make a regular "appointment" or "family meeting time" at home. During this time, they may be asked to conduct all or part of a problem-solving discussion, to rehearse specific communication skills (e.g., clear, nonaccusatory expression of criticism coupled with reflective listening), or to complete problem-solving discussions initiated during the therapy hour. Third, the family is assigned the task of self-monitoring and correcting deficient communication in daily interchanges and crisis situations. For example, a mother and son who exchange accusations and defensive statements may be asked to practice clear, nonaccusatory criticism statements and reflective responses throughout the week. The therapist times and varies these assignments to fit the family's targets and progress during sessions.

The therapist reviews the assignments and discusses generalization issues during the beginning and end of therapy sessions. Common crisis situations may be analyzed, and plans may be made to help prevent or defuse them before they get out of hand. For example, in a family where the adolescent's coming home past curfew predictably elicits a midnight shouting match, the members may plan to set a cooling-off period and discuss the consequences of breaking curfew the next morning.

Sequencing Problem-Solving Communication Training

PSCT is divided roughly into four stages: engagement, skill building, resolution of intense conflicts, and disengagement. During the engagement stage (usually about three 1-hour sessions), the therapist collects assessment information, establishes rapport, and negotiates a therapeutic contract. The skill-building stage emphasizes learning the five steps of problem solving and correcting deficient communication. In the opening skill-building session, the goals are to (1) introduce problem solving; (2) conduct one problem-solving discussion; and (3) send the family home with an assignment to implement a solution. After problem solving is introduced, a concrete topic of low to moderate intensity is selected (e.g., one with anger intensity ratings of 2 or 3 on the IC). Topics such as chores, curfew, or bedtime are well suited to initial discussions because they are easily operationalized; topics such as lying or talking back are vaguer and better handled in later sessions, when members are more proficient at specifying their problems. During subsequent skill-building sessions, increasingly intense patterns are targeted for change. The therapist makes as many corrections as necessary to encourage acquisition of new skills, becoming increasingly demanding as the family members demonstrate increased proficiency.

Skill building blends naturally into resolution of intense conflicts, when the therapist helps the family solve the most anger-provoking issues they encounter. Here the therapist is more concerned with engineering changes in basic interaction patterns and reaching resolutions than with skill acquisition itself. Skill training is supplemented by cognitive restructuring and structural–functional interventions as needed (these are discussed later). Although sessions are still organized around specific problems to be solved, the format is less rigid than during skill building.

In the final stage, disengagement, the therapist gradually becomes less directive during discussions and schedules longer intervals between sessions. The family assumes greater responsibility for independent problem solving, and the therapist and family review strategies for preventing relapses. Positive changes are attributed to the family's own efforts rather than the therapist's abilities in order to promote maintenance of behavior change. Therapy usually ends with an open-ended contract to return as needed in the future, with follow-up phone calls or booster sessions scheduled at the therapist and family's discretion.

Implementation Issues

Several kinds of roadblocks can interfere with the course of PSCT. Some of these are difficulties that can occur with any kind of treatment, such as noncompliance with home assignments, maintaining control of sessions, and engaging reluctant participants in treatment; these are discussed later. Others are tied specifically to elements of PSCT. These difficulties, together with suggested solutions for coping with them, are presented in Table 14-3.

Applicability and Contraindications

PSCT is applicable when the primary presenting problems involve overt arguments between parents and teenagers. Single-parent, blended, and intact families have been treated successfully with PSCT. Issues of dispute may vary widely, as long as disagreements are acknowledged and overt. Families who avoid open conflict or do not recognize that they disagree (e.g., many families of anorexic teenagers) will not benefit from this form of treatment until they learn to recognize, self-monitor, and accept the presence of disagreements. Similarly, the parents must be willing to accept the teenager's participation in decision making; this makes the approach unacceptable to some highly rigid parents or to members of cultures that emphasize total parental control.

A minimum level of verbal ability and general intelligence is also necessary for participation in family problem-solving sessions. Although individuals with learning disabilities but average ability can learn problem solving, the presence of borderline or lower intellectual ability in one or more members usually precludes effective participation. With teenagers with limited attention spans (e.g., those diagnosed with Attention Deficit–Hyperactivity Disorder), procedures may need to be shortened or otherwise modified to hold the teens' attention. Nonetheless, problem solving has been suc-

TABLE 14-3 Implementation Problems Encountered with Problem-Solving Training and Suggested Solutions

Implementation problem	Suggested solutions
Member thinks problem solving too artificial.	Explain that all new skills seem artificial at first; later sessions will focus on making PSCT fit their life style.
Parent protests that translating a construct ("respect") into a specific problem definition avoids the real problem.	Explain that it is impossible to solve a construct, but it is possible to alter specific patterns that fit together to create the "real" problem; frame the parent's thoughts as a common misconception that prevents reaching good solutions.
Members try to force others to accept their problem definition.	Explain that everyone has a right to his or her own definition; members need not agree; different definitions are important because they clarify the nature of the problem.
Members evaluate solutions during solution listing.	Remind members that they will have a chance to evaluate later; ask critical members to come up with a solution they like better instead of criticizing.
Solutions are too vague.	Prompt members to be more specific.
Too few solutions.	Suggest a crazy idea; ask questions that prompt different classes of solutions.
One member dominates evaluation phase.	Ask members to take turns; direct dominant member to ask others for their evaluation.
Members deadlock, with parents supporting one solution, teen supporting another.	Ask family to try one solution (usually teen's) for a week; other solution will then be implemented if the first one fails.
Member fails to move from initial position.	Assess possible cognitive distortion; discuss with member how failure to compromise leads to continued problem; assess whether problem situation serves important function for resisting member.
Problem seems too complex for problem solving.	Break problem into component parts; solve components one by one.
Too many solutions; discussion drags.	Ask members to review list to see whether there are any solutions no one likes; cross these off list without evaluating them.

cessfully applied with children as young as 10 years of age who are of normal intelligence and attentional skills. Of course, individuals with superior ability may achieve more sophisticated levels of problem solving than individuals with less ability.

Severe marital conflict or individual psychopathology are often contraindications for PSCT. This is particularly important when the adolescent's arguments with the parents may serve some function in the marriage (e.g., the parents avoid marital strife by cooperating to try to cope with the teenager); to eliminate these arguments would interfere with this interlocking contingency-maintained pattern, and the family is likely to sabotage treatment. The therapist must tackle the marital problems prior to or concurrently with the parent–adolescent problems to achieve success. Individual problems (e.g., alcoholism, severe depression) preclude effective PSCT when the individual or other family members are so overwhelmed or disorganized as a function of the individual problem that they will be unlikely to participate in sessions and/or implement solutions.

A crisis situation that requires immediate action (e.g., deciding whether to remove the adolescent from the home or responding to the teen's getting in trouble with the law) also precludes using problem solving, at least initially. Since initial problem-solving sessions focus on learning skills at the expense of solving major problems, PSCT is probably best deferred until some course of action has been decided and the crisis resolved.

A final contraindication is the potential for family violence, when conflict has reached such explosive proportions that physical violence between members is likely to occur if they congregate in one room and attempt to talk about their problems. Family therapy is physically dangerous and should be avoided in such cases; individual therapeutic approaches are preferable here.

Monitoring Response to Treatment

To assess improvements in problem solving and communication skills, the therapist can observe family members' performance in session, attending in particular to how well the family can proceed through the process and self-correct without therapist intervention. Taping discussions of a problem before or after a session can also help the therapist assess change. To assess whether skills have generalized, the therapist can ask family members to audiotape discussions at home, to report how their discussion went, and/or to keep a record of when and how they use problem solving at home. Administering questionnaires such as the IC and the CBQ periodically (e.g., every 6 weeks) can help the therapist see whether treatment is changing members' perceptions of their interactions. Family members can also be asked to keep a daily log of conflicts at home to assess the impact of treatment on a day-to-day basis. A short form of the CBQ (the CBQ-20; Foster & Robin, 1988) can be completed in about 5 minutes prior to treatment, with instructions to think about the past week only, in order to help the therapist see how members perceive family relations from week to week. Responses to interview questions about how members think they are getting along also help the therapist assess progress.

The key to assessing response to treatment is to look for convergence among multiple types of information rather than to rely on a single potentially biased source, such as client self-report during sessions. Convergent information should increase the therapist's confidence in his or her conclusions about the extent of family progress; lack of convergence should lead the therapist to evaluate why information sources do not converge (e.g., family members' self-reports are influenced more by their moods than by actual occurrences) and to adjust his or her judgments accordingly.

Case Example

Mr. and Mrs. Phillips and their 15-year-old daughter Jessica applied for treatment in an outcome study evaluating the effects of PSCT. Jessica, according to the parents, was an academically gifted student who in the past few months had become difficult to handle. Specifically, she argued with and questioned the fairness of a variety of parental rules and refused to accept her parents' reasons for their regulations. The parents reported good teamwork and a happy marriage. Their approach to Jessica's complaints was to tighten the rules and become more strict. Jessica had recently begun staying out past her curfew, and the parents were concerned that this would escalate into more disobedience. Analysis of a communication sample in which the mother and daughter attempted to resolve a current dispute revealed that although the two could focus their discussion on a specific issue, conversations broke down because of high rates of accusations and counter-accusations, with daughter soon withdrawing from the conversation. The combination of arguments over numerous independence-related issues with communication skill problems and few apparent maladaptive structural patterns made this family an ideal candidate for PSCT and the Phillipses readily agreed to the rationale and proposed structure of the treatment program.

The first treatment session focused on Jessica's bedtime, a relatively minor but persistent area of dispute. The session went smoothly, focusing in particular on defining the problem using "I-statements" instead of "you-statements." The triad agreed to the solutions that Jessica would be in bed at 10 during four school nights a week and allowed to stay up until 11 on one night of her choosing. If she broke the rules, she would be awakened early on Saturday (if not, she could sleep late), and she would lose time the night following the infraction. They also agreed to have a trial period of 1 month and then to re-evaluate the success of their plan. Their homework was to implement the agreed-upon solution and to define the problem for the following week without personal attacks.

The next week, the Phillipses came to the session having completed their homework. They had defined the problem of Jessica's eating habits (her parents were concerned that she ate too little and that her food did not contain sufficient nutrition). During this session, Jessica unpredictably became very resistant to compromising on any of the proposed solutions. The therapist encouraged her throughout the session to propose solutions she thought would satisfy herself and her parents. All family members were encouraged to note times that they deviated from the issue and to bring the family back to the topic under discussion. Ultimately, the family decided that Jessica would eat one second helping of her choice during each evening meal and that she would take a vitamin pill each day that her intake did not satisfy the minimum daily requirements for vitamins and minerals. Their homework was to define a new problem and list solutions.

The Phillipses came to the next session without having done their homework. Instead, Mr. and Mrs. Phillips had talked with Jessica about her resistant behavior during the previous session, and they had together agreed on the importance of open-minded compromise. The topic for this week was what Jessica defined as her parents asking her to do household chores when she was already busy. Problem solving went smoothly until the family members became deadlocked with no solutions mutually acceptable; the therapist coached them on listing new solutions to break the deadlock. Their homework was to implement the solutions they agreed upon and to conduct an entire problem-solving discussion at home.

The Phillipses came to the next session reporting that their homework, a discussion of cleaning the bedroom, had worked out very well. During the session they worked on the problem of Jessica's being on time, with communication training focused on decreasing interruptions. Because the therapist had noticed a variety of problem behaviors related to listening failure, she elected to spend the next session on listening skills (instead of problem solving in regard to a particular issue). In preparation for that session, she asked family members to notice which of their behaviors triggered negative responses from the other. During the next session, all family members practiced paraphrasing the others' point of view, and the therapist encouraged Jessica to give her parents (especially her father) feedback when she did not think they were taking her opinion seriously. They were assigned the homework of practicing listening twice.

At the beginning of the seventh and last session of the research program, the family reported having "informally" done their homework. They chose to do problem solving in regard to Jessica's fighting with her 12-year-old brother, Paul. The therapist intervened rarely and the Phillipses arrived at several solutions, including sitting down with Paul and using problem solving to discuss what he could do to help the situation.

Evaluation data are presented in Table 14-4. IC anger intensity and CBQ scores decreased from the clinical to normal ranges. Ratings of audiotaped problem discussions between Jessica and her mother showed decreases in negative and increases in positive behavior. Gains on questionnaire measures were maintained and improved during a 6-week follow-up; negative behavior during the audiotaped discussion increased slightly, but so did positive behavior. All three family members reported that they had achieved their goals for therapy, were much happier with their relationship, and occasionally used problem solving when it was needed.

Research Evaluations of Problem-Solving Communication Training

We (Robin, Kent, O'Leary, Foster, & Prinz, 1977) evaluated an early form of PSCT with mothers and teenagers recruited via newspaper notices. Three sessions of training using modeling, instruction, and behavior rehearsal with hypothetical problems preceded two sessions discussing real problems. Observations of the number of problem definitions, solutions, and evaluations during audiotaped discussions of hypothetical and real problems before and after training demonstrated that, relative to an untrained group, mothers and teenagers improved markedly after treatment. Reports of home behavior, assessed by forerunners of the CBQ and IC, showed only minor evidence of improvement at home, however.

Later research tried to improve on the treatment strategies in the Robin et al. (1977) study by refining the questionnaires and observation codes (Prinz et al., 1979) and by attempting to enhance the impact of treatment in various ways, such as including fathers, focusing on real problems, extending the duration of the treatment program, and incorporating general-

ization strategies into treatment. Foster et al. (1983) evaluated this more in-depth treatment package; this study also compared treatment with versus without a generalization component (consisting of assignments to practice problem solving at home and discussions of this practice in sessions). Relative to untrained control families, participants in both treatments improved on the IC, CBQ, and ratings of their personal goals for therapy. Audiotapes of mother–teen discussions evaluated via the IBC showed little evidence of change, however. Interestingly, the families in the generalization-programming group did not report greater use of problem solving at home or greater conflict reduction than the group trained without the generalization strategies. Indeed, at a 6- to 8-week follow-up, the generalization group showed some declines from the time treatment ended, whereas the other treatment group appeared to maintain its gains.

These results were difficult to interpret, especially in light of the fact that Foster et al. (1983) could not document that families had actually improved their communication skills. Robin (1981) evaluated a similar PSCT approach, and documented the improvement Foster et al. failed to show. Robin included a second treatment condition, termed a "best alternative treatment control," in which families were treated by a therapist using any of the

TABLE 14-4 Pre-Treatment, Post-Treatment, and Follow-Up Data for the Phillips Family

Measure	Mrs. Phillips			Mr. Phillips			Jessica		
	Pre	Post	Follow-up	Pre	Post	Follow-up	Pre	Post	Follow-up
Conflict Behavior Questionnaire									
Report of other	17	5[a]	3[a]	13	1	5	13/16[b]	7[a]/8[b]	4[a]/3[b]
Report of dyad	7	1[a]	0[a]	7	2	1	7/8[b]	6[a]/5[b]	0[a]/1[b]
Issues Checklist									
Frequency	26	20[a]	15[a]	12	4	5	11[a]	6[a]	8[a]
Anger intensity	2.50	1.10[a]	1.91[a]	2.25	1.00	1.60	1.55[a]	1.00[a]	1.00[a]
Frequency × intensity	2.91	1.17[a]	1.93	2.51	1.00	1.62	3.44	1.00[a]	1.00[a]
Interaction Behavior Code									
Positive behavior	.376[a]	.500[a]	.619[a]	NA	NA	NA	.197	.286[a]	.310[a]
Negative behavior	.287	.047[a]	.132	NA	NA	NA	.198	.036[a]	.118

Note. The Interaction Behavior Code was used to rate mother–daughter discussions only.
[a]Score is within one standard deviation above or below the mean for nondistressed dyads. Means for questionnaires from Robin and Foster (1984). Means for Interaction Behavior Code for Prinz and Kent (1978). Mr. Phillips's data were not compared with means for nondistressed fathers because of insufficient normative data.
[b]Scores preceding the slash represent Jessica's reports of relations with her mother; those following the slash pertain to her father.

alternative family approaches available at the clinic where the study was conducted. After seven treatment sessions, families in the PSCT group improved more in audiotaped communication than did waiting-list or alternative treatment families, but families in both treatment conditions reported improved relationships on the CBQ and IC. About 60% of the treated families completed questionnaires by mail at a 3-month follow-up, generally reporting that their gains had been maintained. Again, the two treatment groups did not differ.

Stern (1984) evaluated PSCT with and without an additional anger control component, taught to groups of parent–adolescent dyads. Mothers and teenagers in both groups improved on the CBQ, and mothers improved on the IC. Observations of videotaped discussions of real problems showed gains in communication skills for parents and teens in both treatment groups.

Together, these studies suggest that PSCT can produce positive results, but that the results can be quite variable. This variability points to the importance of assessing whether families acquire and use the problem-solving skills being taught; how these skills affect the resolution of the problems families bring to treatment; and, finally, the impact of training on short- and long-term indices of the quality of family relationships.

Research on Related Treatment Approaches

Research on interventions similar to PSCT also demonstrates that training parents in negotiation and/or communication skills can change both their communication styles and their reports of interaction at home. Several approaches with parents and teenagers focus at least in part on negotiating solutions to parent–teen problems. In an early study, Kifer, Lewis, Green, and Phillips (1974) demonstrated that mothers and teens increased their problem clarification and option-listing skills in communication samples taken immediately after training and in the home setting, following an intervention comprised of praise and instructions. Unfortunately, Kifer et al. (1974) failed to assess whether these skills were ever used outside of the assessments, and what their impact was on the parent–adolescent relationship.

Besalel and Azrin (1981) combined behavioral contracting with communication skills training and overcorrection and showed that the treatment package resulted in improved ratings of problems in the family, relative to ratings of a waiting-list control group. Treating the waiting-list group replicated the findings, and gains were maintained at a 6-month follow-up. Unfortunately, Besalel and Azrin employed only an unvalidated questionnaire to assess treatment outcome.

Evaluations of functional family therapy (FFT) have assessed changes in both family process and recidivism rate, and provide stronger corroborative findings. In its early form, descriptions of FFT emphasized distinguishing rules from requests, negotiating contracts for resolving family disagreements, and training communication skills (Alexander & Barton, 1976; Alexander & Parsons, 1973). Later writings elaborate a conceptual scheme for exploring the intimacy, distancing, and regulation functions that each family member's behavior serves in problematic interactions, and emphasize deploying therapeutic tactics in ways that alter behavior while preserving important functions produced by problematic behavior (Alexander & Parsons, 1982).

A series of group outcome studies conducted primarily with families with teenagers referred for status offenses showed that FFT, conducted over about 8 weeks, increased supportive communication, reduced defensive communication (as assessed in communication samples), and reduced recidivism rates over 3–15 months after treatment, relative to no-treatment controls (Alexander & Barton, 1976; Alexander & Parsons, 1973; Barton, Alexander, Waldron, Turner, & Warburton, 1985; Parsons & Alexander, 1973). In comparison with forms of client-centered and psychodynamic treatment, families showed greater improvement after FFT (Alexander & Parsons, 1973), although FFT appeared to be more systematically implemented and supervised than the alternative approaches. Furthermore, Klein, Alexander, and Parsons (1977) showed that fewer siblings of teens who had participated in FFT had court records 2½–3 years after termination than siblings of teens treated with client-centered or psychodynamic therapies. Despite these impressive findings, studies of FFT have not employed measures of parent–teen interaction in the home, leading to questions about whether daily interactions change as the treatment model specifies they should.

Most of the studies described above examined treatment packages bearing some similarity to PSCT. Although their results support the use of skill-oriented, problem-focused interactional approaches to treatment, specific elements of therapy responsible for treatment gains cannot be isolated without component analyses. Although such analyses have yet to be done, results of other investigations bear on this issue when interventions similar to components of PSCT are examined in isolation.

Blechman (1974) developed a family contract game that provides a structured format for eliciting problem descriptions, specifications of alternative behaviors, contingencies for altered performance, and systems for monitoring behavior. This intervention, like PSCT, involves solution-oriented negotiation. Unlike PSCT, it does not actively train conflict resolution or communication skills. Single-subject research using ABA designs showed that the game produced more on-task verbalization when the game was being used; also, parents' ratings of child problems on the Devereux Child Behavior Questionnaire decreased from pre-treatment to posttreatment (Blechman, 1974; Blechman & Olson, 1976). These results suggest that even in the absence of specific skill training, reaching agreements to problems may prove useful.

Support for the communication training components of PSCT comes from evaluations of a relationship enhancement program for parents and teenagers (Guerney, 1977; Guerney, Coufal, & Vogelsong, 1981). In this program, therapists teach communication skills aimed at enhancing sharing and understanding. Training utilizes modeling, instruction, behavior rehearsal, and feedback, implemented with small groups of parent–adolescent dyads. Relative to waiting-list controls, mother–daughter and father–son nonclinic families reported improved relationships after training on questionnaires designed by Guerney and his colleagues. Ratings of their communication (sampled in the clinic) also improved (Ginsberg, 1971; Guerney et al., 1981). Vogelsong (1975) followed up mother–daughter dyads in the Guerney et al. (1981) study, and demonstrated that treated dyads' gains were maintained and enhanced with "booster" weekly phone calls and meetings every 6 weeks during the follow-up interval.

Together, the outcome studies examining PSCT and related approaches point to the effectiveness of directive, skill-oriented treatments for reducing parent–adolescent conflict. None of these treatments can claim universal

success, and impressive statistics become more difficult to amass as family problems become more complex (e.g., Barton et al., 1985). In general, skill-oriented approaches appear extremely useful for some families, useful but needing supplementary interventions for others, and extremely difficult to implement for the most severely distressed families. Empirically based predictors for judging who will benefit from these types of therapy would greatly assist in treatment planning, but are presently not available.

Cognitive Restructuring

Cognitive restructuring techniques teach families to become aware of, challenge, and correct distorted cognitions. The cognitive restructuring strategies described here blend Beck's collaborative empiricism (Beck, Rush, Shaw, & Emery, 1979) with Ellis's rational–emotive therapy (Ellis & Grieger, 1977). From Beck's approach comes therapist collaboration with the family to design and execute experiments that test the credibility of various beliefs, with the results of these experiments intended to disconfirm the beliefs. From Ellis's approach come therapist challenges of the veracity of distorted cognitions, and use of persuasive authority to suggest alternative, more suitable beliefs.

Eight themes (described previously) subsuming many of the unreasonable beliefs and misattributions expressed by families constitute the usual cognitions targeted for change (Robin & Foster, 1984, 1989). For parents, these include ruination, obedience, perfectionism, self-blame, and malicious intent. Adolescents' common irrational beliefs include fairness, ruination, malicious intent, and autonomy. One additional theme applies to parents and teens alike: love/approval. Table 14-5 summarizes some of these themes in terms understandable to families, and may be used as a handout in therapy.

In addition to these common content themes, the process by which parents and adolescents reason may be distorted and targeted for change. For example, family members may reason in absolute ways, dichotomizing relationship events in an overgeneralized all-or-none fashion, as when a mother concludes that because her daughter stayed out past curfew and came home with a "hicky," the girl is a tramp.

Teenagers display similarly overgeneralized reasoning when, for example, they conclude that they will never have any friends if their parents do not let them participate in some proscribed activity.

Two forms of cognitive restructuring are useful in treating parent–adolescent problems. The first is used primarily to relabel negative attributions attached to the causes of other family members' behavior. The second is reserved for pervasive distortions that are central to family problems.

Misattributions

Family members often make inferences about why others in the family behave as they do. Negative attributions induce unnecessary anger and limit problem solving. For example, attributing rebellious adolescent behavior to malicious motives ("She stayed out late to get even with me for grounding her") may lead to a very different outcome than attributing the same rebellious behavior to normal developmental processes ("This is her way of testing the normal limits that parents set for teenagers").

TABLE 14-5. Common Unreasonable Beliefs and Alternatives

Unreasonable belief	Reasonable alternative
Parents	
Ruination	
If my teenager is given freedom and/or rules are relaxed, catastrophic consequences will result that will ruin the teenager's future.	Come on! Many teenagers are given additional freedom without any bad reactions. Am I really being realistic?
Obedience	
My teenager should always do what I ask or demand, and it is catastrophic if he or she fails to obey me.	Did I always listen to my parents? Have I turned out terribly? What is the worst thing that can happen?
Perfectionism	
My teenager should always know the right thing to do and should always make the right decision.	Teenagers, like parents, make mistakes and have a right to learn from their mistakes. No one is perfect.
Self-Blame	
It is my fault if my teenager acts badly or makes mistakes. If only I had raised the child differently, this would never have happened.	We can only guide our children. We cannot ultimately be responsible for all of their behavior. Many other people have also influenced my teen.
Malicious Intent	
My teenager is misbehaving on purpose to annoy, hurt, and anger my spouse and me.	Teenagers don't generally plan their misbehavior in advance. What are some other explanations for why it appears as if my teen is trying to hurt me?
Teenagers	
Fairness	
It is terribly unfair for my parents to enforce rules.	Parents have a right to let me know how they feel. Who promised life will always be fair?
Ruination	
Parents' rules will ruin my life by stopping me from having a good time, having friends, or doing what other teenagers do.	When was the last time a parental rule interfered with my plans? Did everything fall apart? Did I lose all my friends? Come on! What is the worst thing that can really happen?
Autonomy	
I should be permitted total freedom to do whatever I want without any parental interference.	Does anyone really have such freedom? Don't I really want help sometimes? Parents have a right to guide me, just as I have a right to let them know how I feel. We need to respect each other's rights.
Approval	
It is terrible for me to do things that upset my parents.	I can't please everyone all the time. Sometimes I must say what I think, even if my parents don't agree.

Note. From *Negotiating Parent–Adolescent Conflict: A Behavioral–Family Systems Approach* by A. L. Robin and S. L. Foster, 1989, New York: Guilford Press. Copyright 1989 by The Guilford Press. Reprinted by permission of the authors and the publisher.

When negative attributions are clearly verbalized, they can be treated like negative communication habits and changed through correction, instructions, modeling, and behavior rehearsal. When the attributions are not clearly verbalized, they can be elicited and corrected via either reframing or verification.

With reframing, the therapist provides a family member with a benign alternative to the malevolent attribution. Overprotective parental behavior can be reinterpreted as concern for the teenager's welfare; adolescent disobedience can be reframed as limit testing or as unskilled attempts to become an independent adult; angry adolescent outbursts can be labeled as attempts to communicate. The absolute truth of a reframe is less important than finding an explanation that neutralizes the negative attribution in a socially acceptable and believable manner, thus facilitating more adaptive communiction.

Correcting misattributions through verification involves asking the member to whom the intent is attributed to comment on its truth or falsity. For example, if Sally believes that her mother is restricting her curfew because her mother does not want her to have any fun, the therapist can ask the mother whether or not Sally's attribution is accurate. If Sally's mother responds by indicating that she wants her daughter to have fun but is worried about Sally's ability to withstand peer pressure to drink and take drugs, the misattribution stands corrected. The success of verification depends upon the willingness of the second member to correct and not endorse the misattribution; this typically limits its utility to interactions characterized by mild to moderate degrees of overall conflict.

Major Cognitive Distortions

The therapist follows six steps to correct serious cognitive distortions: (1) Provide a rationale linking thoughts, feelings, and negative interaction; (2) identify the unreasonable belief; (3) challenge it; (4) suggest a more reasonable alternative; (5) design an experiment to disconfirm the unreasonable belief; and (6) prepare the family to conduct the experiment.

The therapist's rationale introduces cognitive restructuring by indicating how thoughts about relationship events can elicit strong negative feelings, impede effective resolution of issues, and promote cycles of negative communication. Using an imaginary situation can make these points relevant and believable to family members. For example, the therapist may ask the family to imagine a recent rule infraction (e.g., John's failing to clean up his room on time). The therapist asks the parent to imagine all of the ruinous consequences of failure to clean up the room and asks John to think about how unfair the rule is. The therapist then asks members to report their emotional reactions, relating their growing negative feelings to their thoughts. Presenting the rationale for cognitive restructuring via this kind of exercise also sets the stage for the collaborative empiricism later involved in disconfirming unreasonable beliefs.

Identifying unreasonable beliefs can be done in different ways. When a problem interaction has been audiotaped, the therapist can review the tape, ask members to reconstruct their thoughts, and pinpoint examples of unrealistic beliefs drawn from Table 14-5. Alternatively, the therapist can wait until an unreasonable belief interferes with a problem-solving discussion. Either a family member will clearly express the belief (as when an authoritarian father asserts that all adolescents should obey their parents), or a problem-solving impasse will cue the therapist to investigate the possibility of underlying cognitive distortions (as when the mother of an innocent 13-year-old girl inappropriately resists compromises about permitting her daughter to go to shopping malls with peers, suggesting possible ruinous beliefs). Once the belief is identified, the therapist clearly restates the unreasonable belief and asks the family member to self-monitor it.

To challenge unreasonable cognitions, the therapist should focus on gently but persuasively undermining the illogical premises of the belief. It is often helpful to exaggerate the belief to absurd proportions and examine its consequences, making liberal use of humor. Alternatively, the family can be asked to marshal evidence for and against the veracity of a particular belief; their inability to make a convincing case is thus permitted to serve as the challenge.

Logical challenges blend naturally into suggestions of more flexible alternative cognitions. The therapist may ask the family to brainstorm a list of possible alternative beliefs or may make specific suggestions. Extremist phrases such as "should," "must," and "always" can be replaced with more tentative phrases such as "it would be nice if," "I would like you to," and "as often as possible."

As the family members become increasingly aware of more flexible beliefs, the therapist arranges an experiment that helps them convince themselves, based upon personal experience rather than external authority, of the veracity and utility of the flexible beliefs. Such experiments may take the form of implementing a solution irrationally feared by a family member and determining whether the dire consequences predicted by the illogical beliefs occur; surveying other parents to determine whether their experiences confirm or disconfirm the irrational belief; or reading a book or collecting other objective published data to assess the validity of the belief. A mother who ruinously believes that her son's failure to clean up his room will result in his growing up to be an irresponsible, lazy adult might by instructed to consult five "model adults" and inquire whether they ever failed to clean up their rooms as adolescents; she is likely to discover that they did occasionally leave a messy room, and this did not detract from their success as adults.

Further discussion and review of the "experiment" typically help the family members understand their lack of logic. At this stage, they may admit that they have been overreacting or thinking unrealistically, but may still have difficulty integrating the more realistic cognitions into their daily routines, given habitual, "automatic" irrational thinking. A father may say, "I know Sally is not staying out 2 hours past curfew on purpose to hurt me, but it still feels this way each time I have to confront her." The therapist can use the metaphor of "learning a new skill" to plan a strategy for family members to rehearse and incorporate cognitions into their daily thinking. Rehearsal strategies may include (1) writing the reasonable beliefs or the arguments against the unreasonable beliefs on a 3-by-5 card and reviewing them periodically throughout the day; (2) keeping a diary of situations and one's reactions to them; or (3) asking others to cue the individual when they suspect that a cognitive distortion is underlying his or her behavior.

Another useful strategy for incorporating new cognitions into daily routines is to teach a family member to focus on the difference between "feelings" and "knowledge" in a situation that has previously elicited unreasonable thinking. The therapist legitimizes the individual's feelings as a natural response to the situation, but teaches the individual to act on the basis of his or her more rational "knowledge," even though the "feeling" is still in accord with problem cognitions, In the earlier example, the therapist can reassure Sally's father that for some time he may continue to "feel" as if his daughter is purposely trying to hurt him, but since previous discussion has demonstrated that he "knows" her intent is not malicious, perhaps he can act upon his knowledge, accepting his feeling but not allowing it to influence his behavior. Furthermore, the therapist can use an old principle of behavior change strategically by explaining that feelings usually change after behavior and thoughts change; thus, as long as the father reacts rationally, the negative feeling will eventually extinguish.

Applicability and Contraindications

Cognitive restructuring is applicable for those families whose beliefs, expectations, attributions, and cognitive processes promote conflict. Often such families know how to communicate positively and solve problems effectively, but they become so enraged by their overreactions to others' unreasonable expectations and attributions that they cannot utilize their skills. Dogmatic parental demands for obedience and perfection, refusal to compromise during problem solving, adolescent insistence upon total removal of parental controls, expectations out of line with normal adolescent development, consistently malevolent attributions about motives, and dire needs for approval are signs that a therapist should consider introducing cognitive restructuring.

There are two contraindications for conducting cognitive restructuring in the family context. The first occurs when a member's beliefs are extremely rigid and the member resists considering their veracity. Some beliefs represent such automatic, overlearned cognitive processes and/or serve such central functions in an individual's intrapersonal and interpersonal life that they are not easily subject to modification. Extremely authoritarian fathers are sometimes unwilling to change their demands for obedience or perfectionism. This is particularly likely when further assessment reveals that demands for rigid adherence to rules serve the function of avoiding the father's (1) perceptions of catastrophic consequences that will follow from any compromise, (2) anxiety about his incompetence as a parent, and/or (3) perceptions of his own areas of skill deficits. In such cases the therapist's attempts to use cognitive restructuring, particularly in a family context where discussing beliefs may be perceived as an admission of "weakness," will evoke a hostile, defensive reaction. It is more fruitful to work in individual therapy with the father to address the underlying self-blameful cognitions before using cognitive restructuring in family sessions. Unfortunately, we know of no reliable, valid predictors of these kinds of negative responses to cognitive restructuring. At present, the therapist must simply try cognitive restructuring, carefully gauge the response, and modify the approach as needed.

The second contraindication to cognitive restructuring occurs when the unreasonable belief is actually realistic. Some adolescents and parents do in fact behave in the extreme fashions suggested by such themes as ruination, obedience, malicious intent, and so on. Some adolescents do commit illegal acts if unsupervised, drink and take drugs, become pregnant, and get in trouble with the police. Some parents are in fact so restrictive and abusive that adolescents cannot enjoy this period of their life. It is clearly important not to mistake concern over extremely antisocial, negative behavior for unreasonable beliefs. Careful review of assessment information collected through clinical interviews, self-report inventories, and direct observation usually helps the therapist to pinpoint cases where the unreasonable is realistic. In these cases, plans geared at modifying the behavior that provokes the conclusion, rather than the conclusion per se, become the preferred treatment options.

Monitoring Response to Treatment

To assess changes in cognitive processes, the therapist can observe family members' flexibility during problem-solving discussions, attending in particular to how willing they are to compromise and negotiate. Pinpointing daily situations that elicit unreasonable beliefs, and asking family members to monitor their thoughts and feelings via daily logs or diaries, provide another source of information about the effects of cognitive restructuring. Repeated administration of self-report measures such as the FBI or beliefs scales of the PARQ can also corroborate changes in thought patterns, although these measures are so new that they have not yet been used systematically for this purpose.

Case Example

Mr. and Mrs. Dalton and their 16-year-old son Andrew were referred for family treatment because of the parents' concerns about Andrew's excessively angry outbursts, malicious verbalizations, and increasing withdrawal from family activities. Andrew's negative behaviors had escalated after the Daltons recently forbade him to see his close friend of many years, Robert. Robert had gradually drifted toward antisocial behavior, including alcohol and marijuana abuse, truancy and school failure, shoplifting, and running away. The Daltons felt that Robert's recent changes forced them to break off the relationship before Andrew turned antisocial. Andrew became moody and lashed out at his parents in an unexpected, abusive manner, refused to talk to them for days, and spent much of his time in his room. He did not, however, disobey their order to stop seeing Robert. Andrew felt that his parents had acted arbitrarily and extremely unfairly by forbidding him to see Robert. Although he agreed that Robert had some problems, he viewed himself as helping Robert overcome these difficulties, He did not believe that he would imitate his friend's antisocial behaviors, and in fact there was no evidence of such imitation at the time of the first session.

The therapist judged that the parents were unrealistically expecting their 16-year-old to accept without protest a very difficult situation—being deprived of his best friend—and that they needed education about normal adolescent responses to such restrictions. Furthermore, the therapist hypothesized that although there was reason for concern about Andrew's association with Robert, totally breaking off contacts between the two boys was an overreaction based upon ruinous beliefs about Andrew's suggestibility and inability to say no to antisocial temptations. This action suggested more underlying distorted thinking in need of examination. Andrew, for his part, was unable to perceive the legitimacy of his parents' concerns, focusing instead only on the unfairness of their actions and his blind trust in Robert. Since the primary problems revolved around beliefs, expectations, and attributions, the therapist chose cognitive restructuring as the major intervention. Some communication skill training was also included as part of treatment, as cognitive restructuring alone could not deal with Andrew and his parents' recent negative interactions; however, the discussion that follows is limited to the cognitive restructuring elements of treatment.

Following two assessment sessions, the therapist began to focus on the parents' unrealistic expectations and attributions about Andrew's angry outbursts. The angry outbursts and sullen, withdrawn behavior were reframed as a normal adolescent response to a difficult family situation, rather than a malicious action directed at the parents. The therapist appealed to his own experience with hundreds of adolescents and the literature on adolescent development to bolster this interpretation. Mr. and Mrs. Dalton were surprised, but upon reflection found the therapist's explanation plausible. The therapist also corrected these misbeliefs through verification by asking Andrew whether he was trying to punish his parents through his outbursts. He replied "No" emphatically, stating that he cared about his parents but occasionally became very angry and lost control without knowing why. His parents believed his explanation.

In later sessions, the theme of overprotective parental concern about the ruinous consequences of too much freedom served as the basis for invoking the five steps of cognitive restructuring. The parents explicitly indicated that they had no intentions of rescinding the order for Andrew to stop associating with Robert. Even though the therapist felt they had acted in haste, he decided that it was strategically best not to challenge this *fait accompli;* this belief was probably too entrenched to challenge without jeopardizing the therapist's credibility in the parents' eyes. Instead, he targeted other related ruinous beliefs: (1) the mother's belief that if she stopped daily nagging about homework, Andrew would fail at school and grow up aimless and unemployed; (2) the father's belief that Andrew's refusal to complete all of his chores meant that he no longer loved his parents and wanted to punish them for their actions towards him; and (3) the mother's belief that Andrew should constantly express his appreciation for everything she did for him (driving him places, etc.), inferring that he was an ungrateful, insensitive person if he did not. With regard to the first belief, the family agreed to try an "experiment" where Mrs. Dalton said nothing to Andrew about his homework for 2 weeks, Andrew handled it on his own, and then she checked with his teachers to verify whether the assignments had been completed. The check proved positive; Mrs. Dalton reduced her nag-

ging further, and her ruinous belief dissipated somewhat. Other experiments for the remaining beliefs followed, with similar results.

By the end of the seventh session, significant changes had taken place. Andrew and his parents communicated more positively, the angry outbursts had diminished, and Andrew felt that his parents were more fair. Although Andrew was still unhappy about not seeing Robert, his anger passed; he accepted this rule, and he made new friends. Mrs. Dalton reflected that her whole attitude toward her son had changed: She did not get as "uptight" about every minor problem he encountered, and she was more willing to give him the benefit of the doubt. The effectiveness of the cognitive restructuring with the mother had been a catalyst that changed the entire family interaction pattern. At a 2-month follow-up, the positive changes had maintained.

Research

No studies have evaluated the effectiveness of cognitive restructuring as the primary intervention for parent–adolescent conflict. One study, however, examined the contribution of cognitive restructuring to PSCT with parent–adolescent conflict. Nayar (1985) randomly assigned 27 families to PSCT without cognitive restructuring, PSCT with cognitive restructuring (PSCT/CR), or a waiting-list control. Families within each condition met in groups of two or three for seven 90-minute sessions of a highly structured treatment. In the PSCT/CR condition, the steps of cognitive restructuring were interwoven into a basic PSCT intervention in a didactic manner. Each family also identified and challenged illustrative unreasonable beliefs with the help of the the therapist and the group. The PSCT group received the standard PSCT intervention. Content analysis of session audiotapes indicated that the two treatment groups received the appropriate interventions, with cognitive restructuring activities restricted to the PSCT/CR condition. Measures included the CBQ-20, the IC, goal attainment ratings, audiotaped discussions coded with the IBC, and the FBI. Measures were administered before and after treatment; the self-report measures were readministered 2 months following termination.

Results were mixed. Both treatment groups improved on mother and adolescent scores on the IBC and the CBQ-20, with a trend toward similar effects on the father scores of the CBQ-20. The PSCT/CR group was superior to the PSCT group and/or the control group on goal attainment ratings, maternal malicious intent and self-blame scores from the FBI, and paternal CBQ scores. Most treatment effects were maintained at follow-up, but subject attrition during follow-up limited the interpretation of these results.

These results suggested some superiority of PSCT/CR to PSCT (particularly in terms of selected maternal beliefs, communication, and conflict), and replicated to a certain extent the positive results of previous investigations with PSCT, but the overall magnitude and consistency of the results was weaker than in previous investigations. Perhaps the group format limited the outcome; Nayar (1985) commented anecdotally that many of the families had problems that went beyond what could be effectively handled in a group. Thus, at the present time, there are no clear-cut, unambiguous data to support the effectiveness of cognitive restructuring. A factorial investigation crossing cognitive restructuring with PSCT, treating one family at a time, is needed to obtain such information, as are intensive single-subject designs evaluating cognitive restructuring for clients with identified, documented irrational beliefs.

Structural–Functional Interventions

Problem-solving communication skills and cognitions are like atoms; in joining together, they produce the molecules of family interaction—structural and functional patterns. Structural and functional analyses of interactions represent pictures of molar-level, repetitive sequences of behavior that include the family's presenting problem. If one thinks of the family's life as a motion picture, structure is analogous to the view when one stops the projector and examines a single frame; function is based on the view over time as the frames move through the projector.

Parent–adolescent arguments, rebellious adolescent behavior, family fights, and distorted cognitions are events that occur in the context of ongoing sequences of interactions. Particularly with severely distressed, multiproblem families, altering these molecular events through skills training and cognitive restructuring is often insufficient to produce lasting change unless the more molar-level sequences also change. Treatment plans that

consider structure deploy skills in ways to improve problematic structural configurations. Thus, problem-solving discussions for enmeshed families should include solutions that allow the teen age-appropriate autonomy; discussions with disengaged families should encourage communication, monitoring where the child is, increasing parental involvement in discipline, and the like. Parents who fail to work as a team may need coaching in negotiating mutually agreeable solutions, supporting each other's decisions, and preventing the teenager from manipulating their differences to his or her advantage. Finally, triangulated patterns should be restructured in favor of more direct communication among disagreeing family members.

The therapist should also consider the function or purpose of each family member's behavior in problem interaction sequences. Changing any one member's responses will influence the entire family, and seemingly positive changes in one person's behavior may prove aversive to another. Similarly, a family member is unlikely to change a richly reinforced behavior unless sufficient reinforcement is available for the alternative. Unless the therapist anticipates these possibilities, family members may react to others' new behavior by sabotaging therapeutic efforts. In the following pages, we apply selected concepts and interventions from family systems therapy (Gurman & Kniskern, 1981) in addressing structure; we integrate concepts from operant approaches and FFT in considering function. In so doing, we consider four problem sequences that recur reasonably often in treating parent–adolescent conflict: (1) weak parental coalitions; (2) cross-generational coalitions; (3) triangulation; and (4) adolescent misbehavior preventing marital conflict.

Weak Parental Coalitions

A weak parental coalition occurs when a spoiled, omnipotent adolescent manipulates two parents who cannot take strong, joint action to establish and enforce rules. The adolescent usually avoids or escapes either the rules or the consequences of failing to comply with the rules. The following sequence exemplifies the weak parental coalition: (1) Two parents agree about a rule governing a specific issue; (2) the adolescent misbehaves in ways that involve the issue/rule; (3) one parent attempts to impose consequences; (4) the other parent attempts to impose different consequences or fails to support his or her spouse's discipline; and (5) the adolescent ignores both parents' interventions and continues to misbehave. The key points here are the parents' inability to function as a team in setting and enforcing rules, ordinarily because one or both avoids the teen's inevitable negative responses to discipline attempts. This leaves a vacuum in which the teenager exerts undue influence, committing inappropriate acts without being checked.

The therapist's goal is to strengthen the parental coalition—that is, to put the parents effectively in charge of their adolescent, by teaching the mother and father to reach and impose agreements concerning rules and discipline. The method of achieving this goal involves a departure from the usual democratic stance of problem solving: The parents are clearly instructed to use their authority. In less severe cases, parents may be required to propose and come to some agreement about consequences for each misbehavior discussed during a problem-solving discussion. During the planning phase, the therapist and parents together engage in troubleshooting, deciding how to handle potential problems in implementing the strategy. The therapist must then follow up carefully from week to week to insure that parents use the strategies they decide upon.

When weak coalitions are more pervasive and the adolescent's manipulations are more potent, more stringent tactics may be required. In these cases, parents are asked repeatedly to reach agreements concerning how to handle specific issues, with the therapist suggesting possible disciplinary steps. The therapist may ask the parents to use the steps of problem solving in their own discussion to reach such agreements, or to hold a more open-ended discussion. The adolescent is prohibited from participating in this portion of the discussion.

The therapist assertively blocks the adolescent's inevitable objections and attempts to sidetrack the discussion, modeling appropriate authority for the parents. The therapist tells the adolescent that the parents need to reach an agreement first, and that this will continue as long as the adolescent's behavior is out of control; when the teen exhibits responsible behavior, more democratic problem solving will resume. Through persuasion, directive prompting, discussion of how to handle feared consequences resulting from disciplining the

adolescent, and supportive modeling, the therapist helps the parents specify a detailed plan to exert control over the adolescent's acting-out behavior, including anticipating and preparing for adolescent sabotage of their plan. The discussion culminates in the parents' jointly presenting the plan to their son or daughter, who is then given a brief opportunity to comment, but no choice about compliance.

Cross-Generational Coalitions

A cross-generational coalition is a situation in which one parent consistently sides with the adolescent against the other parent on matters of rules and consequences regarding disputes. In single-parent families, cross-generational coalitions may develop across three generations, as when a grandmother consistently takes an adolescent's side against a mother. Cross-generational coalitions are an inevitable feature of family life. Nonetheless, rigid persistence of such patterns in the face of developmental change undermines the parents' effectiveness as disciplinary agents, since their mutual influence is divided, with the adolescent's influence thrown in one direction. A common sequence of events is this: (1) The adolescent disobeys a rule; (2) one parent issues a punishment; (3) the adolescent appeals to the other parent, who sides with the adolescent, softening the punishment or undermining it; and (4) the adolescent continues to disobey the rule. The adolescent's intervention is negatively reinforced by lessening the punishment; the lenient parent's behavior is reinforced by the adolescent's expressions of approval and positive behavior toward that parent.

The therapist's goal is to break up problem cross-generational coalitions and strengthen within-generational coalitions, particularly the mother–father coalition. Explaining the detrimental effects of cross-generational coalitions and using feedback, modeling, instructions, and behavior rehearsal to change coalitional behavior are often useful strategies. When a mother and adolescent gang up on a father, for example, the therapist can stop the interaction and ask the mother to discuss the issue with her husband before agreeing with her teenager. Strategically planned homework assignments can also induce changes in coalitional behavior. For example, if a mother refuses to discipline a daughter who is rebelling against the father's rules, the therapist could encourage the mother to support her husband, not her daughter, to promote effective, joint parental action. The mother may be asked to telephone her husband at work whenever she is faced with a specific disobedient act, and the couple together will decide how to handle it. The couple may also be required to have a brief discussion each evening reviewing the day's events concerning their adolescent. This will insure that the mother receives positive attention from her mate to replace the attention lost from the adolescent when she "toughens up." To insure that the adolescent still has some influence on the parents' behavior, the teenager may be allowed to participate in problem-solving discussions involving both parents. Each parent, however, should be told never to modify a problem-solving agreement at the teen's request without discussing it with the spouse.

Dealing with situations in which parents need to assume greater authority as a team often requires that the therapist deviate from the usual pattern of attempting to involve and "win over" the adolescent. Instead, the therapist models forceful but appropriately assertive imposition of rules during the discussion, stopping the teen from maneuvers that interfere with parental teamwork. This strategy can be softened once the parents take greater charge of directing discussions with the teen. The risk to this approach, however, is that the teen will refuse to attend sessions, escalating his or her attempts to maintain the structure of the family system. When the therapist predicts that this will happen, he or she can choose to work with the parents individually for a few sessions with the goal of improving teamwork, then reintroduce the adolescent into the process.

Triangulation

Triangulation involves an interactive sequence where two family members disagree over an issue or action, and each tries to enlist the support of a third member; the third vacillates between supporting each of the others, not consistently taking one side (otherwise, the pattern would be a coalition). There are three possible triangles with triads: mother–father with adolescent in the middle; mother–adolescent with father in the middle; and father–adolescent with mother in the middle. Often all three occur in rapid succession. As with coalitions, it is the rigid persistence rather than the mere occurrence of triangulation that promotes conflict and

hampers effective problem solving. Triangulation is especially likely to be a problem in blended families, where the natural parent gets caught in the middle between the stepparent/spouse and the natural child.

The therapist tries to break up the pattern of triangulated interactions so that no one member gets caught in the middle. Triangulated interactions can be treated as analogous to a negative communication interaction, since they are manifested in the session in terms of a sequence of verbalizations putting someone in the middle. The therapist can clearly target triangulated interactions for change; provide a rationale to the family; and use feedback, modeling, instructions, and behavior rehearsal to correct specific instances by encouraging direct communication about disagreement between the two members who are triangulating the third. As with cross-generational coalitions, strategic homework assignments can supplement in-session corrections.

Adolescent Misbehavior Preventing Marital Conflict

An adolescent's noncompliant, rebellious behavior may function to reduce open marital conflict between his or her parents, preventing the associated threats of separation and divorce. Marital conflict is aversive to all family members, and divorce is aversive to most children. Behaviors that reduce these aversive stimuli are maintained through negative reinforcement. Misbehavior is one way to redirect the parents' attention (and anger) onto the adolescent and reduce marital disagreements. A typical sequence follows: (1) The parents have a serious argument, which the adolescent overhears; (2) the adolescent begins to break rules, fail to complete schoolwork, or engage in antisocial behavior; (3) the parents become concerned about their adolescent's problem, focus their efforts on helping the adolescent, and stop discussing their own disagreements; (4) the adolescent ceases misbehaving until the next serious parental argument. This sequence is problematic because the underlying marital conflict is not addressed and the adolescent gets into serious trouble.

It is difficult to untangle interlocking contingency arrangements linking marital and adolescent conflicts, because if the adolescent is successful, marital disagreement will not be apparent. When the therapist successfully intervenes to reduce parent–adolescent conflict by teaching problem-solving and communication skills, however, the mechanism by which the parents previously avoided marital conflicts is removed; the couple begins to experience aversive interactions; and resistance or sabotaged interventions quickly result. If the therapist attempts to focus directly on the marriage, the parents may deny their marital problems.

To circumvent resistance, the therapist may simultaneously address parent–adolescent and marital problems, usually in the guise of addressing parent–adolescent conflict. It is often useful to adopt the framework of FFT (Alexander & Parsons, 1982; Barton & Alexander, 1981). Functional family therapists do not attempt to change the functions served by interlocking sequences of behavior. Instead, they try to teach families less aversive mechanisms for creating desired relationship outcomes of intimacy or distance; that is, they change the topography of behavior. For example, suppose a mother and daughter argue about the daughter's curfew violations, and the mother later gains closeness by discussing the problems with her husband. The therapist does not attempt to reverse the mother–daughter distancing or the husband–wife closeness. Instead, the daughter may be taught less aversive mechanisms for becoming independent from her mother while indirectly encouraging increased contact between her parents. Her parents may be taught mechanisms for increasing their level of contact following positive rather than negative mother–daughter interaction. The sequence of payoffs is maintained, but is now accomplished in a less aversive manner, and both parent–adolescent and marital goals are addressed simultaneously without a spoken commitment from the couple to work on marital problems. When intervening within an FFT framework to change interlocking parent–adolescent and marital contingencies, the therapist follows two general steps: (1) Use cognitive restructuring and reframing techniques to indicate explicitly how the presenting problem is really part of an interlocking sequence of behavior involving the entire family (Alexander & Parsons, 1982); and (2) use problem-solving, communication, and contracting techniques to produce changes in the topography of the sequences of behavior while maintaining their functions.

In some cases, the therapist may eventually be able to broach the topic of marital conflict directly without meeting resistance from the family. Clinical experience suggests that after progress in reducing parent–adolescent conflicts, a distressed couple is often ready to acknowledge the need for marital sessions. The parents now trust the therapist, have seen some positive results of treatment, and no longer experience intense conflict with their adolescent. In some cases, couples spontaneously mention to the therapist in about the third or fourth session that they now need help with their marriages, not their teenagers. By teaching skills for effective resolution of parent–adolescent arguments and disagreements, the therapist may neutralize the avoidance function of rebellious adolescent behavior in the marital relationship, and some parents may react to the resulting vaccum by recognizing their need for marital therapy. When a couple requests help with the marriage, the therapist can either conduct marital therapy concurrently with family therapy or gradually phase out family sessions if parent–adolescent conflict has been ameliorated (see Jacobson & Margolin, 1979, and Stuart, 1980, for information on behavioral marital therapy).

Intervening with Function

Even when problematic structural patterns are not evident, the therapist must consider the functions of behavior in planning intervention. Intervening in ways that consider the functions of behavior in family interactions requires first that the therapist hypothesize the primary functions target behaviors and interaction sequences serve for each family member. Having done this, the therapist can either attempt to change the valence of particular functions, or encourage more adaptive behaviors serving the same short-term functions but with fewer negative long-term effects.

Alexander and Parsons (1982) argue strongly that therapy should preserve the functions of behaviors, as these functions represent the fundamental preferences of individuals in the family for interpersonal closeness, distance, and regulation (balancing closeness and distance). In more operant terminology, family members should be taught more adaptive ways to gain access to their reinforcers, without attempting to change the valence or nature of the reinforcers.

Although the idea of retaining the outcomes

produced by behaviors while changing the means of attaining those outcomes has intuitive appeal for increasing treatment success, this hypothesis has yet to be empirically tested. We speculate that in some cases, changing the nature of the consequences individuals receive may also be important. This is likely to be the case when family members say that they actively want more of certain types of interactive outcomes, but assessment shows that they fail to obtain them because they lack requisite interpersonal skills for obtaining what they want. In these cases, teaching these skills may be important.

In other cases, changing the valence of specific consequences may be a useful strategy, particularly when avoidance patterns predominate in the family. Avoiding disagreements, avoiding discussion of problems, avoiding giving permission for the teenager to have age-appropriate responsibilities, and avoiding provision of consequences all run counter to the rationale underlying PSCT intervention, and thus family members should be encouraged to stop avoiding these situations. This may involve examining family members' fears and thoughts about the consequences of avoiding or not avoiding the situation, as well as encouraging the family to try an alternative to avoidance to test the current contingencies. At the same time, the therapist should insure that when avoidance is blocked, family members experience positive consequences for new patterns, in order to reduce the likelihood of continued avoidance.

Whether the therapist chooses to restructure or retain current functions produced by problem behaviors in the family, guidelines from current learning theory indicate that greater reinforcement must be available for adaptive than for maladaptive behaviors if the new behaviors are to be maintained (see McDowell, 1982). Since short-term contingencies control behavior more strongly than long-term outcomes, immediate payoffs for behavior are particularly important to consider. To gauge the functional implications of a proposed intervention, the therapist should ask, "What is the primary function of interactions concerning the particular target problem for *each involved family member?* How will the proposed changes in these interactions affect these functions?" If the proposed changes will not result in improved outcomes (i.e., enhanced reinforcement), failures

in change and maintenance should be expected, and alternative plans should be created.

Applicability and Contraindications

Elements of the structural and functional concepts and interventions reviewed here are applicable to the majority of cases treated by behaviorally oriented family therapists. Even though problem coalitions or triangulation may not be the central issues for most cases, most therapists encounter families where parents discipline inconsistently and fail to work as a team, or where marital and parent–child problems interact. We believe that failure to consider molar concepts of hierarchy or sequence limits the effectiveness of behavioral family therapy, and that integration of these constructs into behavior therapy practice will increase positive outcomes and overall effectiveness, particularly with severely distressed families.

Resistance to direct skills training interventions by one or more family members is a first sign to a therapist that structural–functional patterns within the family may not be sufficiently addressed. The therapist should ask himself or herself who is resisting and what function the resistant behavior serves for this family member. Often the family member who stands to lose important sources of reinforcement from any changes in the status quo resists the most. For example, adolescents who will lose freedom if their parents begin to work as a team resist attempts to strengthen the parental coalition. Couples who avoid unpleasant time together by focusing on adolescent misbehavior may resist attempts to reduce adolescent misbehavior.

Probably the major contraindication for structural–functional interventions is when there is a strong possibility of sabotage from family members or significant others not participating in therapy. A related contraindication is the strong likelihood of interference from outside legal or social agencies. Finally, severe individual pathology in one or more family members is likely to interfere with the effectiveness of structural–functional interventions. One manic–depressive father became very permissive, lavished extravagant gifts on his teenage daughter, and bought her pornographic magazines each time he was entering a manic state. His wife was naturally horrified, but the adolescent developed a strong coalition with her father, evading her mother's disciplinary attempts. Structural interventions clearly might not have been effective when dealing with this parent, particularly since his disturbance was part of a cyclical, biologically based disorder. Instead, the therapist worked on ways of removing the father from all child-rearing responsibility during periods of loss of control.

Monitoring Response to
Structural–Functional Interventions

Many of the comments made throughout this chapter about monitoring response to other intervention components also apply in the case of structural–functional interventions. The therapist can look for changed interactions in the session, ask family members to keep written records, periodically readminister self-report inventories, or use analogue observational tasks. Because of the profound effect of structural changes on the entire family, the therapist can also look for indirect effects of change: For example, has the marriage changed? Are siblings perceiving family interactions differently? Have friends and neighbors noticed changes? Finally, the therapist can try to recreate the problem patterns (as in a single-subject reversal design) and see whether the family resists these attempts or not; resistance would be expected with altered structural patterns.

Research on Structural–Functional
Interventions

The structural and functional considerations described above highlight conceptual notions that can, in our opinion, make a skill-oriented treatment program more effective. Unfortunately, research addressing these hypotheses has not been done. Although a few studies attest to the efficacy of structural family therapy with families with drug-dependent teenagers (Szapocznik, Kurtines, Foote, Perez-Vidal, & Hervis, 1983, 1986), the interventions used in these studies were not clearly specified, and thus their comparability to the strategies advocated here is dubious. Similarly, data supporting the efficacy of FFT (e.g., Alexander & Parsons, 1973) pertain to a treatment package; to what extent the conceptual framework underlying the technology enhances the effectiveness of the technology per se is unclear. Studies testing the effects of specific structural manipulations upon family interactions would provide much-needed documentation of the effects of particular interventions designed to alter family structure. Similarly, examining whether taking functional considerations into account adds to the effectiveness of PSCT technology would provide evidence that these suggestions are useful. Until additional evidence accumulates, however, these guidelines should be considered hypotheses.

Implementation Issues

Regardless of the treatment approach, difficulties in managing sessions and gaining clients' cooperation with therapy will hamper the course of treatment and frustrate both therapist and clients. Among the most problematic of these can be (1) reluctance to attend sessions or resistance to the family focus of treatment; (2) runaway, out-of-control sessions where the agenda disappears; and (3) persistent noncompliance with therapeutic directives.

Unfortunately, research specifically focusing on the therapist skills needed to deal effectively with the first two of these problems is sorely lacking. Nonetheless, Alexander, Barton, Schiavo, and Parsons (1976) and Patterson and Forgatch (1985) reported studies linking therapist behavior to the outcome of FFT with parents and adolescents in the first study and behavioral parent training in the second. Alexander et al. (1976) related supervisors' ratings of therapist behavior at the conclusion of training to indices of therapy outcome, including clients' remaining in treatment and showing changes in interaction patterns. Regression analyses showed that supervisors' ratings of both relationship skills (comprised of warmth, humor, and relating the interdependence of affect and behavior) and structuring skills (directiveness and self-confidence) accounted for significant portions of the variance in family therapy outcome. Both sets of behavior differentiated therapists who produced good versus poor outcomes, suggesting that both types of skills are needed to produce changes in families.

Whereas Alexander et al. (1976) examined global indicators of therapist characteristics and overall treatment outcome, Patterson and Forgatch (1985) examined mothers' responses to therapist behaviors on a more molecular level. In the first of two studies, observers coded therapist antecedents to maternal noncompliance (comprised of the categories "interrupt, negative attitude, confront, own agenda, and not tracking"; Patterson & Forgatch, 1985, p. 847). In apparent contrast with Alexander *et al.'s* (1976) findings, therapist confrontation and teaching behaviors were significantly associated with increased likelihood of non-compliance for three and four (respectively) of the six families observed. Interestingly, for two families, different patterns emerged. In one, teaching was associated with decreased non-compliance; in the other, confrontation was an antecedent for reduced noncompliance. Reframing had mixed results, being associated with reduced noncompliance for one family and increased noncompliance with two others.The categories of facilitation and support were con-sistently associated with lowered probabilities of noncompliance for all six families. In the second study, therapists manipulated teaching and confrontation in an ABAB design; in-creases in these behaviors produced increased noncompliance.

The seeming discrepancy between Alexander *et al.'s* (1976) and Patterson and Forgatch's (1985) results may result from different pop-ulations, data sources, levels of analyses, or therapeutic intervention procedures. It points, however, to the complexity of analyzing thera-pist behavior. Therapist behaviors such as reframing and teaching occur in the context of numerous ongoing therapist–family sequences. Establishing whether a context of certain types of therapist–client interactions is necessary to promote client compliance with therapeutic di-rectives could assist in resolving the seeming paradox inherent in Patterson and Forgatch's findings. Alexander and Parsons (1982), for example, hypothesize that initial sessions should focus on reframing and gaining client cooperation, and that teaching interventions will be successful only after these goals have been met.

Both Alexander *et al.'s* (1976) and Patterson and Forgatch's (1985) data suggest that im-plementation problems will arise with some families during the course of behavioral family treatment. The following discussion describes strategies for dealing with common clinical problems encountered in treating parent–ado-lescent conflict.

Reluctant Participants

Family members do not always enter therapy equally committed to treatment. Parents may want the therapist to act as a mechanic and fix their teenagers' problems; teenagers may see the therapist as another authority figure who will blame, cajole, threaten, and not listen to them while attempting to change their behavior.

Early attention to possible reluctance can alleviate this treatment impasse. Inviting all potentially involved family members to attend intake and assessment sessions includes all members from the outset. The therapist can frame the invitation in terms of the need to understand everyone's views of the problem, rather than as an implicit commitment to treat-ment. During the initial contact with the family, the therapist should notice and discuss reluc-tance, acknowledging it rather than trying to persuade reluctant family members that they "shouldn't" feel that way. Asking reluctant par-ticipants for a commitment to only the assess-ment phase of treatment allows the therapist time to assess and intervene to reduce the re-luctance.

Misinformation or mistaken assumptions fre-quently lie at the heart of teenagers' reluctance. Parents may have lied to them about where they are going and why. Teenagers may fear that they are crazy, that they will be forced to lie on a couch and talk about their dreams, or that their friends will discover they are seeing a therapist. Straightforward statements describing the therapy process and correcting mistaken assumptions can often alleviate these problems.

Other antecedents for reluctance lie in family members' thoughts about the source of the dif-ficulty and the conclusions they draw about what their participation should be. An un-involved parent who considers the teenager and/or the other parent to be wholly responsible for the difficulty, or a teenager who is content with family life as it is, often resists the idea of change. In such cases, the therapist can reduce reluctance by asking questions and reflecting family members' answers in ways that enable reluctant members to discover their unwitting involvement in interaction problems, and the potential personal benefits they can gain from participating in therapy. These reframing strat-egies should reflect the interdependence of family members' behavior and the problems that interdependent patterns cause for individual members, in order to change the mistaken assumptions about the problem that promote reluctance. Asking reluctant participants to ex-press the ways they would like to see the family get along better, and to talk about their own negative feelings and how they would like these to change, may help these members to see the possible personal benefits of therapy. Therapist questions designed to get reluctant members to state their desire to support others in the family can also be used to encourage continued participation. Finally, judiciously planned, nonjudgmental reflection and feedback emphasizing the interaction patterns that characterize family problems can help family members to see that, like it or not, they are integrally involved in the situations that led the family to seek help. Besides altering family members' views of the problems they present, these strategies help teenagers to see that the therapist is fair to all family members and to experience the differences between the therapist and other adults in their lives; this promotes increased rapport and motivation to participate in treatment.

The Silent Teenager

A teenager who answers questions in monosyllables or with stony silence poses special difficulties in handling reluctance. The therapist can often avoid this problem by focusing on establishing rapport with the adolescent in early sessions. Using language the teenager understands; treating the teen's concerns and opinions seriously; preventing the parents from turning the session into a vehicle for unproductive, hostile complaints about the teenager; and reflecting the mutual interdependence of problems without assigning blame all contribute to good rapport with adolescents. A teenager who is anxious may open up if the therapist begins the session with easy, open-ended questions about less sensitive areas, such as school activities or the teenager's interests.

If an adolescent's silence persists despite these efforts, the therapist should assess carefully the functions of the teen's refusal to participate. Silence that only occurs occasionally in sessions can be treated as a communication problem with communication training. Silence that occurs persistently is more difficult to handle. By seeing the adolescent alone, the therapist can assess whether the parents' presence suppresses the teen's verbalization. If the teenager talks in the parents' absence, the therapist can discuss the problem of silence with the teenager, in order to assess its antecedents and consequences more fully. The therapist can also

ask the parents whether the teenager is silent at home and under what conditions this occurs, in order to gather information about the antecedents and consequences of silence.

This information provides the basis for hypotheses about the functions of silence for the teenager. These hypotheses are used to formulate strategies designed to increase the adolescent's verbal participation. For example, if the therapist believes that silence is reinforced by parental and therapist attention, the therapist may instruct the teenager to remain silent and tell the parents to continue their discussion without the teenager, only allowing the teenager to participate once he or she has interrupted with a full sentence. With a teenager whose silence leads to discussions being terminated and rules going unenforced, the therapist may work with the parents to block the avoidance function by negotiating solutions and insuring that rules are enforced, while making it clear to the teenager that he or she can be involved in a renegotiation of the rules at a later date (thus building in reinforcement for participation via the contingency that participation may produce more acceptable rules and consequences). The key elements here lie in formulating reasonable hypotheses, using these hypotheses to devise a creative way to try to increase the teen's verbal participation, and assessing the results.

Runaway Sessions

A runaway session occurs when family members persistently and successfully interrupt, change topics, argue with other members, and/or engage the therapist in long-winded discussions of their viewpoints. The therapist's feelings of frustration, anxiety, or anger, together with frequent concerns about the direction of the session, may indicate that a runaway session is in progress.

Runaway sessions call for firm, consistent, and courteous redirection back to the topic at hand, preferably as early as possible. Nonverbal cues that encourage runaway interviews, such as polite head nods, "uh-huhs," and pulling back physically when the family ignores attempts to slow the pace of the session, should be replaced with nonverbal cues that signal the therapist's turn to speak: breaking eye contact, leaning forward, making forceful gestures. On occasion the therapist must consistently rebuff interruptions to gain the floor and regain session control. Setting an agenda and establishing and enforcing rules for the session (e.g., "Only one person speaks at a time") can help prevent out-of-control sessions.

The therapist can also handle persistent runaway sessions by specifying the negative behaviors that elicit and maintain runaways, then treating these as communication targets. Sticking to the topic, talking more slowly, paraphrasing others' statements, and using "I-statements" to express negative feelings are frequent communication targets for families prone to runaway sessions (and to runaway discussions at home). When easily provoked, intense anger characterizes runaway sessions, anger control strategies may also prove useful in reducing session disruption.

Noncompliance with Homework

Skill-based interventions require change efforts outside the session. To encourage such efforts, the therapist should (1) stipulate that the family members will be expected to practice what they are learning and do other kinds of tasks at home between sessions in the treatment contract; (2) describe homework tasks clearly, specifically, and assertively; (3) check that family members agree to do the task; (4) explain the rationale for the task; (5) explore in advance potential problems that may interfere with the homework; and (6) reinforce compliance by going over the homework at the beginning of the next session and making it an integral part of treatment (see Shelton & Levy, 1981, for an extended discussion of therapeutic compliance).

An occasional failure to complete an assigned task may be due to unanticipated events that interfered with the task; reassigning the same or a similar task and discussing with the family possible future difficulties with completing the task should result in compliance. When a family persistently fails to comply, however, the therapist should examine the antecedents and consequences of noncompliance and intervene on the basis of his or her hypotheses. Such interventions might include, for example, making the consequences of compliance more immediate by calling the family immediately after the task is to have been done, or asking the family to complete the task in the therapist's office (if this is feasible) before the session can begin. A creative alternative involves introducing the topic as a problem for the therapist, then asking the family to assist the therapist in arriving at a solution to the problem using the problem-solving model.*

CONCLUSIONS AND FUTURE DIRECTIONS

Interventions aimed at increasing productive communication between parents and teenagers have a good empirical track record for improving family relationships. Nonetheless, allusions to the need for greater empirical scrutiny of clinically relevant issues abound in this chapter, and indicate to numerous areas warranting further attention.

Among the most important of these is the need to evaluate specific strategies for enhancing the impact of PSCT approaches on parent–adolescent conflict. Data showing moderately successful outcomes, coupled with clinical experience, suggest that although PSCT is very useful for some families, this intervention is often insufficient for severely distressed multi-problem families. These conclusions have led to attempts to include cognitive strategies when appropriate, on the one hand, and to incorporate functional and structural considerations into treatment planning, on the other. Unfortunately, the research base for these additional treatment components is meager.

Other treatment technologies besides those described here may be useful in treating parent–adolescent conflict. Stern (1984), for example, evaluated the effects of adding anger control and stress management strategies to PSCT, delivered in group treatment sessions. Stern hypothesized that adding skills for managing anger and stress would help parents and teenagers handle negative affect more productively, thus increasing the likelihood that they could effectively use problem-solving and communication skills learned in treatment. Her results failed to support this hypothesis, however, with groups receiving PSCT alone and PSCT supplemented with anger management improving equally. Nonetheless, Feindler and her colleagues (Feindler, Ecton, Kingsley, & Dubey, 1986; Feindler, Marriott, & Iwata, 1984) have successfully used anger control strategies with

---

*We are indebted to Ian Falloon for this suggestion.

adolescents in school and in inpatient settings; this suggests their potential utility on a case-by-case basis for families who encounter difficulty controlling negative affect even after problem-solving training.

Unfortunately, the few studies that have examined the additive effects of various strategies designed to enhance the impact of PSCT have failed to demonstrate convincingly that strategies such as cognitive restructuring, generalization programming, and anger control substantially increase family improvement (Foster *et al.*, 1983; Nayar, 1985; Stern, 1984). In retrospect, however, the designs of these investigations may have been inadequate to demonstrate such effects. In outcome studies like these, families are assessed for the presence of parent–teen conflict, then randomly assigned to treatment. Yet the approach advocated here implies that only families with cognitive distortions should benefit from cognitive restructuring; similarly, only those unable to manage anger should benefit from anger control. Using research samples that include only families for whom the respective treatments should be appropriate would make negative results easier to interpret.

It is also important to evaluate the mechanisms of treatment on more molecular bases than has been done in the past. Ways of handling common implementation problems offer a fruitful area for future research, and may be particularly well suited to single-subject designs. In addition, therapists could evaluate more systematically the effects of intervention on day-to-day interactions; they could look, for example, at the effects of cognitive restructuring on thoughts (as assessed by logs kept by family members), and at attempts to decrease triangulation on communication patterns in family problem-solving sessions.

Finally, descriptions of the kinds of therapeutic interactions that lead to successful acquisition and sustained use of new interaction styles in the home setting are essential. Contemporary behavior therapists concur that training families in specific skills does not occur in an interactional vacuum. How the interactions between the therapist and family members affect the training process remains to be established, but this is crucial to know if we are ever to specify the necessary and sufficient conditions for establishing clinically significant change in parent–adolescent relationships.

REFERENCES

Alexander, J. F. (1973). Defensive and supportive communications in normal and deviant families. *Journal of Consulting and Clinical Psychology, 40,* 223–231.

Alexander, J. F., & Barton, C. (1976). Behavioral systems therapy with families. In D. H. Olson (Ed.), *Treating relationships* (pp. 167–187). Lake Mills, IA: Graphic.

Alexander, J. F., Barton, C., Schiavo, R. S., & Parsons, B. V. (1976). Systems–behavior intervention with families of delinquents: Therapist characteristics, family behavior, and outcome. *Journal of Consulting and Clinical Psychology, 44,* 656–664.

Alexander, J., & Parsons, B. V. (1973). Short term behavioral intervention with delinquent families: Impact on family process and recidivism. *Journal of Abnormal Psychology, 81,* 219–225.

Alexander, J., & Parsons, B. V. (1982). *Functional family therapy.* Monterey, CA: Brooks/Cole.

American Psychiatric Association. (1987). *Diagnostic and statistical manual of mental disorders* (3rd ed., rev.). Washington, DC: Author.

Aponte, H. H., & VanDeusen, J. M. (1981). Structural family therapy. In A. S. Gurman & D. P. Kniskern (Eds.), *Handbook of family therapy* (pp. 310–360). New York: Brunner/Mazel.

Barnes, H. L., & Olson, D. H. (1985). Parent–adolescent communication and the circumplex model. *Child Development, 56,* 438–447.

Barton, C., & Alexander, J. F. (1981). Functional family therapy. In A. S. Gurman & D. P. Kniskern (Eds.), *Handbook of family therapy* (pp. 403–443). New York: Brunner/Mazel.

Barton, C., Alexander, J. F., Waldron, H., Turner, C. W., & Warburton, J. (1985). Generalizing treatment effects of functional family therapy: Three replications. *American Journal of Family Therapy, 13,* 16–26.

Beck, A. T., Rush, A. J., Shaw, B. F., & Emery, G. (1979). *Cognitive therapy of depression.* New York: Guilford Press.

Besalel, V. A., & Azrin, N. H. (1981). The reduction of parent–youth problems by reciprocity counseling. *Behaviour Research and Therapy, 19,* 297–301.

Blechman, E. A. (1974). The family contract game: A tool to teach interpersonal problem-solving. *Family Coordinator, 23,* 269–281.

Blechman, E. A., & Olson, D. H. (1976). The family contract game: Description and effectiveness. In D. H. Olson (Ed.), *Treating relationships* (pp. 133–149). Lake Mills, IA: Graphic.

Doane, J. A., & West, K. L., Goldstein, M. J., Rodnick, E. H., & Jones, J. E. (1981). Parental communication deviance and affective style. *Archives of General Psychiatry, 38,* 679–685.

D'Zurilla, T. J., & Goldfried, M. R. (1971). Problem solving and behavior modification. *Journal of Abnormal Psychology, 78,* 197–226.

Ellis, A., & Grieger, R. (1977). *Handbook of rational–emotive therapy.* New York: Springer.

Feindler, E. L., Ecton, R. B., Kingsley, D., & Dubey, D. R. (1986). Group anger-control training for institutionalized psychiatric male adolescents. *Behavior Therapy, 17,* 109–123.

Feindler, E. L., Marriott, S. A., & Iwata, M. (1984). Group anger control training for junior high school delinquents. *Cognitive Therapy and Research, 8,* 299–311.

Foster, S. L. (1978). *Family conflict management: Skill training and generalization procedures.* Unpublished doctoral dissertation, State University of New York at Stony Brook.

Foster, S. L., Prinz, R. J., & O'Leary, K. D. (1983). Impact of problem-solving communication training and generalization procedures on family conflict. *Child and Family Behavior Therapy, 5,* 1–23.

Foster, S. L., & Robin, A. L. (1988). Family conflict and communication in adolescence. In E. J. Mash & L. G. Terdal (Eds.), *Behavioral assessment of childhood disorders* (2nd ed., pp. 717–775). New York: Guilford Press.

Genest, M., & Turk, D. C. (1981). Think-aloud approaches to cognitive assessment. In T. V. Merluzzi, C. R. Glass, & M. Genest (Eds.), *Cognitive assessment* (pp. 233–269). New York: Guilford Press.

Gilbert, R., Christensen, A., & Margolin, G. (1984). Patterns of alliances in nondistressed and multiproblem families. *Family Process, 23,* 75–87.

Ginsberg, B. G. (1971). *Parent–adolescent relationship development: A therapeutic and preventive mental health program.* Unpublished doctoral dissertation, Pennsylvania State University.

Gordon, T. (1970). *Parent effectiveness training.* New York: Wyden.

Guerney, B. G., Jr. (1977). *Relationship enhancement.* San Francisco: Jossey-Bass.

Guerney, B. G., Jr., Coufal, J., & Vogelsong, E. (1981). Relationship enhancement versus a traditional approach to therapeutic/preventative/enrichment parent–adolescent programs. *Journal of Consulting and Clinical Psychology, 49,* 927–939.

Gurman, A. S., & Kniskern, D. P. (Eds), (1981). *Handbook of family therapy.* New York: Brunner/Mazel.

Haley, J. (1976). *Problem-solving therapy.* San Francisco: Jossey-Bass.

Haley, J. (1980). *Leaving home: The therapy of disturbed young people.* New York: McGraw-Hill.

Hollon, S. D., & Bemis, K. M. (1981). Self-report and the assessment of cognitive functions. In M. Hersen & A. S. Bellack (Eds.), *Behavioral assessment: A practical handbook* (2nd ed., pp. 125–174). New York: Pergamon Press.

Jacobson, N. S., & Margolin, G. (1979). *Marital therapy.* New York: Brunner/Mazel.

Kelsey-Smith, M., & Beavers, W. R. (1981). Family assessment: Centripetal and centrifugal family systems. *American Journal of Family Therapy, 9,* 3–12.

Kendall, P. C., & Hollon, S. D. (Eds.). (1981). *Assessment strategies for cognitive–behavioral interventions.* New York: Academic Press.

Kifer, R. E., Lewis, M. A., Green, D. R., & Phillips, E. L. (1974). Training pre-delinquent youths and their parents to negotiate conflict situations. *Journal of Applied Behavior Analysis, 7,* 356–364.

Klein, N. C., Alexander, J. F., & Parsons, B. V. (1977). Impact of family systems intervention on recidivism and sibling delinquency: A model of primary prevention and program evaluation. *Journal of Consulting and Clinical Psychology, 45,* 469–474.

Loeber, R., & Dishion, T. J. (1984). Boys who fight at home and school: Family conditions influencing cross-setting consistency. *Journal of Consulting and Clinical Psychology, 52,* 759–768.

McDowell, J. J. (1982). The importance of Herrnstein's mathematical statement of the law of effect for behavior therapy. *American Psychologist, 37,* 771–779.

Minuchin, S. (1974). *Families and family therapy.* Cambridge, MA: Harvard University Press.

Montemayor, R. (1983). Parents and adolescents in conflict: All families some of the time and some families most of the time. *Journal of Early Adolescence, 3,* 83–103.

Moos, R. H., & Moos, B. S. (1983). Clinical applications of the Family Environment Scale. In E. E. Filsinger (Ed.), *Marriage and family assessment: A sourcebook for family therapy* (pp. 253–273). Beverly Hills, CA: Sage.

Nayar, M. (1985). *Cognitive factors in the treatment of parent–adolescent conflict.* Unpublished doctoral dissertation, Wayne State University.

Olson, D. H., & Portner, J. (1983). Family Adaptability and Cohesion Evaluation Scales. In E. E. Filsinger (Ed.), *Marriage and family assessment: A sourcebook for family therapy* (pp. 299–315). Beverly Hills, CA: Sage.

Parsons, B. V., & Alexander, J. F. (1973). Short-term family intervention: A therapy outcome study. *Journal of Consulting and Clinical Psychology, 41,* 195–201.

Patterson, G. R. (1982). *Coercive family process.* Eugene, OR: Castalia.

Patterson, G. R., & Bank, L. (1986). Bootstrapping your way in the nomological thicket. *Behavioral Assessment, 8,* 49–73.

Patterson, G. R., & Forgatch, M. S. (1985). Therapist behavior as a determinant for client noncompliance: A paradox for the behavior modifier. *Journal of Consulting and Clinical Psychology, 53,* 846–851.

Prinz, R. J., Foster, S. L., Kent, R. N., & O'Leary, K. D. (1979). Multivariate assessment of conflict in distressed and nondistressed mother–adolescent dyads. *Journal of Applied Behavior Analysis, 12,* 691–700.

Prinz, R. J., & Kent, R. N. (1978). Recording parent–adolescent interactions without the use of frequency or interval-by-interval coding. *Behavior Therapy, 9,* 602–604.

Robin, A. L. (1981). A controlled evaluation of problem-solving communication training with parent–adolescent conflict. *Behavior Therapy, 12,* 593–609.

Robin, A. L. (1988). The Parent-Adolescent Interaction Coding System. In A. S. Bellack & M. Hersen (Eds.), *Dictionary of behavioral assessment techniques* (pp. 334–336). New York: Pergamon Press.

Robin, A. L., & Canter, W. (1984). A comparison of the Marital Interaction Coding System and community ratings for assessing mother–adolescent problem-solving. *Behavioral Assessment, 6,* 303–314.

Robin, A. L., & Foster, S. L. (1984). Problem-solving communication training: A behavioral–family systems approach to parent–adolescent conflict. In P. Karoly & J. J. Steffen (Eds.), *Adolescent behavior disorders: Foundations and contemporary concerns* (pp. 195–240). Lexington, MA: D.C. Heath.

Robin, A. L., & Foster, S. L. (1988a). The Conflict Behavior Questionnaire. In A. S. Bellack & M. Hersen (Eds.), *Dictionary of behavioral assessment techniques* (pp. 148–149). New York: Pergamon Press.

Robin, A. L., & Foster, S. L. (1988b). The Issues Checklist. In A. S. Bellack & M. Hersen (Eds.), *Dictionary of behavioral assessment techniques* (pp. 278–279). New York: Pergamon Press.

Robin, A. L., & Foster, S. L. (1989). *Negotiating parent–*

adolescent conflct: A behavioral–family systems approach. New York: Guilford Press.

Robin, A. L., Kent, R., O'Leary, K. D., Foster, S. L., & Prinz, R. J. (1977). An approach to teaching parents and adolescents problem-solving communication skills: A preliminary report. *Behavior Therapy, 8,* 639–643.

Robin, A. L., & Koepke, T. (1985). *Molecular versus molar observational coding systems for assessing mother–adolescent problem-solving communication behavior*. Unpublished manuscript.

Robin, A. L., Koepke, T., & Moye, A. (1986). *Multidimensional assessment of parent–adolescent relations*. Unpublished manuscript.

Robin, A. L., & Weiss, J. G. (1980). Criterion-related validity of behavioral and self-report measures of problem-solving communication skills in distressed and nondistressed parent–adolescent dyads. *Behavioral Assessment, 2,* 339–352.

Shelton, J. L., & Levy, R. L. (1981). *Behavioral assignments and treatment compliance*. Champaign, IL: Research Press.

Stern, S. (1984). *A group cognitive–behavioral approach to the management and resolution of parent–adolescent conflict*. Unpublished doctoral dissertation, University of Chicago.

Stuart, R. B. (1980). *Helping couples change: A social learning approach to marital therapy*. New York: Guilford Press.

Szapocznik, J., Kurtines, W. M., Foote, F. H., Perez-Vidal, A., & Hervis, O. (1983). Conjoint versus one-person therapy: Some evidence for the effectiveness of conducting family therapy through one person. *Journal of Consulting and Clinical Psychology, 51,* 889–899.

Szapocznik, J., Kurtines, W. M., Foote, F. H., Perez-Vidal, A., & Hervis, O. (1986). Conjoint versus one-person therapy: Further evidence for the effectiveness of conducting family therapy through one person with drug-abusing adolescents. *Journal of Consulting and Clinical Psychology, 54,* 395–397.

Vincent Roehling, P., & Robin, A. L. (1986). Development and validation of the Family Beliefs Inventory: A measure of unrealistic beliefs among parents and adolescents. *Journal of Consulting and Clinical Psychology, 54,* 693–697.

Vogelsong, E. L. (1975). *Preventative–therapeutic programs for mothers and adolescent daughters: A follow-up of relationship enhancement versus discussion and booster versus no-booster methods*. Unpublished doctoral dissertation, Pennsylvania State University.

Weiss, R. L., Hops, H., & Patterson, G. R. (1973). A framework for conceptualizing marital conflict, a technology for altering it, and some data for evaluating it. In L. A. Hamerlynck, L. C. Handy, & E. J. Mash (Eds.), *Behavior change: Methodology, concepts and practice* (pp. 309–342). Champaign, IL: Research Press.

15

ANOREXIA NERVOSA AND BULIMIA NERVOSA

JOHN P. FOREYT
Baylor College of Medicine

JILL K. McGAVIN
University of Houston

norexia nervosa and bulimia nervosa are increasingly common, complex disorders that are often perplexing to therapists, frequently resistant to treatment, and often difficult to cure. The purpose of this chapter is to review the history, nature, etiology, assessment, and treatment of these disorders. Assessment strategies, including individual psychotherapy, inpatient approaches, outpatient programs, and specific therapeutic techniques and components, are presented. Throughout the chapter, we emphasize that treatment of these disorders is most effective when therapists utilize comprehensive, multicomponent intervention programs. We welcome the growing trend away from treatment by a single therapist in favor of intervention programs involving many disciplines. We believe that treatments of anorexia and bulimia should be considered experimental in nature. However, with the increasing interest in these disorders by researchers and clinicians, we hope that in the near future the merits of some of the methods described in this chapter will be empirically established.

HISTORY

Anorexia Nervosa

Cases of self-inflicted starvation and weight loss were recorded as early as the 4th century A.D. To a young, "well-bred" girl, St. Jerome wrote, "Let your companions be women, pale and thin with fasting" (Lacey, 1982). This young woman's sister, also under St. Jerome's tutelage, died of the regimen. Evidence suggests that, in the 11th century, Princess Margaret of Hungary may have had anorexia nervosa (Halmi, 1982). In the 13th century, there is an account of a nun who claimed to ingest nothing but the Eucharist for 7 years (Hammond, 1879), and in the 14th century a female saint is said to have existed for years on nothing but a small piece of apple (Hammond, 1879). In those times, the women's behavior was not interpreted as indicating the presence of a psychological or physical disorder. The unusual abstinence was seen as a sign of spiritual power and saintly self-denial (Bell, 1985).

Richard Morton's account in 1694 generally is credited as the first clinical description of anorexia nervosa. He described a state of "nervous consumption" characterized by decreased appetite, amenorrhea, food aversion, emaciation, and hyperactivity. He wrote:

> I do not remember that I ever did in all my Practice see one, that was conversant with the Living so much wasted with the greatest degree of Consumption (like a Skeleton only clad with skin) yet there was no Fever, but on the contrary a coldness of the whole body. (quoted by Powers & Fernandez, 1984, p. 2)

This patient died 3 months later, after refusing the medication offered.

The disorder gained recognition with the report of Charles Laseque (1873) and the coining of the term "anorexia nervosa" in 1874 by Sir William Gull. Gull noted that the condition typically has its onset in adolescence, occurs predominantly in females, and is characterized by a "morbid mental state." He further discussed the effects of prolonged starvation and calorie depletion on metabolic functioning, and emphasized the importance of timely intervention.

Laseque (1873) independently described the cognitive/perceptual distortions in regard to health and body image, as well as the role of the family. He noted, "The family has but two methods at its service which it always exhausts—entreaties and menaces" (quoted by Strober, 1986, p. 235). He wrote that the family attempts to lead the sufferer to eat by enticing her with delicacies and asking for proof of her affection, and that the "excess of insistence begets an excess of resistance" (quoted by Strober, 1986, p. 236).

The accounts of Gull and Laseque, not surprisingly, provoked a debate regarding the involvement of the family in treatment. Some argued that the patient must be removed from her domestic environment for treatment to be successful (Playfair, 1888); others claimed that such removal constituted unnecessary cruelty and cost too much (Myrtle, 1888).

Views about the disorder changed when, in 1914, Simmonds described a patient who suffered from ill health and malnutrition ("cachexia"). At autopsy, the patient was found to have pituitary destruction. Consequently, in the following 10–20 years there was a tendency to view anorexia nervosa as a medical disorder caused by pituitary abnormalities.

With the spread of psychoanalytic thought in the 1940s and 1950s, anorexia nervosa came to be seen as a psychiatric disorder. Simmonds's original cases were reanalyzed, and several important distinctions were drawn between "Simmonds disease" and anorexia nervosa. Patients with Simmonds disease have only a mild degree of weight loss and are often hypoactive. Furthermore, Simmonds's patients did not have a drive for thinness, deny their illness, show body image disturbance, or make vigorous efforts at weight loss, including purging behavior (Sheehan & Summers, 1949). The two disorders share only two features: the amenorrhea and a low basal metabolic rate. With this distinction clarified, anorexia nervosa was viewed as a psychological disorder. Within the psychoanalytic tradition, then, anorexia nervosa was hypothesized to be related to fixated unconscious conflicts regarding oral–sadistic fears, oral impregnation, regressive wishes, and primitive fantasies.

This viewpoint was challenged by the clinical studies of Hilde Bruch (1973), which spanned three decades. Bruch brought about a major rethinking of the treatment and conceptualization of the disorder. She believed that the falsification of early developmental learning experiences is of primary importance in the etiology of anorexia nervosa. The core problems consist of faulty learning regarding the discrimination of internal states and body boundaries, a deep sense of ineffectiveness, and lack of autonomy. Treatment, consequently, should be aimed at girding up and nurturing feelings of effectiveness and autonomy.

Minuchin, Rosman, and Baker (1978) have spurred a more recent conceptual shift in the understanding and treatment of anorexia nervosa. Anorexia nervosa, in their view, is a family disorder that is caused by the family's structure (e.g., boundaries, roles, and alliances) and its inability to establish appropriate conflict resolution strategies. The developmental stasis of such families and the intergenerational difficulties or changes also have been emphasized in bulimia (Schwartz, Barrett, & Saba, 1985).

Cultural factors (e.g., Crisp, Palmer, & Kalucy, 1976; Schwartz, Thompson, & Johnson, 1982) have received recent emphasis; most significant is the observation that the incidence of these disorders appears to be on the rise (Jones, Fox, Babigian, & Hutton, 1980; Willi & Grossman, 1983) and corresponds to pressure placed on women by the society at large to be thin (Schwartz et al., 1982).

Biological theories also have reappeared.

These focus on hormonal changes that accompany puberty (Garfinkel & Garner, 1982; Leibowitz, 1983; Strober, 1986) and on central nervous system functioning (Wurtman & Wurtman, 1984). The statistical relationship found between eating disorders and affective disorders in first-degree relatives has been used to argue for a genetic component to the disorders (Hudson, Pope, Jonas, & Yurgelun-Todd, 1983).

Bulimia Nervosa

Bulimia, or binge eating, occurs both as a symptom of anorexia nervosa and as a syndrome in itself. Binge eating varies greatly in terms of severity. Some persons consider any overeating to be "binge eating." Operational definitions are needed in order to clarify the meaning of the term. It is difficult, except in the case of the bulimic anorexic, to make judgments regarding historical accounts of bulimic behavior. In early Roman times, vomitoria (public places where people could go to vomit) were described, and Seneca, a Stoic philosopher who lived about 65 A.D., wrote, "Men eat to vomit and vomit to eat" (quoted in Lowenberg, Todhunter, Wilson, Savage, & Lubawski, 1974, p. 45). The public nature of the vomiting, however, is not consistent with the secretiveness of the purging (and bingeing) of today's bulimics. The Babylonian Talmud (see Kaplan & Garfinkel, 1984), written around 400 A.D., describes bulimia as a symptom of various illnesses. Gull (1874) mentioned that a patient with anorexia nervosa had an occasional "voracious" appetite. Janet (1919) noted the occurrence of a cluster of symptoms, including vomiting, bulimia, and mood lability, in one group of anorexic patients. Binswanger's (1958) classic account of Ellen West presents a detailed picture of a life characterized by extreme cycles of gorging and purging, laxative abuse, dramatic vomiting, and violent diarrhea in a woman who was not underweight, although she wished to be.

NATURE OF THE DISORDERS

Definitions and Occurrence

Anorexia nervosa and bulimia nervosa are currently recognized by specific sets of symptoms, according to the revised third edition of the *Diagnostic and Statistical Manual of Mental Disorders* (DSM-III-R) of the American Psychiatric Association (1987). These symptoms are presented in Table 15-1. The central characteristic of anorexia is "drive for thinness." Persons with anorexia strive to lose weight beyond the point of social desirability, attractiveness, and good health. At very low weights, they *deny* that they are too thin and instead declare themselves "too fat." Secondary to this weight loss and near-starvation condition are preoccupation with food, amenorrhea, and a variety of psychological and physiological disturbances. Anorexics are afraid of becoming obese, are often hyperactive, and develop odd

TABLE 15-1. DSM-III-R Diagnostic Criteria for Anorexia Nervosa and Bulimia Nervosa

---

Anorexia Nervosa

A. Refusal to maintain body weight over a minimal normal weight for age and height, e.g., weight loss leading to maintenance of body weight 15% below that expected; or failure to make expected weight gain during period of growth, leading to body weight 15% below that expected.

B. Intense fear of gaining weight or becoming fat, even though underweight.

C. Disturbance in the way in which one's body weight, size, or shape is experienced, e.g., the person claims to "feel fat" even when emaciated, believes that one area of the body is "too fat" even when obviously underweight.

D. In females, absence of at least three consecutive menstrual cycles when otherwise expected to occur (primary or secondary amenorrhea). (A woman is considered to have amenorrhea if her periods occur only following hormone, e.g., estrogen, administration.)

Bulimia Nervosa

A. Recurrent episodes of binge eating (rapid consumption of a large amount of food in a discrete period of time).

B. A feeling of lack of control over eating behavior during the eating binges.

C. The person regularly engages in either self-induced vomiting, use of laxatives or diuretics, strict dieting or fasting, or vigorous exercise in order to prevent weight gain.

D. A minimum average of two binge eating episodes a week for at least three months.

E. Persistent overconcern with body shape and weight.

Note. From *Diagnostic and Statistical Manual of Mental Disorders* (3rd ed., rev.) (pp. 67–69), by American Psychiatric Association, 1987, Washington, DC: Author. Copyright 1987 by the American Psychiatric Association. Reprinted by permission.

eating rituals. Underneath these concerns, according to Bruch (1973), is a deep sense of ineffectiveness and a lack of autonomy.

The salient characteristic of bulimia nervosa is an excessive intake of food, usually high in calories, in a relatively short period of time. The binge eating is generally done in secret; bulimics regard their binge-eating as shameful and perceive their eating behavior as "out of control" while they are bingeing.

Anorexia nervosa begins in early to late adolescence, with a bimodal risk for onset highest at ages 14 and 18 (Halmi, Casper, Eckert, Goldberg, & Davis, 1979), whereas the mean age of onset for bulimia is 17–19 (Agras & Kirkley, 1986; Fairburn & Cooper, 1982; Mitchell, Hatsukami, Eckert, & Pyle, 1985). Both disorders occur in females approximately 90% of the time (Halmi, 1974, 1982; Hay & Leonard, 1979). Anorexia nervosa is most frequently found in the upper socioeconomic classes, although in recent years there has been a shift toward more equal distribution among classes (Eckert, 1985). Approximately 1% of young women have anorexia nervosa (Crisp et al., 1976), and approximately 4%–19% of all young women engage in clinically significant levels of bulimic behavior (Halmi, Falk, & Schwartz, 1981; Pyle et al., 1983; Strangler & Printz, 1980). These rates seem to have increased significantly in the past 10–20 years (Jones et al., 1980; Willi & Grossman, 1983). According to Beumont, Booth, Abraham, Griffiths, and Turner (1983), concern about body weight and fairly reasonable weight control efforts, including dieting, tend to precede the development of eating disorders.

Differential Diagnosis

It has been noted that a variety of psychiatric disorders, although they may involve changes in weight and/or eating behavior, should not be considered eating disorders, and particularly should not be confused with anorexia nervosa (Garfinkel & Kaplan, 1986). In conversion disorders, schizophrenia, and depression, changes in appetite and attitudes toward food are sometimes evident. These disorders can usually be distinguished from anorexia nervosa by the absence of an intense drive for thinness, of a disturbed body image, and of an increased activity level. These symptoms are unique to anorexia nervosa, and thus are the best discriminators. For example, although both anorexics and schizophrenics may avoid specific foods, anorexics will avoid foods because they are high in caloric content, and schizophrenics will avoid foods because they are thought to be "poisoned." Amenorrhea, on the other hand, may occur in each of the disorders.

A reliable classification system for eating disorders does not exist at present; however, a number of diagnostic labels have been popularized. Labels currently used include "anorexia nervosa" (Casper, Eckert, Halmi, Goldberg, & Davis, 1980), "bulimia" (Mitchell & Pyle, 1982), "bulimia nervosa" (Russell, 1979), "bulimarexia" (Boskind-Lodahl & White, 1978), "binge eating" (Abraham & Beumont, 1982), "binge–purge syndrome" (Hawkins, Fremouw & Clement, 1984), "self-induced vomiting" (Rich, 1978), "dietary chaos syndrome" (Palmer, 1979), "psychogenic vomiting" (Rosenthal, Webb, & Wruble, 1980), and "laxative abuse syndrome" (Oster, Materson, & Rogers, 1980). The validity of each as a separate syndrome or entity has not been established. The interrelationships between these possible diagnostic entities are not well known. Of these, only Anorexia Nervosa and Bulimia Nervosa are currently listed as diagnoses in the DSM-III-R (American Psychiatric Association, 1987), and the overlap between these two disorders is significant. Approximately 16%–47% (Casper et al., 1980; Theander, 1970) of anorexia nervosa patients engage in binge eating. Normal-weight and underweight binge-eaters tend to be similar on a number of demographic, clinical, and psychometric variables and to differ from non-binge-eating anorexics (Garner, Garfinkel, & O'Shaughnessy, 1983). Compared to nonbingeing anorexics, bingeing anorexics appear to have greater problems with impulsive behavior and self-control in the form of shoplifting, alcohol and other substance abuse, self-mutilation, sexual activity, and lability of mood (Garfinkel, Moldofsky, & Garner, 1980). Bingeing anorexics are more extraverted (Beumont, 1977), whereas nonbingeing anorexics are more socially withdrawn. Bingeing anorexics have histories of obesity both personally and in their families, show greater childhood maladjustment, have higher rates of familial alcoholism and affective illness, and experience greater conflict and negativity in family relationships (Strober, 1986). Not surprisingly, bingeing anorexics are more difficult to treat and have poorer outcomes

(Garfinkel *et al.*, 1980). As a group, bingeing anorexics have *not* been found to be characterized by low body weight, body image distortion, or marked denial of illness (Casper *et al.*, 1980). In the future, we expect that anorexics routinely will be separated into nonbingeing (or restricting) anorexics and bingeing anorexics.

ETIOLOGY

Given that eating disorders generally begin during the adolescent years, most etiological theories incorporate adolescence and its concomitants as causal factors. "Adolescence" involves biological, social, and psychological changes. Biologically, there are physical changes involving the maturation of the reproductive system, along with a growth spurt. Socially, adolescence is a time of transition between childhood and adulthood. Adolescents begin to assume greater responsibility for their actions and are allowed a larger range of independent action and greater freedom. Not only are they "allowed" greater responsibility and freedom, it is *expected* that they begin to be more self-sufficient and more helpful toward others. New demands and expectations (e.g., a first interpersonal relationship involving sexuality and intimacy, and situations requiring new accomplishments) arise. The impact of these experiences may be thought to be heightened as well, in that, psychologically, adolescence is a time of intense self-scrutiny and awareness. Furthermore, adolescents become more capable of higher levels of abstract thought. It is a time during which identity concerns are of foremost importance; adolescents attempt to answer the question "Who am I?" The biological and social changes and new relationships form a part of the answer to this question. In short, adolescence is a time of great change. Bulimics have a difficult time coping with transitions, including changes in settings, going from school to work, and going from work to home. Certainly the passage from childhood to adulthood—adolescence—is a time of *transition,* in a larger sense of the word. Perhaps this is the difficulty of anorexics as well. Many theorists have focused on particular transitions as being problematic for anorexics—the biological, the social, or the psychological.

The disorders also have been reported as being triggered by traumatic separations and losses (Garner, Garfinkel, Schwartz, & Thompson, 1980; Kalucy, Crisp, & Harding, 1977; Strober, 1981). These have included the breakup of the parental home, death of a parent, going away to college, summer vacation, parental illness, pregnancy in parent or sibling, "family scandal," parental infidelities, or sibling promiscuity (Beumont, Abraham, Argall, George, & Glaun, 1978; Kalucy, Crisp, & Harding, 1977; Theander, 1970). Imagined or actual instances of personal failure have also been noted to precede the illness (Dally, 1969; Halmi, 1974; Rowland, 1970).

Any etiological theory must account for the fact that eating disorders occur predominantly in females. Adolescence is a time of transition for males as well as females, but very few males develop eating disorders. The pressure placed upon females to be thin and attractive may provide a partial explanation; males tend to be evaluated in terms of their actions, or what they do, whereas females tend to be evaluated in terms of their appearance, or how they look. Arguments have also been made regarding the ambivalent, "mixed" messages given females regarding their proper role in society. Although girls are encouraged to be autonomous, they are treated differently from boys from early childhood, and are taught that femininity involves "dependency."

Some physiological or even psychiatric conditions may predispose certain individuals toward these extreme conditions, which may then be compounded by societal contingencies for weight control, particularly in females. Even this may not fully determine who will become anorexic or bulimic; the contribution of cognitive distortions these females may have concerning these societal values for thinness, as well as of family variables that may create or exacerbate these distortions, must also be acknowledged. In sum, we are doubtful that the occurrence of these complex disorders will be explained without an understanding of many relevant dimensions, including the physiological, societal, familial, psychiatric, and psychological. Furthermore, it is highly probable that no narrow definition of the psychological dimension will suffice; our behavioral–systems view includes a recognition and assessment of cognitive factors, emotional regulation and coping skills, and behavioral/environmental contingencies. This view should increase our understanding of the causes of these extreme conditions.

ASSESSMENT

Eating disorders are complex and thus require comprehensive assessment (Foreyt & McGavin, 1988). There is at present no single standardized instrument which thoroughly evaluates each and every one of the components or determinants of the disorders. Figure 15-1 illustrates the range of factors that seem to be relevant to the disorders (Johnson & Pure, 1986).

There are at least four general areas to assess in addition to the eating behavior. Anorexics and bulimics have difficulties with (1) self-regulation, particularly affect regulation (including the identification and expression of feelings); (2) interpersonal skills and relationships; (3) personal identity, self-esteem, and sexual identity; and (4) distorted beliefs and cognitions. These difficulties are generally connected to the disordered eating in rather direct ways. In bulimia, for example, feelings of sadness and anger accompanied by negative, distorted thoughts (self-referential) following negative interpersonal interactions are typical triggers for binges. A thorough analysis of the binge behavior should uncover such associations. In the case of the nonbulimic anorexic, thoughts and feelings associated with the need to lose weight and have control over food reflect similar, basic difficulties, insofar as they equate self-worth with weight loss and deprivation.

The instruments listed below focus primarily on the macroanalysis and microanalysis of the abnormal eating behavior, and also give some attention to individual differences or "personality" factors. Although some of the instruments are quite comprehensive, normative data are not yet available.

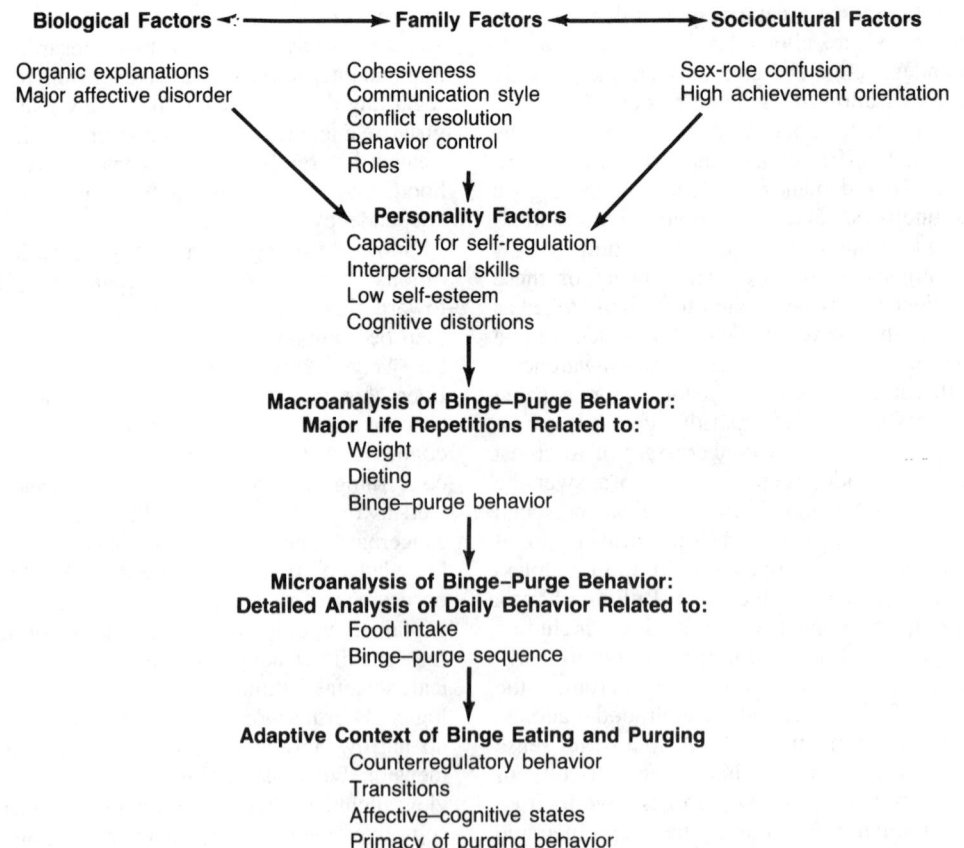

FIGURE 15-1. Assessment outline. From "Assessment of Buiilimia: A Multidimensional Model" (p. 406) by C. Johnson & D. L. Pure, 1986, in K. D. Brownell and J. P. Foreyt (Eds.), *Handbook of Eating Disorders: Physiology, Psychology, and Treatment of Obesity, Anorexia, and Bulimia* (pp. 405–449), New York: Basic Books. Copyright 1986 by Basic Books, Inc. Reprinted by permission.

Eating Disorders Instruments

Several semistructured questionnaires are available to assess the presence and severity of eating disorders. They can be used as self-report or standardized interview instruments. Thus far, there have been no widely available instruments for use with parents or teachers. The Diagnostic Survey for Eating Disorders (DSED) was designed by Johnson (1985) and his colleagues at Northwestern University Medical School. It is a 16-page questionnaire that collects demographic information, as well as information regarding weight and body image, dieting behavior, binge-eating behavior, purging behavior, exercise and related behavior, sexual functioning, menstrual history, and family history. The DSED—Revised (Johnson & Pure, 1986), a somewhat lengthier version (21 smaller-sized pages), is also available. The DSED—Revised contains no new sections, but has additional questions regarding family, feelings during weight loss and gain, physical symptoms, and others. The Eating Disorders Questionnaire (EDQ) of the University of South Florida (Powers, 1984a) is a 24-page instrument that collects demograpahic data, weight history, information on binge-eating and purging, medical history, social history, weight profile, and autobiographical information. The Eating Attitudes Test by Garner and Garfinkel (1979) is also included as a part of the EDQ.

More specialized self-report instruments for anorexia nervosa and bulimia include the Hunger–Satiety Questionnaire by Monello, Seltzer, and Mayer (1965); the Situational Discomfort Scale by Goldberg, Halmi, Casper, Eckert, and Davis (1977); the Goldberg Anorectic Attitude Scale by Goldberg et al. (1980); the Eating Disorders Inventory by Garner, Olmsted, and Polivy (1983); the Binge Eating Scale by Gormally, Black, Daston, and Rardin (1982); and the Binge Scale by Hawkins and Clement (1980). Most of these instruments have been used only for diagnostic/screening or theoretical/research purposes.

For clinical purposes, food diaries can be invaluable. The Self-Monitoring Form (Figure 15-2) by Johnson and Pure (1986) is an expanded version of a food diary that explores mood, activities, physical state, interpersonal climate, feelings about eating, and alcohol intake, as well as food intake. Patients are encouraged to fill out this questionnaire four times daily for at least 1 week during the assessment phase of treatment and periodically thereafter.

Two instruments utilize professional reports. The Anorexic Behavior Scale (ABS) by Slade (1973) is a 22-item scale that requires professionals to make judgments ("yes," "no," or "?") regarding hospitalized patients' resistance to eating, disposal of food, and activity. The Psychiatric Rating Scale for Anorexia Nervosa by Goldberg et al. (1977) is a 14-item scale that is typically completed by nursing or other professional staff members. Most of the items on these scales assume a psychiatric or psychodynamic orientation. The items on the ABS are intended to reflect the major descriptive and psychopathological features of anorexia nervosa: denial of illness, fear of fat, thin ideal body image, loss of appetite, selective appetite, fear of becoming a compulsive eater, desire for activity, desire to control, manipulativeness, depression, obsessiveness, immaturity, purgative and diuretic abuse, and exaggerated cheerfulness (Slade, 1973).

Assessment of the Family Environment

The family unit is perhaps the most critical learning place for the development of interpersonal roles and skills. The roles within the family need to change as children grow and mature. As children reach and progress through adolescence, they struggle with identity concerns and need to see themselves as separate, independent persons. In order to do that, they begin to reject childish roles and dependency upon parents and family and to assert themselves. Frequently this happens in a rebellious fashion. This is a difficult time for all concerned, parents as well as children/adolescents. Eating disorders halt or twist this developmental process. The bingeing or food refusal can serve to meet the needs of a child to grow and become more independent, and at the same time preserves and tightens close parent–child ties. In fact, eating problems typically bring forth increased involvement between parents and children. Conceptualized in this way, eating problems represent a pseudosolution to the task of adolescence.

The question remains, however, why some children (usually girls), who are entering adolescence or progressing from adolescence into young adulthood adopt this pseudosolution while others do not. These families seem to differ from families without eating-disordered adolescents in their cohesiveness, roles, com-

Date:_____ Time:_____ A.M./P.M.

What were you thinking about?_____

_____

Where are you?_____

_____

What was the *main* thing you were doing?_____

	Not at All	Somewhat	Quite	Very
How much choice did you have in selecting this activity?	+ --- + --- + --- + --- + --- + --- + --- + --- + --- +
Did you feel in control of your activity?	+ --- + --- + --- + --- + --- + --- + --- + --- + --- +
How guilty did you feel?	+ --- + --- + --- + --- + --- + --- + --- + --- + --- +
How vulnerable did you feel?	+ --- + --- + --- + --- + --- + --- + --- + --- + --- +
How self-conscious were you?	+ --- + --- + --- + --- + --- + --- + --- + --- + --- +
How much were you concentrating?	+ --- + --- + --- + --- + --- + --- + --- + --- + --- +
How satisfied did you feel with yourself?	+ --- + --- + --- + --- + --- + --- + --- + --- + --- +

    0   1   2   3   4   5   6   7   8   9

Describe your mood:

	Very	Quite	Some	Neither	Some	Quite	Very	
Alert	0	o	.	—	.	o	0	Drowsy
Happy	0	o	.	—	.	o	0	Sad
Irritable	0	o	.	—	.	o	0	Cheerful
Strong	0	o	.	—	.	o	0	Weak
Angry	0	o	.	—	.	o	0	Friendly
Active	0	o	.	—	.	o	0	Passive
Lonely	0	o	.	—	.	o	0	Sociable
Adequate	0	o	.	—	.	o	0	Inadequate
Free	0	o	.	—	.	o	0	Constrained
Excited	0	o	.	—	.	o	0	Bored
Proud	0	o	.	—	.	o	0	Ashamed
Confused	0	o	.	—	.	o	0	Clear
Tense	0	o	.	—	.	o	0	Relaxed
Fat	0	o	.	—	.	o	0	Thin

Describe your physical state:

	None	Slight	Moderate	Severe
Hungry	+ -- + -- + -- + -- + -- + -- + -- + -- + -- + --
Tired, slowed down	+ -- + -- + -- + -- + -- + -- + -- + -- + -- + --
Aches and pains	+ -- + -- + -- + -- + -- + -- + -- + -- + -- + --

Who were you with?

( ) Alone
( ) Brother(s), sister(s)
( ) Mother
( ) Father
( ) Strangers
( ) Coworkers

( ) Friend(s) :
    Number _____
( ) Male
( ) Female
( ) Other(s): _____

Describe how you feel about one of the persons you are with. (If alone and thinking about someone, describe feelings about that person.)

	Very	Middle	Very	
Close to	+ --- + --- + --- + --- + --- + --- + --- + --- + --- +	Distant from
Inferior to	+ --- + --- + --- + --- + --- + --- + --- + --- + --- +	Superior to
Friendly toward	+ --- + --- + --- + --- + --- + --- + --- + --- + --- +	Angry with
In control of	+ --- + --- + --- + --- + --- + --- + --- + --- + --- +	Controlled by

(Identify the person you are referring to: _____)

	Not at All	Somewhat	Quite	Very
How preoccupied were you with eating?	+ --- + --- + --- + --- + --- + --- + --- + --- + --- +			
Do you feel your eating has been out of control since the last report?	+ --- + --- + --- + --- + --- + --- + --- + --- + --- +			
How confident did you feel that you could resist the urge to binge-eat?	+ --- + --- + --- + --- + --- + --- + --- + --- + --- +			

0   1   2   3   4   5   6   7   8   9

Indicate your alcohol intake since the last report:

Beer		_Wine_		_Liquor_	
Number of Units		Number of Units		Number of Units	
_____	cans (12 oz.)	_____	glasses (10 oz.)	_____	shots (1½ oz.)
_____	bottles (12 oz.)	_____	fifths (26 oz.)	_____	drinks (1½ oz.)
_____	glasses (10 oz.)	_____	quarts (32 oz.)	_____	pints (16 oz.)
				_____	fifths (26 oz.)
				_____	quarts (32 oz.)

Indicate your food intake since the last report:

Type	Quantity
_____	_____
_____	_____
_____	_____
_____	_____

How many times have you binged since the last report? _____

How many times have you purged since the last report? _____

FIGURE 15-2. Self-monitoring form. From "Assessment of Bulimia: A Multidimensional Model" (pp. 440–441) by C. Johnson and D. L. Pure, 1986, in K. D. Brownell and J. P. Foreyt (Eds.), *Handbook of Eating Disorders: Physiology, Psychology, and Treatment of Obesity, Anorexia, and Bulimia* (pp. 405–449), New York: Basic Books. Copyright 1986 by Basic Books, Inc. Reprinted by permission.

munication style, and conflict resolution (Johnson & Pure, 1986). Thus, it seems prudent to assess these characteristics. "Cohesiveness" refers to how close family members are to one another—how much independence or "separateness" is encouraged/permitted. If family members have little privacy and there is little distinction between roles and functions, this adds confusion and conflict. Roles and functions should be somewhat different, given the inevitable differences in terms of age and talents of family members. On the other hand, if the boundaries are very rigid and family members have little in common, this can mean little sense of community and—for the children—a push toward autonomy and independence before they are ready for it. "Communication" refers to the way information is sent and received. Messages can be delivered and responded to directly or indirectly. Indirect communication is often used to invalidate or qualify overt messages. For example, with anorexics,

parents may tell their daughters to "grow up" and "obey us" at the same time, perhaps not recognizing that one way of growing up is to become less obedient and more independent. "Conflict resolution" refers to the manner in which conflict is handled; assessment of conflict resolution generally focuses on the conflict within the marital unit. The eating-disordered patient may not know how to cope with conflict in a direct manner and may have been taught to avoid conflict (and anger) at all costs. Parents frequently are in conflict over how to "help" the eating-disordered patient. Fathers frequently take a harsh, disciplinary role, while mothers take a more nurturant, appeasing role. In order to avoid direct conflict, parents may each try to appeal to the child to support their posture ("triangulation"), or parents may set aside their conflicts superficially in order to protect or blame their sick child ("detouring").

Strober and Yager (1985) assess the following when meeting with parents and families:

- Individual perceptions of their children (e.g., strengths, weaknesses) and aspects of each child's behavior they admire or find troublesome.
- Their aspirations for the children.
- Their views on adolescence (e.g., emancipation, contacts outside the home, sexuality).
- Impact of their daughter's illness on the family life style, marital relationship, and family relations generally (e.g., activation of separation fears, abandonment, etc.).
- Their own personal–developmental histories (early self-esteem and maturational problems, relationship with parents and siblings, ongoing intergenerational problems).
- Familial psychiatric disorders.
- General organizational structure of the family (e.g., power structure, parental coalitions, clarity of boundaries, efficiency of problem solving and negotiation, clarity of expression of individual thoughts and emotions, responsibility for individual actions, degree of emotional closeness among members, expressiveness, general emotional tone, degree and intensity of conflict, and degree of empathic responsiveness; see Lewis, 1978). (p. 377)

In most cases, the patient's actions and abilities (or inabilities) have considerable impact upon the family, and vice versa. Thus, it is useful for the therapist to entertain the question "How might X symptom function in an adaptive way in this family?" Obviously, the disordered eating of a family member is going to be experienced by or have some impact on the rest of the family. The role the family plays in the maintenance of the problem, and how family members might be involved in treatment, should also be considered. If the problematic behavior is seen to be maintained by the reactions it engenders, or if stimuli for problematic behavior are identified within the family, family therapy should be considered. This may mean that the parents are simply worried about their child's medical status and that worry may play an important role in the parents' marital relationship, or that the problem child may *perceive* her eating behavior to play a role in their relationship.* More obviously, when parents' willingness to comply with treatment is questionable, family therapy is indicated.

Before concluding this section, it is crucial to note that the manner in which these dimensions are assessed is of the utmost importance. Fami

---

*Because the vast majority of patients with eating disorders are females, feminine pronouns are used in this chapter to refer to such patients.

lies, particularly parents and the afflicted child, are frightened that they are to blame for the disorder. Questions about the areas listed above, if poorly worded or delivered, can arouse thoughts and feelings that are very counterproductive to the establishment of a working therapeutic alliance with patient or parents. Thus, at the outset, the clinician may be wise to tell the family that he or she does *not* view them as deserving blame, but that if therapy is to succeed, all of their support and guidance will be needed. Even if they are not part of the "problem," they may be part of the "solution."

Assessment of Relationships and Environment Outside the Family

Although adolescence and adulthood imply leaving the family, they also imply going to or joining outside networks, girlfriends, boyfriends, peers, colleagues, and the world at large. It is reasonable to assume that there is an underinvolvement in this realm corresponding to the overinvolvement at home. Moreover, interpersonal effectiveness outside of one's family of origin may become increasingly important as one enters adolescence and adulthood. There are data to suggest that anorexics and bulimics have serious interpersonal difficulties. Of 102 consecutive patients seen by Crisp, Hsu, Harding, and Hartshorn (1980), 23 were excessively shy, and 43 had few or no friends during childhood. This difficulty may persist during and after the illness. A review of 700 outcome studies of anorexics (Schwartz & Thompson, 1981) found that only 47% of anorexics had married or were maintaining active heterosexual lives. Bulimic patients report that their problems with eating and weight interfere "a great deal" with their social relationships (94%) and school or job performance (84%) (Leon, Carroll, Chernyk, & Finn, 1985). Bulimic behavior also leads to decreased social contact (Johnson & Larson, 1982). If these disorders are to be thoroughly assessed, it consequently becomes important to assess the level and extent of a client's current social functioning.

Medical Assessment

All eating-disordered patients should be assessed medically. A complete review of the medical assessment of anorexia nervosa and bulimia nervosa is beyond the scope of this chapter. For such, the reader is referred to excellent comprehensive reviews by Mitchell (1985, 1986a, 1986b). A standard medical assessment should include physical examination, standard laboratory tests, multiple-channel chemistry analysis, complete blood count, and urinalysis. The systems that should be reviewed include endocrinological/metabolic, cardiovascular, renal, gastrointestinal, hematological, and pulmonary. The clinician should be alert to complaints of weakness, tiredness, constipation, and depression, which can be produced by electrolyte abnormalities (Webb & Gehi, 1981)—a complication of vomiting and purgative abuse.

The medical assessment is used, among other things, to determine whether hospitalization is necessary. Hospitalization is useful for nutritional rehabilitation and general medical care. Criteria for inpatient treatment have been outlined by Andersen (1986) and Powers (1984b):

1. Significant weight loss (15%–25% below normal weight or more), particularly if the weight loss has been recent and rapid, and severe starvation symptoms.
2. Medical instabilities and metabolic abnormalities, especially hypokalemic alkalosis from bulimic complications.
3. Overriding psychiatric problems involving clinical depression and/or thoughts or intents of suicide.
4. Nonresponsiveness to outpatient treatment (after 3–4 months).
5. Demoralized, nonfunctioning family.
6. Lack of outpatient facilities.

TREATMENT

The treatment of eating disorders is in its infancy; the scientific merit of the various approaches remains to be explored and established. We review here approaches that have and have not been rigorously examined, in the hope that future research will be done to validate and refine the methods of some of our experienced clinicians. Treatments range from individual approaches (including individual psychotherapy and psychopharmacology) to family therapy, group psychotherapy, and intensive programs involving all of the preceding plus coping skills training, assertiveness training, training in women's issues, and nutritional education— either in inpatient settings, outpatient settings, or both. Team approaches are becoming in-

creasingly popular. The primary issues in each of these modalities, along with adjunctive techniques, are reviewed.

The approaches and techniques listed below are designed specifically for the treatment of anorexia nervosa and bulimia nervosa, although some have been used with other target problems as well. At present, little evidence exists regarding the comparative efficacy of any of these techniques, either combined or used separately. We advocate the use of multicomponent, multidisciplinary approaches to the treatment of eating disorders. Although various components of these programs have been highlighted here, it should not be assumed that any of these components represents an entire treatment, unless this is stated explicitly. Future research will be needed to refine the use of these techniques.

Ethical issues surrounding assessment and treatment of eating-disordered patients, such as involuntary commitment, tube feeding, consultation with professionals in other disciplines, patients' rights regarding information about treatment, and specialized competency of therapists, have yet to be resolved. Not every clinician should attempt to treat these patients without specific training in these disorders.

Individual Psychotherapy

In individual psychotherapy, we believe that the cornerstones of the treatment, both philosophically and pragmatically, are flexibility and sensitivity. Therapeutic programs need to be tailored to individuals in terms of speed, content, and style. Anorexic patients can be quite recalcitrant or even excessively dependent in therapy. These patients can be especially draining on therapists, particularly on those who carry a heavy caseload of them. Their treatment is often long-term and may involve periodic regressions. The therapist must respond flexibly to changes in patients' level of organization and maturity (Goodsitt, 1985). Although patients should be allowed as much independence as they can possibly manage, the therapist should not make the mistake of assuming a false mask of self-sufficiency to be real, and should be ready to step in and take over as necessary.

The therapist must also be continually aware of the trust-building aspects of the relationship (Levenkron, 1983). The patient must experience that the therapist is interested in helping her and listens to what *she* has to say (Bruch, 1985). If the patient is pressured into therapy by her family, for example, motivation and trust will be essentially nonexistent until the patient sees therapy as helpful to her. Thus, one of the initial steps in the establishment of a therapeutic relationship is the development of a frame for therapy that is acceptable to the patient and to the therapist. This can only be done by listening closely to the patient's concerns and presenting therapy in a way that is perceived as benefiting the client. Inquiry into the side effects of starvation, such as sleep disturbance, irritability, depression, preoccupation with food, and social withdrawal; and alienation, may help establish a common ground between a therapist and an unwilling patient. The therapist should take care to provide a rationale that does not place blame upon either the patient or the patient's family for the disorder. Bruch (1985) tells patients early in therapy that their illness—their preoccupation with eating and weight—is a cover-up for their doubt about their own self-worth and value. As Goodsitt (1985) describes it, the therapist explains

> that he [sic] is asking her to give up a major defense that has served important protective functions for her. He expects her to feel anxious. He asks her to sit with her anxiety (while he sits with her). He explains that asking her to give up an adaptive defense is like asking a person who cannot swim to let go of the life preserver and try swimming. The danger is drowning. . . . The therapist may point out that it is really a choice she must make. She may continue to desperately hold on to what seems a life preserver to her (i.e., her illness), and continue to feel some temporary relief in not eating. She can also expect to continue her lonely, miserable, suffering life unchanged. On the other hand, . . . she can choose to let go and take a chance on eating—and life. Clearly, by doing so, she is entering a forbidden unknown. He knows that she has little faith in her capacity to relate to others or to live an enjoyable or satisfying life of her own. She may have good reason, based on past experience, not to be optimistic about her future. If this is the case, the therapist should acknowledge that. But the therapist tells the patient that he is committed to seeing that she learn the skills (ego and self functions) she needs to make her life better. (p. 64)

In addition to supporting the patient by pointing out the positive, and in some ways adaptive, functions of the symptoms, we emphasize an additional five components of therapy: (1) thorough information gathering regarding the parameters and history of the disorder, ranging from concrete data regarding weight and amounts of food consumed to social and family functioning; (2) the need to help the eating-disordered patient learn to become aware of, identify, and express her emotional and inner life in more constructive ways; (3) the need to bolster self-esteem and to take into account the severe self-doubts and low self-esteem of the eating-disordered patient; (4) education of the patient regarding the physiology and psychology of starvation, purging, and binge eating; and, as mentioned above, (5) emphasizing therapy as a way to help the patient get what she wants and thereby minimize issues of coercion and control.

Inpatient Approaches

Hospitalization is not so much an approach as it is a setting in which many therapeutic techniques and procedures can be conducted under close supervision. Most hospital programs are multidisciplinary and obviously have many therapeutic components, including outpatient therapy and follow-up services. Psychiatry, psychology, nursing, dietetics, occupational therapy, physical therapy, social services, and general medicine services may be involved with the same patient using a team approach. Several programs have been described in the literature, including the Eating Disorders Program at the University of South Florida College of Medicine (Powers, 1984b; Powers & Powers, 1984); the Meyer 4 Unit at Johns Hopkins Medical School (Andersen, 1986; Andersen, Morse, & Santmyer, 1985); the program at Toronto General Hospital and the University of Toronto (Garfinkel & Garner, 1982); and the Teenage Eating Disorders Program and Adult Outpatient Eating Disorders Program, Neuropsychiatric Institute, University of California at Los Angeles (Strober & Yager, 1985). Treatment programs that explicitly combine both outpatient and inpatient components include the Eating Disorders Clinic, Psychiatry Department, University of Cincinnati Medical Center (Wooley & Wooley, 1985) and the Eating Disorders Clinic, Department of Psychiatry, University of Minnesota (Eckert & Labeck, 1985).

Each member of the team contributes to the therapy and management of the patient. In reviewing the different hospital programs, one finds, however, that each takes a different approach to the questions of what professions or disciplines are represented on the team and what roles the different professionals play. The roles are not neatly dictated by disciplines. With this in mind, we present the "roles" of each of the members on a typical treatment team.

1. Psychiatrists prescribe and monitor psychotropic medications, do intake evaluations, and, depending upon training and interest, may provide individual and family therapy. Given the structure and tradition of hospitals, psychiatrists also tend to occupy administrative and directorial positions on such wards.

2. Psychologists provide psychological and family evaluations, devise treatment plans, and conduct individual, group, and family therapy. If behavioral management contracts are developed, it is often a psychologist who does this. Powers and Powers (1984) recommend that the person administering the behavioral management program *not* be responsible for the anorexic's psychotherapy. The anorexic is often very angry about the program and may well have difficulty relating positively to the person administering it.

3. A medical consultant is needed to take careful histories and conduct physical examinations as a part of the evaluation process (especially in cases of atypical presentation), to conduct laboratory screenings and possibly neurological assessments, and to monitor patients' medical stability.

4. The nursing staff implements the treatment plans, enforces the rules, supervises the meals, and monitors the patients after eating (to prevent purging). The nursing staff has the most difficult and often the least rewarding role, and consequently should be given periodic progress reports to foster enthusiasm (Powers & Powers, 1984).

5. Dietitians and nutritionists help patients to plan meals and educate patients regarding nutrition and calories. Kalucy, Gilchrist, Mc-Farlane, and McFarlane (1985) have found the role of dietitians to be a problematic one, but not one without solutions. Dietitians, because of the milieu of their profession, tend to endorse a nutritional philosophy very similar to that held by anorexics; the profession emphasizes the deleterious effects of being overweight, the "badness" of refined carbohydrates, and the "goodness" of bran, fruit, and fresh vegetables, for example. Kalucy et al. (1985) conclude that dietitians must develop some psychotherapeutic skills and learn to ignore some of the traditional philosophies of their profession. They also

point out the danger of hiring a female dietitian—as well as a nurse, social worker, or doctor—who is herself anorexic.

Hospitalization generally lasts between 2 and 4 months (Andersen et al., 1985; Powers, 1984b; Powers & Powers, 1984). The admission process involves negotiation with the patient and family. Toward this end, preadmission tours and contracts (Andersen et al., 1985; Powers & Powers, 1984) help to allay concerns and smooth the transition. The program should be clearly explained so that patients and their families know what to expect. They should be given an opportunity to talk with other patients, and are allowed to ask the staff questions. They should be told what to expect in terms of their diet and its management, in particular. Some programs require that patients sign statements promising that they will comply with all aspects of the programs, and are told that they will be expected to "take food" as if it were a prescribed medication (Andersen et al., 1985). Patients may also be more ready to enter the program if they are assured that the staff will not allow them to become overweight.

Refeeding tends to begin with a diet of 1,200–1,500 calories per day, distributed across three meals. This is gradually increased by 500–750 calories a week to 3,500–5,000 calories per day. Powers (1984b) reports that the University of South Florida program has established limits on the duration of meals, and that if a meal is not consumed in an appropriate amount of time, patients may be given a liquid meal for their next meal. If patients fail to consume the liquid, they can be tube-fed. Andersen et al. (1985) claim never to have needed to use tube feedings with their more than 170 patients; others (Powers, 1984b) report using tube feedings infrequently and almost never more than once with any particular patient. If this procedure is to be used, this plan should be clearly explained to the patient upon admission.

Goal Weights

Staff members typically set an initial goal weight for a patient by consulting weight charts (e.g., Frisch & McArthur, 1974; Metropolitan Life Insurance Company, 1984). When set, the goal weight takes the form of a 3- to 5-pound range. Andersen et al. (1985) make this decision as a staff after several weeks of treatment, and modify the goal weight range depending upon the patient's appearance. However, patients are not informed of their goal weight until they are in the middle of the established range. It is helpful to keep patients hospitalized for approximately 2 weeks after they have reached their goal weight, in order to help them become comfortable maintaining that weight, and to provide a supportive environment when they fear they may continue to gain weight and become obese.

Special Problems

Special problems associated with hospitalization have been discussed in detail by Garfinkel, Garner, and Kennedy (1985). These are outlined below.

Problems with Patients.
1. Patients may refuse to cooperate with the treatment program, because they feel they have no problem and do not want to change.
2. Patients may believe that others want to control them rather than help them; they may also mistrust themselves or fear that they cannot control themselves.
3. Severe depression may be present.
4. Anorexic patients may compete for staff time or "specialness" by virtue of being the most seriously ill.
5. Attitudes of nonanorexic patients toward anorexic patients may be problematic. Since anorexic patients require more staff time, other patients tend to feel neglected and angry.
6. Medical complications may arise. Anorexic patients are, or can become, seriously physically ill; consequently, they pose special concerns to staff members accustomed to dealing primarily with psychiatric problems.

Problems with Families.
1. Families may encourage the patient to resist treatment or push for a premature discharge.
2. Patients and parents may fear separation.

Staff Problems.
1. Staff members may become frustrated and angry with a patient's resistance and repeat the family's attempt to punish the patient; or, conversely, they may avoid confrontation, may not be consistently firm, or may allow the patient to be manipulative.
2. Staff members may become polarized around various issues because of the

anorexic's tendency to view people and situations as "all good" or "all bad."

Admission Problems.
Problems with admission to the hospital have been discussed by Kalucy et al. (1985). Their group typically conducts preadmission assessments over several weeks, and states that patients and families often try to circumvent this process by presenting in a state of crisis. The support system may have been driven to a state of rage, despair, and impotence, or the patient may feel that she has lost control of her eating and will become obese if not admitted immediately. Kalucy et al. have found that these families and patients will agree to anything to escape the crisis, but that once hospitalization has occurred and the crisis has been smoothed over, motivation and compliance are minimal. Thus, except in cases of medical and psychiatric emergencies, they insist that routine assessment procedures be followed. If the patient is in a medical crisis characterized by confusion, disorientation, and memory disturbance, or in a psychiatric emergency (e.g., a suicidal depression), then she is hospitalized on an emergency basis and is stabilized. She is not admitted into the eating disorders program, however; after she is stabilized, she is re-evaluated and may or may not be admitted to the program. In some cases, patients are discharged with outpatient services.

Some admission problems can be circumvented by not considering hospitalization as an "all-or-none" decision. Kalucy et al. (1985), for example, describe four hospitalization alternatives, each with different aims, ranging from very short-term stays with limited goals to protracted inpatient stays. If a patient is in an extreme state of emaciation, a short-term admission is recommended as a life-saving procedure. A second option is presented to patients whose eating behavior is "substantially out of control" and who are psychologically and socially in a state of chaos. They are considered for a short-term admission in order to stabilize and restore physical and metabolic well-being (e.g., to treat hypokalemia). A third alternative is a 1-month hospitalization, which is used to establish a therapeutic alliance, complete a thorough assessment, and establish a reasonable set of rules about eating and diet for orderly weight gain. This alternative is considered as a prelude to outpatient therapy, as a compromise for patients who need more than a short stay but less than a protracted stay. Finally, the fourth option involves a protracted inpatient stay with strict bed rest until target weight is reached, followed by progressive mobilization, psychological work, and relaxation of controls dependent upon the quality of the psychotherapeutic relationship. One-third of Kalucy's group's patients (Kalucy *et al.*, 1985) then pursue intensive individual psychotherapy for 6–24 months after hospitalization, while 10% receive longer and more intensive therapy.

Multicomponent Outpatient Treatment Programs

Intensive, multicomponent outpatient treatment programs are becoming increasingly popular for the treatment of bulimia and anorexia (Lacey, 1985; Mitchell, Hatsukami, Goff, *et al.*, 1985; Wooley & Kearney-Cooke, 1986). These programs typically combine educational seminars, group psychotherapy, individual psychotherapy, family therapy, and body image therapy, incorporating many of the themes discussed above and utilizing many of the techniques outlined below.

The Eating Disorders Clinic in the Psychiatry Department of the University of Cincinnati Medical Center offers an intensive treatment program (Wooley & Kearney-Cooke, 1986). The women are seen daily for 6–8 hours of therapy, in groups of six, for 3½ weeks while they are housed in a nearby hotel. (The program is designed for women who are from out of town.) One group of 18 patients treated in this program was followed up 12 months after termination; of the 16 patients contacted, 7 were entirely free of binge–purge behaviors. The other 9 showed an average reduction in binge behavior of 85% (range, 63% to 94%). These patients also showed improvement on psychometric tests and general life adaptation.

Techniques and Therapy Components

Operant Conditioning Techniques

Operant conditioning techniques have been used to facilitate weight gain (Bachrach, Erwin, & Mohr, 1965; Lang, 1965; Leitenberg, Agras, & Thompson, 1968) in hospital settings. These techniques use positive and negative contingencies (either social praise, hospital rewards, and/or earlier or later discharge) in association with a performance criterion (either eating or weight gain). In the case of anorexia nervosa, this criterion is generally a predetermined weight. This requires that the therapist have control over the contingencies, and hospitalization is thus necessary. Although it can produce initial and rapid weight gains, this procedure has not been shown to be any more effective than other treatments in long-term weight maintenance, nor to be any better than simple hospital programs with discharge contingent on weight gains (Garfinkel *et al.*, 1977). It has been concluded that operant conditioning techniques are helpful but inadequate (Bemis, 1978).

Treatment must also deal with the personal problems regarding feelings, thoughts, and interpersonal relationships. For these problems, many of the techniques employed in outpatient treatment programs have been recommended, including social skills training, assertiveness training, relaxation exercises, and video techniques (Agras & Werne, 1977); these are reviewed in a later section of this chapter.

Cognitive Techniques

Cognitive retraining or restructuring techniques combat distorted body image, erroneous beliefs and assumptions, and misinterpretations of environmental "messages" (Beck, 1976). Anorexics and bulimics may judge their self-worth solely in terms of shape and weight. Examples of cognitive distortions (Fairburn, Cooper, & Cooper, 1986) include the following:

- "To be fat is to be a failure, unattractive, and unhappy."
- "To be thin is to be successful, attractive, and happy."
- "To exert self-control is a sign of strength and discipline."

These ideas are obviously present in the culture; therapy consequently involves questioning of social values. It is helpful to emphasize that these statements are overgeneralizations, and that although they may be true to some degree, they are not absolute or universal truths. Common categories of cognitive disturbances have been detailed by Garner (1986), Garner and Bemis (1982), and Fernandez (1984). These are presented in Table 15-2. Teaching patients to label cognitive distortions as such can help them combat these thoughts.

An extensive listing of cognitive techniques

is provided by Garner and Bemis (1985). These include articulation of beliefs, decentering, de-catastrophizing, challenging the "shoulds," challenging beliefs through behavioral exercises, prospective hypothesis testing, reattribution techniques, palliative techniques (parroting and distraction), and challenging cultural values regarding shape (see Table 15-3). Garner and Bemis (1985) also help patients to improve their self-esteem by encouraging them to explore their interests and to develop a more complex view of self. To accomplish this, these authors praise small signs of independent and competent functioning, including risk taking, reasonable self-expression, assertiveness, flexibility, the pursuit of purely pleasurable activities, and even "healthy" noncompliance. Once deficits in emotions, sensations, and thoughts are identified, new responses are practiced.

Self-monitoring, stimulus control, and cognitive restructuring have been used by Grinc (1982), who reported a case of a 26-year-old normal-weight bulimic woman. Each of the

TABLE 15-2. Cognitive Distortions

Cognitive disturbance	Examples in regard to food
Selective abstraction, or basing a conclusion on isolated details while ignoring contradictory and more salient evidence.	"I just can't control myself. Last night when I had dinner in a restaurant, I ate everything I was served although I had decided ahead of time that I was going to be very careful. I am so weak." "The only way that I can be in control is through eating." "I am special if I am thin."
Overgeneralization, or extracting a rule on the basis of one event and applying it to the other dissimilar situations.	"When I used to eat carbohydrates, I was fat; therefore, I must avoid them now so I won't become obese." "I used to be a normal weight, and I wasn't happy. So I *know* gaining weight isn't going to make be feel better."
Magnification, or overestimation of the significance of undesirable consequent events. Stimuli are embellished with surplus meaning not supported by an objective analysis.	"Gaining five pounds would push me over the brink." "I've gained two pounds, so I can't wear shorts any more." "If others comment on my weight I won't be able to stand it."
Dichotomous or all-or-none reasoning, or thinking in extreme and absolute terms. Events can be only black or white, right or wrong, good or bad.	"If I'm not in complete control, I lose all control. If I can't master this area of my life, I'll lose everything." "If I gain one pound, I'll go on and gain a hundred pounds." "If I don't establish a daily routine, everything will be chaotic and I won't accomplish anything."
Personalization and self-reference, or egocentric interpretations of impersonal events or overinterpretation of events relating to the self.	"Two people laughed and whispered something to each other when I walked by. They were probably saying that I looked unattractive. I *have* gained three pounds." "I am embarrassed when other people see me eat." "When I see someone who is overweight, I worry that I will be like her."
Superstitious thinking, or believing in the cause–effect relationship of noncontingent events.	"If I eat a sweet it will be converted instantly into stomach fat." "I can't enjoy anything because it will be taken away."

Note. From "A Cognitive–Behavioral Approach to Anorexia Nervosa" by D. M. Garner and K. M. Bemis, 1982, *Cognitive Therapy and Research, 6,* 123–150. Copyright 1982 by Plenum Publishing Corporation. Reprinted by permission.

components was introduced sequentially. Treatment lasted 7 months; sessions were weekly at first and became less frequent later. Self-monitoring and stimulus control procedures were introduced in the second session, and vomiting decreased from 12 episodes per week to 3 per week; then, at the fifth session, cognitive restructuring was introduced. Two weeks after this introduction (by week 9), the vomiting had ceased altogether. There were several relapses 3 months later (weeks 18–22), but at a follow-up 1 year after the beginning of therapy (week 52), the patient reported that she had not vomited in 5 months.

Systematic Desensitization

Systematic desensitization has been used to decrease anxiety related to fears of gaining weight and/or being criticized (Hallsten, 1965; Lang, 1965; Ollendick, 1979), self-deprecating thoughts (Monti, McCrady, & Barlow, 1977), and changes in physical appearance concomitant with weight gain (Schnurer, Rubin, & Roy, 1973).

Social Skills Training

Social role identification and skills training are used to help correct the deficits in social skills,

TABLE 15-3. Cognitive Techniques

Articulation of beliefs

The therapist simply asks the patient to state her belief(s). The therapist may then need to clarify and condense the statement. The irrationality of some beliefs becomes obvious merely upon verbalization; in other cases, challenges to distorted beliefs will require repetition and repeated reinforcement.

Decentering

With patients who feel that others are constantly aware of and evaluating their weight or behavior, decentering involves asking them whether they are as aware of others as they think others are of them. The therapist may ask whether the patient is aware of how much the therapist's weight has fluctuated over the past session or two and what such changes mean to the patient, or whether the patient scrutinizes what others eat.

Decastrophizing

To combat anxiety resulting from the exaggeration of the negative consequences of an event, the therapist can ask what realistically might happen if the particular event were to occur.

Challenging the "shoulds"

This involves questioning the oppressive, tyrannical internal imperatives generated by patients, often using the words "must," "ought," and "should."

Challenging beliefs through behavioral exercises

Behavioral assignments or personal experiments can be used to point out the inaccuracy of various beliefs.

Prospective hypothesis testing

Beliefs can be translated into formal hypotheses, and experiments can be designed to evaluate the validity of the hypotheses, perhaps by asking people their views.

Reattribution techniques

Patients can be taught to recognize that certain of their beliefs are a consequence of their illness, and therefore that they cannot trust their own thoughts or feelings around certain issues about which their illness causes them to be inaccurate.

Palliative techniques

In "parroting," patients are taught to repeat positive coping statements regarding themselves and their capabilities, and to engage in distracting activities when they become anxious.

Challenging cultural values regarding shape

Patients are encouraged to examine for themselves the validity of the cultural preferences for thinness among women and encouraged to develop more realistic attitudes toward shape by persuasion, questioning, or review.

Note. Adapted from "Cognitive Therapy for Anorexia Nervosa" (pp. 118–124) by D. M Garner and K. M. Bemis, 1985, in D. M. Garner and P. E. Garfinkel (Eds.), *Handbook of Psychotherapy for Anorexia Nervosa and Bulimia* (pp. 107–146). New York: Guilford Press. Copyright 1985 by Guilford Press. Adapted by permission.

assertiveness, interpersonal communication, and basic problem-solving capabilities frequently observed in anorexics and bulimics. Improving such skills may be necessary for patients to develop a greater sense of self-control and become more effective in living. A first step is to identify their basic roles and postures in life and what those roles communicate to and elicit from others. Before giving up the old ways of interacting, they may need to become clearer on how their current nonassertiveness (and aggressiveness) is both beneficial and protective.

Social skills training was used in one study to try to modify the social isolation and interpersonal anxiety of anorexics (Pillay & Crisp, 1981). Anorexics have difficulty distinguishing their own motivations and desires from the expectations of others; social skills training can be useful in exploring this distinction. In the study, one group of hospitalized anorexics received the social skills training, and another group was placed in a placebo condition. At 1-year follow-up, the social skills group did not differ significantly from the placebo-treated group in terms of weight, but they were less likely to terminate treatment and reported a more rapid decrease in their levels of anxiety, depression, and fear of negative evaluation.

Pharmacological Treatment

Anorexia Nervosa. Pharmacological treatments typically have been used as one component of multicomponent programs for anorexia nervosa. Andersen et al. (1985), for example, use antianxiety medication (usually 0.5 mg of lorazepam [Ativan]) during the first 2 weeks of hospitalization with approximately half of their patients. Patients are told that the medication is used to help them to be able to make choices with less anxiety. Andersen et al. (1985) argue that the use of medications to stimulate appetite is misguided, in that appetite is not disturbed in anorexics. They refrain from using antidepressant medications until a patient has attained normal weight, and then use them only if the patient meets the criteria for a major depressive disorder.

A recent double-blind inpatient drug study compared cyproheptadine (a weight-inducing antidepressant drug) to amitriptyline hydrochloride (a tricyclic antidepressant) and a placebo (Halmi, Eckert, LaDu, & Cohen, 1986). The overall lack of effect of cyproheptadine on the number of days it took for the anorexic patients to reach a normal weight obscured a differential response to the drug. Cyproheptadine shortened treatment for nonbulimics and lengthened treatment for the bulimic subgroup, compared to the amitriptyline- and placebo-treated groups. The authors recommend cyproheptadine as a therapeutic adjunct to a structured milieu and psychotherapeutic treatment program, and emphasized the absence of serious side effects. The study, unfortunately, failed to comment on the long-term outcome of these patients, and it is not clear that speeding up weight gain (in an absolute sense) is an important treatment goal.

Bulimia Nervosa. Pharmacological treatment of binge eating has been explored using the anticonvulsant medication phenytoin sodium (Dilantin) and antidepressants. The rationale for using Dilantin is that binge eating may be a symptom of epileptic convulsions. Abnormal electroencephalograms (EEGs) have been found in some individuals with compulsive eating disorders (Green & Rau, 1974; Rau & Green, 1975). Treatment successes as high as 90% have been reported using Dilantin (Green & Rau, 1974); however, the criteria for improvement were unclear, and there were no controls for placebo effects. Wermuth, Davis, Hollister, and Stunkard (1977) used a double-blind crossover study with Dilantin and a placebo ($n = 19$); although binge frequency was significantly reduced during the Dilantin phase compared to the placebo phase, improvement continued during the placebo phase. Overall, only 40% of subjects experienced marked or moderate improvement. Studies by Weiss and Levitz (1976) and Greenway, Dahms, and Bray (1977) of the effects of anticonvulsant medication on compulsive eating indicated a lack of response to medication. With further study, Green and Rau (1977) concluded that a neurophysiological element is evident in some, but not all, compulsive eaters.

Antidepressant medications such as the monoamine oxidase inhibitors (MAOIs) have been tried because of data suggesting a link between bulimia and affective disorders (Hudson, Laffer, & Pope, 1982; Walsh et al., 1982). Results have been mixed. Russell (1979) reported that antidepressants failed to have an effect on eating behavior. By contrast, Walsh *et al.* (1982) reported dramatic improvement in both mood and eating behavior in six women who met the DSM-III criteria for Bulimia Nervosa as well as Atypical Depression (Liebowitz, Quitkin, & Stewart, 1981). Unfortunately, there was no control group, the sample size was small, the method for measuring improvement was not specified, and follow-up data were not presented.

Later treatment studies by Pope and Hudson (1982), Pope, Hudson, and Jonas (1983), Stewart, Walsh, Wright, Roose, and Glassman (1984), and Brotman, Herzog, and Woods (1984) have shed further light on the potential use of antidepressant medications for bulimia. Pope and Hudson (1982) reported moderate (defined as 50%) to marked (75%) decreases in bingeing within 3 weeks in six of eight cases treated using tricyclics (mainly imipramine hydrochloride); these improvements were maintained at follow-up at 2 and 6 months. On an expanded sample of 65 bulimic patients, which was reduced to 49 (after those who were judged to have had an inadequate trial of medication were excluded), 10 showed remission, 15 showed marked improvement, 12 showed moderate improvement, and 12 experienced no improvement (Pope *et al.*, 1983). The authors stated, however, that half of the remitted cases reported an occasional binge or cluster of binges. Stewart *et al.* (1984) reported that 10 of 12 bulimic patients showed a rapid decrease in binges (from 14 to 1 per week on the average) after treatment with MAOIs; 6 of the 12 patients met the DSM-III criteria for Major Depression, and 4 patients had had an episode of major depression. At follow-up approximately 9 months later, 6 of the initial 10 responders had maintained their improvement; 5 of these had continued to take their medication. Three patients who continued their medication had relapsed within 2–3 months.

Pope *et al.* (1983) assigned 22 bulimic patients to treatment with imipramine or placebo in a double-blind study. Patients who were suicidal, had anorexia nervosa, or had been previously treated with antidepressant drugs were screened out of the study. Of the 22 subjects, 19 completed the 6-week treatment (2 experimental subjects withdrew for side effect problems, and 1 placebo subject withdrew from the study). The drug group showed a 70%

reduction in bingeing at posttreatment, whereas the placebo control group showed no improvement. At follow-up 2–8 months later, 90% continued to report at least a moderate or marked reduction in binge eating, and 35% had ceased binge eating altogether.

Walsh, Stewart, Roose, Gladis, and Glassman (1984) randomly assigned patients to either phenelzine sulfate or a placebo for 8 weeks, using a double-blind methodology. Screened out were subjects who were suicidal, had recent alcohol or drug abuse problems, or were judged to be unable to follow a tyramine-free diet. Of the 35 subjects entered in the study, 15 were excluded from data analysis because they failed to adhere to the diet, keep appointments, or take the medication as instructed, or because they responded to the placebo treatment in the first 2 weeks. Only 15 patients completed the full 8-week course of treatment; however, data were analyzed for all 20 patients. All of the phenelzine-treated patients had reduced their binge eating by 50% or more, and 5 of these 9 patients stopped binge eating entirely. Only 2 of the 11 placebo-treated patients reduced their binge frequency by 50% or more, and none stopped binge eating completely. The selectivity of this sample must be kept in mind, however. At follow-up (between 3 and 15 months), only 3 of the phenelzine-treated group had continued to take the medication. Of those who discontinued the medication, 3 had relapsed and 2 were binge-free; of those who continued the medication, 2 were binge-free and 1 had had a partial relapse.

Sabine, Yonace, Farrington, Barratt, and Wakeling (1983) tested the effects of mianserin hydrochloride compared to a placebo on 50 patients with bulimia nervosa for 8 weeks, using a double-blind procedure. Although both groups showed significant improvement on attitudes toward eating and bingeing, depression, and anxiety, no changes occurred in the number of days per week that subjects binged.

Another drug tested, with fewer side effects than the ones described above, is desipramine. An advantage of desipramine is that it does not require that patients be placed on diets with rigid restrictions. Furthermore, in one study using a double-blind, placebo-controlled partial crossover trial, desipramine hydrochloride reduced binge frequency by 91%, whereas the placebo group increased binge frequency by 19% (Hughes, Wells, Cunningham, & Ilstrup,

1984). Of the 22 patients on the drug, 15 attained complete abstinence from bingeing and purging after 6 weeks of treatment.

Family Therapy

Family therapy ranges from supportive, informational counseling to more intensive work focused on changing the structural and/or functional patterns of the family. Family therapy has been used as a treatment by itself (Minuchin *et al.*, 1978) and as an element of multicomponent treatment packages (e.g., Strober & Yager, 1985). Although the goals of both approaches are quite similar, the varieties and techniques are extensive and sometimes mutually exclusive. In general, family therapy aims at encouraging the anorexic's gradual disengagement from the family, her progress toward adolescence and adulthood, and the realignment of family roles and boundaries along more developmentally appropriate and adaptive lines. The agenda of family therapy as an element of a treatment package (Wooley & Kearney-Cooke, 1986) is (1) to help the patient find a way to achieve the necessary separation from the family without the feared loss of all connection to her family; (2) to help the patient state personal needs and feelings clearly; (3) to help the patient get permission from the mother to be separate or different from her; and (4) to facilitate communication between the parents so that the daughter is not needed as a facilitator.

Physical Therapy

Moderate exercise (walking, stretching) is thought to promote a healthy distribution of weight gain and is a source of encouragement to patients. A graduated exercise program is begun within a week or two after admission at the Johns Hopkins program (Andersen, 1986). However, strenuous exercise (e.g., aerobics) is generally not allowed until near discharge time. The concern is that the exercise may become compulsive and used as a weight reduction strategy. Thus, close supervision of such activities may be necessary.

Body Image Work

Body image work helps patients become more accepting of their bodies and more aware of them. Photographs, videotapes, various types of role playing, movement, expressive art, and guided imagery therapies can be employed. Wooley and Kearney-Cooke (1986) discuss the use of a combination of such techniques. In particular, they describe using deep muscle relaxation along with the suggestion of images or guided imagery. They focus on three major vignettes. One is the transition from childhood to puberty: Patients are asked to recall and develop pictures in their minds of what their bodies were like at age 5, first grade, prepuberty, when they first menstruated, adolescence, and the time they first left home. They may be asked to draw these images or to sculpt them in clay. The second concerns early sexual experiences. Patients are asked to recall early sex play with peers, early sex play with adults, sexual encounters during adolescence, and recent sexual experiences. They visualize the actual settings in which these experiences took place and the feelings they had at the time. Again, sculptures and drawings may be used to capture these images. In the third vignette, the patient compares her own body image to that of her mother. The patient is asked to imagine herself as her mother preparing for a social event and then at the actual event, copying her movements and gestures. These exercises help to uncover feelings and beliefs, as well as traumatic experiences that have shaped the lives of these women and their attitudes about their bodies.

Self-Monitoring Techniques

Self-monitoring techniques are quite helpful, particularly when patients binge. Patients are encouraged to monitor and record the parameters of their binge eating; associated and preceding thoughts, feelings, and events; presence or absence of others; and the particular environment involved. Fairburn (1980) used elaborate self-monitoring in conjunction with cognitive techniques with four severely bulimic women who engaged in vomiting. The self-monitoring was used as a vehicle whereby the clients and therapist could explore ways to increase self-control over eating and to decrease food avoidance.

Stimulus Control Strategies

Stimulus control strategies are used to limit or negate the environmental cues that lead to inappropriate eating. These include removal of binge foods from the household and avoidance of problematic eating situations (e.g., particular restaurants or being alone in the house during specific hours).

Antecedent Control

Antecedent control involves the manipulation of factors preceding the binge. These factors often include particular feeling states (e.g., boredom or anxiety), difficulty with interpersonal relationships, and dietary deprivation. These strategies are very similar to coping skills training, which teaches patients to cope with difficult situations.

Emotional Regulation Training

Emotional regulation training consists of keeping diaries of feelings and the exploration of reasons behind demands and actions. Such diaries can be used to help patients become more aware of their inner experiences. Also, when the therapist takes the patient's thoughts and feelings seriously, this helps the patient to take her own thoughts and feelings seriously. Wooley and Kearney-Cooke (1986) argue that "the central task of therapy is to push patients outside their range of comfort into expression of meaningful emotion" (p. 486). In order to do this they employ six strategies, described in Table 15-4.

Education

Education is an important component of all treatment programs for eating disorders. Learning about the physiological and psychological effects of starvation and the process of weight maintenance and gain can increase patients' sense of control and understanding and can help decrease their fears.

TABLE 15-4 Range of Emotional Regulation Training Techniques

1. *Interrupting whitewashing*—in order to avoid strong feeling, patients typically whitewash problems or rescue other patients. The therapist must block these attempts and teach that discomfort is acceptable and can be productive.
2. *Exploring ambivalence*—intense contradictory feelings are common, and their exploration can lead to greater resolution. Gestalt-style dialogues in which the two sides of the ambivalence are allowed to "talk" to each other can be helpful. Patients can switch chairs to express each side or can coach another person to act out the other side of the ambivalence and engage in a live dialogue.
3. *Exploring relationships*—feelings toward family members or significant others, sometimes deceased, can be explored by having the therapist or another patient play the role of the other person. The role play can allow the patient to say things to the person that she has always wanted to say, and the therapist and group can provide useful feedback in terms of what the other person may not be able to say—feelings or fears that that person may find too threatening.
4. *Re-enacting past events*—events from the recent or remote past can be re-enacted, with the goal of doing something different or experiencing the event differently. Sometimes, this is with an eye toward future events that may be expected to be a repeat of past events. Returning to an experience in childhood that one was inadequately equipped to deal with, with all of the knowledge and skills acquired later in life, can often bring one to perceive the events differently. One may be better able to experience and express feelings of anger or frustration, for example, and one also may be much less apt to blame oneself.
5. *Dramatizing future events*—it may be particularly helpful to envision and enact what life will be like with and without the symptom in 1, 5, 10 or 20 years. It is helpful to imagine what one's life will be like in the future, particularly in terms of relationships and major life events, marriage, children, deaths of parents, career moves, and so on.
6. *Amplifying expression with movement*—roles can be translated into physical postures and actions. The woman who feels "pushed around" can become aware of her feelings about this by having a member of the group literally push her around. There are obvious positions and actions that express begging and pleading, being stepped on, ignored, hung onto, blamed, and pulled in two directions. Group members can act out the roles of different family members simultaneously for an integrated experience of the family climate. Following this, the patient can explore what postures and positions would be more comfortable and more satisfying for her, and have group members act these out as well.

Note. Adapted from "Intensive Treatment of Bulimia and Body-Image Disturbance" (pp. 486–488) by S. C. Wooley & A. Kearney-Cooke, 1986, in K. D. Brownell and J. P. Foreyt (Eds.), *Handbook of Eating Disorders: Physiology, Psychology, and Treatment of Obesity, Anorexia, and Bulimia* (pp. 476–502), New York: Basic Books. Copyright 1986 by Basic Books, Inc. Adapted by permission.

Symptom Prescription

Programmed bingeing or symptom prescription is used to help patients experience their problem behavior in a new and different way (Haley, 1976; Loro, 1984; Weeks & L'Abate, 1982). The therapist and client typically review previous binge behavior and identify preferred binge foods, as well as thoughts and feelings that accompany the binge. The bulimic or bingeing anorexic may be instructed to bring the binge foods into the therapist's office and to consume them in the therapist's presence, or the therapist and client may contract together for the client to go on a binge. Amount of food, time of day of binge, location, and so on may be specified. The client may or may not be directed to keep detailed records of calories consumed, thoughts, and feelings. The client may be encouraged to eat slowly and to think about the number of calories in each bite, the taste of each bite, and the sensations of eating, or to binge-eat in her usual fashion.

Since the binge behavior is typically seen as something over which clients lack control, having clients engage in binge behavior voluntarily as opposed to "involuntarily" changes the experience of the binge. Clients typically experience that they have more control than they formerly perceived themselves to have, and that the self-recriminations that generally follow their bingeing are not a necessary consequence of bingeing (they do not blame themselves, because they are merely doing as the therapist requested). Furthermore, when the binge behavior loses its "forbidden" status, it sometimes loses its desirability. In Loro's (1984) experience, many clients report being unable to follow through on the binge because they become uninterested in eating or are unable to eat as much as anticipated. Such experiences can be used to identify tactics the client can use later to resist bingeing.

Positive Connotation

Positive connotation can be used with binge behaviors and interpersonal problems for anorexics and bulimics and their families. Loro (1984) suggests to bulimics that their counter-dependency and rebelliousness is "smart when you have to deal with all the undependable people around today" (p. 202). When the undesirable behavior is judged to be positive, it is much easier to approach the frightening topics of vulnerability, rejection, and exposure that

dependency may have come to mean. Thus, rather than trying to reduce the counter-dependency, the therapist can encourage bulimics to refine their methods for finding dependable people. Positive connotation allows the therapist to tread on sensitive ground without causing the client to feel criticized.

Although Coffman (1984) does not discuss his therapeutic techniques in terms of positive connotation, what he does with his clients could easily be considered to involve positive connotation. He interprets binge behavior as "a statement of determination and integrity" (p. 216), which is called forth by a significant relationship in which the client is pressured to conform to a controlling "master's" expectations. With this understanding, the client is then encouraged to be her own master—to choose to do whatever *she* wishes, to eat or not eat, to binge or not binge. Emphasis shifts to replacing the goals of the old master with the goals of the new master. Many of the client's desires, wants, needs, and values may be hidden, and the therapist's help may be needed in order to bring them forth. Johnson, Lewis, and Hagman (1984) emphasize the "adaptiveness" of binge eating as a relatively safe way of regulating tension and being impulsive, aggressive, erotic, oppositional, or "out of control."

Exposure plus Response Prevention

Exposure plus response prevention procedures have been systematically studied by Rosen and Leitenberg (1982). They hypothesized that vomiting is a response to overeating that decreases anxiety related to an intense fear of gaining weight. As a result, the individual learns that vomiting after eating leads to anxiety reduction. These authors proposed that binge eating might not occur if the bulimic individual were prevented from vomiting afterward. They treated a 21-year-old, normal-weight female college student with bulimia of 6 years' duration. The subject was instructed to eat "binge" foods from three categories until she felt the urge to vomit (exposure), but then was not allowed to vomit and instead was directed to focus on the anxiety and discomfort created by not being allowed to vomit (response prevention). This attention to the discomfort was continued until the urge to vomit had receded. Vomiting ceased in 1½ months and recurred only once during a 10-month follow-up. Binges ceased also, even though they were never targeted in therapy. Rosen and Leitenberg argued that the subject habituated to the experience of having overeaten, which dissipated the felt anxiety and thus decreased the intensity of the urge to vomit.

Response Delay

Response delay procedures are based on the theory that if an impulse can be delayed it can be resisted, and that, at least initially, delaying an act is easier than resisting one. After time has passed, the urge is thought to subside and become more manageable. Furthermore, the sequence or chain of events will be altered by the delay. The delay tactic can involve allowing some predetermined length of time to pass or engaging in some particular activity. For example, the client may choose to make herself wait 20 minutes, call a friend, wash a load of laundry, or perform some other activity. It is important that the activity be selected ahead of time and be something of the client's choosing, perhaps something pleasurable and esteem-building. Garner and Beamis (1985) suggest that some clients find it helpful to have a "mnemonic card" listing prebinge delay tactics, so that they can consult it if and when their thinking becomes confused in the face of post-meal anxiety. They also state that this tactic is particularly helpful with clients who have not yet made a commitment to stop vomiting.

Aversion Techniques

Aversion techniques were used by Kenny and Solyom (1971) on a female patient who binged and vomited an average of three times daily. The subject formed a mental image of the eight steps leading to a vomiting episode and raised her finger when each image was clearly perceived. An electric shock at pain threshold intensity was delivered to her middle finger. Each of the eight steps was punished individually, and the procedure was repeated five times each session for 22 sessions. The subject stopped vomiting after 15 sessions and reported that she had not resumed vomiting at follow-up 3 months later.

Psychoeducational Approaches for Bulimics

Psychoeducational approaches for bulimics have been reported by Lacey (1983), Johnson, Connors, and Stuckey (1983) and Connors, Johnson, and Stuckey (1984). These approaches are most appropriately considered to be "multicomponent." Lacey's treatment approach included both group and individual therapy. Sixty women who met the DSM-III criteria for Bulimia Nervosa were assigned to a treatment or an assessment-only control group. The treatment lasted for 10 weeks; subjects received 1½ hours of group therapy and 30 minutes of individual therapy per week. Subjects contracted to attend sessions, maintain their weight, and follow a prescribed diet. Each subject kept a food diary in which she recorded eating behavior, thoughts, and feelings. Of the 30 subjects in the treatment group, 24 stopped bingeing and vomiting completely by the end of the treatment, and an additional 4 stopped within a month after the end of treatment. Two-year follow-up data were available on 28 patients; of these, 20 were completely free of bingeing, 8 had had occasional episodes (an average of three per year).

Johnson et al. (1983) and Connors et al. (1984) treated two groups of 10 bulimic women over a 12-week period. Therapy included didactic presentations as well as group process interventions. The presentations focused on challenging beliefs about the value of thinness and distorted ideas about food, weight, and dieting. Subjects were also taught behavioral strategies to reduce bingeing and purging and to normalize eating by means of self-monitoring and self-graduated goal setting. Binge–purge episodes were reduced by 70% at posttreatment and at a 6-month follow-up. Three subjects had ceased bingeing, eight had reduced their frequency by more than 50%, six had reduced their frequency by between 30% and 50%, and three patients were unchanged.

Group Therapy

Group Approaches for Anorexics. Group therapy for anorexics is rarely advocated, compared to group approaches for normal-weight bulimic patients (Hall, 1985). Conducting group therapy for anorexics can be a lonely, draining experience for therapists and requires many special considerations. Most anorexics are simply not suitable for group therapy. Group work may be beneficial for those anorexics who are not severely ill (i.e., who are gaining weight or are stable), are highly motivated, have benefited psychologically from other treatments, are not totally isolated or withdrawn, are psychologically minded, are able to reveal feelings, are sensitive to others, are liked by the therapist, and have the potential to be liked by other group members. Additional considerations are whether other treatments are indicated (inpatient treatment or family therapy) and/or whether it is practical to combine other treatments with group work (Hall, 1985). Careful consideration must also be given to group size and composition, preparation of clients for the group, length of session, duration of treatment, the admittance of new members, and therapist characteristics and tenure. From her experience and those of others, Hall has developed very specific guidelines for therapists regarding the structuring of groups through the various stages of treatment—from preparatory phases to the first session, to early stages, and on to termination. Hall also advises against the use of gestalt techniques such as role plays and others that facilitate emotional expression, as such experiences tend to be refused by anorexics because of their self-consciousness, fears of failure, and fears of loss of control.

Experiential Group Therapy For Bulimics. Experiential group therapy has been advocated for the treatment of normal-weight bulimic women. This type of therapy may incorporate a feminist perspective and take the position that eating disorders are caused in part by the conflicted role demands placed upon today's women. Accordingly, bulimia is considered to be "related to the struggle to achieve a perfect, stereotypic female image in which women surrender most of their self-defining powers to others" (White & Boskind-White, 1981, p. 501). Treatment consequently questions these standards (Boskind-Lodahl & White, 1978). In their earlier report (Boskind-Lodahl & White, 1978), of 12 of 13 women who completed treatment, 4 ceased bingeing, 6 reduced the frequency and length of their binges, and 2 had no change. Follow-up 1 year later suggested that the successes had been maintained. A similar treatment procedure was followed with a separate sample of 14 women (White & Boskind-White, 1981); 6 months after treatment, 3 of the women reported a cessation of binges, 7 reported reduced frequency and decreased duration of binges, and 4 reported little change in binges. All of the 10 women who found the treatment helpful in reducing their binge behavior also reported that they no longer engaged in purge behavior, despite a high frequency of purges prior to treatment.

Treatment Recommendations

Experienced clinicians have come to classify eating-disordered patients along a continuum of intrapsychic structure (Johnson, 1985; Swift & Stern, 1982) ranging from "borderline" at one extreme through "false self" in the center to "identity conflicted" at the other end. Patients who fall in the "borderline" range (Masterson, 1977) usually have multiple symptoms reflected in chaotic and impulse-ridden personal histories. These patients respond best to highly structured, directive, supportive interventions that aim at life management. With these patients, Johnson (1985) and his colleagues have found that "more is better"; they consequently integrate individual, group, family, and medical treatment in such a way that the patients feel securely "held" by the treatment setting. Patients with a "false self" are second in terms of the severity of their problems. They are compliant and nondemanding patients who try not to become too involved in treatment. Although these patients seem to be functioning adequately in their present lives and report uneventful personal backgrounds, they find discussion of their personal lives painful and threatening, to the point that the therapist may be reluctant to pursue the inquiry. They seem to maintain a superficial accommodation to the therapist and to their interpersonal world. These patients were forced to develop psychological autonomy too early in their development, and they have developed a "pseudo-" identity to present to the world while hiding the part that experiences neediness and a loss of control (Johnson, 1985). The treatment of choice for "false self" patients is long-term, relationship-oriented, individual psychotherapy using a nondirective, nonintrusive approach. The last group, "identity conflicted" patients, are those for whom clear precipitants for the abnormal food behavior can be identified. This group functions well interpersonally and is responsive to short-term, symptom-focused interventions. Johnson (1985) advocates the use of "both individual and group interventions that challenge their beliefs about dieting behavior, the pursuit of thinness, achievement, guilt, failure, rejection, assertiveness, approval, and sexuality" (p. 33). Further work is needed to explore the validity of these guidelines and to develop diagnostic schemas that are sensitive to the distinctions.

Kalucy *et al.* (1985) have identified six subgroups that differ in symptomology, duration, family involvement, and prognosis. They recommend different treatment methods accordingly. All but the last group can contract to gain weight in an orderly and slow manner on a diet with no high-calorie supplements, three meals (one midevening), and a morning and afternoon snack. The first type, patients with nonbulimic anorexia nervosa of less than 2 years' duration, represents 18% of patients. Patients between 10 and 14 years of age who fit this description are very difficult, because their families resist treatment and collude in the patients' denial of the problem. Given the difficulty and lack of success, treatment recommendations are not given for this group. Those between the ages of 15 and 25 who fit into this category usually report a precipitating event related to a family crisis. These women are more open and acknowledge that they have a problem. For these women, outpatient psychotherapy and direct advice regarding eating and weight are recommended.

A second group consists of those women with nonbulimic anorexia nervosa of between 2 and 10 years' duration. This accounts for the largest group (32%) of patients. For these, treatment includes protracted inpatient stays that begin with strict bed rest until goal weight is attained, followed by psychotherapy and training in eating and living skills. The third group includes normal-weight women with chronic anorexia nervosa; these women, accounting for 6% of patients, are characterized by a preoccupation with issues of control, diet, and weight so extreme that it permeates all aspects of the patients' lives. They have a history of classical anorexia nervosa with amenorrhea of 3 to 5 years. These women are "very controlling" and have only superficially satisfactory social and marital relations. In each case, Kalucy et al. have recommended marital therapy, only to have it rejected in favor of individual therapy. Opportunities for family and marital therapy with these women can be arranged when short hospitalizations are deemed necessary for other reasons.

The fourth group consists of patients with anorexia nervosa with bulimia, vomiting, and laxative abuse; in all, 22% fit this description. Four-fifths of these women are within ± 10% of their normal weight; the remainder are "remarkably underweight." This is the group with which Kalucy et al. have had the least success, with only 30% of patients in this category

achieving reasonable gains. They are now experimenting with an outpatient program for these women, which gives permission to binge-eat as long as a diary is kept; they emphasize both the physical and emotional aspects of the disorder. Hospitalization for these women is reserved for those who become acutely suicidal or whose eating behavior is grossly out of control.

Male anorexia nervosa patients, the fifth group, form 6% of Kalucy et al.'s population. These boys have severe gender identity problems and are much more difficult to treat than abstaining female anorexics. Hospitalization is recommended. The last final group consists of chronic anorexia nervosa sufferers—those with anorexia nervosa of longer than 10 years' duration. Most of these women refuse to consider a program that involves significant weight gain, and thus do not attend such programs. If they do enter such programs, they deteriorate psychologically to a severe degree, and the rate of suicide among patients and their families is high. With these patients, the therapist or treatment team should be satisfied with minimal weight gain and minimal increases in social functioning, and should expect continued eccentric, rigid, and boring diets.

Prediction of Outcome

There are very few data suggesting that different treatments have better and worse outcomes, and almost no differential outcome data based upon treatment and symptom characteristics. For the most part, treatment effectiveness has been explored in relationship to *patient,* not *treatment,* characteristics.

Eckert (1985) has provided a concise review of prognostic indicators. Favorable long-term prognosis has been found to be related to early age of onset of illness (Halmi, 1974; Halmi, Brodland, & Rigas, 1975; Hsu, Crisp, & Harding, 1979; Morgan & Russell, 1975; Pierloot, Wellens, & Houben, 1975; Sturzenberger, Cantwell, Burroughs, Salkin, & Green, 1977; Theander, 1970). Poor outcomes have been associated with longer duration of illness and previous hospitalizations (Garfinkel, Moldofsky, & Garner, 1977; Hsu et al., 1979; Morgan & Russell, 1975; Pierloot et al., 1975; Seidensticher & Tzagournis, 1968); very low weight during illness (Dally, 1969; Hsu et al., 1979; Morgan & Russell, 1975); and the presence of such symptoms as bulimia, vomiting, and laxative abuse (Garfinkel et al., 1977; Halmi, 1974; Halmi et al., 1975; Hsu et al., 1979; Theander, 1970).

Less commonly mentioned negative prognosticators include overestimation of body size (Garfinkel et al., 1977; Kalucy, Crisp, Lacy, & Harding, 1977), premorbid personality difficulties and family relations (Dally, 1969; Hsu et al., 1979; Morgan & Russell, 1975), depressive and obsessive–compulsive symptoms (Halmi, Brodland, & Loney, 1973), high rates of physical complaints (Halmi et al., 1973), neuroticism (Dally, 1969; Pierloot et al., 1975), psychological tests suggesting psychosis (Pierloot et al., 1975), and lower social class (Garfinkel et al., 1977; Halmi et al., 1973; Hsu et al., 1979; Seidensticher & Tzagournis, 1968).

Factors predictive of weight gain during a 35-day treatment program include greater hyperactivity and exercising, less denial of illness, greater expressed anger and appetite, less psychosexual immaturity, less tendency to overestimate actual body size, and less sleep disturbance (Garfinkel et al., 1977).

Strober (1983) discriminated three types of anorexia nervosa that were related to outcome at 30, 60, and 90 days. This study was based upon 130 females between the ages of 15 and 19, who were diagnosed as having anorexia nervosa and admitted to a hospital for at least 3 months, with a duration of symptoms (indexed as the number of months past onset of compulsive dieting) between 4 and 22 months. Type 1 patients were characterized by a high need to conform and exercise control, but were self-accepting and maintained a sense of well-being without frank psychopathology. Type 2 patients had high levels of anxiety, self-doubt, and social isolation, with premorbid histories of social avoidance and obsessionality and intermediate levels of intrafamilial tension. Type 3 patients had low ego strength, were impulsive, were prone to addictive behaviors, and had turbulent interpersonal dynamics. There was significant family pathology and disharmony, both present and past, with histories of obesity and binge eating. Outcomes were best for Type 1 and worst for Type 3, with Type 2 falling in the middle.

CONCLUSIONS

This chapter has reviewed the considerable controversy and complexity surrounding the treatment of the eating disorders, anorexia nervosa and bulimia nervosa. The field is currently one of intense activity and interest; yet few questions about the disorders have been answered definitively. Why young women, predominantly, engage in such apparently self-defeating, irrational behaviors centered around such a basic life activity is no longer a complete mystery. There are many indications, perhaps each a part of the "truth." It is now time for a comprehensive view of these disorders—one that recognizes the interplay among biological, social, behavioral, and psychological factors. The importance of cultural factors such as the changing nature of women's roles is increasing, at the same time that biological factors such as neurological functioning are being explored. The *Zeitgeist* encourages clinicians to incorporate recognition of these different spheres in their treatment of clients with eating disorders.

Acknowledgment

Preparation of this chapter was supported in part by Grant No. 1 RO1 HL 33954-01 from the National Heart, Lung and Blood Institute of the National Institutes of Health.

REFERENCES

Abraham, S. F., & Beumont, P. J. V. (1982). How patients describe bulimia or binge eating. *Psychological Medicine, 12*, 625–635.

Agras, W. S., & Kirkley, B. G. (1986). Bulimia: Theories of etiology. In K. D. Brownell & J. P. Foreyt (Eds.), *Handbook of eating disorders: Physiology, psychology, and treatment of obesity, anorexia, and bulimia* (pp. 367–378). New York: Basic Books.

Agras, S., & Werne, J. (1977). Behavior modification in anorexia nervosa. In R. A. Vigersky (Ed.), *Anorexia nervosa* (pp. 291–304). New York: Raven Press.

American Psychiatric Association. (1987). *Diagnostic and statistical manual of mental disorders* (3rd ed., rev.). Washington, DC: Author.

Andersen, A. E. (1986). Inpatient and outpatient treatment of anorexia nervosa. In K. D. Brownell & J. P. Foreyt (Eds.), *Handbook of eating disorders: Physiology, psychology, and treatment of obesity, anorexia, and bulimia* (pp. 333–352). New York: Basic Books.

Andersen, A. E., Morse, C., & Santmyer, K. (1985). Inpatient treatment for anorexia nervosa. In D. M. Garner & P. E. Garfinkel (Eds.), *Handbook of psychotherapy for anorexia nervosa and bulimia* (pp. 311–343). New York: Guilford Press.

Bachrach, A. J., Erwin, W. J., & Mohr, P. J. (1965). The control of eating behavior in an anorexic by operant conditioning techniques. In L. Ullmann & L. Krasner (Eds.), *Case studies in behavior modification* (pp. 153–163). New York: Holt, Rinehart & Winston.

Beck, A. (1976). *Cognitive therapy and the emotional disorders*. New York: International Universities Press.

Bell, R. M. (1985). *Holy anorexia*. Chicago: University of Chicago Press.

Bemis, K. M. (1978). Current approaches to the etiology

and treatment of anorexia nervosa. *Psychological Bulletin, 85,* 593–617.

Beumont, P. J. V. (1977). Further categorization of patients with anorexia nervosa. *Australian and New Zealand Journal of Psychiatry, 11,* 223–226.

Beumont, P. J. V., Abraham, S. F., Argall, W. J., George, C. W., & Glaun, D. E. (1978). The onset of anorexia nervosa. *Australian and New Zealand Journal of Psychiatry, 12,* 145–149.

Beumont, P. J. V., Booth, A. L., Abraham, S. F., Griffiths, D. A., & Turner, T. R. (1983). A temporal sequence of symptoms in patients with anorexia nervosa: A preliminary report. In P. L. Darby, P. E. Garfinkel, D. M. Garner, & D. V. Coscina (Eds.), *Anorexia nervosa: Recent developments in research* (pp. 129–136). New York: Alan R. Liss.

Binswanger, L. (1958). The case of Ellen West. In R. May, E. Angel, & H. F. Ellenberger (Eds.), *Existence: A new dimension in psychiatry and psychology* (pp. 236–363). New York: Basic Books.

Boskind-Lodahl, M., & White, W. C. (1978). The definition and treatment of bulimarexia in college women: A pilot study. *Journal of the American College Health Association, 27,* 84–86.

Brotman, A. W., Herzog, D. B., & Woods, S. W. (1984). Antidepressant treatment of bulimia: The relationship between binging and depressive symptomatology. *Journal of Clinical Psychiatry, 45,* 7–9.

Bruch, H. (1973). *Eating disorders: Obesity, anorexia nervosa and the person within.* New York: Basic Books.

Bruch, H. (1985). Four decades of eating disorders. In D. M. Garner & P. E. Garfinkel (Eds.), *Handbook of psychotherapy for anorexia nervosa and bulimia* (pp. 7–18). New York: Guilford Press.

Casper, R. C., Eckert, E. D., Halmi, K. A., Goldberg, S. C., & Davis, J. M. (1980). Bulimia—its incidence and clinical importance in patients with anorexia nervosa. *Archives of General Psychiatry, 37,* 1030–1040.

Coffman, D. A. (1984). A clinically derived treatment model for the binge–purge syndrome. In R. C. Hawkins II, W. J., Fremouw, & P. F. Clement (Eds.), *The binge–purge syndrome: Diagnosis, treatment, and research* (pp. 211–226). New York: Springer.

Connors, M. E., Johnson, C. L., & Stuckey, M. K. (1984). Treatment of bulimia with brief psychoeducational group therapy. *American Journal of Psychiatry, 141,* 1512–1516.

Crisp, A. H., Hsu, L. K., Harding, B., & Hartshorn, J. (1980). Clinical features of anorexia nervosa: A study of a consecutive series of 102 female patients. *Journal of Psychosomatic Research, 24,* 179–191.

Crisp, A. H., Palmer, R. L., & Kalucy, R. S. (1976). How common is anorexia nervosa: A prevalence study. *British Journal of Psychiatry, 218,* 549–554.

Dally, P. J. (1969). *Anorexia nervosa.* New York: Grune & Stratton.

Eckert, E. D. (1985). Characteristics of anorexia nervosa. In J. E. Mitchell (Ed.), *Anorexia nervosa and bulimia: Diagnosis and treatment* (pp. 3–28). Minneapolis: University of Minnesota Press.

Eckert, E. D., & Labeck, L. (1985). Integrated treatment program for anorexia nervosa. In J. E. Mitchell (Ed.), *Anorexia nervosa and bulimia: Diagnosis and treatment* (pp. 152–170). Minneapolis: University of Minnesota Press.

Fairburn, C. G. (1980). Self-induced vomiting. *Journal of Psychosomatic Research, 24,* 193–197.

Fairburn, C. G., & Cooper, P. J. (1982). Self-induced vomiting and bulimia nervosa: An undetected problem. *British Medical Journal, 284,* 1153–1155.

Fairburn, C. G., Cooper, Z., & Cooper, P. J. (1986). The clinical features and maintenance of bulimia nervosa. In K. D. Brownell & J. P. Foreyt (Eds.), *Handbook of eating disorders: Physiology, psychology, and treatment of obesity, anorexia, and bulimia* (pp. 389–404). New York: Basic Books.

Fernandez, R. C. (1984). Disturbances in cognition: Implications for treatment. In P. S. Powers & R. C. Fernandez (Eds.), *Current treatment of anorexia nervosa and bulimia* (pp. 133–142). Basel: S. Karger.

Foreyt, J. P., & McGavin, J. K. (1988). Anorexia nervosa and bulimia. In E. J. Mash & L. G. Terdal (Eds.), *Behavioral assessment of childhood disorders* (2nd ed., pp. 776–805). New York: Guilford Press.

Frisch, R. D., & McArthur, J. W. (1974). Menstrual cycles: Fatness as a determinant of minimum weight for height necessary for their maintenance or onset. *Science, 185,* 949–951.

Garfinkel, P. E., & Garner, D. M. (1982). *Anorexia nervosa: A multidimensional perspective.* New York: Brunner/Mazel.

Garfinkel, P. E., Garner, D. M., & Kennedy, S. (1985). Special problems of inpatient management. In D. M. Garner & P. E. Garfinkel (Eds.), *Handbook of psychotherapy for anorexia nervosa and bulimia* (pp. 344–362). New York: Guilford Press.

Garfinkel, P. E., & Kaplan, A. S. (1986). Anorexia nervosa—diagnostic conceptualizations. In K. D. Brownell & J. P. Foreyt (Eds.), *Handbook of eating disorders: Physiology, psychology, and treatment of obesity, anorexia, and bulimia* (pp. 266–282). New York: Basic Books.

Garfinkel, P. E., Moldofsky, H., & Garner, D. M. (1977). The outcome of anorexia nervosa: Significance of clinical features, body image and behavior modification. In R. A. Vigersky (Ed.), *Anorexia nervosa* (pp. 315–330). New York: Raven Press.

Garfinkel, P. E., Moldofsky, H., & Garner, D. M. (1980). The heterogeneity of anorexia nervosa: Bulimia as a distinct subgroup. *Archives of General Psychiatry, 37,* 1036–1040.

Garner, D. M. (1986). Cognitive therapy for anorexia nervosa. In K. D. Brownell & J. P. Foreyt (Eds.), *Handbook of eating disorders: Physiology, psychology, and treatment of obesity, anorexia, and bulimia* (pp. 301–327). New York: Basic Books.

Garner, D. M., & Bemis, K. M. (1982). A cognitive–behavioral approach to anorexia nervosa. *Cognitive Therapy and Research, 6,* 123–150.

Garner, D. M., & Bemis, K. M. (1985). Cognitive therapy for anorexia nervosa. In D. M. Garner & P. E. Garfinkel (Eds.), *Handbook of psychotherapy for anorexia nervosa and bulimia* (pp. 107–146) New York: Guilford Press.

Garner, D. M., & Garfinkel, P. E. (1979). The Eating Attitudes Test: An index of the symptoms of anorexia nervosa. *Psychological Medicine, 9,* 273–279.

Garner, D. M., Garfinkel, P. E., & O'Shaughnessy, M. (1983). Clinical and psychometric comparison between bulimia in anorexia nervosa and bulimia in normal weight women. In *Understanding anorexia nervosa and bulimia: Report of Fourth Ross Conference on Medical Research* (pp. 6–14). Columbus, OH: Ross Laboratories.

Garner, D. M., Garfinkel, P. E., Schwartz, D., & Thompson, M. (1980). Cultural expectations of thinness in women. *Psychological Reports, 47,* 483–491.

Garner, D. M., Olmsted, M. P., & Polivy, J. (1983). Development and validation of a multidimensional Eating Disorder Inventory for anorexia nervosa and bulimia. *International Journal of Eating Disorders, 2*(2), 15–34.

Goldberg, S. C., Halmi, K. A., Casper, R., Eckert, E., & Davis, J. M. (1977). Pretreatment predictors of weight change in anorexia nervosa. In R. A. Vigersky (Ed.), *Anorexia nervosa* (pp. 31–42). New York: Raven Press.

Goldberg, S. C., Halmi, K. A., Eckert, E. D., Casper, R. C., Davis, J. M., & Roper, M. (1980). Attitudinal dimensions in anorexia nervosa. *Journal of Psychiatric Research, 15,* 239–251.

Goodsitt, A. (1985). Self psychology and the treatment of anorexia nervosa. In D. M. Garner & P. E. Garfinkel (Eds.), *Handbook of psychotherapy for anorexia nervosa and bulimia* (pp. 55–82). New York: Guilford Press.

Gormally, J., Black, S., Daston, S., & Rardin, D. (1982). The assessment of binge eating severity among obese persons. *Addictive Behaviors, 7,* 47–55.

Green, R. S., & Rau, J. H. (1974). Treatment of compulsive eating disturbances with anti-convulsant medication. *American Journal of Psychiatry, 131,* 428–432.

Green, R. S., & Rau, J. H. (1977). The use of diphenylhydantoin in compulsive eating disorders: Further studies. In R. A. Vigersky (Ed.), *Anorexia nervosa* (pp. 377–382). New York: Raven Press.

Greenway, F. L., Dahms, W. T., & Bray, G. A. (1977). Phenytoin as a treatment of obesity associated with compulsive eating. *Current Therapeutic Research, 21,* 338–342.

Grinc, G. A. (1982). A cognitive–behavioral model for the treatment of chronic vomiting. *Journal of Behavioral Medicine, 5,* 135–141.

Gull, W. W. (1874). Anorexia nervosa (apepsia hysterica, anorexia hysterica). *Transactions of the Clinical Society of London, 7,* 22–28.

Haley, J. (1976). *Problem-solving therapy.* San Francisco: Jossey-Bass.

Hall, A. (1985). Group therapy for anorexia nervosa. In D. M. Garner & P. E. Garfinkel (Eds.), *Handbook of psychotherapy for anorexia nervosa and bulimia* (pp. 213–239). New York: Guilford Press.

Hallsten, E. A. (1965). Adolescent anorexia nervosa treated by desensitization. *Behaviour Research and Therapy, 3,* 87–91.

Halmi, K. A. (1974). Anorexia nervosa: Demographic and clinical features in 94 cases. *Psychosomatic medicine, 36,* 18–25.

Halmi, K. A. (1982). Pragmatic information on the eating disorders. *Psychiatric Clinics of North America, 5,* 371–377.

Halmi, K. A., Brodland, G., & Rigas, C. (1975). A follow-up study of 79 patients with anorexia nervosa: An evaluation of prognostic factors and diagnostic criteria. *Life History Research in Psychopathology, 4,* 290–298.

Halmi, K. A., Brodland, G., & Loney, J. (1973). Prognosis in anorexia nervosa. *Annals of Internal Medicine, 78,* 907.

Halmi, K. A., Casper, R. C., Eckert, E. C., Goldberg, S. C., & Davis, J. M. (1979). Unique features associated with age of onset of anorexia nervosa. *Psychiatric Research, 1,* 209–215.

Halmi, K. A, Eckert, E., LaDu, T. J., & Cohen, J. (1986). Anorexia nervosa: Treatment efficacy of cyproheptadine and amitriptyline. *Archives of General Psychiatry, 43,* 177–181.

Halmi, K. A., Falk, J. R., & Schwartz, E. (1981) Binge eating and vomiting: A survey of a college population. *Psychological Medicine, 11,* 697–706.

Hammond, W. A. (1879). *Fasting girls: Their physiology and pathology.* New York: Putnam.

Hawkins, R. C., II, & Clement, P. F. (1980). Development and construct validation of a self-report measure of binge eating tendencies. *Addictive Behaviors, 5,* 219–226.

Hawkins, R. C., II, Fremouw, W. J., & Clement, P. F. (Eds.). (1984). *The binge–purge syndrome: Diagnosis, treatment and research.* New York: Springer.

Hay, G. G., & Leonard, J. C. (1979). Anorexia nervosa in males. *Lancet, ii,* 574–575.

Hsu, L. K., Crisp, A. H., & Harding, B. (1979). Outcome of anorexia nervosa. *Lancet, i,* 61–65.

Hudson, J. I., Laffer, P. S., & Pope, H. G. (1982). Bulimia related to affective disorder by family history and response to the dexamethasone suppression test. *American Journal of Psychiatry, 139,* 685–687.

Hudson, J. I., Pope, H. G., Jonas, J. M., & Yurgelun-Todd, D. (1983). Family history study of anorexia nervosa and bulimia. *British Journal of Psychiatry, 142,* 133–138.

Hughes, P. L., Wells, L. A., Cunningham, C. J., & Ilstrup, D. M. (1984, May 9). *Treating bulimia with desipramine: A double-blind placebo-controlled study.* Paper presented at the annual meeting of the American Psychiatric Association, Los Angeles.

Janet, P. (1919). *Les obsessions et la psychastheuie.* Paris: Alcan.

Johnson, C. (1985). Initial consultation for patients with bulimia and anorexia nervosa. In D. M. Garner & P. E. Garfinkel (Eds.), *Handbook of psychotherapy for anorexia nervosa and bulimia* (pp. 19–51). New York: Guilford Press.

Johnson, C., Connors, M., & Stuckey, M. (1983). Short-term group treatment of bulimia. A preliminary report. *International Journal of Eating Disorders, 2*(4), 199–208.

Johnson, C., & Larson, R. (1982). Bulimia: An analysis of moods and behavior. *Psychosomatic Medicine, 44,* 341–353.

Johnson, C., Lewis, C., & Hagman, J. (1984). The syndrome of bulimia: Review and synthesis. *Psychiatric Clinics of North America, 7,* 247–273.

Johnson, C., & Pure, D. L. (1986). Assessment of bulimia: A multidimensional model. In K. D. Brownell & J. P. Foreyt (Eds.), *Handbook of eating disorders: Physiology, psychology, and treatment of obesity, anorexia, and bulimia* (pp. 405–449). New York: Basic Books.

Jones, D. J., Fox, M. M., Babigian, H. M., & Hutton, H. E. (1980). The epidemiology of anorexia nervosa in Monroe County, New York: 1960–1976. *Psychosomatic Medicine, 42,* 551–558.

Kalucy, R. S., Crisp, A. H., & Harding, B. (1977). A study of 56 families with anorexia nervosa. *British Journal of Medical Psychology, 50,* 381–395.

Kalucy, R. S., Crisp, A. H., Lacey, J. H., & Harding, B. (1977). Prevalence and prognosis in anorexia nervosa. *Australian and New Zealand Journal of Psychiatry, 11,* 251–257.

Kalucy, R. S., Gilchrist, P. N., McFarlane, C. M., & McFarlane, A. C. (1985). The evolution of a multi-therapy orientation. In D. M. Garner and P. E. Garfinkel (Eds.), *Handbook of psychotherapy for anorexia nervosa and bulimia* (pp. 458–487). New York: Guilford Press.

Kaplan, A. S., & Garfinkel, A. H. (1984). Bulimia in the Talmud. *American Journal of Psychiatry, 141,* 721.

Kenny, F. T., & Solyom, L. (1971). The treatment of compulsive vomiting through faradic disruption of mental images. *Canadian Medical Association Journal, 105,* 1071–1073.

Lacey, J. H. (1982). Anorexia nervosa and a bearded female saint. *British Medical Journal, 285,* 1816–1817.

Lacey, J. H. (1983). Bulimia nervosa, binge eating, and psychogenic vomiting: A controlled treatment study and long term outcome. *British Medical Journal, 286,* 1609–1613.

Lacey, J. H. (1985). Time-limited individual and group treatment for bulimia. In D. M. Garner & P. E. Garfinkel (Eds.), *Handbook of psychotherapy for anorexia nervosa and bulimia* (pp. 431–457). New York: Guilford Press.

Lang, P. J. (1965). Behavior therapy with a case of anorexia nervosa. In L. P. Ullmann & L. Krasner (Eds.), *Case studies in behavior modification* (pp. 217–221). New York: Holt, Rinehart & Winston.

Leibowitz, S. F. (1983). Hypothalamic catecholamine systems controlling eating behavior: A potential model for anorexia nervosa. In P. L. Darby, P. E. Garfinkel, D. M. Garner, & D. V. Coscina (Eds.), *Anorexia nervosa: Recent developments in research* (pp. 221–229). New York: Alan R. Liss.

Leitenberg, H., Agras, W. S., & Thompson, L. E. (1968). A sequential analysis of the effect of selective positive reinforcement in modifying anorexia nervosa. *Behaviour Research and Therapy, 6,* 211–218.

Laseque, C. (1873). On hysterical anorexia. *Medical Times Gazette, 2,* 265–266.

Leon, G. E., Carroll, K., Chernyk, B., & Finn, S. (1985). Binge eating and associated habit patterns within college student and identified bulimic populations. *International Journal of Eating Disorders, 4*(1), 43–57.

Levenkron, S. (1983). *Treating and overcoming anorexia nervosa.* New York: Warner Books.

Lewis, J. M. (1978). The adolescent and the healthy family. In S. C. Feinstein & P. L. Giovacchini (Eds.), *Adolescent psychiatry* (Vol. 6, pp. 156–170). Chicago: University of Chicago Press.

Leibowitz, M. R., Quitkin, F., & Stewart, J. W. (1981). Phenelzine and imipramine in atypical depression. *Psychopharmacological Bulletin, 17,* 159–161.

Loro, A. D., Jr. (1984). Binge eating: A cognitive–behavioral treatment approach. In R. C. Hawkins II, W. J. Fremouw & P. F. Clement (Eds.), *The binge–purge syndrome: Diagnosis, treatment, and research* (pp. 183–210). New York: Springer.

Lowenberg, M., Todhunter, E., Wilson, E., Savage, J., & Lubawski, J. (1974). *Food and man* (2nd ed.). New York: Wiley.

Masterson, J. F. (1977). Primary anorexia nervosa in the borderline adolescent: An object relations view. In P. Hartocollis (Ed.), *Borderline personality disorders* (pp. 475–494). New York: International Universities Press.

Metropolitan Life Insurance Company. (1984). 1983 Metropolitan height and weight tables. *Statistical Bulletin, 64,* 2–9.

Minuchin, S., Rosman, B. L., & Baker, L. (1978). *Psychosomatic families: Anorexia nervosa in context.* Cambridge, MA: Harvard University Press.

Mitchell, J. E. (1985). Medical complications. In J. E. Mitchell (Ed.), *Anorexia nervosa and bulimia: Diagnosis and treatment* (pp. 48–77). Minneapolis: University of Minnesota Press.

Mitchell, J. E. (1986a). Anorexia nervosa: Medical and physiological aspects. In K. D. Brownell & J. P. Foreyt (Eds.), *Handbook of eating disorders: Physiology, psychology, and treatment of obesity, anorexia, and bulimia* (pp. 247–265). New York: Basic Books.

Mitchell, J. E. (1986b). Bulimia: Medical and physiological aspects. In K. D. Brownell & J. P. Foreyt (Eds.), *Handbook of eating disorders: Physiology, psychology, and treatment of obesity, anorexia, and bulimia* (pp. 379–388). New York: Basic Books.

Mitchell, J. E., Hatsukami, D., Eckert, E. D., & Pyle, R. L. (1985). Characteristics of 275 patients with bulimia. *American Journal of Psychiatry, 142,* 482–485.

Mitchell, J. E., Hatsukami, D., Goff, G., Pyle, R. L., Eckert, E., & Davis, L. E. (1985). Intensive outpatient group treatment for bulimia. In D. M. Garner & P. E. Garfinkel (Eds.), *Handbook of psychotherapy for anorexia nervosa and bulimia* (pp. 240–256). New York: Guilford Press.

Mitchell, J. E., & Pyle, R. L. (1982). The bulimic syndrome in normal weight individuals: A review. *International Journal of Eating Disorders, 1*(2), 61–73.

Monello, L. F., Seltzer, C. C., & Mayer, J. (1965). Hunger and satiety sensations in men, women, boys and girls: A preliminary report. *Annals of the New York Academy of Sciences, 131,* 493–602.

Monti, P. M., McCrady, B. S., & Barlow, D. H. (1977). Effect of positive reinforcement, informational feedback and contingency contracting on a bulimic anorexic female. *Behavior Therapy, 8,* 258–263.

Morgan, H. G., & Russell, G. F. M. (1975). Value of family background and clinical features as predictors of long-term outcome in anorexia nervosa: Four-year follow-up study of 41 patients. *Psychological Medicine, 5,* 355–371.

Morton, R. (1694). *Phthisiologica: Or a treatise of consumptions.* London: S. Smith & B. Walford.

Myrtle, A. S. (1888). Letters to the editor. *Lancet, i,* 899.

Ollendick, T. H. (1979). Behavioral treatment of anorexia nervosa: A five-year study. *Behavior Modification, 3,* 124–135.

Oster, J. R., Materson, B. J., & Rogers, A. I. (1980). Laxative abuse syndrome. *American Journal of Gastroenterology, 74,* 451–458.

Palmer, R. L. (1979). The dietary chaos syndrome: A useful new term? *British Journal of Medical Psychology, 52,* 187–190.

Pierloot, R., Wellens, W., & Houben, M. (1975). Elements of resistance to a combined medical and psychotherapeutic program in anorexia nervosa. *Psychotherapy and Psychosomatics, 36,* 101–107.

Pillay, M., & Crisp, A. H. (1981). The impact of social skills training within an established in-patient treatment program for anorexia nervosa. *British Journal of Psychiatry, 139,* 533–539.

Playfair, W. S. (1888). Note on the so-called anorexia nervosa. *Lancet, i,* 817.

Pope, H. G., & Hudson, J. (1982). Treatment of bulimia with antidepressants. *Psychopharmacology, 78,* 167–169.

Pope, H. G., Hudson, J. I., & Jonas, J. M. (1983). Antidepressant treatment of bulimia: Preliminary experience and practical recommendations. *Journal of Clinical Psychopharmacology, 3,* 274–281.

Powers, P. S. (1984a). Eating Disorders Questionnaire. In P. S. Powers & R. C. Fernandez (Eds.), *Current treatment of anorexia nervosa and bulimia* (pp. 302–325). Basel: S. Karger.

Powers, P. S. (1984b). Multidisciplinary approach to treatment and evaluation. In P. S. Powers & R. C. Fernandez (Eds.), *Current treatment of anorexia nervosa and bulimia* (pp. 166–179). Basel: S. Karger.

Powers, P. S., & Fernandez, R. C. (1984). Introduction. In P. S. Powers & R. C. Fernandez (Eds.), *Current treatment of anorexia nervosa and bulimia* (pp. 1–17). Basel: S. Karger.

Powers, P. S., & Powers, H. P. (1984). Inpatient treatment of anorexia nervosa. *Psychosomatics, 25*, 512–527.

Pyle, R. L., Mitchell, J. E., Eckert, E. E., Halverson, P., Neuman, P., & Goff, G. (1983). The incidence of bulimia in freshmen college students. *International Journal of Eating Disorders, 2*(3), 75–85.

Rau, J. H., & Green, R. S. (1975). Compulsive eating: A neuropsychologic approach to certain eating disorders. *Comprehensive Psychiatry, 16*, 223–231.

Rich, C. L. (1978). Self-induced vomiting: Psychiatric considerations. *Journal of the American Medical Association, 239*, 2688–2689.

Rosen, J. C., & Leitenberg, H. (1982). Bulimia nervosa: Treatment with exposure and response prevention. *Behavior Therapy, 13*, 117–124.

Rosenthal, R. H., Webb, W. L., & Wruble, L. D. (1980). Diagnosis and management of persistent psychogenic vomiting. *Psychosomatics, 21*, 722–730.

Rowland, C. V., Jr. (1970). Anorexia nervosa—a survey of the literature and review of 30 cases. *International Psychiatric Clinics, 7*, 37–137.

Russell, G. (1979). Bulimia nervosa: An ominous variant of anorexia nervosa. *Psychological Medicine, 9*, 429–448.

Sabine, E. J., Yonace, A., Farrington, A. J., Barratt, K. H., & Wakeling, A. (1983). Bulimia nervosa: A placebo controlled double-blind therapeutic trial of mianserin. *British Journal of Clinical Pharmacology, 15*(Suppl), 195S–202S.

Schnurer, A. T., Rubin, R. R., & Roy, A. (1973). Systematic desensitization of anorexia nervosa seen as a weight phobia. *Journal of Behavior Therapy and Experimental Psychiatry, 4*, 149–153.

Schwartz, D. M., & Thompson, M. G. (1981). Do anorectics get well? Current research and future needs. *American Journal of Psychiatry, 138*, 319–323.

Schwartz, D. M., Thompson, M. G., & Johnson, C. L. (1982). Anorexia nervosa and bulimia: The socio-cultural context. *International Journal of Eating Disorders, 1*(3), 20–36.

Schwartz, R. C., Barrett, M. J., & Saba, G. (1985). Family therapy for bulimia. In D. M. Garner & P. E. Garfinkel (Eds.), *Handbook of psychotherapy for anorexia nervosa and bulimia* (pp. 280–310). New York: Guilford Press.

Seidensticher, J. F., & Tzagournis, M. (1968). Anorexia nervosa: Clinical features and long-term follow-up. *Journal of Chronic Diseases, 21*, 361–367.

Sheehan, H. L., & Summers, V. K. (1949). The syndrome of hypopituitarism. *Quarterly Journal of Medicine, 18*, 319–378.

Simmonds, M. (1914). Uber embolische prozesse in der hypophysis. *Archives of Pathology and Anatomy, 217*, 226–239.

Slade, P. D. (1973). A short Anorexic Behaviour Scale. *British Journal of Psychiatry, 122*, 83–85.

Stewart, J. W., Walsh, T., Wright, L., Roose, S. P., & Glassman, A. H. (1984). An open trial of MAO inhibitors in bulimia. *Journal of Clinical Psychiatry, 45*, 217–219.

Strangler, R. S., & Printz, A. M. (1980). DSM-III: Psychiatric diagnosis in a university population. *American Journal of Psychiatry, 137*, 937–940.

Strober, M. (1981). The significance of bulimia in juvenile anorexia nervosa: An exploration of possible etiological factors. *International Journal of Eating Disorders, 1*(1), 28–43.

Strober, M. (1983). An empirically derived typology of anorexia nervosa. In P. L. Darby, P. E. Garfinkel, D. M.

Garner, & D. V. Coscina (Eds.), *Anorexia nervosa: Recent developments in research* (pp. 185–196). New York: Alan R. Liss.

Strober, M. (1986). Anorexia nervosa: History and psychological concepts. In K. D. Brownell & J. P. Foreyt (Eds.), *Handbook of eating disorders: Physiology, psychology, and treatment of obesity, anorexia, and bulimia* (pp. 231–246). New York: Basic Books.

Strober, M., & Yager, J. (1985). A developmental perspective on the treatment of anorexia nervosa in adolescents. In D. M. Garner & P. E. Garfinkel (Eds.), *Handbook of psychotherapy for anorexia nervosa and bulimia* (pp. 363–390). New York: Guilford Press.

Sturzenberger, S., Cantwell, P. D., Burroughs, J., Salkin, B., & Green, J. K. (1977). A follow-up study of adolescent psychiatric inpatients with anorexia nervosa. *Journal of the American Academy of Child Psychiatry, 16*, 703–715.

Swift, W. J., & Stern, S. (1982). The psychodynamic diversity of anorexia nervosa. *International Journal of Eating Disorders, 2*(1), 17–35.

Theander, S. (1970). Anorexia nervosa: A psychiatric investigation of 94 female patients. *Acta Psychiatrica Scandinavica, 214*(Suppl.), 1–194.

Walsh, B. T., Stewart, J. W., Wright, L., Harrison, W., Roose, S. P., & Glassman, A. H. (1982). Treatment of bulimia with monoamine oxidase inhibitors. *American Journal of Psychiatry, 139*, 1629–1630.

Walsh, B. T., Stewart, J. W., Roose, S. P., Gladis, M., & Glassman, A. H. (1984). Treatment of bulimia with phenelzine: A double-blind placebo-controlled study. *Archives of General Psychiatry, 41*, 1105–1109.

Webb, W. L., & Gehi, M. (1981). Electrolyte and fluid imbalance: Neuropsychiatric manifestations. *Psychosomatics, 22*, 199–202.

Weeks, G. R., & L'Abate, L. (1982). *Paradoxical psychotherapy: Theory and practice with individuals, couples, and families.* New York: Brunner/Mazel.

Weiss, T., & Levitz, L. (1976). Diphenylhydantoin treatment of bulimia [Letter to the editor]. *American Journal of Psychiatry, 133*, 1093.

Wermuth, B., Davis, K., Hollister, L., & Stunkard, A. (1977). Phenytoin treatment of the binge-eating syndrome. *American Journal of Psychiatry, 134*, 1249–1253.

White, W. C., & Boskind-White, M. (1981). An experiential–behavioral approach to the treatment of bulimarexia. *Psychotherapy: Theory, Research, and Practice, 18*, 501–507.

Willi, J., & Grossman, S. (1983). Epidemiology of anorexia nervosa in a defined region of Switzerland. *American Journal of Psychiatry, 140*, 564–567.

Wooley, S. C., & Kearney-Cooke, A. (1986). Intensive treatment of bulimia and body-image disturbance. In K. D. Brownell & J. P. Foreyt (Eds.), *Handbook of eating disorders: Physiology, psychology, and treatment of obesity, anorexia, and bulimia* (pp. 476–502). New York: Basic Books.

Wooley, S. C., & Wooley, O. W. (1985). Intensive outpatient and residential treatment for bulimia. In D. M. Garner & P. E. Garfinkel (Eds.), *Handbook of psychotherapy for anorexia nervosa and bulimia* (pp. 391–430). New York: Guilford Press.

Wurtman, R. J., & Wurtman, J. J. (1984). Nutrients, neurotransmitter synthesis, and the control of food intake. In A. J. Stunkard & E. Stellar (Eds.), *Eating and its disorders* (pp. 77–86). New York: Raven Press.

INDEX